Dictionary of the Middle Ages

AMERICAN COUNCIL OF LEARNED SOCIETIES

The American Council of Learned Societies, organized in 1919 for the purpose of advancing the study of the humanities and of the humanistic aspects of the social sciences, is a nonprofit federation comprising forty-six national scholarly groups. The Council represents the humanities in the United States in the International Union of Academies, provides fellowships and grants-in-aid, supports research-and-planning conferences and symposia, and sponsors special projects and scholarly publications.

MEMBER ORGANIZATIONS

AMERICAN PHILOSOPHICAL SOCIETY, 1743
AMERICAN ACADEMY OF ARTS AND SCIENCES, 1780
AMERICAN ANTIQUARIAN SOCIETY, 1812
AMERICAN ORIENTAL SOCIETY, 1842
AMERICAN NUMISMATIC SOCIETY, 1858
AMERICAN PHILOLOGICAL ASSOCIATION, 1869
ARCHAEOLOGICAL INSTITUTE OF AMERICA, 1879
SOCIETY OF BIBLICAL LITERATURE, 1880
MODERN LANGUAGE ASSOCIATION OF AMERICA, 1883
AMERICAN HISTORICAL ASSOCIATION, 1884
AMERICAN ECONOMIC ASSOCIATION, 1885
AMERICAN FOLKLORE SOCIETY, 1888
AMERICAN DIALECT SOCIETY, 1889
AMERICAN PSYCHOLOGICAL ASSOCIATION, 1892
ASSOCIATION OF AMERICAN LAW SCHOOLS, 1900
AMERICAN PHILOSOPHICAL ASSOCIATION, 1901
AMERICAN ANTHROPOLOGICAL ASSOCIATION, 1902
AMERICAN POLITICAL SCIENCE ASSOCIATION, 1903
BIBLIOGRAPHICAL SOCIETY OF AMERICA, 1904
ASSOCIATION OF AMERICAN GEOGRAPHERS, 1904
HISPANIC SOCIETY OF AMERICA, 1904
AMERICAN SOCIOLOGICAL ASSOCIATION, 1905
AMERICAN SOCIETY OF INTERNATIONAL LAW, 1906
ORGANIZATION OF AMERICAN HISTORIANS, 1907
AMERICAN ACADEMY OF RELIGION, 1909
COLLEGE ART ASSOCIATION OF AMERICA, 1912
HISTORY OF SCIENCE SOCIETY, 1924
LINGUISTIC SOCIETY OF AMERICA, 1924
MEDIAEVAL ACADEMY OF AMERICA, 1925
AMERICAN MUSICOLOGICAL SOCIETY, 1934
SOCIETY OF ARCHITECTURAL HISTORIANS, 1940
ECONOMIC HISTORY ASSOCIATION, 1940
ASSOCIATION FOR ASIAN STUDIES, 1941
AMERICAN SOCIETY FOR AESTHETICS, 1942
AMERICAN ASSOCIATION FOR THE ADVANCEMENT OF SLAVIC STUDIES, 1948
METAPHYSICAL SOCIETY OF AMERICA, 1950
AMERICAN STUDIES ASSOCIATION, 1950
RENAISSANCE SOCIETY OF AMERICA, 1954
SOCIETY FOR ETHNOMUSICOLOGY, 1955
AMERICAN SOCIETY FOR LEGAL HISTORY, 1956
AMERICAN SOCIETY FOR THEATRE RESEARCH, 1956
SOCIETY FOR THE HISTORY OF TECHNOLOGY, 1958
AMERICAN COMPARATIVE LITERATURE ASSOCIATION, 1960
MIDDLE EAST STUDIES ASSOCIATION OF NORTH AMERICA, 1966
AMERICAN SOCIETY FOR EIGHTEENTH-CENTURY STUDIES, 1969
ASSOCIATION FOR JEWISH STUDIES, 1969

The Anastasis Mosaic. St. Mark's, Venice. COURTESY OF BYZANTINE PHOTOGRAPHIC COLLECTION, DUMBARTON OAKS, WASHINGTON, D.C.

Dictionary of the Middle Ages

JOSEPH R. STRAYER, *EDITOR IN CHIEF*

Volume 1

AACHEN—AUGUSTINISM

CHARLES SCRIBNER'S SONS
MACMILLAN LIBRARY REFERENCE USA
NEW YORK

Library of Congress Cataloging in Publication Data
Main entry under title:

Dictionary of the Middle Ages.

Includes bibliographies and index.
1. Middle Ages—Dictionaries. I. Strayer, Joseph Reese, 1904–1987

D114.D5 1982 909.07 82-5904
ISBN 0-684-16760-3 (v. 1) ISBN 0-684-18169-X (v. 7)
ISBN 0-684-17022-1 (v. 2) ISBN 0-684-18274-2 (v. 8)
ISBN 0-684-17023-X (v. 3) ISBN 0-684-18275-0 (v. 9)
ISBN 0-684-17024-8 (v. 4) ISBN 0-684-18276-9 (v. 10)
ISBN 0-684-18161-4 (v. 5) ISBN 0-684-18277-7 (v. 11)
ISBN 0-684-18168-1 (v. 6) ISBN 0-684-18278-5 (v. 12)

Charles Scribner's Sons
1633 Broadway, New York, NY 10019-6785

7 9 11 13 15 17 19 20 18 16 14 12 10 8

PRINTED IN THE UNITED STATES OF AMERICA.

The *Dictionary of the Middle Ages* has been produced with support from the National Endowment for the Humanities.

The paper in this book meets the guidelines for permanence and durability of the Committee on Production Guidelines for Book Longevity of the Council on Library Resources.

Maps prepared by Joseph Stonehill.

Editorial Board

Advisory Committee

Editorial Staff

Preface

Interest in the Middle Ages has grown tremendously in the last half-century. In the 1920's Charles Homer Haskins was genuinely concerned when he could not recognize the name of a fellow medievalist, whatever his specialty. Now it is difficult to know all the workers in one's own specialty. No single publication can keep fully abreast of the current activity in this burgeoning discipline; no single center—not even the great consortiums at Toronto and Los Angeles—can cover every field in which medievalists are now working.

This situation is difficult enough for mature scholars; it is bewildering and at times disheartening to younger people who, no matter how wide their reading has been, constantly encounter unfamiliar medieval names and terms. Although teachers can help, no teacher can be equally familiar with the terminology of the history of art, law, literature, music, numismatics, philosophy, theology, and technology. Even after a lifetime of reading one still finds unfamiliar names and ideas, and each generation adds to the list.

Moreover, as the study of the Middle Ages has delved deeper into old problems, it has also expanded geographically and in subject matter. The first medievalists were aware, of course, that western Europe in the Middle Ages was only a fragment broken off from an older civilization that had centered on the Mediterranean. Indeed, contacts had always existed between the western European fragment and the Muslim fragment (Syria, Egypt, and North Africa). Except for the Crusades, which involved all three areas, students of western European medieval history have paid little attention to the work of Byzantinists and Arabists or to the role of the Jews in transmitting ideas from east to west.

This intellectual isolation was possible, though hardly commendable, so long as medievalists were concerned mainly with political, legal, and institutional history. But with the emergence of economic history, the history of philosophy, and, above all, the history of science as important fields of investigation, it has become impossible to ignore the Byzantine, Jewish, and Muslim contributions. They were the sources from which western Europe drew its material and intellectual luxuries—silks and spices, algebra and astronomy—and even an undergraduate finds himself confronted by references to the scholars and techniques of these civilizations.

Recognizing these problems, the American Council of Learned Societies called a conference early in 1978 to discuss the possibility of preparing a *Dictionary of the Middle Ages,* which would not only be a practical guide for the novice and a useful reference work for the advanced student but would also serve as a valuable tool for the professional scholar. The conference decided that such a work was indeed necessary, and the ACLS undertook to organize the project. A grant was secured from the National Endowment for the Humanities, and Charles Scribner's Sons agreed to act as publisher. An editorial board representing various disciplines and interests was formed. It was charged with drawing up lists of articles to be commissioned and with reviewing them in order to ensure that no important topic had been omitted.

It was decided that the chronological limits of the *Dictionary* should be roughly A.D. 500 to 1500 and that its geographical scope would be limited to the Latin West, the Slavic world, Asia Minor, the lands of the caliphate in the East, and the Muslim-Christian areas of North Africa. A scale of article lengths was established comprising major articles of 10,000 words to definitions and identifications of 50 to 100 words. Although in some cases an editor felt that a topic had been given inadequate—or excessive—attention, on the whole there was unexpected unanimity on the assignment of word lengths.

After all these factors had been taken into account, it became evident that the *Dictionary* would run to approximately twelve volumes of about 600 pages each. The next task was to find authors for the 5,000 or so articles that had emerged. Colleagues were most helpful in accepting the often onerous job of condensing the knowledge acquired in years of study into a few pages, and in suggesting other scholars competent to write on topics that they themselves could not undertake. Each editor assumed responsibility for finding authors in his or her own area of specialization. The overlapping among topics dealing with ecclesiastical, intellectual, and political institutional history proved a decided asset: it is most helpful to examine the same personage or event from different perspectives.

That the great majority of contributors to the *Dictionary* are teachers at American or Canadian universities is not a manifestation of chauvinism but, rather, recognition that our first obligation was to students in North America. Nevertheless, if the ranking authorities on particular subjects are European we have not hesitated to ask for their help; we are especially grateful to Professor Charles Verlinden, among others, for his series of remarkable articles.

Another recurrent problem concerned bibliographies. Many students, even at an advanced level, can read only one foreign language, and some do not possess even that ability. This lack is especially unfortunate with regard to German, since so many important contributions to medieval scholarship have been made in that language. The bibliographies, therefore, are made up largely of works in English, but we have tried to select those works that include bibliographical references to important works in other languages.

The work is illustrated where necessary, particularly in the articles dealing with the history of art. We have also made liberal use of maps, attempting to combine a modern rendering with representations of geographical areas as they were at the time under discussion.

It should be clear that the *Dictionary* is intended for use at three levels. High school students will find definitions and explanations of medieval terms and ideas that arise in their reading. Those at the university level will find further information on the people, events, and concepts of the Middle Ages. Finally, there is the specialist, and every medievalist is a student throughout his career, for the deeper one digs, the wider the gaps. By combining previously fragmented areas of medieval studies, the *Dictionary* renders the field readily surveyable to scholars, offering them a singular means of coordinating the various branches of medieval scholarship into an accessible and coherent whole.

Many people have played important roles in the production of the *Dictionary.* R. M. Lumiansky and James Settle of the American Council of Learned Societies were unfailingly enthusiastic and supportive. The Editorial Board labored long, often at the sacrifice of their own work, to produce the list of topics, commission articles, and read the manuscripts. The National Endowment for the Humanities, of course, has made the *Dictionary* possible through its generous subvention. The publisher, Charles Scribner, Jr., has been an enthusiastic partner in this enterprise from its inception, as have the editorial staff led by Marshall De Bruhl, the Managing Editor, and Janet Hornberger, the Production Supervisor. And we are all deeply indebted to Carolyn Patton, the Administrative Editor, for her unstinting efforts on behalf of the project.

JOSEPH R. STRAYER
Princeton, N.J.

Contributors to Volume 1

ROBERT W. ACKERMAN
Stanford University
Ancrene Riwle; Arthurian Literature

DOROTHY AFRICA
Aidan of Lindisfarne; Armagh

JUDSON BOYCE ALLEN
Marquette University
Accessus ad Auctores

GORDON A. ANDERSON
University of New England, New South Wales
Ars Antiqua; Ars Subtilior

THEODORE M. ANDERSSON
Stanford University
Atlakvida; Atlamál

S. G. ARMISTEAD
University of Pennsylvania
Alfonso XI, Poema de

YOM TOV ASSIS
Hebrew University of Jerusalem
Abrabanel, Isaac ben Judah

BERNARD S. BACHRACH
University of Minnesota
Alamanni; Alani; Alaric

TERENCE BAILEY
University of Western Ontario, Talbot College
Ambrosian Chant

DEIRDRE BAKER
University of Toronto, Centre for Medieval Studies
Altfrid of Münster; Apollonius of Tyana

CARL F. BARNES, JR.
University of Michigan
Abiell, Guillermo; Achard or Aichardus; Amiens Cathedral; Antiquarianism and Archaeology; Archaeology of Medieval Monuments

STEPHEN A. BARNEY
University of California, Irvine
Allegory

ROBERT BEDROSIAN
Aristakēs Lastivertcʿi

JEANETTE M. A. BEER
Purdue University
Allegory, French

A. F. L. BEESTON
University of Oxford
Arabia, Pre-Islamic; Arabic Language

HUGO BEKKER
Ohio State University
Albrecht von Johansdorf

HANS BEKKER-NIELSEN
Odense University
Árna Saga Biskups

JOHN F. BENTON
California Institute of Technology
Abelard, Peter; Arnald of Villanova

JANE BISHOP
Columbia University
Anastasius Bibliothecarius

THOMAS N. BISSON
University of California, Berkeley
Aragon (800–1137); Aragon, Crown of (1137–1479)

N. F. BLAKE
University of Sheffield
Ars Moriendi

JONATHAN M. BLOOM
Harvard University
Aghlabid Art

RENATE BLUMENFELD-KOSINSKI
Columbia University
Aubade (Aube)

SÁNDOR BÖKÖNYI
Hungarian Academy of Sciences, Archaeological Institute
Animals, Draft; Animals, Food

DIANE BORNSTEIN
Queens College, City University of New York
Antifeminism

C. E. BOSWORTH
University of Manchester
Alamūt; Alptigin

CALVIN M. BOWER
University of Notre Dame
Agnus Chant

JOHN F. BOYLE
University of Toronto, Centre for Medieval Studies
Apollinarius; Apostolic Constitutions

CHARLES M. BRAND
Bryn Mawr College
Alexios I Komnenos; Andronikos I Komnenos; Angelos

MICHAEL BRETT
University of London, School of African and Oriental Studies
Aghlabids; Almohads

CONTRIBUTORS TO VOLUME 1

MARIANNE G. BRISCOE
Newberry Library, Chicago
Ars Praedicandi

LESLIE BRUBAKER
Wheaton College
Absidiole; Aedicula; Agape; Agnus Dei; Alburanus; Aléaume; All'Antica; Alpha and Omega; Altar, Portable; Alternation (or Alternating Supports); Ambo; Ambulatory; Ampulla; Anastasis; Ancient of Days; Andachtsbild; Andrea da Firenze; Angel; Angilbert of Milan; Aniconism; Animal Style; Anno; Annunciation; Antependium; Anthemios of Tralles; Apocalypse, Illustration of; Apse; Apse Echelon; Arabesque; Arch; Archangel; Archivolt; Arcosolium; Ark of the Covenant; Arma Christi; Arts, Seven Liberal; Ascension; Assumption of the Virgin; Atelier; Athos, Mount, Monuments of; Atrium

GENE A. BRUCKER
University of California, Berkeley
Alberti, Leon Battista

ANTHONY BRYER
University of Birmingham, Centre for Byzantine Studies
Alexios I of Trebizond

BONNIE BUETTNER
Cornell University
Athis und Prophilias

RICHARD W. BULLIET
Columbia University, Middle East Institute
Abode of Islam—Abode of War

ALLEN CARBANISS
University of Mississippi
Agobard

ANGUS CAMERON
University of Toronto, Centre for Medieval Studies
Anglo-Saxon Literature

AVERIL CAMERON
University of London, King's College
Agathias

COLIN CHASE
University of Toronto, Centre for Medieval Studies
Acrostics—Wordplay; Alfred the Great; Alfred the Great and Translations; Anglo-Latin Poetry

ROBERT CHAZAN
Queens College, City University of New York
Anti-Semitism; Ashkenaz

FREDRIC L. CHEYETTE
Amherst College
Albigensians

WANDA CIŻEWSKI
Pontifical Institute of Medieval Studies, Toronto
Adam of the Little Bridge

MARSHALL CLAGETT
Institute for Advanced Study, Princeton
Archimedes in the Middle Ages

WILLIAM J. COURTENAY
University of Wisconsin
Accident; Actualism

WILLIAM CRAWFORD
University of Toronto, Centre for Medieval Studies
Audradus Modicus

GEORGE G. P. CUTTINO
Emory University
Aquitaine

JOSEPH DAN
Hebrew University of Jerusalem
Apocalyptic Literature and Movement, Jewish

PETER F. DEMBOWSKI
University of Chicago
Ami et Amile; Assonance

LUCY DER MANUELIAN
ałtʿamar; Ani, Monuments of; Armenian Art; Aštarak (Ashtarak)

ROBERT DESHMAN
University of Toronto
Anglo-Saxon Art

H. W. DEWEY
University of Michigan
Agriculture and Nutrition (Slavic)

WACHTANG DJOBADZE
California State University at Los Angeles
Alaverdi; Atenis Sioni

JERRILYNN D. DODDS
Columbia University
Asturian Art

CHARLES DOHERTY
University College, Dublin
Áedán mac Gabráin

MICHAEL W. DOLS
California State University at Hayward
Alchemy, Islamic

FRED M. DONNER
Yale University
al-ʿAbbās ibn ʿAbd al-Muṭṭalib ibn Hāshim; ʿAbd al-Muṭṭalib; ʿAbd Allāh ibn al-Zubayr; Abū Bakr; Abū Sufyān; Abū Ṭālib; ʿĀʾisha; ʿAmr ibn al-ʿĀṣ

PETER W. EDBURY
University College, Cardiff
Assizes of Jerusalem

CHRISTIAN EWERT
Deutsches Archäologisches Institut, Madrid
Almohad Art; Almoravid Art

ANN E. FARKAS
Alimpi

JERE FLECK
University of Maryland
Alvíssmál

CLIVE FOSS
University of Massachusetts
Anatolia; Antioch

KLAUS GAMBER
Liturgiewissenschaftliches Institut, Regensburg
Aquileia, Rite of

NINA G. GARSOÏAN
Columbia University
Ałc; Ani in Daranałikʿ; Ani in Širak; Armenia, Geography; Armenia: History of; Armenia, Social Structure; Armenian Muslim Emirates; Arsacids/Aršakuni, Armenian; Aršak II; Artašat (Artaxata)

CONTRIBUTORS TO VOLUME 1

ADELHEID M. GEALT
Indiana University
AGNOLO DI VENTURA; AGOSTINO, GIOVANNI D'; ALTARPIECE; ALTICHIERO; ANGELO DA ORVIETO; ANTONIO DA VICENZO; ANTONIO VENEZIANO; ARENA CHAPEL; ARNOLDI, ALBERTO; ARNOLFO DI CAMBIO; ARRICCIO; ASSISI, SAN FRANCESCO

C. J. GELLINEK
University of Florida
ANNOLIED

OWEN GINGERICH
Smithsonian Astrophysical Observatory
ALFONSINE TABLES; ASTROLABE

THOMAS F. GLICK
Boston University
AGRICULTURE AND NUTRITION (THE MEDITERRANEAN REGION)

PETER B. GOLDEN
Rutgers University
ALP ARSLAN; AQ QOYUNLU; ARGUN; ATABEG

GORDON K. GREENE
Wilfrid Laurier University
ARS NOVA

ROBERT HALLEUX
University of Liège
ALCHEMY

ANDRAS HAMORI
Princeton University
ABŪ NUWĀS; AKHṬAL, AL-; ARABIC LITERATURE, PROSE; ARABIC POETRY

ERIC P. HAMP
University of Chicago, Center for Balkan and Slavic Studies
ANEIRIN

EMILY ALBU HANAWALT
Boston University
ANNA KOMNENA

CONRAD HARKINS
Saint Bonaventure University, Franciscan Institute
ALEXANDER OF HALES

L. P. HARVEY
University of London, King's College
ALJAMIADO LITERATURE

EDWARD R. HAYMES
University of Houston
ALPHARTS TOD

R. H. HELMHOLZ
Washington University, St. Louis
ANNULMENT OF MARRIAGE

HEATHER HENDERSON
University of Toronto, Centre for Medieval Studies
AREITHIAN PROSE: PROSE RHETORICS

JOHN BELL HENNEMAN
University of Iowa
AGINCOURT, BATTLE OF

JOHN HENNIG
ANGELUS

MICHAEL HERREN
York University
ALDHELM

ROBERT H. HEWSEN
Glassboro State College
ALBANIA (CAUCASIAN); ARAKS RIVER; ARARAT, MOUNT; ARČĒŠ; ARCN; ARMENIAN PENTARCHY

ROBERT HILLENBRAND
University of Edinburgh
ALHAMBRA

MICHAEL J. HODDER
Sotheby Parke Bernet, Inc.
ALLOD

JASPER HOPKINS
University of Minnesota
ANSELM OF CANTERBURY

GEORGE F. HOURANI
State University of New York at Amherst
ASHᶜARĪ, AL-

ANTONÍN HRUBÝ
University of Washington
ACKERMANN AUS BÖHMEN, DER

PETER HUENINK
Vassar College
AACHEN, PALACE CHAPEL

ANDREW HUGHES
University of Toronto
ADAM DE LA BASSÉE; AEVÍA; ANTIPHON; ANTIPHONAL (ANTIPHONER, ANTIPHONARY)

SHAUN F. D. HUGHES
Purdue University
ÁNS SAGA BOGSVEIGIS

MOSHE IDEL
Hebrew University of Jerusalem
ABULAFIA, ABRAHAM BEN SAMUEL

EPHRAIM ISAAC
Institute for Advanced Study, Princeton
ABYSSINIA (ETHIOPIA)

ALFRED L. IVRY
Brandeis University
ABRAHAM IBN DAUD

W. T. H. JACKSON
Columbia University
ALEXANDER ROMANCES

JAMES J. JOHN
Cornell University
ABBREVIATOR; ALPHABETS

D. W. JOHNSON
Catholic University of America
ADOPTIONISM; ARIANISM

WILLIAM CHESTER JORDAN
Princeton University
ANGEVINS: FRANCE, ENGLAND, SICILY

PETER A. JORGENSEN
University of Georgia
ÁLA FLEKKS SAGA

WALTER EMIL KAEGI, JR.
University of Chicago
AKRITAI; ANATOLIKON, THEME OF; ARMENIAKON, THEME OF

RICHARD W. KAEUPER
University of Rochester
ADMIRALTY, COURT OF; ALDERMEN; ARCHES, COURT OF; ASSIZE; ASYLUM, RIGHT OF

STEPHEN J. KAPLOWITT
University of Connecticut
ANEGENGE

LLOYD KASTEN
Hispanic Seminary of Medieval Studies
ALFONSO X

ALEXANDER P. KAZHDAN
Dumbarton Oaks Research Center
AGRICULTURE AND NUTRITION (BYZANTIUM)

CONTRIBUTORS TO VOLUME 1

THOMAS KEEFE
Appalachian State University
ANTRUSTIONES

MARILYN KAY KENNEY
University of Toronto, Centre for Medieval Studies
ARTHURIAN LITERATURE, WELSH

ANGELIKI LAIOU
Harvard University
ANDRONIKOS II PALAEOLOGOS; ANDRONIKOS III PALAEOLOGOS

IRA M. LAPIDUS
University of California, Berkeley
ALEPPO

JOHN LARNER
University of Glasgow
ART, COMMERCIAL TRADE OF; ARTIST, STATUS OF THE

JACOB LASSNER
Wayne State University
ABBASIDS

DAMIAN RIEHL LEADER
University of Toronto, Centre for Medieval Studies
ARNOBIUS THE ELDER; ARNOBIUS THE YOUNGER

R. WILLIAM LECKIE, JR.
University of Toronto, Centre for Medieval Studies
ALBRECHT VON SCHARFENBERG

RICHARD LEMAY
City University of New York, Graduate Center
ARABIC NUMERALS

ROBERT E. LERNER
Northwestern University
ALEXANDER OF ROES; ANTICHRIST

ARCHIBALD R. LEWIS
University of Massachusetts
ADMIRAL

BERNARD LEWIS
Princeton University
ASSASSINS

LESTER K. LITTLE
Smith College
ADRIAN IV, POPE; ANTHONY OF PADUA, ST.; ANTIPOPE

LARS LÖNNROTH
Aalborg University
ALEXANDERS SAGA

H. R. LOYN
University of London, Westfield College
ANGLO-SAXONS, ORIGINS AND MIGRATION

GEARÓID MAC EOIN
University College, Galway
AISLINGE MEIC CON-GLINNE

R. D. McCHESNEY
New York University
AFGHANISTAN

MICHAEL McCORMICK
Dumbarton Oaks Research Center
ALGER OF LIÈGE

RALPH McINERNY
University of Notre Dame, Medieval Institute
AQUINAS, ST. THOMAS

JOHN W. McKENNA
ACCLAMATIONS; ANOINTING

MARTIN McNAMARA
Sacred Heart Missionaries, Dublin
AIRDENA BRÁTHA

WILLIAM MACOMBER
St. John's University, Hill Monastic Manuscript Library
ALEXANDRIAN RITE; ANTIOCHENE RITE

JOHN C. MAGEE
Pontifical Institute of Medieval Studies, Toronto
ANGELA MERICI, ST.; ANGELA OF FOLIGNO; ANTONINUS, ST.

GEORGE P. MAJESKA
University of Maryland
ANALOI

ALAN MAKOVSKY
Princeton University
ANKARA

KRIKOR H. MAKSOUDIAN
Columbia University
ANANIA ŠIRAKAC^C^I; ARCHON TON ARCHONTON; ARCRUNIS; ARMENIAN ALPHABET; ARMENIAN CHURCH, DOCTRINES AND COUNCILS; ARMENIAN CHURCH, STRUCTURE; ARMENIAN HELLENIZING SCHOOL; ARMENIAN LANGUAGE; ARMENIAN LITERATURE; ARMENIAN SAINTS; AŠOT I MEC (THE GREAT); AŠOT II ERKAT^C^; AŠOT III OŁORMAC (THE MERCIFUL)

JOAQUÍN MARTÍNEZ-PIZARRO
Oberlin College
ADAM OF BREMEN; ÁSMUNDAR SAGA KAPPABANA

THOMAS F. MATHEWS
New York University, Institute of Fine Arts
ARCHITECTURE, LITURGICAL ASPECTS

E. ANN MATTER
University of Pennsylvania
ANGEL/ANGELOLOGY

BRIAN MERRILEES
University of Toronto
ADGAR; AMADAS ET YDOINE; ANGIER; ANGLO-NORMAN LITERATURE; ANONIMALLE CHRONICLE; ARUNDEL PSALTER

JOHN MEYENDORFF
Fordham University
ALEXIS OF MOSCOW; ARCHIMANDRITE; ARSENIUS AUTORIANUS; ATHANASIUS OF ALEXANDRIA, ST.; ATHOS, MOUNT

MARK D. MEYERSON
University of Toronto, Centre for Medieval Studies
ADALBOLD OF UTRECHT

MARILYN S. MILLER
Pontifical Institute of Medieval Studies, Toronto
ARNOLD OF BRESCIA

M. MORONY
University of California, Los Angeles
ALIDS

DANA A. NELSON
University of Arizona
ALEXANDRE, LIBRO DE

HELMUT NICKEL
Metropolitan Museum of Art, New York
ARMS AND ARMOR

MÁIRÍN NÍ DHONNCHADHA
University College, Cork
ADAMNAN, ST.

CONTRIBUTORS TO VOLUME 1

MARGARET F. NIMS
Pontifical Institute of Medieval Studies, Toronto
ARS POETICA

TIMOTHY B. NOONE
University of Toronto, Centre for Medieval Studies
ADALBERT OF BREMEN; ADALBERT, ST.; AGNELLUS OF PISA; AMALRIC OF BÈNE

FRANCIS OAKLEY
Williams College
AILLY, PIERRE D'

DONNCHADH Ó CORRÁIN
University College, Cork
ÁED SLÁNE

BRIAN Ó CUÍV
Dublin Institute for Advanced Studies
ACALLAM NA SENÓRACH

NICHOLAS OIKONOMIDES
University of Montreal
AUGUSTA

PÁDRAIG P. Ó NÉILL
University of North Carolina at Chapel Hill
AIRBERTACH MAC COISSE; APOCRYPHA, IRISH

PETER D. PARTNER
Winchester College
ALBORNOZ, CARDINAL GIL; ANNATE

OLAF PEDERSEN
University of Aarhus
ARMILLARY SPHERE; ASTROLOGY/ASTRONOMY, EUROPEAN

FRANKLIN J. PEGUES
Ohio State University
ASSIZE, ENGLISH

DAVID A. E. PELTERET
University of Toronto
ADBO (ABBO) OF ST.-GERMAIN-DES-PRÉS; ADELMAN OF LIÈGE; ADÉMAR OF CHABANNES; AEDDI (EDDIUS STEPHANUS); AGIUS OF CORVEY; ASSER

EDWIN B. PLACE
AMADÍS DE GAULA

ELIZABETH WILSON POE
Tulane University
ALBA; ARNAUT DANIEL

NANCY A. PORTER
University of Toronto, Centre for Medieval Studies
ANGELOMUS OF LUXEUIL; ANGELRAM OF ST. RIQUIER; ANGILBERT, ST.; ANSELM OF BESATE; ANSELM OF LIÈGE; ARATOR

DAVID S. POWERS
Cornell University
ALMS TAX, ISLAMIC

JAMES F. POWERS
College of the Holy Cross
ALFONSO I OF ARAGON

WADĀD AL-QĀḌĪ
American University of Beirut
ᶜALĪ IBN ABĪ ṬĀLIB

MARY LYNN RAMPOLA
University of Toronto, Centre for Medieval Studies
ALEXANDER III, POPE

GEORGE RENTZ
The Johns Hopkins University
ARABIA, ISLAMIC

ROGER E. REYNOLDS
Pontifical Institute of Medieval Studies, Toronto
ADVENT; ALL SAINTS' DAY; ALL SOULS' DAY; ALTAR—ALTAR APPARATUS; ASCENSION, FEAST OF THE

D. S. RICHARDS
University of Oxford
ATHĪR, IBN AL-

A. G. RIGG
University of Toronto, Centre for Medieval Studies
ANTHOLOGIES

LINDA ROSE
ADRIANOPLE (EDIRNE); ALLELENGYON; AMORIANS; AMORION

MARY A. ROUSE
University of California, Los Angeles
ALPHABETIZATION, HISTORY OF

RICHARD H. ROUSE
University of California, Los Angeles
ALPHABETIZATION, HISTORY OF

TEOFILO F. RUIZ
Brooklyn College, City University of New York
ALMOGÁVARES; ANDALUSIA; ASTURIAS-LEÓN (718–1037)

JAMES R. RUSSELL
Columbia University
ARDEŠĪR (ARDASHIR, ARTAXERES) I

GEORGE SALIBA
Columbia University
ASTROLOGY/ASTRONOMY, ISLAMIC

PETER SCHÄFFER
University of California, Davis
ALBRECHT VON HALBERSTADT

RAYMOND P. SCHEINDLIN
Jewish Theological Seminary of America
ABRAHAM BEN MEÏR IBN EZRA

NICOLAS SCHIDLOVSKY
Dumbarton Oaks Research Center
AKATHISTOS; ASMATIKON

ANNEMARIE SCHIMMEL
Harvard University
ANGEL, ISLAMIC

JANICE L. SCHULTZ
Canisius College, Buffalo
ADAM OF ST. VICTOR; ADELARD OF BATH

ALBERT SEAY
Colorado College
ANONYMOUS IV

HARVEY L. SHARRER
University of California, Santa Barbara
ARTHURIAN LITERATURE, SPANISH AND PORTUGUESE

LON R. SHELBY
Southern Illinois University
ARCHITECT, STATUS OF

LAURENCE K. SHOOK
Pontifical Institute of Medieval Studies, Toronto
ABBO OF FLEURY; ALCUIN OF YORK; AUGUSTINE OF CANTERBURY

LEAH SHOPKOW
University of Toronto, Centre for Medieval Studies
AGNELLUS OF RAVENNA, ST.; ALBERIC OF MONTE CASSINO; ALPERT OF METZ; ALPHANUS OF SALERNO; ARBEO OF FREISING

CONTRIBUTORS TO VOLUME 1

BOAZ SHOSHAN
Ben-Gurion University of the Negev
ALEXANDRIA

CYRIL SMETANA
York University
AUGUSTINIAN CANONS; AUGUSTINIAN FRIARS

ROBERT SOMERVILLE
Columbia University
ALEXANDER II, POPE

PRISCILLA SOUCEK
New York University, Institute of Fine Arts
AGHKAND WARE; AḤMAD MŪSĀ; ASCENSION OF THE PROPHET

MARY B. SPEER
Rutgers University
ADENET LE ROI

RUTH STEINER
Catholic University of America
AGNUS DEI (MUSIC)

ALAIN J. STOCLET
University of Toronto, Centre for Medieval Studies
ADALBERO OF LAON; AIMOIN DE FLEURY; AMALARIUS OF METZ; AMMIANUS MARCELLINUS; ANDRÉ DE FLEURY; ARNULF

M. ALISON STONES
University of Minnesota
ANGLO-NORMAN ART

JOSEPH R. STRAYER
Princeton University
ADVOCATE; ALBERT OF SAXONY; APOSTASY; ATHANASIANS

RICHARD E. SULLIVAN
Michigan State University
AACHEN

RONALD G. SUNY
University of Michigan
AMIRSPASALAR

RONALD E. SURTZ
Princeton University
APOLONIO, LIBRO DE

E. A. SYNAN
Pontifical Institute of Medieval Studies, Toronto
ANSELM OF LAON; ATTO OF VERCELLI; AUGUSTINE OF HIPPO, ST.; AUGUSTINISM

JOSEPH SZÖVÉRFFY
ARCHPOET

ALICE-MARY M. TALBOT
Hiram College
ANNA (MACEDONIAN PRINCESS); ATHANASIUS I, PATRIARCH OF CONSTANTINOPLE; ATTALEIATES, MICHAEL

ELAINE C. TENNANT
University of California, Berkeley
AMBRASER HELDENBUCH

CLAIBORNE W. THOMPSON
AESIR

PAULINE A. THOMPSON
University of Toronto, Centre for Medieval Studies
AMARICIUS; AMATUS OF MONTE CASSINO; ANSELM II OF LUCCA

R. W. THOMSON
Harvard University
AGAT^c ANGEŁOS

RICHARD TOPOROSKI
University of Toronto, St. Michael's College
AMBROSE, ST.

PETER TOPPING
Dumbarton Oaks Research Center
ASSIZES OF ROMANIA

DAVID R. TOWNSEND
University of Toronto, Centre for Medieval Studies
AELFRIC BATA; ANTHOLOGIA LATINA; ARNULF OF MILAN

ISADORE TWERSKY
Harvard University
ABRAHAM BEN DAVID OF POSQUIÈRES

KARL D. UITTI
Princeton University
AUCASSIN ET NICOLETTE

KRISTINE T. UTTERBACK
University of Toronto, Centre for Medieval Studies
ARNOLD OF ST. EMMERAM

GEORGES VAJDA
Centre National de la Recherche Scientifique, Paris
ABRAHAM BAR ḤIYYA

ANNE HAGOPIAN VAN BUREN
Tufts Univeristy
AUBERT, DAVID

JEANETTE A. WAKIN
Columbia University
ABŪ ḤANĪFA

WILLIAM A. WALLACE
Catholic University of America
ARISTOTLE IN THE MIDDLE AGES

ANN K. WARREN
Case Western Reserve University
ANCHORITES; APOSTOLIC SUCCESSION

ANDREW M. WATSON
University of Toronto
AGRICULTURE AND NUTRITION (THE ISLAMIC WORLD)

W. MONTGOMERY WATT
University of Edinburgh
ALLAH

JAMES A. WEISHEIPL
Pontifical Institute of Medieval Studies, Toronto
ALBERTUS MAGNUS

WINTHROP WETHERBEE
University of Chicago
ALAN OF LILLE

ESTELLE WHELAN
New York University
ABBASID ART AND ARCHITECTURE; AJÍMEZ

LYNN WHITE, JR.
University of California, Los Angeles
AGRICULTURE AND NUTRITION (NORTHERN EUROPE)

NIGEL WILKINS
University of Cambridge
ADAM DE LA HALLE

DANIEL WILLIMAN
State University of New York at Binghamton
ARCHIVES

GABRIELE WINKLER
St. John's University
ARMENIAN RITE

KLAUS W. WOLLENWEBER
Memorial University of Newfoundland
ARISTOTELES UND PHYLLIS

CONTRIBUTORS TO VOLUME 1

CHARLES T. WOOD
Dartmouth College
APPANAGES

BASIL S. YAMEY
University of London
ACCOUNTING

JAMES L. YARRISON
Princeton University
ALMORAVIDS; ATLAS MOUNTAINS

DAVID YERKES
Columbia University
AELFRIC

MARK A. ZIER
University of Toronto, Centre for Medieval Studies
ALEXANDER V; ANDREW OF ST. VICTOR

RONALD EDWARD ZUPKO
Marquette University
ACRE; ALNAGE, AUNAGE; ARPENT

Dictionary of the Middle Ages

Dictionary of the Middle Ages

AACHEN-AUGUSTINISM

AACHEN, a city in west central Germany in the modern state of North Rhine-Westphalia, was significant during the Middle Ages because of its association with the Carolingian and Holy Roman empires and the German rulers who tried to carry on the Carolingian tradition of a unified Europe. First occupied by the native Celts of Gaul, Aachen became a modest Roman military establishment in the first century A.D., especially attractive because of the baths made possible by the warm springs rising there. The Romans named the site Aquae Grani ("waters of Granus") after a Celtic god worshipped there. After the Franks occupied the area in the fifth century, Aachen's history was obscure for about three centuries.

In the late eighth century the recently established Carolingian rulers of the Frankish kingdom gave Aquae Grani (or Aquisgranum as it was now called) new prominence. Attracted by the springs, the site's strategic advantages as a base for his efforts to subdue the Saxons, and the existence of large family landholdings in the area, Charlemagne decided to develop a major royal residence there. Between about 785 and 805 several important structures were built, including a chapel (still standing), a great hall containing royal living quarters and facilities for governmental activities, and a large bath. This complex, known as the palace *(palatium),* remained the focal point of life in Aachen during most of the Middle Ages.

As the chief royal residence during the first half of the ninth century, Aachen was the center of intense activity. Emperors were crowned there, and popes and foreign emissaries visited the palace, from which a major part of the administrative activity for the huge empire was conducted. Royal vassals constantly came, especially to take part in the royal assemblies and ecclesiastical synods, which helped shape legislation on matters affecting all aspects of life in the empire. The royal chapel was the center of the vigorous religious activity that provided models for the reforms being promoted by the emperors and the popes. Charlemagne gathered at Aachen a circle of scholars (sometimes called the Palace Academy), whose efforts stimulated the cultural revival known as the Carolingian renaissance. Especially important for the future was the burial of Charlemagne in the royal chapel in 814.

With the collapse of the Carolingian empire in the late ninth century, Aachen ceased to be a royal residence and lost its importance. As a result of the partitions of the empire arranged between 843 and 870 to provide kingdoms for various members of the Carolingian family, the city became a royal outpost on the extreme western fringe of the kingdom of the East Franks in the duchy of Lotharingia (Lorraine). It was rescued from obscurity by Otto I, whose family had replaced the Carolingians as rulers of Germany in 919. In 936 Otto decided to hold his coronation in the royal chapel, an action intended to link his dynasty with the fame and accomplishments of Charlemagne. From then until 1531 almost every Holy Roman emperor was crowned at Aachen, giving it a powerful symbolic role in the history of medieval German monarchy.

Several king-emperors took special steps to exalt the memory of Charlemagne. After exhuming and reburying his remains in a splendid sarcophagus, Otto III chose the royal chapel as his own burial place. Frederick I Barbarossa arranged to have Charlemagne canonized in 1165; the fame of the new saint, along with many relics linked to his memory, began to attract numerous pilgrims. The monarchs favored Aachen's churches and monasteries with rich endowments, extended privileges to its residents, and protected it against the efforts of local princes to absorb it into their principalities. The interest of German rulers in Aachen extended beyond its symbolic value in linking monarchy to the glorious memory of the Carolingians. From Carolingian times on Aachen lay at the center of important royal estates, which the German monarchs took an active interest in exploiting, acting through royal officials who exercised considerable direct authority over the town's inhabitants. In short, during much of the Middle Ages Aachen enjoyed special status as an imperial city.

In the later Middle Ages the citizens of Aachen played an increasingly important role in the direction of civic affairs. A small community of merchants and artisans had already developed in Charlemagne's time. It grew slowly in succeeding centuries, partly because of imperial favors but more importantly because of Aachen's involvement in the expanding trade between the Low Countries and the Rhine Valley. The growing influence of the merchant-artisan group was recognized in 1166 when Frederick I granted the city an important charter giving personal freedom to its citizens and constituting them as a legal corporation entitled to certain rights of self-government. Later concessions from the monarchs expanded their control over taxation, judicial affairs, economic regulation, and relationships with local princes. A town government, featuring a council and elected burgomasters, developed in the thirteenth century.

Growing commerce and increasing control over the agricultural production of the surrounding countryside brought considerable prosperity to Aachen in the fourteenth and fifteenth centuries and made possible important building projects: a major enlargement of the city walls (1326), the replacement of the old Carolingian residence hall with an impressive city hall (1334–1349), and the addition of a Gothic choir to Charlemagne's chapel (1355–1414). Urban life was sometimes disturbed by conflicts between rich merchants, who controlled the city council, and the increasingly exploited craftsmen acting through their guilds. Despite these tensions, Aachen enjoyed its most affluent days as an imperial city. As the Middle Ages ended perhaps the most ominous threat was the growing power of local princes, anxious to gain independence from the weakening imperial government and to enlarge their territorial holdings by absorbing locations that had long enjoyed imperial protection and favors.

BIBLIOGRAPHY

Karl Faymonville, *Die Kunstdenkmäler der Stadt Aachen,* 2 vols. (1916–1922); Dietmar Flach, *Untersuchungen zur Verfassung und Verwaltung des Aachener Reichsgutes von der Karolingerzeit bis zur Mitte des 14. Jahrhunderts* (1976); Josef Fleckenstein, *Die Hofkapelle der deutschen Könige,* 2 vols. (1959–1966); Robert Folz, *Le souvenir et la légende de Charlemagne dans l'Empire germanique médiéval* (1950); H. Hoeffler, "Die Entwicklung der kommunalen Verfassung und Verwaltung der Stadt Aachen bis zum Jahre 1450," in *Zeitschrift des Aachener Geschichtsverein,* **23** (1901); Walter Kaemmerer, *Geschichtliches Aachen,* 2nd ed. (1957); Aloys Schulte, *Die Kaiser- und Königskrönnungen zu Aachen, 813–1531* (1965); Richard E. Sullivan, *Aix-la-Chapelle in the Age of Charlemagne* (1963).

RICHARD E. SULLIVAN

AACHEN, PALACE CHAPEL. Charlemagne's palace chapel, situated on the southern edge of the palatine complex at Aachen, is the major Carolingian building still standing. Construction on the chapel began probably in the early 790's, and by 799 it was well on its way to completion. On its consecration, allegedly in 805 by Pope Leo III, or earlier perhaps, the chapel was dedicated to Christ and the Virgin. Charlemagne was buried there in 814. The chapel was once the center of a larger ceremonial program, now known only in plan, which included chapel annexes to the north and south, and an atrium to the west. Although later additions crowd around and over it, the chapel itself remains, from a structural viewpoint, virtually unchanged.

The chapel plan condenses central and axial space. A sixteen-sided exterior mass encloses an octagonal shaft of space that constitutes the chapel's core. Secondary spaces of the ambulatory and gallery turn round the periphery of the octagon. The axis across the central space is fixed at the east side by a rectangular sanctuary (replaced in the fourteenth century by the present Gothic choir), and at the entrance side by a westwerk of identical depth. The emperor's throne was placed in the gallery, or tribune, of the westwerk, on axis with the altars in the two-story sanctuary.

The limits of interior space are clearly stated in structural terms. The central core is marked off at points of the octagon plan by heavy piers, by flat elevation walls of arcades and cornices at ground level, and by column screens inserted into the gallery openings above. It is covered by an eight-sided cloister vault and lighted directly by windows in the drum from which the vault springs. The lower spaces outside the core are vaulted by a rigorously

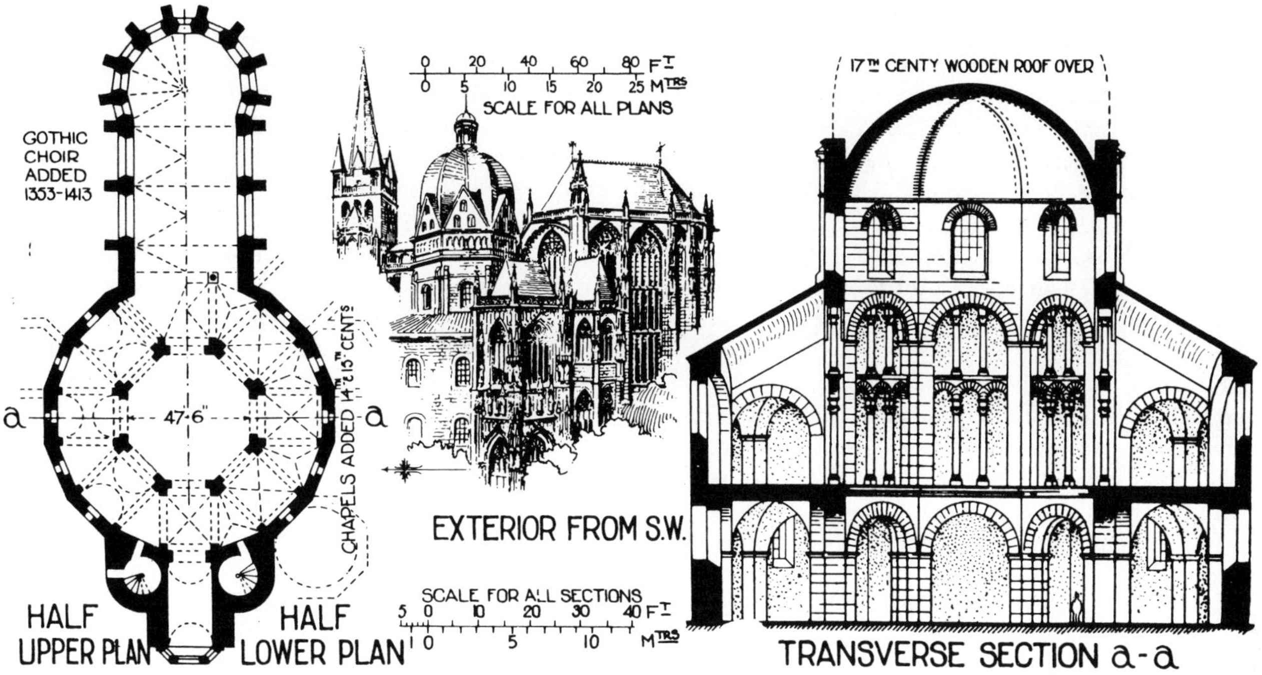

Palace Chapel. Aachen. SIR BANISTER FLETCHER'S A HISTORY OF ARCHITECTURE

geometric system of alternating square and triangular compartments: the ambulatory is covered by an annular groin vault, and the gallery by barrel-vaulted cells on diaphragm arches. The axes of the gallery vaults point to the center of the plan. They rise in height from outside in and brace the drum of the central octagon. A rich array of surfaces and furnishings originally created an impression of Byzantine magnificence. Little of this survives today, but some idea of the wealth of furnishings may be gathered from Angilbert's and Hariulf's accounts of the imperial church of St. Riquier.

The palace chapel is an eminently Byzantine architectural type, and San Vitale at Ravenna has long been the most frequently proposed model. But such derivation from a model does not imply that the chapel is an exact copy. This holds, as well, for the many progeny that the Aachen chapel itself inspired after the year 800. Charlemagne's chapel is a northern building both from the standpoint of construction, as a freestone building of immense structural strength, and from that of design, as an assemblage of separate surfaces and spatial units. It has recently been demonstrated that its schematic design is based on a rule of modular prime relationships. The palace chapel is also an architectural symbol of Charlemagne's imperium. Its pride of place was understood by his successors, for whom the chapel continued to be the focal point of German kingship.

BIBLIOGRAPHY

Charlemagne, Council of Europe exhibition catalogue (1965); Walter Horn and Ernest Born, *The Plan of St. Gall*, I (1979), 104–111; Leo Hugot, "Die Pfalz Karls des Grossen in Aachen," in Wolfgang Braunfels, ed., *Karl der Grosse*, III (1965–1967), 534–572; W. Eugene Kleinbauer, "Charlemagne's Palace Chapel at Aachen and Its Copies," in *Gesta*, **4** (1965), 2–11; and Felix Kreusch, "Kirche, Atrium und Portikus der Aachener Pfalz," in Braunfels, ed., 463–533.

PETER HUENINK

ABACUS. See **Mathematics.**

ABASGIA. See **Georgia.**

ᶜABBĀS IBN ᶜABD AL-MUṬṬALIB IBN HĀSHIM, AL-(*ca.* 567–*ca.* 653), merchant in the Meccan tribe of Kuraysh, paternal uncle of the prophet

Muḥammad, and eponymous ancestor of the Abbasid dynasty. He is said to have traded with the Yemen in aromatics, which he then sold to pilgrims to Mecca. He appears to have been close to his nephews Nawfal ibn al-Ḥārith ibn ᶜAbd al-Muṭṭalib and Rabīᶜa ibn al-Ḥārith, who may have been his commercial and financial partners. Though never the formal chief of the clan of Hāshim (a position held successively by his half brothers al-Zubayr, Abū Ṭālib, and Abū Lahab), al-ᶜAbbās was nonetheless an influential member of the clan, presumably because he was financially better off than many others.

His relative wealth seems to have enabled him to purchase from Abū Ṭālib the *siqāya*, the right to distribute water to the pilgrims to Mecca's sacred enclave from the well of Zamzam, although some claim that he inherited this cultic office directly from his father. Some accounts state that he controlled the *rifāda*, the distribution of food to pilgrims (lucrative because it included the right to tax the Ḳuraysh in order to purchase the food), but others put this function in the hands of his nephew Nawfal.

Al-ᶜAbbās' relations with the Prophet and his attitude toward early Islam are very difficult to discern clearly. Many of the historical accounts of his life were set down in writing under the first caliphs of the Abbasid dynasty (749–1258), who naturally had a vested interest in demonstrating that their ancestor al-ᶜAbbās was an early and pious follower of Muḥammad, and in effacing any accounts that suggested otherwise. On the other hand, after the accession of the Abbasids, al-ᶜAbbās also became the target of an intense counterpolemic generated by the Abbasids' main rivals for political legitimacy, the descendants of ᶜAlī ibn Abī Ṭālib, and their supporters, the Shīᶜa. The majority of the accounts about al-ᶜAbbās thus tell us more about the Abbasid-Shiite polemic of the eighth and ninth centuries than they do about the life of al-ᶜAbbās himself.

It does not appear, however, that al-ᶜAbbās was an early adherent of Islam. He participated on the Meccan side at the battle of Badr (624), was taken prisoner by the Muslims, and ransomed himself; traditions to the effect that he (and indeed the whole clan of Hāshim) went to battle hesitantly may be efforts to erase the stigma of this episode. Accounts claiming that he gave quiet protection to Muḥammad early in the latter's prophetic career, or that he converted secretly at an early date, seem likewise to be apologetic efforts to offset traditions placing his conversion only relatively late in Muḥammad's life, at the battle of the Trench (627) or after the conquest of Khaibar (628). Indeed, he may well figure among those prominent Meccans who joined Muḥammad in the year or so after the Treaty of al-Ḥudaybiya (628), during which time the political tide in western Arabia was turning rapidly in Muḥammad's favor.

Muḥammad acknowledged al-ᶜAbbās' importance and helped secure his allegiance by recognizing his right to the *siqāya* and by awarding him 200 camel loads of dates from Khaibar per annum upon his conversion to Islam. He made al-ᶜAbbās and his nephew Nawfal "foster brothers" and assigned them tracts of land adjacent to the mosque in Medina, where they took up residence. Al-ᶜAbbās is said to have participated in the Muslims' conquests of Mecca in 630 (where he may have helped persuade some of the defenders to submit), Ḥunayn, Al-Ṭā'if, and Tabūk.

After Muḥammad's death (632) his successors continued to grant al-ᶜAbbās recognition as a key elder member of the Prophet's clan of Hāshim. A dispute between al-ᶜAbbās and the second caliph, ᶜUmar, over al-ᶜAbbās' house, which the caliph wanted to purchase in order to expand the mosque, was resolved amicably when al-ᶜAbbās donated it; ᶜUmar eventually awarded al-ᶜAbbās a very high stipend—second only to those received by the Prophet's widows—when he set up the *dīwān* (stipend register) to distribute the booty and tax receipts gathered from the conquests in Syria and Iraq.

In general, however, al-ᶜAbbās is not mentioned often during the conquest period. Certain accounts suggest that he went to Syria with the Muslim high command in his final years, but it seems more likely that, being too old to undertake the rigors of a military or administrative post, he spent most of his last years in Medina as an influential and informal adviser to the first caliphs.

BIBLIOGRAPHY

Ibn Hishām, *Sīra* (Alfred Guillaume, tr., *The Life of Muhammad* [1955]), index; al-Wāqidī, *Kitāb al-maghāzī* (1966), index; al-Ṭabarī, *Annales* (1879–1901), index; Ibn Saᶜd, *Ṭabaqāt*, IVA (1906), 1–22; Ibn Ḥajar al-ᶜAsqalānī, *al-Iṣāba fī tamyīz al-ṣaḥāba*, s.n.; Theodor Nöldeke, "Zur tendenziösen Gestaltung der Urgeschichte des Islāms," in *Zeitschrift der deutschen morgenländischen Gesellschaft* 52 (1898).

FRED M. DONNER

[See also **Abbasids; ᶜAbd al-Muṭṭalib; Badr; Hāshim; al-Ḥudaybiya.**]

ABBASID ART AND ARCHITECTURE

ABBASID ART AND ARCHITECTURE, falls into three phases.

The first, 750–836, was characterized by continuity with the preceding Umayyad period. The most important monument was the capital city of Baghdad (Madinat al-Salam), the defensive walls of which followed a circular plan, with four main gates. The caliphal palace and the Great Mosque were located in the center. These monuments are known entirely through detailed descriptions in Arabic texts. Other monuments that have been convincingly attributed to this phase include a stone miḥrab (prayer niche), now in the Iraq Museum, and four panels from a wooden minbar (pulpit), in the Metropolitan Museum of Art, New York. The carving, in both stone and wood, is noteworthy for its three-dimensional, organic quality, characteristic also of Umayyad sculpture.

The second phase, 836–883, is considered the "classical" period of Islamic art, not only reflecting continuity with earlier periods but also establishing the pattern for artistic development throughout the Islamic world for some time to come. It spanned the brief interval in which the city of Samarra supplanted Baghdad as the Abbasid capital.

Stucco panel in beveled style. Samarra, ninth century. IRAQ MUSEUM, BAGHDAD

The structures excavated at Samarra include two congregational mosques, two caliphal palaces, and many private houses. Special mention is owing to the Great Mosque (848–852), with its detached spiral minaret, and to the palaces, which were built on the same triple-tract plan that had characterized late Umayyad palaces. The palace known as al-Jawsaq al-Khāqānī (begun in 836) yielded a number of wall paintings. The characteristic features of the human figures that constitute the "Samarra figure style" had already appeared under the Umayyads: disproportionately large heads with round chins and staring eyes, the pupils as if suspended from the upper lids; scalloped hairlines; locks curling before the ears; hieratic postures; and tiny feet. The impact of this style can be observed in the approximately contemporary wall paintings from Nishapur in Iran, in the ceramics of Fatimid Egypt, in twelfth-century wall and ceiling paintings from Cairo and Palermo, and in manuscript miniatures from Iran and Spain.

Carved stucco decoration was particularly prominent at Samarra ranging from fairly naturalistic plant forms reminiscent of the Umayyad period to the "beveled" style, in which curvilinear forms interlock so that it is impossible to distinguish figure from ground. The latter was subsequently adopted for media as disparate as wood, ceramics, rock crystal, and glass throughout the Islamic world. In addition, the ceramics of the Samarra phase reflect particular inventiveness. Beside imitations of Tang Chinese wares, designs in cobalt blue on white glaze and in metallic luster stand out. Both the latter show close ties with much earlier Nabatean painted pottery, particularly in the famous "peacock's eye" pattern so characteristic of Abbasid lusterware. The appeal of the luster technique was so great that an Iraqi craftsman was sent to make luster tiles for the Great Mosque of Qayrawān in Tunisia (862–863). Imitations of lusterware were produced in northeastern Iran.

The impact of the Samarra court styles can be measured not only by their longevity and geographical scope but also by their acceptance in segments of society outside the court. A series of wine bottles painted with "trademarks" in the Samarra figure style were made at nearby Christian monasteries, thus by craftsmen outside court circles. Furthermore, designs related to those on luster ceramics and Koran illumination occur in a Jewish manuscript illumination at Tiberias in 895.

ABBASIDS

Miḥrab (prayer niche), *ca.* 800. IRAQ MUSEUM, BAGHDAD

The third phase of Abbasid art, 883–1055, is represented by few surviving monuments. Most prominent are the northern and southern gates of the city of Amid (now Diyarbakir, Turkey) in northern Mesopotamia, with their carved inscriptions and animal reliefs, produced under the patronage of the caliph al-Muqtadir in 909–910 and reflecting designs current in the capital at about the same time.

Al-Muqtadir also issued two splendid silver medallions of a type introduced by al-Mutawakkil in the ninth century. Such medallions continued to be struck in gold or silver; the last inscribed example was issued by the caliph al-Qa'im between 1038 and 1063.

Although the Abbasid caliphate lasted until 1258, most works of art and architecture produced after 945 are designated by the names of the princely families that held secular power in various parts of the empire (for example, Buyids, Artuqids, Zankids, Seljuks, Ayyubids). Only from the reign of the caliph al-Nāṣir li-Din Allah (1180–1225), when the caliphate enjoyed a resurgence of power, has evidence of Abbasid artistic patronage survived, most notably the Talisman Gate at Baghdad, now destroyed.

BIBLIOGRAPHY

J. Lassner, *The Topography of Baghdad in the Early Middle Ages* (1970); K. A. C. Creswell, *Early Muslim Architecture*, II (1940), 35–36, chaps. IX, XI, XIII; M. S. Dimand, "Studies in Islamic Ornament, I. Some Aspects of Omaiyad and Early ᶜAbbāsid Ornament," in *Ars Islamica*, **4** (1937), 293–337, esp. figs. 1–3; *Die Ausgrabung von Samarra*, I–VI (Berlin, 1923–1948); E. J. Grube, *The Classical Style in Islamic Painting* (1968), 11–13; Ettinghausen, "The 'Beveled Style' in the Post-Samarran Period," in G. C. Miles, ed., *Archaeologica Orientalia in Memoriam Ernst Herzfeld* (1952), 72–83; A. Lane, *Early Islamic Pottery* (1947), chaps. 3–5; E. Kühnel, "Die ᶜabbāsidischen Lüsterfayencen," in *Ars Islamica*, **1** (1934), 149–159; D. S. Rice, "Deacon or Drink: Some Paintings from Samarra Re-examined," in *Arabica*, 5 (1958), 15–33; J. Walker, "A Unique Medal of the Seljuk Tughrilbeg," in H. Ingholt, ed., *Centennial Publication of the American Numismatic Society* (1958), 691–695.

ESTELLE WHELAN

ABBASIDS, the second Islamic dynasty of caliphs, which ruled from 750 to 1258. At the zenith of their power the Abbasids governed domains that extended from central Asia to North Africa. The dynasty took its name from al-ᶜAbbās ibn ᶜAbd al-Muṭṭalib, a member of the clan of Hāshim and the paternal uncle of the prophet Muḥammad. The Abbasid branch of the Banū Hāshim does not seem to have played a very prominent role in the political affairs of the early Islamic state. No member of the family was seriously considered for supreme rule during the

ABBASIDS

early caliphate, and when the Umayyads seized control from the Banū Hāshim and established the first dynasty of caliphs, the Abbasid response was muted. It was left for their kinsmen, the Alids, to take up the challenge against the usurpative regime in power.

One of the Alid pretenders, a certain Abū Hāshim ibn Muḥammad ibn al-Ḥanafiyyah, was about to die without any surviving male offspring. He was apparently unwilling to turn over the sacred authority that he held to other members of his own family, and instead transferred this authority, together with his revolutionary cadres, called the Hāshimiyya, to his Abbasid kinsman Muḥammad ibn ^{c}Ali ibn ^{c}Abd Allāh ibn al-^{c}Abbās around 716. The latter organized a clandestine revolutionary movement with centers in Iraq and Khorāsān.

This movement was but one of several revolutionary groups that sought the overthrow of the Umayyads. It ultimately succeeded where others had failed, because the Abbasid leadership preferred to keep a low profile. The name of the hidden Abbasid leader, or imam, was known to but a few trusted operatives. Moreover, the Hāshimiyya eschewed open revolt, preferring instead to wait for a propitious moment when the proper combination of forces could be assembled to bear against the armies of the Umayyads. This policy created tensions within the movement, for there were those who desired to promote a more activist stand. In the end, the more guarded approach to revolution won out. It was not until 747 that the Abbasids were prepared to act decisively. The internal breakdown of order in the Umayyad state, and more particularly the outbreak of tribal warfare in Khorāsān, produced the necessary preconditions for an open revolt.

The Abbasid client Abū Muslim, who had served the family in Khorāsān, co-opted the disaffected local Iranian populace, although it is clear that the major fighting units of the Abbasid army were Arab tribesmen and that the political and military leadership was drawn largely from the old Arab settlers in Khorāsān. To what extent the coalition of forces raised by Abū Muslim was guided by ideological concerns and to what extent their allegiance was determined by economic self-interest cannot be determined with certainty. In any event the Abbasid armies, displaying the black banners of revolution, moved triumphantly from Khorāsān to Iraq, and then into Syria, the heartland of the Umayyad regime. After several bitterly fought engagements, the Umayyad army was broken and the dynasty was subsequently ended. The entire ruling family (with one exception) was put to death in a series of executions, and the bodies of their forebears were exhumed.

The Abbasids emerged from the conflict with almost their entire revolutionary apparatus intact. As their army displaced the Umayyads in region after region, the revolutionary cadres became an acting government according to a plan originally conceived during the phase of clandestine operations. Since the Abbasid family was enjoined to remain in the background, inordinate power thereby accrued to two particular agents, Abū Muslim in Khorāsān and Abū Salama, the director of revolutionary operations in Iraq. The discourteous treatment meted out by Abū Salama to the Abbasid leadership, which had not yet emerged from hiding, and the suspicion that his ties to the Abbasid cause were not total and hence suspect, alerted the Abbasids to seek action. Once he was formally invested with power, Abu 'l-^{c}Abbās, the first caliph of the new line, sought to remove certain revolutionaries and to replace them with various relatives, who along with Abu 'l-^{c}Abbās, now came out into the open. Abū Salama was assassinated along with several others. Abū Muslim was to be killed somewhat later.

With the death of Abu 'l-^{c}Abbās in 754, the Abbasid house was plunged into civil conflict. The two contenders for the caliphate were the nondescript elder brother and heir-apparent Abū Ja^{c}far al-Manṣūr, and his paternal uncle ^{c}Abd Allāh ibn Alī, the conqueror of Syria and "extirpator" of the Umayyad line. Objective realities seemed to predict a victory for the uncle over Abū Ja^{c}far, who was a last-minute choice for the caliphate. ^{c}Abd Allāh ibn Alī, however, miscalculated and sought to rely on the old tribal army of the Umayyads that had gone over to the Abbasids following the collapse of the old regime. He turned against the Khorāsān army under his command, in effect forcing them into his adversaries' camp. Rallying behind Abū Muslim, who had not yet been eliminated, the Khorāsānis brought Abū Ja^{c}far to power, and became the prop upon which his regime came to rest. Abū Muslim, who now controlled the army and the treasuries to support it, had emerged as both the savior of the new regime and the greatest potential threat to it. After some difficult diplomatic maneuvering, Abū Ja^{c}far had his former ally put to death.

Following the civil conflict Abū Ja^{c}far took off on a bold path to restructure Abbasid government. The caliph's relatives, who were so prominent in the earliest years of the regime, were slowly but surely removed from positions of importance, particularly in the provincial government, lest they use some regional sinecure in an attempt to promote their own interests. The government itself was greatly expanded and staffed with a highly centralized bureaucracy very often made up of clients, or *mawālī*. With this change came a distinct decline of Arab leadership and privilege. In effect, the Abbasid caliphs beginning with Abū Ja^cfar preferred to conduct the business of government through agents tied exclusively to themselves rather than to rely on persons with well-established affiliations to tribal and other political units of importance.

The clients at court and within the imperial bureaucracy certainly wielded considerable influence, but the substantive power of the regime continued to reside in its military forces. It was, therefore, only a question of time before the caliphs also applied the principles of clientage to that most central of institutions. The free army could not be manipulated as an entity, but it was possible to establish personal ties with important elements of the military establishment. This was accomplished by dispensing patronage in a manner beneficial to both subject and sovereign. Within two decades, a loose coalition of tribal forces from Khorāsān was transformed into a well-disciplined professional army. By planting a Khorāsāni force in the new Abbasid capitals in Iraq, principally at Baghdad, the Abbasids were able to instill an esprit de corps in military contingents previously wracked by tribal dissensions. The Abbasid army found cohesiveness in unfamiliar surroundings by stressing the common geographical affiliations of the past.

The Umayyad ruling institution, which was predicated on the special privilege of a relatively small Arab aristocracy, soon gave way to a polity that was more broadly defined. A universal outlook displaced the narrow tribalism that hindered the previous dynasty and helped bring about its downfall. The displacement of anarchic tribal sentiments allowed for the creation of a highly centralized authority. The governmental structures created by al-Manṣūr reflected the incredible complexity and breadth of a great imperial regime. Rank, and the privileges of rank, were clearly defined in a highly elaborate and carefully encoded protocol.

The geographical epicenter of Abbasid authority was al-Manṣūr's great capital at Baghdad, an agglomeration of urban settlements that dwarfed anything that had been erected previously in the Near East. This "navel of the universe" contained the magnificent Round City, an administrative complex that featured the caliph's palace, the mosque, the government bureaus, and the residences of various public officials. According to the original conception, the civilian populace was generally denied access to the Round City, and the innermost area, containing the residence of the caliph, could be approached only through an elaborate series of gateways protected by an imperial guard, which was used as well for ceremonial purposes. In every respect, the Round City was the metaphor for Abbasid rule. Here was the caliph encased within walls of monumental architecture and surrounded with a highly centralized bureaucracy of staggering dimensions. He was thus situated in the center of a round structure, equidistant from the agencies of government, which were in turn centered within a wider urban setting that was at the center of a province (Iraq), which bisected the domains of the Abbasid state.

The creation of an Abbasid imperial style stemmed from a keen awareness of the desirability of integrating image and function in conducting the affairs of government. Some see this as a residual influence of Iranian origins. At the extreme, such views lead to the picture of an Abbasid state that was essentially a new Iranian empire, albeit one dressed in the formal attire of Persianized Islam. These attributions seem at best vague, and at worst irrelevant. With or without a Persian past, the Abbasid ruling institution had to be significantly enlarged and increasingly centralized. The Abbasid imperial style may therefore be seen as resulting from the internal dynamics of Abbasid rule.

The early Abbasid caliphs paid careful attention to the ideological foundations of their rule and generally sought to imbue their office and their government with a religious significance that had not been stressed under the Umayyads. It has been maintained that the Abbasids generally championed orthodoxy and conformity in order to weld a cosmopolitan empire into a unified polity based on a common faith and a common way of life. Orthodox thinkers were thus wooed, and the religious establishment generally received the benefit of the caliphs' favor. Conversely, movements deemed heretical were fully persecuted. The occasional juxtaposition of heretical groups and social protest would seem to indicate that religion and politics could not be considered separate concerns even when extremist views were formulated.

But the real threat to Abbasid rule was their own

ABBASIDS

kinsmen. The Alids had never reconciled themselves to the Abbasid dynasty and rejected the claim of Abbasid legitimacy through the dying Alid Abū Hāshim. They maintained that the sacred authority was transferred through the Fatimid line of their family, and they emphasized their political activism vis-à-vis the Umayyads. They thus called attention to dramatic cases of martyrdom that had no parallel in the house of al-ᶜAbbās. The high political profile of the Fatimids during the years of Umayyad rule had a powerful emotional appeal among the general populace, particularly in Iraq. In order to counter these arguments, the Abbasid caliphs, in particular Abū Jaᶜfar al-Manṣūr, encouraged the creation of a revisionist history that established them with proper credentials to rule. Much of this historiography that was assembled under official patronage has become part of the historical record. Nevertheless, the sentiment on behalf of the Alids would not dissipate. Fortunately for the Abbasids, the Alids more often than not accommodated themselves to the ruling dynasty; but, on occasion, various Alid pretenders encouraged followers to take up arms on their behalf. These efforts invariably ended in failure. From the outset, the Abbasid regime was also beset by various provincial uprisings about which little is known. In any case, such local revolts do not seem to have seriously threatened the rule emanating from Baghdad.

Although the successors of al-Manṣūr confidently built on the foundations that he had established, the internal contradictions of the Abbasid ruling institution led to a period of incipient decline. The continuous loyalty of the military was not a foregone conclusion. Unlike clients in government service, the army commanders, backed by their professional contingents, had the means to effect significant action. The imperial army had a vested interest in the affairs of the Abbasid state and was particularly sensitive to economic and political stresses. Difficulties that could not be resolved in localized court intrigues often required the direct intervention of the army, thereby adding a new and volatile dimension to the existing structure of Abbasid society.

The highly personalized system of transferring power within the ruling family (an outgrowth perhaps of the revolutionary experience) served to exacerbate existing tensions. The internal cohesion of the Mansurid family began to crack with the death of the third caliph, al-Mahdī, in 785, as his sons Hārūn al-Rashīd and Mūsā al-Hādī were pitted against each other by ambitious court figures. Attached as they were to a particular prince of the ruling line, many leading clients acted as provocateurs in an effort to enhance the positions of their patrons and thereby their own fortunes. Shadow governments were created to serve young Abbasid princes who were considered for rule, and the once-reliable army of al-Manṣūr's creation became a vested interest group available to the highest bidder with the prerequisite credentials to rule.

It would appear that al-Rashīd, who came to power when his brother and rival was murdered, was aware of the internal problems besetting the house of al-ᶜAbbās. In order to ensure that the tumultuous events surrounding his father's succession were not repeated, he laid down a rather elaborate scheme of succession. Muḥammad al-Amīn, the eldest son, was nominated as heir-apparent; he was in turn to be followed by ᶜAbd Allāh al-Maᵓmūn and a third son, who, it turned out, never became a serious contender for the caliphate.

The unique feature of the plan was that each of the latter sons was given the governorship of a vast region while the caliph still lived. Al-Amīn remained at the capital in Baghdad and hence was able to secure the support of central administration. Al-Maᵓmūn more than balanced his brother's potential power, by controlling the vast territories to the east known collectively as Khorāsān. Egypt and the west were left to the third brother in the line of succession. In such fashion each brother had a power base to maintain his rightful claim should the rival brother wish to displace him from the line of succession in favor of his own progeny. It may well be that al-Rashīd also sought in this fashion to decentralize the empire, which had grown administratively cumbersome, while at the same time maintaining family control over all its domains. The caliph himself left Baghdad for the regional capital at al-Rāfiqah, although his reasons for this move are not clear.

The reign of Hārūn al-Rashīd is generally regarded as the zenith of Abbasid glory, and yet it may be thought of as an edifice of rotting wood covered by a lustrous shellac finish. The provinces to the west, although they continued to recognize the caliph's suzerainty, became in effect local hereditary governorships, thereby setting a pattern that was to engulf the dynasty over a wide geographical area in years to come. To the east, a series of regional conflicts was a cause of concern. Moreover, the campaigns against the Byzantines, which were pursued by al-Rashīd with more vigor than his predecessors, proved inconclusive. Toward the end of his rule, al-Rashīd, already disenchanted with the politics of

ABBASIDS

Baghdad, incarcerated the entire Barmakid family, a group of distinguished civil servants who had been in the employ of the regime since the clandestine stages of the revolution. The consequences of this act are not entirely clear, but, given its unprecedented scope, it is likely to have seriously affected the daily functioning of the administrative agencies of the government.

In any event, the caliph's successor al-Amīn immediately sought to remove his brother al-Maʾmūn from the line of succession. The plan was to bring him to Baghdad, thus isolating him from his regional power base in Khorāsān. The latter vacillated, but on the advice of his client-confidants, he stood firm, thereby setting into motion a long and debilitating civil war which ended with the death of al-Amīn in 813.

The war between the brothers has been viewed as a conflict between the Persians of Khorāsān and the Arabs of Iraq. Such an interpretation is not supported by the available data. The conflict, which lacked an ideological dimension, must be understood in terms of economic and political considerations. At the heart of the issue were the benefits that were derived from caliphal patronage: which army and which bureaucracy was to be favored by the brother who ultimately became the uncontested *amir al-umarāʾ* (Commander of the Faithful). The war only served to underscore a basic weakness of the Abbasid ruling institution. The army would not betray the caliph on behalf of a non-Muslim enemy, but its primary responsibility was the preservation of order within the boundaries of Islam. Here the issues of loyalty and authority could become exceedingly complex, particularly when the caliphate was contested by two parties that carried bona fide credentials to rule. In such circumstances, the military came to be governed by strong attitudes of self-interest. Since periods of conflict often resulted in augmented service pay, the agency of government whose primary charge it was to preserve public order had developed a vested interest in continuing chaos.

The emergence of al-Maʾmūn's caliphate marked the beginning of a new era in the history of the Abbasid state. Political life would never be as it was in the past. A fine line had been crossed, pointing to the inherent weakness of the caliph and the ruling institution that served him. The army, which formed the backbone of the Abbasid military, was divided into rival factions. The Baghdad regiments, defeated but not crushed, retained the capacity to undermine the foundations of Abbasid rule. As a result al-Maʾmūn did not return to Baghdad until six years after his accession to the caliphate, and even then it cannot be said that Baghdad became his permanent capital. It was in Khorāsān that the caliph dispensed his favor upon his loyal followers. Following their success in battle, the military commanders were given provincial governorships which in time became hereditary fiefdoms. Although they recognized the suzerainty of the caliph, they eventually limited his effective authority. In the course of time they would siphon off the manpower necessary to field the Abbasid armies, and limit the revenues available to the central administration by withholding taxes.

But the effects of al-Maʾmūn's policies would not be felt for some time. He was a vigorous ruler who still commanded respect, as did his brother and successor al-Muʿtaṣim. An innovation begun by the former and more fully implemented by the latter nevertheless created an institution that was to shake the foundations of the regime. The conduct of the war had taught the Abbasid sovereigns a lesson about the reliability of the free armies. The notion of creating a client army was understandably extremely attractive. This led ultimately to the introduction of Turkish slave regiments. Although the further subjugation of Transoxiana under al-Maʾmūn had brought significant numbers of Turkish slaves to the center of the Islamic empire, it was left to al-Muʿtaṣim to form them into elite fighting units.

It should be made clear that the Turks were not recruited exclusively to guard the caliph but were brought in relatively large units to join the fighting commands. As such they did not replace, but supplemented, the contingents of the regular army. The attractive features of these units were their absolute ties to the caliph as a result of their servile status and their well-known prowess, particularly as cavalry. The bonds between the Turks and the caliph superseded all previous ties of loyalty, which were torn asunder when the Turks entered a servile status. The slave army, beginning with al-Muʿtaṣim, became a central factor in the formation of an Islamic military society.

Despite the caliph's various attempts at establishing the personal loyalty of the Turks, it was perhaps inevitable that the Turkish commanders would come to define their loyalty to the regime in terms of self-interest, and that the slave army of the caliphs would intervene directly in the affairs of the state, just as the free Khorāsānis had done before them. The personal ties between the caliph and his military clients were lessened by the general malaise within the ruling society. The successors of al-Muᶜtaṣim were not his equals, but, beyond that, the empire itself had undergone serious dislocation.

Beset by economic difficulties, al-Muᶜtaṣim and his successors drained the imperial treasuries, building a second massive administrative center at Samarra. The new capital, which rivaled Baghdad in size and splendor, was a conceptual monstrosity. Each major construction scheme begat its successor and none proved adequate to the caliph's needs. The city was an economic anachronism which could not sustain itself. Since the allegiance of an army, professional or otherwise, is bought with substantial monies, the declining state revenues only forced the army to intervene still further in affairs normally falling to the civilian administration. As a result, the Turkish generals went so far as to exercise veto power on the succession and to eliminate caliphs not to their liking. Internal bickering among the military aggravated further the already chaotic situation.

The caliph still retained the prestige of his office; it was inconceivable that the universe could exist without an Abbasid caliph. The military would never go so far as to provoke public sentiment by establishing one of their own as Commander of the Faithful, even if they were so inclined. The caliph, hitherto the center of Abbasid rule, was reduced to one of three elements in the power structure, the others being the bureaucracy and the military. The caliphate nevertheless retained a certain vitality, and when conditions allowed room for political maneuver, the Commander of the Faithful managed to reassert his position—for example, the regent al-Muwaffaq and the caliphs al-Muᵓtaḍid and al-Muktafī. But the process that began with the great civil war was degenerative; the caliphate never fully recovered, and the military dimension in the affairs of government became awesome.

In the first half of the tenth century, the leading military figure assumed the title *amīr al-umarāᵓ* and eventually took on the responsibility for civil authority. His name was also mentioned in public prayer along with that of the caliph, although the de jure status of the sovereign was never questioned. Concurrent with the decline of caliphal fortunes, the areas actually controlled by the central administration shrank to parts of Iraq and Syria. The power vacuum created by the Abbasid retrenchment served to stimulate militant Alid partisans. The Abbasid state was thus buffeted by a series of insurrections which occasionally led to the creation of independent ministates. In 945 Baghdad itself was captured by the Buyid prince Muᶜizz al-Dawla. Although the Buyids were Alids they recognized the Abbasid caliph as their sovereign. Nevertheless, temporal rule was effectively taken out of the caliph's hands. An elaborate protocol protected the caliph's theoretical status, but in every other respect, the Buyids asserted themselves as masters of Iraq. The Buyids were replaced in 1055 by the Seljuks who were Sunnis, but this had little bearing on the status of the Abbasid caliph. From then until the end of the dynasty, the caliph never was able to fully reestablish the preeminence of his office.

To the west, Egypt came under the control of a Fatimid dynasty in 969. The militant Alids soon extended their power into Syria and the Arabian peninsula. The emergence of the Fatimids was quite a different threat from that of the Buyid hegemony at Baghdad, and may indeed explain why the Buyids, although themselves Alids, never tampered with the caliph's status. For the first time, an independent dynasty bearing legitimate claims to rule was created. The Fatimids did not recognize even the titular authority of the Abbasids. To the contrary, they actively sought to replace them, and to this purpose they organized a powerful and widespread revolutionary apparatus to subvert the Abbasid state from within, while at the same time the Fatimid armies challenged the Abbasid supporters in the field of combat.

After the breakup of the Buyid empire, the Fatimid ruler was briefly recognized in Baghdad, but the appearance of the Sunni Seljuk Ṭughrīl Bak restored Abbasid sovereignty. This did not mean, however, a resurgence of caliphal authority. The Seljuk leader further institutionalized the civil authority that had accrued to the military leadership by creating the office of sultan. The rise of the military leadership to power, a process that had become irreversible in the tenth century, led to a new social and fiscal order, which was quasi-feudal. One result of this development was the weakening of the government bureaucracy; a second was the breakdown of agriculture in Iraq and severe fiscal crises. In Baghdad, there were frequent outbreaks of civil strife among diverse urban groups. The city itself shrank to a hollow shell of its former self. Where once there were contiguous areas of occupation within the legal boundaries of the city, there were now barren fields separating truncated neighborhoods that took on the characteristic features of distinct settlements.

The tensions felt within contemporary society

during the Abbasid decline were the result of far-reaching changes brought about by social and economic dislocation. In such times discontent was expressed in religio-political terms. This served the purpose of a religious establishment that was anxious to promote its influence, and was now encouraged to do so by the military rulers, whose power, although absolute, was never covered with the symbolic trappings of authority that accrued to the caliph. The support of the religious establishment was politically desirable. For their cooperation with the temporal authorities, religious functionaries were granted the license to supervise an ever-growing network of religious institutions. The caliph, as usual, continued to enjoy the fiction of his de jure suzerainty. Indeed, when the Great Sultanate collapsed, the caliph al-Nāṣir (1180–1225) attempted to reestablish the lost authority of the caliphate and partially succeeded. His success was limited geographically to Iraq, and was only possible because the major powers were preoccupied with one another. When the Mongols conquered Persia, opening the gates to Iraq, the independence of Abbasid authority, such as it was, was destined to come to an end.

The Mongol conquest of Baghdad brought a dramatic end to the Abbasid caliphate in its native region. Unlike the past conquerors of the city, the Mongols did not favor the Abbasid caliph by paying lip service to his authority. The caliph al-Mustaᶜṣim was executed, and the house of al-ᶜAbbās at Baghdad came to an end. The sultans now appropriated for themselves the titles and prerogatives that had formerly been reserved for the Abbasid sovereigns. The fiction of Abbasid authority ended, and with it the five-hundred-year-old dynasty.

There was a resurgence of rump caliphs in Egypt beginning in 1261, but the Egyptian Abbasids were no more effective than their more recent Baghdad predecessors. The Egyptian caliphate continued until 1517, but the Abbasids ruled in name only. De facto control was in the hands of the Mamluk sultans. The caliph was essentially limited to ceremonial duties. With the Ottoman conquest of Egypt, the Abbasid caliphate was finally abolished.

BIBLIOGRAPHY

Harold Bowen, *The Life and Times of ᶜAli ibn ᶜIsa* (1928); Jacob Lassner, *The Shaping of Abbasid Rule* (1980); B. Lewis, "Abbasids," in *Encyclopedia of Islam*, 2nd ed.; Adam Mez, *The Renaissance of Islam* (1938); Farouk Omar, *The ᶜAbbāsid Caliphate, 132/750–170/786* (1969); M. A. Shaban, *The ᶜAbbāsid Revolution* (1970); and *Islamic History: A New Interpretation*, 2 vols. (1971–1976); Dominique Sourdel, *Le Vizirat ᶜAbbāside de 749 à 936*, 2 vols. (1959–1960); Julius Wellhausen, *The Arab Kingdom and Its Fall* (1927).

JACOB LASSNER

[See also **Abū Jaᶜfar Al-Manṣūr; Abū Muslim; Alids; Baghdad; Fatimids; Hārūn Al-Rashīd; Al-Mahdī; Mamluk Sultans; Muḥammad; Mongol Conquest; Ottoman Conquest; Seljuks; Sultanate; Sunnis.**]

ABBESS; ABBOT. See **Clergy.**

ABBO OF FLEURY (FLORIACENSIS) (*ca.* 945–1004) was born near Orléans. His parents handed him over as oblate to the Benedictines in the Abbey of Fleury-sur-Loire (Saint-Benoît-sur-Loire) when Wulfad was abbot; two relatives of Abbo's mother were monks and presbyters there. Abbo began his studies in Fleury's monastic school surrounded by rare books and excellent scribes. For advanced studies in theology and the sciences he went to Paris and Rheims. His most distinguished teacher was Gerbert of Aurillac, who had studied under Arab scholars in Spain.

Abbo taught in Fleury both before and after his advanced studies. Back in Fleury he also started to write. Attributed to him from this time are a *Commentary on the Calculus of Victurius,* a short treatise on astronomy, and a *computus.* Like Gerbert, Abbo was possibly aware of the existence of Aristotle's *Prior* and *Posterior Analytics,* and he wrote a *Syllogismi dialecti.* Not all of Abbo's early work has yet been found, nor has all that has been identified been published. Some of his work has been wrongly included in Bede's *dubia.* These items, however, are significant for the history of medieval science.

After Abbot Wulfad died, three abbots held office in rapid succession: Richard (died 979), Amalbert (died 985), and Oylbold (died 987 or 988). Abbo was a candidate when Oylbold was chosen. Following Oylbold's election, Abbo went to England for two years, possibly to avoid embarrassment, and certainly because Fleury had English connections: Archbishop Oswald of York and Abbot Germanus of Ramsey had been monks at Fleury, and Oswald invited Abbo to Ramsey.

Abbo taught at Ramsey for two years, acting also as consultant for Oswald, who was introducing Cluniac reforms into English monasteries. While in

England, Abbo was ordained presbyter by Oswald. As at Fleury, he continued to write. His important book at this time was *Quaestiones grammaticalae,* dealing with matters of prosody and pronunciation, and dedicated to his "dilectissimis in Christo Ángligenis fratribus." Abbo was much quoted by, and dear to, Englishmen: to Dunstan, for whom he wrote a *Vita sancti Eadmundi;* to Oswald; to Aelfric of Eynsham; and to others.

In 988, Abbo returned to France and was elected abbot of Fleury. He was a scholarly abbot, a reformer, an adviser of kings and popes, and became a canonist of sorts, defending the rights of kings against popes, of bishops against kings, of monks against bishops. He twice visited Rome for King Robert II (995, 997), bringing cases before popes John XV and Gregory V; he also appeared at synods in Saint-Denis, Saint Basle, and Mousson. In these contexts he prepared his *Apologeticus,* addressed to King Hugh and King Robert, in response to Arnulf, bishop of Orléans, and his *Collectio canonum.* In Rome, Abbo assembled an *Epitome of Popes' Lives Down to Gregory I,* and on another occasion made *Excerpts from the Fathers.* His works also include important correspondence and some poems (two in the manner of Porphyry).

Still preoccupied with reform, Abbo journeyed in 1004 to Gascony, to the Abbey of La Réole, placed under Fleury some years before when disturbances had broken out between the French and Gascons. There was trouble on this occasion too, and Abbo received a wound from which he died on 13 August, as recorded by Aimoin (Aimoinus Monachus), who accompanied him on this last journey. The circumstances of Abbo's death, and the edifying character of his life, generated a cult. His feast is celebrated in Benedictine liturgies on 13 August. His finest eulogy is by Fulbert of Chartres: "Supreme among abbots for his love of wisdom and most renowned authority in all France in divine and earthly jurisdiction."

BIBLIOGRAPHY

Abbo's works are in Jacques P. Migne, ed., *Patrologiae cursus completus, Series latina,* **139** (1880), 417–578 (incomplete). A biography is Aimoinus Monachus, "Vita Abbonis Floriaci," in J. P. Migne, **139,** 375–414. Also see Henry Bradley, "On the Text of Abbo of Fleury's *Quaestiones Grammaticalae,*" in *Proceedings of the British Academy,* **10** (1921–1923), 126–169; Patrice Cousin, *Abbon de Fleury-sur-Loire: un savant, un pasteur, un martyr à la fin du xe siècle* (1954); Augustin Fliche, *La réforme grégorienne et la reconquête chrétienne (1097–1123)* (1950); Étienne Gilson, *La philosophie au moyen âge,* 2nd ed. (1952), 227; Maximilianus Manitius, *Geschichte der lateinischen Literatur des Mittelalters,* II (1923; repr. 1976), 664–672; George Sarton, *Introduction to the History of Science,* I (1927), 671f.; André van de Vyver, "Les oeuvres inédites d'Abbon de Fleury," in *Revue bénédictine,* **47** (1935), 126–169.

LAURENCE K. SHOOK

ABBREVIATOR, an official of the papal chancery who composed the drafts and corrected the final form of apostolic letters. Although the formal title, *abbreviator litterarum apostolicarum,* may not have come into use until the fourteenth century, abbreviators were apparently already working directly for the vice-chancellor from the latter thirteenth century. Earlier the abbreviators were private employees of the papal notaries rather than of the chancery itself, and the notaries continued to hire their own abbreviators as private assistants even after some of the abbreviators had achieved an independent status in the chancery. There were also abbreviators connected with other departments of the papal curia: the datary, for example, had an *abbreviator de curia* until 1908. The rules under which the abbreviators lived, always subject to at least minor changes, were spelled out most fully in the constitution *Divina aeterni* issued by Pope Sixtus IV in 1479.

The abbreviators' task began when the petitions to which the pope or his delegate had decided to reply were distributed among them. They then drafted and signed responses, called minutes, making use of the text of the petition itself as well as chancery formularies. After the draft had been copied in its final form by a papal scriptor, or scribe, it received a first reading by an *abbreviator de prima visione* and then a more careful examination and correction by "abbreviators assisting the vice-chancellor in the dispatch of apostolic letters." One or two of these abbreviators signed the letter before it was sealed by a *bullator* and dispatched. The fees that the abbreviators received for each of their tasks were established in minute detail by Pope John XXII in 1331. If a letter had to be recopied because of an abbreviator's mistake, the recopying was done at his expense.

A limit of twenty-four abbreviators was set by

Pope Benedict XII (1334–1342), but the number kept increasing and reached seventy-two under Sixtus IV, who, after a previous attempt by Pius II in 1463 had been undone, organized the abbreviators into a college with numerous important rights and privileges. Although all the chancery abbreviators belonged to this college, there were three different classes of membership. Of the seventy-two members in 1479, the highest class in terms of competence, responsibilities, and income consisted of twelve abbreviators called presidents of the greater enclosure *(presidentes de parco maiori);* a second class included twenty-two abbreviators of the lesser enclosure *(de parco minori),* whose duties were sometimes hard to distinguish from those of the thirty-eight members of the third class called abbreviators of the first reading *(de prima visione).* According to Pope Calixtus III in 1458, no one should normally be made a member of the highest class until he had served at least three years in the third class and five years in the second. Many of the recruits had originally been scriptors, and some continued in both roles.

The college of abbreviators gradually lost its functions, and in 1908 it was definitively suppressed and its remaining duties transferred to the apostolic prothonotaries.

BIBLIOGRAPHY

Geoffrey Barraclough, "Minutes of Papal Letters (1316–1317)," in *Miscellanea archivistica Angelo Mercati* (1952), 109–127. Harry Bresslau, *Handbuch der Urkundenlehre für Deutschland und Italien,* 2nd ed., repr. I (1912, 1958), 274–275; Édouard Fournier, "Abréviateurs ou abréviateurs des lettres apostoliques," in *Dictionnaire de droit canonique,* I (1935); Peter Herde, *Beiträge zum päpstlichen Kanzlei- und Urkundenwesen im dreizehnten Jahrhundert,* 2nd ed. (1967); Michael Tangl, ed., *Die päpstlichen Kanzleiordnungen von 1200–1500* (1894, repr. 1959).

JAMES J. JOHN

ᶜABD AL-MALIK. See **Marwān, ᶜAbd al-Malik ibn.**

ᶜABD AL-MUṬṬALIB, proper name Shayba ibn Hāshim ibn ᶜAbd Manāf ibn Quṣayy (died *ca.* 578), chief of the Hāshim clan of the Meccan tribe of Ḳuraysh and paternal grandfather of the prophet Muḥammad. His father Hāshim arranged to marry a woman of the al-Najjār clan of the Khazraj tribe during a stopover in Yathrib (Medina) on his way to Syria for trade, agreeing that she might bear children only among her own people. When she became pregnant, she was accordingly returned to Yathrib, where ᶜAbd al-Muṭṭalib was born and was raised until the age of seven or eight. At this point he caught the attention of a visiting Meccan, who noted his prowess in archery and his claim to be a son of Hāshim, since deceased. Learning this, his uncle al-Muṭṭalib decided to raise the boy, especially as he seemed to be a talented youth, and took him to Mecca. Traditional accounts claim that the boy acquired the name ᶜAbd al-Muṭṭalib ("slave of al-Muṭṭalib") because people in Mecca at first thought him to be his uncle's slave. Al-Muṭṭalib served as the boy's guardian and raised him to maturity.

When the uncle died while trading in the Yemen, ᶜAbd al-Muṭṭalib succeeded him as head of the clan of Hāshim. He also inherited from his uncle the cultic offices customarily held by the descendants of ᶜAbd Manāf: the *siqāya* (distribution of water to pilgrims to Mecca) and the *rifāda* (distribution of food). These offices were lucrative, partly because they involved collection of a tax from the Ḳuraysh to purchase food. When Abraha, the Aksumite commander who had seized control of the Yemen, marched north to destroy Mecca's shrine, ᶜAbd al-Muṭṭalib lost some 200 camels to an Abyssinian raiding party and had to negotiate with Abraha himself to get them back. This suggests that he was quite prosperous at the time. In these negotiations ᶜAbd al-Muṭṭalib is portrayed as the chief of Ḳuraysh, the master of Mecca's caravans, and a paragon of traditional virtues.

It is probable, however, that ᶜAbd al-Muṭṭalib's authority did not embrace the whole of Ḳuraysh. Some accounts describe a quarrel between him and other branches of Ḳuraysh over their demands for a share in the waters of the copious well of Zamzam, which ᶜAbd al-Muṭṭalib is said to have discovered. Similarly, he seems to have been in a dispute with his uncle Nawfal ibn ᶜAbd Manāf over some property, and with another clan chief, Ḥarb ibn Umayya, for reasons that remain obscure. It may be that all these accounts, as well as others describing a dispute between ᶜAbd al-Muṭṭalib and a chief of the Thaqīf tribe over a well of which ᶜAbd al-Muṭṭalib took possession in the town of Al-Ṭā'if, are echoes of a struggle for control of the cultic office of *siqāya* among different clans of Ḳuraysh, but the record remains unclear. In any case, ᶜAbd al-Muṭṭalib concluded an alliance between the clan of Hāshim and the tribe of Khuzāᶜa, apparently to counterbalance the opposition of his uncles Nawfal and ᶜAbd Shams. In fact, ᶜAbd al-Muṭṭalib seems to have led the clan of Hāshim quite effectively through a time when the old clan relationships within the Ḳuraysh were changing, as commercial prosperity brought some clans (Umayya, Makhzūm) greatly increased wealth and influence.

The prophet Muḥammad was born to one of ᶜAbd al-Muṭṭalib's ten sons, ᶜAbdullāh, about 570, but ᶜAbdullāh died before Muḥammad's birth. Consequently the boy was raised by his mother, Āmina, and ᶜAbd al-Muṭṭalib, until his mother's death when Muḥammad was about six. Two years later ᶜAbd al-Muṭṭalib died, at an advanced age (some accounts say that he was 120 years old), bequeathing to his son al-Zubayr the cultic offices he had held. The orphaned Muḥammad was cared for thereafter by another of ᶜAbd al-Muṭṭalib's sons, Abū Ṭālib. Other sons of ᶜAbd al-Muṭṭalib, Muḥammad's uncles—notably Ḥamza, al-ᶜAbbās, and Abū Lahab—played important parts in Muḥammad's later life.

BIBLIOGRAPHY

Ibn Hishām, *Sīra* (Alfred Guillaume, tr., *The Life of Muhammad* [1955]), index; Ibn Saᶜd, *Ṭabaqāt* (partial transl. S. M. Haq and H. K. Ghazanfar (1967–1972), index; al-Ṭabarī, *Annales* (1879–1901), index; William M. Watt, *Muhammad at Mecca* (1953), index.

FRED M. DONNER

[See also **Abū Ṭalib; Hāshim; Kaaba; Mecca; Ḳuraysh.**]

ᶜABD ALLĀH IBN AL-ZUBAYR, (624–692) prominent Islamic aristocrat and rival claimant to the caliphate during the reigns of the Umayyad caliphs Yazīd I, Marwān I, and ᶜAbd al-Malik. Born in Medina shortly after the prophet Muḥammad's arrival there, he was the son of al-Zubayr ibn al-ᶜAwwām, an early convert to Islam from the ᶜAbd al-ᶜUzzā clan of Ḳuraysh, and his wife Asmāᵓ, daughter of Abū Bakr, Muḥammad's closest confidant and eventual successor. He was close to his mother's sister ᶜĀᵓisha, the Prophet's favorite wife, who, being childless, seems to have been especially fond of her nephew and went by the name "Umm ᶜAbd Allāh" (mother of ᶜAbd Allāh). His grandmother was the Prophet's paternal aunt Ṣafiyya, and he was also related to Muḥammad's first wife, Khadīja. His close family ties to Muḥammad and Abū Bakr, the political activity and influence of his father and his aunt ᶜĀᵓisha, and the great wealth accumulated by his father and passed on to him, assured him a leading position in the early Islamic aristocracy.

As a youth ᶜAbd Allāh is said to have participated with his father at the battle of Yarmuk in Syria (*ca.* 636), in campaigning in Egypt shortly thereafter, and in the offensive launched by the governor of Egypt, ᶜAbd Allāh ibn Saᶜd ibn Abī Sarḥ, against Byzantine forces in Ifrīqīyya (Tunisia) in about 647. Somewhat later he campaigned in northern Iran with the forces of Saᶜīd ibn al-ᶜĀṣ. According to traditional accounts ᶜAbd Allāh was one of several companions charged by the third caliph, ᶜUthmān, with copying and collating the vulgate of the Koran from materials available in Medina.

During the rebellion against ᶜUthmān, ᶜAbd Allāh was among those who tried unsuccessfully to defend the aged caliph. After ᶜUthmān's murder in 656, ᶜAbd Allāh joined the Meccan party (which included his father, his aunt ᶜĀᵓisha, and ᶜĀᵓisha's close kinsman Ṭalḥa ibn ᶜUbaydallāh) in opposition to ᶜAlī ibn Abī Ṭālib, who had been proclaimed caliph in Medina. With the rebellious party he went to Basra, where they had some support. He commanded the foot soldiers at the Battle of the Camel (656) against ᶜAlī's forces, and is said to have suffered many wounds. After ᶜAlī's victory he, like other members of the Meccan party, withdrew from active participation in politics for the time being; although present at the arbitrations intended to settle the dispute between ᶜAlī and the Umayyad pretender, Muᶜāwiya ibn Abī Sufyān, he played no important role in them. Thereafter he recognized Muᶜāwiya as caliph and returned to Medina.

Only at the end of Muᶜāwiya's reign (661–680) did ᶜAbd Allāh again enter politics openly, by joining several other notables of Medina who refused to recognize Muᶜāwiya's designation of his son Yazīd as heir-apparent. Upon Yazīd's accession in 680, ᶜAbd Allāh fled to the sanctuary of Mecca to evade arrest by Yazīd's governor in Medina, and from there directed what became a protracted struggle against the Umayyads. Yazīd, finding negotiation with ᶜAbd Allāh fruitless, directed his governor to dispatch a troop to Mecca led by ᶜAbd Allāh's brother ᶜAmr ibn al-Zubayr, with whom ᶜAbd Allāh had long been on bad terms. When his plan to seize the rebel failed, ᶜAbd Allāh captured his brother and had him cruelly executed. Thereafter both ᶜAbd Allāh and Yazīd bided their time.

In 683 the population of Medina withdrew their allegiance from Yazīd, besieged his relatives in the Umayyad quarter of the town, and declared themselves loyal to ᶜAbd Allāh. Yazīd consequently decided to dispatch a large Syrian army to establish his authority in the Ḥijāz. After defeating the Medinese insurgents, this army took up positions before Mecca, which was strongly reinforced by Medinese refugees and even by Khārijites from eastern Arabia. A siege was begun—during which fire damaged the Kaaba—but it was abruptly halted when the commander received news of Yazīd's death in Syria.

The death of Yazīd left the Umayyad house with no clear leadership, and many Muslims turned their allegiance to ᶜAbd Allāh ibn al-Zubayr, who was recognized as caliph in Egypt, the Ḥijāz, South Arabia, the important garrison town of Al-Kufa in Iraq, and even by part of the population of Syria. ᶜAbd Allāh duly set about naming his governors for the various provinces. But his consolidation of power was stalled by the emergence of Marwān ibn al-Ḥakam as the leader of the reunited Umayyad family. Marwān quickly restored Syria and Egypt to allegiance to the Umayyads. Meanwhile the rebellion of al-Mukhtār ibn Abī ᶜUbayd in Al-Kufa weakened ᶜAbd Allāh's grip on Iraq; and although ᶜAbd Allāh's brother and governor in Basra, the talented Musᶜab ibn al-Zubayr, eventually managed to defeat al-Mukhtār, the struggle prevented ᶜAbd Allāh from consolidating his position in Iraq sufficiently to withstand the Umayyad onslaught that was to come. Moreover, ᶜAbd Allāh's position was weakened by the loss of eastern Arabia and even Al-Ṭā'if (near Mecca), seized by the ᶜKhārijite rebels of the Ḥanīfa tribe.

After the death of Marwān the new caliph, ᶜAbd al-Malik (685–705), vigorously prosecuted the struggle against ᶜAbd Allāh ibn al-Zubayr. An army led by the caliph's general, al-Ḥajjāj ibn Yūsuf, defeated and killed Musᶜab ibn al-Zubayr and reoccupied Iraq in 691. Al-Ḥajjāj then marched on Mecca, which was besieged for six months. In the end, abandoned by most of his supporters, ᶜAbd Allāh chose to meet certain death on the battlefield rather than surrender.

ᶜAbd Allāh ibn al-Zubayr's rebellion was the last, and most serious, attempt by the old aristocracy of early converts to Islam to wrest the caliphate from the Umayyad family. Depending on their attitude toward the Umayyads, later historians either praise him for his piety or vilify him for his bad temper and cruelty.

BIBLIOGRAPHY

ᶜAbd al-Ameer ᶜAbd Dixon, *The Umayyad Caliphate, 65–86/684–705* (1971); al-Balādhurī, *Ansāb al-ashrāf,* ivB (1938) and v (1938); al-Ṭabarī, *Taᵓrīkh al-rusul wa-al-mulūk;* Henri Lammens, *Le califat de Yazid Ier* (1921), 182ff.; Julius Wellhausen, *The Arab Kingdom and Its Fall* (1927, 1963).

FRED M. DONNER

[See also **ᶜAbd Al-Malik; Abū Bakr; ᶜĀᵓisha; Second Civil War.**]

ABELARD, PETER (*ca.* 1079–*ca.* 1142), philosopher, teacher, author, and lover, was born at Le Pallet, near Nantes, the oldest son of Berengar, lord of a small border castle that defended the county of Nantes against Anjou, and of his wife Lucie. He took his cognomen (in Latin *Abaelardus*) from neither his father, his family, nor his place of origin; its meaning is uncertain. Abelard studied under the celebrated nominalist philosopher Roscelin of Compiègne at Loches, in Anjou. After moving to Paris he continued his studies with the realist philosopher William of Champeaux, with whom he soon quarreled. In his twenties and early thirties Abelard taught philosophy at Melun, Corbeil, and Paris, as well as on Mont Sainte Geneviève, just south of Paris. During this period he began to publish commentaries on Aristotelian logic as transmitted by Cicero and Boethius.

Not long after 1112 Abelard expanded his horizon from logic to theology. At this time the venerable Anselm had made the cathedral school of Laon preeminent as a center for scriptural study. Abelard's training led him to combine the skills of logic and disputation with those of biblical commentary, and as a student at Laon he quickly set himself up as a rival to Anselm, as he had with William of Champeaux. After returning to Paris he became a teacher at the cathedral school of Notre Dame about 1113 and was widely sought by students from England, Germany, and Italy as well as France.

When he was almost forty Abelard became the tutor of Heloise, the niece of a canon of Notre Dame cathedral named Fulbert, and twenty years his junior. The tutor and pupil fell passionately in love, and their affair, vividly described in Abelard's autobiographical *Historia calamitatum,* became a celebrated theme in European literature, inspiring Petrarch, Alexander Pope, and Rousseau. A child was soon born, baptized Peter after his father, and known as Astralabe. He grew to manhood in unrecorded circumstances, and we last hear of him in the 1140's, when Heloise asked for help in finding him an ecclesiastical position.

After the birth of Astralabe had revealed their illicit love to Fulbert, Abelard offered to marry Heloise. According to Abelard it was Heloise who presented the arguments against marriage, but he persisted and a clandestine ceremony was performed. Outraged by the secrecy and suspecting that no marriage had taken place or that Abelard was preparing to abandon Heloise in a convent, Fulbert took vengeance by hiring a pair of ruffians to castrate Abelard. That event probably took place in 1118. Publicly humiliated, Abelard retired from the world, seeking seclusion at the Benedictine monastery of St. Denis and insisting that Heloise take the veil at the nearby convent of Argenteuil.

The great royal abbey of St. Denis was probably the richest and most prestigious in France. He held very high monastic ideals, but in practice Abelard found conventual life hard to bear and sought a large degree of independence. After leaving the mother house of St. Denis, he established a school at one of the abbey's dependencies, possibly at St. Blaise de Grandpuits in the territory of Thibaut IV of Blois. There he wrote a work on the Trinity for his students known from its opening words as *Theologia "Summi Boni."*

Abelard's book attacked his old master Roscelin, who replied in a vicious letter deriding Abelard after his castration as an *imperfectus Petrus.* Two students of Anselm of Laon also attacked Abelard, charging him with heresy for his teachings on the nature of the Trinity. In 1121 at the Council of Soissons the unrepentant Abelard was found guilty and condemned to cast his book into a fire. After a short imprisonment in the abbey of St. Médard of Soissons, he returned to St. Denis, where he quickly embroiled himself with his fellow monks by jesting about the authenticity of the abbey's traditions about its patron saint.

Threatened with further discipline, Abelard fled to the priory of St. Ayoul of Provins. Supported by powerful advocates, he received permission in 1122 from the new abbot of St. Denis, Suger, to leave his abbey on the condition that he not become a monk of another house. On the territory of a vassal of St. Denis, the lord of Nogent-sur-Seine, in the parish of Quincey, sixty miles southeast of Paris, Abelard built an oratory that he named Le Paraclet, meaning comforter or Holy Spirit, and established a school that drew students from far and wide.

About 1125 Abelard was chosen abbot by the monks of St. Gildas of Rhuys, on the coast of Brittany near Vannes. No more suited by temperament to govern monks than he had been to live under monastic rule, Abelard quickly became critical of his monks and soon concluded that they were trying to murder him. At this point the tone of his autobiographical letter suggests the author was paranoid, though other evidence shows him traveling honorably in highly respectable circles. He probably preached in the presence of a papal legate at the abbey of Redon in 1127 and was at Morigny with Pope Innocent II in January 1131, when he was called "monk and abbot and rector of a most excellent school." It is not known when he returned to teaching on Mont Ste. Geneviève, where John of Salisbury heard him lecture in 1136.

Despite his miserable experience at St. Gildas, Abelard possessed considerable talent for spiritual direction, which he demonstrated at the convent that he and Heloise created at Le Paraclet. After Suger claimed the property of Argenteuil for St. Denis and expelled the nuns in 1129, Abelard offered Heloise and her companions his oratory; the foundation charter of Pope Innocent II is dated 28 November 1131. Abelard was known as *magister,* or master, of the house, while Heloise was installed first as prioress and then as abbess in a fashion that parallels Robert of Arbrissel's foundation at the convent of Fontevrault.

It is unclear how much time Abelard spent at Le Paraclet, but in the 1130's he wrote extensively for Heloise and the nuns there. The *Historia calamitatum* is the opening letter of a collection that continues with a dramatic exchange between Heloise and Abelard and concludes with a rule that Abelard wrote for the convent, and which Heloise appears not to have followed in all its particulars. Abelard also prepared a collection of more than 140 hymns for the nuns, wrote some of the music, and oversaw their liturgy in general. He sent Heloise a collection of sermons, answered questions for her in the *Problemata,* and dedicated to her such works as his commentary on the six days of Creation, the *Hexaemeron.* At the same time he continued to polish his treatises on logic and to work on revisions of his textbook *Sic et non* and his *Theologia Christiana.*

Although distinguished among her contemporaries for her learning, Heloise emerges most clearly from the surviving historical record as a monastic administrator. Her abbey soon reached its ideal size of sixty nuns, and it was she who was in charge at

ABELARD, PETER

the time of the establishment of all its dependencies, new houses which continued to be built even after Abelard's death: Ste. Madeleine de Traînel about 1142, the abbey of La Pommeraie about 1147, Laval before 1154, Noëfort and St. Flavit before 1157, and St. Martin de Boran before 1163. At her death in 1164 (or possibly 1163) Heloise was known as a pious and effective abbess honored by popes and by such an abbot as Peter the Venerable.

Not only was Abelard involved with Le Paraclet and in teaching at Paris, but in the middle and late 1130's he produced challenging new works, a new edition in several versions of his *Theologia,* known as the *Theologia "Scholarium,"* a commentary on Paul's Epistle to the Romans, and his *Ethica,* also called *Know Thyself.* His new treatises and the enthusiastic activity of his students, who used his methods to draw conclusions beyond those of their master, attracted the critical attention of William of St. Thierry and his Cistercian colleague, Bernard of Clairvaux.

William wrote an attack, Bernard preached before Abelard's students and appealed privately to Abelard to change his ways, but no accommodation was reached and Abelard brought the dispute before a church council at Sens in June 1140. This was not, however, the occasion for a great debate, for Abelard then appealed to Rome, perhaps fearing that Bernard's preparations for the council, especially his lobbying, had been too effective for him. The council condemned him anyhow and sent its judgment to Pope Innocent II, who quickly confirmed it. Abelard, who had left Sens to go to Rome in person but traveled with surprising slowness, received the news of his papal condemnation at Cluny, where he fulfilled his sentence by becoming a monk of Cluny and refraining from public teaching.

His new abbot, Peter the Venerable, later wrote that Abelard in this period was unkempt, retiring, abstemious, and taciturn, qualities that he considered an indication of humility but that also can be seen as signs of deep depression. If, as now seems likely, Abelard's uncompleted *Dialogue of a Philosopher with a Christian and a Jew* was written before the Council of Sens, then we have no evidence of any literary productivity at Cluny. Ill health began to affect him seriously, so that Peter the Venerable sent him to the priory of St. Marcel near Chalon-sur-Saône, where he died on 21 April, perhaps as early as 1142 or as late as 1144. According to a medieval tradition, both Abelard and Heloise were sixty-three when they died. His body was moved to Le Paraclet, and Heloise was later buried beside him. In 1792 their remains were moved and were finally reinterred at Père Lachaise Cemetery in Paris in 1817.

More than any other master, Abelard created the reputation of Paris as an intellectual center in the first half of the twelfth century. Brilliant, witty, learned, supremely confident of his own ability, and contemptuous of less talented rivals, Abelard was adulated by his students. Though it is a serious error to consider him a rationalist, Abelard believed that reason could clarify matters of faith, particularly in cases where authorities disagreed. Following his conviction that words are tools for human discourse, with different meanings in different contexts, he taught his students to resolve difficulties with sophisticated linguistic analysis. *Sic et non* is a challenging and stimulating textbook; its introduction states, "By doubting we come to questioning, and by questioning we learn truth." His predecessor, Ivo of Chartres, and his slightly younger contemporaries, Gratian and Peter Lombard, also produced compilations of contradictory authorities, but Abelard's *Sic et non* differs from their works by not including an orthodox solution to protect the reader from possible heresy.

In the great debate over the nature of universals that preoccupied the early Scholastics, Abelard staked out a moderate nominalist position between Roscelin, and William of Champeaux. Roscelin supposedly claimed that only individuals (Peter, Paul) exist and that a universal (man) is just a vocalized breath of air, or *flatus vocis.* William, at least according to Abelard, argued that individuals differ only by their accidents, not their substance, so that humanity or "man-ness" is wholly present in both Peter and Paul. Abelard taught that only individual objects exist, but that since a universal names things that really exist, it is not a *flatus vocis* but a word that bears meaning, a *vox significativa.* In this respect Abelard may correctly be called a logical or, better, epistemological nominalist. On the other hand, he was, like Augustine, a philosophical or metaphysical realist in accepting the existence of reality independent of the human mind, as in the case of mathematical truths known only to God. The label "conceptualist" applied to Abelard's thought by some historians of philosophy unfortunately conflates these two positions; Abelard did not argue that the locus of reality is in the concepts conceived by the human mind.

Abelard's stated goal in writing on the Trinity was to defend orthodox doctrine from the attacks of "pseudo-logicians." In order to do so he introduced a number of analogies for which he was in turn attacked. To give one example, his discussion of the three Persons in terms that equated the Father with power *(potentia)*, the Son with wisdom *(sapientia)*, and the Holy Spirit with goodness *(benignitas)* easily led to the charge that he was denying or at least minimizing the power of the Son and Holy Spirit, the wisdom of the Father and Holy Spirit, and so on. In later books and subsequent reeditions Abelard qualified some statements, revised others, and denied having ever said or written others with which he was charged. He also held that such critics as Bernard of Clairvaux were not sufficiently learned to understand what he was doing. Theologians today are still discussing whether Abelard's doctrine was really orthodox or at least harmless; probably it was. What seems to have outraged his contemporaries the most is not what he said—they often did not bother to determine this in detail—but how he said it.

In ethics and the study of redemption Abelard made a more significant contribution. Anselm of Canterbury had argued a contract theory of redemption through substitute suffering, which Abelard countered by teaching that the devil held no rights over man, whom he had seduced; for Abelard the atonement should be seen in terms of the revelation of God's love through the life and death of Christ. In his *Ethica,* Abelard argued quite originally for the central role of intention in the determination of sin. Adultery, for example, might not necessarily be a sin if a man honestly but mistakenly believed that another woman was his own wife; but knowingly consenting to adultery was sinful.

In popular literature, poetry, and drama Abelard's fame rests on his reputation as a romantic lover. If the letters to Abelard attributed to Heloise were actually written by her, then we have her testimony that Abelard had been an unforgettable lover and that years after his castration she still fantasized about him during mass and preferred him to God. On the other hand, if the letters came from Abelard's pen, then the words attributed to Heloise were filtered through his mind and may in some sense be considered a projection of his own self-image onto his wife, an image of eroticism and power—which he denied in his own letters.

Despite several attempts, no convincing case has yet been made that the whole correspondence is a fabrication by a third party. Historians are still divided, however, over whether Heloise's letters are her own, and until this matter is resolved any evaluation of their relationship must remain uncertain. Two things are nevertheless clear: in the *Historia calamitatum* Abelard depicted their relationship in terms of carnal desire and passion; and in his later years he treated Heloise, "once his wife, now his sister in Christ," with solicitude and loving care.

A contemporary epitaph said of Abelard that "he knew all there was to know." He was without question a man of genius who made significant contributions to logic, influenced the study of theology, and enriched the world with his writing. He was, however, also too smart for his own good, he gloried in intellectual disputes, and he provoked conflicts; and since he left many of his books unfinished, the full structure of his thought is often unclear. The consequence of his condemnation for heresy was that by the thirteenth century his works were little studied, and his fame as a philosopher was eclipsed by his reputation as a lover until his rediscovery as a philosopher in the nineteenth century.

Although he wrote one of the rare autobiographical statements of the twelfth century, it is uncertain just how self-aware or self-critical Abelard actually was. Like most of his contemporaries, he considered those who differed with him to be envious rivals. He dwelt on his own misfortunes in more detail than any of his contemporaries, so that it is easy to conclude that he was proud, pugnacious, flamboyant, and at times chillingly self-centered. But it must also be remembered that he earned the love of Heloise and of some of his students and the respect of such men as Peter the Venerable, and that the *Historia calamitatum* is the opening letter of a correspondence that concludes in the spiritual peace of Le Paraclet.

BIBLIOGRAPHY

Most of Abelard's works appear in *Patrologia latina,* CLXXVIII (1855), and in *Petri Abaelardi Opera,* Victor Cousin, ed., 2 vols. (1849–1859). Éloi M. Buytaert published critical editions of some theological works in *Petri Abaelardi Opera theologica,* 2 vols. (1969), which contains a bibliography to 1967. For translations see *Abelard's Christian Theology,* J. R. MacCallum, trans. (1948); *Peter Abelard's Ethics* (1971), David E. Luscombe, ed. and trans.; *Peter Abelard. A Dialogue of a Philosopher with a Jew and a Christian,* Pierre J. Payer, trans. (1979); and *Du bien suprême (Theologia Summi boni),* Jean Jolivet, trans. (1978).

For Abelard's logical works see *Peter Abaelards philosophische Schriften,* 4 pts. (1919–1933; 2nd ed. 1973); *Scritti filosofici,* Mario dal Pra, ed. (1954); Lorenzo Minio-Paluello, ed., *Abaelardiana inedita* (1958); and *Dialectica,* Lambertus M. de Rijk, ed., 2nd ed. (1970). The *Logica "In-*

gredientibus" was partially translated by Richard McKeon in his *Selections from Medieval Philosophers,* I (1929).

The best edition of *Historia calamitatum* is by Jacques Monfrin (1959, repr. 1978). For the rest of the correspondence with Heloise, see Joseph T. Muckle, *Medieval Studies,* **12** (1950), **15** (1953), and **17** (1955). Muckle translated the *Historia calamitatum* as *The Story of Abelard's Adversities* (1954). The only complete English translation of the correspondence is that of Charles K. Scott Moncrieff (1925, repr. 1974), but Betty Radice's ed. (1974) is more reliable.

David E. Luscombe, *Peter Abelard* (1979), is a judicious survey with succinct bibliography; for sharply differing views see Étienne Gilson, *Heloise and Abelard,* L. K. Shook, trans. (1960); and Durant W. Robertson, Jr., *Abelard and Heloise* (1972).

See also Mary M. McLaughlin, "Abelard as Autobiographer," in *Speculum,* **42** (1967); David E. Luscombe, *The School of Peter Abelard* (1969); Leif Grane, *Peter Abelard,* Frederick Crowley and Christine Crowley, trans. (1974); and Peter Dronke, *Abelard and Heloise in Medieval Testimonies* (1976).

JOHN F. BENTON

[See also **Anselm of Laon; Philosophy-Theology; William of Champeaux.**]

ABGITIR CRABHAI. See **Fenian Poetry.**

ABIELL, GUILLERMO, master mason responsible for a number of churches in Barcelona, Spain, around 1400, most notably Nuestra Señora del Pino, Nuestra Señora del Monte Carmelo, Santiago, and Montesión—and, after 1407, master of the Hospital de Santa Cruz. Abiell was one of twelve masters summoned by the bishop and chapter of Gerona in 1416 to recommend how the cathedral there should be completed. Seven of the twelve, including Abiell, recommended a basilican triple-nave scheme, but a single-nave format was adopted.

BIBLIOGRAPHY

"Abiell," in *Allgemeines Lexikon der bildenden Künstler,* ed. Ulrich Thieme and Felix Becker (1907), I, 23; and Leopoldo Torres Balbás, *Arquitectura gótica* (1952), 271–272, 319–320.

CARL F. BARNES, JR.

ABKHAZIA. See **Georgia.**

ABODE OF ISLAM—ABODE OF WAR. In its most rigid and widely repeated understanding, the Abode of Islam *(Dār al-Islām)* is that part of the world where the law of Islam, the *sharīᶜa,* prevails. The rest of the world is the Abode of War *(Dār al-Ḥarb),* that is, territory whose inhabitants are to be warred against until they accept Islam or, for People of the Book (Jews, Christians, and, by interpretation, Zoroastrians and others), accept the status of being protected subjects, *dhimmīs,* under Islamic rule without change of faith. Portrayed in this way, the division of the world into an Abode of Islam and an Abode of War seems to go hand in hand with the concept of *jihād* (holy war), and reinforces the image of Islam as an inherently warlike faith. However, there are reasons for regarding this portrayal as oversimplified and unrealistic.

The dichotomy between Abode of Islam and Abode of War does not appear in the Koran nor is it mentioned more than rarely in medieval Arabic geographical works. The concepts arose in the course of the evolution of Islamic legal thinking, and their relationship to actual political practice and territorial demarcation has varied greatly over the centuries from one Muslim regime to another. War and peace, domination and subordination, have tended to be governed by the exigencies of given situations more than by the requirements of legal theory. This holds true of many other aspects of Islamic political theory as well.

On the legal plane the reasons underlying the emergence of the concepts have as much to do with financial relations as with military activities. In the aftermath of the Arab conquests in the seventh century, a new ruling group, the Muslims, inherited the financial traditions of the Sassanid and Byzantine empires along with myriad treaties and other agreements made by Arab military commanders in terminating hostilities in various areas. It took more than a century for Muslim legists and administrators to bring order to the confusing financial picture and to sanctify a taxation system that would be consistent, easily understandable, and based upon the Koran or the deeds or words of the prophet Muḥammad. It is in this context more than any other that the concern over the nature of treaties and the status of peoples in territories gained or lost in war was felt.

As in most other areas of Islamic law, particularly in the absence of specific Koranic revelation, there is a broad range of legal opinion regarding the Abode of Islam and the Abode of War. The most rigid interpretation holds that there can be no middle term between these two. But even then disagreement can arise as to what constitutes a lapse in the application of Islamic law in a territory passing from the first category to the second. Some have maintained that a land can remain in the Abode of Islam as long as a single provision of the *sharīᶜa* remains in force.

The more important divergent opinions revolve around the existence of an Abode of Truce *(Dār aṣ-Ṣulḥ)* or Abode of Covenant *(Dār al-ᶜAhd)* constituting a third and even fourth category of territorial division. The concept of an Abode of Truce is rooted in an agreement reached between Muḥammad and the Christians of Najrān in the Yemen and another entered into by an early Muslim governor of Egypt and the Nubians of the northern Sudan. The former had little practical effect, but the latter governed relations between the parties for many years. In return for certain obligations that could be construed as payment of tax or tribute, the non-Muslim party to such a truce may live in peace and independence. Whether this truce (*ṣulḥ* or *hudna*) is inherently temporary, and therefore not truly an alternative to the primary dichotomy, remains an issue for legal debate.

The concept of Abode of Covenant is not greatly different; but the non-Muslim party to the covenant, particularly during the Ottoman period, when such agreements were commonly made with the non-Muslim princes of newly conquered regions, is more clearly a tributary client of the Muslim party, with definite limitations upon total sovereignty. The model for this type of relationship is the agreement between Caliph Muᶜāwiya (661–680) and certain Armenian princes who retained their land and autonomy in return for a yearly payment.

It is noteworthy that the legal acceptance of these intermediary states hinges upon the interpretation of the tribute payment as a form of legally and religiously sanctioned Islamic taxation, regardless of how the payment is interpreted by the party paying it. The importance of fiscal systematization as a factor underlying the creation of the categories is here quite evident.

It is not surprising, therefore, that the salience of these categories was slight in the thinking of the medieval geographers, who usually portrayed borders as being easy to cross and open to trade. The categories also took on a more symbolic than legalistic complexion during times of weakness or disruption, when orderly financial exploitation of the land deteriorated. For the medieval period, therefore, the Abode of Islam and Abode of War were most important as strict legal categories under the early Abbasid caliphs.

BIBLIOGRAPHY

Majid Khadduri, *War and Peace in the Law of Islam* (1955); Majid Khadduri, tr., *The Islamic Law of Nations: Shaybānī's Siyar* (1966); and Frede Løkkegaard, *Islamic Taxation in the Classic Period* (1950).

RICHARD W. BULLIET

ABRABANEL, ISAAC BEN JUDAH (1437–1508), statesman, biblical commentator, philospher, and one of the pioneer Jewish scholars whose works reflect their acquaintance with emerging Renaissance ideals and concepts. Abrabanel received a broad education and was equally well versed in Talmudic, classical, and Christian theological literature. In 1471 he succeeded his father as treasurer of King Alfonso V of Portugal. His political career in Portugal ended abruptly in 1483, when King John II accused him of conspiracy in an unsuccessful rebellion led by aristocrats.

Abrabanel fled to Castile and began a brief but productive period of devotion to biblical exegesis. In 1484 he entered the service of Ferdinand and Isabella and contributed much to the efficient administration of the royal treasury. Following the expulsion of Jews from Spain in 1492, Abrabanel settled in Naples, where he managed to combine his literary and political activities. When the French attacked Naples in 1494, he followed the royal family to Messina. After the death of Alfonso II he left for Corfu; and after the French withdrew, he settled in Monopoli.

During this period he wrote commentaries on Deuteronomy, the *Haggadah,* and *Avot,* as well as messianic and philosophical works. In 1504 he settled in Venice, where he completed his biblical commentaries and participated in negotiations between Venice and Portugal for a commercial treaty to regulate the spice trade.

Abrabanel's most original contribution to philosophy was his defense of the rabbinic concept of salvation and of prophecy. He opposed Maimonides' ascription of scientific and imaginative qualities to prophets and, rejecting his naturalism, saw human behavior and destiny as consequences of either man's free will or divine forces. His interpretation of Jewish history is completely traditional.

Abrabanel's commentaries on the Pentateuch and the Prophets were largely influenced by earlier scholars. His characteristic innovation was the division of Scripture into chapters with prefatory introductions in which he analyzes the difficulties in the spirit of medieval Scholasticism. His refutations of Christological interpretations and his consolatory words to his suffering and exiled brethren are noteworthy characteristics of Abrabanel's exegetical works, some of which were quite influential in humanistic circles.

YOM TOV ASSIS

ABRAHAM BAR ḤIYYA (died *ca.* 1136), Jewish theologian and encyclopedist, was born in Barcelona. His theological work consists of two treatises in Hebrew. *Hegyon ha-Nefesh,* translated by Geoffrey Wigoder as *The Meditation of the Sad Soul* (1969), is an exhortation to penance in which traditional Jewish wisdom is combined with a Neoplatonic outline of metaphysics and psychology. It had an influence on the thirteenth-century cabala of Gerona, in Catalonia. *Megillat ha-Megalleh (The Scroll of the Revealer)* is a messianic treatise in which the idea of the divine spark in man transmitted down from Adam (an idea that Abraham bar Ḥiyya's contemporary Judah Halevi was inspired by and adopted in his own teaching) is joined with astrological calculations and with a philosophy of history that owes much to Isidore of Seville.

Thoroughly versed in Arabic, Abraham bar Ḥiyya devoted the bulk of his career to the dissemination to coreligionists, in Hebrew, of Greco-Arabic mathematics, astronomy, astrology, and cosmography. In addition, thanks to his collaboration with the Christian translator Plato of Tivoli, he contributed to the transmission of Arabic science to western Christendom.

BIBLIOGRAPHY

Georges Vajda, "Abraham bar Ḥiya," in *Hebrew Union College Annual,* **43** (1972), 143–144; J. M. Millas-Vallicrosa, "La obra enciclopedica de R. Abraham bar Ḥiya," in *Estudios sobre historia de la ciencia española* (1949), 219–262.

GEORGES VAJDA

ABRAHAM BEN DAVID OF POSQUIÈRES (*ca.* 1125–1198), usually referred to by the acronym *Rabad* (Rabbi Abraham ben David), was born in Narbonne and died in Posquières. He is best known for his original, enduring contributions to halakic literature and methodology; indeed he is one of the great architects of halakic reasoning, having helped to develop a critical-conceptual approach to talmudic literature. He was a creative practitioner of this abstract method of talmudic study—probing into the inner strata of talmudic logic, defining fundamental concepts, and formulating disparities as well as similarities among various passages in the light of conceptual analysis. Complex concepts, which were discussed fragmentarily in numerous, unrelated sections of the Talmud, are defined by Rabad with great rigor and precision. Many of his interpretations and innovations were endorsed and transmitted by subsequent generations of talmudists and incorporated into standard works of Jewish law up to the *Shulḥan Arukh* and its later commentaries.

Rabad's literary activity in the field of rabbinic literature is noteworthy for its creativity and originality. His versatility is seen in the range of his compositions: codes of rabbinic law, commentaries on various types of talmudic literature (on Mishnah [e.g., *Eduyyot* and *Kinnim*], Talmud [e.g., *Avodah Zarah* and *Bava Kamma*], halakic midrash [e.g., *Sifra*]), responsa (recent edition by Yosef Kafaḥ, 1964), homiletic discourses, and critical annotations and glosses *(hassagot)* on standard works of rabbinic literature. The most important and influential of his codes, which include *Hilkot Lulav, Hibbur Harsha'ot,* and *Perush Yadayim,* is the *Ba'alei ha-Nefesh* (first ed. Venice, 1602; most recent and complete ed. by Yosef Kafaḥ, 1964). The last chapter of the work, entitled "Sha'ar ha-Kedushah" ("Gate of Holiness"), formulates and analyzes the moral norms and religious attitudes which enable one to achieve self-control in sexual matters and to attain purity of heart and action.

Rabad's name is linked historically with the *hassagot,* critical scholia and glosses, which he composed toward the end of his life, on the *Halakhot* of Alfasi, the *Sefer ha-Ma'or* of Zerahiah ha-Levi, and the *Mishneh Torah* of Maimonides. These glosses combine criticism and commentary; they are not exclusively polemical, and the polemical emphasis varies in intensity and acuity from one to the other. Rabad and his Provençal contemporaries refined the *hassagot* into a special, expressive, and repercussive

ABRAHAM BEN MEÏR IBN EZRA

genre of pointed, precise, and persuasive critique. The *hassagot* constitute a wide-ranging form of writing based on broad information and a firm, self-assured erudition, on a sharp style and polemical skill. They were a major factor in the continuation of the intellectual freedom and criticism which are so important for rabbinic literature.

Rabad's writing is characterized by a dynamism and openness. He kept rethinking interpretations, reassessing inferences, introducing stylistic and substantive changes which reflect either subtly varying nuances or genuinely divergent emphases—partly in response to the penetrating, often persuasive criticism of Zerahyah ha-Levi and partly as a manifestation of the nature of halakic study, which favored intellectual growth and necessitated unflagging alertness and intellectual dynamism.

His milieu, twelfth-century Provence, was marked by (1) an efflorescence of rabbinic literature, a real golden age of creativity; (2) the introduction of the philosophic-scientific literature of Spanish Jews, especially in Arabic, into a Hebrew-speaking environment; and (3) the appearance of medieval cabala. Rabad was a major figure in the first development. He encouraged and benefited from the second; for example, he urged Judah ibn Tibbon to complete the translation of Baḥya ibn Paquda's *Ḥovot ha-Levavot (Duties of the Heart)* from the original Arabic into Hebrew, and his own writing reflects traces of philosophy and philology. He is described by later cabalists as one of the fathers of cabala.

BIBLIOGRAPHY

Isadore Twersky, *Rabad of Posquières,* rev. ed. (1980), includes complete bibliography.

ISADORE TWERSKY

ABRAHAM BEN MEÏR IBN EZRA (1089–1164), Hebrew poet, grammarian, Bible commentator, and philosopher, was born in Tudela, Spain. Ibn Ezra left Spain in 1140, in the wake of the invasion of the Almohad Berbers, he wandered thereafter in Italy, Provence, France, England, and perhaps Palestine.

As a liturgical poet, Ibn Ezra cultivated the traditional strophic forms as well as the typically Hispano-Judaic monorhymed meditation. Many of the latter show a Neoplatonic tendency, as does the long philosophical prose poem *Ḥai ben Mekiẓ*. His secular poetry is notable for its witty epigrams and rueful reflections on the writer's life as a wandering scholar.

Ibn Ezra seems to have composed commentaries on every book of the Old Testament—several in the case of some books—which enjoyed great popularity and wide dissemination. Terse often to the point of obscurity, they aim above all to expound the plain meaning of Scripture by means of a careful examination of grammatical and lexical matters in the tradition of Hispano-Judaic linguistic studies, and by careful distinction between the plain meaning of the text and the traditional rabbinic exegesis.

The commentaries are of great interest for Ibn Ezra's occasional references to a variety of other topics: hints of a Neoplatonic allegorical interpretation of the Garden of Eden and Jacob's ladder, allusions to a heterodox view of the Mosaic authorship of certain passages in the Pentateuch, intimations of the existence of a Deutero-Isaiah, as well as digressions on philosophical and scientific topics. Some of Ibn Ezra's hints bearing on the authorship of the Pentateuch and his rationalistic approach in general have lent him the reputation of a freethinker or even the forerunner of modern biblical criticism. Actually his commentary seems simply to epitomize the way in which the Bible was customarily understood by cultivated Spanish Jews of the courtier class.

Ibn Ezra's treatises deal with a variety of subjects, particularly Hebrew grammar, but also mathematics, astronomy, philosophy, and theology. As in the case of the Bible commentaries, these works epitomize the views current among the Spanish-Jewish aristocracy of the Golden Age (*ca.* 950–*ca.* 1250). Composed in Hebrew during Ibn Ezra's wanderings, they provided the Jews of Christian Europe with access to the attainments of Sephardic scholarship.

He returned to Spain where he died in 1164.

BIBLIOGRAPHY

Wilhelm Bacher, *Abraham Ibn Esra als Grammatiker* (1882); Naftali Ben-Menahem, *Inyene Ibn Ezra* (1978); Max Friedländer, *Essays on the Writing of Abraham Ibn Ezra,* 4 vols. (1873–1877); Isaac Husik, *History of Mediaeval Jewish Philosophy* (1916); R. Levi, *The Astrological Works of Abraham Ibn Ezra* (1927); Israel Lewin, *Abraham ibn Ezra, ḥayyav ve-shirato* (1969); Ḥayyim Schirmann, *Shirim Ḥadashim min ha-geniza* (1965), 267–276.

RAYMOND P. SCHEINDLIN

ABRAHAM IBN DAUD (*ca.* 1110–1180), also known as Rabad I, is one of Spanish Jewry's celebrated historians, polemicists, and philosophers. Born in Muslim Spain, he settled in Christian Toledo after the Almohad conquests and died a martyr's death there. In his historical work he extolled the rabbinic tradition in Judaism, while philosophically he was a committed—and pioneering in Judaism—Aristotelian of an Avicennian sort.

BIBLIOGRAPHY

For Abraham ibn Daud's historical work, see *Sefer Ha-Qabbalah: The Book of Tradition by Abraham Ibn Daud*, Gerson D. Cohen, trans. (1967). A German translation and edition of his philosophical work (known in the Hebrew extant translation as *Ha-Emunah ha-Ramah*) is by Simson Weil (1852).

ALFRED L. IVRY

ABSIDIOLE. A small chapel, often semicircular, that opens from an apse. Absidioles, also called apsidioles, are similar to but smaller than apsidal chapels; they are characteristic of French Gothic architecture.

LESLIE BRUBAKER

ABŪ BAKR (*ca.* 572–634), called al-Ṣiddī, "the veracious," father-in-law of the prophet Muḥammad and the first caliph (632–634). Born about three years after the Prophet Muḥammad, his parents were of the clan of Taym of the Meccan tribe of Ḳuraysh. Little is known of his early life; he was evidently a respected merchant, but whether he engaged in caravan trade with Syria or the Yemen, like some aristocrats of Ḳuraysh, is not known. At the time of his conversion to Islam, around 612, he is said to have had 40,000 dirhams, but whether this was a large or modest sum in contemporary terms remains a matter of disagreement.

Abū Bakr was one of the first converts to Islam, and became Muḥammad's closest adviser and confidant. His intimate ties to the Prophet and key position in the early community of Muslims were sealed when the Prophet married Abū Bakr's daughter, ᶜĀᵓisha, after the death of his first wife, Khadīja, in about 618. He is said to have spent much of his wealth purchasing from the Ḳuraysh the freedom of slaves who had embraced Islam. During the years of persecution that Muḥammad and his followers endured in Mecca, Abū Bakr remained in the city with Muḥammad while some Muslims chose to go to Abyssinia to escape this abuse. Even when Muḥammad had arranged for all his supporters to take refuge in Medina, Abū Bakr stayed behind with the Prophet and was the only Muslim to accompany him on his hegira, or emigration to Medina in 622. He settled in Medina with a man of the Khazraj tribe, whose daughter he later married. He seems to have had close ties of respect and affection to another early and influential Muslim, ᶜUmar ibn al-Khaṭṭāb, who became the second caliph.

Abū Bakr played an important role in Muḥammad's political career in Medina. His extensive knowledge of tribal genealogy made him a valuable asset in the Prophet's effort to build a base of support among the many tribal groups in western Arabia. Furthermore, he accompanied Muḥammad on all his military engagements. Sometimes he appears to have been more involved in planning strategy than in actual combat, as at the battle of Badr in 624, where he seems to have been with Muḥammad in a kind of command post. In other cases, however, he took a more active part in campaigning. At Khaibar he was given a banner by the Prophet and charged with leading the assault on one of the Jewish forts; at Ḥunayn it was Abū Bakr and some other stalwarts who stood fast against an enemy ambush and prevented the Muslims' momentary disarray from becoming a rout; at Tabūk he carried a standard into battle. On one occasion, Muḥammad sent him to the Najd at the head of a small force directed against the Hawāzin tribe.

Abū Bakr's unwavering loyalty to Muḥammad (and, perhaps, his participation in the formulation of strategy) are reflected in his steadfast backing of Muḥammad's treaty with the Ḳuraysh at al-Ḥudaybiya, an agreement that many Muslims at first opposed. He was appointed by the Prophet to lead the pilgrimage to Mecca in 631; and, when Muḥammad entered his final illness, he instructed Abū Bakr to take his place as leader of the communal prayers in the mosque in Medina.

Muḥammad's death in 632 plunged the Islamic community into a severe crisis, because there was no consensus about who should succeed him—or, indeed, whether he could have a successor. The Medinese were on the verge of choosing a leader of their own and urged the Ḳuraysh to do likewise; for they had come to resent the early Meccan emigrants and, even more, the late converts from the aristocracy of Ḳuraysh, toward whom Muḥammad had shown great favor in his final years despite their early opposition to him. After intense deliberations Abū Bakr was finally elected Muḥammad's political successor (*khalīfa,* caliph), probably with the backing of the Ḳuraysh aristocracy, which was sufficient to overcome the opposition of many Medinese and of factions of the Meccan emigrants, who either favored another of their number or feared that Abū Bakr would continue Muḥammad's policy of favoritism toward the late converts from Ḳuraysh. Many were doubtless swayed by Abū Bakr's mature age, steady character, loyal service to Islam, and intimate ties to the Prophet. Still, some important figures withheld the oath of allegiance (*bay^{c}a*) for a time, notably ^{c}Alī ibn Abī Ṭālib, whose displeasure was doubtless increased by the new caliph's decision to bar the Prophet's daughter Fāṭima, ^{c}Alī's wife, from inheriting the oasis of Fadak.

Abū Bakr faced a serious challenge from many tribal groups that upon Muḥammad's death attempted to establish their independence from Medina and Muslim rule. They had seen their opportunity in the disagreements over succession that divided the community, and not long after Abū Bakr's election a raiding party from the Ḥijāzī tribe of Sulaym began to move closer to the city, hoping to plunder it. Medina's precarious situation was further weakened by Abū Bakr's insistence, against all advice, on sending a force under Usāma ibn Zayd to raid in southern Syria; this he felt bound to do because the Prophet had ordered such an expedition just before his death. Fortunately, the remaining Medinese were able to repulse the raiders at the battle of Dhū$^{\supset}$l-Ḳaṣṣa.

With the return of Usāma's raiding party, Abū Bakr began to organize troops to deal with the larger and more distant tribal rebellions. Shortly before his death, Muḥammad had dispatched agents to collect a tax from many tribes in western and northern Arabia; but some tribes, learning of his death, withheld payment. In other cases, tribal chiefs claiming to be prophets like Muḥammad organized resistance to the Muslims. Crushing these movements of opposition, collectively called *ridda* ("apostasy") by the Islamic sources, became Abū Bakr's main task, as he was determined to collect Muḥammad's tax from delinquent tribes and to extend Medina's hegemony over all tribes of the Arabian Peninsula. To this end he dispatched several armies, which during his caliphate subdued the main centers of opposition in the Najd, eastern Arabia, and southern Arabia. He assigned the leadership of these campaigns mainly to aristocrats of Ḳuraysh, most of them late converts to Islam, in keeping with Muḥammad's policy of favorable treatment of them in his last years.

Having completed the subjection of the Arabian Peninsula, Abū Bakr sent a small force to the Euphrates region to subdue the Arab tribes there and drew up several large armies to march against Syria, over which Muḥammad and the Muslims apparently had long wanted to establish their control for religious, political, and economic reasons. These forces soon became embroiled in confrontations with the Sasanian and Byzantine authorities, which controlled Iraq and Syria; the Muslims were seriously engaged in battling the Byzantines in Syria when Abū Bakr suffered his final illness in 634. Remembering the crisis that had ensued upon Muḥammad's death two years earlier, he designated as his successor his close associate, ^{c}Umar ibn al-Khaṭṭāb, who took office as the second caliph upon Abū Bakr's death. Abū Bakr's body was buried beside that of the Prophet in the mosque in Medina.

Abū Bakr is remembered in Islamic tradition for his simple ways, unassuming manner, devotion to the Prophet, and disdain for wealth and fame. His election as caliph, made possible by his personal qualities, saved the nascent Islamic community from political dissolution at a critical moment, and his forceful policy of consolidation in Arabia—doubtless in accordance with Muḥammad's wishes—made his two-year reign one of the most important in Islamic history, because it laid the foundations for the Islamic conquests that were, soon after his death, to engulf most of the Middle East and North Africa.

BIBLIOGRAPHY

Primary sources are Ibn Ḥajar al-^{c}Asqalānī, *al-Iṣāba fī tamyīz al-ṣaḥāba,* s.n. "Abū Bakr"; Ibn Hishām, *The Life of Muhammad,* Alfred Guillaume, trans. (1955); and Ibn Sa^{c}d, *Ṭabaqāt,* S. M. Haq and H. K. Ghazanfar, trans., 2 vols. (1967–1972). Secondary sources include Fred M. Donner, *The Early Islamic Conquests* (1981); Muhammad A. Shaban, *Islamic History, A.D. 600–750 (A.H. 132)* (1971); Elias S. Shoufani, *Al-Riddah and the Muslim Conquest of Arabia* (1973); al-Ṭabarī, *Ta$^{\supset}$rīkh al-rusul wa l-mulūk,* index; al-Wāqidī, *Maghāzī,* Marsden Jones, ed. (1966), index; William Montgomery Watt, *Muhammad at Mecca* (1953) and *Muhammad at Medina* (1956).

FRED M. DONNER

[See also **Islamic Conquests.**]

ABŪ ḤANĪFA AL-NUʿMĀN IBN THĀBIT IBN ZŪṬĀ (699–767), Islamic lawyer and religious scholar, after whom the Hanafi school of religious law is named, was born in Al-Kufa. His forebears are known for two generations only, for his grandfather, Zūṭā, had come to Al-Kufa as a slave from Kabul and was manumitted by a member of the Arab tribe of Taym-Allāh. Thus his grandfather's descendants, including Abū Ḥanīfa's father Thābit, were born free members and clients of that tribe. The Arabic biographical sources preserve many legends concerning Abū Ḥanīfa's life, but little is known for certain. He made a comfortable living as a silk merchant and, unlike some of his contemporaries, had no need for—or refused to accept—a government appointment as a *qāḍī*, or judge. He was educated in religious law mainly under Ḥammād ibn Abī Sulaymān, whose lectures and discussions he attended over many years. After Ḥammād's death in 737, Abū Ḥanīfa took his place as the leading Kufan authority on religious law, and gathered around him several illustrious disciples who later transmitted his doctrine. He died in prison in Baghdad, where his mausoleum still stands.

The biographers seek to account for some aspects of Abū Ḥanīfa's life that seemed anomalous and even inexplicable to later generations. One was his death in prison; another was the fact that he never held the post of *qāḍī*. Both are explained by the story that the Abbasid caliph al-Manṣūr (or, in a variant, the Umayyad governor of Kufa) asked him to accept an appointment as a *qāḍī* but that he persistently refused; for this he was flogged and imprisoned. However, independent Zaidi sources offer another reason for his imprisonment: covert sympathy (shared by several other well-known scholars) with an Alid uprising against the Abbasids in 762. Further, the fact that Abū Ḥanīfa did not apply his learning in a salaried professional capacity was not unusual during this early period of development in Islamic law.

The question of Abū Ḥanīfa's writings is more difficult. Although he was the leader of the Iraqi school of religious law and is represented as the head of an important tradition in religious doctrine, it is virtually certain that he left no legal writings and only one short treatise in dogmatics. The many works attributed to him actually originated in the circles of his later followers, part of a not uncommon literary convention by which an author or scholar puts his own work under the authoritative name of a master. Yet, we know a great deal about Abū Ḥanīfa's legal doctrines through the work of some of his more prolific immediate disciples—in particular, Abū Yūsuf and Muḥammad ibn Ḥasan al-Shaybānī. His opinions, which he discussed and dictated to these scholars, are preserved in their works as well as in the polemical writings of later jurists such as al-Shāfiʿī.

Abū Ḥanīfa's jurisprudence can be assessed by comparing his thought with that of two famous contemporaries, Ibn Abī Laylā, the *qāḍī* of Kufa, and Mālik ibn Anas of Medina, the eponym of the Maliki school of law. Generally, Abū Ḥanīfa's reasoning is regarded as much more systematic and consistent, and more highly developed technically. In keeping with the legal method of his time, he used his personal judgment *(raʾy)* and analogical reasoning *(qiyās.)* Perhaps because he was not a *qāḍī*, he was less concerned with the practical application of the law and could give more scope to theoretical considerations.

After the beginning of the ninth century, when al-Shāfiʿī established the idea that the precedents of the Prophet should be the over-riding authority for determining the law, Abū Ḥanīfa was accused of neglecting these traditions, but it has been shown that such accusations were unfounded and the result of polemical positions. Just as stricter analogical reasoning was feasible because of Abū Ḥanīfa's efforts, it was only after his time that opposition to it and to its application became possible.

Abū Ḥanīfa also holds an important position in the history of religious thought, especially as the proponent of the trend known as Murjiʾism, which emphasized the unity of the Muslim community against various divisive tendencies. Faith is defined as intellectual assent to, and public profession of, certain doctrines (knowledge of God, acknowledgment of His Messenger and of the revelation). Faith is integral and does not increase or decrease; thus a man's acts—even sinful ones—do not exclude him from membership in the community of believers.

This doctrine had obvious implications for a view of Islam that entailed a moderate and unifying approach, stress on scriptural authority, and reliance on the views of the majority. It formed the most important stream of thought that later contributed to what became known as Sunni Islam. Abū Ḥanīfa's dogmatic views are contained in works by later writers; in a series of creeds or short treatises written by followers but that, for the most part, contain his essential ideas; and in a letter by him to ʿUthmān al-Battī defending his Murjiʾite views, which is considered to be his one authentic composition.

BIBLIOGRAPHY

See Joseph Schacht, *The Origins of Muhammadan Jurisprudence* (1953), for Abū Ḥanīfa's legal thought; Fuat Sezgin, *Geschichte des arabischen Schrifttums,* I (1967), 409–419, the basic biobibliographical source; William Montgomery Watt, *The Formative Period of Islamic Thought* (1973), on the Murjiʾite movement; and Arent J. Wensinck, *The Muslim Creed* (1932; repr. 1965), which contains the creeds attributed to Abū Ḥanīfa.

JEANETTE A. WAKIN

ABŪ JAʿFAR. See **al-Manṣūr.**

ABULAFIA, ABRAHAM BEN SAMUEL (1240–*ca.* 1292), Jewish mystic and the most important representative of ecstatic cabala, was born in Saragossa and educated in Tudela in Navarre. From 1260 he wandered in Greece, Palestine, Italy, Spain, and Sicily, mostly because of persecutions resulting from his claim to be both prophet and Messiah. After 1271 he received revelations, one of which persuaded him to seek a meeting with the pope in 1280. The meeting never took place, but Abulafia continued to propagate his doctrines among Jews and Christians. His many books, most of which survive in manuscript, describe techniques, reminiscent of both Yoga and Sufic practices, to arrive at ecstatic experiences. Some of his most important works were translated into Latin and Italian in the Renaissance and had a deep influence on Christian cabalists.

BIBLIOGRAPHY

Moshe Idel, *Abraham Abulafia's Works and Doctrines* (Ph.D. diss., in Hebrew, Hebrew University, Jerusalem, 1976); Gershom G. Scholem, *Major Trends in Jewish Mysticism* (1967), 119–155; F. M. Tocci, "Una tecnica recitativa e respiratoria di tipico sufico nel libro 'La Luce dell'intelletto' di Abraham Abulafia," in *Annale della Facolta di Lingue e Letterature Straniere di ca'Foscari,* **14** (1975), 221–236.

MOSHE IDEL

ABŪ NUWĀS. By this sobriquet is known al-Ḥasan ibn Hāniʾ, one of the finest Arab lyric poets of the Middle Ages. He was born in Ahvāz, Iran, to an Arab father and Persian mother, between 747 and 762, and died in Baghdad between 813 and 815. His education to the poet's trade began early, when a minor poet of dissolute verse, Wāliba ibn al-Ḥubāb, took him under his wing. Among his teachers in Basra and Al-Kufa were Abū ʿUbayda, a scholar of ancient wars, genealogies, and other tribal traditions—"a skin stuffed with knowledge," Abū Nuwās said of him—and Khalaf al-Aḥmar, the famous collector of pre-Islamic Arabic verse. Abū Nuwās is known to have memorized a vast body of such verse. He no doubt received instruction on linguistically or historically difficult points. He also studied the Koran and hadith, Arabic grammar, and lexicography. It is reported, perhaps correctly, that he spent a year among the bedouins to perfect his command of pure Arabic.

In 786/787, at the beginning of the reign of Hārūn al-Rashīd, Abū Nuwās settled in Baghdad, the newly founded capital of the Islamic empire. Folktales, especially those in the Thousand and One Nights, link his name with Hārūn's and at times present him in the character of a court prankster. In fact Abū Nuwās was disappointed in his hope of becoming a court poet to this caliph. Because of his openly licentious life, other likely patrons too admired him with caution, but he did gain the favor of some illustrious families. As his profession demanded, he wrote poems to extol his patrons, but unlike many later Arab poets he was never first and foremost a panegyrist. The chief task he set himself was to accumulate pleasures: the love of boys and slave girls; drinking parties in taverns or gardens; poetry and music. The best poets of the time were among his friends. Politics did not interest him much. In religion he was perhaps a Murjiʾite, believing that in the next world a Muslim might suffer painful punishment but would at length be forgiven. He took two long trips: in his youth he went on pilgrimage to Mecca; later, in search of a patron, he spent some time in Egypt.

With the accession to the throne of Hārūn's son Amīn in 809, Abū Nuwās' luck improved. He enjoyed not only the patronage but the intimacy of this politically inept but liberal and pleasure-loving ruler. Their friendship ended with Amīn's death in 813 at the hands of his brother Maʾmūn's soldiers. Abū Nuwās died not long after. One report has it that he was poisoned by victims of his sharp tongue; another sets his death in a tavern; a third, in prison. No evidence confirms these tales. He did spend a few brief terms in jail: once or twice under Hārūn (a too sharply agnostic verse is reported as one cause of imprisonment, the violence of his satire against the northern Arab tribes as another) and once under Amīn. This last was from political expediency, for the dangerous Maʾmūn had made propaganda out of the debauched company his brother the caliph was keeping. Apparently Abū Nuwās was soon released and received back into favor.

Abū Nuwās' best poetry is characterized by limpidity of diction, a sharp and lively imagery, and a sense of humor ranging from the ironic hint to the scurrilous joke. His reputation rests chiefly on his sparkling drinking songs, but his love poems—courtly or erotic, and written alike to boys and women—are also remarkable for their vigor and charm. His hunting poems too are highly regarded. The drinking songs are usually built on a variety of conventional motifs: now it is spring, prompting descriptions of blooming earth, mild air, and birdsong; now it is black night, with a small band of friends setting forth on a quest for wine. As in all Arabic verse, a role of the first importance is played by descriptions: of the boy or girl who fills the cups, of the play of light in the wine, of the cups themselves. There are frequent snatches of dialogue. Drunkenness is celebrated as not only a pleasure but a refuge from the evils of the world. The passage of years and the mutability of fortune and affections often set the tone. In these poems much hangs on the prohibition, in Koranic law, of intoxicating drink. Some poems contain notes of an ostentatious libertinism ("Come let us rebel against the Despot of Heaven"); some end with phrases of fear or repentance. Imagery and wording may parody or usurp the styles of religious yearning and religious admonition. Eyes are rarely shut to the conflict between seeking, with all one's heart, the brief refuge of sensual pleasure and throwing off, knowingly and dangerously, the revealed laws. Whether this conflict reflects emotional turmoil or a polished skill at setting up lyric tensions it is impossible to tell.

In many of Abū Nuwās' love poems we meet the stock apparatus of medieval Arabic love poetry. There are tear-stained cheeks and burning hearts; the emaciated lover submits to a lush beauty's implacable teasing. Often, however, a witty twist refreshes the courtly manner. Some of his poems delight in ribaldry. Some, through abrupt self-contradiction or deft punning, combine the delicate and the ribald, creating the witty dissonant effect on which Abū Nuwās' poetry thrives.

In his love and pleasure poems, Abū Nuwās' language is lively, musical, and free of linguistic or rhetorical mannerisms. He makes fun of some conventions of the much admired old bedouin poetry but, like all his contemporaries, makes copious use, in theme, image, and phrase, of the conventions of his own consciously refined age. Despite their conventional aspects, his best poems have an uncommon freshness and fiber thanks to Abū Nuwās' gift for integrating invention and convention, his compositional skill at cross-weaving images, and the verve of his syntax and rhythm.

BIBLIOGRAPHY

Of the two chief medieval recensions of Abū Nuwās' poetry, that of Ḥamza al-Iṣfahānī contains many pieces of dubious authorship, some of them no doubt conscious imitations of the poet's manner. The other, by al-Ṣūlī, retains only about a third of Ḥamza's material and, excessively cautious, probably excludes authentic texts. A modern critical edition is being prepared by Ewald Wagner, who also provides an excellent introduction in *Abū Nuwās* (1965), in German. See also A. Hamori, *On the Art of Medieval Arabic Literature* (1974), 47–77; 101–118.

ANDRAS HAMORI

ABŪ SUFYĀN ibn Ḥarb ibn Umayya (*ca.* 560–*ca.* 653), proper name Ṣakhr ibn Ḥarb. A prominent contemporary of Muḥammad from the clan of ʿAbd Shams (Umayya) of the Meccan tribe of Ḳuraysh, Abū Sufyān, like many prosperous men of his clan, made his living by commerce and seems to have had close ties to Syria, where he owned land and where his grandfather, Umayya, had lived for ten years. Little is known of his early life, and many details of his later life are difficult to verify because his biography became the grafting-place for many tendentious traditions whose aim was, by praising or discrediting him, to bring praise or discredit upon the Umayyad dynasty of caliphs.

By the time the prophet Muḥammad began to receive his revelations in about 610, Abū Sufyān was already the chief of the clan of ʿAbd Shams, one of the wealthiest and most powerful among the Ḳuraysh. As opposition to Muḥammad's preaching in Mecca grew, it gradually took the form of a boycott of the Prophet's clan of Hāshim; in this boycott the ʿAbd Shams, led by Abū Sufyān, and the Makhzūm, which included Muḥammad's bitterest opponent, Abū Jahl, played a major role.

After the Prophet's hegira, or emigration from Mecca to Medina in 622, Abū Sufyān appears to have been the main chief of the Meccans in the Prophet's struggle against his native town. This seems to have been especially the case after the battle of Badr in 624; Abū Sufyān, who was leading a caravan back to Mecca from Syria when it was threatened by Muḥammad's men, managed to lead the caravan to safety, but the Meccan force hastily summoned to defend the caravan suffered a severe defeat at the hands of the Muslims. The effect may have been to bolster Abū Sufyān's position of leadership in Mecca and to weaken the position of some of the more impetuous chiefs whose poor judgment had led to the Meccan defeat.

Abū Sufyān responded to the demands of those who wished to see vengeance done for the defeat at Badr by organizing a campaign against Medina, which culminated in the battle of Uḥud in 625. Abū Sufyān commanded the Meccan forces at Uḥud, and evidently considered the engagement a Meccan victory. Similarly, it was Abū Sufyān who led the Meccans in the inconclusive foray to Badr al-Maw^{c}id (626) and in the grand alliance which besieged Medina during the battle of al-Khandaq, or the Trench, in 627. The enmity between Muḥammad and Abū Sufyān during these years seems to have been intense, as indicated by reports that each tried (unsuccessfully) to arrange the other's assassination.

At the time of the expedition to al-Ḥudaybiya in 628, Abū Sufyān seems still to have been the paramount leader in Mecca, as Muḥammad sent "to Abū Sufyān and the chiefs of Ḳuraysh" to arrange a truce; and after the Ḳuraysh had broken the truce some time later, it was Abū Sufyān who came to Muḥammad to try to put things aright. Finally, on the eve of Muḥammad's conquest of Mecca in 630, it was Abū Sufyān who came to the Prophet, embraced Islam, and secured favorable terms for almost all the population of his town, even though he was reviled for having done so by some of the Ḳuraysh diehards. Any Meccan who remained in Abū Sufyān's house, in the mosque, or locked in his own house, was guaranteed security of life and property.

Shortly after the conquest of Mecca, Abū Sufyān joined the Muslims in the battle of Ḥunayn, and he was one of the former enemies of Muḥammad singled out by the Prophet to receive a special share of booty as "conciliation of hearts," to help assure his continued cooperation. He also took part in the conquest of Al-Ṭā'if, and was sent by the Prophet along with an early convert from that town to destroy its idol, al-Lāt. Most sources state that Abū Sufyān was in Mecca when the Prophet died in 632, but a few allege that he was serving as Muḥammad's tax collector at Najrān, in South Arabia, at the time.

Toward the end of his life, Abū Sufyān went to Syria, where his sons Yazīd and Mu^{c}āwiya, the future caliph, were prominent in the Islamic conquest. He is said to have witnessed the battle of the Yarmuk, where he exhorted the troops before battle. He died during the caliphate of ^{c}Uthmān, aged between 88 and 93 years, sometime between 650 and 654.

BIBLIOGRAPHY

Ibn Ḥajar al-^{c}Asqalānī, *al-Iṣāba,* s.n. "Ṣakhr b. Ḥarb"; Ibn Hishām, *Sīra* (Alfred Guillaume, tr., *The Life of Muḥammad* [1955]), index; Ibn Sa^{c}d, *Ṭabaqāt,* index; Al-Ṭabarī, *Ta$^{\supset}$rīkh al-rusul wa$^{\supset}$l-mulūk,* (1941), index.

FRED M. DONNER

[See also **Badr, Battle of; Hegira; Al-Ḥudaybiya; Uḥud, Battle of; Umayyad Dynasty; Yarmuk, Battle of.**]

ABŪ ṬĀLIB, proper name ^{c}Abd Manāf ibn ^{c}Abd al-Muṭṭalib ibn Hāshim (died *ca.* 619), clan chief in the tribe of Ḳuraysh in Mecca and uncle of the prophet Muḥammad. He became the chief of the clan of Hāshim, succeeding his brother al-Zubayr, but does not appear to have had the ability to arrest the decline in the fortunes of the clan, which around 600 was rapidly losing ground to other clans such as Makhzūm and ^{c}Abd Shams (Umayya). Tradition records that he engaged in commerce with Syria, and he also composed poetry, some of which survives.

When Muḥammad was about eight, Abū Ṭālib became the boy's guardian following the death of his mother and grandfather (the Prophet's father, Abū Ṭālib's brother ^{c}Abdullāh, had died before Muḥammad's birth). Muḥammad's claim to prophethood, first voiced when he was in his early forties, and his attacks on the religious beliefs and mores of his fellow Meccans, scandalized the Ḳuraysh, and Abū Ṭālib was required to summon the clan of Hāshim and the closely affiliated clan of al-Muṭṭalib to secure their agreement to stand as one in protecting Muḥammad from insults and other abuse by his opponents. This protection was rooted not in any particular sympathy on the part of Abū Ṭālib for Islam—he appears never to have embraced the new religion—but in the old Arabian concept of clan solidarity.

Abū Ṭālib led the two clans successfully through a two-year boycott by other clans of Ḳuraysh, who refused to do business or intermarry with them as long as they continued to protect the Prophet. Ultimately the boycott collapsed, but the scarcity of information about it frustrates attempts to establish exactly why it failed or even whether factors other

ABYSSINIA (ETHIOPIA)

than Muḥammad's religious activities, such as economic rivalries, may have played a part in it in the first place.

Shortly afterward Abū Ṭālib died. Leadership of the clan of Hāshim seems to have passed to his brother Abū Lahab, who, though also an uncle of the Prophet, was one of his bitterest enemies. With the death of Abū Ṭālib, Muḥammad and his followers lost their main protector. Abū Lahab revoked the clan's protection of Muḥammad and ushered in a trying period in Muḥammad's life that culminated in his emigration to Medina in 622.

Among Abū Ṭālib's sons, ᶜAlī and his descendants through the Prophet's daughter Fāṭima rose to great political prominence in the Islamic community. Because of the political quarrel between the Alids and the descendants of another of Muḥammad's uncles, al-ᶜAbbās, beginning in the eighth century, a considerable amount of spurious biographical material about Abū Ṭālib was circulated with polemical intent. Some of it attempted to show that he had converted to Islam secretly, or openly, and hence died a Muslim. Other accounts stressed his affiliation to the Prophet, such as making him a participant in the Baḥīrā episode, during which a Syrian monk by that name predicted to Abū Ṭālib an illustrious future for the boy Muḥammad. In fact, however, very little can be known about Abū Ṭālib's life with any certainty, except that he died in Mecca.

BIBLIOGRAPHY

Ibn Ḥajar al-ᶜAsqalānī, *al-Iṣāba fi tamyīz al-ṣaḥāba,* s.n. "Abū Ṭālib"; Ibn Hishām, *The Life of Muhammad,* Alfred Guillaume, trans. (1955); Ibn Saᶜd, *Ṭabaqāt,* S. M. Haq and H. K. Ghazanfar, trans., 2 vols. (1967–1972); and al-Ṭabarī, *Taᵓrīkh al-rusul wa l-mulūk,* index, are primary sources. See also Fred M. Donner, "The Death of Abū Ṭālib," in John H. Marks, ed., *Love and Death: Near Eastern Studies Presented to Marvin H. Pope* (1981); and William Montgomery Watt, *Muhammad at Mecca* (1953).

FRED M. DONNER

[See also **Alids; Hāshim; Muḥammad; Shiᶜa.**]

ABYSSINIA (ETHIOPIA). While the origin of Ethiopia as a political state goes back to remote antiquity, it was during the first millennium B.C., according to our present knowledge, that a centralized government with Aksum as its capital came into being in the north. According to the extensive archaeological and epigraphical evidence—gathered from the surroundings of Aksum and from such sites as Maṭārā, Qasqasē, Tacondā, Qohāyto, and others in the region now known as Eritrea—Ethiopia, from about the fifth century B.C. until the early Christian period, was an area comprising the wedge-shaped, northernmost Ethiopian plateau, including the seacoast where the cosmopolitan port of Adulis was located. This primordial state gradually expanded, moving far into the interior highlands and eventually giving rise to a much larger kingdom, which came to be known as Ethiopia in early Christian times.

At the dawn of the period known as the Middle Ages in Europe, this ancient African kingdom reached the zenith of its power, growing into an empire that extended from the island of Meroë to the heart of the Arabian peninsula, a territory almost the size of Western Europe. From Adulis, it controlled the important international maritime trade moving through the Red Sea and established extensive cultural contact not only with the East but also with the Mediterranean world. It was probably at Adulis that the early Christian missionaries who came with the Red Sea traders and travelers began their evangelizing activities.

During the reign of Emperor Ezana (*ca.* 325–*ca.* 360), when Aksum was still at the height of its political, military, and economic power, Ethiopia adopted Christianity as the state religion. In a highly Africanized form, Christianity gave rise to the dominant culture of Ethiopia—its literature, art, music, law, and architecture. During the fourth and fifth centuries the entire Ethiopian plateau in the north was so thoroughly Christianized that Cosmas, the famous Egyptian monk who visited Ethiopia about 525, returned impressed that there were "everywhere churches of the Christians, bishops, martyrs, monks, and hermits, by whom the gospel . . . is proclaimed."

After about the middle of the seventh century, with the rise of Islam as a world power, Ethiopia lost control over the Red Sea trade, which had been a major source of economic and international strength, and entered a period of isolation. The decline of its maritime trade became one of the main reasons why Ethiopia began to look to its hinterland for other areas of economic wealth and stability. Probably in the tenth century the capital was moved to Agaw land in the middle highlands, where Christianity, translated into indigenous African cultural terms, triumphed once again. The north still remained the spiritual center of the nation and Aksum the national holy city. All succeeding rulers legiti-

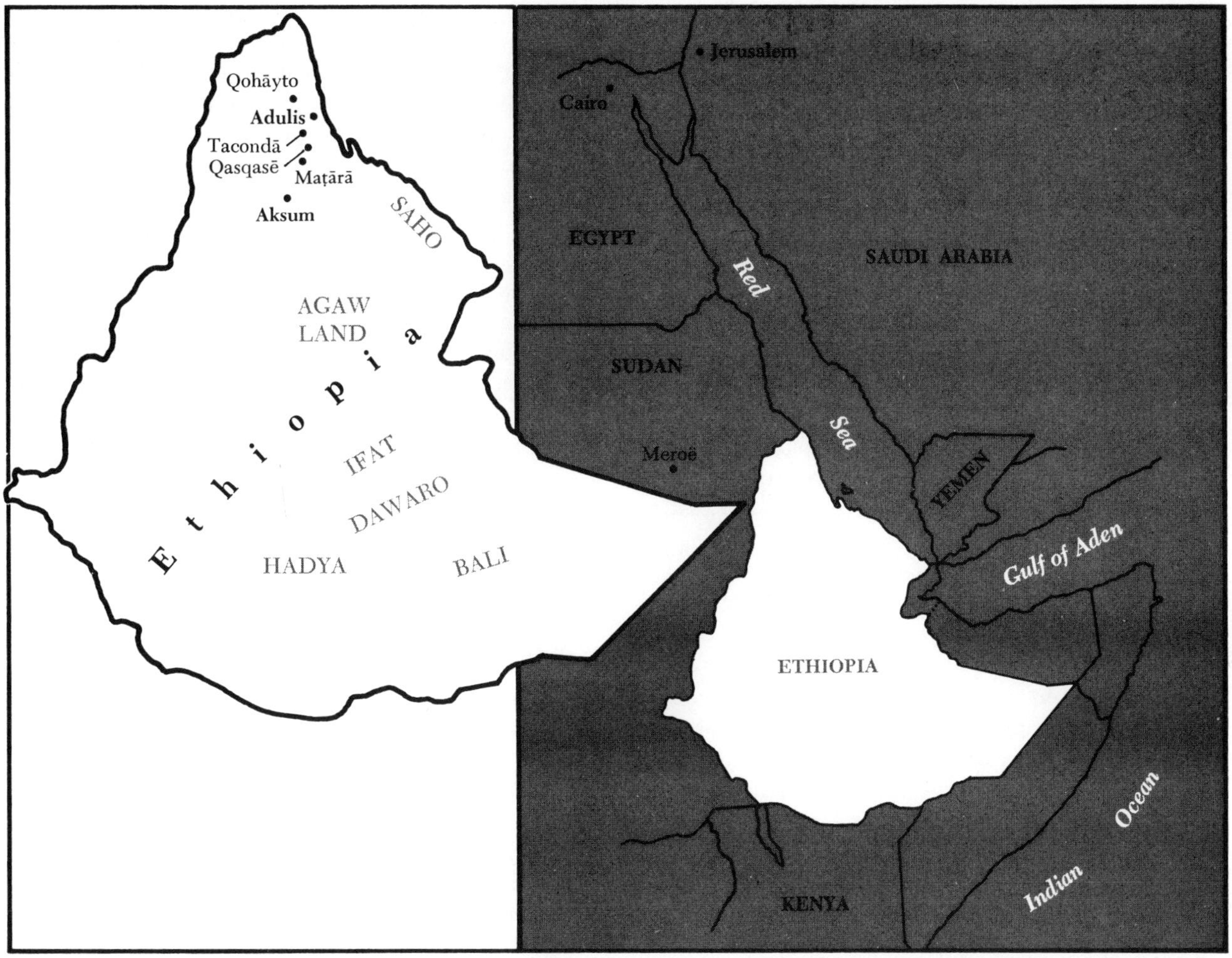

Medieval Ethiopa

mized their thrones by tracing their ancestry to the Aksumite rulers and by going to Aksum to be crowned and to receive political authority in the church of that mother city.

About this time some of the coastal population (particularly the Saho) began to embrace Islam, further adding to the cultural eclipse of Ethiopia with respect to the contemporary Christian world. It is ironic that Ethiopia, which suffered decline and internal setbacks due to the rise of the new religion, also served as an important midwife in its birth. It was in this country that some of Muḥammad's first disciples, following his advice to go to the "land of righteousness," found religious tolerance and refuge in a world dominated by Christianity.

Islam subsequently spread to Ethiopia through *jihad* (holy wars) as well as by migrations and nomadic movements. Thus, though Christianity remained the official religion during the period of the European Middle Ages, Muslim states such as Ifat, Dawaro, Hadya, Saho, and Bali were given full recognition and were federated into the Ethiopian empire. Despite the continual conflict between the Christian and Muslim states, at times joined by a Falasha Jewish state, the relative tolerance of the states toward each other gave the Ethiopian rulers some semblance of authority as protectors of Christians in Muslim lands—particularly in Egypt—as was the case during the reign of Emperor ᶜAmda Ṣeyyon (1314–1344).

ETHIOPIA AND GRECO-ROMAN CHRISTIANITY

Christianity came to Ethiopia directly from Syro-Palestine. The fourth-century Syro-Palestinian monk Frumentius, who played an important role in the creation of the Christian state, studied with Atha-

ABYSSINIA (ETHIOPIA)

nasius, and upon returning to Ethiopia became its first *abuna* (bishop). During the Arian controversy, Emperor Constantius II felt it important enough to seek the support of Ethiopian Christianity that he wrote to the Ethiopian rulers Ezana and She^{c}azana. Addressing them as his "esteemed brothers," he asked them to expel Athanasius, who was rumored to have fled to Ethiopia, and to accept an Arian bishop. But Ethiopian Christian leaders were apparently not eager to be drawn into the various theological controversies and even after settlement of the Monophysite controversy at the Council of Chalcedon in 451, remained on good terms with all parties. Thus the large-scale Ethiopian expedition to South Arabia during the reign of Emperor Kaleb (514–542) to rescue the Christians of Najran was carried out in full cooperation with Emperors Justin I and Justinian, and points to an alliance with anti-Monophysite Christians against the Persians and their allies.

Even in pre-Christian times, the author of the *Periplus maris Erythraei,* who visited Aksum around the second century and wrote of its important commercial relations with the Greco-Roman world, observed that the Ethiopian king "Zoskales" was well acquainted with Greek literature. Numerous Greek inscriptions, including the important trilingual inscription of Ezana, have also been found in northern Ethiopia. From the fourth to sixth centuries many early literary works (*Physiologus,* Rules of Pachomius, Cyril of Alexandria) were rendered into Geez (classical Ethiopic) from the Greek; the translation of biblical, apocryphal, and pseudepigraphic works had taken place at an even earlier time. It is only in Ethiopic that we have the complete versions of such works as the *Book of Enoch, Jubilees,* and the *Ascension of Isaiah;* and the Alexandrian Jewish calendar of the Hellenistic period is best preserved in Ethiopic calendaric literature.

ETHIOPIA AND EUROPE IN THE MIDDLE AGES

From early Christian times, Ethiopian monks flocked to the Holy City of Jerusalem, which became the focal point of contact between Ethiopia and the rest of Christendom. In his letter to Leta, Jerome wrote, "Every day we receive large numbers of monks from India, Persia, and Ethiopia." The concept of *Aethiopia credet Deo* ("Ethiopia believes in God") preoccupied the great minds of the early church from Origen to Augustine, from Cyril of Alexandria to Gregory of Nyssa, particularly in their exegetic works. During the Crusades and immediately thereafter European Christian interest in Ethiopia intensified. This era overlaps the periods of Ethiopian ecclesiastical revival during the Zagwe dynasty (1137–1270) and the period of the rise and growth of the so-called Solomonid dynasty (1270–1527). It also involved fact and fiction concerning Prester John, a legendary Christian priest and ruler of a vast kingdom in the East.

Beginning in the fourteenth century, when it emerged that John resembled the emperor of Ethiopia more than any other temporal leader, European monarchs tried to win the political alliance of the Ethiopian emperor, and popes his spiritual allegiance. After the fall of Acre in 1291, a plan for another crusade to "exterminate the Saracens" by blockading the Gulf of Aden with Ethiopian cooperation was espoused in 1317 by Guillaume Adam, the Dominican monk who became the archbishop of Sultaniyah; this idea was also presented to King Philip V of France. As the fourteenth-century Egyptian chronicler al-Maqrīzī indicates, the Muslims were aware of the quest for this Euro-Ethiopian "great alliance against Islam" and feared it. Ethiopian rulers themselves sought to organize their own "crusades" to liberate Jerusalem—an objective that lingered on in Ethiopian history until the mid nineteenth century.

From the fourteenth to the sixteenth century, European leaders sustained interest in Ethiopia for various reasons: John II of Portugal, for instance, desired to divert the spice trade from Venice. But the religious objective always remained important, as is attested by the missions that these leaders sent to Ethiopia and the messages they received from its rulers. An important reason underlying the systematic explorations of Henry the Navigator was the hope of discovering a sea route to Ethiopia.

During major religious reform in Ethiopian history, under the reign of Emperor Zar^{c}a Ya^{c}qob (1434–1468), representatives of the Ethiopian monasteries of Jerusalem arrived at the Council of Florence in 1441 to entertain the idea of Christian unity. (It is unknown whether they came with official Ethiopian approval, either imperial or ecclesiastical.) Thereafter the Holy See acquired a house (Santo Stefano dei Mori) behind St. Peter's for Ethiopian pilgrims; documents of the pontifical archives also reveal additional financial support. The pilgrims contributed not only to Ethiopian studies in Europe but also to scholarly interest in the study of Semitic languages and Eastern Christendom. As the European Middle Ages drew to a close, an even more intensified contact with Ethiopia continued to stimulate the intellectual development of the times in the free marketplace of ideas.

BIBLIOGRAPHY

Francisco Alvares, *The Prester John of the Indies,* Charles F. Beckingham and George W. B. Huntingford, trans. (1961); Athanasius, *Apologia ad imperatorum Constantium,* in *Patrologia graeca,* XXV (1857), 636; and *Historical Tracts,* John Henry Newman, trans. (1843), 182–183; Enrico Cerulli, "Documenti arabi per la storia dell'Etiopia," in *Memorie della Reale Accademia dei Lincei,* 6th ser., **4** (1931); "Eugenio IV e gli Etiopi al concilio di Firenze nel 1441," in *Rendiconti della Reale Accademia dei Lincei,* 6th ser., **9** (1933); and *Etiopi in Palestina,* 2 vols. (1943–1947); Cosmas Indicopleustes, *The Christian Topography,* John W. McCrindle, ed. and trans. (1897); August Dillmann, "Zur Geschichte des Axumitschen Reichs im vierten bis sechsten Jahrhundert," *Abhandlungen der Königlichen Akademie der Wissenschaften zu Berlin* (1880); Abraham J. Drewes, *Inscriptions de l'Éthiopie antique* (1962); and Ibn Hisham, *Sīrat Rasūl Allah,* F. Wüstenfeld, ed. (1858–1860; 1937); Ephraim Isaac, *A New Text-Critical Introduction to Maṣḥafa Berhān* (1973); Enno Littmann, *Deutsche Aksum Expedition,* 4 vols. (1913); Al-Maqrīzī, *Historia regum Islamiticorum in Abyssinia,* Friedrich T. Rinck, ed. and trans. (1790); William Muir, *The Life of Moḥammad* (1923); *The Periplus of the Erythraean Sea,* Wilfred H. Schoff, ed. and trans (1912); Procopius, *De bello Persico,* Henry B. Dewing, trans. (1914); Carlo Conti Rossini, "Sulle missioni domenicane in Etiopia nel secolo XIV," in *Rendiconti della Reale Accademia dei Lincei,* 7th ser., **1** (1940); Rufinus, *Historia ecclesiastica,* in *Patrologia latina,* XXI (1878), 478–480; and John Spencer Trimingham, *Islam in Ethiopia* (1965).

Major editions of works in Geez (classical Ethiopic) are to be found in the Corpus Scriptorum Christianorum Orientalium: Scriptores aethiopici and in the Patrologia Orientalis. *Rassegna di studi etiopici* and *Annales d'Éthiopie* are also useful aids to research.

EPHRAIM ISAAC

ACALLAM NA SENÓRACH, the most extensive text of the Finn cycle of storytelling, is a product of the Irish literary renaissance of the eleventh and twelfth centuries. During that time Finn mac Cumaill, known earlier as a mythological warrior-hunter possessing magical powers, had been given a place in pseudohistorical tradition as leader of the soldiers of Cormac mac Airt, a supposed third-century king of Tara. And so, from being a figure popular with tellers of folktales, Finn became the focal point of a new literary activity.

It was about this time that the ballad was coming into vogue in Europe, and the Irish innovators who adopted it as a narrative medium used it almost exclusively to tell of Finn and his companions. In the course of a few centuries, a rich ballad literature about the Fiana was produced; and, like the many new tales about Finn, it proved popular and enduring at all levels of society.

Acallam na Senórach ("The Colloquy of the Old Men") is a very different kind of production, and in its form and scope it reflects a truly original mind, for its author conceived the idea of combining various branches of Irish tradition in a vast new literary compilation of an encyclopedic nature. Basic to his plan was the interest in *dinnshenchas* ("lore about places"), which had developed in the preceding two centuries. This interest had been manifested at a literary level in a number of prose and verse anecdotes explaining the derivation of place names, and it is virtually certain that this sort of lore was circulating widely in oral form.

The *Acallam* consists of a "frame-tale" having a very simple plot, together with a large number of "in-tales" in prose with verse interludes, some narrative and some lyrical. The basic story is laid in the time of St. Patrick and, according to it, a few survivors of the Fiana meet the saint and his fellow missionaries. According to some traditions Finn's son Oisín had been enticed by a fairy lover to the otherworld where no one grows old, and he had returned to Ireland not knowing that centuries had passed and that his companions were long since dead. In the *Acallam* the great age of the Fiana heroes is reflected in the term *senórach* ("ancient"), but there is no explanation of how they came to survive so long. Furthermore, although Oisín is one of the surviving heroes, it is Caílte mac Rónáin who is the main character. In their first encounter the Fiana and the Christian missionaries establish a good relationship, and the rest of the text deals with their wanderings around Ireland, with St. Patrick inquiring about the origin of the names of the places they visit and, in reply, Caílte or Oisín recounting anecdotes about figures and events of the past.

In all there are more than two hundred such anecdotes, presented in the typically Irish form of prose interspersed with verse. Some of them relate to members of the mythological Tuatha Dé Danann, some to persons who are familiar from the "historical" cycles, and there is mention occasionally of heroes of the Ulster cycle. But most of the in-tales are about Finn and the Fiana, with emphasis on the qualities of bravery, loyalty, and generosity that were held to be characteristic of them. One of the most moving stories is the tragic death of Cael and Créd, which is also found as an episode in an independent story, *Cath Finntrága* ("The Battle of Ventry"). There is also a fine version of the story of Fithir and Dáirine that forms part of the pseudohistorical *Bóraime Laigen* ("The Leinster Tribute").

Sufficient variety is maintained in the broken narrative of the frame-tale to keep it from becoming in any way tedious. There is, for instance, the description of the doubt that St. Patrick has about the propriety of listening to pagan tales and the advice he is given by his guardian angels to commit all the tales to writing, "to be a delight for companies and nobles to the end of time." At another point in the narrative, the Fiana and St. Patrick separate for a year—Patrick to go with the king of Tara; Oisín, with the king of Leinster; and Caílte, with Conall mac Néill, ancestor of Cenél Conaill of Ailech. Sometimes there is variation by having one of the kings as interrogator instead of Patrick. In addition the framing narrative itself has romantic interludes, such as that between Aillenn of the Túatha Dé Danann and the king of Connacht.

Although manuscript copies of the *Acallam* from the fifteenth century on show that it was very popular, no complete text has survived. There are four principal manuscripts (fifteenth and sixteenth centuries) of the oldest recension, which dates from about the end of the twelfth century. A shorter version, which is also fairly old, is found in one of these manuscripts. And there is a later version, dating from the fourteenth or fifteenth century, that represents a conflation of the two earlier ones and is known from manuscripts of the seventeenth century and later. (Detailed information about these manuscripts is given in the edition by Nessa Ní Shéaghdha, which is listed in the bibliography.) The end of the *Acallam* is missing in all versions. It may have described how Oisín and Caílte, both previously baptized by St. Patrick, departed from this life at the festival known as *Feis Temrach* ("The Feast of Tara").

The *Acallam,* which runs to about 80,000 words, contains a great deal of legend that is not found elsewhere. If, as seems likely, the original compiler had witnessed the advent of the Anglo-Normans to Ireland, factors that motivated him in his great work of collecting and synthesizing may have included fear of a threat to Irish traditions and a desire to ensure that the advice supposedly given to St. Patrick by the angels would be put into effect.

BIBLIOGRAPHY

Standish Hayes O'Grady, *Silva Gadelica* (1892), I, 94–233 (text), and II, 101–365 (translation); Whitley Stokes, *Acallamh na Senórach,* Irische Texte, IV, 1 (1900); Eoin Mac Neill and Gerard Murphy, *Duanaire Finn,* 3 vols. (1908–1953); Douglas Hyde, "An Agallamh Bheag," in *Lia Fáil,* 1 (1924); Nessa Ní Shéaghdha, *Agallamh na Seanórach,* 3 vols. (1942–1945); Cecile O'Rahilly, *Cath Finntrágha* (1962); Myles Dillon, *Stories from the Acallam* (1970); and Gerard Murphy, *The Ossianic Lore and Romantic Tales of Medieval Ireland,* rev. ed. (1971).

Brian Ó Cuív

[See also **Irish Literature.**]

ACCESSUS AD AUCTORES, an introduction, usually to a text received as authoritative, which discusses a small number of topics, taken as canonically specified, in conventional and broadly uniform terms. Thus, beyond preserving information and opinion about a specific text, the *accessus* in use defines culture as something bookish, cognitive, and subject to primarily philosophical analysis.

Medieval reference to the procedure of Boethius in his *In Isagogen Porphyrii commenta* probably identifies the most important single source, both of the *accessus* procedure and of its major topics. Medieval writers also admitted the influence of Servius' commentary on Virgil and of the *De inventione* of Cicero. In the topics themselves there was much variation within a rhetoric of obligatory items *(quae consideranda sunt).* A major change came in the thirteenth century, when topics based on the four Aristotelian causes generally replaced ones verbally resembling Servius and Boethius.

According to ninth-century formulations, the commentator considered the circumstances *(circumstantiae)* of a text, answering the questions: who, what, why, in what manner, where, when, and whence (or by what means). Outmoding these, categories like those of late classical sources were dominant through the twelfth century. They specified discussion of title, author, intention, material, mode of treatment, order of the book, utility, and the part of philosophy to which the book belonged. Under the influence of Aristotle, author, material, and utility and intention were covered by efficient, material, and final cause. Mode of treatment and order were considered under a double formal cause, specified as the form of the treatment *(forma tractandi)* and the form of the treatise *(forma tractatus).* Title and part of philosophy continued to be treated as such. Since to consider a topic was normally to deal with a textbook, *accessus* procedure was applied to many fields, including canon and civil law, medicine, theology, and exegesis, as well as to the curricular arts.

Accessus discussion of intention and final cause expressed the medieval willingness to receive all respected books as a part of one unitary and often explicitly Christian culture. Discussion of mode of treatment and form, by defining a great many modes around a central attention to definition, logical and rhetorical proof, analysis by division, and exemplification, heightened the significance of language as a model for thought as well as its instrument. Attribution of a work to its proper part of philosophy refined understanding of what distinguished verbal arts (such as grammar, rhetoric, and logic), which had no "content," from speculative disciplines (such as metaphysics), which were cognitive, and from practical disciplines (such as ethics and politics), whose end was action. The need to fit all books into these schemes of analysis, and the related need to distinguish discussion of some text from the practice of the art it described (*de arte* from *per artem* or *ex arte*), helped make the resulting commentaries characteristically medieval.

BIBLIOGRAPHY

Judson B. Allen, "Commentary as Criticism: Formal Cause, Discursive Form, and the Late Medieval Accessus," in J. IJsewijn and E. Kessler, eds., *Acta Conventus Neo-Latini Lovaniensis* (1973), 29–48. R. W. Hunt, "The Introductions to the 'Artes' in the Twelfth Century," in *Studia Mediaevalia in honorem admodum reverendi patris Raymundi Josephi Martin, O. P.* (n.d.), 85–112. R. B. C. Huygens, *Accessus ad Auctores, Bernard d'Utrecht, Conrad d'Hirsau Dialogus super Auctores* (1970); Alastair J. Minnis, *Medieval Theory of Authorship: Scholastic Literary Attitudes in the Later Middle Ages* (in press); Gustaw Przychocki, *Accessus Ovidiana* (1911); Franz Quadlbauer, *Die antike Theorie der genera dicendi im lateinischen Mittelalter* (1962); Edwin A. Quain, "The Medieval Accessus ad Auctores,"in *Traditio,* 3 (1945), 215–264. Bruno Sandkühler, *Die frühen Dantekommentare und ihr Verhältnis zur mittelalterlichen Kommentartradition* (1967), 16–46.

JUDSON BOYCE ALLEN

ACCIDENT. In medieval philosophy an accident is the derivative, less important aspect of a thing or event; a nonessential attribute. It can be a feature present by chance *(per accidens).* More technically, it is one of the sense-perceptible qualities of a substance, which in turn is the imperceptible, unchanging substrate in which the sensible qualities inhere. In the doctrine of transubstantiation the accidents are the sensible qualities of bread and wine after consecration.

WILLIAM J. COURTENAY

ACCLAMATIONS, the oral judgments of medieval assemblies, were important elements in the development of the electoral process and in the ceremonial confirmation of temporal and spiritual leaders. As a form of popular election, acclamation derives from Germanic tribal politics. Kings and war leaders were selected by the spontaneous hailing of the assembled adult males, possibly by prearrangement. The Viking custom of holding a candidate up on a shield to be acclaimed preserved this traditional ritual by the assembly of freemen with its fiction of unanimity. An analogous elevation of the Byzantine emperors was rooted in Roman legal notions of popular consent.

Among the Franks, the Goths, and the Anglo-Saxons the introduction of hereditary monarchies weakened the force of election, but an acclamation or "recognition" introduced into the coronation ceremonies preserved the principle. At the coronation of Otto the Great in 936 the bishops presented the emperor to the people asking that they indicate approval of his election by the princes. Anglo-Saxon kings and their successors were similarly presented on the coronation dais for popular acclamation. When William the Conqueror was crowned, however, the new king's Norman soldiers unfortunately mistook the acclamatory cheering for a revolt and set about burning houses in the area. At the coronation of King John, in 1199, Archbishop Hubert Walter pointedly noted the electoral nature of this ritual confirming the unanimous approbation of the kingdom.

A related form of political acclamation, the formulaic chanting of laudatory phrases, originated in a separate Latin tradition. Roman political and theatrical figures hired paid claques to provide an enthusiastic chorus, and customary phrases hailed festal, familial, or political triumphs. Byzantine imperial ceremonies of the sixth century already incorporated these sacerdotal affirmations of majesty, and such formalized lauds were widely imitated by Western rulers. Like their counterparts for the investiture of popes and bishops, these royal lauds emphasized the origins of the ruler's authority.

As the preferred form of voting in medieval assemblies, acclamation derived from both Germanic tribal and Roman senatorial roots. Ecclesiastical councils and monastic houses assented or dissented orally (saying *placet* or *non placet*; *yay* or *nay*) as did legislative assemblies such as parliaments and Estates-General. This process allowed for the expression of dissent while preserving the appearance of a consensus for the eventual decision.

French and English kings from at least the thirteenth century were greeted with set phrases, devised by royal publicists, for use at ceremonial royal crown-wearings on principal feastdays and formal royal entries into the chief towns of the realm. The famous royal salute of the French heralds, *Vive le roi!*, was first conjoined with the funerary valediction *Le roi est mort!* at the entombment of Charles VI in 1422. Thereafter, "The king is dead ... long live the king" became the final acclamation of a king's reign and the first hailing of his successor.

BIBLIOGRAPHY:

The tradition of Germanic acclamations was studied in the early treatise of Arthur Jones, *The Glory of Regality* (1820), while royal and liturgical aspects are traced in Ernst H. Kantorowicz, *Laudes Regiae* (1946).

JOHN W. MCKENNA

ACCOLADE ARCH. See **Arch, Types of.**

ACCOUNTING. Accounts and accounting statements take a variety of forms, vary greatly in scope and content, and may serve a variety of purposes. They range from records of detailed information useful for the control and administration of money or debts, to statements that summarize and classify receipts and expenditures, profits and losses, or assets and liabilities—synoptic statements conceivably helpful in the formulation of major financial or economic decisions.

Surviving medieval accounts display considerable variety as regards account keeper (cleric or layman), content, order or lack of it, regularity, numeral system (Roman or Arabic), language (Latin or vernacular), form (roll, book, or loose records), and material (parchment, paper, or wax tablet). They were generated in a variety of contexts and within a diversity of institutions. Nevertheless, excluding those of commercial enterprises, most of the remaining accounting materials exhibit one common feature: they were created as part of a process in which a subordinate agent or steward "accounted" to his superior or principal—that is, a process in which the subordinate from time to time sought to justify his activities on behalf of his superior, and to determine the remaining debt owed to or owed by the superior.

Stewardship accounting was likely to exist wherever the delegated activities were extensive or complex, the superior or principal often was absent, and literate clerks were available to compose the accounts. The purpose of such accounting was the same as that ascribed by de Ste. Croix to Greek and Roman accounting: "The whole purpose of ancient accounting was ... to keep accurate records of acquisitions and outgoings, in money and kind, and to expose any losses due to dishonesty and negligence" (de Ste. Croix, p. 38).

Accounts alone would not be satisfactory for this purpose. Entries in the accounts would have to be examined to determine what lay behind them, and to establish that all revenues due to the principal had been collected or otherwise satisfactorily accounted for, and that all expenditures by the agent had been properly incurred or authorized. This examination of the stewardship accounts was the audit. As the word indicates, the examination of the accountant (agent) by the auditor(s) was oral: this was so partly because accountants or auditors might be illiterate, and also because "reading was still primarily oral rather than visual" (Clanchy, p. 215).

Basically a stewardship account was an account of the reporting steward's receipts and expenditures of money or goods on behalf of his principal. But it was not invariably quite so simple. An account might record among "receipts" the full amount of an item that should have been received even though it had not been received in full. Or an entry on the "receipts" side might record the unspent part of an authorized item of expenditure entered in full on the "payments" side. Thus, the terms "charge" and "discharge" are more accurate than "receipts" and "payments." The balance on an account represented the amount due to or from the steward, and was in no sense the profit or loss on his activities.

Stewardship accounting was prescribed in the Carolingian *Capitulare de villis* (*ca.* 800), issued partly in an attempt to eliminate improprieties in the administration by the stewards *(iudices)* of the royal estates and partly to encourage production. Several paragraphs in the capitulary concern quantitative returns to be submitted to the palace—for instance, "Let the stewards give us an accounting of the male and female goats and of their horns and skins. . . ." Since many of the stewards were illiterate, Wolfgang Metz believes that accounts were not rendered to the palace, but given verbally to the traveling *missi.* The *missi* or their clerks would draw up the accounts from the information supplied (Metz, p. 82). Later instructions required additional returns from the stewards—for example, of the wool and flax issued to women on the royal domain and of the number of garments produced. It is not known how scrupulously these various instructions were carried out.

The papal accounting system serves to illustrate several points. Outside the patrimonies and the states of the Church, revenues were collected by officials appointed by the pope. They had wide powers: "The responsibility of the collectors was enforced mainly by the accounts which they were compelled to render to the camera" (Lunt, I, p. 47). They had to submit their accounts in person at Rome (or Avignon), at first whenever summoned and later commonly every two years. They had to produce vouchers and other evidence to support their accounting. Members of the college of clerks responsible to the *camerarius,* or chamberlain, audited the accounts in detail and prepared them for final approval by the *camerarius* or the cameral council.

The collector had some incentive to keep accurate records because his personal assets were at risk as security, a feature of personal responsibility also found in other administrative systems, such as municipal government and the English manorial system. There were ample opportunities for fraud in the collectorates, and the camera was aware of them. A papal bull of 1404 recounted possible types of fraud, including reporting as arrears to be collected sums that already had been collected, and making vacant benefices available to accomplices at low prices. Multiplicity of currencies also facilitated the duping of cameral officials. Moreover, the requirement of regular accounting at the camera was widely disregarded, and the camera found it necessary from time to time to send envoys to conduct audits and investigations on site. There were several collectors, like Jean de Palmis in southern France, who began as poor men and soon became wealthy. One is reminded of Chaucer's reeve of the manor, who, although also subject to account and audit, "koude bettre than his lord purchace./Ful riche he was astored pryvely."

The cameral treasurer, responsible for the receipt and payment of moneys, had to account annually to the *camerarius* on the basis of his account book, the *introitus et exitus,* the entries in which were based on a journal. The depository, usually a firm of bankers appointed by the pope, stored and handled the cash, and had to render accounts regularly to the camera. The *camerarius,* the highest financial officer and a person close to the pope, in turn had to render an account when he gave up the office; and if this was satisfactory, he was released by the pope from further financial responsibility.

"In medieval administrative systems finance and judicature went hand in hand" (Lunt, I, p. 21). This was true of the papal camera. It was also true, for example, of the royal exchequer in England and of corresponding institutions in western Europe, such as the *Chambre des comptes* in France.

Much is known about accounting in the exchequer of the English kings because copious records have survived and there is available the manuscript *Dialogus de scaccario,* written toward the end of the twelfth century by Richard Fitzneale, treasurer of England and bishop of London. Some features of early exchequer accounting may have been superimposed upon a pre-Conquest illiterate method of account keeping by means of notches on sticks (Johnson, p. xxxv). Other features of the functioning of the exchequer may have been influenced by the constitution and operations of the *duana* of King Roger of Sicily, which in turn may partly have been derived from the practices of the Fatimid *dīwān.*

The English medieval exchequer developed out of the *curia regis,* and was entrusted with financial and judicial responsibilities. The accounting and audit arrangements are of interest here. The sheriffs and other royal officers annually rendered their accounts before the barons of the exchequer and their specialist staff. Proceedings took place around a large table covered with a cloth marked into squares. This was the "chessboard" or abacus on which an officer, the calculator, placed counters, the number and location of which indicated sums of money. Additions and subtractions were performed on the exchequer board in a manner visible and comprehensible to all present, the object being to establish, in effect, the accountant's balance vis-à-vis the crown. The accountant produced supporting vouchers and tallies, and his explanations could be challenged and adjudicated. The resulting accounts were enrolled to form the pipe rolls, many of which have survived, the earliest being that of 1130.

The contents of the exchequer rolls underwent modifications from time to time. Thus, when the number of debtors to the crown had increased greatly, space was saved and greater clarity achieved in the pipe rolls by consolidating many otherwise separate receipts as single entries, and by removing details of certain categories of revenue to separate rolls.

Just as the sheriffs had to account to the exchequer, so the treasurer and chamberlains of the exchequer from time to time had to account to special commissioners appointed by the king. At first these commissioners were men of high rank in the court, but by the fourteenth century this type of audit was being performed by an official of the treasury.

The main accounting and auditing features of the early exchequer system were found also in Flemish, Capetian, and Norman financial institutions. It appears that by the eleventh century, written accounts and elaborate financial administration, previously unnecessary, had to be introduced. Common problems and links between the countries ensured that basically similar solutions came to be adopted, although there were minor differences in early practice. For instance, in France accounts were rendered three times a year; in England, Normandy, and Flanders, the final account only once yearly (though there was usually a semiannual preliminary account).

The Teutonic Knights had elaborate accounting and auditing arrangements, two features of which are of interest. First, from the middle of the fourteenth century the officers of the various establishments of the order had to compile inventories of the assets and liabilities to be handed over to their successors. Copies were sent to the headquarters in Marienburg (now Malbork, Poland), where the information was entered in a book. Second, the *Treszler* (treasurer) in Marienburg kept detailed records of the money transactions he handled. Annual accounts were prepared from preliminary records, which were probably made on wax tablets and destroyed when no longer required. These annual accounts, partly organized according to the type of transaction and partly chronological, were submitted to the *Groszkomtur* (grand commander) for approval.

Many accounts of the finances of town and city administrations survive from the thirteenth century on. The elected or appointed treasurers and other accounting officials submitted their accounts periodically to the magistrates, to other scrutineers, or in some cases to assemblies of citizens. Like the similar accounts of other governmental institutions, these accounts, written on rolls or in books, tended to improve in terms of systemization and order in the course of the later Middle Ages. It may be noted in passing that Leonardo Fibonacci, author of an influential work on arithmetic, *Liber abaci* (1202), probably at one time was examiner of the Pisan municipal accounts. The account books of the *biccherna,* the Sienese treasury, are notable in that they have wooden covers adorned with paintings by local artists.

For effective audit the examiners of papal, royal, or municipal accounts required independent information about the receipts due from the accountants. For this purpose, as well as for other administrative reasons, lists of amounts due from tenants, revenue farmers, and taxpayers were prepared. For example, following a practice initiated in ancient Egypt, land registers were compiled for revenue administration in the Byzantine Empire. Several Carolingian surveys or inventories of manors have survived—the polyptych of the estates near Paris belonging to the abbey of St.-Germain-des-Prés, compiled early in the ninth century, is an elaborate example. A copy of the Domesday Book of 1086 (itself developed in an Anglo-Saxon administrative context) was kept in the English exchequer, although the extent of its use is debatable. In Sicily a similar record was compiled in 1140.

The auditors in the English exchequer also used information contained in earlier pipe rolls as a basis for checking entries in the current accounts under audit. In the Normandy of the Angevin dukes, the *extractus memorandorum* listed under each district certain debts and revenues from land to be collected by the officer in charge. In 1192 the papal *camerarius* Cencio compiled the first *liber censuum,* which listed by provinces and dioceses those who owed census and the amounts due.

How well informed about the state of their finances were the central headquarters of such far-flung organizations as the papacy and the royal states? Evidently the numerous accounts rendered by local agents and others provided a mass of detailed information. But the content and form of these accounts reflected their limited purpose, and not all revenues or expenditures necessarily flowed into or out of the various treasuries. The French exchequer rolls of the twelfth century and the summary accounts of 1202 "are very confused. . . . It would be difficult from these rolls to find the total revenue collected by one man or the total revenue given by one

ACCOUNTING

source" (Strayer, p. 36). During the reign of Louis IX the centralization of authority in the hands of the *baillis* and the gradual development of classification of revenues and expenditures in the accounts represented substantial improvements.

The camera of the Avignon popes had no "clear and immediate knowledge of the overall state of the papal finances," but "it had a detailed, if delayed knowledge of its revenues, and had absolute control over their use" (Favier, p. 92).

This centralization of papal finance and accounting did not last, "since in the fifteenth century the centralised system of book-keeping" of Avignon broke down (Partner, p. 256). But summaries of the accounts, comprehensive in scope, could be compiled when required. The "budget" of the Roman church of 1480–1481 is an example. A surviving fragment of an account reveals that in 1221, toward the end of the reign of Philip II, a general recapitulation of the French royal receipts and payments was drawn up. Unlike that of the surviving French account of 1202, it was not the purpose of the account of 1221 to control the payments made by *baillis* and other accountants; rather, it was to provide a review of the royal finances, and may well be the earliest surviving "budget" of northern Europe. The emperors of the Holy Roman Empire, by contrast, generally seem to have displayed "remarkable ignorance of the imperial domains and the royal revenues" (Schubert, p. 147).

The preceding discussion should dispel any erroneous impression that accounting information was recorded and compiled solely for the purpose of rendering accounts of stewardship. Two more commonplace examples may be useful here. The murage and pavage accounts of Shrewsbury, England, have survived from as early as 1256. It is evident that each account is "a public record, not a private justification; it is, so to speak, itself part of the works for which the murage pays" (Martin, p. 135). And the administration of the duke of Brabant in 1358 kept a ledger of current accounts.

A much-studied class of stewardship accounts are the manorial accounts of ecclesiastic and lay owners of large estates in England. Many have survived, and are valuable sources for economic historians. The accounts of the thirteenth and fourteenth centuries are especially useful because demesne farming (the direct conduct by the owner of agricultural activities through local agents) was widespread in England, unlike the rest of Europe. Agricultural estate accounting of continental Europe has not attracted systematic study, and does not appear to have followed any particular pattern.

In England the local agent was the reeve or bailiff responsible for a manor. He was in charge of the manorial demesne and also collected rents from tenants. He rendered an annual written account, examined locally by itinerant auditors responsible to the owner. The system of written accounts probably developed out of an earlier system of oral accounting.

In the period from (roughly) 1270 to 1350, manorial accounts were fairly standardized, the result of exchanges of ideas and methods among owners and officers, the circulation of specimen accounts and manuscript treatises, and possibly also the regular courses for clerks taught at Oxford and elsewhere, which almost certainly included instruction in the compilation of manorial accounts. The typical account roll was as follows (Harvey, 1976, p. 19):

> It opens with a heading naming the manor and the reeve or bailiff . . . and the period covered by the account, usually one year running from one Michaelmas (29 September) to the next. On the front [of the parchment membrane] are the cash receipts and payments, with cash balance; both are divided by subject-matter into a series of paragraphs, each with a marginal heading and a sub-total. On the dorse are first the corn, then the stock accounts; each category of corn or stock has a marginal heading and two paragraphs, one of receipts, one of expenditures, with a total following each and a concluding balance.

The entries on the dorse referred to quantities, not money values. Surviving manorial accounts have markings that bear witness to the thoroughness of their auditors' scrutiny. And it is likely that an efficient auditor had a good enough understanding of conversion ratios in agricultural activities to enable him to challenge dubious entries.

Appendages to the stock account sometimes included a works account, recording labor services due from tenants and rendered by them, or a land account, listing the lands of the demesne and their use during the accounting year.

Manorial accounts were often drawn up by clerks. The reeve supplied the detailed information, partly from written records if he were literate and partly from tallies. "Much may have been stored in the astonishing memories which countryfolk develop when they cannot write" (Plucknett, p. 6).

Other accounting documents used included manorial "extents." These were detailed surveys of demesne lands and of tenants' obligations, with the annual value "set on every piece of property and every service" (Harvey, 1976, p. 75). An inventory of livestock and equipment was often added to the manorial account when there was a change of reeve. On larger estates household accounts were also compiled at the center, such as those kept in connection with what Smith has called the *regimen scaccarii* in certain English monasteries (Smith, p. 54).

Some manorial accounts after 1350 contain notes on the manor's profits for the year. These notes rarely indicate the basis of the profit calculation. Terms used for profit include *proficuum, clarum,* and *valor.* According to E. Stone, such profit calculations for Canterbury and Norwich cathedral priories influenced decisions whether to lease particular manors or to run them in demesne. Stone writes that these accounts of profit represent, in concept, "an intellectual effort of an altogether higher order than that which can be associated with the ordinary manorial account or with, say, the older series of exchequer accounts" (Stone, p. 48). P. D. A. Harvey suggests that the need to make decisions of this kind on a better-informed basis may have been among the reasons for the introduction of written manorial accounts (Harvey, 1976, pp. 56–57).

Reference to profit measurement leads naturally to the accounts and accounting practices of medieval merchants, bankers, and manufacturers, although often a calculation of profits was not performed in their accounts.

Surviving medieval commercial accounting records are diverse. They fall into two groups: accounts not kept on the double-entry system, often unhelpfully lumped together as "single entry," and those kept on double-entry lines. A large number of surviving European account books up to 1500 are discussed in Raymond de Roover's survey of 1956.

Early examples of accounting in business can be attributed to credit transactions, or to relationships of accountability, or to partnerships. The earliest surviving European business accounts are fragments of an account book dated 1211. The sheets record in paragraph form details of loans made by an unknown firm of bankers to customers (sometimes with the names of witnesses or guarantors) and details of repayments. There are no totals nor balances; the entries relating to a particular loan were crossed through when it was fully repaid. Several other surviving medieval account books are likewise restricted to recording indebtedness by and to the merchant. In some places account books had probatory value in law courts under certain circumstances; and merchants came to have less need of notarized instruments.

The accounts of commerical agents or factors, sedentary or itinerant, constitute another category of records. Some account books of factors employed by the commercial wing of the Teutonic Knights have survived. Partnership enterprises also generated accounts; in partnerships, credit and accountability relationships occur in combination. Partners' capital accounts were often included, showing what each partner put into or drew out of the enterprise or was due from the enterprise.

Accounting records served other purposes as well. A cash account or cashbook provided some check on the cash or the cashier. Records of goods received and delivered helped control the warehouse keeper and gave information on stocks on hand. The monitoring of goods through accounts was especially important in the operation of the putting-out system in textile manufacturing (although the system worked even without written accounts). Finally, some account books included classified information on particular kinds of incomes or expenses, or on particular trading ventures.

Accounting entries were arranged in various ways. The paragraph form of entry was probably the earliest. The account form presented information more clearly and accessibly: opposing types of entry (such as receipts and payments, creation and discharge of debt) were separated from each other, but those relating to a particular asset or person were united in a single "account." The "debit" and "credit" sections of an account were sometimes one above the other on the same ledger page, or were segregated in the two halves of the ledger. Eventually the bilateral form of ledger account came to prevail. A page was divided vertically into debit and credit sides, or the two pages of a ledger opening were given to debit and credit entries, respectively. In Italy the latter type of bilateral account was known as "alla Veneziana."

Profit calculations are found in many account books not kept on the double-entry system (see de Roover, pp. 125, 128, 130, 172). From time to time assets were examined and listed, their values summed, and the amounts owing to creditors deducted; the difference between the current and the preceding totals of the net assets was the profit for the intervening period.

Today the double-entry method is overwhelmingly the dominant accounting method. Its precise origins cannot be ascertained. Suggestions that it was of Arabic or Indian origin lack supporting evidence. Bearing in mind that there is a large element of chance in the survival of records, and that the surviving records of early enterprises tend to be incomplete, it is safest to locate the origin of double entry—generally known throughout Europe until the nineteenth century as the "Italian" method—in Italy (Genoa, Florence, and Venice have had their champions), and to date it toward the end of the thirteenth century.

It is not known whether the system emerged by a process of slow evolution out of less complete systems, or whether a particular individual or firm consciously pioneered the system and made it known to others. Although it is sometimes claimed that "double entry developed in response to the needs of nascent capitalism" (de Roover, p. 174), this explanation of its origins is unsatisfactory because the particular needs, supposedly not met by other accounting arrangements, are not distinctly specified.

But whatever the circumstances of its birth, by 1500 double entry was widely employed by Italian business enterprises. There is evidence also of the use of the system by some nonbusiness organizations, including hospitals, monasteries, and communes. The account book of the *massari* of Genoa, dated 1340, was long thought to be the earliest extant specimen of double entry. In 1494, Luca Pacioli's *Summa de arithmetica* included the first published exposition of the system. The claim that Pacioli plagiarized a Venetian manuscript used in *scuole di abaco* may be true, but the particular evidence adduced in its support is weak.

There is no convincing evidence that any non-Italian merchant or banker kept his books by double entry before 1500. Non-Italian businessmen or their bookkeepers could have acquired a knowledge of the system in Italy or from Italian businessmen and bookkeepers in their midst. Knowledge of double entry was not protected as an Italian trade secret.

The minimum requirements for accounts to qualify as double entry are as follows [de Roover, 1956, p. 114]:

> A necessary prerequisite is that all transactions be recorded twice, once on the debit and once on the credit side [of the ledger]. . . . This principle also involves the existence of an integrated system of accounts, both real [property, goods, debts] and nominal [incomes and expenses], so that the books will balance in the end, record changes in the owner's equity [capital] and permit the determination of profit or loss.

The system as described by Pacioli made use of three account books: the memorial, in which transactions were noted chronologically by whoever was involved; the journal, in which the transactions were transcribed chronologically in proper form, with the debit and credit elements clearly identified; and the ledger, in which the information in the journal was entered in the appropriate debit and credit sections of the relevant accounts.

In practice, arrangements were usually more elaborate, with, say, the ledger subdivided to facilitate the bookkeeping operations of large firms or of complex businesses. Thus there could be separate ledgers for different groups of debtors or creditors. Many of the larger firms had secret ledgers, reserved for the partners' accounts and other sensitive accounts. The variety and degree of subdivision of ledger accounts also varied according to circumstances. Voyage accounts featured prominently in Venetian mercantile ledgers. In the ledgers of Tuscan textile manufacturing concerns, separate accounts for each process permitted the accounting control of the flow of materials.

The double-entry system was more comprehensive in scope than alternative methods. Further, it had the potential to organize information systematically; it provided for a check on the arithmetical accuracy of the ledger; and it permitted the production of summary accounts: the profit-and-loss account and the balance account, containing the balances on asset, liability, and capital accounts.

Did the introduction of double entry improve business organization and administration, and entrepreneurial decisions? Order, clarity, and accuracy in accounts evidently were useful. But these features could not be guaranteed by double entry itself. For example, eight of the ten published fifteenth-century balance accounts of the Medici bank do not balance, an indication that errors in the ledger were not tracked down and corrected, as Pacioli was to specify should be done. Further, comprehensiveness in business recording was an advantage, but was achieved at the cost of clerical effort.

It has been argued that double entry made possible or materially facilitated the development of sedentary trading, the use of agents or factors, the operation of partnerships or companies, and even the development of banking. Such claims for double entry are amply refuted by the historical record and by simple consideration of the relevant business needs (Yamey, 1975).

More generally, the view is sometimes expressed that double-entry bookkeeping was one of the business techniques developed and used in Italy that help to explain why medieval Italian business enterprises were more efficient than their counterparts in the rest of Europe. This view has been challenged on various grounds. The fact or extent of the superiority of Italian accounting techniques has been questioned (for instance, by F. Blockmans and R. S. Lopez in *Finances et comptabilité urbaines,* 1964, pp. 217–218). Moreover, the Datini, Bardi, Peruzzi, Alberti, and Medici enterprises in Italy cannot be shown to have been less efficiently run before they adopted double entry in their accounting than after they did so. And the German Welser and Fugger operated large, dispersed enterprises in the fifteenth century without having double-entry records. Apparently they and others like them did not introduce the Italian system, although it must have been accessible to them.

Caution is necessary, therefore, when appraising even more sweeping and more general historical claims for the double-entry system and for its introduction, such as those made by the German historian Werner Sombart. He asserted that "Capitalism without double-entry bookkeeping is simply inconceivable. They hold together as form and matter." He wrote also that "with this [double-entry] way of thinking the concept of capital is first created" (Sombart, pp. 118–120).

More recently Federigo Melis wrote: "It is capitalism which begets the method [double entry], creating the necessary conditions for its existence; and it is capitalism, on the other hand, which requires this perfect instrument to attain its objectives" (Melis, 1950, p. 598).

Sombart's more detailed discussion of the interconnections between capitalism and double entry is interesting, but not persuasive. Among other considerations, one may note that it is difficult to discern any systematic relationship between the mentality of businessmen and their accounting methods and practices; that Sombart was wrong in supposing that the "rationalistic" pursuit of profits or effective decision making depended upon systematic calculation of past profits, notably so when markets were volatile and communications slow; that, insofar as profit figures might have been relevant for rational decision making, double entry was not essential for their production; that the concepts and accounting quantification of profits and capital preceded the adoption of double entry; and that the recognition of the firm as an entity distinct from its owners did not depend upon double-entry accounting or have the far-reaching consequences attributed to it by Sombart.

Double-entry bookkeeping or accounting is an intellectually satisfying and interesting achievement of medieval Italian business. It had real but nevertheless modest practical utility.

BIBLIOGRAPHY

M. T. Clanchy, *From Memory to Written Record in England, 1066–1307* (1979); Franz Dölger, *Beiträge zur Geschichte der byzantinischen Finanzverwaltung besonders des 10. und 11. Jahrhunderts* (1960), 92–112; Jean Favier, *Les finances pontificales à l'époque du grand schisme d'occident, 1378–1409* (1966), 41–135; *Finances et comptabilité urbaines du XIIIe et XVIe siècle, colloque international: Actes* (1964). François Louis Ganshof, *Frankish Institutions Under Charlemagne* (1968), 34–35; P. D. A. Harvey, "Agricultural Treatises on Manorial Accounting in England," in *Agricultural History,* **20** (1972); P. D. A. Harvey, ed., *Memorial Records of Cuxham, Oxfordshire, Circa 1200–1359* (1976). Charles H. Haskins, "England and Sicily in the Twelfth Century," *English Historical Review,* **26** (1911); John Bell Henneman, *Royal Taxation in Fourteenth Century France* (1971), Appendix 1.

Charles Johnson, ed. and trans., *The Course of the Exchequer, by Richard, Son of Nigel* (1950); Geoffrey Lee, "The Oldest European Account Book: A Florentine Bank Ledger of 1211," in *Nottingham Mediaeval Studies,* **16** (1972); and "The Development of Italian Bookkeeping 1211–1300," in *Abacus,* **9** (1973); William E. Lunt, *Papal Revenues in the Middle Ages,* I (1934), 3–51; Bruce Lyon and Adrian Verhulst, *Medieval Finance: A Comparison of Financial Institutions in Northwestern Europe* (1967); G. H. Martin, "The English Borough in the Thirteenth Century," in *Transactions of the Royal Historical Society,* 5th ser., **13** (1963); Federigo Melis, *Storia della ragioneria* (1950), 381–602; and *Documenti per la storia economica dei secoli XIII–XVI* (1972), 49–74, 377–462; Wolfgang Metz, *Das karolingische Reichsgut: Eine verfassungs- und verwaltungsgeschichtliche Untersuchung* (1960), 18–25, 77–87.

Christopher Nokes, "Accounting for Bailiffship in the Thirteenth Century," in *Accounting and Business Research,* **11** (Spring 1981); Michel Nortier and John W. Baldwin, "Contributions à l'étude des finances de Philippe Auguste," in *Bibliothèque de l'École de Chartes,* **138** (1980); Dorothea Oschinsky, *Walter of Henley and Other Treatises on Estate Management and Accounting* (1971); Peter Partner, "The 'Budget' of the Roman Church in the Renaissance Period," in Ernest F. Jacob, ed., *Italian Renaissance Studies* (1960); Hans Patze, "Neue Typen des Geschäftsschriftgutes im 14. Jahrhundert," in Hans Patze, ed., *Der deutsche Territorialstaat im 14. Jahrhundert,* I (1970); Balduin Penndorf, *Geschichte der Buchaltung in Deutcshland* (1913), 3–36; Theodore F. T. Plucknett, *The Mediaeval Bailiff* (1954); Reginald L. Poole, *The Exchequer in the Twelfth Century* (1912); Raymond de Roover, "Aux origines d'une technique intellectuelle: La formation et l'expansion de la comptabilité à partie double," in *Annales d'histoire économique et sociale,* nos. **44–45** (1937).

"The Development of Accounting Prior to Luca Pacioli according to the Account-Books of Medieval Merchants," in Ananias C. Littleton and Basil S. Yamey, eds., *Studies in the History of Accounting* (1956), Ernst Schubert, *König und Reich: Studien zur Spätmittelalterlichen deutschen Verfassungsgeschichte* (1979), 147–150; Reginald A. L. Smith, "The *Regimen Scaccarii* in English Monasteries," in his *Collected Papers* (1947); Werner Sombart, *Der moderne Kapitalismus,* II (1924), 110–125; Geoffrey E. M. de Ste. Croix, "Greek and Roman Accounting," in Litteton and Yamey, *op.cit*; E. Stone, "Profit-and-Loss Accountancy at Norwich Cathedral Priory," *Transactions of the Royal Historical Society,* 5th ser., **12** (1962); Joseph R. Strayer, *The Administration of Normandy Under Saint Louis* (1932); Peter Gerrit Thielen, *Die Verwaltung des Ordensstaates Preussen vornehmlich im 15. Jahrhundert* (1965); Basil S. Yamey, "Accounting and the Rise of Capitalism: Further Notes on a Theme by Sombart," in *Journal of Accounting Research,* **2** (1964), 117–136; reprinted in his *Essays on the History of Accounting* (1978); "Notes on Double-Entry Bookkeeping and Economic Progress,"in *Journal of European Economic History,* **4** (1975), reprinted in Yamey's *Essays on the History of Accounting* (1978); Tommaso Zerbi, *Le origini della partita doppia* (1952).

BASIL S. YAMEY

[See also **Bailli; Domesday Book.**]

ACHAIA-MOREA. See **Latin Principalities.**

ACHARD or AICHARDUS (died *ca.* 1170). Received into the Cistercian Order around 1125, Achard was sent by St. Bernard of Clairvaux to build the order's church at Himmerod in the diocese of Trier. Modeled after Clairvaux II, of which Achard may also have been the architect, Himmerod was consecrated on 1 June 1178. Achard's church was replaced between 1731 and 1750 by a Baroque church. Achard is commemorated on 15 September as blessed in the Cistercian calendar.

BIBLIOGRAPHY

Marcel Aubert, *L'architecture cistercienne en France* (1947); Ambrosius Schneider, *Die Cistercienserabtei Himmerode im Spätmittelalter* (1954); Carl Wilkes, *Die Zisterzienserabtei Himmerode im 12. und 13. Jahrhunderts* (1924). Himmerod is not included in Anselme Dimier, *Recueil de plans d'églises cisterciennes* (1949).

CARL F. BARNES, JR.

ACKERMANN AUS BÖHMEN, DER ("The Plowman from Bohemia"), a masterpiece of German literature unsurpassed for its time, was written shortly after 1400 in Saaz, in northwestern Bohemia (now Žatec, Czechoslovakia). Its authorship, by Johannes of Teplá (or von Tepl), has been considered proven since 1934, when Konrad Heilig discovered a dedicatory letter written in Latin in the so-called Freiburg formulary, in which Johannes refers to himself as the author of an *Ackermann* written in German. By 1383 at the latest, Johannes (who also used the name Johannes Henslini de Sitbor) was serving as city scribe, notary, and school rector in Žatec. He died early in 1415 in Prague, where he had been notary and imperial notary since 1411.

Comprising thirty-two chapters of dialogue, the *Ackermann* is a prose debate between a widower, who appears allegorically as a plowman *(Ackermann),* and the personified character of Death. The widower indicts Death before God's tribunal, accusing him of being an enemy of mankind and of God. He charges Death with arbitrarily destroying the divine order of the world by allowing evil men to live while prematurely snatching away the just, who, like his wife, might obtain God's grace.

The plaintiff rebels against Death's hostile assaults, which abjectly debase art, knowledge, and all human aspiration. He defends beauty, nobility, and human dignity: man, he says, is the only free creature possessing the capacity to comprehend the nature of God. Death counters by presenting himself as the universal ordering principle of the world. He asserts that God himself granted him irrevocable sovereign dominion over the world and entrusted him with the task of destroying mankind, a corrupt creature ruined through original sin, as punishment for his Fall. But the Plowman holds firmly to his argument that what God has created is good, and consequently immortal, because He will always love virtue. His conviction is based on the authority of Plato and others who from time immemorial taught that the recur-

ACKERMANN AUS BÖHMEN

rent cycles of heaven and the changes in earthly phenomena that are subject to them, are eternal. Holding steadfast to his accusation, he begs God to destroy Death, the false judge and the greatest malefactor of creation.

God pronounces judgment in the thirty-third chapter, saying that Death's power on earth is only temporary, while adding that the Plowman has no inherent claim to the pleasure of earthly life; the question on which the argument has centered is thus left without an unequivocal answer in terms of Christian eschatology. In the thirty-fourth, and concluding, chapter the Plowman submits to the unfathomable will of the Creator, praying for the salvation of his wife Margreth.

Because the plaintiff is identified as a scribe from Saaz and, in the concluding prayer, as Johannes, literary historians such as Krogmann have asserted that the work was occasioned by the death of Johannes' first wife. Stylistically, the *Ackermann* combines the three genera of Aristotelian rhetoric. Burdach, Strothmann, and Borck have shown that the lawsuit format, which is not always consistently realized, recalls such works as Jacobus Palladinus' *Processus Belial.* Through its dialectic form the *Ackermann* is linked to the tradition in Latin and vulgar literature of the widespread genre of debates and poems questioning the pros and cons of a specific question. The style is thematically related to such works as Helinandus' *Vers de la mort,* the *Vado mori* poems, *Visio Policarpi,* and the *Totentanzversen.* Blaschka showed that the fourth lesson of an office to St. Jerome, which Johannes instituted for the St. Niklas Church in Cheb in 1404, forms the intellectual nucleus of the work; Doskočil has proven that the *Tractatus de crudelitate mortis* is a direct source of thematic inspiration.

The sixteen extant manuscripts as well as the seventeen early printed editions (including two by Albrecht Pfister illustrated with woodcuts)—which represent only a part of the tradition destroyed by the Hussite Revolution—testify to the work's popularity during the fifteenth and sixteenth centuries. It subsequently fell into oblivion and was not mentioned again until 1748, by Johann Christoph Gottsched. At the beginning of the nineteenth century Dobrovský and Hanka asserted that the *Ackermann* was an abridged translation of its old Czech counterpart *Tkadleček;* and German literary critics, including Grimm, Hagen, and Wackernagel, turned their attention to the ensuing debate. In 1877 Knieschek proved that the *Ackermann* could not be derived from *Tkadleček* and offered an opposing theory that is now generally accepted.

The *Ackermann* engenders questions of philology, aesthetics, and cultural history that became the center of international research in Germanic studies at the beginning of the twentieth century. Its importance is attested by Burdach's unremitting attention to the origin of literary New High German and the beginnings of early German humanism in Bohemia; by his monumental collection of studies, texts, and documents published with numerous co-workers under the title "Vom Mittelalter zur Reformation" (1893–1939); and especially by Bernt's and Burdach's critical edition (1917).

Burdach considered the *Ackermann* an important step in the development of the language of the imperial Prague chancery into literary New High German, a thesis moderated by more recent philologists, and regarded it as the first work of German humanism, revealing the influence of Plato, Seneca, Boethius, and Petrarch alongside unorthodox Waldensian and Wycliffian characteristics. For him the figure of the Ackermann was the poetic prototype of the plowman, a literary character in which the Renaissance ideal of free, aspiring, industrious man was anticipated. Schafferus, on the other hand, sought to explain the work completely in terms of the Middle Ages, tracing its theological content to Augustine, Thomas Aquinas, and sacred literature. Joachimsen had already called into question the new spirit of the dialogue, and literary historians like Hübner, Blaschka, and Bäuml attempted to diminish the work's ideological validity by interpreting it as a primarily rhetorical exercise. Nevertheless, the *Ackermann* is generally understood as an intellectual work of art and, in the interpretation of Brand-Sommerfeld and Hahn, is explained along the lines of its philosophical and theological assertions.

In fact, the *Ackermann* reveals intellectual influences of the medieval sermon and of mysticism, and has its formal and stylistic roots in the Latin rhetorical tradition. Its flowing free-rhythmic prose is permeated with numerous metaphors and rhetorical figures, and as Thieme demonstrated, also shows a tendency to transpose the Latin *cursus* into the German language alongside an inclination toward triple articulation of syntactical, rhythmical, and other elements. The work's particular stylistic characteristics are based on the notarial literary mannerism and clearly attest to the influence of the poetic and literary endeavors of the early humanist Johannes of Středa (also known as Johannes Noviforensis and Johannes of Neumarkt), who headed the Prague chancellery of Emperor Charles IV. Thematically and motivically the work grows out of the medieval tradition of the *memento mori* literature and, as Hübner demonstrated, contains parallels to other medieval genres, especially to chivalric love poetry and to the early *Minnesang*. Hrubý pointed out that from a philosophical and theological point of view the debate takes up the Peripatetic doctrine of the eternity of the world which was frequently discussed in Scholastic disputations, tracts, and *quaestiones*.

Although the *Ackermann* is indeed formally based on medieval stylistic traditions and in its conception of life consolidates Jewish, Arabic, and Scholastic speculation on the nature of God, its genre, style, and content cannot be completely explained in terms of the past. As Tschirch has shown, it breaks through the boundaries of the medieval debates and of the stylistic tradition of rhythmic chancellery prose: individual chapters are connected with word ties, the composition is multilateral both in its parts and when considered as a whole, the work is unified into an integrated structure, and word and sentence parallelisms extend both forward and backward. The *Ackermann* is a transitional work in which the direct influence of Petrarch and of early Italian humanism cannot be clearly ascertained but in which, nevertheless, are germinating the ideas that—nourished in biblical soil—came to fruition with the late humanists, Renaissance thinkers, and religious reformers. In the *Ackermann aus Böhmen* the author has composed an integral poem that in the power of its language, its intellectual import, and its beauty towers over the literature of its time and in whose formal perfection the human experience of death has found a universally valid expression.

BIBLIOGRAPHY

Editions of the *Ackermann* include those of Alois Bernt and Konrad Burdach (1917); *The Plowman from Bohemia*, Alexander Henderson and Elizabeth Henderson, trans. (1966), a bilingual edition; Günther Jungbluth (1969); Johann Knieschek (1877); and Willy Krogmann (1964).

See also Isaac Bacon, "A Survey of the Changes in the Interpretation of *Ackermann aus Böhmen*," *Studies in Philology*, 53 (1956); Franz H. Bäuml, *Rhetorical Devices and Structure in the Ackermann aus Böhmen* (1960); Renée Brand-Sommerfeld, *Zur Interpretation des "Ackermann aus Böhmen"* (1944); Konrad Burdach, *Der Dichter des Ackermann aus Böhmen und seine Zeit*, 2 pts. (1926–1932); Gerhard Hahn, *Die Einheit des Ackermann aus Böhmen* (1963); Antonín Hrubý, *Der Ackermann und seine Vorlage* (1971); and "The Plowman from Bohemia," in Gerhart Hoffmeister, ed., *The Renaissance and Reformation in Germany* (1977), 17–32; Ernst A. Philippson, "Der Ackermann aus Böhmen: A Summary of Recent Research and an Appreciation," *Modern Language Quarterly*, 2 (1941); *Tkadleček*, Hynek Hrubý and František Šimek, eds. (1923); and Maurice O'Connell Walshe, "Der Ackermann aus Böhmen. A Structural Interpretation," *Classica et mediaevalia*, 15 (1954).

ANTONÍN HRUBÝ

ACOLYTE. See **Clergy.**

ACRE, an area or superficial measure for land in the British Isles, which in its earliest usage probably referred to the amount of land which one yoke of oxen could plow in a day. In England the acre was standardized during the High Middle Ages at 160 square perches of 16½ feet each, or 4,840 square yards, or 43,560 square feet (0.405 hectares). This statutory acre was 40 perches in length and 4 in breadth and was equal to 4 roods of 40 square perches each. Since the size of the acre was defined in terms of the linear perch, regional variations arose whenever the length of the perch (16½ feet [5.029 meters] by statute) or the number of square perches in the acre (160 by statute) differed from the statutory standards. The largest acre appeared in Cheshire, 10,240 square yards (*ca.* 0.86 hectares); the smallest in Leicestershire, 2,308¼ square yards (*ca.* 0.19 hectares).

RONALD EDWARD ZUPKO

ACROSTICS-WORDPLAY. Man's fascination with the physical and semantic properties of words can be illustrated in all ages, from the most ancient biblical puns to James Joyce's elaborate experiments with paronomasial imagery and symbolism. More difficult to parallel is the technical complexity sometimes achieved in medieval Latin examples and the apparent seriousness with which literate society treated works frequently dismissed by modern commentators as frivolous excess.

Early examples of such extreme ingenuity are found in the work of Publilius Optatianus Porfyrius, a fourth-century court poet and Roman prefect under Constantine. He managed, for example, to compose acrostic Latin hexameters in which each verse had the same number of letters (thirty-five or thirty-seven) as the poem had lines. This created a crossword grid thirty-five or thirty-seven spaces square, in which additional hexameters could be identified by reading the first letters (the usual sense of *acro-stich*), the last letters *(tele-stich),* or the eighteenth or nineteenth letters *(meso-stich).* In addition, various combinations of diagonals expressing intelligible hexameters were interwoven to form crosses and parallelograms within the verse. Surviving manuscripts are rubricated to aid the reader in discovering these *versūs intexti.*

Though Optatianus probably worked with thirty-five and thirty-seven for the practical reason that these numbers provide a mean for the Latin hexameter, Venantius Fortunatus, the sixth-century bishop of Poitiers, tells us that he chose thirty-three out of devotion to Christ, crucified at that age. For easily understandable reasons this way of writing never became popular, but during the Carolingian period several authors tried their hand at it, including Alcuin, Theodulf, Josephus Scotus, Rabanus Maurus, and Ermoldus Nigellus. An impressive instance of the form brought to an admittedly limited kind of perfection is the thirty-five-line poem of Josephus, "Primus avus vivens, en, nos in morte redegit" (See how our first father's life has brought us to death), in which a narrative of the Fall contains an interwoven acrostic quatrain that both forms an elaborate cruciform pattern and provides a succinct exegesis of the incident.

Behind such tours de force is a belief that language has power and significance beyond man's capacity to endow it with meaning by conventional agreement. The most complete and influential didactic work of the Middle Ages was Isidore of Seville's *Etymologies,* an encyclopedia organized on the principle that a study of words will reveal the true nature of things (*etymon,* "true" + *logos,* "idea, principle"). In this sense an etymology is not an attempt to describe the linguistic history of a word but an analysis of the true nature of the thing designated. Frequently, therefore, names are seen as reliable indicators of the nature of their bearers, and a common entry into the life of a saint is to comment on the way in which his name is prognostic of his life. Similarly, the names of beasts, stones, planets, and stars are felt to reveal their essential nature (as in bestiaries, lapidaries, and calendars). This attitude to the relation between meaning and being gives a more serious intent to the activity of wordplay found in punning, rhyming, or the forming of alliterative connections.

BIBLIOGRAPHY:

Texts. Ernst Dümmler, ed., *Poetae Latini aevi Carolini,* I–II (1881–1884); Wallace M. Lindsay, ed., *Isidori Hispalensis episcopi Etymologiarum siue Originum libri XX,* 2 vols. (1911).

Commentary. Ernst Robert Curtius, "Etymology as a Category of Thought," in *European Literature and the Latin Middle Ages,* Willard R. Trask, trans. (1953); Fred C. Robinson, "The Significance of Names in Old English Literature," in *Anglia,* **86** (1968); Dieter Schaller, "Die karolingischen Figurengedichte des Cod. Bern. 212," in *Medium aevum vivum,* Hans Robert Jauss and Dieter Schaller, eds. (1960).

COLIN CHASE

[See also **Isidore of Seville; Latin Literature.**]

ACTUALISM describes the Greek notion that pure act is fully realized being, without any unrealized potentiality, and is therefore beyond change. One encounters the notion in the Middle Ages wherever the presence of Aristotle is felt. In a Neoplatonized version, such as that of Avicenna, pure act is understood as the source from which all being emanates. In Christianized Aristotelianism, such as that of Thomas Aquinas, God is pure act. Actualism can be used to describe the view that all things and events in the created universe result from God as both prime cause and conserving cause.

WILLIAM J. COURTENAY

ADALBERO OF LAON (*ca.* 955–1031), also known as Ascelin, bishop of Laon and chancellor at the court of Lothair. An opportunistic and unscrupulous politician, pro-Ottonian by family tradition, he supported Hugh Capet against the last Carolingians and became, toward the end of his life, an open ally of the Capetians following their establishment on the throne. Adalbero is also known as a satirist, whose *Carmen ad Robertum regem* attacks Robert II for raising humble clerics to the rank of bishop.

BIBLIOGRAPHY

Adalbero's poem to Robert was translated by Claude Carozzi as *Poeme au roi Robert* (1979). See also Robert T.

Coolidge, *Adalbero, Bishop of Laon* (1965); and O. G. Oexle, "Die funktionale Dreiteilung der 'Gesellschaft' bei Adalbero von Laon," in *Frümittelalterliche Studien,* **12** (1978).

ALAIN J. STOCLET

[See also **France, 987–1223; Germany to 1125.**]

ADALBERT OF BREMEN (*ca.* 1000–1072), archbishop of Hamburg-Bremen and royal adviser, was born of noble parents in Thuringia and was educated at Halberstadt. He rose quickly in the ecclesiastical hierarchy, becoming canon and, by 1032, provost of Halberstadt. He was appointed archbishop of Hamburg-Bremen with royal approval from Emperor Henry III in 1043.

Adalbert's ecclesiastical activities consisted largely of his attempted evangelization of the Scandinavians and northern Slavs. Despite his efforts both King Harald III of Norway and King Edmund of Sweden remained indifferent and occasionally hostile to evangelization. Adalbert enjoyed greater success in Denmark, where he assiduously cultivated and largely obtained the favor of King Svend II Estridsen and, likewise, received the support of the Slavic leader Gottschalk in eastern Germany.

Adalbert's political goal, to enrich his archbishopric and widen its influence, led to protracted controversy with the Billunger dukes of Saxony and continuing efforts to placate political leaders in northern Europe. One rather enigmatic event, given Adalbert's political ambition, was his decision to decline Henry III's offer of the papacy after the Council of Sutri (1046); perhaps he was content with the lower but more independent post of archbishop. Adalbert recommended a friend, Suidger of Bamberg (Clement II), and his recommendation was accepted.

The influence thus secured was used to full advantage to resolve difficulties with northern kings or gain ecclesiastical benefits. Adalbert strove to acquire the title of patriarch for his archbishopric, but the honor was denied him; his friend Pope Leo IX later granted him the status of papal vicar in 1057. The height of his wordly prestige was his patronage of young Henry IV between 1063 and 1066, during which time Adalbert virtually ruled the imperial government, obtained control of the lands that he had always wanted, and realized his economic goals.

In January 1066 Adalbert's rivals at court convinced Henry IV to banish him and diminish his territorial holdings. After a three-year period of declining health and "exile" in Hamburg-Bremen, Adalbert was recalled to court and spent the last three years of his life traveling in the imperial retinue.

BIBLIOGRAPHY

Adam von Bremen, *Hamburgische Kirchengeschichte,* Bernhard Schmeidler, ed. (1917), is the major primary source. See also Edgar N. Johnson, "Adalbert of Hamburg-Bremen: A Politician of the Eleventh Century," in *Speculum,* 9 (1934); and Otto Heinrich May, *Regesten der Erzbischöfe von Bremen,* I (1937).

TIMOTHY B. NOONE

ADALBERT, ST. (*d.* 981), first archbishop of Magdeburg, spent his early years, and was educated, at the monastery of Trier. He remained in the monastic life until 962, when he was appointed archbishop of Mainz by William, the son of the Holy Roman Emperor Otto I. Adalbert found difficulty in evangelizing Mainz and, after several of his companions were killed, he returned to Germany. In 966 he became abbot of the monastery in Wissembourg, and in 968 he was chosen archbishop of Magdeburg, where he died.

BIBLIOGRAPHY

Acta sanctorum, Godefridus Henschenius et al., eds., V (20 June), 27–33; Adolphe Regnier, "Adalbert (Saint)," in *Dictionnaire d'histoire et de géographie ecclésiastiques,* I (1912), 443.

TIMOTHY B. NOONE

ADALBOLD OF UTRECHT (*ca.* 970–1026). Educated at Liège, he was bishop of Utrecht from 1010 until his death and supported the monastic reform of St. Poppo of Stavelot. A friend of Pope Sylvester II (Gerbert), to whom he dedicated a work on the measurement of a sphere, Adalbold also wrote a commentary on a passage of Boethius' *Consolation of Philosophy* (III, 9) and a biography of Emperor Henry II.

BIBLIOGRAPHY

Texts include "De ratione inveniendi crassitudinem sphaerae," in Nicholaus Bubnov, *Gerberti Opera mathematica* (1899); "Commentarius in Boethii Consol. III, 9," in Kist and Moll, *Kerkhistor. Archief,* III (1862), 163–221; biography of Henry II, in *Monumenta Germaniae Historica, Scriptores,* IV , 679–694.

MARK D. MEYERSON

[See also **Sylvester II.**]

ADAM DE LA BASSÉE (*d.* 1286), priest of St. Pierre in Lille, known only as author of *Ludus super Anticlaudianum* (*ca.* 1280), a poetic paraphrase of Alan of Lille's famous allegory *Anticlaudianus.* The plot concerns nature's creation of a perfect man, imbued with arts and virtues. During a journey to heaven to complement the earthly body with a soul, the music of the spheres is heard. Although written in Latin, the *Ludus* is more like a *roman* and is simpler than Alan's learned work. Adam emphasizes the arts and the music of the spheres by inserting musical pieces with sacred or semisacred texts, two of which are polyphonic compositions. Twenty of them are modeled on preexisting pieces, which are often identified, including dances, popular monophonic songs by famous trouvères, and widely known liturgical chants. The collection is a minianthology of current musical styles, chosen with great care for the symbolic meaning. In one section, for example, the pieces resemble those of the canonical hours; in another, chants of the Mass are suggested, using models from Pentecost, where the new, perfect man receives his soul.

BIBLIOGRAPHY

Guido M. Dreves, ed., *Analecta hymnica,* **48** (1897), gives only the texts; P. Bayart, *Ludus super Anticlaudianum* (1930), has facsimiles of the leaves, with music; Andrew Hughes, "The *Ludus super Anticlaudianum* of Adam de la Bassée," in *Journal of the American Musicological Society,* **23** (1970).

ANDREW HUGHES

ADAM DE LA HALLE (*fl.* 2nd half 13th c.) came from Arras. He was perhaps the most important of the bourgeois poets writing in the Picard dialect, in both lyric and dramatic genres. He also played a key rôle in the history of music, for he was a skillful composer as well as an active performer and singer.

The little certain information we have about his life is to be deduced from his own works. In particular we read in his poem of leave-taking, *Li congé,* and his satirical play, *Le jeu de la feuillée* (dated 1276), about the conflict of interests he experienced between his love for Marie, whom he married, and his desire to study in Paris in order to widen his knowledge, improve his technique, and make a firmer base for the future. He names some of his family and certain wealthy citizens of Arras who had aided him in his endeavors. It seems likely that he did indeed study for some time in the capital, for certain of his motets are contained in a famous manuscript now at Montpellier, along with a repertory from Notre Dame, and one of them, "Entre Adan et Hanikiel," conveys a jolly impression of student life.

Later Adam, who also came to be known as Le Bossu (the Hunchback), probably because of his wit rather than a physical deformity, or as Adam d'Arras when away from home, certainly entered the service of Robert II, comte d'Artois. He accompained Robert's suite on campaigns and eventually to the Angevin Kingdom of Naples, where the trouvère celebrated Charles d'Anjou in a rather individualistic "epic poem" entitled *Le roi de Sicile.* Only the opening of this poem seems to have survived, but it is enough to betray Adam's professional and personal enthusiasms for amours, minstrelsy, and, above all, high standards of technical perfection.

Further details of Adam's career are given in the short play *Le jeu du pèlerin.* The attribution of this work to Adam has been disputed, but it seems likely that the "Pilgrim," who arrives in Arras and tells of the poet's talents and how he had been shown his "tomb" by the comte d'Artois in person, is no other than Adam himself; he teases his friends, and himself, by his portrayal of local citizens who claim never to have heard of him, and to know better songs than those the Pilgrim quotes.

Our knowledge that Adam was a professional singer ("Et s'estoit parfais en chanter," says the Pilgrim) makes it seem possible that the "Maistre Adam le Boscu" paid among many other entertainers at an English royal feast at Westminster in 1306 might be Adam de la Halle. The only serious objection to this possibility is the testimony of a scribe who, at the end of his copy of the *Roman de Troie,* dates his work as 1288, names himself as Jehan Mados, and says Adam le Bossu was his uncle who is now dead. The reference is a passing one, with criticism of Adam as being foolish to leave Arras, and it is perfectly possible that the poet's death was here merely assumed in the absence of news. At all events, we should be wary of accepting the conventional view that Adam died in 1288 and the facetious suggestion that a grand tomb was erected for him in Naples.

Adam's plays are entirely secular and worthy representatives of the great literary traditions of thirteenth-century Arras. *Le jeu de la feuillée* is sharply satirical in its depiction of the citizens of Arras, including Adam's own father, shown as profligate and a miser. Contemporary abuses are revealed, particularly in the figure of a monk trading fake holy relics who has to pay for a large round of drinks in the local tavern when he has awoken from drunken slumber. Basic humor is derived from the antics of a madman, also significantly accompanied by his father, and superstition is mocked in the crazy tea party attended by three grotesque fairies, Morgue, Maglore, and Arsile.

Le jeu de Robin et de Marion, composed possibly for the court at Naples or possibly earlier at Arras, is a dramatized version of the traditional *pastourelle* story of the knight out riding who presses his attentions on the pretty shepherdess he meets. Adam, in line with many of the lyric versions of this theme, causes the knight to beat a retreat, though more because of the spirited showing made by Marion than because of her timid rustic love. Exuberant high spirits pervade the play, especially in the scenes of peasant picnics, games, and dancing. It is above all in the introduction into the text of a large number of contemporary popular sung refrains that the special flavor of Adam's treatment resides.

Adam must have been prized by his patrons mainly for his songs: rondeaux, motets, *chansons d'amour,* and *jeux-partis,* many of which had been elaborated in the poetic contests of the Puy, or trouvères' guild, in Arras. His lyrics set to music fall into two distinct groups. The single-melody settings of thirty-six *chansons* (text alone survives for one of these) and eighteen *jeux-partis* (no music survives for two of these) are entirely in the trouvère tradition of the twelfth and thirteenth centuries. Adam displays considerable skill in metrical variation. But whereas the *chansons* adhere strictly to courtly convention, the debating songs, most of which are in contest with Jehan Bretel, allow some bourgeois humor to enter in.

The polyphonic works, on the other hand, are particularly significant. The five motets for voices over an instrumental foundation are typical enough of thirteenth-century style, but the application of three-voice conductus-style writing to the sixteen simple rondeaux texts was a new departure. Popular song is thereby made into a more serious art form, and this is the germ from which much of the lyric art of the following two centuries was to spring.

BIBLIOGRAPHY

Editions. Rudolf Berger, *Canchons . . . des altfranzösischen Trouvère Adan de la Hale le Bochu d'Aras* (1900); Edmond de Coussemaker, *Oeuvres complètes du trouvère Adam de la Halle* (1872, repr. 1965); Jean Dufournet, *Le jeu de la feuillée* (1977); A. Jeanroy, "Trois dits d'amour du XIIIe siècle," in *Romania,* **22** (1893); 50–53; Ernest Langlois, *Adam le Bossu: Le jeu de la feuillée,* 2nd ed. (1965); and *Adam le Bossu: le jeu de Robin et Marion suivi du jeu du pèlerin* (1924, repr. 1965); J. Marshall, *The Chansons of Adam de la Halle* (1971); Léon Nicod, *Les jeux partis d'Adam de la Halle* (1917, repr. 1974); G. Raynaud, "Deux jeux-partis inédits d'Adam de la Halle," in *Romania,* **6** (1877), 590–593; Pierre Ruelle, *Les congés d'Arras (Jean Bodel, Baude Fastoul, Adam de la Halle)* (1965); Nigel Wilkins, *The Lyric Works of Adam de la Hale* (1967).

Critical Works. N. Cartier, "La mort d'Adam le Bossu," in *Romania,* **89** (1968), 116–124; and *Le Bossu désenchanté: Etude sur le "jeu de la feuillée"* (1971); Jean Dufournet, *Adam de la Halle à la recherche de lui-même ou le jeu dramatique de la feuillée* (1974); F. Gégou, "Adam le Bossu était-il mort en 1288?" in *Romaina,* **86** (1965), 111–117; and *Recherches biographiques et littéraires sur Adam de la Halle, accompagnées de l'édition critique de ses chansons courtoises* (diss. University of Paris-IV, 1973); and Henri Guy, *Essai sur la vie et les oeuvres littéraires du trouvère Adam de Le Hale* (1898).

NIGEL WILKINS

ADAM LOCK. See **Lock, Adam.**

ADAM MARSH. See **Marsh, Adam de.**

ADAM OF BREMEN (*ca.* 1040–*ca.* 1081). Information about Adam's life is scarce, making conjecture inevitable. Born probably in eastern Franconia, he may have been educated in Bamberg. In 1066/1067 he went to Bremen to become a canon of the cathedral and teacher at the cathedral school. Of the northern lands about which he wrote, it is certain only that he visited Denmark, where he had occasion to meet and converse with King Sweyn Estrithson.

His *Gesta Hammaburgensis ecclesiae pontificum (History of the Bishops of the Church of Hamburg),* written between 1073 and 1076, is the cornerstone of

ADAM OF BREMEN

our knowledge of north German and Scandinavian history in the tenth and eleventh centuries. Adam stresses the missionary role of the church of Hamburg, placed at the northern limits of the Christian world and in charge of the conversion of Scandinavian and Slavic pagans.

The *History* is divided into four books. Book I opens with an outline of the early history and culture of the Saxons, going on to survey the progress of Christianity in Lower Saxony, the mission of Boniface, the forcible conversion of the natives by Charlemagne, the union of the sees of Bremen and Hamburg under Ansgar, and the succession of patriarchs of the church up to Archbishop Unni's death at Birka in 936. Book II covers the careers of the various archbishops of Hamburg-Bremen from Adaldag (937–988) to Alebrand (1035–1045), gives a survey of the Slavic nations and their territories, and offers a brief account of the conflicts between the church and the Saxon aristocracy, on which Adam takes a strongly clerical position.

The third book is dedicated in good part to the episcopate of Adalbert (1043–1072) and to a sketch of his character. Nowhere else does Adam impress us with his psychological penetration, but here his achievement is remarkable. Echoing Sallust, he undertakes to write his account of Adalbert in such a way "that everything shall be understood from his character." The description of Adalbert's *grandeur et misère,* colored as it is by the admiration, pity, and moral reproof of the writer in equal proportions, constitutes an admirable personal biography, a unique performance in its time and in the tradition of historiography within which Adam was working. In this book more attention is given to Nordic history than to the affairs of the Holy Roman Empire. Adam describes the Danish expansion under Canute the Great; the careers of St. Olaf, Magnus the Good, and Harold Hardråde in Norway; and the battle of Stamford Bridge and the Norman Conquest. He tells the story of the Slavic prince Gottschalk and his missionary labor among his people, describing also their later relapse into paganism and the killing of Gottschalk and his followers.

The fourth book, *Descriptio insularum aquilonis,* is a description of Scandinavia and its peoples, the most factual and critical in Western literature until that time. Adam does mention the Amazons, unipeds, cyclopes, and dog-headed men of late antique ethnography, since he uses the works of Solinus, Orosius, and Martianus Capella, but these references are made with marked skepticism. He describes Denmark, Sweden, Norway, the Baltic and its shores, then the Orkneys, Iceland, Greenland, and Vinland. The book ends with the account of a Frisian expedition to the legendary confines of the Northern ocean. Sailing beyond Iceland "toward the farthest northern pole," the Frisians reach an island populated by cyclopes, from which they barely escape with their lives. For ethnography and religious history, Book IV contains priceless information: a description of the heathen temple at Uppsala, its cult and the sacrifices performed in it every nine years, as well as Adam's own interpretation of the Northern gods.

In method Adam's work is closer to modern standards than that of most medieval historians; he is factual and objective, interested in establishing an exact chronology and in pointing to discrepancies in various versions of the same events. Lauritz Weibull's work on Adam has served to establish the *History* as a far more dependable source for the Nordic history of that period than the Norse sagas and Scandinavian chronicles.

Adam was exceptionally well read and used numerous sources, both written and oral, including both the works of his great predecessors, Gregory of Tours, Bede, and Einhard, and books of more immediate relevance to his subject, such as the *Vita Anskarii, Vita Liudgeri, Vita Willibrordi,* the annals of Corvey and Fulda, and also many documents, bulls, and capitularies. Most of his oral informers remain anonymous ("a certain man," "a certain Christian"), but the most important one was Sweyn Estrithson, whom Adam always mentions with esteem and admiration. Though Adam's Latin is undistinguished, echoes of Vergil, Lucan, Juvenal, Horace, Terence, and Persius are extremely frequent in his prose.

Manuscripts of the *History* have been divided by Bernhard Schmeidler into families A, B, and C. A-manuscripts represent the work as first completed by the author around 1076. Later, probably between 1076 and 1080, Adam undertook a revision, making many additions to the text. According to Schmeidler, the B and C families go back to the revised version, which he calls X. New research has shown that there is extensive mutual contamination between A, B, and C, and that the manuscript tradition may be understood better in terms of four families, A, B_1, B_2, and C.

BIBLIOGRAPHY

Standard Edition. Adam von Bremen, *Hamburgische Kirchengeschichte,* Benhard Schmeidler, ed., 3rd ed.(1917);

English translation by F. J. Tschan, *History of the Archbishops of Hamburg-Bremen* (1959).

Literature. Georg Misch, *Geschichte der Autobiographie,* III (1959); Bernhard Schmeidler, *Hamburg-Bremen und Nordost Europa vom 9. bis 11. Jahrhundert; Kritische Untersuchungen zur Hamburgischen Kirchengeschichte des Adam von Bremen, zu Hamburger Urkunden und zur nordischen und wendischen Geschichte* (1918); Lauritz Weibull, *Kritiska undersökningar i Nordens historia omkring år 1000* (1911).

JOAQUÍN MARTÍNEZ-PIZARRO

ADAM OF ST.VICTOR (*ca.* 1110–*ca.* 1180), liturgical poet, canon regular of the Abbey of St. Victor, Paris, was born probably in Britain or Brittany. According to tradition he entered the monastery of St. Victor in 1130 and died during the prelacy of Guérin, abbot from 1173 to 1193.

Adam is celebrated as the master of the final Sequence form, developed in the late eleventh or early twelfth century. A *Sequence* is a chant that follows the Alleluia in the Mass; the text that sometimes accompanies it is called a *prose.* Three prose styles were recognized in the twelfth century. The final, "regular," Sequence style is characterized by regular (uniform) rhythm based on word accent, regular pauses *(caesuras)* that break each line, and regular two-syllabled rhyme. The strophes or stanzas are generally composed of two or three eight-syllable trochaic lines followed by a trochaic line of seven syllables.

Precise identification of Adam's Sequences remains a problem. Since other Sequence writers of Adam's time occasionally employed an earlier prose style, Adam may have done the same. Further, some predecessors and contemporaries probably wrote in his peculiar fashion. Misset lists forty-five Sequences judged authentic on stylistic criteria; although such standards are not wholly reliable, Raby holds that a portion of this list can with relative certainty be ascribed to Adam.

The following attributes belong to Sequences most likely to be Adam's: a variety of strophes and meters, a preponderance of alliteration and play upon words, objective rather than personal expression, and Old Testament typology germane to the allegorical biblical interpretation characteristic of the School of St. Victor, which held that the visible both reveals and conceals the invisible. Examples of typology abound: the Christ who brought the world joy is said to be prefigured by Isaac, whose name signifies laughter; Joseph's removal from the pit typifies Christ's resurrection (Seq. XIV in Wrangham); Eve, formed from Adam's side, signifies the Church, which emerged from the wounded side of the Redeemer, her Bridegroom (Seq. XXVI). Adam's work is also replete with Marian typology. As the virgin mother, Mary is the sealed fountain and enclosed garden of the Canticles (Seq. LXXIV); she is the temple of God (Seq. V) and the throne of Solomon (Seq. LXXII).

In Adam's teacher, Hugh of St. Victor, one finds a spokesman for mystical theologizing in the manner of Augustine and Pseudo-Dionysius. All these threads are present in poetry attributed to Adam. For example, among Misset's list of sequences is a hymn to St. Denis, the first bishop of Paris, who was identified by Adam and others of his day with Dionysius the Areopagite (Seq. LXXX). In "S. Michael et omnes angeli" (Seq. LXXVII), Adam follows the Dionysian division of the angels and suggests a similar classification for the glorified dead.

BIBLIOGRAPHY

Léon Gautier, ed., *Oeuvres poétiques d'Adam de Saint-Victor,* 2 vols. (1858–1859), 1 vol. (1894); trans. by D. S. Wrangham as *The Liturgical Poetry of Adam of Saint Victor,* 3 vols. (1881); Eugène Misset and Pierre Aubry, eds., *Les proses d'Adam de Saint-Victor: Texte et musique* (1900); Hildebrand Prévost, ed., *Recueil complet des célèbres séquences du vénérable maitre Adam le Breton* (1901); Clemens Blume *et al.,* eds., *Liturgische Prosen des Übergangsstiles und der zweiten Epoche insbesondere die dem Adam von Sanct Victor zugeschriebenen,* in *Analecta hymnica medii aevi,* LIV (1915); John F. Benton, "Nicolas of Clairvaux and the Twelfth-Century Sequence," in *Traditio,* **18** (1962), 149–179; *Histoire littéraire de la France,* XV (1869), 40–45; Frederic J. E. Raby, *A History of Christian-Latin Poetry from the Beginnings to the Close of the Middle Ages,* 2nd ed. (1953), 345–375, esp. bibl., p. 486; Hans Spanke, "Die Kompositionskunst der Sequenzen Adams von St. Victor," in *Studi medievali,* n. s., **14** (1941).

JANICE L. SCHULTZ

ADAM OF THE LITTLE BRIDGE (Adam of Balsham, Adamus Parvipontanus, Adam de Parvo Ponte), was born at Balsham near Cambridge, a member of the Beverley family, which originated in Beauvais. The name Parvipontanus (of the Little Bridge) is taken from the location in Paris of his school, near a small bridge over the Seine. Very little is known of his earlier life and training. He studied at Paris under Matthew of Angers and Peter Lombard, and taught there from about 1132, in which year he produced his textbook of logic, the *Ars disserendi.* John of Salisbury became acquainted with him in England or Paris, around 1136 to 1138, or as late as 1140, and may have been one of his pupils.

Around 1145, Adam became a canon of Notre Dame. He was present in April 1147 at the consistory convened by Pope Eugene III at Paris, where he testified against Gilbert de la Porrée. In March 1148 he was present with Peter Lombard, Thierry of Chartres, and several other masters at the Council of Rheims, where Gilbert's teachings came once more under discussion.

Adam of the Little Bridge has been identified with the Adam, canon of Paris and master, who became bishop of St. Asaph in Wales around 1160, but this is now considered unlikely by some scholars. In 1179, Adam was present at the Lateran to defend a proposition of his former teacher, Peter Lombard, According to an entry in the necrology of the abbey of Val, he died on August 6, probably in 1181.

In his *Metalogicon* (especially 4:3) John of Salisbury portrays Adam as clever, learned, a keen student of Aristotle, and an intricate stylist. Adam had several pupils in logic, including William of Soissons. His *Ars disserendi* was described by Lorenzo Minio-Paluello as "a bold, not wholly unsucessful, attempt at establishing a completely modern textbook of the art of logic," at a time when training in the arts of the trivium consisted mainly in the study and explanation of ancient authors. Adam's sources were the Aristotelian logic translated by Boethius, especially the *Topics* and *Sophistici elenchi,* and Boethius' own logical writings. The work was also known as the *Dialectica Alexandri,* possibly because it may have been re-edited by Alexander Nequam, the most distinguished of Adam's followers.

Adam also wrote a manual of lexicography entitled *De utensilibus,* or *Phaletolum,* in the form of a letter to a friend Anselm. Here he relies on some passages from Aulus Gellius' *Noctes Atticae* and St. Isidore's *Etymologiae* to compile a treatise on rare Latin words for common objects, within an account of a return visit to England after several years of teaching in Paris. The work retained some popularity well into the thirteenth and perhaps also the fourteenth century. It was imitated by Alexander Nequam, who also wrote a *De nominibus utensilium,* following Adam's model.

BIBLIOGRAPHY

Adam Balsamiensis Parvipontani Ars disserendi (Dialectica Alexandri), Twelfth Century Logic Texts and Studies, Vol. 1, Lorenzo Minio-Paluello, ed. (1956). *Epistola Adami Balsamiensis ad Anselmum,* A. H. Hoffmann von Fallersleben, ed. (1853), is the best edition of the *De utensilibus.* Lorenzo Minio-Paluello, "The '*Ars disserendi*' of Adam of Balsham 'Parvipontanus,' " in *Mediaeval and Renaissance Studies* (London), 3 (1954), provides information on the manuscripts as well as additional biographical material. See also Ivo Thomas, "A Twelfth Century Paradox of the Infinite," in *Journal of Symbolic Logic,* 23 (1958).

WANDA CIŻEWSKI

ADAMNAN, ST. (*ca.* 624–704), was the ninth abbot of Iona, and like all his predecessors but one, was a descendant of Conall Gulban and a kinsman of the founder St. Columba (Colum Cille). He was an eminent Church statesman and scholar, and his life is well documented in his own writings, those of his younger contemporary Bede, and the Irish Annals.

He succeeded to the abbacy of Iona in 679, at a time when the prestige of the Columban church in Britain and Ireland had been greatly diminished by the Easter controversy. The main points of dissention were the Paschal dating and the method of tonsure. The Roman party, which included the ecclesiastics in southern Ireland and the Northumbrian church, had conformed to the teaching from Rome, but the northern ecclesiastics and the Columban church in Scotland still adhered to the Celtic customs. Adamnan was on good terms with King Aldfrid and had maintained the Columban links with Northumbria. On his second visit to the Northumbrian court in 688, he was induced to adopt the Roman Easter. Thereafter he became the principal agent in converting the northern Irish, who conformed shortly before his death in 704, but he failed to win over his own recalcitrant monks on Iona, and the greater part of the Columban community in Scotland held out until 716. Another indication of Adamnan's involvement in political affairs is the law that was enacted in his name for the protection of noncombatants and church property. The *Lex innocentium,* or *Cáin Adamnáin,* was enjoined upon the "people of Ireland and Britain" at the Synod of Birr in 697.

Adamnan's greatest literary work is his biography of St. Columba, which he wrote on Iona almost certainly between the years 688 and 692. The historical references are incidental rather than systematic, but the *Vita Columbae* is still the best record of the old Celtic monastic church. Although written almost a century after the saint's death in 597, it drew on an uninterrupted oral tradition, and since conditions had not changed essentially in the intervening years, it is accepted as a fair representation of the monastic regime on Iona during the founder's time. There are many other works attributed to Adamnan, for the most part spuriously: prayers, poems, two visions, and a commentary on Vergil; he is cited as one of the authors of the *Collectio canonum Hibernensis.* One genuine attribution is his treatise on the holy places, *De locis sanctis.* Although Adamnan probably traveled no farther east than Northumbria, he compiled a work from the limited resources of his own library and from notes which he took from the Gallic pilgrim-bishop Arculf which treats of Palestine, Tyre, Crete, Constantinople, and Sicily. It is a testimony to the breadth of vision of this scholar-abbot of Iona.

BIBLIOGRAPHY

Modern editions of Adamnan are William Reeves, ed., *The Life of St. Columba* (1857); A. O. Anderson and M. O. Anderson, eds. and trans., *Adomnan's Life of Columba* (1961); and D. Meehan, ed., *Adamnan's De Locis Sanctis* (1958).

Works by contemporaries include Kuno Meyer, ed. and trans., *Cáin Adamnáin, an Old-Irish Treatise on the Law of Adamnán* (1905); Bede, *Historia ecclesiastica gentis Anglorum,* 2 vols., C. Plummer, ed. (1896); *A History of the English Church and People,* L. Sherley-Price, trans. (1975); and William Hennessy and B. MacCarthy, eds., *Annals of Ulster* (1887; 1901).

Adamnan's later life is discussed in R. I. Best, ed., "Betha Adamnáin," in *Anecdota from Irish Manuscripts,* II (1908); and Maud Joynt, trans., "The Life of Adamnán," in *Celtic Review,* **18** (1908).

See also J. F. Kenny, *The Sources for the Early History of Ireland: Ecclesiastical* (1966).

Máirín Ní Dhonnchadha

ADBO (ABBO) OF ST.-GERMAIN-DES-PRÉS, author of a historical poem in three books describing the Viking siege of Paris in 885 and other events down to the year 896. His Latin diction (especially in the final book) displays the excessively learned vocabulary characteristic of glossaries. He also composed a number of sermons, five of which have been published.

BIBLIOGRAPHY

Bella Parisiacae urbis, Paul Carl Rudolf von Winterfeld, ed., in *Monumenta Germaniae historica, poetae latini aevi Carolini,* IV. 1 (1899), 72–122; the sermons are in *Patrologia latina,* CXXXII (1880), cols. 761–778.

David A. E. Pelteret

ADELARD OF BATH (*ca.* 1070–after 1142–1146), English Scholastic philosopher, author of scientific treatises, and translator. He studied at Tours, taught at Laon, and traveled in Italy, Sicily, Asia Minor, Syria, possibly the Holy Land, and probably Spain. English records reveal that he had returned to England by 1130.

Among his scientific works are *Quaestiones naturales* (1111–1116) and translations, from Arabic, of astrological treatises, astronomical tables, and other texts of the Islamic scientific tradition, including an *Introduction* by Muḥammad ibn Mūsā al-Khwārizmī dating from the first half of the ninth century. Manuscript evidence assigns this last work either to astronomy or to the whole quadrivium. Adelard also produced, working from an Arabic translation, the first Latin version of Euclid's *Elements.*

It has been shown that the early thirteenth-century superiority of English scholars in physical science over their counterparts on the Continent was owing to a generation of twelfth-century English investigators of whom Adelard was the first. These men had turned their attention to the physical rather than to the metaphysical and logical treatises of Aristotle, a movement that reached its peak in the thirteenth century with Roger Bacon and Robert Grosseteste.

The *Quaestiones naturales,* or 76 *Questions on Nature,* embraces Aristotle's demonstration of an unmoved mover, Democritean atomism, and the indestructibility of matter; the work also treats other issues expounded in the Arabic scientific tradition. Adelard extols the value of reason over authority and defends ingeniously the "natural place" account of gravity.

Adelard's original metaphysical thought is found in his main work, *De eodem et diverso* (*On the Identical and the Diverse,* 1105–1110), written as a dialogue between Philosophia, the domain of the immutable (*idem,* identical) and Philocosmia, the sphere of the mutable (*diversum,* diverse). The former probably stands for the realm of reason; the latter represents the varying world grasped by sense experience.

Adelard recognized that Aristotle considered universals such as genus and species to be "only in sensibles," whereas Plato located them in the unchanging world, "outside sensibles." Still Adelard was convinced that "although these men might seem opposed in words *(verbis),* in reality *(re),* however, they are of the same opinion." (Willner, p. 12). He justified Aristotle's position by noting that both a specific name *(nomen),* such as "human being," and a generic name, such as "animal," are applicable to individuals. He justified Plato by recognizing that these individuals can be examined "more profoundly" *(altius)* not inasmuch as they are "diverse in the sensible order" but because they are designated by specific and generic terms which stand for realities preexisting "in the Divine Mind" (*ibid.,* pp. 11–12). Thus Adelard echoes Question 46 of Augustine's *Book of 83 Different Questions,* according to which Platonic universals become divine ideas. He also restricts Aristotle's analysis of universals to the realm of physical science, while reserving for Plato the higher metaphysical domain.

Other works of Adelard include *Rules for the Abacus, Functions of the Astrolabe* (*ca.* 1141–1146), and *On Falconry.*

BIBLIOGRAPHY

Hans E. Willner, ed., *Des Adelard von Bath Traktat De eodem et diverso* (1903); M. Müller, ed., *Die Quaestiones naturales des Adelardus . . .* (1934); Hermann Gollancz, ed. and trans., *76 Questions on Nature,* in Berechiah ben Natronai, *Dodi ve-nichdi (Uncle and Nephew)* (1920); Franz J. P. Bliemetzrieder, *Adelhard von Bath* (1935); Daniel A. Callus, "Introduction of Aristotelian Learning to Oxford," in *Proceedings of the British Academy,* **29** (1943); Meyrick H. Carré, *Phases of Thought in England* (1949); Alistair C. Crombie, *Augustine to Galileo* (1952); Eduard J. Dijksterhuis, *The Mechanization of the World Picture,* C. Dikshoorn, trans. (1961); Étienne Gilson, *History of Christian Philosophy in the Middle Ages* (1955); Charles Homer Haskins, *Studies in the History of Mediaeval Science,* 2nd ed. (1927); John E. Murdoch, "The Medieval Euclid: Salient Aspects of the Translation of the *Elements* by Adelard of Bath and Campanus of Novara," XIIe Congrès international d'histoire des sciences, *Revue de synthèse,* **89** (1968), 49–52, 67–94; Lynn Thorndike, *A History of Magic and Experimental Science,* II (1923).

JANICE L. SCHULTZ

ADELELMUS. See **Aleaume.**

ADELMAN OF LIÈGE was a favorite pupil of Fulbert of Chartres, under whom he studied with Berengar of Tours about 1025. He later addressed an orthodox letter to Berengar on the Eucharist. After being a teacher at Liège, he was in Speyer (a letter from a Speyer resident opposing the misuse of general absolution may be his), and then became bishop of Brescia (*ca.* 1050–*ca.* 1061).

BIBLIOGRAPHY

Rythmi alphabetici de viris illustribus sui temporis, in *Patrologia latina,* CXLIII (1882), cols. 1295–1298; *Ad Berengarium epistola, ibid.,* cols. 1289–1296; and *Epistola A. civis Spirensis ad Heribertum Coloniensem archiepiscopum, ibid.,* CLI, cols. 693–698.

DAVID A. E. PELTERET

ADÉMAR OF CHABANNES (*ca.* 988–*ca.* 1035), educated in the monastery of St. Martial at Limoges and wrote histories of the region and of the abbots of his monastery. A skilled copyist, illustrator, and musician, he was influential through his writings and by assiduous forgery in the establishment of the cult of St. Martial as an apostle.

BIBLIOGRAPHY

Adémar's published works are *Historiae,* G. Waitz, ed., in *Monumenta Germaniae historica, scriptores,* IV (1841), 106–148; *Commemoratio abbatum Lemovicensium,* in *Patrologia latina,* CXLI (1880), cols. 79–86; *Epistola de Apostolatu Sancti Martialis, ibid.,* cols. 87–112.

See also D. F. Callahan, "The Sermons of Adémar of Chabbanes and the Cult of St. Martial of Limoges," in *Revue Bénédictine,* **86** (1976), 251–295.

DAVID A. E. PELTERET

ADENET LE ROI (*ca.* 1240–after 1297), a thirteenth-century musician and poet, called both Adam and Adenet in contemporary documents. Contrary to current convention, *le Roi*—a professional title, not a surname—preceded the given name: "Ce livre de Cleomadés / rimai je, li rois Adenés."

Born about 1240, Adenet was trained as a minstrel (instrumentalist and reciter of poems) at the court of

Henry III, duke of Brabant. After his patron's death in 1261, he entered the service of Guy of Dampierre, count of Flanders, becoming *roi des ménestrels,* chief of the court minstrels. In this capacity, he accompanied the count to Tunis on the Eighth Crusade (1270–1271) and on frequent visits to the Parisian court of Philip III the Bold. His literary activity coincided with the prosperous years (1269–1285) of Guy's reign. As political troubles overwhelmed Flanders, Adenet faded from the public record; he is last mentioned in a document of 1297.

Adenet composed four French narrative poems. *Buevon de Conmarchis,* a colorless reworking in dodecasyllabic monorhymed stanzas of the *Siège de Barbastre,* is judged the earliest on stylistic grounds; its 3,947 verses lack an ending in the single manuscript. Adenet wrote his second epic, *Les Enfances Ogier* (8,229 decasyllabic verses), for Guy of Dampierre. Handling his source, an unknown version of the *Chevalerie Ogier,* with increasing independence, he transformed his robust model through an infusion of the courtly manners and idealized chivalry of his own time. With *Berte aus grans piés* (3,486 dodecasyllabic verses), Adenet moved from epic toward romance in retelling the legendary adventures of Charlemagne's mother. Noted for its sympathetic depiction of women, *Berte* tends to pit virtuous characters against evil ones in systemic oppositions. The romance *Cleomadés* (18,698 verses, octosyllabic couplets with interpolated lyrics) was rhymed for Queen Marie of France and her sister-in-law, Madame Blanche Anne. Based on a Hispano-Arabic tale, this action-filled love story featuring a flying wooden horse is Adenet's most successful and influential work.

BIBLIOGRAPHY

Albert Henry, ed., *Les oeuvres d'Adenet le Roi,* 5 vols. (1951–1971); Urban T. Holmes, Jr., ed., *Adenet le Roi's "Berte aus grans piés"* (1946); André Adnès, *Adenès, dernier grand trouvère: recherches historiques et anthroponymiques* (1971); Margaret Munroe Boland, *Cleomadés: A Study in Architectonic Patterns* (1974); Renée Colliot, *Adenet le Roi, "Berte aus grans piés": Étude littéraire général,* 2 vols. (1970).

MARY B. SPEER

ADGAR (*fl.* last third 12th c.), also called Willame, an Anglo-Norman writer who translated into verse a collection of forty-nine miracles about the Virgin Mary called the *Gracial.* The work is dedicated to an otherwise unknown Gregory and to a Lady Maud, who may have been the natural daughter of Henry II of that name. She was abbess of Barking from 1175 to 1195. The miracles are found in three manuscripts, which could represent three different versions.

BIBLIOGRAPHY

Carl Neuhaus, ed., *Adgars Marienlegenden* (1886); Pierre Kunstmann, ed. *Le Gracial* (1981); M. Dominica Legge, *Anglo-Norman Literature and its Background* (1963).

BRIAN MERRILEES

[See also **Anglo-Norman Literature.**]

ADMIRAL. The title of admiral is derived from the Arabic *emir* or *amir-al,* which refers to officials who seem to have commanded a fleet or a naval shore installation or bureau in Ommiad Spain during the tenth century. We find the title first used in Latin Europe a little later during the twelfth century in Norman Sicily where Admiral Eugenius was the most famous commander who bore it. Soon thereafter the title spread to Genoa, and by the thirteenth century was found in all the major Spanish realms. We find it used in Aragonese lands during the reign of James the Conqueror (1208–1276) and that of his immediate successors, while soon after the fall of Seville in 1248 Castilian monarchs appointed admirals who were in charge of their new fleet based on their arsenal on the Guadalquivir. At about the same time, Portuguese rulers also began to choose admirals, often Genoese, to command their warships.

Though English kings from the time of John regularly chose commanders of their fleets in time of war, the first use of this title for such an officer seems to date from 1303. At about the same time, their French rivals began to appoint admirals as commanders of their fleets, too. And from England and France, the title spread throughout the northern seas of Europe.

Curiously in the Byzantine Empire the title of admiral was never used to designate a naval commander, and it was rarely employed in medieval times in the Muslim world of the eastern Mediterranean until quite late. This may explain why Venice never called its fleet commanders admiral but reserved the title, rendered as *armirao,* for the manager of their famous *Arsenal* or for navigators on fourteenth- and fifteenth-century galleys. The last famous medieval admiral was Columbus, who was given the title of Admiral of the Ocean Seas by his royal mistress, Queen Isabella of Spain.

Our earliest full account of the duties of an admiral is from that Catalan collection of maritime laws known as *The Consulate of the Sea,* whose earliest provisions date from the thirteenth century. This code carefully enumerates the rights and duties of an admiral in relation to naval vessels and personnel and merchant ships and seamen under his command. It formed the basis of similar laws in late medieval England promulgated under the title of *The Black Book of the Admiralty.*

BIBLIOGRAPHY

Stanley Jados, *Consulate of the Sea and Related Documents* (1975); Evelyn Jamison, *Admiral Eugenius of Sicily, His Life and Work* (1957); Frederic Lane, *Venice, A Maritime Republic* (1973); Évariste Lévi-Provençal, *L'Espagne musulmane au Xème siècle* (1932); Travers Twiss, *Monumenta juridica, The Black Book of the Admiralty* (1871–1876).

ARCHIBALD R. LEWIS

ADMIRALTY, COURT OF. The English kings who from earliest times had vigorously pressed their jurisdictional claims within the realm were much slower in dealing with the complex problems of maritime law, piracy, and spoil. Although the late medieval Black Book of the Admiralty ascribed the creation of a distinct admiralty jurisdiction to Edward I (1272–1307), modern scholarly opinion holds that the court did not come into existence until the reign of Edward III, sometime between 1340 and 1357.

By the mid fourteenth century, the convergence of several lines of development in maritime law, problems over piracy, and royal power in England and France favored the creation of an admiralty court. The law maritime existed in northwest Europe as a body of rules based on the "laws of Oléron," a codification of decisions made in the maritime courts of the Île d'Oléron off the western coast of France. Merchants carried this law with them almost like cargo and settled cases in seaport towns in England and elsewhere. In fact the laws were closely associated with Aquitaine, ruled since 1199 by the English king as duke (although the attribution of the laws to Eleanor of Aquitaine seems to be a myth), and were particularly concerned with regulating the lively wine trade between the duchy and England.

But issues related to piracy were more difficult to settle, especially when they involved the subjects of rival kings already standing with eyes fixed on each other and hands fixed on swords. The diplomatic correspondence of the late thirteenth and first half of the fourteenth centuries was swelled by a constant stream of complaints from victims of illegal acts on the seas. The common-law courts of England were not the most favorable setting for a foreigner seeking redress over incidents of piracy or spoil committed by Englishmen; kings tried various forms of arbitration and treaty but these efforts likewise failed to solve the problem. From 1293 the maritime complaints reached a new level of seriousness and, in fact, contributed to the outbreak of war between England and France. Documents surviving from this period (collected in the fourteenth-century *Fasciculus de superioritate maris*) record specific claims by Englishmen that the king of England rightfully had guardianship of the sea or admiralty jurisdiction; these claims seem intended to counter French assertions that certain acts of spoil were carried out under the command of an admiral of the seas acting under orders of the French king. These English claims to guardianship of the seas appeared, in parliamentary petitions and letters patent, for example, at various times in the fourteenth century. But such claims were, at least for a time, translated into reality in 1340 following the great naval victory of Edward III over the French at Sluis; the French fleet was almost completely destroyed and the king of England indeed became the sovereign of the seas that he had claimed to be.

Sometime in the following decade or two, Edward III granted to his admiral full judging powers in piracy and other maritime cases. The office of admiral itself was not new. The title appears half a century earlier and the admirals had long exercised the disciplinary and administrative jurisdiction necessary for operating a major naval command. But the early admirals had held commands of short duration, often for a particular expedition, or had authority only within a specific district (there were admirals for the north, south, and west). Questions of piracy and spoil had been left to the courts of common law, the Council, special commissions, such as *oyer* and *terminer*, or to the arbitrations established in negotiations with foreign governments. But in 1360, a single admiral, John Pavely, was appointed to command all the king's fleets; he was empowered to hear pleas and to appoint a deputy who was obviously intended to be a judge in the new court. His letter patent of appoint provided, in language used throughout the rest of the century, "full power by the tenor of these presents of hearing plaints of all and singular the matters that touch the office of the admiral and of taking cognizance of maritime causes and of doing justice and of correcting and punishing offenses and of imprisoning and of setting at liberty prisoners who ought to be set at liberty and of doing all other things that appertain to the office of admiral as they ought to be done of right and according to the maritime law."

But the new court, which did not operate on common-law principles, quickly generated opposition. A parliamentary petition of 1371, for example, complained that men were put to answer charges otherwise than by jury presentment as required by the common law. Perhaps even more serious were the irregularities committed by the court under John Holland, earl of Huntingdon, who was appointed admiral in 1389. His actions led to two statutes under Richard II in 1389 and 1391 that defined and restricted admiralty jurisdiction. A similar statute followed in 1400, during the reign of Henry IV. In the early fifteenth century, dissatisfaction led to decentralization of admiralty jurisdiction. Conservators of truces, appointed in the seaports by statutory authority from 1414, basically took on the jurisdiction of the admiral, although capital crimes were formally reserved to him or his judge. Throughout the fifteenth century most piracy cases were in fact dealt with by the local officers or by commissioners with similar delegated powers. "It would appear," as Reginald Marsden wrote, "that the working of the Admiral's Court had not been altogether satisfactory." Yet the court was revived by Henry VIII and had a more successful postmedieval history.

BIBLIOGRAPHY

Frederic L. Cheyette, "The Sovereign and the Pirates, 1332," in *Speculum,* 45 (1970); Hubert Hall, *Select Cases Concerning the Law Merchant, A.D. 1239–1633* (1930); Reginald G. Marsden, *Select Pleas in the Court of Admiralty,* vol. I (1894); Timothy Runyan, "The Rolls of Oléron and the Admiralty Court in Fourteenth-Century England" (Conference on Medieval Studies, Western Michigan University, 1971).

RICHARD KAEUPER

ADOPTIONISM, the heresy that appeared in Spain in the latter part of the eighth century and taught that Jesus Christ is the Son of God only by adoption. The controversy arose when Migetius, about whom nothing is known except what he wrote, taught the threefold historical manifestation of the Trinity: the Father as David, the Son as Jesus the offspring of David, and the Holy Spirit as the apostle Paul. Elipandus, archbishop of Toledo from about 780, responded to this by arguing for the immanence of the Trinity, but in such a way that he drew a radical distinction between the divinity and humanity of Christ. Thus Christ could be properly called the Son of God only according to his divine nature. According to his manhood he was the adopted Son of God.

From the orthodox perspective this doctrine destroys the unity of person in Christ and appears to posit two persons. There are several theories about what occasioned Elipandus's teaching. Expressions in the old Spanish liturgy and the writings of Hilary of Poitiers and Isidore of Seville might have suggested such a conclusion. The similarity between Elipandus's views and those of Nestorianism are remarkable, and a direct influence through some Nestorian writings has been suggested. Accommodation to the religious sensibilities of Islam might suggest itself, but the basic opposition of Islam to any Trinitarian doctrine would seem to rule this out.

The defense of adoptionism was taken up by Felix, the bishop of Urgel. Felix defended his doctrine before Charlemagne at Regensburg (Ratisbon) in 792. Adoptionism was rejected by the bishops, and Felix was sent to Rome, where he was imprisoned until he recanted. Alcuin entered the dispute in an attempt to dissuade Felix and Elipandus from using the term "adoption" about Christ. At the insistence of adoptionist Spanish bishops, a rehearing was convened by Charlemagne at Frankfurt in 794. Two documents from this synod, together with one issued by Pope Adrian I, again condemned adoptionism. In 798, Felix, who apparently was back in Urgel, wrote to Alcuin, defending the doctrine, and Alcuin replied with the seven-book treatise *Contra Felicem* (Against Felix). In 798 or 799, Pope Leo III called a synod in Rome that anathematized Felix. Throughout this period efforts were being made to counteract the heresy and to recover the heretical provinces for the orthodox church. Finally, a meeting was arranged at Aachen, probably in 799, with Charlemagne again presiding. Felix was finally induced to recant, and called upon his diocese to follow suit.

The heresy gradually died out, and was extinct in

Spain by the mid ninth century. A recurrence of mitigated adoptionism took place in the twelfth century in the teachings of Peter Abelard. It again centered on a rational distinction between the two natures of Christ. Abelard was accused of Nestorianism, and his supporter Eberhard, bishop of Bamberg, accused opponents of the opposing heresy, Eutychianism. Attempts by these and later medieval theologians, such as Duns Scotus and Durandus, to give an orthodox interpretation to adoptionism were finally rejected as unsound.

BIBLIOGRAPHY

For the works of Elipandus of Toledo and Felix of Urgel, see J. P. Migne, *Patrologia latina,* XCVI (1851). The following studies are also useful: M. Menéndez y Pelayo, *Historia de los heterodoxes expañoles,* I (1880; repr. 1956), 265–305; the article "Adoptionisme," in *Dictionnaire de théologie catholique* (1930), I.1: pt. 1, "Adoptionisme au VIIIe siècle" (H. Quilliet), cols. 403–413, and pt. 2, "Adoptionisme au XIIe siècle" (E. Portalié), cols. 413–421, both with full bibliographies; and J. F. Rivera, *Elipando de Toledo* (1940).

D. W. JOHNSON

[See also **Abelard, Peter.**]

ADRIAN IV, POPE (*ca.* 1100–1159), was born Nicholas Breakspear and was the only Englishman ever to serve as pope. He was elected 4 December 1154 and crowned the following day. His father was a minor royal official who in time became a monk at St. Albans.

Nicholas went to France, perhaps to study, and joined the community of regular canons at St. Rufus near Avignon. He became their abbot but soon had such strong disagreements with them that complaints and counter-complaints were fired off to Rome. In this way Nicholas came to the attention of the papal court, in particular to Pope Eugenius III, who around 1149 named him cardinal bishop of Albano.

With the full authority of a legate, Nicholas undertook a major mission to reorganize the church in Scandinavia. In Norway he set up a new archdiocese at Trondheim, and in Sweden one at Uppsala; these territories had previously been under the ecclesiastical supervision of the archbishop of Hamburg-Bremen. He also arranged for the regular payment of Peter's Pence by the Scandinavian churches.

The city of Rome was in the turmoil of a communal revolution when Anastasius IV died and Nicholas was elected unanimously to succeed him. During Holy Week in 1155, the new pope placed the city under an interdict for the first time in its history. That was too much for the Romans to bear at Easter: the revolution collapsed; its leader Arnold of Brescia left the city; and the interdict was lifted. Arnold was shortly afterward caught and turned over to the prefect of Rome (a papal official), who had him hanged.

Frederick Barbarossa supported Adrian in opposing the commune because he wished to be crowned as Holy Roman emperor by the pope; the coronation took place on 18 June 1155. But then Frederick withdrew from the city and thereafter opposed the pope on virtually every issue. The pope had also to contend with King William I of Sicily over their respective rights. For a while he supported Norman rebels and Greeks in William's lands, but at Benevento in June 1156 he restored the alliance established a century before by Leo IX with the Norman rulers of southern Italy.

For three months at Benevento, Adrian had the company of John of Salisbury, who had come to seek approbation of Henry II's plan to invade Ireland. By the bull *Laudabiliter* (whose authenticity is still questioned by some scholars), Adrian approved the plan and granted Henry lordship over Ireland.

Signs of the coming, protracted struggle between the papacy and the Hohenstaufen emperors first appeared in 1157 at Besancon in a dispute over papal claims concerning the empire and in 1158 at Roncaglia, where Frederick's lawyers elaborated a full statement of imperial claims in Italy. Both sides became increasingly adamant and started to seek out allies among the other's enemies. They stood at such an impasse when Adrian died suddenly at Anagni.

Highly regarded as a preacher and singer, Adrian was apparently a most capable administrator. Although not a lawyer, he was served throughout his reign by a chancellor, Orlando Bandinelli, who succeeded him as Alexander III and initiated the line of lawyer-popes that ran uninterrupted from 1159 to 1303. Adrian's career was based upon his own talent; indeed Sir Richard Southern has called him "the Dick Whittington of the twelfth century."

BIBLIOGRAPHY

Adrian, letters and privileges, in *Patrologia latina,* vol. CLXXXVIII; Boso, *Vita Adriani IV,* in *Liber pontificalis,* ed. L. Duchesne, vol. II; Michele Maccarrone, *Papato e impero dalla elezione di Federico I alla morte di Adriano*

IV (1152–1159) (1959); Horace K. Mann, *Nicholas Breakspear* (1914); Richard W. Southern, *Medieval Humanism and Other Essays* (1970); W. Ullmann, "The Pontificate of Adrian IV," in *Cambridge Historical Journal,* **11** (1953–1955); Edith M. Almedingen, *The English Pope* (1925).

LESTER K. LITTLE

[See also **Alexander III, Arnold of Brescia, Frederick I, John of Salisbury.**]

ADRIANOPLE (EDIRNE). Lying about 130 miles northwest of Constantinople, Adrianople was on the main highway from the Byzantine capital to the Danube and was therefore a vital military city that changed hands often throughout Byzantine history. It was the capital of the Macedonian theme and an important Byzantine border fortress. It was taken by the Bulgars in the ninth and tenth centuries, by the Venetians during the Fourth Crusade, again by the Bulgars in the thirteenth century, and finally by the Ottomans in 1362.

BIBLIOGRAPHY

George Ostrogorsky, *History of the Byzantine State,* Joan Hussey, trans. (1957; rev. ed., 1969).

LINDA ROSE

ADVENT, the season preceding the coming of Christ, has been part of the liturgical calendar of the Western church since the fourth century. It seems to have appeared first in those areas in which the ancient Gallican liturgical rite and its derivatives were used. By the time of Perpetuus of Tours (*d.* 491) Christians were bidden to fast three days a week from the feast of St. Martin (11 November) to the feast of Christ's nativity—the six- or seven-week Lent of St. Martin. Pope Gregory I is often said of have consolidated the Roman tradition of Advent by reducing the number of Sundays to four and by composing a number of homilies and perhaps musical pieces for Advent. By the eighth century the four-Sunday tradition had become normative throughout Europe.

The penitential features of the ancient Gallican practice eventually penetrated the Roman rite, so that fasting and abstinence were enjoined and marriages forbidden during Advent. Hence, by the late thirteenth century Gulielmus Durandus was stressing the ambiguity of the season as a time not only of joy in expectation of Christ's birth but also of penance in expectation of the Second Coming.

BIBLIOGRAPHY

Walter Croce, "Die Adventsliturgie im Lichte ihrer geschichtlichen Entwicklung," in *Zeitschrift für katholische Theologie,* **76** (1954); Josef Andreas Jungmann, "Advent und Voradvent: Überreste des gallischen Advents in der römischen Liturgie," *ibid.*, **61** (1937); Francis X. Weiser, *Handbook of Christian Feasts and Customs* (1958), 49–59.

ROGER E. REYNOLDS

[See also **Durandus, Gulielmus; Gallican Rite.**]

ADVENTUS. See **Entry Into Jerusalem.**

ADVOCATE. During the Carolingian period many gifts of land, and rights annexed to land, were made to cathedrals and monasteries. To profit from these gifts bishops and abbots would have had to engage in secular business, such as holding courts, arresting disturbers of the peace, and repulsing invaders. Kings, popes, and councils thought this unseemly. Thus it became customary to appoint an advocate (*avoué* in French, *vogt* in German) or, for a bishop, a vidame (*vice-dominus,* vice-lord) to handle these secular affairs. The advocate was rewarded by a grant of part of the lands and revenues that he protected. As time went on, advocates began to think of these holdings as their own possessions and rendered little service to the church from which they held them. At their worst they oppressed the churches they were supposed to protect, but even when they were not oppressive they were, in fact, independent feudal lords. The vidame of Amiens was a faithful servant of Philip the Fair of France but was considered an enemy of the church by Pope Boniface VIII. In England, where royal control of both the church and the nobility were tighter, there were no advocates.

BIBLIOGRAPHY

Jan F. Niermeyer, *Mediae latinitatis lexicon minus* (1976), has good examples under the heading *advocatus.* See also Eberhard Otto, *Die Entwicklung der deutschen Kirchenvogtei im 10 Jahrhundert.* (1933); Charles Pergameni, *L'avouerie ecclésiastique belge* (1907); and Félix Senn, *L'institution des avoueries ecclésiastiques en France* (1903).

JOSEPH R. STRAYER

ADVOWSON. See **Presentation.**

ÁEDÁN MAC GABRÁIN (*d.* 609), was born into a royal line of the Dál Riata, a kingdom occupying the glens of Antrim in northeast Ireland with colonies in Kintyre, Argyll, and neighboring islands. On the death of his cousin Conall in 574 he succeeded to the kingship, which straddled both Ireland and Scotland. He was reluctantly "ordained" king by St. Columba of Iona, who, in the following year at the convention of Druim Cett, was instrumental in securing an alliance between Áedán and Áed mac Ainmuirech, king of the northern Uí Néill. This was to offset pressure on Dál Riata by Báetán mac Cairill of Ulaid, who reputedly received Áedán's hommage at Rinn Seimne (Island Magee, near Larne). Báetán's overseas ambitions were crushed two years after his death in 582, when Áedán expelled the Ulaid settlement from the Isle of Man.

Continuing a policy of his precedessor, Áedán led an expedition to the Orkney Islands in 580–581 to put pressure on the Picts—an aggression maintained throughout his reign. His expansionist ambitions won him a costly victory against the Miathi settled on each side of the Forth River, in which battle he lost two sons and 303 men. Two other sons were killed by the Angles in Northumbria in 598.

Áedán's mother was reputedly British, and the tradition of his marriages with British, Pictish, and Saxon women reflect his political embroilment. Although an ally of the Britons, he may have attempted to expand at their expense in Strathclyde—hence their epithet "wily" for him.

Unsupported by his British allies, Áedán was heavily defeated in the battle of Degsastán in Northumbria in 603. In his army was a discontented faction from the Bernician royal house and contingents from the Cenél nEógain and Dál nAraide.

He retired from the kingship in 608 and died the following year.

BIBLIOGRAPHY

Marjorie O. Anderson, *Kings and Kingship in Early Scotland* (1973), 145–157; John Bannerman, *Studies in the History of Dalriada* (1974), 80–90; Francis John Byrne, *Irish Kings and High-Kings* (1973).

CHARLES DOHERTY

ÁED SLÂNE (*d.* 604?) according to the unreliable seventh-century annals and genealogies, the son of the legend-encrusted Diarmait mac Cerbaill (*d.* 565?) and the brother of Colmán Már (*d.* 555–558?). These dynasts belonged to the midland branch of the great Uí Néill dynasty. In the later king-lists, Áed Sláne is accounted king of Tara (that is, overking of the whole Uí Néill dynasty), but the seventh-century *Baile Chuind* accords him no such title. The annals for the seventh century have two entries concerning him. The first, under 600, states that he killed Suibne son of Colmán Már, his nephew; and the second, under 604, records his own murder at the hands of Conall son of Suibne, with whom he had shared the kingship of Tara. Adamnán (*d.* 704), in his life of Columba, records a tradition that the saint warned Áed Sláne against the crime of kin-slaying *(fingal),* for by so doing he would lose "the prerogative of monarchy over the kingdom of all Ireland"; nonetheless, Áed slew his nephew Suibne, and as a result his reign was brief and his dominion limited. Adamnán and the annals are unlikely to be independent, and all the sources cited belong to the end of the seventh century, when the success of the descendants of Áed Sláne encouraged a rewriting of the story of their eponymous ancestor.

In fact, Áed Sláne had greater success as an ancestor than as a ruler, and it is probably true that the real establishment of Uí Néill power in the midlands was due to his descendants (Sil nÁeda Sláne), who excluded the descendants of Colmán Már (Clann Cholmáin) until the early eighth century and supplied some eight kings of Tara. They ruled the rich coastland kingdom of Brega (in which Tara lay), and their kings were among the most powerful in Ireland. The last of the dynasty to be king of Tara (apart from a brief interlude in the tenth century) was Cináed (*d.* 728), and henceforth their rivals excluded them from the overkingship.

In the middle of the eighth century the dynasty resolved itself into two mature and mutually hostile segments, descended, according to the genealogical scheme, from two sons of Áed Sláne, Congal (*d.* 634?) and Diarmait (*d.* 665). The one established itself at Knowth on the Boyne to the north, the other at the island fortress of Lagore to the south of Tara. Clann Cholmáin, now the holders of power in the midlands, dominated them in the ninth century, and apart from the brief but brilliant reign of Congalach of Knowth, who was king of Tara from 944 to 956, they rapidly declined in status. From the middle of the tenth century to the Norman invasion in the twelfth they were petty local kings and vassals of Clann Cholmáin.

BIBLIOGRAPHY

Francis John Byrne, "Historical Note on Cnogba (Knowth)," in George Eogan, "Excavations at Knowth, Co. Meath, 1962–1965," in *Proceedings of the Royal Irish Academy* **66** Section C (1968); and *Irish Kings and High-Kings* (1973); Gerard Murphy, "*Baile Chuind* and the Date of *Cín Dromma Snechtai,*" in *Ériu* **16** (1952). See also A. O. and M. O. Anderson, eds., *Adomnan's Life of Columba* (1961) and M. A. O'Brien, ed., *Corpus Genealogiarum Hiberniae,* vol. I (1962). For a later literary birth tale of Áed Sláne, see Richard I. Best and Osborn J. Bergin, *Lebor na hUidre* (1929).

DONNCHADH Ó CORRÁIN.

AEDDI (EDDIUS STEPHANUS). A Kentishman invited to Northumbria by Bishop Wilfrid (634–709) to teach chanting, Aeddi wrote a biography of Wilfrid, probably within a decade of his death. Despite its bias and inaccuracies, it is an invaluable source on one of the most important and controversial figures in the early Anglo-Saxon church.

BIBLIOGRAPHY

The Life of Bishop Wilfrid by Eddius Stephanus, text, translation, and notes, Bertram Colgrave, ed. (1927). See also D. P. Kirby, ed., *Saint Wilfrid at Hexham* (1974), esp. 35ff.

DAVID A. E. PELTERET

AEDICULA. An ornamental frame formed by columns or pilasters supporting an entablature, canopy, or lintel. It surrounds a niche, window, or door. A shallow niche formed in this fashion is also called an aedicula.

LESLIE BRUBAKER

AEGIDIUS ROMANUS. See **Giles of Rome.**

AELFRIC (*ca.* 955–1010 or 1015), the finest prose stylist of the Anglo-Saxon (Old English) period and one of the finest of any period of the language. Aelfric influenced writers for two hundred years after his death and has grown steadily in importance since his rediscovery in the sixteenth century by Anglican apologists looking to the early English church for precedents for their customs and beliefs that differed from those of Rome. Born in Wessex, Aelfric entered the Old Minster at Winchester, the monastery attached to the cathedral, as a boy or young man. Ordained as a priest at the age of thirty, he was sent out to the new monastery at Cerne Abbas, Dorset, in 987. In 1005 he became abbot of another new community, at Eynsham, near Oxford, where he died. Though not of pronounced originality as a theologian, Aelfric was a great teacher, selecting and making available in the vernacular much of the learning of the church fathers.

At Winchester, Aelfric studied under Ethelwold, bishop from 963 until his death in 984 and, along with Dunstan and Oswald, one of the reformers of English monasticism during the reign of King Edgar. Aelfric's own literary career began at Cerne Abbas, where he completed two collections of forty homilies each—the so-called first and second series of *Catholic Homilies*—for the church year; a series of saints' lives; miscellaneous homilies and theological treatises; a Latin grammar (the first in English); a *Colloquy*, or elementary instructional conversation; translations of parts of the first eight books of the Old Testament; and translations of two long sermons attributed to St. Basil: the *Hexameron* on the six days of creation and the *Admonitio ad filium spiritualem* ("Admonition to a Spiritual Son"). During the 990's, Wulfsige, the bishop of Sherborne, had asked Aelfric to write a letter of advice and instruction to the clergy of his diocese; Archbishop Wulfstan of York made a like request in 1005, about which time Aelfric wrote at length to his monks of Eynsham on their duties and to a layman, Sigeweard, on how to read and study the Bible. Aelfric also prepared a Latin life of Ethelwold and continued to revise and expand his earlier English works, particularly the homilies.

Translating the Bible troubled Aelfric. On the one hand he feared that uninstructed readers might take

Old Testament figures as models (in his preface to Genesis he cites Jacob and his four wives in this connection); on the other hand, to translate other than literally would be to substitute one's own words for God's. Homilies offered a happy solution. After quoting in Latin and then translating a passage from Scripture, Aelfric could devote the rest of the homily to explaining the spiritual meaning.

The opening sentence of his account of St. Benedict, one of the second series of *Catholic Homilies*, exemplifies Aelfric's clear, straightforward style:

> Benedict the holy abbot on this present day went from this deadly life to that eternal one which he had deeply earned with holy demeanor.

The elements of the complex sentence follow so logically and naturally that it needs no commas. The simple diction includes two strings of alliterating words: "abbot," *andwerdum* (here rendered as "present"), "eternal," "earned" and "day," "deadly," "deeply," "demeanor." A little later, still at Cerne Abbas, Aelfric started to shape and arrange his phrases for them to fall into alliterating pairs, in the manner of Old English verse:

> After *Au*gustine had come to *E*ngland,
> there was a *n*oble king *n*amed Oswald
> in the *l*and of Northumbria who be*l*ieved in God.

In this the opening sentence from Aelfric's life of Oswald, the first half of each rhythmic line has at least one stressed word or syllable that alliterates with one in the second half-line.

But the formal demands of Aelfric's newfound "rhythmic prose" did not prevent him from composing either richly patterned paragraphs or sentences as syntactically intricate as this one from the preface to his translation of St. Basil's *Admonitio*:

> Basil the blessed, about whom we have written,
> was a very saintly bishop in the city of Caesarea
> in the land of the Greeks; loving God greatly,
> living in cleanness in the service of Christ,
> father of many monks, a monk himself.

More difficult to follow for a reader than for a listener, the closing string of nominative participles ("loving," "living") and appositives ("father," "monk") makes for difficult punctuating but good preaching.

BIBLIOGRAPHY

Peter Clemoes, ed., *The Anglo-Saxons* (1959), 212–247; and "Aelfric," in Eric G. Stanley, ed., *Continuations and Beginnings* (1966), 176–209; Malcolm Godden, *Aelfric's Catholic Homilies: The Second Series* (1979); James Hurt, *Aelfric* (1972); John C. Pope, ed., *Homilies of Aelfric: A Supplementary Collection*, 2 vols. (1967–1968); Caroline L. White, *Aelfric: A New Study of His Life and Writings* (1898), repr. with a supplementary bibliography by Malcolm Godden (1974).

DAVID YERKES

AELFRIC BATA, a disciple of Aelfric of Eynsham, is known to us from rubrics in two eleventh-century English manuscripts and from an anecdote in Osbern's life of St. Dunstan. He made additions to his master's *Colloquy*, a lively dialogue for beginners in Latin grammar, and composed others of his own. Osbern's anecdote, written in the time of Lanfranc, suggests that Bata was still living after the Norman Conquest.

BIBLIOGRAPHY

Thomas Wright, *Biographia Britannica literaria,* I (1842); Neil R. Ker, *Catalogue of Manuscripts Containing Anglo-Saxon* (1957); George N. Garmonsway, ed., *Aelfric's Colloquy,* rev. ed. (1978); William H. Stevenson, *Early Scholastic Colloquies* (1924).

DAVID R. TOWNSEND

AELRED. See **Ethelred.**

ÆSIR. A group of gods in the Old Scandinavian pantheon. In the systematized mythology of the post-pagan age, the Æsir dwell in Ásgarðr with the god Odin as their patriarch (Allfǫðr) and leader. Though they are able to resist old age by eating the apples of the goddess Iðunn, they are not immortal. At the "doom of the gods" *(ragnarǫk)* they and their arch-enemies—giants, monsters, and other forces of evil and chaos—will meet and destroy each other.

Lexically, *Æsir* is the nominative plural of *áss* (god), a word of disputed etymology, though we can trace it in a number of Germanic languages. The sixth-century historian Jordanes, for example, confirms (in Latin) its existence among the Goths, and it is found as a personal name element (*Ans-*, *Ás-*, *Ōs-*) in Gothic, Old English, Old Norse, Old High German, Old Saxon, Burgundian, and Langobardic, and in some early North Germanic runic inscriptions. The word is also attested in the later rune lore as the name of the fourth letter of the runic alphabet (Proto-Germanic **ansuz*), representing the vowel /a/. In literary Old Norse, a feminine equivalent is found: *ásynja,* plural *ásynjur* (goddess).

Although the word *Æsir* generally seems to encompass all the gods (as opposed to giants, elves, etc.), in some myths a distinction is made between the Æsir and another race of gods called Vanir. In both his *Edda* and his *Ynglingasaga,* Snorri Sturluson tells of a primordial conflict between the Æsir and Vanir that is probably also the subject of some obscure verses in the Eddic poem *Vǫluspá* (stanzas 21–24). According to Snorri's account, the war ended in a truce; as part of the peace agreement the Vanir god Njǫrðr and his children, the twins Freyr and Freyja, joined the Æsir in Ásgarðr.

Some scholars have been tempted to accord a historical significance to this mythical war, interpreting it as a distant reflection of an actual conflict between adherents of a Vanir cult (indigenous?) and an invading Æsir cult (Indo-European?). In the absence of real evidence, such a view remains largely speculative. In Snorri's euhemeristic and learned framework, the Æsir were men, later worshipped as gods, who migrated to the North from Asia (Troy).

Unlike the Vanir, who are quintessentially fertility gods, the Æsir represent a number of divine functions. Odin, for example, grants victory as god of war, receives sacrifices as lord of the dead, and lends divine inspiration as patron of poets. He is by nature aristocratic, cerebral, magical, ecstatic, and rather undependable. In a complementary role, the god Thor provides comfort to gods and men as the dependable protector of the divine order. In the literary sources, Thor's immense physical strength is contrasted, often humorously, with his limited intellectual capabilities. Other Æsir include Týr, a somewhat obscure god but probably very important at an earlier stage of Germanic religion; Baldr, portrayed as a beautiful and innocent victim in the literary sources; and Frigg, consort of Odin, whose importance is attested in the name of the day "Friday" (as Týr's, Odin's, and Thor's names appear in "Tuesday," "Wednesday" [English *Woden* for Norse *Odin*], and "Thursday").

In the system proposed by Georges Dumézil, the first function (sovereignty) is filled by Odin and Týr, the second (force) by Thor, and the third (fecundity) by the Vanir. This is presumed to reflect a social system of kings and priests, warriors, and peasant cultivators, though such clear distinctions are not very apparent in Old Scandinavian society.

BIBLIOGRAPHY

Most of the standard primary sources of Scandinavian myth are available in convenient Old Norse editions and in English translations. The most frequently cited edition of the Eddic poems is by Gustav Neckel (revised by Hans Kuhn), *Edda Saemundar. Die Lieder des Codex Regius* (1962). A fairly reliable English translation is by Henry A. Bellows, *The Poetic Edda* (1923). Snorri's Edda has been edited by Finnur Jónsson (1931) and is available, with certain parts omitted, in English translations by Arthur G. Brodeur (1916) and by Jean I. Young (1954). Snorri's *Ynglingasaga* is the first saga in his *Heimskringla,* edited by Bjarni Aðalbjarnarson, 3 vols. (1941–1951) and translated into English by Lee M. Hollander (1964).

General surveys for the student of Scandinavian mythology and religion include Hilda R. Ellis Davidson, *Gods and Myths of Northern Europe* (1964); Jan de Vries, *Altgermanische Religionsgeschichte,* 2 vols. (1935–1937; rev. ed. 1956); and Edward O. G. Turville-Petre, *Myth and Religion of the North* (1964). Georges Dumézil's views have appeared in many publications, such as *Les dieux des germains* (1959), translated into English by Einar Haugen *et al.* (1973).

CLAIBORNE W. THOMPSON

AETHELWOLD. See **Ethelwold.**

AEVIA, a word occasionally used in liturgical books as an abbreviation, formed by extracting the vowels of the word "Alleluia." It is perhaps an imitation of the similarly formed word "Evovae."

ANDREW HUGHES

AFFLIGHEM, JOHN OF. See **John of Afflighem.**

AFGHANISTAN, the modern (nineteenth-century) political term for the mountainous zone between the Indian subcontinent, the Central Asian steppe, and the Iranian plateau. In the Middle Ages the territory of present-day Afghanistan was divided among at least five distinct regions: Khorāsān, Sistan, Badakhshan, Kabulistan, and Zabulistan. The pattern of the region's political history in the Middle Ages is one of repeated foreign conquest periodically interrupted by the emergence of local dynasties, a few of which (for example, the Saffarids and Ghaznevids) achieved world prominence. In the late pre-Islamic era (*ca.* 500–650) western Afghanistan was subject to the Sassanid state in Iran while the eastern part was held by a Hunnic people, the Hephthalites and by remnants of the earlier Kushano-Kidarite dynasty. After the middle of the sixth century, eastern Afghanistan came under the control of the Hindu-Shahi dynasty whose roots appear to have been Kushano-Kidarite. The Hindu-Shahids endured for more than four-hundred years in eastern Afghanistan, staving off Muslim control until the late tenth century.

Western Afghanistan followed a very different course. By the middle of the seventh century, Arab Muslim armies had toppled the Sassanid state and were raiding in Khorāsān and Sistan. By the mid eighth century, the towns of western and northern Afghanistan including Herat, Zaranj, Bushanj, Farah, Shibarghan, Maymanah, and Balkh were Muslim although the conversion of the countryside took much longer. As a frontier of the Umayyad (661–750) and Abbasid (750–1258) caliphates, Muslim Afghanistan tended to be culturally provincial and ideologically populist. Out of this milieu a local family in Sistan, the Saffarids, rose to power in the middle of the ninth century. Although of proletarian origin, the Saffarids attempted to revive the pre-Islamic Iranian imperial tradition exemplified by the Achaemenids and Sassanids. From the ninth century to the early eleventh century, the Saffarid state spread over much of Iran until in 1003 its ambitions expired at the hands of the Ghaznevids.

The Ghaznevid period (*ca.* 977–1186) was one of political expansion and cultural florescence. Under the Ghaznevids, who were Turks of slave origins, state patronage attracted such renowned artists and

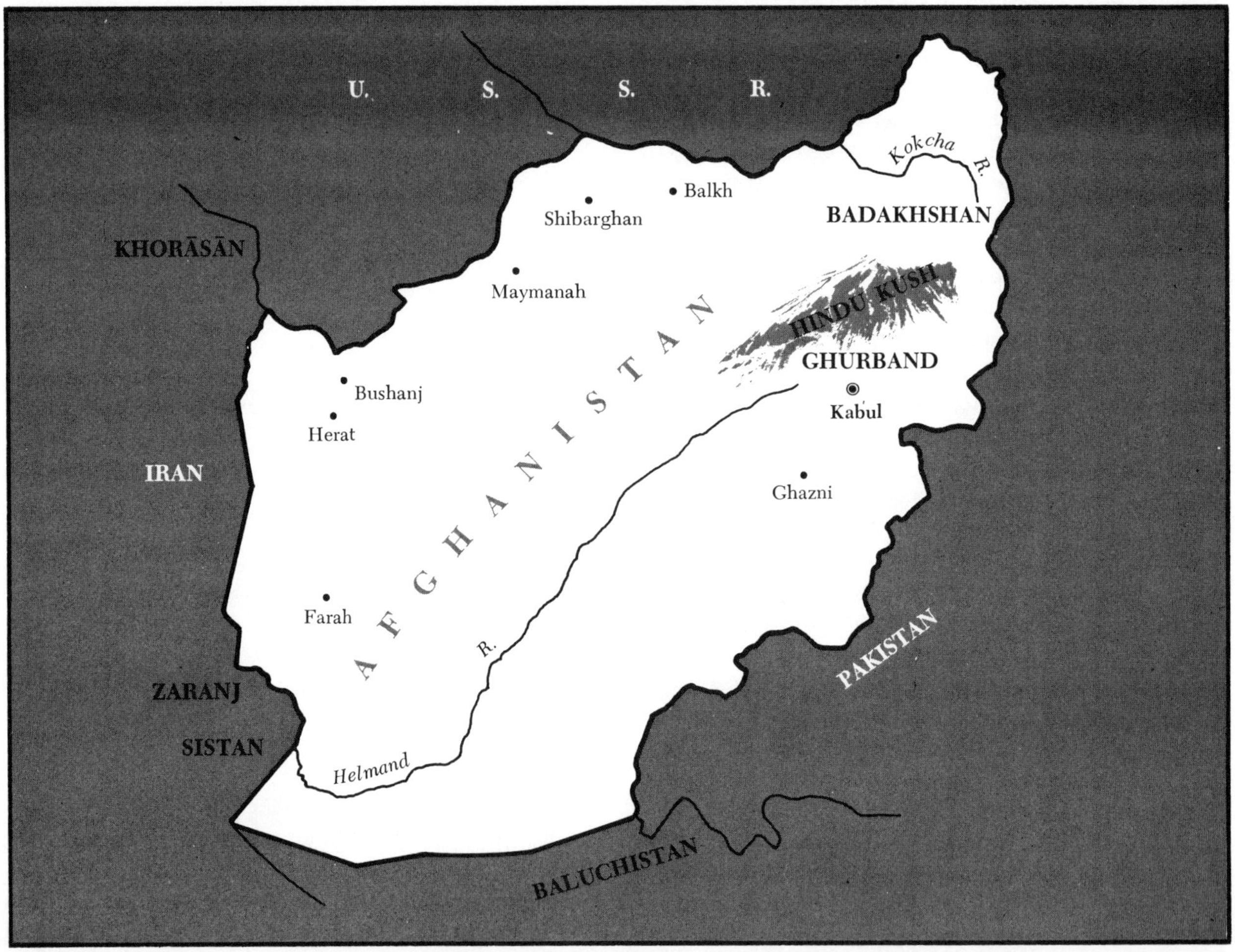

AFGHANISTAN

scholars as al-Biruni, Unsuri, Manuchihr Damghani, and Firdawsi. The city of Ghazni in eastern Afghanistan became an imperial capital and the center of Islamic civilization in the east. During the reign (998–1030) of Maḥmūd ibn Sebuktegin, the Ghaznevid state reached its political apogee. He ended the Hindu-Shahi dynasty, expanded north and west against the Saffarids, Qarakhanids, and Ziyarids, and invaded northern India establishing Islam there.

The next major autochthonous dynasty in Afghanistan was the Shansabani family of Ghur in the Hindu Kush massif. Originally vassals of the Ghaznevids, the Shansabanids, or Ghurids, eventually overthrew their liege lords and sacked Ghazni in 1174. Like the Ghaznevids, the Ghurids were great patrons of the arts. But unlike their former masters, the Ghurids held to an appanage form of state, in which eligible male Shansabanids claimed and received territorial hares thereby effectively decentralizing political authority. This form of state was an obstacle to imperial expansion and led to a breakup of Ghurid territory by the end of the twelfth century. A branch of the family, the Karts, established itself at Herat shortly after the Mongol conquests in the 1220's. The Karts held Herat as Mongol vassals until 1389.

From the beginning of the thirteenth century, most of Afghanistan except for Herat was subject to foreign domination—the Khwārizm-shāhs at the beginning of the thirteenth century, the Mongols until the late fourteenth century, and the Tīmūrids until the beginning of the sixteenth century. The latter dynasty made the western region of Afghanistan the center of Islamic high culture in the east and there fostered a major renaissance of art, literature, and scholarship.

The intellectual history of Afghanistan in the Middle Ages, with the notable exceptions of the Ghaznevid and Timurid periods, is a provincial one. Afghanistan's mountains and isolated regions protected ideological movements considered dangerous by conventional Muslim thinkers. One such movement was Ismāᶜīlism. Nāṣir-i Khusraw, one of Ismāᶜīlism's most famous ideologues, settled in the isolated Kokcha River valley of Badakhshan in the second half of the eleventh century. There he produced numerous theological and cosmological works and established a thriving Ismāᶜīli community which survives to the present. Another movement, the Karramiya, was especially widespread in the cities of western Afghanistan in the tenth century. Like the later Ismāᶜīlis, the Karramiya struck a responsive chord in society as much for the quality of its leaders and their identification with local problems as for its ideological tenets. In Timurid times, intellectualism was more conservative and conventional. Shāhrukh ibn Tīmūr (reigned 1397–1447) made Herat the cultural capital of the Iranian world, which it remained under his successors, most notably Husayn Bayqara (reigned 1473–1506). To the Timurid era belong such well-known artists and scholars as Sayyid-i Sharif Jurjani, Mir Khwand, ᶜAbd al-Rahman Jami, Mir Ali Shir Nawa'i, Ubayd Allah Ahrar, Khwandamir, Abd al-Razzaq Samarqandi, Kamal al-Din Bana'i, Qasim-i Anwar, Dawlatshah, and Bihzad.

Economically Afghanistan in the Middle Ages was an important part of the Mediterranean-Chinese-Indian economic sphere. Two major international trade routes traversed it and its commercial interests and involvements were correspondingly cosmopolitan. Domestically, agriculture, animal husbandry, mining, textile manufacturing, and metallurgy were the region's main industries. Individual areas had their own specialties: Balkh its melons; Herat its grapes and figs; Badakhshan rubies and lapis lazuli; Ghur silver, gold, and mercury; Sistan palm fiber; and Kabul the astringent myrobalan and Bactrian camels.

BIBLIOGRAPHY

For a general study of the history, culture, ethnography, and archaeology of Afghanistan see Louis Dupree, *Afghanistan* (1980).

For the late pre-Islamic history of Afghanistan see especially the papers collected in B. G. Gafurov *et al.* eds., *Central Asia in the Kushan Period,* Proceedings of the International Conference on the History, Archaeology, and Culture of Central Asia in the Kushan Period, Dunshanbe, 1968, 2 vols. (1974); also A. D. H. Bivar, Chapters 1–4 in Gavin Hambly, ed., *Central Asia* (1969).

V. M. Masson and V. A. Romodin, *Istoriia Afganistana,* vol. I (1964), and ᶜAbd al-Ḥayy Ḥabībī, *Afghanistan ba'd az Islam,* vol. 1 (1967), provide general surveys of Afghanistan's history in the Middle Ages (Ḥabībī's work covers only the seventh through ninth centuries). For the early Islamic period see also E. Daniel, *Khurasan under Abbasid Rule* (1979); Hamilton A. R. Gibb, *The Arab Conquests in Central Asia* (1923); Clifford E. Bosworth, *Sīstān under the Arabs* (1968); anon., *The Tārikh-e Sistān* (1976), Milton Gold, trans; V. V. Bartold, *Turkestan down to the Mongol Invasions* (1968).

For the Ghaznevid era, Clifford E. Bosworth, *The Ghaznavids* (1963), and *The Later Ghaznavids* (1977), are especially important. Many of his articles have also been collected in his *The Medieval History of Iran, Afghanistan, and Central Asia* (1977).

For the Mongol and Tīmūrid periods see V. V. Bartold, *Sochineniia,* 9 vols. in 10 (1963–1977); and especially "Mir Ali Shir," vol. III, and "Ulugh Beg," vol. II, of *Four Studies on the History of Central Asia,* V. Minorsky and T. Minorsky, trans. (1962–1963).

For the intellectual history of Afghanistan, see C. E. Bosworth, "The Rise of the Karramiya in Khurasan," in *Muslim World,* **50** (1960); H. Corbin, "Nasir-i Khusrau and Iranian Isma^cilism," in *Cambridge History of Iran,* vol. IV (1975); and Vladimir A. Ivanov, *Nāṣir-i Khusraw and Ismailism* (1948).

A survey of the geography, toponymy, and economy of Afghanistan in the Middle Ages will be found in Guy Le Strange, *The Lands of the Eastern Caliphate* (1905; repr. 1966). For modern locations see Ludwig W. Adamec, *Historical and Political Gazetteer of Afghanistan,* 5 vols. (1972–); and M. H. Nahiḍ, *Qāmūs-i Jughrāfiyā-yi Afghānistān,* 4 vols. (1957–1961).

R. D. McChesney

[see also **Ghaznavids, Ghurids, Timurids.**]

AGAINST THE SECTS/DE DEO. See **Eznik.**

AGAPE. Greek for brotherly love or, in the plural *agapai,* lovefeast. A meal shared by the congregation in the early Christian church service until the third century, after which agapai were offered to the poor as charity suppers. The practice gradually died out after the fourth century, although agapai are still mentioned in the Acts of the Trullan Council (692). The agape is sometimes represented in catacomb paintings (for example, Catacomb of Peter and Marcellinus, Rome).

Leslie Brubaker

AGAT^cANGEŁOS (Greek for "good messenger") is the name of the supposed author of a *History of the Armenians* which describes the life of St. Gregory the Illuminator (*ca.* 257–332) and the conversion of Trdat (Tiridates), king of Armenia, to Christianity in the early fourth century. Although "Agat^cangełos" claims to be an eyewitness, the *History* received its present form well after the invention of the Armenian script at the beginning of the fifth century. The first reference to this work in other Armenian sources occurs in the *History* of Łazar of P^carpi, who was writing *ca.* 500.

The *History* of Agat^cangełos is a compilation of various traditions welded into a more or less coherent whole. It begins with the revolution in Iran that brought the Sassanian dynasty to power in 224. Since the Armenian royal family was Arsacid, related to the deposed Parthian line, war between Armenia and Iran ensued. King Khosrau was murdered by a Parthian, Anak, and the Persians occupied Armenia. These events set the scene for Agat^cangełos' main story. Trdat (Khosrau's son) was eventually restored to the Armenian throne with Roman help. Gregory (the son of Anak) was brought up as a Christian; he returned to Armenia with Trdat and was thrown into a dungeon when he refused to join in pagan worship. Thirteen (or fifteen) years later Trdat put to death a young Roman nun Hrip^csimē with her companions, who had fled to Armenia to escape Diocletian. In retribution Trdat was transformed into a wild boar and was cured only when Gregory, rescued from the dungeon, converted him to Christianity. At this point an immense sermon, the "Teaching of St. Gregory," longer than the rest of the text together, is inserted into the story.

The rest of the book describes the burial of the martyrs at sites revealed in a vision to Gregory (including that of the present cathedral at Ējmiacin in the Armenian S.S.R.); the destruction of pagan temples throughout the country; Gregory's consecration as the first bishop of Armenia; the building of churches and missionary activity in Armenia; the visit of Trdat and Gregory to the newly converted emperor Constantine; and the attendance of Gregory's son and successor, Aristakes, at the council of Nicaea in 325.

Although the *History* of Agat^cangełos is full of legendary material and compresses the events of nearly a century into the period of a single generation, it preserves information about pre-Christian Armenia not found elsewhere, most notably details about pagan deities and their shrines. The consecration of Gregory took place in Caesarea of Cappadocia, probably in 314. But the Armenian populace was not converted as rapidly as Agat^cangełos implies, for later Armenian sources draw attention to the continuation of pagan practices. And Gregory's missionary travels as here described are based on the fifth-century activity of Maštoc^c, the inventor of the Armenian script, as described by the latter's pupil Koriwn. Even when the Armenian text of Agat^cangełos received its present form, probably in the second half of the fifth century, little was known of Gregory's last days. His death and burial and the discovery of his relics were elaborated by later hagiographers.

Of all Armenian historical works Agat^c angełos' has the most complicated textual history. From the surviving Armenian, a Greek version was made soon after the Armenian received its present form; on that Greek version depend others in Arabic and numerous later adaptations in Greek, Latin, and other languages. Furthermore, two Greek, two Arabic, and one Syriac version derive from a lost Armenian text of Agat^c angelos which has left no direct trace in the later Armenian tradition. These versions are less homogeneous than those deriving from the extant Armenian.

The great importance of the *History* of Agat^c angełos is that it became the standard, "authorized" account of the conversion of Armenia, the most significant event in Armenian history. The traditions enshrined in this work have had a profound influence on Armenian life and literature for the past 1,500 years.

BIBLIOGRAPHY

The Armenian Text. The Armenian text of the *History* was first printed in 1709 at Constantinople. Since then many editions have appeared, but the only critical text is that printed at Tiflis, edited by Galowst Tēr-Mkrtch^c ian and St. Kanayeanc^c, *Agat^c angełay Patmut^c iwn Hayots^c* (1909). The text without the apparatus was reprinted at Tiflis in 1914 in the Łukasean library. A photographic reprint of that 1914 text (excluding the "Teaching of Gregory") is included in the English translation and commentary by R. W. Thomson (1976).

Translations. Italian: The Mechitarist Fathers, revised by Niccolò Tommaseo, *Storia di Agatangelo* (1843). French: Victor Langlois, *Collection des historiens anciens et modernes de l'Arménie,* vol. I, Paris (1867). English: R. W. Thomson, *Agathangelos, History of the Armenians* (1976). None of these translations includes the long section (§§259–715 of the Armenian) known as the "Teaching." For that see R. W. Thomson, *The Teaching of Saint Gregory: An Early Armenian Catechism* (1970).

Texts Derived from the Extant Armenian. Greek: *La version grecque ancienne du livre arménien d'Agathange,* édition critique par Guy Lafontaine (1973). It has full references to the MSS and to earlier editions, plus a detailed study of the style and date of this early translation. Arabic: A. Ter-Ghłevondyan, *Agat^c angełosi arabakan nor xmbagrut^c yun* (1968). This translation was made from the Greek and not directly from the Armenian.

Texts Derived from a Lost Armenian Version. Greek: Gérard Garitte, *Documents pour l'étude du livre d'Agathange* (1946); and "La vie grecque inedite de saint Grégoire d'Arménie," in *Analecta Bollandiana,* **83** (1965). Arabic: N. Marr, "Kreshchenie Armjan, Gruzin,' Abkhazov' i Alanov' svjatym' Grigoriem'," in *Zapiski Vostochnago Otdelenija Imperatorskago Russkago Arkheologicheskago Obshchestva,* **16** (1905). Translations in Garitte, *Documents.* A. Ter-Ghłevondyan, "Agat^c angełosi arabakan xmbatrut^c yan norahayt bnagirə," in *Patmabanasirakan Handes* **60** (1973). Syriac: M. van Esbroeck, "Le résumé syriaque de l'Agathange," in *Analecta Bollandiana,* **95** (1977). Karshuni: M. van Esbroeck, "Un nouveau témoin du livre d'Agathange," in *Revue des études arméniennes,* n.s. 8 (1971).

For bibliographies of secondary literature see Garitte, *Documents,* and Thomson, *Agathangelos* and *Teaching.*

R. W. THOMSON

[See also **Armenian Alphabet; Armenian Language; Armenian Literature.**]

AGATHIAS (*ca.* 531–*ca.* 580), poet and historian, was from Myrina (in Asia Minor). He practiced law in Constantinople where he was known as Agathias Scholasticus. Agathias wrote erotic poems, now lost, called *Daphniaca* and assembled a collection of mainly contemporary epigrams (the *Cycle*), in seven books, published early in the reign of Justin II (565–578). His *Histories,* in five books, were composed in the 570's, the writing evidently being interrupted by the author's death. The finished portion continued Procopius's *Wars* from 553 to 559.

Agathias' own epigrams in the *Cycle* (now split up and dispersed in the *Greek Anthology*) are correct and learned, and include erotic subjects. But he wrote on Christian themes also (*AP* I.34–36), and a Christian tone has been detected in some of his other poems. There is no good reason to suppose that Christian poems were deliberately excluded from the *Cycle,* even though most of the epigrams are on classical themes. Agathias' preface to the *Cycle* (*AP* IV.3) displays the same imperial ideology as Corippus' panegyric (566–567) on Justin II.

The *Histories* cover Justinian's wars in Italy and Lazica up to 559, though Agathias had intended to carry the narrative up to his own day. The work is on an ambitious scale, with long and learned digressions on the Franks and the Sassanians, whose now-lost archives he may have consulted. The literary style is more elaborate and poetic than that of Procopius; and while Agathias observes the same conventions, imitating the classics and excluding specif-

AGHKAND WARE

ically ecclesiastical material, he nevertheless attributes a heavily religious and clearly Christian interpretation to events. Agathias was not a military man and did all he could to embellish his work with ornamental and discursive passages, yet he was well informed and did a good deal of research. The work was continued by Menander Protector.

BIBLIOGRAPHY

Text. Historiarum libri quinque, Rudolfus Keydell, ed. (1967).

Translation. Joseph D. Frendo, *The Histories of Agathias* (1975).

Secondary Literature. B. Baldwin, "Four Problems in Agathias," in *Byzantinische Zeitschrift,* **70** (1977); Averil Cameron, *Agathias* (1970); "Agathias on the Early Merovingians," in *Annali della Scuola normale superiore di Pisa,* 2nd ser., **37** (1968); and "Agathias on the Sassanians," in *Dumbarton Oaks Papers,* **23–24** (1969–1970); Herbert Hunger, *Die hochsprachliche profane Literatur der Byzantiner,* I (1978); Ronald C. McCail, "The Earthquake of A.D. 551 and the Birth-Date of Agathias," in *Greek, Roman and Byzantine Studies,* **8** (1967); and "On the Early Career of Agathias Scholasticus," in *Revue des études byzantines,* **28** (1970); Z. V. Udaltsova, *Ideyno-politicheskaya borba v ranney Vizantii* (1974); and "Mirovozzrenie vizantyskogo istorika VI v. Agafia Mirineyskogo," in *Vizantysky vremennik,* **29** (1968).

Cycle. Averil Cameron and Alan Cameron, "The 'Cycle' of Agathias," in *Journal of Hellenic Studies,* **86** (1966); and "Further Thoughts on the 'Cycle' of Agathias," *ibid.,* **87** (1967); Axel Mattsson, "Untersuchungen zur Epigrammsammlung des Agathias" (diss., University of Lund, 1942); Ronald C. McCail, "The *Cycle* of Agathias: New Identifications Scrutinised," in *Journal of Hellenic Studies,* **89** (1969); "Poetic Reminiscence in the 'Histories' of Agathias," in *Byzantion,* **38** (1968); and "Three Byzantine Epigrams on Marital Incompatibility," in *Mnemosyne,* **21** (1968).

AVERIL CAMERON

[See also **Procopius.**]

AGHKAND WARE is a term used by modern authors to designate a type of lead-glazed ceramics with incised decoration said to have been found near the village of Aghkand in northwest Iran. Best known are two examples signed by a single potter named (A) bū Ṭālib, one in the Louvre and the other in the Art Institute of Chicago. The discovery of such vessels in Iran led scholars to conclude that they were of Persian manufacture, but archaeological investigations in the Azerbaijan, Georgian, and Armenian S.S.R.'s have demonstrated that "Aghkand ware" was used and produced over much of the southern Caucasus. The bowls signed by Abū Ṭālib are particularly close in decorative repertoire and shape to vessels excavated at Orenkala/Bailakan in the Azerbaijan S.S.R. that are assumed to be of local manufacture. Kilns producing similar vessels are also said to have been discovered at Dwin in Turkey and Tbilisi in Georgia.

Interior detail of an Aghkand Ware bowl by Abū Ṭālib. COURTESY OF THE ART INSTITUTE OF CHICAGO

Decorative schemes used on the Abū Ṭālib bowls and related examples also have links with the Caucasian region. The Louvre bowl's interior is decorated with the incised and painted design of a rabbit standing on its hind legs and surrounded by vegetal scrolls. Similar compositions appear in the carved decoration of a church at Ani built in 1215. The quadripartite medallion scheme of the Chicago bowl resembles decorative panels used on Georgian and Byzantine cloisonné enamels. Thus, despite their discovery in Iran, Aghkand ware vessels were probably produced in the southern Caucasus, where the Muslim population favored designs used also by their Christian neighbors to the north and west.

BIBLIOGRAPHY

Arthur Lane, *Early Islamic Pottery* (1948), 25–26.

P. SOUCEK

[See also **Islamic Art.**]

AGHLABID ART. The art of the Aghlabid dynasty (800–909) of eastern North Africa is known almost entirely through its architectural monuments, of which the major one is the Great Mosque of Qayrawān (Kairouan). Although the first mosque was founded on the site in 670 and was continuously embellished and reconstructed by later rulers, the building is essentially the work of three Aghlabid emirs—Ziyādat Allāh I, Abū Ibrāhīm Aḥmad, and Ibrāhīm II—between 836 and the end of the century. On three sides double arcades surround a huge courtyard, and on the fourth side a deep hypostyle prayer hall shows the classical formulation of the so-called T-plan—a wider and higher axial aisle leads to a dome before the mihrab, where it intersects an equally wide and high transverse qibla aisle. This plan, probably the result of the successive building campaigns of the Aghlabid emirs, became the standard mosque plan for the Aghlabid realm, as seen in the mosques of Tunis, Sousse, and possibly Sfax. While the plan and support system of the mosque were inspired by foreign models, the use of stonemasonry is a distinctly local feature, as is the shape of the three-story minaret, which is now thought to be modeled on the ancient lighthouse at nearby Salakta.

Excavations have produced tantalizing evidence of court life in Qayrawān. Apart from the major hydraulic installations throughout the interior region, the most important secular monuments are the coastal *ribāṭs* (fortress monasteries), notably those of Sousse and Monastir. Each of these two-storied square structures has circular towers at its corners and a single entrance into its central courtyard. The courtyard is surrounded by galleries, small cells, and an oratory for the use of the religious warriors on this frontier of Islam.

Fortuitous remains at the Great Mosque of Qayrawān provide evidence for the "minor arts" of the period. The minbar (pulpit) is the earliest extant in the Islamic world; made about 863 under Abū Ibrāhīm Aḥmad out of teak imported from Baghdad, it is covered with splendid carving of geometric interlaces and vegetal forms. The equally splendid mihrab is lined with similarly carved marble panels as well as epigraphic decoration. Its hood is of wood painted with vine motifs, and the surrounding wall is inlaid with square luster tiles in a diaper pattern. A cache of rare Koran manuscripts discovered by chance in the mosque has provided precious documentation of Aghlabid manuscripts and particularly of early medieval bookbinding technique in embossed leather.

Generally speaking, Aghlabid art exhibits the characteristics of contemporary Abbasid art—the addition of Mesopotamian and Persian forms to a Syrian Umayyad vocabulary—along with the local artistic traditions of this once-important province of the Roman Empire.

BIBLIOGRAPHY

K. A. C. Creswell, *Early Muslim Architecture,* vol. II (1940; repr. 1979); Alexandre Lézine, *Architecture de l'Ifriqiya; recherches sur les monuments aghlabides* (1966);

Great Mosque at Qayrawān. PHOTO S. BLAIR/J. BLOOM

Georges Marçais, *L'Architecture musulmane d'occident* (1954); Georges Marçais and Louis Poinssot, *Objets Kairouanais,* 2 vols. (1948–1952).

JONATHAN M. BLOOM

AGHLABIDS. The Aghlabid dynasty (800–909) was the first to lead a province of the Abbasid Empire into virtual independence. In 800 an Arab soldier, Ibrāhīm ibn al-Aghlab, was confirmed as emir of Ifrīḳiya by the caliph Hārūn al-Rashīd, on terms that made him a hereditary monarch in exchange for acknowledging the suzerainty of the caliph in the Friday prayer and in the coinage, and for defending the western regions of the empire against the Umayyads in Spain and the Idrisids at Fès. His appointment completed a process that had begun in 759, when the Abbasids commenced the reconquest of the province from the Kharijite rebels of the Ibadite sect, who had seized it in the confusion following the fall of the Umayyad dynasty at Damascus. The Abbasids were to be frustrated by the continual revolts of the *jund,* the Arab troops stationed in the country. The success of the governor, al-Muhallabī (772–788), depended upon his use of a retinue of clients, slaves, and guards to dominate the Muslim community in Ifrīḳiya. Further revolts in the 790's made it necessary to elevate this kind of regime to a formal monarchy.

The power of Ibrāhīm ibn al-Aghlab was based on his command of the army in the Zāb, the western frontier district of Ifrīḳiya. It was consolidated by the construction in 800 of al-ᶜAbbāsiyya, "the city of ᶜAbbās," built in honor of the caliphs and in imitation of their imperial capital, Baghdad. Situated two miles south of Qayrawān, the capital of Ifrīḳiya, al-ᶜAbbāsiyya replaced the Dār al-Imāra, or "government house," at the Great Mosque in the center of the city as the seat of government. The transfer marked the final stage in the evolution of the provincial governor from commander of the Muslim army in the garrison city of Qayrawān to a monarch.

Al-ᶜAbbāsiyya contained Ibrāhīm's palace, court, household, and retinue; his chancellery and his treasury; and his army of several thousand bodyguards. Called ᶜ*abīd* ("slaves") because of their slave origin, these troops are usually said to be blacks from the central Sudan, but were probably *ṣaqāliba* ("Slavs")—that is, Europeans. The fortified wall around the palace city enabled Ibrāhīm to defy and defeat the rebellion of the *jund* in 810. Quartered in fortresses mainly in the north and west of the country, the *jund* remained quiet during the reign of Ibrāhīm's son ᶜAbd Allāh I (812–817), but between 822 and 826 it rebelled against ᶜAbd Allah's brother Ziyādat Allāh I. The revolt, led by al-Tunbudhī, centered on Tunis and enlisted the support of the populace at Qayrawān. It was suppressed only with the greatest difficulty.

Popular unrest was diverted by the invasion of Byzantine Sicily in 827, led from the port of Sousse by the qadi of Ifrīḳiya, the great jurist Asad ibn al-Furāt. Palermo was captured in 831, and the conquest of the entire island—marked by the taking of Messina in 842–843, Castrogiovanni (Enna) in 859, Syracuse in 878, and Taormina in 902—continued for the rest of the century. The conquest of Sicily was a profitable enterprise under Aghlabid command, yielding land for settlement and opportunities to trade and raid as far as Rome (846) and the Adriatic, from bases in Calabria and Apulia. Ifrīḳiya meanwhile enjoyed fifty years of comparative peace and prosperity under Ziyādat Allah I (817–838); his brother Abū ᶜIḳāl (838–841), the third and last son of Ibrāhīm ibn al-Aghlab to succeed to the throne; Abu ᶜIḳāl's son Muḥammad I (841–856); Muḥammad's nephew Aḥmad (856–863); Aḥmad's brother Ziyādat Allah II (863–864); and the latter's nephew Muḥammad II (864–875).

The route of the Arab conquest along the coast of North Africa had become an artery of trade and communication from Egypt through Ifrīḳiya to Spain. Other routes branched northward from Ifrīḳiya across the Mediterranean and southward across the Sahara to the central Sudan and the bend of the Niger River. The cities of Ifrīḳiya grew in size, and a corresponding increase in agricultural activity occurred. The Aghlabids and their principal officers owned vast estates, with herds of horses in the steppe country to the south of Qayrawān.

Syrian and Iraqi craftsmen and materials were imported to build reservoirs and to reconstruct the Great Mosque of Qayrawān in the style of that at Samarra. Begun in 836, the rebuilding was completed in 862–863. The Great Mosques of Sfax and Sousse data from 849–850, and that of Tunis was rebuilt in 864. Aḥmad provided Qayrawān with a water supply from two huge tanks fed by a stream and an aqueduct. This evident affluence may have been accompanied by indifference to the growing independence of the *jund* stationed in the hills to the west. The Ibadite kingdom of Tāhert in the direction of Tlemcen, established by the Kharijite rebels ex-

AGHLABIDS

pelled from Ifrīḳiya in the 760's, was no longer a threat, nor were the Idrisids of Fès, and the emirs paid little attention to the western frontier.

Constitutional conflict took the form of an attempted coup against Muḥammad I by his brother Abū Ja^{c}far in 846–847, in which the powerful ministerial family of the Banū Ḥumayd was overthrown. The Banū Ḥumayd had patronized and protected the jurists of the Maliki school of jurisprudence against the qadi of Ifrīḳiya, Ibn Abi 'l-Jawād. Having succeeded Asad ibn al-Furāt as the chief religious and judicial officer of state, Ibn Abi 'l-Jawād upheld the doctrine that the Koran had been created, a doctrine endorsed by the Abbasids in opposition to the majority of Muslim jurists.

The ultimate defeat of Abu Ja^{c}far by Muḥammad I led to the dismissal of the qadi, who was replaced by the leading Maliki scholar, Saḥnūn. Saḥnūn, author of the *Mudawwana,* the definitive treatise on the jurisprudence of his school, had his predecessor flogged to death. This vindication of the authority of the jurists in matters of holy law was offset in the administration of justice by the reluctance of Saḥnūn to accept the post and by the appointment of a second qadi to control his zeal. The restriction of the qadi's competence to "civil" matters of family law, commercial transactions, and so forth, was beginning here, as elsewhere in the Muslim world.

Besides the jurist, a second type of holy man was appearing. As a defense against the Byzantine fleet, the ribat, a kind of small square fortress, had been built at intervals along the Ifriḳiyan coast at the end of the eighth century. The invasion of Sicily reduced the need for these castles, and the archers who manned them gradually turned from soldiers into pious ascetics. These *murābiṭūn,* or "men of the ribat," were distinguished less for their learning than for their piety, zeal, and holiness. After the scholarly theologian, they completed the range of religious types with which North Africa was familiar from the previous example of Christian, Jewish, and pagan priests, monks, hermits, rabbis, preachers, zealots, and visionaries. To them should be added the sheikhs of the Ibadite sect based in the oases and hills of the Djerid and the Jabal Nafūsa in the south. They had their own version of the law, but among tribal peoples who governed themselves with little interference from the Aghlabid state, they were more than scholars, becoming arbiters, judges, leaders, and patriarchs.

Native Christians may have been employed in the financial administration, but their numbers were dwindling. The Berber majority had been nominally Muslim since the conquest. In the eighth century the process of Islamization had centered on the army and produced the Ibadites; under the Aghlabids the process centered on the cities. Their populations multiplied not only with the importation of slaves and the arrival of immigrants from Spain and the Middle East, but also with the influx from the countryside. Sicily, where a new Muslim community was established in a new country, provided this expansion with a new outlet and a further stimulus.

The cities themselves controlled an extensive hinterland—especially Qayrawān, which drew grain from the region of Bādja to the north. The satisfaction of their demand for goods and services was not wholly commercial, the work of merchants traveling on and off the main caravan routes to draw the most remote peoples into the market economy. Tax collection, which brought tribal peoples face to face with the agents of Muslim government, was equally important. Meanwhile, the men of religion were moving out of the cities to colonize the countryside and provide a Muslim presence in the midst of tribal communities.

The tensions within this developing society became apparent during the reign of Ibrāhīm II (875–902), the elder brother of Muḥammad II, who set aside Muḥammad's infant son and heir with a dispensation from the jurists of Qayrawān. His reputation for insane cruelty may be part of the legend surrounding his death. In contrast with his immediate predecessors, he was a determined tyrant and an active warrior, alarmed perhaps by the rapid decay of Umayyad power in Spain and envious of the achievements of Ibn Ṭulūn in Egypt. Having massacred the guardsmen of his predecessor, he recruited a whole new army of ^{c}*abīd,* this time black. Al-^{c}Abbāsiyya was replaced in 878 by the new palace city of Raḳḳada, about a mile away from Qayrawān. Ibrāhīm's administration was effective: he restored the value of the silver coinage and gained a reputation for administering justice that did not spare the rich. Turning his attention to the *jund,* in 893 he massacred the warriors of Balazma, near Batna, northwest of the Aurès Mountains. The revolt that followed in 894, comparable with that of al-Tunbudhī in 824–825, confined him briefly to Raḳḳada. In 896 he attacked and put to death his cousin Muḥammad at Tripoli, advancing as far as the Egyptian frontier. He died in 902 during the siege of Cosenza in Calabria, having mounted a great expedition that had captured Taormina, the last Byzantine stronghold in Sicily.

This last campaign, in which Ibrāhīm met a martyr's death in battle against the infidel, is said to have been undertaken in expiation of his many sins and monstrous crimes, after he had abdicated in favor of his son ᶜAbd Allah II at the behest of the Abbasid caliph. The account is most probably derived from contemporary Abbasid propaganda, preparing the world for the reconquest of Egypt from the Ṭūlūnids in 905 and using the edifying end of the Aghlabid emir to reinforce the moral and political authority of Baghdad. It was required, among other things, to counteract the propaganda of the Ismaili Mahdi, who was predicted to manifest himself about the year 902–903.

Abū ᶜAbd Allah, a *dāᶜī* (emissary) of the mahdi, had worked for ten years among the Kutāma, a Berber people of the mountains beyond Constantine in the northwest of Ifrīḳiya. Harassed by the Arab *jund* in the citadels of Mila and Sétif, the tribesmen were ready for a prophet who preached the damnation of the Aghlabids at the approach of a savior destined to rule the world. They banded together under the direction of the *dāᶜī* in a new Muslim community and a new army. In 903, ᶜAbd Allah II was murdered by his son, Ziyādat Allah III. The new emir proclaimed himself champion of the Abbasids in the west but was unable to halt the progress of Abū ᶜAbd Allah, who conquered the western region of Ifrīḳiya between 904 and 907. In March 909 the Aghlabid army protecting Qayrawān was defeated at Laribus. Ziyādat Allah III fled from Raḳḳada to the Middle East, where he died about 917. Ifrīḳiya was taken by the Mahdi ᶜUbayd Allāh, the founder of the Fatimid dynasty.

BIBLIOGRAPHY

Michael Brett, *The Moors: The Arabs in the West* (1980); *The Cambridge History of Africa,* II (1978), chs. 8, 10; Charles André Julien, *History of North Africa,* John Petrie, trans. (1970); George Marçais, *La Berbérie musulmane et l'Orient au moyen âge* (1946); Mohamed Talbi, *L'émirat Aghlabide* (1966).

MICHAEL BRETT

AGINCOURT, BATTLE OF (25 October 1415), a decisive victory for the troops of Henry V of England over a French army more than three times as large. The Agincourt campaign opened the Lancastrian phase of the Hundred Years War. The English invaders, trying to extricate themselves from France by reaching Calais, were blocked near the Picard village of Agincourt. They took superior positions and used their archers effectively against French men-at-arms, who advanced on a narrow, muddy plain bounded by woods. The thousands of French casualties included many nobles of northwestern France, whose unprotected lands the English conquered in the next few years.

BIBLIOGRAPHY

John Keegan, *The Face of Battle* (1976); Albert A. Nofi, *Agincourt: The Triumph of Archery over Armor* (1978).

JOHN BELL HENNEMAN

AGIUS OF CORVEY. A priest and monk, probably of Corvey (a daughter house of Corbie), Agius wrote (*ca.* 876) a *Life* of Hathumoda, the first abbess of Gandersheim, for the nuns of her house. Later he produced a verse dialogue about her in elegiac distichs. The latter reflects on Hathumoda's early death in alternating discussion between Agius and the sisters. One of several Carolingian works whose form is derived ultimately from Vergil's *Eclogues,* its immediate literary antecedent is the *Ecloga duarum sanctimonialium* of Paschasius Radbertus. Agius earlier wrote some (as yet unedited) verses to accompany a table of Paschal letters and Easter dates, and a set of seven computistical poems.

BIBLIOGRAPHY

Vita et obitus Hathumodae, Georg Heinrich Pertz, ed., in *Monumenta Germaniae historica, scriptores,* IV (1841), 165–175; *Dialogus Agii,* Ludwig Traube, ed., in *Monumenta Germaniae historica, poetae latini aevi Carolini,* III (1896), 369–388; *Versus computistici,* K. Strecker, ed., *ibid.,* IV. 3 (1923), 937–943; unpublished computistical verses in Dijon, Bibliothèque Municipale, MS 440 (269), fol. 80r, v, and London, British Library, Royal MS 13 A XI, fol. 145r. Ewald Könsgen, "Agius," in *Die deutsche Literatur der Mittelalters. Verfasserlexikon,* I, (1978), cols. 78–82.

DAVID A. E. PELTERET

AGNELLUS OF PISA (*ca.* 1194–1236), the first Franciscan minister provincial in England, was born at Pisa; little is known of his early life. He probably was received into the order when St. Francis passed through Pisa in October 1211, and he is known to have become a deacon between 1211 and 1217. Agnellus was among the group of Franciscans that arrived in Paris in 1217 and was custos of Paris from 1218 to 1223. Appointed by St. Francis to introduce the order into England, Agnellus traveled there in 1224; and under his leadership the order grew quickly, with establishments at London, Oxford, Cambridge, and York.

A great supporter of poverty among Franciscans, Agnellus considerably restricted their acquisition of property. He considered it the order's task to acquire erudition and hired Robert Grosseteste as lecturer to the house of studies in Oxford, thus helping to shape the eminent intellectual tradition for which the English Franciscans became famous. He also defended the order in the mendicant controversy and attempted a reconciliation of Henry III with the earl of Pembroke, who challenged royal authority in western England. He died at Oxford.

BIBLIOGRAPHY

Andrew G. Little, *The Grey Friars in Oxford* (1892); John R. H. Moorman, *A History of the Franciscan Order from Its Origins to the Year 1517* (1968); Thomas of Eccleston, *Tractatus de adventu Fratrum Minorum in Angliam*, Andrew G. Little, ed., 2nd ed. (1951).

TIMOTHY B. NOONE

AGNELLUS OF RAVENNA, ST. (*ca.* 487–569/570), was born into a noble family and pursued a military career before becoming bishop of Ravenna in 556. To him fell the task of reorganizing Arian lands into a system of parishes; these lands had been granted to the bishops of Ravenna by Justinian I. Agnellus' most famous work was the redecoration and rededication of formerly Arian churches, particularly S. Apollinare Nuovo. Agnellus is also credited with the composition or supervision of a letter-tract on the orthodox faith, *De ratione fidei,* which argued against both Arian and patripassian theologies. He is not to be confused with the ninth-century Andreas Agnellus, author of a *Liber pontificalis ecclesiae Ravennatis*.

BIBLIOGRAPHY

Agnello arcivescovo di Ravenna: Studi per il XIV centenario della morte (570–1970) (1971) contains *De ratione fidei.* The *Liber pontificalis* is in *MGH: Scriptores rerum langobardorum VI-IX* (1878), 265-391.

LEAH SHOPKOW

AGNOLO DI VENTURA (*fl.* 1312–1349), Sienese sculptor and architect, and the collaborator of Agostino di Giovanni, with whom he was first active in Volterra, working on scenes from the lives of SS. Regolo and Ottaviano (now in the Museo dell'Opera del Duomo). Together with Agostino he signed the tomb of Bishop Guido Tarlati in the Duomo of Arezzo, for which Agostino is documented to have received payment between 1329 and 1332; Cino de' Sinibaldi's tomb (*d.* 1337) is also attributed to them. The Tarlati tomb remains their most important work, standing together with Ambrogio Lorenzetti's frescoes for the Palazzo Pubblico in Siena as significant and political images of the Trecento.

BIBLIOGRAPHY

John Pope-Hennessy, *Italian Gothic Sculpture,* I (1970); John White, *Art and Architecture in Italy, 1250–1400* (1966).

ADELHEID M. GEALT

AGNUS CHANT. A chant with the text *Agnus Dei, qui tollis peccata mundi, miserere nobis* was introduced into the Roman Mass by Pope Sergius I (687–701) as a chant to be sung at the fraction. The formula of the text can be found in the *Gloria in excelsis* and in the Roman litany, although these archetypes need not be considered sources of the Agnus chant. By the ninth century the Agnus chant seems to have taken on the familiar threefold repetition, and it came to be sung following the fraction as a communion chant. The earliest musical sources usually present the *Agnus Dei* in conjunction with tropes, both introductory and interlinear. By the eleventh century the form of the Agnus chant was consistently tripartite, and the last *miserere nobis* had been changed to *dona nobis pacem.*

BIBLIOGRAPHY

Charles M. Atkinson, "The Earliest Agnus Dei Melody and Its Tropes," in *Journal of the American Musicological Society,* **30** (1977); Gunilla Iversen, *Tropes de l'Agnus Dei,* Corpus Troporum IV (1980); J. A. Jungmann, *The Mass of the Roman Rite,* F. A. Bounner, trans., 2 vols. (1951–1955); M. Shildbach, *Das einstimmige Agnus Dei und seine handschriftliche Ueberlieferung vom 10. bis zum 16. Jahrhundert* (1967).

CALVIN M. BOWER

AGNUS DEI. Latin for Lamb of God. A symbol of Christ, based on John 1:29 ("Behold the Lamb of God, which taketh away the sins of the world"), used in Christian writings and art beginning in the early Christian period and symbolizing Christ's sacrifice and resurrection (1 Corinthians 5:7) and his eternal victory (Revelation 5, 6, 14, and 21). The Lamb is usually shown in profile with a cruciform nimbus and is often enclosed in a clipeus. It may hold a banner or cross, representing Christ's victory over death, or a scroll that refers to the Apocalyptic Lamb of Revelation.

During the early Christian period, the Agnus Dei was frequently depicted with twelve lambs symbolizing the apostles (for example, Sant' Apollinare in Classe, Ravenna). The Agnus Dei was a predominantly western theme throughout the medieval period since its use was banned in Byzantium in 692. During the Carolingian period the Apocalyptic Lamb was most common, worshiped by the twenty-four elders of Revelation 5 and 8 (for example, the Codex Aureus of Saint Emmeram) or accompanied by the symbols of the four evangelists; during the later Middle Ages the Agnus Dei was often identified with the host of the eucharist as a symbol of Christ's sacrifice.

LESLIE BRUBAKER

AGNUS DEI (music), a chant (derived from John 1:36) of the Ordinary of the Mass addressed to Christ: "O Lamb of God, that takes away the sins of the world, have mercy on us." This is repeated and said a third time, when the supplication changes to "give us peace" (in masses for the dead, "grant them rest"). Its place is in the Liturgy of the Faithful, as part of the Communion rite, where it follows the Lord's Prayer, the commingling, and the kiss of peace.

The earliest reference to the Agnus Dei as a chant of the Roman rite occurs in the *Liber pontificalis I,* where Pope Sergius I (687–701) is referred to as follows: "Hic statuit ut tempore confractionis dominici corporis 'Agnus Dei qui tollis peccata mundi, miserere nobis' a clero et populo decantetur." This is taken to mean that it was Sergius who made the Agnus Dei a regular part of the Ordinary of the Mass. (He came from a Syrian colony in Palermo; and as early as the sixth century the words "lamb of God" had been used in the Syrian liturgy to refer to the Host.)

From references to the Agnus Dei in ordinals, sacramentaries, and commentaries on the Mass of the period up to the tenth century, it is evident that local practices still varied with regard to the placement and repetition of the words. Two different sacramentaries of *ca.* 900 specify that "Agnus Dei, qui tollis peccata mundi, miserere nobis" should be said three times; but in other sources the number of repetitions is left open. In this period, the position of the chant in the Communion rite also varies: in Germany it was sung at Communion itself, but further west (in France) and in Italy it was sung during the Fraction (the breaking of the consecrated loaves of bread prior to distribution—which, if communicants were numerous, might take an appreciable length of time).

When musical notation is provided in manuscripts of the late tenth and eleventh centuries, the text is often amplified and extended. (These added words and phrases are now spoken of as tropes, though the medieval terminology for them was not consistent.) Thus, the text of one chant in a late tenth-century troper (collection) from Prüm (Paris, B.N., lat. 9448) reads: "*Agnus Dei, qui tollis peccata mundi, miserere nobis.* Christe redemptor orbisque factor, *miserere nobis.* Omnipotens pater pius et clemens, magnus et magnificus, *miserere nobis.*" In this, according to the interpretation of Gunilla Iversen, the basic liturgical text is progressively amplified, while remaining Christocentric. However, in a later version from the north of France, it has become a prayer to the Trinity: "*Agnus Dei qui tollis peccata mundi,* Omnipotens pater, pius et clemens, magnus et magnificus, *miserere nobis. Agnus Dei qui tollis peccata mundi,* Christe redemptor orbisque factor, *miserere nobis. Agnus Dei qui tollis peccata mundi,* Spiritus in cunctis radians et cuncta reformans, *dona nobis pacem.*"

For tropes from further east (Switzerland), as early as the late tenth century, there is a set form, exemplified in the following of *ca.* 965 (St. Gall, Stiftsbibliothek, MS 484): "*Agnus Dei qui tollis peccata mundi,* Qui sedes ad dexteram patris solus invisibilis rex, *miserere nobis. Agnus Dei qui tollis peccata mundi,* Rex regum, gaudium angelorum, deus, *miserere nobis. Agnus Dei qui tollis peccata mundi,* Lux indeficiens, pax perpetua hominumque redemptio sancta, *miserere nobis.*"

The remarkable diversity of forms for the troped Agnus Dei until around the middle of the eleventh century has been surveyed by Iversen. She has also demonstrated that later sources, even those from France, tend increasingly to present troped versions of the chant in a tripartite form paralleling that outlined in the first paragraph of this article. Commentators on the Mass after the mid eleventh century refer to a tripartite form ending "dona nobis pacem." Then the tropes fell out of use, again at different times in different places; and where the chant had once accompanied the Fraction, it no longer did so—perhaps because the bread, no longer made with leaven, came in the form of small particles rather than loaves, perhaps because of a sharp decline in the number of communicants.

For the standard untroped text, musical settings in several forms are provided; in the most preferred form, the first and last sections have the same melody, and the second contrasts with them. Often all three sections have the same ending. The *Liber usualis* contains a selection of chant settings of the untroped Agnus Dei; Martin Schildbach catalogued 267 melodies and gave an overview of their style, but there is still no critical edition. An edition of the troped versions is now being prepared by Charles Atkinson.

BIBLIOGRAPHY

Charles M. Atkinson, "The Earliest Agnus Dei Melody and Its Tropes," in *Journal of the American Musicological Society,* 30 (1977); Gunilla Iversen, *Tropes de l'Agnus Dei* (1980); Josef A. Jungmann, *The Mass of the Roman Rite,* Francis A. Brunner, trans., II (1955), 332–340; Martin Schildbach, "Das einstimmige Agnus Dei und seine handschriftliche Überlieferung vom 10. bis zum 16. Jahrhundert" (dissertation, University of Erlangen, 1967).

RUTH STEINER

AGOBARD (769–840), forty-seventh bishop of Lyons, was probably born in Spain. At the age of thirteen he took up residence at the monastery of St. Polycarp near Narbonne. A decade later he was in Lyons. In the meanwhile he entered Holy Orders and by 804 he received consecration as *chorepiscopus* (rural bishop, possibly a suffragan), succeeding Leidrad as bishop of Lyons in 816. There he remained until his death, except for an interval (834–838) of exile in Italy under the protection of King Lothair I, the son of Emperor Louis the Pious, and except for his absence on an imperial mission at the time of his death.

Agobard's episcopal life was one of broad and vigorous interests. He was a stalwart opponent of superstition and folk paganism, using against it both rational argumentation and texts of Scripture. He was opposed, as most of Frankland was, to the employment of art in the service of religion. He discouraged going on pilgrimage to secure merit, deplored trial by ordeal, advocating instead the weighing of evidence before a judicial decision was reached, and urged a unified system of law for the entire Frankish realm instead of the Teutonic principle of plurality of laws for particular ethnic groups. Contrary to royal encouragement, Agobard resisted the growing importance and influence of Jews in the empire. He protested the early Carolingian practice of sequestering church lands and bestowing them upon laymen. Although he excoriated churchmen who entered clerical status to secure worldly honors, he recognized that the sacerdotal functions of such clergy were not thereby rendered invalid. He urged the convening of provincial synods to correct abuses in the church. He argued persistently for the visible unity of the church and for its superiority to the empire. From the foregoing it is obvious that Agobard was a man who was liable to evoke strong friendships and equally strong hostilities.

Between 820 and 840 the government of the Frankish state underwent much tribulation and became embroiled in a significant division. There were some leaders who constituted a court party, incipient absolutists, and other leaders who constituted a baronial party, incipient constitutionalists. Agobard gradually aligned himself with the latter. Although in the revolt of 830 he was able to remain neutral, in that of 833 he became an open partisan of the rebellious sons of Louis the Pious. In the spring of 834, when Louis was restored, Agobard took refuge in Italy.

In 835 the Council of Thionville deprived Agobard of the revenues of his diocese but did not depose him. Administration of the church of Lyons seems to have been entrusted to one Amalar, once bishop of Trêves and a loyal courtier. Amalar's revision of the liturgy of Lyons aroused the opposition of clergymen faithful to Agobard, who wrote from Italy pointing out Amalar's errors. In the autumn of 838 Amalar's teachings were declared heretical by the Council of Kierzy, and Agobard quietly resumed possession of the see, but he chose to remain thereafter unobtrusive. In the spring of 840, during a mission for the emperor, he died at Saintonge.

Agobard is venerated in Lyons as a saint with approved cult, but he established no school of thought. His writings are preserved mainly in one major ninth-century manuscript, which was not rediscovered until the early years of the seventeenth century.

Agobard's works were placed on the very first Index of Prohibited Books until they could be corrected. Since then he has been slowly rehabilitated and restored to a position of prominence for his time and place. He has attracted special attention because of his opposition to veneration of artistic representations, because of his common-sense approach to superstitions, because of his dislike of Jewish influence, and because of his anti-allegorical interpretation of the liturgy. His insistence on the liberties of the church, on unity of law, and on constitutionalism have been relatively neglected until recently since they were not emotional issues.

Agobard's prose treatises may be classified under eight topics: (1) two on superstitions; (2) two on phases of Frankish law; (3) three on theological subjects; (4) five, probably his best known, on Jewish influence in the empire; (5) three on diocesan administration; (6) two on pastoral care; (7) six on political matters; and (8) three on liturgy and liturgical theory.

Agobard's authorship of some of the works attributed to him has been questioned, but without convincing evidence. Three short poems may be his and his hand may be discerned in several statements in *Annales Lugdunenses.* Much of his work was citation of authorities (the Bible, church fathers, councils, the liturgy), as was typical of the time and situation. Agobard disclaimed anything but "rustic simplicity," but he made effective use of many rhetorical devices (parallelism, rhythm, rhyme, apostrophe, hyperbole). It is obvious that a few of his works may have been partially drawn up in his chancery, but it is equally obvious that he put a finishing touch to them making them authentically his own. He was able to employ his keen observation of life to lift some of his writing to incisive expression and occasional sparkle.

BIBLIOGRAPHY

Agobard, *Sancti Agobardi Archiepiscopi Lugdunensis Opera* (1666); Egon Boshof, *Erzbischof Agobard von Lyon* (1969); A. Bresolles, *Saint Agobard évèque de Lyon* (1949); Allen Cabaniss, *Agobard of Lyons: Churchman and Critic* (1953); and J. P. Migne, *Patrologia latina,* CIV.

ALLEN CABANISS

AGOSTINO, GIOVANNI D', Sienese architect and sculptor, active 1310–*ca.* 1350. Collaborated with Agnolo di Ventura on Bishop Tarlati monument in the Duomo of Arezzo (1329–1332). Also tomb of Cino de' Sinibaldi in Pistoia. Active Palazzo Pubblico, Siena (*ca.* 1331) and in 1339 worked with Lando di Pietro and others on Fonte Gaia. In 1340 helped to reconstruct Palazzo Sansedoni. Influenced by Tino di Camaino, Agostino was a notable minor Sienese sculptor.

BIBLIOGRAPHY

Werner Cohn-Goerke, "Scultore senesi del Trecento," in *Rivista d'Arte,* **20** (1938); John Pope-Hennessy, *Italian Gothic Sculpture* (1972); W. R. Valentiner, "Observations on Sienese and Pisan Trecento Sculpture," in *Art Bulletin,* **9** (1927); John White, *Art and Architecture in Italy: 1250–1400* (1966).

ADELHEID M. GEALT

AGRICULTURE AND NUTRITION. The following article is in five sections: I. **Byzantium;** II. **The Mediterranean Region;** III. **Northern Europe;** IV. **The Slavic World;** V. **The Islamic World.**

I

BYZANTIUM. The major sources of grain supply for the Latin Roman Empire were Egypt and North Africa. Both provinces were conquered by the Arabs, in the mid seventh century and at the beginning of the eighth century respectively. Sicily was lost by 902. The steppes of the northern shore of the Black Sea also ceased to be an imperial granary: Pope Martin I, exiled to Cherson in 655, complained of constant famine and bread shortage in this area. The core of medieval Byzantium was thus restricted to Asia Minor, the Balkans, and southern Italy; the latter region was finally lost by 1071. Despite the loss of the most fertile provinces, the Byzantines managed to produce considerable amounts of agricultural products. Western chroniclers stressed the opulence of grain, wine, olives, and so on in Byzantium, and from the twelfth century on, the Byzantines exported grain, wine, and meat to Italy. Even in the fifteenth century the Peloponnese was still famous for its grain, wine, and meat.

Asia Minor and the Balkans presented a comparatively uniform landscape: mountains covered with forests, and highlands which provided summer pas-

AGRICULTURE AND NUTRITION

tures for flocks and the tertiary soils suited for crops. As a rule, the higher land was planted, and the lower sown. Both large plains and lush meadows were rare, and in many regions stony lands prevailed.

According to a description of the island of Patmos from 1088, only a little more than 16 percent of its territory was arable, while the greater part of the land was rocky, "rough," and impassable; moreover only 4 percent of the land could be tilled with a plough, the other fields being worked with spades and hoes. In the coastal areas summers were hot and dry, and the seasonal rainfall irregular and frequently violent, coinciding with the autumn and spring sowing. Some regions were swampy and needed drainage, while in others cultivation was impossible without irrigation. Evidence concerning forest clearing is scanty, and there are no precise data on the extension of arable lands. Occasional mentions of the sower who scatters seeds over untilled soil might be related to the practice of slash-and-burn.

Agricultural technique remained, in general traits, the same as in ancient Rome. The works of ancient agronomists were read in Byzantium, and in the tenth century the so-called *Geoponica* was compiled. A collection of fragments from ancient agronomic writers, it presents a picture of very developed agriculture. It remains questionable whether we can take the recommendations of the *Geoponica* at face value for the characteristics of Byzantine horticulture, manuring, and so on. The two-field rotation continued to prevail; fallowing not only gave a rest to the soil but also preserved its reserves of moisture. The Byzantines knew both autumn and spring sowing, and in the fall ripe grain and green shoots could be seen simultaneously.

The wheelless breaking plow of the so-called sole-ard type was still in use. It consisted of a sole, or share beam, of hard wood set horizontally, a curved beam which was dowelled into the sole, and a stilt. It was fitted with an iron-socketed plowshare and drawn by a pair of oxen *(zeugarion)*. The Byzantine ard-plow differed essentially from the turning, or moldboard, plow used north of the Danube, which was drawn by up to eight oxen. The ard was ideal in semiarid zones where a light and frequent stirring of the surface soil was needed. It was also very suitable to the individualistic organization of labor in the Byzantine village.

Though the horse collar and horseshoe were known in Byzantium since the tenth century, the Byzantines did not attempt to use the horse for tillage in order to increase the speed of labor. Hand-working was used both for tillage of small and rocky allotments and as a complement of plowing. The Byzantines knew different kinds of spades and mattocks, either plain or two-pronged (*liskarion, dikella, axine georgike, tzapion,* etc.). Hoeing was particularly important in gardens and vineyards.

For harvesting, sickles *(drepana)* were used and not scythes. As a rule, the stalk was cut halfway up, so that only the ears were taken off, the straw being regarded more valuable for the land as fertilizer than for the stock as food. After harvesting, peasants grazed their stock on fields or even on vineyards, but holdings were not transformed into "open fields," being surrounded (in accordance to Byzantine individualistic agriculture) with ditches or brick fences.

The Byzantines did not use flails for threshing; the crops were threshed either by treading oxen or by a special animal-drawn implement, which consisted of a wooden board embedded with flints or iron on the underside. To separate the grain from the chaff, the peasants tossed up the mixture with shovels so that the straw was carried away by the wind, and the Byzantines constantly recommended placing threshing floors on hills open to the wind. Water-powered grain mills, which were still uncommon during the time of Palladius (the fourth century), appeared to be a normal device in the Byzantine countryside from the seventh century onward: they are mentioned in the Farmer's Law (articles 78–80).

Nonetheless animal-operated mills were well known and remained in use even in Constantinopolitan mansions of high dignitaries and in monasteries; moreover the traditional hand quern was never completely displaced by mills using more efficient sources of power. Windmills were introduced in Byzantium later than in Western Europe—not earlier than the late thirteenth century. Among rare Byzantine mechanical innovations was a machine for preparing dough operated by animal power; this device seems to have been invented in the Lavra of St. Athanasius at the end of the tenth century.

Byzantine agriculture was characterized by polyculture, but grain and grapes were the most important crops. It is probable that the Balkans remained primarily a land of barley production while wheat was abundantly harvested in Asia Minor, but the figures are scanty and comparatively vague. On the estates of Michael Akominates on Euboea, 14 *medimnoi* of barley and 11 *medimnoi* of wheat were collected. Akominates also testifies that the Athenians have rarely seen wheat bread; normally they

AGRICULTURE AND NUTRITION

baked their bread of barley flour. On the contrary, on the Asia Minor estate of Baris, according to the inventory of 1073, the seed grain consisted of 260 *modioi* of wheat, 150 of barley, 5 of beans, and 5 of flax seed. In the testament of 1192 from the region of Smyrna (İzmir), 120 *modioi* of wheat are listed as well as 39 *modioi* of beans, whereas barley is not mentioned at all. On the other hand, Psellus proposed to collect on the lands of the monastery of Medikion, located in the theme of Opsikion (the northwest area of Asia Minor), twice as much barley as wheat. Millet was used mostly for animals, and Symeon Seth in the eleventh century called it bad food causing stomach diseases. We know, however, that in the surroundings of Serdica (Sofia) bread was baked from millet and bran. Vetch and oat were eaten primarily by animals, rye is mentioned rather rarely (for instance, in the will of Theodore Skaranos, from Macedonia, of *ca.* 1270–1274).

Vineyards and olive trees are referred to frequently in different sources. According to Symeon Seth, olive trees did not grow at a distance greater than 300 stadia from the sea, and we have no traces of olive planting in the Farmer's Law. Fruit trees (apple, peach, pear, fig, walnut, cherry, almond, mulberry, pomegranate, chestnut, and in the latest period even lemons) were planted in orchards, which included sometimes truck gardens (with cabbage, onions, leeks, carrots, garlic, squashes, melons, cucumber, etc.) and vines, which were often trained up trees. In some cases legumes were also cultivated in fields as part of two-field rotation. Flax, cotton, and sesame were cultivated, too, and South Italy remained the most important area of sericulture.

The Byzantines did not eat much: Kekaumenos in the eleventh century recommended a square breakfast and abstemiousness at dinner time. Monastic rules had the same principle, allowing only one or two meals a day: boiled food was served only in the morning (fish, beans, or cabbage), while at the evening meal the monks got only some bread and wine, if anything. As for the bread ration, a person consumed about a *litra* (325 grams) a day.

Evidence concerning the crop capacity is scanty and vague. In the estates of the Acciajuoli family in 1380 the yield per measure sown oscillated between 1.6:1 and 5:1, while Eustathius of Thessalonica boasted that he had harvested fifty-nine *medimnoi* from the field where he had sowed only three *medimnoi* of grain. Even more fantastic figures are given in an unpublished speech by Gregory Antiochos to Andronicus Kamateros: the rhetor mentioned there thirty-, sixty-, and hundredfold harvests. Fertile soil and mild climate allowed two harvests in some regions. In any case, Gregory Antiochos treated disdainfully the area of Serdica where the soil produced only one crop a year.

Did the Byzantine yield really increase after the loss of Egypt and North Africa? And if so, what causes might account for this? There are some facts which suggest that the role of cattle breeding grew after the seventh century. The later Roman Empire seems to have suffered from "understocking": the fragments of cadastral records from Thera, Mitylene, and Lydia show quite insignificant amounts of stock per acre. On the contrary, the Farmer's Law presents Byzantine peasants as deeply engaged in pasture, and in the twelfth century, the Russian pilgrim Daniel was amazed at the amount of stock he came across in the islands of Patmos, Rhodes, and Cyprus.

Kantakouzenos, in the fourteenth century, deploring his losses during the civil war, listed 5,000 cows in herds, 1,000 yokes of oxen, 1,500 mares, 200 camels, 300 mules, 500 donkeys, 50,000 swine, and 70,000 sheep (and goats?). In the tenth century, stock was particularly cheap beyond the Sangarios. After the annexation of Bulgaria this region was regarded as the richest in the empire in cattle and famous for its cheese, pork, wool, and poultry. Akropolites called Bulgaria the first among the provinces with regard to breeding sheep, swine, and oxen.

Bone evidence of the eighth to twelfth centuries uncovered at a site in the Bulgarian village of Popino indicates that the percentage of cattle among livestock increased in the area during the eleventh and twelfth centuries. Indoor maintenance of stock was known to the Byzantines, and stalls and pigsties are referred to in different sources. Dung was used for manuring: young Theodore of Studios is said to have carried on his shoulders baskets of mule dung, in all probability to the fields; and in a later Latin inventory from Morea "fimus qui ibidem ponitur" (dung which is laid down there) is explicitly mentioned.

The relative scarcity of stock-raising lands favored the practice of transhumance on varying scales. Many lives of saints relate how peasant boys were sent at dawn to nearby pastures with their swine or sheep, returning in the evening. Long-distance migrations are also mentioned: the herds moved from winter to summer pastures. In the thirteenth-century cartulary of the Lembiotissa monastery, an agreement between two landowners is preserved, according to which they could use in

AGRICULTURE AND NUTRITION

common a distant pasture for their herds in winter, but with the spring, "when grass shoots up," animals had to be driven off and the meadow was reserved for hay. In some regions it was ethnic minorities, particularly the Vlachs and Polovtzi, or Cumans, who practiced transhumance and supplied the Greeks with meat and cheese.

Poultry, apiculture, and fishing had an important place in many regions. Fourteenth-century peasants in the village of Doxompous (Macedonia) owned boats and fishponds besides yokes of oxen, vineyards, and livestock, and of their rent of 660 *hyperpera,* 300 were levied for fishing activity. The Jewish writer of the twelfth century, Samuel ben Meir, affirmed that beekeeping in the "Greek kingdom" stood on a higher level than in northern France where he lived.

Social changes may also have contributed to Byzantine agrarian prosperity. The decrease in urban population in the seventh century reduced the number of consumers and diminished the constant demand for bread, which had been the great problem of the late Roman city. On the other hand since the seventh century, free or state peasantry predominated in the Byzantine countryside; slave labor was restricted mostly to pasture. Cultivation of the soil assumed signally individualistic features, evidently different from the temperate zone of Europe. The household had a central building, usually two-story, with a roof of thatch; it was surrounded by sheds and stalls and had its own well; its land sometimes consisted of dozens of small allotments scattered in different parts of an area. In the fourteenth-century village of Aphetos, belonging to the Athonite monastery of Khilendar, the individual holdings were divided into five to thirty-three lots.

The countryside settlement was not a complete unit: the houses were dispersed, the settlements comparatively large, especially in Asia Minor; and, because of the mountainous landscape, they were scattered sometimes from the sea to hilltops without any clear pattern. This substantially hampered the internal cohesion of the village. Common lands served primarily as border zones between two villages or as a fund for arranging new holdings. It remains questionable whether these so-called *zeugologia,* large stripes of land, could be used collectively as common arable fields by the village community.

The organization of village community was relatively loose and consisted above all in neighbors' and relatives' rights *in re aliena:* the peasants could make hay or collect chestnuts on the neighboring holdings; they had the right of preemption, if the neighboring land was sold; and they were liable for the taxes of their impoverished or absconding neighbors by virtue of the law of "common responsibility." In other words, the solidarity of the Byzantine village appeared as a sum of different individual links connecting independent owners. The solidarity also appeared in the existence of some village officials, in the celebrating of common feasts, and in common actions against robbers.

In spite of its comparative prosperity, the Byzantine countryside frequently endured hardships caused by natural phenomena (drought or inundation, hail or heavy winds, locusts or cattle disease) and political circumstances, particularly foreign invasions. Famines are registered in many Byzantine chronicles: especially disastrous was the unusually long and hard winter of 927–928, which caused a serious failure in the harvest and a grave famine. In contrast, the twelfth century was a period when our sources are silent about great famines within the empire; moreover, during the twelfth century Byzantium started to export grain to Italy, suggesting that the feudal development of the Comnenian era did not have so serious an impact on the Byzantine countryside as has been traditionally assumed.

BIBLIOGRAPHY

M. Blagojević, *Zemljoradnja v srednjovekovnoj Srbii* (1973); *The Cambridge Economic History of Europe,* I (1966), 89–102; J. Čangova, "Srednovekovni orŭdija na truda v Bŭlgarija," in *Izvestija na Archeologičeskija institut,* 25 (1962); A. P. Kazhdan, "Iz ekonomičeskoj žizni Vizantii XI–XII vv.," in *Vizantijskie očerki* (1971); Ph. Koukoulès, *Vie et civilisation byzantines,* V (1952), 245–343; Angeliki E. Laiou-Thomadakis, *Peasant Society in the Late Byzantine Empire* (1977); John W. Nesbitt, *Mechanisms of Agricultural Production on Estates of the Byzantine Praktika* (Ph.D. Diss., Univ. of Wisc., 1972); J. L. Teall, "The Byzantine Agricultural Tradition," in *Dumbarton Oaks Papers,* **25** (1971); and "The Grain Supply of the Byzantine Empire, 330–1025," in *Dumbarton Oaks Papers,* **13** (1959); G. Weiss, "Antike und Byzanz. Die Kontinuität der Gesellschaftsstruktur," in *Historische Zeitschrift,* **224** (1977).

ALEXANDER P. KAZHDAN

[See also **Weights and Measures, Byzantine.**]

II

THE MEDITERRANEAN REGION. As a natural region, the Mediterranean is best defined by its climate, which is typified by hot, dry summers and

AGRICULTURE AND NUTRITION

warm, humid winters, with an abrupt autumn break marking the passage between the two. The natural vegetation is distinguished by certain typical species, notably the holm oak *(Quercus ilex),* whose range is nearly coterminous with that of the olive. As a practical definition, therefore, the limits of olive cultivation may be taken as the boundaries of a distinctively Mediterranean agricultural region.

The present discussion is limited to the western Mediterranean, which includes the Iberian peninsula, the Midi, or French Mediterranean littoral, Italy, Sardinia, Sicily, and the Balearic islands. Under the Romans, the area was developed with a common agricultural technology, whose primary feature was the Roman plow (or family of plows), and with common agronomical principles. The precise technological zonation has not been historically defined, but Richard Bulliet has detected, on the basis of a comparative study of harnessing techniques and terminology, a broad zone, including Spain, Italy, Malta, and North Africa, which was technologically distinct from southern France.

The distribution map of the three major types of ard, or Roman plow, adds a note of complexity to this generalization. The deep-share ard, which appears to have evolved from a digging stick, was found in Portugal, Galicia, parts of Morocco and Algeria, Italy, Sardinia, Corsica, and Sicily. The crook plow, which does not cultivate as deeply, was used on drier soils. One subfamily was used in most of Spain and Tunisia; the other was found in the Moroccan Rif, in areas of Spain opposite it which were settled by Berbers, and in Majorca. The Midi is a technologically complex region, connected in some ways with Sardinia (plow type) and in others to eastern Spain (the *forquier,* pitchfork, whose form is related to the *forqueta* of the Segre valley and Castellón de la Plana). However, it contains virtually all varieties of the Roman plow, with a sharp demarcation in types on either side of the lower course of the Rhône, a historically effective linguistic and technological barrier (related to the settlement of Visigoths to the west, Ostrogoths to the east).

The Arab invasions of the early Middle Ages and subsequent "Green Revolution," stimulated by the introduction of new crops and the intensified practice of irrigation, lent further homogeneity to the agriculture not only of those areas under Islamic rule but also, through a slow process of diffusion, those of central and northern Italy and southern France toward the end of the medieval period.

With the Arab contribution superimposed upon the Roman base, medieval Mediterranean agriculture bore a number of distinctive characteristics. First, it favored labor-intensive technologies: irrigation, terracing, more complex rotations, and painstaking horticultural methods. Although the Romans had been familiar with many of the irrigation techniques later diffused by the Arabs, their agriculture was not dependent upon summer crops and thus irrigation remained a supplementary technique.

On the other hand, the contrast between the new intensive irrigation agriculture and extensive dry-farming regimes, a pattern readily detectable in classical Mediterranean agriculture, was also pronounced in the Middle Ages. Indeed, the emerging pattern of densely populated towns surrounded by irrigated garden belts, with sparsely populated hinterlands given over to dry farming, grazing, or arboriculture, tended to accentuate the contrast. The Roman biennial rotation, with fallowing in alternate years, was a relatively intensive technique in spite of its low yields. The Castilian *cultivo al tercio,* a triennial rotation with one course of wheat followed by two of fallow, was a typical response in one of the numerous Mediterranean regions where summer aridity was pronounced. Only in the Midi could one find a generalized dry-farming regime which did not emphasize lengthy fallowing.

Thus although the open-field system, where peasants had strips scattered in each of two, three, or more open fields, cultivated collectively, was widely known, the Mediterranean dry-farming regime must not be confused with the open-field agriculture of northern Europe. In virtually the entire area, summer aridity seems to have been an effective impediment to the introduction of a northern-style three-course rotation which included a summer crop. Still, the biennial rotation proved to be quite amenable to modifications in the direction of greater intensity. In the Midi and in Italy, spring crops were often planted on a portion of the fallow field. Moreover, especially in Italy, the great variety of winter grains raised was in part a compensation for the lack of spring planting; barley, a typical summer crop in northern Europe, was planted in the winter in the Mediterranean region.

Another distinguishing feature of medieval Mediterranean agriculture was that it was based upon variegated planting regimes, some of Roman inspiration (for example, intercultivation, the Italian *coltura promiscua*), others the result of Arab innova-

AGRICULTURE AND NUTRITION

tions (for example, the introduction of a long roster of irrigated summer crops and the utilization of a wider variety of soil types than the Romans had used). The tendencies towards intensification and the use of a larger variety of plants were systemically linked. To cultivate two crops yearly on land that had previously produced but one (or even one every other year) demanded both more labor and more water; thus the need for irrigation, whose labor requirements were also high. Polyculture, involving, for example, the interplanting of fruit trees, grapevines, and vegetables or cereals, was a way of intensifying agriculture in the face of habitually low cereal yields.

THE ARAB GREEN REVOLUTION

The Arab conquests resulted in the diffusion of a series of new crops, mainly of Indian origin, to the Islamic Middle East and the Mediterranean. Since these crops originated in tropical regions whose climate was characterized by a season of heavy summer rains, most could not be grown in the Middle East or Mediterranean basin without irrigation. Among the most significant of these plants were sugar cane, rice, the sour orange and other citrus varieties, the banana, watermelon, artichoke, eggplant, and an industrial plant, cotton. The new edible crops combined with the classical "triad" of winter wheat, grapevines, and olives to enrich substantially the food base of Mediterranean lands, making possible the provisioning of the dense urban populations of the early Islamic empire.

The Arabs also introduced two nonirrigated cereals, hard wheat *(Triticum durum),* which by the end of the Middle Ages had become the staple cereal throughout most of the region, and sorghum. Sorghum, like rice, is normally a summer crop, and could be planted in novel rotations; thus dry farming, as well as irrigation agriculture, benefited from the new labor-intensive style. The rotations which emerged, according to the Andalusi (Hispano-Muslim) school of agronomists, were biennial with some fallowing. These rotations were highly varied, with only the winter wheat crop appearing in a fixed period. With irrigation, a great variety of crops was grown in succession, with no methodical order. Fallowing was reduced, although not altogether eliminated, and the length of fallowing between crops varied.

Under the Arabs, the variety of soils deemed tillable was greater by far than what had been customary for the Romans. As a result, lands previously considered marginal or unfit for agriculture were brought under cultivation. Like the English agronomists of the eighteenth century, Arab agricultural writers recommended dressing the soil with different kinds of fertilizers and additives in order to correct its natural deficiencies. Among the newly introduced crops, sorghum, hard wheat, and watermelon could be grown on sandy soils, and sugar cane, Colocasia, and eggplant, among others, tolerated salinity well. It is not uncommon to find a dozen or more gradations of soil, according to fertility and physical quality, listed in medieval Islamic administrative manuals, indicating that the prescriptions of the agronomists reflected actual practice.

Islamic Spain was a full beneficiary of the Arab Green Revolution. Nearly the entire roster of new crops was introduced, and new varieties were acclimated in botanical gardens, such as those of Toledo and Seville, under the direction of agronomists. Sugar cane, a plant of Indian origin, reached Persia in Sassanian times and, in the early Islamic period, was cultivated in a wide band extending from northern India to the Tigris and Euphrates valleys. By the tenth century it was grown throughout the Mediterranean, from Lebanon and Palestine in the East, in Egypt and across North Africa, and abundantly in Spain wherever irrigation was practiced: in the Guadalquivir Valley, along the southeastern coast, in Granada, and on the eastern coast as far north as Castellón de la Plana. Sugar cane was deemed to have high water requirements and was commonly irrigated every four to eight days in Islamic Spain. Discarded cane was used for animal fodder.

The banana, or plantain, was of Southeast Asian origin and may have reached Mesopotamia before the Islamic era. It had already appeared in Spain by the ninth century and was prominent in the agriculture of Granada and the southern coast around Almuñécar, whose bananas were famous throughout the Arab world. The Castilian word for watermelon, *sandia,* indicates the origin of this variety in the Sind, or northwest India. The *Calendar of Córdoba* documents its presence in Spain in 961. Spinach, of central Asian origin, was mentioned by the Hispano-Muslim agronomists of the eleventh century, as were Colocasia, a tuber of Southeast Asian provenance, and eggplant, which originated in India. The latter was extremely popular in Spain and is the only one of the Indian plants to be mentioned in the *Obra de agricultura* of Gabriel Alonso de Herrera (1513).

AGRICULTURE AND NUTRITION

To this list must be added cotton, a fiber of Indian origin, which had been cultivated in certain areas of the classical Near East, although the precise contours of its early diffusion cannot be stated. By the ninth century it was grown in Spain, apparently spreading from the south (Seville, Algarve) northward to Valencia and Majorca. Ibn Baṣṣāl states that it was irrigated every two weeks from the time it sprouted until 1 August. Islamic Spain was self-sufficient in cotton and exported it, according to al-Ḥimyarī, as far east as Tunisia and as far south as Sijilmāsa.

Roman Baetica (centered in the Guadalquivir Valley) was one of the breadbaskets of the empire, famed for the high quality of its wheat. Under the Arabs, the soft varieties grown there were replaced by hard wheat, and references to its durability in storage in the works of medieval Muslim historians and geographers document its presence in places as widely seprated as Saragossa, Lorca, and, particularly, Toledo. The plains around Córdoba were still famous for the high quality of their wheat, as were the plain of Cartagena and that between Cintra and Lisbon. Yet Al-Andalus appears not to have been self-sufficient in wheat, which it imported from North Africa from the ninth century on and, in the twelfth century, from Christian León. One must posit a steady decline in wheat production, owing to a complex play of cultural factors. As wheat-growing Christians immigrated to northern Spain they seem not to have been replaced, and the agricultural balance shifted away from dry farming, in favor of irrigation and arboriculture.

Wheat was also displaced by the high favor enjoyed by two other cereals introduced by the Arabs, sorghum and rice. Sorghum not only replaced millet as the staple cereal of the poor, but also seems to have played the same social and nutritional role as that played by rye in Christian Spain and other areas of Europe. Sorghum arrived somewhat late, probably not until the eleventh century, when wheat production was already in decline. Wheat, when dry-farmed, was grown in biennial rotation with fallowing, following the standard practice in Islamic North Africa. In open-field areas of the Tunisian plain, there was a fairly strict adherence to classical biennial rotation, although in some areas of Algeria, hard wheat was rotated with a spring cereal, *bechna,* one of the few examples of a summer cereal in the traditional agriculture of the western Mediterranean.

Rice, of Indian or Southeast Asian origin, was, of course, the irrigated crop par excellence, since it was continuously submerged during its growing season. It was grown in Islamic Valencia, particularly in the swampy areas south of the city, and in Majorca, whence it was exported to Flanders.

Cereals and irrigated field crops were complemented by the standard Mediterranean combination of fruit trees, olives, and grapes. Literary sources record the efforts of individuals, both the lowly and the prominent, in the introduction of eastern varieties. A chief judge of Córdoba introduced a species of pomegranate from Damascus, for example, and the poet al-Ghazāl returned to his native Jaén from a mission in the East with the *doñegal* fig, one of the most important of the numerous varieties grown in Islamic Spain. The *Calendar of Córdoba* translates the Latin *ficus* as, simply, *shajar,* "trees," a vivid indication of the fig's universality. Málaga was an important fig-growing center, and its figs were sold as far away as India and China.

The best-known olive-growing region was al-Sharaf (Aljarafe), an area forty miles square to the west of Seville which, it was said, could be traversed without leaving the shade of olive and fig trees. Aljarafe oil was of high quality and was exported to the East. The region between Lérida and Mequinenza was called by the geographer al-Idrīsī "the land of the olives" *(iqlīm al-zaitūn).* In spite of the Koranic prohibition of wine-drinking, grapes were widely grown, including a number of new varieties developed by Andalusi horticulturists. In the larger cities, before the emigration of Christians and, later, Jews, the production of grapes must have in part been attuned to the needs of these communities. But wine was consumed by Muslims as well, and the agricultural districts of Málaga, Ubeda, and Córdoba were renowned for their grapes.

Turning now to the state of agriculture in Christian Spain, Portugal, the Midi, and Italy, one can note that in general the new crops and techniques introduced by the Arabs diffused there only slowly. (The crops and techniques diffused at different rates, to be sure. In the Midi, irrigation, with some indirect Muslim influence, developed from the tenth century on, while most of the new Arab crops appeared only in the sixteenth.) To explain the slowness of diffusion, Andrew Watson suggests a number of cultural and economic factors: "the lack of skills of the European peasantry, which may have been a serious barrier since some of the crops were difficult to grow; the lack of agricultural manuals which could teach Europeans how to grow the new crops; the in-

AGRICULTURE AND NUTRITION

ability of feudal landholding arrangements to receive certain of the new crops . . . the limited use of irrigation in European agriculture and in particular the near absence of heavy or perennial irrigation; and the lower population density which made it unnecessary." Climatic factors seem to have been secondary, given the similarities between Islamic and Christian regions.

CHRISTIAN SPAIN

The development of agriculture in medieval Castile, León, Aragón, and Catalonia was conditioned by a number of cultural factors. First, the migration of a mountain people to the plains entailed a shift from a herding economy to a fully Mediterranean-style agriculture. In León, this shift was furthered by the migration of Christian dry farmers from Islamic Spain, from the mid ninth to the mid tenth centuries. This early phase was characterized by the steady replacement, in a southward direction, of wood and grazing lands by cereal and vine cultivation, whose pace and rhythm were determined by the upward movement of population. Second, the pace of agricultural change increased when, from approximately 1050 on, large areas of Islamic territory came under Christian control. In this second phase, the Christian kingdoms participated directly in the benefits of the Arab Green Revolution.

The center and east of Old Castile and much of the Leonese plain were good wheat lands. Cereal production expanded steadily there, increasing in pace in the course of the eleventh and twelfth centuries when population pressure forced the conversion of flax fields and vineyards into wheat cultivation in some areas. Cereals were grown in open fields under a cultivation system called *año y vez,* the classical Roman biennial rotation, whereby one of a village's two fields was planted in wheat and the other left fallow, in alternate years. In a two-course system, local herds grazed on half the fields annually. (This stratagem had not been needed in earlier centuries when there was plenteous scrub land, or *monte,* both for grazing and perhaps for temporary agriculture on fields cleared by burning.)

Whether for reasons of aridity or in order to provide more grazing for local herds, a three-course rotation (though not of the northern European type), *cultivo al tercio,* was particularly widespread. Under this regime, two-thirds of a village's fields were always available for fallow grazing. The increasing trend toward transhumant herding, which deprived wheat fields of local sources of fertilizer, increased the dependence of cultivators on fallowing. As a result, yields were low. Thirteenth-century figures from Silos indicate returns on wheat and barley ranging from 3:1 to 4:1, which compare unfavorably with the standard northern European yields of 5:1 for wheat and 8:1 for barley.

As for other cereals, they appear typically in especially humid areas like Galicia or those with intensive irrigation, like Valencia. In the sandy soils of the Galician littoral, rye grew better than wheat (although the lords forced increased cultivation of wheat, with correspondingly low yields, by demanding it in payment of manorial dues). By the twelfth century, sorghum and millet were cultivated in Galicia, according to the Arab geographer al-Bakrī. In fourteenth- and fifteenth-century Valencia, sorghum fields *(dacçars)* were irrigated, and rice, of course, was the staple cereal in the areas watered by the royal canal of Alcira and other derivations of the Júcar River. Christian settlers continued to cultivate rice in Majorca from the mid-thirteenth century on.

Data from the Valencian region raise the issue of continuous cropping under irrigation, including both winter cereals and summer crops. Documents from fifteenth-century Castellón indicate an intensive regime, with wheat planted in the winter, and beans, peas, and garlic in the summer. It should be noted, first, that the same rotation could be found in a nonirrigated regime and, second, that the Indian crops cultivated by the Arabs were notably absent. The same records indicate fallowing throughout the year, which reflects, in part, the practice of interspersing short periods of fallowing between the harvest of one crop and the sowing of the next.

Some grain, grown in enclosed plots called *herrenales* (*ferraginers,* in Catalan), was harvested green for forage. Oats were rarely grown before 1100, but increased dramatically in Catalonia in the early twelfth century. Another important fodder was the turnip, which made a great impact in Galicia in the late thirteenth century when its cultivation made possible a substantial reduction in fallowing. The climatic situation there made possible a genuine, northern European style of rotation: winter corn was harvested in the summer; then turnips were planted and harvested in the spring, when barley and millet were planted. The cycle repeated itself every two years.

Wheat was one cornerstone of Christian agricultural expansion; the other was the grapevine. The growth of monasticism resulted in the progressive conversion, first of wasteland, then of wheat fields, to vineyards, until the end of the twelfth century in

AGRICULTURE AND NUTRITION

Castile and León. Then, as demand for wheat increased, so did the value of vineyards, which offered the small proprietor an economically attractive alternative to open-field cereal cultivation. In Catalonia, grapevines tended to invade the hill country where, from the tenth century on, extensive terracing was carried out. Throughout the early Middle Ages, grapes were grown in areas where their cultivation ceased later on. Peasants were unwilling to invest in vineyards too close to the Islamic frontier, and the lack of commercialization made consumers dependent upon local supplies. Thus grapes were the most important crop in León, in spite of the acidity of the soil; and elsewhere they were grown in regions now considered either too high or too cold for their cultivation—the Arlanzón-Upper Ebro region of Old Castile, the Pyrenean foothills of the upper Segre and Ribes Valley in Catalonia, and the plain of Cerdagne.

Fruit trees also provided an important complement to the daily diet. In the northwest of the peninsula, particularly the Basque country, the apple was the most popular fruit, and the southward migration of Basques entailed the diffusion of the apple. In wine country, apples and other fruit trees were intercultivated with vines or used as vineyard borders. Figs, pears, cherries, peaches, and plums were also widely grown and, where possible, irrigated, as was the carob, whose bean provided a staple fodder.

The epoch of the great Christian conquests of Islamic Spain (eleventh through thirteenth centuries) set in motion substantial currents of change in the agricultural regimes of the center and south of the peninsula. After the conquest of Toledo in 1085, the irrigated gardens and vineyards surrounding the town continued to be farmed by Christian (Mozarab) peasants. Olive production decreased until the fourteenth century, because the Muslim arboriculturists fled and the new settlers were unaccustomed to growing this crop. The entire central meseta was given over to cereal cultivation, with grants made to new settlers of fields to be worked under the traditional biennial rotation—not in open fields, however, but in individual parcels, each divided in two. This proved to be an interim arrangement, as transhumant sheepherding steadily replaced cereal cultivation and had, by the end of the thirteenth century, become the dominant form of agrarian enterprise in the central meseta.

The agriculture of the heartland of Andalusia suffered a radical transformation when it fell into Christian hands in the mid-thirteenth century, inasmuch as most of the Muslim population fled. Fields were abandoned for pasture; some cereals were cultivated in biennial rotation; and a high level of olive production was maintained. Towns like Seville and Córdoba which before the conquest had enjoyed a mixed agriculture based on wheat, olives, and gardens irrigated by *norias* (hydraulic wheels) were now converted into sheepherding centers.

In Valencia, on the other hand, continuity with the Islamic agricultural regime was pronounced. The irrigation systems developed by the Muslims survived intact and were used to water the entire range of crops grown, including some introduced in the course of the Arab conquests: oranges (grown mainly for ornamental use), lemons, limes, sorghum, and rice. (Rice cultivation is now concentrated to the south of the city, but in the later Middle Ages it was grown not only in the huerta of the city itself but also in irrigated villages upstream of Valencia.) Vineyards were either irrigated or not, as was the case with carobs and figs.

The conquest of Murcia produced a more complex pattern. The Muslims, who cultivated both the irrigated gardens of the city and the rich cereal lands of the plain of Cartagena, steadily migrated to Granada. As a consequence, some irrigated areas turned to marsh, although the huerta continued to produce figs, cereals, hemp, and flax. Christian settlers were granted cereal lands in the Cartagena plain at *año y vez*. But as Muslims departed, the value of the land fell and the new settlers also abandoned their fields, leaving the area as a vast pasture for sheep.

PORTUGAL

Portugal practiced a distinctive kind of agriculture because the Suevi who settled there in the early fifth century brought with them an agricultural technology quite different from that which predominated in the rest of the peninsula. Its characteristic features included the wheeled plow and rye cultivation, which resulted, in northern Portugal, in agricultural regimes more similar to those of northern Europe than was the case elsewhere in the peninsula, Galicia excepted. Later, the Arabs implanted an equally idiosyncratic regime in the south, one of whose legacies was the creation of a dual agricultural terminology, whereby many elements of Portuguese agrarian technology can be described either by an Arabism or by a term of Romance origin.

The Portuguese northwest was characterized by extensive arboriculture and pasture, a regime not unlike the French *bocage* except that here irrigation

AGRICULTURE AND NUTRITION

was practiced. There appears to have been a slow changeover from pure *bocage* to a more varied agricultural landscape with a strong component of vineyards in the years following the conquest of the area from the Muslims. The interior north (Trás-os-Montes) was open-field country, with a biennial rotation and where rye was the staple grain. The central zones (Beira, Ribatejo, Alentejo) were also an open-field area, but characterized by more extensive rotations, such as triennial, with one year of fallow, or quadrennial, with two or three years of fallow.

In Portuguese Estremadura, the agricultural regimes were more varied and a kind of *coltura promiscua* prevailed—grapes, olives, and apples grown in conjunction with each other, or with wheat or with vegetable gardens. Meadowlands were absent. In the irrigated alluvial zones, irrigated crops of Arab origin made their appearance at the end of the Middle Ages, notably rice and sugar cane.

Finally, in the extreme south, the Algarve, the typical regime of the Islamic Mediterranean persisted. This was a region of towns surrounded, as in southern Spain, by irrigated gardens. The terraced hillsides of the hinterlands were given over to dry-farming polyculture—notably grapevines, olives, figs, almonds, and carobs. As in Estremadura, cereals and vegetables were grown in spaces between the trees.

THE FRENCH MIDI

The Midi was an area where cereal was cultivated in open fields in biennial rotation, with important enclaves of triennial. The two types of rotation coexisted in the same regions, and the distribution of the two systems did not seem to obey any geographical rules. Paradoxically, the biennial form was used (according to fourteenth-century sources) on the most fertile soils and produced higher yields than the triennial.

From a document of 1338 listing agricultural holdings of the Hospitalers throughout Provence, Thérèse Sclafert was able to reconstruct a complicated pattern of field systems. In places as widely separated as the valley of Argens, Nice, Arles, and Marseilles, a two-course rotation of cereal and fallow produced yields of 4:1, and as high as 7:1. The cereals grown were soft wheat (hard wheat was unknown until the sixteenth century), rye, *conseigle* or *méteil,* which was wheat and rye mixed, barley, or oats. Various modifications of the two-course rotation were also practiced. The most common variation was to plant a small portion of the fallow field in oats or other summer crops, such as peas or beans. (The wheat-bean rotation had been described by Columella, the Roman agronomist.) In this way, in places like the valley of the Molle or the Auvezère, a great variety of grains were grown, because the sown field was divided among a number of cereals (wheat, rye, and barley in the same planting, for example). Yields ranged from 4:1 to 6:1.

In a small number of cases, fallowing was completely eliminated. Such fields were called *annulae,* indicating that they were sown the year round. There were also a number of examples of three-course rotations with fallowing, all with yields of 4:1. In such cases, one field was planted with wheat; one with *conseigle,* barley, or oats, or divided among them; and the third field lay fallow. In the Midi, the presumption is that the field containing "spring corn" was in fact sown in the winter. The fallow field was plowed up to four times. Weeds grow throughout the winter in the Mediterranean region and must be controlled.

As elsewhere, Midi polyculture was typified by the association of fruit trees, olives, and grapes. In certain areas, such as the lower Rhône valley, terraced polyculture was characteristic of the hill country, with the plains devoted to market gardens. Parcels in Provence, called *oulières,* were elongated strips, separated by the two or three rows of grapes, mixed with olives, almonds, or fruit trees. Although grapes were widely grown, few areas were known for wine. An exception was the Bas-Languedoc, where grapevines became economically important with the commercialization of its wine in the course of the fourteenth century.

In Roussillon, cerealculture manifested a characteristic pattern of rye at high altitudes (such as Vallespir and Cerdagne), with barley the most frequent cereal on the plain. Wheat was eaten only by the aristocracy; millet was the staple of the poor. Roussillon is not now noted for grapes, but frequent citations attest that they were grown in medieval Cerdagne (Cerdaña), where they are not grown now, and in late thirteenth-century Collioure they were grown almost exclusively. Irrigated gardens *(hortas)* were grouped together near towns in typical Catalan style, an example being the *horta nova* of Perpignan (1225). These gardens produced vegetables, but also cereal grains, olives, and grapes. From the twelfth century on, Roussillon also produced vegetable dyes: madder, woad, and yellowweed.

The agriculture of the Toulouse region was very similar. Biennial rotations were the rule, although

AGRICULTURE AND NUTRITION

not without variation. A late fifteenth-century contract reveals an atypical rotation of wheat-fallow-woad-fallow, and the existence of numerous share-cropping contracts for periods of three or nine years indicates that triennial rotations were practiced in some areas. Flax and grapes completed the panorama.

Of course, irrigation was practiced in the Midi, intensively so in Roussillon, where, by the thirteenth century, rice was cultivated. The introduction of new plants into the region was always from the south, with the new plants of the Arabs reaching Roussillon from Spain and the eastern Midi from Italy. One of the earliest introductions was romaine lettuce, a variety of Persian origin, which reached Avignon from Italy in the late fourteenth century. The artichoke's history was more normative: it did not reach the Midi until the 1530's.

ITALY

The Italian agricultural landscape was a distinctive mixture of cereals grown in biennial rotation, irrigated huertas and meadows, lands in polyculture (in its most complete form, figs, grapevines, and vegetables), and specialized vineyards. Because of the peninsula's extremely varied landscape, it is difficult to formulate generalizations concerning the nature of its agriculture, and the often-mentioned dichotomy between a well-irrigated north and an underirrigated south must be adjusted to account for atypical areas.

Northern Italian cerealculture in the ninth and tenth centuries, the subject of a study by Massimo Montanari, was characterized by a striking anomaly in comparison with most other Mediterranean areas: rye was the dominant grain, by a healthy margin over wheat (39.44 percent rye vs. 20.21 percent wheat, 15.92 percent millet, 11.62 percent barley and oats mixed, and 5.09 percent oats alone, with minor varieties and vegetables accounting for the rest of the crops grown on the lands of Santa Giulia di Brescia). The incidence of rye remained high: in the Piedmont of the late thirteenth century, mills were taxed in kind, half in wheat and half in rye.

Northern Italian documents distinguished between *grani grossi* and *grani minuti*—great and lesser grains. The distinction was not one of size but of quality. The *grani grossi* were winter grains—wheat, rye, and, in the case of northern Italy, barley and even oats. The *minuti* were spring cereals—sorghum, millet, and panic, all of which were sown substantially earlier than was customary in northern Europe (March rather than May), and which in any case were not highly valued. Barley was apparently unimportant in northern Italy, increasing in significance towards the south. Tenth-century grain yields from Lombardy ranged from 1.75:1 to a high of 3.3:1, with an average yield of 2.2:1.

A common adaptation to the lack of summer crops and one which, according to Pierre Toubert, conferred a kind of genetic plasticity upon the total cereal pool, was the planting of cereals in mixtures—wheat and millet, millet and rye, wheat and rye, oats and barley. In the Piedmont, the oat crop became increasingly important. Its price was extremely low, and it could grow where wheat and rye could not. During the fourteenth century it advanced markedly into marginal lands because it was the only grain that could be grown there. Moreover, the broad bean *(fava)*, another typical summer crop of northern Europe, was widely used as a grain substitute and sown in the winter. The beans were ground into flour and mixed with wheat. Sorghum was known from the tenth century on (it appears as *melega* or *suricum,* in a document of 910), but citations become frequent in the thirteenth century. Hard wheat arrived late. *Pasta* emerged in the late thirteenth century, with a veritable florescence in the fourteenth of many varieties, with the generic name of *tria.*

In thirteenth-century Latium, a kind of triennial rotation was practiced, with two winter cereals planted in consecutive years (wheat and spelt, or wheat and winter barley), followed by one year of fallow. From the mid tenth century, it was common for part of the fallow to be planted with broad beans.

One more facet of the dry-farming regime of northern Italy is worth noting. Certain vegetables typically associated with huerta cultivation were grown as field crops—the chick-pea, the vetch (a fodder), the green bean, and the pea, although the latter is cited less than the others in documents of the ninth through thirteenth centuries.

Polyculture, or interculture, generally refers to unirrigated regimes. However, huerta cultivation in medieval Italy was based on an association of fruit trees and vegetables which, as in dry-farming polyculture, was designed to prevent evaporation and to encourage the growth of the smaller plants by casting shade on them in summer. Thus in Latium, until the fourteenth century, one found the common association of cherry, apple, and pear trees on the one

AGRICULTURE AND NUTRITION

hand, and peas, green beans, cabbage, squashes, and aromatic herbs on the other. Citrus trees appeared early in Sicily (*pomi citrini* in a document of 1002) but not until the fourteenth century farther north. Then, in Tuscany, the full range of varieties was found—citrons, oranges, limes, and lemons. The artichoke, another plant associated with the Arabs, was introduced in northern Italy from Naples in the mid-fifteenth century, reaching Venice around 1480.

Filling an intermediate role between cereal lands and huertas were irrigated meadows *(ferraginalia),* whose introduction resulted in the reduction or elimination of fallowing. In Latium, they tended to be prime targets for conversion into huertas in response to growing market demand. A different kind of land use was the flax field, found from the tenth century on but, in the course of the thirteenth, moving into marginal lands with gravelly soil, frequently intermixed with vineyards and olive groves. The latter were particularly notable in subalpine Lombardy, according to documents of the early tenth century.

Vineyards followed a distinct pattern of development: first, ecclesiastical and seignorial vineyards; then a phase of bourgeois viticulture around the year 1000, when suburban vineyards became common throughout north and central Italy; and then a long process of retreat (conversion of vineyards to cereal lands in response to rising urban populations) and change (fewer specialized vineyards, with more grapevines in polyculture). For example, the suburbs of tenth-century Rieti had been densely planted in vineyards. Towards the end of the century, these tended to yield to irrigated gardens, with vineyards reappearing in peripheral zones. Thirteenth-century documents from the Bologna area still reveal a large number of specialized vineyards (49.04 percent of agricultural land), typically suburban, with the rest of the grapes grown in various forms of interculture. A large number of varieties of grapes were grown. Pietro de' Crescenzi mentions twenty-one varieties grown in the Bologna region, thirteen white and eight red.

In its most complete form, interculture, or "vertical polyculture," included a cereal or grass, grapevines, and then, at the highest level, fruit trees. The idea was to interplant species whose root systems occupied the soil at different depths and for the lower plants to benefit from the shade of the higher. Grapevines were frequently planted on the fruit trees, with the grapes suspended in an arbor or canopy between two trees. The most typical associations were figs and grapes, grapes and chestnuts, or grapes and olives. However, the model seems rarely to have been found in reality. In medieval Latium, Toubert found grapevines juxtaposed with arboriculture, but never fully integrated with it. Trees seem to have been planted around vineyards, as borders, but never fully integrated within them. The region appears to have been too dry in the summer to have supported full polyculture.

The fifteenth century saw the culmination of trends begun in earlier times. Data from lower Lombardy (Pavese) from around 1550 may be taken as representative of the growth pattern of the previous century. Thirty-eight percent of the land was in cereal cultivation, with only 0.7 percent in irrigated fields, presumably of the garden variety. Meadows (many of which were irrigated) occupied 27.4 percent of the area, with 26.3 percent in vineyards. A new irrigated crop, rice, accounts for 1.6 percent of total land use and also reflects the canal-building activity of the later Middle Ages. Leaving aside the 3.2 percent of forest, less than one percent of the land in this region was uncultivated, which attests to the trend towards intensive land use demanded by the dense urban concentrations of northern and central Italy of the Renaissance.

SICILY AND SARDINIA

The agriculture of medieval Sicily was a faithful reflection of the new Arab style. The typical medieval huerta crops had been introduced under Islamic rule; sugar, cotton, citrus, artichokes, spinach, and eggplant were all irrigated by systems with a strongly Arab technological and institutional imprint. It can be presumed that, as was the case in southern Spain, a diminution in land area devoted to cereals had taken place under Islamic rule as compared to Roman times. Twelfth-century documents from the monastery of Monreale whose lands to the south of Palermo had a large Muslim population reveal a mixed agrarian regime: wheat in open fields, some of which were set aside for pasture; zones of specialized agriculture near villages where hemp, flax, mulberry, and cotton were grown, along with the dye plants, henna, woad, and saffron; and irrigated gardens. The Muslims also grew sugar cane for domestic consumption, but appear not to have commercialized the crop. In the course of the thirteenth century, the agricultural landscape was altered sharply as the Muslim population left. By the fourteenth century a wheat and grazing pattern had

AGRICULTURE AND NUTRITION

replaced the more variegated agricultural regime of the Muslims. Mid-fourteenth-century Sicily, according to a contemporary source, grew the standard range of grain varieties, including a new, fast-growing wheat variety called *diminia.* Besides cereals, grapevines, grown in enclosed parcels, were the most important crop, and new plantations of sugar cane were found in littoral zones in response to the commercialization of Sicilian sugar.

Sardinia presents a similar perspective. In the thirteenth century, oranges, lemons, and melons (including the *sandria,* or watermelon) were grown on irrigated parcels, the melons on fields (called *isclas*) which were cultivated only in April, May, September, and October. Grapes were the island's most important crop, grown almost exclusively in interculture with apples, figs, pears, or olives. Cereals were grown on clayey soils, in long rotations of two or three years in crops and then three in fallow or pasture. The typical south Sardinian rotation of two years in grain and one in beans had not yet emerged. Peas, lentils, and oats (called "horse barley," *orzo de cavallos*) were also grown.

BIBLIOGRAPHY

The Western Mediterranean as a Region. James M. Houston, *The Western Mediterranean World* (1964). On technology, see M.-C. Amouretti, "A propos de l'histoire de l'outillage agricole," in *Monde alpin et rhodanien,* **4** (1976); Richard W. Bulliet, *The Camel and the Wheel* (1975); Jorge Dias, "Arado," in *Dicionário de história de Portugal,* ed. Joel Serrão (1963).

Islam and the Arab Green Revolution. Lucie Bolens, *Les méthodes culturales au moyen-âge d'après les traités d'agronomie andalous* (1974); Mounira Chapoutot-Remadi, "L'agriculture dans l'empire Mamluk au moyen âge d'après al-Nuwayrī," in *Cahiers de Tunisie,* **22** (1974); Thomas F. Glick, *Islamic and Christian Spain in the Early Middle Ages* (1979); J. Poncet, "Les champs et l'évolution du paysage agraire en Tunisie," in *Annales de géographie,* **71** (1962); Andrew M. Watson, *New Crops in the Early-Islamic Period: A Study in Diffusion* (in press); "A Medieval Green Revolution: New Crops and Farming Techniques in the Early Islamic World," in *Land, Population and Society: Studies in the Economic History of the Middle East,* ed. A. Udovitch, (1980); and "Towards Denser and More Continuous Settlement: New Crops and Farming Techniques in the Early Middle Ages," in *Pathways to the Medieval Peasant,* ed. Ambrose Raftis (1980).

Christian Spain. Thomas F. Glick, *Irrigation and Society in Medieval Valencia* (1970).

Portugal. Orlando Ribeiro, "Agricultura," in *Dicionário de história de Portugal,* ed. Joel Serrão (1963); Albert Silbert, *Le Portugal méditerranéen à la fin de l'ancien régime,* 2 vols. (1966).

Southern France. Jean-Auguste Brutails, *Étude sur la condition des populations rurales du Roussillon au moyen âge,* reprint ed. (1975); Roger Dion, *Essai sur la formation du paysage rural français* (1934), stressing continuity with Roman agriculture; and *Histoire de la vigne et du vin en France* (1959); Daniel Faucher, "L'assolement triennal en France," in *Études rurales,* **1** (1961); *Géographie agraire; Types de cultures* (1949); and "Polyculture ancienne et assolement biennal dans la France meridionale," in *Revue géographique des Pyrénées et du Sud-Ouest,* **5** (1934); Emmanuel Le Roy Ladurie, *Les paysans de Languedoc,* I (1966); Thérèse Sclafert, "Usages agraires dans les régions provençales avant le XVIIIe siècle," in *Revue de géographie alpine,* **29** (1941); Germain Sicard, "Les techniques rurales en pays Toulousain aux XIVe et XVe siècles d'après les contrats de métayage," in *Annales du Midi,* **71** (1959).

Italy. Henri Bercher, Annie Courteaux, and Jean Mouton, "Une abbaye latine dans la société musulmane: Monreale au XIIe siècle," in *Annales: Economies, Sociétés, Civilisations,* **34** (1979); Pietro de' Crescenzi, *De omnibus agriculturae* (1548); Giovanni Cherubini, "L'agricoltura e il mondo rurale siciliano tra il 1337 e il 1361," in *Rivista di storia dell'agricoltura,* **6** (1966); Felice Cherchi Paba, "Lineamenti storici dell'agricoltura sarda nel secolo XIII," in *Studi storici in onore di Francesco Loddo-Canepa,* II (1959); Carlo M. Cipolla, "Per la storia delle terre della 'Bassa' Lombarda," in *Studi in onore di Armando Sapori,* I (1957); and "Repartizione delle colture nel Pavese secondo le 'Misure Territoriali' della metà del 500," in *Studi di economia e statistica, Università di Catania,* **1** (1950–1951); Georges Duby, "Sur l'histoire agraire de l'Italie," in *Annales: Economies, Sociétés, Civilisations,* **18** (1963); Vito Fumagalli, "Note per una storia agraria alto medioevale," in *Studi medievali,* 3rd ser., **9**, pt. 1 (1968); and "Rapporto fra grano seminato e grano raccolto, nel polittico del monastero di S. Tommaso di Reggio," in *Rivista di storia dell'agricoltura,* **6** (1966); Ildebrando Imberciadori, "Agricoltura italiana dall'XI al XVI secolo," with useful bibliography, *ibid.,* **11** (1971); and "Vite e vigna nell'alto Medio Evo," *ibid.,* **6** (1966).

Philip Jones, "Medieval Agrarian Society in its Prime: Italy," in *Cambridge Economic History of Europe,* ed. M. M. Postan, I, 2nd ed. (1966); Maurice Le Lannou, *Pâtres et paysans de la Sardaigne* (1941); Massimo Montanari, "Cereali e legumi nell'alto medioevo; Italia del nord, secoli IX–X," in *Rivista storica italiana,* **87** (1975); Gianfranco Pasquali, "Olivi e olio nella Lombardia prealpina," in *Studi medievali,* 3rd ser., **13**, pt. 1 (1972); Antonio Ivan Pini, "La viticoltura italiana nel Medioevo," *ibid.,* 3rd ser., **15**, pt. 2 (1974); Claudio Rotelli, *Una campagna medievale: Storia agraria del Piemonte fra il 1250 e il 1450* (1973); Emilio Sereni, *Storia del paesaggio agrario italiano* (1961); Pierre Toubert, *Les structures du Latium médiéval,* I (1973); Renato Zangheri, "L'agricoltura dell'Italia medievale," in *Studi storici,* **8** (1967).

THOMAS F. GLICK

AGRICULTURE AND NUTRITION

III

NORTHERN EUROPE. This article deals with the development of husbandry in the northern half of medieval Europe and with the sorts of food thus made available. Because wine is so largely a southern product, it is not discussed here. We shall not include vegetable and animal fibers or dyes used for textiles and cordage, or large-scale herding separate from agriculture, or leather, furs, fishing, and salt. Likewise, this article omits conditions of tenure and forms of village settlement. Hunting and falconry are relevant to nutrition, but are treated separately.

Patterns of agriculture reflect the interplay of terrain, soil, precipitation and its distribution over the year, temperatures (especially in the growing seasons), the availability of power (whether human, animal, or mechanical) for cultivation, the varieties of food sources known and their appropriateness to the context, the amount and suitability of fertilizer, and both the food-producing traditions and the food preferences of the population. New patterns are produced by local inventiveness and by borrowing from elsewhere.

Europe is divided into two major agricultural regions by natural factors and by dietary and farming habits. The line of separation runs very roughly along the Loire and the Alps, then eastward into the Ukraine. Around the Mediterranean and in the Near East, summer rains are generally too sparse or infrequent to permit summer crops without irrigation, the landscape is irregular, and most soils are light and sandy. Diets rely chiefly on cereals, with relatively little meat. Most fat comes from olive oil and from a small amount of sheep and goat cheese.

By contrast, on the great rolling plain of northern Europe that extends with minor breaks from the Atlantic deep into the Soviet Union, precipitation is considerable, summer rains are frequent, and soils are often claylike and heavy. As in the south, the popular diet has centered on cereals, but from early times more meat has been consumed than in any other society above the hunting-gathering level. Fats have consisted far less of vegetable oils than of butter, cheese, suet, and lard.

The Near Eastern tradition of agriculture and animal husbandry spread to Europe, both north and south, during the Neolithic. The crops (notably certain varieties of wheat, barley, and legumes) and animals (horned cattle, horses, sheep, goats, swine, geese, pigeons, and eventually chickens from India) were immigrants arriving chiefly through the Balkans and up the Danube basin. The first European plant domestications were rye and oats, which the Romans regarded as weeds in wheat fields. During the early Middle Ages, northern peasants recognized that in their cool climate these weeds were often more productive of edible seeds than wheat was, and began to cultivate them.

A major reason for the relatively high level of urbanism and for the cultural resilience of the Near East was the fact that its agricultural style was indigenous, well suited to the regional ecology. By contrast, the growth of cities and high culture lagged in northern Europe largely because its agriculture was an exotic transplant into an alien environment, and consequently was less productive than in its native soil. The history of agriculture and of nutrition during the Middle Ages in northern Europe is that of the development of modes of food production suited to the northern environment. The process was so successful that eventually the focus of European vitality shifted from the shores of the Mediterranean to the northern plains.

This agricultural revolution of medieval northern Europe—no milder term does it justice—was composed of several elements that gradually fused into a distinctive system of agrarian technology that spread wherever it proved viable and profitable. But remember that we are dealing with innovations among illiterate peasants; upper-class documents dealing with rural matters are far more concerned with who owns the land and with what revenues he gets from it than with the methods of husbandry that make it worth owning. Moreover, agrarian archaeology is still rudimentary. Naturally there are notable variations of soil, climate, and tradition in a region as large as the great European plain, and these produced many different combinations of farm implements, crops, and customs. The result is that while the fact of a profound mutation in medieval northern European styles of husbandry is now universally accepted, specific information is so fragmentary that no two experts seem to agree entirely on the origins, datings, diffusions, and implications of the new methods.

THE HEAVY PLOW, OPEN FIELDS, AND MIXED FARMING

The basic agricultural tool is the plow. Its first form was invented in the Near East as a digging stick drawn by a yoke of two oxen. This simple plow does not turn over the soil, but merely stirs it in the line of the furrow. In the relatively arid climate of the Near East, cross-plowing to pulverize the soil is

AGRICULTURE AND NUTRITION

essential, both to preserve the moisture just below the surface and to fertilize the land by the capillary attraction that draws up minerals from the subsoil. Cross-plowing produces fields squarish in shape. In the Near East and Mediterranean basin, with their generally light soils, this plow worked fairly well and is still in wide use.

But when agriculture reached northern Europe from the Near East, the scratch plow proved inappropriate to both soil and climate. Only sandy and chalky upland soils could normally be cultivated with it; it did not cope well with the more fertile alluvium of the river bottoms and adjacent plains. While the Near Eastern farmer wanted to retain water in his soil, the northern cultivator needed to drain it out. Moreover, capillary attraction does not operate in very moist soils: to refresh his fields the northern plowman wanted his plowshare to cut deep into the earth and turn up lower layers of dirt. To do all this he eventually created a bigger and heavier plow that generally needed wheels for easy mobility and more than two oxen to draw it.

The first hint that something was happening to plow design appeared in the writing of Vergil, who mentioned wheels on a plow in the first century B.C. In the early fifth century Servius, Vergil's great commentator, wrote that in Vergil's time plows in the Po valley, where Vergil was reared, had wheels. (South of the Loire-Alps line there are pockets—northern Portugal and Galicia, Catalonia, parts of Provence, Tuscany, and the Po valley—where moisture-saturated westerly winds strike mountains and produce enough rain to provide an environment somewhat like that of the north.) A century after Vergil, Pliny the Elder wrote that in Italy—presumably the Po region—often eight oxen pulled a plow. But, strangely, he also spoke of the "recent" invention, in eastern Switzerland, of putting two wheels on a plow. Despite these experiments, however, the Romans did not achieve the heavy wheeled plow with a moldboard.

In the Celtic, Romanic, and Germanic tongues, the vocabulary surrounding the heavy plow and its use is confused. However, in all three of the Slavic linguistic groups—eastern, western, and southern—philologists find twenty-six technical terms connected with the fully developed, heavy, wheeled plow and methods of plowing with it, including ridging and drainage. All of these words, except the enigmatic new word *plug* (English *plough,* American *plow*) come from Slavic roots. This means that at least scattered groups of Slavs were employing the heavy wheeled plow before the Avar invasion of Pannonia (modern Hungary) in 567–568 seriously reduced contact between the southern Slavs and the rest. Since a vocabulary can—indeed, must—be built up rapidly to surround any novelty, we should not assume that the Slavs had the new plow before the early sixth century. Some did not start using it until later; in Moravia, for example, the transition from scratch plow to heavy plow seems to have occurred between the seventh and the ninth centuries.

When did the Germans get it? The word "plow," as Latin *plovum,* appeared in 643 in north Italy in an edict of the Lombard King Rothar. The Lombards, expelled from Pannonia into Italy by the Avar invasion of 567–568, may have brought the new plow with them. The most common medieval Latin word for the heavy plow, *carruca,* originally meant a two-wheeled cart; and in the Salic Law, formulated in the Rhineland about 507–511, it still had that meaning. But the Alemannic Law of southwest Germany, produced in 724–730, used *carruca* for the wheeled plow, and by the ninth century this new meaning had generally obliterated the older one, at least in the northern parts of the Frankish empire.

In the context of this chronology, the Angles, Saxons, Jutes, and Frisians who invaded Britain between 449 and 584 can scarcely have brought the heavy plow with them. It was long thought that the laws of King Ine of Wessex (about 690) indicated use of the new plow, but now it is recognized that we have this text only in a presumably updated version issued by King Alfred (died 899). The derivation of English "plough" from Old Norse *plógr* perhaps indicates that the object itself was introduced to England, or popularized there, by the ninth-century Scandinavian invaders and settlers.

The new heavy plow offered several advantages in the north European environment, but it also placed new demands on the peasants using it. The old scratch plow was cheap to make—even its conical plowshare was often wooden—and inexpensive to operate. The new plow was larger, with two costly wheels; an iron knife, the colter, fixed vertically beneath the plow beam to cut the line of the furrow; a flat iron share set horizontally to undercut the soil at the desired level; and a wooden moldboard to scoop up and turn over the ribbon of sod thus loosened, either to the right or to the left, according to which way it was set. The friction of colter, share, and moldboard with the soil was much too great to

AGRICULTURE AND NUTRITION

be overcome by a pair of oxen; it was deliberately greater because the idea behind this new invention was to create a plow that could cultivate the richer, stickier, bottomland soils. Although no medieval picture shows more than four oxen pulling a plow, there is massive documentary evidence that often eight were employed. In plowing recently cleared land, still full of roots and rocks, a big team would have been needed. As reclamation declined and fields became clear of snags and less resistant to the plow, the average size of the plow team doubtless became smaller. In estimating additional costs of the new means of tillage, we must not forget that while one man could manage a scratch plow, it took a plowman and an ox driver to handle the heavy plow.

On the other hand, the heavy plow broke the soil with such violence that the cross-plowing needed when the scratch plow was used became unnecessary; a rapid harrowing served to break up the larger clods and cover the seeds. After cross-plowing was eliminated, the most efficient shape for a field was not a square but a long strip, because time was wasted turning a big team about at the end of a furrow. The turf was turned by the moldboard toward the center line of the strip so that strips gradually became long, gentle ridges, with channels for drainage of surplus water between them. This was precisely what the northern European peasant needed if, in his drippy climate, he intended to exploit the most fertile soils yielding the best crops. The increased costs of the new system were far outweighed by the larger returns.

The result is today physically visible in Britain. Celts, Romans, and presumably the first Teutonic invaders all cultivated primarily the more meager upland soils. When, at some time not yet ascertained, the new plow arrived, their squarish, "Celtic" fields on thin soils were abandoned. Most have not been tilled since; yet their outlines often can still be clearly seen. In the bottomlands, forests were felled and strip cultivation became habitual. The England depicted in *Domesday Book* (1086) reveals an agricultural prosperity without precedent.

Although the profits from the new mode of tillage were great, the heavy plow nevertheless demanded drastic revisions of the ways peasants worked if good results were to be achieved. The scratch plow was a tool for a man laboring alone and owning his simple implement. The heavy plow could scarcely be used except by the cooperation of a sizable group, perhaps less in actual labor than in supplying equipment. Welsh laws, once ascribed to the tenth century but now known to be later, provided that a plow team must not break up before it had plowed twelve strips; these were assigned in turn to the plowman, the driver, the owner of the plow irons, the owner of the plow frame, and one to the owner of each of the eight oxen. Since cultivated strips were often bought and sold, divided among heirs, or given to the church, these provisions reflect no reality found in other documents. Yet they indicate what late medieval Welsh legists thought must have been the origin of the intensely cooperative style of cultivation found in "open-field" villages.

The squarish fields produced by the scratch plow could be fenced or hedged fairly economically. The long strips resulting from the heavy plow could not, yet fencing was essential if animals were to be kept from damaging the crops. The only solution was to fence the entire arable area of the village as a unit. Peasants, however, had always known that land constantly cultivated is soon worn out; during at least one year in two it must lie fallow, but be carefully plowed in order to put the weeds into the soil as fertilizer, so that the following year it can produce a decent crop. Where, therefore, the heavy plow was adopted, the need for fallowing initially resulted in the organization of villages with two great open fields of strips that were planted to crops in a two-year rotation. Obviously, deciding what should be planted, and when and where, and when and how to harvest, required much talking in the village council. In scratch-plow regions there was less need for such councils; only in highly irrigated areas of the south did institutional habits of group discussion emerge among the peasantry. In heavy-plow northern regions the exigencies of agriculture, by contrast, provided deep roots for rural democracy.

The new system of tillage was labor-saving and capital- and energy-intensive. The increased energy came from oxen, which was one reason why the peasants tried to raise more cattle. But also, to get better returns from their fields, they needed more animal manure.

The Romans had recognized that the northern barbarians, both Celts and Germans, ate much more meat than did the Mediterranean peoples. This was partly because, as we have noted, the cereal-growing system introduced from the Near East was unsuited to the northern climate and soil and, consequently, not very productive. The Romans themselves never systematically integrated herding and agriculture;

 AGRICULTURE AND NUTRITION

plow oxen, pigs, geese, and chickens were found, of course, around farm buildings, but meat production was conducted on wild ranges where the animal droppings were lost. When the northern peasants adopted the heavy plow, they quickly combined their ancestral tradition of herding with the newly successful methods of grain culture. Since the early Middle Ages this mixed farming has been distinctive of northern Europe and of temperate regions elsewhere that have been colonized by northern Europeans.

The symbol of this change is the scythe. The Romans had scythes, but they were little used until Frankish times. The sickle was the preferred tool for harvesting grain because it cut the stalk more gently than the scythe, and thus lessened the risk of shattering the head of grain. Not until the end of the Middle Ages does one find scythes (for example, in Pieter Brueghel's pictures) used for cutting grain; presumably by 1500 another millennium of natural selection of grains had reduced shattering. The scythe was the tool for haying. Its presence indicates strong interest in meadows, in stall-feeding during the winter, and in the collection of manure from barns to be spread on fields. What Charlemagne thought of all this is shown by his effort to rename the months: July was to be "Haying Month" and August, "Harvest Month." In addition to eating cut hay, animals grazed on fallow fields and on the stubble after harvest on cropped fields, thus helping both to feed themselves and to fertilize the fields. Naturally animals continued to browse on the wild land beyond the fields when necessary.

THE THREE-FIELD ROTATION AND THE USE OF HORSES ON FARMS

Under the old Roman, and the more systematized early medieval, rotations, plowing for winter grains was done in October or November and the harvest came in June or July. But in Charlemagne's new nomenclature, August, as we have noted, was "Harvest Month." The emperor was thus celebrating a recent mutation in the pattern of the agricultural year in northern Europe that he obviously felt was of prime importance for the prosperity of his realm: the three-field system of rotation. Peasant communities were beginning to divide their arable land into three, rather than two, open fields of strips. One field was left fallow, and merely plowed to put the weeds under the soil. A second, in the old style, was planted with grain in late autumn, and the harvest came in the late spring or early summer. The third field—which was the novelty—was planted with oats, barley, peas, or broad beans in the spring and reaped in the autumn. In the second year of the three-year cycle, the previous fallow field would be planted with winter crops, the previous winter-crop field would be used for summer crops, and the previous summer-crop field would remain fallow. In the third year the second year's fallow would go into winter crops, the winter-crop field into summer crops, and the summer-crop field would lie fallow. In the next year the cycle would start over again.

The new arrangement appears suddenly in the records, the earliest firm dates being 763, 783, and 800; thereafter references to it are common. For obvious reasons the three-field system could be adopted only in areas of adequate summer rains, so that most Mediterranean regions remained confined to autumn plantings. And even though the legumes that now were regularly a part of the spring planting fertilized the soil by means of nitrogen-fixing bacteria in nodules on their roots, only a rich soil could sustain the more rapid rotation of crops. Nevertheless, the advantages of the triennial rotation were so considerable that many two-field northern villages, with soil so poor that the swifter rotation over three open fields would quickly have proved ruinous, achieved some of the benefits of the new agrarian system by dividing their single planted fields in half each year, sowing one part in the autumn and the other in the spring. What were these benefits?

First, the increased production of legumes not only improved the fertility of the soil—adequate fertilizer is always one of the major problems of a farmer—but also provided a better diet for the lower classes (a topic to which we shall return).

Second, having two seasons of sowing and of harvest each year reduced the risk of famine: it was unlikely that both crops would fail.

Third, the new cycle of crops distributed the labor of plowing more evenly over the year, and kept men, plow animals, and costly plows from standing idle for long periods. This was advantageous not only to lords but also to peasants, who after paying the established manorial dues would keep for themselves much of the new surplus produced.

Fourth, the shift from biennial to triennial rotation enabled a group of peasants to cultivate considerably more hectares annually with the same labor. Modern scholars have generally stressed changes in production per unit of arable land, but the more realistic measure is production per peasant.

In the eighth through the tenth centuries there

AGRICULTURE AND NUTRITION

were two plowings each year in two-field villages, and three a year in three-field villages. Fallow was plowed in June, the winter field in autumn, and (in a three-field cycle) the summer field in March. Thus, a village cultivating 600 hectares in two fields would annually plow 600 hectares and plant 300 hectares in crops. Under the three-field system the same village would plow the same amount and plant 400 hectares in crops, an increase of one-third in production.

By the twelfth century it had been found advantageous to plow the fallow twice in order to keep weeds down and to maintain fertility. This intensification of plowing increased the advantage of the triennial rotation even more. Peasants handling 600 hectares according to the two-field plan would annually plow 300 + 600 = 900 hectares and have 300 hectares yield crops. Under the three-field plan, again plowing the fallow twice, they would plow 200 + 200 + 400 = 800 hectares and have 400 hectares yield crops. Since, however, this involves 100 fewer hectares of plowing, the villagers might add 75 hectares (plowed as 25 + 25 + 50) to their arable land without extra labor if such land could be got by reclamation from the wild. The same number of peasants would thus, under the three-field rotation, be cultivating not 600 but 675 hectares, with 225 lying fallow and 450 annually in crops. Their production advantage over a two-field village of the same population would be 50 percent. It is no wonder that much land was cleared and many swamps were drained, while food production per peasant soared.

Fifth, the increased growing of oats under the three-field system was an essential element in enabling northern peasants in the more favored areas to change from the ox to the horse as their chief draft animal. Oats are the best food for horses, but climatic obstacles to a spring planting prevented most Mediterranean peasants from shifting their scheme of rotation so as to raise more oats. The horse had been generally an animal for battle or for sport, rather than for labor, in Europe because the ancient yoke harness, although well suited to the anatomy of an ox, was entirely wrong for that of a horse. About 800 two new forms of horse harness (the breast strap and the rigid collar, both provided with lateral traces) appeared in Europe. They presumably came out of Asia, and were so efficient that they increased the pulling power of a horse by four or five times. The first news of the habitual use of horses for plowing comes out of Norway toward the end of the ninth century. At just that moment an astonishing invention, nailed iron horseshoes, began to become common, thus greatly increasing the staying power of horses for heavy hauling.

An ox was a slow, grass-burning tractor; the horse burned a more expensive fuel, oats. A horse, however, could work more hours in a day than an ox, and it moved twice as rapidly. In terms of human labor, it was worth its cost if the investment could be afforded. Western Slavic regions in the twelfth century measured plowlands in units that could be worked by a pair of oxen or by one horse—an advantage of 100 percent for the horse.

It is no wonder, then, that wherever enough oats could be raised to fuel horses, peasants substituted horses for oxen. The border of the Bayeux Tapestry, probably made in Kent *ca.* 1077, shows a horse harrowing and a single mule drawing a heavy wheeled plow (probably a medieval joke), and a conversation recorded in the Ukraine in 1103 indicates that in that region all plowing was done with horses. By 1095 plow horses were so common in the north that, in his famous sermon at the Council of Clermont launching the First Crusade, Pope Urban II placed not only oxen and plow horses, but also horses that harrow, under the protection of the Peace of God.

In some northern areas—the region around the university city of Marburg in Hesse, for example—peasants still plowed with oxen well into the twentieth century. But on more fertile lands the shift to horses occurred generally in the eleventh and twelfth centuries. Doubtless no village was ever ideally situated, but it is instructive to refer again to our model village of 600 arable hectares that switched from the biennial to the triennial rotation, thus gaining 75 arable hectares without additional plowing, and increasing its annual yield by 50 percent. Let us assume that such prosperity permitted the peasants to replace oxen with horses, which plow twice as fast. We would then have an agrarian utopia in which, with the same annual expenditure of human labor, the same number of peasants can raise their arable 675 hectares with 450 in crops to 1,350 hectares with 900 in crops, always assuming that the added cultivable land could be reclaimed from adjacent wilds. This is an improvement of 200 percent over what the same number of peasants in the village could have produced under the two-field system. The productivity per peasant is vastly greater than that of the era before the heavy plow, the strip system, and the biennial rotation of crops between two open fields emerged, probably in the early sixth century.

The sixth century was a time of dreadful epidem-

AGRICULTURE AND NUTRITION

ics in all of Europe; it is probable that the low point of European population in historical times came about 600. There is evidence that this shrinkage affected even small hamlets and thinly settled regions. Yet, as we have seen, the heavy plow demanded cooperation among several peasants. A small settlement was too fragile a base for adoption of so elaborate a system of tillage. In the seventh century population appears to have begun to increase; by the eighth century the density of settlement in more and more northern areas was making feasible the adoption of the new agrarian plan. Before the end of that century the even more intricate and profitable three-field rotation was spreading quickly. By producing more food, it encouraged population increase; and that increase stimulated adoption of more efficient agricultural methods.

A setback came in many areas during the ninth and early tenth centuries, when first the Norsemen and then the Magyars launched prolonged and disruptive raids over much of northern Europe. The extent of the damage is much debated, but undoubtedly thousands of villages were burned, plow animals were slaughtered, and countless peasants perished from deprivation if not by the sword. After the Norsemen began to settle down, however, and after the Magyars were tamed at the Battle of Lechfeld (955), the forward surge of both population and agriculture was swift.

The earliest detailed picture of northern European peasant life under the new dispensation is from the southern German lands. *Ruodlieb* (*ca.* 1050) is a picaresque story in Latin verse composed by a cleric for the amusement of his fellows. He had no intention either of romanticizing the peasants or of arousing compassion for them. What he wrote about them was purely incidental to his narrative and presumably was recognizable by his audience. In this work the peasants are crude, vigorous, at times dirty; not infrequently they are disrespectful toward their social betters. We are shown two prosperous peasant establishments in a fairly big village. Houses are built around courtyards that include stables, storerooms, barns, and latrines. There are many cattle, horses, sheep, goats, hogs, chickens, geese, and bees, not to mention dogs and cats. The peasants have not yet made the transition from oxen to horses as plow animals, but they use mares for harrowing. There is no lack of food, including meat. To celebrate, one drinks wine or mead. Surplus production is sold for money; spices are twice mentioned. The wife of one farmer has a fur cloak. The other farmer owns a splendid cup carved of walnut wood and ornamented with gold that he brings out on special occasions. There are several hired servants. This is a thriving, self-confident, rapidly developing peasant society, flushed with the affluence brought by its new agricultural technology.

That technology continued to spread for another 200 years, into the late thirteenth century, and population likewise kept growing. But by about 1300 there was little wasteland left that could profitably be reclaimed; indeed, marginal soils that rashly had been put under the plow were relapsing to the wild. Population began to outstrip food supply. Standards of living among the peasants decayed swiftly. At the same time the climate was changing, and both drought and flood led to great famines. Life expectancy was apparently declining even before the tragedy of the Black Death (1347–1350) wiped out probably 30 percent of Europe's inhabitants. Its return every few years combined with other catastrophes to lower Europe's population in 1400 to roughly half of what it had been in 1347. Thousands of villages were abandoned while the surviving peasants gradually retreated to the areas of the best soils. This, and the scarcity of labor, meant a general improvement in conditions of peasant life over what they had been since the middle 1200's. But there were no major new ideas for agricultural expansion. It was not until the seventeenth and eighteenth centuries, when novel crops from the New World combined with original agrarian techniques, that Europe experienced its second agricultural revolution and its second demographic explosion.

NUTRITION

The carbohydrate food of medieval northern Europeans was overwhelmingly derived from cereals: several varieties of wheat, rye, oats, barley, and buckwheat, the last having been introduced from central Asia about the middle of the fifteenth century. (The highly glutinous durum wheat needed for pasta products appears not to have been grown north of the Alps, although today it is adapted to cold climates.) These cereals were consumed as bread, porridge, dumplings, and beer. The rapid spread of water-powered mills during the early Middle Ages undoubtedly shifted the emphasis from porridge to bread. The only major medieval advance in the handling of these foods was the introduction of hops to the making of beer in the time of Charlemagne.

AGRICULTURE AND NUTRITION

Hops have an antibiotic action against the bacteria producing acetic acid, and therefore assist the storage of beer.

In the analysis of a culture, negative as well as positive facts should be noted. Europe is filled with forests of oaks and beeches. In times of extreme famine Europeans occasionally ate beechnuts, but seldom, it seems, acorns. These were left to the pigs. Yet in precolonial California the densest population north of central Mexico was maintained without agriculture: it largely depended on acorns for its carbohydrates and fats. Leaching the tannin out of acorn meal, and thus making it edible, is considerably simpler than curing olives. The concept of "resource availability" demands more thought.

Cereals contain proteins, but in varying sets and proportions. An adequate diet demands that these be combined with amino acids from other sources. Northern Europe in the Middle Ages was not well endowed with protein-rich legumes; both chick-peas and lentils do better around the Mediterranean than in the north, and—despite close contacts with China during the Yüan dynasty—the soybean, with its 35 percent protein content, did not reach Europe until the nineteenth century, presumably because in East Asia it is consumed largely as bean curd and soy sauce, and the West had no analogous traditions of transforming legumes to improve their edibility. The staple vegetable proteins of the north were peas and broad beans. Their production was greatly increased by the spring planting of the triennial rotation that spread from about 800 onward, and especially after about 950. Together these legumes were known as pulse, and their greater availability did much for the diet of the common people.

The history of ceramics confirms this conclusion. In the early Middle Ages the most common form of cooking pot was small and cylindrical. In northern archaeological strata of the later ninth and early tenth centuries considerably larger, globular pots have been found that to modern Americans are bean pots, and that a modern Frenchman would use for cooking a cassoulet; they clearly were designed to simmer legumes in quantity over a low fire.

We may be confident that normally these pots contained not only pulse and herbs but also some bits of pork. Dietetically it was fortunate that Charles Martel turned back the armies of Spanish Islam, for if Europe had become Muslim, the pig would have been banned and the West would have placed greater dependence on the goat, which is a far worse peril to its ecology. To be sure, in the ninth century the Latin church reduced the inventory of permissible proteins by prohibiting the eating of horses, because horse sacrifices, followed by ceremonial banquets of horsemeat, had been the great festivals of Indo-European paganism. Horses, however, breed slowly; and, if devouring them had not been made taboo, being large animals they would doubtless have graced the spits of nobles' kitchens, as did cattle and sheep, more often than the stewpots of peasants. The pig, by contrast, was prolific; a sow could produce at least two litters a year, of perhaps seven each, and piglets grew quickly, ranging the forests surrounding the villages, crunching acorns and beech mast. Traditional illustrated calendars showing the "works of the months" exist from the ninth century. Invariably they show, in midwinter, a peasant slaughtering a pig. This detail was constant for the next 600 years.

In addition to pigs, the peasants could depend for protein upon another rapid reproducer, the free-range, omnivorous chicken. Finally, in the Middle Ages the rabbit, the most recent edible animal to be brought under man's dominion, was domesticated. In wild form it was found in Spain and North Africa. The rabbit is not listed in Charlemagne's careful inventory of the possessions of his domains. In England it was first mentioned in 1186, in terms indicating that it was a recent arrival. Aristocrats kept rabbits in warrens; peasants kept them in hutches. In 1341 a Milanese chronicler wrote that the city and all the neighboring villages were filled with rabbits. Rabbits have a specialized way of using internal bacteria to turn grass that they chew into a high-protein excretion, which they then eat. Even the poorest peasant could gather weeds by the road to feed his rabbits. Moreover, rabbits are proverbial for their fecundity. They are meaty and their fur is useful. Incidentally, to flush rabbits out of warrens into waiting nets, a specialized form of the European polecat, the ferret, was also domesticated. With a muzzle on its jaws, the ferret was released into rabbit holes, then rewarded by the warrener with the livers of the captured rabbits. The European ferret, altered by domestication, no longer exists in wild form.

In notable contrast with antiquity, the Middle Ages, especially in the north and in northern Italy, developed cheese as a major source of protein and fat. Cheeses were often part of feudal dues, and because many sorts shipped well, they became a considerable item of commerce. English cheeses early

AGRICULTURE AND NUTRITION

won great repute: Philip II of France purchased them to provision his fortress at Falaise even after he had seized Normandy from the English. During the reign of King John of England, a noble lady boasted of owning 13,000 milking cows for producing cheese.

The most puzzling aspect of medieval nutrition is the problem of the availability of the vitamins and minerals so often derived from vegetables and fruit. Attached to every peasant house was a kitchen garden. The produce from it belonged almost entirely to the peasant, and much manure and labor went into it. Similarly, there were both scattered fruit trees and orchards. As yet, however, we know little about these important sources of food—what was grown, in what regions, and in what periods. We can be certain that selective breeding occurred; but when we hear of apples, pears, plums, and cherries, or of cabbages, garlic, turnips, and onions, we do not know in any detail what they were like or what their nutritive value was. Considerable changes seem to have occurred. The brassica family doubtless started in antiquity as a leafy kale. By the twelfth century both red and white head cabbages were grown in Germany, followed by kohlrabi, cauliflower (perhaps developed by the Muslims), and, in Flanders in 1472, Brussels sprouts. Spinach seems to have worked its way northward from Islamic Spain, adapting to a chill climate by the thirteenth century; and romaine lettuce is supposed to have been brought to Avignon from Rome by the popes a century later. When carrots reached northern Europe from Afghanistan in the fourteenth century, they had an unpleasant purple or yellowish color; they did not become orange, and a standard vegetable, until the seventeenth century in the Netherlands. Celery seed had been used since the ancient Greeks as a flavoring and a medicine, but celery is not mentioned as a food until the seventeenth century. The celery with fleshy stalks that is taken for granted today emerged not long before 1800. Much is known scientifically about human nutrition, but little is known historically.

BIBLIOGRAPHY

Georges Duby, *L'économie rurale et la vie des campagnes dans l'Occident médiéval,* 2 vols. (1962); Roger Grand, *L'agriculture au moyen âge de la fin de l'empire romain au XVe siècle* (1950); Michael M. Postan, ed., *The Cambridge Economic History of Europe,* vol. I: *The Agrarian Life of the Middle Ages,* 2nd ed. (1966); N. W. Simmonds, ed., *Evolution of Crop Plants* (1976); Bernard H. Slicher van Bath, *The Agrarian History of Western Europe, A.D. 500–1850,* trans. Olive Ordish (1963).

LYNN WHITE, JR.

IV

THE SLAVIC WORLD. In discussing medieval Slavic agriculture we may conveniently begin with the West Slavs (today's Poles, Czechs, and Slovaks), say a few words about the South Slavs (today's Yugoslavs and Bulgarians), and turn finally to the East Slavs (today's Ukrainians, White Russians, and Great Russians). All Slavs shared certain features, but each major group had its own geography and history, which sometimes affected its agriculture in a distinct fashion.

The West Slav homeland had been between the Dnepr River, the Carpathian Mountains, the Bug River, and the Pripet Marshes. From this area many moved westward into lands earlier tilled and then abandoned by German tribes, which had moved farther west. Perhaps the West Slavs had been "mobile cultivators"—often changing their sites of cultivation—before the medieval era, but they were not nomads, and by the sixth century some had become sedentary farmers.

That agriculture played a central role in their lives may be seen from their calendar: the month we call August was known as Sierpień ("sickle") in Polish; September was Wrzesień ("threshing"), and these names are still in use today. The harvest was a major event for West Slavs, who awaited the ripening of crops with impatience, especially in hungry years. Some scholars, using such evidence as descriptions of pre-Christian harvest rituals, believe that grain was already a basic item of subsistence.

But Slavic agriculture in the early medieval era was quite backward. The West Slavs used primitive farming implements and techniques: their "hook" plow (*uncus* in Latin) barely scratched the soil, and a common method of preparing an area for tillage was to "slash and burn" a forested area, a system described below. In nonforested regions they engaged in field-grass husbandry. Regular rotation of crops was unknown.

The situation began to change after the West Slavs embraced Christianity and their princes introduced German colonists, a process that was well under way after 1100 and continued vigorously for over two centuries. Thus German migrants were flooding Poland and Eastern Bohemia in the first half of the thirteenth century, at approximately the same time the Mongols were invading Russia to the east, but with radically different consequences. The Mongol invasion (and subsequent occupation) was a disaster for Russia, whereas the German colonists

AGRICULTURE AND NUTRITION

made a number of positive contributions to West Slavic agriculture. They did this in return for certain concessions, such as greater autonomy under German law and fewer fiscal dues and obligations. With the German influx came an enormous expansion of cultivated area in territories east of the Elbe, from Estonia in the north to Transylvania in the south. The Germans brought their superior farming implements and techniques with them as they moved eastward.

The West Slavs, under their princes, were quick to imitate the Germans in their own organization of agriculture and village life. From the thirteenth century on, the native populations of Poland, Silesia, and Bohemia began enjoying some of the privileges and freedoms first extended to the Germans. Profiting from German technology and management skills, the West Slavs now acquired better implements, including heavy plows and water-driven mills (supplementing the older manually operated querns and the animal-driven mills). They learned to drain marshes and to build dikes; and they adopted the three-field system of tillage. As a result of such innovations, the West Slavs turned to settled farming with regular field systems and an accompanying expansion of grain cultures. New markets, towns, and cities sprang up.

All Slavs, it seems, had earlier engaged in slash-and-burn agriculture; old place names like Żary ("fires"), Praga (Prague) (prażiti = "burn"), and Trzebnica ("offering") may well have originated with it. In slash-and-burn tillage, a large number of trees were chopped down and allowed to dry. (Sometimes the trees were killed ahead of time, by stripping bark around the trunk, for example, and were then chopped down the next year.) When dry, the felled trees and underbrush were burned. Farmers now had a clearing on which to raise crops, and its ash-covered surface was ideal for planting seeds. Iron-bladed axes had been used to fell the trees; primitive rakes, forked wooden hoes, or harrows were employed to till the clearing.

Although slash-and-burn tillage gave an excellent yield in the first year (later centuries recorded yield ratios as high as 1:75 for crops like millet), it produced so little thereafter that the clearing had to be abandoned after two or three years. New trees had to grow there before slash-and-burn methods would again prove effective. Scholars have characterized this method of tillage as laborious and wasteful; chopping the trees, removing the stumps, and so on required great effort by as many people as could be assembled for the task, yet the soil quickly became exhausted and had to be given back to the forest. Hence it is not surprising that Slavs turned from such primitive methods to the more advanced techniques used by the Germans, culminating in the "three-field" system of crop rotation.

Witold Hensel has identified five stages in the evolution of tillage among the Slavs. The first four were associated with the slash-and-burn method. In the earliest, most primitive stage, pointed sticks and hoes were used to loosen the surface; in the second, a wooden "furrowing stick" that dug long rows was added; the third was marked by the development of a wooden scratch plow that could be pulled by man or draft animal; the fourth was ushered in by forked plows, usually with metal tips (seventh and eighth centuries). These stages were followed (after the tenth century) by a fifth, no longer associated with slash-and-burn tillage, that involved "plow agriculture" on regularly tilled fields. Some form of crop rotation (two-field or three-field) became common.

Under the three-field system a given area of land was divided into three plots. In one season the first plot or field lay fallow, the second was planted with a crop like oats or rye, and the third with a crop like winter wheat. The next season the first field was planted with wheat, the second lay fallow, and the third was sown with oats or rye. In the third season the first field was planted with oats or rye, the second with wheat, and the third lay fallow. Thus a regular rotation of crops took place every three seasons, preventing or retarding the soil exhaustion that occurred when a single crop was raised year after year, intensively, in the same field. Besides varying the types of planted crops, the three-field system, by keeping two-thirds of the total land in production, made possible a greater annual yield than the two-field system, where only half the land was under cultivation at any given time.

The chief implements in Hensel's fifth stage were light and heavy plows. Employed earlier on the estates of large landholders, the heavy plow *(plug)* was in general use among the West Slavs by the twelfth century. There has been controversy over its origins, but the consensus is now that it was introduced to the Slavs by the Germans; the very term *plug* appears to derive from the German *Pflug*.

The advent of this heavy plow, drawn by two or more draft animals, marked an important step forward for Slavic agriculture, and production increased dramatically with its use. The *plug* differed from the light plow *(ralo, sokha)* in that it had two

AGRICULTURE AND NUTRITION

front wheels and a colter to cut the sward ahead of the plowshare, which furrowed the soil, thus making it easier for the plowshare to pass through. The larger, heavier plowshare was placed so that it not only opened up the earth but also turned it over, aided by an attached moldboard. Around 1300 in Bohemia, and later elsewhere, the plowshare evolved to acquire an asymmetrical shape, and the moldboard was no longer needed.

With such a plow, deep furrows could be easily laid. Turning up the earth aerated the soil, improved water retention, and made mineral nutrients more accessible to the plants. It also destroyed the habitats of insects and other pests, and it buried many weeds so far down that they could not germinate, while permitting plant roots to grow deep rather than broad, thus enabling more plants to occupy a given space.

The Slavs continued to use other types of equipment, sometimes with improved design, such as iron-tipped harrows. They harvested cereal grains and cut cattle fodder with sickles and scythes similar to those of our day. Slav women did much of this work. The sickle preceded the scythe; the larger scythe was harder to wield, but with it less grain fell off to be lost during the reaping.

Milling equipment also got bigger and better. Apparently the Slavs had hand-operated mills (querns) in the early Middle Ages and larger mills, driven by animals, but of unknown design, by the ninth century. By the twelfth century at the latest, West Slavs had water-driven mills. The first reference to a windmill (based on a West European model) dates from 1325.

The earliest fertilizer had been ash, common in slash-and-burn tillage. Later the West Slavs learned the value of organic (animal) fertilizer. Poles had begun to apply manure, often mixed with straw, in the early Middle Ages; some of their fellow Slavs remained unaware of its benefits for centuries to come. By the late medieval era all Slavs had learned the value of enriching the land with manure from domestic animals in enclosures. Chemical fertilizers of the type used today were, of course, unknown.

The West Slavs, particularly the Poles, were blessed with an abundance of rich soil, and by the Middle Ages grain-raising had become an important occupation. Their pagan religious rites were partly based on agricultural cycles. Archaeologists have discovered threshing flails dating from the fifth century, although we cannot say how grain was cleansed of chaff at that time.

Millet, an Oriental contribution to the European diet, was universally popular, from the Danube delta to north China. Wheat and barley (originally from East Asia and North Africa) were also important crops. The Slavs also raised oats and rye (from Persia and Asia Minor), buckwheat, legumes (especially peas and lentils), flax, and hemp. Organized fruit-growing was introduced from Rome, via German intermediaries, in the eleventh and twelfth centuries; and the need for wine in the Christian liturgy led to the planting of vineyards east of the Elbe.

From earliest times Slavs had fished, hunted with traps and bows and arrows, and raised livestock. Falconry, learned from the Orient, was largely an aristocratic pastime. Slavs have always been famous for their honey and wax; in the medieval period they obtained these products primarily from the forest or raised bees in tree-trunk hives. More modern techniques of apiculture were not needed.

During much of the medieval period, animal husbandry was far less important in the Slav economy than hunting and crop raising, but it came to play an increasingly significant role; and as more domestic animals were raised, more natural fertilizer became available. Improved harnesses and connecting gear enabled the Slavs to make better use of some livestock as draft animals. When wool became a valuable trade item, sheep-raising increased to the point where grain-growing lost its dominance in the economy of certain regions.

Slavs were newcomers to the Balkans in the early Middle Ages. It is difficult to make general statements valid for all sections of that demographic crazy quilt, where some lived mainly by agriculture while others herded sheep and bred horses. Some areas of the Balkans had fine soil (but locust plagues could cause major crop failures, as in Bulgaria in 927); other regions were rocky and mountainous. In some areas the temperature was mild, in others it could become very cold—and so on.

Still, South Slavs shared some features with their western and eastern brothers. Balkan Slavs had also been engaged in slash-and-burn tillage at the beginning of the medieval era, and they began making the transition to plows with iron shares at about the same time as the West Slavs (eighth and ninth centuries). By the tenth century they may well have adopted the light plow *(ralo)* with a "foot" to throw aside the sod. If the West Slavs owed much to the Romans and Germans, the South Slavs picked up innovations from the East Roman (Byzantine) Empire and sometimes earlier than the other Slavs: although

AGRICULTURE AND NUTRITION

the West Slavs learned fruit-growing from the Germans in the eleventh and twelfth centuries, the Balkan Slavs were already planting vineyards (to meet liturgical needs) by the eighth and ninth centuries.

But information on early Balkan agriculture remains woefully sparse. Historians suspect that the so-called Farmer's Law, thought by some to reflect Slavic norms, was actually a Greek compilation for Greek villages. Its Slavic translation probably dates from the tenth century and suggests Byzantine influence on the Balkan Slavs rather than the other way around.

We possess only fragmentary sources for East Slavic agriculture in the early Middle Ages, but we know that then, as now, farming conditions were far from ideal throughout much of their vast homeland. Many areas lay too far north or had poor soil; even the fertile "black earth" (*chernozem*) regions of the south often lacked sufficient rainfall. There were years of drought and (in the north) years of flood or early frost. Locusts periodically ravaged the land. As a result of these natural disasters (as well as the devastations of war) Old Rus chronicles abound with accounts of crop failure and famine.

We also know now that East Slavs engaged in agriculture throughout the medieval period. A few decades ago some historians still believed that the East Slavic population had been highly mobile in the early Middle Ages, engaging more in hunting and fishing than in farming; few hold this view today. Archaeological findings such as large cemeteries in present-day Ukraine have shown that many East Slavs lived in settled farming communities, and medieval Russian law (the eleventh-century *russkaya pravda*) mentions fields with definite boundaries and enclosures. So it seems that farming, hunting, fishing, and forest industry all coexisted in Kievan Rus from the beginnings of its recorded history.

Kievan Russians also traded on a large scale. In fact, some historians formerly insisted that most Kievans supported themselves by trade. This theory too has given way to evidence that by far the greatest number of Kievans were engaged in agriculture, with trade an upper-class activity practiced largely by the rulers and the aristocracy, along with some professional, or "full-time," merchants.

East Slavic farming was undeniably primitive, in both its tools and its methods of tillage. Yet this agriculture was less backward in some areas than in others. The most primitive farming took place in the north, where the population was relatively sparse and the temperature often frigid. There even the soil differed: the north's sandy, loamy podzols lent themselves less readily to agriculture than did the south's black earth. Much of the north, furthermore, lay in a forest zone, which provided a less favorable setting for agriculture. It was a region where slash-and-burn methods (*podseka* or *podsechnoe zemledelie*) were widely used. Preplow agriculture, carried on without draft animals, began to give way to plow agriculture, using horses or oxen as draft animals, by the tenth century.

Early crops in the north included millet, wheat, vetch, various beans, and peas. Grain crops were harvested with sickles and the grains ground by manually operated querns. In addition to raising crops, the population of North Russia had early learned to hunt, fish, and raise livestock. The forests were full of elk, bear, and hare; the rivers and lakes teemed with fish. Although hunting was more important in the north than in the south, archaeological digs have turned up twice as many bones of domestic livestock as of wild animals in the north, suggesting that livestock breeding played a greater role than hunting in the economy.

Agriculture was somewhat more advanced in the south. Farmers used a two-field system of tillage, whereby each field lay fallow in alternate years. Apparently the three-field system did not come into use in Russia until the fifteenth century, long after the Kievan era, as did the application of manure as fertilizer.

Farm tools included both the hoe plow or light plow *(ralo, sokha)* and the heavy plow *(plug)*. Unfortunately many small farmers could not afford the heavy plows or the horses and oxen to pull them. The ax, sickle, and scythe were widely used; by the twelfth century, Kievan Rus had water mills as well, but no windmills.

Farmers raised a wide variety of field crops: oats, wheat, millet, rye, buckwheat, five types of flax, poppies, and hemp. Archaeologists have unearthed many spades and shovels used by Kievans in gardening. The gardens produced cabbage, beans, malt, onions, garlic, and turnips, which were as essential to the Kievan diet as potatoes later became to the imperial Russian fare. Apples and cherries grew in the orchards, and grapes were raised in the Crimea.

Throughout the medieval era, Russia's urban population also engaged in agriculture. Although for townfolk it was a secondary occupation, many managed to feed themselves from their gardens and orchards, even producing surpluses, sold in the marketplace, in good years.

AGRICULTURE AND NUTRITION

Kievans hunted not only for food but for amusement; indeed the word for "hunting" *(okhota)* also meant "cheer," "goodwill," and "recreation." Hunting with falcons was a princely pastime. The forests abounded with elk, lynx, aurochs, bear, wild boar, and hare, as well as beaver, sable, and fox, whose furs were prized as items of trade or tribute. For all this, it seems that the meat that Kievans consumed came mostly from domesticated animals. Sturgeon, pike, carp, bream, and herring were plentiful; and the consumption of fish increased with the spread of Christianity and fasting days. Beekeeping remained a forest industry for the most part, with bees kept in trees rather than man-made hives. Often mentioned as a trade item, honey was collected by "tree-climbers" *(drevolaztsy)* and consumed in its natural state or fermented into mead.

Two major events of the tenth century—the unification of the East Slavic tribes under the Rurik dynasty (whose princes originally came from Scandinavia) and Russia's official conversion to Orthodox (Byzantine) Christianity in 988—had profound influences on the socioeconomic aspects of Kievan agriculture. One of the reasons for the rapid expansion of Christianity, incidentally, was the resourceful way in which it "adopted and adapted" certain East Slavic agricultural festivals and deities.

The changes did not occur at once, of course. Although the eleventh century saw three major groups of private landholders emerge (the princes of the ruling house, their boyar retainers, and the church), most land still belonged to peasant communes (for a survey of the controversy over communes, see Blum, *Lord and Peasant*). Still, the subjugation of Russia's peasantry definitely began at this time. Even at this early date (eleventh and twelfth centuries) the large landholders enjoyed certain advantages: they could afford to use more draft animals to pull heavy plows, for example, whereas a common peasant was fortunate to own a horse and could do little more than scratch at the earth with his wooden *sokha* or *ralo.* If some of the large landholders were using fertilizer, the ordinary peasants were not. Soon the major landholders had slaves, peons, and indigent *smerdy* (whose precise status remains controversial) working their estates.

The Russian church, unlike its West European counterparts, tolerated slavery for Christians, with the result that some of the slaves who worked for private landholders (monasteries as well as princes and boyars) were native Kievans. A debate has long raged over "feudalism" in Russia, but one thing seems certain: Kievan retainers (as opposed to their West European counterparts) owned their estates outright and did not have to give them up if they left their princes' service.

Russia suffered a great calamity in the thirteenth century when it was conquered by the Mongols (Tatars). Kiev, the capital, fell in December 1240. Its population was massacred and the city so thoroughly destroyed that a foreigner traveling through the site declared it full of skulls and bones; only 200 dwellings remained, and the inhabitants had become enslaved. Many other areas shared Kiev's fate.

Although George Vernadsky claims that agriculture suffered less from the Mongol conquest than did the industrial crafts, there is no question about the invasion's initial impact on the peasantry. Throughout the devastated countryside Russian peasants fled, died, or were captured. Mongol-Tatar raids recurred throughout the fourteenth and fifteenth centuries, and the Asiatic overlords through their vassals, the Russian princes, imposed heavy burdens of tribute and obligatory services on the agricultural population. This terrible era of the "Tatar yoke," which did not officially end until 1480, brought depopulation and severe economic depression to Russia; cities declined and many rural communities were abandoned. Recovery came slowly.

Under the circumstances it is hardly surprising that systems of tillage made little progress—yet some progress did take place, especially toward the end of this period. Agricultural tools improved gradually, especially in areas of the northwest such as the Novgorod region, that had been spared from direct Tatar conquest. The heavy plow *(plug),* drawn by horses or oxen, came into greater use; it did not replace the light plow *(sokha, ralo),* but the light plow underwent improvement, with larger and heavier plowshares. Methods of milling with water-driven mills, threshing, and storage were all refined. Agriculture remained the dominant branch of the Russian economy, with rye, wheat, millet, oats, and barley the prime crops. With the gradual recovery, gardens and orchards regained their importance as sources of vegetables (turnips, cabbage, beets, legumes) and fruits (apples, plums, cherries, various berries).

Livestock included cows, sheep, rams, and many kinds of horses although there were few thoroughbreds. Harnesses and horseshoes were essentially of the types used in later centuries as well. The Russians also raised pigs and goats (more of the former than the latter). Fishing, hunting, beekeeping, and other

AGRICULTURE AND NUTRITION

forest industries all prospered again after the initial decades of Tatar conquest.

A major problem in medieval Russian agriculture had been the exhaustion of soil through intensive cultivation. At some point during the Mongol rule this problem began to be solved through the increased use of organic fertilizer *(unavazhivanie)* and wider adoption of the three-field system of crop rotation.

There was plenty of land during the era of the Tatar yoke, and anyone—even a slave—could own it. But some landholders did better than others. Thanks to the Mongol policy of religious tolerance, and to their practice of granting extensive immunities to the church, monasteries prospered almost from the outset. Clashes occurred between monasteries and communal peasants, some of whose lands had been appropriated by monasteries.

Secular seigniors, even those who were princes, often fared less well. After the Mongol conquest much of Russia had split into appanages or "patrimonial principalities" *(udely),* all subservient to their Asiatic overlords and each largely dependent on its own resources. Foreign trade had declined precipitously even before the Mongol invasion, thanks in part to the Crusaders' capture of Constantinople in 1204. The commercial city republics of Novgorod and Pskov continued to engage in trade with the West, but most principalities now had few contacts with the outside world.

Trade among the various principalities also shrank. In the resulting economic stagnation, landholders strove for self-sufficiency; agricultural production went largely to meet the landlords' own needs. The situation gradually improved in the fourteenth century, but one may speak of an economic depression that continued until the fifteenth century. Russia had no rule of primogeniture in land inheritance, and the lack of such a rule affected the system of land tenure profoundly. Many large estates were subdivided into ever smaller shares with each generation, until eventually some descendants got no land at all. Blum speaks of "poverty-stricken royalty" among princely houses whose patrimonies had dwindled in this fashion.

The burden of Russia's slow recovery fell on its agricultural population. Communal peasants on "black lands" (those not held by private seigniors) paid quitrent to the ruling prince and performed services for him. A total sum of dues and obligatory services (carting, post-station and relay maintenance, building and upkeep of roads and fortifications) was levied on the commune as an entity; the members were collectively responsible for the total amount, although individual assessments and work assignments varied according to the circumstances.

In 1500 perhaps one-half, perhaps only one-third of Russia's arable land still qualified as "black," but each ruling prince had always regarded "black" lands as his patrimony, parcels of which he could grant to whomever he pleased, either as an alodial "ancestral" estate *(votchina)* or, by the fifteenth century, as a "service tenure estate" or benefice (*pomestie,* a life estate that the grantee held in return for service to the prince). Peasants on formerly black lands now became seignorial peasants. Unless specifically exempted (usually by princely immunity charter), they had to continue paying dues and rendering services to the prince as well as to their new "private" landlord.

Free seignorial peasants, those who had not fallen into slavery or debt servitude, theoretically retained the right to move from one principality (or locality within the principality) to another. Quite a few took advantage of this right, wandering about in search of better living and working conditions. For the landlord, whether a great monastery or a humble *pomestie* holder, the departure of too many peasants naturally brought economic loss, and the peasants' freedom of movement began to be restricted. Early portents of serfdom appeared—"binding" the tiller to the land he cultivated and subjecting him to the direct jurisdiction of his seignior, rather than to that of the crown or "state." There were local decrees prohibiting peasants from moving except at certain times of the year. Around 1460 Muscovite Grand Prince Basil II issued charters to the Trinity Sergius Monastery, by which that monastery's peasants were temporarily forbidden from leaving at any time of the year. The 1497 law code *(sudebnik)* restricted peasant transfer nationwide, to one annual period in November.

Throughout most of the fourteenth and fifteenth centuries the princes had granted *pomestie* estates from their own patrimonies; not until the end of the medieval period did rulers like Ivan III of Moscow bestow confiscated patrimonies as *pomestie* estates to favored grantees. By then Moscow had reunited much of Russia under its rule; the same Ivan III overthrew the Tatar yoke in convincing fashion (1480). Grantees of *pomestie* estates, which varied from 300 to 800 acres in the late fifteenth century, were known as *pomeshchiki.* They came from all levels of Russian society, but most had relatively humble

AGRICULTURE AND NUTRITION

backgrounds. Many were members of the lesser nobility, but even slaves could become *pomeshchiki* if they rendered useful service to the crown in that capacity. When a *pomeshchik* died or otherwise left his royal patron's service, the estate reverted to the crown, at least in the early decades. The symbiotic relationship between the grand prince/tsar and his *pomeschiki* is obvious.

As the *pomestie* estates increased, the old, hereditary *votchina* estates declined, partly through subdivision among heirs and partly through the *votchina*-holders' *(votchinniki)* practice of giving land to monasteries in return for prayers for the donors' souls. The time was coming when *votchina*-holders would have to turn to the Muscovite grand prince/tsar for help; they too would receive estates contingent upon service to Moscow. In the seventeenth and eighteenth centuries the distinction between hereditary *votchina* and service-tenure *pomestie* would disappear: *all* landholders would have to serve the crown if they wished to retain their estates. But those developments lie beyond our time frame, as does the related process of "full enserfment" of all seignorial peasants, formally completed in 1649.

Peasants made up the majority of the population in all Slav countries, and their lot grew worse by the end of the Middle Ages. While serfdom declined in Western Europe, it spread rapidly east of the Elbe (its progress is harder to measure in the Balkans).

Slav peasants had originally considered the land their own, held by the commune, family, or individual farmer. But conditions of land tenure changed with the emergence of princely power: the Rurik dynasty in Russia (ninth century), the Piasts in Poland (tenth century), and the Přemyslids in Bohemia and Moravia (tenth and eleventh centuries). Thus, halfway through the medieval period, the various Slav countries found themselves ruled by monarchs who regarded the land as their property, which they could freely grant to loyal retainers and, after Christianization, to churches and monasteries. Three major groups of landholders now emerged: the princely house, the royal retainers or boyars, and the ecclesiastical grantees.

The spread of serfdom among the Slavs at the same time as it was declining in Western Europe apparently resulted from the fact that the Slavic landed nobility (aristocrats and petty gentry) was able to have its way, sometimes with the monarch's backing (as in Russia or Serbia) and sometimes independently of the monarch (as in Poland or Bosnia). Slavic landholders acquired enormous political influence, unchecked by a strong bourgeoisie such as existed in Western Europe. They acquired jurisdiction over the peasants living on their estates and proceeded to reduce them to a position of almost total dependence.

Meanwhile, as we have seen in the case of Russia, more and more free peasants fell under the power of private seigniors as the sovereign made grants of "his" land to boyars, *pomeschiki,* and monasteries. Members of the petty gentry, with modest estates, had to demand more of their peasants just to survive. Even the large seigniors, as they began producing more grain for the market, drove their peasants harder and harder. While cities continued to grow in the West, those in the East declined, thanks to antiurban policies of the great nobility. Russian cities failed to develop an influential bourgeoisie because trade remained in the hands of the monarch, the landholders, and associations of traveling merchants.

Peasants on state lands in countries like Poland or Russia paid taxes in cash or in kind and performed obligatory services such as maintenance of roads and bridges, postal and transport duties, and public safety. When they fell under the jurisdiction of a private seignior, they owed their new lord rent and corvée. Although some lords held "immunity grants" from the monarch (thus reducing the taxes due from that lord's peasants), and although other lords exempted newcomer peasants from fiscal obligations for limited periods, the heavy burden of manorial and state imposts and duties grew constantly heavier. Peasants were often held collectively responsible for a set quota of payments and services; if some fell behind, their fellows had to make up the difference.

The peasants sometimes responded violently (many Czech peasants, for example, joined the Hussites and fought beside them), but their reactions tended more often to be sporadic, poorly organized, and ineffective. Individual peasants most frequently sought to better their lot by running away. This led to laws restricting their mobility or prohibiting their departure—and to measures for recovering runaways. By 1500 the process was well under way.

BIBLIOGRAPHY

Walter Ashburner, "The Farmer's Law," in *Journal of Hellenic Studies,* 30 (1910); Jerome Blum, *Lord and Peasant in Russia from the Ninth to the Nineteenth Century* (1961); and "The Rise of Serfdom in Eastern Europe," in *American Historical Review,* 62 (1957); *The Cambridge Economic History of Europe,* vol. II, *The Agrarian Life of the Middle Ages,* 2nd ed. (1966), 57–62, 449–547; N. A.

 AGRICULTURE AND NUTRITION

Gorskaya, "Zemledelie i skotovodstvo," in *Ocherki russkoy kultury XVI veka,* pt. 1 (1977); A. D. Gorsky, "Selskoe khozyaystvo i promysly," in *Ocherki russkoy kultury XIII–XV vekov,* pt. 1 (1969); Witold Hensel, *Die Slawen im frühen Mittelalter; ihre materielle Kultur* (1965); Lubor Niederle, *Manuel de l'antiquité slave,* II (1926); Marc Szeftel, "Aspects of Feudalism in Russian History," in Rushton Coulborn, ed., *Feudalism in History* (1956); Petr Nikolaevich Tretyakov, "Selskoe khozyaystvo i promysly," in *Istoria kultury drevney Rusi* (1951).

H. W. DEWEY

V

THE ISLAMIC WORLD. In the Islamic world of the Middle Ages agriculture embraced two distinct activities, the growing of crops and the raising of animals. The former was concentrated on areas of better soil where rainfall was sufficient (generally over 250 or 300 mm., or 10–12 in.) or irrigation could be provided; while the latter prevailed in steppe lands, deserts, mountains, and on rocky or poor soils.

There appears to have been relatively little integration of the two types of agricultural activity. Sedentary farmers who grew crops kept few or no large animals, often hiring draft animals for plowing or cartage, and they usually did not sell stubble or fodder to herdsmen. Similarly, pastoralists planted few crops, depending almost entirely on natural pasture lands for the feeding of their animals. In consequence, two distinct ways of life developed, each with its social and political systems, its culture and values, and with markedly different diets. They competed in many spheres throughout the Middle Ages and later. At the margins they competed for land, and the frontier between crop land and pasture land shifted back and forth as one activity or the other was favored by changes in rulers, laws, institutions, security, demography, technology, soil cover, and perhaps climate.

As a general rule the early centuries of Islam (until around 950 or 1000 in most places, later in a few regions) saw an extension of sedentary agriculture and a retreat of pastoralism. Perhaps from an instinctive bias and perhaps in order to increase revenues from the land tax, the Prophet and the early rulers seem to have favored city life and settled agricultural communities. The legal systems that they developed strongly supported private rather than collective control of land (giving full ownership to those who reclaimed unused lands), while preferential rates of taxation encouraged both the intensification of tillage and its spread onto new lands. The construction, repair, and improvement of irrigation systems also led to the cultivation of lands that had earlier been grazed, as did an apparent rise in rural population and the growth of many large cities, each needing to be fed from a hinterland. New crops such as sorghum and hard wheat allowed the penetration of farming into regions previously thought to be too dry or too infertile, while other new crops—sugarcane, rice, colocasia, and coconut palms—could be grown on lands too saline for the crops of antiquity.

Grazing was thus pushed back onto relatively arid lands. Although the sources throw little light on the pastoral economies that evolved, they do allow us to glimpse peoples in many regions who herded large flocks of sheep, goats, camels, horses, and cattle. These produced meat, milk, hair, and hides for the use of the pastoral peoples themselves and for sale to villagers and city dwellers. Wool and hides were raw materials for the large and growing textile and leather industries that appeared in many parts of the Islamic world; and they were exported to Europe in raw, semiprocessed, or fully finished form. The lives of pastoral peoples were dominated by the need to find adequate pasture for their animals, a problem that became acute in the dry summer season and in drought years. Generally they were forced to slaughter or sell large numbers of animals in the spring and to move the remainder long distances—either in a highly organized transhumance or in less regular migrations—in search of grazing lands. Overgrazing was to some extent prevented by an institution known as the *ḥimā,* which gave tribes in some regions collective rights over defined pasture lands. But this appears not to have been fully effective. High and growing demand for animal products from urban consumers and villagers—and perhaps from the pastoralists themselves—seems to have led to excessive use of pasture lands, which probably had especially serious consequences in years of low rainfall. These lands deteriorated, if they were not altogether destroyed, as the vegetative cover was damaged and soil was eroded by wind and rain. The pressure of pastoral peoples to move onto cultivated lands, either as settlers or as grazers, may thus have grown.

Although crops were grown in regions with higher rainfall or with artificial irrigation, the choice of crops and intensity of land use were primarily limited by the availability of water; secondary constraints were imposed by soil quality and tempera-

AGRICULTURE AND NUTRITION

ture of soil and air. The great majority of crop lands in the medieval Islamic world lay in the Mediterranean climate zone, which is characterized by low and variable rainfall confined almost exclusively to the winter months. Today the average rainfall of these areas typically ranges between 300 and 600 mm. (12–24 in.), although a few areas receive up to 1,000 mm. (40 in.) or as little as 200 mm. (8 in.). Where rainfall is lower it is also more variable. (The principal exceptions were the crop lands in the southern and southeastern parts of the Arabian peninsula and in southwestern Iran, which received monsoon rains in summer.)

To meet the challenge of low rainfall, farmers resorted to a number of expedients: choice of crops that require little water, some of which (such as fig and olive trees) have extensive root systems and low rates of transpiration; frequent plowing with the ard or "Mediterranean plow," which by crumbling the surface soil increased the penetration of rainfall and limited evaporation; frequent fallowing, which allowed soil moisture to accumulate in winter months; terracing on hillsides, which also served to reduce erosion; and artificial irrigation of various kinds.

The extension and improvement of irrigation, apparent almost everywhere in the early Islamic world, promoted both the extension of tillage and its intensification. Although the lands that the Arabs conquered had irrigation systems of great antiquity, most of these were in disrepair at the time of the conquests and most—even when operating at full capacity—watered land only during one part of the year.

By the end of the eighth century there is much evidence of the repair and extension of old irrigation systems and the construction of new ones. Through the diffusion of irrigation technology, much of it ancient in one region or another but some of it seemingly new, farmers had at their disposal a wide range of methods for capturing, storing, lifting, channeling, and spreading water. These could be combined in many ways, some of them new, to put more water on the land and to prolong the season of irrigation—in some cases to make it yearlong. Among the devices diffused in this period were the *qanāt,* an underground canal that captured groundwater and carried it by gravity flow over long distances; apparently new types of storage dams and older types of diversion and spreading dams; the *nā*ᶜ*ūra* or noria, a wheel powered by the currents of rivers or canals, which could lift water great distances in boxes, buckets, or pots; and similar animal-powered devices that raised water out of rivers, canals, cisterns, or wells.

By the end of the tenth century most regions had irrigation systems that took nearly full advantage of the available water. These ranged from low dams, which spread flash floods onto cropland once or twice in a season, to elaborate systems in the larger river valleys, which provided heavy irrigation during much or all of the year.

Wider and more intensive cultivation was also promoted by the judicious use of the crops of antiquity and their combination with many new crops—mostly of eastern origin—that were diffused across the Islamic world in the centuries following the Arab conquests. The principal crops grown by the ancients were permanent crops such as olives, figs, and grapes (the last of which declined in importance because of the Muslim prohibition of wine); and annual crops, virtually all grown in the winter months, including cereals (emmer, bread wheat, and millet), legumes (chick-peas, lentils, faba beans, and peas), and a small number of fruits and vegetables. Among the new crops introduced into early Islamic agriculture were other cereals that were to become of great importance (hard wheat, sorghum, and rice); a large number of fruits and vegetables (including sour oranges, lemons, limes, grapefruits, bananas, plantains, watermelons, colocasia, artichokes, spinach, and eggplants); sugarcane, which replaced honey as the main sweetener; cotton, which became the principal fiber crop in most of the Islamic world; and various other industrial crops used as sources of dyes, condiments, perfumes, medicines, and so on. As pointed out above, some of the new crops could be grown in difficult conditions and therefore encouraged the extension of farming into new areas.

Annual crops, new and old, could be combined with one another to obtain a great variety of rotations suitable for a wide range of conditions. These allowed the abandonment of winter fallowing in many regions and the introduction of multiple-cropping where moisture permitted. Particularly important in this intensification of land use were new summer crops—sorghum, rice, watermelons, colocasia, eggplants, and cotton—which opened up a virtually new agricultural season. Although some required artificial irrigation, sorghum, cotton, watermelons, and eggplants could be grown with only the residue of winter rains.

Using land of all categories—good and bad, irrigated and unirrigated—to the full or nearly full potential depleted the soil of its nutrients and, in the

AGRICULTURE AND NUTRITION

case of unirrigated land, of its moisture; such heavy tillage could continue over the years with satisfactory results only if strenuous efforts were made to maintain the productivity of the soil. The problem was all the more acute since the sedentary farmers kept few animals and what manure they could get was often used for fuel.

Islamic manuals of farming advise the careful application of almost every available kind of animal manure, each having its own virtues and uses. Night soil (human excrement) was also collected almost everywhere and put on crops. Other animal products recommended for certain soils included blood, urine, and powdered bones, horns, and ivory. Vegetable matter of many kinds was applied, such as sediment from olive oil, lees, straw, husks, leaves, rags, shavings, and ashes. Mineral matter also had its role: the manuals recommended adding different kinds of soil, gravel, dust, chalk, marl, lime, crushed bricks, and broken tiles. They also urged much plowing (normal and occasionally deeper plowing), hoeing, digging, and harrowing. Finally, the right choice of rotations was important, since it was recognized that crops depleted the soil to different degrees, at different levels, and of different nutrients; and it was known that legumes—much emphasized in intensive rotations—restored some fertility to the soil.

Despite these measures it seems likely that by the tenth or eleventh centuries agriculture in many parts of the Islamic world was overdeveloped, making excessive use of too much land. Overcultivated dry lands were probably eroded by winds; some wetter lands were mined of their fertility or eroded by rain; and some irrigated lands, especially those that were poorly drained, became saline. Whatever the explanation, by the eleventh century a period of prolonged agricultural decline seems to have begun in many regions—although the agriculture of Egypt and many parts of Muslim Spain remained prosperous until the later Middle Ages.

Decline proceeded at different rates in different places and was at times interrupted or temporarily reversed. It appears to have been particularly rapid following the invasions of various (mostly non-Arab) peoples: the Seljuks, Crusaders, Ayyubids, Mongols, and Ottomans in the East, and the Banū Hilāl, Almoravids, Almohads, Normans, and the conquistadores of Spain in the West. The invasions themselves often damaged irrigation works and caused peasants, especially in frontier regions, to take flight; and the conquerors, familiar with agricultural systems that made less intensive use of land, brought with them attitudes, laws, and institutions less favorable to the kind of agriculture that the early Islamic world had created.

A decline in rural security, a shrinkage of the money economy, a falloff in trade, and plagues probably all contributed at one time or another to agricultural decay. So did new institutions that became widespread in the later Middle Ages: tax farming; immunities granted to notables and tribal groups (*muqāṭaʿa* and *īghār*); military benefices (*iqṭāʿ*), whose grantees were given far-reaching rights of tax collection; commendation of landowning and landless peasants to landowners (*taljiʿa*); and the inexorable growth of land owned in mortmain by pious foundations (*waqf*). Decline continued in many regions until the late nineteenth or twentieth century. Its visible signs were the abandonment of cultivation in some frontier regions, its deintensification elsewhere, the decay of irrigation, the spread of pastoralism, and rural depopulation.

On the modes of agricultural exploitation the sources throw only a dim light. Geographers and other travelers describe large areas of market gardens surrounding the major cities; these appear to have consisted of small irrigated farms operated by single families, producing mainly fruits and vegetables for urban markets. Elsewhere, on irrigated or unirrigated land, the size of a landholding could vary all the way from small owner-operated farms to very large and extensively farmed estates. Competition among undertakings of various sizes may have contributed to the vitality of early Islamic agriculture.

Labor for the larger farms was generally provided by sharecropping tenants on short-term contracts, although wage labor—unknown in ancient agriculture—was also common. Except perhaps in Tunisia in the eighth and ninth centuries, slave labor does not seem to have been used in Islamic agriculture. In the centuries of agricultural decline, however, smaller ownerships declined in importance as the large estates came almost everywhere to predominate. In many parts tenants saw their freedom of movement—and their incentive to produce—reduced as taxes, rents, and other exactions rose, and as they became tied to the land, its owner, or both.

The medieval Islamic world produced a considerable number of farming manuals, which—along with encyclopedic works, poems, travel accounts, and books of geography, botany and medicine—are our principal documentary sources. The earliest of these were translations of pre-Islamic works, to which new material was added in Islamic times. Two that have survived are the *Greek Book of Agriculture (Kitāb al-filāḥa al-rūmīya)* compiled by Qusṭūs, who may be the sixth-century Cassianus Bassus, and translated into Arabic by Sarjīs ibn Ḥilya; and the *Nabatean Book of Agriculture (Kitāb al-filāḥa al-nabaṭīya)*, preserving the agricultural traditions of the Nabateans of Iraq, which was compiled, translated, and enlarged by Ibn Waḥshīya at the beginning of the tenth century. At about the same time several more original works seem to have been composed, but these have not survived. From a slightly later period we have a large number of treatises written in Muslim Spain, including those by Abū al-Qāsim al-Zahrāwī (= Albucasis, *d.* 1010), Abū al-Khair (*fl.* eleventh century), Ibn Wāfid (= Abenguefith, *ca.* 1007–1074), Ibn Ḥajjāj (wrote 1073), Ibn Baṣṣāl (*d.* 1105), al-Ṭighnarī (*fl.* eleventh–twelfth century), and Ibn al-ᶜAwwām (*fl.* twelfth century), the last of whom wrote what must be regarded as the summa of the Hispano-Muslim agricultural school. In the thirteenth and later centuries other important agricultural works were written in Egypt, Persia, and the Yemen. Although the Arab writers were often familiar with the writings of the ancients, they were critical of them—expurgating from the *Nabatean Book of Agriculture,* for instance, much of its religion, magic, and superstition—and frequently relying on their own experience and observation. In their knowledge of soils, waters, fertilizers, and plants they surpassed—sometimes to a great extent—the writers of classical Greece and Rome.

BIBLIOGRAPHY

Sources. Kitāb al-filāḥa al-nabaṭīya, of which manuscripts exist in London, Oxford, Paris, Leyden, Istanbul, etc., and of which an edition, edited by T. Fahd, will be published in three volumes over three years in the E. J. W. Gibb Memorial series, beginning in the summer of 1982; *Kitāb al-filāḥa al-rūmīya* (1876); "La traducción castellana del 'Tratado de agricultura' de Ibn Wāfid," José M. Millás Vallicrosa, ed., in *Al-Andalus,* 8 (1943); "Un capítulo de la obra agrónomica de Ibn Hajjāj," José M. Millás Vallicrosa and Leonor Martínez Martín, eds., in *Tamuda,* 6 (1958); Ibn Baṣṣāl, *Libro de agricultura,* José M. Millás Vallicrosa and Mohamed Aziman, eds. and trans. (1955); Ibn al-ᶜAwwām, *Kitāb al-filāḥa,* José A. Banqueri, ed. (1802), also exists in a French translation by Jean-Jacques Clément-Mullet, 2 vols. (1864–1867).

Studies. Articles by A. K. S. Lambton, I. Lapidus, A. M. Morony, H. Rabie, M. Talbi, and Andrew M. Watson in Abraham Udovitch, ed., *The Islamic Middle East, 700–1900: Studies in Economic and Social History* (1981); articles by R. Arié, L. Bolens, R. C. Cooper, T. Fahd, and A. K. S. Lambton in Bertold Spuler, ed., *Geschichte der islamischen Länder,* Handbuch der Orientalistik Part I, 6, (1977); Lucie Bolens, *Les méthodes culturales au moyen-âge d'après les traités d'agronomie andalous: traditions et techniques* (1974); Claude Cahen, "Notes pour une histoire de l'agriculture dans les pays musulmans médiévaux," in *Journal of the Economic and Social History of the Orient,* **14** (1971); Thomas F. Glick, *Irrigation and Society in Medieval Valencia* (1970); Xavier de Planhol, *Les fondements géographiques de l'histoire de l'Islam* (1968); Andrew M. Watson, "The Arab Agricultural Revolution and Its Diffusion, 700–1100," in *Journal of Economic History,* **34** (1974); and *Agricultural Innovation in the Early Islamic World: The Diffusion of Crops and Farming Techniques* (1982).

ANDREW M. WATSON

AḤMAD MŪSĀ is mentioned in an essay on Persian painting written in 1544 as a leading painter of fourteenth-century Iran. The essay's author, a painter named Dūst Muḥammad, credits Aḥmad Mūsā with creation of the type of painting still in vogue during the sixteenth century. The essay serves as preface to an album of paintings now in the Topkapi Palace Museum Library, Istanbul, that contains several attributed to Aḥmad Mūsā. According to Dūst Muḥammad, Aḥmad Mūsā was active during the reign of the Īlkhān ruler Abū Sa ᶜid (1317–1335) and illustrated several manuscripts for him, including two texts glorifying the Mongols—the *Chingiz-nama* and the *Abu Sa ᶜid-nama*—as well as copies of *Kalīla u Dimna* and a *Mi ᶜraj-nama.* The album to which Dūst Muḥammad's essay is attached contains ten paintings illustrating the *mi ᶜrāj* (ascension) of the Prophet Muḥammad, and four of these are labeled as the work of Aḥmad Mūsā. It is probable that Dūst Muḥammad was responsible for this identification.

Using the information given by Dūst Muḥammad, modern scholars have attributed to Aḥmad Mūsā such important anonymous fourteenth-century paintings as a fragmentary copy of *Kalila u Dimna* now mounted in an album belonging to the Istanbul University Library and a dispersed *Shāhnāma* manuscript often designated as the "Demotte *Shāhnāma*" after a former owner. In the absence of any further documentary evidence, these attributions remain hypothetical.

BIBLIOGRAPHY

Laurence Binyon, J. V. S. Wilkinson, and Basil Gray, *Persian Miniature Painting* (1933), 139, 184; and E. Schroeder, "Ahmad Musa and Shams al-Dīn: A Review of Fourteenth Century Painting," in *Ars Islamica,* 6 (1939).

P. SOUCEK

[See also **Manuscript Illumination, Byzantine, Islam; Shāhnāma/Book of the King.**]

AID (FEUDAL). See **Feudalism.**

ÂIDÂN. See **Âedán.**

AIDAN OF LINDISFARNE (*d.* 651), monastic bishop. Most of what is known of him comes from the eighth-century *History of the English Church and People* by Bede, who says that Aidan was a monk at Iona but reports nothing of his early life. In the later Irish martyrologies he is identified as Aedan m Lugar of the Fothairt of Leinster, bishop of Scattery Island and Lindisfarne. This is probably due to a conflation of Aidan of Lindisfarne (August 31) with Aedan m Lugar, bishop of Clontarf (August 27) and another Aedan of Scattery, since Aed and the diminutive Aedan are very common names. Iona was an Irish monastery, however, and Bede certainly considered Aidan to be Irish.

Bede's account of Aidan begins with the foundation around 635 of Lindisfarne in Northumbria by Aidan and his monks. King Oswald of Northumbria had requested Iona to send a mission to his kingdom, which had relapsed into paganism after the death of King Edwin in 633. During Edwin's reign Oswald had been in exile in the Irish colony of Dal Riata (Scotland) and the Pictish kingdoms of the north. Therefore, when he became king he turned to the monks of Iona rather than to the southern Christian community in Kent. The first mission, led by Corman, was brief and unsuccessful. Upon his return to Iona, Abbot Seghine and the community chose Aidan in his stead, consecrated him a bishop, and sent him to Oswald. The king gave them land at Lindisfarne, which Aidan and his mission used as a base.

Though the youngest of Aidan's contemporaries was the oldest of Bede's, the force of Aidan's personality left such an impression that memories of him were still vivid when Bede wrote. Only Aidan's observance of the Celtic calculation of Easter marred him in Bede's eyes as an exemplary ecclesiastic. The personal example that Aidan set in Northumbria typified Irish Christianity. Though a bishop, he lived in a monastery. He had a private retreat on Farne Island, to which he retired for prayer and meditation. He traveled extensively and on foot to take advantage of any opportunity to preach or instruct, and rode only when forced by necessity. He observed a rule of fasting, prayer, and personal poverty, distributing the gifts he received to the poor or to churches and monasteries. Some of the donations were used to ransom slaves as well, many of whom were then educated and entered the church. Aidan had a part in the foundation of numerous churches and of monasteries at Lastingham, Tynemouth, Barrow, Coldingham, and Hartlepool.

A number of Aidan's pupils and protégés were important in their own right. Eata became prior of Lindisfarne and later bishop of Bernicia. Cedd and Chad, two brothers, had great success as missionaries among the Mercians and East Saxons. Hilda, abbess of Hartlepool, had returned to Northumbria from Gaul at Aidan's request. Whitby, the house she founded in 657, was the site of the famous synod in 664 and a thriving school.

In 641 King Oswald was killed in battle at Maserfelth. Northumbria briefly split into its component parts, with Oswald's brother Oswy ruling in Bernicia and his cousin Oswin in Deira. Oswin and Aidan were on good terms until Oswin was assassinated at Oswy's instigation in 651. Aidan died twelve days later, on 31 August.

The Synod of Whitby in 664 officially ended the supremacy of the Celtic church in Northumbria, but the cultural influences of Aidan and the monks of Iona and Lindisfarne endured. Certainly, the flowering of Northumbria in Bede's time had its roots in Aidan's.

BIBLIOGRAPHY

George W. O. Addleshaw, *The Pastoral Structure of the Celtic Church in Northern Britain* (1973); Peter Hunter Blair, *An Introduction to Anglo-Saxon England* (1956); Nora K. Chadwick, ed., *Celt and Saxon* (1963), 323–352; Gareth Dunleavy, *Colum's Other Island* (1960); Kathleen Hughes, "Evidence for Contacts Between the Churches of the Irish and English from the Synod of Whitby to the Viking Age," in Peter Clemoes and Kathleen Hughes, eds.,

AILLY, PIERRE D'

England Before the Conquest (1971), 49–68; Henry Mayr-Harting, *The Coming of Christianity to Anglo-Saxon England* (1972); John T. McNeill, *The Celtic Churches* (1974); Margaret Pepperdene, "Bede's *Historia ecclesiastica*," in *Celtica*, 4 (1958); Charles Thomas, *Britain and Ireland in Early Christian Times, AD 400–800* (1971).

DOROTHY AFRICA

[See also **Celtic Church.**]

AILLY, PIERRE D' (Petrus de Alliaco; Cameracensis) (1350–1420) was born at Compiègne and died at Avignon. The son of a prosperous butcher, Colard Marguerite d'Ailly, he rose to prominence successively as a leading figure in Parisian academic circles, as an important and versatile contributor to the intellectual life of his day, as a vigorous proponent of churchwide reform in "head and members," and as one of the distinguished group of ecclesiastical statesmen who helped bring to an end the intractable schism that, since the disputed papal election of 1378, had divided Latin Christendom into two, and then into three, rival obediences.

D'Ailly entered the University of Paris in 1363 or 1364 as bursar at the Collège de Navarre. Clearly a student of extraordinary capacity, he was four years below the usual minimum age when, in 1381, he completed his studies and received the magisterium in theology. His entry into positions of university leadership was equally rapid. Chosen as proctor of the French nation in 1372, he was appointed rector of the Collège de Navarre twelve years later. Under his leadership, and through the pioneering efforts of Jean Gerson, Nicholas of Clémanges, and Jean de Montreuil, Navarre became the cradle of French humanism and in prestige came to rival the Sorbonne. During those years d'Ailly's prominence in academic affairs in general became equally marked, and in 1389 he was named chancellor of the University of Paris.

His entry into public life, therefore, coincided with the onset of the Great Schism. After the disputed election of 1378, and under pressure from King Charles V of France, the University of Paris had recognized the Avignon claimant, Clement VII, as pope. But after Charles's death in 1380, and with the succession to the throne of his minor son, the university shifted its position and, in 1381, advocated the summoning of a general council to end the schism. In the same year d'Ailly defended that position (the so-called *via concilii*) before the royal court and also advanced it in his *Epistola diaboli Leviathan.* It appears to have been the solution closest to his heart, for he returned to it in the years after 1403, when other solutions had failed and the obduracy of the rival claimants was becoming increasingly apparent.

During the intervening years, d'Ailly fluctuated in his attitude toward the Avignon papacy and the problem of ending the schism. In 1394, after a referendum had revealed it to be overwhelmingly the opinion of the university, he committed himself to supporting the *via cessionis*—the simultaneous abdication of the rival pontiffs—as the way most likely to succeed. This approach, adopted by the French court, was for the next few years the focus of the national ecclesiastical policy. In what proved to be an unsuccessful attempt to coerce him into abdicating, it led in 1398 to the unilateral French withdrawal of obedience from Benedict XIII, who had succeeded Clement VII at Avignon.

Though sent to the papal court at Avignon by both the university and the king, and charged with the task of securing the adoption of the *via cessionis,* d'Ailly seems to have become somewhat less than enthusiastic in his advocacy of that cause—possibly, or so his critics suggested, because of favors heaped upon him by the Avignon popes: first, a group of minor benefices (along with a dispensation to hold them in plurality), then the bishopric of Le Puy in 1395 and the more important see of Cambrai in 1397, an office he retained until Pope John XXIII made him cardinal in 1411.

Nonetheless, the years of fruitless negotiation in which he himself was deeply involved finally led him in 1408 to break with Benedict XIII and to embark on a campaign to marshal support for the attempt by dissident cardinals from both obediences to summon the general council that met finally at Pisa. Absent on a diplomatic mission for that council during the two fateful sessions that witnessed the deposition of the Roman and Avignon pontiffs and the election of their successor, Alexander V, he cannot be said to have played the prominent role at Pisa that he certainly played at the subsequent Council of Constance. There his role during the council's early sessions was clearly a dominant one. From his first sermon on 2 December 1414 to the election of Martin V in 1417, d'Ailly was involved in most of the council's great events—notably in the condemnations of John XXIII, of the propositions of Jean Petit, the apologist of tyrannicide, and of Jan Hus. At the close of the council in 1418, Martin V sent him as papal legate to Avignon, where he died.

Long after his contributions as a public figure had been forgotten, d'Ailly's numerous writings helped preserve his memory. Some 170 in number—books, tracts, letters, poems, sermons covering an astonishing variety of subjects—the bulk of them were printed in the late fifteenth and sixteenth centuries, and some reappeared in successive editions into the eighteenth century. The largest group of these writings is devoted to matters relating to the Great Schism and to ecclesiastical reform (such as *Tractatus de materia concilii generatis; Tractatus de reformatione ecclesiae*). Between this group and an impressive group of philosophical and theological works (such as *Tractatus de anima* and his commentary on Peter Lombard's *Sentences*) are works on biblical and pietistic topics and an imposing set of tracts on geography and astronomy. His theological, conciliarist, and reform treatises were the ones most often cited in subsequent centuries, but the best-known of all his writings is the highly derivative *Imago mundi,* which Christopher Columbus studied and annotated before embarking on his historic voyage.

BIBLIOGRAPHY

The standard general biographical studies of d'Ailly are P. Tschackert, *Peter von Ailli* (1877), and L. Salembier, *Le Cardinal Pierre d'Ailly* (1932). Both contain listings of d'Ailly's works, but the most recent and careful listing is P. Glorieux, "L'oeuvre littéraire de Pierre d'Ailly: Remarques et précisions," in *Mélanges de science religieuse,* 22 (1965). The principal source for his general theological and philosophical point of view is his *Quaestiones super I, III, et IV Sententiarum* (1500); and, for his reforming views in general and conciliarist views in particular, his *Propositiones utiles* and *Tractatus de ecclesiastica potestate,* in Jean Gerson, *Opera omnia,* Louis Ellies du Pin, ed., 6 vols. (1706), II, 112–113, 925–960, as well as his *Tractatus de materia concilii generalis,* in *The Political Thought of Pierre d'Ailly,* Francis Oakley, ed., (1964), App. III, pp. 244–342. A modern edition of his *Imago mundi* is *Ymago mundi de Pierre d'Ailly,* E. Buron, ed., 3 vols. (1930–1931).

The most recent of the studies devoted to particular aspects of d'Ailly's life is Alan E. Bernstein, *Pierre d'Ailly and the Blanchard Affair: University and Chancellor of Paris at the Beginning of the Great Schism* (1978).

FRANCIS OAKLEY

[See also **Paris, University of; Schism, Great.**]

AILRED OF REIEVAULX. See **Ethelred of Rievaulx.**

AIMOIN DE FLEURY (*ca.* 960–*ca.* 1010) was born at Périgord to a family of the aristocracy. He entered the monastery of Fleury at an early age. He took the habit sometime between 979 and 987, under the abbot Amalbert. As a friend and disciple of Abbo, the second successor of Amalbert, Aimoin accompanied him on his last voyage to the monastery of La Réole, though he does not seem to have witnessed his assassination. He died around 1010.

Of his copious writings, the most important are the *Historia (Gesta) Francorum,* the *Vita Abbonis,* and books II and III of the *Miracula sancti Benedicti.* The *Gesta* is dedicated to Abbo (d. 1004). It traces the history of the Franks from their origins to the accession of Pepin the Short. Compiled between 997 and 999, this history of the Franks marshals the entire Frankish tradition on behalf of the Capetian kingdom alone. It was conceived with a view toward bolstering the historical argument for the dynastic change of 987. According to R. H. Bautier, "It may well be said that true French historiography was born in the abbey of Fleury, and the credit for this is due to Aimoin."

Indeed, his method was notably innovative—a unified presentation with a single dominant theme: the historical consciousness of a Frankish nation in the making in the central part of the kingdom. In the elaboration of the story there is both genuine methodology and literary art. The sources are not transcribed literally and each passage rests upon a varied documentation brought together by the preparatory work of Abbo's disciples.

The *Historia* ends in 654. We do not know whether Aimoin was ordered to cease work or died before finishing it. Nevertheless, the *Historia* had an illustrious posterity, since it seems to have been the original source for the subsequent chronicles of St.-Denis and, consequently, for the Grand Chronicles of France.

Aimoin likewise belongs at the peak of the French literary renewal for his *Vita Abbonis,* written between 1005 and 1008 for Hervé, treasurer of St. Martin de Tours and formerly a monk of Fleury. Based on Aimoin's own recollections and on the correspondence of his master, it is a work of outstanding quality. The *Vita* is distinct from the History of the

AIRBERTACH MAC COISSE

Abbots of Fleury, and does not constitute, as some have claimed, the conclusion of that work.

And, at the end of the tenth century, Aimoin wrote a continuation of the first book of the *Miracula sancti Benedicti,* composed after 865 by Adrevald de Fleury and ending around the period of the Norman invasions. In book II, Aimoin followed a roughly chronological order, and in book III he recounts the miraculous events that occurred during the abbacy of Abbo (988–1004). Despite its disorderly composition, the work is of great interest, for the author most often deals with things he has seen himself. When this is not the case, Aimoin sometimes discusses his sources, pointing out, when relevant, the disparities between the diplomatic sources and tradition.

BIBLIOGRAPHY

See R.-H. Bautier, *L'historiographie en France aux Xe et XIe siècles (France du Nord et de l'Est),* in *La storiografia altomedioevale, 10–16 aprile 1969* (1970), pp. 793–850; A. Vidier, *L'historiographie à Saint-Benoît-sur-Loire et les Miracles de Saint Benoît* (1965). On the *Historia,* see the bibliography in *Repertorium fontium historiae medii aevi,* II (1967), pp. 158–159; and a dissertation by Christiane Le Stum, *L'"Historia Francorum" d'Aimoin de Fleury. Étude et édition critique,* summarized in *Positions et thèses de l'École Nationale des Chartes* (1976), pp. 88–93, and, more briefly, by G. Grand in *Scriptorium,* 32 (1978).

ALAIN J. STOCLET

[See also **Hagiography; Historiography**.]

AIRBERTACH MAC COISSE (*d.* 1016), master of studies at the Irish monastic school of Ros Ailithir (Rosscarbery, County Cork) in the late tenth century and subsequently *airchinnech,* or superior, of the same monastery, a position that he held until his death. In his role of teacher, the Annals of Inisfallen (990) refer to him as *fer légind,* an Irish title that replaced the Hiberno-Latin term *scriba* to designate a learned ecclesiastic and that reflects the shift of emphasis from Latin to Irish in the monastic schools, which was completed by the tenth century. Significantly, the four works attributed to Airbertach are all in Irish, although the bulk of their contents depends on Latin sources. They occur together in Bodleian MS Rawlinson B 502 (fols. 45r–46v) at the end of a long tract on the Six Ages of the World, in the following sequence:

(a) A versified geography of the ancient world based on late Classical sources, especially Pomponius Mela's *De situ orbis.* This poem of sixty-six stanzas describes the five zones into which the earth is divided; to the north temperate zone belongs the known inhabited region of the world, comprising Europe, Asia, and Africa. Another version of this poem, in sixty-eight stanzas, occurs in the twelfth-century Book of Leinster.

(b) A poem (sixty-one stanzas) on the twenty kings who ruled Jerusalem from the time of David to the Babylonian Captivity, compiled from the biblical narrative of the books of Paralipomenon and, in small part, Esdras.

(c) A poem (fifty stanzas) on the Psalms, outlining the history of their composition, the four ways of interpreting them (including a curious "second historical" interpretation) and their prophetic character, and based on the introduction to the early ninth-century *Old-Irish Treatise on the Psalter.* Stanzas 18–25 on the chronologies of the prophets Isaiah, Jeremiah, and Ezekiel are probably an interpolation; stanzas 41–44 treat of the creation of Adam; and stanzas 45–50 conclude with an incident from the apocryphal *Acts of Thomas* on whose feast day (21 December 985) the poem was composed.

(d) A versified account (twenty-five stanzas) of the Jewish victory over the Midianites, based on Numbers, chapter 31.

All of these works probably constituted basic subject matter for the curriculum taught at Airbertach's school in the late tenth century: the Psalter (the beginner's first Latin text in the Irish school system), Old Testament history and chronology, and world geography—simplified and versified to facilitate memorization.

In 1960 it was suggested that Airbertach also composed *Saltair na Rann,* a versified account of sacred history from the Creation to the Day of Judgment. Although both the subject matter and the proposed date for the *Saltair* (late tenth century) would suit Airbertach, the arguments for attributing the poem to him have not won general acceptance.

That Airbertach was a person of some consequence is shown by the account in the Annals of Inisfallen (990) of his capture by the Danes and subsequent ransoming by Brian Boru, king of Munster. Airbertach mac Coisse (or Coisi-dobráin) is not to be confused with another poet, Erard mac Coise, who is said to have lived about the same time.

BIBLIOGRAPHY

Editions of Airbertach's Poems. Poem (a): Thomas Olden, "On the Geography of Ros Ailithir," in *Proceed-*

ings of the Royal Irish Academy, 2nd ser., **2** (1884); Poem (b): Gearóid S. Mac Eoin, "A Poem by Airbertach mac Cosse," in *Ériu,* **20** (1966); Poem (c): Pádraig Ó Néill, "Airbertach mac Cosse's Poem on the Psalter," in *Éigse,* **17** (1977); Poem (d): Kuno Meyer, "Mitteilungen aus irischen Handschriften," in *Zeitschrift für celtische Philologie,* **3** (1899), 23–24 (text only).

For the suggestion that Airbertach also composed *Saltair na Rann,* see Gearóid Mac Eoin, "The Date and Authorship of Saltair na Rann," in *Zeitschrift für celtische Philologie,* **28** (1960); on the later legends surrounding Airbertach's name, see Colm Ó Lochlainn, "Poets on the Battle of Clontarf-I," in *Éigse,* **3** (1941).

PÁDRAIG P. Ó NÉILL

[See also **Saltair na Rann**.]

AIRDENA BRÁTHA, Gaelic for "the signs of Doomsday." The early Irish commentary material (A.D. 630–800), whether in Latin or Gaelic, shows no particular interest in the signs of the end of the world; interest in the subject is evident from other sources. In some Priscillianist Latin fragments, probably of the eighth century and apparently of Irish origin, the signs to occur the three days before Doom are given. While this three-day list is unique, the text seems to depend on the *Apocalypse of Thomas.* In the Irish vernacular hymn to Our Lady by Blathmac (*ca.* A.D. 750), there are six quatrains listing some twelve signs preceding Doomsday. Although some of the signs are identical with those of the *Apocalypse of Thomas,* the signs are not apportioned by days and do not appear to follow any particular tradition. "The Celtic Catechesis," probably of Irish origin and from the ninth century, contains the signs of the seven days preceding Doomsday, and the first sign coincides with that of the *Apocalypse of Thomas.*

In *The Evernew Tongue,* an Irish apocryphal writing probably composed in the tenth century, there is a description of Doomsday and of the signs accompanying it (nos. 122–138). No formal list of signs is given, nor are the signs assigned to particular days. It is hard to determine to which, if any, tradition this particular text belongs. It is an important text in its own right, and also influenced later Irish tradition (for example, the text *Airdena inna Cóic Lá nDéc ria mBráth*).

A most important text in the development of the Signs of Doomsday tradition in Ireland (and possibly elsewhere) is that found in the extra cantos (nos. 153–162) of *Saltair na Rann* ("The Psalter of the Quatrains"), composed, like the *Saltair,* about the year 1000. This text spreads the signs over nine days, from Sunday to "the Monday of Judgment," Monday in Irish tradition being reckoned as the Day of Doom (even today in Gaelic it is called *Lá an Luain*—"the Day of Monday"). The *Saltair* text depends heavily on the *Apocalypse of Thomas* but also uses other sources, and introduces signs not found in the *Apocalypse.*

The Pseudo-Bedan text "On the Fifteen Signs Preceding Judgment Day," part of the collection of disparate pieces known as the *Collectanea,* is attested independently of the *Collectanea* in about twenty manuscripts, of which about twelve are from the twelfth century. This text, like many of the *Collectanea,* has Irish associations and may have originated in Ireland, possibly in the tenth or eleventh century. A poem on Doomsday by the Irish poet Donnchadh Mór ó Dálaigh (Donogh Mór O'Daly), who died in 1244 (begins: *Garbh éirghidh iodhna an bhrátha),* follows the Pseudo-Bedan type very closely, either because it uses the actual text or because it depends on the tradition that gave rise to it. The "Fifteen Signs," in a form very close to the Pseudo-Bedan type, is incorporated into the later recension (no. III) of *The Evernew Tongue* (found in a fifteenth-century manuscript), replacing most of the signs of the earlier recension (no. I).

An important text in the "Fifteen Signs" tradition is the prose piece entitled *Airdena inna Cóic Lá nDéc ria mBráth,* found in the fifteenth or sixteenth-century manuscript B. Lib Add. 30, 512, fol. 95–96, and in Dublin, TCD MS 1291, fol. 26. Here the signs are given, unusually, in reverse order. The author has used the *Saltair na Rann* text, and his text is closely related to that of *The Evernew Tongue* (early recension). He also uses such earlier Irish texts as *Tidings of Doomsday* and *Tidings of the Resurrection.* He seems to have known the Pseudo-Bedan text but is closer to the form known as the Damian type of the legend found in Peter Damian's work (11th c.) *De novissimis et Antichristo.*

A short unpublished prose piece on the "Fifteen Signs" *(Cúicc comurdha .x.* brátha) is found in the fifteenth-century *Liber Flavus Fergusiorum* (Dublin, RIA, MS 476, vol. I, fols. 12ra9–12rb10). The long Irish poem (forty-nine verses) on the Judgment and its attendant signs by the Irish Franciscan Philip Bocht Ó Huiginn (*d.* 1487) presumably derives from Irish tradition, but does not follow any of the known types.

The Irish tradition on the signs of Doomsday began partly dependent on the *Apocalypse of Thomas* and partly independent of it. It went beyond the *Apocalypse* particularly in the additional cantos of *Saltair na Rann,* then developed into the well-formed "Fifteen Signs" tradition (particularly as found in the Pseudo-Bedan type), which became widespread in England and on the Continent. W. W. Heist, who has made a detailed study of the question, believes that the English and European legend of the fifteen signs before Doomsday has its key in the additional cantos (153–162) of *Saltair na Rann.* Here, he believes, is the probable primary source of the legend of the fifteen signs, with *The Evernew Tongue* serving as the most important secondary source.

BIBLIOGRAPHY

Priscillianist Fragments. D. de Bruyne, "Fragments retrouvés d'apocryphes priscillianistes", in *Revue bénédictine,* **24** (1907), reproduced in *Patrologiae latina scripturae,* II (1960), 1512; Montague R. James, "Irish Apocrypha, II" in *Journal of Theological Studies,* **20** (1919).

Blathmac Poem. James Carney, ed. and trans., *The Poems of Blathmac Son of Cú Brettan,* Irish Texts Society, XLVII (1964).

Pseudo-Bedan Text. Bernard Lambert, *Bibliotheca Hieronymiana manuscripta,* III B (1970), no. 652 (manuscript listing of Pseudo-Bede's *De Quindecim Signis,* in *Patrologiae latina,* XCIV, col. 555).

The Celtic Catechesis. André Wilmart, "MS Vat. Reg. 49," in *Studi e testi,* **59** (1933), on which see Paul Grosjean, "A propos du manuscrit 49 de la Reine Christine," in *Analecta Bollandiana,* **54** (1936); a new edition by Robert McNally is in preparation.

Studies. Brian O'Dwyer Grogan, "The Eschatological Doctrines of the Early Irish Church," Ph.D. dissertation (1973), ch. 11; William W. Heist, *The Fifteen Signs Before Doomsday* (1952); Martin McNamara, *The Apocrypha in the Irish Church* (1975), 128–138; St. John D. Seymour, "The Signs of Doomsday in the Saltair na Rann," in *Proceedings of the Royal Irish Academy,* **36** C (1923).

MARTIN MCNAMARA

AIRNE FINGEIN. See **Irish Literature.**

ʿĀʾISHA (*ca.* 614–678), third wife of the prophet Muḥammad, was born at Mecca. She was the daughter of Abū Bakr, one of Muḥammad's earliest and most trusted followers and his ultimate successor, by his wife Umm Rūmān of the West Arabian tribe of Kināna. Her marriage to the Prophet, arranged when she was only about six, was doubtless intended, like many marriages at that time, to confirm social and political ties: in this case, to bolster the bonds between Muḥammad and Abū Bakr, who though of a lesser clan (Taym) of the Meccan tribe of Ḳuraysh, was highly respected for his judgment and forceful character, and probably controlled considerable wealth as well. As ʿĀʾisha grew to maturity, she developed not only great personal attractiveness but also the vivacity, wit, intelligence, and determination that, together with her devotion to Muḥammad himself, made her the undoubted favorite among his several wives. The marriage seems to have been consummated only some time after Muḥammad's hegira to Medina in 622.

In Medina, ʿĀʾisha, like the rest of Muḥammad's consorts, occupied a modest apartment, opening onto the court of the main mosque, and also directly adjoining Muḥammad's own quarters. The other wives thus constituted (along with her parents, sisters, cousins, and other close relatives) the company in which she passed much of her time, and relations among them seem generally to have been congenial. Nevertheless, it was inevitable that some rivalries should arise among the different members of the harem, both over the affections of the Prophet and over the interests of their respective parents and families. ʿĀʾisha seems frequently to have had an ally in Ḥafṣa, daughter of another of the Prophet's staunchest supporters, ʿUmar ibn al-Khaṭṭāb, whereas Umm Salama and Umm Ḥabība, members of the two aristocratic Meccan clans of Makhzūm and Umayya, respectively, appear often to have joined together in opposition to them, perhaps because they resented the high esteem that ʿĀʾisha and Ḥafṣa, both of less august lineage, enjoyed. The Prophet's daughter Fatima, and her husband, the Prophet's cousin ʿAlī ibn Abī Ṭālib, seem sometimes to have figured as the nucleus of a third "party" in these intrigues.

There is, however, no evidence to show that ʿĀʾisha or any of his other wives dominated Muḥammad or caused him to alter his basic opinions on matters of policy relating to the early Islamic community. Indeed, ʿĀʾisha, though lively and outspoken, is portrayed as being devoted and obedient to her husband, and it is unlikely that she would have wished to interfere in his judgment on political matters, or that Muḥammad's other wives would have permitted such influence to go unchallenged.

ʿĀʾisha's position as Muḥammad's favorite wife was severely tested only once, in the "affair of the lie" *(ḥadīth al-ʾifk),* when she was accused of committing adultery with a young man who returned her to one of the Muslims' raiding parties after it had inadvertently left her behind. ʿĀʾisha's rivals and the leader of Muḥammad's political opposition in Medina encouraged the gossip, which for a time caused Muḥammad to act coldly toward his former favorite, until she was finally absolved by a special revelation (Koran 24:11–16) declaring her to be above suspicion, much to Muḥammad's (and her own) relief. She soon resumed her preeminent position among his wives. The incident left her with favorable feelings toward another of the Prophet's wives, Zaynab, who had spoken well of her during the affair, and with a dislike of ʿAlī ibn Abī Ṭālib, who had hinted that her virtue might be suspect. Muḥammad's affection for ʿĀʾisha was undiminished, however, and when he contracted his final illness in 632, he requested that he be taken to her apartment, where he died in her arms. His body was interred beneath the floor of ʿĀʾisha's chamber, in accordance with Arabian custom.

After Muḥammad's death, ʿĀʾisha continued to live in her apartment in the mosque, along with the other "mothers of the believers," as Muḥammad's wives came to be called (compare Koran 33:6); and though only eighteen when widowed, she was, like all Muḥammad's wives, forbidden to remarry after his death (Koran 5:53). At first she drew close to her father, Abū Bakr, to whom she had always been bound by ties of affection and loyalty. When he died in 634, ʿĀʾisha truly became mistress of her own affairs, and seems also to have been charged with supervising her brothers and sisters and the family interests in general, which may have included the management of some family properties on which they probably relied for income. Her financial situation was made very secure when, after the success of the first wave of Islamic conquests outside Arabia, booty began to flow into Medina, for from that time on, she and the Prophet's other widows received handsome stipends, hers being the largest of all.

With the second caliph, ʿUmar ibn al-Khaṭṭāb, ʿĀʾisha seems to have been on cordial terms; so too with the third caliph, ʿUthmān, for the first years of his reign. As opposition to his rule increased, however, ʿĀʾisha too found cause to criticize him; but when the furor against the aged caliph reached its climax, she discreetly left Medina on pilgrimage to Mecca, and was there when ʿUthmān was murdered in 656. Thereafter, she took the position that the regicides (who had appointed ʿAlī ibn Abī Ṭālib as caliph) had to be punished, and seems to have been very active in holding together a faction of Meccan aristocrats who opposed ʿAlī, under the nominal leadership of her close kinsmen Ṭalḥa ibn ʿUbaydallāh and al-Zubayr ibn al-ʿAwwām. With them and about a thousand men, she went to Basra in hope of finding support against ʿAlī, and after a time they were able to occupy the city; but ʿAlī and his forces, arriving shortly thereafter, engaged the Meccan party outside the city and defeated them at the Battle of the Camel (December 656), so called because the camel on which ʿĀʾisha's litter was mounted became the focus of the fighting. Ṭalḥa and al-Zubayr were both killed, and ʿĀʾisha, graciously treated by ʿAlī, was persuaded to return to Medina and to retire from active participation in politics.

In later years ʿĀʾisha managed to keep on good terms with both ʿAlī and his archenemy, the Umayyad caliph Muʿāwiya ibn Abī Sufyān, who paid her respectful visits during his trips from Syria. Though no longer a force in politics, she was always very influential and eagerly sought out by many for personal, religious, and sometimes political guidance. She died at Medina in July, 678.

In Arabic literature ʿĀʾisha is remembered for her great eloquence and knowledge of verses, as well as for the great number of traditions about the words and deeds of the prophet that later transmitters attributed to her. She is also said to have possessed one of the first copies of the Koran text, and to have been the source of a few variant readings.

BIBLIOGRAPHY

Nabia Abbott, *Aishah, the Beloved of Mohammed* (1942), contains references to primary sources.

FRED M. DONNER

[See also **Muḥammad**.]

AISLINGE MEIC CON-GLINNE ("The Vision of Mac Con-Glinne"), a Middle Irish prose tale, with verse inserts satirizing various institutions of pre-Norman Ireland (the Church, the nobility, and the learned classes, both lay and clerical), as well as parodying many literary forms and customs. Set in the seventh or eighth century, the story records the journey of the goliardic cleric Aniér mac Con-Glinne from the north of Ireland to the monastery of Cork in the south, where he is ill-treated by the abbot and monks. For daring to satirize the monastery over his ill-treatment, he is condemned to death. He purchases a stay of execution by undertaking to rid the king of Munster, Cathal mac Finguine, of his possession by a demon of gluttony, which threatens to ruin the kingdom. By various subterfuges he succeeds in getting the king to fast, thus starving the demon. Then he recounts a long vision of a land consisting entirely of foodstuffs. Finally, by passing tasty food in front of the king's mouth, he entices the demon to leave the king. The demon is trapped in a house that is burned, destroying the demon. Mac Con-Glinne's life is spared, and he is honored by the king.

The tale has survived in two versions, a shorter that may be dated on linguistic grounds to about 1100, and a longer that has had new material added, including a reference to tithes, which indicates a date after 1150. The original, from which both versions derive, must have been composed in the eleventh century in the same spirit as *Airec Menman Uraird meic Coisse* ("The Stratagem of Urard mac Coisse"), a satire/parody on the learned classes and their literature dated about 1000. The similarity of the description of the land of food to the Land of Cockaigne has been frequently mentioned, but no close relationship has been established. The tale is also a social document of some importance, portraying in burlesque form the mores of Irish society just before the Norman invasion.

BIBLIOGRAPHY

An edition is Kuno Meyer, ed., *Aislinge Meic Conglinne: The Vision of Mac Conglinne* (1892), from which the English translation is reprinted in Tom P. Cross and Clark H. Slover, eds., *Ancient Irish Tales* (1936; repr. 1969). Also see B. Ó Buachalla, "Aislinge meic Conglinne," in *Galvia: Irisleabhar Chumann Seandálaíochta is Staire na Gaillimhe,* VII (1960).

GEARÓID MAC EOIN

AIX-LA-CHAPELLE. See **Aachen.**

AJÍMEZ (Spanish, possibly derived from Arabic *al-shimāsah,* "window"; cf. Andalusian *ajiméz*), originally a screened balcony from which residents could observe the street without being seen. Since the early eighteenth century, *ajímez* has also come to denote a window composed of two arched openings separated only by a colonnette; such windows were known in Visigothic Spain from the seventh century onward. The earliest surviving Islamic examples are on the church tower of San Juan de los Caballeros in Cordova, formerly a minaret, of the first quarter of the tenth century, and in Morocco on the minaret of al-Qarawiyyīn mosque in Fez (956). *Ajímeces* became characteristic of the Islamic architecture of the Iberian peninsula and Morocco, as well as of Mudéjar architecture; when found elsewhere they usually reflect some form of influence from the peninsula.

BIBLIOGRAPHY

Ars Hispaniae, II–III (1947–1951); J. Dodd, "Mozarabic Architecture of the Resettlement and the Spirtual Reconquista" (diss., Harvard University, 1979); Reinhart Dozy and W. H. Engelmann, *Glossaire des mots espagnols et portugais dérivés de l'arabe,* 2nd ed. (1869); F. Hernández Giménez, *El Alminar de ᶜAbd al-Rahman III en la Mezquita Mayor de Córdoba* (1975), 134–155; Georges Marçais, *L'architecture musulmane d'Occident* (1954), 197–200; Leopoldo Torres Balbás, "Ajímeces," in *al-Andalus,* **12** (1947).

ESTELLE WHELAN

AKATHISTOS, an anonymous Byzantine hymn in the genre of the kontakion. The term ("not sitting," "standing") indicates the special honor in which it was held. While it may have been composed as early as the sixth century, the first manuscripts with complete musical settings are from the thirteenth century and show a usage in the florid melodic style of the *psaltikon.* As one of the most celebrated of all hymns in the Eastern Church, traces of it are also known in the West. Singing of the akathistos is reported in connection with the sieges of Constantinople in the seventh and eighth centuries as well as on other historic occasions. The text, which praises the Incarnation and the Virgin, is found in the services for the fifth Saturday of Lent and is composed of two introductory strophes (*koukoulia* or *prooimia*) followed by twenty-four metrically imitated strophes *(oikoi)* linked in an alphabetic acrostic.

BIBLIOGRAPHY

Egon Wellesz, *The Akathistos Hymn,* vol. IX of Monumenta Musicae Byzantinae, Transcripta (1957), includes a transcription of the music from the Middle Byzantine notation; Michel Huglo, "L'ancienne version latine de l'hymne acathiste," in *Muséon*, **64** (1951); Gilles Meersseman, *Der Hymnos Akathistos im Abendland*, (1958–1960).

NICOLAS SCHIDLOVSKY

[See also **Hymns, Byzantine: Kontakion; Psaltikon.**]

AKHLAT. See **Xlat.**

AKHṬAL, AL- (*ca.* 640–*ca.* 710). The poet Ghiyāth ibn Ghawth ibn al-Ṣalt, known by the nickname al-Akhṭal ("the chatterer") was born at Hira on the Euphrates. Of the Monophysite Christian tribe of Taghlib, he never converted to Islam, but his religion did not keep him from a splendid career at the Umayyad court. The Caliph ᶜAbd al-Malik is reported to have said: "Each clan has a poet [to praise its glory]; the poet of the Banū Umayya is al-Akhṭal."

In the struggle between the Umayyads, whose power was at first secure only in Syria, and the rival caliphate of ᶜAbd Allāh ibn al-Zubayr, based in Mecca and Medina, the Taghlib were the Umayyads' allies. According to a plausible tradition, al-Akhṭal began his career at court with a poem ridiculing the Anṣār (the descendants of the clans that had been the Prophet Muḥammad's Medinese helpers). Ridicule made memorable by verse was a dangerous weapon. It affected prestige, and therefore power. "I silenced the Banū Najjār on your behalf," al-Akhṭal reminds his Umayyad patrons, ". . . so that they were brought low and sorely grieved by me. Words prick sharper than pinpoints." Al-Akhṭal, like his younger contemporaries Jarīr and al-Farazdaq, did a great deal of sharp pricking. Of his long exchange of insults in verse with Jarīr, the latter, no humble man, reportedly said: "When we joined battle, al-Akhṭal was already old, with only one canine tooth left. With two, he would have eaten me up." The weapon of satire might on occasion hurt the satirist: the sonorities of verse made propaganda more memorable, but also less easily unsaid. There may be truth in the tradition that certain verses by al-Akhṭal rekindled, with bitter results for the Taghlib, the bloody war between them and the tribe of Qays.

Al-Akhṭal was praised by many medieval critics for his pure and forceful Arabic, and for the justice of his descriptions. The verses came to him easily, but he took pains to discard and revise. Many agreed with him that he was the foremost poet of his time. He certainly understood how to adapt the ancient conventions of Arabic poetry to the religio-political style of the quarrels of his day. The Caliph ᶜAbd al-Malik, one anecdote relates, once showed delight in a verse by the poet Kuthayyir, which praised the dynasty for having gained preeminence by the sword. Al-Akhṭal had little difficulty persuading the caliph that his phrase "possessors of kingship neither newfangled nor usurped"—it was something of both—was a handsomer compliment.

The Bedouin virtues are still present in al-Akhṭal's verse: the Umayyads feed the hungry; in generosity "their hands are above the hands of mankind" (with allusion to Koran 48:10). They are "implacable till submitted to, but having the upper hand, they are of all men the firmest in self-control," a verse that Hārūn al-Rashīd is said to have admired. Umayyad triumphs are related with cheerful vivacity—"the post-horses gallop with the heads [of Muṣᶜab ibn al-Zubayr and his companions], the stakes have been fixed for them. . ."—and with righteous enthusiasm—the dynasty holds "the lead-rope of whatever is true and rightful [ḥaqq]." The caliph, addressed in language of religious coloring, "illuminates the land after a darkness has settled over it, in which other guides might lose the right path."

Despite such words, al-Akhṭal's verse stresses that he is a Christian and not a Muslim. Anecdotes testify to his submission to ecclesiastic authority. Nevertheless, his poetry is not Christian in any significant sense: those of his judgments that are not dictated by loyalty to the dynasty or to his tribe are descended from the traditional wisdom of the pre-Islamic poetry. This poetry had been the cultural stock all the Arabs shared—al-Akhṭal's Christian tribe, established in northern Syria well before the Muslim conquest, no less than the pagans of Arabia.

BIBLIOGRAPHY

Henri Lammens, "Le chantre des Omiades," in *Journal asiatique,* ser. 9, **4** (1894). On the literature of the Umayyad period, see also Carlo Nallino's lectures, originally in Arabic, transl. into Italian in his *Raccolta di scritti,* VI (1948), and into French by Charles Pellat in *La littérature arabe dès origines à l'époque de la dynastie umayyade* (1950).

ANDRAS HAMORI

AKRITAI (singular, *akritēa)* were Byzantine border guards who took their name from the Greek word for limit or heights. These soldiers, whose total number and precise relationship to the regular Byzantine armies are unclear, were primarily of Greek or Armenian origin. They were especially prominent as guardians of the Byzantine Empire's eastern frontiers against Muslim raids and invasions. They received important tax exemptions from the government, but their specific terms of service and compensation lack documentation. They were criticized by some regular Byzantine officers for their lack of formal military knowledge and discipline, but they supplied valuable reports (including advance warning of raids) on conditions at and across the eastern frontiers, and they could offer some armed resistance to smaller contingents of invaders.

Sources about the *akritai* include the complex literary epic *Digenis Akritas,* military treatises of the tenth century, the *Strategikon* of Kekaumenos, and the history of Michael Attaleiates in the eleventh century. The *akritai* are most frequently mentioned in the tenth and eleventh centuries, but their origins date at least from the ninth century. Their organizational structure was loose. Many of them developed informal contacts with Muslim authorities on the other side of the border. Governmental mistrust, neglect, and even hostility to the *akritai* contributed to their decline in the eleventh century on the eve of major Turkish invasions, and their decline probably contributed to the rapidity and dimensions of Turkish victories.

Although some contemporaries resented them and criticized their effectiveness, the *akritai* contributed to the development of an effective Byzantine frontier policy against the Arabs and, consequently, to the endurance and security of the empire.

BIBLIOGRAPHY

See the articles published in the section entitled "Frontières et régions frontières du VIIe au XIIe siècles," *Rapports,* II, in *Actes, XIVe Congrès International des Etudes Byzantines* (1971).

WALTER EMIL KAEGI, JR.

[See also **Attaleiates, Michael; Digenis Akritas; Kekaumenos.**]

AKSUMITE ART. See **Axumite Art.**

AL-. See next element of name.

ÁLA FLEKKS SAGA is a native Icelandic blend of folktale and romance *(lygisaga)*, probably composed in its present form just prior to or around 1400. It has been preserved in two vellum manuscripts from the fifteenth and sixteenth centuries and in some thirty-three paper manuscripts. Numerous motifs in the saga enjoy widespread distribution, but direct borrowing from *Finnboga saga ramma* and from *Ynglingasaga* is probable.

The bewildering array of thematic elements in the saga are loosely tied together by four *álög,* or curses, that plague the hero. Áli flekkr, a prince exposed as a child, is found by a poor couple who raise the boy as their own. Each time they give him a name, they forget it during the ensuing night, until they arrive at Áli flekkr. The child is recognized at a dinner by his real parents and taken back and raised by them until the servant Blátönn ("black tooth") places the curse on him to marry her sister, the troll Nótt. On his journey to her, Nótt's daughter, Hlaðgerðr, gives him advice that allows him to escape from Nótt's cave. Áli subsequently saves Thornbjörg, the maiden king of Tartaríá, from an attack by two earls of Indíáland and marries her.

During the wedding night, Nótt's brother transforms Áli into a marauding wolf. Finally caught by his father, he regains his human form after his foster-mother is struck by the resemblance of the wolf's eyes to Áli's. The hero returns home and is beaten in a dream by Nótt, who tells him that his wounds must be cured by her brothers within ten years or he will die. By promising to marry Jötunoxi, one of the brothers, Thornbjörg has him cure Áli and kill his own sister. Áli kills Jötunoxi and numerous other trolls but is cursed a fourth time to enjoy no peace until finding Hlaðgerðr. Áli does so just in time to save her from being burned as a witch and marries her to the king of England.

Ála flekks saga has been edited on two occasions, but the *rímur* versions, two composed in the seventeenth and one in the nineteenth century, are as yet unedited.

BIBLIOGRAPHY

Otto Jiriczek, "Zur mittelisländischen Volkskunde," in *Zeitschrift für deutsche Philologie,* **26** (1894); Finnur Jónsson, *Den oldnorske og oldislandske litteraturs historie,* 2nd ed., III (1924), 109–110; Åke Lagerholm, ed., *Drei lygisögur,* in *Altnordische Saga-Bibliothek,* XVII (1927); Margaret Schlauch, *Romance in Iceland* (1934); Finnur Sigmundsson, *Rímnatal,* I (1966), 13–15; Bjarni Vilhjálmsson, ed., *Riddarasögur,* V (1961), 123–160; Jan de Vries, *Altnordische Literaturgeschichte,* II (1964), 540.

PETER A. JORGENSEN

ALAIN DE LILLE. See **Alan of Lille.**

ALAMANNI, a confederation of German-speaking peoples that probably included, among others, the Juthungi, Lentienses, and Bucinobantes. Also, if the Suevi are to be identified with this group, as most scholars believe, then we may perhaps include the Quadi, the Charudes, and the Eudusii as well. This confederation of "All Men" was first mentioned in the West by the historian Cassius Dio, who recounts their conflict with the emperor Caracalla in A.D. 213. The Alamanni appear to have taken advantage of the civil wars that bedeviled the Roman Empire following the death of Maximianus Thracianus in 236, and they were particularly successful during the period from 260 to 270. These raids focused on Italy. However, in 277 the emperor Probus finally halted the Alamannic expeditions with a decisive victory. During much of the fourth century the Alamanni tried to establish settlements on the banks of the Rhine, but were consistently thwarted by Constantius II, Julian, and Gratian. Julian's campaigns in particular illustrate the great military superiority of the Roman Empire over the barbarians.

By the early fifth century, the breakdown of the Rhine defenses permitted the Alamanni to position themselves, along with the Alani, the Vandals, and the Burgundians, for a breakthrough into imperial territory. On the last day of 406, the freezing of the Rhine provided the opportunity, and a large mass of barbarians crossed the river. However, imperial diplomacy was successful in gaining the Burgundians and some Alani as allies. These people were settled on the Rhine and, along with the Franks, were used to prevent the majority of Alamanni from breaking through. (A minority of Suevi eventually got through into Spain.) However, when the Burgundians were moved south in 443 and the Hunnish invasion of 450 further disrupted imperial defenses along the Rhine, the Alamanni were able to move further west, where they came into serious conflict with the Franks. In about 495, Clovis, ruler of a Salian Frankish band that had conquered much of Gaul north of the Somme, advanced toward the old Roman stronghold of Bonn and clashed with the Alamanni at Zülpich (Tolbiac). Clovis won a decisive victory, and the main body of Alamanni submitted to Frankish authority. A remnant of the Alamanni fled south and placed themselves under the protection of Theodoric the Ostrogoth. Theodoric kept Clovis from extending his domination over them.

Under Frankish domination the Alamanni gradually extended their area of settlement into southern Germany and northern Switzerland. They moved into the region around Basel, Zurich, and the foothills of the Jura. The extent and pace of these movements are problematical, and knowledge of them depends to a large degree on archaeological evidence that at the present time is inconclusive. The difficulty in coming to a sound understanding of the Alamanni internal history is also illustrated in the written sources. For example, in the fourth century the Alamanni are said to live under the rule of *reges,* but by the sixth century they are said to live under the rule of *duces.* This has led some scholars to hypothesize various scenarios of radical constitutional change associated with one or another major historical event, such as settlement in Roman territory or conquest by the Franks. However, it is very likely that the above-mentioned titles illustrate the differing perceptions of the external observers rather than any substantial change in the Alamannic constitution.

Although the *duces,* like the *reges,* were of Alamannic stock, it appears that the Merovingian ruler of Austrasia played a key role in determining which members of the leading families would hold a ducal title. In the mid sixth century two Alamanni *duces* led a large army into northern Italy against the Byzantines in support of Frankish policy. However, despite Frankish influence Christianity did not make great headway among the Alamanni during the sixth century. Real strides in Christianization began late in the century, when St. Columban, who had been exiled by the Merovingian queen Brunhilda, was welcomed in Alamannic terrirory. When Columban moved on into Italy, several of his disciples carried on his work.

The Alamanni who came under Frankish domination west of the Rhine and to the south had their laws codified and written down late in the sixth or early in the seventh century. This was probably done under the aegis of Parthenius, a descendant of the emperor Avitus, who served as a minister of the Merovingian king Theuderic II.

During the later seventh and early eighth centuries, while the Carolingian mayors of the palace were busy consolidating their power in the west after their victory at the battle of Tertry in 687, the Alamanni threw off Frankish rule. With the exception of the period from about 709 to 712, when Pepin II reimposed control, and for a brief period following Charles Martel's victory in 730, the Alamanni remained free of Frankish domination until Pepin III defeated them in 744 and 748. During this half-century or so of virtual independence, they redrew their laws under the leadership of Duke Lantfrid in 719 and resisted the adoption of a Romance language.

BIBLIOGRAPHY

Bruno Behr, *Das alemannische Herzogtum bis 750* (1975); F. Beyerle, "Der Alemannenfeldzug des Kaisers Constantius II. von 355 und die Namengebung Constantia (Konstanz)," in *Zeitschrift für die Geschichte des Oberrheins,* 65 (1956); H. Büttner, "Franken und Alemannen in Breisgau und Ortenau. Ein Beitrag zur Geschichte des Oberrheins im 8 Jahrhundert," *ibid.,* 52 (1959); T. Mayer, "Alemannien im fränkischen Reich," in *Berichte über die Vorträge des Württembergischen Geschichts- und Altertumsvereins* (1956–1958); *Quellen zur Geschichte der Alamannen,* C. Dirlmeier and K. Sprigade, trans. and ed., 5 vols. (1976–1981).

BERNARD S. BACHRACH

ALAMŪT, a fortress in northern Persia in the district of Rūdbār and in the heart of the Elburz Mountains to the north of Qazvīn. Situated at a height of more than 6,000 feet (1,800 m.) and approached through the narrow gorge of the Alamūt River, the fortress was perched on an almost inaccessible rock and could be approached only by a narrow path.

The castle owed its fame in medieval Islam to its role as the seat of local, Caspian-region Shiite potentates from the eighth century onward. From the later eleventh to the mid thirteenth century Alamūt was the headquarters of the extremist Shiite "Ismaili" sect known in Western sources from the Crusading period as the Assassins (Arabic *Ḥashīshiyya,* "hashish eaters") from an almost certainly legendary attribution to the sect's leaders of the use of narcotics to induce daredevil feats of bravery by the rank and file.

The building of Alamūt is attributed to one of the local princes of the Caspian region of medieval Dailam (the mountainous region of modern Gilan), in whose dialect the name is said to have meant "eagle's nest" or "eagle's teaching." In 860 the Shiite propagandist al-Ḥasan ibn Zaid, called al-Dā^{c}i ilā$^{\supset}$l-Ḥaqq, rebuilt the castle. Then in 1090 Ḥasan ibn-al-Sabbah, head of the extremist Nizārī branch of the Ismailis, seized it as a valuable and inaccessible base for the dissemination of Ismaili doctrines throughout Persia and for the deployment of the weapon of political assassination attributed, at least in the popular mind, to him and his followers.

Alamūt then became the nerve center of the Ismaili movement. It survived a siege by the sultan Malik Shah in 1092 and attacks by other Seljuk rulers in the course of the twelfth century. It became an intellectual center of Ismailism, with a celebrated library frequented by scholars from outside, especially as the later grand masters of the early thirteenth century relaxed the intransigence of their Ismaili beliefs. The Grand Master Rukn al-Dīn Khūrshāh faced the invasion of northern Persia by Hulagu's Mongol hordes; he decided to surrender Alamūt and other fortresses to them, hoping thereby to preserve something of his power. Thus at the end of 1256, Alamūt was given over to the Mongols, who wrought considerable destruction; the gleeful orthodox Sunni Muslims were now able to destroy all the heretical books in its library. It was recovered by the Assassins in 1275 but was finally lost soon afterward. Ismailism was henceforth reduced to the status of a minor sect in certain outlying parts of Persia only, disappearing completely from the Caspian region.

Various remains of walls and buildings of the fortress of Alamūt can still be seen. The first European traveler in modern times to describe them was the British officer Justin Shiel (1838). Other travelers have subsequently described Alamūt; a classic account remains that of Freya Stark.

BIBLIOGRAPHY

The primary sources include the general Arabic and Persian histories, such as Ibn al-Athīr, Rāwandī, Bundārī, and especially the Persian history of the Mongol conquests, Juwainī's *History of the World-Conqueror,* John A. Boyle, trans. (1958). The extensive secondary literature includes Marshall G. S. Hodgson, *The Order of Assassins* (1955); W. Ivanow, "Alamut," in *Geographical Journal,* 78 (1931); Guy Le Strange, *The Lands of the Eastern Caliphate* (1905); Bernard Lewis, *The Assassins* (1967); Justin Shiel, "Itinerary from Teheran to Alamut," in *Journal of the Royal Geographical Society* (1838); Freya Stark, *The*

Valleys of the Assassins (1934); and Peter Willey, *The Castles of the Assassins* (1963).

C. E. Bosworth

[See also **Assassins; Heresies, Islamic.**]

ALAN OF LILLE (Alain de Lille, Alanus de Insulis), poet and theologian, was born at Lille around 1120. His mastery of the liberal arts, for which he became known as *doctor universalis,* was probably acquired at one or more of the cathedral schools of the Loire valley and perhaps also at Chartres. Alan may have studied with the great metaphysician Gilbert de la Porrée at Paris or Chartres; he was clearly well grounded in the methods introduced by Gilbert, whose commentaries on Boethius explored the relation between God and the created world in dialectical terms. After the mid century Alan taught at Paris, spent some time in Provence (probably at Montpellier), and evidently returned to Paris at the end of the century. He entered the Cistercian order in his old age and died at Cîteaux in 1202 or 1203.

Alan was unquestionably one of the most learned and versatile figures of the twelfth century. The major Latin poet of his day, he was also an influential theologian and one of the founders of systematic theology. He was an apologist whose treatises against heretics not only attacked the errors of the Cathars and Waldensians but also defended Christianity in broader terms against Jews and Muslims. As a teacher, Alan was concerned with the cure of souls and was author of a treatise on preaching and a penitential manual that are among the first of their kind. His writings vary widely in subject and emphasis, but they are unified by a theologian's concern with the relations between nature and the divine and with the problem of expressing such relations in human language.

These concerns began taking shape in what was probably Alan's first major work, *De planctu naturae* (1160–1175). This work consists of a Boethian dialogue between the poet-narrator and the "goddess" Nature, who appears to the poet in a vision, gives a long account of her role in the cosmos and in human life, and explains the "perversion" that has corrupted human speech, social mores, and sexuality, alienating man from his proper place in Nature's domain. The work ends with the appearance of Nature's "priest," Genius, who administers the natural sacrament uniting matter and form and pronounces a concluding anathema against all those who refuse to obey Nature's laws.

A striking feature of the work is its establishment of Nature as the essential link between God and man, a characteristic twelfth-century attitude for which Alan was an eloquent spokesman and that had important implications for ethics, law, and political theory. But equally significant is Nature's delineation of the limits of her authority. She acknowledges her ignorance of the theological implications of human sinfulness and her inability to apply any but natural remedies. At the end of *De planctu naturae* man remains alienated, and the implicit message is the need for redemptive grace.

The point is reinforced in Alan's most famous work, the *Anticlaudianus* (1182–1183), an epic poem in nine books that is largely a sequel to *De planctu naturae.* Here, Nature resolves to overcome the problem of sin by creating a perfect man. Prompted by the Virtues, she sends Prudence to petition God to create a soul for this "new man," and the bulk of the poem develops Prudence's journey as an allegory of the mind's ascent to God. A chariot is created by the Liberal Arts. With Reason as charioteer and drawn by the five senses, Prudence ascends as far as the empyrean, where the senses and Reason can no longer make headway. Theology then appears in order to guide Prudence to Faith, and at last she reaches the throne of God. Her prayer granted, Prudence descends to earth, the new man is created, and his regenerative role is dramatized in a climactic *psychomachia* in which the Virtues defeat the Vices and restore the Golden Age.

Alan's principal theological work, the untitled summa known from its opening words as the "Quoniam homines," complements the two allegories in stressing the radical separation of theological discourse and method from those of philosophy and the liberal arts. Alan's *Theologicae regulae* is largely an attempt to establish a set of principles for theological language comparable to the self-consistent methodologies of the other arts. Both works follow the Greek patristic tradition as conveyed by Dionysius the Areopagite and John Scotus Erigena in their emphasis on the "negative" character of the true theology and the need to divorce its terms and paradigms from all natural reference in order to render them applicable to the supernatural. The emphasis on epistemology and method and the recourse to the Dionysian tradition are characteristic of the followers of Gilbert de la Porrée; but Alan's extreme stress on the negative, symbolic character of theological language is his own distinctive contribution, as is his tendency to contrast post-lapsarian existence with a pristine state in which Adam, had he not sinned, would have merited eternal life through natural virtue alone. The same vivid sense of the opposition of nature and grace informs Alan's short treatise *De virtutibus et vitiis et de donis Spiritus sancti* and the occasionally eccentric elaborations of symbolic meanings in the *Distinctiones,* a dictionary of biblical terms.

Although Alan's methodological innovations and his imaginative adaptation of the Dionysian tradition were important for later theologians, the direct influence of his strictly theological writings was short-lived. On the other hand, his handbooks and manuals, the *Theologicae regulae, Distinctiones, Ars praedicandi,* and *Liber poenitentialis,* were copied and recopied throughout the Middle Ages. Still more influential were *De planctu naturae* and the *Anticlaudianus,* each of which survives in more than 100 manuscripts. Nature's complaint was a central motif in the *Romance of the Rose* and was still a vital issue for Chaucer and Spenser. The *Anticlaudianus* was treated as virtually the equivalent of a classical text. It was accompanied in manuscripts by elaborate glosses and by the full-scale commentary of Ralph of Longchamp, was imitated in the vernacular by the French poet Ellebaut, and constituted perhaps the most important medieval prototype for Dante's *Divine Comedy.*

BIBLIOGRAPHY

Sources. Patrologia latina, CCX (1855), contains all of Alan's major works except "Quoniam homines" and *De virtutibus; Anticlaudianus,* Robert Bossuat, ed. (1955); *De planctu naturae,* Nikolaus M. Häring, ed., in *Studi medievali,* 3rd ser., **19** (1978); *De virtutibus et vitiis et de donis Spiritus sancti,* Odon Lottin, ed., in *Psychologie et morale aux XIIe et XIIIe siècles,* VI (1960), 45–92; *Summa "Quoniam homines,"* Palémon Glorieux, ed., in *Archives d'histoire doctrinale et littéraire du moyen âge,* **28** (1953). See also Radulphus de Longo Campo, *In Anticlaudianum Alani commentum,* Jan Sulowski, ed. (1972); and Ellebaut, *Anticlaudien,* Andrew J. Creighton, ed. (1944).

Secondary Literature. Alain de Lille, Gautier de Châtillon, Jakemart Giélée et leur temps, H. Roussel and François Suard, eds. (1980), contains eleven essays on Alan; Marie-Thérèse d'Alverny, *Alain de Lille: Textes inédits* (1965), includes the best survey to date of Alan's life and works; Vincenzo Cilento, *Alano de Lilla, poeta e teologo del secolo xii* (1958); Andrea Ciotti, "Alano e Dante," in *Convivium,* **28** (1960); G. R. Evans, *Old Arts and New Theology. The Beginnings of Theology as an Academic Discipline* (1980); Richard H. Green, "Alan of Lille's *De planctu naturae,*" in *Speculum,* **31** (1956); and "Alan of Lille's *Anticlaudianus:* Ascensus mentis in Deum," in *Annuale mediaevale,* **8** (1967); Johan Huizinga, *Über die Verknüpfung des Poetischen mit dem Theologischen bei Alanus de Insulis* (1932); Linda E. Marshall, "The Identity of the 'New Man' in the "Anticlaudianus" of Alan of Lille," in *Viator,* **10** (1979); Christel Meier, "Zum Problem der allegorischen Interpretation mittelalterlicher Dichtung," in *Beiträge zur Geschichte der deutschen Sprache und Literatur,* **99** (1977), includes a thorough review of recent scholarship on Alan's literary works; Peter Ochsenbein, *Studien zum Anticlaudianus des Alanus ab Insulis* (1975); Guy Raynaud de Lage, *Alain de Lille, poète du XIIe siècle* (1951), provides an inventory of manuscripts of Alan's major works and a review of manuscripts of minor works attributed to him; Cesare Vasoli, "Le idee filosofiche di Alano di Lilla nel *De planctu* e nell'*Anticlaudianus,*" in *Giornale critico della filosofia italiana,* **40** (1961); "La 'Theologia apothetica' di Alano di Lilla," in *Rivista critica de storia della filosofia,* **16** (1961); and "Il 'Contra haereticos' di Alano di Lilla," in *Bullettino dell'Istituto storico italiano per il medio evo archivio Muratoriano,* **75** (1963); Winthrop Wetherbee, *Platonism and Poetry in the Twelfth Century* (1972), is largely concerned with the intellectual and literary background of Alan's poetry.

WINTHROP WETHERBEE

[See also **Allegory, French; Gilbert de la Porrée; John Scotus Erigena.**]

ALAN OF WALSINGHAM. See **Walsingham, Alan of.**

ALANI, an Indo-Iranian nomadic people who moved across central Asia into the south Russian steppes. The earliest extant written notice of their existence in the West comes from the Latin author Seneca. Until the later fourth century Alani contacts with the Roman Empire were of minor importance. Perhaps this was because the Alani were never formed into a horde. They were, however, used as interpreters and, several times, were Roman allies. On one occasion this pattern was substantially altered and the Roman general Flavius Arrianus was forced to launch a major campaign against the Alani. He was so impressed by the Alani that he wrote a

ALANI

book about them, which unfortunately survives only in fragments.

With the coming of the Huns, the Alani, like their more sedentary neighbors the Ostrogoths and the Visigoths, suffered severe military setbacks. Remnants of the Alani fled west toward the imperial frontiers, while other small groups were absorbed into the Hunnish horde. One group of Alani allied with the Goths and played a crucial role in the barbarian victory at Adrianople. Another group joined the Romans and served under the emperor Gratian. A part of this latter band ultimately settled in northern Italy, and left substantial evidence of this in the toponymy.

The great influx of Alani into the West, however, came at the end of 406. At this time several important groups of Alani that were allied with the Vandals crossed the Rhine and entered Gaul. After defeating an army of Rome's Frankish allies, one of these Alani bands, under the leadership of King Goar, was detached from the invading force by Roman promises of land and gold. This group was settled in the area of Worms, and a few years later participated in the abortive effort of Jovinus to take imperial power. In the early 440's this group was moved to the Orléanais by Aetius.

Other groups of Alani remained with the Vandals and entered Spain in 409, after ravishing Gaul for several years. In Spain, Alani kingdoms were established in Lusitania and Cartagena, where the land was shared with the Hispano-Roman proprietors. Within a decade, however, the Visigoths, operating under imperial orders, conquered these kingdoms and a greater part of the Alani in Spain. The Alani lost their political identity and joined the Vandals, whose kings thereafter were styled *rex Vandalorum et Alanorum.* Ultimately these Alani settled with the Vandals in North Africa, where they survived until Justinian's reconquest consigned them to oblivion by 535.

The Alani groups that had remained with the Visigoths entered Gaul after Alaric's sack of Rome in 410, and served under the leadership of Athaulf. In 414, however, they defected to the Roman side in return for substantial lands in southern Gaul around Narbonne and as far west as Toulouse. Their settlements, which were based on a division of the land with Roman proprietors, appear to have survived for a long time, at least in cultural terms, despite the Visigothic domination of the region.

In the East the Alani played an important military role, and at Constantinople particular Alani leaders played a dominant political role. At various times Alani forces were used by the East Roman emperor to thwart both Germanic and Hun military efforts. Among the several Alani who rose to high military command, Aspar, the son of the general Ardaburius, was the most important; for some two decades he was the real power behind the imperial throne. In 468, however, he was murdered at the order of Emperor Leo I; thereafter, Alani influence at Constantinople ceased to be of significance.

By the early sixth century, Alani tribal units in the West ceased to exist as recognizable entities. Their rapid acceptance of Christianity and abandonment of their nomadic habits would seem to have facilitated their assimilation. The subsequent history of the Alani in the West rests upon such evidence as place names—for instance, Alancourt and Alanville—of which more than fifty can be identified, elements of folklore, and artistic motifs that have survived in artifacts. In several areas the place-name evidence correlates with the use of Alani personal names in the same region and with archaeological finds and mentions in the written sources. One such case is that of a youth named Goar who grew up in the southern part of Aquitaine during the sixth century. In the same general area we can identify a church dedicated to Sanctus Alanus, animal style artifacts of central Asian inspiration, and place names that suggest Alani habitation.

Bits and pieces of Alani culture survived well into the Middle Ages. It is likely, for example, that some aspects of the Arthurian legends preserve Alani influences. The same may be said for the celebrated Aquitanian style of decoration. Perhaps most lasting has been the fame of the *canis Alani,* the now extinct hunting dog of the Alani.

BIBLIOGRAPHY

Bernard S. Bachrach, "The Alans in Gaul," in *Traditio,* **23** (1967); "Another Look at the Barbarian Settlement in Southern Gaul," *ibid.,* **25** (1969); "The Origin of Armorican Chivalry," in *Technology and Culture,* **10** (1969); "Two Alan Motifs in Åberg's Aquitanian Style," in *Central Asiatic Journal,* **16** (1972); and *A History of the Alans in the West* (1973); L. Franchet, "Une colonie Scytho-Alaine en Orléanais au Vᵉ siècle," in *Revue scientifique,* **78** (1930); Iu. Kulakovskiĭ, *Alany po svedeniiam klassicheskikh i vizantiiskikh pisatelei* (1899); E. Täubler, "Zur Geschichte der Alanen," in *Klio,* **9** (1909); and George Vernadsky, "Sur l'origine des Alains," in *Byzantion,* **16** (1943).

BERNARD S. BACHRACH

ALARIC (*ca.* 370–410), a Visigothic ruler, is believed to have been born on the island of Peuce (Romania), just where the Danube enters the sea. He entered Roman territory and settled with other Visigoths in Moesia about 376. In 395, or perhaps a bit earlier, he became the head of a band of Visigoths and demonstrated the intention of pursuing an aggressive and perhaps even overtly hostile policy toward the Roman Empire. Following the death of Theodosius I, Alaric advanced on Constantinople, on the pretext that subsidies owed to the Goths had not been paid. Alaric's path to the capital of the East was blocked, so he moved against northern Greece. Between 397 and 403 he led expeditions into Greece, Illyria, and Italy.

By 401 he was *magister militum* for Illyria, but this did not keep the Visigoths from their plundering expeditions. However, he was rarely successful in these efforts, for the Roman general Flavius Stilicho always seemed to turn up and blunt the Visigoths' offensive after they had gathered some plunder. It would seem that Stilicho had some sort of working agreement with Alaric, as a result of which the Visigoths were permitted to do a modicum of damage while Stilicho earned the credit for stopping their advances. It was probably because of these arrangements between Alaric and Stilicho that the Roman Senate paid the Visigoths a bribe of some 4,000 pounds of gold in 407.

In 408, after the murder of Stilicho, an effort was made to purge Italy of barbarians. The families of many tribesmen serving in the Roman army were killed, and Alaric's band was much increased by the survivors and defecting tribal soldiers. These elements, as well as a large band of Alani that had joined the Visigoths before the battle of Adrianople in 378, both highlight the multiethnic nature of Alaric's force and may suggest why there was a diversity of opinion concerning what policies the group should follow. Alaric appears to have wanted to take his followers to North Africa, where they would have no trouble finding adequate food, but others appear to have wanted to plunder Italy, particularly Rome. Between 408 and 410, Alaric was in almost constant negotiations with the emperor and the authorities in Rome. On two occasions prior to the summer of 410, he laid siege to Rome, but withdrew when he apparently thought that his demands would be met. Finally, in August of 410 negotiations again broke down, and during the last week of the month, the Visigoths entered the city and sacked it.

After the sack of Rome, it was Alaric's plan to cross to North Africa. He took with him hostages who included Placidia, the emperor's sister. The Visigoths managed to gather a fleet of sorts at Reggio in the south, but before the main body of Alaric's forces could reach the port, the boats were destroyed in a storm. Alaric, forced to alter his plans, moved his band north. He died at Cosentia (Cosenza), apparently of natural causes, probably no more than forty years of age. Leadership of the Visigoths passed to his brother-in-law Athaulf.

BIBLIOGRAPHY

Dietrich Claude, *Geschichte der Westgoten* (1970); F. Dahn, *Die Könige der Germanen,* V (1870); L. Musset, *The Germanic Invasions* (1975), E. and C. James, trans; and O. Seeck, *Geschichte des Untergangs der antiken Welt,* V (1913), index, and VI (1921), index.

BERNARD S. BACHRACH

ALAVERDI cathedral, located in Kakhetia, the eastern province of Georgia, is an early eleventh-century triconch dedicated to St. George and bearing close resemblance to the cathedrals in Oshki and Kutaisi. It is distinguished by its enormous dimensions (exterior height 50 m.), its clearly defined interior cruciform space, and its emphasis on vertical masses. Architectural sculpture and ornamental embellishments are lacking, but the exterior walls are articulated by slender blind arcades. Originally it was equipped with galleries on three sides. The cathedral was restored in the fifteenth, eighteenth, and nineteenth centuries. Removal of the whitewash in the interior revealed the original wall paintings.

BIBLIOGRAPHY

Georgy N. Chubinashvili, *Arkhitektura Kakhetii,* 2 vols. (1956–1959).

WACHTANG DJOBADZE

ALB. See **Vestments.**

ALBA ("dawn song"), a lyric genre that takes for its constant theme the separation of two lovers at daybreak. Although undoubtedly popular in its origins—every culture seems to have its dawn songs—the alba in medieval southern France became in the hands of certain troubadours a highly specific courtly genre. It appears from manuscript evidence that the genre was cultivated far more in southern than in northern France during the twelfth and thirteenth centuries, for more than fifteen albas survive in Old Provencal as compared to fewer than five Old French *aubes.* It is significant too that thirteen of the albas are signed, whereas only one aube bears a poet's name, Gace Brulé, and even this attribution is questionable. In the Old Provençal texts, the word "alba" occurs in the final verse of each stanza, but in Old French there is no indication that aube ever became a technical term descriptive of a literary genre or that it necessarily functioned within the poem as part of a refrain.

Typically the alba assumes the form of a dialogue between a watchman and one of a pair of lovers who have spent the night together. The approaching light of dawn stirs the watchman to consternation, for as their friend and protector he must now arouse the sleeping couple and prevail upon them to end their tryst lest the secret of their love be exposed. The first lover to awaken responds to the watchman's cries and sings a lament on the dawn, which marks the conclusion of these brief hours of nocturnal bliss. The absent figure of the *gilos,* or jealous husband, conspires with the dawn as an ally of those forces opposed to *fin amors.* The most famous alba is *Reis glorios,* by the twelfth-century troubadour Giraut de Bornelh, for which, quite exceptionally, two musical settings have been preserved.

BIBLIOGRAPHY

Arthur T. Hatto, ed., *Eos: An Enquiry into the Theme of Lovers' Meetings and Partings at Dawn in Poetry* (1965), 344–389; Alfred Jeanroy, *La poésie lyrique des troubadours,* II (1934), 292–297, 339–341; Dietmar Rieger, "Zur Stellung des Tageliedes in der Trobadorlyrik," in *Zeitschrift für romanische Philologie,* 87 (1971); and Jonathan Saville, *The Medieval Erotic Alba: Structure as Meaning* (1972).

ELIZABETH WILSON POE

ALBANIA (CAUCASIAN) (Armenian, A^{c}łwank^{c}; Georgian, Rani; Persian, Ṙan; Syriac, Aran; Arabic, al-Rān [which became Arrān]), an ancient and medieval state of southeastern Caucasia, which at first consisted of some eighteen districts located between the Caucasus Mountains on the north, the Kura River on the south, the Caspian Sea on the east, and eastern Georgia (Iberia) on the west.

Originally a federation of twenty-six Caucasian tribes formed under the Aṛanšahikid dynasty in the first century B.C., Albania in the next century came under the control of a branch of the Parthian Arsacids that ruled until about 510. A remote and backward country little touched by Hellenism, Albania possessed a social structure virtually identical to that of Armenia and Iberia.

Together the three states may be said to have formed a single south Caucasian society characterized by a relatively weak king presiding over a turbulent class of dynastic princes who regarded their sovereign as little more than first among equals. Beneath the princes and subject to them were the gentry (*azat* class). A small urban population of merchants and craftsmen also existed. The great mass of the people were either peasants increasingly bound to the land or nomadic or seminomadic herders. A major factor in the Albanian state, however, must have been a number of mountain tribes poorly integrated into the mainstream of national life.

Briefly a Roman province under Trajan from 114 to 117, Albania was usually a vassal of Iran. Ptolemy cited twenty-nine localities in the country, but apart from the capital, Qabala (Armenian, Kapaḷak), Khamekhia (perhaps Shemakha), and Albana (perhaps Derbent), none can be identified. Christianized in the fourth and fifth centuries through Armenian missionary endeavor, Albania rapidly became culturally Armenized, especially after the twenty districts of the Armenian principalities of Utik^{c}, Šakašēn, Gardman, and Koł̓t^{c} were ceded to Albania in 387, along with the land of Arc^{c}ax and the city of P^{c}aytakaran (Arabic, Baylaqān) and its district. This process accelerated after St. Mesrob (Maštoc^{c}), inventor of the Armenian and Iberian scripts, provided the Albanians with a fifty-two-letter alphabet of their own, and especially after the mid fifth century, when the capital of Albania was moved south of the Kura, to Perozapat (Pērōz-Kawādh; Armenian, Partav; Arabic, Bardha^{c}a, now Barda).

The closest ties existed between the Armenian and Albanian churches. The primate (later Katholikos) of Albania had to be consecrated by the primate of Armenia, and the Albanian church followed the Armenian church into the anti-Chalcedonian schism, probably accepted at the second Synod of Dwin (555). After the fall of its Arsacid dynasty, Albania was ruled directly by a Persian viceroy *(marzpan)* until emperor Heraclius established the

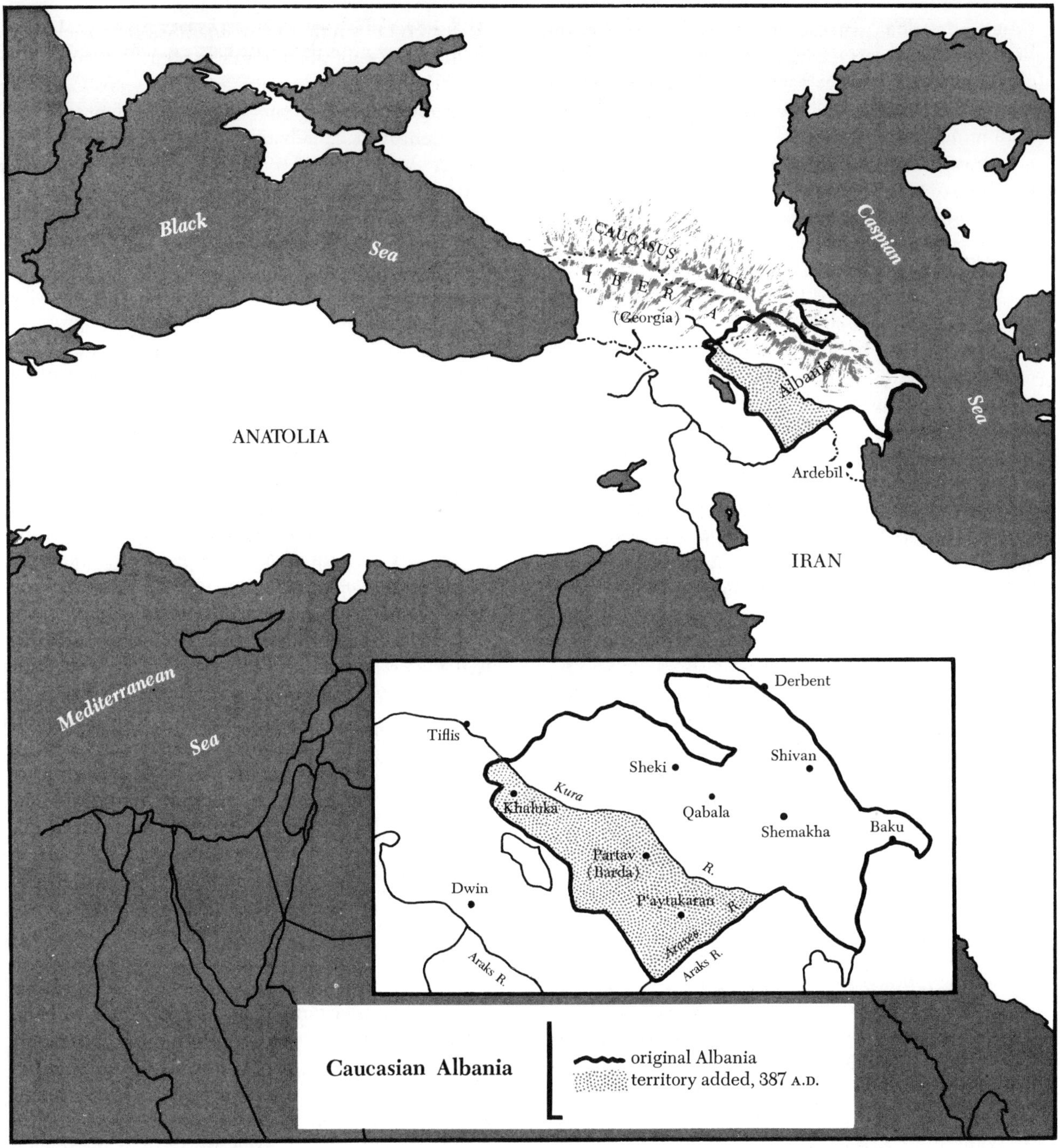

Mihrānids of Gardman as hereditary "presiding princes" of the country (628), a position they held under Arab suzerainty from about 643 to 821. From the sixth to the eighth century, Albania was subjected to ravages by the powerful Khazar state north of the Caucasus, the raids of 552, 626, 681, and 709 being especially destructive. In the following decades, these incursions ceased as a result of successful Arab counterattacks.

Under Arab domination, trade flourished in Caucasia; Bardha^{c}a and Baylaqān both became important commercial centers with well-built houses, bazaars, mosques, and fortifications. Roads linked both cities to Tiflis (Tbilisi) in eastern Georgia, Dwin in

Armenia, Ardebīl in Iran, and Derbent to the northeast. The Armenians, Georgians, and Albanians were vassals of the Arabs rather than an integral part of the caliphate. Repeated insurrections against Muslim domination led to Arab reprisals, and in Albania the native princes were gradually dispossessed from the lowlands. All of the original Albanian territory north of the Kura was early lost to the Muslim states of Shirvan, Derbent, and Sheki, while south of the river the term Arrān came to refer only to the lands between the juncture of the Kura and the Aras, with its center around Bardha^{c}a. Conversions to Islam were numerous in Albania, and the surviving Christian population appears to have taken refuge in the mountains of eastern Armenia. The last Mihrānid, Varaz-Tiridates II, was slain in 821, after which Albania ceased to exist as a Christian political entity.

In 943/944 Bardha^{c}a was destroyed, and the center of Arrān shifted west to Gandzha (Kirovabad), which was ruled by the Kurdish Shaddādids until they were ousted by the Seljuk Turks in 1075. The Mongol and Tartar invasions of the thirteenth through fifteenth centuries completed the Islamification and Turkification of Albania; its catholicate became a subdivision of the Church of Armenia until suppressed by the Russians in 1828. The terms Arrān and Ałwank^{c} lingered long in Muslim and Armenian sources but were gradually replaced by the name Azerbaidzhan, formerly used only for the lands south of the Aras. Occupied by the Russians in 1805–1806, the territory of Caucasian Albania now lies wholly within the Azerbaijan Republic of the Soviet Union.

The Albanian alphabet, a variant of Aramaic script but with its letters arranged as in Greek, was discovered in 1938. Although it cannot yet be read, it reveals that Albanian was a Caucasian language.

BIBLIOGRAPHY

Nikolay G. Adontz, *Armenia in the Period of Justinian,* Nina G. Garsoïan, trans. (1970), *passim;* Akademia nauk Azerbaydzhansky SSR. Institut istorii, *Voprosy istorii Kavkazskoy Albanii* (1962); Georges Dumézil, "Une chrétienté disparue: les Albaniens du Caucase," in *Journal asiatique,* **232** (1940–1941); Sowren T. Eremyan, *Hayastanĕ ĕst "Ašxarhac^{c}oyc^{c}"-i* (1963); C. Toumanoff, *Manuel de généalogie et de chronologie pour l'histoire de la Caucasie chrétienne (Arménie-Georgie-Albanie)* (1976), *passim,* and *Studies in Christian Caucasian History* (1963), *passim;* Kamilla V. Trever, *Ocherki po istorii i kulture Kavkazskoy Albanii* (1959).

ROBERT H. HEWSEN

ALBERIC OF MONTE CASSINO (*d.* 1105) was a major figure in the revival of classical culture in southern Italy that spread from the monastery at Monte Cassino. He entered Monte Cassino in 1060 as an adult. Like many of his contemporaries, his interests were diverse. His letters to Peter Damian concern Berengar of Tours and the investiture controversy. Alberic wrote devotional pieces, hymns to saints and rhythms for Easter (his authorship of some of the hymns and rhythms is disputed); a sermon on St. Scholastica; and a new version of the life of St. Dominic of Sora. He also produced a treatise on astronomy and a dialogue on music (neither extant). However, his most important literary contribution was his *Liber dictaminum et salutatione,* a three-book treatise on metrics, rhythm, grammar, and letter composition, one of the first works of the *ars dictaminis* genre.

BIBLIOGRAPHY

Alberic's published writings include "Alberici Diaconi sermo in sanctam Scholastica," in *Patrologia latina,* LXVI (1866); *Rationes dictandi* and *De dictamine,* in *Briefsteller und Formelbücher des elften bis vierzehnten Jahrhunderts,* L. Rockinger, ed., I (1961); "Vita sancti Dominici," in *Acta sanctorum,* Jan. 22 (1863), and *Alberici Casinensis flores rhetorici,* D. M. Inguanez and H. M. Willard, eds. (1938). See also H. H. Davis, "The 'De rithmis' of Alberic of Monte Cassino: A Critical Edition," in *Mediaeval Studies,* **28** (1966); P. F. Gehl, "Monastic Rhetoric and Grammar in the Age of Desiderius: The Works of Alberic of Monte Cassino" (Ph.D. diss., University of Chicago, 1976); and A. Lentini, "Alberico di Montecassino nel quadro della riforma gregoriana," in *Studi gregoriani,* **4** (1952).

LEAH SHOPKOW

ALBERT OF SAXONY (*ca.* 1316–1390), teacher, philosopher, and bishop, was born in or near Rickmersdorf, Lower Saxony. He studied and taught at the University of Paris and was its rector in 1357 and 1362. He helped found the University of Vienna and was its first rector in 1365. The following year he was named bishop of Halberstadt, where he remained until his death.

A prolific author, Albert helped spread Ockham's ideas in Germany through his well-organized treatise on logic. He was also interested in physics as a result of his studies with Buridan, and he knew something of the work of Bradwardine and other members of the Oxford group of mathematicians. He was especially concerned with problems of motion and accepted the doctrine of impetus, which points toward the later concept of inertia. Albert also tried to work out a rule for the increased velocity of falling bodies, which, he believed, depended on distance rather than time. His studies of a projectile led him to believe that it was affected both by its initial velocity and by what we would call gravity, but he thought that these forces worked sequentially rather than simultaneously. Like his fellow bishop Oresme he considered, but rejected, the idea that it was the earth that revolved and not the heavens.

Albert saw that mathematical solutions could be found for problems in physics. Most of his treatises were published in the Renaissance and had some influence on scientists of that period.

BIBLIOGRAPHY

The best discussion of Albert's work is by Ernest A. Moody, in *Dictionary of Scientific Biography*, I (1970). For translations of his texts, see Marshall Clagett, *The Science of Mechanics in the Middle Ages* (1959); and *Archimedes in the Middle Ages*, I (1964). There are some useful remarks by Alistair C. Crombie in his *Medieval and Modern Science*, 2nd ed., II (1959).

JOSEPH R. STRAYER

[See also **Bradwardine, Thomas; Buridan, Jean; Ockham, William of; Oresme, Nicole; Physics.**]

ALBERTI, LEON BATTISTA (1404–1472), Italian humanist and architect, was born in Genoa, the illegitimate son of an exiled Florentine merchant–banker. He received a humanist education in Padua and Bologna, and obtained a doctorate in canon law in 1428. He then went to Rome and was employed in the papal chancery as an abbreviator. A papal dispensation allowed him to take holy orders despite his illegitimacy, and he held two Tuscan benefices while living in Rome. His early writings were in the classical Latin style then in vogue at the Roman curia.

In 1434, Alberti went with Pope Eugenius IV to Florence, and established close relations with the leading humanists and artists there: Bruni, Gian Francesco Poggio Bracciolini, Marsuppini, Filippo Brunelleschi, Donatello. His intellectual interests broadened while he was in Florence, and after he returned to Rome in 1443 Alberti concentrated upon scientific and artistic problems. He advised Pope Nicholas V (1447–1455) on problems of urban renewal and the restoration of Roman churches. Though he spent most of his later life in Rome, he maintained close contact with prominent Florentine intellectuals: Paolo Toscanelli, Marsilio Ficino, Cristoforo Landino, and the young Lorenzo de' Medici.

Alberti was both a theorist and a practitioner of the classical revival in architecture. His 1452 treatise *De re aedificatoria* (published 1485) formulated the principles of the new style. His major building projects were the following: in Florence, the Palazzo Rucellai and its loggia, and the facade of Santa Maria Novella; in Rimini, the Tempio Malatestiano (Church of San Francesco), and in Mantua, the churches of San Sebastiano and Sant'Andrea.

In addition to his treatise on architecture, Alberti wrote essays on painting and sculpture: *De pictura* (1435) and *De statua* (*ca.* 1464). He used classical models in composing many of his Latin works, such as the comedy *Philodoxios* and the satirical essay *Momus.* His most famous Italian work, *Della famiglia* (*ca.* 1432–1445), was an analysis of the social, moral, and cultural problems of Italian (and specifically Florentine) urban society in the mid fifteenth century. He died in Rome.

BIBLIOGRAPHY

Texts. Opere volgari di Leon Battista Alberti, A. Banucci, ed., 5 vols. (1843–1849); *Opera inedita Leon Battista Alberti,* G. Mancini, ed. (1890); *Momus; o, Del principe,* G. Martini, ed. (1942); *Opere volgare,* C. Grayson, ed., 3 vols. (1960–1973).

Translations. The Family in Renaissance Florence, trans. of *Della famiglia* by R. Watkins (1969); *On Painting; and, On Sculpture,* ed. and trans. Cecil Grayson (1972).

Studies. Joan Gadol, *Leon Battista Alberti: Universal Man of the Renaissance* (1969); Girolamo Mancini, *La vita di Leon Battista Alberti,* 2nd ed. (1911); Paul Henry Michel, *La pensée de Leon Battista Alberti* (1930).

GENE A. BRUCKER

ALBERTUS MAGNUS, Saint (*ca.* 1200–1280), Dominican scholastic, bishop, Doctor of the Church, patron of natural scientists, and philosopher, was born at Lauingen, Germany, and died at Cologne. He is variously referred to as Albert the Great, Friar Albert the German *(Frater Albertus Teutonicus),* Albert of Cologne *(de Colonia),* or as Albert of Lauingen *(de Lauinga),* as well as by the scholastic titles *Doctor universalis* and *Doctor expertus.* Although in his own day Albert was esteemed as the outstanding scholastic of the High Middle Ages, he is best known today as the teacher of St. Thomas Aquinas. His importance lies mainly in having made Aristotelian thought "intelligible to the Latins" through systematic paraphrase of the entire corpus and in opening new areas of study to scientific research.

The first forty years of Albert's life are relatively obscure. Lauingen is a small town in Swabia situated on the Danube between Ulm and Dillingen in the diocese of Augsburg, Bavaria. An elder son of a military lord (knight) in the service of the counts of Bollstädt loyal to the Hohenstaufens, Albert was sent as a young man to the incipient University of Padua, while his father fought in the service of Frederick II in Lombardy. Despite earlier misgivings he joined the Order of Preachers (Dominicans) early in the summer of 1223, receiving the habit from Jordan of Saxony, successor to St. Dominic (died 1221). Albert was then sent to the priory at Cologne for his novitiate and early theological studies, in the future Province of Germany (Teutonia). After becoming a lector (lecturer) in theology in 1228, he taught at Cologne; Hildesheim and Freiberg in Saxony; Regensburg in Bavaria; and Strassburg in Alsace. During these years he wrote *De natura boni* (Cologne (C.) ed. 25), which is based mainly on twelfth-century sources.

MASTER IN THEOLOGY

When John Teutonicus of Wildeshausen was elected master general of the Dominicans in 1241, Albert was sent to Paris to prepare for the mastership in theology. His task at the university was to participate in disputations and to lecture on the *Sentences* of Peter Lombard at the Dominican convent of St. Jacques at the University of Paris. The intellectual climate of Paris was vastly different from that of Albert's native Germany, for here he encountered the "new Aristotle," recently translated from Greek and Arabic, and the wealth of Arabic learning introduced from Spain. Albert arrived in Paris just as Averroës' commentaries on Aristotle were becoming available.

By the spring of 1245, Albert had met all university requirements for the degree of master in theology, the first German Dominican to earn that degree. That fall Thomas Aquinas arrived in Paris to begin his novitiate and theological studies. For the next three years Albert lectured on Pseudo-Dionysius, resolved disputed questions (unedited), and preached university sermons (largely unedited), all the while writing a *Summa Parisiensis* in six parts *(De sacramentis; De incarnatione; De resurrectione; De IV coaequaevis; De homine; De bono)* and revising his commentary on the *Sentences* for publication (completed in 1249). In 1248 he was sent to Cologne to establish a *studium generale* for the Dominicans, open to all clerics, the first of its kind in Germany.

In August 1248, Albert and a group of Dominican students, including Thomas, arrived in Cologne. The priory of Heilige Kreuz on the Stolkgasse was enlarged to receive students from all parts of the order, following the pattern of St. Jacques in Paris. At Cologne, Albert lectured on *De divinis nominibus* (reported by Thomas, C. 37, 1) and on the rest of the Dionysian corpus (C. 37, 2), as well as on the ten books of Aristotle's *Ethics* (C. 14), which had been translated into Latin by Robert Grosseteste about 1246–1247.

Toward the end of 1249, acceding to the pleas of Dominican students, Albert embarked upon his huge paraphrase of Aristotelian philosophy, beginning with the *Physics.* His intention was, first, to present the whole of natural science, even parts that Aristotle did not write about or that had been lost, and, second, to make all the books of Aristotle "intelligible to the Latins" by rephrasing arguments, adding new ones, and resolving difficulties encountered by other schools of philosophy, notably Platonist and Epicurean. The entire Albertinian corpus of Aristotelian paraphrases, completed by 1270, was deliberate, systematic, and consecutive with Aristotle's books; it included the whole of logic, natural philosophy, moral philosophy, and First Philosophy *(Metaphysics* [C. 16] and *Liber de causis).* Albert is one of the very few Scholastics to have commented on *De plantis* (ed. E. Meyer and C. Jessen, 1867) and on the whole of *De animalibus* (ed. H. Stadler, 1916, 1920).

From March 1252 until fifteen months before his death, Albert was frequently called upon to arbitrate difficult litigations. In the first case he and Cardinal Hugh of St. Cher were appointed by Pope Innocent IV to arbitrate the litigation between Conrad von Hochstaden, archbishop of Cologne, and the burghers of the city.

By August 1252, Albert, with the help of Hugh of St. Cher, had convinced the Dominican master general, John of Wildeshausen, to send Thomas Aquinas, Albert's teaching assistant, to Paris to lecture on the *Sentences* for the master's degree.

PROVINCIAL OF TEUTONIA

In June 1254, at the provincial chapter in Worms, Albert was elected prior provincial of the Dominican province of Teutonia, which then had thirty-six

 ALBERTUS MAGNUS

priories (including the mission house at Riga, Latvia) and more than twenty cloisters of nuns. During his term three new priories were founded: Strausberg in the mark of Brandenburg (1254), Seehausen in the Altmark (1255), and Rostock on the Baltic (1256), as well as a number of cloisters for nuns, the most famous of which was the Paradisus near Soest in Westphalia. As provincial, Albert made canonical visitations of each priory, including the one at Riga, always traveling on foot. He presided at three provincial chapters and attended the general chapters at Milan (1255), Paris (1256), and Florence (1257).

The most significant event in Albert's provincialate was his summons in 1256 to the papal curia at Anagni, where he and Master General Humbert of Romans (1254–1263) represented the order in its struggle against William of St. Amour and his colleagues from Paris, who saw mendicant orders, particularly Dominicans and Franciscans at the University of Paris, as precursors of Antichrist before the Last Days. St. Bonaventure, minister general of the Franciscans, and Albert played the decisive role: the controversy was temporarily resolved with the condemnation of William's *De periculis novissimorum temporum* on 5 October 1256, and insistence on the earlier bull *Quasi lignum vitae* of 14 April 1255. At the papal curia of Alexander IV, Albert seems to have debated publicly against the Averroist doctrine of one intellect for all men, later (about 1263) working his arguments into a treatise called *De unitate intellectus contra Averroistas* (C. 17, 1).

During his term as provincial, Albert wrote his paraphrase of Aristotle's *De anima,* which he considered one of his most important works. This was followed by a collection of nine short works, grouped as *Parva naturalia,* which include both Aristotle's treatises and Albert's own supplementary treatises on nutrition, intellection, aging, dying, and other matters. This was followed by *De plantis,* a paraphrase of Pseudo-Aristotle with Albert's own additions, including an herbal in two books.

Albert remained in Italy, possibly expounding "the Gospel of John and all the canonical Epistles" until the general chapter of Florence in June 1257, when he resigned. Following the provincial chapter of Augsburg that summer, he returned to Cologne to resume teaching, which included a series of disputations on Aristotle's *De animalibus* (C. 12).

In 1259, Humbert of Romans appointed Albert head of a commission on studies that included Bonhomme Brito, Florent de Hesdin, Thomas Aquinas, and Peter of Tarentaise. This group drew up what might be called the first *ratio studiorum* of the Dominicans, consisting of twenty-two clear statements dealing with the behavior of lectors and students, the importance of philosophy for theology, and requisites for *studia solemnia* (where there should be bachelors teaching under masters, "repetitions" of lectures by students, instruction in philosophy) and for every priory (where there should be instruction in Scripture, salvation history, and cases of conscience).

BISHOP

A letter from Alexander IV, dated 5 January 1260, appointed Albert bishop of Regensburg in the ecclesiastical province of Salzburg, which was in a deplorable state both financially and spiritually. Despite his own reluctance and the plea of Humbert of Romans that he refuse, he was consecrated at Cologne and invested as a temporal prince in March. Surviving documents show him to have been very solicitous and farsighted. Known to the local Bavarians as "Boots the Bishop," he continued to travel everywhere by foot. As bishop he continued his paraphrases, writing book VII of *De animalibus* at the episcopal castle of Donaustauff. By the end of 1260 he was ready to seek release from this unwanted burden.

In December, having placed the diocese in charge of Henry as vicar, Leo Torndorf as dean of the chapter, and Ulrich as pastor of the cathedral church, Albert set out for the papal curia at Viterbo. He arrived in July 1261, only to learn that Alexander IV had died the preceding May. A new pope was elected on 29 August and consecrated at Viterbo on 4 September, taking the name of Urban IV. By that date Thomas Aquinas had arrived at the Dominican priory of San Domenico to take up duties as lector. Albert's resignation was accepted around November, elections were ordered at Regensburg, and Leo Torndorf was elected and confirmed as his successor on 11 May 1262. During this period Urban IV kept Albert at Viterbo and Orvieto. In February 1263 he ordered Albert to preach the crusade in all lands that spoke the German language, conferring on him extraordinary powers for the successful prosecution of the mission. By March, Albert set out in the company of Friar Berthold, a German Dominican. With Urban's death in October 1264, Albert's commission came to an end.

Residing in the Dominican priory at Würzburg with his brother Henry from the end of 1264 until 1269, Albert wrote his paraphrase of Aristotle's *Me-*

taphysics and the anonymous *Liber de causis,* which brought the mammoth project to an end. In 1269, John of Vercelli, master of the order (1264–1283), asked Albert to live in Cologne as lector emeritus, which he did, writing, performing paraepiscopal functions, arbitrating complex litigations, and serving as an example to all. He was in Cologne when news reached him of Thomas' death in 1274, and he seems to have gone to Paris three years later to defend the teachings of Thomas, then being attacked. In his last will and testament, dated January 1279, he was "of sound mind and body." From 18 August 1279, the date of the last arbitration document, Albert seems to have become progressively senile until his death on 15 November 1280, at the age of "eighty and some."

INFLUENCE

Not only was Albert the only man of the High Middle Ages to be called "the Great," but this title was used even before his death. Before the canonization of Thomas in 1323, the prestige of Albert was higher than that of any other Scholastic of the thirteenth century. In the words of Ulrich of Strassburg, a disciple, Albert was "a man so superior in every science, that he can fittingly be called the wonder and miracle of our time." According to Roger Bacon, a younger contemporary, Albert was quoted in the schools on a par with Aristotle, Avicenna, and Averroës, even though he was still living. Siger of Brabant, a contemporary of Thomas at Paris, considered Albert and Thomas "the principal men in philosophy."

The cult of Albert long existed in Germany among both laity and clergy; numerous miracles were attributed to him and an incredible number of spurious works, both devotional and magical, were ascribed to him. Late in the fifteenth century the cause of his canonization was well advanced until the charge of sorcery and magic was raised; to refute these charges, Peter of Prussia wrote the first really critical biography of Albert (about 1487). Albert was beatified by Gregory XV in 1622. By the decree *In thesauris sapientiae* (16 December 1931) Pius XI declared him a saint with the additional title of doctor. By the decree *Ad Deum* (16 December 1941) Pius XII constituted him the heavenly patron of all who cultivate the natural sciences. His body is buried in Cologne, and his feast is observed on November 15.

Among Albert's immediate disciples, besides Thomas and Ulrich of Strassburg, should be mentioned Hugh of Strassburg, John of Freiberg, John of Lichtenberg, and Giles of Lessines. Through these men and his writings, Albert's teaching influenced Dietrich of Freiberg, Berthold of Mossburg, Meister Eckhart, Johannes Tauler, Heinrich Suso, and Nicholas of Cusa. A distinctive school of "Albertists" (opposed to Thomists) developed in Paris under Jean de Maisonneuve (Joannes de Nova Domo) early in the fifteenth century, and was promulgated by Heymerich van den Velde (Heimericus de Campo, died 1460) both at Paris and at Cologne; it quickly spread throughout German, Bohemian, and Polish universities. At Italian universities in the late Middle Ages it was not so much Albertism as the philosophical opinion of Albert himself that was kept alive.

BIBLIOGRAPHY

Early printed versions of both authentic and spurious writings ascribed to Albert abound; on the other hand, many works known to have been written by him have not yet been discovered. Two editions of "complete works" have been published: Peter Jammy, O.P., ed., 21 folio vols. (1651); Abbé Auguste Borgnet, 38 quarto vols. (1890–1899). A critical edition under the auspices of the Albertus-Magnus-Institut of Cologne began appearing in 1951 and is far from finished; when completed, it will number 40 volumes, some in several parts. The following list gives the volume of the Borgnet edition (B) and the projected volume of the Cologne edition (C); the dates in brackets are the certain or probable dates of composition.

Logic. *Super Porphyrium de universalibus,* B. 1, C. 1; *De praedicamentis,* B. 1, C. 1; *De sex principiis,* B. 1, C. 1; *De divisione,* C. 1; *Peri hermeneias,* B. 1, C. 1; *Analytica priora,* B. 1, C. 2; *Analytica posteriora,* B. 2, C. 2; *Topica,* B. 2, C. 3; *De sophisticis elenchis,* B. 2, C. 3 [all between 1260 and 1271].

Natural Science. *Physica,* B. 3, C. 4 [1249–1250]; *De caelo et mundo,* B. 4, C. 5 [1250–1254]; *De natura locorum,* B. 9, C. 5 [1250–1254]; *De causis proprietatum elementorum,* B. 9, C. 5 [1250–1254]; *De generatione et corruptione,* B. 4, C. 5 [*ca.* 1253]; *Meteora,* B. 4, C. 6 [1253–1254]; *De mineralibus,* B. 5, C. 6 [*ca.* 1254]; *De anima,* B. 5, C. 7 [*ca.* 1254]; *Parva naturalia,* B. 9, C. 7 [1254–1257]; *De plantis,* B. 10, C. 8 [before 1260]; *QQ. super De animalibus,* C. 12 [1258]; *De animalibus* B. 11–12, C. 9–11 [1258–1263]; *De natura et origine animae,* B. 9, C. 12 [*ca.* 1262–1264]; *De principiis motus processivi,* B. 10, C. 12 [1262–1264].

Moral Sciences. *Super Ethica commentum et quaestiones,* C. 14 [between 1248 and 1252]; *Ethica,* B. 7, C. 13 [before 1261]; *Politica,* B. 8, C. 15 [1264–1274].

Metaphysics. *De unitate intellectus,* B. 9, C. 17 [*ca.* 1255; 1263]; *Metaphysica,* B. 6, C. 16 [between 1262 and 1267]; *De causis,* B. 10, C. 17 [between 1267 and 1271]; *De 15 problematibus,* C. 17 [*ca.* 1270]; *43 Problemata determinata,* C. 17 [April 1271].

Scripture. *Super Lucam,* B. 22–23, C. 23 [1261–1262; revised 1270–1275]; *Super Ioannem,* B. 24, C. 24 [*ca.*1256; revised 1270–1275]; *Super Job,* C. 18 [1272 or 1274]; *Super Isaiam,* C. 19; *Super Ieremiam* (fragment), C. 20; *Super Threnos,* B. 18, C. 20; *Super Baruch,* B. 18, C. 20; *Super Ezechielem* (fragment), C. 20; *Super Danielem,* B. 18, C. 20; *Super prophetas minores,* B. 19, C. 20; *Super Mattheum,* B. 20–21, C. 21 [definitive version after 1270]; *Super Marcum,* B. 21, C. 22 [definitive version between 1272 and 1275]. Albert's commentaries on St. Paul and on Apocalypse have not yet been found; the printed Apocalypse is spurious.

Systematic Theology. *De natura boni,* C. 25 [before 1241]; *Super 4 Sententiarum,* B. 25–30, C. 29–32 [revised version completed in 1249]; *QQ. theologicae,* C. 25 [1245–1248]; *De 4 coaequaevis,* B. 34, C. 26 [1245–1248]; *De homine,* B. 35, C. 27 [1245–1248]; *De sacramentis, De incarnatione, De resurrectione,* C. 26 [1245–1250]; *De bono,* C. 28 [1246–1248]; *In corpus Dionysium,* B. 14, C. 36–37 [1247–1260]; *Summa theologiae,* B. 31–33, C. 34–35 [doubtful; after 1270]; *De mysterio missae, De corpore domini,* B. 38, C. 38 [doubtful; after 1270].

Sermons and Letters. C. 39.

Spurious and Dubious Works. C. 40. It is certain that Albert wrote on mathematics, astronomy, and poetics, but these works have not yet been found. Among the many spurious works, the best known are the *Compendium theologicae veritatis,* B. 34, which is by Hugh of Strassburg; *Philosophia pauperum,* B. 5, which is by Albert of Orlamünde; *De laudibus B. Mariae Virginis,* B. 36; *Mariale,* B. 37; *Biblia Mariana,* B. 37; *De secretis naturae, De secretis mulierum,* and many occult books of wonders. The authenticity of many other works, notably the *Speculum astronomiae,* is still disputed among scholars.

The only authentic work of Albert's translated into English is *Book of Minerals,* Dorothy Wyckoff, trans. (1967).

Also see Heinrich Balss, *Albertus Magnus als Biologe: Werk und Ursprung* (1947); Martin Grabmann, "Der Einfluss Alberts des Grossen auf das mittelalterliches Geistesleben," in *Mittelalterliches Geistesleben,* II (1936); Francis J. Kovach and Robert W. Shahan, *Albert the Great: Commemorative Essays* (1980); Marie-Hyacinthe Laurent and Yves Congar, eds., "Essai de bibliographie albertinienne," in *Revue thomiste,* **36** (1931); Paulus von Loë, "De vita et scriptis B. Alberti Magni," in *Analecta bollandiana,* **19** (1900), **20** (1901), and **21** (1902); Gilles Meersseman, *Introductio in opera omnia B. Alberti Magni* (1931) and *Geschichte des Albertismus,* 2 vols. (1933–1935); Franz Pelster, *Kritische Studien zum Leben und zu dem Schriften Alberts des Grossen* (1920); Angiolo Puccetti, *San Alberto Magno dell'Ordine dei Predicatori* (1932); Heribert C. Scheeben, *Albert der Grosse: Zur Chronologie seines Lebens* (1931) and *Albertus Magnus* (1955); Michel Schooyans, "Bibliographie philosophique de Saint Albert le Grand (1931–1960)," in *Revista da Universidade católica de São Paulo,* **21** (1961); Thomas M. Schwertner, *St. Albert the Great* (1932); Lynn Thorndike, *A History of Magic and Experimental Science,* II (1923), 517–592, 692–750; and James A. Weisheipl, ed., *Albertus Magnus and the Sciences: Commemorative Essays 1980* (1980).

JAMES A. WEISHEIPL

[See also **Aquinas, St. Thomas; Aristotle in the Middle Ages.**]

ALBIGENSIANS, the name given in late twelfth-century France to the Waldensian and Cathar heretics. First used at the Council of Tours in 1163 as a geographical adjective, the term came to be used during the Albigensian Crusade, by Matthew Paris among others, as a noun meaning "heretic." Albi (county of Toulouse) was taken as the see of the first Cathar bishop in Occitania, although he generally resided in a village.

FREDERIC L. CHEYETTE

[See also **Cathars; Waldensians.**]

ALBORNOZ, CARDINAL GIL. Gil Álvarez Carillo de Albornoz (1302/1303–1367) was the son of García Albornoz of Cuenca, head of a lineage favored by Alfonso XI of Castile. Gil was Alfonso's councillor, and his nomination as archbishop of Toledo in 1338 marked the entry of his family into the front rank of Castilian politics; after that year the family continued to advance in power, especially during the Trastamara triumph in Castile and Aragon in the 1360's.

However, the death of Alfonso XI in 1350 made Gil fear disgrace at the hands of Alfonso's successor, Pedro the Cruel. Gil withdrew to the papal court at Avignon, where he was made cardinal-priest (12 December 1350) and named papal legate and vicar-general in the Papal States and northern and central Italy (30 June 1353). He owed his nomination to his earlier military and administrative experience in Castile. Gil's appointment showed the intention of Pope Innocent VI to renew the great effort of the Avignon popes to impose firm government on the Papal States and to dominate central Italy, which had been virtually abandoned after the failure of John XXII's Italian policies in 1334.

The political and military activity of Albornoz in Italy falls into two periods: 1353–1357, during which he broke the resistance of the petty lords in the Papal States and prepared for a renewal of strong government there, and 1358–1364, during which he fought a great war with the Visconti and the Ghibelline lords of Lombardy in order to plant papal power firmly in Emilia and the lower Po valley.

Albornoz's accomplishments during the first period were more successful and lasting than those during the second. The subjection of some of the more unruly "tyrants" of the Papal States, especially of the Ordelaffi of Forlì, opened the way in 1357 to the enactment of a collection of laws, the *Constitutiones Aegidianae,* which served as the basic legal and administrative ordinance of the Papal States until the time of Napoleon. The *Constitutiones* was a recapitulatory collection of earlier laws, modified and harmonized, and not an authoritarian law code, as has sometimes been said. Whether Albornoz aimed at the imposition of what could be called papal sovereignty over the communes of the Papal States, or whether he merely wanted to suppress abuses or derogations of church liberty in communal laws, is a question that scholars have not yet settled.

Albornoz's attempt to revive the great Angevin-Guelph alliance of the 1320's at the expense of the Lombard lords was very costly in blood and money, and arguably unsuccessful. Between 1353 and 1360 the papal treasury in Italy spent well over a million and a half gold florins on war and fortification, and the expenses in the subsequent Lombard war were certainly no less. This huge expenditure of church money failed to pacify Italy, perhaps because the French monarchy was no longer strong enough or willing to give the support it had given the popes in the past.

Albornoz died near Viterbo. He was not merely a ruthless warlord but also an educated prince of the church, as was shown by his work as apostolic penitentiary in 1357–1358, and by his founding of the Spanish College at Bologna.

BIBLIOGRAPHY

"El cardenal Albornoz y el Colegio de España," in *Studia albornotiana,* E. Verdera y Tuells, ed., 4 vols. (1972, 1979); P. Colliva, *Il cardinale Albornoz: Lo stato della chiesa: Le Constitutiones aegidianae (1353–1357)* (1977); Francesco Filippini, *Il cardinale Egidio Albornoz* (1933); Berthe M. Marti, *The Spanish College at Bologna in the Fourteenth Century* (1966); Peter Partner, *The Lands of St Peter* (1972).

PETER D. PARTNER

ALBRECHT VON HALBERSTADT. The literary reputation of Albrecht von Halberstadt rests upon a single but monumental achievement, the translation of Ovid's *Metamorphoses* into the contemporary idiom of Middle High German, the first complete translation of any monument of classical literature into German, possibly into any European vernacular. What little information is extant about his life and work derives from the prologue to his translation, according to which he was a Saxon—a native of Halberstadt—and a cleric resident at the provostship of Jechaburg near Sondershausen in Thuringia, the latter supported by documentary evidence of one *magister Albertus* as a canon in 1217 and 1231. The translation was probably begun in 1210 and completed within the following decade.

Equally fragmentary is our knowledge of the translation itself. It was the basis of a further adaptation into sixteenth-century German by Jörg Wickram, published in 1545 in Mainz and frequently reprinted. After this there is no trace of Albrecht's version until two fragments of it came to light in the nineteenth century. Both were part of the same parchment manuscript, dating from the end of the thirteenth century, which was cut up for binding purposes in Oldenburg around 1625.

The two leaves discovered in 1859 (later designated as Fragment B) contain the 279 verses from the King Midas story to the reception of Peleus by Ceyx, corresponding to Ovid 11: 156–290. On the foundation of this brief excerpt but with the boundless philological self-confidence of the nineteenth century, the renowned medievalist Karl Bartsch undertook to turn the Wickram adaptation back into what he presumed to have been its original form and published the result in 1861. Four years later another leaf from the same Oldenburg manuscript was discovered, containing 144 verses of the tale of Procne and Philomela, Ovid 6: 440–482, which demonstrated the futility but did not repudiate the grandeur of Bartsch's attempted reconstruction.

Albrecht's work does not meet today's criteria for an accurate translation but is, rather, an adaptation of the Ovidian material to the cultural horizons and literary conventions of his own times. While necessarily directed by the general story lines, he drew in his choice of vocabulary and moral values upon the tradition of the courtly epic, transforming the scenes as well as the characters of classical mythology into such medieval counterparts as were available, amplifying here and deleting there, as seemed advisable to render the work intelligible and appealing to a prospective audience. The fundamental and ultimately insurmountable difficulty in the achievement of this purpose, as Karl Stackmann observed, lay in the fact that the original did not offer Albrecht the basic element of the courtly epic that was the model for his translation: the single victorious hero who at the end of the tale emerges as the exemplary knight. Conversely, the definitive transformation of the principals from their human shape into objects of nature fell entirely outside the realm of the imaginable in contemporary medieval literature.

These difficulties may account for the apparent lack of response in his own time to Albrecht's work and for its complete disappearance, except for the fragments mentioned, in later centuries. But what remains is a milestone in the compendious Ovidian tradition of the Latin Middle Ages and demonstrates the creative determination of one resourceful scholar to share his fascination with the original *Metamorphoses* in the vernacular long before there was at hand a vehicle equal to the task.

BIBLIOGRAPHY

Texts. The full text of both fragments is in Friedrich Neumann, "Meister Albrechts and Jörg Wickrams Ovid auf Deutsch," in *Beiträge zur Geschichte der deutschen Sprache und Literatur* (Halle), 76 (1954); Wickram's version of Albrecht's translation is in Johannes Bolte, ed., *Georg Wickrams Werke*, VII–VIII (1905–1906).

Studies. Karl Bartsch, *Albrecht von Halberstadt und Ovid im Mittelalter* (1861); Frederick Norman, "Albrecht von Halberstadt," in Wolfgang Stammler, ed., *Die deutsche Literatur des Mittelalters, Verfasserlexikon*, II (1936); Otto Runge, *Die Metamorphosen-Verdeutschung Albrechts von Halberstadt* (1908); Karl Stackmann, "Ovid im deutschen Mittelalter," in *Arcadia*, 1 (1966); and "Albrecht von Halberstadt," in Wolfgang Stammler, *op. cit.*, rev. ed., I (1978).

PETER SCHÄFFER

ALBRECHT VON JOHANSDORF. Little is known about Albrecht von Johansdorf. Documents from 1185 to 1209 mention that he was in the service of the bishop of Passau in northern Austria and that he went on the Third Crusade in 1190. With Johansdorf, the courtly lyric in Austria came fully into its own, and he put his very personal stamp on the genre. His oeuvre consists of six love songs, a poem with a pastoral theme, and four lyrics associated with the Crusades.

Deliberate ambiguity, comical or humorous effects, irony at the cost of the persona ("Swaz ich nu gesinge"), of the audience, or even of the lady of whom he sings ("Wize rote rosen") are the characteristics of the four short love songs. Each creates an environment inhospitable to the concept of courtly love *(hohe Minne)*. Love does not stand at the center of the poet's attention but is subservient to the task of providing entertainment. Thus Johansdorf's ambiguities, humor, and irony are verbal games with his listeners.

In "Ich vant si ane huote" the poet's alleged courtly love proposal to his lady is presented in the framework of a pastoral in which she mocks his plea for rapprochement in a manner that has nothing to do with courtly demeanor. Her closing statement that the poet's persistence is its own reward, since it will bring him worthiness and will fortify his joyful disposition, makes a plaything without substance of the courtly tenet involved and treats it farcically. His love songs depart from the lofty system of thought of traditional elucidations of courtly love.

Johansdorf's Crusade songs breathe a totally different spirit. True piety is at work here, together with what we may conceive of as true, abiding love. "Wie sich minne hebt" is a stirring, dramatic lyric in which the lady feels vulnerable and states what genuine love ought to amount to before she will engage in it. Her self-protective, fearful thoughts center on the threat of separation from the beloved who may depart for the Crusade. Her muted delivery questions God's will, should He call her partner to go on that Crusade. Potentially pitted against the deity, the lady is full of potential tumult, even revolt.

In "Die hinnen varn" the poet argues with himself about his choices: go on the Crusade and separate from his lady or stay with her and incur God's wrath. In "Mich mac der tot von ir minnen wol scheiden" the lady demands an explanation as to how the poet will depart and yet remain with her. His answer is not an answer but a claim that he must go on the Crusade for the welfare of his soul. "Ich unde ein wip, wir haben gestriten" is a more general and objective scrutiny of the difficulties to be faced by the would-be crusader.

"Min erste liebe der ich ie began" is tantamount

ALBRECHT VON SCHARFENBERG

to the poet's endeavor to explain to his lady that her way of thinking leads away from God and salvation, that she pits herself against God if she perseveres in her view. He is full of missionary zeal and seeks to convert her, to lead her to rearrange her priorities, to put the service of God first.

"Guote liute, holt" starts on a general niveau in order to center on the problem of the lady who is about to be left behind. Again the poet fails to come forth with a satisfactory answer. He can only promise to take the beloved with him in his heart and imputes to her that if he fails to return, God is to take care of him.

Thus the lady's unresolved problem recurs throughout Johansdorf's Crusade songs. Devotion to God's cause, whether it stems from contrition (love of God) or attrition (fear of punishment), becomes the overriding principle; but it can bring no peace to the lady, who at best can acquiesce but may be bitter. The concept of love in these poems goes far beyond courtly love. Genuine love, abiding and true, is involved; it is of all times and places. Only the accidents of history affecting such love are time-bound.

BIBLIOGRAPHY

The lyrics of Albrecht von Johansdorf are available in the collection *Des Minnesangs Frühling.* See Hugo Bekker, *The Poetry of Albrecht von Johansdorf* (1978); Wilhelm Braune, "Zu Albrecht von Johannsdorf," in *Beiträge zur Geschichte der deutschen Sprache und Literatur,* 27 (1902); Ulrich Fülleborn, "Die Motive Kreuzzug und Minne und das Gestaltungsprinzip in den Liedern Albrechts von Johansdorf," in *Euphorion,* 58 (1964); J. Hornoff, "Der Minnesänger Albrecht von Johansdorf," in *Germania,* 34 (1889); Dietrich Müller, "Albrecht von Johansdorf: Ein Beitrag zur mittelhochdeutschen Metrik," in *Programm Osnabrück* (1894); Ulrich Pretzel, "Die Kreuzzugslieder Albrecht von Johansdorf," in *Festgabe für L. L. Hammerich* (1962); David Sudermann, "The *Minnelieder* of Albrecht von Johansdorf: Edition, Commentary, Interpretation" (Diss., Univ. of Chicago, 1973).

HUGO BEKKER

ALBRECHT VON SCHARFENBERG. Albrecht von Scharfenberg's name and condensed versions of two of his works *(Seifrid de Ardemont* and *Merlin)* have survived only in Ulrich Füetrer's *Buch der Abenteuer,* a late fifteenth-century compilation of romance materials. Füetrer places Albrecht's stylistic achievement on a par with the artistry of Gottfried von Strassburg and Wolfram von Eschenbach (strophes 17–18). A third title, *fraw Eren hof,* is mentioned in the warmest terms (strophe 838), and the identification of this work has long dominated scholarship on Albrecht von Scharfenberg.

Two possibilities continue to be discussed: (1) *fraw Eren hof* refers to a lost work, perhaps an allegory, that Füetrer omitted from his compilation of romances; (2) the title refers to all or part of the *Jüngerer Titurel,* a text used extensively by Füetrer.

Although a poet named Albrecht did compose the *Jüngerer Titurel,* serious objections have been raised to the identification of his widely read work with *fraw Eren hof.* Among the numerous manuscripts of the *Jüngerer Titurel* there is no evidence to corroborate the use of such a title; indeed, the expression *frou Eren hove* occurs only once in the H text (strophe 682). More important, Albrecht pretends to be Wolfram von Eschenbach until very near the end of the composition. Only after Albrecht's three patrons withdrew their financial support from the mammoth undertaking did the poet drop the long-sustained fiction, and take credit for the entire work (strophes 5767–5768). Throughout the later Middle Ages and even into the nineteenth century the *Jüngerer Titurel* was universally attributed to Wolfram. Albrecht came to be regarded as a redactor and continuator, responsible only for the concluding segments. It is simply not reasonable to assume that Füetrer, alone among all his contemporaries, saw through Albrecht's posturing. Furthermore, Füetrer explicitly attributes both *Seifrid de Ardemont* and *Merlin* to Albrecht von Scharfenberg but does not do so for the material from the *Jüngerer Titurel.*

In all likelihood *fraw Eren hof* is the title of a lost work, but this does not exclude the possibility that only one Albrecht, Albrecht von Scharfenberg, composed the four texts in question. The *Jüngerer Titurel* can be dated with considerable accuracy. The Heidelberg *Verfasserfragment* reveals that, following the withdrawal of support by his original patrons, Albrecht rededicated the *Jüngerer Titurel* to Ludwig II of Bavaria in a belated attempt to capitalize on his candidacy for the crown of the Holy Roman Empire. This shift in patrons came to naught with the election of Rudolf von Hapsburg on 1 October 1273, an event to which Albrecht alludes in the text proper (strophe 5883). Neither *Seifrid de Ardemont* nor *Merlin* admits of such precise dating, but both could conceivably belong to the second half of the thirteenth century. Differences in sources notwithstanding, the *Jüngerer Titurel* and *Merlin* attempt to reconcile Wolfram's account of the Grail's history with the Old French tradition of Joseph of Arimathea. It would seem highly improbable that two Albrechts were engaged simultaneously in such similar projects, especially since the use of Old French models diminished considerably toward the end of the thirteenth century. The fact that Füetrer to some degree reworked all his romance sources makes the textual footing extremely uncertain. At present Albrecht von Scharfenberg's authorship of the *Jüngerer Titurel* must be regarded as an open question.

BIBLIOGRAPHY

Der jüngere Titurel, K. A. Hahn, ed. (1842), is still the only complete edition; *Jüngerer Titurel,* Werner Wolf, ed. (1955–); *Merlin und Seifrid de Ardemont,* Friedrich Panzer, ed. (1902), should be used only for *Seifrid;* Ulrich Füetrer, *Die Gralepen in Ulrich Füetrers Bearbeitung (Buch der Abenteuer),* Kurt Nyholm, ed. (1964), includes the text of *Merlin* on pp. 18–62 (strophes 121–383).

Dietrich Huschenbett, "Albrecht von Scharfenberg," in *Die deutsche Literatur des Mittelalters: Verfasserlexikon,* 2nd ed., I (1978), provides a convenient and very balanced overview of the controversy; Hans-Georg Maak, "Zu Füetrers *fraw Eren hof* und der Frage nach dem Verfasser des *Jüngeren Titurel,*" in *Zeitschrift für deutsche Philologie,* **87** (1968), argues against the identification of *fraw Eren hof* with the *Jüngerer Titurel;* Kurt Nyholm, "Albrechts von Scharfenberg Merlin," in *Acta Academiae Aboensis, Ser. A: Humaniora,* **33,** no. 2 (1967), also disputes this identification and examines *Merlin* in the context of the authorship controversy; Werner Wolf, "Wer war der Dichter des *Jüngeren Titurel*?" in *Zeitschrift für deutsches Altertum und deutsche Literatur,* **84** (1953), argues that *fraw Eren hof* and the *Jüngerer Titurel* are one and the same work and has served as the point of departure for all subsequent discussions.

R. William Leckie, Jr.

ALBURANUS, a Mozarabic scribe who, as was customary in medieval Spain, recorded his name with a request for the reader's prayers—"O pious reader, pray for Alburanus the scribe"—in a manuscript now in Paris (Bibliothèque Nationale, nouv. acq. lat. 2170).

Leslie Brubaker

AŁC [AGHTS], (44°10′E. × 40°15′N.), locality some 19 miles northwest of present-day Erevan. Site of the hypogeum of the Armenian Arsacid kings built *ca.* 364, probably to replace the earlier royal necropolis at Ani in Daranałik^c devastated by the Persian invasion at that time. The underground chamber is decorated with crude reliefs dominated by hunting themes symbolic of the king's inherently heroic character. The ruins of an early basilica adjoining the hypogeum probably belong to the same funerary complex.

BIBLIOGRAPHY

Sirarpie Nersessian, *The Armenians* (1969), 120, 125, and fig. 31.

Nina G. Garsoïan

ALCHEMY. The word "alchemy" *(alchimia, alchemia, alquimia)* as used in the Middle Ages covers a complex group of operations and theories. The most common definition, used by medieval scholars, is "the art and science of transforming base metals into the noble metals, silver and gold." This fits the probable etymology, which derives *alchimia* from the Arabic article *al-* and the Greek *chem(e)ia* or *chym(e)ia,* which came from *cheo,* "to melt"; alchemy means working with melted metals.

This definition also corresponds with the content of most treatises on alchemy, which describe processes for producing the philosopher's stone *(lapis philosophicus),* or the elixir (from the Arabic *al-iksīr,* derived in turn from the Greek *xerion,* "dry tincture"). This is the substance that, when applied to base metals, causes transmutation. In this sense alchemy also has medical connections, since the elixir effects a similar transformation in the human body, incorruptibility and hence longevity. This theory of macrobiosis originated in China.

Discussions about alchemical procedures are often complemented in medieval treatises by speculations on the structure of matter that provide the theoretical basis for research. Among other topics, the subject matter comprises the nature of the universe and of mineral and organic substances, and the classification of the elements. A standard treatise usually has a theoretical section preceding the technical recipes.

A view that was not very common in the Middle Ages, but that became extremely powerful in the sixteenth century, regarded alchemy as a spiritual and mystical experience that transformed the experimenter himself. The experience might be buttressed by solid laboratory work but was usually an internal

ALCHEMY

phenomenon. Treatises based on this definition are often couched in allegorical and symbolic language.

Early historians of alchemy considered it as the prehistory of chemistry. Indeed, the subject matter of alchemy did comprise inorganic and organic chemistry, but it also dealt with pharmacy, geology, theoretical physics, cosmology, and, in a broader sense, natural philosophy. Its allegorical side has appealed to historians of religion as well as to psychoanalysts.

ORIGINS AND DEVELOPMENT

Alchemy is the least-known area of medieval science. There are no critical editions of alchemical works; and the major sixteenth-, seventeenth-, and eighteenth-century collections *(Artis chemicae principes, Artis auriferae, Theatrum chemicum, Bibliotheca chemica curiosa)* give texts that have been seriously distorted. There is no complete list of manuscripts, and the manuscript tradition is very uncertain because of additions and revisions.

Determining the dates and authors of these works is hindered by the established practice of false attribution. Alchemists delighted in attributing their works to the great scholars of antiquity (Hermes Trismegistus, Plato, Aristotle) or of the Middle Ages (Roger Bacon, Albertus Magnus, Thomas Aquinas, Arnald of Villanova, Ramón Lull), and even to the wealthy or well-born (Nicolas Flamel, Jacques Coeur). Their aim seems to have been to vouch for the efficacy of the alchemical procedure by citing well-known authorities and also to compensate for the marginal status of alchemy. In the enormous collections produced in this way, one must distinguish those works that might be authentic—or at least close to the author's ideas—from those that are merely forgeries of later date. The real history of alchemy can be written only when these treatises can be dated with certainty.

GRECO-EGYPTIAN ORIGINS

Alchemy emerged from the craft of artisans. In China, Mesopotamia, and Egypt the alchemist's techniques originated in the work of imitating not only gold and silver but also precious stones and the rare purple dye. Thus, precious metals could be imitated by surface corrosion and enrichment of low-grade alloys; by gilding or plating base metals; by varnishing with colored substances; or by tinting copper, tin, or lead with various cements (salt, sulfur) or corrosive liquids (sulfur water). Joseph Needham has called such processes "aurifiction."

To natural philosophers interested in craftsmanship, these processes may have inspired the idea that, by perfecting them, the natural substance itself could be reproduced. This transition from aurification (imitation) to aurifaction (transmutation) was favored by two ideas. All ancient philosophers regarded metals as compounds; and every technique was considered imitative of nature itself and thus capable of equaling—or even excelling—it.

Good examples of these procedures can be found in the early fourth-century Leiden Papyrus and Stockholm Papyrus. These collections of Greek recipes for making gold, silver, precious stones, and purple dye mix industrial processes with laboratory research that seeks to perfect the processes and extend the range of their usefulness. Thus the "production" of precious stones by applying a mordant and dye to rock crystal is derived from the procedure for dyeing cloth; the transmutation, in this case, is a change in color. Many recipes from these papyri can be found in Latin in the eighth-century *Compositiones Lucenses* and in the *Mappae clavicula* of the ninth and twelfth centuries.

They are also found in the earliest treatise that can properly be called a work on alchemy, the *Physika kai mystika* of an author who wrote under the name of Democritus and who may have been Bolos of Mendes (*fl.* first century B.C.). In this work, large sections of which are preserved in the *Collection des anciens alchimistes grecs,* chemical relations are explained by the doctrine of universal sympathy, supposedly revealed by the magus Ostanes (nature enjoys nature, nature dominates nature, nature triumphs over nature). In the same tradition, the technical treatises called *To Leucippus Book V, Chemistry of Moses, Work of the Four Elements, The Eight Tombs,* and *The System of Iamblichus* appeared during the first centuries of the Christian era. At the same time a mystical and speculative trend inspired the texts attributed to Cleopatra, Comarius, Isis, Agathodemon, Mary the Jewess, and Sophia the Egyptian, which presented theories on the soul, growth, and resurrection of metals, on the elements, and on sexual symbolism. These treatises also included technical methods for sublimation and distillation.

The peak of Greek alchemy coincided with the important work of Zosimus of Panopolis (before A.D. 400), who improved the apparatus for sublimation and distillation, especially for compounds of sulfur and arsenic. Influenced by Neoplatonism and Gnosticism, he worked out allegories of the sacrifice, death, resurrection, and salvation of matter. After Zosimus, there were only commentators: Synesius (fourth century) on Democritus; Olympiodorus (sixth century) reconciled alchemy with Neoplatonism and the theory of the four elements; Stephen of Alexandria (seventh century) declared that transmutation was a spiritual process and set it in a Christological perspective. The so-called "Christian philosopher" (seventh century) and "anonymous philosopher" (seventh century), as well as Pelagius and John the Archpriest merely collected fragments of earlier writers in an attempt to understand them.

ARABIC ALCHEMY AND ITS RECEPTION IN THE WEST

Arabic alchemy was influenced not only by the Greeks but also by the Persians and Chinese, and the Syrian city of Harran was clearly an important center. According to a ninth-century legend, Prince Khālid ibn Yazīd (*d.* 704) learned alchemy in Egypt from a Byzantine monk named Morienus (or Marianos), who had been a student of Stephen of Alexandria. In fact, since the eighth century the Islamic world had known translations from the Greek and apocryphal writings attributed to Greek philosophers; the best known was the *Book of the Secrets of Creation* by Balīnās (Apollonius of Tyana), written between 600 and 750. It discussed the formation of metals by sulfur (the combustible—that is, oxidable—principle) and mercury (principle of fusibility and of the properties of the metallic state). It also included the *Tabula smaragdina,* which was both a cosmology and a transmutation process.

The works attributed to Jābir ibn Ḥayyān (*d.* 815 and also known as Geber) date from the ninth and tenth centuries, as Paul Kraus has shown; they are the *Liber misericordiae* (mid ninth century), the *One Hundred Twelve* and the *Liber de septuaginta* (late ninth century), the *Book of Balances* (early tenth century), and the *Five Hundred Books* (mid tenth century). According to these treatises, metals are composed of the four elements (fire, air, earth, water), of their basic qualities, of sulfur, and of mercury; the relationships among these are expressed in arithmetic terms (the principle of balances). In order to decompose matter and create elixirs, distillation was used, especially for organic substances (discovery of sal ammoniac).

Arabic alchemy reached its highest point in the tenth century. Abū Bakr Muḥammad ibn Zakarīyyā al-Rāzī (865–923/924) in his important *Liber secretorum* improved the description and classification of mineral substances, especially salts of mercury and corrosive liquids. The *Turba philosophorum* tried to reconcile the basic principles of alchemy with Greek philosophy and the Koran. Muḥammad ibn Umail al-Tamimī (Senior Zadith), influenced by Zosimus and Hermes Trismegistus, tended toward allegorical explanation in his *Epistola solis ad lunam crescentem.* Ibn Sīnā in the *Kitāb al-Shifā*ᵓ ("Book of Remedy") explained the formation of metals by sulfur and mercury but rejected attempts at transmutation that are not based on reducing metals to the common primal matter ("The artisans of alchemy should know that metallic compounds cannot be changed if they are not reduced to their primal matter"). The *Epistola ad Hasen regem* may or may not be authentic; but in any case, the *De anima in arte alchemie,* a twelfth-century Spanish work attributed to Ibn Sīnā, was influenced by it.

Although the recipes passed on from the early Middle Ages often transmitted the basic techniques of alchemy, and some infiltration of Arabic material can be seen by the end of the eleventh century, Arabic texts on alchemy did not reach the West until the twelfth century. Hugh of Santalla (*fl.* 1119–1151) translated Balīnās; Robert de Ketene (Robert the Englishman) dated his translation of Morienus 11 February 1144. Gerard of Cremona translated the *Libri de septuaginta;* the *De aluminibus et salibus,* an Arabic text from twelfth-century Spain influenced by Rāzī; the *Lumen luminum,* also attributed to Rāzī, as well as to Michael Scot and to Aristotle under the title *De perfecto magisterio;* and perhaps also the *Lapidary of Aristotle,* a text of Syriac origin with alchemical additions.

Around 1200 Alfred of Sareshel (Alfred the Englishman) translated three chapters of the *Kitāb al-Shifā*ᵓ concerning metals and alchemy as *De mineralibus.* In manuscripts these chapters accompany the *translatio vetus* of Aristotle's *Meteorology,* that is, books I–III translated from Arabic by Gerard of Cremona and book IV translated from Greek by Henricus Aristippus. These chapters, and especially the *Sciant artifices alkimie,* were considered to be Aristotle's work and played an important role pro and con in discussing alchemy. The authors of the other translations are unknown, but most of the texts seem to have been assimilated by 1200.

EUROPEAN ALCHEMY IN THE THIRTEENTH AND FOURTEENTH CENTURIES

Michael Scot mentions alchemy in his *Liber introductorius* and *Liber particularis;* the *Ars al-*

ALCHEMY

chemie is, at least in part, authentic. After presenting some general ideas—the four spirits (volatile substances), seven metals, relations to the planets—this basically practical treatise gives procedures for fixing mercury and projecting it on copper. Contemporaneous work on alchemy was done by Brother Elias of Cortona, minister general of the Franciscans and in the *Correctorium alchemiae* of Richard Anglicus (perhaps Richard of Wendover, who died in 1252 or 1256).

The work of the thirteenth-century encyclopedists reveals the progress of this new subject in European science. In their descriptions of the mineral kingdom Bartholomew Anglicus and Arnold of Saxony use a technical work attributed to Hermes Trismegistus and related to the *Liber sacerdotum.* Vincent of Beauvais cites at length the *De anima in arte alchemiae* and the *De aluminibus et salibus*; Thomas of Cantimpré cites the *Lumen luminum.*

It is in this framework that the attitudes of Albertus Magnus and Roger Bacon can be understood. Between 1250 and 1254 Albert discussed alchemical problems in his *Meteora* and *De mineralibus.* In book IV of the former work he examined several alchemical techniques (the fixing of mercury, the fusion of iron) that seemed to contradict Aristotle's chemistry. He drew his knowledge from the partially alchemical collection of the *Quaestiones Nicolai Peripatetici.*

Having been unable to find the *Lapidary of Aristotle,* which he believed was authentic, Albertus turned to alchemy in *De mineralibus* to explain the origin and properties of metals. Rejecting the opinions of Democritus and Ibn Juljul, as well as of Callisthenes (Khālid's *Liber trium verborum*), he agreed with Ibn Sīnā that metals are made of sulfur and mercury, which in turn are composed of the traditional elements in the form of Aristotelian exhalations. Like Ibn Sīnā he denied the possibility of transmutation except through a return to primal matter. In describing the individual properties of each metal, he took from Albert of Saxony the technical experiments of the *Liber alchimie Hermes.* Of the twenty-eight works attributed to Albertus Magnus, the *Semita recta,* although interpolated, and the *Alkimia minor* are based on the same sources and theoretical principles as the *De mineralibus.* They are perhaps authentic or emanate from the group of Cologne.

The same attitude was held by Roger Bacon, who sought from alchemy what was lacking in the natural philosophy of Aristotle. In his *Opus tertium* he defined *alkimia speculativa* as the study of the inanimate world, an indispensable foundation for studying the living world and theoretical medicine. *Alkimia practica* must be the experimental confirmation of the former and also has socially useful applications: transmutation, industrial chemistry (metals, colors), and pharmaceutical chemistry (prolonging life). Bacon was well acquainted with Rāzī's work, with the *Clavis sapientiae* of al-Tughra^{c}i (eleventh century), and with the *De anima* ascribed to Ibn Sīnā or his school. The same sources were used in the treatises *Breve breviarum, Speculum secretorum,* and *Verbum abbreviatum,* which although possibly authentic are collections of extracts and not very original.

By the end of the thirteenth century a large number of alchemical treatises, both translations from Arabic and original works, existed in the Latin West. One can get an idea of this corpus by looking at the Palermo Catalog of 1325 (MS Palermo 4 Qq A 10), which lists seventy-two titles, including the key works of Albertus and Roger Bacon, owned by Brother Dominic of the Convent of San Procolo of Bologna.

At the same time, alchemy was beginning to arouse suspicion and evoke condemnation because of the economic threat that it posed and the numerous forgeries to which it gave rise. Thomas Aquinas conceded that it was lawful to sell gold made by alchemists as long as it was as pure as real gold. Dominicans, Franciscans, and Cistercians were forbidden to practice alchemy. Pope John XXII's decretal *Spondent quas non exhibent divitias pauperes alchymistae* (1317), which prescribed severe punishment for alchemy, was concerned above all with counterfeiting. The attribution of apocryphal writings to the great scholars of the Middle Ages may have been an attempt to compensate for this situation.

The effort to clarify and organize alchemical material led to the development of *summae* that were both theoretical and practical, and that applied Scholastic reasoning to alchemy. The *Summa perfectionis magisterii* of Jābir ibn Ḥayyān (pseudo-Geber) dates from around 1300. The first book lists the difficulties of the art and the moral qualities of an alchemist, refutes attacks on alchemy and erroneous theories, and states the basic principles of matter. Book II discusses furnaces, instruments, and techniques; book III describes and classifies minerals and metals. Book IV explains the specific elixir that affects each metal and presents tests for verifying the results. Geber's *De investigatione perfectionis* was written for the same reason and complements the work.

Along the same lines, the *Pretiosa margarita novella* (1330) of Petrus Bonus attempts to show not only that alchemy can be considered epistemologically a science in the Aristotelian sense but also that it is nobler, since the success of the endeavor is dependent on divine grace. The work itself is a compilation of many sources.

The earliest treatises attributed to Arnald of Villanova were written late in his life and may be authentic: the *Rosarius,* the *Quaestiones tam essentiales quam accidentales,* the *Epistola ad Bonifatium Papam,* the *Epistola ad regem neapolitanum,* and the *Flos florum.* Believing that philosophical mercury contains its own sulfur as a congealing principle, Arnald elaborated a technique based on this metal alone. John Dastin in his *Desiderabile desiderium, Verbum abbreviatum,* and *Epistola ad papam Joannem XXII* maintained that sulfur and ideal mercury are contained in gold and silver and that the only requisite substances are gold, silver, and mercury. Walter of Odington in his *Icocedron* attempted to give a mathematical description in degrees and minutes of alchemical changes, especially those concerned with the mixture of elements, and of the relationship between primary and secondary qualities—as al-Kindī and Arnald of Villanova had done for compound medicines.

In his encyclopedic *Philosophia*, Philip Elephant gave a numerical structure to an alchemical account derived from the *Summa* of Jābir ibn Ḥayyān. In *De consideratione quintae essentiae* (1351–1352) John of Rupescissa systematized the technical research on the distillation of alcohol that had been going on for two centuries, associating alcohol with the Aristotelian fifth essence by giving it the incorruptible qualities of the elixir. In his *Liber lucis* he derived philosophical sulfur from the quintessence of Roman vitriol (iron sulfate), and he also produced calomel and corrosive sublimate. The *De multiplicatione* formerly attributed to Thomas Aquinas was based on work on amalgams. In 1385 Thomas of Bologna exchanged letters with Bernard of Trier on the major theoretical difficulties of alchemy. The works of the Carmelite Guillem Sedacer (1378) and John Dombelay (1386) are less original.

The oldest treatises of the Lull corpus, first cited by Sedacer, date from the late fourteenth and fifteenth centuries. All of them are apocryphal, since Lull consistently condemned alchemy and never mentions any book on the subject in his autobiography. The *Testamentum,* the *Codicillus,* and the *Lapidarius* seem to be the work of his French or Italian followers, who applied to alchemy the logicomathematical methods of his *Ars magna*—designation of real objects by letters of the alphabet, wheels, diagrams, and so forth.

By the end of the fourteenth century alchemy was being practiced throughout Europe by men from all walks of life. In his notebook of formulas (1394) the alchemist Leonard of Maurperg reflects not only the diversity of procedures and the abundance of scientific exchanges, carried on in a scholarly community that extended as far as Persia, but also the widespread disappointment that followed the pursuit of so many fruitless procedures.

ALCHEMY IN THE FIFTEENTH CENTURY

Although the majority of alchemical manuscripts date from the fifteenth century, this was not a period of great originality. The surviving corpus comprises mainly revisions of famous texts, collections of quotations classified by subject (the *Rosarius* type), and commentaries, such as the *Elucidarius* of Christopher of Paris, compiled in the 1470's.

This period did see, however, a considerable development of allegorical alchemy, which had formerly received much less attention. The use of Christian symbolism, already evident in the *Tractatus parabolicus* of Arnald of Villanova, became systematic in the late fourteenth-century *Aurora consurgens,* formerly attributed to Thomas Aquinas, in which alchemical and religious symbols are interlaced in the description of a mystical experiment; and in the early fifteenth-century *Dreyfaltigkeit* of Ulmannus. This important tendency, which emerged in the spiritual alchemy of the sixteenth century, produced many manuscripts with allegorical illustrations beginning in the late fourteenth century.

Moreover, a body of alchemical poetry appeared. While most secular writers such as Petrarch, Chaucer, and Langland ridiculed alchemy, it had already found a place in didactic poetry as early as the thirteenth century, when Jean de Meun introduced it into the *Roman de la Rose* (verses 16,065–16,148), as did Heinrich von Mügeln in *Der Maide Kranz.* An early example of alchemical poetry in France is the *Sommaire philosophique,* linguistically dated soon after 1400 and wrongly attributed to Nicolas Flamel—who never wrote on alchemy; another example is the *Fontaine des amoureux de science* (1413) by Jean de la Fontaine. Fifty-three poems from

England survive, most of them short; the best known are the *Componde of Alkemy* or *Book of the Twelve Gates* (1471) by George Ripley and the *Ordinal of Alchemy* (1477) by Thomas Norton. On the whole these works are of very poor scientific quality. Thanks to Paracelsus an improvement in technique as well as theory occurred in the sixteenth century.

TECHNICAL AND PHILOSOPHICAL CONTENT

To summarize the techniques and doctrines of medieval alchemy is even more difficult and hazardous than to outline the history of the subject. Because of the lack of critical editions, the obscurity of the language, and the frequent use of *Decknamen* (aliases) we must limit ourselves to generalizations and to enumerating a list of problems requiring separate investigation.

There did not exist in the Middle Ages two alchemies, one theoretical and the other experimental. Even the laboratory manuals give concrete form to the subjacent theoretical structure, and the most freely speculative texts take into account the results of practical procedures. It is, rather, the relationship between theory and practice that governed the development of the art.

MATERIALS, APPARATUS, AND OPERATIONS

Sharing a common origin in the methods of metallurgists, dyers, and pharmacists, the materials, apparatus, and operations of alchemy were improved and refined in the course of efforts to achieve transmutation. Most of the substances employed came from the materia medica of antiquity: salt, sulfur, alum, mercury, vitriols or *atramenta* (sulfates of copper and iron), white lead, litharge, *magnesia* (black and white), urine, and vinegar. Some were of Arabic origin: alkali salt, borax, talc, marcasite (pyrites), and tutty (zinc oxide). Others were first developed by the alchemists themselves: sal ammoniac, artificial cinnabar, calomel, corrosive sublimate, aqua vitae (*aqua ardens* or *quinta essentia vini,* our alcohol), and aquae acutae (impure mineral acids).

Alchemists used heat in varying degrees—sunlight, double boilers, rotting manure, hot sand, hot ashes, and charcoal fires. The oven *(furnus philosophicus)* became more specialized with the evolution of crucible and reverberatory furnaces, and the athanor, from the Arabic *tannūr.* The alembic, an upside-down cup used as a cover, was perfected during the first centuries of the Christian era. Used for distillation, it was refined by improving the condensation apparatus and made possible the isolation of substances with a low boiling point, such as alcohol. Other alchemical equipment included circulating vessels allegedly intended to purify matter indefinitely; "hermetic sealing" was important in working with volatile substances.

Alchemical procedures sought to break down substances, to refine and make them subtle, and to transmute them through reconstitution. Geber cites seven operations, Ripley twelve. The most important were sublimation (applying heat to a dry substance to effect evaporation and adhesion to the vessel); distillation (extracting a liquid, which flowed drop by drop higher or lower); calcination (pulverizing a dry substance using heat or salts); solution (dissolving a dry substance in a liquid, sometimes in an *aqua acuta*); coagulation (reconstituting a dry substance from a liquid); fixation (rendering a volatile substance heat-resistant); and ceration (softening a substance that could not be melted). To these procedures should be added fusion, putrefaction, fermentation, and so on.

The various phases of the process of transmutation are marked by changes of color in the substance. *Nigredo* (black) corresponds to a return to the common, undifferentiated substratum of matter; *albedo* (white) is linked to silver, and *rubedo* (red) to gold. The last phases of the alchemist's work—producing the philosophical stone, projecting it on base metals, multiplication of tinctures—are pure thought experiments and are generally couched in obscure and puzzling language.

THEORETICAL PROBLEMS

It is true that the alchemists described themselves as philosophers; and, indeed, they wrote on problems of epistemology (reasoning by analogy, experience and experiment, theory and practice), morality (work, silence, asceticism, moral responsibility), and religion (the role of grace, inspiration, and of the gift of God). But alchemy, above all, was a chapter in the history of natural philosophy.

All alchemists believed in the idea of the unity of all matter, which permitted decomposition and recomposition, a process symbolized by the *ouroboros*—the mythical dragon that swallows its own tail. Metals had their own place in nature; and their special components, sulfur and mercury, endowed them with particular properties. The number of metals was limited—sometimes seven to correspond to astrological principles and six if mercury was excluded (gold, silver, iron, copper, tin, and lead, quicksilver). They formed a hierarchy, ever more perfect until one attained the mystical perfection of gold. The base metals, correspondingly, were imperfect and lacking, suffering from a kind of illness for which the philosopher's stone was a medicine.

All alchemists followed a biological model. Metals mature in the earth's womb, but base metals have not ripened. Art imitates nature and hastens its work. The constituent elements of metals were likened to male and female seed, volatile and fixed respectively, which could be united by the menstruum. Hence there are repeated comparisons to germination, coitus, marriage, and the philosopher's egg.

Most medieval alchemists followed the general theories of Aristotelian-Galenic philosophy: the action of the four elements, the four humors, active and passive qualities, species, substantial forms, and the like. Claude Gagnon has shown that alchemy only appeared to be at the fringes of medieval thought; much of its philosophy can be explained within the general framework of Scholasticism.

BIBLIOGRAPHY

Bibliographies. Denis I. Duveen, *Bibliotheca alchemica et chemica* (1949, repr. 1965); John Ferguson, *Bibliotheca chemica,* 2 vols. (1906, repr. 1954); Jost Weyer, *Alchemiehistorische Bibliographie* (1974).

General Studies. Guy Beaujouan, "L'histoire des sciences et la philosophie au moyen âge," in *Miscellanea mediaevalia,* **13** (1981), 314–327; M. Berthelot, *La chimie au moyen âge,* 3 vols. (1893, repr. 1967); M. Berthelot and C.-E. Ruelle, *Collection des anciens alchimistes grecs,* 3 vols. (1887–1888, repr. 1967), the only published collection to date—a new edition of these texts is in preparation under the auspices of the Union Académique Internationale by Henri D. Saffrey, Rainer Walther, and Robert Halleux; E. Brehm, "Roger Bacon's Place in the History of Alchemy," in *Ambix,* **23** (1976); John Sherren Brewer, ed., *Fr. Rogeri Bacon Opera quaedam hactenus inedita, Opus Tertium* (1859), 39–42; C. S. F. Burnett, "A Group of Arabic-Latin Translators Working in Northern Spain in the Mid-12th Century," in *Journal of the Royal Asiatic Society* (1977), 62–108; Allen G. Debus, *The Chemical Philosophy* (1977), the best study to date on the technical and theoretical improvements of the sixteenth century; Wilhelm Ganzenmüller, *Die Alchemie im Mittelalter* (1938); and *Beiträge zur Geschichte der Technologie und der Alchemie* (1956); Robert Halleux, *Les textes alchimiques* (1979); E. J. Holmyard, *Alchemy* (1957, repr. 1968); Julius L. Ideler, *Physici et medici Graeci minores,* II (1842), 199–253; Hermann F. M. Kopp, *Beiträge zur Geschichte der Chemie,* 3 vols. (1869–1875); and *Die Alchemie in älterer und neuerer Zeit,* 2 vols. (1886, repr. 1962–1971); Edmund Oskar von Lippmann, *Entstehung und Ausbreitung der Alchemie,* 3 vols. (1919–1954); Robert P. Multhauf, *The Origins of Chemistry* (1966); Emil E. Ploss et al., *Alchimia: Ideologie und Technologie* (1970); Lynn Thorndike, *A History of Magic and Experimental Science,* vols. I–IV (1923–1934).

ROBERT HALLEUX

ALCHEMY, ISLAMIC. The medieval period marks a significant stage in both the transmission of Greco-Roman alchemy to Islamic society and its development by Muslim adepts. The classical texts were translated into Arabic probably from the late eighth century and served as the basis for a copious literature. In turn, Arabic alchemical writings were the impetus for western European alchemy and its cultural ramifications; this process began with the Latin translations of the twelfth century. Alchemical terminology is indicative of the cultural transference. The Greek vocabulary for alchemical notions, procedures, and apparatus was translated into Arabic; the transliteration of the Arabic terms often entered directly into European terminology.

"Alchemy" is derived from *al-kīmiyāʾ*, which goes back through Syriac to Greek χυμεία, χημεία, meaning "the art of casting or alloying metals." Arabic writers give various derivations, synonyms, and definitions for *al-kīmiyāʾ*; however, its basic intent is the transformation of base metals into precious ones.

This definition does not suggest the highly complex nature of Islamic alchemy as an exoteric and esoteric subject. It was the heir to a rich tradition of Greek alchemical literature that was produced mainly in Egypt from the second century B.C. To this literature was eventually added a bewildering heterogeneity of ideas: Egyptian magic, Greek philosophy, Gnosticism, Neoplatonism, Hermetism, Jewish and Christian theology, Babylonian astrology, and Far Eastern metaphysics. The disparate sources point to the divergent purposes of alchemy. This disparity was due, generally, to the belief that the transformation of base metals into gold and silver was also the potent symbol of man's spiritual regeneration. The alchemical works were written in the form of theoretical dialogues, allegorical stories, myths, visions, and poems. Moreover, the writings were characterized by pseudonymous authorship and very obscure language because the knowledge was esoteric and intrinsically secret. On the exoteric level, the obfuscation protected the authors or practitioners of alchemy from competition and social criticism. All these features also distinguished the Arabic alchemical works.

ALCHEMY, ISLAMIC

It appears that Greek alchemy followed the same course of transmission to the Muslim world as Greek medicine, being translated into Syriac and then Arabic. Islamic alchemy seems to have been more closely associated with medicine than in antiquity and to have developed considerably beyond its classical antecedents. There is a greater uncertainty, however, about the dating and authorship of Arabic alchemical works than for the medical writings, so that the early history of Islamic alchemy is virtually legendary. Nevertheless, the early Arabic works are quite important because the original Greek texts are lost or poorly preserved. Unfortunately, the Arabic material has not been studied sufficiently; therefore, many difficulties remain concerning pre-Islamic alchemy and its evolution in the Islamic period.

Despite these difficulties, the broad outline of Islamic alchemy can be traced. According to legend, it was initiated by the Umayyad prince Khālid ibn Yazīd, who died about 704. Reportedly, he ordered the translation into Arabic of Greek and Coptic works on alchemy, medicine, and astrology and was instructed in alchemy by Morienus (Maryānos), a Byzantine monk. Historically, the first major figure was Djābir ibn Ḥayyān (d. *ca.* 812), who established himself as an alchemist at the court of Hārūn al-Rashīd in Baghdad. A large body of alchemical-scientific writings, the *Corpus Gabirianum,* was attributed to him, but it is actually a composite work formed in the late ninth and early tenth centuries. The collection, incorporating the original work of Djābir, is marked by its strong Ismaili orientation. Scientifically, the corpus is distinct from ancient alchemy in its avoidance of hermetic allegorism, which was revived by later Arabic alchemists. The alchemy of the collection was an experimental science based primarily on the physics of Aristotle. Apart from the complicated theorizing, the corpus contains observations of practical chemistry, which probably benefited medicine and other crafts. An emphasis on experimentation over speculation is even clearer in the second major corpus of Islamic alchemy that was contemporary with the Djābirian compilation—the writings of the physician al-Rāzī.

About 900 originated the *Turba philosophorum,* the Latin translation of the lost Arabic work; it is a discussion of the problems of alchemy by nine pre-Socratic philosophers. The objective of the Arabic work was to connect cosmological with alchemical theory: God had created the world with a uniform nature, which is completely composed of the four elements.

Beside the philosophical tradition was the popular hermetic-allegorical tradition that accounts for the numerous religious, mystical, and magical tenets that intermingled with alchemical doctrine. In particular, it stressed the influence that heavenly bodies were supposed to exert on metals and their transformation. This alchemical dogma is given in the famous "emerald table," or *Tabula smaragdina,* the earliest known versions of which are in Arabic. The tradition is well represented in the tenth century by the works of Ibn Umayl.

Over the following centuries alchemical works continued to be written, comprising original contributions and many compilations. It is noteworthy that the Egyptian Aydamir ibn ᶜAlī al-Djildakī (d. 1342) wrote a large number of books in which he summarized and commented upon everything that had preceded him on alchemy and magic. Thus, alchemical beliefs and practices persisted throughout the medieval period, but they provoked a wide range of responses, being strongly defended by al-Fārābī, al-Rāzī, and al-Ṭughrāʾī, while being condemned by others, such as Ibn Sīnā, al-Tawḥīdī, al-Jawziyyah, and Ibn Khaldūn (d. 1406). The validity of alchemy was disputed largely on a theoretical level.

The theoretical foundation for alchemy was a natural philosophy that upheld the uniformity of nature, conceived as composed of the four elements and their four qualities. The elements were believed to be reducible to a prime matter. Alchemy was based on the logical but erroneous belief that any substance can be created from this prime matter by the proper combination of the elementary qualities. Gold was the perfect equilibrium of the qualities in the prime matter. In nature, the qualities were combined over a long period to produce the material world, especially the precious metals deep inside the earth; the alchemist telescoped or imitated this process by using chemical techniques.

The innumerable recipes for gold may be distinguished according to three main methods: the quicksilver-sulfur theory; the principle of balance *(mīzān)* of the four elementary qualities; and the application of an elixir *(al-iksīr)* or philosophers' stone to base metals. The projection of the elixir was the most important method. To the metallic elixirs of antiquity, Islamic alchemy appears to have added vegetable and animal substances as ingredients. The elixir also seems to have assumed a greater medical potency in the Islamic period as well as a reputation for conferring immortality, which was possibly due to Chinese influence.

Islamic alchemy, therefore, displayed a number of divergent trends that were richly cultivated. Most conspicuous to us was the empirical tradition of Greco-Roman science represented by al-Rāzī. In this regard, alchemy may have played a greater part in the development of experimental science than medicine, pharmacology, physics, or astronomy. Distinct but closely related to the empirical tradition was the spiritual or allegorical view of alchemy, which was greatly promoted by poets and mystics.

BIBLIOGRAPHY

The older literature on Islamic alchemy is summarized by E. Widemann, "Al-Kīmiyāʾ," in *The Encyclopaedia of Islam,* first ed. (1913–1934). The more recent literature is reviewed by Manfred Ullmann, "Al-Kīmiyāʾ," in *The Encyclopaedia of Islam,* new ed. (1960–). A fuller treatment of the subject is given by Ullmann in his *Die Natur- und Geheimwissenschaften im Islam, Handbuch der Orientalistik,* B. Spuler, ed., VI (1972), 145–270, and *Wörterbuch der klassischen arabischen Sprache,* I (1970), 512–516.

See also D. Brandenburg, *Medizin und Magie* (1975), 103–137; T. Burckhardt, *Alchemy* (1967); E. J. Holmyard, *Alchemy* (1968); M. Plessner and F. Klein-Franke, *Vorsokratische Philosophie und griechische Alchemie in arabisch-lateinischer Überlieferung; Studien zu Text und Inhalt der Turba Philosophorum* (1975); J. Ruska, "Die Alchemie ar-Rāzī's," in *Islam,* **22** (1935); F. Sezgin, *Geschichte des arabischen Schrifttums,* IV (1971), 1–299; V (1974), 416–426 (on which see M. Plessner, *Ambix,* **19** [1972]); L. Stavenhagen, ed. and trans., *A Testament of Alchemy* (1974); O. Temkin, "Medicine and Graeco-Arabic Alchemy," in *Bulletin of the History of Medicine,* **29** (1955); M. Ullmann, "Ḫālid ibn Yazīd und die Alchemie: eine Legende," in *Der Islam,* **55** (1978).

MICHAEL W. DOLS

[See also **Rāzi, al-.**]

ALCUIN OF YORK (*ca.* 730–804), educator and theologian known in Anglian as Ealhwine ("sanctuary friend"), as Albinus among churchmen, and as Flaccus in Charlemagne's circle, became the dominating figure in the great ninth-century *translatio studii* (transference of learning) to York, Aachen, and Tours.

Alcuin was born in Northumbria and educated at the cathedral school of York when it was Christendom's leading center for ecclesiastical and classical studies, and began teaching there in 768. In 778, when Aethelberht, archbishop of York and headmaster of the school, resigned, he gave his see to Eanbald I, his headmastership to Alcuin. As Alcuin puts it in his long poem on the Church of York, he thus took possession of the "insignia of wisdom: school, chair, library" (line 1582). He held this position until 782.

Alcuin visited the Continent with Aethelberht at least twice, buying books and meeting scholars. In 768 they stopped at Pavia to hear Peter of Pisa and Lullus of Malmesbury debate, and at Aachen to meet Paulinus of Aquileia and Charlemagne. A lifelong deacon, whose service was to teach, Alcuin never became a priest and was perhaps not a professed monk. Several of his students became famous: Luitger the Frisian, Joseph of Ireland, Eanbald II of York, Putul, Beornrad, Sigulf, and Fridigus. While at York, Alcuin had already become a bibliophile; in the same poem (lines 1535–1561) he lists Christian and classical authors with books in his library. He loved Virgil—more than the psalms, according to his biographer—although he later halfheartedly condemned the study of his works. When Aethelberht died in 780, Alcuin, then at his peak, was sent to Rome for Eanbald's pallium. On his return journey to England he stopped at Parma, where Charlemagne invited him to head his palace school at Aachen.

From 782 to 796, Alcuin resided at Aachen as head of the palace school, visiting England in 782 and 790–792. The school, which predated Charlemagne, attracted visiting scholars, including Peter of Pisa, Paul the Deacon, and Paulinus. Alcuin consciously instituted the *translatio studii* there: "Perhaps the new Athens was even a far finer thing in Frankland" (Epistola 170) because it sought "to please God by right speaking," Charlemagne's formula in *De litteris colendis,* a circular that Alcuin may have written.

Alcuin's program at Aachen comprised the trivium with selections from the quadrivium, all with scriptural and ecclesiastical orientation. He later memorialized his trivium with derivative textbooks: *De grammatica, De rhetorica et virtutibus,* and *De dialectica,* to which he added a *De orthographia,* a "scribe's companion" alphabetized like a dictionary, and a *Disputatio Pippini cum Albino,* a conversational exercise. But Alcuin never memorialized the quadrivium. Although a *De musica* and a *Propositiones ad acuendos juvenes* have been ascribed to him, the former has never been found and the latter (consisting mainly of mathematical teasers), formerly classed among Bede's doubtful works, is now thought to be Alcuin's. His letters reveal more about his quadrivium: that he taught chant, witnessed by advice to Eanbald II (Epistola 114) and to Arnulf of Salzburg (Epistola 169), and astronomy, as evidenced by his correspondence with Charlemagne.

The broad spectrum of students at the palace school included Charlemagne, his sons, daughter, queen, sister, and courtiers. Also there were such scholars as Angilbert, Adalhard, Rigbod, Arnulf, and those who followed Alcuin from York: Joseph of Ireland, Putul, Sigulf, and Fridigus. Einhard (or Eginhard), Alcuin's successor, was not his student but came under his influence through Baugulf of Fulda. Alongside the school program were other projects: to remove errors of transcription from scriptural and liturgical texts and to assemble a uniform lectionary and sacramentary including Frankish masses and feasts, upgrading liturgy yet introducing non-Roman customs (the sung Creed) and feasts (All Saints). Alcuin's precise role in these projects is not easily identified. Largely his own from this period is a *liber comitus* (epistle book) and the *hucusque* preface linking a Frankish supplement to a Gregorian sacramentary.

Alcuin also became involved in theological controversy over adoptionism and iconoclasm. Charlemagne summoned him from England to present the royal positions on these issues at the Council of Frankfurt (794). Alcuin is sometimes said to have been the author of royal communications, such as the *Epistola ad Elipantum* condemning adoptionism and the *Libri Carolini* condemning decisions made at Constantinople in 754 and at the Second Council of Nicaea in 787. Scholarship now favors attributing the latter work to Theodulf of Orléans. Charlemagne rewarded Alcuin for his services by giving him revenues from monasteries at Ferrières, Troyes, Flavigny-sur-Ozerain, and St.-Josse-sur-Mer. In 796, Alcuin was entrusted with the Abbey of St. Martin at Tours, where he passed the remaining eight years of his life.

At Tours, Alcuin was a resident abbot responsible for the spirituality of the monks. He continued to teach, provided for the library, and eagerly followed the development of the scriptorium, where competent scribes were already using the new Carolingian minuscule calligraphic script and were working on so-called Alcuin Bibles. He completed corrections on a personal Bible (now lost) and sent it as a coronation gift to Charlemagne. There has been speculation by Francois Ganshof, among others, about his involvement in the coronation. That he foresaw and approved it is certain; that he contrived it is probably not, since his influence over Charlemagne was exerted in a different sphere.

At Tours, Alcuin had a listening post, a pulpit, and time to write; little happened in Europe that he did not hear about. He had long distributed moral counsel to bishops and to kings (Ethelred of Northumbria, Offa of Mercia). He now wrote even to badger Pope Leo III. The total of his known epistles exceeds 300. He continued to write scriptural commentaries, poetry, and both formal and informal treatises. He was also author of saints' lives, notably of St. Willibrord of Utrecht, composed both in prose, for reading in the monks' refectory, and in verse, for posterity. His lives of St. Martin, St. Vedast of Arras, and St. Richarius were reworkings of earlier vitae. Alcuin died at Tours on 19 May 804, having composed his own epitaph: *Alchuine nomen erat, sophiam mihi semper amanti* ("Alcuin was my name and wisdom always my love").

BIBLIOGRAPHY

Texts. Alcuin's works are in *Patrologia latina,* XC (1862), 667–676, C (1863), and CI (1863); his poetry, in *Monumenta Germaniae historica,* Poetae latini aevi Carolini, I (1881; repr. 1978), 160–350; his letters, *ibid.,* Epistolae, IV (1895), 1–493, 614–616, and V (1899), 643–645; and an anonymous biography is in *Patrologia latina,* C (1863), 89–106.

Literature. Stephen Allot, *Alcuin of York* (1974); Bernhard Bischoff, *Mittelalterliche Studien,* II (1967); 227–245; Eleanor S. Duckett, *Alcuin, Friend of Charlemagne, His World and His Work* (1951); Wolfgang Edelstein, *Eruditio und sapientia: Weltbild und Erziehung in der Karolingerzeit* (1965); Gerald Ellard, *Master Alcuin, Liturgist* (1956); François L. Ganshof, *The Carolingians and the Frankish Monarchy,* Janet Sondheimer, trans. (1971); Wilbur S. Howell, ed and trans., *The Rhetoric of Alcuin and Charlemagne* (1965); Geoffrey G. Willis, *Further Essays in Early Roman Liturgy* (1968).

L. K. SHOOK

[See also **Adoptionism; Councils; Hagiography; Iconoclasm.**]

ALDERMEN. By the late Middle Ages the standard form for a charter that incorporated a town provided for a mayor and aldermen (from Old English *ealdor,* elder or chief) to govern it. The model was clearly drawn from London, where the aldermen represented and governed the twenty-four wards of the city and formed a council for the mayor, who was always chosen from among the aldermen. The office of alderman existed in London by at least the mid tenth century, and the wards were all in existence before the early twelfth century; the city had virtual self-government from the early thirteenth century. The aldermen were essentially lawmen whose presence was required for the meeting of every court; they presided over their own wardmotes, and with the mayor acted as judges in the Husting, the chief London court.

Provincial towns may have had an alderman as head of an original merchant guild, but separate wards and a council of aldermen cannot be assumed before the fourteenth and fifteenth centuries.

BIBLIOGRAPHY

Susan Reynolds, *An Introduction to the History of Medieval English Towns* (1977); Gwyn Williams, *Medieval London. From Commune to Capital* (1963).

RICHARD W. KAEUPER

ALDHELM (before 650 [640?]–709/710), the first English man of Latin letters and the most influential figure of pre-Conquest Anglo-Latin literature, judged by the frequency with which his works were copied and studied, as well as imitated, by later writers.

Aldhelm's life can be reconstructed from his own letters and from the biography by William of Malmesbury (Faricius' biography is of little value). He was born and educated at Malmesbury, according to William, by an Irishman named Máeldubh. Aldhelm tells us that he studied law, prosody, computus, and astrology (that is, astronomy) under Hadrian at Canterbury. He may have attended the Council of Hertford in 672 or 673 and not long afterward, as Abbot of Malmesbury, wrote a letter to Geraint, king of Domnonia (modern Devon and Cornwall) on the dating of Easter and certain divergent practices of the Celtic church. During his abbacy (*ca.* 673–705) Aldhelm made a pilgrimage to Rome and sided with Wilfrid, bishop of Northumbria, on the occasion of his expulsion from England by Archbishop Theodore and King Aldfrith of Northumbria. He also was active in founding churches and in teaching. In 705 he became bishop of Sherborne, and held that office until his death.

Aldhelm's genuine works include a prose and a poetic treatment of virginity—an *opus geminatum* in the fashion of the *Carmen Paschale* of Caelius Sedulius; a treatise addressed to Aldfrith dealing with mystical meanings of the number seven, a treatise on meter, and a collection of Aldhelm's own hexameter riddles; five short poems consisting of church dedications; one of the five *carmina rhythmica* attributed to his disciple Æthelwald; letters to Leuthere, Hadrian, Geraint, Cellanus of Péronne, Wilfrid's monks, and several students. The letters are invaluable sources for the study of the early history of education in the British Isles. Aldhelm's hermeneutic prose style has long been a subject of scholarly interest.

BIBLIOGRAPHY

Edition. Rudolf Ehwald, ed., *Aldhelmi opera omnia* (1919), supersedes the 1844 edition by Giles.

Translations. F. Glorie, ed., *Collectiones aenigmatum Merovingicae aetatis,* 2 vols. (1968), I, 359–540, reprints Ehwald's text of the *Enigmata* with facing English translation by J. H. Pitman; Michael Lapidge and Michael Herren, eds., *Aldhelm: The Prose Works* (1979).

Studies. Whitney F. Bolton, *A History of Anglo-Latin Literature,* I, *597–740* (1967), 68–100; Michael Lapidge, "Aldhelm's Latin Poetry and Old English Verse," in *Comparative Literature,* **31** (1979); and "The Hermeneutic Style in Tenth-Century Anglo-Latin Literature," in *Anglo-Saxon England,* **4** (1975); Maximilianus Manitius, "Zu Aldhelm und Baeda," in *Sitzungsberichte der österreichischen Akademie der Wissenschaften,* philosophisch-historische Klasse, **112** (1886); Michael Winterbottom, "Aldhelm's Prose Style and Its Origins," in *Anglo-Saxon England,* **6** (1977).

MICHAEL HERREN

ALE. See **Brewing.**

ALÉAUME (Adelelmus), French cleric at Clermont-Ferrand under Bishop Stephen II who designed at least the crypt of the cathedral dedicated there in 946. Aléaume's plan was one of the earliest examples to incorporate an ambulatory with radiating chapels, a scheme that became central to the development of the Gothic chevet. The major document detailing Aléaume's activities, a tenth-century manuscript still at Clermont (MS 145), describes him as a sculptor and goldsmith as well as an architect; with his brother Adam, he is known to have created a gem-encrusted gold statue of the Virgin for the cathedral at Clermont. Aléaume has also been credited with the gold reliquary of Saint Foy at Conques, where Stephen, his patron at Clermont, was abbot (940–984).

BIBLIOGRAPHY

Louis Bréhier, *L'art en France dès invasions barbares à l'époque romane* (1930), 141–143; H. du Ranquet, *La cathédrale de Clermont-Ferrand,* Petites monographies des grands édifices de la France, 2nd ed. (1928).

LESLIE BRUBAKER

ALEPPO, now the principal city of northern Syria, was first mentioned in historical sources in the twentieth century B.C. In ancient times it was a defensive site with a strong citadel, at times under Hittite, Mitannian, or Egyptian rule; but with the collapse of the Hittite regime around 1200 B.C., Aleppo was reduced to a cluster of villages. Under the Macedonian ruler Seleucus Nicator (301–281 B.C.) the city was rebuilt as Beroia, with a rectangular plan and fortified walls. This reurbanization permanently restored its city form. Beroia was incorporated into the Roman province of Syria in 64 B.C. The Romans added an agora and a colonnaded avenue. In Roman and Byzantine times Aleppo was a regional trading town second to Antioch in northern Syria.

In the early Islamic era Aleppo remained of secondary importance. Upon its capture by the Arabs in 636 a treaty agreement guaranteed Aleppans freedom of religion in return for tribute, and Aleppo maintained its Christian population for many centuries. In the ninth and tenth centuries it became a pawn in the struggles between the Abbasid caliphate and the independent governors of Egypt. Aḥmad ibn Ṭūlūn took the town in 888; in 936–937 it was captured by the Ikhshīd dynasty of Egypt. In 944 Aleppo became the center of the northern Syrian principality of Sayf al-Dawla, who made it the capital of a frontier kingdom defending Muslim principalities against Byzantine attack. Aleppo then enjoyed its first era of historical greatness and flourished as a center of Arabic poetry and philosophy until it was taken in 969 by Nicephorus Phocas.

Until the end of the eleventh century, Aleppo was the object of struggle among Arab Bedouin tribes, the Byzantine Empire, and the Fatimid Empire of Egypt. The Fatimids seized the town in 1015; the Bedouin Mirdāsid dynasty took it in 1023; and it was surrendered to the ᶜUkaylids in 1079 and finally annexed by the Seljuks in 1085. Independent Turkish chieftains governed the town from 1085 until 1129, when Aleppo was conquered by Zangī, the Seljuk governor of Mosul.

Zangī and his successors, Nūr al-Dīn, Saladin, and the Ayyubid princes, restored the prosperity and culture of Syria, and Aleppo became one of the new centers of a reorganized Muslim society in Syria. From the middle of the twelfth century a pattern of government and society was established that lasted until the modern era. Aleppo was ruled by a foreign, usually Turkish, military elite that made itself overlord of the town society and also the patron of a revived Muslim religious community. Under state auspices Muslim religious leaders established numerous colleges and schools for the study of hadith and law, systematized Muslim religious scholarship, and instructed the masses in the ideas and practices of Islam. Henceforth, an alien military elite in conjunction with the religious notables ruled Aleppo.

From 1129 to 1260 Aleppo enjoyed a period of prosperity and revitalized cultural life. Nūr al-Dīn rebuilt its walls and canals, provided it with colleges and hospitals, and made it a center of the revival of religious learning. Scholars were invited from Iraq and Iran to resume the traditions of Muslim scholarship in northern Syria. The Crusades made Aleppo the center of a lively international trade.

The new prosperity was again destroyed. Sacked by the Mongols in 1260, Aleppo did not fully recover for centuries. Aleppo came under the rule of the Mamluks of Egypt and Syria. For half a century Aleppo was abandoned by its new rulers and exposed to further Mongol attack. Only after 1300 did it become the base for Mamluk counterattack in northern Syria, Mesopotamia, and Anatolia. Some rebuilding began, but it was interrupted by the Black Death of 1348. In the late fourteenth and through most of the fifteenth centuries, Aleppo remained a small provincial town subject to the constant factional wars among the Mamluk elite and to fiscal and economic exploitation. To the woes of Aleppo, the late fifteenth century also brought Turkoman migration and the extensive bedouinization of northern Syria.

The late fifteenth century also brought new forms of prosperity. The destruction of the Genoese Black Sea ports and the consolidation of the Ottoman Empire redirected international trade routes through Aleppo. In 1517, Aleppo, Syria, and Egypt were absorbed into the Ottoman Empire, and Aleppo became one of the leading commercial cities of the Levant.

BIBLIOGRAPHY

Ibn al-ʾ Adīm, Zubdat al-halab fī taʾrīkh Ḥalab, S. Dahan, ed., 2 vols. (1951–1954); Ira M. Lapidus, *Muslim Cities in the Later Middle Ages* (1967); Jean Sauvaget, *Alep, essai sur le développement d'une grande ville syrienne* (1941); and *"Les tresors d'or" de Sibṭ ibn al-ʾAjami* (1950); Dominique Sourdel, *La description d'Alep d'Ibn Šaddād* (1953); and "Les professeurs de madrasa à Alep aux XIIe–XIIIe siècles," in *Bulletin d'études orientales,* **13** (1949–1950).

IRA M. LAPIDUS

[See also **Syria.**]

ALEXANDER II, POPE (1010/1015–1073), was born Anselm, to a noble family at Baggio (near Milan). He was educated at Milan, but in all probability did not study with Lanfranc at Bec, as often is alleged, and was ordained a priest at Milan in 1055. In that city Anselm undoubtedly became acquainted with the reforming efforts of the Patarines, but in view of his social background, it is unlikely that he was a participant in their activities.

Anselm was elected bishop of Lucca between May and October of 1056, and continued to hold that see while pope. As bishop he was a reformer in the spirit of the 1050's, opposing simony and clerical incontinence, but at the same time assuming a moderate stance on issues involving relations between the empire and the papacy. He shared much in this regard with his countryman Peter Damian, with whom he served as papal legate to Milan in 1060 under Pope Nicholas II. That Anselm was a supporter of the program of reform centered on the papacy is clear from the fact that he knew and worked closely not only with Damian but also with Archdeacon Hildebrand (later Gregory VII).

After the death of Nicholas II in the summer of 1061, Anselm drew Hildebrand's support for the papal office. Despite a series of disorders that resulted in the election of an antipope (Honorius II), Anselm was enthroned as Alexander II on 30 September or 1 October of that year.

Alexander's pontificate often has been seen as a lull between the important events of the reign of Nicholas II and the momentous years of the pontificate of Gregory VII. The monograph by Tilmann Schmidt (1977) has done much to correct this misimpression and to evaluate Alexander's reign in its own terms. Aside from laboring to gain an advantage in the schism with Honorius, who was abandoned after the Council of Mantua in 1064, Alexander presided over an important reforming council at Rome in 1063. He continued to press throughout his pontificate both for ecclesiastical elections free from simony and for clerical celibacy. The matter of lay investiture was not an issue. His twelve-year reign saw a constant effort to increase respect for the papacy throughout Christendom, as a series of legatine activities under his sponsorship and a large volume of surviving letters testify.

The exact relationship between Alexander and the powerful Hildebrand cannot be known in detail, but probably should be understood as one of like-minded reformers rather than as pawn and master. The great conflicts that were to erupt during the pontificate of Gregory VII had only begun to appear—in the church at Milan, and in the attitudes of Henry IV toward the papacy—when Alexander died at Rome.

BIBLIOGRAPHY

Tilmann Schmidt, *Alexander II (1061–1073) und die Römische Reformgruppe seiner Zeit* (1977), contains a full bibliography of both primary and secondary sources, and is indispensable. See also Philipp Jaffé, *Regesta pontificum Romanorum,* 2nd ed., I (1885), 566–594; and Friedrich Kempf, "Progress of the Reform: The Lotharingian and Tuscan Popes (1057 to 1073)," in *The Church in the Age of Feudalism* (1969).

ROBERT SOMERVILLE

ALEXANDER III, POPE (*ca.* 1105–1181), the first great lawyer pope, was born Rolando Bandinelli in Siena, Italy. A professor of canon law at Bologna, he was brought to Rome in 1148 by Pope Eugene III and rapidly rose to prominence, becoming chancellor of the Apostolic See in 1153. Following the death of Adrian IV in 1159, he was raised to the pontificate by a majority of the cardinals, but his election was opposed by a minority who chose the antipope Victor IV. The latter received the support of Emperor Frederick Barbarossa at the Council of Pavia in 1160, and the resulting schism lasted for seventeen years.

Despite his role as papal legate at Besançon in 1157, when Pope Adrian had aroused suspicions that he was claiming the Holy Roman Empire as a fief, Alexander made no broad assertions of papal authority. Conflicting territorial ambitions in Italy were a more important cause of the breach between pope and emperor. Alexander was supported by most of Western Christendom, especially by the Lombard cities, who opposed imperial claims in Italy. Frederick's defeat by the Lombard League at Legnano led to the Peace of Venice in 1177, in which he finally recognized Alexander.

Despite the schism, and the conflict between Becket and Henry II over clerical rights in England, the papacy was not weakened during Alexander's pontificate. Rather, ecclesiastical administration was strengthened, and important legislation was promulgated; Alexander's decretals are the largest contribution of one pope to the body of medieval canon law.

BIBLIOGRAPHY

Primary Sources. Cardinal Boso, *Alexandri III vita*, L. Duchesne, ed., *Liber Pontificalis*, II (1892, repr. 1955) 397–446. *Boso's Life of Alexander III*, G. M. Ellis, trans., with an intro. by Peter Munz (1973); J. P. Migne, ed. *Patrologiae latinae cursus completus*, CC (1855).

Secondary Sources. M. W. Baldwin, *Alexander III and the Twelfth Century* (1968); M. Pacaut, *Alexandre III, Étude sur la conception du pouvoir pontifical dans sa pensée et dans son oeuvre* (1956).

M. L. RAMPOLLA

[See also **Frederick I Barbarossa; Law, Canon.**]

ALEXANDER V (*ca.* 1340–1410), theologian and antipope, was born Peter of Candia (or Petros Philargos) in Crete (Candia) and was orphaned at an early age. He was taken in by an Italian Franciscan and joined the order when he was about seventeen. He studied at the Franciscan *studium* at Padua before going in the 1360's to Oxford, where he became a bachelor in theology. After studying in England Peter apparently taught at various Franciscan convents in Russia, Bohemia, and Poland, before going to Paris to teach at the Franciscan convent of St. Mary Magdalene. Here he lectured on Lombard's *Sentences* from 1378 to 1380. At the outset of the Western Schism, he remained faithful to the Roman obedience, and in 1381 he received his licentiate in theology following the direct intervention of the antipope Clement VII.

By 1385 Peter returned to northern Italy, where he became a close advisor to Gian Galeazzo Visconti, duke of Milan and his long-standing patron. In 1386 he was appointed bishop to the see of Piacenza, from which he proceeded in 1388 to that of Vicenza and in 1389 to that of Novara. In 1402 he was elevated to the strategic archiepiscopal see of Milan, where finally in 1405 he became cardinal priest of the Church of the Twelve Apostles. As the "cardinal of Milan" Peter also served as papal legate to Lombardy.

In 1409 a council to end the Western Schism was convoked at Pisa, attended by the cardinals of both the Roman and Avignon popes, delegations from nearly every land, and hundreds of lawyers and theologians, although the popes themselves refused to come. The council acted to depose both popes (Gregory XII and Benedict XIII) and thereupon elected Peter, who took the name of Alexander V. Not only did the West welcome this move to end the schism, but the election of the first Greek pope in 700 years also elicited a warm response from the Byzantine Emperor, Manuel II Palaeologus. But since neither of the deposed popes could be compelled to accept the council's decisions, Peter's election in effect created a third pope. This dilemma was not finally resolved until the Council of Constance.

Peter died at Bologna, his pontificate having lasted less than a year (26 June 1409 to 3 May 1410), marred by what his detractors claimed to be inordinate favoritism and a way of life more befitting a prince than a prelate.

Peter's commentary on the *Sentences* treats only selected questions inspired by Lombard's text, as was the style at his time. He was among the first to mention by name the authors whose opinions he cited. His work shows a familiarity with the most important thinkers of the fourteenth century.

Peter's personality comes to the fore in his *principium* lectures, given at the beginning of each academic term. His *Principia* are important because of the rare coincidence of their survival together with his lectures on Lombard. Peter was also author of theological opuscula and of some liturgical works that seem to date from his stay in Italy. The records of the Council of Pisa give the texts of some sermons that he preached there, but the bulk of his works exist only in manuscript.

BIBLIOGRAPHY

P. Victorin Doucet, *Commentaire sur les Sentences: Supplément au répertoire de M. Frédéric Stegmueller* (1954), no. 665. Published as a monograph containing Doucet's articles found in *Archivum franciscanum historicum* **47** (1954): 88–170, 400–427; Franz Ehrle, *Der Sentenzenkommentar Peters von Candia, des Pisaner Papstes Alexanders V* (1925); Willibrord Lampen, "Prosae seu poemata Petri de Candia O. F. M.," in *Archivum franciscanum historicum,* **23** (1930); Giovanni Domenico Mansi, *Sacrorum conciliorum nova, et amplissima collectio,* XXVI (1784), 1136–1256; XXVII (1784), 1–502; Friedrich Stegmüller, *Repertorium biblicum medii aevi,* IV (1954), 248; and *Repertorium commentariorum in Sententias Petri Lombardi,* I (1947), 318–321; Noël Valois, *La France et le grand schisme d'occident* IV (1902); Luke Wadding, *Annales minorum,* 3rd ed., IX (1932).

MARK A. ZIER

[See also **Antipope; Schism, Great.**]

ALEXANDER OF HALES (*ca.* 1185–1245), called *doctor irrefragabilis* ("irrefutable teacher"), was probably born at Halesowen, Shropshire (now Worcestershire), England.

He studied philosophy and theology at the University of Paris, where from around 1220 until his death he was a regent master of theology. By 1231 he had been appointed both canon of Lichfield and archdeacon of Coventry. His contemporary, Roger Bacon, called him "a good and rich man, . . . and also a great master of theology in his time."

In 1231 he represented the University of Paris at the Roman Curia, and in 1235 he took part in the peace negotiations between Henry III of England and Louis IX of France. The next year, to the surprise and edification of his contemporaries, he abandoned his worldly possessions and became a Franciscan Friar Minor, while retaining his chair of theology at Paris. In 1245 he was active at the General Council of Lyons.

As a theologian, Alexander introduced the *Sentences* of Peter Lombard as the textbook for theology. He divided the work into "distinctions" according to the principal problems discussed in it, and between 1225 and 1229 he wrote a commentary on it in the form of glosses. He is also the author of some 200 "disputed questions" in which he tries to elucidate practically all the theological problems debated in the first half of the thirteenth century. After he became a friar he undertook, with the help of other learned Franciscans, the composition of a very extensive theological synthesis, the *Summa Fratris Alexandri.* It is a systematic investigation in four books, concerning God, the Creation, incarnation, and sacraments. The fourth part was composed after his death, in Paris, by William of Militona. Although Alexander of Hales had some limited knowledge of the philosophy of Aristotle, his theology was not influenced by it. It is based on the sacred Scriptures and on the teachings of the church fathers, especially of St. Augustine.

BIBLIOGRAPHY

Editions of Alexander's works include the *Summa theologica,* with prolegomena, 4 vols. (1924–1948); *Glossa in quatuor libros sententiarum Petri Lombardi,* 4 vols. (1951–1957); and *Quaestiones disputatae "Antequam esset frater,"* 3 vols. (1960). See also Ignatius Brady, "The *Summa theologica* of Alexander of Hales," in *Archivum Franciscanum historicum,* **70** (1977); Irenaeus Herscher, "A Bibliography of Alexander of Hales," in *Franciscan Studies,* **5** (1945); Kevin P. Keane, *The Logic of Self-diffusive Goodness in the Trinitarian Theory of the "Summa Fratris Alexandri"* (unpub. diss., 1978); Walter H. Principe, *Alexander of Hales' Theology of the Hypostatic Union* (1967), which contains a good bibliography; and Meldon C. Wass, *The Infinite God* and *the "Summa Fratris Alexandri"* (1964).

CONRAD HARKINS, O.F.M.

ALEXANDER OF ROES, a German political theorist of the late thirteenth century, expounded the view that proper order in the Western Christian world had to rest on a collaboration among Italians, Germans, and French in which the Italians would control the papacy; the Germans, the Holy Roman Empire; and the French, mastery over learning. He was a canon of Cologne who resided in Italy in the retinue of Cardinal Giacomo Colonna from at least 1281 until at least 1288. During those years he wrote three works: *Memoriale de prerogativa Romani imperii* ("Treatise on the Prerogatives of the Roman Empire") (1281), *Pavo* ("Peacock") (1285), and *Noticia seculi* ("Notes on the World") (1288). The first and third are prose treatises; the second is an allegorical poem which alludes to events at the First Council of Lyons (1245); the "peacock" (the pope) deposes the "eagle" (the German emperor) with the aid of the vain "rooster" (France), but a vindication of the "eagle" is intimated.

Alexander sought primarily to defend the dignity of the German empire at a time when its prestige was ebbing and its independence greatly threatened by the papacy and the French. He was inspired to write the *Memoriale* after he noticed that a prayer for the emperor customarily said during Mass was missing from papal missals and after hearing the French who were present at the coronation of the French pope Martin IV proclaim that the empire should be taken away from the incompetent Germans and given to France. Alexander's response, which he set forth in both the *Memoriale* and the *Noticia seculi,* was that the empire belonged by right to the Germans, and that the Italian papacy, German empire, and French studium (preeminence in studies) were equally necessary for the well-being of the Western Christian commonwealth.

Alexander developed these ideas by appealing to history, eschatology, analogy, and collective psychology. From the historical perspective, he argued that Charlemagne had been a Frank, and thus a German rather than a Frenchman, for the French were a mixture of Franks and Gauls. An Italian pope had transferred the empire by right to the Germans through the crowning of Charlemagne, and the empire should remain with the Germans until the end of time. Eschatological wisdom concorded with this, for the Bible said that Antichrist would come when there was a "falling away" from the empire; thus, all who worked to weaken the empire were Antichrist's minions.

Confident that the German empire would regain its former greatness, Alexander was certain that there would be a wondrous Christian future on earth before Antichrist's reign and the end of the world. Drawing on analogy, he argued that there was need for a triumvirate of priesthood, empire, and learning just as humans were created with soul, body, and spirit; the Church, moreover, was a building with a foundation of the priesthood (located in Rome), four walls comprising the empire (located in Aachen, Arles, Milan, and Rome), and a roof of learning (located in Paris). Finally, from the psychological point of view, the Germans were the natural bearers of empire because they were natural aristocrats who took a joy in ruling. Alexander's ideas were without influence on the actual course of events, but his works contain many interesting observations and are valuable sources, above all for the history of German national self-consciousness.

BIBLIOGRAPHY

Herbert Grundmann and Hermann Heimpel, eds., *Alexander von Roes, Schriften* (1958), critical edition of three works, and *Die Schriften des Alexander von Roes* (1949), Latin and facing-page German translations of three works; Herbert Grundmann, "Ueber die Schriften des Alexander von Roes," in *Deutsches Archiv für Erforschung des Mittelalters,* 8 (1950); Hermann Heimpel, "Alexander von Roes und das deutsche Selbstbewusstsein des 13. Jahrhunderts," in *Archiv für Kulturgeschichte,* 26 (1935).

Robert E. Lerner

ALEXANDER ROMANCES are found in almost all the literatures of medieval Europe, and constitute one of the most extensive and involved narrative complexes, in both prose and poetry, of the whole period. The career of Alexander the Great formed the subject of romances—that is, part historical, part fictional narratives—very soon after his death in 323 B.C. None of these early works is extant, but there are numerous redactions, in various languages, of a Greek prose romance usually referred to as the Pseudo-Callisthenes. The earliest extant Greek version is in an eleventh-century manuscript, but there are earlier adaptations by Julius Valerius, *Res gestae Alexandri Macedonis* (*ca.* 320); in Armenian (fifth century); and particularly in Latin by Archpresbyter Leo (*ca.* 950), later reworkings of which version contributed substantially to many of the best-known vernacular works on Alexander. Leo's translation is based on a lost Greek manuscript and is known by the title that appeared in early printed editions, *Historia de preliis.*

Other works based either on the Pseudo-Callisthenes or on its Latin version are found in Bulgarian, Armenian, Hebrew, Serbian, modern Greek, Syriac, Persian, and Ethiopic. Another account of the deeds of Alexander that was of great importance for the writers of medieval works was the Latin prose history written by Quintus Curtius Rufus, *Historiae Alexandri* (early first century). There are considerable lacunae in the medieval manuscripts, particularly in the early books, and in the so-called *Interpolated Quintus Curtius* these are supplied from other sources. This group of works was the closest thing to a strictly historical account available to medieval writers.

Two other works, both fictional, were of considerable significance. The *Espistola Alexandri Macedonis ad Aristotelem* is a letter from Alexander to his tutor Aristotle, describing his travels and especially the wonders of India. It became known chiefly through its incorporation into many of the works already mentioned, although independent versions exist, and it was translated into several western European languages, including Old English (before 1000) and Middle Irish. The other work, the *Iter ad Paradisum* (Journey to Paradise), is definitely of Hebrew origin, as are other stories connecting Alexander with Jerusalem and Daniel the prophet. It appeared before 500, but the earliest Latin version is from the twelfth century. It tells of the accidental arrival of Alexander at the gates of the earthly paradise. When he asks for tribute, he is given a stone with mysterious markings that are interpreted by an aged Jew in Babylon as portraying Alexander's power but also its impotence in the face of death, and as warning him of the danger of avarice. In some versions the stress is on humility.

These sources and many minor ones contributed to the development of the vernacular Alexander romances. Only 105 lines survive of the earliest of these, that of Alberic de Bisançon (early twelfth century), which was translated into German by a priest, Lamprecht of Trier, before 1155. The earliest extant version of the German work, that in the Vorau manuscript, gives a good idea of Alberic's work. Both authors are concerned to stress Alexander's weaknesses as a pagan, in spite of his successes, and Lamprecht goes so far as to reproach Alberic for not pointing out that Alexander was inferior to Solomon. Both works connect his career, quite unhistorically, with biblical locations. Lamprecht's poem ends, as Alberic's probably did, with Alexander's killing of Darius in battle, a deliberate departure from the usual account, but one stressing the destruction of the pride of the Persian empire. The Vorau version is only 1,527 lines long. It was much expanded in a Strassburg manuscript of 1187 and in a Basel manuscript of the fifteenth century. Both make much use of the *Historia de preliis* and add such stories as that of the flower maidens of India, of Alexander's ascent into the air, and of his descent into the ocean in a glass barrel.

The most important medieval poems on Alexander are the Latin *Alexandreis* of Gautier de Châtillon and the French *Roman d'Alexandre.* Gautier's poem, written between 1178 and 1182, consists of ten books of Latin hexameters and is a conscious imitation of classical Latin epic. A summary will give an idea of the Alexander story in its least fantastic form, since Gautier used Quintus Curtius, rather than the fictional material already mentioned, as his main source.

Alexander is introduced as a youth eager to prove his manhood and kingly qualities, but a long speech put in the mouth of his tutor Aristotle stresses the need for wisdom and, particularly, justice. After the death of his father Philip, Alexander defeats but spares Athens, whereas Thebes is destroyed; the verdict in each case is dependent on the city's role in earlier history. The move to Asia and the Persian empire, described in considerable detail, is expressed in epic terms. Some places, such as Jerusalem and the tomb of Achilles, receive special mention, and in a dream Alexander is asked by a Hebrew priest to spare Jerusalem. There is a great deal of comparison between Alexander and Darius, always to the former's advantage, with particular stress on Alexander's superb management of his soldiers. His courtesy is stressed too in his treatment of the wife and mother of Darius, captured after the battle of the Issus, behavior that is in marked contrast with that of Darius when he accuses Alexander of complicity in the entirely natural death of his wife while in captivity.

Before Darius' defeat at Arbela (Erbil), there are two revealing incidents: Alexander's pacification of the terror of his troops during a lunar eclipse and his determined persistence at the long siege of Tyre. Book 5 ends with the entry into Babylon, a highly significant event, for the next five books tell of gradual degeneration. The power is still there, and so is the control of the soldiers, but incidents of cruelty and injustice multiply—for example, the merciless destruction of Persepolis and the almost barbarous investigation into the plot against Alexander's life, in which the innocent are punished with the guilty. Darius is killed by his own followers and duly avenged by Alexander. The long march to India continues, and this time Alexander has to subdue a near mutiny among his troops when a return to Macedon is rumored.

After the defeat of Porus and dreams of further conquests, Alexander returns through the desert to Babylon. The place is significant, for Book 10 opens with a description of an indignant Nature summoning the gods below to destroy him, and he falls victim to a plot engineered by his Greek general Antipater. Gautier shows Alexander as the ideal pagan prince. This is not to say that Alexander is perfect. Indeed, the poem shows him as gradually corrupted by power after the capture of Babylon. But in spite of this, the scope of his ambition, his control of his men, his magnanimity to beaten enemies, and his cultural aims make him a model to imitate.

ALEXANDER ROMANCES

The role of Fortune is constantly emphasized: Alexander almost dies by merely bathing in a river, and recovers from severe wounds, only to fall victim to men who were allegedly his friends. Unlike many authors, Gautier does not stress the absence of Christian virtues, although he does try to make some connections with the Judaic tradition. The epic is well written and may be regarded as an attempt by a scholarly writer of the twelfth century to use epic form and an epic hero as a mirror and a warning to secular princes, particularly against the abuse of power and loss of friends.

There are few marvels in Gautier's work, but they are an essential element in the French *Roman d'Alexandre* and its derivatives. The work of Alberic was remodeled, and appears as the first part of the romance. It is usually called the *Decasyllabic Alexander* (1165–1175) and is 785 lines long. Lambert le Tort, at about the same time, wrote a poem on Alexander's adventures in the East; and these two, with another poem, *Mort Alixandre* (Alexander's Death), form the basis of the *Roman,* from which the twelve-syllable alexandrine line takes its name.

One of the best-known versions is that of Alexandre de Paris, whose four branches are as follows: Alexander's youth, including the capture of Athens; the capture of Tyre, including an independent episode of the siege, the *Fuerre de Gadres,* and Darius' first defeat; the pursuit of and death of Darius, the descent into the ocean and ascent into the heavens, India and its marvels, capture of Babylon, the Amazons, and the plot by Antipater; the death and burial of Alexander.

In this work Alexander is an ideal courtly prince, and he and his "knights" behave like the heroes of an Arthurian romance. The historical events found in Gautier's work are modified or eliminated in favor of fantastic exploits that illustrate the chivalric nature of the king and his men. There is no criticism of his morals, nor is the question of his religion of any importance. Only in the *Prise de Defur* (Capture of Defur, *ca.* 1250) and in the *Prose Romance of Alexander* (between 1206 and 1290) is he criticized for cupidity, an attitude clearly derived from the *Iter ad Paradisum,* since most works stress his generosity. The courtly tradition was continued in such purely fictional works as *Venjance Alixandre* (Jean de Nevelon, before 1181) and *Vengement Alixandre* (Gui de Cambrai, before 1191), which tell of the avenging of his death. The *Voeux du paon* (Vows of the peacock) of Jacques de Longuyon (*ca.* 1312) is an adventure story, connected only loosely with the Alexander romances, as are its continuations *Restor du paon* (Jean Brisebarre, 1338) and *Parfait du paon* (Jean de la Mote, 1340).

There are Alexander books in all the major western European languages that are derived in varying degrees from the works already mentioned: Jakob von Maerlant, *Alexanders Geesten* (twelve books, Dutch, 1256–1260); *Libro de Alexandre* (derived largely from Gautier, Spanish, mid thirteenth century); *Buik of Alexander* (a translation of the *Voeux du paon,* Scots, fifteenth century); *Buik of King Alexander* (by Sir Gilbert Hay, *ca.* 1456, a long work including *Fuerre de Gadres* and *Voeux du paon*); *Roman de toute chevalerie* (Thomas of Kent, second half of the twelfth century, French, later expanded to its present Anglo-Norman form); and *Alexander* (Ulrich von Eschenbach, 1270–1287, German). *Alexanders Saga* (Brand Jónsson, *ca.* 1260, Icelandic) and a Czech poem of about 1265 are both largely dependent on Gautier's poem. A monumental work is that by Rudolf von Ems (1230–1250), which incorporates the account by Quintus Curtius and many of the fictional works in its 21,643 lines, but it is essentially a historical account that emphasizes Alexander's role as a successful conqueror while intimating that he was really an instrument of God's providence.

There is immense variety in the medieval romances of Alexander, but certain elements are constant. He is always admired as a secular ruler, especially because of his bravery, generosity, and magnanimity. In the romances and their derivatives these qualities are part of his characterization as the ideal courtly prince, but in other works they do not make up for the fact that he is a pagan king, motivated by the vanities of this world, who was doomed to perish and who illustrates better than anyone the vanity of all earthly success when compared with the glories of a truly Christian king such as Charlemagne.

BIBLIOGRAPHY

The best account of the medieval works on Alexander is George Cary, *The Medieval Alexander* (1956). There are few translations into English: Elizabeth H. Haight, ed. and trans., *The Life of Alexander of Macedon by Pseudo-Callisthenes* (1955); Immanuel ben Jacob Bonfils, *The Book of the Gests of Alexander of Macedon,* Israel J. Kazis, ed. and trans. (1962), Hebrew trans. of *Historia de preliis* with English text; Rosalie Reich, ed. and trans., *Tales of Alexander the Macedonian* (1972); Albert M. Wolohojian, trans., *Romance of Alexander the Great* (1969), an Armenian version of Pseudo-Callisthenes translated into

English; Marvin L. Colker, *Galteri de Castellione Alexandreis* (1978), is a superb edition of the work of Gautier de Châtillon with the glosses.

W. T. H. JACKSON

ALEXANDERS SAGA, a Norse adaptation in prose of *Alexandreis,* a twelfth-century Latin poem by Gautier de Châtillon about the life and conquests of Alexander the Great. The Norse version is preserved in a thirteenth-century Icelandic manuscript (AM 519a, 4° in the Arnamagnæan collection in Copenhagen) and is generally attributed to the Icelandic bishop Brandr Jónsson of Hólar, who died in 1264, though this attribution has been contested by Widding. The translation was probably made *ca.* 1260.

The Latin rhetoric and didacticism of the original have been transformed into a sober saga style, emphasizing dramatic action and presenting Gautier's own reflections, mainly in the form of abbreviated quotations introduced by *segir meistari Galterus* ("Master Galterus says") or a similar formula. In spite of such attempts to make the narrative more "objective," in the tradition of sagas, the main purpose of the translation is clearly didactic: it provides a sermon for a traditional Norse saga audience about the futility of war and secular honor, and presents lessons in ancient history and mythology in the spirit of the "twelfth-century renaissance." The adaptation probably had some influence on the native Icelandic saga production of the thirteenth and fourteenth centuries.

BIBLIOGRAPHY

Editions. Alexanders saga: Norsk bearbeidelse fra trettende aarhundrede af Philip Gautiers latinske digt Alexandreis, C. R. Unger, ed. (1848); *Alexanders saga: Islandsk oversættelse ved Brandr Jónsson,* Finnur Jónsson, ed. (1925).

Criticism. Lars Lönnroth, "Hetjurnar líta bleika akra; Athuganir á Njáls sögu og Alexanders sögu," in *Skírnir,* **144** (1970); Elinar Ó. Sveinsson, "*Alexandreis* et la Saga d'Alexandre," in *Rencontres et courants littéraires franco-scandinaves* (1972); T. Þórhallsson, "Brandur Jónsson, biskup á Hólum," in *Skírnir,* **107** (1923); O. Widding, "Það finnur hver sem um er hugað," in *Skírnir,* **134** (1960).

LARS LÖNNROTH

[See also **Alexander Romances.**]

ALEXANDRE, LIBRO DE, an early-thirteenth-century Castilian romance on the life of Alexander the Great and an excellent example of European Alexander lore, reflects the enormous prestige accorded the Macedonian conqueror throughout Europe from the twelfth century on. The skeletal structure derives directly from the *Alexandreis* written in Latin hexameter by the French poet Gautier de Châtillon between 1178 and 1182. Second in importance is the *Historia de Preliis* (recensions J^1 and J^2), attributed to Leo of Naples. Other principal sources include the *Roman d'Alexandre* (B) by Alexandre de Bernay and Lambert li Tors, the *Ilias Latina* of Pseudo-Pindarus Thebanus, and the *Origenes* of St. Isidore of Seville, with briefer and perhaps indirect reflections from Pseudo-Callisthenes, Julius Valerius' *Epitome,* the *Physiologus,* and Flavius Josephus.

Composed in 2,675 Alexandrine quatrains, the work survives in two fairly complete manuscripts. The Madrid manuscript reveals Leonese dialectical tendencies and bears a final signature strophe of Juan Lorenzo de Astorga. The Paris manuscript has Aragonese leanings and ends with a signature strophe attributing the work to Gonzalo de Berceo, the first identified Castilian poet. Recent scholarship has discredited the candidacy of Juan Lorenzo, who is clearly no more than a scribe.

Tutored as a youth by Aristotle, Alexander epitomized the perfect prince to the medieval mind: magnanimous, valorous, and well-lettered. But he was also dominated by an insatiable restlessness that drove him ever forward in his quest for new experiences, wider dominions, and glory. In his unbridled ambition lay the seeds of his destruction. Perceiving the humanity of this historical figure, the author communicates the ambivalence of his personality with consummate mastery.

After subduing rebellious Greek principalities, Alexander launches his campaign against the Persian tyrant Darius; here the poet's mastery of the medieval techniques of amplification, particularly in the form of digression, are revealed. On reaching Troy, Alexander recites a lengthy version of the Trojan War, thus evoking ancient Greek heroes as models for emulation by his army. The poet describes the splendors of Babylon and the precious stones found in its rivers; and the death of Darius introduces the *memento mori* theme with a critique of medieval society. After consolidating his Asiatic conquests by marrying Roxane, who in the poem is Darius' daughter, Alexander moves against Porus. The Indian campaign, which gives rise to a disquistion on the behavior of elephants, culminates in the exploration of the Indian Ocean, where the world conqueror, installed in a primitive bathyscaphe, confronts the denizens of the deep.

Allegory plays an important role in the poem's culmination, when Nature, who has been observing Alexander with alarm, intervenes to thwart his unbridled desire to master all peoples and all things. She enlists the aid of Beelzebub during a journey to hell, a juncture that inspires the first detailed description in Spanish of the infernal regions. Envy, a minion of the devil, is dispatched to inspire disloyalty in Jobas, who poisons his master on the occasion of Alexander's triumphant return to Babylon.

BIBLIOGRAPHY

Sources. Dana A. Nelson, ed., Gonzalo de Berceo, *El libro de Alixandre: reconstrucción crítica* (1979); Raymond S. Willis, ed., *El libro de Alexandre: Texts of the Paris and the Madrid Manuscripts* (1934).

Studies. Emilio Alarcos Llorach, *Investigaciones sobre El Libro de Alexandre* (1948); Ian Michael, *The Treatment of Classical Material in the Libro de Alexandre* (1970); Dana A. Nelson, "The Domain of the Old Spanish *-er* and *-ir* Verbs: A Clue to the Provenience of the *Alexandre,*" in *Romance Philology,* **26** (1972); Raymond S. Willis, *The Relationship of the Spanish Libro de Alexandre to the Alexandreis of Gautier de Châtillon* (1934); and *The Debt of the Spanish Libro de Alexandre to the French Roman d'Alexandre* (1935).

DANA A. NELSON

[See also **Alexander Romance.**]

ALEXANDRIA, an important Egyptian port city that, under late Roman and Byzantine rule, became a major seat of Christian learning, was taken by Arab forces on 17 September 642. Although an agreement between ᶜAmr ibn al- ᶜĀṣ, commander of the Arab troops, and the defeated Byzantine garrison allowed the Christian inhabitants to maintain their churches and administer their communal affairs, it is reported that 30,000 Greeks left the city at that time. In 645 a Byzantine force regained control of Alexandria for one year. The legend of the destruction of Alexandria's library by the Arabs upon the conquest is almost certainly apocryphal. It first appears in the thirteenth century and probably preserves the memory of an incident of that nature in Caesarea. The so-called Alexandrian academy was transferred to Antioch several decades after the conquest.

The sources are generally silent about the history of the city from then until the ninth century. In 815, Arab exiles of Spain, who are reported to have numbered 15,000, occupied Alexandria for twelve years and made it a base for piratical activities. In later periods Alexandria occasionally provided a stage for political and military conflicts. In 1167, while being governed by Saladin, it was besieged by the Crusader Amalric. In 1365 it was partly destroyed during the invasion of Peter of Lusignan, who took 5,000 prisoners. The city apparently never fully recovered from that raid.

Under Arab rule Alexandria had ceased to house the seat of Egyptian government, which moved to Al-Fusṭāt. Two of the Umayyad governors, however, temporarily resided in the city. In the tradition of the Roman administrative division, Alexandria either had an administration of its own or was part of the western coastal region of Egypt. Thus during the governorship of Ibn Ṭūlūn (868–884) the city was not under his authority. Even the budget for Egypt was in 958 divided between Al-Fusṭāt and Alexandria. The city's special position was also maintained during the Fatimid period. In Ayyubid and Mamluk times Alexandria was governed by a military officer (emir), whose seat was in a presumably Roman citadel at the northwestern corner of the city. Mamluk sultans very rarely visited Alexandria, using it as a place of imprisonment for political adversaries. Like some other ports, Alexandria was considered a frontier fortress *(thagr)* and is often referred to in the sources as such. Besides Cairo, Alexandria was the only Egyptian city having a chief judge *(qadi'l qudāt).* He was almost always of the Maliki school of law, due to the city's proximity to North Africa and the migration of Maghrebi and Spanish Muslims to it in the course of the *reconquista.* In the Mamluk period there existed a house of justice *(dār al-ᶜadl),* where complaints against the administration were treated.

According to the brief and incomplete medieval accounts of Alexandria's topography, the Arab city occupied only a fraction of the area of the Roman. Eight straight streets intersected eight others at right angles, producing a chessboard pattern of direct and continuous thoroughfares. As in antiquity, houses were built on columns, rising one above the other in as many as three tiers. Alexandria had four main gates and was well fortified. It is reported that al-

Mutawakkil (848–861) furnished it with a wall suitable for resisting a siege.

The medieval seaport consisted of an eastern harbor, reserved for Christian shipping, and a western harbor for Muslim vessels. They both flanked the island of Pharos with its famous lighthouse, which survived the Arab conquest. After the Pharos had been destroyed in a series of earthquakes a second lighthouse was completed in 1365. In 1477 a tower was built on the ruins of the old Pharos.

Under Arab rule Alexandria played an important role in Mediterranean trade. It served as a port from which many Levantine goods were exported to the Christian West. In 828, Venetian merchants were arriving in the city despite a ban by the Byzantine emperor Leo V. The emergence of Alexandria as a center of trade in the twelfth and thirteenth centuries is attested by contemporaries such as Benjamin of Tudela, William of Tyre, and Ibn Batuta. European merchants, being forbidden to trade in Cairo, were confined mainly to Alexandria and resided in *funduqs* (caravanserais), where they also conducted business.

Their presence in the city continued throughout the period of the Crusades. In 1345 Venice concluded a treaty with the Mamluks by which it established regular service with Alexandria. Merchants of Genoa, Pisa, and other maritime cities were also active in the Egyptian port. The trade season in Alexandria lasted up to two months, compared to one or two weeks in the Egyptian interior.

According to a twelfth-century source the city's annual revenue from duties was close to 30,000 dinars; fourteenth-century estimates put the sultan's daily benefits from the city's revenues at 1,000 dinars. By the eleventh century, there were both a customs house *(dār al-wakāla)* and a bureau of commerce *(matjar)*, the latter serving the regime's right of preemption on imported goods. As in every large Islamic city, each major trade had its own market in Alexandria; those of spices, slaves, and linen were especially important. Some markets were reserved for merchants of a specific nationality or ethnic origin.

Besides being an international trade center, Alexandria had always been a center of textile industry. In the medieval period the city housed a large brocade workshop *(dār al-tirāz)*, which worked primarily for the court and for export. Alexandria's mats were world-renowned and its textiles were exported as far as India. The city also served as an entrepôt and bourse for the silk trade. In 1365 the *dār al-tirāz* was burned but was later restored. According to one report there were some 14,000 looms in the city in the early fifteenth century.

Estimates of Alexandria's population in the early Islamic period appear unreliable. About 670 Arculf remarked that it accommodated innumerable people, and Ibn ᶜAbd al-Ḥakam in the ninth century gives conflicting figures (200,000 and 600,000) for the time of the Arab conquest. Later estimates put the population in the thirteenth century at 65,000. Following the outbreak of the Black Death the city seems to have suffered a significant decline, but the population was probably restored to some extent afterward. Lionardo Frescobaldi in 1384 mentions 60,000 inhabitants, and other travelers give similar figures. Demographic decline was renewed during the fifteenth century, and Emmanuel Piloti tells that the city was almost abandoned. According to one report the number of looms declined to no more than 800 around 1435. The Venetian ambassador to Cairo, Domenico Trevisan, reported in 1512 that 90 percent of Alexandria was in ruins and that he had never seen such decay. The destruction of the population by plague, coupled with the discovery of the southern sea route to India in the closing years of the fifteenth century, dealt Alexandria a blow as a center of trade.

The Christian community in Islamic Alexandria consisted of both Copts and Melchites. In the first half of the eleventh century the Coptic patriarch had to transfer his seat from Alexandria to Cairo. Saladin decided to remove the Cathedral of St. Mark for fear that it might serve the Crusades, and the Copts failed to ransom it.

By 1100 most of Alexandria's Jews were Maghrebi whose ancestors had emigrated from Iraq. Inflated figures from Arab sources put the Jewish population at the time of the conquest at 40,000. More reliable estimates from medieval sources give a figure of 3,000 in the twelfth century. Travelers in the last decades of the fifteenth century report fewer than 100 families.

BIBLIOGRAPHY

Sources. Muḥammad ibn Qāsim al-Nuwayrī, *Kitāb al-Ilmām,* II (1969), contains information on the invasion of 1365; Emmanuel Piloti, *L'Égypte au commencement du quinzième siècle* (1950); Ghars al-Dīn Khalīl ibn Shāhīn al-Zāhirī, *Zoubdat kachf el-mamâlik,* Paul Ravaisse, ed. (1894), 39–41.

Studies. Sālim ᶜAbd 'l-ᶜAzīz, *History and Civilization of Islamic Alexandria* (in Arabic), 2nd ed. (1969); Alfred J.

Butler, *The Arab Conquest of Egypt*, 2nd ed. (1978), includes a critical bibliography and added documentation by P. M. Fraser; C. Cahen, "Douanes et commerce dans les ports méditerranéens de l'Égypte médiévale d'après le Minhādj d'al-Makhzūmī," in *Journal of the Economic and Social History of the Orient*, 7 (1964); Aḥmad Darrāg, *L'Égypte sous le règne de Barsbay* (1961); Solomon D. Goitein, *A Mediterranean Society*, 3 vols. (1967–1978), treats mainly the Jewish community; Paul E. Kahle, "Die Katastrophe des mittelalterichen Alexandria," in *Mélanges Maspero*, III (1935), 137–154, deals with the Crusade of 1365; Subhi Y. Labib, *Handelsgeschichte Ägyptens im Spätmittelalter (1171–1517)* (1965); and "Egyptian Commercial Policy in the Middle Ages," in M. A. Cook, *Studies in the Economic History of the Middle East* (1970), 63–77; Muḥammad ᶜAbd al-ᶜAzīz Marzūq, *History of Textile Industry in Alexandria (1955)*.

Subhi Labib, "Al-Iskandariyya," in *Encyclopedia of Islam*, IV, has a good bibliography.

BOAZ SHOSHAN

ALEXANDRIAN RITE. The liturgical usages of the patriarchal see of Alexandria are observed today with variations by the Coptic Orthodox church in Egypt, by the Ethiopian Orthodox church in Ethiopia, and by their Catholic counterparts. They were also observed until the early Middle Ages by the Greek Orthodox church of Alexandria but were gradually replaced by the usages of Constantinople. Presumably they were likewise followed by the churches in Nubia and Libya until Islam submerged those centers of Christianity by the eleventh and sixteenth centuries, respectively.

In Egypt, there was no liturgical uniformity during the early Christian centuries. Tantalizing remnants of local liturgical rites have survived, especially the euchologion attributed to Bishop Serapion of Thmuis, the friend of Athanasius, and the seventh-century anaphoral fragments of *Dair Balāᵓizeh*. Even these witnesses to local liturgical autonomy, however, show a strong family resemblance to the usages of Alexandria. The twelfth-century missal of the White Monastery contains a large number of eucharistic anaphoras that were not accepted in Alexandria; but by the middle of the following century, local usages seem to have succumbed to the pressure exerted by the example and prestige of the patriarchal see and by formal liturgical ordinances of the patriarchs.

The process of uniformization was also at work in Ethiopia, but it did not proceed quite as far. The basic order of ceremonies and most of the ordinary prayers used for the Mass and the sacraments are the same as those used in the Coptic church, but there are noteworthy divergences. All of the prayers of the ordinary of the Coptic Mass occur in the Ethiopian ordinary, but the latter has preserved other prayers that have disappeared in Egypt, for example, the formula for the dismissal of the catechumens. On the other hand, the fourteen eucharistic anaphoras in common use in Ethiopia today are, with the exception of the Anaphora of Basil, unknown in Egypt. Although at least two of them, the Anaphoras of the Apostles and of our Lord Jesus Christ, have come to Ethiopia through Egypt, most of the others appear to be local compositions, especially from the fourteenth and fifteenth centuries. From the same period derives the horologion of Abba Giyorgis of Gaseç̣ç̣a; it has replaced the Coptic horologion that seems to have prevailed in earlier times. The *Deggʷa*, the Ethiopian antiphonary, on the contrary, is ancient, being traditionally ascribed to Yared, a sixth-century saint; its relationship to the corresponding Coptic *Difnar* does not seem to have been studied as yet.

Besides expanding at the expense of local usages, the Alexandrian rite has also undergone changes. The practice reported by Socrates of separating on certain days the Liturgy of the Word from the Liturgy of Sacrifice has long disappeared. When the source of pagan converts dried up after the Islamic conquest, the *disciplina arcani* was abandoned and with it the need to dismiss the catechumens. The eucharistic gifts could be prepared in the sanctuary at the beginning of Mass, and they could then be placed directly on the altar instead of being transferred there in procession just before the anaphora.

Another influence on the Alexandrian rite came from the monks, from whose ranks the bishops have been traditionally drawn. It is not easy to point to specific elements that are due to monasticism, but the actual eucharistic service does have a clearly penitential tone that is exemplified by its two formal absolutions and its frequent use of incense. One reason, moreover, why the traditional Alexandrian Anaphora of Mark has been replaced by the non-Egyptian Anaphora of St. Basil as the ordinary anaphora of the Coptic church may have been that the anaphora was composed by a great monastic legislator and was widely used by monasteries throughout the Middle East.

The liturgical language of Alexandria was originally Greek. The churches of the country districts and many, if not most, of the monasteries of Egypt, on the other hand, used local dialects of Coptic. After the Islamic conquest, Greek ceased to be the language of administration and culture and was gradually abandoned for the liturgy, although it rather curiously survives today in many responses of the people and deacon. Its place was taken by the Bohairic dialect of Coptic, to which Arabic was added as an alternative in the Middle Ages. In Ethiopia, on the other hand, Geez, the classical language, has always been used. Only in the most recent period have efforts been made to introduce Amharic, the official vernacular.

Certain characteristics of the Alexandrian eucharistic liturgy should be mentioned. This is the only rite in which all of the actions, prayers, and chants concerning the gifts—that is, their preparation, transfer, and blessing—take place at the beginning; no vestige of what was formerly done after the dismissal of the catechumens has been left there. The scheme of scriptural readings is also peculiar, namely, four readings drawn exclusively from the New Testament: one reading each from the Pauline Epistles, the Catholic Epistles, the Acts of the Apostles, and the Gospels. Furthermore, after the reading from Acts a reading from the nonscriptural synaxary is inserted. The Coptic liturgy also adds on occasion other nonscriptural readings, but they are commentaries on the scriptural readings or substitutes for homilies. The Alexandrian rite has its own characteristic form for the prayers of the faithful, corresponding to the litanies of other rites. First, the priest or assistant priests invite the faithful to pray for a particular intention; this is next echoed in the imperative by the deacon, to which the people reply, Kyrie Eleison; then the priest offers a prayer for the intention, and the people conclude with an Amen.

Because many of the anaphoras in use in the Coptic and Ethiopian churches derive from non-Alexandrian sources or models, their structure is variable. The ancient Alexandrian Anaphora of Mark, however, does have a very particular structure that is repeated, to a greater or lesser extent, in other anaphoras of purely Egyptian origin. Three principal characteristics should be mentioned. First, the thanksgiving portion of the anaphora is not split by the Sanctus into two parts but is recited as one, uninterrupted prayer immediately after the initial dialogue. Second, the intercessions follow the thanksgiving directly, without any transition; the Sanctus with its preceding transition follows the intercessions. Third, the Narration and the Anamnesis are preceded by one Epiclesis, which follows the Sanctus, and are followed by a second Epiclesis, which terminates in the Doxology. It is the second epiclesis that is today considered consecratory, but some speculate that it may represent an imitation of non-Alexandrian anaphoras and may have replaced a prayer for the acceptance of the sacrifice and the fruits of communion that would have been analogous to the prayer *Supplices te rogamus* of the Roman canon.

The structural similiarities between the Roman rite and the Anaphora of Mark should be emphasized. The Roman rite also places all of the thanksgiving at the beginning of the anaphora, immediately after the prefatory dialogue, and it also has an epiclesis before the Narration. The biggest difference lies in the position of the intercessions, which the Roman rite divides into two parts, one placed between the Sanctus and the Epiclesis and the other placed between the prayer for the fruits of communion and the concluding doxology.

The preparation for communion contains all the main elements found in other rites: the fraction, Our Father, a blessing, the admonition "Holy things to the holy!" and the consignations. However, the consignations are singularly separated from the fraction by the other elements, perhaps on account of the elevation of the sacred species that accompanies the "Holy things to the holy!" Furthermore, the Alexandrian rite introduces two new elements, an absolution before the Sancta Sanctis and a solemn profession of faith in the Real Presence just before communion.

The communion, thanksgiving, final blessing, and dismissal show only minor differences from other rites. The consecrated elements are distributed separately, and the purification of the communion vessels is performed before a lengthy final blessing that invokes a long list of martyrs and saints. One peculiarity may be mentioned, however: after the ablutions, the celebrant sprinkles water over the altar, the ministers, and the faithful as a kind of blessing.

Alexandrian baptism includes most of the elements found in other rites. There is a fusing of ceremonies that were formerly separate associated with the catechumenate and the preparation of adults for baptism. There is an exorcism, a renunciation of Satan and an adhesion to Christ, a solemn blessing of the water during the baptismal ceremonies, and a joining of confirmation and communion to the baptismal rites. Peculiarly Alexandrian, however, is the use of three oils for three anointings: one at the end of the rite for making a catechumen; one before not the baptism itself but the blessing of the baptismal water; and one in the rite of confirmation, in which there is no imposition of hands. The blessing of the baptismal water takes the form of an anaphora, as in other rites, but here the imitation of the Mass ceremonies is notably more complete. In the course of the blessing, each of the three oils is poured at different times into the baptismal water. The baptism itself is by triple immersion, with an active formula similar to the one used in the Roman rite; an insufflation follows each immersion. As in other oriental rites, the chrism used for confirmation is applied not only to the forehead but also to the other principal members and senses.

The Alexandrian divine office does not seem to have been thoroughly studied. Alphonse Raes notes the predominantly monastic character of the Coptic office, especially of vespers according to the horologion, which lacks the service of incense and the *lucernarium* common to other rites. Instead, there are distinct rites of evening and morning incense that are without parallels in other rites.

A final word may be said about the traditional form of Coptic and Ethiopian churches. The former are usually in the form of a basilica, with three apses and three aisles in the nave. The three apses usually contain three altars, permitting more than one liturgy to be celebrated as needed on the same day. The aisles are cut crosswise by numerous divisions. First, the sanctuary is divided from the rest of the church by an iconostasis; next comes a choir separated from the rest by a lattice screen; beyond this comes the men's section; finally there is the women's section, which is traditionally located either behind another lattice screen separating it from the men's section or above it in a gallery suitably shielded by screens. Finally, at the back of the church and separated from the nave by a wall is a narthex that often contains a covered pool for the blessing of the waters on Epiphany. Although the basilica form seems to have been characteristic also of ancient churches in Ethiopia, it is a circular form that is typical of more recent churches. In the center is the holy of holies with the altar, separated from the rest of the church by a concentric wall; then comes the choir, separated from the people by a second concentric wall; finally, beyond the choir wall, the roof extends its eaves and provides shelter for at least some of the faithful attending the liturgy.

BIBLIOGRAPHY

Frank E. Brightman, *Liturgies Eastern and Western,* I (1896), lxiii–lxxvii, 112–244, 461–464, 504–511; Oswald H. E. Burmester, *The Egyptian or Coptic Church* (1967); Heinrich J. D. Denzinger, *Ritus orientalium, Coptorum, Syrorum et Armenorum, in administrandis sacramentis,* 2 vols. (1863–1864); M. Daoud and M. Hazen, *The Liturgy of the Ethiopian Church* (1954); Amédée Gastoué and Henri Leclercq, "Alexandrie (liturgie)," in *Dictionnaire d'archéologie chrétienne et de liturgie,* I (1907), 1182–1204; Ernst Hammerschmidt, "Some Remarks on the History of, and Present State of Investigation into, the Coptic Liturgy," in *Bulletin de la Société d'archéologie Copte,* **19** (1967–1977), 89–113; Alphonse Raes, "Alessandria di Egitto. 3. Il rito alessandrino," "Copti," and "Etiopia," in *Enciclopedia cattolica,* I (1948), IV (1950), and V (1950); and his *Introductio in liturgiam orientalem,* 2nd ed. (1962); Eusèbe Renaudot, *Liturgiarum orientalium collectio,* 2nd ed., I (1847); J.-M. Sauget, *Bibliographie des liturgies orientales (1900–1960)* (1962).

William F. Macomber

[See also **Copts, Coptic Church.**]

ALEXIAD. See **Anna Komnena.**

ALEXIOS I KOMNENOS (*ca.* 1048–1118), Byzantine emperor from 1081 until his death, was the son of John Komnenos and Anna Dalassena; his uncle had ruled as Isaac I Komnenos (1057–1059). During Michael VII Doukas' reign (1071–1078), the young Alexios married Irene Doukaina. When he rebelled in February–March 1081, Alexios had the support of the army and the powerful Doukas family. After he gained entrance to Constantinople, his troops subjected it to several days of plundering.

Once crowned (4 April 1081), Alexios faced serious challenges. The Turks controlled Anatolia, raiding even the suburbs of the capital. Robert Guiscard, leader of the Normans of southern Italy, was preparing to launch an attack on the empire from the west. The Petchenegs, who inhabited the plains of the lower Danube, repeatedly raided into Byzantine Thrace. The empire's internal conditions required reform and renewal.

With a combination of force and diplomacy, Alexios induced the Turkish sultan of Nicaea to make peace; Turkish troops were made available to the emperor. Guiscard posed a serious threat; having defeated the Byzantines in southern Italy, he now hoped to seize the whole empire. In May–June 1081

ALEXIOS I KOMNENOS

his forces occupied Kerkyra (Corfu) and began a siege of Dyrrachium (now Durrës, Albania). Alexios was defeated there in October, and the city fell early in 1082.

In the meantime, Alexios had incited Guiscard's vassals in Italy to revolt and, by heavy subsidies, inuced the German emperor, Henry IV, to attack Italy and Rome. Dutifully responding to Pope Gregory VII's appeal for help, Guiscard left his forces under the command of his son Bohemond, who won a victory over Alexios near Ioannina in May 1082. Norman forces spread over Epirus and besieged Larissa in Thessaly, and Alexios was unable to relieve the city until the following year. Thereafter, he worked to detach Norman garrisons from their allegiance; several nobles came over to his side. Bohemond was forced to return to Italy, and a Venetian fleet retook Dyrrachium. Robert Guiscard's attack on the Byzantine Empire, renewed in 1084, was ended by his death on Kerkyra in July 1085.

Having utilized the Germans to check the Normans, Alexios enlisted Cumans against the Petchenegs and in 1091, with their help, defeated them. In 1093, he used the sultan of Nicaea's aid to rid both rulers of Tzachas, Turkish emir of Smyrna, whose fleets had ravaged many Aegean coasts and islands.

In November 1095, Pope Urban II, partly in response to Alexios' requests for aid against the Seljuk Turks, summoned the First Crusade. The following year bands of peasants, led by Peter the Hermit and others, reached Constantinople. On the way, they had repeated conflicts with the Petcheneg archers whom Alexios had employed to prevent plundering. Against Alexios' advice, Peter's followers plunged into Turkish territory, where most of them were killed.

When the well-equipped armies of the nobles (including Bohemond) began to arrive in 1097, they also experienced difficulty with Byzantine defense forces. By gifts and promises of assistance, Alexios induced most of the Crusade leaders to swear an oath of fealty to him, binding them to restore to him any formerly Byzantine city that they might capture. A joint Crusader-Byzantine siege regained Nicaea, and a small Byzantine force accompanied the Crusaders across Anatolia to besiege Antioch, the metropolis of northern Syria, while Alexios used the opportunity to reconquer western Asia Minor. Bohemond tricked the Byzantine force into leaving the Crusader army; then, after the capture of Antioch in June 1098, he claimed it for himself.

The ensuing six years were dominated by Alexios' efforts to regain Antioch. Harassed by repeated Byzantine attacks, Bohemond returned to Italy, where he gained papal support for a Crusade against Byzantium. In October 1107 Bohemond landed on the coast of Epirus (modern Albania) and attacked Dyrrachium. But Alexios' forces soon blockaded him, and in September 1108 Bohemond gave in. By treaty he acknowledged Byzantine sovereignty over Antioch and became Alexios' vassal. To avoid formally surrendering the city, he returned to Italy, leaving Antioch in the hands of his successor, who did not honor the treaty. The Turks continued their raids on Byzantine territory; in his final years Alexios made a number of campaigns (1112–1116), the last of which attained Philomelion and recovered a crowd of captives.

Women had an important place in Alexios' palace. In the early years of his reign, his mother, Anna Dalassena, shared imperial power with him. His wife Irene at times seemed such a threat that he took her with him on many campaigns, fearing a palace coup if he did not. His daughter Anna was long considered his prospective successor. His brothers, especially Isaac, played important roles, and Alexios sought to link members of the aristocracy (Doukas, Palaiologos, Angelos) to his family by marriage.

From his earliest years, Alexios was firmly orthodox. In 1082, he forced the philosopher John Italus to recant his Neoplatonic beliefs. He toiled to effect the conversion of the "Manichaean" (apparently Paulician) heretics in Thrace and eventually burned the obstinate Bogomil leader, Basil, at the stake.

The hiring of mercenaries and the payment of subsidies to foreign rulers cost Alexios immense sums. During his reign he tried to make taxation more equitable, and the currency attained relative stability. Venetian and Pisan merchants were admitted to trade in the empire on terms advantageous to them. Alexios founded a large philanthropic institution in Constantinople for orphans and maimed veterans.

As Alexios' death drew near, plots thickened around him. Empress Irene and her daughter Anna wished the latter's husband, Nikephoros Bryennios, to succeed Alexios; but Alexios authorized his son John to seize the palace and have himself proclaimed emperor. The aged emperor could die content, for the coup was successful.

By his military and diplomatic skill Alexios I restored the Byzantine Empire when it seemed on the verge of extinction. His dynasty gave Byzantium a century of stable government and a fresh opportunity for cultural creativity.

BIBLIOGRAPHY

The essential bibliography is J. M. Hussey, "The Later Macedonians, the Comneni and the Angeli, 1025–1204," in *Cambridge Medieval History,* 2nd ed., vol. IV, pt. 1 (1966), 858–867. The principal source is *The Alexiad of Anna Comnena,* Edgar R. A. Sewter, trans. (1969, repr. 1979). See also Bernard Leib's "Introduction générale" to his edition and French translation of the *Alexiad,* I (1937, repr. 1967). Georgina Buckler, *Anna Comnena* (1929), is the best work in English on Alexios' reign.

CHARLES M. BRAND

ALEXIOS I OF TREBIZOND (b. *ca.* 1181) was the grandson of the Byzantine emperor Andronikos I Komnenos (1182–1185). Alexios I and his brother David seized most of the Black Sea coastland of Asia Minor, with Georgian help, in a bid for the Byzantine throne in 1204. But the capture of Constantinople by the Fourth Crusade in that year supervened, and Alexios I founded the independent empire of Trebizond as its first grand komnenos, or ruler (1204–1222). His dynasty controlled the coastlands until the Grand Komnenos David surrendered Trebizond to the Ottoman sultan Mohammed II in 1461. Distinguished grand komnenoi were Manuel I (1238–1263) in local Mongol politics and Alexios III (1349–1339) in local Turkmen politics.

BIBLIOGRAPHY

W. Miller, *Trebizond. The Last Greek Empire* (1926; repr. 1969); Metropolitan Chrysanthos [Philippides] of Trebizond, *He Ekklesia Trapesountos* (1933), and *Archeion Pontou* (1933); A. A. M. Bryer, *The Empire of Trebizond and the Pontos* (1980).

ANTHONY BRYER

[See also **Trebizond.**]

ALEXIS OF MOSCOW, metropolitan of Kiev and all Russia (1354–1378) and head of the Orthodox church in Russia during the period of Mongol occupation. Appointed by the patriarch of Constantinople, he resided not in his cathedral city of Kiev but in Moscow. From 1355 to 1361 his authority was challenged by a rival metropolitan, Roman, a protégé of the Lithuanian grand prince Algirdas, who resided in Lithuanian-occupied Kiev. In 1359, Alexis became regent of the Moscovite state, as the grand prince, Dmitri Donskoy, was a minor. In close association with St. Sergius of Radonezh, the leader of northern Russian monastic revival, Alexis contributed greatly to the political and spiritual prestige of the Muscovite principality.

BIBLIOGRAPHY

E. E. Golubinsky, *Istoriya Russkoi Tserkvi,* I (1901); John Meyendorff, *Byzantium and the Rise of Russia* (1981).

JOHN MEYENDORFF

ALEXIUS. See **Alexios.**

ALFONSINE TABLES. Commissioned by Alfonso X, King of Castile, these planetary tables were finished around 1272 by two Jewish astronomers, Yehuda ben Moses Cohen and Isaac ben Sid. The original tables are now lost, so their precise form can only be conjectured, but they were propagated throughout Europe in an arrangement probably established by John of Lignères or John of Murs in Paris around 1320; in this version the mean motions of the sun, moon, and planets were cast in a convenient form that took natural advantage of the sexagesimal place notation. With the Alfonsine Tables, an astronomer could readily compute positions of the celestial objects for any moment as well as eclipses, and all of the printed ephemerides before 1550 were based on them. The tables also included a variety of calendrical conversions and sometimes Ptolemy's star catalog and geographical coordinates as well. Although today the term Alfonsine Tables refers to such a set, various other forms including the so-called *tabulae resolutae* may also be derived from the Parisian Alfonsines.

The completion of the tables is said to have been the occasion of King Alfonso's remark that had he been present at the Creation, he could have given God some hints—the implication being that he thought the scheme needlessly complicated. Actually, the underlying planetary models are purely

ALFONSO I OF ARAGON

Ptolemaic, essentially a single epicycle for each planet except Mercury and the moon, and unembellished except for combining an additional movement into the so-called eighth sphere. This outer circle carried the trepidational motion to correct for Ptolemy's erroneously small rate of precession. The parameters of the tables are essentially Ptolemaic except for an improved eccentricity for the orbits of the sun and Venus and a less accurate eccentricity for Jupiter, idiosyncratically and inconsistently applied.

Well over a hundred manuscript copies survive. The printed *editio princeps* of 1483 (Venice) carries the explanatory canons written by John of Saxony in 1327, whereas the 1492 (Venice) version has a set by the editor, Joannes Lucilius Santritter. The canons written by John of Lignères and by John of Murs remain unpublished. Further printed editions include those of 1518 (Venice), 1524 (Venice), and 1545 (Paris). In the mid sixteenth century, the Alfonsines were swiftly replaced by Erasmus Reinhold's Prutenic Tables (1551), based on the models and parameters of Copernicus, but the computational arrangement of the Alfonsines continued to influence the form of astronomical tables well into the seventeenth century.

BIBLIOGRAPHY

There is no single comprehensive article, but explicit instructions for calculating a planetary position are in Emmanuel Poulle and Owen Gingerich, "Les positions des planètes au moyen âge: Application du calcul electronique aux Tables Alphonsines," in *Comptes rendus des séances de l'Académie des inscriptions & belles-lettres* (Nov.–Dec. 1967); and for calculating a lunar eclipse in Victor E. Thoren and Edward Grant, "Extracts from the Alfonsine Tables and Rules for Their Use," in Edward Grant, ed., *A Source Book in Medieval Science* (1974). See also John D. North, "The Alfonsine Tables in England," in Yasukatsu Maeyama and Walter Gabriel Saltzer, eds., *Prismata* (1977). The original form of the canons is given in Manuel Rico y Sinobas, *Libros del saber de astronomia del rey D. Alfonso X de Castilla,* IV (1866), 111–183, but the associated tables bear no relation to the Alfonsine Tables.

OWEN GINGERICH

[See also **Astronomy/Astrology.**]

ALFONSO I OF ARAGON (*ca.* 1073–1134) was the second son of King Sancho Ramírez by his second wife. Alfonso's half brother Pedro I ruled from 1094 to 1104, when his premature death placed Alfonso on the combined throne of Navarre and Aragon. Known for his skill as a great warrior, Alfonso earned the sobriquet *el Batallador,* the quality for which he is best remembered.

In 1109 a spectacular opportunity for expanding the realm of Aragon appeared when the aged king of Castile, Alfonso VI, sought Alfonso I as a spouse for his recently widowed daughter, Urraca. She had a young son, Alfonso Raimúndez, who for the time being was effectively disinherited. Since Castile was by far the larger state, a major step toward the unification of the Iberian Peninsula had seemingly been achieved. However, marital incompatibility and genetics intervened. Alfonso I produced no issue by this marriage or any other known liaison. This deficiency did not prevent him from pressing his claims in Castile, even after Pope Paschal II annulled the marriage to Urraca on the ground of consanguinity.

Alfonso utilized the title "Imperator totius Hispaniae," long identified with the rulers of Leon and Castile, and garrisoned towns and fortresses along the Santiago pilgrimage route across Castile from La Rioja to Sahagún, and garrisoned Toledo and Soria as well. It required years of continuing warfare waged by Urraca and her allies to contain Alfonso and wrest these territories from his grip, a project not well advanced when Alfonso found a new source of interest, the principality of Zaragoza.

While the conquest of Zaragoza from the Muslims had long been a goal of the Castilian state, the invasion by the North African Almoravids in 1086 had forestalled a successful siege by Alfonso VI. Now, Alfonso I of Aragon, with the aid of Aragonese, Catalan, Castilian, and French warriors, placed Zaragoza under siege in May 1118, capturing it the following December. With this victory the entire principality was opened to Aragonese conquest. Such towns as Tudela, Tarazona, Calatayud, and Daroca had fallen by 1120. Alfonso spent the next several years exploiting these conquests, settling the frontier lands, and making a renowned but largely unfruitful expedition to support a revolt of the Mozarabic community in Granada.

Alfonso's last years were spent struggling to retain his conquests. When Alfonso VII Raimúndez came of age in Castile, he drove his former stepfather from his Castilian holdings, reclaiming the imperial title. Alfonso I attempted to recoup these losses by assaulting the central Ebro valley toward Lérida. The Ebro campaign was decisively reversed at Fraga on 17 July 1134, when the Muslims inflicted a costly defeat upon the Aragonese king. Alfonso I died, leaving the realm of Navarre and Aragon to the crusader military Orders of the Hospital, the Temple, and the Holy Sepulchre in a controversial will. This will was soon thwarted by the Navarrese, who broke free from Aragon, and by the Aragonese nobles, who drew Alfonso's brother Ramiro from his monastery and elected him King Ramiro II of Aragon.

BIBLIOGRAPHY

The most important single work is José M. Lacarra, *Vida de Alfonso el Batallador* (1971), a very general study of the king and his reign. Shorter general accounts are Joseph F. O'Callaghan, *A History of Medieval Spain* (1975); Derek W. Lomax, *The Reconquest of Spain* (1978); and in Bernard Reilly, *León-Castile in the Reign of Queen Urraca* (in press).

For articles on particular aspects of Alfonso's reign, see José M. Ramos y Loscertales, "La sucesión del Rey Alfonso VI," in *Anuario de historia del derecho español,* **13** (1936–1941); P. Kehr, "El papado y los reinos de Navarra y Aragón hasta mediados del siglo XII," in *Estudios de edad media de la corona de Aragón,* **2** (1946); A. Huici Miranda, "Los Banu Hud de Zaragoza, Alfonso I y los almorávides (nuevas aportaciones)," *ibid.,* 7 (1962); José M. Lacarra, "Los franceses en la reconquista y repoblación del valle del Ebro en tiempo de Alfonso el Batallador," in *Cuadernos de historia,* **2** (1968); Elena Lourie, "The Will of Alfonso I 'El Batallador,' King of Aragón and Navarre: A Reassessment," in *Speculum,* **50** (1975); James F. Powers, "Frontier Competition and Legal Creativity: A Castilian-Aragonese Case Study Based on Twelfth-Century Municipal Military Law," *ibid.,* **52** (1977).

JAMES F. POWERS

[See also **Aragon; Castile; Navarre.**]

ALFONSO X (the Learned) (1221–1284), king of Castile and León from 1252. As son of Ferdinand III and Beatrice of Swabia he inherited León and Castile and rights to election to the imperial throne of the Holy Roman Empire. His reign was one of great political complexity and turmoil. At that time Christian expansion southward had gained for Castile the greater part of southern Spain, with the major exception of the Moorish kingdom of Granada. To the east Jaime I (the Conqueror) of Aragon was cooperating in the latter stages of the Reconquest. His daughter Violante was married to Alfonso, who maintained an interest in the affairs of the Aragonese line.

In 1254 the death of Emperor Conrad IV opened up possibilities of Alfonso's election to the imperial throne. After an election marked by corruption, Alfonso was declared winner in 1257, and he prepared to go to Germany for the coronation. However, troubles in Spain, intrigues in Italy, and the decline of the Ghibellines, whom Alfonso represented, prevented it, and the election of Rudolf I in 1273 put an end to Alfonso's imperial aspirations. Domestically his reign was marred by family strife. His indecision, particularly in connection with the succession to the throne, created international problems with France and Aragon, and ultimately strife at home. He died in the midst of civil war, with his son Sancho in open rebellion over the question of the succession.

Despite the dismal political situation, cultural developments at the Alfonsine court made it a significant cultural center in western Europe. In imitation of the celebrated twelfth-century Toledo school of translators, the king gathered learned men to engage in a program of translation and compilation. Christians, Muslims, and Jews alike participated in this literary court, as did the monarch himself. The language employed was Castilian, an early recognition of the vernacular as having equal status with Latin for learned purposes. Because of the broad scope of Alfonso's preserved works, we possess a remarkably well-documented language, which at the literary court became standardized and polished. It set the pattern for the Spanish language (Castilian) until the sixteenth century.

It has been pointed out that Alfonso's varied production was built around his concept of man and the universe. Historical man—man as he had been—was depicted in the *Crónica general,* a history of Spain, and in the *Grande e general estoria,* an attempt at a world history. Moral man—man as he should be—was described in the code of laws. The effects of the planets on man were studied in astronomical and astrological works.

The *Crónica general* details the events of the Iberian Peninsula from traditional beginnings up to the thirteenth century. In its approach it is similar to the Latin chronicles, though fleshed out considerably. Among its sources are epic poems, which are accepted as true historical data. The history, left incomplete at the time of Alfonso's death, was continued in the reign of his son Sancho IV.

The *Grande e general estoria* was conceived in truly monumental terms. Surviving are five huge parts and a fragment of a sixth, covering all history from the Creation to the time of the mother of the

Virgin Mary. Chief among its sources are the Bible and the *Chronicon* of Eusebius of Caesarea (as translated and extended by St. Jerome), the framework of the latter opening the way to the inclusion of purely literary and mythological sources, such as Ovid's *Metamorphoses* and Lucan's *Pharsalia.* Among other sources employed were Arabic, Latin, and French histories, compilations, and poems, which gives an idea of the breadth of culture of the Alfonsine literary court.

The seven books of the legal code, the *Siete partidas,* were an attempt to describe and make uniform the laws and customs of Castile. The presence of peoples of many origins and customs in the kingdom made desirable an official description of the law, all phases of which were treated. The code remains one of the foundations of Spanish law; survivals can be found in the laws of some American states originally colonized by Spain. In addition to this general code, several special legal treatises, which have not yet been accorded appropriate study, are extant.

The fields of astronomy and astrology were represented mostly by translations from Arabic originals. Alfonso's original astronomical tables, calculated on the meridian of Toledo, were standard in Europe for centuries.

Alfonso was known to the troubadours of his day as a patron of the arts. He welcomed these poets to his court and even composed poetry after their fashion. His fame as a poet rests primarily on the *Cantigas de Santa María,* a collection of songs in praise of the Virgin. The preserved manuscripts of the *Cantigas* are outstanding examples of the art of the miniature, and they reveal Alfonso as a generous patron of pictorial art as well.

The activities of Alfonso's court link it to the school of Toledo during the twelfth-century renaissance. The court gave a new meaning to the use of Castilian and presented a softer view of life than that which had prevailed during the more active stages of the Reconquest. Regardless of the calamitous political situation during his reign, the learning and art sponsored by Alfonso were a bright spot in thirteenth-century Spain.

BIBLIOGRAPHY

Editions. Cantigas de Santa María, 4 vols., Walter Mettmann, ed. (1959–1972); *Concordances and Texts of the Royal Scriptorium Manuscript of Alfonso X el Sabio,* Lloyd Kasten *et al.*, eds. (1978); *General estoria,* pt. 1, Antonio García Solalinde, ed. (1930); pt. 2, 2 vols., Antonio García Solalinde *et al.*, eds. (1957–1961); *Lapidario and Libro de las formas & ymagenes,* Roderic C. Diman and Lynn W. Winget, eds. (1980); *El Libro conplido en los iudizios de las estrellas,* by Aly Aben Ragel, Gerold Hilty, ed. (1954); *Libro de las cruzes,* Lloyd A. Kasten and Lawrence B. Kiddle, eds. (1961); *Libros de aeedrex, dados e tablas. Das Schachzabelbuch König Alfons des Weisen,* Arnold Steiger, ed. (1941); *Opúsculos regales del rey don Alfonso el Sabio,* 2 vols. (1836); *Primera crónica general de España,* 2 vols. Ramón Menéndes Pidal, ed. (1955); *Setenario,* Kenneth H. Vanderford, ed. (1945); *Las siete partidas,* Samuel Parsons Scott, trans. (1931).

Secondary Works. John E. Keller, *Alfonso X, el Sabio* (1967); Gardiner R. London, "Bibliographía de estudios sobre la fida y obra de Alfonso X el Sabio," in *Boletín de Filología Española,* 6 (1960); Evelyn S. Proctor, *Alfonso X of Castile* (1951).

LLOYD KASTEN

ALFONSO XI, POEMA DE, a lengthy rhymed chronicle of the fourteenth-century king of Castile and León, from the death of the regents Pedro and Juan on the plain of Granada (1319) to the taking of Algeciras from the Moslems (1344). The poem was written after January and before September 1348 by Rodrigo Yáñez, probably first in Leonese dialect, and consists of some 2,459 verses in predominantly octosyllabic quatrains rhyming ABAB. It survives in two lacunous manuscripts: the fourteenth-century *E* (Escorial Y.III.9) and *M* (Real Academia Española), a fifteenth-century copy of *E,* of limited value and dubious authority in filling a few of *E*'s minor gaps.

Yáñez was probably a witness to, or at least a contemporary of, the events he narrates. The exact relationship of his poem to the complex prose historiography of Alfonso XI needs further study, but Diego Catalán has shown that the *Gran Crónica* used the *Poema* as one of its major sources; the prose text even helps fill some of the poem's lacunae. Yáñez's style was influenced by the oral epic: Cid Ruy Díez, Torpín, Roldán, and Oliveros are mentioned, and jongleur themes (the hero's prayer before battle) and formulas (*veríedes mucha lançada; ojos que bos bieren ir; mill vezes dezir oí*) are used. Also in evidence are Arabic literary commonplaces, such as the elegiac invocation of Algeciras and the city as damsel wooed by a besieger. Among Yáñez's known sources are the mid-thirteenth-century clerical poems *Libro de Alixandre* and *Poema de Fernán González,* as well as an Arthurian text (for Merlin's prophecy) and perhaps also the *Historia troyana po-*

limétrica (*ca.* 1270). Surviving fragments of Afonso Giraldes' Portuguese *Poema del Salado,* concerning the deeds of King Afonso IV of Portugal, are so short that we cannot know who imitated whom; however, Giraldes' poetry seems more prosaic than Yáñez's.

Though the *Poema de Alfonso XI* is not without its dull passages, it is enlivened by impressive battle scenes, heroic epithets (*escudo sin pavor / castiello e fortaleza*), and vivid animal metaphors (*commo un bravo león*), some of which are drawn from the medieval chase (*fuxo commo conejo; commo el falcón a la garça*). Lively descriptions of cities, festivals, and armed knights offer a further attraction. There are occasional humorous notes and an interesting preoccupation with social injustice.

The *Poema*'s attention is concentrated on the Christian reconquest. Religion is another major theme, but paradoxically the king's illicit amours with his beautiful mistress, Leonor de Guzmán, are praised. Perhaps the most successful passage—doubtless influenced by *Alixandre*—is the splendid evocation of May, with its traditional flowers, fruit trees, singing birds, damsels intoning songs of praise, and a host of minstrels playing various instruments (verses 401–414). Though the *Poema* owes a certain debt to the traditional epic, it is ultimately closer to clerical poetry. Diego Catalán has characterized it as a *gesta erudita,* the last learned attempt at narrative poetry as opposed to the popular epic.

BIBLIOGRAPHY

The most recent edition of the *Poema* is by Yo ten Cate (1956); see also S. G. Armistead's review in *Romance Philology,* **12** (1958–1959). Studies by Diego Catalán Menéndez-Pidal include *Poema de Alfonso XI: fuentes, dialecto, estilo* (1953); *Un cronista anónimo del siglo XIV* (1955); "Las estrofas mutiladas en el MS. *E* del *Poema de Alfonso XI,*" in *Nueva revista de filología hispánica,* **13** (1959); "Hacia una edición crítica del *Poema de Alfonso XI* (El cerco de Algeciras)," in Francis W. Pierce, ed., *Hispanic Studies in Honor of I. González Llubera* (1959); *La tradición manuscrita en la "Crónica de Alfonso XI"* (1974), a complete reappraisal of *Un cronista anónimo;* and *La Gran Crónica de Alfonso XI,* 2 vols. (1976). See also G. Davis, "The Debt of the *Poema de Alfonso Onceno* to the *Libro de Alexandre,*" in *Hispanic Review,* **15** (1947); and "National Sentiment in the *Poema de Fernán Gonçalez* and in the *Poema de Alfonso Onceno,*" *ibid.,* **16** (1948); and Yo ten Cate, *Estudio preliminar y vocabulario* (1942), a lexicon.

S. G. Armistead

[See also **Alixandre, Libro de; Spanish Epic Poetry**.]

ALFRED THE GREAT (849–899), an Anglo-Saxon king of the house of Wessex, known for his accomplishments in war, law, and education. In each of these areas, Alfred began with little and laid a foundation upon which later generations could build. Hence the title "Great," given to him since the sixteenth century, describes neither the immense power nor the prodigious learning associated, for example, with Charles the Great (Charlemagne) or Albert the Great (Albertus Magnus), but the quality of greatness ascribed to a founder.

Alfred was born at Wantage in Berkshire, the fifth son and sixth child of Æthelwulf, king of Wessex. Alfred went to Rome twice as a young boy: in 853, to be received as godson by Pope Leo IV, and, in 855, on a pilgrimage that also took him and his father to the court of Charles the Bald. Although Alfred did not learn to read until after he was twelve years old, according to his biographer Asser he loved to listen to native vernacular verse, on one occasion winning from his mother Osburh a handsome book of Old English poems by memorizing them before his brothers did. According to Asser he was afflicted with illness all his life, but as a boy and young man he was nonetheless a capable and enthusiastic hunter.

By the time Alfred came to power in 871, each of his older brothers had been king and had died. Alfred himself first appeared in a public role alongside his brother King Æthelred in 868, in a minor military engagement at Nottingham in support of their brother-in-law Burhred of Mercia against the Danes Ivar the Boneless and Halfdan. As foreshadowed by the meeting at Nottingham, Alfred's reign coincided with the fiercest years of the early wave of Viking raiding. His military campaigns, which occupied virtually every year of a three-decade rule, can be divided between the long series (871–886) undertaken against the sons of Ragnar Lothbrok and the shorter sequence (892–896) against a large force led by Hæsten and other Viking leaders whose names are not known.

The *Anglo-Saxon Chronicle* states that in the year of Æthelred's death and Alfred's accession to power, there were nine major battles "without counting the numberless raids which the king's brother Alfred and one particular ealdorman and the king's thanes rode out on." This gives an accurate impression of the guerrilla warfare that Alfred and his followers were forced to wage in the early campaigns. Though most of the pitched battles in 871—at Basing, at Merantune, at Reading, and at Wilton, for example—went against the English, Alfred was able to carry out an effective policy of constant harassing raids. Nonetheless, the situation had so deteriorated that by the end of 871 Halfdan was having his own coins struck at London.

Not until 878 was there any clear change. After seven weeks of incessant raiding from his base at Athelney in the remote marshes of Somerset, Alfred brought together a large army made up of men from Somerset, Wiltshire, and Hampshire, and forced a battle at Edington that the English won decisively. The Peace of Chippenham, negotiated with Guthrum, the Danish king who had taken over the fighting in Wessex when Halfdan was attacking Northumbria, required an exchange of hostages, the permanent departure of the Vikings from Alfred's kingdom, and the baptism of Guthrum, whom Alfred took as his godson. Only in 886, however, when Alfred's forces occupied London after some bloody fighting, was this long phase of his military campaigns brought to an end. Most scholarly opinion accepts that the remarkable legal document known as the Treaty with Guthrum was drawn up after the occupation of London.

The tactics that Alfred employed against the large Danish army that appeared in 892 under the command of Hæsten and other Vikings whose names are unrecorded were clearly those of a ruler resisting invasion, for he organized his military levies on a practical system of rotation, began construction of the forts that were to cover the countryside of southern England, and ordered larger, faster ships built to counter the swift Viking vessels. As a result of these and other strategies, in 896 he was finally able to trap the Danish ships some twenty miles upstream of London. By blocking the Lea River and constructing forts on either side of it, Alfred cut off escape and the Viking army had to disperse, leaving the ships behind. This did not terminate hostile Scandinavian activity in Wessex, but it did mark the end of concerted effort to invade the area in Alfred's day.

Alfred's main legal accomplishments were two: the Treaty with Guthrum and the new law code based on earlier codes of Ine of Wessex, Offa of Mercia, and Æthelbert of Kent. The Treaty with Guthrum is especially remarkable in that it describes, and is intended to guarantee, the existence of parallel but distinct systems of rights, not only for adjoining geographical areas (the Danelaw, largely in East Anglia, and Alfred's Wessex, with its dependent areas in Kent and Mercia) but also for different populations in the same kingdom (that is, pagan and Christian in the Danelaw). The document is also important for its description of the geographical extent of the Danelaw and for its correlation of Anglo-Saxon and Danish class structures.

Perhaps Alfred's most remarkable accomplishment, given the circumstances of his life and time, was intellectual. Illiterate until his teens and able to read only English until his late thirties, Alfred began to study Latin in 887, and about 890 initiated a series of translations from Augustine, Gregory the Great, Bede, Boethius, and Orosius which were intended to reverse a dangerous decline in learning he had observed in his kingdom.

Although Alfred's kingdom was small, his rule troubled, and his scholarship—by the standards of either eighth- or tenth-century England—unremarkable, when he died he had laid a solid foundation for his country's physical, moral, and intellectual well-being by his tenacity in war, his prudence in law, and his perseverance in learning.

BIBLIOGRAPHY

William H. Stevenson, ed., *Asser's Life of King Alfred,* in Latin (1904), repr. with article by Dorothy Whitelock on current Asser scholarship (1959), translated by L. C. Jane (1966). Charles Plummer, ed., *Two of the Saxon Chronicles Parallel* (1892–1899), an edition of the Anglo-Saxon text. Dorothy Whitelock *et al., The Anglo-Saxon Chronicle,* 2nd ed., corrected (1965), is a translation. Another translation is George N. Garmonsway, *The Anglo-Saxon Chronicle* (1953).

See also "The Age of Alfred," in Frank M. Stenton, *Anglo-Saxon England*, 3rd ed. (1971), 239–275; E. S. Duckett, *Alfred the Great* (1956); Peter J. Helm, *Alfred the Great* (1965).

COLIN CHASE

[See also **Anglo-Saxon Literature; Translations and Translators, Western Europe.**]

ALFRED THE GREAT AND TRANSLATIONS. A notable accomplishment of the reign of Alfred of Wessex (871–899) was a series of translations from Latin into Old English sponsored, and in the main executed, by the king himself. All the translations were completed in the final ten to twelve years of his life, when periods of relative peace were more frequent and the kingdom was more stable.

According to Alfred's biographer Asser, the king began translating bits of Latin into Old English in 887, when he was thirty-eight years old. Between

ALFRED AND TRANSLATIONS

this year and 890 the idea took shape that Alfred and a group of scholars at his court should, in his words, select "some books that are most important for men to know and translate them into that language we are all able to understand." This idea is elaborated in the preface to the earliest translation, the *Pastoral Care* of St. Gregory the Great, quoted here. Alfred explains that he has often reflected on the number of learned men there used to be in England and how their glory in warfare was matched by a wealth of wisdom, so that travelers used to come to England in search of learning. "Now," he laments, "we have to go abroad to find it." At his own accession learning had so declined that very few in southern England could paraphrase their Latin service books or even turn a letter from Latin into English—and he doubts there were many in the north. With translations of the most important books, however, every free-born youth in the country with sufficient talent could be taught to read English, and those destined for a higher calling, Latin as well. For this reason, with the help of Archbishop Plegmund, Bishop Asser, and the Continental priests Grimbold and John, he has translated Gregory's *Pastoral Care* and is sending a copy to each episcopal see.

From internal evidence we know that Alfred was personally responsible for our surviving Old English translations of the *Pastoral Care* and of Boethius' *Consolation of Philosophy,* though no contemporary source mentions the works. This list is supplemented by William of Malmesbury, writing in the early twelfth century, who also ascribes to Alfred translations of Orosius' *Universal History (Seven Books of History against the Pagans)*, Bede's *Ecclesiastical History of the English Nation,* and an anthology called Alfred's *Encheiridion* (handbook). Of these three, only the Orosius appears to have survived in Alfred's version; the extant Old English Bede is a Mercian work, and nothing corresponds to the book described in Asser's *Life* as Alfred's *Encheiridion.* A free translation of St. Augustine's *Soliloquies* can be credited to Alfred with reasonable confidence on the basis of its stylistic similarities to his other work and a copyist's ascription in the concluding sentence of the unique manuscript. Finally, a work that deeply influenced Alfred and possibly led him to conceive his own translation project is the Old English version of Gregory the Great's *Dialogues* made for Alfred by Wærferth, bishop of Worcester.

The sequence and dates of the translations are partly conjectural. One copy of the *Pastoral Care* was sent to Swithulf, bishop of Rochester, who died in 896; and Plegmund, who was consecrated to Canterbury in 890, is referred to in the preface as archbishop. The *Pastoral Care,* therefore, was completed after 890 but before 896. Further, a dependence of the *Anglo-Saxon Chronicle* on the Old English Orosius for the entry at A.D. 81 suggests that that translation was in circulation near the year 890. Hence, the two earliest works must have been the *Pastoral Care,* the preface of which seems to initiate the project, and the Orosius, both probably completed near 890. Generally, scholars accept that Wærferth translated the *Dialogues* before any of Alfred's translations, since it is the only translation mentioned in Asser's *Life* (completed in 893), and that the Boethius and the *Soliloquies* are later work. A probable sequence, therefore, is: the *Dialogues, Pastoral Care,* Orosius, Boethius, *Soliloquies.* If Alfred also translated Bede's *Ecclesiastical History,* he could have done it at any time, but the non-Alfredian version extant may conveniently be considered with the Orosius.

The only part of the Old English *Dialogues* attributable to Alfred is a brief preface explaining that he has had the translation made because he knows how necessary it is for a king occasionally to interrupt his worldly concerns and to contemplate divine things. This motive parallels the occasion for the original *Dialogues,* written about 593, for as Gregory puts it in his introductory section, he was sitting by himself one day, reflecting sadly on the burdens of the papal office and yearning for the peace of the monastery, when his deacon Peter approached and began to question him about the lives and, especially, the miracles worked by Christians of their own time and country. The work that follows is divided into four books, the first and third describing the virtuous lives and miracles of a variety of men and women of sixth-century Italy. The second book answers the same purpose by narrating the life of St. Benedict of Nursia. The fourth is a consideration, also told with many examples, of the immortality of the soul and of life after death. Like the Old English Bede, Wærferth's *Dialogues* is a very literal translation of the original text.

The first translation that Alfred claims for himself, though with acknowledgment to his advisers, is Gregory's *Pastoral Care.* Probably composed when Gregory was still at Saint Andrew's monastery, the *Liber regulae pastoralis* is a practical handbook for bishops published soon after Gregory became pope. The Latin original is divided into four parts, the first

 ALFRED AND TRANSLATIONS

describing the dangers of seeking episcopal office, particularly for the ignorant, the ill-motivated, or the ambitious. The second book considers the qualities needed by the bishop, particularly those of the spirit. The third is the longest and most immediately practical book. Its forty chapters detail the various kinds of people the bishop will be called on to serve—the downcast and the happy, masters and slaves, men and women, rich and poor—and suggest how each might be admonished or encouraged. For example, the timorous person can be corrected rather gently, while the bold one will need strong words and perhaps more. The final book briefly reminds the bishop that he must always remember his own weakness, or his elevated station is liable to turn his head.

While Alfred's translation follows this sequence, the fourfold arrangement is replaced by sixty-five chapters, corresponding roughly but not exactly to Gregory's chapters. Further, though the translation is close, a detailed comparison of the Latin and the Old English reveals a constant process of modification. Chapter titles, in the Latin, for example, are subject headings, while the Old English titles usually state the conclusion. Brief explanations are added for the benefit of English readers. And frequently the implicit imagery of Gregory's prose is made more explicit and concrete, though on occasion Alfred renders a concrete figure with an abstraction. Finally, the use of words such as *aldordom* ("lordship") or *reccendom* ("governance") to translate more specifically ecclesiastical terms gives to the whole of Alfred's translation a secular application not found in the original.

For many scholars the principal value of Alfred's *Pastoral Care* is philological, since two of its manuscripts were copied during Alfred's lifetime and represent the most extensive example extant of early West Saxon prose. Though this important aspect of Alfredian scholarship dominated interest through the early twentieth century, recent commentators have begun to pay attention to the content of this and other Alfredian translations.

Much freer with the original Latin text is the translation of Orosius' *Universal History.* Originally written by the Spanish or Portuguese priest Paulus Orosius, at St. Augustine's request, in order to counter the charge that the evils plaguing the Roman Empire in the early fifth century were caused by the advent of Christianity, its text is largely an uncritical selection of passages from various Latin authors covering the history of the world from the creation to A.D. 417. The whole is prefaced by a geographical survey and unified by the recurring theme that plague, warfare, natural catastrophe, and social upheaval were known to men long before the coming of Christianity.

All of this the Alfredian translation edits, annotates, and reshapes. Orosius' seven books become six, and each of those remaining is drastically reduced, particularly the last three. The most famous annotation or addition comes in the introductory geographical section, in which the Old English includes a survey of Germanic lands not found in the Latin and adds a wonderful account of the voyages of the Norwegian Ohthere and the Englishman Wulfstan, complete with detailed descriptions of the geography of the Baltic Sea, interesting customs of the Lapps, and some fascinating funeral practices of the Estonians. This process of trimming and adding shifts the emphasis of the book away from Orosius' original polemic intent, making of it an encyclopedia of history celebrating the wonderful providence of God in all ages.

Though long attributed to Alfred, the Old English translation of Bede's *History* is today known to be the work of an unidentified Mercian contemporary of the king. As in Wærferth's *Dialogues,* the rendering is very literal, but the Bede translator has omitted much more of his original. This often slavish fidelity mars the style of the work but gives it a special value for Old English lexicography.

Certainly the most challenging, and in many respects the most successful, of Alfred's translations is his version of Boethius' *Consolation of Philosophy.* The original was composed in prison shortly before its author's execution on the order of Theodoric the Great about 524. Its purpose was to express Boethius' belief that the human spirit that is free of attachment to possessions, power, or honor can transcend the most unexpected reversals of fortune. Though Boethius is known from his other works to have been a Christian, the *Consolatio* abstracts from faith and revelation, considering only the comfort that philosophy provides.

Alfred translates Boethius freely and intelligently. Earlier scholarly commentary explained substantial differences between the two versions by supposing Alfred's ignorance of Latin grammar and philosophical discourse, but recent work indicates that such departures more probably reflect genuine philosophical differences attributable both to Alfred's background in patristic thought and to his particular view of the world. An example is his revision of Boethius' elaborate correlation of human freedom with the Neoplatonic chain of being in book V of the *Consolatio.* In the corresponding place in Alfred's text—he substitutes forty-two chapters for Boethius' five books—we find the reflection that men have greater freedom the more they dwell on divine things and less freedom the more they are attached to the world, a thought strikingly reminiscent of major themes in Alfred's preface to Wærferth's *Dialogues,* in Gregory's *Pastoral Care,* and in the *Soliloquies* of St. Augustine. Current discussion of Alfred's Boethius concerns the degree to which such alterations are his own or derive from one of the many medieval commentaries on Boethius.

The final translation to be considered, the *Soliloquies,* is also the freest, for while major dependence throughout the first two of its three books is clearly on Augustine's *Soliloquies,* the third bears almost no relation to that work, collecting ideas, rather, from Augustine's *De videndo Deo* and other unidentified sources. Moreover, throughout Alfred's text ideas from a variety of authors are mingled with Augustine's—the principal ones so far identified being Gregory in his *Dialogues, Pastoral Care,* and the homily on the story of Dives and Lazarus from Luke (16:19–31), and Jerome in his commentary on Luke. Despite these alterations and additions, the work remains, in Old English as in Latin, a dialogue between the author and his reason (hence soliloquies) concerning the soul's awareness of itself, its immortality, and its knowledge of God after death. Even with its lack of fidelity to Augustine's thought and the multiplicity of its sources, Alfred's *Soliloquies* betrays greater confidence in interpreting and reformulating patristic thought than any of his other translations.

BIBLIOGRAPHY

Editions and Translations. Dialogues: Hans Hecht, *Bischof Waerferths von Worcester Übersetzung der Dialoge Gregors des Grossen,* in C. W. M. Grein and R. P. Wülker, eds., *Bibliothek der angelsächsischen Prosa,* V (1900, 1907; repr. 1965), trans. by Robert M. Lumiansky as *A Modern English Version of the Old English Dialogues of Gregory* (1942). *Pastoral Care:* Henry Sweet, *King Alfred's West-Saxon Version of Gregory's Pastoral Care,* 2 vols. (1871–1872; repr. 1958), with translation; and Ingvar Carlson, *The Pastoral Care Edited from British Museum Ms. Cotton Otho Bii,* 2 vols. (1975–1978). Orosius: Janet M. Bately, *The Old English Orosius* (1980), trans. by Benjamin Thorpe in R. Pauli, *The Life of Alfred the Great* (1853). Old English Bede: Thomas Miller, ed., *The Old English Version of Bede's Ecclesiastical History of the English People,* 4 vols. (1890–1898; repr. 1959, 1963), with translation. Boethius: W. J. Sedgefield, ed., *King Alfred's Old English Version of Boethius' De Consolatione Philosophiae* (1899), trans. by W. J. Sedgefield, *King Alfred's Version of the Consolation of Boethius* (1900). *Soliloquies:* Thomas A Carnicelli, ed., *King Alfred's Version of St. Augustine's Soliloquies* (1969), trans. by Henry L. Hargrove (1904). [Accessible, though generally dated, editions of the Latin originals are in J. P. Migne, ed., *Patrologia latina.*]

Studies. William H. Brown, Jr., *A Syntax of King Alfred's Pastoral Care* (1970); Kurt Otten, *König Alfreds Boethius* (1964); F. Anne Payne, *King Alfred and Boethius* (1968); Dorothy Whitelock, "The Old English Bede," in *Proceedings of the British Academy,* **48** (1963); "The Prose of Alfred's Reign," in E. G. Stanley, ed., *Continuations and Beginnings* (1966), 67–103; and "William of Malmesbury on the Works of King Alfred," in Derek A. Pearsall and R. A. Waldron, eds., *Medieval Literature and Civilization: Studies in Memory of G. N. Garmonsway* (1969), 78–93; David Yerkes, *The Two Versions of Waerferth's Translation of Gregory's Dialogues: An Old English Thesaurus* (1979).

COLIN CHASE

[See also **Asser; Anglo-Saxon Literature.**]

ALGAZEL. See **Ghazali, Al-.**

ALGEBRA. See **Mathematics.**

ALGER OF LIÈGE, born around 1050, served as a deacon and *scholasticus* at St. Bartholomew's in Liège; about 1101 he became a canon at St. Lambert's. In 1121 he retired to a monastic life at Cluny, where he died some ten years later. His main writings, *On Mercy and Justice* and *On the Sacrament of the Lord's Body and Blood,* contributed to the development of canon law and sacramental theology. He provoked controversy with Rupert of Deutz and influenced Gratian. He may also have written *On the Dignity of the Church of Liège* and the *Letters,* on various canonical problems.

BIBLIOGRAPHY

Alger's main writings are in *Patrologia latina,* CLXXX (1855), 739–972; *On the Dignity,* S. Bormans and E. Schoolmeesters, eds., in "Le *Liber officiorum ecclesiae Leodiensis,*" in *Bulletin de la Commission royale* [*belge*] *d'histoire,* 5th ser., **6** (1896); *Letters,* P. Jaffé, ed., in *Monumenta Bambergensia,* Bibliotheca Rerum Germanicarum, V (1869), 262–267, 373–379. On the main writings see N. M. Haring, "A Study in the Sacramentology of Alger of Liège," in *Mediaeval Studies,* **20** (1958). Further details and bibliography are in Michael McCormick, *Index scriptorum operumque Latino-Belgicorum Medii Aevi: Nouveau répertoire des oeuvres médiolatines belges,* pt. III, vol. II (1979), 20–28, 169–170.

MICHAEL MCCORMICK

[See also **Gratian; Law, Canon; Rupert of Deutz.**.]

ALHAMBRA. The Alhambra, the most fully preserved medieval Islamic palace and the undisputed masterpiece of western Islamic art, is situated on a high plateau—the Sabīka—measuring 740 meters by 220 meters (an area of thirty-five acres), located outside the city of Granada in southeastern Spain. The setting is typical of Islamic citadels, though its verdant location against the backdrop of the Sierra Nevada is exceptionally beautiful: Moorish poets called the Alhambra "a pearl set in emeralds." The name of the site is probably a corruption of *qal^{c}at al-hamra* ("the red castle," from the color of the multitowered enclosing wall).

The earliest Islamic structure on this natural citadel was the ninth-century Alcazaba, which covers Iberian and Roman remains and was originally surrounded by a wall with twenty-four towers. This lone fort was enlarged in the mid eleventh century by construction of the palace of Jehoseph bar Najralla, the Jewish vizier of Granada, a building now lost but minutely described in contemporary panegyric poetry (notably by the Jewish bard Ibn Gabirol) that emphasizes the Solomonic associations of its architecture. These associations were deliberately heightened and exploited in subsequent buildings.

The Alhambra is in fact a palimpsest of successive royal residences. In its final form it could be described as a Moorish acropolis, or as a self-contained royal city that functioned as a seat of government, like the Medinat al-Zahra (near Córdoba) or the Almohad casbah of Marrakech. But it is equally an array of villas set amid gardens and parks, many of them stocked with animals—in short, a vast paradise. As such it fits into a late antique tradition widespread throughout the Mediterranean world, in which palaces were casually composed aggregates of individual, carefully designed parts (such as Piazza Armerina, Sicily, or Hadrian's palace at Tivoli). The Topkapi Palace in Istanbul is a late example of the genre.

Serious work on the Alhambra in its present form began with Muḥammad I, who from 1238 built the aqueduct that supplies the site with water from the River Darro. The enclosing walls were constructed largely in the reign of his son Muḥammad II, and are datable between 1273 and 1303. Later work is well documented by inscriptions. From 1333 to 1354, Yusuf I expanded, decorated, and fortified the Alhambra on a heroic scale, thereby setting the tone for its later buildings. He was responsible for the huge Tower of the Women, the Court of the Myrtles, and the Gate of Justice (1347–1348), a feature with ancient associations in the Islamic world. But the principal patron was Muḥammad V, who, especially in his second reign (1362–1391), built such masterpieces as the Court of the Lions (begun 1377). The years after the Christian reconquest in 1492 saw much refashioning of the buildings in various European styles, as well as great neglect. New palaces and churches were also erected. However, serious restoration and conservation of the Islamic structures have been practiced consistently only since 1828.

The Alhambra has three divisions, which from west to east are citadel, palace complex, and residential annex. The Alcazaba is a fortified keep independent of the rest of the site, with its own gateway. The annex, known as the Alhambra Alta (Upper Alhambra), has been largely destroyed, but traces of important towers, gateways, and another citadel remain. The rambling core of the Alhambra is its group of palaces, which themselves can be classified into three elements. The first clusters around the Mexuar *(mishwar),* a public reception hall or tribunal, and includes guardrooms or barracks, stables, and an oratory. The second, the *diwan,* features accommodations for court officials arranged around a great court of honor, the Court of the Myrtles, which leads to a vast audience chamber (the Hall of the Ambassadors) enclosed in a bastion. The third component is the *harim,* the focus of which is the Court of the Lions. It also contains the private domestic quarters of the sultan, complete with two large chambers—the Hall of the Two Sisters and the Hall of the Abencerrajes—smaller rooms, a modest oratory, and gardens. The relationship between these two great courts recalls that of the public *atrium* and the private *tablinum* in Roman houses. The *harim* led to the royal funerary precinct *(rauda)* and to the Great Mosque. A similar tripartite disposition is found in palaces in Tunisia and Morocco (such as the Badī^c Palace in Marrakech, 1578–1593) and in the Alcázar of Seville (decorated in 1364 by artists from Granada at the behest of King Pedro I).

Despite its tripartite layout, the Alhambra carefully avoids symmetry. Instead, it exploits contrasts of closed and open; occupied and empty spaces; light and darkness; private and public functions; massive towers and insubstantial colonnades. Unexpected views abound, often opening from belvederes placed to catch the breeze, and the perspectives change constantly. The keynote is surprise. The two big courtyards that form the hub of the design are set at right angles to each other. The buildings that cluster around them seem to be the result of organic growth, not planning. Bent entrances are a standard feature. The discrete, additive nature of the buildings, their continually changing axes, and the rectangular form that transcends their varieties of shape and ornament all invite the eye to wander freely, within well-defined boundaries. Despite its spectacular views, the Alhambra is an essentially inward-looking creation, emphasizing seclusion and privacy. Seen as a whole, it is a labyrinth; but its constituent parts are coherent and well-ordered.

Space permits only a brief discussion of the major buildings. The Court of the Myrtles takes its name from the low hedges flanking the central pool that dominates the marble-paved courtyard and reflects the huge mass of the tower to the north. Thus the great size of the courtyard (36.6 meters by 23.5 meters) is magnified illusionistically. Galleries borne on columns of alabaster and jasper embellish its long sides.

Its natural pendant is the Court of the Lions, named for its central fountain with an alabaster basin atop twelve marble lions that probably came from the eleventh-century palace. The lions represent a late but self-conscious reminiscence of the "brazen sea" carried by twelve oxen in Solomon's temple (I Kings 7:23–26), and may also have zodiacal significance. They function as aquamaniles, spouting

Court of the Lions. Alhambra, Granada. YALE PHOTO COLLECTION

water into a marble canal linked to watercourses in adjoining chambers. The courtyard itself (28.5 meters by 15.7 meters) is divided by two water channels in cruciform disposition. The four quarters thus created—perhaps a cosmological reference—were, it seems, originally planted with orange trees. An ethereal arcade of 124 slender columns of white marble bears a low gallery. Gabled porticoes with filigree ornament project from the arcade on the cardinal axes, a Moorish version of the classical four-*īwān* plan of Eastern Islam. The massed volumes of the roofs offer a vigorous contrast to the fragile beauty of the court below.

Several large halls functionally related to the two major courts are grouped around them. The Hall of the Abencerrajes is a perfect square lit by latticed windows. The cells of its pendant *muqarnaṣ* (stalactite) ceiling seem to explode outward and downward like comets, but also serve to trap and filter light. The Hall of the Ambassadors, a subtly illuminated throne room, occupies most of the Tower of Comares (al-Qamariyya), and is notable for its ceiling, some seventy-five feet high, with inlaid work in white, blue, and gold forming crowns, circles, and stars to imitate the seven heavens of the Koran. The Hall of the Two Sisters has arguably the finest *muqarnas* dome in the Islamic world—a technical tour de force comprising a lacy, insubstantial mass of more than 5,000 individual cells that appear to be in continuous motion and—to judge by the poetic inscriptions in the chamber—are intended to evoke the revolving heavens.

The many poetic inscriptions in the Alhambra address the visitor directly and purport to express the thoughts of the buildings themselves:

"Nothing can match this work. . . ."
(Tower of the Captives)

"Incomparable is this basin! Allah, the exalted one, desired
That it should surpass everything in wonderful beauty!"
(Court of the Lions)

"I am a garden full of beauty, clad with every ornament . . .
The stars would gladly descend from their zones of light
And wish they lived in this hall instead of in heaven."
(Hall of the Two Sisters).

Such verses, many of them by the Grenadan poet Ibn Zamrak, are typical of the self-conscious, literary, and somewhat precious flavor of the Alhambra. They extol the princely patron in language echoing with Koranic and cosmological resonances.

The site, besides being a fortress and a monument to the Islamic faith—not least to its last great victory on Spanish soil, the Battle of Algeciras in 1369—is a celebration of water and fertility. Water, whether in static pools or dynamic fountains and canals, is as integral to the buildings as the brick and stone of which they are constructed. It serves obvious practical and aesthetic functions, but also psychological ones, for it fosters a sense of peace and spiritual tranquillity. Indeed, the Koran describes paradise as "a garden flowing with streams." This atmosphere is best savored in the Generalife (probably ca. 1319), a summer villa outside the Alhambra proper but really an extension of it, and a chance survival of the many such villas that once graced the hillsides around Córdoba and Granada.

Typically, its gardens are far more extensive than its buildings—though the latter included baths and a group of palaces—but are integral to the overall conception. Along the length of the principal garden runs a canal flanked by a series of fountains whose quiet splashing adds the dimension of pleasurable sound to the visual opulence of the garden. Shaded parterres, clipped hedges, pavilions, reflecting pools, sunken flower beds and a network of intersecting alleys are enclosed by a wall. Together these elements create the sense of a jeweled private world removed from the pressures of daily life, a true *hortus conclusus* and thus an image of paradise. The many pavilions, too, evoke the canopies *(rafraf)* of paradise described in the Koran. In the midst of this seclusion, remote perspectives of the distant plain and mountains may suddenly unfold. Some faint echo of these splendors, as detailed by Frankish travelers and Crusaders, may have inspired the potent Western medieval legends of the magic gardens of Klingsor and Armida.

The spatial ingenuity, airy vistas, modulations of light, and sensitivity to color that characterize the Alhambra gardens typify the architecture of the palace as well. Externally, at roof level, continually varied vistas are revealed, as in the intersecting angles of the glazed tile roofs—a study in solid geometry—or in the domes of the baths, with their multiple star-shaped skylights. Evidence that the architects delighted in contrasts is legion: the austere exteriors give no clue to the opulence within, ponderous ceilings are miraculously borne on latticed walls, massive piers alternate with matchstick columns, and tiled dadoes give way to panels of filigree stucco in subtly changing tonal harmonies further enlivened by the play of light. It is a paradox—indeed, a minor miracle—that a palace of such fragility should be the unique survivor of the storied tradition of Muslim royal residences.

A few decorative motifs are used consistently, on many scales, and with an exquisite sensitivity to nuance. They include elaborate, stilted, round-headed arches, and *muqarnas* for domes, capitals, and the intrados of arches. Similarly, doorways, windows, miradors, and other openings are so placed as to mark the different levels of the building and to maintain its essentially human scale—for the constituents of the Alhambra are those of the typical Maghribi house writ large. Cuerda seca and mosaic tilework are used extensively for floors and dadoes. It employs a palette of white, ocher, brownish violet, green, and occasionally light blue. Stucco in rectangular panels, much of it molded and painted in red, blue, and yellow-gold, fills the area above the tiles. Wood is often used for the ceilings, which frequently display decoratively interlaced beams *(artesonados).* Other materials include carved stone (for doorways), polished marble (for columns and sometimes floors), engraved or pierced bronze plating (for doors), and stained glass windows set in lead frames or plaster grilles.

Apart from the scenes of hunting, courtly life, and fighting painted by Christian artists in the Hall of Justice, the human figure is absent from the decorative repertoire, though it seems to have been featured significantly in frescoes now lost. Instead, the standard themes of Islamic ornament are deployed in such density as to deserve the hackneyed term horror vacui. They include geometric patterns, often interlaced designs on multiple levels; floral motifs, with particular emphasis on the pinecone, the palmette, and the palm leaf; and epigraphy. A cursive script of great plasticity is prominent, most often used for a single phrase set in a heraldic cartouche and repeating the motto "There is no victor except God." It is a peculiarly appropriate sentiment for this monument to a doomed civilization.

In architecture and decoration alike, the Alhambra offers little that was not explicit or implicit in earlier Moorish and Maghribi art. To that extent its art is stagnant if not decadent. But in its poised and lyrical classicism and its consciously antiquarian quality with numerous Greco-Roman reminiscences, it encapsulates the many centuries of Moorish art and brings that art to its final flowering. In that sense it is an extended elegy. Washington Irving captured this spirit intuitively in his meditations on the building, and his work ensured that the Alhambra still evokes such associations in a Western mind.

BIBLIOGRAPHY

K. A. C. Creswell, *A Bibliography of the Architecture, Arts, and Crafts of Islam* (1961); H. Gómez Moreno, *El arte arabe espanol hasta los Almoravides,* in *Ars Hispaniae* (1951); T. Gowry and Owen James, *Plans, Elevation, Sections and Details of the Alhambra,* 2 vols. (1842, 1845); Washington Irving, *Tales of the Alhambra* (1832); L. Torres Balbás, *Arte Almohade, arte nazari, arte mudejar,* in *Ars Hispaniae* (1949), *La Alhambra y el Generalife* (1952).

ROBERT HILLENBRAND

[See also **Almohad Art; Almoravid Art; Córdoba; Granada; Islamic Architecture; Islamic Art.**]

ᶜALĪ IBN ABĪ ṬĀLIB (nicknamed Ḥaydara [lion] and Abū Turāb [dustman]), cousin and son-in-law of the prophet Muḥammad, the fourth caliph after Muḥammad's death, and the first imam according to the Shiites, was born at Mecca about 600. He grew up in Muḥammad's house and was among the first to believe in his mission, being at that time a boy no more than eleven years old—perhaps even younger. Whether he was the second, after Muḥammad's wife Khadija, or the third, after Khadija and Abū Bakr (the first caliph), to adopt Islam, is a matter of dispute among historians. There is, however, no doubt that he was a staunch defender of the Prophet's cause. Tradition has it that he slept in Muḥammad's bed on the night the Prophet fled to Medina, thereby deluding the Meccan conspirators who sought to murder him and delaying them in their search. ᶜAlī later joined Muḥammad in Medina, where he married his daughter Fatima. Their sons were Ḥasan and Ḥusayn.

During Muḥammad's stay in Medina, ᶜAlī played an outstanding role among his companions *(sahaba).* Among other things, he was one of the Prophet's secretaries, he was charged by the Prophet with diplomatic missions, on two occasions he was deputed to destroy idols, and in 631 he was asked by the Prophet to read the opening verses of sura 9 of the Koran.

However, ᶜAlī's main role during this period was military: he fought in all but one of the battles of the

Prophet. In this one battle he was asked by Muḥammad to stay behind with his wife—an unusual move that provoked rumors among the Prophet's companions. In order to quell any suspicion, Muḥammad said to ᶜAlī, "You are to me as Aaron was to Moses—except that there is no Prophet after me." This saying was later subjected to heavy interpretation by the Shiites. The same group similarly handled what the Prophet said when he took ᶜAlī, Fatima, Ḥasan, and Ḥusayn under his mantle *(kisaᵓ)* and named them "the People of the House, free from every impurity." At any rate, ᶜAlī showed outstanding valor in his military undertakings, and it was principally this characteristic that led the Shiites to credit him with extraordinary qualities.

When Muḥammad died in 632 and Abū Bakr was elected first caliph, ᶜAlī was busy with the Prophet's burial. Though asked expressly to support Abū Bakr, and through him the Hashimites, his own clan, ᶜAlī refused and did not give his oath of allegiance to Abū Bakr until six months later. By that time his position had become more complicated by a question of inheritance on which ᶜAlī's wife, Fatima, and Abū Bakr disagreed, Fatima claiming the inheritance of her father's—the Prophet's—land in Fadak and Abū Bakr refusing to give it to her, quoting Muḥammad's saying,"We prophets do not inherit nor are we inherited."

ᶜAlī did not participate in any of the military expeditions of the first three caliphs: Abū Bakr, ᶜUmar, and ᶜUthmān. During the rule of ᶜUmar, he was consulted on matters related to Islamic law. On major issues, however, ᶜUmar often held legal and administrative opinions that differed from ᶜAlī's. Although ᶜAlī was a member of the Council of the Six that was to choose the caliph to succeed ᶜUmar, he was not elected; indeed, the election took place when ᶜAlī was away from Medina.

The relations between ᶜAlī and ᶜUthmān were not good, and they deteriorated as the years went on. ᶜAlī, among others of the Prophet's companions, accused ᶜUthmān of deviating from the Koran and the tradition of the Prophet, of changing the prescriptions for legal punishments, and of nepotism. He also differed with ᶜUthmān on political and economic questions. When, in 656,ᶜUthmān's opponents besieged his house in Medina, they asked ᶜAlī to be their leader. Although ᶜAlī refused, his general attitude gave strong moral support to their demand for ᶜUthmān's abdication. The siege led to the assassination of ᶜUthmān. ᶜAlī could not have participated in this bloody event, but he accepted the invitation to become caliph that was supported mainly by ᶜUthmān's opponents, who controlled Medina and were ready to use force against anyone not ready to take the oath of allegiance to ᶜAlī.

Nevertheless, some of the leading companions of the Prophet refused to yield and left Medina. ᶜAlī's election seems not to have been unanimous. His position was further weakened by his immediate acquiescence to measures demanded by ᶜUthmān's opponents, the most obvious being removal of the governors appointed by ᶜUthmān and their replacement by people of ᶜAlī's own party. Although ᶜAlī tried to satisfy the public by distributing the money in the state treasury, he could not secure wide support for himself among all Muslim factions. Resentment toward him grew, especially in Syria and Egypt.

The first challenge to ᶜAlī came from Muᶜāwiya ibn Abī Sufyān, the Ummayad governor of Syria under ᶜUthmān who was also ᶜUthmān's cousin. Muᶜāwiya refused to acknowledge ᶜAlī as caliph, accused him of being an accomplice to ᶜUthmān's murder, and announced that he was going to fight him on this ground, since, according to the Koran, he was the legal claimant to the blood of ᶜUthmān. Muᶜāwiya then prepared for war.

ᶜAlī was responding to this challenge when another serious problem arose. Two of Muḥammad's companions, Ṭalḥa and al-Zubayr, and his wife ᶜĀᵓisha, began assembling an army in Mecca, then moved swiftly to Basra, Iraq, in rebellion against ᶜAlī. ᶜĀᵓisha had been spreading propaganda against ᶜAlī; and Ṭalḥa and al-Zubayr, though opposed to ᶜUthmān, could not accept the drastic change in policy as undertaken by ᶜAlī. The rebels' slogan was "reform" *(iṣlāḥ),* their inner motive being the fear of the influence of the extremists on ᶜAlī. ᶜAlī reacted quickly. With Syria out of hand and Egypt in confusion, he could not afford to lose Iraq. He sent an army to meet the rebels at Basra, following them shortly thereafter. The subsequent Battle of the Camel *(al-Jamal)* took place in 656. ᶜAlī was victorious, Ṭalḥa and al-Zubayr were killed, and ᶜĀᵓisha was forced to return to Medina.

ᶜAlī was less fortunate in his encounter with Muᶜāwiya. After the failure of negotiations, they met with their armies at Ṣiffīn, Iraq, in 657. After fighting in which both armies suffered heavy losses (about 70,000 killed), the battle seemed to be going in favor of ᶜAlī. To avoid defeat, Muᶜāwiya, acting

ᶜALĪ IBN ABĪ ṬĀLIB

on the advice of his shrewd lieutenant ᶜAmr ibn al-ᶜĀṣ, asked his men to raise copies of the Koran onto their lances. The intent of the gesture was to stop the fighting and make the Koran the judge of the conflict. ᶜAlī's men dropped their arms, and forced him to accept arbitration.

Subsequently, ᶜAlī agreed with Muᶜāwiya that an arbitrator should represent each of them and that the two arbitrators should meet in seclusion, discuss the conflict in the light of the Koran and the tradition *(sunna)* of the Prophet, and reach a decision binding on both parties. It is not fully clear from the sources exactly what the arbitrators were to examine. Recent scholarship has suggested that they were to determine whether ᶜUthmān's actions went against the Divine Law, and hence whether his murder was just. This judgment was to serve as the basis for deciding whether ᶜAlī's or Muᶜāwiya's cause was the right one.

Meanwhile, as the arbitration *(ḥukūma)* was starting, ᶜAlī had to face still another crisis. A few thousand of his supporters, discontented with his decision to accept arbitration, and considering that acceptance placed doubt on his rightful position—indeed, was an act of disbelief *(kufr)*—asked ᶜAlī to withdraw his acceptance of arbitration. He refused. Crying *"lā ḥukm illā li-Allāh"* ("no judgment except God's"), this group, later known as the Kharijites *(al-Khawarij),* left ᶜAlī's army. ᶜAlī tried to reenlist them, but they refused unless he declared he was guilty of disbelief. ᶜAlī staunchly refused but promised safe passage to those who returned to his fold. Only a few did, while the rest declared him an unbeliever. ᶜAlī attacked this group at Nahrawān, Iraq, in 658, and in the ensuing battle many pious Kharijites were killed. General bitterness against ᶜAlī increased, and there were more defections from his army.

Meanwhile, the arbitrators had come to a decision. Abū Mūsā al-Ashᶜari, representing ᶜAlī, and ᶜAmr ibn al-ᶜĀṣ, representing Muᶜāwiya, agreed that ᶜUthmān had committed no breach of the Divine Law, but this verdict was announced only to a very few. The Syrians immediately pronounced their allegiance *(bayᶜa)* to Muᶜāwiya. ᶜAlī's supporters objected and prepared for war. In the meantime, Muᶜāwiya had occupied Egypt. Thus, by the time the decision was officially announced in 659, the situation had completely changed for ᶜAlī: no more was he facing a rebel, but a rival caliph; his army was weakened by dissention; and he was accused of the massacre of the Kharijites and, in general, of following a vacillatory policy.

The two arbitrators had agreed on deposing both ᶜAlī and Muᶜāwiya, with a caliph to be chosen by a committee. During the public announcement of this decision, Abū Mūsā observed this agreement, but ᶜAmr deposed ᶜAlī and confirmed Muᶜāwiya. The arbitration, however, had only negative results, for no decision on the caliphate was taken by the participants.

The situation remained uncertain in 659. ᶜAlī enjoyed the homage of his partisans as caliph but was virtually confined to Kūfa, Iraq. Though he had the support of Mecca and Medina, he could not prevent Muᶜāwiya from sending small expeditions to Yemen, Arabia, and Iraq. In 660/661 a Kharijite called ᶜAbd al-Raḥmān ibn Muljam al-Murādī, revenging the Kharijites killed by ᶜAlī, mortally wounded ᶜAlī with a poisoned sword at the mosque of Kūfa. ᶜAlī died a few days later and was buried secretly. His grave was identified, some miles from Kūfa, more than 150 years later, and a sanctuary was subsequently built. Around this sanctuary the city of Najaf grew, with a large cemetery where pious Shiites request burial.

ᶜAlī was short, broad-shouldered, and bald with a long white beard. By nine wives he had fourteen sons and nineteen daughters. During the lifetime of his first wife, Fatima, the Prophet's daughter, he took no other wives. Besides his two sons by her, Ḥasan and Ḥusayn, the only one of his children to play a significant historical role was Muḥammad ibn al-Ḥanafiyya. All Shiite sects name their imams from progeny of Ḥusayn (such as Imaamiyya and Ismaᶜiliyya) or of Ḥasan and Ḥusayn (for instance, Zaydiyya). The only exception is the Kaysaniyya sect, whose imam was Muḥammad ibn al-Ḥanafiyya.

ᶜAlī was a gifted orator whose speeches, letters, and discourses were collected by al-Sharīf al-Radī in a book entitled *Nahj al-balagha* (Path of Eloquence). He was also an outstanding reader of the Koran and extremely knowledgeable in Islamic law, brave in voicing his opinions in it, and rigorous in its application. Piety and religiosity were his outstanding qualities; political maneuvering was not. It is because of this, at least partially, that he was not successful as head of the Muslim state. He inherited a complex and turbulent situation that he faced with religious zeal and military courage, but those virtues were not enough. Although there is much difference of opinion in the evaluation of his achievements, there is generally a consensus that he stood for the religious ideal he believed in but lacked the political flexibility needed by the Muslim community at that time.

BIBLIOGRAPHY

Among the basic biographical sources are Ibn Saʿd, *Kitāb al-Ṭabaqāt al-kabīr*, E. Sachau, ed., III, pt. 1 (1904), 11–27; al-Balādhurī, *Ansāb al-Ashrāf,* M. B. Mahmudi, ed., I (1974), 89–512; Ibn ʿAbd al-Barr, *Kitāb al-Istīʿab*, A. M. Bajawi, ed. (n.d.), 1089–1134; Ibn al-Athīr, *Usd al-ghāba,* IV (1957), 16–40; Abū Nuʿaym al-Iṣfahānī, *Ḥilyat al-Awliyāʾ*, I (1967), 61–87; Yaqut al-Hamawi, *Irshad al-Arib,* D. S. Margoliouth, ed., V (1929), 262–267; Ibn Hajar al-'Asqalani, *Tahdhib al-tahdhib,* VII (1948), 334–339; and *al-Isaba,* II (1950), 507 (no. 5688); Abūʾl-Faraj al-Iṣfahānī, *Maqātil al-Ṭālibiyyīn*, A. Saqr, ed. (1949), which presents the Shiite point of view; Da'i Idriss, *Uyun al-akhbar,* M. Ghalib, ed., IV (1973), which presents the Ismaili point of view.

ʿAlī's early participation in the call of the Prophet is detailed in the *Sira* of the Prophet, a recommended edition of which is *Sira,* M. M. ʿAbd al-Hamid, ed. (1963); an English translation is Sir William Muir, *The Life of Mohammed* (1912). The main historical works on ʿAlī's caliphate are Abū Jafar Muhammad ibn Jarir al-Ṭabarī, *Annals of the Apostles and the Kings,* M. J. de Goeje, ed. (1879–1901). Ya'qubi, *Ta'rik,* Dar Sader, ed. (1960); al-Dīnawarī, *Akhbār al-ṭīwal*, 'A. 'Amir, ed. (1960); Ibn Aʿtham, *Kitāb al-Futūḥ* (1968–1978); Mas'udi, *Muruj al-dhahab,* C. Pellat, ed. (1966–1979), vol. I, pp. 93–180.

Much of the material was translated or abridged by Caetani in his *Annali,* IX and X (1926). Further historical material is in Naṣr ibn Muzāḥim al-Minqārī, *Waqʿat Ṣiffīn*, ʿAbd al-Salam Muḥammad Hārūn, ed. (1945). ʿAlī's speeches, letters, and discourses (many of questionable authenticity) are in al-Sharif al-Radi, *Nahj al-balagha,* of which the most reliable edition is by M. ʿAbdu (1890). This book has several exegeses, the most famous and comprehensive of which is Ibn Abī al-Ḥadīd, *Sharh Nahj al-balagha,* A. Ibrahim, ed., 20 vols. (1965).

Western studies on ʿAlī include Julius Wellhausen, *Die religiös-politischen Oppositionsparteien* (1901); Wilhelm Sarasin, *Das Bild Alis bei den Historikern der Sunna* (1907); Henri Lammens, *Études sur le règne du calife omaiyade Moʿâwia Ier* (1908); Laura Veccia Vaglieri, *Il conflitto ʿAlī–Muʿāwiya e la secessione khārigita riesaminati alla luce di fonti ibāḍite* (1952), 1–94. Among Arabic works on the subject are Ṭāhā Ḥusayn, *al-Fitna al-Kubrā,* II (1954), which presents the Sunnite point of view; and M. Bahr al-ʿUlum, *Fi rihab a'immat al al-bayt: al-Imam amir al-mu'minin* (1978), which presents the Shiite point of view. Also see M. A. Salmin, *Ali the Caliph* (1931); and 'A. M. 'Aqqad, *'Abqariyyat al-Imam* (1967).

WADĀD AL-QĀḌĪ

[See also **ʿĀʾisha; Muʿāwiya; Muḥammad.**]

ʿALĪ IBN HILAL. See **Bawwab, Ibn al-.**

ALIDS are the descendants of ʿAlī ibn Abī Ṭālib, the cousin of Muḥammad and his son-in-law by virtue of his marriage to Muḥammad's daughter Fatima. Their status is based on their membership in Muḥammad's family *(ahl al-bayt).* The Koran states that "God will remove the stains from you, O people of the house and purify you completely" (33:33), and requires Muslims to love Muḥammad's family (43:22). In addition, they were exempted from paying *ṣadaqa.*

They also were the political rivals of early Islamic rulers for the leadership of the community. ʿAlī himself was Commander of the Faithful from 656 until 661, and his party *(Shīʿa)* supported the political ambitions and claims to religious authority of his descendants. His eldest son by Fatima, Ḥasan (died 669), abdicated and recognized Muʿāwiya as Commander of the Faithful in 661 in return for a pension. ʿAlī's second son by Fatima, Ḥusayn, died at Karbala in 680, in a vain attempt to become the ruler of the community. A third son, Muḥammad ibn al-Ḥanafiyya, was recognized by the Shiite rebel, Mukhtār ibn Abī ʿUbayd in 687 as the living Mahdi. Muḥammad's son Abū Hāshim (died 700) provided a focus for the extremist Kaysanid sect and its subgroups in the eighth century.

The grandson of Ḥusayn, Zayd ibn ʿAlī, who rebelled unsuccessfully at Al-Kufa in 740, is the eponym of the Zaydite Shiite sect that survived his rebellion. But the descendants of Ḥasan were more active politically. His grandson, Muḥammad ibn ʿAbdullāh al-Nafs al-Zakiyya, known as "the Pure Soul" (718–762), rebelled unsuccessfully against the Abbasid ruler al-Manṣūr at Medina in 762, while his brother Ibrāhīm rebelled at Basra with Zaydite support. Mansūr's successor, al-Mahdī (775–785) tried to make peace with the family of Ḥasan by giving amnesty to their supporters and by making an Alid, Yaʿqūb ibn Dawūd, his *wazīr.* But the Alids rebelled under his successor, al-Hādī (785–786), in 786 and were massacred at Fakhkh (near Mecca).

Idrīs ibn ʿAbdullāh, the brother of Muḥammad al-Nafs al-Zakiyya, escaped to Morocco, where he founded the Idrisid dynasty. The successor of al-Hādī, Harūn al-Rashīd (786–809) harassed and persecuted the Alids. The Zaydites fled to Daylam in 791; Yaḥyā ibn ʿAbdullāh, another brother of Muḥammad al-Nafs al-Zakiyya, fled to Ṭabaristān but was forced to accept a safe conduct back to Baghdad, where he died in prison.

In the early Abbasid period the descendants of Ḥasan were the most important Alids, and the most dangerous politically; they were therefore eliminated because they posed a threat to the Abbasids. They perished in revolt or were forced to flee, leaving the field to the descendants of Ḥusayn, who survived because of the strategic decision of Jaᶜfar al-Ṣādiq (died 768) about 760 to disassociate himself from the extremists. Nevertheless, his family was persecuted. His son Mūsā al-Kāẓim was brought from Medina to Baghdad, imprisoned, and executed in 799.

By the early ninth century the descendants of Ḥusayn were the most important branch of ᶜAlī's family in the central parts of the Islamic empire. Beginning with Jaᶜfar's father, Muḥammad al-Bāqir (died 731), the claim to leadership and authority (imamate) was passed from father to son by designation *(naṣṣ)*. But by the ninth century, rival groups disagreed over the chain of designation. The rise of Shiite and Alid revolts in the Jazīra and at Al-Kufa, Baṣra, Mecca, and Medina in support of an unnamed "chosen one" *(al-Riḍā)* between 812 and 816 induced the Abbasid ruler al-Maʾmūn to designate a descendant of Ḥusayn, ᶜAlī ibn Mūsā al-Riḍā (died 818), as his successor in 817, which won him the support of the Zaydites and of some Alids. The suppression of these rebellions drove the remaining Alids out of Iraq.

In the ninth century the descendants of Ḥasan emerged as the leaders of the Zaydite movement, and by the early tenth century they established states in northern Iran and a Zaydite imamate in the highlands of Yemen. About the middle of the tenth century, Jaᶜfar ibn Muḥammad, a descendant of Mūsā ibn ᶜAbdullāh (a brother of Muḥammad al-Nafs al-Zakiyya), established himself as Zaydite sharif of Mecca. Mūsa was the ancestor of four dynasties of sharifs who ruled Mecca until 1924. The sharif of Mecca became Sunni in the late twelfth century. Mūsā's son Ibrāhīm was the ancestor of the Ukhaydirid dynasty of the Yamāma.

By the late ninth century the Imamite or Twelver Shiite sect had formed. It recognized the authority of the descendants of ᶜAlī al-Riḍā down to his great-great-grandson, who disappeared about 878. The Fatimid dynasty that established its own caliphate in northern Africa, Egypt, and Syria from the ninth until the twelfth centuries claimed descent from Ismāᶜīl ibn Jaᶜ far al-Ṣādiq (died 760).

ᶜAlī's descendants by all of his children were accorded varying degrees of nobility. They were popular objects of reverence and respect, and sources of blessing, and they possessed the ability to curse. Their tombs became objects of visitation for intercession. As members of the Banū Hāshim, Alī's descendants were included among the *ashrāf* in the Abbasid period when their affairs were administered locally by one of themselves as agent *(naqīb al-ashrāf)*. One of the earliest was an Alid, ᶜAlī ibn Muḥammad ibn Jaᶜfar al-Himmānī (died 873 or 874) at Al-Kufa. The *naqīb* was responsible for checking the genealogies of the *ashrāf,* preserving their claims on the treasury, seeing that their behavior and marriages would not hurt their prestige, and seeing that the endowments *(awqāf)* that were made for their support were properly administered.

The Fatimids restricted the term "sharif" to descendants of Ḥasan and Ḥusayn, and this remained the custom in Egypt. *Sayyid* (master) was also used, especially of Ḥusayn. Alids were allowed to wear green (the color of the prophet and of paradise). In fourteenth-century Egypt they wore a green badge on their turbans, and in sixteenth-century Egypt they wore green turbans.

BIBLIOGRAPHY

Aḥmad al Sibāᶜī, *Ta'rīkh Makka* (1952/1953); Toufic Fahd, *Le Shīᶜisme imāmite* (1970); Ibn Isfandiyār, *An Abridged Translation of the History of Tabaristān,* E. G. Browne, trans. (1905); Ibn Muhanna al-Ḥasanī, *ᶜUmdat al-ṭālib fī ansāb Āl Abī Ṭālib* (1900/1901); Abū'l-Faraj al Iṣfahānī, *Maqātil al-Ṭalībiyyin,* A. Saqr, ed. (1949); Syed H. Jafri, *The Origins and Early Development of Shiᶜa Islam* (1979); Aḥmad al-Nasāʾī, *Khaṣāᶜis Amīr al-Muʾminin ᶜAlī ibn Abī Ṭālib* (1890/1891); Hasan ibn Muḥammad Qummī, *Tārīkh-i Qumm* (1934); M. H. Tabāṭabāᶜi, *Shiᶜite Islam* (1974); Heinrich Ferdinand Wüstenfeld, ed., *Die Chroniken der Stadt Mekka* (1857), *passim;* Yaḥyā ibn al-Ḥusain ibn al-Muʾaiyad al Yamanī, *Jaḥjā ibn al-Ḥusain ibn al-Muʾajjad al-Jamanī's "Anbāʾ az-zaman fī Aḥbār al-Jaman"—Anfänge des Zaiditentums in Jemen* (1936).

M. Morony

[See also ᶜ**Ali Ibn Abi Ṭālib.**]

ALIMPI (died 1114), the first Russian icon painter known by name, was a monk in the Pecherskaya Lavra at Kiev during the late eleventh and early twelfth centuries. He is mentioned in the Laurentian Chronicle and in later Russian liturgical literature. Alimpi was said to be not only a painter but also a mosaicist; he supposedly created very large icons. Although no existing works can be certainly attributed to him, he may have been taught by Greek artists who came to Kiev; the large icon of the Virgin Orans (Tretyakov Gallery, Moscow; twelfth century) may reflect the influence of Alimpi or may actually be from the hand of this master.

ANN E. FARKAS

ALIXANDRE, LIBRO DE. See **Alexandre, Libro de.**

ALJAMIADO LITERATURE (from Arabic *al-ᶜajamiyya,* "non-Arabic") was written in an adaptation of the Arabic script, but in Hispanic dialects (almost always deeply impregnated with Arabisms).

The earliest examples of Arabic characters used in writing a Romance vernacular are refrains *(kharjas)* to eleventh-century Arabic strophic poems *(muwashshaḥāt)* from Spain, but the term "aljamiado literature" is usually restricted to writings produced at the end of the Middle Ages, when the system of Islamic education in Spain had broken down, so that Muslims in areas where Arabic was not spoken needed to translate their sacred texts.

A pioneer was the imam of Segovia, Içe (ᶜIsā) de Gebir (*fl.* 1454–1462), whose religious manual entitled *Brebario sunnī* ("Orthodox Breviary") or *Kitāb segobiano* ("Segovian Book") was widely read. Very few aljamiado manuscripts can be dated with certainty before Içe's work, and the early dates ascribed to the composition of some (for example, the *Poema de Yūsuf* placed by R. Menéndez Pidal in the late fourteenth or early fifteenth century) rest largely on linguistic criteria alone.

Besides all the legal and doctrinal material, there were verse and prose narratives and literature intended for entertainment; a version of the Islamic Alexander legend, the *Rrekontamiento del Rrey Ališandere;* prose as well as verse accounts of the story of Joseph; the *Libro de las batallas,* with accounts of heroic deeds in the early history of Islam; the *Historia de los amores de París y Viana* (a fragment transposed from a Christian novel of chivalry); a verse account of a pilgrimage to Mecca; and other texts. There are collections of spells, recipes for medical potions, and writings on an extensive range of topics.

Aljamiado literature continued to flourish in the sixteenth century, but was brought to an abrupt conclusion by the expulsion of the Moriscos from Spain in 1609.

BIBLIOGRAPHY

Real Academia de la Historia, Madrid, *Memorial histórico español,* V (1853), contains Içe de Gebir's *Suma de los principales mandamientos (Kitāb segobiano)*; Pablo Gil *et al., Colección de textos aljamiados* (1888), a selection of specimen texts in Arabic script; Alois R. Nykl, "El Rrekontamiento del Rrey Ališandere," in *Revue hispanique,* 77 (1929), prefaced by a useful "Compendium of Aljamiado Literature"; and Reinhold Kontzi, *Aljamiadotexte,* 2 vols. (1974), perhaps the most carefully edited texts available. Alvaro Galmés de Fuentes has edited the following volumes of the *Collección de literatura aljamiado-morisca:* I, *Historia de los amores de París y Viana* (1970); II, *El libro de las batallas* (1975); III, *Actos del coloquio internacional sobre literatura aljamiada y morisca* (1978), the last containing studies by a wide range of modern specialists and copious further references.

L. P. HARVEY

ALL SAINTS' DAY. Several anniversaries honoring the saints were celebrated in the early Church, notably 13 May and the first Sunday after Pentecost; it is not clear how 1 November became the feast of All Saints in the Western church. According to John Hennig, this day was first chosen in Ireland. Another theory has it that Pope Gregory III dedicated an oratory in St. Peter's basilica to all the apostles, martyrs, and confessors on that day and that Egbert of York, who was particularly close to Gregory, accepted that day, whence it passed into Bede's *Martyrology.*

In any event, by the end of the eighth century 1 November seems to have been well established throughout Europe as the date commemorating all the saints. Alcuin of York, a liturgical expert in Charlemagne's service, commended Archbishop Arno of Salzburg for celebrating the feast on that day; and Pope Gregory IV asked Louis the Pious to extend the feast of 1 November throughout the empire. Finally, in numerous liturgical books of the ninth century 1 November is given as the *natale omnium sanctorum.*

BIBLIOGRAPHY

John Hennig, "The Meaning of All the Saints," in *Mediaeval Studies,* 10 (1948); Karl Adam Heinrich Kellner, *Heortology* (1908), 323–326.

ROGER E. REYNOLDS

ALL SOULS' DAY. Although the Church has always encouraged prayers for the faithful departed, it was somewhat slow in instituting a specific day for commemoration. In the Spain of Isidore of Seville, Pentecost Monday was set aside for remembering the dead, and around 980 Widukind of Corvey mentions a tradition in Germany of prayer for the dead on 1 October.

But not until the Cluniac movement was in full bloom was 2 November singled out as a special day of remembrance. The choice is attributed to Odilo, abbot of Cluny, but his contemporary, Pope Sylvester II, approved of the day also, and under Bishop Notgar the feast was celebrated in the diocese of Liège.

The Cluniac feast spread gradually throughout Europe and came to involve the use of texts and formulas from the Office of the Dead, the black vestments of Good Friday, and the sequence *Dies irae.* The practice of trination, or the celebration of three masses, perhaps originated with the Dominicans in Spain in the fifteenth century.

BIBLIOGRAPHY

Karl Adam Heinrich Kellner, *Heortology* (1908), 326–328; C. A. Kneller, "Geschichtliches über die drei Messer am Allerseelentag," in *Zeitschrift für katholische Theologie,* **42** (1918).

ROGER E. REYNOLDS

[See also **Dead, Office of the.**]

ALL'ANTICA, Italian for "in the antique way." A phrase used by Italian artists, architects, and art critics of the Renaissance to describe art that consciously revived classical style and was considered superior to the Gothic and, especially, the Italo-Byzantine style *(maniera greca)* that dominated Italian art in the trecento.

LESLIE BRUBAKER

ALLAH, the Arabic word for God, used not only in the Koran and in Islamic literature but also by Christian Arabs. The term is widely held to be contracted from *al-ilāh,* "the deity," which has cognates in other Semitic languages; but the ultimate derivation is obscure. In intention Muslims are referring to the same Being as Jews and Christians, but their conception of God differs in some respects.

In pre-Islamic times many Arabs believed in Allah as a "high god" or supreme god—a form of belief widespread among Semitic peoples. Other deities, sometimes regarded as angels, were thought to be able to intercede with the "high god" on behalf of their worshippers. A number of passages in the Koran have arguments against believers in Allah as a "high god" (for instance, 10:18; 29:61–65; 39:3, 38).

The earliest passages of the Koran to be revealed emphasize God's omnipotence and beneficence. Various natural phenomena are mentioned as "signs" *(āyāt)* of God's creative power, which he exercises to promote the welfare of mankind. These signs include the light that men get from sun, moon, and stars; the creation of animals that are useful to man; the creation of man himself by stages in the womb; the rains that revive dead land; and the crops and fruits that are then produced. Since this is the nature of God, men should acknowledge the fact by worshipping him and showing gratitude.

In later passages of the Koran, the immediacy of God's creative power is emphasized by the assertion that a thing comes into being as soon as He pronounces the word "Be." "When He decrees a thing, He merely says to it 'Be,' and it is" (2:117; also see 6:73; 16:40). This corresponds to the *fiat* of creation in Genesis 1. There are also passages in which it seems to be asserted that God's power works through human activity or even overrides it. Thus it is said to those who fought at Badr, "You [Muslims] did not kill them, but God killed them, and you [Muḥammad] did not shoot [arrows] when you shot, but God shot" (8:17). With regard to believing in God and the Koran, men are told, "You will not so will unless God wills" (76:30; also see 81:29). God also is said to place a lock on men's hearts and to harden them.

These and similar verses gave rise to vigorous discussions by later theologians. Some maintained that man is essentially free in his actions, but the great majority held that God has absolute control of the course of events, so that, as later creeds put it, "What reached you could not have missed you, and what missed you could not have reached you." The acts of men were said to be created by God, but at the same time they were in some sense the men's own acts, for which they were responsible.

The Koran also teaches that God has power to restore men to life so that they can come before him on the Last Day to be judged. There is mention of a balance on which deeds are to be weighed; and this is interpreted to mean that if the good deeds outweigh the bad, the man will go to paradise (or heaven), whereas, if the bad are heavier, he will go to hell. This doctrine came to be modified by the ideas of forgiveness and intercession. Soon after Muḥammad's death, it came to be held that on the Last Day he would intercede with God on behalf of Muslims, and that all would eventually be forgiven except those who "gave partners" to God (that is, worshipped other deities).

God is also described as giving mankind revelations through prophets or "messengers" in which he communicates to them something of his nature and his commands for them. Muḥammad is regarded as following a long series of prophets that included Abraham, Moses, and Jesus, all of whom brought to their peoples revelations that were the same in essentials. Muḥammad is called "the seal of the prophets" *(khātam an-nabiyyīn)* in the Koran (33:40). Originally this probably meant that the Koran confirmed previous revelations, but it is now taken to mean that there will be no prophet after Muḥammad. God's commands to men constitute the *sharīʿa* ("revealed law"), which covers every aspect of human life. Where there is no explicit rule on some novel point, God's will may be discovered by properly qualified jurists using various forms of inference.

In the earliest passages of the Koran, there is no special emphasis on the first half of the Islamic profession of faith *(shahāda)* that "there is no deity but God"; this emphasis appeared in the course of the Meccan period of Muḥammad's activity, and then became one of the distinctive features of Islamic belief. This doctrine was originally directed against the idea of Allah as "high god" and other forms of paganism, but it was also used against Christians, in that they were regarded as saying that "God is the third of three" (5:73).

Despite the emphasis on God's uniqueness or oneness, Muslims give much attention to many attributes of God, especially in the form of his names. The suras (chapters) of the Koran begin with the formula "In the name of God, the Merciful, the Compassionate," and many verses end with such words as "and God is knowing, wise." From the Koran later Muslims collected ninety-nine "beautiful names" of God; these are associated with the Islamic chaplet or rosary, which commonly has thirty-three beads, so that three times around completes the ninety-nine names.

Some of the earlier theologians selected seven attributes for special attention: power (omnipotence), knowledge (omniscience), will, speech, hearing, seeing, life. Important schools of Sunnite theologians gave these attributes a hypostatic character; this was specially relevant in the case of the Koran, the outward expression of God's speech, which was held to be eternal and uncreated. Christian apologists took advantage of this and claimed that the three hypostases of the Trinity corresponded to three of these attributes of God.

Following the Koran, Muslims have emphasized God's transcendence and absolute difference from created things—"nothing is like Him" (42:11)—but this does not prevent the Sufis (mystics) from speaking about men being "characterized by the characters of God" *(takhalluq bi-akhlāq Allāh).*

BIBLIOGRAPHY

Charles J. Adams, "Islamic Religious Tradition," in Leonard Binder, ed., *The Study of the Middle East* (1976); Louis Gardet, *Dieu et la destinée de l'homme* (1967); Louis Gardet and M.-M. Anawati, *Introduction à la théologie musulmane* (1948); Toshihiko Izutsu, *God and Man in the Koran* (1964); Daud Rahbar, *God of Justice* (1960); W. Montgomery Watt, *What Is Islam?* (1968; repr. 1979); *The Formative Period of Islamic Thought* (1973); and "The Qur'ān and Belief in a 'High God,'" in *Der Islam,* 56 (1979); and Arent J. Wensinck, *The Muslim Creed* (1932).

W. Montgomery Watt

[See also **Islam; Muḥammad.**]

ALLEGORY. The Greek term *allegoria* compounds the bases of two words, *allos* (other) and *agoreuein* (to speak publicly—that is, to speak in the *agora,* the marketplace). Allegory is "other speech"; indeed, Latin writers sometimes translated the term as *alieniloquium.* This derivation implies that in an allegory, when a writer says one thing, he also says something other. Dante speaks of allegory as being "polysemous," of multiple meaning. In its use in literary criticism, "an allegory" indicates a narrative whose elements mean something other than what the narrative obviously narrates, and the narrative encourages interpretation in order to uncover what that other may be.

Of the many kinds of allegory, we can usefully distinguish two large classes. The sentence "Allegory took root in the early Christian era, but it flowered in the Middle Ages" points to the first class of allegory, in which the obvious statement about the early

ALLEGORY

emergence and medieval development of allegory is complicated and enriched by a parallel, "other" statement about the emergence and development of a tree. To speak of anything that has no actual roots as "taking root" is to speak metaphorically, to "translate" the attributes of one thing (tree) to another (allegory). (The Latin version of the Greek term *metaphora* is *translatio*: both mean "carry across.")

When a speaker or writer sustains such a metaphor, continues it through the discourse for a certain hard-to-define time, we begin to call it allegory. If the speaker omitted the "other"—in this example, the term "allegory"—and just told a story about a tree, referring in detail to its roots, bark, trunk, branches, leaves, nourishment, reproduction, photosynthesis, stature, uses, death in such a way that if we were stupid, we would think he merely described a tree, but that if we were discerning, we could translate all the "literal" statements about the tree into statements about allegory—then we would have (to shift the metaphor) a full-fledged allegory.

The speaker, we could say, reifies ("makes a thing of") an abstract notion, translates "allegory" into "tree." This class of allegory—reification allegory, because it merely develops a common figure of speech (metaphor)—fell into the province of the experts in figurative speech, the rhetoricians. The most important, because so often repeated, statement about reification allegory is that of Quintilian, the first-century rhetorician who wrote in his *Institutio oratoria* (8.6.44):

> Allegoria, quam inversionem interpretantur, aut aliud verbis aliud sensus ostendit aut etiam interim contrarium. Prius fit genus plerumque continuatis translationibus, ut
> O navis, referent in mare te novi
> Fluctus; o quid agis? fortiter occupa
> Portum,
> totusque ille Horatii locus, quo navem pro re publica, fluctus et tempestates pro bellis civilibus, portum pro pace atque concordia dicit.

> *Allegory,* which in Latin is *inversio,* presents in words one thing, and in sense some other thing, sometimes even a contrary thing. The first kind usually consists of continued metaphors, as
> O ship, new waves will drive you back to sea;
> O what are you doing?
> Bravely take port,
> and the rest of the passage in Horace [*Odes* 1.14], in which he speaks of a ship for the state, of waves and storms for civil wars, of port for peace and concord. [The second kind of allegory to which Quintilian refers is irony.]

A little later Quintilian says "*ἀλληγορίαν* facit continua *Μεταφορὰ*": continued metaphor makes allegory. We should remember that Quintilian had never read a prolonged, free-standing allegory, a form that emerged three centuries later. When he speaks of "continuous" or "continued" *(continua, continuata)* metaphor as making allegory, he means continuous as opposed to the usual single use of metaphor in a discourse. His words do not imply that every element in a reification allegory need be translated into the other sense.

Two equally famous statements about allegory lead us to the second class, typology. The first, from the thirteenth century or before (see de Lubac 1.1, 23–24), is this distich:

> Littera gesta docet, quid credas allegoria,
> moralis quid agas, quo tendas anagogia.

> The literal [sense] teaches the events; the allegorical, what you should believe; the moral, what you should do; the anagogical, whither you are tending.

The second statement is the fuller account from Dante's epistle to Can Grande della Scala, in which he claims that the meaning *(sensus)* of his work is not simple, but

> ymo dici potest polisemos, hoc est plurium sensuum; nam primus sensus est qui habetur per litteram, alius est qui habetur per significata per litteram. Et primus dicitur litteralis, secundus vero allegoricus sive moralis sive anagogicus. Qui modus tractandi, ut melius pateat, potest considerari in hiis versibus: "In exitu Israel de Egipto, domus Iacob de populo barbara, facta est Iudea sanctificatio eius, Israel potestas eius." Nam si ad litteram solam inspiciamus, significatur nobis exitus filiorum Israel de Egipto, tempore Moysis; si ad allegoriam, nobis significatur nostra redemptio facta per Christum; si ad moralem sensum, significatur nobis conversio anime de luctu et miseria peccati ad statum gratie; si ad anagogicum, significatur exitus anime sancte ab huius corruptionis servitute ad eterne glorie libertatem. Et quanquam isti sensus mistici variis appellentur nominibus, generaliter omnes dici possunt allegorici, cum sint a litterali sive historiali diversi. Nam allegoria dicitur ab "alleon" grece, quod in latinum dicitur "alienum," sive "diversum."

> Rather, it may be called "polysemous," that is, of many senses. A first sense derives from the letters themselves, and a second from the things signified by the letters.

We call the first the "literal" sense, the second the "allegorical" or "moral" or "anagogical." To clarify this method of treatment, consider this verse: "When Israel went out of Egypt, the house of Jacob from a barbarous people: Judea was made his sanctuary, Israel his dominion" [Psalm 113 Vulgate, Douay translation]. Now if we examine the letters alone, the exodus of the children of Israel from Egypt in the time of Moses is signified; in the allegory, our redemption accomplished through Christ; in the moral sense, the conversion of the soul from the grief and misery of sin to the state of grace; in the anagogical sense, the exodus of the holy soul from the slavery of this corruption to the freedom of eternal glory. And although these mystical senses are all called by various names, they can all be generally called allegorical, as other than the literal or historical, because the term "allegoria" derives from the Greek *alleon,* which means "other" or "diverse."

Dante and the author of the distich merely repeat a division of the various senses of allegory that originated among commentators on the Bible in the early Christian era. Their "fourfold" allegory had become traditional by the sixth century. In this division the literal or historical sense (the plain sense of the narrative) is distinguished from the "mystical" or "spiritual" or "allegorical" (other) senses: the allegorical, the moral, and the anagogical. With some medieval authority we can substitute "typological" for "allegorical" to avoid confusion with the general term for the mystical senses. Biblical exegetes also used the term "tropological" for "moral."

The three allegorical senses, then, are as follows: *typological,* which refers the narrative to the deeds and circumstances of Christ, especially by connecting Old Testament events (the Exodus) with New Testament events (the redemption of mankind); *moral* or *tropological,* which refers the narrative to the state and progress of the soul; *anagogical* ("leading up"), which refers the narrative to the final things, or the *eschaton,* and the final events of Christian history, and to cosmic circumstances: heaven, hell, judgment, apocalypse, glorification, damnation. Because these three senses connect the narrative with other events and circumstances in time—past to present, present to future, all to the time of Christ—the typological sense subsumes them.

The interpretation of allegory, "allegoresis," oddly preceded what we now think of as its full and complex flowering in the *Psychomachia* of Prudentius (*ca.* A.D. 400). The rhetoricians, following a sophistic tradition of analyzing language for the sake of political power, ranged "allegory" among the figures of speech: close to irony, on a par with epithets and periphrases. The biblical exegetes, following Jewish traditions, attempted for religious reasons to reconcile the archaic and sometimes embarrassing material in the Old Testament with the more modern sense of dignity and the overriding revelation of the New. Everywhere in the Old Testament they found types, foreshadowings, of the New: David was king like Christ; Jonah was submerged three days like Christ; the tree of knowledge adumbrated the cross; Jerusalem, the heavenly city; the lovers in the Song of Songs, the Church and Christ. Both kinds of allegories—reifications and typologies—involve transference of meaning from the plain present text, the "literal," to something other: reification tends to refer to an abstract paradigm (the nature of the universe, the creation of the state, the war within the soul), whereas typology refers to the single crucial narrative of the history of Christ.

Rhetorical analysis and biblical exegesis dominate, but they are not the only sources of allegory. An important source precedes them in time: the tradition of interpretation of mythology. The pagan gods, by a prerational identification or by metonymic association, could be taken as the things of which they were gods. If Bacchus showed the way to Venus, wine led to love. Not far removed from the allegorical use of classical deities was the personification of abstractions—Fame as a goddess, Victory as an eagle. Such uses are ancient, but may have been encouraged by Stoic rationality and a cheapening of the sense of divinity (as the Caesars were made gods).

Hence a tradition of mythography—interpretation of mythology—grew up in classical times, interpreting the gods of Homer, for instance (Athena as wisdom), and rationalizing the pantheon. The motives of early mythography resemble the motives of early typology: as the culture changed, the early narratives (Homer, the Old Testament) became irrelevant or embarrassing, and were modernized by interpretation. By the first century, poets and mythographers concurred. In the Christian era the principles of mythography developed robustly, and by the time Boccaccio set to work on his *Genealogy of the Pagan Gods* (*ca.* 1350–1370), a substantial tradition of Christian mythography sanctioned his work. Vergil's *Aeneid* and Ovid's *Metamorphoses,* textbooks throughout the Middle Ages, each sustained an elaborate tradition of allegorical interpretation.

Another tradition that influenced medieval allegory sprang from philosophical speculation. Plato's Myth of Er, which concludes the *Republic,* was the exemplar; the tradition went through Cicero's account, in his *Republic,* of the *Dream of Scipio,* and was handed on to the Middle Ages by Macrobius' *Commentary on the Dream of Scipio.* In this tradition of moral allegory, the physical structure of the universe, the relations of the starry spheres and of such cosmic forces as Necessity, Chance, Nature, Love, and Change, were brought to bear on the nature of man, on his place in the universe, and on the ultimate meaning of his conduct. Such allegories often adopted the form of visions—the Revelations that conclude the Bible are an example—and journeys to the other world. The fourth-century mythographer Sallustius typifies this philosophical allegoresis. Interpreting the myth of Kronos swallowing his children, he developed a fourfold allegory: *theologically* it represents the divine intellect returning to itself; *physically* it represents the absorption of the divisions of Time by Time itself; *psychically* it represents the Soul's retention of thoughts even though the thoughts extend to other objects; *materially* Kronos represents water.

These traditions of poetic usage and schoolish interpretation were mingled during the early Christian centuries, when rhetorical training flourished, when the classics of mythology were still the texts of school instruction, when the Stoic and Neoplatonic philosophies encouraged cosmological speculation, when the Greek and Roman pantheons of divinities retained their visible forms if not their numinous force among the learned populace, and when the new religion constructed its own typology, and vigorously assimilated or rejected pagan religion by adopting or ridiculing pagan allegoresis. Most of the overtly pagan material fell into the mode of reification allegory, yet some of the greater myths could inform Christian narrative almost as biblical typology did—such myths as those of Narcissus, Aeneas, or Orpheus.

The *Psychomachia* ("Soul-War") of the Spaniard Prudentius, written in Latin hexameters around the year 400, almost too neatly combines the various currents of allegory and allegoresis that preceded it. It is the first pure, freestanding, extensive allegory. Its plot is simple: various personified virtues—Hope, Sobriety, Chastity, Humility, and so forth—battle in matched pairs various vices—Pride, Wrath, Paganism, Avarice, and so forth. The poem is a pure reification of the *bellum intestinum.* The virtues are victorious, and at the end enter the holy city with its temple of Christ.

Prudentius had (probably) earlier written the *Hamartigenia* ("Origin of Sin"), in which personified vices wage battle. The new thing about the *Psychomachia* was the extension of the personifications' activity to the whole plot. Except for its preface (and its important title) the poem has no frame of explanation. Prudentius does include, somewhat inconsistently, human beings as part of the trappings of virtues and vices (Job accompanies Patience), and he refers occasionally to biblical persons and events, but on the whole the fiction remains an *enigma,* a "dark conceit" that could, to some theoretically ultra-naïve reader, be taken for an adventure story about some angry women. (The vices and virtues, like most personifications, are female because most Latin words for abstract concepts are of feminine gender. The effects of allegory's use of female persons on the public consciousness of women is hard to assess; in Chaucer and Spenser we find sophisticated exploitation of the matter.)

No allegory of any length is all of one kind. The simple narrative of combats in the *Psychomachia* is much enriched by two systems of typological allegory. In the first, Prudentius—like many Latin poets of that Silver Age—constantly quotes phrases and lines from Vergil, especially from the last six books, the war books, of the *Aeneid.* The siege and entry into the holy city parallel the epic actions that founded Rome, and the *Psychomachia* by verbal allusion makes itself a Christianized and interiorized *Aeneid.* In a literary culture that still took Vergil as archpoet—St. Augustine as a youth taught Vergil for a living—this redefinition of the sense of epic violence had an impact we can no longer feel. In the same generation in which Augustine contrasted Rome with *The City of God* (*ca.* 413–426), Prudentius made it a figure of the human soul.

Still more powerful is Prudentius' adoption of the large outlines of biblical typology. In the preface he tells the story of Abraham, emphasizing his military rescue of the captive Lot, and says:

> haec ad figuram praenotata est linea,
> quam nostra recto vita resculpat pede.

> This picture has been marked down beforehand as a type [*figura*] that our life should trace again with right foot [ll. 50–51].

The poet goes on to give a typological and moral interpretation of the life of Abraham as a prefiguration of Christ's salvation. The allusions throughout the poem to Old Testament figures who were already taken as traditional types of New Testament actions (the heroic Judith and the heroic Mary) reinforce the typological matrix of the poem: the war of the soul takes place in a context of Christian history. Culminating the poem, the holy city to which the victorious virtues retire, a reification of the sanctified soul, is furthermore the New Jerusalem, the heavenly city described in Revelation, the end of history. The typology of the poem concludes in anagogy, a vision of the heavenly abode of the redeemed soul.

During the same period—the turn of the fifth century—in which Prudentius and Augustine wrote, there emerged three other writers of special importance to the history of allegory: Claudian, Macrobius, and Martianus Capella. All were bookish and decadent writers from the point of view of the Golden Age of Vergil, Ovid, and Horace. All are of great importance as transmitters of mythological information and a taste for allegory to later ages. The political disintegration of the Roman Empire, which ushered in the Middle Ages, paralleled a transformation of the literary culture that made medieval allegory possible. Claudian's *In Rufinum,* an invective against the vicious Rufinus, provided the model for Alan of Lille's twelfth-century *Anticlaudianus,* an allegory of the making of a virtuous man. Claudian's unfinished *Rape of Proserpine* is full of allegorized locales, full of mythological figures and personifications of the sort that had already become traditional, and the whole text may be construed as a cosmographic allegory.

We have already mentioned Macrobius' *Commentary on the Dream of Scipio,* which was to provide the Middle Ages with a favorite allegorical topic—the journey to the spheres—and with an authoritative treatment of the nature of dreams, which influenced the idea of making allegories in the form of dream-visions. Martianus, influenced by the allegorical episode of Cupid and Psyche in Apuleius' *Metamorphoses* (late second century), wrote the *Marriage of Philology and Mercury,* a mixture of difficult Latin verse and prose in a form derived from Menippean satire; its title refers to the allegorized union of intelligent learning and the love of letters. Because it contained short treatises on the seven liberal arts—grammar, rhetoric, dialectic, geometry, arithmetic, astronomy, and music—it became a textbook, and greatly influenced later educators who compiled compendia of the arts.

Little is known about Claudian, Macrobius, and Martianus; for instance, we cannot say whether any was, even nominally, a Christian. What is certain is that all come from a schoolish culture, and all were thoroughly Latin in their education and interests. They handed down Roman rhetorical, mythological, and philological learning to the medieval schools, and with these an inclination to express learned material in allegorical form, principally by means of personification. The half-century from about 390 to 440 saw the rise of allegory as the form was known to the Middle Ages.

Boethius (*ca.* 480–524) took it upon himself to translate the works of Plato and Aristotle into Latin, but died before completing his project. He must have been conscious, as the earlier writers were not, of the cultural decline that accompanied the political turmoil of the Roman Empire (a turmoil that caused his execution). Probably his last work, *The Consolation of Philosophy,* had an enormous impact on medieval letters. It seemed to solve the problem of evil and the conflict of human free will and divine providence without specific recourse to Christian revelation. It is a learned work, full of references to pagan themes and myths, that helped to authorize the use of non-Christian culture by medieval Christians (who assumed, as modern scholarship does again, that Boethius was a Christian).

For us the chief importance of the *Consolation* is its form. A dialogue, again a mixture of prose and verse, its speakers are the imprisoned Boethius and Lady Philosophy, whom he sees in a vision. The theme of a knowledgeable woman who descends from a watchtower *(specula)* to advise a visionary poet had already become traditional—the *Shepherd of Hermas* (late first or early second century), the book of Revelation, passages in Ovid, and the *Symposium* of Methodius are forebears—and Boethius' personified Philosophy is the source of innumerable later such figures, whom the modern scholar Paul Piehler aptly calls *potentiae.* To Boethius we owe the medieval allegorists' delight in the dialogue form and their use of a visionary narrator in need of information and correction, a narrator who resembles the Socratic naïf.

The sixth to the eleventh centuries are dark from allegory's point of view. Although allegorical ways of thinking and allegorical ornament abounded in poetry and exegesis of the period, no major single allegory was composed. European literature had to undergo the development of vernacular languages and the return, with the universities, of a large and leisured class of students of the arts, to produce again sustained allegories. It is arguable that Boethius' *Consolation* is the last great work of belles lettres in Latin, at least until the Renaissance, and the techniques and resources of allegorical writing began to affect vernacular writing—primarily French—on a large scale only in the eleventh century. The progress of allegory in Latin after Boethius has never been traced; it would be a prolonged excursion in minor poetry.

But in the twelfth century there arose two Latin poets whose work, astonishingly, continues almost immediately from the sixth century, as if Neoplatonic cosmography were still a lively tradition, and as if Prudentius, Claudian, Boethius, and Martianus were of the preceding generation. These poets, Bernard Silvestris and Alan of Lille (Alanus de Insulis), drew from a revival of interest in Plato (whose *Timaeus,* and an important commentary by Calcidius, were available in Latin) and in Neoplatonic speculation on cosmology and psychology, in a movement associated with the flourishing cathedral school at Chartres, especially with the masters Thierry of Chartres and William of Conches. Their voracious interests likewise drew on the influx of speculative scientific thought pouring into Europe from the Arab world. They mixed poetry and prose after the manner of Martianus and Boethius; it is perhaps unlucky that they adopted the deliberately difficult style of Martianus, rather than Boethius' good, clear Latin. Both poets were given to encyclopedic summaries of various cosmic phenomena, and both made fundamental use of reification allegory.

Bernard wrote his *Cosmographia* (formerly called *De mundi universitate*) in or before 1147. It tells of the plea by Nature to Noys (the Greek *νοῦς*, the divine mind) that the chaotic mass Silva be shaped into a noble form. The first part, "Megacosmos," describes the creation of the universe, largely by cataloguing. The second part, "Microcosmos," comes to the creation of man (the pattern is of course that of the first chapters of the Bible), in which Nature, Urania, and Physis cooperate. Alan's *Plaint of Nature* (before 1170), a dream vision, again treats of the goddess Natura and of cosmology, now in a more satiric spirit. Natura's complaint is the imperfection of man, especially his sexual perversions (which run contrary to her design of generation) that underlie the other vices. The poem concludes with the figure of Genius, deity of procreation, excommunicating vicious man. In his *Anticlaudianus* (*ca.* 1182)—written, unlike the other works, in hexameters—Alan refers to Claudian's *In Rufinum,* the poem about a vicious man: Alan will write a poem about a virtuous man. Again in the footsteps of Bernard, Natura oversees the poem. Phronesis (Prudence), Reason, Theology, and Faith cooperate in getting a soul from God; Nature makes a body from the elements; and Concord joins body and soul. The work concludes with a little psychomachia, as the personified vices attack the virtues of the New Man, and lose. The Golden Age ensues.

These works are rightly called cosmographic epics. They are immensely learned and difficult; their influence on later allegory was to be largely at second hand (by way of Jean de Meun). But between them Bernard and Alan made possible the notion that allegorical forms, principally personification, could put into narrative the most abstruse speculation on metaphysical and scientific questions. Their spiritual successors were Dante and the Neoplatonists of the Renaissance. As the Italian humanists and their successors in the fifteenth and sixteenth centuries prepared the way for Spenser's great allegory, *The Faerie Queene,* so these French poets of the twelfth century profoundly influenced *The Romance of the Rose,* whose impact on medieval literature rivaled that of Ovid and the Bible.

The influence of Ovid, as his works were filtered through the Middle Ages, had a double effect on the rise of vernacular allegory in the eleventh and twelfth centuries. First, there was a new flurry of mythographic activity, much of it based on the *Metamorphoses,* which had become (as it remains) the standard reference book for information about classical mythology. Borrowing from the sixth-century *Mythologies* of Fulgentius and from the Vatican mythographers (so called because their three treatises are deposited in the Vatican Library), Arnulf of Orléans compiled his *Allegories on the Metamorphoses* (twelfth century), which worked through Ovid's text, summarizing it and then allegorically interpreting it. This was followed by the thirteenth-century *Integumenta Ovidii* (Ovid's Surfaces Interpreted) of John of Garland, and in the fourteenth century by the *Allegories on Ovid* of Giovanni del Virgilio, the anonymous *Ovide moralisé* in French octosyllabics, the *Fulgentius metaphoralis* of John of Ridewall, the *Ovidius moralizatus* of Pierre Bersuire, and Boccaccio's *Genealogies.* Certainly by the thirteenth century, allegorical interpretations of Ovid's myths were common knowledge among the well educated. As allegorical meanings of figures from mythology developed and spread, their use in literature by Christians grew apace, and the writers could take for granted a habit of mythographic allegoresis in their readers.

The other, more profound influence of Ovid on high medieval letters came from his love poetry—

especially the *Amores,* the *Ars amatoria,* the *Remedia amoris,* and the *Heroides.* Ovid's ways of expressing love (doubtless along with other influences; the question is controversial) deeply affected the new lyric poetry that arose in Provence during the eleventh century. This poetry, notably self-searching and interior in its focus, naturally seized on any means available of expressing complex psychological states; and it early adopted allegory, chiefly in the form of personification, to analyze the muddled emotions of loving. Personifications of these faculties (Reason, Desire, Hope) joined with a mock religion of love, which had Venus and Cupid as the principal deities. Hence reification allegories—psychological and mythographic—entered a powerful stream of literature that was new, popular, often associated with court patronage, secular, and, perhaps most important, vernacular: first Provençal, then French, Italian, German, Spanish, English. By the time of Chrétien de Troyes in the late twelfth century, the allegorical expression of the sense of love was inevitable. The new genre he begot, chivalric romance, absorbed the allegory of love at the outset; romancers easily turned to personifications when their knights turned from their violent quests to their loves.

By the 1230's, when Guillaume de Lorris wrote the first part, in French octosyllabic couplets, of *Le Roman de la Rose,* the use of allegory in secular love poetry was familiar. What was new in Guillaume's work was the persistence and extensiveness of the allegory. His work was left unfinished. What we have is a transparent allegory of an aristocratic love affair, which Guillaume wittily claims is obscure and in need of explication, in the form of a dream-vision. The dreamer enters a garden of delight, or *Deduit,* whose gatekeeper is Leisure, from which the vices of love are excluded. The vices are portrayed as a series of paintings on the garden wall—Hate, Felony, Villainy, Avarice, Envy, Old Age, and the rest, an amalgam of Christian and courtly vices.

In the garden the dreamer encounters the virtues of love—Courtesy, Beauty, Youth, Generosity, Wealth, and others—in a dance led by the God of Love. The dreamer wanders through the garden, comes to the fountain of Narcissus, sees in it two crystal stones that magically reflect the whole garden, and falls in love with a rose, the allegorical image of the lady's favor. The God of Love shoots the dreamer with his arrows—Beauty, Simplicity, Independence, Companionship, Fair Seeming—and takes the dreamer as his liegeman, enjoining him to obey the ten commandments of love and to worship in love's religion. There follows a series of dialogues between the dreamer and Fair Welcome, Haughtiness, Reason, Friend, Evil Tongue, Jealousy, and others, personified features of the progress of his suit. Guillaume's work breaks off as the rose is imprisoned by Jealousy in a castle. His fragment extends to 4,058 lines.

Here the refined sensibility and the delight in detailed exposition of aristocratic manners and love psychology reached its fruition. The dreamer lingers on rhetorically correct descriptions of the formally arranged figures he meets, and he unfolds the landscape of the garden in long catalogues of species. The garden itself was a traditional visionary setting, the classical *locus amoenus* or "pleasance," influenced by the image of the *hortus conclusus,* the "enclosed garden" of the Song of Songs. The whole world of Guillaume's poem—as dream, as traditional landscape, as rhetorical set piece, as allegory of love—constitutes a leisurely, set-apart, ideal world of aristocratic courtship. Nearly untainted by contact with reality, it is, as its chief critic (Jean de Meun) called it, a Mirror for Lovers, a cleansed and glittering image of what might be. At its heart is the fountain of Narcissus, already allegorized by the mythographers as an emblem of vanity, here the source of the self-contemplation and the somewhat morbid feelings induced by love.

Some forty years later Jean de Meun exploded Guillaume's dream. *The Romance of the Rose*, already extremely popular, was incomplete, and Jean set out to finish it. He added more than seventeen thousand lines. In his continuation Jean took each element of Guillaume's poem and, principally by magnifying it out of proportion, made it an object of humor, often of satire. He brought to bear on the tradition of love allegory the academic learning and intellectual playfulness of a Schoolman. The delicate rhetoric explodes into parodic catalogs of oxymorons and other standard conceits of love poetry; the religion of love is crushed in confrontation with Christianity and with Neoplatonic cosmography issuing from the poems of Bernard Silvestris and Alan of Lille; the dance of love and wounding of the lover burst out in a pitched psychomachia of hostile forces, personifications of the attributes and maneuvers of courtship; the Garden of Delight is set against the Fair Park, whose core is not the fountain of Narcissus but a jewel symbolizing the Trinity.

To the delicate train of virtues and vices of love Jean adds the figures Genius (universal generation), Venus (mythical and cosmic eros), and Nature, in allegories drawn directly from the twelfth-century cosmographies. He also introduces the Old Woman (prime source of Chaucer's Wife of Bath) and False Seeming (who lies behind Chaucer's Pardoner), who embody the satiric spirit alien to Guillaume. Jean's countermyth to Guillaume's Narcissus is the myth of Pygmalion, a myth that concludes not in self-indulgent death but in successful procreation. And while Guillaume's poem allegorized the courteous play of courtship, Jean rudely concludes his poem with a transparent allegory of sexual intercourse. Jean deflowers the *Rose.*

Both poets' *Romance of the Rose* was well known throughout western Europe. More than two hundred manuscripts survive; it was among the earliest vernacular works printed. Among its early effects are four. First, it stimulated the production of vernacular works in a new genre, the extended allegorical dream-vision. Second, it fostered many direct imitators, who adopted the strategy of telling of an amorous affair in an allegory based on some courtly activity. As the story of *The Romance of the Rose* itself is based on a stroll in the garden, so its successors based their plots on a game of chess, a siege, a tourney, an imprisoning, a hunt, a lawsuit. Third, by its example the *Romance* sanctioned a new collusion of the special poetics and erotic sensibility of the love poetry that arose in Provence with the encyclopedic learning, metaphysical wrestling, and moral, satiric, truth-seeking tone of academic intellectualism. It joined Provence to Paris. Finally, because of its length and breadth, it served as a *summa* of characters, strategies, devices, conceits, attitudes, and topics from which later poets could draw.

The French poets whom Chaucer knew and used—Guillaume de Machaut, Eustache Deschamps, Jean Froissart, Oton de Granson—constantly echo *The Romance of the Rose;* the poem was to them what the *Aeneid* was to Prudentius. Chaucer himself translated the *Romance* (a fragment of the translation remains), and his work everywhere shows its profound influence. When Chaucer adopts the techniques of allegory, as he does in his dream-visions and occasionally elsewhere, his attitudes and conventions can usually be traced back, directly or through the medium of Boccaccio and Dante, to *The Romance of the Rose.*

Allegory inevitably reveals itself as a literary strategy, a somewhat bookish, artificial mode of expression. This is certainly true of many allegories of love in the later Middle Ages: even the most ardent Provençal lyric, the most serious argument by a figure like Guillaume de Lorris' *Reason,* shows a gamefulness and lurking sense of the potentially comic that Jean de Meun brought into the open. But alongside this tradition, which flourished in the vernacular and remained relatively secular (for we can never entirely distinguish religious and secular poetry in the Middle Ages), there arose a more solemn tradition of allegory, again especially in France, that took up the topics of the vices and virtues, after Prudentius, and of the last things: death, judgment, heaven, and hell.

These moral and religious allegories regularly adopted the visionary mode, and often took the form of a journey, a *voie,* to some otherworldly place, paradise or hell. They joined the reification techniques of the *Psychomachia* with the old tradition of the journey to the otherworld, a tradition loosely associated with the "Scipio vision" literature emerging from Plato's Myth of Er. The Christian versions probably originated in apocryphal New Testament writings: the Revelation of Peter (perhaps second century), the Gospel of Nicodemus (fourth and fifth centuries), and especially the Vision of St. Paul, which was translated into Latin in the eighth century. These influenced the widely popular Irish visions of hell, the *Voyage of St. Brendan* (perhaps tenth century), the *Vision of Tundal* (after 1148), and *St. Patrick's Purgatory* (late twelfth century).

The joining of the plot of these *voies* to personification allegory, so that the pilgrim visioner sees in hell or paradise such things as the River of Gluttony or a banquet of allegorical foods, was made early in the thirteenth century in Raoul de Houdenc's *Songe d'enfer* (Dream of Hell). In this tradition follow, for example, Jehan de le Mote's *Voie d'enfer et de paradis,* Rutebeuf's *Voie de paradis,* Guillaume de Deguileville's *Pilgrimage of Human Life, Pilgrimage of the Soul,* and *Pilgrimage of Jesus Christ* (mid fourteenth century), and John Bunyan's *Pilgrim's Progress* three centuries later. The overtly moralizing, rather homiletic cast of these allegories naturally associates them with clericalism and satire. Their formal concern with the last things connects them with the anagogical sense of biblical allegoresis, and because their action recapitulates the type of Christ's harrowing of hell, they augment personification allegory with typology. Other plots inform these moralizing allegories, notably the psychomachian siege and battle, as in *The Tournament of Antichrist.*

The two traditions here surveyed can be only roughly defined, since they interact with each other and each tradition is composed of uniquely variant poems. The one, whose great example is *The Ro-*

mance of the Rose, makes persistent use of figures from classical mythology, wittily focuses on the subject of love, and adopts the dream-vision form and the mode of reification allegory. The other, the great example of which is of course Dante's *Divine Comedy,* develops especially out of the Christian apocrypha; solemnly focuses on moral obligations, usually in terms of personified vices and virtues (Dante recasts the personifications into the soul of dead persons); and adopts the dream-vision form and the mode of typological allegory.

Only four allegories besides *The Romance of the Rose* deserve to be called great. *The Faerie Queene* belongs to the Renaissance; the other three are all of the fourteenth century: the *Divine Comedy,* William Langland's *Piers Plowman,* and the anonymous English poem *The Pearl.* From the point of view of the traditions we have surveyed, *Piers Plowman* is the most conservative of these. It mixes an encyclopedic array of allegorical devices and topics—dream-vision, pilgrimage and *voie,* personification, satire (including satire on the social estates), the allegorical banquet, psychomachia, vices and virtues, the *potentia* addressing the naïf dreamer from her *specula,* a disruptive figure (the liar or *mendax*) often found in allegories that point toward the apocalypse, even a variant (in the Tree of Charity episode) of the enclosed garden. More than any other allegory, except perhaps for the somewhat tedious work of Guillaume de Deguileville, it makes use of specific commonplaces of biblical exegesis—for instance, the notion that Abraham represents Faith. But underlying its sometimes confusing spray of knotty dialogues, abrupt transitions, dreamlike locales, and baroque figures is a typological structure that holds the poem together: the dreamer's progress recapitulates the progress of biblical history from Fall to Apocalypse. In many ways *Piers Plowman* is the chief precursor of the most original development of allegory in the fifteenth century, the morality plays like *The Castle of Perseverance* and *Everyman,* which likewise project a scheme of human weakness, in the form of personifications, against a background of divine providence expressed in the more historical, time-full form of typology.

The Pearl is just as firmly based on a typological view of history. Its whole plot constitutes an anagogical allegory, in which a translated soul, the *potentia,* the pearly maiden, introduces the dreamer to the heavenly Jerusalem. Where *Piers* attempts to assess the meaning of human society and individual vice against the truth of Christianity, *The Pearl* focuses, with amazing poetic virtuosity, on the single issue of the meaning of death. It is a religious and beautiful response to Boethius' *Consolation of Philosophy.*

In his *Divine Comedy,* the finest product of the Middle Ages, Dante so perfectly integrated the allegorical mode with the whole design that it scarcely seems to be allegory: the literal sense and the "other" sense are hard to distinguish. His own account of the four senses aptly describes the way the poem means: literally it tells of Dante's vision, and in this case the literal story is also the anagogical level, because his vision is of the afterlife. The moral sense is the purification of the moral state of the people Dante encounters—the stripping away in death of everything accidental, nonmoral, about them, so that their place perfectly defines their being. Because Dante reenacts in himself the moral ascents and descents he makes, the external plot is an allegory of internal changes in him (and, if the art has its effect, in us). The typological sense is Dante's imitation of all the great quests, especially (as he hints when he says that he is not Aeneas, not St. Paul) the descent to the underworld of Aeneas, the classical type of Christ's harrowing of hell, and the visionary ascent to the spheres of St. Paul, in imitation of Christ's ascension.

Dante's choice of a subject matter, a pilgrim's vision of the places of the afterlife, of course draws on the tradition of the *voies* of hell and paradise, but he was the first to see how intricately the relationships of typological allegory could be knotted. Each of the four traditional senses is the basis for all the others: for instance, the anagogy (the vision of the afterlife) obviously coincides with the literal sense, but it is also the typology (as Dante imitates in vision what Christ did); the moral sense (the whirlwind of desire) is the literal sense (Dante sees the whirlwind; hell really is this way). Dante saw through what allegory could do, and realized its full potential as an instrument of discovery and of intellectual liberation.

BIBLIOGRAPHY

Texts (in the order quoted). Quintilian, *Institutio oratoria,* H. E. Butler, ed., 4 vols. (1920–1922); the distich on the four senses, Henri de Lubac, *Exégèse médiévale: Les quatre sens de l'Ecriture,* 4 vols. in 2 pts. (1959–1964); Dante's epistle to Can Grande is quoted in Robert Hollander, *Allegory in Dante's "Commedia"* (1969), p. 45, n.; Prudentius, *Psychomachia,* H. J. Thomson, ed. (1949).

Editions of texts (in the order cited). Giovanni Boccaccio, *Genealogie deorum gentilium libri,* V. Romano, ed. (1951); Sallustius, *Concerning the Gods and the Universe,*

A. D. Nock, ed. and trans. (1926); Prudentius, *Hamartigenia,* H. J. Thomson ed. and trans. (1949, 1953); Claudian, *In Rufinum* and *De raptu Proserpinae,* M. Platnauer, ed. (1922); Macrobius, *Commentarii in somnium Scipionis,* J. Willis, ed. (1963, 1970), trans. by W. Stahl as *Commentary on the Dream of Scipio* (1952); Apuleius, *Metamorphoses,* S. Gaselee, ed. (1915); Martianus Capella, *De nuptiis philologiae et Mercurii et de septem artibus liberalibus,* Adolph Dick, ed. (1925); Boethius, *De consolatione philosophiae,* H. F. Stewart and E. K. Rand, eds. (1926); *Shepherd of Hermas,* K. Lake, ed. (1919); Methodius, *Symposium,* H. Musurillo, ed. (1963); Bernard Silvestris, *Cosmographia,* C. S. Barach and J. Wrobel, eds. (1876), trans. into English by W. Wetherbee (1973); Alain de Lille, *De planctu naturae,* N. M. Häring, ed., in *Studi medievali,* 3rd ser., **19** (1978), also trans. into English by J. J. Sheridan (1980); and *Anticlaudianus,* R. Bossuat, ed. (1955), trans. into English by J. J. Sheridan (1973); Fulgentius, *Mitologie,* R. Helm, ed. (1898).

Vatican mythographers, *Scriptores rerum mythicarum Latini tres Romae nuper reperti,* G. H. Bode, ed. (1834); Arnulf of Orléans, *Allegoriae super Ovidii Metamorphosin,* F. Ghisalberti, ed., in *Memorie del Reale Instituto Lombardo di Scienze e Lettere,* **24,** no. 4 (1932); John of Garland, *Integumenta super Ovidium Metamorphoseos,* F. Ghisalberti, ed. (1933); Giovanni del Virgilio, *Allegorie librorum Ovidii,* F. Ghisalberti, ed., in *Giornale Dantesca,* **34** n.s. **4** (1933); *Ovide moralisé,* C. de Boer et al., eds., in *Verhandelingen der Koninklijke Akademie van Wetenschappen: Afdeeling Letterkunde,* n.s. **15** (1915), **21** (1920), **30** (1931), **37** (1936), **43** (1948); John of Ridewall, *Fulgentius metaforalis,* Hans Liebeschütz, ed. (1926); Pierre Bersuire (Petrus Berchorius), *Ovidius Moralizatus,* J. Engels, ed. (1962); fully printed by Badius Ascensius, Paris, 1509, and later Renaissance printings; Guillaume de Lorris and Jean de Meung, *Le roman de la rose,* E. Langlois, ed., 5 vols. (1914–1924), and F. Lecoy, 3 vols. (1966–1970), also trans. into English by H. W. Robbins (1962) and by C. Dahlberg (1971).

Revelation of Peter, trans. by M. R. James in *The Apocryphal New Testament* (1924), 504–521; *Gospel of Nicodemus,* C. Tischendorf, ed., in *Evangelia apocrypha* (1853), trans. by M. R. James in *The Apochryphal New Testament* (1924), 117–146; *Visio Sancti Pauli,* H. Brandes, ed. (1885), and H. T. Silverstein, ed. (1935); *Navigatio Sancti Brendani,* C. Selmer, ed. (1959); *Visio Tnugdali,* A. Wagner, ed. (1882); *St. Patrick's Purgatory, Tractatus,* K. Warnke, ed., (1938); Raoul de Houdenc, *Le songe d'enfer suivi de la voie de paradis,* P. Lebesgue, ed. (1908); Jehan de le Mote, *La voie d'enfer et de paradis,* Sister M. E. Pety, ed. (1940); Rutebeuf, *Oeuvres complètes,* E. Faral and J. Bastin, eds. (1960); Guillaume de Deguileville, *Le pélegrinage de l'âme,* J. J. Stürzinger, ed. (1895); G. Wimmer, ed., *Le tournoiement de l'antécrist* (1888); William Langland, *Piers Plowman,* B-Text ed. by A. V. C. Schmidt (1978), and C-Text ed. by D. Pearsall (1979); *The Pearl,* E. V. Gordon, ed. (1953); *The Castle of Perseverance,* in *The Macro Plays,* **3,** F. J. Furnivall and A. W. Pollard, eds. (1914); *Everyman,* A. C. Cawley, ed. (1961).

General books on allegory. C. S. Lewis, *The Allegory of Love* (1936); John MacQueen, *Allegory* (1970); Paul Piehler, *The Visionary Landscape* (1971); Angus Fletcher, *Allegory: The Theory of a Symbolic Mode* (1964); Stephen A. Barney, *Allegories of History, Allegories of Love* (1979); Maureen Quilligan, *The Language of Allegory* (1979); Rosemond Tuve, *Allegorical Imagery* (1966); A. D. Nuttall, *Two Concepts of Allegory* (1967); Gay Clifford, *The Transformations of Allegory* (1974); Edwin Honig, *Dark Conceit* (1959).

Typology. Alan C. Charity, *Events and Their Afterlife* (1966); Jean Daniélou, *Sacramentum futuri* (1950), trans. into English by D. W. Hubbard (1961); Robert M. Grant, *The Letter and the Spirit* (1957); G. W. H. Lampe and K. J. Woollcombe, *Essays on Typology* (1957).

Early allegoresis. Johan Chydenius, *The Theory of Medieval Symbolism* (1960); Erich Auerbach, "Figura," trans. by Ralph Mannheim in *Scenes from the Drama of European Literature* (1959); Isaak Heinemann, *Altjüdische Allegoristik* (1935); Harry A. Wolfson, *The Philosophy of the Church Fathers,* I (1956; 3rd ed., rev., 1970), esp. chs. 2 and 3, an excellent survey of allegoresis in the Church fathers; Joseph Bonsirven, *Exégèse rabbinique et exégèse paulinienne* (1939); R. P. C. Hanson, *Allegory and Event* (1959); Beryl Smalley, *The Study of the Bible in the Middle Ages* (1952).

Mythography. Don Cameron Allen, *Mysteriously Meant: The Rediscovery of Pagan Symbolism and Allegorical Interpretation in the Renaissance* (1970); F. Wehrli, *Zur Geschichte der allegorischen Deutung Homers in Altertum* (1928); Jean Seznec, *The Survival of the Pagan Gods,* B. F. Sessions, trans. (1953; 1972); Jean Pépin, *Mythe et allégorie* (Paris, 1958).

Full-length studies of individual works. Only recent studies are included; see their bibliographies. For current bibliography consult the *MLA Bibliography,* issued annually. *Psychomachia:* Macklin Smith, *Prudentius' "Psychomachia": A Reexamination* (1976); Reinhart Herzog, *Die allegorische Dichtkunst des Prudentius* (1966); Christian Schwen, *Virgil bei Prudentius* (1937). Bernard Silvestris: Winthrop Wetherbee, *Platonism and Poetry in the Twelfth Century* (1972); Brian Stock, *Myth and Science in the Twelfth Century* (1972); Peter Dronke, *Fabula: Explorations into the Uses of Myth in Medieval Platonism* (Leiden, 1974). *Le Roman de la Rose:* Alan M. F. Gunn, *The Mirror of Love* (1952); Marc-René Jung, *Études sur le poème allégorique en France au moyen âge* (1971); H. R. Jauss and Uda Ebel, *La littérature didactique, allégorique, et satirique* (1968), with excellent bibliography (1970); John V. Fleming, *The "Roman de la Rose": A Study in Allegory and Iconography* (1969). *Piers Plowman:* Morton W. Bloomfield, *"Piers Plowman" as a Fourteenth-Century Apocalypse* (1961); Durant W. Robertson, Jr., and Bernard F. Huppé, *"Piers Plowman" and Scriptural Tradition* (1951; 1970); Robert W. Frank, Jr., *"Piers Plowman" and the Scheme of Salvation* (1957; repr. 1969); Elizabeth D. Kirk, *The Dream Thought of "Piers Plowman"* (1972); Mary Carruthers, *The Search for St. Truth* (1973). *The Pearl:* Ian Bishop, *Pearl in its Setting* (1968); Patricia M. Kean, *The Pearl: An Interpretation* (1967). On *voies* see D. D. R. Owen, *The Vision of Hell* (1970).

Spenserians who present important materials on medieval allegory are Harry Berger, Jr., *The Allegorical Temper* (1967); and James Norhnberg, *The Analogy of "The Faerie Queene"* (1976).

STEPHEN A. BARNEY

[See also **Alan of Lille; Boethius; Dante; Exegesis; Jean de Meun; Langland, William; Macrobius; Martianus Capella; Ovid in the Middle Ages; Pearl, The; Plato in the Middle Ages; Prudentius; Rhetoric (Western Europe); Romance of the Rose; Visions, Literary Form.**]

ALLEGORY, FRENCH. Allegory, deriving from the Greek *allegoria* (ἀλληγορία, the uttering of something otherwise), represents abstract ideas by symbolic means in what is, in effect, extended metaphor. The term is used also for a work that employs the allegorical method. Obvious analogies may be seen between allegory, parable, and fable. Each genre exploits implied comparison, usually for didactic purposes, and each necessitates the simultaneous appreciation of a surface representation and its signification. The form of allegory, however, is less fixed than that of the parable or fable. It employs either prose or verse or a mixture of both, and may be found also in the various manifestations of medieval art.

Allegory was not an invention of the Middle Ages. Hindu and Buddhist scriptures, Persian and Arabian legend, Jewish, Greek, and Roman sources all contributed precedents and themes. However, allegory became a favored didactic medium from the time of the early Christian apologists: Jerome and Augustine both made allegorical interpretations of Scripture, and Augustine maintained that a hidden meaning was to be found there in everything not directly concerned with faith and morals. Isidore of Seville in his scriptural handbook *Allegoriae* catalogued the main allegories that had been uncovered in the Old and New Testaments.

The *Psychomachia* (Battle of the Soul) of the fourth-century poet Prudentius pitted the Seven Deadly Sins against the Seven Virtues. Martianus Capella's *De nuptiis Philologiae et Mercurii,* written *ca.* 400, made an impressive assemblage of allegorical figures and their attributes for the wedding of Philology to Mercury. The sixth-century statesman and scholar Cassiodorus in his *De artibus ac disciplinis liberalium litterarum* identified those grammatical and rhetorical figures (including allegory) that were common to Scripture and antiquity. In Boethius' early sixth-century *De consolatione philosophiae,* Philosophy, clothed in a robe featuring Praxis and Theoria, brought consolation to the imprisoned philosopher.

Boethius provided much of the inspiration for the twelfth-century *Liber de planctu naturae* by Alan of Lille. Nature there appeared to the Poet to discuss her work in comparison with God's. Not only did Alan personify such abstractions as Nature, Genius, and Chastity, but he also borrowed antiquity's heroes to serve as the quintessence of such ideas as strength (Hercules), cunning (Ulysses), and eloquence (Cicero). Nature was again portrayed in Alan's *Anticlaudianus* as she planned, with the help of her heavenly sisters Concord, Abundance, Favor, Youth, Laughter, Modesty, Discretion, Reason, Chastity, Adornment, Prudence, Piety, Faith, Liberality, and Nobility to create a perfect man. Nature's House and Wisdom's Chariot allowed further didactic complexities as the sum of their various symbols was brought together into composite allegorical figures.

Allegorical works in the vernacular were many and varied. Some, like Jean de Meun's prose translation of Boethius' *De consolatione philosophiae* and Philippe de Thaon's early twelfth-century *Bestiaire* (from the fourth-century Latin translation of the second-century Alexandrian *Physiologus*), derived directly from Latin sources. In this category were the bestiaries, herbals, lapidaries, and other learned treatises that incorporated allegorical commentaries into their enumeration of the properties of things.

Some didactic allegories in the vernacular owed a less direct debt to Latin. Jean le Teinturier's *Mariage des sept arts* imitated Martianus Capella's *De nuptiis Philologiae et Mercurii;* Guillaume de Normandie's *Bestiaire divin* borrowed from the *Liber de bestiis et aliis rebus* (probably written by Hugh of St. Victor), and Richard de Fournival adapted the bestiary to new purposes in his erotic treatise *Bestiaire d'amour.* Huon de Méri's *Tournoiement de l'Antéchrist* was inspired by Prudentius' battle between the vices and the virtues.

Even more distinctive were those works that used allegory for chivalric literature. In the late twelfth-century *Roman des eles* by Raoul de Houdenc the two wings of Prowess, Generosity, and Courtliness each comprised seven wondrous feathers representing various abstractions of chivalry. In the anonymous poem *Ordene de chevalerie,* Hue de Tabaire, while imprisoned by the sultan, listed for him the symbolic ceremonial that made a Christian knight. The late thirteenth- or early fourteenth-century *Songe du castel* portrayed Man as a castle besieged by the Seven Deadly Sins and eventually overcome by Death as the World looked on.

The most influential allegory of the French Middle Ages was the *Roman de la Rose.* A substantial tradition of love allegory preceded it. Ovid had been imitated or translated many times: Andreas Capellanus' *De arte honeste amandi* (between 1174 and 1186), Jacques d'Amiens's *Art d'amour* and *Remedes d'amour,* and Drouart La Vache's *Livre d'amours* (1290) all derived from Ovid. The anonymous *Clef d'amour,* which rejuvenated Ovid's treatise by contemporary allusions, may also have been written by the time Guillaume de Loris began to write—thus providing him with an Ovidian climate. Just as important was the composite tradition of love personification that had been built up by the Provençal troubadour lyric, Chrétien de Troyes's romances, and Gautier d'Arras (for example, in *Ille et Galeron,* written between 1167 and 1170).

Sometime between 1225 and 1237 Guillaume de Lorris composed the 4,058 octosyllabic lines that constitute the first part of the *Roman de la Rose.* The narration of the Rose's conquest begins with a dream that the Poet had five years before: he followed a river to Love's garden *(Le Jardin de Déduit),* which was protected from the outside world by battlements picturing the enemies of Love—among them Avarice, Envy, Poverty, Old Age, and Hypocrisy. Inside the garden the Poet was struck by Love's arrow, and thereafter his symbolic quest for the Rose was alternately aided or thwarted by such various qualities as Fair Welcome, Shame, Pity, or Danger. The first part breaks off before this symbolic representation of new love is complete.

Some forty years later Jean de Meun composed the second part of the *Roman de la Rose* (17,722 lines). Jean adapted Guillaume's narrative to different purpose by his predilection for learned digressions of encyclopedic range. Such abstractions as Nature, Genius, and Reason assumed greater importance at the expense of Guillaume's delicate analysis of the psychology of love. Jean's learned sources included all the classical writers, Alan of Lille, Boethius, and William of St. Amour, among others. The *Roman de la Rose* survives in about 300 manuscripts. It had many imitators, as allegory continued to be a favored vehicle for didacticism.

Social comment was made through the allegorical horse in Gervais du Bus's *Roman de Fauvel* (Book I, 1310; Book II, 1314) whose name is an acronym derived from Flaterie, Avarice, Vilenie, Variété, Envie, and Lâcheté. Eustache Deschamps' *Miroir de mariage* satirized conjugal delights through Franc Vouloir, whose false friends Desire, Folly, Servitude, and Deceit urged him to marry. The *Livre du roy Modus et de la royne Ratio,* probably by Henri de Ferrières, gave instruction in the art of hunting through the allegorical Modus and Ratio. Moral didacticism dominated Guillaume de Deguilleville's *Pèlerinages* (written between 1330 and 1358) and the fourteenth-century *Ovide moralisé,* an amalgam of Ovid's *Metamorphoses* and theological commentary.

In the later Middle Ages allegory remained a favorite medium of three major authors, Guillaume de Machaut, Christine de Pisan, and Alain Chartier. The particular influence of the *Roman de la Rose* was further revealed by the sustained polemic of the well-known "Querelle du *Roman de la Rose.*" Allegory's schematic ordering of the complexities of human existence had been congruent with the Scholastic climate of the Middle Ages, but the allegorical mode continued to thrive in the sixteenth century and even later.

BIBLIOGRAPHY

William Calin, *A Poet at the Fountain* (1974); Alan M. F. Gunn, *The Mirror of Love* (1952); C. S. Lewis, *The Allegory of Love* (1958); Charles Muscatine, "The Emergence of Psychological Allegory in Old French Romance," in *PMLA,* **68** (1953); Henry Osborn Taylor, *The Mediaeval Mind,* 4th ed. (1925, repr. 1966).

JEANETTE M. A. BEER

[See also **French Literature.**]

ALLELENGYON. A tax that represented an extension and variation of late Roman practices, the *allelengyon* originated in the early ninth century when Emperor Nicephorus I (802–811) ordered landowners to be responsible for the full payment of the taxes owed by their poorer neighbors who were unable to pay. In 996, Basil II issued a *novella* that revised the tax: it was now to be paid by the large landowners, since farmers often fled because they could not pay these taxes. The *allelengyon* aroused a great deal of opposition among the magnates and had fallen into disuse by the time of its repeal by Emperor Romanus III (1028–1034).

BIBLIOGRAPHY

George Ostrogorsky, *History of the Byzantine State,* Joan Hussey, trans. (1957; 1969).

LINDA ROSE

ALLELUIA. See **Eucharist.**

ALLOD (Latin *alodis,* after eleventh-century *allodium*), a word of Frankish origin, used in the *Lex salica* to describe personal property (movable property) as distinguished from real property (land or other property in which the owner's family had an interest). In the *Formulary of Marculf* the word is applied as well to real property, and in this sense it finds its primary usage from the middle of the seventh century.

An allod is property or the right to that property over which there is no right of lordship other than that of the immediate possessor. It could take the form of a parcel of land or a collection of rights or dues accruing from a lordship or a possession. The allodialist had an absolute right in law to dispose of his alod in any way he wished. In practice, as with every other right in medieval times, the allodialist was constrained to recognize the interests of others in his property, such as his family or kin group, neighbors, or tenants. Most allods were small peasant holdings, encompassing a dwelling and kitchen garden, but some were quite large, especially in Germany.

The origins of the allod are uncertain, and references to them before 1100 are rare. Characterized by independence from external lordship and supported by the widely recognized right of alienation at will, the allod has roots that reach back to the Merovingian settlement of Gaul.

Small peasant allods were found throughout western Europe with the exception of England, where the allod was unknown. Allodial tenure was more common in those areas that were less subject to feudalism or where geographical or military considerations encouraged isolation and the need for independent action. These areas included the Mediterranean littoral of France and its river valleys, the great marches lordships in Spain and Germany, the kingdom of Arles, and the duchies of Aquitaine and Burgundy.

After 1100 the allod declined in number and significance in the legal and economic life of Europe. Subject to disintegration through the effects of partible inheritance, prey to the encroachments and economic competition of larger neighboring lordships, the allodialist was under constant pressure to translate his freehold into a dependent tenure.

BIBLIOGRAPHY

There is no useful general discussion of the allod; the following bibliography is intended only to introduce a difficult subject to the interested student. Marc Bloch, *Feudal Society,* 2 vols. (1964); Georges Duby, *La société aux XIe et XIIe siècles dans la région mâconnaise* (1953); *Rural Economy and Country Life in the Medieval West* (1968); *The Early Growth of the European Economy: Warriors and Peasants from the Seventh to the Twelfth Century* (1974).

MICHAEL J. HODDER

[See also **Land Tenure, Western Europe.**]

ALMOGÁVARES, a term thought to derive from the Arabic *al-Mughāwir* (raider). Bernat Desclot (*fl.* 1300), a Catalan chronicler, thought they were Catalans, Aragonese, and Saracens (probably Mozarabs). The Almogávares, according to Desclot, shunned the cities, preferring to live in the mountains and forests. They hired themselves as professional soldiers, serving primarily as light infantry but also as cavalry. Almost Spartan in dress and physical endurance, they were armed with two or three javelins which they hurled at the enemy, and a sword for combat at close quarters.

Almogávares were among the Catalan and Aragonese armies that accompanied Jaime I (1213–1276) in his conquest of Valencia. They are also mentioned in the legal code of Alfonso X of Castile and León (1252–1284), the *Siete partidas,* and appeared prominently among the armies harassing the French after Philip III's invasion of Aragon in 1284. The Almogávares are better known, however, for their feats of arms and unruly behavior in Sicily and, above all, in the East during the fourteenth century.

In 1303, after their campaigns in Sicily were over, one of the Almogávares' captains, Roger de Flor

ALMOHAD ART

from Sicily, entered the service of the Byzantine emperor Andronicus II. Joined by Catalan and Aragonese noblemen, some 4,500 Almogávares sailed east to fight the Turks. Their campaigns in Asia Minor, which proved to be successful but were marked by many excesses and cruelties, have been described with vivid and at times exaggerated detail by the Catalan chronicler Ramón de Muntaner, an eyewitness and participant.

The Almogávares did not take very long to develop ambitions of their own. Roger de Flor demanded and received concessions that were onerous to the Byzantine emperor: the title of caesar, a large fief in Asia Minor, and extensive rights in the lands to be conquered from the Turks. Led by Michael IX Paleologus, son of Andronicus II, the Byzantines soon claimed their revenge. Roger de Flor and 130 of his men were assassinated in 1306 by order of the emperor's son, and this was followed by the Catalans' swift and brutal revenge.

The Almogávares found a new leader in Berenguer de Entenza and in the early 1300's served, in succession, Charles of Valois; John II, lord of Thessaly; and Walter of Brienne. As hired mercenaries they played an important role in the complex political world of Byzantium and Asia Minor, a history punctuated by switching alliances, betrayals, and heroic feats of arms. In 1311, this time fighting for their own interests, the Almogávares defeated the Byzantines at the battle of Cephissus, near Lake Copais, Boeotia, and shortly afterward established their rule in the duchy of Athens. They made the duchy an outpost of Catalan culture and commercial interests in the East. Catalan became the official language, and the ancient medieval law code of Barcelona, the *Usatges,* became the law of the land. The Almogávares held the duchy of Athens until 1380, when it reverted to the crown of Aragon before finally passing to Florentine hands eight years later.

BIBLIOGRAPHY

Kenneth M. Setton, *Catalan Domination of Athens, 1311–1388,* rev. ed. (1975); Fernando Soldevila Zubiburu, *Els almogàvers* (1952).

TEOFILO F. RUIZ

ALMOHAD ART. The Almohads were the artistic as well as the political heirs of the Almoravids. The fundamentally puritanical character of their religious reform can also be perceived in the art of the period, especially in the architecture of the mosques, although in the decoration it is somewhat softened by the predominant role that Andalusian and Andalusian-influenced workshops continued to play. As with Almoravid art, the preeminent form of Almohad art is architecture, and the most important innovations are to be found in the mosques.

Mosque Typology. Three works within the artistic orbit of the capital Marrakech summarize all the characteristic features of the classic Almohad type: the so-called first Kutubīya Mosque, probably built immediately after the city was conquered (1146); the memorial mosque erected for the founder of the movement, Ibn Tūmārt, in the locality where he worked and died, the village of Tinmal in the Atlas Mountains (1153–1154); and the so-called second Kutubīya Mosque, placed at an oblique angle against the first structure, the schema of which it copies almost exactly. The pier mosque with longitudinal aisles, a type already developed in the Almoravid period (for example, at Algiers, around 1097), was purified and enriched, especially in the *qibla* zone. The longitudinal arcades of the normal aisles end at the transverse arcade in front of the *qibla* (as was already the case in the Aghlabid rebuilding of the Great Mosque of Qairawān, around 836). A wider nave and a *qibla* transept gave rise to the characteristic T-shaped plan familiar from the Great Mosques of Qairawān and Córdoba. With the lengthening of the nave and of the outermost aisle of each group of four side aisles appear compartments vaulted with *muqarnas* cupolas which serve to accentuate the *qibla* transept. In elevation, the hierarchy of arches found in prototypical form among the Almoravids is perfected and canonized: pointed horseshoe arches for the arcades of the normal aisles, arches with plain pendants or with real *muqarnas* around the cupola compartments, and polylobed arches in the other bays of the transept arcade. The great seventeen-aisle-type of the Kutubīya Mosque was repeated in the new Great Mosque of Seville (around 1175), on the site on which the cathedral was later erected. Its famous tower (the Giralda), closely related to both of the Almohads' great Moroccan minarets (at the second Kutubīya Mosque in Marrakech and the Ḥassān Mosque in Rabat) is conserved, transformed into a campanile.

The Casbah Mosque in Marrakech (around 1185–1190), with its unusual group of four-sided courts, which are separated from the main court only by ar-

Second Kutubīya Mosque, Marrakech (*ca.* 1150). Prayer hall (*left*) and the *qibla* transept arcade (*right*). PHOTO DEUTSCHES ARCHÄOLOGISCHES INSTITUT, MADRID, WISSHAK

Gate of the Casbah of Udaya, Rabat (*ca.* 1195). PHOTO DEUTSCHES ARCHÄOLOGISCHES INSTITUT, MADRID, WISSHAK

cades, and the uncompleted, twenty-one-aisle Ḥassān Mosque in Rabat (around 1195) are special types without successors. On the other hand, the classic type survived even among the Merinids, and the Saᶜdites revived it in an exact, restorative manner (al-Muwassīn Mosque in Marrakech, 1562–1573).

Secular Architecture. In this domain, the monumental character of Almohad art is most clearly reflected in the richly decorated gates of the newly founded city of Rabat (around 1195). The Bāb ar-Ruwāḥ and the gate of the Casbah of Ūdāya transform a fortified type ("porte à chicane") into wide-hall-structures.

Decoration. The prayer hall, especially, deviates from the established Islamic ideal of densely applied, intricate decoration. Adornment is concentrated on essential points, and a graduation, a real hierarchy is worked out, culminating in the prayer niche, the *miḥrāb.* The decorated surfaces evoke a feeling of purification. Bands of geometric patterns, which are often very broad, accentuate essential structural members. They appear, for example, as borders on the *miḥrāb* facades and as crowning friezes under the visible roof structure, the beams of which repeat the motif of interlacing geometric bands.

In a singularly contrasting manner, however, tectonic members are also dissolved into vegetable forms: the development of the foliated arch terminated in a series of half palmettes growing into and around each other. This motif receives its most monumental treatment in the broad, reticular surfaces which henceforth cover West Islamic minarets (for example, the Giralda in Seville).

Not only is the background of geometric and vegetable patterns made flat; their surfaces are treated in the same fashion. The smooth fillet band is typical, as is the use of a smooth or only slightly crenate leaf instead of a pinnate leaf. This is perhaps the first time in Islamic art that decoration and smooth background are balanced against each other. The monoplanar sgraffito patterns represent the extreme limit of this tendency toward simplified decoration.

BIBLIOGRAPHY

H. Basset and H. Terrasse, *Sanctuaires et forteresses almohades* (1932); C. Ewert and J. P. Wisshak, *Forschungen zur almohadischen Moschee.* I, *Hierarchische Gliederungen westislamischer Betsäle des 8. bis 11. Jahrhunderts: Die Hauptmoscheen von Qairawān und Córdoba und ihr Bannkreis* (1981); L. Golvin, *Essai sur l'architecture religieuse musulmane,* IV (1979), 243–296; G. Marçais, *L'architecture musulmane d'occident. Tunisie, Algérie, Maroc et Sicile* (1954), 200–212; H. Terrasse, *L'art hispano-mauresque des origines au XIIIᵉ siècle* (1932), 249–395; L. Torres Balbás, *Arte almohade. Arte nazari. Arte mudéjar,* Ars Hispaniae, IV (1949), 9–70; and *Artes almorávide y almohade* (1955).

CHRISTIAN EWERT

ALMOHADS (al-Muwaḥḥidūn, "those who proclaim the Oneness of God") originated in the High Atlas Mountains of Morocco as a religious community opposed to the regime of the Almoravids at Marrakech. They were founded by Muḥammad ibn Tūmart, a native of the Sūs, to the south of the mountains. He had been educated in the Middle East, and returned to the Maghrib sometime between 1117 and 1121, preaching against immorality and teaching a return to the scriptural "roots" of the Islamic law. This was in conformity with the ideas put forward by al-Ghazālī in Iraq, but in opposition to the jurisprudence of the Maliki school upheld by the Almoravids, which concerned itself exclusively with the "branches" or traditional interpretations of the law. Among the Berber peoples of southern Morocco, Ibn Tūmart went further, assuming the role of Mahdi, the Rightly Guided One sent by God to restore the reign of the law on earth. As Muḥammad ibn ᶜAbd Allah, he claimed descent from the Prophet through ᶜAlī and his son Ḥasan, in fulfillment of the tradition that the Mahdi would be of the House of the Prophet and would bear his name.

Recognized as Mahdi by the Maṣmūda peoples of the High Atlas, Ibn Tūmart established himself at Tinmel in the mountains south of Marrakech. He converted the Berber tribes into the elements of a community bound together by belief in his mission, adherence to the doctrines that he expounded in Berber as well as Arabic, and strict religious discipline. In order of precedence, the member tribes were directed by the Mahdi through his personal attendants, a group of about ten of his principal disciples, and a council of some fifty tribal leaders. About 1125 or 1126 the community was purged of all opposition to Ibn Tūmart by the massacre of the halfhearted by their kinsmen, and toward 1130 it launched an unsuccessful attack upon Marrakech. Command of the army fell to ᶜAbd al-Muᵓmin, an early disciple of Ibn Tūmart from the region of Tlemcen. Though a stranger to the Maṣmūda, he was accepted by the community as the caliph (successor to the Mahdi) following the death of Ibn Tūmart about 1130.

For ten years ᶜAbd al-Muᵓmin fought to preserve the community and to extend its control over the peoples of the High Atlas. The military organization progressed with the development of tribal regiments, each commanded by a *muḥtasib;* discipline was maintained by collective prayer. Senior leaders, preeminently Abū Ḥafṣ ᶜUmar of the Hintāta tribe, formed an aristocracy of sheikhs, and a tradition of scholarship grew up around the Mahdi's writings. About 1140, ᶜAbd al-Muᵓmin led his forces toward Tlemcen, where, following the death of the old Almoravid emir ᶜAlī ibn Yūsuf in 1142, he was victorious over his successor Tāshufīn in 1145. The fall of Fez at the end of the year, and of Marrakech in 1147, after protracted sieges eliminated the Almoravids from the Maghrib. Their power in Spain collapsed in the face of rebellion and Christian invasion, although the Almoravid Banū Ghāniya survived as rulers of the Balearic Islands.

The Almohads, however, took possession of little more than Seville and Córdoba. ᶜAbd al-Muᵓmin turned instead to the systematic conquest of the central and eastern Maghrib. An expedition in 1151–1152 overthrew the Hammadid dynasty at Bijaya (Bougie), and defeated the Arab tribes of the Banū Hilāl, who provided the princes of Ifrīḳiya with the bulk of their armies, in battle at Sétif. In 1159, ᶜAbd al-Muᵓmin advanced to Tunis, and laid siege to the Normans of Sicily in Mahdia. The fall of Mahdia in 1160 entailed the expulsion of the Normans from Sousse, Sfax, Gabès, and Tripoli, which they had occupied since 1146. At the battle of Jabal al-Qarn, the Banū Hilāl were finally beaten, and Ifrīḳiya was incorporated into the Almohad empire.

In Spain the Almohads had been unable to prevent the loss of Lisbon to the Portuguese, and of Tortosa and Lérida to the Catalans, although they recovered Almería from the Castilians in 1157. Their position was threatened by the growing power of Ibn Mardanīsh at Murcia. In 1161, ᶜAbd al-Muᵓmin crossed briefly to Gibraltar, and in 1163 was preparing a major expedition when he died at Ribāṭ al-Fatḥ (the Fortress of Victory, now Rabat), which he had built for the purpose of launching the invasion.

The conquests of the Almohads converted their community into a ruling group separated from the Muslim population of North Africa and Spain by doctrine and by membership in a military and political body whose nucleus was provided by the tribes of the High Atlas. Their regiments were called up for tours of duty at Marrakech, the capital; their leaders and commanders became the principal generals and senior counselors of the caliph. The vital training of students of the Mahdi's doctrines was used by ᶜAbd al-Muᵓmin to produce a corps of scholars with a military and political education who could serve as administrators. The result was a government of remarkable efficiency, within the framework of a conventional monarchy.

About 1155, ᶜAbd al-Muᵓmin secured the designation of his son as heir to the throne; the dynasty thus established, the provinces were entrusted to the young princes of the royal family under the supervision of the older sheikhs. The army was enlarged to include a troop of ᶜAbd al-Muᵓmin's own Kūmiya tribesmen, ᶜ*abīd* (slave) soldiers, and levies from the cities and tribes of the empire. Because they did not belong to the Almohad community, the subject peoples were classified as unbelievers, even though the vast majority were Muslim. Their lands were held to belong to the Almohads, and as occupants they were liable for the *kharāj,* the tax upon property owned by the community of the faithful. ᶜAbd al-Muᵓmin is reputed to have surveyed the Maghrib for this purpose, allowing one-third for mountains and deserts, and fixing what was due from the remainder. Military tribes of nomads were employed in the central Maghrib to collect these taxes, in return for their own exemption.

The dynasty's future was not assured until ᶜAbd al-Muᵓmin's son Abū Yaᶜqūb Yūsuf (1163–1184) was firmly on the throne, having dispossessed his brother, the designated heir, and won the approval of the sheikhs under Abū Ḥafṣ ᶜUmar. Rebellion among the tribes of the Rif in northern Morocco, and the defiance of the royal princes in Ifrīḳiya and Spain, were not overcome for several years. Abū Yaᶜqūb's eventual success was followed by an expedition to Spain in 1171–1172, as a result of which the power of Ibn Mardanīsh at Murcia was finally broken and the whole of Andalus-Muslim Spain (larger than Andalusia) was incorporated into the empire. The caliph made his capital at Seville, where he had among his physicians and ministers the philosophers Ibn Ṭufayl and Ibn Rushd. In 1180 he marched into Ifrīḳiya to drive Qarāqūsh, a Mamluk of Saladin's who had invaded the country from Egypt, back to Tripoli. In 1184, faced by renewed attack from Christian Spain, he was killed by the Portuguese at the siege of Santarém.

Abū Yaᶜqūb Yūsuf's son and successor, Abū Yūsuf Yaᶜqūb, inherited this war on two fronts. In 1184 the Almoravid rulers of the Balearics, ᶜAlī and Yaḥyā ibn Ghāniya, seized Bijaya, and in alliance with Qarāqūsh at Tripoli and the Arab tribes of Ifrīḳiya, conquered the eastern Maghrib except for Tunis. An expedition led by Abū Yūsuf in 1187–1189 recovered the bulk of the province, but left Yaḥyā ibn Ghāniya and Qarāqūsh in control of Tripoli and the Djerid of southern Tunisia. Abū Yūsuf returned to Morocco and Spain to campaign against the Portuguese in 1190 and 1191, and to win the great victory of Alarcos over Castile in 1195, taking the title al-Manṣūr (the Victorious).

Meanwhile Abū Yūsuf turned his attention to doctrine and the question of his relationship to the Almohad community. His father's success in gaining the throne, and the support of the dynasty by the great sheikh Abū Ḥafṣ ᶜUmar (*d.* 1175/76) and his sons, had deferred but not avoided the problem of authority. When Abū Yūsuf denounced the Maliki school of jurisprudence and ordered the burning of its books, he was thinking less of the populace whose law this was, and more of the Almohads. His command that jurists should go straight to the scriptural sources of the law, as demanded by Ibn Tūmart, was not so much directed at a general reformation of Islam in the Maghrib as at depriving the writings of the Mahdi of any authority as a source of wisdom in themselves. The target was those sheikhs and scholars among the Almohads who might claim, as the trustees of a new scriptural revelation in addition to the Koran and the standard Traditions, the right to subject the caliph to their guidance.

The matter rested with the death of Abū Yūsuf in 1199. Concerned about doctrine, he had been less tolerant than his father, living at Marrakech rather than Seville, withdrawing his favor from Ibn Rushd, and discriminating against the Jews. His son and successor, Muḥammad al-Nāṣir (1199–1214), was a scholarly and conscientious man who freed himself from the war in Ifrīḳiya only to be disastrously defeated in Spain. At his accession a rebellion at Mahdia enabled Yaḥyā ibn Ghāniya to reconquer Ifrīḳiya. Tunis was taken, but in 1203 the Almohad fleet captured the Balearic Islands, and in 1205 al-Nāṣir finally reconquered the eastern Maghrib. In 1207 he appointed Abū Muḥammad ᶜAbd al-Wāḥid, the son of Abū Ḥafṣ ᶜUmar, as his viceroy at Tunis, with plenipotentiary powers to govern in his name. With Ifrīḳiya thus largely independent, al-Nāṣir prepared to meet a concerted attack by the Christian kings of Spain. In 1212 the Almohads were slaughtered at the battle of Las Navas de Tolosa. Al-Nāṣir returned to Marrakech, where he died in 1214.

The empire, however, did not collapse immediately. The heavily fortified cities of Andalus did not fall. At Marrakech the young son of al-Nāṣir was recognized as caliph with the title al-Mustanṣir. The tradition of obedience to the Almohad monarch, and acknowledgment of his right to rule the Maghrib, was still strong. The administration functioned until the death of al-Mustanṣir in 1224, when rivalry among members of the royal family for the throne, combined with the assertion by the Almohad sheikhs of their right to choose the caliph, brought about a civil war. Following the murder of the caliph al-ᶜĀdil in 1227, the sheikhs installed their own candidate at Marrakech, while al-ᶜĀdil's brother, the governor of Seville, proclaimed himself caliph in Spain, with the title al-Maᵓmūn.

The Andalusian Muḥammad ibn Ḥūd rebelled at Murcia and occupied the greater part of Andalus as al-Maᵓmūn, with a force of Castilian knights in his army, crossed to Morocco, denouncing the Mahdi and proclaiming himself an orthodox Muslim of the Maliki school. In 1230 he captured Marrakech and massacred the sheikhs. His son al-Rashīd (1232–1242) returned to the doctrine of the Almohads, and made his peace with the survivors of the Marrakech massacre. At Tunis, however, the Hafsid viceroy declared himself an independent ruler, and from 1236–1237 onward claimed the leadership of the Almohad community. Tlemcen became the capital of the Ziyanid chieftain Yaghmurāsin. Andalus was overrun by the Christian kings, so that after 1248 only Granada remained as a vassal of Castile.

At Marrakech the son and successor of al-Rashīd, al-Saᶜīd al-Muᶜ taḍid, attempted to restore by conquest the empire the dynasty had lost by al-Maᵓmūn's repudiation of its religious origins, but his attack on Tlemcen in 1248 ended in his death and the defeat of his army by the tribal forces of the Banū Marīn (Marinids) in northern Morocco. The Marinids went on to establish a new dynasty at Fès, and the two last caliphs, al-Murtaḍā (1248–1266) and al-Wāthiq, survived as their tributaries until in 1269 they captured Marrakech.

Despite the strong organization of the Almohad community, and its adaptability to the task of governing a large empire, its exclusiveness severely restricted the social base of the regime; the caliphate lacked the support to survive military defeat and constitutional conflict. On the other hand, the ideal of empire that it established in the Maghrib helped to ensure that the Almohad regime was in fact renewed, partly from within by the Hafsids and partly from without by the Ziyanids and the Marinids, who shared the Almohad dominions between them.

BIBLIOGRAPHY

Jamil Abun-Nasr, *A History of the Maghrib,* 2nd ed. (1975); Michael Brett, *The Moors: The Arabs in the West* (1980). Rachid Bourouiba, *Abd al-Muᵓmin* (1974) and *Ibn Tūmart* (1974); Charles André Julien, *Histoire de l'Afrique du Nord,* 2nd ed., II, R. Le Tourneau, ed. (1952), translated by J. Petrie and edited by C. C. Stewart as *History of North Africa: Tunisia, Algeria, Morocco, from the Arab Conquest to 1830* (1970); Roger Le Tourneau, *The Almohad Movement in North Africa in the Twelfth and Thirteenth Centuries* (1969); and Henri Terrasse, *Histoire du Maroc,* I (1949).

MICHAEL BRETT

ALMOIN OF FLEURY. See **Aimoin de Fleury.**

ALMORAVID ART. Starting out from Morocco, the Almoravids brought about the political unification of substantial portions of the Maghrib and of entire al-Andalus. In al-Andalus they overcame the *muluk aṭ-ṭawāᵓif* (*taifas*), but the latter's art, heir to that of the caliphate of Córdoba, proved a decisive stimulus to their own artistic activity. Consequently, from the end of the eleventh century, the Maghrib became wide open to Andalusian influence. West Islam was now unified artistically too, and the repertoire was elaborated from which the puristic Almohads selected the most important elements of their art around the middle of the twelfth century.

The principles of Almoravid art and the tendencies in its development can be seen most clearly from its architectural monuments and their decoration.

Mosque Typology. The prayer hall with aisles oriented perpendicularly to the *qibla* had already appeared, though still in the form of a columned mosque, among principal monuments of early West Islam (Great Mosque of Córdoba, *ca.* 785; Aghlabid rebuilding of the Great Mosque of Qairawān, 836), probably derived from eastern models in the basilica tradition (al-Aqṣā Mosque in Jerusalem). After the supply of columns from pre-Islamic monuments was exhausted, the brick pier mosque was introduced in the Maghrib as well. Tulunid and Fatimid Cairo (mosque of Ibn Ṭūlūn, 876–879; mosque of al-Ḥākim, founded in 990), acted as an intermediary be-

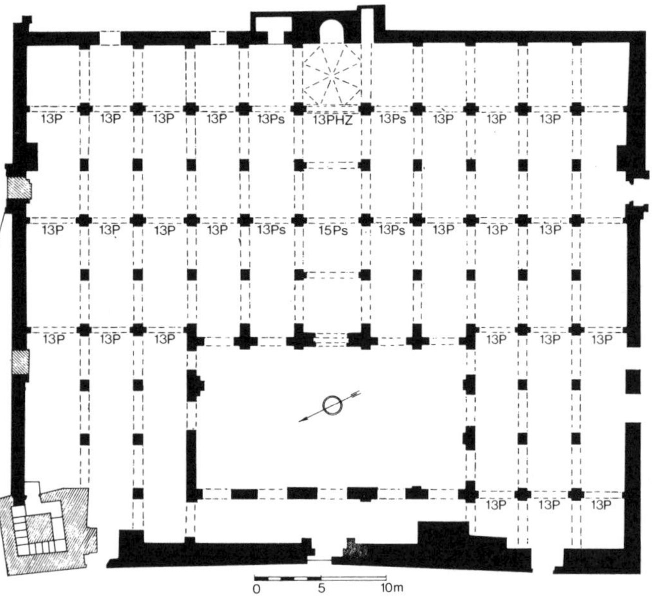

The Great Mosque of Algiers. Ground plan (*above*). GOLVIN AND EWERT-WISSHAK. View through the nave to the *miḥrāb* (*right*). PHOTO EWERT

Stucco detail in customary interlaced structure. Al-Qarawīyīn Mosque, Fès. PHOTO BIBLIOTHÈQUE GÉNÉRALE ET ARCHIVES

tween the Abbasid East (for example, mosque of Abū Dulaf in Sāmarrā, *ca.* 860) and of the Maghrib. The overpowering pillar profile of the Abbasid structures, which perhaps stemmed from ancient Oriental tradition, was, however, considerably reduced in the Maghrib; the almost standardized dimensions of Almohad structures were elaborated.

The Great Mosque of Algiers (*ca.* 1097) shows most clearly how the new type led from the Umayyad tradition to the Almohad mosque, which is foreshadowed by the narrow court, the T-type of the prayer hall, and the pillar profiles, as well as by the arcade arches and their gradually enriched, hierarchical distribution. The longitudinal arcades have simple, pointed horseshoe arches, while the transverse arcades are characterized by polylobed arches, which are enriched in the three central aisles, most especially in the nave. The characteristic T-shape in the plan, formed by the broadened nave and the *qibla* transept, can already be found in the enlargement of the mosque of Córdoba undertaken by al-Ḥakam II (*ca.* 961–965). Later the Almohads simply eliminated the penetration of the side aisles and of the transept. The two other most important new foundations of the Almoravids, the Great Mosque of Tlemcen (completed in 1136) and the much smaller building at Nedroma, possess a reduced form in terms of typology; for they have no *qibla* transept and only a compartment in front of the prayer niche or *miḥrāb.*

The Qarawīyīn Mosque at Fès was enlarged and decorated in this period (1134–1144), but typologically the plan conserves the schema of the founding era of the ninth century, probably influenced by the Great Mosque of Damascus; it consists of a transverse prayer hall with a perpendicular, longitudinal nave.

Secular Architecture. In the Almoravid capital city of Marrakech, founded around 1070, traces of a ruler's palace have been uncovered under the first of the two Kutubīya mosques built by the Almohads.

Up to the twentieth century the complete ground plan of a rural palace was conserved near Murcia ("Castillejo," first third of the twelfth century). The perfectly symmetrical, double-axis structure was built around a garden court. The gate and chamber projections in the rectangular enclosure-wall are related to similar structures in North African palaces of the tenth and eleventh centuries (Ashīr and Qalᶜat Banī Ḥammād).

Decoration. Andalusian elements clearly predominate. Within the vegetable decoration several tendencies may be discerned. One current employs the pattern of pinnate-leaf tendrils developed in the eleventh century. Another displays a penchant for a fleshier molding (for example, Qubba of ᶜAlī ibn Yūsuf at Marrakech; Palacio de Pinohermoso at Játiva). Acanthus ornament inspired by pre-Islamic antiquity should be considered a special case (cupola of a nave compartment in the Qarawīyīn Mosque at Fès).

The *muqarnas* vault made its first appearance in the Maghrib at this time. After a few hesitant trials in the traditional designs of ribbed cupol (Great Mosque of Tlemcen; Qubba of ᶜAlī ibn Yūsuf at Marrakech), it was used to cover entire areas (as in the nave compartments of the Qarawīyīn Mosque at Fès). Its rapid development to maturity points to the existence of Eastern influences.

BIBLIOGRAPHY

R. Bourouiba, *L'art religieux musulman en Algérie* (1973), 67–103; L. Golvin, *Essai sur l'architecture religieuse musulmane,* IV (1979), 167–241; M. Gómez-Moreno, *El arte árabe español hasta los almohades. Arte mozárabe,* Ars Hispaniae, III (1951), 279–296; G. Marçais, *L'architecture musulmane d'occident. Tunisie, Algérie, Maroc et Sicile* (1954), 191–200; J. Meunié, H. Terrasse, and G. Deverdun, *Nouvelles recherches archéologiques à Marrakech* (1957); H. Terrasse, *L'art hispano-mauresque dès origines au XIIIe siècle* (1932), 211–245; and "La mosqueé d'al-Qarawīyīn à Fès et l'art des Almoravides," in *Ars Orientalis,* 2 (1957), 135-147. L. Torres Balbás, *Artes almorávide y almohade* (1955).

CHRISTIAN EWERT

ALMORAVIDS, anglicized Spanish rendering of Arabic *al-murābiṭ,* meaning "inmate of a *ribāṭ*" (Muslim religious hermitage). *Ribāṭs* in the Muslim West were usually located on borders with non-Muslim lands (in Spain) or on seacoasts. *Murābiṭs* (Arabic plural *murābiṭūn*) were volunteers who led pious lives and fought invading unbelievers in defense of their faith. The name Almoravids *(al-Murābiṭūn)* was given to the members of the puritanical Berber religious movement and tribal dynasty that ruled much of West Africa and Spain for extended periods between 1054 and 1147.

The history of the Almoravids falls into several discrete parts: their founding, then their involvements in the Sahara and sub-Saharan Africa, in western North Africa (the western Maghrib), in Muslim Spain (al-Andalus), and in the Balearic Islands. The discovery, publication, and interpretation (since the mid-1950's) of previously lost sources has changed and clarified much that was formerly accepted about the African aspects of this history.

The decaying Umayyad caliphate (fell 1031) of al-Andalus fragmented into numerous small kingdoms (*mulūk al-ṭawā*ᵓ*if* or *taifas*—kings of factions or parties) in the first third of the eleventh century. This fragmentation had its counterpart among the caliphate's Berber clients in the Zanāta "confederation" of the western Maghrib. After 1031 these tribes were particularly in conflict with members of the Ṣanhāja "confederation." While most Zanāta tribes were sedentary or transhumant, most Ṣanhāja tribes were transhumant or fully nomadic, moving about in the southern reaches of the Atlas Mountains and across the Sahara. The Islamization of most tribes of both confederations was imperfect; several heresies flourished, protected by isolation and distance from centers of orthodoxy. Ignorance of much about Islam beset other tribes, and it was this ignorance that brought about the founding of the Almoravids.

Around 1036 the titular head of the Ṣanhāja, Yaḥyā ibn Ibrāhīm al-Judālī (of the Judāla tribe), returned from the pilgrimage (ḥajj) to Mecca through Qayrawān (in Tunisia). Concerned with his people's ignorance of Islam, he sought out an eminent jurist, Abū ᶜImrān al-Fāsī, and asked him to send a teacher to instruct his tribes in the tenets of Islam. Instead, Abū ᶜImrān requested a former student, Wajjāj ibn Zalwah al-Lamṭī, who had returned after study to the western Maghrib and established a center for Islamic scholarship, to provide such a teacher.

The teacher was ᶜAbd Allāh ibn Yāsīn al-Jazūlī, who imposed a rigidly enforced observance of Muslim law and ritual that included severe punishment of any infractions. A disagreement arose between him and a faction of the Gudāla following Yaḥyā ibn Ibrāhīm's death (*ca.* 1048), causing Ibn Yāsīn's expulsion. He moved to the territory of the Lamtūna, a neighboring Ṣanhāja tribe, to whom he became religious teacher and disciplinarian.

Interpretations based largely on fourteenth-century sources, held that Ibn Yāsīn then retired with a band of followers to an island off the Atlantic coast or in the Senegal River, where he constructed the *ribāṭ* from which the movement took its name and where the group's religious solidarity was confirmed. Scholarship based on more contemporary sources casts considerable doubt on the existence of such a hermitage, and suggests that the epithet *Murābiṭūn* derived from Ibn Yāsīn's thus naming his followers in honor of their newly acquired piety and fierce religious devotion. The precise origin of the term, however, remains uncertain. The various sources also call the group Lamtūna, from the name of the movement's leading tribe, or *Mulaththamūn* (veiled ones), from the *lithām* (veiling face muffler) the tribesmen wore.

Over the next few years the Lamtūna chief, Yaḥyā ibn ᶜUmar, and Ibn Yāsīn embarked on a campaign to subject and proselytize the Ṣanhāja tribes, among them the Judāla. Having accomplished this, they attacked and conquered Zanāta-controlled Sijilmāsa in 1053 or 1054. Ibn Yāsīn directed the destruction of all musical instruments and wine shops, and the abolition of uncanonical taxes. This conquest also removed a long-lasting pocket of Khārijīte heretics. In 1055 the Almoravids pushed south and conquered Awdaghost in the *bilād al-Sūdān* (lands of the black people), the southern terminus of the western trans-Sahara caravan route to Sijilmāsa.

While the Almoravids were thus engaged to the south, the Zanāta of Sijilmāsa revolted and massacred their garrison. The Judāla also rebelled, and in 1056, Yaḥyā ibn ᶜUmar was killed in the Mauretanian Adrar while trying to subdue them. His brother, Abū Bakr ibn ᶜUmar, became chief of the Lamtūna. The wars continued: the Sijilmāsan and Judālan revolutions were quelled, the Sūs was conquered, and a lengthy campaign was begun against the heretic Barghawāṭa in southern Morocco. Ibn Yāsīn was martyred in 1058 or 1059 while fighting the Barghawāṭa on the Tāmasnā Plain, but Abū Bakr continued the war until that heresy was extirpated.

In 1068, Abū Bakr married Zainab, the wealthy widow of the Zanāta ruler of Āghmāt. The next year, after the construction of Marrakech had begun, he was recalled to the desert to put down a revolt among the tribes. He left his cousin and second in command, Yūsuf ibn Tāshfīn, as his deputy, and advised him to marry Zainab, whom he had divorced. During Abū Bakr's absence Yūsuf, counseled by his new wife, built an army and governmental apparatus, and established himself as the effective ruler of the Almoravid territories in Morocco. When Abū Bakr returned in 1071 or 1072 and saw both Yūsuf's new power and the fact that he intended to keep it, he agreed to return to the desert. Yūsuf continued to strike money in Abū Bakr's name until the latter's death, and in other ways acknowledged his titular leadership.

From Abū Bakr's return to the desert, the history of the Almoravids splits. His activities in the desert and the *bilād al-Sūdān* occur independently of the better-known struggles of the Banū Tāshfīn-led group to the north. Abū Bakr continued the *jihād* against the recalcitrant Saharan tribes and the unbelieving Sudanis from his base at Azūqī, an oasis fifteen miles north of Atar in the Mauretanian Adrar. This campaign drove the Sudanis south from the desert, effected the firm islamization of the Saharan tribes, and helped to install Islam in sub-Saharan West Africa. After Abū Bakr died fighting Sudanis from Ghana in the Tagant region of southern Mauretania in 1087, the southern movement of the Almoravids disintegrated through lack of leadership and through Ghanaian pressure. Their religious zeal remained, however, and many eventually formed groups that provided religious instruction and moral guidance to the inhabitants of the desert and the western Sudan, communicating their militant, fundamentalist Islam.

In Morocco, Yūsuf ibn Tāshfīn continued to consolidate his hold on the Moroccan Meseta (coastal plain) and the surrounding mountains. By 1069 his armies had conquered Fès, and moved north and east through the Rif chain, campaigning in the Moulouya River valley (1070–1072). By 1084 he ruled Tangier and the rest of the coastal and inland population centers and tribes as far east as Algiers, and had established relatives as military governors in these places. The Abbasid caliph in Baghdad, to whom Yūsuf deferred as the religious leader of Sunni Islam, proclaimed him *amīr al-muslimīn* (commander of the Muslims) in 1073, a title that succeeding Almoravid rulers retained.

Yūsuf's reputation for rectitude and military ability had long since reached al-Andalus, where the *taifas* were finding themselves increasingly unable to resist the Christian kings bent on reconquering Muslim lands. By the 1080's many of the remaining *taifas* had become vassals of Alfonso VI of León and Castile in order to maintain a semblance of independence. Alfonso had alarmed all remaining Muslims with his armed progress through al-Andalus to Tarifa (1083), and had made clear his intent to overcome al-Andalus with his seizure and subsequent fortification of Toledo in 1085. Embassies of notables from the *taifas* therefore sought Almoravid assistance from Yūsuf against the Christian menace. Yūsuf may have consented to these appeals as early as 1083, but he did not cross to al-Andalus until June 1086, after both Ceuta and Algeciras were under his control.

Yūsuf and his army moved to Seville, where a plan of action was developed with that city's ruler, al-Mu^{c}tamid ibn ^{c}Abbād (one of the leading *taifas*), and several lesser princes. The combined Almoravid and Andalusian forces then marched north and met Alfonso's (which had come from supporting a Muslim puppet in Valencia) at Zallaqa (or Sacralias) on 23 October 1086, winning a resounding victory. Yūsuf then returned with his army to the Maghrib. In the spring of 1088, the Almoravids were again in Spain, responding to the Andalusians' call to eliminate the menace that the Christian fortress at Aledo was said to represent. The four-month siege failed, and Yūsuf was impressed by the *taifas'* inability to cooperate, even against what proved to be a minimal threat. When he returned to the Maghrib, he left behind a force commanded by one of his generals to assist the Andalusians.

From his experiences with the Andalusians and the reports of his general, Yūsuf concluded that in order to preserve al-Andalus, he must eliminate the bickering *taifas* and unite the country's Muslims under Almoravid governance. Having secured *fatwās* (legal opinions) that encouraged his war against these Muslim enemies of Islam, Yūsuf crossed to al-Andalus in 1090. By 1094 he had disposed of most of the opposition and erected a military government geared to fighting the Christian enemy. Al-Mu^{c}tamid ibn ^{c}Abbād of Seville, who fruitlessly attempted to call Alfonso VI to his rescue, ended as an exile in the Sūs. The Almoravid armies then pushed toward Valencia, where they engaged El Cid (Rodrigo Díaz de Bivar) for the first time, and suffered their first defeat. The Cid (*d.* 1099), and then his widow, withstood the Almoravid assaults until 1102, when the defenders burned Valencia, then abandoned it.

ALMORAVIDS

Yūsuf ibn Tāshfīn died in 1106 and was succeeded by his son ^{c}Alī. The Almoravid work of unification continued with wars against both the Christian kingdoms and the remaining *taifas;* the final subjugation of the Muslim kingdom of Saragossa came in 1110, and the seizure of the Balearics in 1115. Subsequent battles with the Christians assumed a desultory character, victories often seeming to be balanced by defeats.

Much has been made of the decline of the Almoravids during the last half of ^{c}Alī ibn Yūsuf's reign, a decline attributed variously to ^{c}Alī's inability, the physical and spiritual decadence of the Almoravids under Andalusian influence, and their slavish adherence to the advice of legal scholars. A great deal of this attribution derives from Almohad propaganda. Perhaps contributing more to the Almoravid decline were the rise of the Almohads in the shelter of Morocco's High Atlas Mountains, the general failure of the Andalusians to participate greatly in their own defense, the temporary resolution of several internal conflicts that had weakened the Christian kings, and the comparatively small size of the Almoravid forces.

This part of ^{c}Alī's reign coincided with the appearance and growth of the Almohads as serious military foes, the first independence of Portugal under Alfonso I Henriques (1128), and the Reconquest campaigns of Alfonso the Battler of Aragon (reigned 1104–1134) and of Alfonso VII of León and Castile (reigned 1126–1157). Thus, the Almoravids found themselves more heavily engaged in al-Andalus while, from the first Almohad attack on Marrakech (1129), an intensifying war with these Muslim rivals diverted scarce resources from Iberia and led ultimately to their downfall in both areas. Their use in Morocco of significant forces of Christian mercenaries (begun by Yūsuf ibn Tāshfīn) provided the Almohads with a potent propaganda weapon among the Berber tribes at the same time it helped hold back the Almohad advance. Despite his efforts, when ^{c}Alī ibn Yūsuf died in 1143, he left a crumbling empire, under attack from within and without, in the hands of his courageous but unlucky son.

Tāshfīn ibn ^{c}Alī ibn Yūsuf had been fairly successful for more than ten years as one of ^{c}Alī's military governors in al-Andalus, but he succeeded to a demoralized and disintegrating empire. With the death of the able Christian general, Reverter (1145), the Almoravid armies in the Maghrib lost the source of much of their discipline and cohesion. In the same year Tāshfīn, attempting to reach al-Andalus in order to organize Almoravid resistance, was killed when his horse fell from a cliff near Oran. The Almoravids continued fighting under Tāshfīn's son Isḥāq, but by this time the Almohad tide was overwhelming. Isḥaq and Marrakech were submerged in 1146 by ^{c}Abd al-Mu$^{\supset}$min, the Almohad caliph.

With the death of Isḥāq and the capture of Marrakech, Almoravid rule in the Maghrib ended. Only the Banū Ghāniya, the governors of the Balearics, continued as remnants of the former Almoravid empire. After a period of reorganization and internal quarrels in the 1150's, the survivor, Isḥāq ibn Muḥammad ibn ^{c}Alī ibn Yūsuf ibn Ghāniya, managed to form a principality that survived for a time as a corsair state, then as a way station for European traders.

Isḥāq ibn Ghāniya died in 1183 or 1184, leaving a weak state and several competing sons, the second of whom, ^{c}Alī, deposed his older brother and seized power (1184). On finding that the Almohad fleet was about to descend upon him, he mounted a diversionary invasion of the Maghrib that struck Bougie late in 1184. The Almohads counterattacked and drove the invaders through the Atlas ranges into the desert, where they joined forces with an Ayyubid mercenary band from Egypt and harassed Almohad Tunisia with raids and ambushes. The Balearics finally fell to the Almohads in 1203, and the Almoravid heirs there were executed. Those in the deserts of the eastern Maghrib menaced Almohad territory to the north until the Almohads made Abū Muḥammad ibn Abī Ḥafṣ their governor there (1207) and directed him to extirpate this pest. He succeeded, driving the remnants of the Banū Ghāniya deep into the desert, where they ended their days wandering among the oases their ancestors had left a century and more earlier.

The effects of the Almoravid reign were several. Their presence and earlier successes in sub-Saharan Africa seem greatly to have furthered the spread of Islam there. Their initial campaigns and long rule served to eradicate several heresies that had subsisted in the western Maghrib since the eighth century and to accustom the inhabitants to orthodox Islam. Their rule over the tribes of Morocco is said to have accustomed them, as well, to the habit of obeying a single master, facilitating their successors' efforts in that regard. Their descent upon al-Andalus postponed the ultimate downfall of that Muslim region until the Almohads replaced them. Their importation of Andalusian Muslims, Jews, and Christians brought a cultural enrichment in thought, letters, art, and architecture that flourished most under their Almohad successors. Finally, the disruptive effects of the Banū Ghāniya's presence in the eastern Maghrib brought about the establishment of the first Ḥafṣid there and set a pattern of independent government that would lead to the dismemberment of the Almohad empire in the 1230's.

BIBLIOGRAPHY

Almoravid historiography has been hindered until recently by the loss of most of the contemporaneous Arabic sources, which has forced modern historians to rely on al-Bakrī (*ca.* 1068), *Description de l'Afrique septentrionale,* MacGuckin de Slane, ed. and trans. (2nd ed., 1911–1913; repr. 1965); ᶜAbd al-Wāhid al-Marrākushī (thirteenth-century), *Histoire des Almohades,* E. Fagnan, trans. (1893); Ibn al-Athīr (thirteenth century), *Annales du Maghreb et de l'Espagne,* E. Fagnan, trans. (1901); and these fourteenth-century works: Ibn Abī Zarᶜ, *Rawḍ al-Qirṭās,* A. Huici Miranda, trans. (1964); Ibn Khaldun, *Histoire des Berberes,* MacGuckin de Slane, trans., 4 vols. (1925–1926); and the unsigned *al-Ḥulal al-Mawšiyya,* A. Huici Miranda, trans. (1952). Among the authors whose interpretations reflect this limited source material are Jamil M. Abun Nasr, *A History of the Maghrib* (1971), pp. 92–103; Charles-André Julien, in *History of North Africa,* R. Le Tourneau and C. C. Stewart, eds., John Petrie, trans. (1970), pp. 76–93 and bibliography, pp. 351–421; Henri Terrasse, in *Histoire de Maroc,* I (1949), pp. 211–260 (no footnotes).

The *Index Islamicus* lists many articles on the Almoravids, most in French or Spanish. The only recent book-length treatment of the Almoravids in a Western language is Jacinto Bosch Vila, *Historia de Marruecos: Los Almoravides* (1956).

Since the 1950's newly available sources have caused the modification of most earlier interpretations. These include the Almoravid portion of Ibn ᶜIdhārī's *Bayan al-mughrib,* published by Huici Miranda as "Un fragmento inedito de Ibn ᶜIdārī sobre los Almoravides," *Hespéris-Tamuda,* 2 (1961); Qāḍī ᶜIyād, *Tartīb al-madārik,* Aḥmad Bakīr Maḥmūd, ed., 5 vols. (1967–1968); part of Ibn al-Qaṭṭān's *Naẓm al-juman,* M. ᶜA. Makkī, ed. (n.d.); and a number of Almoravid letters published in the *Revista del Instituto de Estudios Islamicos*—all in Arabic.

Articles embodying the newer sources and their interpretation are listed in Nehemia Levtzion, "The Sahara and the Sudan from the Arab Conquest of the Maghrib to the Rise of the Almoravids," in *Cambridge History of Africa,* II, J. D. Fage, ed. (1978); and "The Western Maghrib and Sudan," *ibid.,* III, Roland Oliver, ed. (1977). A treatment of the Banū Ghāniya is Alfred Bel, *Les Benou Ghānya* (1903).

JAMES L. YARRISON

[See also **Almohads; Atlas Mountains; Castile; Cid; Spain, Christian–Muslim Relations; Spain, Moorish Kingdoms of.**]

ALMS TAX, ISLAMIC. The *zakāt* (alms tax) is one of the five pillars of Islam. The verb *zakā* in Arabic means "to increase" or "to augment," and also "to be pure" or "to become pure." In the opinion of the Koran commentators, alms are called *zakāt* either because they increase a man's store by drawing down a blessing upon him, or because they purify the remaining part of one's property from pollution and the soul from avarice.

The obligation to pay *zakāt* is mentioned frequently in the Koran, often in connection with the duty of prayer (for instance, 2:43, 2:83, 2:110, 2:177, 2:277). The payment of *zakāt,* which symbolizes the solidarity of the Muslim community, is thought to pave the way for salvation; the caliph ᶜUmar II (717–720) is reported to have said, "Prayer carries us halfway to God; fasting brings us to the door of His palace; and alms procures for us admission."

The Islamic doctrine regarding the *zakāt* developed rapidly during the time of the Prophet and the first four caliphs. The obligation to pay it was at first only vaguely defined, and it did not represent a tax demanded by religion. The organized distribution of charity was not necessary in Mecca, where Muḥammad had only a small number of followers, and it became so only after the emigration (hegira) to Medina, where the first Islamic polity was established. As increasing numbers of tribes agreed to pay tribute to Muḥammad, charitable funds grew more and more abundant; these funds were used to support the Meccans who had immigrated to Medina and to equip the Muslim troops for raids. During the lifetime of Muḥammad, the *zakāt* remained primarily a voluntary and individual offering, distributed directly by the donor.

The institutionalization of the *zakāt* as a regular tax during the reign of the first caliph, Abū Bakr, promoted the expansion of Islam by providing the armies with funds. As the authority of the state increased and the fiscal administration was centralized under the first caliphs, the collection and distribution of the *zakāt* was taken away from individual donors and placed in the hands of tax collectors, in order to insure equitable distribution among the beneficiaries.

The following is a brief account of the main prescriptions regarding the collection and distribution of the *zakāt*. It is required from any person who is free, sane, adult, and a Muslim, provided that person is in possession of the *niṣāb,* or minimum amount of property upon which the tax is due, and has been in full possession of that property for one complete year. *Zakāt* is payable on crops, fruit, livestock, precious metals, and merchandise. Crops and fruit are taxed at a rate of one-tenth the annual yield, payable at harvest time. Only members of the family of the Prophet are exempt from paying this tax, which is levied on both private land and public estates. The tax on livestock, which is computed according to the number and type of animals possessed, is due in kind; this tax, which reflects the nonurban character of seventh-century Arabia, mainly affected the nomadic herdsmen. Precious metals and merchandise are taxed at a rate of 2½ percent.

An important distinction with regard to the assessment of taxes is that between *ẓāhir* ("openly visible") articles, such as crops, fruit, and livestock, and *bāṭin* ("hidden") articles, such as precious metals and merchandise. The right of the government to demand the *zakāt* is limited to the former; the amount of tax due on these items may be determined by the tax collector on the basis of personal observation. The latter category, however, is not subject to such control, and the determination of the amount of tax due is left to the discretion of the individual.

Although it is permitted to give the *zakāt* directly to the beneficiaries, it is preferable to hand it to the authorities for proper distribution. Eight categories of people are mentioned in the Koran (9:60) as being entitled to receive *zakāt*: the poor, the needy, tax collectors, "those whose hearts are to be reconciled," slaves, debtors, volunteer soldiers, and wayfarers. The tax collectors receive a fixed salary, and whatever remains is distributed in equal parts among the other seven categories.

These regulations, which reflect the values of a primarily nonurban society, were fixed relatively early in the development of Islamic society, and thus could not keep pace with the rapidly changing economic reality. Social and economic changes caused by the urbanization of the Muslim state under the Umayyads and Abbasids brought the norms of *zakāt* into conflict with the fiscal interests of the state. The only way for the state to take advantage of supplementary sources of income in an age of economic prosperity was to impose extralegal taxes (*mukūs*) such as tolls, rents, and trade imposts. The importance of *zakāt* as a source of state income decreased significantly in comparison with these noncanonical taxes.

The gap between the Islamic ideal and political and economic reality was extended by the conquest of the eastern lands of the Muslim world by the Mongols, who established a new system of rural and urban taxation. The *zakāt,* which was replaced by Mongol taxes on livestock, land, trade, and commerce, ceased to function as a fiscal institution. This development did not, of course, affect the continuing validity of the private, voluntary alms tax, such as the *zakāt al-fiṭr,* the alms given to the poor on the day the fast of Ramadan is broken.

Beginning in the eleventh century, the term *zakāt* took on a secondary meaning, which it has retained. *Zakāt* became the symbol of the lost order of early Islam, of the divine state on earth that had been destroyed by worldly kings. A number of reformers called for a return to *zakāt*—that is, abolition of the noncanonical taxes and reintroduction of the *zakāt* as the primary source of state income. These movements invariably failed, because few people voluntarily chose to pay their tribute to the state, especially on "hidden" items. In the twentieth century, in such countries as Pakistan and Libya, efforts have been made to revive the *zakāt* as an integral element of a modern taxation system.

BIBLIOGRAPHY

John Thomas Cummings *et al.,* "Islam and Modern Economic Change," in John L. Esposito, ed., *Islam and Development: Religion and Sociopolitical Change* (1980); U. Haarmann, "Islamic Duties in History," in *Muslim World,* **68** (1978); Robert Roberts, *The Social Laws of the Qurʾan* (1977); Arent J. Wensinck, *Handbook of Early Muhammadan Tradition* (1927).

D. S. POWERS

[See also **Taxation, Islamic.**]

ALNAGE (French *aunage*), the testing of manufactured cloth by designated officials, originated at various places in Europe during the thirteenth century, although some of the actual operations and the fees involved (also called alnage) may date back even further. Throughout the Middle Ages, alnagers, a highly trained, full-time, permanent officer corps, performed two principal services: they enforced laws governing cloth measurements, and they collected levies on cloth sales. Their duties extended to examining foreign cloths with special cords, strings, or rods marked in ells (*aunes*), marking and sealing (thus, verifying) cloths of assize (cloths having legal dimensions), and seizing defective pieces or bolts on behalf of their government or regional/local authorities. They made certain that buyers were not deceived by sellers, that the quality of cloth in commercial transactions remained at a consistent level, and, like other weights and measures officials, that fraudulent practices were kept to a minimum.

By the sixteenth century, in most places alnagers had been forced to relinquish their searching and measuring duties, and to devote all of their time to collecting fees and fines; the cloth industry had become too large and complex for one set of officials to handle all of these operations. They became part of the machinery of taxation, while other personnel (principally searchers and measurers) acquired their other functions.

RONALD EDWARD ZUPKO

[See also **Weights and Measures.**]

ALOVANIA. See **Albania.**

ALP ARSLAN (1029–1073), ruler of the Seljuk Empire. He succeeded his father, Chaghri-Beg, as ruler of the eastern portion of the realm around 1058 and assumed supreme political authority in September 1063, upon the death of his heirless uncle, Toghril-Beg. The attempts of various kinsmen to contest this authority throughout the 1060's ended in failure. Alp Arslan amplified those tendencies in the new state that were moving away from the steppe and nomadic traditions, a pattern already established by his father and uncle. With the assistance of the brilliant Iranian statesman Niẓām al-Mulk, his closest advisor, the Seljuk realm was further transformed into a traditional Near Eastern monarchy.

This development found little favor with the Oghuz Turkic tribes that had formed the military base upon which Seljuk power had grown. The resultant sharp dichotomy in attitudes created a constant tension between the increasingly splendiferous, centralizing Seljuk sultanate and the anarchic, centrifugal Turkoman tribes. Thus, while pursuing his goal of supreme political leadership in the Islamic world, an objective that required the conquest of the Fatimids, Alp Arslan directed the restless tribes toward the Christian frontiers in Transcaucasia and Anatolia. Their successes there, only in part guided by the central government, brought prestige to the Seljuk dynasty as ghazis, satisfied the booty-hungry tribesmen, and lessened potential friction with the Islamic communities. Thus in 1064 Ani, the former Armenian capital, was annexed and in 1068 Georgia was invaded.

Turkoman raiding into Asia Minor, over which Alp Arslan had little control, finally provoked a Byzantine counteroffensive in 1071. Sidetracked from his Fatimid expedition, he turned to face Romanus IV Diogenes at Manzikert, where the Byzantines were routed. Anatolia, which had never been a goal of the Seljuk ruler, now lay open. Alp Arslan, who appeared content not to press the advantage, was assassinated in central Asia in 1072 and was succeeded by his son, Malik Shah I.

BIBLIOGRAPHY

ᶜAli el-Ḥüseynī, *Akhbār ad-Dawlat as-Saljūqīya*, Muḥammed Iqbāl, ed. (1933), *Ahbār üd-Devlet is-Selçukiyye*, Necati Lügal, Turk. trans. (1943); Ibn al-Athīr, ᶜIzz al-Dīn, *Ibn-el-Athirs Chrönika*, Carl J. Tornberg, ed., 12 vols. (1851–1876), vol. IX; ᶜImād al-Dīn al-Kātib al-Iṣfahani, abridgment in al-Bondārī, *Zubdat an-Nuṣra wa Nukhbat al-ᶜUṣra*, Martijn T. Houtsma, ed., *Recueil de textes relatifs à l'histoire des Seldjoucides*, II (1889); Matthew of Edessa, *Zhamanakagrowtᶜiwn* (1898), French trans. in Edouard DuLaurier, *Bibliothèque historique arménienne* (1858); Niẓām al-Mulk, *Siyāsat-nāma;* or, *Siyar al-mulūk*, Muḥammad Qazvīnī, ed. (1956), *The Book of Government;* or, *Rules for Kings*, Hubert Darke, ed. and trans. (1960).

PETER B. GOLDEN

[See also **Seljuks.**]

ALPERT OF METZ (*fl.* 1005–1025), a monk of St. Symphorian at Metz. He continued Paul the Deacon's history of the bishops of Metz up to the reign of Bishop Theodoric II (*d.* 984). Only two fragments of this history remain: one concerns the death of Bishop Theodoric I and the disastrous Calabrian campaign (982–983) of Emperor Otto II, while the other contains details on Bishop Adalbero II and Bishop Theodoric II. Alpert later left Metz for a monastery near Utrecht; his second work, *De diversitate temporum*, written in 1024 or 1025, contains many references to local places and events, and to events in his own life.

BIBLIOGRAPHY

Alpert's published works are *De diversitate temporum libri duo* and *De episcopis Mettensibus libellus*, G. H. Pertz, ed., in *Monumenta Germaniae historica, Scriptores*, IV (1841), 697–723. They are translated in *Des Alpertus von Metz zwei Bücher über verschiedene Zeitereignisse nebst zwei Bruchstücken über Bischöfe von Metz,* A. Dederich, trans. (1859).

LEAH SHOPKOW

ALPHA AND OMEGA, the first and last letters of the Greek alphabet (A and Ω). Based on Revelation 1:8—"I am the alpha and omega, the beginning and the end, saith the Lord . . ."—the two letters have been used in Christian art since the earliest period to express the eternity of the Lord. In medieval art, they occur most commonly flanking representations of the cross or the Crucifixion, as a signal of Christ's resurrection, and in apocalyptic imagery.

LESLIE BRUBAKER

ALPHABET OF PIETY. See **Fenian Poetry.**

ALPHABETIZATION, HISTORY OF. The Roman (Latin) alphabet has always possessed a fixed sequence, borrowed from the Greek alphabet, which in turn had preserved the previously established order of the Phoenician alphabet. Thus, the Latin Middle Ages inherited the only piece of equipment necessary for alphabetization, an ordered alphabet. The history of alphabetization, therefore, depends upon two other elements: a conscious need for an artificial structure and the choice of alphabetical order to provide that structure.

Isolated examples of alphabetization date from antiquity. Occasional Greek inscriptions bearing alphabetized lists of names (subscribers to a monument or members of a cult, for instance) survive from as early as the second century B.C. A few instances of alphabetized Greek bibliographic lists—of authors, or of an author's works—have been somewhat tenuously traced back to the arrangement of the *Pinakes* of Callimachus (*d. ca.* 240 B.C.) at Alexandria. It was also evidently at Alexandria, or under Alexandrian influence, that the earliest alphabetized glossaries, including lists of medical terms, were compiled; and from Ptolemaic and Greco-Roman Egypt, beginning as early as 112 B.C., there survive alphabetized accounts, principally tax rolls.

Curiously, the Roman state, for all its size and complexity, never adopted the practice of arranging such things as tax rolls, army rosters, or accounts in alphabetical order. But the Romans did adopt, on the basis of Greek models, the practice of alphabetizing glossaries and lexical material—grammatical examples; unusual terms used by a given author or in a specific genre; medical terms; lists of animals, of precious stones, of botanical specimens—all relatively brief.

This limited heritage from Rome had a two-edged effect in the Latin Middle Ages. On the one hand, the Middle Ages regarded it as acceptable, though never obligatory, that one should arrange materia medica and lists of words-out-of-context in alphabetical order. On the other hand, for much of the Middle Ages it was tacitly assumed that alphabetization was useful for little else. Florilegia, and especially collections of proverbs, were the occasional addition to tradition; and these were alphabetized, rather perversely, by initial word, including such unhelpful ones as *de* and *quidam.* For some of these collections, it is clear that alphabetization was in no way intended to help a reader locate the proverb sought; on the contrary, the proverbs were intended to serve the alphabet: that is, they were used to form a satisfying pattern—one proverb beginning with *A,* one beginning with *B,* and so on. Several versions of the so-called Proverbs of Seneca were of this type.

An exception of sorts are the *apophthegmata,* Greek collections of sayings of the Desert Fathers, compiled by the fourth or fifth century and soon translated into Latin. Although initially arranged by topic, they were eventually alphabetized according to the supposed authors of the quotations; the alphabetical collection existed at least by the ninth century and probably much earlier. In the Latin West, however, the rough topical arrangement persisted.

The principal types of alphabetical works produced in the Latin Middle Ages prior to 1050 thus comprised glossaries of medical terms, grammatical lexicons, lists (of precious stones, of medicinal herbs, of properties of things), and collections of proverbs. Even for these the lists that were alphabetically arranged were always in the minority—and always brief. The first alphabetized Latin work of any magnitude or complexity was the dictionary of Papias, completed in Italy about 1053. Its prologue contains the first known description of alphabetical arrangement. Papias explains, among other things, that the arrangement he uses is alphabetical not merely according to the initial letter of each word but according to the second and third letters as well.

Alphabetization by first letter only had been the

ALPHABETIZATION, HISTORY OF

nearly universal practice in Latin to this time. Therefore, Papias' dictionary, employing third-letter alphabetization, was an innovation—but one with restricted implications. It was certainly not the first step in an orderly progression toward complete alphabetization (alphabetization through all the letters of the word). For in spite of Papias in 1053, and in spite of the fact that by 1250 complete alphabetization had come into frequent use, first-letter alphabetization remained the norm throughout the Middle Ages—not from ignorance, obviously, but from choice.

Papias, in creating a complex alphabetical tool for scholarly purposes, was ahead of his time; his work did not immediately inspire others to seize upon this device and employ it to different purposes. Instead, the apparatus developed for the pivotal concern of scholarship—scriptural commentary—was the gloss, which followed the order of the biblical text. The notion of an alphabetical apparatus to the Bible was not consciously rejected; the question simply did not arise, even when the Ordinary Gloss, and glosses on the Gloss, reached quite unwieldy proportions.

We can most readily understand this "blind spot" through a simple analogy: to suggest that one should learn the names of the months in alphabetical order (April, August, December, February, . . .) would seem to us patently absurd. It is irrational, because it is divorced from the essential *ratio* of the months, which is chronological; and it is unnecessary, because these names are already indelibly impressed, in a different order, on our consciousness. For some twelve centuries it would have seemed equally absurd, to the literate in the Christian West, to apply alphabetical order to the Scriptures: irrational, because the *ratio* of the Scriptures was divine inspiration; and unnecessary, because the order of the events and, to a surprising extent, the very order of the words in most books of the Bible were known by heart to the literate, whom the Bible served as elementary textbook for learning Latin, central object of study for more advanced scholarship, wellspring of the liturgical cycle, and both object and instrument of lifelong meditation.

Nevertheless, the rigid mold was broken at the end of the twelfth century. An added element, the need of preachers for sermon material, may have been the agent. In any event, alphabetical order is first seen in a scriptural context in the collections of biblical *distinctiones*—handbooks or dictionaries of biblical terms, with their several allegorical meanings as illustrated by various uses in the Bible—that were compiled principally at the University of Paris for use in preaching. At least five major collections date from the last decade of the century; of these, two were arranged alphabetically (rather than in scriptural order), and a third, Peter of Cornwall's (*ca.* 1189), was supplied with an alphabetical apparatus after the fact. Peter realized belatedly that his list of distinctions in topical order was difficult to search; therefore, by about 1200 he added a new list of the contents in first-letter alphabetical order, with a preface explaining "how to find quite easily what is sought, according to a new method, alphabetical order. " Here is clear evidence of one scholar's conscious shift, in a ten-year period, from rational to alphabetical order. It is noteworthy that all the major thirteenth-century collections of distinctions—and they were many—are alphabetized.

The compilers of these collections were seemingly the first to recognize that, far from being detrimental, the nonrationality—hence, neutrality—of alphabetical arrangement was advantageous in some circumstances as an approach to the Scriptures. It was a recognition of the fact that each user of such a work would bring to it his own *ratio,* shaped by needs peculiar to himself. Thereafter, alphabetization became a frequent tool of the thirteenth-century effort to make the written tradition not merely readable but searchable. The application of alphabetical order to new purposes was slow and never inevitable, but it increased steadily from that time onward.

One of the earliest of the thirteenth-century tools deserves to be ranked with Papias' dictionary as a milestone in the history of alphabetization, the verbal concordance to the Latin Bible. This is an attempt to list, in complete alphabetical order, all the words that occur in the Scriptures, with the location of each occurrence. Compiled by the Paris Dominicans at St. Jacques by 1239, it was revised twice by the same group before the 1280's. Another alphabetized biblical tool was the list of "Interpretations of Hebrew Names." The "Interpretations," one version of which dates back to St. Jerome, had previously consisted of a separate list for each book of Scriptures. In the thirteenth century the lists were combined into a single alphabetical sequence for the whole Bible. Few thirteenth-century Bible manuscripts lack this "standard apparatus."

Alphabetical indexes—of topics or of key words—to various patristic works were being compiled by the mid thirteenth century. Alphabetical subject indexes to much of the Latin Aristotle—*Ethics, Old Logic* and *New Logic,* and the *Libri natu-*

ALPHABETIZATION, HISTORY OF

rales—had also been compiled by about 1250. Before 1261, Robert Kilwardby at Oxford had compiled a single composite alphabetical index or concordance to the major works of Augustine, Ambrose, Boethius, Isidore of Seville, and Anselm (in addition to his many indexes of individual works). By the end of the century one finds the first instance of an author himself compiling an alphabetical index as an integral part of his work—John of Freiburg, in his *Summa confessorum* (1297/1298). Beginning in the late thirteenth century, it is not uncommon to find the owner of a manuscript creating an alphabetical index to his volume that is tailored to fit his particular interests and needs. In concept, then, if not always in execution, the thirteenth-century creation of the alphabetical subject index rivals the biblical concordance in importance to the history of alphabetization.

By the early fourteenth century, topical compendiums—collections of exempla and florilegia—were arranged alphabetically by topic, beginning, respectively, with the *Alphabetum narrationum* (1297–1308) of Arnold of Liège and the *Manipulus florum* (1306) of Thomas of Ireland. Many subsequent alphabetical compendiums of both sorts appeared during the fourteenth and fifteenth centuries, but they were slow to achieve parity in numbers with the nonalphabetical compendiums. In this genre the medieval indifference to, or even mistrust of, alphabetization was bolstered by the sense that a diligent compiler should be able to discern a logical order for his topics; the usual schema was a descending hierarchy: *Deus, Christus, Maria, Angeli, Apostoli. . . .* As a result, one sees such anomalies as Johannes de Mirfeld in the fourteenth century giving a logical explanation for beginning his *Florarium* with the topic *Abstinentia* ("Nobody attains to the palm in the spiritual conflict who does not first . . . cleanse away the filthy sins of the body . . . ; therefore it would seem most fitting to [begin] . . . with the chapter on 'Abstinence.'") —when, in fact, *Abstinentia* came first only because the *Florarium* is alphabetical.

Finally, alphabetization began rather tentatively to be employed in library catalogs. This was not a new notion—witness the alphabetization associated with Alexandria in the third century B.C. In addition, there are at least two isolated examples—at the abbeys of St. Bertin and Corbie—of alphabetical book lists in northern France in the twelfth century. Shortly after 1320 the catalog of the contents (as opposed to an inventory of the volumes) of the books in the Sorbonne's chained library was organized by subject; but, as an aid in searching the longer lists under given headings, the authors were listed alphabetically. The *Catalogus scriptorum ecclesiae,* a bibliography/union catalog compiled by Henry of Kirkestede in the late fourteenth century at Bury St. Edmunds, lists its some 670 authors in first-letter alphabetical order; and in the longest entry, that for Augustine, the list of works is also alphabetized by title. In the fifteenth century many additional alphabetical catalogs were produced. Overall, however, the use of alphabetization for catalogs is rather disappointing in both quantity and quality.

If medieval use of alphabetical order for scholarly pursuits was limited to certain purposes—and limited in quantity even for those purposes—its employment in administration was almost nonexistent. Virtually every ecclesiastical institution and every noble household maintained a cartulary, or record of its charters; but of the thousands that survive, less than three percent (mostly fifteenth-century) are provided with an alphabetical index to make the records searchable. Tax rolls or similar lists of tenants and their obligations occasionally presented the names in alphabetical order, beginning in the fourteenth century; but, again, the proportion was minute. The papal chancery, vastly superior in organization to any other administrative unit in the Middle Ages, organized its documents chronologically through the fifteenth century, with one or two alphabetical exceptions. The papal camera, or financial office, however, began to produce alphabetical indexes to its records on a systematic basis in the mid fourteenth century, starting with the payment records of the *Obligationes et solutiones* (1342–1345) and extending to the *Obligationes communes* (1405–1417) and the *Annates* (1421–1459). By the middle of the fifteenth century, several of the larger Italian banking houses regularly produced alphabetical indexes to their account books, perhaps in emulation of papal practice. In contrast, except for two or three isolated examples (in thirteenth-century France), royal and seigneurial accounts had no alphabetical apparatus in the Middle Ages.

It is difficult to summarize the eclectic and sporadic medieval uses of alphabetization. On the one hand, the Middle Ages witnessed either the introduction or the diffusion of alphabetization for virtually all appropriate purposes. In the latter category are the various glossarial lists of things, in a tradition inherited from Roman antiquity. In the former is the application of alphabetical order to such important tasks as the dictionary, the verbal concordance to the Bible, subject indexes, topical compendiums, and, however slightly, administrative records and accounts. On the other hand, alphabetization never quite attained wholehearted acceptance in the Middle Ages. In part, the reasons may have been temperamental, based on the feeling that alphabetical order was not merely nonrational but antirational (a feeling evidently shared by the Enyclopedists of the eighteenth century, for instance). More important, however, must have been the great expense, of both time and material, involved in the process of alphabetizing. Men were occasionally willing to expend the effort and the necessary draft sheets of parchment required to alphabetize even a lengthy work—Papias for his dictionary, the Dominicans for the concordance, Thomas of Ireland for his topical florilegium—when the nature of the work demanded it or when the projected "lifetime" of a work justified the initial investment; but it was the increasing availability of a cheaper medium, paper, that made alphabetical indexing financially feasible for business accounting.

The introduction of the printing press, which could produce hundreds or thousands of copies of a single work, at last ensured a sufficient return on the investment in time that a lengthy alphabetical index represents. Nevertheless, alphabetical works in the era of the printing press had a sound medieval base on which to build. Indeed, medieval alphabetized tools, such as the biblical concordance and the *Manipulus florum,* were printed in the incunabular period. And the edition of the works of St. Augustine by the Benedictines of St. Maur (1679–1700) includes the thirteenth-century alphabetical indexes of Robert Kilwardby, at that late date still the best in existence.

BIBLIOGRAPHY

Lloyd W. Daly, "Early Alphabetic Indices in the Vatican Archives," in *Traditio,* **19** (1963); and *Contributions to a History of Alphabetization in Antiquity and the Middle Ages;* Lloyd W. Daly and Betty A. Daly, "Some Techniques in Mediaeval Latin Lexicography," in *Speculum,* **39** (1964); Richard H. Rouse and Mary A. Rouse, *Preachers, Florilegia and Sermons: Studies on the Manipulus florum of Thomas of Ireland* (1979); and *"Statim invenire:* Schools, Preachers, and New Attitudes to the Page," in Robert L. Benson and Giles Constable, eds., *Renaissance and Renewal in the Twelfth Century* (1982); Christina von Nolcken, "Some Alphabetical Compendia and How Preachers Used Them in Fourteenth-Century England," in *Viator,* **12** (1981).

Mary A. Rouse
Richard H. Rouse

[See also **Books and Book-Making.**]

ALPHABETS, sets of conventional written symbols or letters, of which each letter stands for one or more single speech sounds and with the totality of letters ideally able to represent all the sounds of a language. The wider sense of this term, designating any complex of written symbols, including syllabic scripts and pictorial as well as phonetic word scripts, will be disregarded here. The terms, derived from the first two letters of the Greek alphabet *(alpha, beta),* also meant a dictionary, handbook, or alphabetical acrostic in the Middle Ages.

Universal literacy was not achieved by any medieval civilization; but because Christianity or Islam—each a religion founded on a sacred book—was in some form at the basis of these civilizations, none of them is conceivable without a literate class. This in practice meant the possession and use of an alphabet. There were also relationships of reciprocal causation between the spread of literacy and various medieval political and economic developments. Although some parts of the world that were eventually incorporated into a medieval civilization did not have an alphabet when the Middle Ages began, and were therefore in a position possibly to develop an alphabet completely from scratch, there is no evidence that they did so. During the Middle Ages some new alphabets were invented, but the idea of the alphabet itself came by cultural diffusion—and particularly by religious diffusion—from areas where alphabets were already in use. The question of the ultimate origins of the alphabet, therefore, with all the complications and controversies that still attend the development from pictorial word script to phonetic word script to syllabic script to alphabetic script, need not be treated here.

Alphabets inherited by the Middle Ages included the Hebrew, Syriac, Greek, and Latin from antiquity and the Arabic, Ethiopic, Armenian, Georgian, Coptic, Gothic, runic, and Oghamic from the transitional period overlapping both antiquity and the Middle Ages. Of these alphabets the most widely used were the Arabic, Greek, and Latin. The main new alphabets developed after the Middle Ages were fully under way were the Slavonic ones. None of the inherited alphabets was maintained completely unchanged during the Middle Ages, and several even fell completely out of use. The vicissitudes that some of these alphabets underwent during the Middle Ages included geographical expansion or contraction, the introduction of new letters, changes in the forms of old letters, and applications to various nonliteral uses. The paucity of surviving evidence does not always permit us to say exactly how or when some of these changes took place, and there is also still much disagreement about the origins of many of these alphabets.

Three of the inherited alphabets descended from the Aramaic branch of the twenty-two-letter North Semitic alphabet, namely the Hebrew, Syriac, and Arabic. They shared the Semitic characteristics of being exclusively consonantal and of being written from right to left. All three introduced vowel indicators either in late antiquity or in the early Middle Ages.

With the diaspora of the Jews the Hebrew alphabet in the square form that is still used today (see Figure 1) came to be at home in widely scattered parts of Asia, Africa, and Europe. This dispersion eventually resulted in differing script traditions, with the Sephardic Jews writing a more round and the Ashkenazic a more angular script. A cursive form of the Hebrew alphabet, called the Rashi or rabbinic script, was developed in the eleventh century. The difficulty of maintaining correct pronunciation after Hebrew ceased to be a spoken language led to the development of at least three systems of vowel indicators. The Babylonian system assigned vowel sounds to four consonants—*aleph, he, waw,* and *yod*—and placed miniature forms of these letters over the consonants to represent the vowels. The Palestinian system used dots in place of the vocalic consonants. The Tiberian system (named for Tiberias in Palestine), which also used dots along with short dashes but placed them mainly below the consonants, became the most widely used and is still employed today for printing the Hebrew Bible. The Tiberian system seems to have been fully developed by the end of the eighth century. The Hebrew alphabet was eventually used in the Middle Ages for other languages, including Arabic, Turkish, Yiddish (Judeo-German), and Judezmo or Ladino (Judeo-Spanish).

The Syriac alphabet (see Figure 2), which survives in monuments from as early as the first century A.D., had letter forms that lent themselves to connection with a preceding or following letter. It was used for copying the second-century Peshitta translation of the Bible. Originally at home on the east shore of the Mediterranean in a form called Estrangela, the Syriac alphabet expanded eastward and eventually split into western and eastern branches: the Jacobite remained in the original homeland; the Nestorian, still in use today, developed among the Nestorian Christians who had begun to migrate eastward in the second half of the fifth century and who finally reached India and even China. The Nestorian alphabet was

Fig. 1 Hebrew

Phonetic value	2nd century A.D.	A.D. 916–917	Italian Rashi script
ʾ	אאא	א	ħ
b	ככ	ב	ב
g		ג	ג
d	דד	ד	ד
h	הההּ	ה	ה
w	וו	ו	ו
z	ו	ז	ז
ḥ	חח	ח	ח
ṭ	ϭϭ	ט	ט
j	יי	י	׳
k	ככ	כך	כך
l	ךך	ל	ל
m	מם	מם	מ ס
n	נן	נן	נן
s		ס	ס
ʿ	ע	ע	ע
p	פף	פף	פף
ṣ	צץ	צץ	צץ
q	ק	ק	ק
r	ר	ר	ר
š	ש	ש	ש
t	תתת	ת	ת

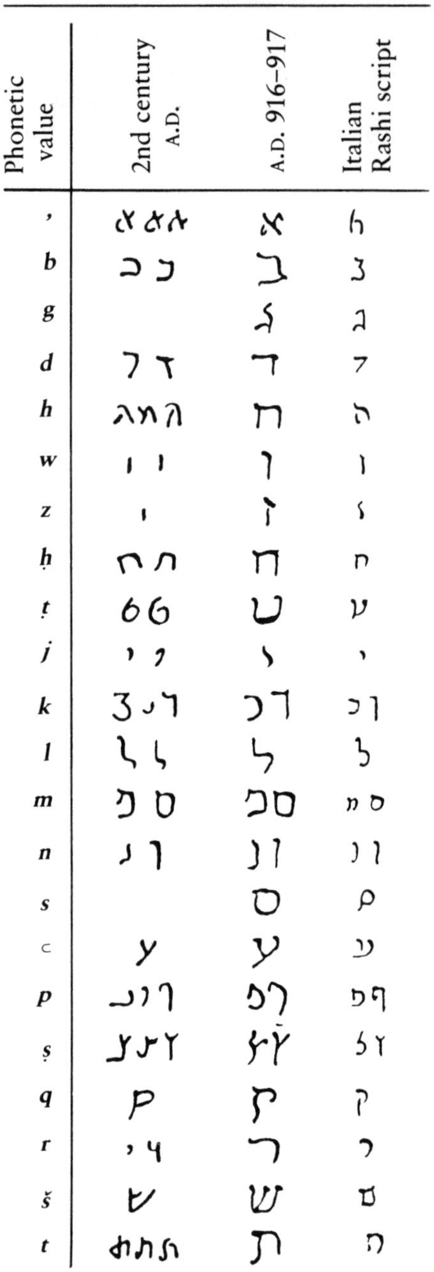

From Hans Jensen, *Sign, Symbol and Script*, 3rd ed. (1969). COURTESY OF THE PUTNAM PUBLISHING GROUP

the main ingredient in the Syro-Malabar alphabet used in southwest India. The vowel indicators that were introduced into the Syriac alphabet and even-

Fig. 2   Syriac

Phonetic value	Inscription of A.D. 512	Estrangelo	Nestorian	Jacobitic
ʾ				
b				
g				
d				
h				
w				
z				
ḥ				
ṭ				
j				
k				
l				
m				
n				
s				
ᶜ				
p·f				
ṣ				
q				
r				
š				
t				

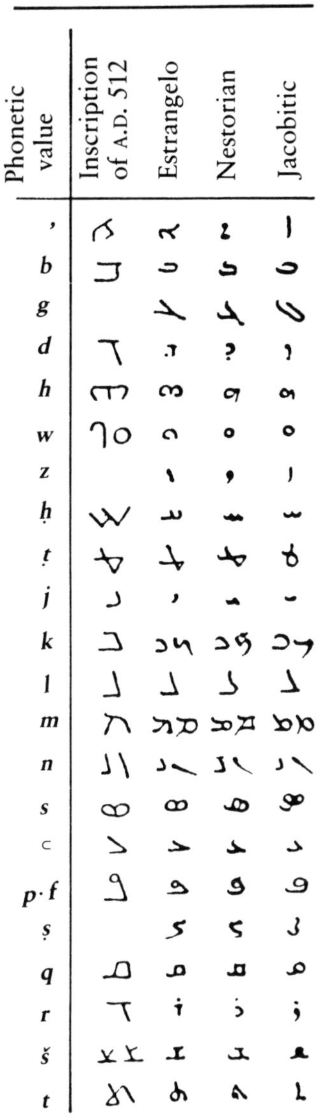

From Hans Jensen, *Sign, Symbol and Script,* 3rd ed. (1969). COURTESY OF THE PUTNAM PUBLISHING GROUP

tually became supralinear or sublinear dots in the Nestorian alphabet and small Greek letters in the Jacobite may have influenced the kind of vowel signs used in the Hebrew alphabet.

The Arabic alphabet (see Figure 3), used over a greater area during the Middle Ages than any other alphabet and second only to the Latin alphabet in the number of users today, owed its popularity to Islam. The alphabet of the Koran, it traveled with Islam from Arabia to India and beyond in the east, to Spain, and in the fifteenth century even into the Balkans. Only a handful of pre-Islamic examples of the alphabet survive. Because Arabic had more consonantal sounds than the standard twenty-two-letter North Semitic alphabet represented, six new letters were added and the order of the letters was changed to bring letters with similar forms or phonetic values together. Two basic types of script developed. The Kufic, originally an angular, epigraphic script, became popular for copies of the Koran. The Neskhi, more rounded and cursive, is the ancestor of the modern Arabic script. A third type, apparently derived from the Kufic, had developed in the Maghreb by the beginning of the tenth century. The indication of vowel sounds by dots, which may have begun in the pre-Islamic period, was well established in the eighth century, though Arabic as a living language had less need of this help than Hebrew. The Arabic alphabet was eventually adapted for use by many other languages, including Persian, Turkish, and Berber.

A fourth Semitic alphabet, which derived around the middle of the fourth century from the South Arabian branch of the South Semitic script, is the Ethiopic or Old Abyssinian (see Figure 4). It had an unusual way of indicating vocalization. The short *a* sound was built into the basic form of each of its twenty-six consonantal letters. By adding a line or circle to a letter, or by lengthening or curving one of its strokes, six further vowel sounds, or even the absence of a vowel, could be indicated. The Ethiopic is unique among Semitic alphabets in being written from left to right, probably under Greek influence. The modern languages of Ethiopia still use the old alphabet, though sometimes together with new signs.

The Greek alphabet (see Figure 5) was among the most important inherited by the Middle Ages, both because of its widespread use and because of the richness of the literature preserved in it. In addition, the inherited Greek alphabet furnished most of the elements for the Coptic, Gothic, and Cyrillic alphabets, and an earlier branch of the Greek family of alphabets furnished the elements for the Latin. The area in which Greek was a "mother alphabet" contracted during the Middle Ages. This contraction was tied to the political fate of the Byzantine Empire, which gradually lost its Near Eastern, African, and Sicilian provinces to the Muslims, its Italian holdings to the Latins, its Balkan holdings to the Slavs, and finally in 1453 its very existence to the Turks.

ALPHABETS

Fig. 3 Arabic

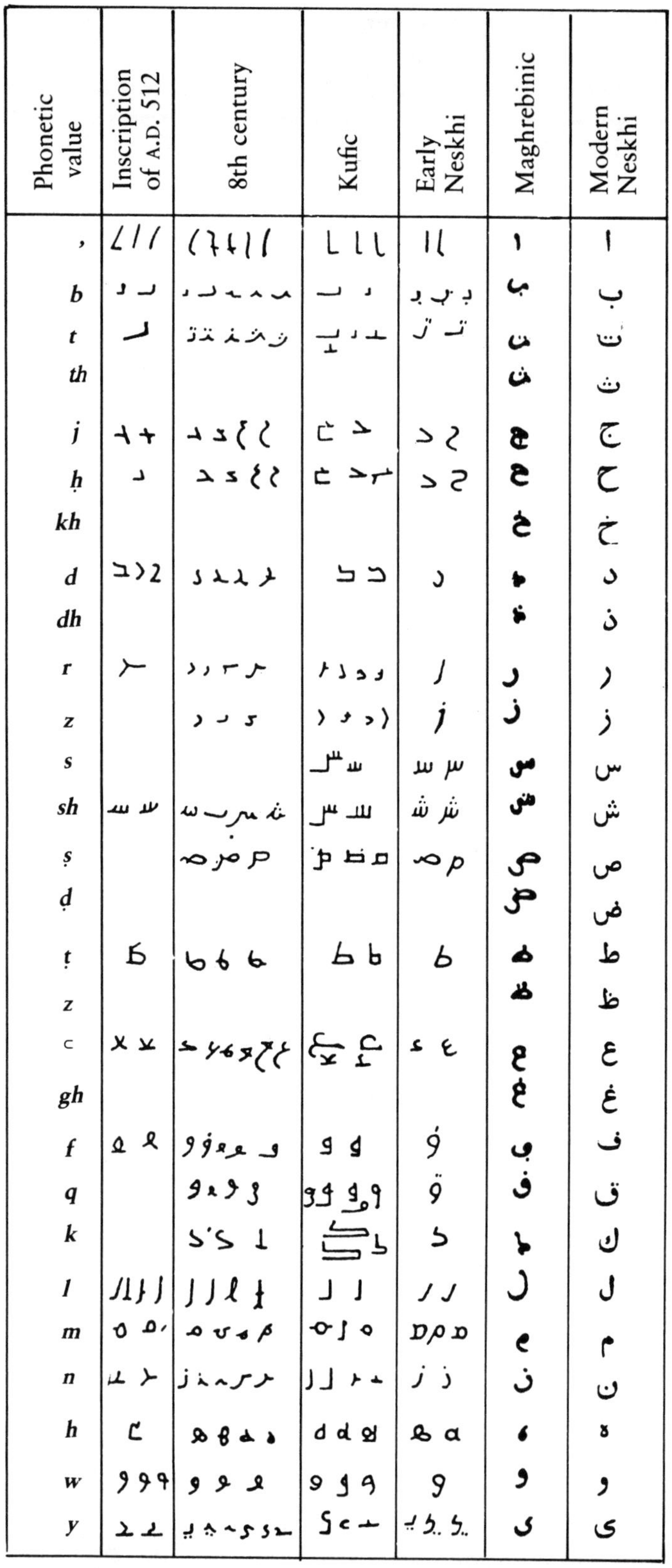

Cols. 2–5: From David Diringer, *The Alphabet: A Key to the History of Mankind,* 3rd ed. (1968). COURTESY OF FUNK AND WAGNALLS, A DIVISION OF READER'S DIGEST BOOKS, INC.

Col. 6: From James G. Février, *Histoire de l'écriture,* new ed. (1959). COURTESY OF ÉDITIONS PAYOT

Col. 7: From Albert Socin, *Arabic Grammar,* rev. by W. H. Worrell (1922). G. E. STECHERT AND CO.

Fig. 4   Ethiopic or Old Abyssinian

Phonetic value	Consonant					+ ē or without vowel	
	+ ā	+ ū	+ ī	+ ā	+ ē		+ ō
h	ሀ	ሁ	ሂ	ሃ	ሄ	ህ	ሆ
l	ለ	ሉ	ሊ	ላ	ሌ	ል	ሎ
ḥ	ሐ	ሑ	ሒ	ሓ	ሔ	ሕ	ሖ
m	መ	ሙ	ሚ	ማ	ሜ	ም	ሞ
š	ሠ	ሡ	ሢ	ሣ	ሤ	ሥ	ሦ
r	ረ	ሩ	ሪ	ራ	ሬ	ር	ሮ
s	ሰ	ሱ	ሲ	ሳ	ሴ	ስ	ሶ
q	ቀ	ቁ	ቂ	ቃ	ቄ	ቅ	ቆ
b	በ	ቡ	ቢ	ባ	ቤ	ብ	ቦ
t	ተ	ቱ	ቲ	ታ	ቴ	ት	ቶ
ḫ	ኀ	ኁ	ኂ	ኃ	ኄ	ኅ	ኆ
n	ነ	ኑ	ኒ	ና	ኔ	ን	ኖ
'	አ	ኡ	ኢ	ኣ	ኤ	እ	ኦ
k	ከ	ኩ	ኪ	ካ	ኬ	ክ	ኮ
w	ወ	ዉ	ዊ	ዋ	ዌ	ው	ዎ
ʿ	ዐ	ዑ	ዒ	ዓ	ዔ	ዕ	ዖ
z	ዘ	ዙ	ዚ	ዛ	ዜ	ዝ	ዞ
j	የ	ዩ	ዪ	ያ	ዬ	ይ	ዮ
d	ደ	ዱ	ዲ	ዳ	ዴ	ድ	ዶ
g	ገ	ጉ	ጊ	ጋ	ጌ	ግ	ጎ
ṭ	ጠ	ጡ	ጢ	ጣ	ጤ	ጥ	ጦ
p	ጰ	ጱ	ጲ	ጳ	ጴ	ጵ	ጶ
ṣ	ጸ	ጹ	ጺ	ጻ	ጼ	ጽ	ጾ
ḍ	ፀ	ፁ	ፂ	ፃ	ፄ	ፅ	ፆ
f	ፈ	ፉ	ፊ	ፋ	ፌ	ፍ	ፎ
p	ፐ	ፑ	ፒ	ፓ	ፔ	ፕ	ፖ

From Hans Jensen, *Sign, Symbol and Script*, 3rd ed. (1969). COURTESY OF THE PUTNAM PUBLISHING GROUP

Fig. 5   Greek

Phonetic value	Classical	Uncial 7th century	Minuscule 10th–11th centuries	Modern	
				Capitals	Small letters
a	A	ᶁ	a	A A	a ɑ
b	B	B	ʙ u	ß	b β
g	Γ	Γ	v γ	ℊ	γ
d	Δ	ᴀ	Δ δ	D	ſ
ĕ	E	Є	є ъ	ℰ ℰ	ε
z	Z	ᴢ	ȝ ʒ	ℤ	ʒʒʃ
ē	H	н	ʰ ʟ н	ℋ	η y
th	Θ	ϑ	θ ϑ	ɑ	ϑ
i	I	ɪ	ɪ ι	ℐ ℐ	ι
k	K	к	к k	ℋ	u ĸ
l	Λ	λ	ℓ λ	ℛ	λ ι
m	M	M	μ μ	ℳ	μ
n	N	ɴ	ν ν	ℕ	v
x	Ξ	̄ξ ̄ʒ	ȝ ȝ	ℤ	ȝ ȝ
o	O	ᴏ	o	ℴ	σ
p	Π	Γ	π ϖ	ℼ	ω
r	P	ρ	ϸeȝ	℘	ρ
s	Σ	ϲ	σ(ϲ	ℒℒ	σ ϲ
t	T	т	τ ℓ	ℐ	τ ι
u(y)	Υ	γ	ν	℣	ν
ph	Φ	Φ	ϕ φ	℘	ɥ γ
kh	X	χ	χ	ℵ	x t
ps	Ψ	ϒ ϯ	ϯ ϯ	ℽ ℽ	γ
ō	Ω	ω	∞	ℳ	ω

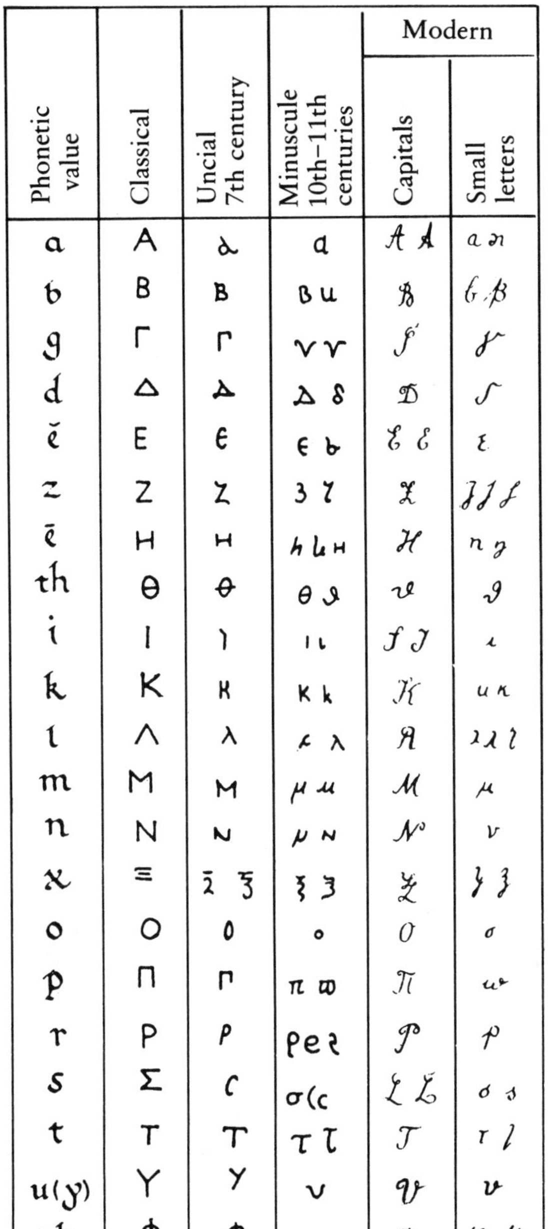

From David Diringer, *The Alphabet: A Key to the History of Mankind*, 3rd ed. (1968). COURTESY OF FUNK AND WAGNALLS, A DIVISION OF READER'S DIGEST BOOKS, INC.

Although Greek did not retain during the Middle Ages the status of international learned language that it had enjoyed during antiquity, some Greek-writing monastic enclaves nevertheless managed to maintain themselves behind the Arabic and Latin lines. There were also scholars in the non-Greek world who possessed a knowledge of at least the Greek alphabet and not infrequently of the Greek language and literature as well. Unlike the Semitic alphabets, the Greek was written from left to right, and its twenty-four letters included vowels as well as consonants. No new letters were introduced during the Middle Ages, but a minuscule form of script, with ascending and descending strokes projecting beyond the body of the letters, was developed by the ninth century to replace the inherited capital and uncial forms. The rough breathing sign, or *spiritus asper*, originally the left half of a capital *eta* (*H*), was transformed during the Middle Ages into the reversed apostrophe (ʽ) still used today. The Greek letters also continued to serve as numerals.

Of the inherited alphabets based on the Greek, the oldest is the Coptic (see Figure 6), surviving examples of which may date from as early as the second century. With the increasing conversion of the Egyptians to Christianity the new alphabet, which was used especially for copying Christian texts, gradually supplanted the native and very ancient hieroglyphic, hieratic, and demotic scripts. Greek, which was already the language of the Egyptian elite classes, provided twenty-five letters in their uncial form (including the digamma for the number 6) for the Coptic alphabet. Seven additional signs were taken over from the demotic script to indicate Egyptian sounds that did not occur in Greek. The Coptic alphabet was in turn gradually supplanted by the Arabic as the Egyptian Monophysite Christians began to convert to Islam after the Muslim conquest starting in the 640's.

A second alphabet based mainly on the Greek and from the transitional period was the Gothic (see Figure 7), devised by the fourth-century Arian Christian missionary Ulfilas for his translation of the Bible into the language of the Visigoths, the first Germanic people to accept Christianity. Of the twenty-seven letters in the Gothic alphabet (of which two had only a numerical value), eighteen or nineteen were borrowed from the Greek alphabet in its uncial form, six from the Latin, and two or three from the runic. The borrowed letters, however, did not always retain their original phonetic values in the Gothic alphabet. Of the few extant monuments in the alphabet, which hardly seems to have survived the demise of the Ostrogothic kingdom in Italy, the most famous is the Gospel book copied on purple parchment in silver ink (and hence called the Codex Argenteus), now preserved in Uppsala and probably copied in the sixth century for Theodoric the Great.

The Latin alphabet (see Figure 8), extremely successful in antiquity and destined eventually for the widest use of all in modern times, also originated from the Greek but mainly in a western Greek form mediated by the Etruscans. It underwent a considerable displacement in areas of use during the Middle Ages. The former southern and eastern Mediterranean provinces of the Roman Empire gradually ceased to use Latin even as a secondary, administrative language after the Islamic conquests and the development of Byzantium as a completely independent empire. The return of Latin to the Middle East with the Crusades in the twelfth century proved to be only a temporary phenomenon.

The losses in the south and east were eventually more than compensated for by gains in the north. The Latin alphabet spread to the Irish by the fifth century, to the Picts in Scotland by the sixth, to the Anglo-Saxons in England in the seventh, to the Germans north of the Danube and east of the Rhine in the eighth, to the western Slavs in the ninth and tenth, to the Hungarians in the tenth, and to the Scandinavians from the ninth to the eleventh centuries. In another dimension of expansion it was adopted during the Middle Ages for writing all of the Western European vernacular languages.

The inherited Latin alphabet had twenty-three letters, to which the only definitive medieval addition was *w*, which can be seen in the eleventh-century Domesday Book and in the Bayeux Tapestry. Although *u* and *v* were used in antiquity and the Middle Ages, both forms were used interchangeably for vocalic as well as consonantal sounds. Not until the seventeenth century did the *u* and *v* become truly distinct letters by taking on an exclusively vocalic and exclusively consonantal value respectively. The same can be said of *i* and *j*. In the late sixth century the Merovingian king Chilperic I ordered the addition of four other letters to the Latin alphabet, doubtless in imitation of the attempted addition in the first century of three letters by the Roman Emperor Claudius, but with no discernible effect.

More successful was the addition in the eighth century of several runes to the Latin alphabet used in England for vernacular texts or for Anglo-Saxon proper names in Latin texts. The runic sign for wen

Fig. 6 Coptic

	Phonetic value		Phonetic value
Ⲁ	a	Ⲣ	r
Ⲃ	v (b)	Ⲥ	s
Ⲅ	g	Ⲧ	t
Ⲇ	d	Ⲩ	y, u
Ⲉ	ĕ	Ⲫ	ph
Ⲍ	z	Ⲭ	ch=kh
Ⲏ	i, ē	Ⲯ	ps
Ⲑ	ṯ	Ⲱ	omega
Ⲓ	i	Ϣ	š
Ⲕ	k	Ϥ	f
Ⲗ	l	Ϧ	ḫ
Ⲙ	m	Ϩ	h
Ⲛ	n	Ϫ	ġ
Ⲝ	x	Ϭ	č (ancient)
Ⲟ	ŏ		
Ⲡ	p	Ϯ	ti

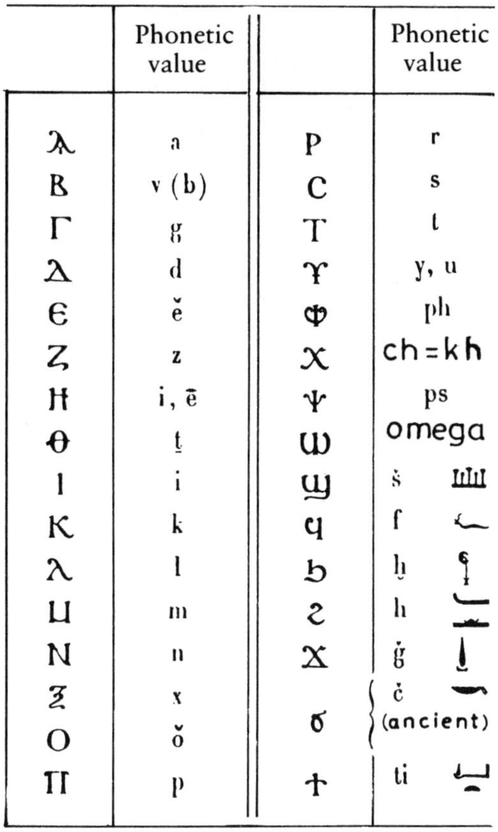

From David Diringer, *The Alphabet: A Key to the History of Mankind,* 3rd ed. (1968). COURTESY OF FUNK AND WAGNALLS, A DIVISION OF READER'S DIGEST BOOKS, INC.

Fig. 7 Gothic

𐌰	a	𐌹, ï	i	𐍂	r
𐌱	b	𐌺	k	𐍃	s
𐌲	g	𐌻	l	𐍄	t
𐌳	d	𐌼	m	𐍅	w
𐌴	e	𐌽	n	𐍆	f
𐌵	q	𐌾	y	𐍇	ch
𐌶	z	𐌿	u	𐍈	hw
𐌷	h	𐍀	p	𐍉	o
𐌸	þ	𐍁	90	𐍊	900

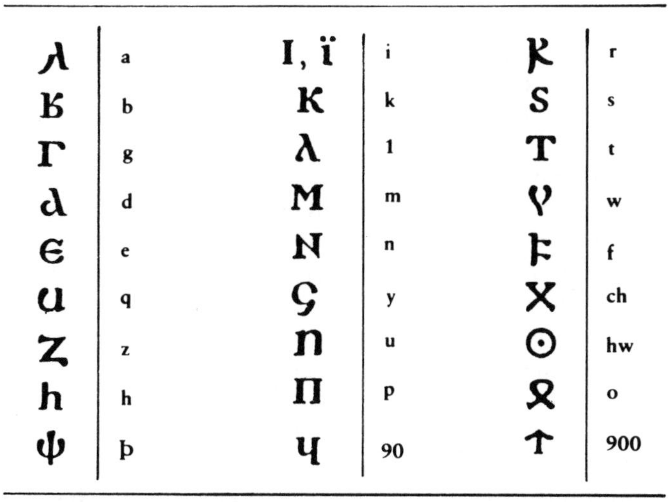

From James G. Février, *Histoire de l'écriture,* new ed. (1959). COURTESY OF ÉDITIONS PAYOT

Fig. 8 Latin

Uncial, *ca.* A.D. 800, with *k* missing:

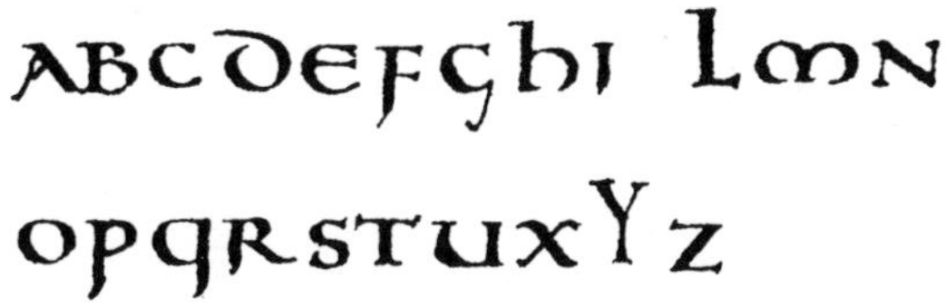

Caroline minuscule, *ca.* A.D. 800:

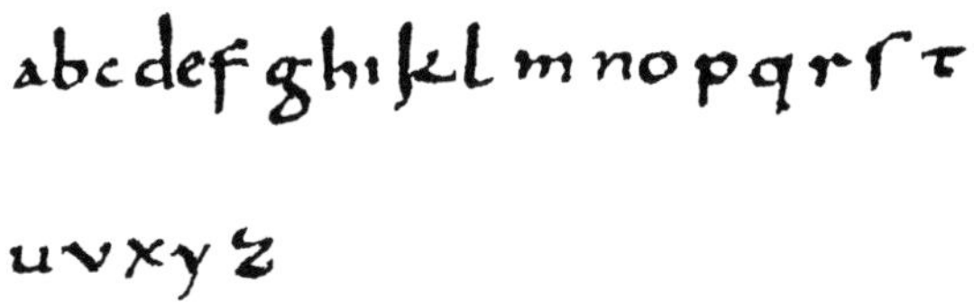

Formal Gothic, *ca.* A.D. 1500:

Col. 1: Uncial, from the Lorsch Gospels, *ca.* 800. From *The Lorsch Gospels* (1967). COURTESY OF GEORGE BRAZILLER

Col. 2: Caroline minuscule, from the Lorsch Gospels. From *The Lorsch Gospels* (1967). COURTESY OF GEORGE BRAZILLER

Col. 3: Formal Gothic, *ca.* 1500, from the Gregorious Bock pattern book for scribes. COURTESY OF THE BEINECKE RARE BOOK AND MANUSCRIPT LIBRARY, YALE UNIVERSITY

ALPHABETS

Fig. 9 Armenian

	Phonetic value		Phonetic value
ա	a	յ	y, j, h,
բ	b – p	ն	n
գ	g – k	շ	š
դ	d – t	ո	o
ե	e	չ	č, č, čh
զ	z	պ	p - b
է	e	ջ	ǧ ǰ, dž
ը	Silent ə e	ռ	ṙ
թ	t'	ս	s
ժ	ž	վ	v
ի	i	տ	t – d
լ	l (Scott. ch)	ր	r
խ	ḫ x	ց	c, t's
ծ	ts z	ւ	u, w
կ	k – g	փ	p, p', ph
հ	h	ք	k, k', x
ձ	d – z	օ	o
ղ	tł gh	ֆ	f
ճ	č		&
մ	m		

From David Diringer, *The Alphabet: A Key to the History of Mankind,* 3rd ed. (1968). COURTESY OF FUNK AND WAGNALLS, A DIVISION OF READER'S DIGEST BOOKS, INC.

Fig. 10 Georgian

Khutsuri		Mkhedruli	Phonetic value	Khutsuri		Mkhedruli	Phonetic value
Majuscule	Minuscule			Majuscule	Minuscule		
Ⴀ	ⴀ	ა	a	Ⴒ	ⴒ	ტ	t
Ⴁ	ⴁ	ბ	b	Ⴓ	ⴓ	უ	u
Ⴂ	ⴂ	გ	g (hard)	Ⴣ	ⴣ	ჳ	wi
Ⴃ	ⴃ	დ	d	Ⴔ	ⴔ	ფ	p'(p
Ⴄ	ⴄ	ე	e	Ⴕ	ⴕ	ქ	k'
Ⴅ	ⴅ	ვ	v	Ⴖ	ⴖ	ღ	ł (g
Ⴆ	ⴆ	ზ	z	Ⴗ	ⴗ	ყ	k̇
Ⴡ	ⴡ	ჱ	h (weak)	Ⴘ	ⴘ	შ	š (s
Ⴇ	ⴇ	თ	t'	Ⴙ	ⴙ	ჩ	č
Ⴈ	ⴈ	ი	i	Ⴚ	ⴚ	ც	t z
Ⴉ	ⴉ	კ	k	Ⴛ	ⴛ	ძ	dz
Ⴊ	ⴊ	ლ	l	Ⴜ	ⴜ	წ	t s
Ⴋ	ⴋ	მ	m	Ⴝ	ⴝ	ჭ	t š
Ⴌ	ⴌ	ნ	n	Ⴞ	ⴞ	ხ	x
Ⴢ	ⴢ	ჲ	i (ie, y)	Ⴤ	ⴤ	ჴ	x h
Ⴍ	ⴍ	ო	o	Ⴟ	ⴟ	ჯ	dz
Ⴎ	ⴎ	პ	p	Ⴠ	ⴠ	ჰ	h (as
Ⴏ	ⴏ	ჟ	ž (zh)	Ⴥ	ⴥ	ჵ	hō
Ⴐ	ⴐ	რ	r			ჶ	f
Ⴑ	ⴑ	ს	s (hard)			ჷ	ə

From David Diringer, *The Alphabet: A Key to the History of Mankind,* 3rd ed.(1968). COURTESY OF FUNK AND WAGNALLS, A DIVISION OF READER'S DIGEST BOOKS, INC.

(*ρ*) was used until the thirteenth century. The runic thorn (Þ) was used until the fifteenth century, by which time it had assumed a form easily confusable with *y.* Middle English also introduced the yogh (ʒ) for several different sounds.

Two other alphabets that developed in the transitional period and that had some connection with the Greek are the Armenian (see Figure 9) and Georgian. Tradition links the invention of both alphabets with St. Mesrob, a fifth-century Armenian missionary who translated the Bible into Armenian and devised an alphabet for this purpose "after the system of the Greek syllables." Greek influence may be evident in the inclusion of vowels, in the rightward direction of the writing, and in the order of the letters; but the forms of the letters in both scripts seem more closely related to those of the Persian or Pahlavi alphabet. Armenian originally had thirty-six letters, later thirty-eight; the letters representing sounds not occurring in Greek were inserted at various places in the original Greek order, thereby changing the numerical values of the letters.

Of the two forms of Georgian alphabets that developed (see Figure 10), only the thirty-eight-letter Khutsuri or ecclesiastical script is credited to Mesrob. The Mkhedruli or military script, of forty letters, which may or may not be older is still used today. The Georgian alphabet is considered a model

ALPHABETS

of accuracy and clarity in representing the sounds of the language.

Two alphabets, very different from any hitherto considered and having origins that are still obscure, are the runic used by the Germans (see Figure 11) and the Oghamic used by the Celts (see Figure 12). Both were used mainly for brief inscriptions on stone, metal, or wood. No extended literary texts survive in Ogham, and the few in runes are mostly late medieval.

The runic alphabet, which survives in about 4,000 inscriptions, mostly from Sweden, probably derived from an Alpine version of the Etruscan script with an admixture, perhaps, of some magical symbols. It may have originated in the pre-Christian era, but no surviving examples seem to antedate the third century A.D. The runes were used by all the Germanic peoples, originally in a form comprising twenty-four letters. Among the Anglo-Saxons in England the number of letters began to increase in the sixth century in response to gradual differentiation of vocalic and a few consonantal sounds; a final total of thirty-three had been reached by the tenth century, when the use of runes began to decline. Eventually English runes survived only in the wen and thorn taken over into the Latin alphabet. On the Continent the use of runes was dying out in the Germanic lands south of Denmark by the eighth century, but their use continued in a sixteen-letter alphabet in Scandinavian lands and in some remote places until well after the Middle Ages. The order of the runic alphabet, which is called the futhark from its first six letters, was unique. The original twenty-four runes were divided into three groups of eight; the sixteen-letter alphabet was divided into three groups of six, five, and five letters respectively. Although the original runes may have been round, their use on wood seems to have favored angular forms and to have dictated the avoidance of horizontal strokes that would run along the grain.

The Ogham alphabet survives in about 375 inscriptions, mostly from Ireland but also from Wales, Scotland, and the Isle of Man. None of these inscriptions, found mainly on tombstones, antedates the fourth century, though the invention of the alphabet may go further back. Only isolated examples, including some marginal notes in manuscripts, postdate the mid seventh century. The inventor of the alphabet, possibly moved by cryptographic intent, was probably of south Irish background and may have known both the runic and Latin alphabets. The original twenty letters of the Ogham alphabet were made

Fig. 11 Runic

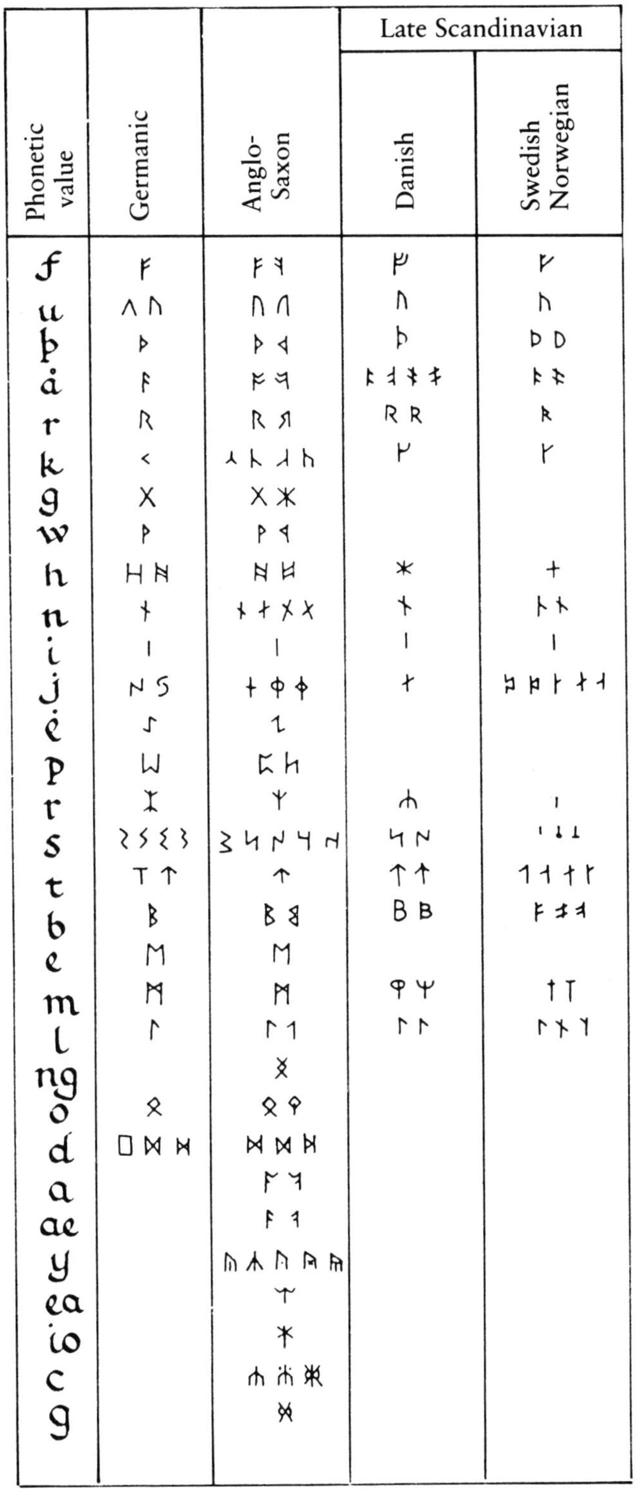

From David Diringer, *The Alphabet: A Key to the History of Mankind,* 3rd ed. (1968). COURTESY OF FUNK AND WAGNALLS, A DIVISION OF READER'S DIGEST BOOKS, INC.

Fig. 12 Oghamic

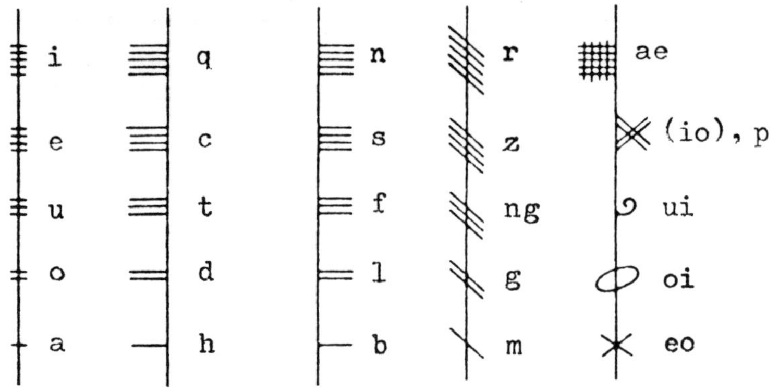

From James G. Février, *Histoire de l'écriture,* new ed. (1959). COURTESY OF ÉDITIONS PAYOT

by cutting or drawing one to five short lines on a vertical or horizontal axis line in four different ways: (1) to the right or below; (2) to the left or above; (3) through at a slant; (4) through at right angles (for the vowels). The vowels were also made with one to five notches on the axis; and because the axis itself was often the edge of the stone, the letters went around corners and eroded more easily. Vertical running inscriptions were read from bottom to top. The division of the letters into four groups may be related to the division of runes into groups. Five supplementary signs were eventually added for diphthongs and the *p* sound.

Of the alphabets invented during the Middle Ages, the Cyrillic had by far the greatest numbers of users and areas of use. One of two basic types of Slavonic alphabet (the other being the Glagolitic), the Cyrillic alphabet (see Figure 13) was named for St. Cyril. A ninth-century Greek apostle to the Slavs, Cyril translated biblical and liturgical texts into Old Bulgarian or Old Church Slavic for the benefit of his Christian converts in Moravia and was credited with having devised a new alphabet for this purpose. However, more scholars connect Cyril with the invention of the Glagolitic than of the Cyrillic alphabet, and some associate him with the invention of both. The question of priority between the two alphabets is still disputed. The earliest surviving Cyrillic inscriptions date from the late ninth or tenth century, and manuscripts from the eleventh; Glagolitic manuscripts survive from the late tenth century and inscriptions from the eleventh. The Cyrillic alphabet had forty-three letters, most of which were borrowed from the Greek alphabet in its uncial form. The remaining letters for Slavic sounds not found in Greek have forms modified from the Greek or similar to Glagolitic. The Cyrillic eventually became far more popular than the Glagolitic, having been adopted by all Slavs professing the Greek Orthodox form of Christianity and by the Russians in particular. The use of Cyrillic in a slightly modified form in modern times spread eastward to the Pacific Ocean and was adapted for the writing of numerous non-Slavonic languages.

The forty letters of the Glagolitic alphabet (see Figure 13) stand for the same sounds and have the same names as the corresponding Cyrillic letters but are rather different in appearance. Some of the letters standing for peculiarly Slavic sounds have similar forms in both alphabets; but the origin of these and the other Glagolitic forms has not yet been satisfactorily explained, even though scholars have looked in almost every conceivable direction and have found Hebrew models for several letters. The Glagolitic alphabet survived in Bulgaria until the twelfth century, when it yielded to the Cyrillic. Further west it eventually yielded to the Latin alphabet used by the Roman Catholic church, and after the Turkish conquest of the Byzantine Empire it yielded in some places to the Arabic. The triumph of the Latin over the Glagolitic occurred very quickly in Moravia, but in the western half of the Balkan peninsula, particularly in Croatia, the process was drawn out. Luxurious Glagolitic manuscripts were still being produced in the fourteenth century, and in some parts of Dalmatia and Montenegro Glagolitic is still used for the Slavonic liturgy. Both the Cyrillic and Glagolitic alphabets reflect the phonetic values of the Slavonic languages more completely and unambiguously than the Greek and Latin alphabets represent theirs.

Although the Middle Ages produced no other al-

Fig. 13 Slavonic

Cyrillic	Glagolitic	Phonetic value
а	Ⰰ	*a*
б	Ⰱ	*b*
в	Ⰲ	*v*
г	Ⰳ	*g*
д	Ⰴ	*d*
є	Ⰵ	*e*
ж	Ⰶ	*ž*
ѕ	Ⰷ	*dz*
з	Ⰸ	*z*
и, і	Ⰹ Ⰺ, Ⰻ	*i*
	Ⰼ	*ġ*
к	Ⰽ	*k*
л	Ⰾ	*l*
м	Ⰿ	*m*
н	Ⱀ	*n*
о	Ⱁ	*o*
п	Ⱂ	*p*
р	Ⱃ	*r*
с	Ⱄ	*s*
т	Ⱅ	*t*
оу	Ⱆ	*u*
ф	Ⱇ	*f*
х	Ⱈ	*ch*
ѡ	Ⱉ	*o*
щ	Ⱋ	*št*
ц	Ⱌ	*c*
ч	Ⱍ	*č*
ш	Ⱎ	*š*
ъ	Ⱏ	*ъ*
ꙑ, ъи	ⰟⰉ, ⰟⰊ, ⰟⰋ	*y*
ь	Ⱐ	*ь*
ѣ	Ⱑ	*ě*
ю	Ⱓ	*yu*
ꙗ		*ya*
ѥ		*ye*
ѧ, ꙙ	Ⱔ	*ę*
ѫ	Ⱘ	*ǫ*
ѩ	Ⱗ	*yę*
ѭ	Ⱙ	*yǫ*
ѯ		*ks* (Greek ξ)
ѱ		*ps* (Greek ψ)
ѳ	Ⱚ	Greek ϑ
ѵ	Ⱛ	Greek υ

Col. 1: Cyrillic. Col. 2: Glagolitic. From August Leskien, *Handbuch der altbulgarischen (altkirchenslavischen) Sprache,* 7th ed. (1955). COURTESY OF CARL WINTER VERLAG

phabet that can even remotely compare in importance with the Slavonic, the invention of the Slavonic by no means exhausted ingenuity on the subject of alphabets. Not only were numerous collections of foreign alphabets made in the Latin world, but a considerable number of fanciful or curious alphabets was also invented, of which that ascribed to Aethicus Ister is perhaps the best known. Various kinds of partial or complete cryptographic alphabets were also devised; the Oghamic, as already noted, may originally have been of this type.

The alphabet was also put to various nonliteral uses or given nonliteral meanings during the Middle Ages. In the dedication of a church, for example, the bishop inscribed a Greek alphabet along a line on the floor and then wrote a Latin alphabet along another line that crossed the first to form an *X*. An alphabet was sometimes used in the making of chirographs. These were original medieval documents copied in duplicate on a single sheet of parchment and then cut apart, often in indentured fashion, so that each party concerned could have a copy. The name is derived from the word *chirographum,* which was often, as part of the means of authentication, written in the space between the copies through which the cut would be made. An alphabet was occasionally written in here and cut through in place of the *chirographum.* The books of the Old Testament were often counted, from at least the time of St. Jerome, in a rather Procrustean fashion as twenty-two, so that their number would accord with the number of letters in the Hebrew alphabet. Individual letters were given mystical meanings. Isidore of Seville in his *Etymologiae* handed on to the Latin Middle Ages knowledge of the five mystical Greek letters: *upsilon* (Υ) symbolized human life and the choice that had to be made in adolescence between virtue and vice; *theta* (Θ) signified death; *tau* (T) symbolized the Lord's cross; and *alpha* (A) and *omega* (Ω) stood for the beginning and the end, as affirmed in the Book of Revelation. These last two letters were already being used in sixth-century manuscripts as a decorative motif hanging from the arms of a cross. Medieval authors would add new spiritual meanings. *A,* for example, because it had three strokes, was a type of the Trinity, as were *E* and *M. X* was a type of the Cross. Other letters could signify the Old and New Testaments. Words were sometimes written to form figures. The body of a centaur, for example, was composed in the ninth century out of Latin rustic capital letters, probably in imitation of the *carmina figurata*, or shaped poems, of the fourth-century poet Publilius Optatianus Porphyrius. Riddles were written about each letter of the alphabet, and alphabetic acrostics were composed by the Venerable Bede and others. Their original inspiration perhaps came from the Hebrew alphabet introduced into the Lamentations of Jeremiah and Psalm 118 (Vulgate numbering).

Familiarity with ancient views on the origin of the alphabet was most easily acquired in the Latin West through Isidore of Seville; direct access was also available to Pliny the Elder's account in *Naturalis historia*. There seems to have been general agreement that the Greeks received the alphabet from the Phoenicians, and the Romans from the Greeks; but there was disagreement about the more remote origins. Allowing that the original inventors may have been the Assyrians, the Egyptians, or the Syrians, Pliny cited one source who claimed that the Egyptians invented the alphabet "15,000 years before Phoroneus, the most ancient king of Greece" and another who attributed writing to the Babylonians at least 490,000 years earlier. Ignoring these extravagant claims, Isidore argued for the priority of the Hebrew alphabet, the source, he said, of the Greek and Latin ones, and he even accorded to the Hebrew the title of "mother of all languages and letters." But he also inconsistently made Moses responsible for the Hebrew while crediting Abraham, much earlier, for the Syriac and Chaldean alphabets. In *De civitate Dei* St. Augustine had pushed the beginning of Hebrew writing back far beyond Moses to Heber. In the fifteenth century Nicholas of Cusa, employing in his *Compendium* a not unusual medieval form of historical reasoning based more on fittingness than on actual evidence, pushed the origin of writing all the way back to Adam.

How knowledge of alphabets was disseminated in the Middle Ages is a subject still in need of further investigation. But much information has nevertheless been assembled about medieval abecedaria and about the pen-trial verses used to familiarize students with all the letters of the alphabet.

The significance of the alphabet was highly appreciated and reflected on rather often in the Middle Ages. Both Christians and Moslems regarded writing as a special gift of God. The Christians of the Latin West in the Scholastic period, in accord with their general obsession with understanding what they had previously accepted on faith if it was capable of being understood, submitted the nature of the alphabet to a rigorous examination in order better to comprehend its metaphysical status. They started from the traditional grammatical teaching about the three "accidents" of a letter: its name, its figure or shape, and its power or phonetic value. But they carried their systematic analysis far beyond previous efforts in this line. A work such as the *Summa gramatica* of Johannes Dacus, written in 1280, attempted to do for the understanding of the nature of the letters of the alphabet something similar to what Thomas Aquinas had tried to do less than a decade earlier in his *Summa theologiae* for understanding of the Bible.

BIBLIOGRAPHY

Bernhard Bischoff, "Übersicht über die nichtdiplomatischen Geheimschriften des Mittelalters," in *Mitteilungen des Instituts für österreichische Geschichtsforschung*, 62 (1954); *Mittelalterliche Studien*, I (1966), 74–87; and *Paläographie des römischen Altertums und des abendländischen Mittelalters* (1979); Centre International de Synthèse, *L'écriture et la psychologie des peuples* (1963); Marcel Cohen, *La grande invention de l'écriture et son évolution*, 3 vols. (1958); René Derolez, "Ogam, 'Egyptian,' 'African' and 'Gothic' Alphabets," in *Scriptorium*, 5 (1951); David Diringer, *The Alphabet: A Key to the History of Mankind*, 3rd ed., 2 vols. (1968); Hans Jensen, *Sign, Symbol and Script*, George Unwin, trans., 3rd ed. (1969); Berthold L. Ullman, *Ancient Writing and Its Influence* (1932, repr. 1969); and "Abecedaria and Their Purpose," in *Transactions of the Cambridge Bibliographical Society*, 3 (1959–1963); Berthold Wolpe, "Florilegium Alphabeticum: Alphabets in Medieval Manuscripts," in A. S. Osley, ed., *Calligraphy and Palaeography* (1965), 69–74, pls. 18–28, and fig. 6.

JAMES J. JOHN

[See also **Acrostics and Wordplay; Alphabetization; Paleography**.]

ALPHANUS OF SALERNO (1015/1020–1085) was born at Salerno and taught at the university there before entering the Benedictine Order at Monte Cassino in 1056 with his friend Desiderius (later Pope Victor III). He returned to Salerno to be abbot and then archbishop (1058). Alphanus was associated with the Gregorian reforms (it was to him that Gregory VII fled in 1084), but his literary legacy belongs to the revival of classical culture and the growth of new learning in southern Italy. He died at Salerno.

Alphanus' poetic work is characterized by a return to metrical verse following the models of Boethius and Prudentius, and a great familiarity with the classical past. Most of his poems are devotional pieces, but some are dedicated to contemporaries.

Alphanus' other main contribution developed from the secular culture of Salerno. He wrote a medical treatise, and he translated the Greek medical text of Nemesios into Latin. Alphanus stands at the beginning of the medical tradition of the University of Salerno.

BIBLIOGRAPHY

Alphanus' published writings include "Carmina, Sermo Alphani super evangelium, vita et passio sanctae Christinae," in *Patrologia latina*, CXLVII (1879); his translation of *Nemesii episcopi Premnon physicon sive* Περὶ φύσεως 'ανθρώπου, C. Burkhard, ed. (1917); and *Il "De quattuor humoribus corporis humani" di Alfano I arcivescovo di Salerno (secs XI), P. Capparoni, ed. (1928). Also see Frederic J. E. Raby, A History of Christian-Latin Poetry,* 2nd ed. (1953), 242–249.

LEAH SHOPKOW

ALPHARTS TOD, a Middle High German heroic poem, was probably composed in southwest Germany sometime in the thirteenth century, but the dating is uncertain because the poem survives only in a late fifteenth-century manuscript. The story is one of the numerous late accretions to the originally historical account of Dietrich von Bern (Theodoric the Great). The Emperor Ermanrich (the historical Ermanaric, who lived a full century before Theodoric) has challenged Dietrich to surrender himself and become his vassal, or be driven from his lands. Dietrich and his retainers decide to resist. The young Alphart insists, against all good advice, on riding out alone to scout the enemy. In a final attempt to dissuade him, his uncle Hildebrant rides out in disguise and fights him, expecting to defeat the inexperienced youngster easily. Instead, Alphart defeats his uncle and is prevented from killing him only when the latter reveals his identity. Alphart then rides on alone and meets eighty of Ermanrich's warriors. He kills all but eight, who return and report on the amazing unknown warrior. Ermanrich sends out Wittege and Heime—men who had previously been in Dietrich's service. Fighting together, they manage to kill Alphart.

At this point the first fragment breaks off. The second fragment begins with Hildebrant's efforts to raise an army to protect Dietrich and to avenge Alphart's death. He is successful in recruiting many men, and begins his return trip to Bern. Scouting ahead of the main group, Hildebrant encounters several of Ermanrich's men and a battle ensues. Only the arrival of the main contingent saves Hildebrant's life. They succeed in driving away Ermanrich's army, and continue their journey. Upon reaching Bern, they prepare for battle. Ermanrich's men decide to attack before Dietrich's men can be ready. In the giant battle that follows, all of Dietrich's most important vassals seek the honor of killing Wittege and Heime, who are forced to flee the battlefield along with Ermanrich and his chief vassal Sibeche. Dietrich's entire army celebrates its victory.

In spite of its fragmentary and distorted transmission, the poem remains of interest. Its relatively uncluttered plot line sets it apart from the wildly prodigal tales found in the other Dietrich epics.

The poem is composed in long-line strophes in which the rhyme scheme of the four lines is AABB. The metrical form of about half of the stanzas can be scanned in the same meter as the strophe of the *Nibelungenlied,* and the other strophes are in the simpler form of the *Hildebrandston.* Many of the lines of the manuscript are very difficult to scan according to either scheme, and the attempts of editors to restore an even scansion have resulted in a text that often is very far from anything attested in the manuscript.

BIBLIOGRAPHY

Ernst Martin, ed., "Alpharts Tod," in *Deutsches Heldenbuch,* II (1866), has a text reconstructed to fit "classical" Middle High German and a regular metrical scheme. Uwe Zimmer, *Studien zu "Alpharts Tod" nebst einem verbesserten Abdruck der Handschrift* (1972), contains a verbatim transcription of a unique manuscript, an exhaustive study of the poem's language, and an extensive bibliography.

EDWARD R. HAYMES

ALPTIGIN (*d.* 963[?]), Turkish military commander in the Samanid emirate of Transoxania and Khurasan in the eastern Islamic world, and founder in the tenth century of a line of Turkish local rulers at Ghazni in east central Afghanistan that later developed into the Ghaznavid dynasty of sultans.

In the course of the tenth century, the Samanid

emirs came increasingly to depend militarily on a corps of Turkish slave guards, recruited from the inner Asian steppes, whose loyalty, it was believed, would be firmer because of their lack of local ties. Alptigin was such a slave, of unknown tribal affiliation, who had begun his career in the guard of Aḥmad ibn Ismāᶜīl (907–914), had been manumitted by Aḥmad's son and successor Naṣr (914–943), and then, under Nūḥ ibn Naṣr (943–954), had become commander-in-chief *(ḥājib al-ḥujjāb)* of the slave troops. An idealized account of Alptigin's early career in the *Siyāsat-nāma* ("Mirror for Princes") of the Seljuk vizier Niẓām al-Mulk states that Alptigin came to have an entourage of 1,700 personal Turkish slaves, among whom was Sebüktigin, future founder of the Ghaznavid dynasty; and this same source describes Alptigin as Sebüktigin's mentor in all praiseworthy habits and skills.

The opportunity for Alptigin's personal ambitions to have free rein came in the reign of ᶜAbd al-Malik ibn Nūḥ (954–961), when the hold of the Turkish commanders grew tight and the waning personal prestige of the emirs plunged the Samanid emirate into a period of disorder and weak rule that culminated, at the end of the tenth century, in the overthrow of the dynasty. Alptigin secured an ascendancy over the youthful emir, replacing the earlier influence in the state of the former governor of Khurasan, Abū ᶜAlī Chaghānī (died 955), and controlling the vizier Abū ᶜAlī al-Balᶜamī. Despite ᶜAbd al-Malik's efforts to free himself from Alptigin's tutelage, he was obliged in 961 to appoint him governor of the province of Khurasan. However, a crisis arose when the emir died suddenly later that year. Alptigin and Balᶜamī placed the deceased emir's young son Naṣr on the throne in Bukhara, but his rule lasted for only a few days. The army, under one of Alptigin's rivals, favored Manṣūr, brother of the former emir. Alptigin's putsch thus failed, and he was abandoned by his former supporters, including Balᶜamī, who went over to the new regime.

Alptigin realized that he could no longer maintain himself in the heartland of the state. The new emir sent an army against him as he fell back through northern Afghanistan, but he defeated it in the spring of 962. He then marched unimpeded into eastern Afghanistan with a few hundred Turkish soldiers, and after a siege captured the town of Ghazni from its local ruler, Abū ᶜAlī (or Abū Bakr) Lawīk. Alptigin's status was that of a semirebel at least, but the state seems to have been prepared to tolerate vassal principalities on its peripheries.

At his death, Alptigin was succeeded in Ghazni by his son and then by other Turkish leaders, from whom, in 977, there emerged Sebüktigin, who inaugurated a policy of raids into the Indus valley and thus laid the foundations of the Ghaznavid empire, the first Muslim power to undertake systematic expansion into northern India.

BIBLIOGRAPHY

The main primary sources are Gardīzī, *Zayn al-Akhbār,* Muḥammad Nāẓim, ed. (1928); Niẓām al-Mulk, *Siyāsat-nāma,* H. Darke, trans. (1961), esp. 107–121; Jūzjānī, *Ṭabaqāt-i Nāṣiri,* H. G. Raverty, trans. (1881–1899); and Ibn al-Athīr, *Al-Kāmil.* Secondary sources include W. Barthold, *Turkestan down to the Mongol Invasion* (1928), 249–251, 261; Muḥammad Nāẓim, *The Life and Times of Sulṭān Maḥmūd of Ghazna* (1931), 24–26; C. E. Bosworth, *The Ghaznavids, Their Empire in Afghanistan and Eastern Iran 994–1040* (1963), 37–38; *Cambridge History of Iran,* IV, R. N. Frye, ed. (1975), 152, 164–165.

C. E. Bosworth

AŁTᶜAMAR. The Armenian Church of the Holy Cross (S. Xačᶜ), on the island of Ałtᶜamar in Lake Van, in what is now southeastern Turkey, is notable as the earliest medieval Christian monument extant that is entirely covered with sculptured reliefs. The palatine church of King Gagik Arcruni of Vaspurakan (908–943), it was built by the Armenian architect Manuel between 915 and 921. The tenth-century Armenian historian Thomas Arcruni describes its splendor in his chronicle of the Arcruni family.

The scope and variety of the sculptural program makes Ałtᶜamar a unique monument in the history of art. The horizontal bands of sculpture on the walls and drum contain large figures of Christ, the Virgin, saints, prophets, apostles who preached in Armenia, historical Armenian personages, and scenes from the Old Testament. There are also scenes of hunting, harvesting, and feasting—an unusual feature in a Christian sculptural program—and a large carved portrait of King Gagik as the founder offering a model of the church to Christ.

The interior frescoes, now in poor condition, are important for the history of East Christian church decoration, since Ałtᶜamar is the earliest church extant in which the wall paintings have survived almost in their entirety. They include a Genesis cycle, unique for this period in both East and West Christian art, and an extensive Gospel cycle.

ALTAR–ALTAR APPARATUS

Aght^{c}amar is constructed in rose-colored sandstone blocks, carefully cut and polished, which face a core of masonry rubble, the typical method of construction in Armenian churches. The church is quatrefoil in plan, with a central square covered by a dome buttressed with four vaulted apsidal niches and, on the diagonal axes, four small cylindrical niches. The plan is a variant of a type used in Armenian architecture as early as the seventh century.

A conical roof covers the dome (repaired in the thirteenth century), giving the church the characteristic silhouette of an Armenian church. The dome rests on a high, circular drum, sixteen-sided on the exterior, and is supported by pendentives.

Above the south portal the royal gallery, reached by an exterior staircase (now destroyed), once had a richly carved stone balustrade.

BIBLIOGRAPHY

Sirarpie Der Nersessian, *Aght^{c}amar, Church of the Holy Cross* (1965), with photographs; Sirarpie Der Nersessian and Herman Vahramian, *Aght^{c}amar* (1974); Mazhar İpşiroğlu, *Die Kirche von Achtamar* (1963); Stepan Mnac^{c}akanyan, "Pahpanič' Xorhrdanšannerė Mijnadaryan Hay K'andakagorcut'yan Meǰ" ("Protective Symbols in Medieval Armenian Sculpture"), in *Patma-banasirakan handes,* 3 (1970); Armenag Sakisian, "Notes on the Sculpture of the Church of Akhthamar," in *Art Bulletin,* **25** (1943); T'oros T'oramanyan, *Nyut'er Haykakan Čartarapetut'yan Patmut'yan,* II (1948), 305–308.

LUCY DER MANUELIAN

[See also **Armenian Art and Architecture.**]

ALTAR–ALTAR APPARATUS. Of all of the spaces in a medieval church none was more holy than the altar. It was there that the bread and wine became the body and blood of Christ and the relics of the saints were venerated. Because of its holiness all care was taken to adorn the altar, the surrounding structures, and the apparatus used to serve it. And because of its importance in medieval cultural practice and theology, the altar was the subject of numerous commentaries on its spiritual significance and the object of numerous laws for its consecration, dedication, and use.

When and how the Christian altar developed is obscure, but it is generally agreed that it developed from the tables around which the early Christians celebrated the Eucharist. Some scholars argue that the earliest altars were simply tables that were symbolically linked to the altars of the Old Testament. But in any event, Christians from the very beginnings of the Church spoke of altars, whether symbolic or real. And by the third century Latin Christians had designated these altars with the term *altare* and the pagan *ara* and later with the term *mensa.*

According to a popular legend reported by Bonizo of Sutri in the eleventh century, the earliest altars, at least in the Rome of St. Peter, were made of wood and were portable so that they could be moved from church to church and house to house during times of persecution. And both Eusebius of Caesarea and St. Augustine describe the use of wooden altars. But even though wooden and portable altars continued to be used in the Middle Ages in the West, altars were generally fixed or quasi-fixed and had to be constructed of stone.

Depictions and extant altars from late patristic antiquity and the early Middle Ages show that the shape of altars was extremely variable. Catacomb frescoes and mosaics depict sigma-shaped and semicircular tables; and there are semicircular *mensae* ("altar table") tops into which identations were made for the eucharistic species. But much more common were the rectangular and square altars, as depicted in the mosaics of Sant'Apollinare in Classe near Ravenna.

Several types of these rectangular and square altars were commonly in use in Europe. The form known as the table altar consisted of a top, or *mensa,* cemented to legs, or *stipes,* that might number from one or two, as in early medieval Spanish and Scandinavian churches, to five or more.

From earliest Christian times altars were often closely associated with the saintly dead and were built in the catacombs or on the site of martyrs' passions or burial places. As a result there developed the so-called chest altar either over or containing the relics of saints and martyrs or confessors. In the former case the altar was raised above the *confessio* that contained the relics and was linked to it by a set of stairs. Thus, the faithful could descend to the *confessio* and insert veils, vials of oil, and other objects through the *fenestellae* ("windows") of the container with the saints' relics. The relics could, on the other hand, be placed in a receptacle immediately below the *mensa* of the altar with *fenestellae* surrounding them.

The most common form, however, was the so-called block altar used widely after the Carolingian period. As its name implies, the *mensa* was set on *stipes* connected with massive blocks. It was from

ALTAR–ALTAR APPARATUS

this form that the so-called sarcophagus altar developed in the sixteenth century.

Antependium or Frontal: During the early Middle Ages it became customary to cover the front of altars with antependia or frontals. Those made of metal, wood, or stone were sculpted with Christian symbols and figures; antependia of wood or cloth were decorated with paintings or embroidery. Probably the most famous of these antependia are the ninth-century golden antependium, which actually encircles the altar, in the basilica of St. Ambrose in Milan; the eleventh-century golden Basel antependium now in the Musée de Cluny in Paris; and numerous brightly painted wooden antependia of the Catalan churches of the eleventh through thirteenth centuries.

Altar Superstructures: Surmounting the altar in patristic and early medieval times was a canopy called a *ciborium* or *umbraculum* supported by four columns. These ciboria were usually made of stone or marble, and occasionally even wood was used. Perhaps the most spectacular ciborium was a decorated one given by the Emperor Constantine to the Lateran basilica in Rome in the fourth century; its roof was made of silver and weighed slightly more than a ton. From the roof of the ciborium a variety of items could be suspended, including chandeliers, votive crowns, crosses, and pyxes, often in the forms of doves or chalices, that contained the reserved Sacrament. From the sides of the ciborium veils were sometimes hung; we know from tenth- and eleventh-century English pontificals that they were drawn at times during liturgical ceremonies.

Another form of altar canopy, the tester, became popular in the later Middle Ages. A gilded or decorated wooden canopy, it was suspended from the ceiling or apse wall over an altar set near or against the wall. The tester was usually suspended over the apsidal window so as not to block light coming into the church and onto the altar. Related to the tester are the strange canopies, such as that in the cathedral at Gerona, set on spindly legs over the altar. Veils could be hung between the side posts, and this would eventually lead to the riddel-curtain "canopy," which consisted of four posts, three of which had veils hung between them.

Altar Screens: In later medieval churches the most imposing structure surmounting the altar is the altar screen, or reredos, which is actually behind the altar. This structure probably developed out of the cult of relics. In the early Church saints' relics were kept under the altar or near it, but by the ninth century they could be placed in chests on the altar. Eventually the relics came to be set on a raised shrine or ledge close to the back of the altar, meaning that the ciborium was moved back over the shrine. To prevent the Mass from being disturbed by those visiting the relics behind the altar, a screen something like the antependium was set up behind the altar. These screens had developed by the fourteenth century into vast structures sometimes reaching to the vault of the church. They were no longer connected primarily to the relics they screened but were connected to the altar by a *predella* ("step") and became the vehicle for ornate decoration, sculpture, and gilding.

Chalices: If the altar and its surrounding structures had a special significance—it was there that the eucharistic sacrifice was offered—the altar apparatus and vessels had, according to some interpreters, even more importance, because they came into physical contact with the elements that were to be or had been consecrated. Of these vessels, none was more precious than the chalice. Not only did it contain the wine, but it was also a vessel specifically mentioned by Christ at the Last Supper; and in the liturgical year of the Church there were two *natales calicis* ("feasts of the chalice"), Epiphany and Maundy Thursday.

Because very few early eucharistic chalices remain, we are heavily dependent on illustrations in mosaics and sarcophagi for their reconstruction. The earliest were large, deep, ovoid cups attached to a knop and a steeply splayed base; some had handles. Chalices were customarily adorned with eucharistic symbols such as vines or doves or with ornate geometrical patterns. Until the eighth century chalices were made of metal, glass, wood, or even horn, but gradually they came to be made exclusively of precious metal befitting their dignity.

In the early medieval Church a variety of sizes of chalice were used. The *calix sanctus* or *calix minor* was used by the priest for the consecration and communion of the clergy. A larger chalice, called the *calix ministerialis (communialis)* or *scyphus,* into which a small amount of the consecrated wine was poured from the *calix sanctus,* was given to the people, who could drink from it directly or through a liturgical straw called a *fistula* or *calamus.* Other types of eucharistic chalices were the *calix offerenda,* in which the offerings of wine were carried to the altar and surrounding tables there to be strained

ALTAR–ALTAR APPARATUS

with a *colatorium,* and the smaller chalices that could be suspended from the ciborium with the sacred species.

From the twelfth century on there was a marked development in the shape of chalices. With refinements in eucharistic doctrine and practice, there was no longer a need for the variety of chalices or for the larger chalices of late patristic antiquity and the early Middle Ages. The deep ovoid cup was replaced by a smaller bowl. This was not attached directly to the knop; but the knop, which would be heavily decorated with geometrical designs, symbols, and gems, was placed midway between the splayed base and the cup. Beginning in the thirteenth century, chalices became much more elongated and architecturally membered through the use of tracery design. Scenes from the life of Christ or eucharistic decorations continued to be used to adorn late medieval chalices.

Patens: Almost as precious as the chalice was the paten, which held the host. Like chalices, patens were at first made of various materials such as metal, wood, horn, or glass, but from the fourth century on it was common to make them in precious metal and decorate them with inscriptions or precious jewels. Patens were almost always circular, and they might have rims or even indentations like the circular or semicircular altar *mensae* on which they are sometimes said to have been modeled. Their size was determined largely by their liturgical function: they had to be large enough to hold as many hosts as were needed and to hold the host of the correct size, which varied throughout the early Middle Ages. Early hosts were relatively large, and hence the patens had to be large too; and on feast days with many communicants larger patens were also needed. But by the eleventh century, when there were fewer communicants and hosts were small, the patens had become smaller. In the later Middle Ages the paten was used to hold only the large host of the celebrant and was generally further reduced in size.

Cruets: Almost from the beginning the Church in the Eucharist has mixed water and wine as a symbol of the water and blood that flowed from Christ's side and as a symbol of the unity of Christ's body in the wine and water signifying his people. To carry the wine and water to the altar, special vessels called *amae, ampullae, fontes,* and *filae* were made. At first these vessels must have been relatively large because of the larger numbers of those offering wine and those being confirmed or communicated by it. But by the eleventh and twelfth centuries the cruets had become much smaller with the decline in lay communion of the wine. Unlike chalices and patens, there seems to have been no standard material from which cruets were made, and examples exist in both precious and base metals as well as glass. Nor was there any standard shape, although occasionally a pair of cruets were varied slightly to signify that one held water and the other wine, or they were marked with *A* and *V* to indicate water and wine.

Pyx: This object could be used to store relics, but its prime function was to hold the host. In the early Church hosts were taken to other churches, to the sick, and even to the houses of laymen in a variety of containers called *saccelli, capsae,* or *arcae.* Moreover, the sacrament itself was reserved in churches in a vessel called a *turris* ("tower"). By the ninth century the pyx became the ordinary vessel in which the host was reserved on the altar or was taken to the sick for the administration of the viaticum. Other terms used to designate containers for the host included *columba* ("dove"), *theca,* and *bustia;* but by the later Middle Ages the term *ciborium* was being used, and in the sixteenth century the term that had once applied to the altar canopy became the common term for the eucharistic container.

In the early Middle Ages the pyx with the host could be kept in the sacristy, on the altar, or above it. But it became common to reserve the host in structures known as ambries and tabernacles, after the Fourth Lateran Council of 1215, which decreed that the sacrament should be kept under lock and key.

The material and shape of pyxes varied greatly. Precious and base metals, wood, ivory, and even cork were used, and shapes varied from boxes and round containers to doves. Probably the best known, however, are the footed dove-shaped pyxes made in the High and later Middle Ages and decorated with Limoges enameling.

Monstrance: Closely related to the pyx is the vessel used for the exposition of the host and known as Melchisedec, *tabernaculum, porte-Dieu,* and *monstrancia.* It seems to have developed from containers used to show relics. With the growth of eucharistic piety in the thirteenth century associated with the elevation of the host in the canon of the Mass and the establishment of the feast of Corpus Christi, reliquaries were fitted with a lunette to hold the host. At first horizontal crystal cylinders on feet were used but were eventually replaced by vertical cylinders. By the later Middle Ages monstrances had developed

ALTAR–ALTAR APPARATUS

into several distinctive types in the forms of crosses, disks, and the familiar tower. Monstrances were always constructed of precious metals and could be decorated with scenes from the life of Christ and eucharistic symbols and verses.

Altar Cloths: At least from the third century the Christian altar was veiled with a cloth, or pall, which covered all four sides of the altar. The antependium or frontal eventually came into use, especially when the altar was moved back to the apse wall. Separate cloths also came to be used over the covering cloth in case of spillage; and because the uppermost cloth came into contact with the sacred species it was called the corporal. Well into the thirteenth century the corporal could be folded back over the chalice and host to serve as a pall, which was eventually to become a separate piece of cloth.

Altar Books: During the very early Middle Ages only the Gospels were permitted on the altar besides the paten and chalice. These books, which might be either evangelaries containing the four gospels in sequence or evangelistaries containing gospel pericopes appropriate to the day, were venerated as the Word of Christ and hence decorated accordingly. The Gospels might rest directly on the altar cloths, but supports of some kind were often used. Stands for the Gospels were in use by the sixth century, and from the thirteenth century cushions were used.

From the ninth century on when it was permitted to have objects other than the sacred vessels and Gospels on the altar, books used in the course of the Mass were placed there. Hence, sacramentaries and missals might either be held by an assistant to the celebrant or placed on a support or directly on the altar cloths.

Altar Cross: In the patristic and early medieval Church crosses were not placed on the altar but were used in processions. In fifth-century Rome stational crosses were used to lead processions to the station churches, and it is known that in early medieval Spain the deacon bore the cross. The processional crosses were generally detachable from the staff on which they were mounted and thus could have been placed on or near the altar. It is sometimes argued that crosses came to be placed on altars as early as the sixth century in France, but the texts used to support this contention are somewhat ambiguous and might even refer to crosses hung from the ciborium. In any event, by the eleventh century there is clear evidence that metal and wood crosses, either with or without a figure of Christ, were placed on altars during Mass. By the fourteenth century these crosses were permanently affixed to the altar.

Altar Candles: Like crosses, candles also were early used in processions and were placed around and above the altar. By the tenth century there is some indication, especially in Cluniac documents, that candles were placed on the altar, and by the eleventh century altars with candles on them are depicted, the most celebrated being the fresco in the lower church of San Clemente in Rome. In the twelfth century Lothario di Segni (later Pope Innocent III) spoke of the custom of having only two lighted candles on the altar, but soon thereafter in papal masses and on important feasts seven altar candles came to be used. In some places from one to seven candles might be used on the altar together with up to fourteen set around the altar.

Pax Brede: On or near the altar was the *osculatorium* by means of which the pax, or kiss of peace, was exchanged during the Mass. At first the *osculatorium* could be any precious object—Gospel books, reliquaries, crosses, or patens. But by the High Middle Ages it was common to use a small panel or board decorated with biblical or eucharistic scenes in precious metal, stone, or paint.

Thurible: In the service of the Christian altar the burning of incense, signifying honor and prayer, was common from the fifth century on, that is, after the practice had lost its connection with pagan devotion. The early vessels in which incense was burned at the altar were open and set on stands near it. By at least the ninth century it is known from such depictions as that on the ivory cover of the Drogo Sacramentary that thuribles were spherical and covered and were hung on chains so that acolytes and other clerics might hold or swing them during Mass. Eventually feet were added so that they could stand alone, and the lids took on such shapes as towers or lanterns. All nonfusible metals were used, but, as sacred vessels, silver and gold were preferred. Perhaps the most spectacular modern successor of large medieval hanging thuribles is the *botafumeiro,* still in use at the Romanesque pilgrimage church of Santiago de Compostela in Spain. Standing as high as a meter or more, this thurible is hung from the crossing of the basilica and belches out clouds of smoke and fire as eight men pull the rope that swings it through the arc of the transept.

Flabellum ("Fan"): Used in antiquity for both practical and ceremonial reasons, fans early became part of Christian altar apparatus. As ceremonial objects they were seen as honoring the sacrifice of the altar and as representing the wings of the angelic beings surrounding it. They were used practically to circulate air around the altar and to disperse insects from the sacred species. Fans ranged from long poles surmounted by ivory holders for sumptuous plumes to small, decorated round disks.

Bells: Besides the large bells hung in medieval church towers and campaniles to ring the hours and the feast days, smaller bells were part of the altar apparatus and were rung (except during penitential seasons) at the Sanctus, the elevation of the host, the Gloria in excelsis, and at the exposition of the Sacrament.

BIBLIOGRAPHY

A. A. Barb, "*Mensa sacra:* The Round Table and the Holy Grail," in *Journal of the Warburg and Courtauld Institutes,* **19** (1956); Joseph Braun, *Der christliche Altar in Seiner geschichtlichen Entwicklung,* 2 vols. (1924); and *Das christliche Altargerät in seinem Sein und in seiner Entwicklung* (1932); David R. Dendy, *The Use of Lights in Christian Worship* (1959); Victor H. Elbern, "Liturgisches Gerät in edlen Materialien zur Zeit Karls des Grossen," in Wolfgang Braunfels and H. Schnitzler, eds., *Karl der Grosse: Lebenswerk und Nachleben,* III (1965), 115–167; *Eucharistic Vessels of the Middle Ages* (1975); Klaus Gamber, *Liturgie und Kirchenbau* (1976), 140–151; and *Ecclesia Reginensis* (1979), 49–66; Robert Lesage, *Vestments and Church Furniture,* Fergus Murphy, trans. (1960), 12–92; Otto Nussbaum, "Zur Problem der runden und sigmaförmigen Altarplatten," in *Jahrbuch für Antike und Christentum,* **4** (1961); Cyril Pocknee, *The Christian Altar in History and Today* (1963); J. L. Schrader, "Antique and Early Christian Sources for the Riha and Stuma Patens," in *Gesta,* **18**, no. 1 (1979).

ROGER E. REYNOLDS

[See also **Architecture, Liturgical Aspects.**]

ALTAR, PORTABLE, an easily movable rectangular or square plaque or box on which a priest celebrates the Mass, consecrated for this use and created for service where a permanent structure is not practical. In the third century St. Cyprian noted the use of portable altars in prisons; in 692 Bede mentioned their usefulness for missionaries; in the *Miracula S. Dionysii* portable altars were described as part of the equipment taken on military campaigns by Charlemagne; and they were used in Byzantium for the coronation ceremony when it took place in the hippodrome at Constantinople. The earliest portable altars were apparently made of wood, often covered with metal. In the Latin West, stone (usually porphyry) was favored in the medieval period, while in Byzantium a square or rectangular cloth called an *antimension* (Greek for "instead of a table") is found from the ninth century and is still used in the Eastern church.

LESLIE BRUBAKER

ALTARPIECE. Between A.D. 900 and 1000 liturgical practices placed priest and congregation to one side of the altar, permitting the back of the altar to be decorated. Decoration in the form of altarpieces soon flourished, in diverse forms and materials. Northern Europe favored sculpted altar decorations. Many were associated with the preservation of relics. The earliest examples were made of precious metals, while later altarpieces, beginning roughly 1300, consisted of stone, marble, alabaster, or polychromed wood. Large carved and painted wooden altarpieces with hinged wings gained popularity in the mid fourteenth century, reaching their fullest potential for powerful theatrical depictions of religious events in the fifteenth century, in Flanders, the Netherlands, and Germany. The Reformation brought the destruction of many examples and slowed the production of altarpieces in Northern Europe.

Italy produced sculpted examples but painted panels were far more popular. Early examples take their form from altar-frontals. Others consisted of large single gabled panels. During the fourteenth century, numerous multipaneled triptychs and polyptychs were produced, complete with elaborate carved and gilded frames, pinnacles, and predellas to accommodate a whole range of sacred subject matter. In the fifteenth century, taste evolved toward large single panels in which sacred figures were grouped in a consistent space.

Throughout Europe, smaller, portable examples of altarpieces (usually painted panels) were produced for private devotions.

ADELHEID M. GEALT

ALTERNATION (or **ALTERNATING SUPPORTS),** the use of regular and repeating configurations of vertical elements to support the ceiling or vaulting of a church: pier–column–column–pier, for example. Alternating supports mirror and accent a modular system of construction and plan, especially in Ottonian architecture (as in St. Michael's, Hildesheim, 1001–1033), or—in the late Romanesque and early Gothic periods—reflect the form of the vaulting (as at Mantes, *ca.* 1170).

Sexpartite vaulting requires the use of alternating supports because the vaulting system spans two bays: the central shaft is a single transverse arch, while the corners sustain transverse and diagonal ribs. The distinction between the corner and central shafts is usually (but not always, as at St. Etienne, Caen) echoed in the vertical responds running through the gallery—for instance, five shafts rise from the nave arcade columns below the corners of each sexpartite vault at Laon Cathedral (*ca.* 1160) while only three shafts surmount the nave columns below the central arch of the vault—and often affects the entire wall elevation, with piers rising uninterrupted from floor to ceiling at the vault corners and columns supporting the central shaft (as at Noyon Cathedral, *ca.* 1150).

Alternating supports occur in conjunction with other vaulting systems as well: at Durham Cathedral (1093–1133), piers and columns alternate in the nave beneath double groin vaults, and at Chartres Cathedral (begun 1194) alternating supports are conservatively retained for quadripartite vaults.

LESLIE BRUBAKER

[See also **Bay System.**]

ALTFRID OF MÜNSTER, third bishop (839–849), succeeded his father Gerfrid; he died April 22, 849 and was buried in Werden where he was once abbot. Probably the nephew of St. Ludger, first bishop of Münster, he wrote a celebrated biography of the saint based on reports of Ludger's relatives. The style of the *Vita* is simple and the work treats Ludger, above all, as a missionary and performer of miracles.

BIBLIOGRAPHY

Life of St. Ludger, Patrologia latina, XCIX (1864), cols. 769–796; *Die Geschichtsquellen des Bistums Münster, IV,* L. Diekamp, ed. (1881), pp. xvff.

DEIRDRE BAKER

[See also **Münster.**]

ALTICHIERO (*fl. ca.* 1330–1395), Veronese painter, known chiefly for his fresco cycles in the Chapel of S. Giacomo (now S. Felice), documented 1370–1379 and the Oratorio of S. Giorgio, documented 1377–1384, both in the basilica of S. Antonio in Padua for the patron Bonifazio Lupi. These frescoes, assisted by Avanzo, illustrate the lives of SS. James, George, Lucy, and Catherine. Inspired by Giotto's Arena Chapel frescoes, Altichiero's work demonstrates remarkable genius and originality. A precocious naturalism, sense of atmosphere, and keen human understanding make Altichiero's frescoes an important link between the work of Giotto and that of Donatello, Masaccio, Bellini, Mantegna, and Titian.

BIBLIOGRAPHY

H. W. Kruft, *Altichiero and Avanzo, Untersuchungen zur oberitalienischen Malerei des ausgehenden Trecento* (1966); Gian Lorenzo Mellini, *Altichiero e Jacopo Avanzi* (1965); Robert Oertel, *Early Italian Painting to 1400* (1968); John White, *Art and Architecture in Italy: 1250–1400* (1966).

ADELHEID M. GEALT

ALUANK. See **Albania.**

ALVÍSSMÁL (The Words of All-Wise) are the tenth and last mythological poem of the *Poetic Edda* according to the sequencing of Cod. reg. 2365 4°, the only manuscript in which the poem is recorded in its entirety; *Alvíssmál* 20 and 30 are quoted in the *Snorra Edda,* where the title is mentioned. The *Alvíssmál* consist of thirty-five *ljóðaháttr* strophes of great metrical uniformity; only the final strophe adds a questionable additional short line. Most scholars agree that it is one of the most recent eddic poems.

The narrative framework (*Alvíssmál* 1–8, 35) identifies Alvíss as a dwarf to whom Thor's daughter has been promised during the god's absence. Alvíss arrives to press his claim and is met by Thor; since neither recognizes the other, the protagonists introduce themselves. Thor rejects the betrothal but offers Alvíss a chance to win his bride by passing a knowledge test. The gnostic core of the poem consists of thirteen questions and answers. Since dwarfs can not stand daylight, it is Thor's intention to prolong the test until the sun rises and turns Alvíss to stone.

The thirteen formulaic questions and answers concern the different words used by men, gods, giants, elves, dwarfs, and sundry others for common objects: earth, sky, moon, sun, clouds, wind, calm, sea, fire, wood, night, grain, and ale. The lexicographic evidence provided is subject to considerable suspicion; some of the synonyms are documented elsewhere but many appear to have been invented for this poem alone.

The *Alvíssmál* are also subject to suspicion regarding the mythological content of the frame: Thor, who usually deals with troublesome giants or dwarfs by using his characteristic physical strength, here turns to deceit masked by a bogus knowledge confrontation. Both the superficial gnostic content and the god's uncharacteristic actions suggest the clumsy construction of a Thor poem based on the model typical for an Odin poem. In any event, the *Alvíssmál* have weaknesses that argue forcefully for late authorship by an epigone; mythological insights based on the evidence of the *Alvíssmál* must be met with scholarly skepticism.

BIBLIOGRAPHY

A text edition is *Edda. Die Lieder des Codex regius nebst verwandten Denkmälern,* Gustav Neckel, ed., 4th rev. ed., Hans Kuhn, ed., I (1962). Translations are *The Poetic Edda,* Henry Adams Bellows, trans. (repr. 1968); *The Poetic Edda,* Lee M. Hollander, trans. (repr. 1962).

Hugo Gering and Barend Sijmons provide a commentary in *Kommentar zu den Liedern der Edda,* 2 vols. (1927–1931). See also Halldor Hermannsson, *Bibliography of the Eddas* (1920); the annual bibliographies (1927–1962) in *Arkiv för nordisk filologi* and *Acta philologica scandinavica;* Jóhann S. Hannesson, *Bibliography of the Eddas* (1955); and Hans Bekker-Nielsen and Thorkil Damsgaard Olsen, eds., *Bibliography of Old Norse-Icelandic Studies* (1964–).

JERE FLECK

AMADAS ET YDOINE, an adventure romance of 7,912 lines written between 1190 and 1220, probably first in Anglo-Norman but surviving in complete form only in Picard. The humbly born hero, Amadas, and the aristocratic Ydoine are idealized lovers who are married only after overcoming numerous obstacles; the story is told with exaggerated courtliness.

BIBLIOGRAPHY

An edition is John Revell Reinhard, ed., *Amadas et Ydoine, roman du XIIIe siècle* (1926). Also see Mary Dominica Legge, *Anglo-Norman Literature and Its Background* (1963), 109–115; Robert Bossuat in *Histoire de la littérature française,* I, *Le moyen age* (1964), 51–52.

BRIAN MERRILEES

[See also **Anglo-Norman Literature.**]

AMADÍS DE GAULA, Arthurian prose romance of chivalry, is a Hispanic creation—its original French sources were in verse. Although it has traditionally been dated late thirteenth century and attributed to one Juan Lobeira, a Portuguese or Galician, it now appears more likely to have been the work of an unknown Spanish (Leonese) author. His work, the primitive Books I and II, has been entirely lost; there remain only fragments of Book III, probably added by a second writer before 1379. It is certain that in it Amadís was killed in a duel with his son Esplandián, who did not recognize his armor-clad parent.

Late in the fifteenth century, Garcí Rodríguez de Montalvo (not Ordóñez) reworked Book III, from which he extracted material for the nucleus of Book IV, in which he planned to deny the slaying of Amadís and have him subordinated to Esplandián, who was already arrayed against knight-errantry motivated by courtly love, and was dedicated to vanquishing infidels, giants, and other sinister characters. Book V is entitled *Sergas* ("Exploits") *de Esplandián,* whose adventures are apparently imitations of those of Amadís in Books I and II.

Montalvo died shortly before 1505. The first printed edition of his Volumes I–IV appeared in 1508, and that of Volume V, the *Sergas,* in 1510. Once in print, the *Amadís* became enormously popular. During the sixteenth century, many continuations of it were published in Spain, and the number of Spanish imitations was legion. But its vogue was even greater abroad; it was translated, in whole or part, into English, French, Italian, German, Dutch, Portuguese, and Hebrew. A collection of courtly speeches culled from its French translation, first published in 1559, went through twenty editions. Cervantes in his *Don Quijote* spoke well of the *Amadís,* even while ridiculing the chivalric genre in general.

BIBLIOGRAPHY

A translation of Books I–IV into English has been done by E. B. Place and Herbert C. Behm, 2 vols. (1974–1975). A critical edition of the Spanish *Amadís* was edited by E. B. Place, 4 vols. (1959–1969). A list of translations and adaptations of Books I–IV is in Place's first volume. The *Ser-*

gas is no. 40 in Biblioteca de autores españoles. Also see N. Alonso Cortés, "Montalvo, el de *Amadís,*" in *Revue hispanique,* **41** (1933); María Rosa Lida de Malkiel, "El desenlace del *Amadís* primitivo," in *Romance Philology,* **6** (1953); and Antonio Rodríguez-Moniño et al., *El primer manuscrito del Amadís de Gaula* (1957).

EDWIN B. PLACE

[See also **Spanish Literature.**]

AMALARIUS OF METZ (*ca.* 775–*ca.* 850), liturgist, was born near Metz and died there. A student of Alcuin of York, he was named bishop of Trier in 811. He served as Charlemagne's ambassador to Constantinople in 813 and was sent by Louis the Pious to Lyons to replace the exiled bishop Agobard. The latter, after having been pardoned and restored to his post, became an opponent of Amalarius' liturgical theories and obtained their official condemnation at the Synod of Quierzy in 838.

Amalarius' works, especially the *Liber officialis* (823), were widely circulated and influential in propagating the allegorical interpretation of the liturgy in the Middle Ages. This mode of interpretation answered a popular need by promoting an immediately comprehensible meaning for the Mass at the expense of the more historical understanding set forth by the hierarchy.

BIBLIOGRAPHY

Amalarius' liturgical works were published by Jean-Michel Hanssens as *Amalarii episcopi, opera liturgica omnia,* 3 vols. (1948–1950). A bibliography of his writings is in James A. Cabaniss, *Amalarius of Metz* (1954), 107–114. See also René-Jean Hesbert, "L'antiphonaire d'Amalaire," in *Ephemerides liturgicae,* **94** (1980), a very technical study.

ALAIN J. STOCLET

[See also **Agobard; Allegory.**]

AMALRIC OF BÈNE (*d.* 1206), theologian, was born at Bène, near Chartres. He was a student of arts in Paris, where he was noted for his subtlety, and later became a master of theology. The only reports of Amalric's writings are contained in condemnatory documents, and therefore what little we know of his teaching must be weighed carefully. Moreover, in these documents, Amalric's doctrine is frequently associated with that of his followers; this leads to further confusion.

Amalric is reported to have thought that God was the substantial form of the universe or the form of all things. The sources for his statements were largely misunderstandings of John Scotus Erigena, Scripture, and Aristotle. This identification of God with the universe led to difficulties with ecclesiastical authorities, and Amalric was called by Pope Innocent III to Rome, where he reportedly retracted his earlier teaching. He died at Paris.

Amalric's followers are thought by most scholars to have worked out the moral and religious implications of his metaphysics. The Amalricians allegedly denied the real distinction between good and evil, the necessity of faith, and the transubstantiation of the Eucharist. The Amalricians reportedly held a threefold division of history corresponding to the Trinity, with the Holy Spirit's reign being ushered in by Amalric.

Both Amalric and his followers were condemned at the Council of Paris in 1210, along with David of Dinant, and later at the Fourth Lateran Council in 1215. The sect soon died out. However, the condemnation identified the source of the heretical teachings in Aristotle, leading to the proscription of his writings (with the exception of the logical and ethical works) in the early statutes of the University of Paris.

BIBLIOGRAPHY

Germaine C. Capelle, *Amaury de Bène* (1932); Heinrich Denifle and Émile L. M. Chatelain, *Chartularium Universitatis Parisiensis,* I (1889), 70–72, 79, 81–82; Félix Vernet, "Amaury de Bène et les Amauriciens," in *Dictionnaire de spiritualité, ascétique et mystique, doctrine et histoire,* I (1937), 422–425.

TIMOTHY B. NOONE

[See also **Aristotle in the Middle Ages; Heresies, Western Europe.**]

AMALU/NORAVANK. See **Noravank at Amalu.**

AMARCIUS (*fl.* 1070). The details of the life of Sextus Amarcius Gallus Piosistratus (a pseudonym) are conjectured to be as follows: he was a German, educated at the cathedral school of Speyer, and attracted to the court of Henry III, perhaps because his knowledge of medicine made him valuable there. Whether he was a monk, a clerk, or a wandering scholar is not clear. He is noted for his four books of *Sermones,* satires modeled on those of Horace but directed against the clergy, nobility, and Jews. They were probably written between 1056 and 1080. He is characterized by Manitius as the greatest satirist of the Middle Ages.

BIBLIOGRAPHY

The most recent ed. of Amarcius' *Sermones* is by Karl Manitius (1969). Secondary literature includes Frederic Amory, "The Satires of Sextus Amarcius," in *Medium Ævum,* 39 (1970); Maximilian Manitius, *Geschichte der lateinischen Literatur des Mittelalters,* II (1923), 569–574; and Frederic Raby, *A History of Secular Latin Poetry in the Middle Ages,* 2nd ed., I (1934), 401–404.

PAULINE A. THOMPSON

AMATUS OF MONTE CASSINO (b. *ca.* 1010). Recent scholarship surmises from the scant sources available that Amatus was born in Salerno, that he was bishop of Pesto-Capaccio (1042–1058), and that he then entered Monte Cassino. He died on 1 March sometime prior to 1105. Two works survive, the *De gestis apostolorum Petri et Pauli* and the *Historia Normannorum* (now extant only in a fourteenth-century French translation). The former is notable both for its support of the Gregorian reform and for its extolling of the glories of ancient Rome. The latter is valuable as a historical source for the Norman involvement in Italy 1016–1078.

BIBLIOGRAPHY

Vincenzo de Bartholomaeis, *Storia de' Normanni di Amato di Montecassino* (1935); Anselmo Lentini, *Il poema di Amato su S. Pietro Apostolo* (1958).

PAULINE A. THOMPSON

AMBO (from the medieval Greek for "pulpit"), a type of pulpit, usually made of stone and often in the form of a large, raised oval platform accessible by a double stairway, located in the nave of a church and connected with the altar by a passageway (*solea*). Ambos were used for the reading of the Gospels in Eastern churches until the eighth century. They occur in some medieval Italian churches as well, but are rare outside the orbit of Byzantine influence.

LESLIE BRUBAKER

AMBRASER HELDENBUCH. The illuminated manuscript (Cod. vind., S. n. 2663) is one of several late medieval *Heldenbuch* collections that transmit postclassical Middle High German heroic, epic, and romance materials. The codex, now in the Österreichische Nationalbibliothek in Vienna, owes its popular title to the designation *heldenpuch* that occurs in its table of contents, and to its many years in the collection of art and curiosities *(Kunst- und Wunderkammer)* at Schloss Ambras in Alto Adige. The immense manuscript (5 + 238 parchment leaves, 18 × 14.5 inches) was penned by a single calligrapher, Hans Ried, and the border illustrations are the work of one artist, perhaps either Ulrich Funk the Elder or Veit Fiedler; the 123 illuminated initials that appear throughout the text may be the work of one of the former or of an anonymous rubricator.

The sumptuous Ambras manuscript was commissioned by Emperor Maximilian I, presumably for his own use. The earliest surviving reference to Maximilian's plans for a *Heldenbuch* dates from 1502. Two years later Hans Ried, then a tariff collector on the Eisack (Isarco) near Bolzano, began work on the manuscript that would occupy him intermittently until his death in 1516. Ried, a calligrapher of some local reputation, probably received his initial training in the chancery of Sigmund of Tirol, and had already served Maximilian for some years in the chancery when he accepted the *Heldenbuch* assignment. Documentary evidence from the period 1504–1516 indicates that Ried continued to have other duties while copying the manuscript, and that disparaging evaluations of his slow progress are quite unjustified.

The Ambras codex, which is devoted exclusively to forms of narrative verse, differs somewhat from other *Heldenbücher* by focusing primarily on works from the twelfth and thirteenth centuries while excluding contemporary adventure romances and adaptations of classical Middle High German courtly works. The collection reflects Maximilian's intense interest in knighthood and in the preservation of monuments of the German chivalric tradition. It contains twenty-five poems, of which more than half (indicated by *) are preserved in this manuscript alone: (1) Der Stricker, "Frauenlob" (MS d); (2) "Moriz von Crâôn"*; (3) Hartmann von Aue, "Iwein" (MS d); (4) Hartmann von Aue, "Das Büchlein"*; (5) "Das [2.] Büchlein"*; (6) Heinrich von dem Türlîn, "Der Mantel"*; (7) Hartmann von Aue, "Erec"; (8 and 9) "Dietrichs Flucht" and "Die Rabenschlacht" (MS d); (10 and 11) "Das Nibelungenlied" and "Die Klage" (MS d); (12) "Kudrun"*; (13) "Biterolf"*; (14) "Ortnit" (MS A); (15) "Wolfdietrich A"*; (16) "Die böse Frau"*; (17, 18, 19, and 20) Herrand von Wildonie, "Die treue Gattin,"* "Der verkehrte Wirt,"* "Der nackte Kaiser,"* and "Die Katze"*; (21) Ulrich von Lichtenstein, "Frauendienst"*; (22) Wernher der Gartenaere, "Helmbrecht" (MS A); (23) Der Stricker, "Pfaffe Amis" (MS W); (24) Wolfram von Eschenbach, "Titurel" (MS H); and (25) "Priester Johannes."*

The immediate sources of the *Ambraser Heldenbuch* remain obscure. Franz Unterkircher suggests that Ried must have copied from at least two works: one that contained shorter verse tales, and one that grouped the courtly romances with the postclassical epics in their present order; *Nibelungenlied* MS O (Preussische Staatsbibliothek Quart. 792) may be a remnant of this latter source.

BIBLIOGRAPHY

A complete facsimile edition is *Ambraser Heldenbuch,* Franz Unterkircher, ed. (1973); for references to published editions of the individual works in the codex, see Unterkircher's "Kommentar" to the facsimile.

General works are Helmut de Boor, *Das späte Mittelalter: Zerfall und Neubeginn* (1962), 136, 141; Johannes Janota, "'Ambraser Heldenbuch,'" in *Die deutsche Literatur des Mittelalters: Verfasserlexikon,* 2nd ed., I (1977), 323–327; Hans Rupprich, *Das ausgehende Mittelalter, Humanismus und Renaissance* (1970), 66–69, a brief summary of the contents of the *Ambraser Heldenbuch* and an explanation of its relationship to other *Heldenbücher;* Franz Unterkircher, "Kommentar," in the facsimile edition, a commentary on all aspects of the codex that also provides material on the genesis of the manuscript and on its history since the sixteenth century; Martin Wierschin, "Das Ambraser Heldenbuch Maximilians I.," in *Der Schlern,* **50** (1976), the most complete study available and the best single bibliographic source.

On Hans Ried see David Schönherr, "Der Schreiber des Heldenbuchs in der k. k. Ambraser Sammlung," in *Archiv für Geschichte und Alterthumskunde Tirols,* **1** (1964); Edward Schröder, "Der Ambraser Wolfdietrich. Grundlagen und Grundsätze der Textkritik," in *Nachrichten von der Gesellschaft der Wissenschaften zu Göttingen,* (1931), which misinterprets Ried's accomplishment as copyist and calligrapher (compare with A. Leitzmann, below); Helmut Weinacht, "Archivalien und Kommentare zu Hans Ried, dem Schreiber des Ambraser Heldenbuches," in Egon Kühebacher, ed., *Deutsche Heldenepik in Tirol* (1979), 466–489, which amplifies Wierschin's material on Ried and further clarifies the scribe's role.

On the illuminator see Erich Egg, "Der Maler des Ambraser Heldenbuches," in *Der Schlern,* **28** (1954) and M. Wierschin, above.

Philological aspects are discussed in Albert Leitzmann, "Die Ambraser Erecüberlieferung," in *Beiträge zur Geschichte der deutschen Sprache und Literatur,* **59** (1935) and in E. Schröder, above. Thomas P. Thornton, "Die Schreibgewohnheiten Hans Rieds im Ambraser Heldenbuch," in *Zeitschrift für deutsche Philologie,* **81** (1962), is a condensation of his 1953 Johns Hopkins dissertation.

Selection and arrangement of texts are treated in Ingeborg Glier, *Artes amandi* (1971), 389–392; and in Hugo Kuhn, *Minnesangs Wende,* 2nd ed. (1967), 183–186.

ELAINE C. TENNANT

AMBROGIO, GIOVANNI D'. See **Giovanni D'Ambrogio.**

AMBROGIO MAITANI. See **Maitani, Ambrogio.**

AMBROGIO TRAVERSARI. See **Traversari, Ambrogio.**

AMBROSE, ST. (*ca.* 340–397). Aurelius Ambrosius was born no later than 340, probably at Trier, the son of an aristocratic and Christian Roman family—his father was probably praetorian prefect of Gaul. After a liberal (including Greek) and legal education at Rome, Ambrose began to practice law at the court of the praetorian prefect of Italy, Illyricum, and Africa (probably at Sirmium), and around 370 was appointed "consular" (governor with honorary consular rank) of Aemilia-Liguria, a combined province whose administrative center was Milan (then the real capital of the Roman Empire in the West).

In 374 the bishop of Milan, Auxentius (an Arian), died, and Ambrose was elected bishop by acclamation after going to the Christian assembly to keep order between the Catholic and Arian parties. Though he tried to avoid the election, it was confirmed by the emperor Valentinian I. Ambrose, who, being in public life, had followed the common custom of not being baptized, was within a week both baptized and admitted, day by day, to the various ministries of the Church until his ordination as bishop on 7 December. His ordination was followed by a swift course of theological training, probably under the presbyter Simplicianus, who later succeeded him as bishop.

Apart from his writings—largely sermons, Scripture commentaries, and letters (important among his sources are Cicero, Origen, and St. Basil)—Ambrose's activities as a bishop can perhaps be condensed into two main categories: his defense of the Catholic faith against the Arians, and his vindication of Christian moral principles and the independence of the Church even against the power of the Roman emperor. Often, however, these two categories overlap. And because his see put him in a position to influence the emperors of his time, Ambrose was even able to persuade them to use their power to advance the Church and its principles. As early as the Council of Aquileia in 381, he was marshaling the authority of the empire against the Arians.

In 383, Ambrose served as envoy for Justina, the Arian mother of Valentinian II, son of Valentinian I. She sent him to treat with Maximus, the Gallic usurper who had murdered Valentinian's half brother, Gratian, the principal emperor in the West after the death of Valentinian I. In spite of this service, Justina tried to reestablish Arianism in Milan. During 385–386 she demanded that churches be surrendered to the Arian community and, using the imperial authority of her young son, tried to compel Ambrose to debate with an Arian pretender to the see, finally besieging him and his congregation in his cathedral. (It was at this time that Ambrose introduced the antiphonal singing of psalms into the Milanese church. He also so successfully introduced metrical hymns into worship in Milan that they spread to the other rites of the West, and all hymns of the type—four-line stanzas of iambic dimeter—became known as *Ambrosiani.* Of the great number attributed to him, four are certainly his, on the evidence of St. Augustine.)

Justina finally gave up (indeed, she again used Ambrose as an envoy to Maximus in 386) when Ambrose remained firm both against Arianism and in his conviction that in matters of faith, the emperor was within the Church but did not command it. In 384, before the conflict with Justina, Ambrose had also successfully argued (in the "Altar of Victory" controversy) against Quintus Symmachus, the prefect of Rome, that Valentinian II should not restore to pagan worship the official and financial support that Gratian had removed.

The great fruit of these years of conflict was the conversion of Augustine, then a skeptical teacher of rhetoric who, in the few years he was in Milan, was so impressed by the way in which Ambrose's preaching answered his difficulties about the Christian faith that he received baptism at his hands in 387. (There is no truth in the legend that on this occasion the two saints spontaneously composed the *Te Deum;* it is possible, however, that Ambrose is the author of the Athanasian Creed.) It was doubtless from Ambrose, Simplicianus, and their circle that Augustine derived at least some of the Christian Neoplatonism that was to influence Latin theology in later centuries.

The other Roman emperor before whom Ambrose defended Christian principles and his beliefs about the emperor and the Church was Theodosius I. Theodosius had been made emperor in the East by Gratian and, after defending Valentinian II against Maximus, lived at Milan for several years. In 388 he commanded that a synagogue at Callinicum in Syria, which Christians had destroyed, be rebuilt at Christian or civil expense and that monks who had burned a Gnostic chapel be punished. Ambrose resolutely insisted that the emperor could not give such orders. For Ambrose the issue was one of God's truth versus error. He conceded that Jews and heretics had been treated unjustly, but that for Christians to support them was no less than apostasy. The emperor reluctantly yielded.

In 390, Theodosius ordered the inhabitants of Thessalonica to be put to the sword indiscriminately for lynching the local commander. His countermanding order was too late, and in a private and compassionate letter Ambrose told him that he was now cut off from the communion of the Church. The emperor clearly felt his guilt (the later picture of Ambrose turning him away from the church is a fiction), and eventually humbled himself in public penance.

Ambrose died on Easter Eve, 4 April 397, the day later observed as his festival north of the Alps and in Britain. The Church of Milan, however, not admitting feasts during Lent, moved his commemoration to the anniversary of his episcopacy, 7 December, an example followed by Constantinople and medieval Rome.

Although Ambrose is a late Roman rather than a medieval figure, his reputation in his own church (its distinctive rite is called Ambrosian rather than Milanese), his role in the career of St. Augustine (with Augustine, St. Gregory the Great, and St. Jerome the Latin Middle Ages reckoned him one of the four Doctors of the Church), and, perhaps most important, the position he took in relation to the Roman emperor, thereby originating the idea that the state had a duty to advance the Church's mission, have

AMBROSIAN CHANT

made him a figure who must stand at the source of any understanding of the Middle Ages.

BIBLIOGRAPHY

There is no complete modern critical ed. of St. Ambrose's works. The most easily accessible earlier complete edition is Migne, *Patrologia latina,* XIV–XVI (1845). (XVII contains the commentary of "Ambrosiaster" on Paul and other pseudo-Ambrosian works.) Several works (the most significant being *Exameron; Expositio Evangelii secundum Lucam* (also in the *Corpus Christianorum,* XIV [1957]); *Expositio Psalmi CXVIII; De Sacramentis; De Excessu Fratris; De obitu Valentiniani; De obitu Theodosii; De fide ad Gratianum Augustum; De spiritu sancto,* and 35 of the 91 extant letters) have been edited in the *Corpus scriptorum ecclesiasticorum latinorum,* XXXII, LXII, LXIV, LXXIII, LXXVIII, LXXIX, LXXXII (1892–). Significant works not yet in this series are *De officiis ministrorum, De virginibus,* and *Contra Auxentium.* Editions and translations of individual works have appeared in the Catholic University of America series Patristic Studies (1925–); English translations of some works are in *A Select Library of Nicene and Post-Nicene Fathers,* 2nd ser., X (1896) and in the Catholic University of America collection *The Fathers of the Church* (1953–).

The basic primary source for Ambrose's life is the biography written for St. Augustine by Ambrose's secretary, Paulinus: *Vita Sancti Ambrosii,* Sister M. S. Kaniecka, ed. and trans., *Patristic Studies,* XVI (1928). The best recent short account of Ambrose, with exhaustive bibliographies, is Maria Grazia Mara, "Ambrogio di Milano," in Angelo di Berardino, ed., *Patrologia,* III (1978), 135–169. The standard large-scale biographies in English remain F. Homes Dudden, *The Life and Times of St Ambrose,* 2 vols. (1935); and Angelo Paredi, *Saint Ambrose: His Life and Times,* M. Joseph Costelloe, trans. (1964).

An important collection of articles is Pierre Courcelle, *Recherches sur Saint Ambroise* (1973). See also Yves-Marie Duval, *Ambroise de Milan* (1974); Giuseppe Lazzati, ed., *Ambrosius Episcopus* (1976); and Giuseppe Toscani, *Teologia della Chiesa in Sant'Ambrogio* (1974).

RICHARD TOPOROSKI

AMBROSIAN CHANT, the ecclesiastical monody of Milan and the surrounding region, a repertory different from those of the Gregorian, Gallican, Visigothic, Beneventan, and other Latin rites, although perhaps sharing a nucleus. The specifically musical activities of St. Ambrose (died 397) cannot be documented, and were probably nowhere nearly as important as the title "Ambrosian" for the chant might suggest. It seems likely that the name of the great Milanese bishop was adopted long after his time, in an analogy with the use of Pope Gregory I's, to distinguish the repertory of Milan from the "Gregorian," which gradually displaced the local chant practically everywhere else in western Europe. It was the political importance of Milan that enabled the city to resist this encroachment (although attempts were made periodically, beginning with Charlemagne early in the ninth century, to enforce conformity) and to remain an Ambrosian island in a Gregorian sea.

The early history of the Milanese chant is difficult to document. The singers seem to have relied on oral transmission of the music long after notation became common elsewhere. In any case, except for a few fragments that are not much older, the earliest musical manuscripts date from the twelfth century. The many similarities between the Roman and Milanese repertories (too numerous to be explained as borrowings by Rome), and St. Ambrose's assurance that he followed the Roman practice very closely, suggest that the early Milanese chant was as much Roman as local.

Both Roman and Milanese chants have undergone changes that obscure their relationship, but the Milanese repertory has had fewer additions and, although its longer chants are in general more florid (which has convinced some that it is later than the Gregorian), it has changed less in its essentials. The filling of melodic intervals and the elaboration of simple lines with ornamental turns and repetitions, developments that may have occurred between the tenth and twelfth centuries (if the Milanese did not always have a predilection for what is so obviously Italian bel canto), did not obliterate the original forms. The ancient structures and logic of Latin chant are more easily to be found in the Ambrosian books of the twelfth century than in the Gregorian of the tenth.

Although much more is shared with Rome, there is evidence of some contact with the Gallican and Visigothic churches (the Ambrosian had special affinities with their liturgies), the Byzantine Church, and even the Church of Jerusalem. Borrowed forms are not always obvious; their melodies (when not replaced by familiar ones) were usually naturalized, altered in detail to conform to the Ambrosian style. It is probable, then, that some relationships have escaped notice. Borrowings between churches were normal, but there are indications that the Milanese, beginning in the ninth century with the first attempts to suppress their rite, made a special effort to resist outside influences and to preserve their characteristically Ambrosian repertory.

But the Gregorian siege was relentless, and the defenses were ultimately breached—in some cases by reformers whose declared purpose was the restoration of Ambrosian chant to its ancient purity. Camillo Perego's *La regola del canto fermo ambrosiano* (1622) incorporates much that is Gregorian, especially for the psalmody, and it imposes an eight-mode classification of the chants that was unknown in the old Ambrosian books. Reform may well have seemed necessary, for the state of the chant may not have been healthy. Polyphony was more and more preferred, and even the liturgical customs may not have been as well observed. Most of the chant remained unpublished until the twentieth century, yet manuscript copies of chant books made after the fifteenth century are rare. Much of what was unique in the Ambrosian liturgy was swept away when the two ancient cathedrals (the Winter Church and the Summer Church) were destroyed and their services consolidated in the present enormous Duomo (begun in 1386).

Modern editions of the chants, inspired by the same zeal that led to the earlier Gregorian restoration, began to appear about the turn of the twentieth century; but although much was published, the editions are not very reliable for scholarly purposes, and much of the music has never been printed. The liturgical reforms of the Second Vatican Council seem to have extinguished all hope that the ancient chants will ever be restored to regular use.

The usual musical categories of the Western liturgies—psalm and recitation formulas, antiphons, responsories, and hymns—are all found in Ambrosian chant. It has, however, a more varied style than the Gregorian: its simple chants and recitations are plainer; its solemn chants, more florid. Although this great stylistic range is found within categories, the simplest chants are among the Psalter antiphons; the most florid, among the Alleluias, with their breathtaking melismas of two hundred to three hundred notes. The florid melodies are overwhelmingly stepwise, their effect wavelike, rising and subsiding gradually with successive undulations. Many of the longer melismas have been extended mechanically with repetitions; others are clearly insertions of favorite vocalizations borrowed from other chants. Such textless insertions represent the earliest stage of troping, and the only one to be admitted to Ambrosian chant. These additions presumably were made about the beginning of the ninth century (when similar interpolations appear in Gregorian chant), before the Milanese hardened their resistance to outside influence.

In general the liturgical function of the Ambrosian chant forms, although the designations differ in some instances (*Ingressa* for Introit, *Cantus* for Tract, and so on), is very much the same as in the Gregorian and in the other Latin rites, this similarity being a striking attestation of their fundamental kinship. Hymns, in spite of the celebrated activity of St. Ambrose, who is known to have written several that survive (the texts, not the music), are not more extensively used in the Ambrosian liturgy than in the Gregorian.

In the old manuscripts, office and Mass chants are found together, but divided into two volumes (the *pars hiemalis* and the *pars aestiva*) for use either in the Winter Church, where the main services were held from Advent to Easter, or in the Summer Church, which was the main venue for the rest of the year. These churches having been destroyed, the latest manuscripts and the printed editions adopt the usual Gregorian division of Mass and office.

BIBLIOGRAPHY

Editions of music and liturgy are M. Magistretti, *Beroldi mediolanensis ecclesiae kalendarium et ordines* (1894); G. Suñol, *Antiphonale missarum juxta ritum sanctae ecclesiae mediolanensis* (1935), and *Liber vesperalis juxta ritum sanctae ecclesiae mediolanensis* (1939).

Studies include A. Gajard, "Ambrosian (chant)," in *Dictionnaire d'archéologie chrétienne et de liturgie* (1903–1953); E. Bishop, *The Mozarabic and Ambrosian Rites: Four Essays in Comparative Liturgiology* (1924); G. Reese, *Music in the Middle Ages* (1940); E. Wellesz, *Eastern Elements in Western Chant* (1947); R. Jesson, "Ambrosian Chant: the Music of the Mass" (Ph.D. diss., Indiana Univ., 1955), and "Ambrosian Chant," in W. Apel, *Gregorian Chant* (1958); P. Borella, *Il rito ambrosiano* (1964); R. Weakland, "The Performance of Ambrosian Chant in the Twelfth Century," in *Aspects of Medieval and Renaissance Music* (1966); M. Huglo, "Relations musicales entre Byzance et l'Occident," in *Eleventh International Congress of Byzantine Studies* (1966); and T. Bailey, "Ambrosian Psalmody: an Introduction," in *Rivista internazionale de musica sacra,* I (1980).

TERENCE BAILEY

AMBROSIAN RITE. See **Milanese Rite.**

AMBROSIUS AURELIANUS. See **Aurelianus, Ambrosius.**

AMBROSIUS AUTPERTUS. See **Autpertus, Ambrosius.**

AMBULATORY (Latin, *ambulatio,* a place for walking), a passageway or aisle surrounding an apse or apsidal chapel; in a baptistry, martyrium, or church with a central plan, the passageway around the central space. The covered walk around a cloister is also called an ambulatory. Ambulatories may be isolated passageways or may contain openings into the apse, shrine, etc., as well as openings through the exterior wall into small chapels. Ambulatories were used in pagan mausoleums but were first merged with the basilican plan by Christian architects of the early fourth century (for example, San Lorenzo Fuori le Mura, Rome). Beginning in the Carolingian period, ambulatories became increasingly elaborate in order to accommodate the crowds who came in steadily increasing numbers to view the relics, which were housed in chapels off the annular corridors. By the first half of the twelfth century the ambulatory was merged with the apse and apsidal chapels (for example, St. Denis, near Paris), to form a single large spatial unit called a chevet.

LESLIE BRUBAKER

AMI ET AMILE, an immensely popular legend, combining both hagiographic and folkloric elements; the story deals with an ideal friendship of two look-alike knights, who, in testing their friendship, go to the point of child sacrifice. The most important medieval versions of the legend are (1) the Latin verse epistle (before 1114) of the French monk Raoul le Tourtier (Radulfus Tortarius); (2) the *Vita sanctorum Amici et Amelii,* in prose (*ca.* 1150); (3) the Old French chanson de geste *Ami et Amile* (*ca.* 1200); (4) the Anglo-Norman adventure romance *Amis e Amilun* (shortly after 1200); (5) the Middle English poem *Amis and Amiloun,* composed soon after its source, the Anglo-Norman romance; and (6) the French miracle play *Amis et Amille* (fifteenth century). Amis in the Anglo-Norman version corresponds to Amile in the Old French; Amilun is the Anglo-Norman counterpart of Ami.

BIBLIOGRAPHY

Francis Bar, *Les epîtres latines de Raoul le Tourtier; étude de sources; la légende d'Ami et d'Amile* (1937); Eugen Kölbing, ed., *Amis and Amiloun, zugleich mit der altfranzösischen Quelle* (1884), which, in addition to the Middle English poem, includes the Anglo-Norman romance and the Latin *Vita;* MacEdward Leach, ed., *Amis and Amiloun* (1937, repr. 1960), an excellent edition of the Middle English version preceded by a thorough discussion of various medieval versions, as well as of the sources and themes of the legend, also offers a translation of Raoul's version; Peter F. Dembowski, ed., *Ami et Amile. Chanson de geste.* (1969); Samuel Danon and Samuel N. Rosenberg, eds., *Ami and Amile* (1980), a prose translation with a good introduction; Gaston Paris and Ulysse Robert, eds., *Miracles de Nostre Dame par personnages* (1897).

PETER F. DEMBOWSKI

[See also **Anglo-Norman Literature.**]

AMICE. See **Vestments.**

AMIDA. See **Diyarbakir.**

AMIENS CATHEDRAL, one of the five "High" or "classic" Gothic cathedrals of France, together with Bourges, Chartres, Rheims, and Soissons. Although considered by many the epitome of Gothic construction, the cathedral contains decorative and structural features that anticipate later developments in Gothic architecture.

Amiens has a fully developed cathedral plan including choir with ambulatory and seven radiating chapels, projecting aisled transept, and a seven bay-aisled nave. The west facade has shallow towers carried on massive buttresses that form the deep portals. The nave vaults are 138 feet high, among the tallest in Gothic architecture. Amiens is noted for the precision of its planning.

The Gothic cathedral was begun after a fire around 1220 had destroyed the Romanesque cathedral, but the chronology of construction is imperfectly known. The generally accepted sequence is nave, *ca.* 1220–*ca.* 1235, under Robert de Luzarches; lower story of transept, choir, and radiating chapels, *ca.* 1235–*ca.* 1240, under Thomas de Cormont; upper parts of the choir, *ca.* 1240–*ca.* 1280, at an er-

Amiens Cathedral, west facade. SCALA/EDITORIAL PHOTOCOLOR ARCHIVES

ratic pace, under Regnault de Cormont. The architect's names are known from an inscription installed in the nave floor in 1288 (original destroyed in 1828; copy installed in 1894) by Regnault de Cormont, Thomas's son.

The cathedral has undergone extensive restoration, most notably by Eugène Emmanuel Viollet-le-Duc from 1849 to 1874, but its interior has been little altered from its original appearance except for the loss of stained glass. Amiens possesses an extensive program of undistinguished sculpture. It has been proposed that its lack of quality is due to an attempt around 1250 to replicate a style of sculpture in fashion a generation earlier.

BIBLIOGRAPHY

Carl F. Barnes, Jr., "Cross-Media Design Motifs in XIIIth-Century France: Architectural Motifs in the Psalter and Hours of Yolande de Soissons and in the Cathedral of Notre-Dame at Amiens," in *Gesta,* **17,** no. 2 (1978); Amédée Boinet, *La cathédrale d'Amiens,* 5th rev. ed. (1959); Alain Erlande-Brandenburg, "La façade de la cathédrale d'Amiens," in *Bulletin monumental,* **135** (1977); Robert Branner, "Paris and the Origins of Rayonnant Gothic Architecture down to 1240," in *Art Bulletin,* **44** (1962); and *St. Louis and the Court Style in Gothic Architecture* (1965), esp. 25–28 and 138–140; Georges Durand, *Monographie de l'église Notre-Dame, cathédrale d'Amiens,* 2 vols. (1901–1903).

CARL F. BARNES, JR.

[See also **Gothic Architecture.**]

AMIRSPASALAR, from *amir,* an Arabic term meaning commander, governor, prince; and *spasalar,* from the Old Persian *spahpat,* the commander in chief of the medieval Georgian army, and one of the highest officials of the Georgian kingdom, and the equivalent of the Armenian *sparapet.* In the early twelfth century the *amirspasalar* was chosen from the Georgian branch of the Orbeli family but in 1155, David, son of Demetre I, overthrew his father and attempted to eliminate Orbeli influence by giving the post to their rival, Tirkash Abuletisdze. The Orbeli succeeded in poisoning King David, restored Demetre, and retained the post of *amirspasalar* until the rebellion of Ivane Orbeli in 1176–1177, when it was given to the Kipchak Turk, Qubasar. In 1184 Queen Tamara removed Qubasar and appointed Gamrakeli. Later the post descended in the Armenized Kurdish family of Zak^{c}arids (in Georgian, the Mxargrdzeli).

BIBLIOGRAPHY

William E. D. Allen, *A History of the Georgian People* (1932; repr. 1971); Robert Bedrosian, "The Turco-Mongol Invasions and the Lords of Armenia in the 13–14th Centuries" (diss., Columbia University, 1979); Mariam D. Lordkipanidze, *Istoria Gruzii XI–nachala XIII veka* (1974).

R. SUNY

AMIS ET AMILOUN. See **Ami et Amile.**

AMMIANUS MARCELLINUS (*ca.* 330–*ca.* 396), historian, was born at Antioch and participated in the Asian campaigns of Ursicinus (354–360) and Julian (363). His *Res gestae* is a major work of great value, which relates in thirty-one books the history of the Roman Empire from the accession of Nerva in 96 to the death of Valens in 378. Only the last eighteen books survive, beginning with the seventeenth year of the reign of Constantinus II (353).

BIBLIOGRAPHY

Ammianus Marcellinus' *Rerum gestarum libri qui supersunt* was edited by Wolfgang Seyfarth, 2 vols. (1978) and includes an extensive bibliography; John C. Rolfe, *Ammianus Marcellinus,* 3 vols. (1935–1939), frequently reprinted, includes an English translation. See also Arnold Hugh Martin Jones, John R. Martindale, and J. Morris, *The Prosopography of the Later Roman Empire,* 2nd ed., I (1975), 547–548; and Guy Sabbah, *La méthode d'Ammien Marcellin* (1978).

ALAIN J. STOCLET

[See also **Gratian; Julian the Apostate.**]

AMORIANS, a dynasty, named from the home city of the rulers, Amorion, which ruled the Byzantine Empire from 820 to 867 and consisted of three emperors: Michael II (820–829), Theophilos (829–842), and Michael III (842–867). Michael II was a soldier whose followers murdered Emperor Leo V, enabling Michael to seize the throne. Although he came from Phrygia, a stronghold of Iconoclasm, he followed a moderate policy on that issue. His son Theophilos, an extremely learned man, was especially interested in Muslim culture and was an Iconoclast. Michael III was six when he came to the throne, and his mother, Theodora II, ruled as regent until 856, supporting the restoration of icons by the Synod of 843. In addition to the Iconoclastic controversy, the main events of the Amorians' reign were the revolt of Thomas the Slav (821–824), campaigns against the Arabs and Paulicians, and the Photian Schism.

BIBLIOGRAPHY

Georgije Ostrogorski, *History of the Byzantine State* (1957; rev. 1969).

LINDA C. ROSE

AMORION, located in Asia Minor at 39° 50′ north latitude, longitude 31° east, the home of the Amorian dynasty and the largest and most important fortress of the Anatolikon theme. It was the base of power of the *strategos* of that theme, who was to become Emperor Leo III, and it was to Amorion that Leo's son Constantine V fled in 742 during a civil war and was welcomed by the population. Amorion was attacked by the Arabs in the seventh and eighth centuries and was captured by them in 838, but it was recaptured by Byzantium during the great Macedonian reconquests.

BIBLIOGRAPHY

Georgije Ostrogorski, *History of the Byzantine State* (1957; rev. 1969).

LINDA C. ROSE

AMPULLA, a small silver flask, often decorated in repoussé, made to contain oil sanctified by contact with a relic in Palestine, such as the cross of Golgotha in Jerusalem. Ampullae were sold to pilgrims to the Holy Land during the sixth century; they are decorated with scenes from Christ's life or the cross of the crucifixion. Most ampullae are now in collections in Italy, at Bobbio or Monza.

BIBLIOGRAPHY

André Grabar, *Ampoules de Terre Sainte* (1958).

LESLIE BRUBAKER

ᶜAMR IBN AL-ᶜĀṢ (*ca.* 575/595–664), prominent companion of the prophet Muḥammad and conqueror of Egypt, was a member of the Sahm clan of the Meccan tribe of Ḳuraysh. Before the advent of Islam he made his living by commerce, notably to al-ᶜArīsh and towns in Palestine; it is possible that he also went to Egypt for trade, although the accounts of his visits there are heavily overlaid with symbolism prefiguring his conquest of the country. At first an opponent of Islam, ᶜAmr is said to have been sent by the Ḳuraysh to Abyssinia, to persuade the negus to return some Muslims who had fled there to escape persecution in Mecca; but some time later, shortly before the conquest of Mecca by Muḥammad in 630, he embraced Islam. The Prophet appointed him to lead the raid against some tribes of the northern Ḥijāz at Dhāt al-Salāsil (629), and toward the end of the Prophet's career ᶜAmr was sent as his representative to Oman, where he appears to have persuaded the leaders of the local nobility to embrace Islam.

Upon the Prophet's death ᶜAmr returned to Medina and was charged by the caliph Abū Bakr with

ᶜAMR IBN AL-ᶜĀṢ

securing the allegiance of the Quḍāᶜa tribes of the northern Ḥijāz during the *Ridda* (tribal defections following the Prophet's death), partly because he had ties with the tribe of Balī, from which his mother had come. When the Muslims embarked on the conquest of Syria, ᶜAmr was put in command of one of the four armies sent there. His forces participated in all the main confrontations with the Byzantines in Syria (Adjnādayn, Yarmūk, siege of Damascus), and some authorities claim that he was also active in northern Syria; but his main sphere of operation was clearly Palestine, where he was largely responsible for the conquest of the main towns (Jerusalem, Caesarea, Ashqelon).

From Palestine, ᶜAmr marched with a small force toward Egypt—whether on his own initiative or on orders from the caliph ᶜUmar being a much disputed question. Between about 640 and 642 his troops, which had been considerably reinforced in the interim, were able to subdue most of Egypt despite stiff resistance from Byzantine garrisons in the main towns of Babylon (near Cairo) and Alexandria. ᶜAmr also launched campaigns from Egypt against North Africa and commanded troops that took the city of Barqa in Cyrenaica and, according to some authors, Tripoli in Libya; but Egypt always remained his main concern. Once the conquest of Egypt was completed, however, the caliph ᶜUmar, concerned lest ᶜAmr should become too independently powerful in his province, placed ᶜAbd Allāh ibn Saᶜd ibn Abī Sarḥ in command of Upper Egypt and the finances of all of Egypt, leaving ᶜAmr control over the delta region and command of the army.

The caliph ᶜUthmān went even further, removing ᶜAmr from office entirely and appointing ᶜAbd Allāh as governor. The new appointee, however, lacked the full support of the army; and when a rebellion broke out among the Greek population of Alexandria in 645, and was followed by the arrival by sea of a large Byzantine army hoping to reconquer Egypt, ᶜUthmān was forced to reinstate ᶜAmr as governor in order to ensure effective resistance. ᶜAmr managed to block the Byzantine advance, defeat the invaders at Nikiu, and reoccupy Alexandria, the city walls of which he ordered razed. No sooner had he restored order than the caliph reinstated ᶜAbd Allāh as governor-general and supervisor of finances, offering to leave ᶜAmr as commander of the army. ᶜAmr refused this sop, declaring that the caliph asked him "to hold the cow by the horns, while ᶜAbd Allāh milked it." He retired to Syria and Palestine, where he owned several properties.

During the first civil war ᶜAmr backed Muᶜāwiya against ᶜAlī; he served as Muᶜāwiya's cavalry commander at the battle of Ṣiffīn and is said to have been the one who devised the stratagem of raising leaves from the Koran on lances when ᶜAlī's troops gained the upper hand, precipitating confusion in ᶜAlī's ranks that led to demands that the dispute be settled by arbitration rather than battle. It was ᶜAmr, again, who was chosen by Muᶜāwiya to represent him at the arbitration at Adhruḥ (658). He seems to have outwitted his pious counterpart, obtaining a verdict that was unacceptable to ᶜAlī, who rejected it. At about the same time Muᶜāwiya appointed ᶜAmr to be his governor in Egypt, which was under the uncertain control of ᶜAlī's governor, Muḥammad ibn Abī Bakr. ᶜAmr, still idolized by his former troops, reestablished his position in Egypt with little difficulty. He remained in office for the rest of his life, and besides organizing Egypt's domestic affairs he launched new raids against the Berber tribes to the west. In 661 he escaped a Khārijite assassin and died at an advanced age in Al-Fustāt (Old Cairo) about 664.

A good commander and administrator, ᶜAmr won the affection of troops and subjects alike. He apparently resisted pressure from the caliphs ᶜUmar and ᶜUthmān to increase the taxes in Egypt, which may have been one reason why they removed him from office. He also showed an interest in developing the country economically, by clearing the freshwater canal that connected the Red Sea and the Nile to facilitate trade. He founded Al-Fustāt, the Muslims' garrison town at the head of the Nile delta, and ordered the construction of the mosque there that, although later rebuilt, still bears his name. He was also renowned and remembered for his political acumen and skills as a negotiator.

BIBLIOGRAPHY

Ibn Hishām, *Sīra,* translated by Alfred Guillaume as *The Life of Muḥammad* (1955); al-Wāqidī, *Maghāzī*; Ibn Ḥajar al-ᶜAsqalānī, *Isābu,* s.n. "ᶜAmr ibn al-ᶜĀṣ"; al-Balādhurī, *Futūḥ al-buldān,* translated by Philip K. Hitti as *The Origins of the Islamic State* (1916); Ibn ᶜAbd al-Ḥakam, *Futūḥ Miṣr;* al-Ṭabarī, *Ta'rīkh al-rusul wa l-mulūk.* The biography in Ibn Saᶜd, *Kitāb al-ṭabaqāt al-kabīr,* Eduard Sachau, ed. (1905–1940), IV, pt. 2, 2–8, is incomplete and should be augmented by material from vols. XII and XIII of the Damascus manuscript of Ibn ᶜAsākir's *Ta'rīkh madīnat Dimashq* (Ẓāhiriyya Library, Damascus, MS Ta'rīkh 11 and 12). On ᶜAmr's activity in the northern Ḥijāz and in the conquest of Syria, see F. M. Donner, *The Early Islamic Conquests* (1981). On activity in Egypt, see Alfred J. Butler, *The Arab Conquest of Egypt and the Last Thirty Years of the Roman Dominion* (1902); Ulrich Luft, "Der Beginn der islamischen Eroberung Ägyptens im Jahre 639," in *Forschungen und Berichte aus dem transeatischen Lebensraum,* **16** (1974); A. Cocatre-Zilgien, "Amr ibn al-Ass et la conquête de l'Égypte par les Arabes," in *Annales africaines* (1959).

FRED M. DONNER

ANALDI. See **Arnoldi, Alberto.**

ANALOI (or *naloi;* Greek *analogion*), a small, slant-topped lectern used in Eastern Orthodox churches to hold service books and, among the Russians, icons. Whereas in Balkan churches these lecterns are often permanently installed, in Russia they were usually portable and consisted of a folding wooden frame with the front, top, and rear covered with a cloth material, as had been the custom in Byzantine times.

GEORGE P. MAJESKA

ANANIA ŠIRAKAC^{c}I (or Anec^{c}i (*ca.* 610–late 680's) was born in Ani, in the district of Širak. The principal source on the early part of his life is his autobiography. In it he states that he studied for eight years with Tychikos, a Greek scientist living in Trebizond. After completing his education, he says, he returned to his native land and attracted many students. His success, however, was short-lived; his pupils left before finishing their studies, and began to compete with their master. Anania was greatly embittered by their actions.

The main historical event connected with the name of Anania was the calendar reform proposed by the Kat^{c}ołikos Anastas in 665. Anania was commissioned to revise the Armenian calendar and make provisions for a leap year. The task of enforcing Anania's revision remained unfinished because of Anastas's death in 667.

As a consequence of the limited nature of our sources, little is known about Anania's later years, his status, or his origins. Some modern scholars have questioned the medieval tradition of his being a priest. Anania probably died in the late 680's, since the second year of the Emperor Justinian II (686) is the last date recorded in his *Chronicle.*

Anania wrote mathematical texts, studies on weights and measures, calendrical tables, cosmographical studies, the *Chronicle,* and several minor works on religious and scientific topics. According to a very recent theory, most of the scientific works formed a textbook of universal scope. The Ašxarhac^{c}oyc^{c} ("Geography of the World"), which occasionally appears under his name, is the work of an earlier author.

In the corpus of Anania's works the mathematical texts occupy an important place. These consist of tables of addition, subtraction, multiplication, and division, and of mathematical problems, which together seem to constitute a general textbook. The tables are among the earliest that have survived. The cosmographical works reflect the state of Greco-Roman science of the post-classical period.

Anania was the first Armenian scientist-astronomer. His works were used as basic textbooks in medieval Armenian monastic universities, and his thought and observations were quite influential in the development of medieval science in Armenia.

BIBLIOGRAPHY

For an extensive bibliography see H. S. Anasian, *Haykakan Matenaqitut^{c}yun,* I (1959), cols. 731–774, 1174. His writings include Iosif A. Orbeli, *Viprosy i resheniia vardapeta Ananii Shirakatsi, armianskogo matematika VII veka* (1918); *Tiezeraqitut^{c}yun ew Tomar* ("Cosmography and Calendar"), A. G. Abrahamyan, ed. (1940); *Anania Širakac^{c}u matenagrut^{c}yunə* ("The Writings of Anania Širakac^{c}i"), A. G. Abrahamyan, ed. (1944); *Lusni parberašrǰannerə* ("Tables of the Motion of the Moon"), A. G. Abrahamyan, ed. and trans. (1962), Armenian text with Russian translation; *Kosmografiia,* preface and Russian trans. by K. S. Ter-Davtian and S. S. Arevshatian (1962); "Autobiographie d'Anania Širakac^{c}i," H. Berberian, trans., in *Revue des études arméniennes,* **1** (1964). An English version of the "Autobiography" is F. C. Conybeare, "Ananias of Sirak," in *Byzantinische Zeitschrift,* **11** (1897).

Articles and studies include Paul Lemerle, "Note sur les données historiques de l'autobiographie d'Anania de Shirak," in *Revue des études arméniennes,* **1** (1964); W. Petri, "Ananija Schirakazi—ein armenischer Kosmograph des 7. Jahrhunderts," in *Zeitschrift der Deutschen morgenländischen Gesellschaft,* **114,** no. 2 (1964); R. H. Hewsen, "Science in VII Century Armenia: Anania of Širak," in *Isis,* **59** (1968); A. G. Abrahamyan and G. B. Petrosian, *Ananiia Shirakatsi* (1970).

KRIKOR H. MAKSOUDIAN

ANASTASIS (Greek for *resurrection*; also known as Harrowing of Hell, Descent into Limbo) commemorates Christ's triumph over death through his descent into hell to redeem the righteous who died before him and thus, not being Christians, could not be admitted into heaven. The Anastasis was elaborated in narrative form by the fourth or fifth century in the Apocryphal Gospel of Nicodemus; it is not described in the New Testament. Celebrated as one of the Great Feasts of the Greek Church (Easter Sunday), the Anastasis was usually represented by Byzantine artists as an autonomous image; in the Latin West, particularly in the late medieval period, it was often incorporated into Passion cycles (Strasbourg Cathedral, central west portal, *ca.* 1280). Representations of the Anastasis show Christ trampling on the broken gates of hell or, especially in the Gothic period, stepping unscathed into an anthropomorphized Mouth of Hell. Christ is depicted either raising Adam and Eve from their graves or leading them out of hell as a symbol of the redemption of all righteous souls. In the earliest versions—for example, the Fieschi reliquary in New York, Metropolitan Museum of Art (*ca.* 700?)—Christ pulls Adam from the tomb while Eve stands or kneels by Adam's side. Especially after the ninth century, apparently influenced by antique images of Herakles dragging Cerberus from Hades, artists emphasized Christ's physical presence by depicting him vigorously striding away from hell while firmly grasping Adam's arm. After the late thirteenth century, particularly in Byzantium, Christ may also pull Eve from her tomb (the Kariye Djami, Constantinople). Rarely, Christ stands frontally and is flanked by Adam and Eve.

LESLIE BRUBAKER

ANASTASIUS BIBLIOTHECARIUS (*ca.* 815–879), Roman scholar and papal official. His stormy early career, including an attempt to become pope by force in 855, earned him three papal anathemas. From late 862 on, he was the letter writer and chief adviser of Pope Nicholas I (858–867). Adrian II (867–872) made him official papal *bibliothecarius* (librarian) and he remained so until his death, except for a period of disgrace in 868–869 for his alleged role in a double murder by his cousin. He was known for his influence on Nicholas and Adrian and for his literary works. These include translations into Latin of contemporary Byzantine writings, notably the minutes of the council of Constantinople IV in 869–870; annotated source collections clarifying episodes in papal history; letters and notes that illumine his own time; and probably the life of Nicholas I in the *Liber pontificalis.*

BIBLIOGRAPHY

Anastasius' letters and prefaces are edited by Ernst Perels and Gerhard Laehr in *Monumenta germaniae historica, Epistolae,* VII (1928), 395–442. His collections and translations are in J.-P. Migne, ed., *Patrologia latina,* CXXIX (1879), 9–743 (vols. CXXVII and CXXVIII contain the *Liber pontificalis,* which is wrongly attributed to him). See the pioneering biography, Arthur Lapôtre, *De Anastasio Bibliothecario sedis apostolicae* (1885); its essential corrective, Ernst Perels, *Papst Nikolaus I und Anastasius Bibliothecarius* (1920); and especially Girolamo Arnaldi, "Anastasio Bibliotecario," in *Dizionario biografico degli italiani,* III (1961), 25–37.

JANE BISHOP

ANATOLIA, or Asia Minor, a broad peninsula stretching almost 800 miles from the Aegean Sea to the Euphrates River and over 400 from the Black Sea to the Mediterranean, consists of a central plateau surrounded by mountains that decline in the west to fertile river valleys and coastal plains. Agricultural and mineral wealth and a strategic location on land and sea routes between Europe and Asia ensured its importance. By 500, Anatolia had enjoyed half a millennium of almost uninterrupted peace, possessed a rich urban economy, and was one of the most populous and prosperous regions of the Byzantine Empire. Its centers were Nicomedia, Nicaea, Smyrna, Ephesus, and Sardis in the west; Attaleia, Side, Seleucia, and Tarsus in the south; Heraclea, Sinope, and Trebizond on the north coast; and Ancyra (Ankara) and Caesarea on the plateau. The cities were foci of trade and economic activities, civil and ecclesiastical administration, and cultural life, which was largely confined to them. Anatolia was divided into some twenty provinces, most of which were ruled by civilian governors. Since the time of Constantine, the cities of Anatolia had maintained much of their ancient splendor with extensive public works and services. Christianity added a vast range of church buildings along with charitable establishments.

Fundamental changes began in the sixth century, under Justinian, who rebuilt the defenses of the eastern frontier and adorned Anatolia with monumental

churches and public works: the cathedral of Ephesus and the bridge over the Sangarius still stand as magnificent examples. Yet brigandage was endemic in many country districts; and special military officials, whose efforts produced no lasting results, replaced the civil government in Pisidia, Galatia, and Pontus. Ruthless exaction of taxes to support the ambitious and extravagant imperial policies ruined many cities and districts; and the bubonic plague of 542 and subsequent years, the greatest catastrophe of the age, decimated the population. Archaeology also suggests incipient decline by revealing little activity after 542. Places on main highways, however, continued to flourish, as did the south coast. The construction of villages and towns in Lycia and Cilicia indicates an unprecedented prosperity, probably from increasing production of olive oil and from their location along the main sea route between east and west.

Collapse followed in the early seventh century. From 611 to 628, Persian armies struck repeatedly: cities and villages were captured, plundered, and destroyed; whole populations were massacred or enslaved. The devastation, which the archaeological record strikingly confirms, can hardly be exaggerated. The network of cities, on which the classical civilization of Anatolia had depended, virtually vanished, and a new age began in which fortresses and villages predominated. Of the major excavated cities, Ephesus and Ancyra were largely destroyed, and Sardis practically disappeared. Only the north coast, protected by high mountains, and perhaps some heavily fortified cities of the south and west seem to have escaped. Since the Persians were soon followed by the Arabs, the country never had a chance to recover.

The Arab invasions left Anatolia the dangerously exposed heartland of a reduced state. In response,

Constans II reorganized the defenses and fortified cities in the west, where a walled hilltop often replaced an ancient metropolis. But no firm frontier was established and Arab raids penetrated incessantly for two centuries, culminating in the sieges of Constantinople in 674–678 and 717–718 and the capture of Ancyra and Amorium in 838. Devastation and looting further reduced and impoverished the population, which suffered a recurrence of the plague from 744 to 747. The needs of defense produced a military administration based on districts called "themes." These apparently originated in the seventh century when the headquarters of the imperial armies were moved to Anatolia: to Amasia (the Armeniac army), Amorium (the Anatolic), and Ancyra (the Obsequium or Opsikion), while the fleet was based on the south coast, probably at Attaleia. During the eighth century, themes replaced the old civil provinces, which disappeared except in ecclesiastical organization. Anatolia was also a cradle of iconoclasm; strife between its adherents and opponents only added to the general insecurity. During the early Middle Ages new or previously obscure fortresses, usually located along the invasion routes, came into prominence while many ancient cities decayed.

In the ninth century, construction of fortresses presaged the recapture of much territory from the heretic Paulicians of the upper Euphrates and from the Arabs. Under the Macedonian dynasty (867–1057) peace returned with a limited prosperity and a modest urban life; a typical Anatolian city comprised a citadel, town walls, a cathedral (usually a much-repaired ancient building), and a crowded network of houses and industrial installations strewn among the ruins of antiquity. Villages grew and flourished, as did monasteries, particularly in Bithynia, Ionia, and Cappadocia whose painted rock-cut churches, along with many substantial buildings elsewhere, reflect the general recovery.

A new enemy found Byzantine Anatolia's borders at their greatest extent. Turkish raids reached the central plateau in 1059 and constantly increased to provoke the Battle of Manzikert (1071). This great Turkish victory marks a fundamental turning point and the beginning of the area's transformation from Greek Christianity to Turkish Islam. Within ten years, the Turks spread to the Aegean and founded a state at Nicaea. Although the First Crusade pushed them back, they retained the center and introduced a period in which several powers contested Anatolia.

The Seljuks of Rum based in Konya and the Danishmendids to the north shared the plateau. Despite long wars, which finally brought Seljuk supremacy in 1174, both states achieved some stability and orderly government. The richer coastal regions, which remained Byzantine, were afflicted by the unceasing raids of the Turks. The Komnenoi (1081–1185) won victories and brought security by constructing fortresses, but lack of other remains suggests that the long period of turmoil had impoverished their lands. In 1176, the ambitious Manuel I attempted to overthrow the Seljuks. His crushing defeat at Myriokephalon weakened the Greeks and allowed the Turkoman nomads, whose gradual infiltration and settlement had long been contested, to advance westward.

The capture of Constantinople in 1204 by the forces of the Fourth Crusade produced further fragmentation. Greek empires arose at Nicaea and Trebizond; the crusaders for a time occupied the northwest; and the Armenians of Cilicia and the Taurus became independent. The greatest power, the Seljuk sultanate, controlled the center and east and gained strategic outlets on the Mediterranean and Black Sea. In the early thirteenth century, under ᶜAlāᵓ al-Dīn Kai-Kobadh I, the state reached its height: mosques, religious schools, charitable institutions, fortresses, and public works reveal its wealth, while caravanserais and bridges show its attention to trade and communications. The monuments of Konya, Kayseri, Sivas, Niğde, and Erzurum suggest a level of prosperity higher than that of the small Christian states. In them also, extensive construction of churches and fortresses reveals considerable economic activity.

In 1243, the Seljuks were crushed by the Mongols at Köse Dağ and entered into a decline, which became precipitous by the end of the century. In 1261, the Nicene empire reconquered Constantinople and turned its attention fatefully toward the west. The Turkoman tribes, freed from restraint, threw off Seljuk control and advanced on the fertile Aegean valleys. By the early fourteenth century only a few walled Byzantine towns were resisting the Turkomans, who now formed independent emirates. The Armenian kingdom was obliterated by the Mamluks, and Cilicia soon fell to the Ramazanids. Other, more powerful states ruled further east. The empire of Trebizond, profiting from its location at the end of the trade route to Persia, maintained its independence, as did the isolated Byzantine enclave of Philadelphia; otherwise the fall of Nicomedia to the Ottomans in 1337 effectively marked the end of Greek rule in Anatolia.

Ottoman expansion began with Orkhan and Murad I, who defeated the Byzantines and annexed Turkoman states, a movement culminating in the conquest of the whole region by Bāyazīd I. His actions provoked a massive attack by Tamerlane, who routed the Ottomans at Ancyra in 1402. After conquering Izmir from the crusaders, he returned to central Asia, leaving behind widespread devastation and chaos. Tamerlane restored the emirates, but those of the west were soon retaken by the Ottomans. It remained for Muḥammad II to establish full Ottoman supremacy by the conquests of Karaman in 1457 and Trebizond in 1461. Selim I reduced the remaining independent states and introduced a unity that has prevailed to the present.

BIBLIOGRAPHY

There is no comprehensive work on medieval Anatolia. In addition to the standard histories of the late Roman, Byzantine, and Ottoman empires, see Claude Cahen, *Pre-Ottoman Turkey* (1968); Clive Foss, "The Persians in Asia Minor and the End of Antiquity," in *English Historical Review,* **90** (1975); *Byzantine and Turkish Sardis* (1976); and *Ephesus After Antiquity* (1979); Paul Lemerle, *L'émirat d'Aydin, Byzance et l'occident* (1957); Speros Vryonis, *The Decline of Medieval Hellenism in Asia Minor* (1971); and Paul Wittek, *Das Fürstentum Mentesche* (1934); and *The Rise of the Ottoman Empire* (1938, repr. 1971).

CLIVE FOSS

[See also **Byzantine Empire** (individual articles); **Cilicia; Ottomans; Seljuks; Trebizond; Turkomans.**]

ANATOLIKON, THEME OF, Byzantine army corps formed from the withdrawal of the Orientales (or Anatolikoi), troops under the *magister militum per Orientem,* from Syria after its conquest by the Arabs. Its headquarters had become Amorion (and later Marj al-Sham) by the early 640's. The *strategos* of Anatolikon acquired responsibility for the defense of central Asia Minor, including Cappadocia and parts of Phrygia, Galatia, and Pisidia. It may not have included the Thracian theme. Originally the theme of Anatolikon was the most important one in court protocol and possessed the largest thematic army until its subdivision. It declined in the tenth century because of its gradual partition into smaller themes, the emergence of the domestic of the schools as the most powerful Byzantine military commander, and because of the theme's increasing distance from the critical eastern frontier, as Byzantium recovered territory from Muslim authority.

WALTER EMIL KAEGI, JR.

ANCHORITES. Derived from the Greek *anachorein* (to withdraw), "anchorite" was, in early Christian writings, synonymous with "hermit." During the High and late Middle Ages these terms became differentiated as part of the process whereby anchoritism and hermitism shifted from purely personal religious expressions to vocations under church organization. The Latin *inclusus,* used as an alternative and equivalent for *anachoreta,* conceptualized the major distinction between anchorites and hermits. Anchorites were persons, most often women, who were ritually enclosed and permanently set apart both from lay society and from the regular religious life, whereas hermits retained freedom of movement. In England medieval anchorites generally lived under episcopal control, in individual cells attached to parish churches. Continental anchorites more frequently were found in clusters of cells under the protection of monasteries.

BIBLIOGRAPHY

Rotha Mary Clay, *The Hermits and Anchorites of England* (1914); *L'eremitismo in occidente nei secoli XI e XII* (1965); H. Mayr-Harting, "Functions of a Twelfth-Century Recluse," in *History,* **60** (1975); Ann K. Warren, "The English Anchorite in the Reign of Henry III, 1216–1272," in *Ball State University Forum,* **19,** no. 3 (1978); and "The Anchorite in Medieval England: 1100–1539" (Ph.D. dissertation, Case Western Reserve University, 1980).

ANN K. WARREN

ANCIENT OF DAYS (Daniel 7:9, 13, 22; Revelation 1:13–14), God or Christ represented as an aged, white-haired man, often as the Apocalyptic Man in Byzantine and Latin imagery. In Byzantium the Ancient of Days is often paired with, or takes on the cross nimbus of, Christ Logos in reference to the Gospel of St. John (1:1), thus assuming additional meaning as a form of God the Father, who exists outside time, as a symbol of eternity and of divine, extratemporal unity.

BIBLIOGRAPHY
André Grabar, *L'art de la fin de l'antiquité et du moyen âge,* I (1968), 51–62.

LESLIE BRUBAKER

ANCRENE RIWLE, or *Ancrene Wisse,* written about 1220 in the southwest Midlands of England, one of the most important and interesting prose works in Middle English literature. Its merit was recognized in its own day, as is shown by the eight manuscripts still extant and by its translation into French and Latin.

The author is not known by name, but according to one theory he was an Augustinian canon. He identifies himself in his work as spiritual counselor to three sisters who had embraced the austere life of anchoresses (religious solitaries). *Ancrene Riwle* was composed in response to a request by these women. Alterations in later copies suggest that it came to be used by larger groups of recluses, and it was probably read by pious laymen as well.

During the Middle Ages the spiritual benefits of solitude exerted an appeal that has since faded. Male and female members of regular orders, such as Benedictines and Cistercians, would sometimes withdraw from the communal life of their abbeys and enter a cell that was then sealed with a solemn rite of enclosure. The recluse was to consider himself or herself dead to the world, and to live with scant opportunity for communication with others, except for a confessor, or for work with the hands, spending the days in almost constant prayer. Lay people also, such as the three sisters of *Ancrene Riwle,* took up the life of seclusion, although their numbers probably were never great at any time. Anchor-holds were commonly annexed to churches, and remains of such structures can still be seen in England. Each of the three sisters occupied her own quarters in such a church annex and was able to observe the celebration of Mass and the Divine Office at the high altar through a special window in her cell.

The author distinguishes between the outer and inner rules, the first of which governs the external life, including diet, personal care, and the proper observance of liturgical obligations. The inner, or "lady," rule pertains to the schooling of the heart and the innermost thoughts. The sole purpose of the outer rule is to maintain the purity of the inner self. Part I of the work explains in detail how the anchoress is to perform the eight "hours" of the Office of Our Lady, with supplementary offices and prayers, a program of perhaps five hours daily. Part VIII, with which the rule closes, dwells on such matters as the recommended frequency of confession and communion. It also contains mundane advice, including the often-quoted admonitions that the anchoress should keep no more than one cat, restrict her sewing to church vestments and clothing for the poor, and refrain from excesses of ascetic self-discipline.

The six interior chapters are homilies or meditations on the bodily senses, the sacrament of penance, and divine love. The deadly sins are strikingly allegorized: for example, pride is represented as a lion, gluttony as a sow, and lechery as a scorpion. All these chapters, but especially that on the love of God, contain some of the most highly prized and most beautifully expressed spiritual insights to be found in Middle English religious writings.

BIBLIOGRAPHY
Robert W. Ackerman, "The Liturgical Day in *Ancrene Riwle,*" in *Speculum,* 53 (1978); *The Ancrene Riwle (The Corpus MS: Ancrene Wisse),* Mary Salu, trans. (1956); Francis D. S. Darwin, *The English Mediaeval Recluse* (1944); and Eric J. Dobson, ed., *The English Text of the Ancrene Riwle* (1972); and *The Origins of Ancrene Wisse* (1976).

ROBERT W. ACKERMAN

[See also **Anchorites; Hermit; Liturgy; Monasticism.**]

ANDACHTSBILD (German, "devotional image"), a sculpture, painting, or tapestry, usually made for private devotional use, that served as a pictorial aid to prayer. *Andachtsbilder* usually showed Christ detached from all spatial and temporal connections, and emphasized his grief and suffering, for example, as the Man of Sorrows. Although some of the images were produced in Byzantium and may have been derived from Eastern liturgical images such as the *epitaphios,* the term refers specifically to Western examples. From the late thirteenth century on, when new themes such as the Pietà were introduced, *Andachtsbilder* were increasingly popular and widespread.

LESLIE BRUBAKER

ANDALUSIA. The etymology of the word is in doubt; some scholars have traced it back to the Vandals' occupation of southern Iberia in the fifth century. Muslim chroniclers and geographers used the term *al-Andalus* to describe the Iberian lands under Islam. Thus, in the mid eighth century *al-Andalus* encompassed almost the entire peninsula, while in the late fifteenth century it was limited to the area around Granada. Andalusia is at present a region of southern Spain that extends from the provinces of Almería and Granada in the east to the Portuguese border and the Atlantic Ocean in the west.

TEOFILO F. RUIZ

ANDRÉ DE FLEURY (d. 1050–1060) entered the monastery of Fleury under the abbot Gauzlin (1004–1030), and made his final vows under Hugh, who was abbot from 1036 until sometime after 1043. He died with the rank of prior, or dean. His *Vita Gauzlini abbatis Floriacensis monasterii* is deemed a masterpiece of biography by R.-H. Bautier. André also compiled books IV–VII of the *Miracula sancti Benedicti* in 1041, dedicating them to Abbot Hugh. A high point of hagiography in this period, these books continue the narratives of Adrevald (ninth century) and Aimoin (early eleventh century).

BIBLIOGRAPHY

André's *Vie de Gauzlin, abbé de Fleury. Vita Gauzlini abbatis Floriacensis monasterii* was edited, translated, and annotated by R.-H. Bautier and G. Labory (1968). Also see R.-H. Bautier, *L'historiographie en France aux Xe et XIe siècles (France du Nord et de l'Est)* in *La storiografia altomedioevale, 10–16 aprile 1969* (1970), pp. 793–850; A. Vidier, *L'historiographie à St. Benoît-sur-Loire et les Miracles de Saint Benoît* (1965); and the bibliography in *Repertorium fontium historiae medii aevi*, II (1967), pp. 227–228.

ALAIN J. STOCLET

[See also **Aimoin; Hagiography; Historiography.**]

ANDREA DA FIESOLE. See **Fiesole, Andrea Da.**

ANDREA DA FIRENZE (Andrea Bonaiuti da Firenze) (*fl.* 1337–1377), a painter active in Florence and Pisa, is best known for his fresco decoration of the Spanish Chapel in the Dominican Friary of Sta. Maria Novella in Florence. He also executed frescoes in the Campo Santo at Pisa (*ca.* 1377). His style reflects a conservative reaction to the innovations of trecento art following the Black Death, which reached its height in Italy in 1348.

BIBLIOGRAPHY

J. Wood Brown, *The Dominican Church of S. M. Novella* (1902); Millard Meiss, *Painting in Florence and Siena After the Black Death* (1951), 94–104; John White, *Art and Architecture in Italy: 1250–1400* (1966), 371–373.

LESLIE BRUBAKER

ANDREAS CAPELLANUS. See **Capellanus, Andreas.**

ANDREW OF ST. VICTOR (d. 1175), exegete. Of English or Anglo-Norman origin, Andrew became a canon at the abbey of St. Victor in Paris sometime before 1141. He was a student of Hugh of St. Victor and composed *expositiones* on most of the books of the Hebrew Scriptures (old testament). He was the abbot of Wigmore, on the Welsh border, from shortly after 1161 until his death.

Andrew kept to the literal-historical meaning of the Bible. He consulted the Jews of Paris, encountered their rationalizing approach, and frequently accepted their interpretations, sometimes even on texts considered as manifest prophecies of Christ.

BIBLIOGRAPHY

Gregorio Calandra, *De historica Andreae Victorini expositione in Ecclesiasten* (1948); Angelo Penna, "Andrea di San Vittore. Il suo commento a Giona," in *Biblica*, 36 (1955); Michael Signer, ed., *Expositio super Ezekielem* (in press); Friedrich Stegmüller, *Repertorium Biblicum medii aevi*, II (1950), nn. 1295–1329; and VIII (1976), nn. 1295–1327.

See also Beryl Smalley, *The Study of the Bible in the Middle Ages*, 2nd ed. (1955).

MARK A. ZIER

ANDRONIKOS I KOMNENOS (*ca.* 1120–1185) made himself Byzantine emperor in 1183 and ruled until he was dethroned on 12 September 1185. The son of John II's younger brother Isaac, he nurtured a lifelong hostility to the ruling branch of the family. After an adventurous career of imprisonment and exile, he was reconciled with his cousin Emperor

Manuel I shortly before the latter's death, and became governor of Pontus. He was ambitious, intelligent, and determined, but also given to luxurious self-indulgence.

Upon Manuel's death (1180) his son Alexios II (aged eleven) became emperor, under the regency of his mother Mary (Xena) of Antioch, her paramour Alexios Komnenos the Protosebastos, and the patriarch. Andronikos kept in touch with discontented aristocrats and the mob in Constantinople; early in 1182, his rebel force arrived opposite the city. Elements of the fleet went over to him, the Protosebastos was arrested, and the mob was allowed to sack the Latin quarters (April 1182); the ensuing massacre widened the breach between East and West. Andronikos assumed the regency.

Andronikos could now give vent to his hatred of the other Komneni. Alexios II's sister Maria and her husband soon perished; Empress Mother Mary went first to a convent, then was put to death. With the way thus cleared, Andronikos had himself crowned as coemperor (September 1183), and soon afterward strangled Alexios. His widow, the French princess Agnes-Anna, was married to the new ruler. Aristocrats who conspired or were suspect suffered mutilation, blinding, or death; many fled. A rebellion in Bithynia (1183–1184) was bloodily suppressed.

Despite his support for their massacre, Andronikos seems not to have hated Latins. To revive his commerce, he had to restore the Venetians to their privileged position in the empire. This action alienated the mob in Constantinople. In the provinces Andronikos sought to provide good governors, end the sale of offices, and reduce taxes; his regime was favorably remembered.

In foreign affairs he did not fare well. Serbs and Cilician Armenians broke away from Byzantium; the Turks and Hungarians sought to expand their frontiers. Cyprus, under its tyrant Isaac Komnenos, revolted, and was never regained. Most serious, William II of Sicily, spurred by refugee nobles and a pretended Alexios II, invaded the Balkans. The Normans besieged and sacked Thessalonica (August 1185).

As the Sicilian army advanced toward Constantinople, terror gripped the populace, already disenchanted with its former favorite. Andronikos determined to rid himself of potential foes, but Isaac Angelos eluded assassination and reached the church of Hagia Sophia. A mob assembled, and on 12 September 1185 proclaimed Isaac II. Andronikos fled, was captured, and was tortured to death by a mob.

Andronikos I is often credited with serious intentions of reforming the evils that beset the empire, but he seems to have been more intent on establishing his own and his family's power.

BIBLIOGRAPHY

Charles M. Brand, *Byzantium Confronts the West, 1180–1204* (1968); W. Hecht, *Die byzantinische Aussenpolitik zur Zeit der letzten Komnenenkaiser (1180–1185)* (1967); J. M. Hussey, "The Later Macedonians, the Comneni and the Angeli 1025–1204," in *The Cambridge Medieval History,* 2nd ed., IV, pt. 1 (1966), 193–249, 858–867; O. Jurewicz, *Andronikos I. Komnenos* (1970).

CHARLES M. BRAND

ANDRONIKOS II PALAEOLOGOS (1260–1332) was crowned co-emperor of Byzantium in 1272 and emperor after the death of his father, Michael VIII, in 1328. He married twice (Anne of Hungary in 1272; Yolanda/Irene of Montferrat in 1284); both alliances were undertaken to strengthen the Byzantine position against the Angevins.

The two main axes of Andronikos II's policy in the early years of his reign were the repudiation of his father's policy of church union with Rome, and his concern with Asia Minor. The union with Rome had already been dissolved by Pope Martin IV in 1281; Andronikos confirmed the repudiation and cleared the Byzantine church hierarchy of those in favor of reunion. The church was still rent by the Arsenite schism, which also had political connotations of opposition to the Palaeologan dynasty, and was healed in 1310.

Andronikos' policy entailed the potential hostility of western powers, which was mitigated until 1302 by the war of the Sicilian Vespers. During this time Andronikos adopted an attitude of disengagement; he signed a peace treaty with Venice (1285), and tried to arrange the marriage of his son Michael IX to the titular empress of Constantinople, Catherine of Courtenay, but had little active involvement in European affairs. His interest was concentrated on Asia Minor, where he resided from 1290 to 1293. He sent there his nephew Alexios Philanthropenos, whose inital success was followed by a rebellion (1295), and in 1298 the Arsenite general John Tarchaneiotes, who carried out some social and economic reforms, but was forced to resign.

The failure of Andronikos' Asia Minor policy became evident in 1302, when his son was defeated by the Turks in Magnesia, while the Ottomans won a major victory at Bapheus, opening the way for their conquest of Bithynia. Meanwhile, part of western Macedonia had been lost to the Serbs. On the other hand, the Byzantine reconquest of Thessaly and Epirus began in the 1310's.

In 1302, after the peace of Caltabelotta, Catalan mercenaries under Roger de Flor offered their services to Andronikos, to help save Asia Minor. After a few victories the Catalans were recalled to Thrace, which they devastated for a few years before leaving for Macedonia (1307), then finally settling in Athens. The Catalan campaign was very expensive in men and resources.

Andronikos, who had scuttled the Byzantine fleet in 1285, became involved in the war between Venice and Genoa, on the Genoese side (1296–1302), and was forced to accept a humiliating peace with Venice. During his reign the Venetians and Genoese established their economic dominance in the Aegean and the Black Sea and were able to extend their hold over the commercial economy of Byzantium.

After the failure both of his Asia Minor policy and of the plans of Charles de Valois to conquer Constantinople, Andronikos revived his father's policy of alliance with the West. He developed friendly relations both with Ghibelline powers (Louis IV of Bavaria in 1328), and with their opponents (Venice), and even tried to promote ecclesiastical union. These efforts were interrupted by the civil war between himself and Andronikos III, which began in 1321. Andronikos II was deposed in 1328, became a monk (Antonios) in 1330, and died at Constantinople two years later. He was a pious and intelligent man, but neither a soldier nor an able diplomat. His advisers (Nicephorus Choumnos, Theodore Metochites, Nicephorus Gregoras) were important intellectuals, but unequal to the political needs of the times.

BIBLIOGRAPHY

Erwin Dade, *Versuche der Wiedererrichtung der lateinischen Herrschaft in Konstantinopel im Rahmen der abendländischen Politik (1261 bis etwas 1310)* (1938); George Georgiades Arnakes, *The First Ottomans* (1947) (in Greek); Angeliki E. Laiou, *Constantinople and the Latins; the Foreign Policy of Andronicus II (1282–1328)* (1972).

ANGELIKI LAIOU

ANDRONIKOS III PALAEOLOGOS (1296–1341), co-emperor (1316–1328) and emperor (1328–1341) of Byzantium. He rebelled against his grandfather, Andronikos II, in 1321, starting a civil war that lasted, with interruptions, until 1328. He had the support of much of the aristocracy, as well as of the people of Thrace (to whom he promised relief from taxes) and of Constantinople. The war was marked by the intervention of the Serbs and the Bulgarians.

Unlike his predecessor, Andronikos III had a martial temperament. He campaigned in Asia Minor, where he was defeated by the Ottomans at Pelecanum (1329); his defeat was followed by the loss of the last cities of Bithynia, Nicaea (1331), and Nicomedeia (1337). To meet the Ottoman danger, Andronikos developed two somewhat contradictory policies. On the one hand, he pursued negotiations for the union of the Greek and Latin churches (1333–1339), which he made contingent upon Western aid against the Ottomans. His wife, Anne of Savoy, and her entourage played a role in the union negotiations. Andronikos also participated in the discussions about the creation of a flotilla that fought the Turks (1331–1334). On the other hand, he and his adviser John Cantacuzenus initiated a policy of alliance with other Turkish emirates, especially Aydin (1335). Both policies proved inadequate.

In other areas Andronikos was more successful. He recovered the splinter states of Epirus and Thessaly in the 1330's. He took Chios from the Genoese in 1329, following an uprising on the island; received the allegiance of the Genoese lord of New Phocaea, and took Lesbos (1336). He also continued his predecessor's efforts to reform the corrupt Byzantine judicial system. After 1329 the highest court consisted of two laymen and two ecclesiastics, appointed by the emperor. These "general judges of the Romans" had jurisdiction on all matters, and their decisions were irrevocable. This reform, although it underwent changes, persisted until the end of the empire.

BIBLIOGRAPHY

Ursula V. Bosch, *Kaiser Andronikos III. Palaiologos. Versuch einer Darstellung der byzantinischen Geschichte in den Jahren 1321–1341* (1965); and Paul Lemerle, *L'émirat d'Aydin, Byzance et l'Occident* (1957).

ANGELIKI LAIOU

ANECDOTA/SECRET HISTORY. See **Procopius.**

ANEGENGE (*Anfang,* "beginning" or "origin"), is a Middle High German poem of 3,243 verses written by an Austrian clergyman around 1160–1170. Directed at a lay audience, it first tells the story of the Creation and Lucifer's fall, then continues with man's creation, his fall from grace, and the story of Adam's descendants down to Noah. The poem concludes with the depiction of man's salvation through Christ. The narrative of biblical events is frequently interrupted by the author's attempts to use his knowledge of theology, most likely acquired in a monastery school, to make intelligible an extensive range of difficult theological questions, including the nature of the Trinity.

BIBLIOGRAPHY

Dietrich Neuschafer, ed., "Das Anegenge," in *Medium aevum,* **8** (1966), contains a comprehensive bibliography through 1966. See also Brian Murdoch, *The Fall of Man in the Early Middle High German Biblical Epic: The Wiener Genesis, the Vorauer Genesis and the Anegenge* (1972).

STEPHEN J. KAPLOWITT

[See also **Middle High German.**]

ANEIRIN, traditionally said to be the author of the *Gododdin,* would have been alive, according to chapter 62 of Nennius' *Historia Brittonum,* in the 560's. The two references to him in the poem occur in stanzas that may not belong to the central material. The *Gododdin,* preserved in the thirteenth-century Book of Aneirin in the Free Library of Cardiff, comprises the archaic forty-two-stanza *B* text, which partly overlaps the later eighty-eight-stanza *A* text. As edited, excluding 223 lines of the four associated lays *(gorchanau)* and 267 lines mostly of overlapping material, the corpus totals about 1,000 lines in 100 stanzas of unequal length. Lines are frequently of nine- and ten-syllable length with end rhyme *(unodl)*, sometimes embellished by internal rhyme and alliteration.

The nucleus was composed in Cumbric, the northern dialect spoken by the Brython (British Celts) of Gododdin, the country and tribe known in the Romano-British period as Votādīnī and so called by Ptolemy. Centered at Eidyn (Edinburgh), they ranged from the Firth of Forth south to County Durham. The poem was transmitted in a Welsh manuscript, and some of the considerably interpolated text can be "translated" only approximately. The *B* text descends from a lost manuscript of the ninth or tenth century, which in turn derives from a still older written source stemming from an oral tradition; the *A* text reflects a different oral descent. All this is consonant with a date of composition of around 600, a bit later than Taliesin's dozen surest poems, although this dating has been contested on syntactic grounds. A late ninth-century transmission to North Wales via Strathclyde seems plausible.

The *Gododdin* is a series of elegies on heroes fallen in battle; we can piece together the events mainly by inference from the stylized vignettes. A king or chief called Mynyddog the Wealthy assembled an army of 300 warriors (360 in one version) and their retainers, totaling perhaps 3,000 men, from what is now Scotland, Yorkshire, and North Wales. He gave food and drink (mead, but also wine in some stanzas) to the retinue for a year before sending them to attack 100,000 encroaching English of Berenicia and Deira; the text implies that he did not lead the expedition, possibly because he was too old. All but three of Mynyddog's men (one in some stanzas) were killed in battle at Catraeth (Catterick, in north Yorkshire), which took place around 588–590. Few of the heroes named in the poem are known from other sources, thus arguing for the historicity of these events.

BIBLIOGRAPHY

Canu Aneirin, Ifor Williams, ed. (1938), in Welsh, is the monumental standard annotated edition and replaces that of William F. Skene, *The Four Ancient Books of Wales* (1868), I, 374–427; II, 62–107. Kenneth H. Jackson, *The Gododdin: The Oldest Scottish Poem* (1969; repr. 1978), is an annotated English rendering with essayistic commentary summarizing recent scholarship. See also M. Miller, "Historicity and the Pedigrees of the Northcountrymen," in *Bulletin of the Board of Celtic Studies,* **26** (1975), on the probable diffusion of the poem in the 870's from Strathclyde to the Conwy-Dee region of North Wales.

ERIC P. HAMP

[See also **Welsh Literature: Poetry.**]

ANGEL. From the Greek ἄγγελος (messenger), an angel is, in Jewish, Islamic, and Christian theology, one of a multitude of beings intermediate between man and deity, a divine messenger and attendant (see Genesis 32:1). In the Old Testament angels appear primarily as messengers (Genesis 16:7), attendants (Isaiah 6), and agents (Daniel 10) of God. Jewish apocrypha, especially the Ethiopic Book of Enoch, developed an extensive angelology and promoted angels to promulgators of divine law, a view accepted by New Testament authors (for example, Acts 7:53). In the Gospel of Matthew, angels are described as spiritual beings who behold God's face in heaven (18:10) and will accompany him at the Last Judgment (16:27); the Gospels also include angels in the narration of most of the important moments of Christ's life (for instance, the Annunciation in Matthew 1:20, 1:24; the Nativity in Luke 2:9–15). Angelology seems to have been of only peripheral interest to the early church fathers except for the fifth-century Pseudo-Dionysius the Areopagite, in whose *Celestial Hierarchy* angels are ranked in the lowest of nine orders, and it was not fully developed until the Scholastics.

Although winged messengers appear in Assyrian art, and are images made by idolators, winged cherubim and seraphim are described in the Old Testament (see Ezekiel 10; Isaiah 6), and winged cherubim adorned the Jewish tabernacle (Exodus 25:17–22) and the Temple of Solomon (2 Chronicles 3:10–13). The earliest Christian representations of angels are wingless (for example, in the catacombs of Vigna Massima and of Priscilla, Rome), presumably because angels are not commonly described as winged in the Bible.

Winged angels appear in the fourth century, but not in scenes derived from the Bible; winged angels modeled on the pagan Nike (Victory) support a Christian wreath on the early fourth-century Sarigürzel sarcophagus (Archaeological Museum, Istanbul), and the man, symbol of the evangelist Matthew, is winged in the mosaics in the apse of Sta. Pudenziana, Rome (*ca.* 320). In the fifth century, angels with wings appear in biblical contexts, though wingless angels are also represented: in the mosaics of Sta. Maria Maggiore, Rome (432–440), the angel of the Annunciation is winged but angels in Old Testament scenes are wingless. By the ninth century, angels are only rarely depicted without wings.

Angels were usually presented as beardless youths and, from the fifth century, often were given halos. They were normally clad in tunic and pallium, though occasionally in early examples (such as the Cotton Genesis [British Library, Cotton MS Otho B.VI]) they appear in the peplos of Roman psychopomps; archangels were normally dressed more sumptuously, often in imperial garments. Attributes given to angels include scrolls, staffs, the labarum of victory, the orb of the world, and, in the late Middle Ages, various instruments of the Passion.

LESLIE BRUBAKER

[See also **Angel/Angelology; Archangel; Arma Christi.**]

ANGEL, ISLAMIC. Angels are mentioned in the Koran in various capacities, and belief in them is an essential of the Muslim creed (sura 2:285). They are subtle, luminous beings created from light, and have a number of occupations: primarily they are messengers *(malāʾika),* who with the Truth (sura 15:8) speak to Mary and to the prophets, and thus are seen as intermediaries between the divine and the human spheres. Two angels are thought to be placed on man's shoulders to record his actions in the book that will be presented at Doomsday (derived from sura 82:11); two other, frightful angels, later called Munkar and Nakīr, will question the dead person in the grave about his faith. One small group, called *al-Zabānīya* (sura 96:18) are guardians of Hell, and the story of the angels Hārūt and Mārūt (sura 2:102) shows that they can inspire witchcraft; their being enticed by the beautiful Zuhra was later poetically elaborated.

Innumerable angels throng around the divine throne (sura 39:75), praising the Lord; some of them are called *al-muḳarrabūn,* "those brought near" (sura 4:172). In general angels are thought of as performing constant acts of worship while remaining in one position of ritual prayer (such as prostration or standing); only man can perform the full circle of adoration. They also join God in uttering blessings over the Prophet (sura 33:56).

The angels objected to Adam's creation, foreseeing the turmoil that would ensue, but finally obeyed the divine command to fall down before mankind (sura 2:30ff., for example). They are thus considered inferior to man. Also, they were not granted the knowledge of the names, worldly and divine, that God inspired to Adam. A special place is given to the four archangels who are surrounded by colorful descriptions in later tradition. Most important is Djabrāʾīl (Gabriel), the bearer of divine revelation (sura 2:97, for instance), called *al-rūh al-amīn,* "the trustworthy spirit." Through him the prophets receive their inspiration, but at the moment of Muḥammad's greatest proximity to God during his heavenly journey, Gabriel had to recede and was not admitted to the divine presence. Michael (Mīkāʾil) dispenses humanity's daily bread, ʿAzrāʾīl takes the soul at the moment of death, and Isrāfīl will blow the trumpet to announce resurrection.

ANGEL/ANGELOLOGY

In some later mystical systems, angels play a central role—for example, in the illuminist theories of al-Suhrawardī al-Maḳtūl (died 1191), who perceived the divine light as reflected to arrays of angels, who are as numerous as the fixed stars. His angelology was inspired to a large degree by Zoroastrian sources, as becomes clear from the names of the angels; among them, Sarōsh in particular became a favorite of later Persian poets and was sometimes equated with Gabriel. In al-Suhrawardī's system Gabriel is the archetype of humanity, and all things come into existence by the sound of his wings.

In popular Islam numerous angels with strange-sounding names are known; they play an important role in mystical and magical practices. Philosophers and modernists, on the other hand, tend to interpret angels as faculties of the human soul.

ANNEMARIE SCHIMMEL

ANGEL/ANGELOLOGY, the study of the heavenly beings known in Jewish, Christian, and Islamic traditions as angels. The Greek word ἄγγελες means "messenger"; in the biblical tradition angels appear as created beings who serve God by proclaiming and overseeing the divine will on earth. Angels are superior to human beings in powers and usually in virtue, although the fallen angels, led by Satan or Lucifer, work against God's will and attempt to influence humans to do likewise. This article, like the main tradition of medieval Christian angelology, will concern itself primarily with the good angels.

In the Hebrew scriptures, angels often appear in human form, and are not always recognized by the recipients of the divine message. The Angel of the Lord, who has a special mission to protect Israel, is present at the sacrifice of Isaac (Genesis 22:11), speaks to Jacob in a dream (Genesis 31:11), in some way helps the Israelites through the Sea of Reeds (Exodus 14:19), and appears to Balaam, Joshua, Gideon, and the parents of Samson. Beginning with the Book of Daniel, presumably as a result of Persian influence, angels acquire specific names and personalities: Gabriel (in human form, 8:16, 9:21) explains the meaning of Daniel's visions, and Michael ("the angel prince," 10:13, 10:21, 12:1) appears as the captain of a heavenly host fighting against the angel prince of Persia.

These angelic personalities are also found in the New Testament: Gabriel prophesies and explains the births of John the Baptist (Luke 1:11–20) and Jesus (Luke 1:26–38), and Michael is the champion against the legions of the fallen angel, Satan (Jude 9, Apocalypse 12:7). Unnamed angels comfort Jesus in the wilderness (Matthew 4:11), testify to the Resurrection (Matthew 28:2–7, John 20:12), and are in charge of the seven bowls, trumpets, and seals of the Apocalypse. Angels also appear several times in the Acts of the Apostles, notably to the centurion Cornelius (10:3–7, 10:22) and to rescue the apostles from imprisonment ("an Angel of the Lord," 5:19, 12:7–10). In the apocryphal Book of Tobit (5:4–11:8), the angel Raphael guides the quest of Tobias, helping him to conquer a demon who had slain the previous husbands of his bride, Sarah, and to restore the sight of his father, Tobit.

From this biblical tradition, medieval Christian thinking on angelology moved in two directions. The first, a part of the transmission of pseudepigraphical literature beginning with Jewish sources of the third century B.C., is marked by a fascination with the personalities of specific angelic figures, both good and bad. Such writings as the Books of Enoch, the Testament of Abraham, and the Apocalypse of Elijah, extant in a number of languages including Greek and, less frequently, Latin, describe the functions of angels named Uriel, Raguel, Sariel, Jeremiel, and others, who serve alongside Gabriel, Michael, and Raphael. Christian noncanonical writings, especially the Nag Hammadi texts, continue and elaborate upon this trend. The association of these writings with Christian Gnostic sects is behind Irenaeus's rejection of a list of the orders of angels (*Adversus haereses,* II, 30, 3). Nevertheless, the vivid angelic traditions of the pseudepigrapha were popular in the medieval Christian world, and were preserved in Greek and Latin hagiographical manuscripts.

The second tradition of medieval angelology is primarily a philosophical one. In it, names and personalities are neglected in favor of speculation about the corporeality and hierarchy of angels. The idea that angels have a spiritual, but not a fleshly, body is found in the writings of Origen and Augustine, and seems to have been widely held in the patristic period. But the Christian authors of the first five centuries were far too concerned with disciplinary and dogmatic issues to give much attention to theories about angels, and it was only with the early sixth-century writings of Pseudo-Dionysius the Areopagite that Christian angelology took on its classical form.

Pseudo-Dionysius is an unknown author who

claimed to be the philosopher converted by St. Paul on the Athenian Areopagus (Acts 17:34). Modern scholarship has placed him in Syria at the turn of the sixth century. His Neoplatonism is evident in both the conception and the terminology of *The Celestial Hierarchy,* the most influential treatise in Christian angelology. The Dionysian scheme describes nine choirs of angels, grouped in three hierarchies. In descending order they are (1) seraphim, cherubim, thrones; (2) dominations, virtues, powers; (3) principalities, archangels, angels. Only the last two choirs have contact with human beings; in them are placed all of the angels, named and unnamed, of the biblical tradition.

According to another Pseudo-Dionysian work, *The Ecclesiastical Hierarchy,* the angelic orders are reflected in the structure of the earthly church, and thus form a continuum between God and the believer. The Dionysian scheme bears a curious resemblance to the Gnostic order of angels criticized by Irenaeus; both systems may reflect Persian angelology passed on through the biblical and rabbinic literature of postexilic Judaism. The Jewish philosophical tradition from Philo to Maimonides included elaborate theories about angels that influenced both Christian and Muslim authors. In turn, the differing angelologies of the Muslim philosophers Avicenna and Averroës left their marks on medieval Jewish and Christian philosophies of angels.

The Celestial Hierarchy took on rather different roles in Eastern and Western Christianity. Byzantine authors, from Maximus the Confessor in the seventh century to the hesychast Gregory Palamas and his opponents in the fourteenth century, adapted, abridged, and used the Dionysian system as part of a mystical theology with roots in the writings of the Alexandrian and Cappadocian fathers. In the Latin West, however, Pseudo-Dionysius stimulated theories concerning the nature of angels. The early medieval authors Gregory the Great and Bede used his writings in essentially pastoral discussions of the role of angels. In the ninth century *The Celestial Hierarchy* was translated into Latin by Hilduin of Saint-Denis and again by John Scotus Erigena. The latter translation, corrected by Anastasius the Librarian in 875, became a standard reference work in the High Middle Ages. In the twelfth century Peter Lombard set forth a Dionysian theory of the nature of angels (*Sentences,* II, dist. x) that was commented on by Scholastic theologians of the following centuries, including Albertus Magnus, Bonaventure, Thomas Aquinas, and John Duns Scotus. All of these authors agreed on a basic definition of angels as spiritual beings, but showed some differences of opinion on the question of angelic corporeality. These opinions are most sharply opposed in the writings of Thomas Aquinas and Duns Scotus.

Aquinas devoted fourteen books of the *Summa theologiae* to the nature and powers of angels (I, 50–63). He held that angels have form but not matter, and are therefore eternal and incorruptible. Angels are able to assume bodies (52, art. 1); these bodies take up space, so only one angel can be in a particular place at a certain time (52, arts. 2–3). In contrast, Duns Scotus asserted that angels consist of both form and a noncorporeal matter particular to them alone, which makes it possible for more than one angel to occupy the same place at the same time (*De anima,* XV; *De rerum principio,* VII–VIII). The ensuing debates over these positions may have given rise to the early modern legend that the Scholastics argued over such questions as how many angels can dance on the head of a pin.

BIBLIOGRAPHY

Alexander Altman *et al.,* "Angels and Angelology," in *Encyclopedia Judaica,* II (1972); B. J. Bamberger, *Fallen Angels* (1952); James D. Collins, *The Thomistic Philosophy of the Angels* (1947); Henry Corbin, *Avicenna and the Visionary Recital* (1960); Jean Daniélou, *Les anges et leur mission d'après les pères de l'église* (1952), English translation by David Heimann (1957); Gustav Davidson, *A Dictionary of Angels* (1967); Evile Peterson, *Das Buch von den Engeln* (1935); Gershom Scholem, *Major Trends in Jewish Mysticism,* 3rd ed. (1955); and *Jewish Gnosticism, Merkabah Mysticism, and Talmudic Tradition* (1965). *The Celestial Hierarchy* of Pseudo-Dionysius the Areopagite, edited by René Roques, is no. 58 bis in Sources Chrétiennes (1970), with introduction, bibliography, and complete French translation.

E. Ann Matter

[See also **Dionysius the Pseudo-Areopagite.**]

ANGELA MERICI (or ANGELA OF BRESCIA), ST. (21 March 1474–27 January 1540), founder of the Ursulines, was born at Desenzano, where around 1506 she received a vision concerning the founding of her society. In 1516 she moved to Brescia to live with the Patengoli family and in 1531 organized a small group of girls who helped in her catechetical work. On 25 November 1535 Angela and twenty-seven companions formed the Company of St. Ursula, which became the Ursulines. The order was created to provide young girls with a Christian education, and its rule emphasized the virtues of virginity and poverty, with Christian family life and the local community being central themes.

BIBLIOGRAPHY
Sister Monica, O.S.U., *Angela Merici and Her Teaching Idea, 1474–1540* (1927); Marie Vianey, *Vers un apostolate de conquête. Sainte Angèle Mérici, fondatrice des Ursulines* (1942).

JOHN C. MAGEE

ANGELA OF FOLIGNO (*ca.* 1248–4 January 1309), mystic, was born into a wealthy family in Foligno, Umbria. After receiving a vision of St. Francis, she entered into a life of self-mortification; and she left her home and disposed of her fortune around 1291, after her mother, husband, and sons had all died within a brief period. Angela became a Franciscan tertiary and lived for some time in a convent, pursuing a life of higher virtue. This life was characterized by a spiritual ascent of eighteen stages and by a sense of penitence that tended to be regarded as extreme even by members of Angela's own society. Although she spent approximately two years in severe self-torment, Angela's life was marked by continual supernatural gifts and visions. Her reputation for sanctity survived her death and helped to foster her cult.

BIBLIOGRAPHY
L. Leclève, *Sainte Angèle de Foligno* (1936); Mary G. Steegmann, trans., *The Book of Divine Consolation of the Blessed Angela of Foligno* (1909, repr. 1966).

JOHN C. MAGEE

ANGELICO, FRA. See **Fiesole, Giovanni De.**

ANGELO DA ORVIETO (Angelus Urbsveterensis) (*fl.* 1317–1352), architect and sculptor from Orvieto. First mentioned 1317, working together with Lorenzo Maitani on fountain in Perugia. From 1332 to 1335 designed and signed the Palazzo dei Consoli; in 1349 the Palazzo Pretorio and Gubbio. Also designed and signed the portal Palazzo dei Priori in Città di Castello (1334–1352). An imaginative engineer and architect, Angelo anticipated many fifteenth-century developments in the design of Florentine palazzos.

BIBLIOGRAPHY
Ottorini Gurrieri, *Angelo da Orvieto, Matteo di Giovanello Gattapone e i palazzi pubblici di Gubbio e di Città di Castello* (1959); Ulrich Thieme and Felix Becker, *Allgemeines Lexikon der bildenden Künstler* (1908); John White, *Art and Architecture in Italy: 1250–1400* (1966).

ADELHEID M. GEALT

ANGELOMUS OF LUXEUIL (d. *ca.* 855), a monk who wrote three exegetical works: the *Commentarius in Genesin* (dedicated to his teacher Mellinus), *Enarrationes in quattuor libros regum,* and *Enarrationes in cantica canticorum* (dedicated to Lothar I, his patron). His works rely heavily on the Church Fathers (especially Gregory, Isidore, and Augustine) and reveal Angelomus' interest in natural phenomena.

BIBLIOGRAPHY
Angelomus' writings are in *Patrologia latina,* CXV, cols. 105–628, and *Monumenta Germaniae Historica Poetae latini aevi Carolini,* II, 675–677.

NANCY A. PORTER

ANGELOS, the ruling family of the Byzantine Empire from 1185 to 1204. Descended from a daughter of Alexios I Komnenos, Isaac Angelos was elevated to the throne by the mob in Constantinople and ruled as Isaac II from 1185 to 1195. He struggled vainly with myriad problems until he was deposed, blinded, and imprisoned by his brother, Alexios III (1195–1203), whose weak regime allowed internal decay. In 1201, Isaac's son Alexios escaped to Italy, where he gained the support of the Fourth Crusade. When the Crusaders attacked in 1203, Alexios III fled; Isaac II was restored (1203–1204) with his son Alexios IV as co-emperor. In January 1204, Isaac died and Alexios IV was overthrown by Alexios V Doukas.

BIBLIOGRAPHY
Charles M. Brand, *Byzantium Confronts the West, 1180–1204* (1968); Georgije Ostrogorski, *Zur byzantinischen Geschichte* (1973), 166–182.

CHARLES M. BRAND

ANGELRAM OF ST. RIQUIER (*ca.* 975–1045), scholar, studied under Fulbert at Chartres and Abbot Ingelard at St. Riquier. After Ingelard's death in 1022, Angelram became abbot. His *Vita Richerii,* a poem in hexameter, is concerned with saints and miracles. Hariulf, abbot of Oldenburg, wrote a biography of Angelram.

BIBLIOGRAPHY

Angelram's *Vita Richerii* is in *Patrologia latina,* CLXXIV (1854), 1305–1330. On his life and work, see Hariulf's biography, *ibid.,* CXLI (1853), 1403–1422; Ferdinand Lot, *Chronique de l'abbaye Saint Riquier* (1894), 178–220; and Maximilian Manitius, *Geschichte der lateinischen Literatur des Mittelalters,* II (1923), 533–535.

NANCY A. PORTER

ANGELUS. An Italian catechism printed at Venice in 1560 is the first record of the introduction of the three Aves said at the ringing (or three strokes) of the church bell by one versicle each (see Luke 1:26–31, Luke 1:38, and John 1:14). From the first words of the first of these versicles the name is derived by which this devotion has since been known, *Angelus Domini* (shortened to Angelus in the English-speaking world). The custom of concluding this devotion by a versicle invoking the Mother of God and by the prayer *Gratiam tuam* (which for a thousand years has been the Post-Communion for the feast of the Annunciation) is even later. These textual additions to the Ave Marias said at the sound of a bell are outside the scope of this dictionary.

By the tenth century, children were called upon to recite three prayers, after which the bell was struck thrice. The custom of saying three prayers three times a day was known in tenth-century England *(Regularis concordia Sancti Ethelwoldi)* and in eleventh-century Germany (Manegold of Lauterbach). In the early thirteenth century the ringing of the bell at sunset attained a deeper meaning than a sign of *couvrefeu*—namely, as a prayer for peace—and the habit of joining an Ave to a Pater noster first appeared. About 1250, Benedict of Arezzo introduced the singing or reciting, at the sound of the evening bell, of the antiphon *Angelus locutus est Mariae,* the first record of eventide being considered the time of the Annunciation. At St. Denis in the early thirteenth century, after Compline the prior rang the bell, and all prayed together. In 1239, Gregory IX ordered the ringing of the evening bell for the salutation of the Blessed Virgin, and Henry of Brixen granted an indulgence for saying three Aves at the evening tolling.

The Franciscan *Chronica XXIV generalium* reports for 1263 that at a chapter in Pisa, the friars were enjoined to exhort the people to greet Mary at the striking of the evening bell, and for 1269 that at the striking of the evening bell, the friars should say three Aves. In 1295 the chapter in Padua stated that *in singulis locis,* when the evening bell is struck in honor of Mary, all friars should genuflect. In the Milan district Bonvicino de Ripa (died 1314) introduced the custom of reciting the Ave Maria at the sound of the evening bell. This custom also became general in the district of Padua. Carthusian and later Benedictine sources say that this devotion was accompanied by prostration.

In 1314, Clement V ordered the bells to be struck after Compline for the recitation of the Pater noster and Ave. On 13 October 1318, John XXII prescribed for the diocese of Saintes that at the strokes of the evening bell, three Aves should be said by all, kneeling; and on 7 May 1327 he introduced this custom in Rome and attached an indulgence. The Synod of Sens prescribed this Roman custom for Paris in 1346. In 1330, John Calderino said that this evening devotion was particularly suitable for the laity.

Although this evening prayer at the striking of the bell was connected with Compline, whereas in practice it followed upon Vespers, the corresponding morning devotion originated from Prime. In 1346, Raoul of Bath ordered the clergy of his cathedral to say five Aves morning and evening. Thomas Arundel, archbishop of Canterbury, recommended in 1399 that a morning salutation to the Blessed Virgin should correspond to the evening one. In 1369, at Béziers, the devotion was fixed at three Paternosters and three Aves. Boniface IX in 1390 asked the clergy of Bavaria to ring the bell *in aurora* for the Ave.

What is known as the midday Angelus had a separate origin. Prayers accompanying the ringing of the bell at noon (or at None) either were said for peace or commemorated the Passion of Christ. At first this devotion was confined to Friday (Prague, 1386; Mainz, 1423).

BIBLIOGRAPHY

Thomas Esser, "Geschichte des englischen Grusses," in *Historisches Jahrbuch der Görres-Gesellschaft,* 5 (1884); W. Henry, "Angelus," in *Dictionnaire d'archéologie chrétienne et de liturgie,* I (1907); E. Longpré, "Angelus," in

Catholicisme hier, aujourd'hui et demain, I (1948), 554–556.

JOHN HENNIG

ANGEVINS: FRANCE, ENGLAND, SICILY. The adjective "Angevin" is applied to two noble lineages that played important roles in the political and cultural history of medieval France, England, and Sicily. The word is derived from the capital of the western French province of Anjou. The rulers of Anjou established themselves as counts in the first third of the tenth century, and their chief accomplishment was the steady growth of their territory and influence, especially northwest into Maine and southeast into Touraine. In the mid eleventh century, however, the prominence of Anjou was severely threatened by the power of the duchy of Normandy. Maine became a battlefield for the two rivals. Simultaneously, the county of Anjou began to chafe under the rigorous rule of Count Fulk Nerra (987–1040) and Count Geoffrey Martel (1040–1060).

The conquest of England in 1066 by Duke William of Normandy might have sounded the death knell of Angevin prominence, but dynastic problems made the bond between England and Normandy precarious during parts of the reigns of the conqueror's sons, William Rufus (1087–1100) and Henry I (1100–1135). Henry I had secured the marriage of his daughter and heir Matilda, the widow of Emperor Henry V, to Geoffrey, the heir of the county of Anjou. (It was this Geoffrey who later bore the nickname Plantagenêt.) He became count in 1129, and on Henry I's death in 1135, Matilda claimed the throne. She was denied the queenship by the usurpation of Stephen of Blois (1135–1154), a younger son of Henry I's sister Adela; but she fought steadily, though with indifferent success, in England to attain it. Her husband, meanwhile, conquered Normandy. On Stephen's death in 1154, their son became King Henry II of England, and thus inaugurated the Angevin (or Plantagenêt) dynasty, which lasted in direct succession until the deposition of Richard II in 1399. At its summit (about 1200) the Angevin king of England was ruler or overlord of an "empire" that included most of the British Isles and half of France (Normandy, Anjou, Maine, Poitou, Touraine, Saintonge, Limousin, Quercy, and Aquitaine).

In 1204 many of the continental possessions of the Angevins, including Anjou, were lost to Philip II of France (1180–1223). Thereafter they came under the direct administration of the French crown. In 1246, Charles, the youngest brother of Louis IX (1226–1270), was invested with the counties of Anjou and Maine as his appanage. Charles and his lineage constitute the second major family known as the Angevins. Also in 1246 he added to his lands by marrying Beatrice, the youngest daughter of the count of Provence, which gave him tutelary authority over the county after the old count's death. In fact, Angevin authority became hereditary in Provence until late in the fifteenth century. In 1266, Charles commanded an army in Italy which defeated Manfred of Sicily, the most formidable of the Hohenstaufen enemies of the papacy. In the next two decades he became senator of Rome (1263, 1265–1278), overlord of Albania (1272) and Tunisia, and king of Jerusalem, and he threatened the Greek Empire. But his fortunes began to ebb after the revolt of the Sicilian people in 1282 (the Vespers). Thereafter, Angevin Sicily was confined to the peninsula of Italy; the Aragonese, who supported the revolt, were in power in Sicily proper.

An Angevin dynasty ruled southern Italy (the kingdom of Naples) until 1435, though with less and less effect during the incompetent reign of Joanna II (1414–1435), whose forces succumbed to the Aragonese. The claims of the family to the "Two Sicilies" were actively pursued thereafter, especially under Joanna's designated successor, the titular king René I and his son John (d. 1470). René was the scion of a rival branch of the Angevin family; he is known as a patron of the arts rather than as a statesman. Also during the fourteenth and fifteenth centuries, his branch of the Angevin family had established itself in Lorraine and Bar. Owing to the support of some Catalan dissidents, René even put forward claims in Spain. Various members of the Angevin line also made serious claims to the throne of Hungary in the fourteenth and fifteenth centuries, in opposition to claimants representing the interests of Bohemia and Poland-Lithuania.

In 1481, a year after René's death, the Angevin line in France died out, and Anjou, Maine, and Provence passed into the royal domain, though not without dispute. The formal settlement was delayed until 1486.

BIBLIOGRAPHY

On the early Angevins, the work of Louis Halphen is still quite valuable, *Le Comté d'Anjou au XIe siècle* (1906). More recent is Olivier Guillot, *Le Comte d'Anjou et son entourage au XIe siècle* (1972). On the "English" Angevins' administration of their Continental lands, Jacques Boussard, *Le Comté d'Anjou sous Henri Plantegenêt et ses fils, 1151–1204* (1938), is standard. On the political situation leading to the intervention of the Angevins in Italy, see the concluding portions of Edouard Jordan's *Les Origines de la domination angevine en Italie* (1909). Later developments in this region and the extension of Angevin interests on the Continent throughout the later Middle Ages are treated by Emile Léonard, *Les Angevins de Naples* (1954).

William Chester Jordan

[See also **England, Norman-Angevin; France; Sicily, Kingdom of.**]

ANGIER. Canon of St. Frideswide's, Oxford, in the early thirteenth century and translator of the *Dialogues* of St. Gregory the Great into French verse (1213). Angier also wrote *Vie de Saint Grégoire* (1216) in octosyllabic rhyming couplets.

BIBLIOGRAPHY

Timothy Cloran, *The Dialogues of Gregory the Great, Translated into Anglo-Norman French by Angier* (1901); Paul Meyer, "La vie de Saint Grégoire le Grand, traduite du latin par Frère Angier, religieux de Sainte-Frideswide," in *Romania,* **12** (1883); Mildred K. Pope, *Étude sur la langue de frère Angier* (1903).

Brian Merrilees

ANGILBERT, ST. (*ca.* 750–814), Carolingian poet, was a student of Alcuin, an official in Charlemagne's court, and an envoy to Rome. He fathered two illegitimate sons by Charlemagne's daughter, Bertha. Two of his poems deal with the royal family, and a fragmentary epic concerns the events of his time. In 781 he became the lay abbot of St. Riquier and wrote on administering a monastery. His feast day is 18 February.

BIBLIOGRAPHY

Angilbert's writings are in *Monumenta Germaniae historica, Poetae latini aevi Carolini,* I (1881, repr. 1978), 355–381; and *ibid., Scriptorum,* XV, pt. 1 (1887, repr. 1963), 173–181. Secondary literature includes J. Carnandet, ed., *Acta sanctorum Februarius* III (1865), 91–108; Ferdinand Lot, *Chronique de l'abbaye Saint Riquier* (1894); Maximilian Manitius, *Geschichte der lateinischen Literatur des Mittelalters,* I (1923), 543–547; and Wilhelm Wattenbach, *Deutschlands Geschichtsquellen* (1952), 236–240.

Nancy A. Porter

ANGILBERT OF MILAN, archbishop of Milan (824–859) who commissioned the golden altar (paliotto) at S. Ambrogio. Angilbert is identified in the inscription that encompasses three sides of the altar, and is portrayed in relief receiving the paliotto from the craftsman Wolvinus and transferring it to St. Ambrose. The altar was built over the tombs of Sts. Ambrose, Gervase, and Protase, with doors set into the side panels to allow access to the tombs.

BIBLIOGRAPHY

Aachen, *Karl der Grosse: Werk und Wirkung,* exhibition catalogue (1965), 559; Peter Lasko, *Ars Sacra 800–1200* (1972), 50–55; K. Weitzmann, ed., *Age of Spirituality* (1979), 682.

Leslie Brubaker

ANGLO-LATIN POETRY. The English composed Latin verse virtually as soon as they learned to write in the seventh century, and continued to do so throughout the Middle Ages. The earliest verse by an Englishman to survive is that of the learned Aldhelm (*ca.* 640–709), the range of whose work extends from the briefest of riddles to his 3,000 line poem on the celibate life, *De virginitate* (sometimes called *De laudibus virginitatis*). Many pre-Conquest Englishmen well-known for other accomplishments have left us poems. Bede's hymn on Judgment Day, Boniface's collection of riddles, and Alcuin's philosophical reflections on the Viking destruction at Lindisfarne are notable examples. Aside from occasional poetry—including epitaphs, church dedications, and monumental inscriptions—interest was focused on liturgical hymns, metrical lives of the saints, and prayers. Unusual for the period was the sort of historical interest shown in Alcuin's poem on the church at York or in Ethelwulf's *De abbatibus,* a metrical history of a monastic cell at Lindisfarne.

The Norman Conquest brought England into more immediate contact with the intellectual life of Europe. Hence, in the twelfth and thirteenth centuries the mainstream of hymns and liturgical poetry was increasingly supplemented by classically inspired epigrams and satiric verse. For a generation after the Conquest the chief poets writing in England had been born elsewhere: for example, Godfrey of Cambrai, the prior of St. Swithin's who composed epigrams in imitation of Martial, or the Frenchman Reginald of Canterbury, who wrote a long epic on St. Malchus. The most famous of the twelfth-century satirists is Nigel Wireker (or Whitacre), whose long *Speculum stultorum* (Mirror of Fools) satirizes ambitious monks and venal clerics alike in telling the story of a donkey who wanted a longer tail. More philosophical is Alexander Neckham's *De laudibus divinae sapientiae;* and emblematic of the period's revitalized concern with Latin poetic tradition is Geoffrey of Vinsauf's *Poetria nova,* devised as a handbook of poetic tropes and topoi.

The coming of the Franciscans and other friars in the thirteenth century added new themes and a new piety to earlier satiric and religious verse. Walter of Wimborne's work, for example, is fairly evenly divided between rather heavily didactic satire and poems of intense, if repetitive, personal devotion to the Virgin Mary. John Peckham, the Franciscan archbishop of Canterbury, composed his *Philomena* to express man's sense of separation from the divine in the plaintive song of the nightingale. Also important were John of Howden, who shows some Franciscan influence, and John of Garland, who wrote many works, including a textbook of poetry, rhetoric, and morality called *Exempla honestae vitae.* Such verse as that written around the exploits of Simon, earl of Leicester, give a more political cast to thirteenth-century poetry.

Although Franciscan piety continued to be expressed in verse in the fourteenth century—for example, by Richard Ledrede—and the period's intense interest in religious mysticism inspired Richard Rolle's composition, Latin played an increasingly subordinate role to the vernacular from the mid fourteenth century on. Chaucer left no Latin verse, while his contemporary John Gower wrote in Latin, Anglo-Norman French, and English.

BIBLIOGRAPHY

W. F. Bolton, *A History of Anglo-Latin Literature 597–1066,* I (1967), 597–740; F. J. E. Raby, *A History of Secular Latin Poetry in the Middle Ages* (1934; 2nd ed. 1957) and *A History of Christian Latin Poetry from the Beginnings to the Close of the Middle Ages* (1927; 2nd ed., 1953); Josef Szövérffy, *Weltliche Dichtungen des lateinischen Mittelalters* (1970).

COLIN CHASE

[See also **Alcuin; Aldhelm; Bede; Gower, John; John of Garland; John of Howden; Latin Language; Latin Literature; Nigel Wireker; Peckham, John; Reginald of Canterbury; Rolle, Richard.**]

ANGLO-NORMAN ART. The term "Anglo-Norman" was first used to designate the dialect of Old French imported into England by William the Conqueror and his followers in 1066, and spoken thereafter in England as the language of the court, the law, literature, education, and trade. Its origins lie not only in Normandy, where Old French resembled the language of northern France in general, but also in William's lands in Brittany and western France. From the mid twelfth century, Anglo-Norman became more and more isolated from its origins, and thus evolved as a regional form distinct in many respects from continental French. When adapted for use by art historians, the term "Anglo-Norman" does not always preserve its original meaning, according to which it would apply only to the art of England.

In the context of medieval art, the term was first used by architectural historians. It commonly refers to the buildings constructed in England during the massive rebuilding campaigns initiated soon after the Conquest and continued into the twelfth century, as well as to the monuments erected under William and his successors in Normandy, which were the stylistic antecedents of the English buildings. Thus the term "Anglo-Norman" is synonymous with Romanesque in England and Normandy.

Several important architectural features are characteristic of the churches built during the second half of the eleventh century in England and Normandy: they are large, with one of two east-end plans—three eastern apses (Bernay; La Trinité, Caen; Westminster; Canterbury Cathedral; Lincoln; Old Sarum; Rochester; Bury St. Edmunds; St. Albans; Ely; Durham) or an ambulatory and radiating chapels (Notre-Dame, Jumièges; Rouen Cathedral; Battle; St. Augustine's, Canterbury; Winchester; Worcester; Gloucester; Norwich); they are wood-roofed with vaulted aisles; and most have three-story elevations vertically articulated by wall shafts, with tribune galleries, often with a setback at the base of the second story, and a clerestory with a wall passage. The latter is the most important and distinctive feature of the Anglo-Norman repertoire.

The influence of Normandy on English building had manifested itself before the Conquest in the use of a triapsidal east end in the 1050's at Edward the Confessor's new abbey of Westminster (consecrated 1065). In architecture, as in the Anglo-Norman language, Anglo-Saxon elements played an important role; their most important manifestation in architecture is in decoration, where the use of chevron, dog-

ANGLO-NORMAN ART

tooth, and other pattern motifs are common on columns or moldings (Durham, Waltham, Romsey, Gloucester), and intersecting arcading is characteristic (Tewkesbury, Exeter, Castle Acre, Durham, Canterbury, Lincoln, and elsewhere). Aspects of this approach to decoration were reflected in Normandy (facade of La Trinité, Caen) and elsewhere in spheres of Norman influence, especially southern Italy and Sicily (Cefalù, Monreale).

In England, Anglo-Norman architecture also shows influences from other regions of Europe: for example, the interior elevations of the churches at Gloucester, Tewkesbury, and Pershore derive the proportions of their tall drum piers from Burgundian buildings like Tournus, while the general predominance in England of the cushion capital suggests that German influence was also an important factor.

In relation to sculpture, the term "Anglo-Norman" is used in its strict sense to refer to the sculpture of the Romanesque period in England. While there is some connection between the sculpture of Normandy and that of England, as shown by the use of the same models for the capitals of St. Eustace at Durham and a capital at Falaise, or capitals at Norwich Cathedral and Cérisy-la-Forêt, there are also differences between Normandy and England, where there was already a rich tradition of monumental sculpture in the Anglo-Saxon period. In Normandy, apart from the capitals of Bernay, which derive from Burgundy, much of the capital decoration of major buildings, such as Notre-Dame at Jumièges, is dependent on illuminated manuscripts. This kind of interrelation between the patterns of illuminated initials and carved capitals is also found in England, where its clearest manifestation is in the manuscripts made at Christ Church monastery and the crypt capitals at Canterbury Cathedral; another example is the parallel between the foliage types of Winchester acanthus in eleventh-century manuscripts and the capitals of Milton Port (Somerset).

Elsewhere in England the regionalism of the Anglo-Saxon period continued after the Conquest, as with the flat relief of the carving at Newton in Cleveland (Yorkshire), Uppington (Shropshire), or Byton (Herefordshire) or the survival of the Viking Urnes style at Kirkburn (Yorkshire) or Jevington (Sussex). In the period roughly between 1130 and 1180, the development of the beak-head motif as a characteristic decoration of roll moldings or columns emerged in Yorkshire (Bridlington) and Oxfordshire (St. Ebbe's, Oxford; Iffley; Barford), and spread from there to such places as Lincoln and Old Sarum.

Influences from western France are evident in the tympanum of St. George at Brinsop (Herefordshire), which is based on the equestrian figure at Parthenay-le-Vieux. Western French influence is also striking in the use of radiating voussoirs (Fishlake, Yorkshire) or corbel tables (Barton-le-Street, Yorkshire) with sculpture. Italian influence is shown in the caryatids at Durham Chapter House, and from Flanders were imported fonts (Winchester, Lincoln) and ready-carved capitals (Old Sarum, at Salisbury and Wiltshire Museum, and Glastonbury, at Glastonbury Abbey Museum). In the second half of the twelfth century, English sculptural programs included elaborate facades at Lincoln, Ely, and Rochester, each influenced by developments in northern Italy and in the emergent Gothic of the Île-de-France. Thus Anglo-Norman sculpture (Romanesque sculpture in England) is highly eclectic in its sources and is a rich and highly varied art form.

In painting, close ties of exchange had existed between England and Normandy at least since the second quarter of the eleventh century in the sacramentary illuminated in the Anglo-Saxon Winchester style and sent to Jumièges by its former abbot, Robert, while he was bishop of London (1044–1051); a late tenth-century Winchester benedictional was in Rouen in the Middle Ages, and belonged to an Archbishop Robert—perhaps the same Robert of Jumièges, who later became archbishop of Canterbury (1051–1052), or Robert, brother of Queen Emma and archbishop of Rouen (990–1037).

The influence of the Winchester style during the tenth and eleventh centuries in Normandy was so considerable that there has been confusion about the provenance of a number of important late eleventh-century manuscripts made for French patrons whose ecclesiastical offices took them to England. For instance, the manuscripts made for William of St. Carilef (St. Calais), bishop of Durham (1081–1096), once thought to be English, are now assumed to be Norman because of the stylistic similarity of their acanthus initials with clambering figures to those in manuscripts at Bayeux and Rouen (such as Bayeux Cathedral Library, MS 57–58, Gregory the Great's *Moralia*). William's books, such as Durham Cathedral Library, MS A II 4 (Bible) and B II 13–14 (St. Augustine on the Psalms) are now thought to have been made for him in Normandy while he was in exile (1088–1091) for having supported Odo of Bayeux's rebellion against William Rufus.

ANGLO-NORMAN ART

Illumination *(right)* from St. Luke's Gospel commissioned by Reginald, abbot of Abingdon (1085–1097). Rouen, Bibliothèque Municipale. PHOTOGRAPH BY THE AUTHOR

Nave, Waltham Abbey *(below, left)*. PETER DRAPER. Door, Barford St. Michael, Oxfordshire *(below, right)*, with beak heads, foliage, and interlace. G. ZARNECKI

ANGLO-NORMAN ART

Also now thought to be of Norman, rather than English, manufacture are the books illuminated by Hugo Pictor (Oxford, Bodleian Library, MS Bod. 717, Jerome's commentary on Isaiah; Paris, B. N. lat. 13765, a liturgical fragment; and Rouen, B. Mun. 1408 [Y. 109], lives of saints), of which the Bodleian manuscript was owned by Osbern, bishop of Exeter (1072–1103). Another case is the Gospels (Rouen, B. Mun. 32 [A. 21]) presented to his former abbey by Reginald, abbot of Abingdon (1085–1097). Although written in England, this manuscript is thought to have been illuminated at Jumièges because of the similarity of its red outline initials to those of the Bible of Jumièges (Rouen, B. Mun. 8 [A. 6]).

The term "Anglo-Norman" is most appropriately used for these groups of manuscripts in which the original stylistic impetus came from the English Winchester style but the development of which took place in Normandy in the late eleventh century—the reverse of the direction in Anglo-Norman architecture.

In England in the late eleventh and early twelfth centuries, the major center of production was Canterbury, where book illumination, especially at St. Augustine's, was characterized (like much of English sculpture of the same period) by the survival of Anglo-Saxon style. In the illuminated manuscripts the nervous, jagged outlines of the figures, most frequently drawn in outline with light color wash, predominated until the St. Albans Psalter (Hildesheim, St. Godard) in the 1120's. From then on, stylistic connections between England and Normandy were no longer as close as those between England and other parts of the Continent; crucial to the formation of the St. Albans Psalter style were influences from Germany and Byzantium.

Later in the twelfth century, parallels between England and northeastern France were so close as to suggest that painters traveled between the two regions. Especially close is the style of the Lambeth Bible (Lambeth Palace Library, MS 3 and Maidstone Museum) and that of the Gospel Book made in 1146 for Abbot Wedricus of Liessie (Avesnes, Société Archéologique, formerly Metz 1151). Also, the work of the painter who worked for Abbot Simon of St. Albans (1167–1183) appears in Continental manuscripts. It has been suggested too that the wall paintings at Sigena in Aragon (founded 1185) were the work of the late painters of the Winchester Bible. To the same stylistic movement of the end of the twelfth century has been ascribed the wall paintings at the Norman chapel of St.-Julien-du-Petit-Quevilly near Rouen, built by Henry II as part of his residence there but converted to a leper hospital in 1183, the likely date of the paintings. By this time the term "Anglo-Norman" has little to contribute as an art historical term, although Anglo-Norman continued to be the language of the English court up to the reign of Henry IV (1399–1413).

BIBLIOGRAPHY

General works include Mildred Katherine Pope, *From Latin to Modern French,* rev. ed. (1952), pt. V, "Anglo-Norman," 420–485; David T. Rice, *English Art, 871–1100,* vol. II of *The Oxford History of English Art* (1952); and T. S. R. Boase, *English Art, 1100–1216,* vol. III of *The Oxford History of English Art* (1953).

On architecture see V. M. C. Ruprich-Robert, *L'architecture normande aux XIe et XIIe siècles en Normandie et en Angleterre,* 2 vols. (1884–1889); Robert C. Lasteyrie du Saillant, *L'architecture religieuse en France à l'époque gothique,* 2 vols. (1926–1927), and *L'architecture religieuse en France à l'époque romane,* 2nd ed. (1929); Alfred W. Clapham, *English Romanesque Architecture After the Conquest* (1934); Jean Bony, "La technique normande du mur épais," in *Bulletin monumental,* **98** (1939); Paul Frankl, *Gothic Architecture* (1952); Geoffrey F. Webb, *Architecture in England: The Middle Ages* (1956); Pierre Heliot, "Les antécédents et les débuts des coursières anglonormandes et rhénanes," in *Cahiers de civilisation médiévale,* **2** (1959); Kenneth J. Conant, *Carolingian and Romanesque Architecture, 800 to 1200,* 2nd ed. (1966); Alan Borg, "The Development of Chevron Ornament," in *Journal of the British Archaeological Association,* **30** (1967); Lucien Musset, *Normandie romane,* 2 vols. (1974); Hans E. Kubach, *Romanesque Architecture* (1975); and W. W. Clark, "The Nave of Saint Pierre at Lisieux: Romanesque Structure in a Gothic Guise," in *Gesta,* **16** (1977).

Anglo-Norman sculpture is discussed in L. Grodecki, "Les débuts de la sculpture romane en Normandie, Bernay," in *Bulletin monumental,* **108** (1950); George Zarnecki, *English Romanesque Sculpture, 1066–1140* (1951), and *Later English Romanesque Sculpture, 1140–1210* (1953); Lawrence Stone, *Sculpture in Britain: The Middle Ages* (1955); George Zarnecki, "The Winchester Acanthus in Romanesque Sculpture," in *Wallraf-Richartz Jahrbuch,* **17** (1955), reprinted in his *Studies in Romanesque Sculpture* (1979); and "1066 and Architectural Sculpture," in *Proceedings of the British Academy,* **52** (1966), reprinted in his *Studies in Romanesque Sculpture* (1979); and *Trésors des abbayes normandes* (1979), catalog of exhibition held at Rouen and Caen.

On painting see Francis Wormald, *The Survival of Anglo-Saxon Illumination After the Norman Conquest* (1944); Otto Pächt, "Hugo Pictor," in *Bodleian Library Record,* **3** (1950); Hanns Swarzenski, "Der Stil der Bibel Carilefs von Durham," in *Form und Inhalt, Festschrift für Otto Schmitt* (1951); Charles R. Dodwell, *The Canterbury*

School of Illumination, 1066–1200 (1954); *Les manuscrits à peintures en France du VIIe au XIIe siècles* (1954), catalog of an exhibition in Paris; François Avril, "Notes sur quelques manuscrits bénédictins normands," in *Mélanges d'archéologie et d'histoire publiés par l'École française de Rome,* 73 (1964); Margaret Rickert, *Painting in Britain in the Middle Ages,* 2nd ed. (1965).

Millénaire du Mont-Saint-Michel, 966–1966 (1966), catalog of an exhibition in Paris; *Millénaire monastique du Mont-Saint-Michel* (1967–1971), catalog of an exhibition at Paris; Jonathan J. G. Alexander, *Norman Illumination at Mont-St.-Michel, 966–1100* (1970); Charles R. Dodwell, *Painting in Europe, 800–1200* (1971); Geneviève Nortier, *Les bibliothèques médiévales des abbayes bénédictines de Normandie,* new ed. (1971); François Avril, *Manuscrits normands, XIe–XIIe siècles* (1975), catalog of an exhibition in Rouen; Charles M. Kauffmann, *Romanesque Manuscripts, 1066–1190,* vol. III of J. J. G. Alexander, ed., *A Survey of Manuscripts Illuminated in the British Isles* (1975); and Elżbieta Temple, *Anglo-Saxon Manuscripts, 900–1066,* vol. II of J. J. G. Alexander, ed., *A Survey of Manuscripts Illuminated in the British Isles* (1976).

M. ALISON STONES

ANGLO-NORMAN LITERATURE. Anglo-Norman is the name given to the French dialect spoken in the British Isles for the nearly three centuries following the Norman Conquest in 1066. The term "Anglo-Norman" is used in a more limited sense by historians to refer to the period up to the accession of the first Plantagenet king of England, Henry II (1154); but its wider use by linguists and historians of literature is now well established, despite occasional preference by some scholars for the term "Anglo-French," particularly when referring to the late thirteenth and fourteenth centuries. French was the dominant vernacular of church and state authorities in England until well into the thirteenth century, and it continued to have substantial currency even in the fourteenth. In law its use extended even later. The first king following the Conquest to have English as his mother tongue was Henry IV (1367–1413). The privileged position of the Anglo-Norman dialect for over three hundred years left irrevocable changes in the grammar, vocabulary, and pronunciation of the English language, and the effects of the Norman-French culture on literature, law, and society at large were scarcely less important.

Anglo-Norman shared many of the characteristics of the northern and western Old French dialects, since many of the invaders came from these two areas, which included the duchy of Normandy; but it also developed its own distinctive traits. Most notably, the palatal *ü* sound, still a feature of modern French, did not survive, first blending with *u* sounds that derived from the Vulgar Latin ọ and later, in the thirteenth century, developing into the *ju* found in the English borrowings *duke, view, pure.* Most diphthongs reduced to a simple vowel (compare the pronunciation of English *chief* < Old French *chief, arrears* < *arriere, fruit* < *fruit*). The nasal vowels *e* and *a* were kept distinct (compare English *gentle* and the later *jaunty,* both from French *gentil*), the latter sound taking a more posterior position in Anglo-Norman than on the Continent (compare English *aunt, avaunt, taunt*). Affricate consonants that became sibilants in central French were maintained as such in the northern dialects (compare English *cherry, chimney, chase, judge, John* and French *cerise, cheminée, chasse, juge, Jean*). Preconsonantal *s* occasionally became *d* (English *meddle* < *mesler*). The relative isolation of the dialect also contributed to the conservation of such features as a final dental sibilant (English *faith*).

In the grammar the two-case system of Old French tended to be reduced, at an earlier stage than on the Continent, by the generalization of oblique forms and the abandonment of a distinct nominative singular except in a few nouns referring to persons (*fiz,* retained in many family names such as Fitzsimmon, Fitzwilliam, *sire*). Increasingly, the ending *-s,* the mark of the nominative singular and the oblique plural, became used for the plural only without distinction of case, a feature adopted by English. The first conjugation became even more dominant than on the Continent, absorbing verbs from other classes (compare English *tender, surrender* with French *tendre, surrendre*), and infinitives of this conjugation were frequently transposed as substantives with the sense of one act or example of the verb in question (compare English *dinner, supper, disclaimer, misnomer, merger, ouster;* and, from what were once third conjugation verbs, *attainder, remainder, rejoinder*). Many of these examples derive directly from the language of law, as do such former past participles as *lessee, grantee, mortgagee.*

The vocabulary of Anglo-Norman was essentially the same as in other Old French dialects except for the adoption of some few words from English (for example *acre, bateau, est, ouest, varech*). The lexicon of the English language, on the other hand, was transformed by the very large number of words that entered from Anglo-Norman and that touched on almost every aspect of life and society (see Middle English Language). If it is possible to see the growth of a fairly unified and coherent Anglo-Norman dialect until the thirteenth century, the period of the later thirteenth and fourteenth centuries witnesses a gradual degeneration as structures and forms become increasingly heterogeneous.

Scholars do not agree on the extent to which French was spoken in England during the post-Conquest and early Plantagenet reigns. No accurate figures can be given of the number of soldiers staying after the Conquest or of the number of immigrants who followed. Intermarriage, usually of immigrant men with English women, was common; and it has been suggested that children might well have learned English first and French later, as was the case of Ordericus Vitalis (b. *ca.* 1075), who was sent to Normandy to learn his "father's language." In his *Speculum duorum* (1209), Giraldus Cambrensis complains of a nephew who had failed to learn Latin and French. Nonetheless, in the twelfth century a considerable part of the population must have been French-speaking or at least effectively bilingual. By the end of the thirteenth century this proportion had diminished, though French by then had become virtually indispensable as the language of law, administration, and, to a lesser extent, commerce.

The use of French in administrative documents began in the twelfth century, when Latin was the normal vehicle for the recording of statutes, charters, writs, pleas, and other legal items. *Magna Carta* (1215) was written in Latin but translated almost immediately into French, probably in order that it might be proclaimed in courts throughout England. The *Provisions of Oxford* (1258) were also translated into French, as well as into English; statute rolls first appear in French in 1278, though the use of Latin continued; and from the reign of Edward II (1307–1327) yearbooks were kept in French. Indeed, the position of French as a language of law and government is enhanced from the last third of the thirteenth century, and a vast array of documents in the language from the thirteenth, fourteenth, and fifteenth centuries may be found. In law the language took on a special character and developed a life of its own, so much so that lawyers in English-speaking countries still use many of the same terms employed in the courts of the late Anglo-Norman period.

From the beginning of the twelfth century Anglo-Norman was a principal language of culture, and for more than 150 years the number of literary texts in French produced in England by far surpassed the number done in English. Anglo-Norman texts were produced throughout the fourteenth century, and when, during that period, English regained its ascendancy in literature, its indebtedness to the literary traditions of Continental and insular French was almost as great as that of the English language itself to the Romance dialect with which it had so long coexisted.

No simple definition can be given of Anglo-Norman literature. If the works to be included are limited to those written in England for an audience residing in England, and that have in their language of composition Anglo-Norman features, it must be recognized that Anglo-Norman writers themselves would not always have made such a distinction, seeing themselves rather as part of a larger sphere and knowing their audiences to have a similarly broad culture. Chardri, a writer active in the early thirteenth century, acknowledges that listeners to his *Vie de Seint Josaphaz* ("The Life of Saint Josaphat") might well have preferred hearing of Roland and Oliver and that he is relating his *Vie des Set Dormanz* ("The Life of the Seven Sleepers") rather than what one can assume were the more popular stories of Tristan, Galeron, Renart, or tales from Ovid. Some writers, such as Marie de France, Béroul, and Guillaume le Clerc de Normandie, are traditionally considered Continental, though they wrote mostly in England.

Inevitably, Anglo-Norman shares in the wide activity abroad. A large number of texts were copied in England, and in some cases the English manuscripts preserve forms lost on the Continent, the best known case being the *Chanson de Roland* in its Oxford version (Bodleian Library, MS Digby 23). There are Anglo-Norman versions of the *Tristan* by Thomas, the *Roman d'Alexandre, Amis et Amiles,* and the *Pseudo-Turpin Chronicle. Guillaume d'Angleterre,* sometimes attributed to Chrétien de Troyes and certainly Continental, was probably written for an English family. The romance *Fergus,* also written in France, was intended for Scottish patrons. Guernes de Pont-Sainte-Maxence came to England to find firsthand details for his second *Vie de Saint Thomas Becket.* The sermon *Deu le omnipotent* appears to be an adaptation or imitation of the Norman *Grant mal fist Adam.* The debate over the origin of *Le Mystère d'Adam* has never been clearly settled.

However, even when texts of disputed provenance are excluded, there remains a large body of texts that are by common consent Anglo-Norman.

In general they fit the definition given above. This insular literature is not merely a reproduction on a smaller scale of what was being written elsewhere; indeed, some texts signal trends that appear later in France. The first chronicle in French, Geffroy Gaimar's *L'estoire des engleis;* the first substantial narrative in octosyllabic rhyming couplets, the *Voyage de Saint Brendan;* the first French drama, *Le Mystère d'Adam*—all are Anglo-Norman. In the Anglo-Norman corpus there is a large proportion of saints' lives and of didactic, religious, and moral works; an important number of chronicles but no epics of its own; a few romances, some of which seem to belong to a genre apart; little theater and lyric poetry; and few fabliaux. There was no lack of productivity, but more serious works outnumber the purely entertaining.

SAINTS' LIVES AND EARLY WRITINGS

The largest identifiable group of texts that can be classified as a genre comprises the saints' lives, which are particularly numerous in the dialect. Of the approximately 250 lives extant in Old French, more than 100 appear in Anglo-Norman, ranging from versions of such well-known legends as those of St. Catherine, St. Mary of Egypt, St. Francis, and the miracles of the Virgin, to texts recounting the deeds of local figures, St. Alban, St. Audrey, St. Osyth, St. Edward the Confessor, St. Edmund the Martyr, St. Edmund of Abingdon, St. Richard of Chichester, and most notably St. Thomas à Becket, archbishop of Canterbury, whose murder in 1170 inspired Latin and French lives that have strongly political overtones. The legendary St. George, patron saint of Crusaders and of England, is the subject of a life by Simund de Freine (late twelfth century). Irish saints honored were St. Modwenna, St. Patrick, and St. Brendan, though the last two are not the subjects of proper lives. Many of the Anglo-Norman saints' lives are translations or adaptations of Latin sources, and few have been praised for their literary merit.

There has, however, been interest shown in the variations brought by Anglo-Norman writers to legends known elsewhere and especially in lives treating British saints. St. Edmund, the ninth-century king of East Anglia, martyred in 869 following a battle against the Danes, is the inspiration for two Anglo-Norman lives: one by Denis Piramus, a court poet turned monk who wrote at Bury St. Edmunds; the other an anonymous twelfth-century *Passiun* based on a tenth-century Latin work by Abbo of Fleury. Edward the Confessor, king from 1042 to 1066, also has two lives bearing his name, both from a source by St. Aelred of Rievaulx. The first, written probably between 1163 and 1170, is by a nun of Barking Abbey (Essex); the other is by the prolific Matthew Paris of St. Albans (Hertfordshire). Both houses belonged to the Benedictine order and were important centers of literary production. The *Life of St. Catherine* was also the work of a nun from Barking, named Clemence, who may also have been the author of the *St. Edward.* At least three other authors of lives of St. Alban are known, Guichard de Beaulieu, Thomas of Kent, and a certain Benoît, author of a life of Thomas à Becket that employs a tail-rhyme stanza. Benoît's life is only one of four in French about the martyred archbishop. The earliest are the poems in Francien by Guernes de Pont-Sainte-Maxence, the first only a draft and surviving in fragments, the second completed in 1174 after the poet visited England to obtain clearer information of events. Around 1240, or soon after, Matthew Paris wrote another version, only fragments of which are extant.

Matthew is also responsible for a life of the patron of his abbey, St. Alban, and a life of another archbishop of Canterbury, St. Edmund of Abingdon, himself a writer *(Merure de Seinte Eglise).* Another Anglo-Norman clergyman celebrated by a life was Richard Wyche, bishop of Chichester who was made chancellor of Canterbury by St. Edmund. He was canonized in 1262 and his life was written by Peter of Peckham. In the late thirteenth and early fourteenth centuries, Nicole Bozon wrote eleven saints' lives, all but two of them featuring female saints. These were saints Agatha, Agnes, Christina, Elizabeth of Hungary, Juliana, Lucy, Margaret, Martha, and Mary Magdalen; the two male saints were Paphnutius and Paul the Hermit. Among other verse lives are those of the saints Clement Pope, Foy, Giles, and Gregory the Great by Angier, Melor, and Thaïs, the last by a templar of Temple Bruer (Lincolnshire) who also wrote a *Vies des pères,* a poem on Antichrist, and a version of *St. Paul's Descent into Hell.* There are a number of versions of *St. Patrick's Purgatory* besides that of Marie de France and a version of the Irish legend, *La Vision de Tondale.*

In the early thirteenth century, Chardri composed two poems with eastern sources, the *Vie des Set Dormanz* ("The Life of the Seven Sleepers") and the *Vie de Seint Josaphaz,* the Christianized story of Buddha. Several prose lives could be included if copies of legendaries that begin to appear in the late thirteenth century are taken into account (see Paul Meyer, in

ANGLO-NORMAN LITERATURE

Histoire littéraire de la France, XXXIII [1906], 33). These tend to be shorter in length, sometimes simply résumés of earlier forms. Many of the legendaries follow the order of the liturgical year.

It is no longer common to class with saints' lives the extraordinary tale of the *Voyage de Saint Brendan,* an adaptation by an unidentified Beneit, writing in the first quarter of the twelfth century, of the *Navigatio Sancti Brendani.* Among the earliest and best of Anglo-Norman works, the *Brendan* recounts in lively and dramatic fashion the voyage of Brendan and his crew of monks from Ireland to the Promised Land. Their fantastic adventures along the way include visits to the Island of Sheep and the Island of Birds, an encounter with a Great Fish mistaken for an island, and their meeting with Judas on a lonely rock near his double hell. The work owes much in its form to the Irish *immram,* a genre in which a voyage serves as a frame tale; and the Anglo-Norman version is a unique example in French of such a type, though derivatives exist. With its quest structure and composition in octosyllabic rhyming couplets, the *Brendan* is regarded as a link between hagiography and romance. A blend of biblical, classical, Oriental, and Irish traditions, it has been the subject of study by historical geographers, some of whom seek evidence that Irish seafarers may have preceded the Vikings to the North American continent.

The texts contemporary to the *Brendan* are of quite different character and have contributed to the reputation of Anglo-Norman for serious works of a religious or moral nature. Philippe de Thaon, a "dull but well-meaning" writer according to M. Dominica Legge, produced possibly as early as 1113 a *Cumpoz* (or *Computus*), which explains the names of days and months, gives moralizing comments on their significance, and describes the calculation of movable feasts, adding "scientific" reasons for the movement of heavenly bodies. His sources include Bede, Helperic of Auxerre, Gerland, Turkil, and Nimrod, and he shows a penchant for proverbial material. His *Bestiaire* (*ca.* 1125–1139), based on the *Physiologus* tradition, recounts the traits of various animals, real and imaginary, usually with a moral interpretation. Also attributed to Philippe are a lapidary, which may be the third part of a tripartite bestiary or volucracy, and a *Livre de Sibylle.*

Possibly the oldest text in Anglo-Norman is the Oxford Psalter, a translation of the Gallican version of St. Jerome that may date from as early as 1100. One of the manuscripts (Oxford, Bodleian Library, MS Douce 320) is known as the Montebourg version; another (Paris Bibliothèque Nationale, MS lat. 768) is sometimes referred to as the Corbie Psalter. A translation of the Hebrew version, also deriving from St. Jerome, is found in the Cambridge Psalter (*ca.* 1115). Two other psalters are known, the so-called Orne fragment and the Arundel Psalter, also fragmentary, both of them Gallican.

During the next 250 years other books of the Bible were translated, though no complete Bible exists. The fourteenth-century Anglo-Norman Bible, apparently intended to be a prose translation of both Testaments, survives in fragmentary form only. From the twelfth century there are the *Proverbs of Solomon,* transposed with commentary in 11,854 lines by Sanson de Nanteuil (*ca.* 1150) and composed as a book of instruction for the adolescent son of Alice de Condet; an excellent prose translation of the *Quatre livre des reis;* and some Bible stories based on the Vulgate and St. Jerome's *Commentaries.* Among thirteenth-century additions are several versions of the Apocalypse, in verse and in prose, with some of the latter illustrated, and a commentary on Proverbs. In a class by itself is the fourteenth-century *Holkham Bible Picture Book,* which illustrates with captions the Old Testament from Genesis to Noah, the New Testament up to the Ascension in a common gospel, and *Last Things,* containing Fifteen Portents and the Day of Judgment. There is a verse Genesis in London (British Library, MS Harley 3775) and stories from Genesis, Exodus, and Numbers (MS Harley 2253, fols. 92v–105r).

HOMILETIC TEXTS

Homiletic literature is represented by sermons in verse and prose. Shortly before 1200 Guichard de Beaulieu wrote a gloomy sermon in alexandrines on the temptations of the world, the *Romaunz de temtacioun de secle* ("The Temptations of the World"). Possibly as early as the mid twelfth century, a sermon known as *Deu le omnipotent* was composed in Normandy, but it survives only in three Anglo-Norman manuscripts. Others to be noted are Robert of Gretham's *Evangiles des domnees* ("Sunday Gospels"), a prose sermon by the Franciscan Thomas of Hales, a rhymed *Sermon on Antichrist* (Oxford, Bodleian Library, MS Rawlinson Poetry 241), John of Howden's (or Hoveden's) *Rossignos* ("Nightingale"), written in 1274 for Eleanor of Provence, and several short metrical sermons by Nicole Bozon. It is unclear how much preaching was done in Anglo-

ANGLO-NORMAN LITERATURE

Norman; most of it would naturally be in Latin, and from the thirteenth century on, much vernacular preaching would have been in English.

The Anglo-Norman dialect was the vehicle for an unusual number of religious manuals and treatises, most of them written in the thirteenth century and many attributable to the influence of the Fourth Lateran Council of 1215 and of the subsequent Council of Oxford held in 1222; both provided for renewed discipline in the church and a renewed emphasis on promulgation of the faith. The Lateran decree *Omnis utriusque sexus fidelis* is especially cited, as it required annual confession and communion for which the laity had to be prepared. The aim of the works was to instruct priests or laity in the rudiments of Christian dogma and morality, and the nature of these texts is thus utilitarian rather than literary. Such *summae* were common in Latin but rarer in the vernacular. Continental French has some works of this kind, the *Somme le roi* ("The King's Summa") written for Philippe III of France being the best known; but in England the type flourished.

Always cited as a prime example is St. Edmund's *Merure de Seinte Eglise* ("Mirror of Holy Church"), a composite text that embodies sermon and lecture material probably written much earlier than the time of the *Merure's* composition, which is presumed to be in the years immediately following St. Edmund's assumption of the archbishopric of Canterbury in 1234. The aim of the *Merure* was to teach the religious life of meditation and contemplation. It deals with obvious points of dogma, the articles of faith, the Commandments, the Beatitutdes, and the Sins, and much significance is attached to numerological explanations. The work, which survives in twenty-three manuscripts, is now thought to have been translated from Latin and was also translated into English.

The anonymous *Manuel des péchés* ("Book of Sins," *ca.* 1260) was another widely used text. Divided into nine books and over 12,000 lines long, it covers some of the material found in the *Merure* but is distinguished by its considerable use of exempla and by its emphasis on confession. Not only, for example, is a precise and concrete list given of transgressions against the Commandments (book II), but fifteen exempla are included as illustration. Of the three later translations into English, the most important is *Handlyng Synne* by Robert Manning of Brunne in 1303. In 1267 Peter of Peckham (or Fetcham), also known as Peter of Abernon, produced a *Lumere as lais* ("Light for Lay People"), the title of which reflects the influence of the *Elucidarium* (before 1108) of Honorius Augustodunensis. The *Lumere* begins as a translation of Honorius' work but develops into a summary of dogma and an examination of the importance of numbers. A fragment of a work presumably similar to the above three, Robert of Gretham's *Corset,* deals with the sacraments only.

Different in content but also instructional is *La petite philosophie* (*ca.* 1230), based on the first book of the *Imago mundi* with some influence from the *Elucidarium.* It surveys Creation, the elements, zones of the earth, heavenly bodies, and signs of the Zodiac, and adds to this information a tirade against sin and an exhortation to repentance, confession, and absolution before death.

Virtues and vices are the subject of a more allegorical work by Robert Grosseteste, bishop of Lincoln, the *Chasteau d'amour.* Grosseteste's other extant French poem is *Le mariage des neuf filles du diable,* an allegory of nine vices, portrayed as women who find appropriate husbands in the world. Sins were often viewed as diseases or wounds to be healed, the image chosen by Henry, duke of Lancaster in 1354 for his *Livre de seyntz medicines* ("Book of Holy Remedies"), a lengthy prose text that shows evidence of social and personal detail among the traditional and the commonplace. The author compares his soul to the vortex of the sea, a nest of foxes, and a marketplace, among other things, and draws on a number of realistic comparisons to render his text more striking.

John Gower also wrote of the vices and virtues in his very long *Mirour de l'omme* ("Mirror of Man" *ca.* 1376–1379), devoting over half of the poem's more than 30,000 lines to their treatment. Gower's contribution to this tradition is to attribute five daughters to each of the seven daughters of Sin. The rest of the text is an examination of human society and its various classes and estates since the court of Rome, concluding that man, a microcosm of the world and the source of all evil, has his only hope of salvation through the intercession of the Virgin. Gower also wrote *Un traitié selonc les auctours pour essampler les amantz marietz* ("A Treatise to Give Examples from Writers to Married Lovers," 1397), praising virtuous love and condemning infidelity.

Nicole Bozon used the vices in his allegory the *Char d'Orgueil* as materials from which Pride's

ANGLO-NORMAN LITERATURE

chariot is built. Bozon's best work, the *Contes moralisés,* is less a manual than a sourcebook for preachers and contains a diversity of exempla, *fabulae,* and *narrationes,* used to teach people "to escape sin, embrace goodness, and above all praise the Lord God." Bozon draws examples from natural science, contemporary events, and collections of fables. Also to be cited among texts giving instruction on religious matters are an anonymous mid-thirteenth-century *Dialogue de Saint-Julien et son disciple,* which is a verse adaptation of St. Julian of Toledo's *Prognosticum futuri saeculi,* and the *Jerarchie* written in 1297 by John Peckham, archbishop of Canterbury, for Eleanor of Castile, wife of Edward I. To all these religious texts can be added a number of prayers and doctrinal poems.

MORAL AND DIDACTIC WRITINGS

Closely related to these instructional texts is a body of writing, diverse in form and content, that can be loosely labeled moral and didactic. It varies from discussion of moral precepts to formulas for proper social behavior and can include Christian values, courtly ideals suitably moralized, or such practical advice as the choosing of days considered lucky for various undertakings. Didactic texts were also common on the Continent, particularly in Normandy, and Continental texts such as the *Vers de la mort* by the Norman Hélinandus de Froidmont, the *Poème moral* composed in Walloon, and the Picard *Doctrinal sauvage* were known in England. Guillaume le Clerc de Normandie wrote all of his works, including his *Besant de Dieu,* based on the parable of the talents, in England. Some well-known texts were adapted or translated into both Continental French and Anglo-Norman. The *Disticha* of Dionysius Cato is found in three Anglo-Norman versions, one by Elie de Winchester, the second by an Everart, otherwise unknown, the third anonymous. Boethius' *Consolatio philosophiae* is found in an adaptation, totally in verse, entitled the *Roman de philosophie* and written by Simund de Freine (*fl.* 1190–1200).

From the same period is a translation into Anglo-Norman of a collection of moral tales by a converted Jew, Petrus Alfonsi, the *Disciplina clericalis* (1106), in which Oriental examples are put to the service of Christian ideals. The form of the work is that of *enseignements,* advice given by a father to his son, a structure related to the debate and popular also in England. It was used by the Norman Robert de Ho in his *Enseignements Trebor* and in England for the anonymous treatise *Urbain le courtois,* also known as the *Ditié (traité) d'Urbain.*

The debate form proper provides the frame for an early thirteenth-century work, the *Petit Plet* ("The Minor Dialogue"), in which the author, Chardri, depicts an old man depressed in spirit by the vicissitudes of the world—death, sickness, poverty, and the loss of loved ones—all commonplace complaints. Chardri's originality in this poem, which is based on the debate of Sensus and Ratio in the *De remediis fortuitorum,* is to accord to a young man the task of comforting, chiding, and persuading his older companion to accept life's events as God's will. Two of the *Petit Plet* MSS (British Library, MS Cotton Caligula A9 and Oxford, Jesus College, MS 29) also contain the Middle English debate, the *Owl and the Nightingale.*

Advice on government, morality, and hygiene is found in the *Secret des secrets,* adapted by Pierre d'Abernun of Peckham (author of the *Lumere as lais*) from the *Secretum secretorum.* This was supposedly an exchange of correspondence between Aristotle and Alexander the Great. Such was the seriousness of Anglo-Norman that even arts of love could provide moral counsel for lovers.

CHRONICLES

The oldest chronicle extant in the French language is Geffroy Gaimar's *Estoire des Engleis,* a verse text of 6,526 lines written about 1140 for Constance, wife of Ralph FitzGilbert of Lincolnshire. The *Estoire* appears to be the second of two parts, the first a now lost *Brut* or *Estoire des Bretuns,* supplanted in surviving manuscripts by the more skillfully told *Brut* of Robert Wace of Jersey. Gaimar's *Estoire des Engleis* begins with the arrival of Cerdic in Britain in 495 (according to the Anglo-Saxon Chronicle) and concludes with the death of William Rufus in 1100. It is generally accepted that two of his principal sources were Geoffrey of Monmouth's *Historia regum Britanniae* and the Anglo-Saxon Chronicle, but these are far from the only ones, as Gaimar admits to having used "many models" in English, French, and Latin.

Until the reign of Edgar (959–975), the *Estoire* is largely based on the Anglo-Saxon Chronicle with the insertion of the stories of Haveloc the Dane and of Buern Bucecarle, a mythical Northumbrian lord who fought against his king Osberht in revenge for the violation of his wife, and the story of Gormont, here not a Danish but a Saracen king credited with leading a Danish force and ravaging Normandy and

 ANGLO-NORMAN LITERATURE

France before being killed at Ghent. There is no Isembart, the Christian renegade usually associated with the name of Gormont. Long episodes are devoted to Edgar and his queen Aelfryth and to the struggle between Harold Godwinson and William the Conqueror. The description of the Battle of Hastings singles out the valiant conduct of the Norman minstrel Taillefer in the fighting. Gaimar refuses to go on to the reign of Henry I (1100–1135) on the grounds that this has elsewhere been sung of, in a book by David, otherwise unidentified. The work is for the most part unoriginal as history; its importance lies in its status as the oldest French chronicle and in the structural pattern it seems to have laid down for later chroniclers. For them a history began with a *Brut,* followed by the story of Anglo-Saxon and Norman kings, and then brought up to date for each author's contemporaries. The *Estoire* also indicates that the Normans were becoming interested in the past of their adopted land.

One other Anglo-Norman chronicle has come down from the twelfth century, an account of the struggle between the English and the Scots in 1173–1174, written by Jordan Fantosme, chancellor of Winchester, in rhymed laisses (2,071 lines). Jordan's chronicle differs considerably from Gaimar's in that it tells only of recent events, the rebellion of the "Young King" Henry, Henry II's eldest son, and of William the Lion of Scotland against King Henry himself and the subsequent capitulation of the Scottish leader. Although Jordan at times gives the impression that he was an eyewitness of events, there is no firm evidence that he took part in the battles.

In the thirteenth century the first prose chronicles appear. *Le livere de reis de Britannie et le livere de reis de Engletere* ("Book of the Kings of Brittany and Book of the Kings of England"), a two-part prose chronicle often dubiously attributed to Peter of Ickham, appears in a number of copies. It covers history from the *Brut* to a time near the date of each copy, the principal copy stopping at 1274. Two continuations are known, the Wroxham (Cambridge, Trinity College, MS R. 14. 7), which brings the chronicle up to 1306, and the Sempringham (an unnumbered Vatican manuscript), which extends to around 1325. A prose *Crusade and Death of Richard I* (mid thirteenth century) following Roger Howden, Roger de Wendover, and Matthew Paris, related the adventures of the Lionheart in the Holy Land, his capture and imprisonment in Austria, his return to England, and his death in the campaign against Philip II of France in 1199. There are also two verse texts of interest. One is the *Song of Dermot and the Earl* (written after 1230), which recounts the conquest of Ireland and breaks off in the middle of the siege of Limerick in 1175. The second is a poem *On the Erection of the Walls of New Ross,* also Irish in origin (1268).

Numerous prose copies of the *Brut*, usually with an updated history, appear in England in the thirteenth and fourteenth centuries. These include the prose *Brute d'Angleterre abrégé,* probably translated from a French verse version, the *Petit Bruit,* which contains many unique details of the *Brut* story along with later material. The *Prophecies of Merlin,* normally part of the *Brut*, also occurs independently in several copies. A text associated with the *Brut* tradition is the *Scalacronica,* written by Sir Thomas Gray of Heton during his imprisonment in Edinburgh Castle from 1355 to 1357. The title derives from a scaling ladder that was part of the family's arms and is the image used to recall earlier writers to whom Gray was indebted and who form the rungs of a ladder to knowledge. The work goes as far as 1362. Though not strictly a chronicle, the thirteenth-century *Grants geanz* is sometimes placed as an introduction to the *Brut.* A lengthy verse chronicle in alexandrine laisses was made around the beginning of the fourteenth century by Peter Langtoft, whose work comprises a *Brut,* a history of Anglo-Saxon and Norman kings to Henry III, and a history of the reign of Edward I. This third section appears independently in five of the sixteen manuscripts and is found in two different redactions, neither of which is totally Langtoft's work.

The prose *Anonimalle chronicle* of St. Mary's Abbey in York also updates a *Brut.* It is a valuable sourcebook for such fourteenth-century events as the Good Parliament, the Peasant's Revolt of 1381, and the plagues of 1374 and 1378. John of Canterbury's prose *Polistorie* follows a similar pattern with the added twist that it was intended to vaunt the claims of the Canterbury see over York and the Monastery of St. Augustine. Another monastic chronicle surviving only in a fragmentary 1723 transcription is the *Geste de Burch,* thought to date from the late thirteenth century. A more universal history is found in the Anglo-Norman *Chronicle* of Nicholas Trivet, author of two Latin chronicles, *Annales sex regum Angliae* and *Historia ad Christi nativitatem.* The *Chronicle* in French is dedicated to Mary, daughter of Edward I, but was probably completed around 1334, two years after her death.

The annals of the city of London survive in

 ANGLO-NORMAN LITERATURE

French for the period 1259–1342, though they were written in the mid fourteenth century presumably as a record; these annals are sometimes entitled the *Chroniques de Londres.* The *History of the Foundation of Wigmore Abbey* (fourteenth century) and the *Delapré Chronicle* (thirteenth century), dealing with the earldom of Huntingdon and the Cluniac house of Delapré (Northamptonshire), were both written in Anglo-Norman. Two important biographies are sometimes credited to Anglo-Norman, the *Histoire de Guillaume le Maréchal* written soon after William Marshall's death in 1219 on commission of his son, and the *Vie du prince noir* (*ca.* 1385). Although intended for English readers, both poems are by Continental writers.

ROMANCES

It is regrettable that the romance generally recognized as the best in Anglo-Norman, and one of the best known in Old French, the *Tristan* of Thomas, should survive only in fragmentary form. No identification has been made of this Thomas, who is neither the author of the *Horn* nor of the *Roman de toute chevalerie.* Thomas's version is sometimes referred to as the *version courtoise* (as opposed to the *version commune* represented by Béroul's *Tristan*), though this label is not as current as it was earlier this century; the work is usually dated between 1150 and 1170. The eight fragments, appearing over five manuscripts, total 3,151 lines and deal with the latter part of the Tristan story; his marriage to Iseut aux Blanches Mains; the persistence of his love for Iseut la Blonde and his attempts with the aid of Kaherdin, brother of Iseut aux Blanches Mains, to regain the other Iseut; and the deaths of the two lovers. All the manuscripts are Anglo-Norman.

Thomas's version was followed by Gottfried von Strasburg for his Middle High German *Tristan und Isolde.* A short text known as the *Folie Tristan d'Oxford,* also insular in origin, is sometimes related to the Thomas poem, but there are no certainties concerning its date and authorship. In the *Folie d'Oxford,* Tristan arrives at the court of Mark of Cornwall disguised as a fool named Trantris, and after revealing to Iseut his knowledge of many of the events of his relationship with her, and after being recognized by the dog Husdent, convinces the queen that he is indeed Tristan.

Another text that shares a wider heritage, the legend of Alexander the Great, is the *Roman de toute chevalerie* attributed to Thomas of Kent. This romance (*ca.* 1175–1181) is independent of Continental French forms of the Alexander story but is based on Latin writings found in England, particularly the so-called *Zacher Epitome,* that are largely identical with Continental sources. The poem is in 8,054 dodecasyllabic lines, the form used by Alexandre de Paris and later known as the alexandrine, and is divided into rhymed laisses. Thomas's version does not fit easily into the French tradition and is characterized by a strong moral tone that would not be out of place in a didactic work. The poem is a source for the Middle English *Kyng Alisaunder.*

Another romance in alexandrine rhymed laisses is the *Romance of Horn* by Master Thomas, a minstrel who shows evidence of wide reading in French and Latin. Thomas claims in the opening lines to have already sung of Horn's father, Aälof. It appears that *Horn* (*ca.*1170) is the central poem in a trilogy that was to be completed by the story of Horn's son Hadermod and composed by Thomas's own son Gilimot. No indication exists that this third poem was ever written. *Horn* begins with the casting adrift of the orphan hero Horn of Suddene (south Devonshire) and fifteen companions in an oarless and rudderless boat that is blown ashore in Brittany. They are taken in by King Hunlaf and kept at his court, where Horn grows to manhood and attracts the love of the king's daughter, Rigmel. Despite his defense of the kingdom against Saracen invaders, Horn is falsely accused of lying with Rigmel and leaves for Ireland, where under the name of Gudmod he earns further glory and the attention of the princess Lenburc. He returns, however, to Brittany to save Rigmel from a forced marriage, eventually recovers his father's kingdom, and finally marries Rigmel. There are many echoes of the epic in the Horn poem, yet it cannot be classed as a *chanson de geste.* Nor can it be placed squarely with the courtly romances, as the love element, if it affects the hero's decisions, neither creates a significant change in his character nor places him in any dilemma.

More courtly is a romance by Hue de Rotelande, *Ipomedon,* composed sometime between 1174 and 1191. The hero, after whom the work is named, is heir to the throne of Apulia. He pursues and finally wins, after seven years of disguises, battles, and adventures, the reluctant duchess of Calabria, known as La Fière Pucelle (the proud maiden), as his bride. This lengthy tale (10,578 lines) was followed by Hue's *Protheselaus* (12,741 lines), named for the younger son of Ipomedon and La Fière, who finds himself dispossessed of Calabria by his elder brother Daunus. With the aid of Medea, queen of Sicily, Pro-

ANGLO-NORMAN LITERATURE

theselaus eventually regains his kingdom, defeats his brother in combat, and marries the queen. In both poems Hue uses the octosyllabic rhyming couplet, the principal romance verse form of the second half of the twelfth century.

A work usually classed as a *roman d'aventures et d'amour,* and one that has many courtly features, is *Amadas et Ydoine,* written between 1190 and 1220. The hero, Amadas, a seneschal's son, becomes sick with love for Ydoine, daughter of the duke of Burgundy. He marries her in the end, but not before suffering illness, separation, her forced marriage to the count of Nevers, and numerous other impediments. Here the love element determines the hero's actions or lack of action, and both hero and heroine are idealized creations. The only entire surviving manuscript is Picard; there are two Anglo-Norman fragments.

The story of *Amis e Amile,* two friends so alike in appearance that they cannot be told apart even by their wives, occurs in Old French as a *chanson de geste.* The Anglo-Norman *Amis e Amilun* (the first named here corresponds to Amile in the French version and Amilun to Amis) is by contrast a romance, at least in traditional terminology. Written near the end of the twelfth century, it appears to be independent of *Amis e Amile* and may be the source for the Middle English *Amis and Amiloun* or derive from a similar version. Roughly contemporary is the very long *Estoire de Waldef* (22,304 lines), which contains elements found in several epics and romances: marriage of the hero's mother to an inimical stepfather; escape of the still young hero from being put to death, exile, or removal to a foreign land; marriage to a king's daughter; siring of sons; separation from his wife; potential remarriage of the hero's wife during his absence or during her abduction; capture of the sons by Saracens; loss of kingdom; return of the sons to regain the lost territory, and crowning of the sons as kings in their own right.

Most of these elements are likewise present in the early thirteenth-century *Boeve de Haumtone,* an adventure romance cast in the form of a *chanson de geste* and that can be linked to the epic cycle of Doon de Mayence. Its beginning is somewhat similar to that of the Hamlet legend, though there is no direct influence. Boeve's mother betrays her husband, Guy of Hampton, in order to marry the emperor of Germany, who in turn seeks to have Boeve killed. Boeve is saved by a faithful retainer, Sabot, and is eventually sold into slavery. A Saracen princess, Josiane, falls in love with him, but Boeve is sent away with a letter that causes the recipient to imprison him for seven years. By the time he escapes, Josiane has been married—chastely as it turns out—to Yvori de Monbrant, and Boeve rescues her. After various adventures that include the recovery of Boeve's lands, the pair is married and twin sons are born to them. But almost immediately the family is separated, again for a seven-year period; Boeve nearly marries again, only to have Josiane arrive in time to prevent this. One son, Miles, becomes king of England; the other, Guy, succeeds Josiane's father, King Hermine, and eventually Boeve himself. The story is told at a frenetic pace and crammed with events that leave no time for reflection or introspection. Notable features are Boeve's magic sword, Murgleie; his horse, Arundel, after whom a castle will be named; and the Saracen giant, Escopart, who is saved by Boeve and will aid him in his struggles. The Bevis legend is also found in a Continental French version and was adapted into Middle English.

Closer in tone to the courtly romances, at least in its first part, is *Gui de Warewic* (*ca.* 1232–1242). Gui falls in love with the better-born Felice and seeks to become worthy of her by proving himself a knight, a process that takes up the first part of the long poem and that ends in their marriage. In the second part Gui seeks to put his knightly prowess at the service of God rather than of his wife and goes abroad to Jerusalem and elsewhere to fight holy battles. A son born to him and Felice meanwhile is sold into slavery. Gui returns to England to defeat a Danish invader, Analf, spends his last years at Warwick unrecognized by his wife (compare the story of St. Alexis), and reveals his identity just before his death, when he sends Felice a ring she had given him. The best-known episode is a battle between Gui and Analf's champion Colebrand. It has been suggested that the poem was intended to glorify the houses of Wallingford and Warwick, whose lands embraced parts of Warwick, Oxford, and Buckingham, where some of the action is located.

Legge has proposed that *Gui de Warewic, Waldef, Boeve de Haumtone, Fouke Fitzwarin,* as well as two poems by Continental writers, *Guillaume d'Angleterre* (also attributed to Chrétien de Troyes) and *Fergus,* might be grouped under the label "ancestral romances," that is, adventure romances written to provide a legendary past for Anglo-Norman families. It is possible that Gui was intended by the author to be passed off as an ancestor of Wigod of Wallingford, cupbearer to Edward the Confessor,

ANGLO-NORMAN LITERATURE

and that some of his exploits may imitate those of Brian Fitzcount, second husband of one of Wigod's daughters, who defended Wallingford in 1139. With this and most of the other texts, except the *Fouke Fitzwarin,* family connections are difficult to demonstrate. *Fouke* is a fourteenth-century prose romance, almost certainly derived from an earlier verse account of the FitzWarin family who played an important role in Anglo-Welsh border history. The most notable of them was Fouke III, who rebelled against King John and who becomes in this legendary form a literary ancestor of Robin Hood.

LAIS

Three lais should be mentioned with the romances. The story of Haveloc the Dane first appears as a virtual prologue interpolated in Gaimar's *Estoire des engleis,* and it was later (*ca.* 1200) adapted as a proper lai, the *Lai d'Haveloc,* probably by a Continental writer living in England. Haveloc is the son of a Danish king, Gunter, and is raised by an English fisherman and his wife after Gunter is dethroned and killed. Haveloc, under the name of Cuarran, works as a scullery boy for the English king Edelsi, who marries him to his niece Argentille to belittle her position. When Haveloc learns of his real origins, he recovers his father's throne with the aid of an old seneschal and returns to England to regain his wife's rightful kingdom.

The *Lai du cor* ("Lay of the Horn") by Robert Biket is a cheerful poem concerning a chastity-testing horn from which no knight in Arthur's court—or Arthur himself—can drink except Caradue, whose wife has never thought of any man but him. A similar motif is treated in the Continental *Mantel mautaillié* ("The Ill-cut Coat"). The date of the *Lai du cor* is uncertain, possibly as early as 1200, possibly nearer the date of its one manuscript, around 1272–1282. The *Lai del Desiré* (late twelfth century), like Marie de France's *Lanval,* which in some scholars' opinions it imitates, uses the theme of the fairy mistress. Desiré, a knight born of previously childless parents, is given a ring as a love token by a beautiful woman whom he meets on his return to his homeland after years of tourneying. His ring disappears when he confesses his love to a forest hermit, and his happiness is not restored until a year later, when his mistress reappears, chiding him for seeing their love as a sin requiring confession. Desiré later finds and attempts to enter his lady's castle, but injury forces him to return to the court of the king of Scotland at Calatir, where his mistress finally arrives with a son and a daughter both of whom she gives over to the king while Desiré departs with her, never to return.

COURTOISIE

Two texts that reflect courtly ideals are *Blancheflor et Florence* and *Melior et Ydoine,* both versions of the *jugement d'amour,* a debate on the relative merits of knights and clerks as lovers. In both, two women are the initial participants, but in each case the question is taken to the court of the God of Love, where it is debated by an assembly of birds. In *Melior et Ydoine* the verdict favors clerks because of their discretion; in *Blancheflor et Florence* a combat of sparrow hawk and lark results in the victory of the former, the champion of the knight's claims and of Florence. Blancheflor dies of grief. *Blancheflor et Florence,* which is very similar, except for its decision, to the Continental *Florence et Blancheflor,* was written at the beginning of the thirteenth century by Brykhulle, who claims to be adapting an English version by an unidentified Banastre.

A more theoretical exposition of *courtoisie* is found in the *Donnei des amanz* ("Lovers' Courtship"). The poet overhears a lover's attempt to persuade his lady to grant him her favors, and in the ensuing debate the pair discusses the question by means of several exempla, including a Tristan episode not found elsewhere; two tales, the *Vilain and the Serpent* and the *Vilain and the Bird;* and references to several *romans.* The text has a number of lacunae and no conclusion is given. It is clear, however, that the risk of being discovered is the lady's chief reason for her reluctance. In the Tristan episode, sometimes called *Tristan rossignol,* Iseut is awakened by Tristan's imitation of bird calls and steals from Mark's bed but is seen by a dwarf, who awakens Mark; the king refuses to follow his wife, on the grounds that Tristan cannot possibly be nearby and that husbands should not be overly constraining.

Only one *art d'aimer* proper exists in Anglo-Norman (London, College of Arms, MS Arundel XIV). This allegorical poem recounts the poet's visit in a dream to the Castle of Love and his instruction in the precepts of love. The God of Love is portrayed as a golden-haired child, naked except for a jeweled crown, armed with a dart and a firebrand, and carrying a box of ointments, that is, the instruments of love's afflictions as well as a remedy for them. Occasionally, definitions of love are found separately. John of Garland (*ca.* 1195–1272) wrote a trilingual

ANGLO-NORMAN LITERATURE

definition, one stanza in Latin translated into French and English; a longer definition from the mid thirteenth century, modeled on the so-called Andreas Capellanus tradition, lists the properties and qualities of love. Less idealistic and certainly more practical is the advice contained for women in a *Letter to a lady containing admonitions concerning behavior to a lover* written in 1299. Here women are enjoined to look to a lover's financial habits as well as to the quality of his love.

LYRIC POETRY

Continental fashions of the late twelfth and early thirteenth centuries in lyric poetry seem to have found only a modest following in England. Lyric poems are not abundant in Anglo-Norman, and most are scattered in several manuscripts rather than collected in *chansonniers.* The Anglo-Norman lyric exploits some of the techniques of composition originally used by the troubadours and imitated by the poets of northern France. These include *coblas unissonans* (the same rhyme in each stanza), *coblas doblas* (two stanzas with same rhyme), *coblas singulars* (a different rhyme in each stanza), *coblas capfinades* (in which a key word from the last line of one stanza is repeated in the first line of the next), and *rimas derivatas* (alternating masculine and feminine rhymes containing the same root). Certain rhetorical techniques, too, are derivative, for example, the *reversarias* or antithesis, as in the poem that begins "Malade sui, de joie espris."

Special mention should be made of the macaronic, in which two or more languages are combined in a single poem. The fifteen known macaronics that contain Anglo-Norman date from the twelfth to the fifteenth centuries and include amatory, religious, and satirical verse. Examples of the various forms used on the Continent are also found in Anglo-Norman: the *pastourelle* ("En mai quant dait e foil e fruit"), the *ballete* ("E! dame jolyve"), the *rondeau* ("Margot, Margot"), the *rotrouenge* ("Quant primes me quintez de amors"), the debate ("Bele mere, ke frai? de deux amanz su mis en plai"), and the *plainte,* the Anglo-Norman examples of which, as noted below, are political. John Gower, around 1350, used the *balade* form in his *Cinkante balades* (actually fifty-one, with two dedicatory pieces to Edward III as an introduction). The love lyrics draw on the usual themes and topoi of courtly love. Spring is a frequent setting ("Quant le tens se renovele," "En averil al tens delits," "En la sesoune que l'erbe poynt"). Poets suffer for their love in service ("Longement me sui pené de servir en lealté"), in sickness ("Malade sui, de joie espris"), in fear of rivals ("E! dame jolyve"), and as prisoners of their beloved ("En la sesoune que l'erbe poynt"). Religious songs, especially those devoted to the Virgin, were popular and often follow the pattern of secular love lyrics, as in "Quant le russinol se cesse." Anglo-Norman has its share of antifeminist pieces as well, such as *De conjuge non ducenda, Le blasme des fames,* and Bozon's *De la femme et de la pye.* A famous Latin hymn "Laetebundus" is parodied in a drinking song "Or hi parra: la cerveyse nos chantera."

A collection of sixteen political songs published in 1953 (Isabel S. T. Aspin, ed.) includes three laments (for Simon de Montfort, Edward I, and Edward II), a complaint against heavy taxation, and satirical pieces on society in general. *Sur les états du monde* comments wryly on the three "orders" of medieval society; the *Ordre de bel ayse* portrays a religious order where the monks are richly fed and dressed and lead lives of ease and pleasure. All of these songs are from the thirteenth and fourteenth centuries; some are macaronic, both bilingual (French-Latin, French-English) and trilingual (the *Proverbia trifaria).*

There are few fabliaux, and only one manuscript (London, British Library, MS Harley 2253) contains more than one example. Some of the fabliaux are redactions of stories also found on the Continent: *Les trois dames qui trouverent un vit, Le chevalier qui faisaient parler les cons,* and *Les quatre souhaits Saint Martin,* though the variations are not always small. One fabliau, *Le chevalier, sa dame et un clerc,* is similar enough to *La bourgeoise d'Orléans* to be considered a variant version. Another, *Le héron* (or *La fille mal gardée*) has a Continental and an Anglo-Norman version and closely resembles another story, *La grue.* Three are found only in Anglo-Norman: *Les trois savoirs, Le chevalier à la corbeille,* and *La gageure.*

DRAMA

The oldest surviving French play wholly in the vernacular is thought to have been written in England. The work of which the Latin title is the *Ordo representacionis Ade* is usually known as the *Mystère d'Adam* or as the *Jeu d'Adam,* though neither title is especially apt, and was written about the middle of the twelfth century. The sole copy is a southwestern French manuscript (Tours, Bibliothèque Municipale, MS 927). Three sections remain of what may have been a fulller production—the

ANGLO-NORMAN LITERATURE

story of Adam and Eve and their expulsion from Paradise, the slaying of Abel by his brother Cain, and a procession of mostly Old Testament prophets who predict the coming of Christ. The last part is based on an *Ordo prophetarum* and its source, the pseudo-Augustinian sermon *Contra Judaeos paganos et Arianos.* The two earlier sections have as their immediate sources various lections and responsories from church services, illustrated with a good dose of dramatic liberty and skill by the author. Probably most successful theatrically are the dialogues between Adam, the Devil, and Eve, which both lend credibility to the story of the Fall and humanize for the audience the temptation of Eve and Adam. Elaborate directions are given in Latin for the staging of the play.

Two sizable fragments survive of the *Seinte Resureccion,* one in a mid-thirteenth-century Paris copy (Bibliothèque Nationale, MS fr. 902), the other in a manuscript copied at Canterbury (London, British Library, MS. Add. 45103). Although the second was copied earlier than the first, it clearly represents a more developed *remaniement* than the Paris version. The original version probably dated from the late twelfth century. The fragments record Joseph of Arimathea's visit to Pilate to request that Christ's body be handed over to him. Pilate dispatches his soldiers to find out whether Christ is really dead, and they use the blind Longinus to thrust a spear into the body for this reason. Longinus' sight is miraculously restored when he touches Christ's blood to his eyes. Pilate imprisons Longinus to keep him quiet, grants Joseph Christ's body, but sends soldiers to guard it. When Joseph arrives to wrap the body for burial, he is apprehended and brought before Caiphas the high priest. The text stops at this point. Scholars presume that a Harrowing of Hell episode would have followed and then the remainder of the Resurrection story, including Joseph's liberation. Two bilingual (French-English) fragments, one from the thirteenth century, the other from the fourteenth, also point to the existence of other plays that are at least partly in French. These fragments are, however, too short to afford any real clues to the nature of their content or form.

FRENCH INSTRUCTION

From the thirteenth century French appears to have become, at least for some of the population, a learned language, and various manuals of instruction testify to this status: grammars, Latin-French vocabularies, and conversation books. The first two works to be noted deal principally, as their titles indicate, with orthography, though both touch upon aspects of pronunciation, grammar, and dialect as well. The first, the *Tractatus orthographiae,* dates from the late thirteenth century and is signed by one T. H. Parisii Studentis, probably an Englishman who had studied in Paris; it is directed at advanced students who have some French and a good knowledge of Latin, as Latin is the language of explanation and terminology. A later version (Oxford, All Souls College, MS 182) was done by Coyfurelly. The better-known *Orthographia Gallica* (*ca.* 1300) is also written in Latin, though one of its manuscripts (London, British Library, MS Harley 4971) has additional rules and comments in French. The *Orthographia* appears to have been intended for educated Englishmen and makes a point of prescribing Continental as opposed to Anglo-Norman usage. One *Donait français* (the "French Donatus," after the fourth-century Latin grammarian) states unabashedly in its introductory paragraph that the intention of the compiler, John Barton, is to "introduce the English to the correct language of Paris and of the regions thereabouts." More like a full grammar, this *Donait* deals not only with pronunciation but with word formation, morphology, parts of speech, and verb conjugations.

The best-known of the vocabularies is Walter of Bibbesworth's *Tretiz pur aprise de langwage (Traité pour apprendre la langue),* written around 1240–1250 for a certain Dionysia of Munchensy and intended to be used to help teach children French. Written in verse, this treatise lists words connected with animals and the sounds they make, cultivation, spinning, brewing, fishing, plants and trees, birds and game animals, the parts of a cart, a harness, and house building and ends by detailing courses for a splendid feast. It is unlikely that the work was intended to be used by children themselves; more probably it was an aid to mothers teaching their children French, by now a learned language for them both, as English glosses aid the interpretation of many of the words. Bibbesworth is particularly fond of pointing out homonyms and near homonyms in the first part of the text and the importance of gender or a single sound in distinguishing words.

Similar in content in many passages to Bibbesworth's treatise is the *Nominale sive verbale in Gallicis cum expositione eiusdem in Anglicis,* a bilingual (French-English) vocabulary also in verse. The composition is less coherent than the *Tretiz* and its educational purpose less manifest. Perhaps most interesting are the various *manières de langage,* or

ANGLO-NORMAN LITERATURE

conversation books, so called because they frequently contain expressions such as "Voici une autre manière de langage pour demander . . ." and "Voici une autre manière de parler." These are not the work of grammarians, and their purpose seems to be to provide colloquial French for Englishmen about to travel in France; their content is hardly suited for instruction to children. One such work in particular depicts various situations from daily life and is composed of stories and dialogues mostly concerning a hypothetical journey to Orléans undertaken by an English traveler and his servant.

Anglo-Norman was also used for a wide variety of nonliterary texts and documents. References to many of these may be found in the bibliographical studies and other surveys listed below.

MODERN SCHOLARSHIP

Modern Anglo-Norman scholarship may be said to have begun with the publication of a series of lectures delivered by Abbé Gervais de La Rue, *Essais historiques sur les bardes, les jongleurs et les trouvères normands et anglo-normands* (1834), in which de La Rue drew attention to the importance of the Anglo-Norman contribution to French literature. At the same time Francisque Michel began an investigation of manuscript holdings in British libraries, later reporting back to the French minister of education. On this mission Michel rediscovered the Oxford version of the *Chanson de Roland,* which he published in 1837. Achille Jubinal and Antoine Jean Victor Le Roux de Lincy also began exploiting Anglo-Norman material about this time, as did an Englishman, Thomas Wright, who beginning in 1839 published a number of Anglo-Norman texts in his various works, including some political songs, Philippe de Thaon's *Cumpoz* and *Bestiaire,* Gaimar's *Chronicle,* and the *Lai d'Haveloc.*

A number of early editions of Anglo-Norman texts may be found in series established by nineteenth-century British literary and historical societies, the Roxburghe Club, the Bannatyne Club, the Surtees Society, the Camden Society, and the Percy Society. Greater interest in the language, as well as in the texts, is shown during the last part of the century, when several journals of Romance philology were founded (*Revue des langues romanes* in 1870, *Romania* in 1872, *Zeitschrift für romanische Philologie* in 1877), and series for Old French texts were begun (Société des Anciens Textes in 1875, Altfranzösische Bibliothek in 1879, Bibliotheca Normannica in 1879). The first independent study of the linguistic traits of the dialect was made in 1882 in an Uppsala dissertation by Johan Vising, *Étude sur le dialecte anglo-normand du XIIe siècle.* Two of France's leading medievalists, Gaston Paris and Paul Meyer, were also attracted to Anglo-Norman, and the latter recorded several surveys of insular French manuscripts in *Romania, Histoire littéraire de la France,* and *Notices et extraits des manuscrits. . . .*

Most texts published in this period (for example, Eduard Mall's edition of Philippe de Thaon's *Cumpoz,* 1873) were reconstructed to bring Anglo-Norman closer to Continental standards in language and versification; but one editor, Robert Atkinson, vigorously defended the text of the *Vie de Seint Auban* (1876) as it stood in its manuscript, an autograph, against the criticism of German and French scholars. Atkinson was virtually alone in his refusal to make sweeping editorial interventions until Joseph Bédier published a preface to his second edition of the *Lai de l'ombre* in 1913, arguing against attempts to reconstruct what were claimed to be original forms of the text.

In 1904 an American scholar, Louis Emil Menger, published *The Anglo-Norman Dialect.* In 1913 Paul Studer, an Anglo-Normanist, was named to a newly created chair of Romance languages at Oxford, and his inaugural lecture, *The Study of the Anglo-Norman* (1920), called for increased attention to the field. Johan Vising, who was already known for his work on the language, published *Anglo-Norman Language and Literature* in 1923. The work surveyed the history of the Anglo-Norman period and gave a list of all known texts with references to editions and cross-references to a list of manuscripts containing Anglo-Norman items. At Cambridge in 1924 Oliver H. P. Prior brought out the first volume of a planned series, *Anglo-Norman Texts,* with an introduction that considered possible English influence on phonology and orthography. Between the two world wars, Oxford was the center of Anglo-Norman studies. Studer was succeeded in the Romance languages chair by Edwin G. R. Waters, whose *The Anglo-Norman Voyage of St. Brendan* (1928) became a standard for other editors. In 1933 Waters was followed by Alfred Ewert, later editor of *Gui de Warewic,* the lais of Marie de France, and of the *Tristan* of Béroul.

The dominant figure, however, was Mildred K. Pope, a fellow of Somerville College, Oxford, and from 1934 professor of French language and Romance philology at Manchester. In 1934 her major work appeared, a remarkable study of the phonology and morphology of Anglo-Norman, *From Latin to Modern French with Especial Consideration of Anglo-Norman;* the work was revised and updated in 1952. Pope was also first secretary of the Anglo-Norman Text Society, founded in December 1937, which published its first volume, *La petite philosophie* (William H. Trethewey, ed.) in 1939. By 1980, thirty-seven volumes had appeared in the series. In 1955 Pope published the first volume of the *Romance of Horn.* Another British scholar, M. Dominica Legge, published two works of great importance for the literature of the dialect, *Anglo-Norman in the Cloisters* (1950) and *Anglo-Norman Literature and Its Background* (1963), which became a standard reference. Following Pope, she also wrote a number of articles that served to make the field better known to scholars.

In the United States, S. H. Thompson and Ruth Dean performed a similar role. Dean also published bibliographical studies, as did Keith V. Sinclair in Australia. Thomas B. W. Reid took the Oxford chair of Romance languages in 1958 and later also became president of the Anglo-Norman Text Society. In 1964 he completed volume II of the *Romance of Horn,* giving particular attention to syntax, previously a much neglected area. In 1949 Louise W. Stone announced an *Anglo-Norman Dictionary* project, and the first fascicle of this work appeared in 1977, coedited by William Rothwell and prepared by Reid.

BIBLIOGRAPHY

Bibliographical Studies. Ruth J. Dean, "Anglo-Norman Studies," in *Romanic Review,* **30** (1939); and "The Fair Field of Anglo-Norman: Recent Cultivation," in *Medievalia et humanistica,* n.s. **3** (1972); Keith V. Sinclair, "Anglo-Norman Studies: The Last Twenty Years," in *Australian Journal of French Studies,* **2** (1965); Johan Vising, *Anglo-Norman Language and Literature* (1923).

Language. Kathleen R. Lambley, *The Teaching and Cultivation of the French Language in England During Tudor and Stuart Times* (1920), ch. 1; Louis E. Menger, *The Anglo-Norman Dialect, a Manual of Its Phonology and Morphology* (1904); Mildred K. Pope, *From Latin to Modern French with Especial Consideration of Anglo-Norman* (1934, rev. 1952); Mildred K. Pope and Thomas B. W. Reid, eds., *The Romance of Horn,* II (1964); William Rothwell, "The Role of French in Thirteenth-Century England," in *Bulletin of the John Rylands University Library of Manchester,* **58** (1976); Louise W. Stone and William Rothwell, *Anglo-Norman Dictionary* (1977–); Frédéric J. Tanquerey, *L'évolution du verbe en anglo-français* (1915); R. M. Wilson, "English and French in England: 1100–1300," in *History,* n.s. **28** (1943); George E. Woodbine, "The Language of English Law," in *Speculum,* **18** (1943).

Literature. Albert C. Baugh, *A Literary History of England* (1948), 135–142; Henry J. Chaytor, *The Troubadors and England* (1923); Ruth J. Dean, "What Is Anglo-Norman?" in *Annuale médiévale,* **6** (1965); Gervais de La Rue, *Essais historiques sur les bardes, les jongleurs et les trouvères normands et anglo-normands,* 3 vols. (1834); Mary Dominica Legge, *Anglo-Norman in the Cloisters* (1950); *Anglo-Norman Literature and Its Background* (1963); and "La précocité de la littérature anglo-normande," in *Cahiers de civilisation médiévale,* **8** (1965); Brian Merrilees, "Anglo-Norman," in A. G. Rigg, *Editing Medieval Texts: English, French and Latin Written in England* (1977), 86–106; Josiah C. Russell, *Dictionary of Writers of Thirteenth-century England* (1936); Paul Studer, *The Study of Anglo-Norman* (1920); Emmanuel Walberg, *Quelques aspects de la littérature anglo-normande* (1936); Constance B. West, *Courtoisie in Anglo-Norman Literature* (1938).

BRIAN MERRILEES

[See also **Alexander Romance; Ars dictaminis; Breton Lays; Chansons de Geste; Fabliaux; French Literature; Middle English.**]

ANGLO-SAXON ART. After the Viking invasions destroyed Hiberno-Saxon culture in the early ninth century, artistic production in England did not revive until the reign of King Alfred (871–899), when the invaders were repulsed and Anglo-Saxon art was born. Little survives from the earlier stages of the artistic renewal. The patronage of Alfred and later rulers seems to have been a major factor, making Winchester, the royal capital, an important center. Books decorated at Alfred's court at first copied modest initials from south English manuscripts of the eighth century, but in the course of the tenth century these indigenous initial types were gradually enriched with a more classicizing foliate ornament derived from the ninth-century Carolingian renaissance.

An analogous process occurred in the representation of the human figure. While reviving decorative Hiberno-Saxon compositional principles, Anglo-Saxon artists turned from relatively abstract Hiberno-Saxon figure representations to more recent and more classicizing foreign ones. The figures on the embroideries made in Durham (909–916) for Bishop Frithestan of Winchester were influenced by posticonoclastic Byzantine art, and the early tenth-

ANGLO-SAXON ART

century English manuscript of Rabanus Maurus' treatise on the Cross (Cambridge, Trinity College, MS B.16.3) copied a Carolingian source from Fulda. A mixture of foreign and indigenous sources also influenced the iconography of the first half of the tenth century. The Winchester pictures in the Athelstan Psalter (London, British Library, MS Cot. Galba A. XVIII) drew upon Carolingian and Byzantine New Testament iconography as well as Hiberno-Saxon eschatalogical and devotional imagery.

The middle of the tenth century ushered in a second phase of Anglo-Saxon art under the aegis of Saint Dunstan (*ca.* 909–988), who initiated a monastic reform at Glastonbury. An exquisite line drawing of him kneeling before Christ (Oxford, Bodleian Library, MS Auct. F.IV.32) displays a more monumental, volumetric style with long, sweeping lines and fluttering folds. Sometimes termed the "first" or "Ada" style, this seems to be a synthesis of the Carolingian court (or Ada) style of Charlemagne and the classicizing style of the Byzantine Macedonian renaissance. The new style spread with the monastic reform to Winchester, which assumed a leading artistic and ecclesiastical position under Bishop Æthelwold (963–984).

Æthelwold's sumptously illustrated benedictional (London, British Library, MS Add. 49598) drew anew upon earlier English, Carolingian, and middle Byzantine art for style and iconography. A highly elaborate iconographic program propagandized the alliance between Æthelwold and King Edgar (reigned 959–975) for monastic reform. Anglo-Saxon figural style was brought to a new expressive pitch with figures depicted in frenzied movement, their drapery agitated in linear patterns of broken zigzag folds.

At Winchester figures in this dynamic style were combined with broad, acanthus-filled frames eclectically derived from Carolingian art. Figures and ornament were subtly assimilated to each other and united in an overall decorative composition. This was a sophisticated solution to an aesthetic problem that had occupied English artists ever since the Hiberno-Saxon period: the reconciliation of the nonfigural, ornamental northern tradition with the figural Mediterranean one. This combination of figures and foliate ornament is often called the Winchester style, even though it soon spread outside Winchester, as evidenced by the Glastonbury line drawings (about 979) in the Leofric Missal (Oxford, Bodleian Library, MS Bodl. 579). These are executed in inks of different colors, an important innovation reflecting the Anglo-Saxon penchant for decorative effects. Painting and line drawing were sister media in Anglo-Saxon art, and the same style was often practiced in both.

By the early eleventh century the Carolingian Utrecht Psalter from Reims had come to Canterbury, where its vibrant drawings were gradually copied in the Harley Psalter (London, British Library, MS Harley 603); other workshops, such as that of Winchester, also fell under the sway of the Reims book. The Anglo-Saxon style influenced by the Utrecht Psalter has been called the "second" or "Utrecht" style, but often there is comparatively little distinction between it and the late phase of the "first" style which continued into the eleventh century. The Utrecht Psalter appealed to the English because they had independently developed an analogous style. Its unusually imaginative iconography also stimulated the Anglo-Saxons' lively fantasy. They created many iconographic novelties, such as the new Ascension imagery of the "disappearing Christ," in which the Lord is shown merely as a pair of feet dangling from heaven.

Canterbury in the eleventh century became a major center for the production of texts illustrated with extensive cycles, such as the *Psychomachia* of Prudentius and two Old English paraphrases of Old Testament books, the Caedmon Genesis (Oxford, Bodleian Library, MS Junius 11) and the Ælfric Paraphrase of the Pentateuch (London, British Library, Cot. Claud. B.IV). Anglo-Saxon craftsmen also worked in other media, such as fresco, ivory and monumental-stone carving, metalwork, enamel, and embroidery, but not much in these media is extant.

Barbaric Viking art brought by the renewed Scandinavian incursions of the late tenth and eleventh centuries greatly affected northern English stone sculpture, but had comparatively slight effect upon southern English art, which became increasingly patterned and ornamented. The Conquest also had little impact; indeed, English artists working in a traditional Anglo-Saxon style for a Norman patron executed the Bayeux Tapestry, a vast embroidered narrative of the Conquest. Only in the early decades of the twelfth century did the tenacious Anglo-Saxon style yield to the new Romanesque one.

BIBLIOGRAPHY

R. Bailey, *Viking Age Sculpture in Northern England* (1980); N. P. Brooks and H. E. Walker, "The Authority and Interpretation of the Bayeux Tapestry," in R. A. Brown, ed., *Proceedings of the Battle Conference on*

ANGLO-SAXON LITERATURE

Anglo-Norman Studies, I. 1978 (1979); Robert Deshman, "Anglo-Saxon Art After Alfred," in *Art Bulletin,* **56** (1974); "The Leofric Missal and Tenth-Century English Art," in *Anglo-Saxon England,* **6** (1977); and *Anglo-Saxon Art* (in preparation); Thomas D. Kendrick, *Late Saxon and Viking Art* (1949); Meyer Shapiro, "The Image of the Disappearing Christ," in *Gazette des beaux arts,* 6th ser., **23** (1943); Elżbieta Temple, *Anglo-Saxon Manuscripts 900–1066* (1976); and Francis Wormald, "The Survival of Anglo-Saxon Illumination After the Norman Conquest," in *Proceedings of the British Academy,* **30** (1944); and *English Drawings of the Tenth and Eleventh Centuries* (1952).

ROBERT DESHMAN

ANGLO-SAXON LITERATURE. If, as Bede and other sources tell us, the Angles, Saxons, and Jutes came to Britain in the middle of the fifth century A.D., then the period of Anglo-Saxon culture extended for over 600 years until its nature and direction were changed by the Norman conquest of 1066. Although both the distance in time and the patchiness of our information tend to foreshorten this period for us, we can get some idea of its length by going back 600 years from our own day, to the fourteenth century, the age of Chaucer. The Celtic languages were replaced by Germanic ones, kingdoms and rulers came and went, religions changed, and Christianity was introduced in a lasting form. There were periods of great prosperity and tranquillity in the seventh, eighth, and tenth centuries, followed by periods of invasion and internal warfare, when civilization itself seemed in peril.

The evidence for Anglo-Saxon culture is intermittent but of many kinds. There is a host of place-names, and many material objects either have remained in place or have been dug up by fortune hunters and archaeologists. There are many fine standing crosses in the north of England and fragments of carved stonework throughout the country. Strikingly beautiful metalwork and jewelry were found in the Sutton Hoo ship burial, and there are even Anglo-Saxon embroideries from the treasures of St. Cuthbert in Durham Cathedral. The many written remains include about fifty short inscriptions in runic characters carved on stone, metal, and bone objects, and an equal number of inscriptions in the Latin alphabet. Above all, there is a large number of manuscripts that tell us about the tastes of the Anglo-Saxons, their intellectual and religious interests, and as much of their recorded history as has survived.

These manuscripts, most of which were written in the last two or three centuries of the Anglo-Saxon period, contain texts both in Latin and in the vernacular, which is usually called Old English. Although the number of Latin texts is considerably greater, those in Old English are our particular concern. They are of great interest, as they make up one of the earliest vernacular literatures in western Europe. Old English literature has been compared with the vernacular literatures that developed later in Germany, Iceland, Ireland, and France. From the linguist's point of view the Old English dialects are important because after Gothic they were among the earliest of the Germanic languages to be written down. Their study played a large part in nineteenth-century comparative work on the Germanic languages.

Although Old English literature has its moments of grandeur, pathos, beauty, and subtlety, it began as a severely practical tool. It was transmitted by churchmen who had the purposes of the church in mind when they took parchment and wrote on it. They used only Old English because they were afraid no one would understand them if they wrote in Latin. King Alfred the Great (871–899) put this very clearly in his preface to the Old English translation, *Pastoral Care,* of the *Liber regulae pastoralis* of Pope Gregory I (540–604). Speaking of the state of learning, he says, "Swæ clæne hio wæs oðfeallenu on Angelcynne ðæt swiðe feawa wæron behionan Humbre ðe . . . cuðen . . . an ærendgewrit of Lædene on Englisc areccean; ond ic wene ðætte noht monige begiondan Humbre næren." ("So general was its decay in England that there were very few on this side of the Humber who could . . . translate a letter from Latin into English; and I believe that there were not many beyond the Humber.") Alfred goes on to note that although reading in Latin had declined badly, many could still read in their own language. He proposes that some of the youth of his kingdom be educated in the vernacular and that the most promising of these should go on to learn Latin.

Many of the texts that have survived would have been useful to such students: documents necessary for evidence, rules to be followed, sermons to be read, or literary texts to be studied in schools. There are also a few traces of the traditions of oral storytelling, which were a feature of Anglo-Saxon society and which are mentioned by historians from Bede to William of Malmesbury. It seems unlikely that large numbers of these stories were ever written down, although *Beowulf* is probably one of them. While

ANGLO-SAXON LITERATURE

large numbers of Old English manuscripts must have been destroyed during the sixteenth century with the dissolution of the monasteries, so far as we can tell from the medieval library catalogue, those that have survived are quite representative.

Of the 400 extant manuscripts containing Old English texts, Neil Ker describes 189 as major manuscripts. Most of them are handsome pieces of work, clear and well-spaced; and the Insular minuscule hands in which they are written are easy to read and pleasing to the eye. Abbreviations are few, and the only special characters are the two "th" letters, þ (thorn) and ð (eth), ƿ (wynn) for "w", and the low front vowel æ (ash). In tenth- and eleventh-century manuscripts runic characters occasionally appear, either in collections of alphabets, singly as a kind of abbreviation for their own rune names, or as acrostics in the poetry. The manuscripts are often decorated. Initial letters are either colored or worked in elaborate zoomorphic or interlace patterns. Psalters, biblical translations, and liturgical manuscripts often have full-page drawings or paintings of great beauty. These illustrated manuscripts have been highly prized by collectors since the sixteenth century, although very few remain in private hands. Most Old English manuscripts are now deposited in public or university and college libraries in Great Britain, Europe, and the United States.

Not all of the surviving texts can be considered as literature. Quite a number of them are interlinear glosses or notes to Latin texts, aids to the study of literature rather than literature itself. Others are lists of various kinds, the boundaries in charters, or scribbles and pen trials. When these are set aside, a considerable body of literature remains. The homilies and saints' lives are the most numerous, followed by biblical translations; the works of the Latin fathers in translation; the Anglo-Saxon chronicles and other historical documents; laws, charters, wills and other legal documents; and treatises dealing with grammar, computus, medicine, and geography. Although there are fewer than 30,000 lines in all, the poetry is of high quality and interest. Old English literature, then, presents a very considerable memorial to the powers of its mostly anonymous creators.

While we will never know the names of more than a few Old English authors, we can try to date their productions. We always have to distinguish between the date of the manuscript and that of the text itself. To take an extreme case, the laws of King Aethelbert of Kent are supposed to date from the end of the sixth century but occur only in the *Textus Roffensis,* a manuscript of the twelfth century. Because of twentieth-century work on the paleography of Old English manuscripts we can, with some confidence, date the manuscripts on the basis of script and appearance. Eighteen of the surviving manuscripts can be dated within close limits, and Ker assigns the 189 major manuscripts as follows: 2 to the eighth century, 6 to the ninth, 21 to the tenth, 133 to the eleventh, and 27 to the twelfth. The earliest poetic text, the Northumbrian version of Caedmon's *Hymn,* was copied into two Latin manuscripts of Bede's *Historia ecclesiastica* that can be dated around the middle of the eighth century. One of these manuscripts, the Leningrad Bede, has been associated with Bede's own monastery of Wearmouth and Jarrow. Among the latest texts that can be considered as Old English is the Hatton manuscript of the West Saxon Gospels, dated around 1200.

The dating of the texts is much more difficult than the dating of manuscripts and depends on internal references and sets of linguistic criteria. At the turn of the century several German scholars worked out chronologies for Old English texts and devised a series of linguistic tests for determining whether texts were early or late. Neither the chronologies nor the tests have proved entirely satisfactory. In some cases, particularly with prose texts, we can date within narrow limits. For instance, with the homilies of Aelfric and Wulfstan we know that the earliest manuscripts were written within the authors' lifetimes, and correcting hands in these early manuscripts have been identified as those of the authors themselves. With the poetry, dating is much more difficult. *Beowulf,* for example, exists in a manuscript written at the end of the tenth or beginning of the eleventh century, yet estimates of the date of composition range from the sixth century to the tenth. While there is still no consensus on the date, many scholars favor the middle of the eighth century. Generally speaking, nineteenth-century scholars preferred early dates of composition for Old English texts. They thought that the texts were more valuable as linguistic evidence if they were early and that they then could be taken as evidence for a Germanic society relatively untouched by Christianity. More recent scholars have preferred composition dates closer to the writing of the manuscripts.

From their scripts and the orthography of the texts we now know where quite a number of Old English manuscripts were written. At least twenty-seven scriptoria have been identified, and as the handwriting of vernacular manuscripts is compared

ANGLO-SAXON LITERATURE

with those of Latin manuscripts, more should come to light. The scriptoria whose productions are most numerous are those of the Winchester houses, Exeter, Worcester, Abingdon, Durham, and the two Canterbury houses, Christ Church and St. Augustine's. An an example of the information we now have, we can take the six surviving manuscripts of King Alfred's translation of Gregory's *Pastoral Care.* We know that one (Bodleian MS Hatton 20) was sent to Worcester and that a second (Corpus Christi College, Cambridge, MS 12) was also at Worcester. A third (Cambridge University Library MS Ii.2.4) was written at Exeter, and a fourth (Trinity College, Cambridge, MS R.5.22) was at Sherborne (on the strength of a sixteenth-century note). The other two manuscripts, both in the Cotton collection now in the British Library, are so damaged by fire that we cannot gather much about their origins from examining them, although one (MS Cotton Tiberius B. xi) was probably written in Winchester. Medieval library marks and annotations are an additional source of information; we know where sixty-two Old English manuscripts were lodged during the Middle Ages. Because of the distinctive annotations of one scribe now known as the "tremulous hand," we can tell that sixteen manuscripts were in the library of St. Mary's, Worcester, in the early thirteenth century.

Old English texts have been carefully studied for their dialects; and, on the basis of orthography and to a lesser extent vocabulary and syntax, four written dialects have been identified. Northumbrian is represented in its early eighth-century state by a few short poems, Caedmon's *Hymn,* Bede's *Death Song,* the *Leiden Riddle,* and the runic inscriptions on the Ruthwell Cross and the Franks Casket. Its later tenth-century form appears in three glossed texts, the Lindisfarne Gospels, the Durham Ritual, and Owun's part of the Rushworth Gospels.

Mercian is represented in its early stages by a small number of English words in the Latin glossaries now known from their present homes as the Leiden, Épinal, Erfurt, and Corpus (= Corpus Christi College, Cambridge) glossaries, and by a few glosses in the Blickling Psalter; in the ninth century by the gloss in the Vespasian Psalter and by a few charters; and in the tenth century by Farman's part of the Rushworth Gospels and the glosses to some prayers in British Library MS Royal 2.A.xx.

Kentish is represented in the ninth century by a few charters and in the tenth century by one manuscript (British Library MS Cotton Vespasian D.vi) that contains two poems, a short prose text, and a set of glosses to the Book of Proverbs. Other later manuscripts show traces of similar spelling conventions.

West Saxon, which becomes the main literary dialect, first appears in the reign of King Alfred at the end of the ninth century. The early entries in the Parker manuscript of the Anglo-Saxon Chronicle, the two earliest manuscripts of *The Pastoral Care* translation, and the Tollemache manuscript of the Orosius translation show the early state of the dialect. Its later state, at the end of the tenth century, is represented by the Corpus Christi College, Oxford, copy of the translation of the Rule of St. Benedict and by the early manuscripts of Aelfric's homilies. This written form of late West Saxon, which is first recorded in the Winchester scriptoria, becomes in the eleventh century a standard for written English throughout the country.

From the tenth and early eleventh centuries there is a group of manuscripts whose orthography shows a mixture of forms from all the attested dialects. These manuscripts include the four collections of Old English poetry, the Blickling homilies, the Old English translations of Bede's and Gregory's dialogues, the *Martyrology,* and a number of other texts. This mixture of forms can be explained by positing a long textual transmission or by assuming that they represent the work of scriptoria where orthographic standards were not rigidly imposed.

Having considered these external manifestations of Old English literature, we can turn to the literature itself. As the poetry has been the most admired and studied, we can begin with it.

POETRY

Anglo-Saxon scribes made no distinction between the ways poetry and prose were set down in the manuscripts. Despite this, and despite the fact that some Old English prose approximates the effects of the poetry, scholars have had no difficulty in distinguishing between them. The strong rhythmical patterns, the heavy alliteration, and the language characteristic of the poetry are quite distinctive.

The Anglo-Saxons left no treatises on their metrical practice in the vernacular, so that our notions of their art are based on a modern analysis of the surviving texts, particularly *Beowulf.* The first widely accepted theory of Old English meter was that of Eduard Sievers (1885), in which he distinguished five basic types of alliterative patterns. It is still used, although he himself repudiated it in his old

ANGLO-SAXON LITERATURE

age. The theory of John C. Pope (1942), which uses a musical notation, has gained acceptance, but the question of metrical practice is still hotly debated and every few years a new theory is launched.

The basic unit of Old English poetry is a four-stress alliterative line, similar to that found in the poetry of the other Germanic languages. As an example we chose the first two lines from *The Wanderer.*

× × / /× /× × / ×
Oft him anhaga are gebideð
/ ×× / × × ×× / / ×
Metudes miltse þeah þe he modcearig

The key syllable for determining alliterative patterns seems to be the first stressed syllable in the second half-line. All vowels alliterate with one another, while each consonant or consonant group alliterates only with itself. In poems such as *The Battle of Maldon* and in the Paris Psalter, the metrical rules, particularly those governing alliteration, are more relaxed than in *Beowulf.* There is also some rhyme in Old English poetry. Where this appears, as in the text in the Exeter Book called *The Riming Poem,* the half-lines rhyme with each other. Other poems such as *The Phoenix* 15–18 or *Elene* 1236–1244 have blocks of rhyme in catalogs or other rhetorical figures of the high style. Anglo-Saxon poets show many signs of their knowledge of the figures of classical rhetoric, particularly the figures of amplification. They make little use of the simile. The metaphor is their favorite figure, and they rejoice in the coining of metaphoric compounds very like the kennings of Old Norse poetry.

Most Old English poetry has survived in four manuscripts. Of these, the Junius manuscript (Bodleian MS Junius 11) and the Exeter Book (Exeter Cathedral MS 3501) are poetic anthologies; the Vercelli Book (Vercelli, Biblioteca Capitolare CXVII) and the Nowell Codex (British Library MS Cotton Vitellius A. xv) are mixtures of poetry and prose. The first poem in the Junius manuscript is illustrated, and there are spaces for illustrations after that. The Exeter Book seems to have been in the library of Exeter Cathedral ever since it was donated by Bishop Leofric in the eleventh century, but how and when the Vercelli Book got to northern Italy has been the subject of lively conjecture. All four manuscripts are available in annotated facsimiles, and their poems are available both in collected editions and in editions of individual texts. Other manuscripts that contain poetry are Corpus Christi College, Cambridge, MS 201 with *The Judgement Day II* and several other shorter poems; Paris, Bibliothèque Nationale, MS Lat. 8824 with the Paris Psalter; and British Library, MS Cotton Otho A.vi with the *Meters* of Boethius.

Most Old English poetry remains anonymous. Only three poets are known by name, Caedmon, Aldhelm, and Cynewulf. Caedmon is much the best-known of these and is regarded as the father of English poetry. He lived at the abbey of Whitby in Northumbria in the seventh century, and his story is told by Bede in the *Historia ecclesiastica* IV, 24. Bede gives a list of his poetic subjects.

> He sang about the creation of the world, the origin of the human race, and the whole history of Genesis, of the departure of Israel from Egypt and the entry into the promised land and of many other of the stories taken from the sacred Scriptures: of the incarnation, passion, and resurrection of the Lord, of His ascension into heaven, of the coming of the Holy Spirit and the teaching of the apostles. He also made songs about the terrors of future judgement, the horrors of the pains of hell, and the joys of the heavenly kingdom.

From their correspondence with the first part of this list, the poems in the Junius manuscript were early associated with Caedmon's name, although scholars now recognize that they must have come from various sources. The only text now assigned to him is the nine-line poem called Caedmon's *Hymn,* which is found in its Northumbrian form in some of the Latin manuscripts of Bede and in a later form in the Old English translation. This poem may be either Caedmon's own hymn or a later poet's response to Bede's paraphrase of the original. Here is the Northumbrian version from the Leningrad manuscript.

Nu scilun herga hefenricæs Uard,
Metudæs mehti and his modgithanc,
uerc Uuldurfadur, sue he uundra gihuæs,
eci Dryctin, or astelidæ.
He ærist scop aeldu barnum
hefen to hrofæ, halig Sceppend.
Tha middingard moncynnæs Uard,
eci Dryctin æfter tiadæ
firum foldu, Frea allmehtig.

Now let us praise the Guardian of the Kingdom of Heaven
the might of the Creator and the thought of his mind,
the work of the glorious Father, how He, the eternal Lord
established the beginning of every wonder.
For the sons of men, He, the holy Creator
first made Heaven as a roof, then the
Keeper of mankind, the eternal Lord,

God Almighty afterwards made the middle world,
the earth, for men.

William of Malmesbury says that Aldhelm, bishop of Sherborne (*d.* 709), performed secular songs to the accompaniment of a harp. His Latin poems and prose works have survived in many manuscripts, but his English compositions have not.

Cynewulf is a shadowy figure by comparison with Caedmon and Aldhelm. His name appears in runes in an acrostic at the end of four poems, *The Fates of the Apostles* and *Elene* in the Vercelli Book, and *Christ II* and *Juliana* in the Exeter Book. Although Cynewulf is a very common Anglo-Saxon name, scholars have made valiant efforts to attach the poems to a particular individual and even to add other poems to his canon. He is now thought to be an Anglican who flourished in the early part of the ninth century. The poems do not have very close stylistic affinities, and were it not for the runic signatures they might not be associated with one poet.

The Old English poetry that has had the most attention is that which deals with subjects from the Germanic heroic past. The most important text is *Beowulf*. This splendid poem of 3,182 lines tells the story of a hero of the remote past in a far country and gives an evocative picture of the societies in which he moved. The narrative is biographical and tells of three great conflicts in Beowulf's career. Woven in and out of the main story are many digressions and allusions to other early tales, some of which we know from other sources. *Beowulf* has been placed at the head of English literature and has been given the epic status of the *Iliad* or the *Chanson de Roland*. The historian, the philologist, the anthropologist, the literary critic, and the collector of folktales have all been interested in the text, and there is an extensive literature on all aspects of the poem.

Two other heroic poems have survived in fragments. *The Fight at Finnsburh* deals with an episode that is also retold at some length in *Beowulf*. The text was copied by George Hickes from a leaf in the Lambeth Palace Library and was printed by him in his *Thesaurus* (1705). The leaf had disappeared by the time that Humphrey Wanley made his catalog of manuscripts a few years later, and it has not been seen since. Hickes's text seems quite defective but gives a vivid battle scene full of action.

Ne ðis ne dagað eastan, ne her draca ne fleogeð,
ne her ðisse healle hornas ne byrnað.
Ac her forþ berað; fugelas singað,
gylleð græghama, guðwudu hlynneð,
scyld scefte oncwyð.

This is neither the dawn from the east, nor does a dragon fly here,
Nor are the gables of this hall here burning;
but here they are attacking; the birds [ravens] are singing
the gray coat cries out, the war wood clashes,
shield answers to shaft.

The relation between the fragment and the episode in *Beowulf* has been much debated.

The second fragmentary poem, *Waldere,* occurs on two separate leaves now in the Royal Library in Copenhagen. They were discovered in the 1860's and were first printed by George Stephens, the noted antiquarian and runologist. Both leaves contain speeches that, from their leisurely style, seem to come from a fairly lengthy English version of the story of Walter of Aquitaine, which we know from the Latin poem the *Waltharius* and other sources.

The last two poems that mention heroic figures are both in the Exeter Book. The longer, *Widsith,* is a monologue in which the singer tells of his adventures, the countries he has visited, and the rulers he has entertained. Although some of the persons and tribes mentioned are clearly fantastic, the information about Eormanric and the Goths in the fourth century is very detailed, and most scholars think that parts of the poem are very old. *Deor* is a Boethian lyric in which the singer names Germanic figures such as Weland and Eormanric in its exempla, and then turns to his own case. Each exemplum ends with the refrain "þæs ofereode, þisses swa mæg." ("That passed away, so may this.")

The various manuscripts of the Anglo-Saxon Chronicle contain a number of poems inserted among the regular annals. The earliest and longest of these is the entry for the year 937, *The Battle of Brunanburh.* This fine example of panegyric celebrates the victory of King Athelstan and Prince Edmund over the combined forces of the Scots and the Norse. It gives a strong sense of the national importance of the battle but is so unspecific in its details that we still do not know where the battle was fought. There are also shorter poems on the capture of the Five Boroughs (942), the coronation of King Edgar (973) and his death (975), the death of Prince Alfred (1036), and the death of King Edward the Confessor (1065).

The finest poem dealing with contemporary

ANGLO-SAXON LITERATURE

events is *The Battle of Maldon,* which celebrates Earl Byrhtnoth of Essex and his men, who fell in a battle against the Vikings in 991. The poem is 325 lines long, but both beginning and end are missing. Furthermore, the only manuscript was destroyed in the fire that damaged the Cotton Library in 1731, and it is now known only through John Elphinston's eighteenth-century transcript and the edition of Thomas Hearne. Perhaps because it is fragmentary, *The Battle of Maldon* seems very direct. The poet uses both description and speeches to give the events of the battle and the deaths of Byrhtnoth and his followers as they occur. Near the end is the well-known speech of the old retainer, Byrhtwold (ll. 312–319).

Hige sceal þe heardra, heorte þe cenre,
mod sceal þe mare, þe aure mægen lytlað.
Her lið ure ealdor eall forheawen,
god on greote. A mæg gnornian
se ðe nu fram þis wigplegan wendan þenceð.
Ic eom frod feores; fram ic ne wille,
ac ic me be healfe minum hlaforde,
be swa leofan men, licgan þence.

Thought shall be the harder, the heart the keener, courage the greater, as our strength lessens. Here lies our leader all cut down, the valiant man in the dust; always may he mourn who now thinks to turn away from this warplay. I am old, I will not go away, but I plan to lie down by the side of my lord, by the man so dearly loved.

Both the Vercelli Book and the Exeter Book contain saints' lives, long narrative poems. Those in the Vercelli Book are *Andreas* and *Elene. Andreas,* a poem of 1,722 lines, is the story of St. Andrew and his adventures in rescuing St. Matthew from the cannibalistic Mermedonians. The story also appears in a prose version in the Blickling homilies. The poem is forceful and is the closest to *Beowulf* in style and tone among the surviving Old English poems. *Elene* is the story of St. Helena, the mother of the Emperor Constantine, and of her discovery of the True Cross. The cult of the True Cross was widely celebrated in Anglo-Saxon England, and this poem is one of its most important testimonials, along with the *Dream of the Rood* in the same manuscript and the Ruthwell Cross poem.

The saints' lives in the Exeter Book are *Guthlac* and *Juliana.* The text called *Guthlac* is actually two poems about St. Guthlac, an English saint of the seventh century, who was honored in the fenlands of the East Midlands. The second poem follows the Latin version of his life by Felix of Crowland. *Juliana* is the story of the virgin martyr of Nicomedia. Although the poet follows the events of her life and death, his main interest is in the long debates between Juliana and the devil, who visits her in prison.

The Junius manuscript contains three paraphrases of Old Testament texts, all of which suffer from gaps because of losses to the manuscript. The first and longest of these, *Genesis,* follows the Bible from the Creation through the sacrifice of Isaac. Scholars now divide the text into two parts on stylistic grounds. They were first distinguished by Sievers (1875), who hypothesized that *Genesis B,* or the *Later Genesis,* was based on a lost Old Saxon original. This hypothesis was triumphantly confirmed in 1894 when fragments of an Old Saxon *Genesis* were discovered in a manuscript in the Vatican Library. *Genesis B* deals with the fall of the angels and the temptation in the Garden of Eden in a way that strikingly anticipates Milton's treatment of the subject in *Paradise Lost.* While *Genesis A* is sober and restrained in its handling of Biblical narrative, *Genesis B* is more expansive and shows lively touches of characterization in its speeches. Satan says (ll. 364–376),

þæt me is sorga mæst,
þæt Adam sceal, þe wæs of eorðan geworht,
minne stronglican stol behealdan,
wesan him on wynne, and we þis wite þolien,
hearm on þisse helle. Wa la, ahte ic minra handa geweald
and moste ane tid ute weorðan,
wesan ane winterstunde, þonne ic mid þys werode—
Ac licgað me ymbe irenbenda,
rideð racentan sal. Ic eom ricesleas;
habbað me swa hearde helle clommas
fæste befangen. Her is fyr micel
ufan and neoðone. Ic a ne geseah
laðran landscipe.

It is the greatest of sorrows to me that Adam,
who was made from earth, shall hold my mighty
throne, dwell in joy, and we suffer this torment,
affliction in this hell! Alas! If I had the
strength of my hands and could be out for a time,
for a winter hour, then I with this troop . . .
But around me lie ironbonds, the chains and
fetters ride me. I am powerless, the hard bonds
of hell have seized me so closely. Here is a
great fire above and below. I never have seen a
more hateful landscape.

Exodus deals mostly with the Children of Israel and their passage out of Egypt but also has references to other biblical events. It is a difficult poem in the high style, full of daring images and metaphors.

ANGLO-SAXON LITERATURE

Daniel is in some ways the most attractive of these biblical poems. It deals briefly with the events of the Book of Daniel down to Belshazzar's feast. At its center are the two beautiful lyrics "Song of the Three Children" and "Song of Azarias." The latter also appears in the Exeter Book after *Guthlac.*

The last of the biblical narratives is *Judith,* which occurs in a fragmentary state in the Nowell Codex just after *Beowulf.* It is a spirited retelling of the story of Judith, quite unlike *Beowulf* in style.

Old English poetry has no paraphrases of New Testament materials to match the Old Saxon *Heliand.* Perhaps as the *Heliand* circulated in England and on the Continent, there was no need.

The other part of the Bible to be paraphrased in Old English verse is the Psalter. Metrical versions of Psalms 51 to 150 are preserved in the Paris Psalter where they follow a prose version of the first fifty psalms. We can suppose that there was once a complete metrical psalter, as bits of the earlier psalms are quoted in a liturgical text called *The Benedictine Office.* There is also an independent paraphrase of Psalm 50 called the *Kentish Psalm.*

In addition to the Biblical paraphrases, there are a number of religious poems that have narrative elements but that are mainly lyrical or meditative in effect. Some of these have liturgical origins, while others are homiletic. One of the most striking sequences of these poems is found at the beginning of the Exeter Book, under the title *Christ.* There are three main sections: *Christ I* is a group of Advent lyrics, based on a series of antiphons; *Christ II,* which concludes with the runic Cynewulf signature, is an Ascension poem based on a homily of Gregory; *Christ III* is a set of visual meditations on the Last Judgment. The three sections are linked by theme and imagery, with the Ascension poem acting as a bridge passage between the Advent lyrics and the Last Judgment. The Last Judgment is a favorite theme in Old English poetry and is the subject of another short poem in the Exeter Book and of a translation and paraphrase of Bede's *De die judicii* in Corpus Christi College, Cambridge, MS 201.

Perhaps the most beautiful of all Old English poems is the *Dream of the Rood* in the Vercelli Book. This meditation on the cross is in the form of a dream vision. The cross is personified and speaks to the dreamer about the crucifixion and the need for seeking the cross as a means of intercession (ll. 50–56).

Feala ic on þam beorge   gebiden hæbbe
wraðra wyrda.   Geseah ic weruda god
þearle þenian.   þystro hæfdon
bewrigen mid wolcnum   wealdendes hræw,
scirne sciman,   sceadu forðeode,
wann under wolcnum.   Weop eal gesceaft,
cwiðdon cyninges fyll.   Crist wæs on rode.

I endured much hardship on that hill. I saw
the God of hosts stretched out cruelly. Darkness
had covered with clouds the body of the Lord,
the bright radiance. A shadow went forth, dark
under the heavens. All creation wept, mourned
the death of the king. Christ was on the cross.

The dreamer resolves to put his trust in the cross, and the poem ends with an ecstatic vision of the Kingdom of Heaven, where the dreamer hopes to join his friends. A shorter, but closely related poem, consisting of lines spoken by the cross itself, is carved in runes on the sides of a Northumbrian standing cross now at Ruthwell in Dumfriesshire.

There are several religious debate poems in Old English, besides *Juliana.* Of these the longest is *Christ and Satan,* a poem added at the end of the Junius manuscript by several later hands. Although the poem deals with the confrontation between Christ and Satan during the forty days in the wilderness, its interest is in the conflict of the speeches rather than the narrative. Another debate poem is the difficult *Solomon and Saturn,* in which Saturn is portrayed as a pagan magician contesting with the wise king. The text survives in two fragments, one copied into the margins of the Old English translation of Bede. The address of the Soul to the Body is the subject of two closely related poems in the Exeter Book and the Vercelli Book. This address is a favorite theme in Old English homiletic literature.

Several Old English poems are adaptations of late classical philosophical texts. The longest of these is the metrical translation of the meters from Boethius' *Consolation of Philosophy* in the tenth-century Cotton manuscript. In the later Bodley manuscript the meters are rendered in Old English prose. Another similar adaptation is *The Phoenix* in the Exeter Book. This is an expansion and allegorization of the *De ave phoenice* by Lactantius. The poem ends with a macaronic passage in which Old English and Latin half-lines are joined. Close to *The Phoenix* in the Exeter Book are the short poems *The Panther, The Whale,* and a fragmentary poem called *The Partridge.* They are derived from the Latin *physiologus* or bestiary tradition.

In the Exeter Book there are a number of short poems that have recently been described as wisdom

ANGLO-SAXON LITERATURE

poetry. They are lyric or sententious and by means of direct exposition and exempla deal with such Boethian and penitential themes as the variability of human fortune and the transitoriness of human life. The best known of these poems are *The Wanderer* and *The Seafarer.* These two monologues, with their somber images of life as an exile or as a sea voyage redeemed only by the hope of joy in heaven, have come to be seen as characteristic of Old English literature. Such poems as *Wulf and Eadwacer, The Wife's Lament,* and *The Husband's Message* are much more personal in tone, and the events of which they speak are very strongly felt. The first two poems seem to be spoken by women.

The Exeter Book ends with a collection of ninety-five riddles. These are similar to the Latin riddles of Symphosius, Aldhelm, and Tatwine, and a few of them are translations of Latin texts. The answers to the Old English riddles are not supplied, and a number of them are still being debated. Some give their answers in runic acrostics; others invite a number of different answers, some of them obscene.

Among the many charms written in the flyleaves and blank spaces of Old English manuscripts are twelve written in verse. These are remedies against a dwarf, a sudden stitch, loss of cattle, delayed birth, swarms of bees, wens, and so on. The longest of these is the mysterious *Nine Herbs Charm,* which seems pagan in its incantations.

The Exeter Book also contains a collection of maxims or gnomes. These one- and two-line proverbs and observations are linked to one another by alliteration, theme, and a number of other structural devices. A similar, shorter collection appears in the Cotton MS, which contains the *Menologium.*

The *Menologium* is one of a whole group of mnemonic poems whose purpose seems to be to keep lists and sequences of various things straight. Other similar poems are *The Fates of the Apostles* in the Vercelli Book, *The Rune Poem, The Seasons for Fasting,* and the *Instructions for Christians.*

Finally there are a number of short occasional poems. Besides the verses from the Psalms, *The Benedictine Office* contains verse translations of the Gloria, the Lord's Prayer, and the Creed, and there are extant a number of other short prayers and hymns, proverbs, and dedicatory poems. King Alfred's translation of *The Pastoral Care* has a metrical preface and epilogue, and Bishop Waerferth of Winchester's translation of Gregory's *Dialogues* has a metrical preface. Even inscriptions can be in verse as they are on two sides of the Franks Casket, on the Brussels Cross, and on the Sutton Hoo disk brooch.

PROSE

The amount of Old English prose that has survived is much greater than that of the poetry. It first appears in the ninth century and continues to be written and copied to the end of the twelfth century, varying greatly in kind and quality. Much of it is simple documentary or expository prose, often translated directly from Latin. At its most polished in the prose homilies and saints' lives, we find examples of well-sustained narrative, of clearly presented theological reasoning, and of the skillful use of rhetorical figures. In the rhythmical and alliterative prose styles developed by two homilists, Aelfric, abbot of Eynsham, and Wulfstan II, archbishop of York, Old English literature shows a precocity not found in other vernacular literatures for several centuries. Both men were products of the great Benedictine reform of the second half of the tenth century. Aelfric was educated at Winchester and served at Cerne Abbas in Dorset before becoming abbot of Eynsham. He was a pupil of the celebrated Abbot Aethelwold, who is now given credit for the Old English translation of the Benedictine Rule. Wulfstan's style is particularly distinctive, and modern scholars have detected his rhythms in the law codes of Ethelred II and Cnut, in several charters, and even in two of the poems in the Anglo-Saxon Chronicle.

While most Old English poems survive only in one copy, a number of the prose texts have been preserved in many. If we can judge fairly by what has survived, the works of Aelfric were the most popular. Some of his Catholic homilies appear in as many as seventeen manuscripts, while his grammar appears in fifteen. By the eleventh century, many of the short Old English prose texts had already been collected into large composite manuscripts. Some examples of these are Cambridge University Library MS Gg 3.28, the collection of Aelfric's two series of Catholic homilies together with several of his other works, and British Library MS Cotton Tiberius A.III, a collection of monastic rules that also contains homilies and many other kinds of texts. Individual texts are found in a number of quite different collections. For instance, one anonymous homily for Tuesday in Rogationtide turns up in the Blickling homilies manuscript; the Vercelli Book; Corpus Christi College, Cambridge, MS 302, one of the large homiliaries containing many of Aelfric's homilies; two smaller eleventh-century collections, Corpus Christi College, Cambridge, MS 421 and Bodleian MS Junius 85 and 86; and finally in Bodleian MS Bodley 343, a late twelfth-century collection.

Another monk who wrote in English at much the

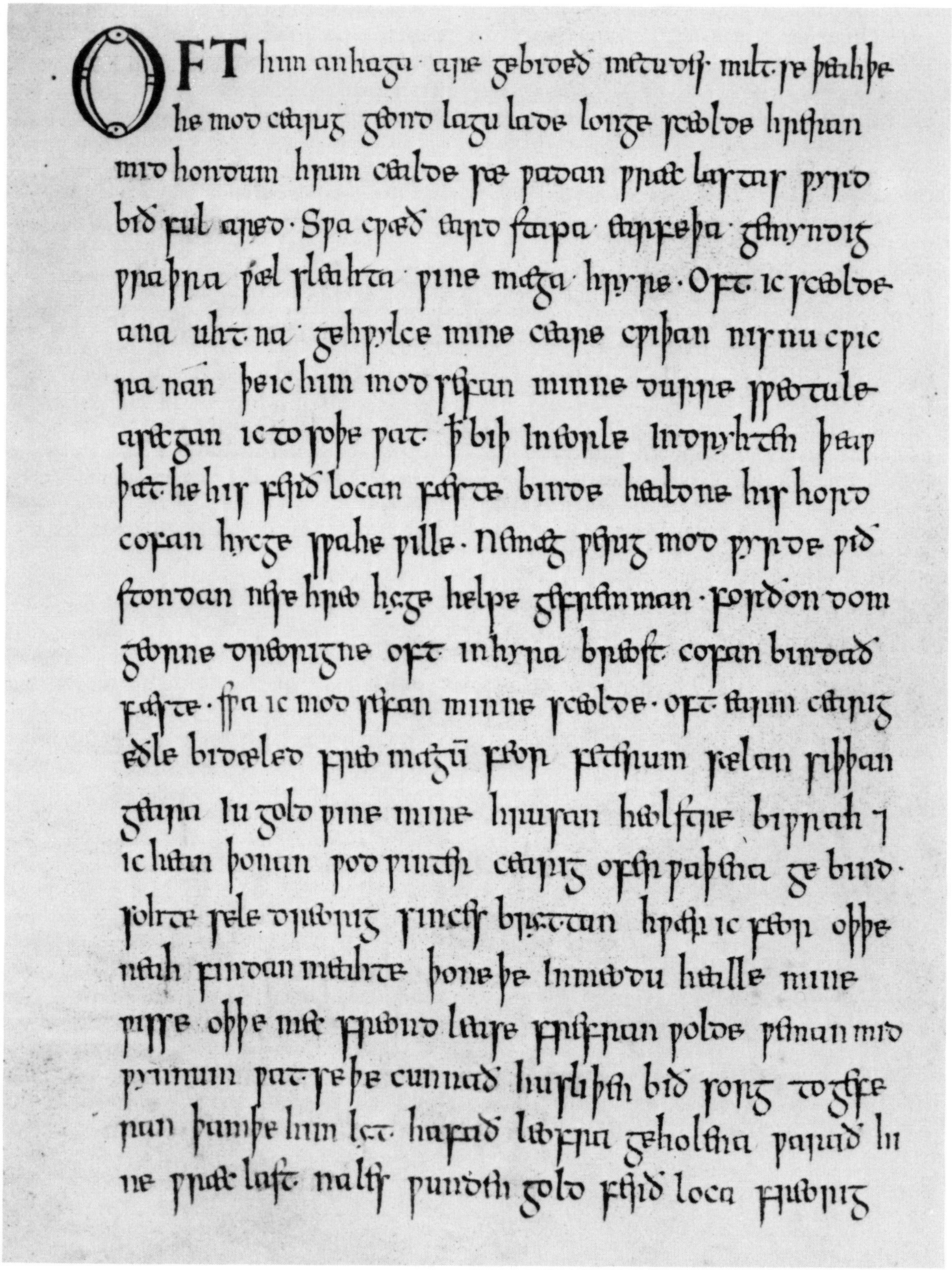

The Exeter Book. fol. 76b. *The Wanderer,* lines 1–33, taken from Raymond W. Chambers, et al., *The Exeter Book of Old English Poetry* (1933).

ANGLO-SAXON LITERATURE

Edition from Dorothy Whitelock, *Sweets' Anglo-Saxon Reader* (1967), 160–161:

Oft him anhaga are gebideð,
Metudes miltse, þeah þe he modcearig
geond lagulade longe sceolde
hreran mid hondum hrimcealde sæ,
wadan wræclastas: wyrd bið ful aræd.
Swa cwæð eardstapa earfeþa gemyndig,
wraþra wælsleahta, winemæga hryre:
"Oft ic sceolde ana uhtna gehwylce
mine ceare cwiþan. Nis nu cwicra nan,
þe ic him modsefan minne durre
sweotule asecgan. Ic to soþe wat
þæt biþ in eorle indryhten þeaw,
þæt he his ferðlocan fæste binde,
healde his hordcofan, hycge swa he wille.
Ne mæg werigmod wyrde wiðstondan,
ne se hreo hyge helpe gefremman.
For ðon domgeorne dreorigne oft
in hyra breostcofan bindað fæste;
swa ic modsefan minne sceolde,
oft earmcearig eðle bidæled,
freomægum feor, feterum sælan,
siþþan geara iu goldwine minne
hrusan heolster biwrah and ic hean þonan
wod wintercearig ofer waþema gebind,
sohte sele dreorig sinces bryttan,
hwær ic feor oþþe neah findan meahte
þone þe in meoduhealle [min] mine wisse,
oþþe mec freondleasne frefran wolde,
weman mid wynnum. Wat se þe cunnað
hu sliþen bið sorg to geferan
þam þe him lyt hafað leofra geholena:
warað hine wræclast, nales wunden gold,
ferðloca freorig, nalæs foldan blæd;

Transliteration:

Oft him anhaga are gebideð metudes miltse þeah þe he mod cearig geond lagu lade longe sceolde hreran mid hondum hrim cealde sæ wadan wræc lastas wyrd bið ful aręd. Swa cwæð eard stapa . earfeþa . gemyndig wraþra wæl sleahta . wine mæga hryre. Oft ic sceolde ana uhtna gehwylce mine ceare cwiþan nis nu cwic ra nán þe ic him modsefan minne durre sweotule asecgan ic to soþe wat þ biþ in eorle indryhten þeaw þæt he his ferð locan fæste binde healdne his hord cofan hycge swa he wille. Ne mæg werig mod wyrde wið stondan ne se hreo hyge helpe gefremman. Forðon dom georne dreorigne oft in hyra breost cofan bindað fæste. swa ic mod sefan minne sceolde . oft earm cearig eðle bidæled freo mægum feor feterum sælan siþþan geara iu goldwine mine hrusan heolstre biwrah and ic hean þonan wod winter cearig ofer waþena gebind. sohte sele dreorig sinces bryttan hwær ic feor oþþe neah findan meahte þone þe in meodu healle mine wisse oþþe mec freondlease frefran wolde weman mid wynnum wat se þe cunnað hu sliþen bið sorg to gefe ran þam þe him lyt hafað leofra geholena warað hi ne wræclast nales wunden gold ferð loca freorig [nalæs foldan blæd.]

Translation:

Often the lonely man prays for the favor,
the mercy of God, though sad at heart
for a long time on the sea ways he must
stir with his hands the ice-cold sea,
walk paths of exile. Man's lot is settled.
So said the wanderer, remembering hardships,
hateful killings, the fall of his kinsmen.
Often alone I must speak of my cares
at the dawn of each day. Now there is no one alive
to whom I can clearly tell
my heart thoughts. I know in truth
that it is in a man a noble custom
to bind fast his spirit
and hold in his heart, think as he will.
The weary mind cannot withstand fate
nor resentful thoughts give help.
And so often those who want glory bind
sadness fast in their hearts
as I often troubled must bind my heart with fetters,
deprived of my home, far from my kinsmen,
since long ago the darkness of earth
covered my generous lord, and I went sadly from there,
desolate as winter over the frozen waves.
Sad from the loss of my hall I looked for
a giver of treasure, where far or near
I could find someone in a meadhall
who would know my thoughts, or would
comfort me, the friendless one,
attract me with happiness. He who has been through it
knows how cruel sorrow is as a companion,
to the one who has few close friends.
Exile obsesses him, not twisted gold;
the frozen heart, not the fruit of the earth.

ANGLO-SAXON LITERATURE

same time as Aelfric and Wulfstan was Byrhtferth of Ramsey, whose *Handboc,* or *Manual,* is a curious mixture of the study of computus and rhetoric.

The most widely known writer of Old English prose is King Alfred, who ruled the West Saxons from 871 to 899. He gives his reasons for translating necessary books from Latin and his method of translation in the celebrated preface to his translation of Gregory's *Pastoral Care.* Most of the early Old English translations of Latin texts have been traditionally associated with Alfred's name, but one, the translation of Gregory's *Dialogues,* has always been assigned to Waerferth.

One of the earliest English texts in continuous prose is the *Martyrology.* A set of short notices of saints and martyrs arranged according to their feasts and anniversaries in the church calendar, this text has survived in six fragments ranging from the ninth to the eleventh centuries. Fortunately, among them we have a nearly complete text for the whole year. These notices are drawn from many sources, and they contain much curious and interesting information. Scholars now think that the *Martyrology* was compiled by a ninth-century Mercian author.

The earliest manuscripts of Alfred's translation of *The Pastoral Care* date from his reign in the last decade of the ninth century. *The Pastoral Care* is a manual for parish priests on the conduct of their duties. The other translations in this group are equally useful. They include the *Dialogues,* a collection of exempla that can be used in sermons. Many of the stories from the *Dialogues* turn up in later Old English homilies by Aelfric and others. The *History of the World* by Orosius is a historical companion piece for St. Augustine's *City of God.* It opens with a description of the geography of the known world to which Alfred has added a description of the tribes of Germany and a well-known account of the Scandinavian journeys of two travelers named Ohthere and Wulfstan. The other three translations are *The Consolation of Philosophy* of Boethius, *The Soliloquies* of St. Augustine, and the *Ecclesiastical History of the English People* by Bede. Although all these works except Gregory's *Dialogues* are traditionally associated with Alfred, they are so varied in style and language that they were probably translated by different men and even at different periods. All of them are really adaptations rather than strict translations, and the writers freely abridge or expand the text.

Our oldest copy of the Anglo-Saxon Chronicle, the Parker Chronicle (Corpus Christi College, Cambridge, MS 173), was first kept in Alfred's reign. This copy was started at Winchester and later moved to Canterbury. Chronicles kept at Worcester (British Library MS Cotton Tiberius B. IV), Abingdon (British Library MS Cotton Tiberius B. I and A. VI), and Peterborough (Bodleian Library MS Laud Misc. 636) have also survived. All have a common beginning but add different materials as they were kept in different places in the tenth and eleventh centuries. Most of the entries for early years are brief, but there is a long entry for the year 755 (the story of Cynewulf and Cyneheard) and for the years of Alfred's reign. Most of the chronicles end in the eleventh century, but the one at Peterborough was started and kept in the twelfth century. It was copied from a Canterbury chronicle after a fire in 1116 and was continued until 1154.

There are more homilies than any other kind of Old English prose. How and where they were used in church services has been the subject of recent investigation. Annotations made in them show that they were also used as reading texts.

The oldest collections of homilies are the Blickling homilies (Princeton University Library) and the prose homilies in the Vercelli Book. Both collections date from the late tenth century and differ from later works in style and in their more extensive use of apocryphal materials.

The greatest and most prolific writer of homilies in Anglo-Saxon times was Aelfric of Eynsham. His earliest works are the two great series of Catholic homilies, each containing more than forty sermons for particular days in the church year. Later in his career he expanded these series, adding further pieces in his alliterative and rhythmical style. In many of Aelfric's homilies he begins with the Bible reading for the particular day and then goes on to explain this text and expand on it. His sources are many. He seems to have known the homilies of Augustine, Gregory, and Caesarius of Arles through the Carolingian homiliaries such as those of Paul the Deacon and Haymo of Auxerre. His use of earlier materials is extremely interesting and various.

Aelfric also wrote exhortatory sermons such as *De falsis deis,* a warning against the worship of the pagan gods, and *De septiformi spiritu.* Both these sermons were reworked and adapted by Archbishop Wulfstan in his own manner. Wulfstan was a great master of the high style. His abrupt two-stress alliterative phrases, building to great heights of impassioned invective, are in sharp contrast with the more relaxed four-stress phrases of Aelfric. Many of Wulfstan's sermons convey the need for repentance and

ANGLO-SAXON LITERATURE

the terrors of the Last Judgment. His best-known work is *Sermo ad Anglos,* in which he castigates the English and blames their sins for the Viking invasions.

Scribes continued to copy and adapt the homilies of Aelfric until well into the thirteenth century. The custom of adapting earlier materials to new homilies is often very interesting. An adapter would fashion a new homily out of sections from three or four older ones. Examples of this can be seen in the homilies in Lambeth Palace Library MS 489, arts. 5–6.

Aelfric included some lives of the saints in the two series of Catholic homilies. He also compiled a cycle of saints' lives to be read on the particular saint's day. This cycle, which is a kind of extension of the martyrology, was his first work in an alliterative style. In the earliest manuscript of the lives of the saints, British Library MS Cotton Julius E. VII, someone has added four additional lives, those of the Seven Sleepers of Ephesus, St. Mary of Egypt, St. Eustace, and St. Euphrosyne. The author of these pieces in each case draws on the traditions of late classical romance in his work and writes with great clarity and sensitivity. There are also many other anonymous saints' lives. Among the most interesting of these are the prose life of St. Guthlac that appears in the Vercelli Book and in one other manuscript, the lives of St. Margaret with their demon called Ruffus, and the life of St. Chad (Ceadda), which exists only in a twelfth-century copy but seems to go back to much earlier Mercian traditions.

Apart from the saints' lives that draw on late classical romance traditions, only one example of a secular romance has survived. This is a fragmentary translation of *Apollonius of Tyre,* which appears in an eleventh-century manuscript (Corpus Christi College, Cambridge, MS 201). It is a competent and straightforward translation of the Latin text.

Another literary form that Aelfric practiced was the pastoral letter. He wrote a number of these on various subjects, including two for Wulfstan. Some of these letters were later adapted as homilies; and others, such as the letters to Sigeweard and Aethelweard, became prefaces to the biblical translations.

There are quite a number of Old English translations of various parts of the Bible. The first six books of the Bible, the Hexateuch, are translated or abridged, and portions of this work have been assigned to Aelfric on stylistic grounds. They exist in several manuscripts, one of which, British Library MS Cotton Claudius B. IV, is splendidly illustrated. Aelfric also made epitomes of a number of books of the Old Testament in his homilies; he treated Chronicles, Kings, Job, Esther, Judith, and Maccabees in this way. There are also glosses and translations of passages from Proverbs, Wisdom, and Ecclesiasticus in the homilies, and in the Paris Psalter the prose translation of Psalms 1 to 50.

Although there are references to most books of the New Testament in the Old English homilies, the actual translation is limited to the Gospels. The West Saxon version of the Gospels probably goes back to an interlinear gloss such as that found in the Lindisfarne or Rushworth Gospels. There are six major manuscripts of the West Saxon Gospels dating from the eleventh and twelfth centuries.

There are also translations or reworkings in homiletic form of a number of the apocryphal New Testament texts. These were very popular in Anglo-Saxon England, although scholars of the Benedictine reform such as Aelfric discouraged their use. The most popular of all was the Gospel of Nicodemus, which appears in one manuscript (Cambridge University Library MS Ii.2.11) as though it were a fifth gospel. Other apocryphal gospels in translation are the *Gospel of Pseudo-Matthew, Vindicta salvatoris, Vision of St. Paul,* and *Apocalypse of Thomas.*

Besides the essential works translated by King Alfred and his circle, there are a number of other treatises and tracts that must have been used in schools. Aelfric wrote a *Latin* grammar and glossary in Old English that has survived in many manuscripts. It was also used later by students whose primary language was French, because in several manuscripts the paradigms are also glossed in Old French. The study of language and rhetoric is also one of the subjects of Byrhtferth's *Manual.* Byrhtferth's other concern is computus, the practical application of arithmetic to the regulation of the calendar. A great many other notes and diagrams on computistic matters have also come down to us. These are rules for finding movable feasts and fast days, and tables for calculating such variables as the tides and the age of the moon. Aelfric also wrote several elementary scientific treatises, two of which, his *Hexameron* and the *Interrogationes Sigewulfi in Genesin,* arose from commentaries on the story of the Creation. The *De temporibus anni* draws on Bede's scientific work as well.

The additions to the geographical description of the world in the Orosius translation show that the Anglo-Saxons had an interest in the world about them. There are several other signs of this. One manuscript, British Library, Cotton Tiberius B. V, con-

ANGLO-SAXON LITERATURE

tains a remarkable map of the world, along with a finely illustrated text of *The Wonders of the East.* This work and *Alexander's Letter to Aristotle* also occur in the Nowell Codex along with *Beowulf.* Some scholars have speculated that this manuscript may have been a collection of materials on exotic places and monsters.

Perhaps the most remarkable group of these scientific texts is the medical literature. The text that has survived in the most copies is the translation of the *Herbarium* of Pseudo-Apuleius, which is usually found together with a second work, the *Medicina de Quadrupedibus.* In the *Herbarium,* which is strikingly illustrated in one manuscript, British Library, Cotton Vitellius C. III, the materials are arranged by plants, and various diseases and their cures are found under them. A second collection of texts is *Bald's Leechbook,* the earliest manuscript of which dates from the mid tenth century. While many of the cures in it are herbal, it also contains directions for several surgical procedures. A third collection, the *Lacnunga,* occurs in one of the manuscripts of the *Herbarium.* In it there is greater reliance on charms, incantations, and white magic than in the other two collections. In 1975 a leaf of medical recipes turned up in the library of the Catholic University of Louvain. It is somewhat earlier than any of the other surviving manuscripts and contains materials found in both *Bald's Leechbook* and the *Lacnunga.*

The Anglo-Saxon laws are a large and important group of texts. Already in the eleventh and twelfth centuries they were being gathered into collections of which the eleventh-century manuscript British Library, Cotton Nero A. I, and the twelfth-century *Textus Roffensis* are the most important. They include the laws of the kings, beginning with those of Aethelbert of Kent and ending with those of Cnut. Beginning in the twelfth century, these same laws were translated into Latin. There are also a number of legal texts that have to do with particular situations, cases, or parts of the country. One of the most interesting of these is *Gerefa,* which sets out the duties of a reeve on a large estate. Besides the civil laws, there are a number of texts dealing with clerical matters. These include the *Institutes of Polity* and the *Canons of Edgar,* now both attributed to Wulfstan, and a large number of penitential texts including the *Penitential* and *Confessional* of Pseudo-Egbert.

Rules for monks and canons were often translated into Old English and presented in bilingual manuscripts in which the text is given first in Latin and then in English. The translation of the Benedictine Rule and the enlarged *Rule of Chrodegang,* together with portions of the *Regularis concordia* and the *Capitula* of Theodulf of Orleans, have survived.

One of the largest bodies of vernacular texts is found among the legal documents collected and preserved by religious houses. These include texts of many kinds; charters or notices of donations by kings, members of the nobility, and bishops; wills; manumissions, or documents of emancipation; lists of books and relics; court cases; and guild rules. These are found as single charters; as items copied on the flyleaves and blank spaces of Gospels, Psalters, and other books that were certain of preservation; and as cartularies, or large collections of documents associated with certain religious institutions.

By the eleventh century most charters were in Old English. One of the largest collections of vernacular documents is the group of writs issued by Edward the Confessor in connection with the establishment of Westminster Abbey. Many charters are bilingual, and even if the text is in Latin, the boundaries of the land described are usually in Old English.

Wills were almost always written in Old English, as were the manumissions. These documents are invaluable for the study of administrative and social history in Anglo-Saxon times, but they are also of literary interest for their use of rhetorical figures and formulas. In the records of court cases the narratives can be quite detailed and effective in their sober language. Many Old English charters and legal documents are preserved in cartularies from the later Middle Ages, but two of the largest—*Textus Roffensis* and Heming's *Cartulary* (British Library MS Cotton Tiberius A. XIII)—come from the twelfth century.

OLD ENGLISH SCHOLARSHIP

Old English literature did not cease to be read or used with the Norman Conquest. Vernacular manuscripts continued to be preserved in monastic and cathedral libraries, and if some of them seemed old and useless to thirteenth- and fourteenth-century cataloguers, others were certainly used and annotated.

With the coming of the Reformation and the disruption of the monastic libraries, we find a new kind of interest in Anglo-Saxon manuscripts. These were collected by such scholars and antiquarians as Laurence Nowell, probably dean of Lichfield, Matthew Parker, archbishop of Canterbury, and Sir Robert Bruce Cotton. Humfrey Wanley described all the manuscripts known to him in the catalog included in George Hickes's *Thesaurus.* His work remained

 ANGLO-SAXON LITERATURE

the standard authority for over 250 years and is still the main source of information for those manuscripts that have since disappeared.

Beginning with Nowell, scholars have compiled glossaries and dictionaries. The first published dictionary was William Somner's *Dictionarium Saxonico-Latino-Anglicum* (1659). The chief Anglo-Saxon lexicographer of the nineteenth century was Joseph Bosworth, who produced his first dictionary in 1838 and continued to revise and enlarge it throughout his life. His final dictionary was completed by Thomas Northcote Toller, who produced *An Anglo-Saxon Dictionary* in 1898 with a supplement in 1921; their work was further supplemented by Alistair Campbell in 1972. Dictionaries and concordances to the poetry, an etymological dictionary, and several student dictionaries are also available.

The tradition of Old English grammars also goes back to the seventeenth century. The earliest separate grammar, by George Hickes (1689), was followed by Hickes's larger grammar in the *Thesaurus* (1705) and by that of Elizabeth Elstob (1715). The standard reference grammar is now that of Alistair Campbell (1959).

William Lambarde, the keeper of the records in the Tower of London, brought out some of the Anglo-Saxon laws in his *Archaionomia* (1568); Abraham Whelock edited the Old English Bede and the Anglo-Saxon Chronicle for the first time in 1643; and Franciscus Junius edited the first collection of Old English poetry (the Caedmon manuscript) in 1655.

In the nineteenth century, interest in Anglo-Saxon studies was first revived on the Continent and was part of the new study of Teutonic antiquities and the comparative study of the Germanic languages. The first edition of *Beowulf* (1815) was produced by Grímr Jónsson Thorkelin. Old English became part of the regular program in universities, and much effort went into the production of texts and textual commentary. Since World War II, there has been a greater interest in the manuscripts themselves, aided by the paleographical work of Neil Ker, whose *Catalogue of Manuscripts Containing Anglo-Saxon* (1957) was a milestone in Anglo-Saxon studies, and by publication of the series *Early English Manuscripts in Facsimile* (1951–). By 1980 nearly all the surviving Old English texts were in print.

There has also been a movement to consider Old English texts as literature and as a subject for literary criticism. Some of the impetus for this has come from J. R. R. Tolkien's celebrated lecture *Beowulf: The Monsters and the Critics* (1936). In comparative work, scholars have turned from looking for Germanic sources and analogues for Old English literature and instead are concentrating on the connections between Anglo-Saxon culture and the Latin Middle Ages.

Since the middle of the nineteenth century, Old English literature has become known to a wider public through being taught in the universities and through translations. Some of the best-known translations are Alfred, Lord Tennyson's version of *The Battle of Brunanburh,* William Morris' translation of *Beowulf,* and Ezra Pound's translation of *The Seafarer.* The influence of Old English poetry on modern poets can be seen in the meters and images of Gerard Manley Hopkins, T. S. Eliot, Pound, and W. H. Auden. The subject matter and vocabulary of the heroic poetry have left their marks on Tolkien's *The Hobbit* (1937) and *The Lord of the Rings* (1954–1955), John Gardner's *Grendel* (1971), and on many other stories for children and adults.

BIBLIOGRAPHY

The bibliography is very selective; for more detailed listings see Greenfield and Robinson (1979), Robinson (1970), Ker (1957), and the annual bibliographies in *Anglo-Saxon England* and the *Old English Newsletter.*

Eleanor N. Adams, *Old English Scholarship in England From 1566–1800* (1917); Christopher F. Battiscombe, ed., *The Relics of Saint Cuthbert* (1956); Jess B. Bessinger, Jr., and Philip H. Smith, Jr., *A Concordance to the Anglo-Saxon Poetic Records* (1978); Walter de G. Birch, ed., *Cartularium saxonicum,* 4 vols. (1885–1899); Joseph Bosworth, *An Anglo-Saxon Dictionary,* edited by Thomas N. Toller (1898), with *Supplement* by Toller (1921) and *Enlarged Addenda and Corrigenda* by Alistair Campbell (1972); Rupert Bruce-Mitford, et al., *The Sutton Hoo Ship-Burial,* I, *Excavations, Background, the Ship, Dating and Inventory* (1975); Angus Cameron, "A List of Old English Texts," in Roberta Frank and Angus Cameron, eds., *A Plan for the Dictionary of Old English* (1973); Alistair Campbell, *Old English Grammar* (1959); Raymond W. Chambers, Max Förster, and Robin Flower, *The Exeter Book of Old English Poetry* (1933); Peter Clemoes, ed., *Anglo-Saxon England,* (1972–); Thomas Oswald Cockayne, ed., *Leechdoms, Wortcunning and Starcraft of Early England,* 3 vols. (1864–1866); Bertram Colgrave, Kemp Malone, Knud Schibsbye, et al., eds., *Early English Manuscripts in Facsimile,* 19 vols. (1951–); William G. Collingwood, *Northumbrian Crosses of the Pre-Norman Age* (1927); Donald K. Fry, *Beowulf and the Fight at Finnsburh: A Bibliography* (1969); John C. Gardner, *Grendel* (1971); Stanley B. Greenfield, *A Critical History of Old*

English Literature (1965); Stanley B. Greenfield and Fred C. Robinson, *Bibliography of Publications in Old English Literature From the Beginning Through 1972* (1979); Christian M. W. Grein and Ferdinand Holthausen, *Sprachschatz der angelsächsischen Dichter,* Johann J. Köhler, ed. (1912); Christian M. W. Grein, Richard P. Wülker, and Hans Hecht, eds., *Bibliothek der angelsächsischen Prosa,* 13 vols. (1872–1933); John R. Clark Hall, *A Concise Anglo-Saxon Dictionary,* 4th ed. with supp. by Herbert D. Meritt (1960); Ferdinand Holthausen, *Altenglisches etymologisches Wörterbuch,* 2nd ed. (1963); Neil R. Ker, *Catalogue of Manuscripts Containing Anglo-Saxon* (1957); and "A Supplement to *Catalogue of Manuscripts Containing Anglo-Saxon,*" in *Anglo-Saxon England,* 5 (1976); Frederich Klaeber, ed., *Beowulf and the Fight at Finnsburg,* 3rd ed., with 1st and 2nd supps. (1950).

George P. Krapp and Elliott Van Kirk Dobbie, eds., *The Anglo-Saxon Poetic Records,* 6 vols. (1931–1953); Felix Liebermann, ed., *Die Gesetze der Angelsachsen,* 3 vols. (1903–1916); Kemp Malone, *The Nowell Codex,* Early English Manuscripts in Facsimile, no. 12 (1963); Hertha Marquardt, *Bibliographie der Runeninschriften nach Fundorten:* I, *Die Runeninschriften der Britischen Inseln* (1961); Bruce Mitchell, *A Guide to Old English,* 2nd ed. (1968); Arthur S. Napier, ed., *Wulfstan* (1883; repr. 1967); Elisabeth Okasha, *Handlist of Anglo-Saxon Non-runic Inscriptions* (1971); *Old English Newsletter* (1967–); Charles Plummer, ed., *Two of the Saxon Chronicles Parallel,* 2 vols. (1892–1899, repr. 1952); John C. Pope, *The Rhythm of Beowulf,* rev. ed. (1966); John C. Pope, ed., *Homilies of Aelfric: A Supplementary Collection,* 2 vols. (1967–1968); Randolph Quirk and Charles L. Wrenn, *An Old English Grammar,* 2nd ed. (1958); Agnes J. Robertson, ed., *Anglo-Saxon Charters,* 2nd ed. (1956); Fred C. Robinson, *Old English Literature: A Select Bibliography* (1970); Peter H. Sawyer, *Anglo-Saxon Charters: An Annotated List and Bibliography* (1968); Kenneth Sisam, *Studies in the History of Old English Literature* (1953); Walter W. Skeat, ed., *The [Four] Gospel ... in Anglo-Saxon, Northumbrian and Old Mercian Versions,* 4 vols. (1871–1887); and *Aelfric's Lives of Saints,* 4 vols. (1881–1900); Eric G. Stanley, ed., *Continuations and Beginnings: Studies in Old English Literature* (1966); Henry Sweet, *King Alfred's West-Saxon Vȩrsion of Gregory's Pastoral Care,* 2 vols. (1871–1872); Henry Sweet, ed., *Anglo-Saxon Reader,* 15th ed., rev. by Dorothy Whitelock (1967); Elżbieta Temple, *Anglo-Saxon Manuscripts 900–1066* (1976); Benjamin Thorpe, ed., *The Homilies of the Anglo-Saxon Church: Part 1, The Sermones catholici, or Homilies of Aelfric,* 2 vols. (1844–1846); John R. R. Tolkien, "*Beowulf:* The Monsters and the Critics," in *Proceedings of the British Academy,* 22 (1936); and *The Lord of the Rings,* 3 vols. (1954–1955); Humfrey Wanley, *Librorum veterum septentrionalium ... catalogus,* vol. II of George Hickes, *Linguarum veterum septentrionalium thesaurus,* 2 vols. (1703–1705); George Watson, ed., *The New Cambridge Bibliography of English Literature,* I (1974); Charles L. Wrenn, *A Study of Old English Literature* (1967).

ANGUS CAMERON

ANGLO-SAXONS, ORIGINS AND MIGRATION. There are many uncertainties of detail in the period of the Anglo-Saxon invasions. Written evidence is scarce and open to diverse interpretation. The historian has to rely heavily on the evidence of the archaeologist and place-name expert, and consensus is not always easy to find. The long stretch of time from the end of Roman Britain in the first half of the fifth century to the beginnings of Christian England in the closing years of the sixth century ranks among the most obscure in the recorded history of the British Isles.

Nevertheless, some broad, general truths emerge with surprising clarity. During the fifth and sixth centuries there was a radical transformation in the composition of the peoples, in the nature of the languages spoken, and in the nature of institutional life in Britain. For close on four centuries Britain up to the line of Hadrian's Wall (from the mouth of the Tyne to Solway Firth) had been an integral part of the Roman Empire. The native Celtic peoples had been romanized, absorbed into or subsisting under Latin civilization and Roman rule.

The Britain to which St. Augustine of Canterbury came in 597 had lost this unity and integrity, and was divided politically into numerous groupings of Celtic and Germanic tribal kingdoms. Most of the more fertile lowlands had been overrun and occupied by Germanic newcomers. Within the eastern lowlands, up to the highland spine of Britain, and spilling over to the fertile Severn valley and toward the southwest beyond Cirencester, Gloucester, and Bath, the predominant language had become a branch of West Germanic. Latin had disappeared along with the Christian faith, which now helped to preserve it among the surviving Celtic communities in western Britain. (Indeed, these troubled centuries saw an extension of Christianity among the Celts, initially to Ireland in the fifth century and then among the Picts and Scots north of Hadrian's Wall.) Roman towns and villas also had disappeared in Britain as significant institutions.

Augustine landed in a world where the economy was overwhelmingly agrarian in nature and coins were virtually unknown. The characteristic institu-

ANGLO-SAXON ORIGINS, MIGRATION

tions were Germanic. Society was dominated by tribal kings surrounded by warrior bands, each bound to its lord by ties of almost religious loyalty. The kings claimed descent from pagan gods, and the peoples worshipped the gods of the German pantheon, Woden and Thor above all.

The origins of these Germanic peoples have always aroused great interest. They are, of course, the ancestors of the modern English, and the basic features of the English language can be traced back firmly through all its accretions to Anglo-Saxon roots. The term "Anglo-Saxon" seems to have been popularized in the eighth century to distinguish the insular West Germans from their continental cousins in Old Saxony; and Bede, the great historian, writing in 731, made efforts to divide them still further into their component groups. He says that they came from the three most formidable races of Germany—the Saxons, the Angles, and the Jutes—and attempts to connect the accepted eighth-century story of their origins with their contemporary geographical and political situation:

> They came from three very powerful Germanic tribes, the Saxons, Angles, and Jutes. The people of Kent and the inhabitants of the Isle of Wight are of Jutish origin and also those opposite the Isle of Wight, that part of the kingdom of Wessex which is still today called the nation of the Jutes. From the Saxon country, that is the district now known as Old Saxony, came the East Saxons, the South Saxons, and the West Saxons. Besides this, from the country of the Angles, that is the land between the kingdoms of the Jutes and the Saxons, which is called *Angulus,* came the East Angles, the Middle Angles, the Mercians, and all the Northumbrian race (that is those people who dwell north of the river Humber) as well as the other Anglian tribes. *Angulus* is said to have remained deserted from that day to this (*Bede's Ecclesiastical History* i.15).

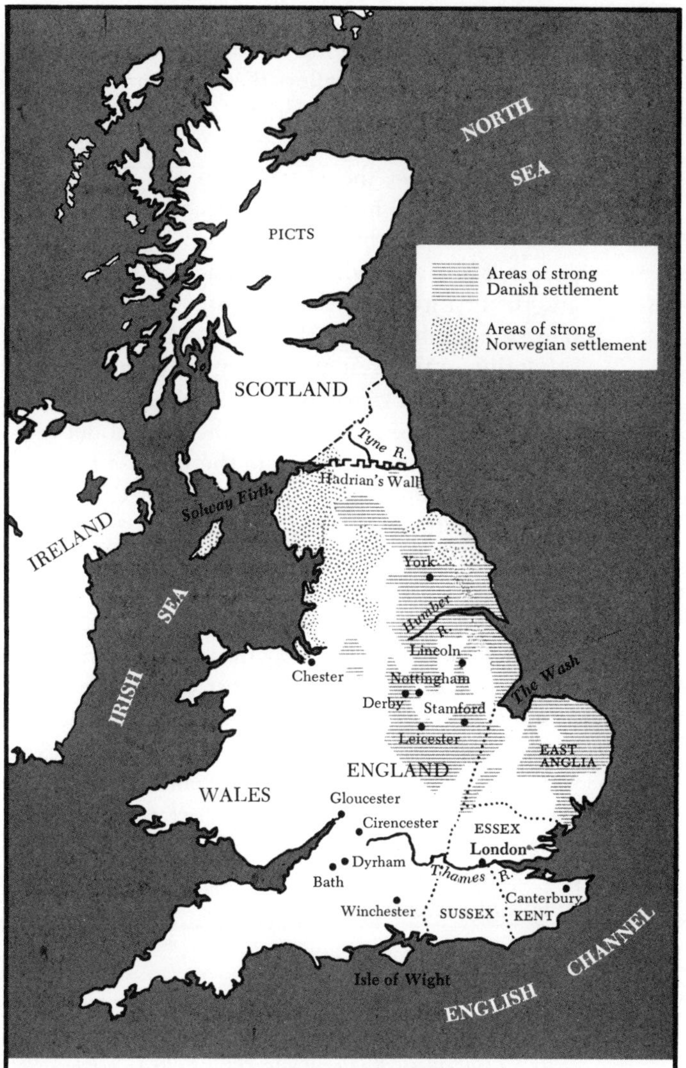

Anglo-Saxon England

Other sources confirm that parts of modern Denmark were the original homeland of the English, but even so, Bede is obviously simplifying. English settlement in Britain must be read as part of the complex movement of peoples known as the German "folk-wandering" of the fourth and fifth centuries. A large Frisian element took part in the enterprise along with the Angles, Saxons, and Jutes. It is reasonable to see peoples of the entire Germanic coastline, from the mouth of the Rhine to Denmark and possibly southern Sweden, contributing to the move into Britain. Given the technical limitations of the boatbuilders of the day, it is clear (and archaeologists and linguists confirm the hypothesis) that Frisia and the Frisian islands were important in the movement, both directly and as staging posts.

The course and pattern of the migration are securely established in broad outline. The presence of Germans as federate troops in the later phases of Roman Britain is well attested, and stories abound of Germans from more backward areas being summoned to help against marauding Picts and Scots in the early fifth century. Probably around 449 or 450 a true migration developed. Political leadership appeared in the southeast as the kingdoms of Kent and

Sussex were formed, but the migrants, seeking arable land to till, entered along the eastern waterways, notably along the river valleys that lead into The Wash, and along the Humber to the Vale of York.

By the end of the fifth century the tribes were well established from the Humber to the Thames and along the eastern half of the south coast. Their progress was halted by a revival of Romano-British power, associated with the legends of King Arthur, and the first half of the sixth century was a period of uneasy equilibrium, with Celtic communities consolidating in the west and Germanic communities in the east. English victories at Deorham (Dyrham) near Bath in 577, and at Chester in the second decade of the seventh century, illustrate the process by which the Celtic peoples were confined politically to the west, to parts of Cumbria, to Wales, and to the southwest. Celtic populations survived to varying degrees and in subordination within the English kingdoms.

Battles and political organization are, however, only externals. The reality is lost unless one always bears in mind the fact that this was a migration, a steady colonizing movement. The Anglo-Saxons were primarily tillers of the soil, men and women exercising skills learned in the forest-clearing and swamp-draining of northwest Germania and in setting up new agrarian communities in the fertile river valleys of eastern Britain.

BIBLIOGRAPHY

The principal primary written sources are available in good translations in B. Colgrave and R. A. B. Mynors, *Bede's Ecclesiastical History of the English People* (1969); F. Winterbottom, *Gildas: de Excidio Britanniae* (1974); and D. Whitelock, *Anglo-Saxon Chronicle* (1961).

For discussion of other sources such as the *Historia Brittonum* (Nennius), attention is drawn to the comments of Whitelock in D. C. Douglas, gen. ed., *English Historical Documents,* 2nd ed., I (1979).

H. R. LOYN

ANI IN DARANALIK^c (modern Kemah, lat. 39°35′N long. 39°02′E), not to be confused with Ani in Širak, the ancient Armenian capital. On the Euphrates in eastern Turkey, it was the site of the main temple of Ahura Mazda in pagan Armenia and of the Armenian royal necropolis sacked by the Persians in A.D. 364. The Persians attempted to take home the royal bones believed to detain the "glory" and "fortune" of the country, but were intercepted by the Armenians, led by the *sparapet* Mušeł Mamikonean, who rescued the royal remains and returned them to Armenia, probably to the new hypogeum at Ałc. In the Arab period Ani-Kamaχ was a citadel of considerable importance.

BIBLIOGRAPHY

Sirarpie Der Nersessian, *The Armenians* (1969), 72; Cyril Toumanoff, *Studies in Christian Caucasian History* (1963), 109, n. 168.

NINA G. GARSOÏAN

ANI IN ŠIRAK (lat. 41°00′N long. 43°05′E), capital of Armenia under the later Bagratids (961–1045), was located in eastern Turkey near the Soviet border, on a narrow, triangular plateau protected on the east and southeast by the deep ravines of the Aχurean/Arpa Čay and its tributary the Alaǰa Čay.

Because of its easily fortifiable position, Ani in the fifth century A.D. was the first fortress belonging to the Kamsarakan lords of the surrounding district of Širak. Early in the ninth century Ani and Širak were bought by the Bagratid prince Ašot Msaker, but Ani did not become the Bagratid royal capital until 961, when King Ašot III chose to be crowned there by the Katolikos Anania who established his seat in the suburban village of Argina. Within forty years the boundary walls had to be complemented by a second line of fortifications that nearly tripled the enclosed area.

Ani remained the administrative and cultural center of the senior Bagratid line until the chaotic period of the mid eleventh century. In 1045, threatened simultaneously by Byzantium and the Shaddādid emir of Dwin, the citizens of Ani sought protection (in the absence of King Gagik II, who had been lured to Constantinople) from the Iberian Bagratid king Bagarat IV or from an Armenian ruler whose identity is still disputed. The Katolikos Peter Getadarj, supported by some of the magnates, preferred to surrender the city to the Byzantine forces. This solution proved brief at best, for on 16 August 1064, Ani was taken from the Byzantine governor by the Seljuk commander Alp Arslan, who soon relinquished the city to the Shaddādids who bought it from him (1065?).

For more than a century thereafter a younger Shaddādid branch ruled Ani with only occasional interruptions. Their dominion was, however, disputed by the Georgian crown, from the capture of the city by David II (IV) the Restorer in 1123–1124 and its recapture in May 1161 under his grandson Georgi III until the establishment of the Georgians in Ani, possibly as early as 1174 although a last Shaddādid inscription dated 1098–1099 has been found in the city. In 1201, Queen T^{c}amar gave Ani as a fief to her viceroys Zak^{c}arē and Ivanē Mχargrdzeli, who had taken it in 1199. The Zak^{c}arids retained their control of Ani even after its capture by the Mongols in 1236, although their power gradually diminished in the later thirteenth century. Tradition ascribes the decline of Ani to the great earthquake of 1319, but recent scholarship has shown that gold coins were still minted there in the fifteenth century. However, by the sixteenth century the city was reduced to the level of a village, and to mere ruins by the eighteenth.

Ani had numerous secular and religious buildings that won it the traditional, if exaggerated, name of "the city of 1,001 churches." Like most Armenian cities of that period, it was laid out according to a Muslim plan, with a walled inner city containing the citadel and the main administrative buildings, fortified industrial and commercial suburbs. The actual area of the city did not exceed some 400 acres, but N. Marr's excavations found traces of churches, baths, and dwellings beyond the outer walls.

The size of the city's population is uncertain. The figure of 100,000 inhabitants and 10,000 dwellings given by the tenth-century Armenian historian Matt^{c}eos Urhayec^{c}i is probably too high, although Marr argued that most of the population lived outside the walls. In H. Manandyan's opinion it was unquestionably much larger than that of contemporary west European cities. The population apparently included "nobles" and "notables," who had some say in the affairs of their city; in later times, at least, rich merchants such as Tigran Honenc^{c}, who detailed his wealth in the dedicatory inscription of his church; and poverty-stricken slum dwellers.

Although Ani began its career as a military and administrative center, its prosperity was primarily due to its position on the great northern trade route linking the Muslim lands on the east with the port of Trebizond on the Black Sea, and by the late tenth century it had replaced Dwin as the main commercial center of Bagratid Armenia. With the end of the Bagratid dynasty, the commercial character of the city came to the fore and its prosperity continued, checked only by the Seljuk invasions of the eleventh century. A number of scholars have considered the Zak^{c}arid period in the early thirteenth century, rather than the Bagratid era, to be the zenith of the city's history, although Manandyan holds this to be an exaggeration. In any case, the Zak^{c}arid era was unquestionably marked by great monetary wealth and building activity at Ani.

In the fourteenth century a combination of heavy Mongol taxation and, especially, the southward shift of the international trade routes, contributed to the gradual ruin of the cities on the northern route controlled by Ani and to the eventual decline of the city.

BIBLIOGRAPHY

The main study on Ani is N. Marr, *Ani* (1934), in Russian. See also Sirarpie Der Nersessian, *The Armenians* (1969); H. Manandyan, *The Trade and Cities of Armenia in Relation to Ancient World Trade,* N. G. Garsoïan, tr. (1965); A. Ter Ghewondyan, *The Arab Emirates in Bagratid Armenia,* N. G. Garsoïan, tr. (1976); J. Shepard, "Scylitzes on Armenia in the 1040's and the Role of Catacalon Cecaumenos," in *Revue des études arméniennes,* n.s. **11** (1975–1976); K. Yuzbashyan, "Skilitsa o zakhvate Aniĭskogo tsarstva v 1045g," in *Vizantiĭskiĭ Vremennik,* **40** (1979); V. Minorsky, "The Shaddādids of Ani," in *Studies in Caucasian History* (1953).

NINA G. GARSOÏAN

[See also **Armenia, History.**]

ANI, MONUMENTS OF. The surviving monuments of the once-splendid medieval Armenian city of Ani are among the finest examples of Armenian architecture, both religious and secular. Although in various states of disrepair, they attest the creativity, mastery of stone construction, and engineering skills of medieval Armenian architects.

Ani, called the city in which Mass was said in a thousand and one churches, is most noted for its church architecture. Approximately two dozen churches dating from the seventh (the Palace Church of the Citadel, 622[?]) to the fourteenth century were documented early in the twentieth century through physical remains, excavations, and inscriptions. Most of the churches now extant, each with a different plan and exterior design, are Bagratid-period structures located mainly between the Citadel and the northern city walls.

One of the most important churches is the Cathedral of Ani (S. Astuacacin), founded by King Smbat II and completed by Queen Katranideh in 1010. The

Ani. Section of fortified walls. Tenth century. THOMAS F. MATHEWS

architect Trdat constructed a domed basilica with clustered piers, pointed arches, ribbed ceiling vaults (which appear a century later in Gothic architecture), and a blind arcade.

The earliest definitely dated Bagratid church is the Abułamrenc^{c} family Church of S. Grigor (domed, with six radiating apses), constructed before 994 by Prince Grigor Pahlawuni. Other Pahlawuni churches include S. Aṙak^{c}eloc^{c} (four apses, four corner chapels, and probably five domes), constructed by 1031, and the Church of S. P^{c}rkič^{c} (domed, with eight radiating apses), completed by 1035, which was commissioned by Abłłarip Pahlawuni, marzpan of Armenia, to house a fragment of the True Cross.

The Church of S. Grigor Lusaworič^{c} (a domed, three-level, aisled tetraconch), erected by King Gagik I, was completed in 1000 by the architect Trdat. Now in ruins, it was patterned after the massive seventh-century Armenian church of Zuart^{c}noc^{c}. The small, three-level Hoviv Chapel, from the eleventh century (domed, with a star-shaped plan), displays an ingenious system of vaulting in which six supporting arches terminate at the hanging keystone at the center of the structure.

Zak^{c}arid churches include the richly ornamented S. Grigor Lusaworič^{c}, commissioned by the merchant Tigran Honenc^{c} and completed in 1215 (noted for its frescoes), and the Kusanac^{c} Monastery church, from the thirteenth century.

Other notable structures include the series of wide-span bridges built with advanced engineering techniques, an effective fortification system of double walls and round towers (by King S^{c}mbat II in 977–989), palaces, baths, and the tenth-century vaulted structure now referred to as the Mosque of Manuč^{c}ē (Minūchihr).

BIBLIOGRAPHY

Marie F. Brosset, *Les ruines d'Ani,* 2 vols. (1860–1861); Harry F. B. Lynch, *Armenia, Travels and Studies,* I (1901; repr. 1965), 367–387; Joseph Strzygowski, *Die Baukunst der Armenier und Europa,* 2 vols. (1918); Nicole Thierry and Michele Thierry, "Ani, ville morte du moyen âge arménien," in *Jardin des arts,* 3 (1960); *Architettura medievale armena, Roma—Palazzo Venezia 10–30 giugno, 1968* (1968), exhibition catalog; Sirarpie Der Nersessian, *The Armenians* (1969); Varaztad Harouthiounian and Morous Hasratian, *Monuments of Armenia* (1975); Paolo Cuneo, *L'architettura della scuola regionale di Ani nell'armenia medievale* (1977); Sirarpie Der Nersessian, *Armenian Art* (1977–1978).

LUCY DER MANUELIAN

[See also **Armenian Art; Zuart^{c}noc^{c}.**]

The Abułamrenc^{c} family church of S. Grigor, Ani. Tenth century. THOMAS F. MATHEWS

ANICONISM (from the Greek ἀν [negative prefix] and εἰκον [image]). Aniconism denotes a preference for nonfigurative art during a given period in a specific area or by a particular group. For example, most Jewish, iconoclastic, and early Islamic art is aniconic.

LESLIE BRUBAKER

ANIMAL STYLE, one of the major styles of the migration period, between the fifth and seventh centuries, associated with Scandinavia, northern Germany, and the British Isles. The animal style is characterized by small objects for personal adornment executed in precious metal and usually representing animals, especially the dragon. The animals are not naturalistically represented, but have sinuous contours and are often interlocked. During the first half of the sixth century, ribbonlike zoomorphic heads appeared on the animals; these led to the interlaced animals associated with the Hiberno-Saxon period. Much Romanesque and Gothic sculptural decoration also descended from the animal style.

BIBLIOGRAPHY

Marvin C. Ross, *Arts of the Migration Period* (1961).

LESLIE BRUBAKER

ANIMALS, DRAFT. The use of animal power (including saddle and pack animals as well as draft animals) seems not to have started before the beginning of the fourth millennium B.C. According to the accepted hypothesis, it started with the traction plow, followed by sledges and slide cars, and reached its high point with the first disk-, and then spoke-wheeled, vehicles. Animal power was thus connected with the cultivation of cereals; with the domestication of herd animals (beginning with cattle); and with the use of paired draft animals. Although such scholars as Jacqueline Murray, and B. Ghetie and C. N. Mateescu, have postulated the use of cattle as draft animals before the fourth millennium, the evidence is not sufficient to prove their assumption.

In medieval times there were five species and one hybrid that served as work animals: cattle, horse, ass, water buffalo, camel, and mule. The importance and role of each species—draft, riding, or pack animal; agriculture; transport; trade; or war—differed according to time and place.

CATTLE

Cattle almost never were saddle or pack animals in medieval Europe, but served as the main draft animals. As such they were the most important work animals for agriculture and short-range transport. The main draft cattle were the oxen. They were docile and quiet, and, being larger than either cows or bulls, had more draft power; and, having longer legs, they also could move somewhat more swiftly. Cows and bulls occasionally were used to pull wagons or plows; however, their use was not practical because cows working under the yoke gave less milk and bulls were uncontrollable.

The fall of the Roman Empire signaled the end of selective breeding in its first European manifestation. This resulted in much smaller sheep, goats, pigs, and particularly cattle. In the period of migrations, this size decrease did not exceed ten centimeters for cattle, but at the beginning of the second millennium, a real dwarfing took place and cattle became the smallest they have ever been.

Interestingly, the dwarfing of cattle was more pronounced in eastern Europe and Scandinavia, territories outside the boundaries of the Roman Empire, than in central Europe and the Balkan Peninsula. This shows that the effect of the conscious animal breeding introduced by the Romans to their colonies apparently survived and influenced at least those colonies and a small area around them. In medieval Russia the average withers height of cattle was between 95.5 and 102 centimeters; it was less than 110 centimeters in Poland and in free Germany. At the same time cattle taller than 110 centimeters were found in Switzerland, France, western Hungary, and other former parts of the Roman Empire.

Medieval oxen were well above this average, having a withers height of 118–120 centimeters or more. Even so, they were very small by modern standards. Thus it is not surprising that one needed an eight-ox team—for breaking virgin land, ten or twelve oxen—to pull a plow. And this was true throughout Europe.

Oxen primarily provided power for agriculture. This is indicated by their relative infrequency in Slavic settlements of eastern Europe that were surrounded by marshes and therefore had very little agriculture. Because of their slowness, oxen were not used in long-distance transport. Draft oxen began to work at the age of four, and their average working life was around four years. Cows were kept to produce replacements for the oxen. Over the four-year working life of a team, two calves were needed as replacements every year. Thus, at least two cows were used to breed animals for each team.

The practice of castrating cattle had begun in the Neolithic period. Its large-scale application in the Middle Ages can be proved by the anatomical changes on numerous remains of such cattle. The most interesting artifacts connected with castration, several sets of tools dating from the seventh to tenth centuries, were found at Staraya Ladoga, in northwest Russia.

Pathological alterations show that these oxen were used under yoke, and chronic arthroses on the extremity bones demonstrate that they worked heavily. A noticeable increase in the size, and consequently in the strength, of the oxen occurred in the fourteenth and fifteenth centuries. Selective breeding was renewed, producing larger cattle that are best exemplified by the gray Hungarian strain. The oxen of this breed were fifteen to twenty centimeters higher at the withers, and four to six of them were enough for a team. Thus they were more valuable draft animals than the smaller breeds, and soon found their way to most of central and southern Europe.

THE HORSE

The horse has probably been the most common work animal for thousands of years. Its domestication in the middle of the fourth millennium B.C. differed from that of the earlier tamed species, in that its aim was both to secure living protein reserves and to obtain work animals with draft or carrying power.

Shortly after its domestication the horse became a draft and saddle animal, and began to play an important role in the development of long-distance transport. In this respect its speed was of decisive importance. While the speed of an ox was about half that of a walking man, a horse equaled the man's performance at a walking pace, and covered three times more at a trot and four to six times more at a gallop. Thus, with the use of the horse, man was able to have transport move faster than he himself could. A horse could cover fifty to sixty kilometers a day, compared with twenty to twenty-five kilometers for oxen and twenty-five to thirty kilometers for man. It also revolutionized warfare, first with the chariot that was a "mobile firing platform," then with riders; nevertheless, the early horse-borne troops were not real cavalry, but more like mounted infantry. Really effective cavalry developed with the invention and the general use of the stirrup around the middle of the first millennium of the Christian era.

Large herds of wild horses lived only in eastern Europe, and consequently their large-scale domestication must have begun there. In prehistoric times four waves of horses invaded central and western Europe from the east, greatly affecting the local horse populations. Even the large Roman military horse originated from eastern horses.

At the fall of the Roman Empire there were three horse groups in central and western Europe: the large, improved Roman breed; small Celtic and Germanic horses of local origin; and somewhat larger Scythian-Sarmatian horses of eastern origin. In the migration period large masses of oriental horses reached Europe in wave after wave, and mixed with the European horses. As a result a uniform type developed, closely resembling the Scythian horse that had arrived in the region about a thousand years earlier. Thus, at the end of the migration period there was no difference between western and eastern horses, at least as far as size, build, and body and extremity proportions were concerned.

These horses averaged 136–137 centimeters at the withers; body and extremities were light and slender, with the proportions of a solid riding horse. The only difference remaining between eastern and western horses was in the form of the skull, the least changed part of the body: while the eastern horse's skull had a broad forehead, the western horse's forehead was comparatively narrow. This latter type was found throughout medieval Europe, and represented the overwhelming majority of the horse population. Smaller local forms appeared, varying with the extent of eastern influence on the local horses, as well as with such factors as soil, climate, and feed. For example, the medieval horses of the Baltic area were quite small, their average height at the withers hardly exceeding 120 centimeters.

Toward the end of the migration period, selective breeding began to reappear. It was in this period that the first large, heavy, coldblood horses appeared. Since they seem to have emerged first in Italy, it must be supposed that the large Roman military horses played a role in their development. In Britain, where the requisite conditions for breeding large horses—plentiful grain and large quantities of hay for winter feed—did not exist until about the time of the Norman conquest, this heavier type emerged as the great English war horse, possibly related to Scandinavian

ANIMALS, DRAFT

horses. These coldblood horses were large, thick-legged animals that were ridden by knights wearing heavy armor. Interestingly, they are far better known from contemporary representations than from archaeological excavations: only a half-dozen sites in all of Europe have yielded their bones. (The reason may be that since they were not eaten, they were buried outside settlements.) It is worth noting that the emergence of the coldblood horse was connected with the appearance of the horseshoe in central Europe in the ninth and tenth centuries—doubtless because the weak hooves of these heavy horses needed shoeing more than those of the light eastern horses.

In Arabia conscious horse breeding started somewhat earlier, in the time of Muḥammad. This resulted in the first modern breed, the Arabian horse. It came into being through a long process of natural and human selection, combined with long interbreeding, tough endurance tests, and careful training and feeding. The Arabian has the features of an excellent riding horse, and has hardly ever been used for anything else.

In medieval Europe the horse was mainly a riding animal. Pack horses were extremely rare. Horses were not used for agricultural work until about 1000. There was even a tenth-century Welsh law that restricted plowing to oxen, though in England horses may have been used for plowing since Saxon times. And up to the fourteenth century Hungarian documents do not refer to horses pulling a plow.

As draft animal the horse was used in long-distance transport, pulling light passenger carriages or heavy wagons. The daily mileage of the former was amazing: one light carriage with six passengers covered the distance between Vienna and Buda (130 km./80 mi.) in a night and a day. The wagons, drawn by six to eight horses, were slower, but were so large that they could easily carry as many as 200 oxhides. The use of horses as draft animals can be proved by excavated remains as well as by documents. For example, at Wolin, Pomerania, chronic, deforming inflammation of the tarsal joint was found in several cases—a condition typical of hard-working, overloaded draft horses.

As a riding animal the horse was mostly used by wealthy people or knights. Therefore, horses in large numbers were kept on royal or noble estates. According to records dated between 1057 and 1248, 710 cattle, 673 horses, 5,605 sheep, and 1,220 pigs were kept on 33 praedia in Hungary. In 810, 272 cattle, 278 horses, 1759 sheep, and 1025 pigs were kept on three royal alodia near Lille, France. In both cases the number of horses in comparison with cattle is conspicuously high.

THE ASS

The other domestic equid, the ass, quickly spread from its earliest domestication center in northeast Africa to southwest Asia, where it has been the most common work animal ever since. It serves mostly as a pack animal, but also pulls plows or primitive, mostly two-wheeled carts. It can also be ridden, but because of its small size it cannot carry a heavy rider with great speed or for a long distance. The ass is adapted to hot climates, and needs less water and food than the horse. All these characteristics make it suited to desert conditions.

The ass reached Europe via Greece around 500 B.C., and was introduced by the Romans throughout their empire, from the Carpathian Basin to Britain. It was brought to eastern Europe by the Greeks, through their colonies on the northern shore of the Black Sea. Being a warmth-loving animal, the ass's distribution in Europe was limited by the cold climate of the northern part of the continent. Thus, it has been found in large numbers only in southern Europe.

After the fall of the Roman Empire, there must have been an extraordinary decline in ass keeping in most parts of Europe, because not a single ass bone dating from the fifth to the tenth century has been found in central Europe. From about 1000, asses occurred again in temperate Europe, and the religious houses had an important role in this new spread. In the Middle Ages the ass retained its role as beast of burden and riding animal of the smallholder; it was also an important work animal in mills, carrying sacks and turning treadmills. In the same manner, it was used to turn water-raising engines, particularly for the deep wells in castles. Most of the asses in medieval Europe were small. The only known exception is a specimen from Garvan (Dinogetia), Romania (ninth–twelfth century), that reached the size of the large Hittite asses of Anatolia.

THE MULE

The mule is a cross between a horse and an ass. The result of breeding an ass with a mare is a mule that is nearer in size to a horse, while breeding a stallion with a she-ass produces a small hinny or jenny. Most of the mules in use belong to the first type, the females of which are fertile.

The origin of the mule was probably southwest

Asia, where horses and asses were first kept together. The first mules reached southeast Europe by the eighth or seventh century B.C. From there the mule spread in two directions: to the north, into the Pontic area, and to the west, to Italy.

From medieval times both pictorial and written evidence exists of mules in Europe. Like asses, mules were rather scarce in the northern and eastern parts of the continent, and where they did exist, were probably imported from southern Europe. For example, from the year 1016 we possess a record of an Italian mule in Russia.

Mules were used primarily as pack and draft animals, but sometimes also as riding animals. In the latter case they served less skillful riders, such as women and church dignitaries.

THE CAMEL

Typical work animals of the desert, two camel species live in the Old World: the one-humped camel, or dromedary, and the two-humped, or Bactrian, camel. The distribution of the former stretches from the Balkans through central Asia as far as Manchuria, and that of the latter from the Caspian to North Africa. To what extent they are independent species is still an undecided question, for recently some researchers have suggested that the one-humped camel is merely a domesticated form of the two-humped one.

Camels are slow breeders, becoming mature only in their fifth year; not really prolific, the females bringing forth a single calf every three years or more; hardly trainable; bad tempered; and sometimes even dangerous. Nevertheless, they have a great advantage: they are extremely well adapted to deserts. With their padded feet they can easily walk on sand or arid soils; they are able to survive on the vegetation of saline areas; and they can go without water for long periods. With these characteristics they became indispensable pack animals in arid zones, and helped man to develop nomadic and seminomadic economic systems in areas that would otherwise have been uninhabitable. As draft animals they are almost exclusively used for pulling the plow. As riding animals, saddle camels played an essential role in warfare up to the twentieth century.

Of the two camel varieties it was the two-humped that reached Europe first. It came from western Asia and reached the lower basin of the Volga River sometime between the fifth and third centuries B.C. Camels were also kept in the Greek colonies, such as Olbia, Panticapaeum, and Phanagoria on the northern coast of the Black Sea, although they were never numerous.

From this region the camel spread westward in the early Middle Ages. Its bones occur in samples from medieval Kiev (sixth–twelfth centuries), from the hill fort of Borshevo I (ninth–tenth centuries) near Voronezh, and in strata excavated at the capital of Volga-Bulgaria (twelfth–fourteenth centuries). Around the year 1000 the camel reached Romania, brought by peoples moving west near the northern coast of the Black Sea, and was introduced into the Carpathian Basin by the conquering Magyars by the end of the ninth century. We know that when Frederick Barbarossa and his crusaders passed through Romania in 1189, King Béla III gave them bread and wine, oats for the horses, and presented them with oxen, sheep, and three camels. A fourteenth-century illuminated chronicle, representing the entry of the Huns, who were thought at that time to have been the Hungarians' ancestors, shows two riding camels. Later the camel disappeared from the Carpathian Basin, but it has survived in Bulgaria, Romania, and the southern parts of the Ukraine and Russia.

The one-humped camel first reached Europe—Switzerland, Germany, Austria, and Hungary—in the time of the Roman Empire, having been brought by military units transferred from southwest Asia or North Africa. When these forces were ordered back, the camels disappeared from the region. At the end of the Middle Ages the Turks brought one-humped camels to their occupied territories in Europe. These camels also disappeared when Turkish rule ended in the area.

In Europe the camel has never been of great importance because it cannot compete with other pack or saddle animals except in desert conditions. Its strange appearance often made the camel an object of mockery in medieval Europe. In 1121, for example, Pope Calixtus II had his captured adversary, the antipope Gregory VIII, bound to the back of a camel, facing the animal's rear parts, and then driven around in a mocking procession.

THE WATER BUFFALO

A typical draft animal, the water buffalo can compete with the horse where heavy loads are to be transported over short distances on bad roads. In terms of speed it certainly lags behind the horse; on the other hand, it can exert unbelievable strength. Albertus Magnus, the eminent natural scientist of

Cow and Camel Meat, from The Tacuinum of Liège, a medieval handbook of the late 14th, early 15th century. UNIVERSITY LIBRARY, LIÈGE.

Ram Meat, from The Tacuinum of Liège, a medieval handbook of the late 14th, early 15th century. UNIVERSITY LIBRARY, LIÈGE.

The Purchase of a Bull, from the Da Costa Hours, Bruges, 1520. PIERPONT MORGAN LIBRARY M399, F. 11V.

The Slaughter of a Pig, from the Da Costa Hours, Bruges, 1520. PIERPONT MORGAN LIBRARY, M399, F. 13V.

ANIMALS, DRAFT

the thirteenth century, stated that one water buffalo matches the power of two horses. He gave an exact description of its appearance and of the way in which it pulled heavy loads and how it sometimes rushed to the nearest pond to submerge up to its mouth. Indeed, as a draft animal the water buffalo is easy to handle. However, if it goes for several days without submerging in a pond, it is likely to run into the water, cart and all.

Shortly after its domestication somewhere in southeast Asia by the Late Neolithic or Copper Age, the water buffalo emerged in Mesopotamia, whence it spread slowly. It reached Anatolia in post-Hittite times (twelfth–seventh centuries B.C.), and the Arabs in the first century of the Christian era. After the second century it is often mentioned in Arabic poetry. In the fourth century it found its way to Persia. In the Near East it soon became one of the most important draft animals in areas where its high water requirements could be met. In tropical and subtropical areas it could replace cattle because of its higher resistance to disease. In Egypt, where it arrived rather late in the Middle Ages, it spread significantly when rinderpest almost completely destroyed the stock of cattle.

From Persia the water buffalo probably went directly to southern Russia, where its remains have been found in fifth-century strata at Olbia. This was only one of the routes by which the water buffalo reached Europe; the other led through Greece, where it appeared sporadically in the sixth century. In fact the water buffalo had already appeared in Europe, in wild form, at the "climatic optimum," the warm wave of the Early Holocene. The Avars brought the water buffalo from southern Russia to the Carpathian Basin in 560 and to Italy in 596. The Bulgarians took it to the Balkan Peninsula in 679.

Apparently only a few reached Italy or Bulgaria. Saint Willibald, while traveling to Palestine in 723, to his great astonishment found water buffalo for the first time in Italy. And an inscription on a marble column reveals that in the peace treaty Khan Omortag concluded with Byzantium in 814, he demanded two water buffalo for every repatriated Byzantine prisoner of war. No doubt the Avars also introduced the water buffalo to Germany, where the earliest place name referring to the animal (Buffileba, near Gotha) dates from 874.

It seems probable that the Hungarians introduced many domestic water buffalo into the Carpathian Basin at the end of the ninth century, because from about 1000 on, references to them are rather frequent. The water buffalo of Transylvania (eleventh-century) also were part of this importation. In King Béla II's foundation deed of Dömös Abbey (1183), water buffalo are mentioned, and from the end of the twelfth century, place names deriving from *bivaly,* Hungarian for water buffalo, occur.

In France the earliest written sources mentioning the water buffalo as a domestic animal date from 1154; in England, from 1252. Water buffalo reached Gdańsk during the rule of the Order of the Teutonic Knights. All these were, however, temporary occurrences; the northernmost point of the permanent distribution area of the domestic water buffalo was the Carpathian Basin.

The few finds of medieval domestic water buffalo bones show that these animals differed from the wild form of the species only in having shorter and thinner horns. However, they do not differ from modern domestic water buffalo with respect to the form and size of their horns. This shows that the recent breeds of water buffalo, at least in terms of horn form, had evolved by the end of the Middle Ages and have not undergone any essential change since then.

BIBLIOGRAPHY

M. Beranová, "The Raising of Domestic Animals Among Slavs in Early Middle Ages According to Archaeological Sources," in *Origine et débuts des Slaves* (1966); Sándor Bökönyi, *History of Domestic Mammals in Central and Eastern Europe* (1974); and "The Importance of Horse Domestication in Economy and Transport," in P. Sörbom, ed., *Transport Technology and Social Change* (1980); B. Ghetie and C. N. Mateescu, "L'utilisation des bovins à la traction dans le néolithique moyen," in *Actes du VIIIe Congrès international des sciences préhistoriques et protohistoriques,* II (1973); M. A. Littauer and J. H. Crouvel, *Wheeled Vehicles and Ridden Animals in the Ancient Near East* (1979); L. Makkai, "Östliches Erbe und westliche Leihe in der ungarischen Landwirtschaft der frühfeudalen Zeit (10.–13. Jahrhundert)," in *Agrartorteneti szemle,* **16** (1974); Jacqueline Murray, *The First European Agriculture* (1970); Stuart Piggott, "The Earliest Wheeled Transport: Technology and Tradition," in P. Sörbom, ed., *Transport Technology and Social Change* (1980); M. L. Ryder, "Livestock," in Joan Thirsk, ed., *The Agrarian History of England and Wales,* I, *Prehistory* (1981); Robert Trow-Smith, *A History of British Livestock Husbandry to 1700* (1957); V. I. Zalkin, "Economy of East European Tribes in the Early Iron Age," in *VIIth International Congress of Anthropological and Ethnological Sciences* (1964); and Frederick E. Zeuner, *A History of Domesticated Animals* (1963).

SÁNDOR BÖKÖNYI

[See also **Agriculture; Animals, Food; Travel and Transport.**]

ANIMALS, FOOD. Throughout Europe in the Middle Ages, the overwhelming majority of food of animal origin—mainly protein and fat, but also milk and eggs—came from domestic animals except in certain heavily forested or swampy areas of eastern Europe and the northernmost regions of the continent, which were unsuitable for agriculture. The last flourishing of hunting as a major food source occurred in the second half of the Bronze Age, when the deteriorating climate undoubtedly diminished agricultural production, and the population turned to hunting as a secondary source of animal food. During the Iron Age, and particularly during the Roman imperial period—when there was a climatic improvement—agriculture surpassed hunting to such an extent that by the Middle Ages the latter no longer played an essential role in providing food. For the nomadic peoples of the early Middle Ages it was a military exercise and an activity of festive occasions.

The quantity of animals raised for meat and the prevalence of hunting, like the use ratio of different kinds of meat, depended on several factors, the most important of which were available animal species, environment and climate, way of life, prohibitions by secular and religious authorities, and social differences.

The lack of bone remains from settlements limits our knowledge of the animal food of the peoples of the migration period, but from animal bones found in graves it seems that they ate meat mostly of domestic species that could be easily herded (cattle and caprids). Although horse bones are rarely found as food remnants in such graves, this does not conclusively rule out the consumption of horseflesh, since the presence of such items depends entirely on burial rites.

In the post-migration period cattle, sheep, goats, and pigs were the most common food animals throughout Europe except in the extreme north. In eastern Europe the horse was also an essential food, as was the water buffalo in southeastern Europe. The importance of these species, as reflected by the frequency with which their bones are found in excavations of settlements and in references in written sources, varied from region to region and also over time.

Caprids (sheep and goats) have always been popular food animals in southern Europe. Little is known in this respect about the Balkans, but it seems likely that the situation was similar there, with perhaps the addition of pork made possible by the heavier forestation of the area.

In central, western, and northwestern Europe pigs and cattle were the main meat animals until about 1000. After that, pigs and cattle remained popular until the Renaissance only in central Europe, while in the western and northwestern areas sheep (and on a smaller scale goats) became the preferred food animals. This was because the great forests in central Europe, which were ideal grazing areas for swine, survived, but in western and northwestern Europe there was heavy deforestation. In some towns, such as Haithabu in Schleswig-Holstein, northern Germany (in the example of Reichstein and Tiessen), the proportion of beef consumed increased during the period, a sign of the consolidation of the town economy throughout Poland, the Baltic countries, White Russia, Russia, and the Ukraine.

In eastern Europe—with the exception of the southern steppes—cattle and pigs were the main domestic food-producing species. By contrast, on the steppes and in Hungary, cattle, horses, and capriforms provided the bulk of the meat consumed.

Compared with environment and climate, the ethnic group does not play an essential role in food habits. The best proof of this is that there was no difference between the Germanic and Slavic settlements in this respect or between those of the early Hungarians and the Pontic steppe peoples north of the Black Sea. Instead, the way of life—which is closely connected with the environment and climate—is of decisive importance. Settled peoples eat swine, animals that cannot be driven easily but that can be fed in towns, with remnants of human food, or that can live in forest pastures during most of the year. Where large forests did not exist, sheep and goats were likely to thrive. Nomadic peoples ate animal species that could be easily driven, and they tried to continue their original animal husbandry centuries after they settled in one location.

Animals raised for their meat were generally killed before maturity, not only because their flesh was more tender but also because in this way only the valuable breeding stock had to be fed in winter. Sometimes, however, swine were exceptions to this rule. In castles, manors, and cloisters a large number of adult or even mature pigs could often be found: this was because they were kept for compulsory gifts to liege lords and to monks. Written sources mention such gifts. The best proof of this is the high proportion of boars among these animals, since fully grown or mature boars yield more meat. That milk-producing cows and egg-laying hens reached advanced ages is clearly reflected in animal bone remains. The quantity of milk the cows yielded was certainly not great because they were small, poorly fed animals and were also used as draft animals.

The chief meat consumed by European armies was beef. The chronicle of Giovanni and Matteo Villani (1347–1361) vividly describes how the Hungarians prepared and preserved large quantities of beef for their army. According to them it was baked in big pots, then salted, dried in ovens, and finally smashed into a fine powder. Every soldier carried a bag of this beef powder, and more was carried on carts. To eat it they boiled water and threw in one or two handfuls of the powder. The nutritious paste thus formed could be eaten with or without bread. Earlier, the nomadic armies' main food source was their herd of spare horses, whose milk, meat, and blood were mixed and stuffed into sausage skins and fried over an open fire.

In Europe the earliest food taboo dates from the end of the Bronze Age, when the consumption of dog meat ceased. The second prohibition, which came with mass conversion to Christianity, regarded horsemeat. But Christianity was not the only religion that forbade the consumption of horsemeat: Buddhism and Islam did the same. Nevertheless, the prohibition seemingly did not apply to the meat of wild horses, which was eaten even in cloisters. The first evidence of such a ban comes from England, where St. Theodore of Tarsus (archbishop of Canterbury 668–690) forbade the consumption of horsemeat, as a remnant of pagan rituals. In 732, Pope Gregory III instructed Boniface, the apostle to the Germans, to forbid the consumption of horseflesh. We know of no such prohibition in Hungary, but the fact that a chronicle written during Watha's rebellion (1044) condemned eating horsemeat as reversion to pagan customs shows that the church evidently did not approve it. As a result most peoples of Europe stopped eating horsemeat, with the exceptions of the Hungarians and the Irish.

In Hungary, horseflesh was not eaten in settlements near centers of royal or religious power, but it was a common source of food in remote villages. In the animal bone remains from such villages until the fifteenth century, horse bones—among them skulls smashed for the brain and long bones broken up for the marrow, both considered delicacies since prehistoric times—constitute 20 to 25 percent of the total, which means that almost half of the meat eaten by the villagers came from horses.

In medieval Ireland horseflesh consumption was often connected with ancient pagan ceremonies. At the inauguration of a local king in Ulster in the twelfth century, a white mare was killed and a broth prepared from its meat; the king sat in this bath, eating horseflesh and drinking the broth, while his assembled subjects ate and drank too.

Pork prohibitions go back to Babylonian times (about 2000 B.C.). The pork taboo of the Jews started at least several hundred years before Christ, and Muḥammad in the Koran forbade his followers to eat pork. For the Jews the avoidance of pork became an important symbol of their religion, and eating or refusing pork was always a key test whenever a conqueror wanted to force them to forsake their faith. From the time the population of Volga-Bulgaria accepted Islam in the twelfth or thirteenth century, the animal remains of the area contain no pig bones at all. Pig remains appeared there later, and always in very small quantities. Similarly, in the palace of the Turkish pasha at Buda Castle in Hungary, out of nearly 1,500 animal remains only five pig bones were found.

The secular authorities had nothing to do but enforce these religious prohibitions. At the same time, they regulated animal husbandry by ordering deliveries of live animals or animal products to residences and cloisters, for example. In the area of hunting, however, secular authorities gradually exerted greater and greater control.

According to Roman law, wild game was *res nullus*—anyone could kill it, regardless of where or on whose land it was—and this was probably so throughout early medieval Europe. Later hunting became increasingly a privilege of kings and noblemen. In Scotland, for example, David I established hunting reserves as early as the 1130's. They were designated either royal forests or baronial forests, the first by proclamation and the second by free forest grant. He reserved, in principle, all greater game (red deer, roe deer, and wild swine) to himself, although this was never seriously enforced. A body of forest law was probably first written down by the middle of the fourteenth century. By that time only freemen had the right to hunt outside reserves, and then only lesser game. Finally, the Act of 1621 stated that only landholders were allowed to hunt.

The development of restrictions probably followed similar lines in other parts of Europe, because wild animal remains can be found only very rarely in peasant villages. In royal or episcopal residences, noblemen's manors, and the like remains are more common, though not to such an extent that venison would have constituted an important part of the diet. Laws forbidding serfs to hunt are not known before the sixteenth century, but the fact that, for example, István V of Hungary gave special permission in 1272 to German settlers of northwestern Hungary to hunt chamois, wild swine, brown bear, and red deer indicates that such prohibitions existed even earlier. Fishing was no privilege of the noblemen, and on or near the seacoasts or along rivers fish was a staple food both in peasant villages and in larger towns.

The most important game was the red deer, followed by wild swine and roe deer. In eastern Europe, bison was a precious game animal (the Hungarian kings had a whole regiment of bison hunters), while the closely related aurochs was regarded as a royal wild. Although in northern and northeastern Europe the elk was a common game animal yielding a large quantity of meat, in other parts of the continent it was kept in hunting reserves. The fallow deer, introduced from the south, also was found in enclosed reserves. The most common wild game was undoubtedly the brown hare, a creature of the open agricultural areas. By the twelfth century the rabbit was also common. The wild form of this species lived only on the Iberian Peninsula and in southern France, but its domesticated form was introduced in other parts of Europe and a quickly growing feral population developed from individuals that escaped. Wild birds did not constitute a major proportion of the diet, at least considering the quantity of meat each yielded.

Variations in diet among the social classes were not manifested in the consumption or lack of venison alone. The menu of the upper classes was certainly richer and more varied. Meat of newly introduced species—rabbit, peacock, guinea fowl, and perhaps turkey—or imported species—such as oysters in central Europe—often appear in the aristocrats' diet, and new trends, such as the appearance of domestic fowl at the end of the Middle Ages, can first be noticed there. The diet of town dwellers rarely contained the delicacies consumed by the high nobility and also lagged behind in terms of changes in taste. The lower-class people of the suburbs consumed meat parts of lower value, as was observed at Wolin (Pomerania), where head and foot bones were conspicuously more common than in the central part of the town.

The yields of medieval domestic animals were much lower than those of modern breeds, because of their small size and primitive character (comparable with the breeds kept by the peasants of the Balkan Peninsula, the Near East, and the Middle East today). With the fall of the Roman Empire, selective animal breeding disappeared, except for horses used in warfare and dogs serving the sport of the highborn. This resulted in a general decrease in size of all domestic species. This was particularly noticeable in cattle, whose populations were devastated by the frequent wars—the chief meat consumed by the armies was beef, and what soldiers did not eat, they drove off. Mating at too young an age may also have caused the degeneration of cattle, and their use as draft animals certainly decreased their milk yield. As a result a rather uniform breed of dwarf cattle could be found across Europe throughout the Middle Ages until the economic upswing of the Renaissance contributed to the improvement of cattle and other domestic breeds.

A breakthrough came in European beef production with the appearance of the longhorned Hungarian gray cattle in the fourteenth century. In all probability this breed emerged from the cattle population of the Carpathian Basin through selective breeding, and soon became a standard type in the adjacent regions as well: large cattle easily driven a long way, and capable of yielding much more beef than the more primitive breeds (their height was at least fifteen to twenty centimeters greater at the withers). Because they were so easy to drive, a large-scale export of these cattle to Italy and the western part of central Europe started soon after the breed emerged.

The milk yield of medieval cattle was not high. Recent breeds of primitive type produce 4 to 5.5 liters of milk per day for six to seven months, and one can assume that medieval cows did not yield more. According to Dahl and Hjort's observations of African cattle herders, the surplus milk for human consumption after feeding the calf could be somewhere between one-half and two liters per day. Trow-Smith estimates even lower figures for medieval British cows, supposing a lactation period of 150 days and a daily production of about 3.3 liters. After the need of the calf there scarcely remains a liter per day. Thus cow milk could not play an essential role as human food.

The medieval sheep were likewise very small.

Their milk yield would have been negligible, although the milking of sheep was certainly practiced, judging from the mention of cheese used as rent in medieval documents. The goats were only slightly larger, and their milk yield would be about 2.3 liters a day through five to six months.

Medieval pigs were long-legged and long-haired with a hairy crest along the spine, slow-maturing beasts strongly resembling in the form of their skull the wild swine with which they often interbred. Their meat was lean, but their thick layer of back fat was highly esteemed; in Anglo-Saxon England, for example, a pig's value was judged by the thickness of its back fat.

BIBLIOGRAPHY

Sándor Bökönyi, *History of Domestic Mammals in Central and Eastern Europe* (1974); J. Bourdillon and J. Coy, "The Animal Bones," in Philip Holdsworth, ed., *Excavations at Melbourne Street, Southampton, 1971–1976* (n.d.); J. Clutton-Brock, "The Animal Resources," in David M. Wilson, ed., *The Archaeology of Anglo-Saxon England* (1976); Gudrun Dahl and Anders Hjort, *Having Herds: Pastoral Herd Growth and Household Economy* (1976); John M. Gilbert, *Hunting and Hunting Reserves in Medieval Scotland* (1979); Hans Reichstein and Maike Tiessen, "Ergebnisse neuerer Untersuchungen an Haustierknochen aus Haithabu," in *Berichte über die Ausgrabungen in Haithabu,* 7 (1974); M. L. Ryder, "Livestock," in Joan Thirsk, ed., *The Agrarian History of England and Wales,* I, *Prehistory* (1981); Frederick J. Simoons, *Eat Not This Flesh: Food Avoidances in the Old World* (1961); Robert Trow-Smith, *A History of British Livestock Husbandry to 1700* (1957); V. I. Zalkin, "Fauna iz raskopokh arkheologicheskykh pamyatnikov srednego Povolzhya," in *Materialy i issledovania po arkheologii SSSR,* 61 (1958).

SÁNDOR BÖKÖNYI

ANKARA (ancient Greek, Ancyra; modern Greek, Angora), a city of unknown origin in central Asia Minor, a Roman capital from the first century, and the site of the Galatian community addressed by St. Paul around A.D. 51. Located near the border of the Byzantine Empire and fortified by the Romans, it was frequently occupied by invading powers, including the Sasanids (620–627), the Arabs (654), and the Abbasids (early ninth century), but remained under Byzantine rule until 1071, when the Turkish Seljuk sultan Alp Arslan defeated the Byzantines at Manzikert (Malazgert) and opened Anatolia to Turkish settlement. Ankara held out against the Turks for some two years after the battle, and it was briefly reconquered from them during the First Crusade in 1101. But the Christians could not hold the city, and the second Byzantine surrender—the precise date is unknown—definitely marked the end of the empire's involvement with Ankara.

For the next 250 years the city came under a succession of Muslim, mostly Turkish, rulers. Seljuks, Dānishmendids, Mongol Ilkhānids, and Eretnids took their turn as sovereigns. For much of this period, however, the actual administration of Ankara was carried out by indigenous wealthy merchants and craftsmen said to have dominated the city through their commercial-religious-political guilds known as *akhī* associations.

According to Byzantine sources, Ankara came under Ottoman domination in the mid fourteenth century, by conquest in 1354; Ottoman sources claim that *akhīs* turned the city over to Murad I in 1361. Although Tamerlane defeated the Ottoman Bāyezīd I in 1402 on the plains of Chubuk (Battle of Ankara), he withdrew from Anatolia the following year, leaving Ankara to remain under Ottoman domination for more than 500 years.

The city was an important provincial administrative center of the Ottoman Empire. By the close of the fifteenth century a large influx of Turkish settlers and the consolidation of Turkish rule had nearly erased from Ankara the Hellenic and Christian culture of its Byzantine days. Nevertheless, an Ottoman survey of 1522 reveals that despite an overwhelmingly Muslim population, a primary source of income was the manufacture and sale of alcoholic beverages, perhaps indicating that Islam had not taken over all aspects of life. Of course, the Christian population in the surrounding countryside no doubt contributed to the success of this trade.

BIBLIOGRAPHY

Besim Darkot, "Ankara," in *Islam Ansiklopedisi,* I (1940); Avram Galanti, *Ankara Tarihi* (1950); Halil Inalcik, *The Ottoman Empire: The Classical Age 1300–1600* (1973); F. Taeschner, "Ankara," in *The Encyclopedia of Islam: New Edition,* I (1960).

ALAN MAKOVSKY

[See also **Byzantine Empire; Ottomans.**]

ANKH. See **Cross, Forms of.**

ANNA (*fl.* late tenth century), Macedonian princess, daughter of Romanos II (959–963) and Theophano, and the sister of Basil II the Bulgar-Slayer (976–1025). She was married to Vladimir, grand duke of Kiev, in 988 or 989, on condition that he and his subjects convert to Christianity, thus helping to bring Kievan Russia into the Byzantine orbit.

BIBLIOGRAPHY

Georgius Cedrenus, *Historia,* I. Bekker, ed., II (1839), p. 444; Samuel H. Cross and Olgerd P. Sherbowitz-Wetzor, eds. and trans., *The Russian Primary Chronicle* (1953), p. 112.

ALICE-MARY TALBOT

ANNA KOMNENA (1083–*ca.* 1155), the oldest child of the Byzantine emperor Alexios I Komnenos and the empress Irene Doukas, was born in the purple chamber of the imperial palace in Constantinople. To strengthen his tenuous claim to the throne won by coup in 1081, Alexios betrothed the infant to young Constantine Doukas, son and grandson of earlier emperors, and entrusted Anna to the boy's mother, Maria of Alania. Honored as her father's heir, Anna shared the crowd's acclamations, the crown, and the diadem with Constantine. But the birth of her brother John in 1087 or 1088 signaled the approaching end of the glory Anna treasured. By 1092, Alexios had recalled her to the palace and named John as his successor. Anna seems never to have recovered from the shock of disinheritance.

She found some happiness in study, on her own initiative acquiring an exceptional education in ancient Greek literature and history, philosophy, theology, mathematics, and medicine. In 1097, shortly after the death of Constantine Doukas, she married the caesar Nikephoros Bryennios, whose grandfather had been defeated by Alexios when the elder Bryennios rebelled against Nikephoros III Botaniates. (Some say Anna's husband was the son of that Bryennios. For references and a summary of the arguments, see Dalven, p. 81.)

In her extant writing Anna professes only admiration and love for her husband—a scholar, military commander, and the father of her children, four of whom survived to adulthood. Privately she must have lamented his failure to support her claim to the throne. According to historian Niketas Choniates, Anna and Irene planned to seize control at the death of Alexios, but Bryennios subverted the conspiracy by neglecting his crucial role. Niketas reports that Anna, in her rage, cursed God for making her female and Bryennios male. John II honored Bryennios as long as he lived, but relegated Anna to seclusion in the convent Kecharitomene, which Irene had established along the Golden Horn. Deprived of the political power and acclaim she craved, Anna sought consolation in writing the *Alexiad,* the history of her father's rise to power (beginning in 1069) and his reign (1081–1118). She was still writing in 1148. From the probable date of a surviving funeral oration, Browning places her death at 1153–1155.

In the preface to the *Alexiad,* Anna says that she wanted to continue her husband's history, the *Hyle Historias* (III.3), and rescue her father's deeds from oblivion (I.2). To this end she aggressively sought out witnesses and found simple chronicles written by monks who had served as soldiers in Alexios' army before they retired to the monastery. Family connections gave Anna access to archival documents and diplomatic correspondence as well as imperial decrees that she sometimes presents in their entirety. She also consulted the histories of Michael Psellos, Joannes Zonaras, Joannes Scylitzes, and Michael Attaleiates, as well as Euthymios Zigabenos' *Dogmatic Panoply.*

Because of her commitment to truth and attention to detail, Anna has preserved much information otherwise unknown. The *Alexiad* has been especially prized for giving the contemporary Byzantine view of the First Crusade. Anna laments the arrival of greedy, unscrupulous Franks as "all the West and all the barbarous peoples dwelling in the land between the Adriatic and the Pillars of Hercules migrated *en masse* to Asia" (X.5.4). The *Alexiad* is our only source for the Patzinak wars, and provides precious information on activity in Asia Minor. Fond of colorful anecdotes and dramatic expansion, Anna fills her history with rich material on Byzantine life and values. She excels at character portrayal, showing a special interest in the women who exercised influence over Alexios: Anna Dalassena, the ambitious and formidable matriarch of the Komnenoi; the beautiful empress Maria, rumored to be a dangerous rival to Irene for Alexios' affection; Irene Doukas, praised for her severe piety and comprehension of dogmatic theology.

Anna's faith in God and Providence are evident throughout the *Alexiad,* but an even more persistent emphasis on the hero Alexios gives the history an epic flavor that is reinforced by the language and style. While displaying the influence of Herodotus,

Thucydides, and Polybius, the resolute archaizing of Anna's Attic Greek reveals her fond acquaintance with Homer. Despite such stylistic affectations, and despite her prejudices, filial protectiveness toward Alexios, and inevitable gaps in her knowledge, Anna was obviously trying to tell the truth, to write history rather than epic.

Nevertheless, the *Alexiad's* apparent subjectivity arouses the reader's suspicions. Sometimes Anna herself appears as a participant in the action, traveling with her father (XIV.8.2), listening to his counsel (XV.11.1), or nursing him throughout his final illness (XV.11.15); more often she openly injects her own feelings and judgments into the narrative. In one way or another, Anna makes her presence felt on every page of the *Alexiad.*

Anna's personality dominates the work and creates its overwhelming mood of despair. She would like to stress fidelity to the emperor, but finds she must fill her pages with tales of disloyalty and insurrection. A devout Christian, she must often focus her attention on heretics and infidels. Fresh enemies assail the empire from within and without as Alexios fights valiantly to preserve Byzantium. Combined with Anna's own disappointments, these themes help to create the *Alexiad's* embittered, humorless tone.

Annoyance with this self-pity should not be allowed to obscure the frequent soundness of Anna's judgment. For example, the agitated account of the Komnenian revolt of 1081 rings true in its emotional detail of Anna Dalassena's bravery and decisive leadership, George Palaeologos' aggressive protection of his sister-in-law Irene Doukas, and the old caesar John Doukas' feisty reaction to the news of the rebellion. Anna Komnena's access to firsthand information, reverence for her father, and dedication to truth, unite with her intelligence, erudition, piety, and private despair to produce a history no other person might have created.

BIBLIOGRAPHY

Texts. The Alexiad of Anna Comnena, E. R. A. Sewter, trans. (1969); Anna Komnena, *Alexiade,* Bernard Leib, ed. and trans. 3 vols. (1937–1945); Robert Browning, "An Unpublished Funeral Oration of Anna Comnena," in *Proceedings of the Cambridge Philological Society,* **188,** n. s. no. 8 (1962); E. Kurtz, ed., "Das Testament der Anna Komnena," in *Byzantinische Zeitschrift,* **16** (1907).

Studies. Georgina G. Buckler, *Anna Comnena: A Study* (1929); Rae Dalven, *Anna Comnena* (1972); Joan Hussey, "The Byzantine Empire in the Eleventh Century: Some Different Interpretations," in *Transactions of the Royal Historical Society,* 4th ser., **32** (1950); Karl Neumann, *Griechische Geschichtschreiber und Geschichtsquellen im zwölften Jahrhundert* (1888).

EMILY ALBU HANAWALT

[See also **Alexios I Komnenos; Nikephoros Bryennios.**]

ANNALS. See **HISTORIOGRAPHY.**

ANNATE, a tax imposed upon a minor church benefice, representing a portion of the income supposed to accrue to the clerk who had been newly collated to the benefice during the first year. The tax was originally a practice of many patrons of church benefices of taking part of the first fruits (*fructus primi anni*) from the clerk on whom they had bestowed the benefice. Such patrons, many of them laymen, continued to exact annates from certain benefices throughout the medieval period. But from the early fourteenth century onward, the most common use of the term was to describe the payments exacted from certain benefice holders by the Apostolic Chamber on behalf of the Pope.

Papal annates were first exacted in 1306, when Pope Clement V reserved to his own use the first fruits of all benefices becoming vacant in the British Isles during the subsequent three years. Later practice was established by Pope John XXII in 1326, when he imposed the payment of annates on all minor benefices that became vacant "at the Apostolic See." By this were intended benefices that had become subject to reservation or collation by the pope, either because of a general or special reservation, because the holder had died in Rome, because he had renounced the benefice because of the papal rule concerning pluralism, or because of a union of benefices or other things of the kind. Benefices affected by the obligation to payment of annates included capitulary prebends, priories, and granges but excluded chaplaincies or vicariates founded to serve mortuary chapels. In chapters the "daily distributions" to resident canons were excluded from the valuation.

The concordats negotiated by various countries with the Holy See during the later Middle Ages paid scant attention to annates: little was said about them, for example, in the negotiations between Richard II of England and the popes. Nor were annates the object of important provisions in the concordats between various governments and the papacy, made at the end of the Council of Constance in 1418. But after 1418 the outcry against annates was loud, and their incidence was in practice much reduced. In England, for example, the annates between 1349 and 1378 represented about a quarter of the "spiritual" revenues taken by papal collectors; in the following century they shrank to a small fraction of this. In the German-speaking part of the Holy Roman Empire the collection of annates had always been difficult. The Council of Basel by a decree of 9 June 1435 purported to abolish the payment of annates altogether; although the decree had few legal results, its effect on opinion was considerable. In 1438 the Pragmatic Sanction of Bourges reduced the fiscal liability for payment of annates in France from half to a fifth of the sum to which the benefice was assessed for tithe. In England payment of annates withered; there was a brief revival of payments, mostly on unions, in the late fifteenth century, but before the Reformation their amount had shrunk almost to zero.

Annates, a tax on minor benefices, were not levied on bishoprics or regular abbeys conferred in the papal consistory, which were subject to the heavier taxes known as common services. Annates were liable to payment only to the papal Chamber, whereas the common services were shared between the College of Cardinals and the papal Chamber. But with a change of usage at the end of the Middle Ages, the term began to be applied indifferently to annates and also to common services. By the time of the Reformation this changed terminology had become standard.

In the fourteenth century annates were collected in most countries by apostolic collectors to whom fell the duty of identifying and taxing the clergy who owed them. The amount due was based on the assessment of the value of the benefice concerned, made for payment of the clerical tenth. The incumbent was supposed to pay as an annate half the full assessment for the tenth; or, in other terms, he was to pay a quintuple tenth. In the fourteenth century payment was due in one term during the year in which the benefice was collated; in the fifteenth century it was sometimes held to be payable in two terms but still within the first year. Where no assessment of the tax value of the benefice was available, one was to be made; assessments could be reduced on grounds of war damage or of depopulation. Benefices of less than the annual value of six marks of silver or ten pounds tournois (twenty-four gold florins of the Apostolic Chamber, in fifteenth-century usage) were exempt from payment of annates, as were benefices conferred *in forma pauperum.*

Payment of the annate through a proctor at the Roman court had been made quite often during the fourteenth century. From 1379 it became the practice of the papal chancery not to expedite the papal letters conferring a benefice until the relevant "obligation" to pay the annate that was due had been presented on behalf of the clerk concerned to the Apostolic Chamber. In the later period the practice for payment of the annates came increasingly to resemble that for the payment of common services. It became usual for the clerk to whom the benefice had been collated, if he was not present in Rome, to name a proctor who would assume the obligation for payment on his behalf and effect the payment within the term. If, as tended to occur for the payment of larger sums, a banker with offices in Rome was deputed to make the payment, the Apostolic Chamber would hand over to the banker the bulls of provision or whatever other bulls were concerned. These bulls then became in effect a pledge, which the banker held with "faculty of regress," that is, with permission from the Chamber to restore the bulls in case of nonpayment to the banker on the part of the holder of the benefice. The corresponding branch of the bank in the country in which the clerk concerned was resident would then take payment for the bulls, and the bank would then transfer them to the clerk in his own country. Such a complicated and costly practice was not worthwhile for a small sum, and the smaller annates tended to disappear.

BIBLIOGRAPHY

François Baix, "La chambre apostolique et le 'Libri Annatarum' de Martin V," in *Analecta Vaticano-Belgica,* **14** (1942); Émile Brouette, "Les 'Libri Annatarum' pour les pontificats d'Eugène IV à Alexandre VI," *ibid.,* **24** (1963); Johann Peter Kirsch, *Die päpstliche Annaten in Deutschland* (1903); William E. Lunt, *Papal Revenues in the Middle Ages,* (1934), I, 93–99, II, 315–372; Guillaume Mollat, in *Dictionnaire de droit canonique,* I (1935), 533–537; Michele Monaco, ed., *Il De officio collectoris in regno Angliae. Di Pietro Griffi da Pisa (1469–1516)* (1973); Noël Valois, *Histoire de la pragmatique sanction de Bourges* (1906).

PETER PARTNER

[See also **Taxation, Church.**]

ANNO, an Ottonian monk, probably from the monastery at Lorsch, who was the scribe of the Gero Codex, a Gospel lectionary now in Darmstadt (Landesbibliothek, MS 1948) dated *ca.* 950–970. Anno is shown on folio 7v presenting the book to the priest Gero and is also mentioned in the dedication. He probably painted the initials of the Gero Codex as well as copying the text, and may also have been responsible for the initials in the first part of the Peterhausen sacramentary.

BIBLIOGRAPHY

Adolf Schmidt, *Die Miniaturen des Gero Kodex* (1924); Charles R. Dodwell and D. H. Turner, *Reichenau Reconsidered* (1965).

LESLIE BRUBAKER

ANNOLIED. The *Annolied* is a hagiographic poem glorifying Archbishop Anno of Cologne, who ruled that city from 1056 to 1075 and was canonized in 1183.

This poem of 878 lines with end rhymes attributes legendary good deeds to its hero, and has been identified as being written in late eleventh-century Rhenish Middle German. Various criteria call for a dating around 1085. Parts of the *Annolied* were reused in the epic *Kaiserchronik*.

No twelfth-century manuscript is extant at present, the oldest fragment having appeared in 1597. The edition by the Silesian poet Martin Opitz, which now takes the place of a codex unicus, was printed at Breslau in 1639.

BIBLIOGRAPHY

A bilingual (Middle High German-New German) edition of *Annolied* by Eberhard Nellmann, *Das Annolied* (1975), is useful and contains an annotated bibliography. Also see Dorothea Knab, "*Das Annolied:* Probleme seiner literarischen Einordnung," in *Hermaea,* n.s. **11** (1962).

C. J. GELLINEK

ANNULAR VAULT. See **Vault, Types of.**

ANNULMENT OF MARRIAGE has always required a declaration, usually a judicial sentence, that a putative marriage was invalidly contracted and, hence, void ab initio. Annulment must be distinguished from repudiation of a spouse, which is a unilateral and normally a private act, and also from divorce in the modern sense, which admits the existence of a valid marriage but dissolves it prospectively.

It is impossible to speak of annulment in this restricted sense much before the twelfth century; the traditions of Roman law and the habits of the Germanic tribes, both of which treated marriage as a private matter admitting dissolution by mutual consent or even unilateral repudiation, were too strong. The early medieval Church proclaimed the principle of indissolubility of marriage with a vacillating voice, and it was only after the revival of jurisprudence and the organizational strengthening of the Church in the eleventh and twelfth centuries that formal annulment became necessary or even possible. The creation of a unified system of canon law that defined the grounds of invalidity, and the establishment a little later of a regular system of ecclesiastical courts, lay behind this development. Prior to the twelfth century there were certainly private decisions made on questions of validity. There are also occasional references in the sources to annulments declared by bishops in their synods or elsewhere, but they are too scattered to merit describing them as regular practices.

Several grounds for annulment existed in medieval law. Precontract, or the existence of a valid, prior (though not necessarily consummated) marriage, seems to have been the most frequently alleged. Consanguinity and affinity, or close relationship by blood or marriage, came next. Other possible grounds for annulment were coercion of one of the parties; sexual impotence; criminal conversation (adultery) during an existing marriage when coupled with a promise of later marriage or conspiracy to cause death of the first spouse; minority of one of the contracting parties (normally fourteen for boys, and twelve for girls); error of person, that is, mistaken identity, or of condition, that is, the mistaken belief that the other was of free status; solemn religious vows or holy orders; and disparity of cult, or marriage between a Christian and non-Christian. There was also academic opinion in favor of a papal right to annul a valid but unconsummated marriage, though this seems very rarely to have been exercised.

Jurisdiction to grant annulments belonged to the Church throughout the later medieval period, although in some places—for example, France—secular courts encroached on ecclesiastical jurisdiction by hearing cases in which the validity of a marriage was raised indirectly, such as those involving disputed inheritance claims. The frequency and ease with which the Church courts granted annulments has long been debated; court records suggest that annulments were less common than the Church's detractors have sometimes portrayed.

BIBLIOGRAPHY

Adhémar Esmein, *Le mariage en droit canonique,* 2nd ed. (1929); Jean Gaudemet, *Sociétés et mariage* (1980); R. H. Helmholz, *Marriage Litigation in Medieval England* (1974); George H. Joyce, *Christian Marriage: An Historical and Doctrinal Study,* 2nd ed. (1948); Anne Lefebvre-Teillard, *Les officialités à la veille du Concile de Trente* (1973), 147–179.

R. H. HELMHOLZ

[See also **Family.**]

ANNUNCIATION, the announcement by the archangel Gabriel to the Virgin Mary that she would bear the child Jesus, related in Luke (1:26–38). The Annunciation is also described in the Protevangelium of James, an apocryphal second-century book that became very popular in the Middle Ages and is the source of many nonbiblical details in representations of the Annunciation. Although the earliest images simply show a seated Virgin listening to a standing man (as in the fourth-century catacomb of Priscilla at Rome), apocryphal details from the Protevangelium occur in representations of the Annunciation from the fifth century. James writes that Mary was spinning purple wool when Gabriel arrived; the wool is held by the Virgin in the arch mosaics of Santa Maria Maggiore in Rome (432–440) and continued to be included in images of the Annunciation throughout the medieval period, although it became increasingly rare in the Latin West after 1000. Another popular episode from the Pro-

The Annunciation (detail). Simone Martini, 14th century. Uffizi Gallery, Florence. ALINARI

tevangelium was the preliminary Annunciation at a spring or well, which preceded the biblical Annunciation at Mary's house. The Annunciation at the Well is shown on several ivories (for example, the Werden casket) and was especially popular in Byzantine monumental cycles (Daphne; the Kariye Camii) and cycles influenced by Byzantine art.

Other details not derived from Luke include the Virgin's inclined head (Psalm 45:10) and the anachronistic presence of the prophet Isaiah, who foretold the virgin birth (Isaiah 7:14). Sometimes the Annunciation is presented in conjunction with an image of Adam and/or Eve to suggest that Christ's incarnation redeemed Original Sin (Christ is often called the "new Adam," Mary the "new Eve"). On the north portal of Chartres Cathedral, for example, the Annunciation is carved immediately above the Fall of Man.

By the sixth century the standing Virgin began to appear. Later representations may show one or both of the protagonists kneeling (Giotto's frescoes at the Arena Chapel). Until the twelfth century in the Latin West, and throughout the Byzantine period, the biblical Annunciation usually occurs in front of an architectural setting. Northern artists of the fifteenth century often returned the Virgin to an interior setting, either a domestic one (the Merode altarpiece by the Master of Flémalle) or in a church (Jan van Eyck's *Annunciation* at the National Gallery of Art, Washington). These same artists frequently incorporated everyday objects invested with religious symbolism. The bowl of lilies on the table in the center of the Merode altarpiece symbolizes the chastity of the Virgin.

BIBLIOGRAPHY

Edgar Hennecke and Wilhelm Schneemelcher, eds., *New Testament Apocrypha*, I (1963), 370–388; Erwin Panofsky, *Early Netherlandish Painting* (1958), 131–148; Gertrud Schiller, *Iconography of Christian Art*, Janet Seligman, trans. (1971), 33–52.

LESLIE BRUBAKER

ANOINTING, the ceremonial application of olive oil blessed on Holy Thursday, effected the most solemn consecration in ecclesiastical ordinations. Royal unction, the central feature of medieval coronations, was widely regarded as a quasi-sacrament for the legitimation of new rulers. Christian bishops from the seventh century followed biblical accounts of the Hebrew royal and priestly tradition in pouring blessed oil on the head of the new monarch. Wamba, Visigothic king of Toledo, was anointed in 672, and early Anglo-Saxon coronation rites grafted this liturgical ceremony to Germanic traditions of election and acclamation.

Pepin, the first Carolingian, was anointed by St. Boniface and subsequently by Pope Stephen II in 754. The first Holy Roman emperor to receive unction was Ludwig I the Pious in 816. León, Castile, Navarre, and Aragon had introduced versions of the practice by the thirteenth century, when the French and English coronation rites were already well established. These consecrations secured the early reputation of the king as a *persona mixta*, possessing both lay and clerical capacities, and monarchs often reflected this duality by holding canonries and exercising the office of deacon. Such liturgical kingship bound church and state, and reinforced the monarch's Christlike image.

The ninth-century French kings introduced a miraculous coronation vessel called the *sainte ampoule*, said to have been sent from heaven for the baptism of Clovis. This celestial unction became an integral part of the coronation rituals at Rheims, and its exclusive use was a symbolic weapon against claims of imperial authority. Exaggerations of the sacerdotal powers of monarchs reached their fullest expression during the investiture controversy of the late eleventh and early twelfth centuries, when royal propagandists such as the Anonymous of York ascribed godlike qualities to anointed kings.

The Gregorian reformers, attacking such claims, denied the priesthood of kings and refuted the supposed sacramental nature of royal unction. Pope Innocent III reserved to bishops the privilege of anointing on the head with chrism, the more solemn oil mixed with balsam. Imperial coronations from that of Otto IV in 1209 exemplified the new papal deemphasis of mystical kingship. The French and English disregarded these reformist injunctions and alone among Western rulers boasted chrismation on the head, shoulders, and members. Anointing on the hands, always absent from imperial coronations, confirmed their unique claims to cure scrofula with the royal touch.

In 1318 Pope John XXII refused to sanction a newly discovered English oil supposedly furnished to Thomas Becket by the Virgin. Eighty years later Archbishop Arundel denied its use to Richard II on the grounds that royal unction, like baptism, conferred an indelible character and could not be repeated. Henry IV, having deposed Richard in 1399, inaugurated a much publicized use of this English unction, but chroniclers maliciously reported that it infected him with head lice. Both the French and English chrisms developed reputations as miraculous curatives and as touchstones for royal legitimation. Their efficacy in royal anointing, though questioned by reformers, outlasted the Reformation itself.

BIBLIOGRAPHY

Royal anointings have been studied by Eduard Eichmann, *Die Kaiserkrönung im Abendland*, 2 vols. (1942); and Percy E. Schramm, *Der König von Frankreich*, 2 vols. (1939); and *A History of the English Coronation* (1937). Theological and political implications were explored in Ernst H. Kantorowicz, *The King's Two Bodies* (1957); and illustrations can be found in Percy E. Schramm, *Herrschaftszeichen und Staatssymbolik*, 3 vols. (1954–1956).

JOHN W. MCKENNA

[See also **Extreme Unction; Kingship, Theories of in Europe; Tractates of York.**]

ANONIMALLE CHRONICLE, a fourteenth-century Anglo-Norman continuation of the *Brut,* compiled at the Abbey of St. Mary, York. The chronicle covers the years 1333 to 1381 and includes an account of Wat Tyler's rebellion. The first part, 1333–1346, seems to share a source with the Latin *Chronicon de Lanercost,* but the longer section, 1346–1381, has no known source.

BIBLIOGRAPHY

Vivian Hunter Galbraith, ed., *The Anonimalle Chronicle* (1927).

BRIAN MERRILEES

[See also **Brut, The.**]

ANONYMOUS IV is the author of a musical treatise of the late thirteenth century, describing the practices and techniques of musicians at Notre Dame in Paris. The designation as Anonymous IV is due to the publication of the treatise as the fourth in a series of anonymous treatises in volume I of Charles Edmond de Coussemaker's *Scriptorum de musica medii aevi nova series* (1864). From remarks made in the treatise, Anonymous IV was a monk, probably of English origin, who may have been from the Benedictine Abbey at Bury St. Edmunds. The treatise comes from the background of a stay in Paris as a student. It was written after 1272, for the author mentions the death of King Henry III of England. There is some evidence that the work was completed by 1280.

Anonymous IV makes it clear from the beginning of the treatise that his primary concern will be with polyphony and, in particular, with the new kind of polyphony that had been developed at Notre Dame. The essence of this new style lies in the setting up of metrical patterns of long and short notes in six standard groupings known as the six rhythmic modes. In two voices these can be paired with themselves or with one of the other five, giving thirty-six possibilities. The first chapter of the treatise takes up each mode in turn, describing how it may be used in its normal or perfect form, then discussing the possible irregularities or imperfect variations. In much of this, Anonymous IV follows the teachings of John of Garland. The second chapter turns to the question of notation, for it is by the grouping of notes into ligatures or by placement of single notes that one can determine the correct rhythmic mode for a specific section of a polyphonic composition. Again, John of Garland is the authority. Recognition of proper mode through understanding of notational patterns is the goal, as is comprehension of modal irregularities through pattern variation.

The notation of pauses and rests is treated in the third chapter, for their length may vary according to how they are written or where they appear in a specific mode. There are also some remarks on the differences between the notation of plainchant and polyphony, differences depending also on locale and point in time. The fourth chapter is devoted to the proportions of intervals and the definition of consonances as used in polyphony. With these definitions in mind, we are then shown how consonances should be used in simple organum, or note-against-note counterpoint, the least complicated form of polyphony (often improvised during the Middle Ages). Anonymous IV here provides concrete examples, much like those found in earlier treatises. He then turns to the more complicated kind of polyphony developed in Paris: that of descant, in which a lower voice (tenor) in long notes is provided with an upper voice in shorter values, in one of the rhythmic modes described earlier. The rules of where and how consonances between the two voices are to fall are explained, with some remarks on problems encountered in various modal combinations.

The fifth chapter continues the discussion of complex polyphony, extending the medium from two to three or four voices. The method of composition explained is consecutive or additive, in which a second voice is joined to the foundation tenor, then a third, and so on. There are some rules of voice movement to be observed: opposite motion in the upper parts if possible, and certain intervals—sixths, for example—to be avoided as discords.

In the sixth chapter, Anonymous IV attempts to describe and define the various types of compositions in vogue: organa tripla and organa quadrupla, conductus of various kinds, and simple organa for two voices. He explains some of the irregularities one may encounter and the value of these variations to augment beauty. The seventh and final chapter is a study of irregular modes and further rules for the placing of consonances and the introduction of dissonances.

The explanations given by Anonymous IV are not completely clear, and many of the points he makes are debated by scholars. What he has to say about composers and their works is, in some ways, of greater importance. It is from this treatise that we know of the work of Léonin and Pérotin, the first renowned as the composer of the *Magnus liber* (the "Great Book" of polyphonic settings of parts of the *graduale* and the *antiphonale)*, and the second as the composer of substitute *clausulae* and the two four-voiced organa "Viderunt" and "Sederunt." Through these mentions of specific pieces, we have been able to give composers' names to these and other works in the musical sources. Secure identifications have not been possible for many of the names he gives, but Anonymous IV has provided historical continuity while showing the historical progress of the development of the Notre Dame style of polyphony.

As a theorist Anonymous IV gives a viewpoint different enough to allow scholars to compare, and thus understand, some of the more obscure details of modal theory and Notre Dame style that are clearly explained by no one writer. Transcribers of the Notre Dame repertoire have used his information as their foundation for solution of the ambiguities seen in the sources; not all the problems can be resolved, but without the help of this treatise, the areas of doubt would be even greater. Anonymous IV's references to specific composers and works have allowed us to see the body of one composer's compositions and to place the rise of new ideas in a time framework. His book has been, and will remain, a major document in the study of the development of compositional technique and musical style from the closing years of the twelfth century to the middle of the thirteenth.

BIBLIOGRAPHY

John Caldwell, *Medieval Music* (1978); Luther Dittmer, trans. and ed., *Anonymous IV, Musical Theorists in Translation,* I (1959)—use with reviews by Janet Knapp in *Journal of Music Theory,* 3 (1959); and by Gilbert Reaney in *Journal of the American Musicological Society,* **12** (1959); Richard H. Hoppin, *Medieval Music* (1978); and Fritz Reckow, *Die Musiktraktat des Anonymus 4,* 2 vols. (1967), which includes the Latin text in critical edition and a complete bibliography, the latter in II, 92–100.

ALBERT SEAY

[See also **Ars Antiqua.**]

ANONYMOUS OF YORK. See **York Tractates.**

ÁNS SAGA BOGSVEIGIS. The late fifteenth-century Old Norse saga of Án bogsveigir (bow-bender) was very popular and exists in numerous manuscripts. There also survive eight fits of *Áns rímur bogsveigis,* composed in the early fifteenth century and based on an earlier version of the saga. The saga is traditionally classified among the *Fornaldar sögur Norðurlanda* (sagas of the north in ancient times) and is the fourth of the sagas about the men of Hrafnista, along with *Ketils saga hængs, Gríms saga loðinkinna*, and *Örvar-Odds saga*, although its inclusion in this group is probably a relatively late innovation.

Án is something of a *kolbítr* ("coal eater," or unpromising hero) as a child. He goes to the court of King Ingjaldr of Naumdælafylki against the advice of his more worldly brother, Þórir. Án makes no concessions to live at court and is eventually outlawed for killing Ingjaldr's two half-brothers in battle. After a series of adventures Án marries a rich widow, Jórunn, and settles down in the forest to manage his farms. He is able to foil all the king's attempts to assassinate him and is eventually revenged on Ingjaldr through Þórir háleggr (long leg), his son by Drífa, a farmer's daughter. Án returns to Hrafnista to end his days peacefully.

Analogues to this narrative exist in Saxo's *Gesta Danorum* and Snorri Sturluson's *Heimskringla.* The narrative, with its straightforward story line uncluttered by either subplots or superfluous characters, is reminiscent in some ways of the style of the *Íslendingasögur* (family sagas), and attempts have been made to discern the particular influence of *Egils saga.* There is little of the supernatural except for the one appearance of Litr, a dwarf, who teaches Án craftsmanship and gives him a mighty bow and arrows. These arrows are a link with the *Gusisnautar* (gifts of the Finnish King Gusir) and figure in the other *Hrafnistumannasögur.*

Ans saga contains a number of verses, at least one of which may have previously existed as an independent lyric; and in addition to the expected litotes, the author has enlivened his narrative through the frequent use of puns. The saga is also an outlaw saga, and de Lange attempted to show that it was the model for the Middle English outlaw tales, although this position is no longer considered tenable.

BIBLIOGRAPHY

Sources. Carl C. Rafn, ed., *Fornaldar sögur Norðurlanda,* II (1829), 323-362; *Áns saga bogsveigis,* Callum Campbell, ed. (forthcoming).

Studies. Joost de Lange, *The Relation and Development of the English and Icelandic Outlaw-Traditions* (1935); S. F. D. Hughes, "The Literary Antecendents of *Áns saga bogsveigis,*" in *Medieval Scandinavia,* **9** (1976); Leopold F. Läffler, *En kärleksvisa i Áns saga bogsveigis* (1912); Helga Reuschel, *Untersuchungen über Stoff und Stil der Fornaldarsaga* (1933).

SHAUN F. D. HUGHES

ANSELM II OF LUCCA (*ca.* 1036–1086), a nephew of Pope Alexander II, was appointed bishop of Lucca in 1073; he was canonized in 1087. He is noteworthy for his influential collection of canon law supportive of the Gregorian Reform: roughly 1,200 canons, many previously unused, advocating clerical celibacy and papal primacy, and condemning simony and lay investiture.

BIBLIOGRAPHY

Fridericus Thaner, ed., *Anselmi episcopi Lucensis collectio canonum una cum collectione minore,* I, II (1906, 1915) stops at canon 15 of book XI (there are XIII books in all). Also see "Anselme de Lucques," in *Dictionnaire de droit canonique,* R. Naz, ed. (1935); Paul Fournier and Gabriel Le Bras, *Histoire des collections canoniques en Occident,* II (1932), 25ff.; Gilberto Madella, *Sant Inselum Sant in Dom* (1973).

PAULINE THOMPSON

[See also **Law, Canon.**]

ANSELM OF BESATE (also called Anselmus Peripateticus) was an Italian peripatetic philosopher of the eleventh century. He studied rhetoric and Roman law under Drogo at Parma and later became chaplain to Henry III, a post he held from 1048 to 1056. His prose treatise, the *Rhetorimachia,* contains a dream vision in which three maidens—Dialectic, Rhetoric, and Grammar—discuss philosophical problems. His sources are Cicero, Justinian, Boethius, Porphyry, and Aristotle.

BIBLIOGRAPHY

Karl Manitius, ed., "Epistula ad Augiensis von Gunzo und Rhetorimachia von Anselm von Besate," in *Monumenta Germaniae historica, Quellen zur Geistesgeschichte des Mittelalters,* II (1958).

NANCY A. PORTER

ANSELM OF CANTERBURY, ST. (1033–1109), called Anselm of Aosta by Italians because he was born there. He died at Canterbury, where he had been archbishop since 1093. His body was entombed in Canterbury Cathedral and was later relocated (in conjunction with his canonization) to an area of the cathedral subsequently destroyed by fire in 1174. The canonization initiated by Thomas Becket in 1163 may be presumed to have been completed. He was declared a Doctor of the Church by Pope Clement XI in 1720. His feast day is 21 April.

Anselm's father, Gundulf, and his mother, Ermenberga, were both of the noble class. According to Eadmer, a monk at Canterbury and Anselm's biographer, Anselm was close to his mother but did not get along with his father; even less is known of his sister, Richeza. Following his mother's death he left Aosta (1056). After sojourns in Burgundy (his native kingdom) and in parts of France, he arrived in 1059 at the French Abbey of Bec in Normandy, where he intended to study with Lanfranc of Pavia. Within a year, at the age of twenty-seven, he decided to take the monastic vows. When Lanfranc left to become abbot of St. Stephen's monastery at Caen, Anselm was elected to succeed him as prior of Bec (1063); and in 1078, a few days after Herluin's death (26 August), he was elevated to abbot. Toward the end of his priorship Anselm wrote his *Monologion* (completed during the second half of 1076) and probably his *Proslogion* (1077–1078). As abbot he wrote the *Reply to Gaunilo* and the dialogues *De grammatico,*

ANSELM OF CANTERBURY

De veritate, De libertate arbitrii (1080–1085), and *De casu diaboli* (1085–1090).

After the death of Lanfranc (May 1089), who had become archbishop of Canterbury (29 August 1070), the see of Canterbury remained vacant for four years—King William Rufus preferring to profit from its revenues rather than to name a successor. Finally, in 1093, William, believing he was mortally ill, acceded to the urging of the English bishops and barons. On 6 March he named as archbishop the abbot of Bec, then in England to seek a tax reduction on the English lands held by his abbey. Anselm had been invited to William's bedside in Gloucester as spiritual counselor. He seemed surprised, and unwilling, to be presented with the archbishopric. When he would not accept the symbolic staff, the assembled bishops took it from the willing king's hand and pressed it against his clenched fist.

Such was Anselm's investiture. He could not have been as surprised as Eadmer would have us believe. But his reluctance, arising from whatever mixture of motives, was no doubt enormous and unfeigned. Consent having subsequently been obtained from the duke of Normandy, the archbishop of Rouen, and the community of monks at Bec, Anselm was persuaded to accept the office. In September he did homage to the king; his consecration followed on 4 December.

Disputes between William and Anselm commenced even while Anselm was archbishop-elect, and they continued with only intermittent periods of truce. Anselm insisted upon, and obtained, the return of all the lands over which Lanfranc had had jurisdiction—some of which William had enfeoffed to other vassals. And there were additional money disputes. Moreover, when Anselm asked William for permission to go to Rome to receive the pallium from Pope Urban II, William responded that he had not yet recognized Urban in preference to the rival claimant Clement III. (Without the pallium Anselm was forbidden, canonically, from conducting his full duties as archbishop.) William insisted that the archbishop could not hold allegiance to a pope not yet recognized by the king. Anselm asked that a council be called to examine this issue (Rockingham, 25–28 February 1095). Highly politicized, the council's deliberations were inconclusive.

Anselm had threatened to leave England if the decision were that he should withdraw his recognition of Urban. In the end the council arranged a truce between the king and the archbishop. William, hoping to divest Anselm of his office, sent secretly to Rome to ascertain which of the papal claimants was actually in power and to request that the pallium be given to him, as king, to confer upon whom he would; in return he was willing to extend royal recognition. Urban sent the pallium—by his legate Cardinal Walter, bishop of Albano—directly to William; but he did not consent to Anselm's divestment from the archbishopric. When Anselm declined to accept the pallium from the king's hands, because the king should not have the prerogative of bestowing it, a ceremony was arranged at Canterbury Cathedral, where on 27 May 1095, Walter laid the pallium on the altar, from which Anselm took it, as if from St. Peter's hands.

When relations between William and Anselm further deteriorated, Anselm on several occasions asked William's permission to go to Rome to consult with the pope. Each time, William refused. Finally Anselm threatened to go anyhow; and William, in turn, threatened to confiscate the see's properties and revenues if he did. On 15 October 1097, William agreed to give Anselm safe conduct out of the kingdom. Anselm left Canterbury on 25 October. Once he was out of the country, William proceeded to seize the properties even though Anselm had departed with permission. At some point between his departure from England and his conversations with Hugh, archbishop of Lyons, whom he visited en route to Rome, Anselm decided to ask the pope to release him from office. From Lyons he wrote a letter stating this request. When he reached Rome, however, the pope refused to let him resign.

During the tumultuous Canterbury period Anselm managed to complete the final version of *De incarnatione Verbi* (toward the beginning of 1094)—the first recension of which had been written at Bec before 7 September 1092. Sometime between 1094 and 1097 he began his magnificent *Cur Deus homo,* under the prodding of Boso's many questions, as well as under the lingering influence of his former pupil at Bec, Gilbert Crispin. While in exile he finished this work and began thinking about the doctrine of the Holy Spirit's procession from both the Father and the Son—in preparation for the Council of Bari (October 1098). According to Eadmer, whose report in this instance is not altoghether plausible, at this council Urban would have excommunicated William had Anselm not interceded to prevent it. In the end the pope did nothing except grant William a postponement of his case.

ANSELM OF CANTERBURY

At a Vatican Council at St. Peter's in April 1099, Anselm heard Pope Urban sentence to excommunication all laymen who gave ecclesiastical investiture, all clergy who received it from them, all bishops who consecrated such clergy, and all clergy who did homage to laymen as a prerequisite to obtaining ecclesiastical office. The following day he left for Lyons, where he was residing when word came of Urban's death (29 July 1099) and the succession of Paschal II (consecrated 14 August 1099). At Lyons, sometime between the summer of 1099 and that of 1100, Anselm completed *De conceptu virginali et de originali peccato* and *Meditatio redemptionis humanae.*

On 2 August 1100, William Rufus was killed by an arrow in what was reported to be a hunting accident. Learning of his death through messengers, Anselm set out for England, being met en route by emissaries bearing an invitation from the new king, Henry I. Anselm reached Dover on 23 September 1100. He came into conflict with Henry when the latter asked him to be reinvested and to do homage. Anselm explained that, on the basis of the anathemas of the Vatican Council, he could not. Henry deferred the matter and, together with Anselm, sent envoys to Paschal for clarification. The letter from Paschal uncompromisingly reaffirmed Urban's pronouncements. Henry, his kingship now secured, disregarded the papal directive and insisted that Anselm either do homage and consecrate the bishops recently appointed by him or leave the kingdom immediately.

Anselm chose to do neither. After additional and inevitably slow exchanges with the pope, Henry, assuming a conciliatory tone, implored Anselm to go to Rome for clarification and intervention. Accepting the advice of the nobles, Anselm, now close to seventy years old, left England on 27 April 1103 for what was to be another absence of three years. When he reached Rome in October, he learned that Henry had sent an envoy, William of Warelwast, to intervene on his own behalf. At the papal audience William's reasoning carried some weight with the Curia. Though Paschal reiterated the unacceptability of lay investiture, his letter to Henry (23 November 1103), carried by William, was silent regarding homage (as had been the letter of 12 December 1102 to Anselm at Canterbury).

William had lingered after Anselm's departure, hoping to persuade the pope and the Curia. He then overtook Anselm at Lyons and informed him that Henry would not allow him back into England unless he yielded to the king on the very point the pope had just forbidden. Interrupting his journey at Lyons, Anselm slowly came to realize that the pope would never take peremptory action against Henry. He therefore headed north, determined to issue a writ of excommunication on his own authority. Henry, in Normandy on a military expedition, learned of Anselm's intent. Alarmed by the prospect of such a politically untimely edict, he arranged to confer with Anselm at Laigle (22 July 1105). Promising to restore the Canterbury lands and revenues, he convinced Anselm not to issue the writ. But he still refused Anselm readmittance to England unless Anselm agreed to fellowship both with those whom Henry had invested and with the bishops who had consecrated them.

While Anselm went to Bec and the king returned to England, a final round of messages was sent to the pope. In April 1106, Anselm received from Paschal what must be regarded as a letter of compromise, dated 23 March. The pope consented to the practice of homage until such time as God softened the king's heart through Anselm's preaching; but he continued to forbid lay investiture. Anselm was visited by the king in August and returned to England the following month, while Henry concluded his conquest of Normandy. At an assembly at the royal palace in London during August 1107, the king formally renounced the right to invest bishops and abbots with the staff (the symbol of the pastor's office) and the ring (the token of faith); and Anselm agreed that bishops and abbots would do homage to the king regarding their temporal holdings (Concordat of London). In 1108 and 1109, Anselm was troubled by the refusal of Thomas, archbishop-elect of York, to recognize the primacy of the see of Canterbury by accepting consecration there. The issue was resolved in favor of Canterbury only after Anselm's death.

Before his second exile Anselm had written his penetrating *De processione Spiritus Sancti* (completed in the summer of 1102). And after his return to England he penned both his *Epistola de sacrificio azimi et fermentati* and his *Epistola de sacramentis ecclesiae* (1106–1107). During the last years of his life he wrote *De concordia praescientiae et praedestinationis et gratiae Dei cum libero arbitrio* (1107–1108). He seems never to have commenced his projected treatise on the origin of the soul.

The corpus of Anselm's works consists of the aforementioned treatises; 3 meditations; 19 prayers; 375 letters; a collection of philosophical fragments

ANSELM OF CANTERBURY

(*Ein neues unvollendetes Werk des hl. Anselm von Canterbury*); the *Dicta Anselmi,* compiled by Alexander, a monk at Canterbury; and *De morum qualitate per exemplorum coaptationem,* compiled by an unknown member of the Canterbury circle. The last two compilations are published, together with a reedited version of the incomplete work, in *Memorials of St. Anselm.* Anselm's writings are known both for their straightforwardness and for their religious fervor.

The *Monologion,* a soliloquy, purports to establish its conclusions *sola ratione*—by reason alone. It attempts not only to prove the existence of a single Supreme Nature but also to exhibit the rationale of the doctrine of creation ex nihilo. With equal boldness it argues for the triunity of the Supreme Nature, as well as for the immortality of the human soul and the necessity of faith, or trust, in this Nature, which only in the last chapter is identified as God. No other work of Anselm's appears as rationalistic as does the *Monologion.* And yet, even the *Monologion* explicitly acknowledges that the doctrine of the Trinity is incomprehensible and that all discourse about the Supreme Nature is oblique (ch. 65).

Although the *Proslogion,* an address, moves *sola ratione* just as much as the *Monologion,* it does not give the immediate appearance of doing so. (*De incarnatione Verbi* 6 refers to both works as proving by compelling reasons [*necessariis rationibus*] and apart from appeal to scriptural authority.) The many textual and philosophical problems surrounding the formulation and the implications of Anselm's *unum argumentum* to establish God's existence and nature will perhaps never all be settled. But it is clear that the phrase *id quo maius cogitari non potest* ("that than which a greater cannot be thought") is a description (not a definition), that the language of conceivability cannot be simply reduced to the language of possibility, and that the reductio ad absurdum format of Anselm's line of reasoning must not be lost sight of by representing the argument as merely syllogistic. The label "ontological argument" seems first to have been used by Gottfried Leibniz and Christian Wolff in the modern period.

If the *Proslogion* was to be Anselm's most controversial work, the *De grammatico* proved to be his most puzzling one. It owes its philosophical rehabilitation largely to the efforts of Desmond P. Henry (*The De Grammatico of St. Anselm*). It deals with the topic of paronymy—that is, with words (such as *grammaticus,* meaning "expert-in-grammar") that (1) derive from other words from which they differ only in case ending (such as *grammatica,* meaning "expertise-in-grammar") and (2) that function as both adjectives and nouns (for example, we say both that someone is expert-in-grammar and that someone is *an* expert-in-grammar). Anselm wrote this dialogue in order to introduce students to dialectic.

The three other dialogues—*De veritate (On Truth), De libertate arbitrii (Freedom of Choice),* and *De casu diaboli (The Fall of the Devil)*—center, in a highly original way, on the notion of *rectitudo. De incarnatione Verbi (The Incarnation of the Word)* reaffirms, in reply to Roscelin of Compiègne, the teaching of the Christian tradition: Father, Son, and Holy Spirit are one in substance, or nature, but are three relations, or persons—only one of which could have become incarnate. In assuming a human nature, the Son of God became a man—that is, a human being. Accordingly, Jesus is the assumed man (*assumptus homo*), just as He is also the incarnate God. But when the Church makes this profession, advises Anselm, it must remember that only God the Son was incarnate, just as only the human nature that is Jesus's was assumed. Anselm's doctrines of Trinity and Incarnation are thoroughly orthodox.

In the *Cur Deus homo (Why God Became a Man),* whose main lines were summarized in the *Meditatio redemptionis humanae (Meditation on Human Redemption),* Anselm presents his satisfaction theory of atonement and rejects the Augustinian theory of devil ransom. Anselm's central task was to reply to the question of why, if God could have accomplished human salvation by some other means or could simply have forgiven men, He became a man in order to redeem mankind by His death. Though the topic is different from the topics of the *Monologion* and the *Proslogion,* the method is the same, as is evidenced by the statement in the *Cur Deus homo,* I, 20: "Therefore, let us keep proceeding *sola ratione.*" Anselm regards even considerations of fittingness as having the weight of necessity, provided nothing more reasonable opposes them (I, 10).

De conceptu virginali (On the Virgin Conception and on Original Sin) asks how the Son of God could have assumed a sinless human nature from the sinful mass of humanity; it gives an alternative answer to the explanation found in the *Cur Deus homo.*

De processione Spiritus Sancti (The Procession of the Holy Spirit) defends the Latin Church's addition of *filioque* to the Nicene Creed of 381. *De sacrificio azimi et fermentati (The Sacrifice of Unleavened and Leavened Bread)* sets out the reasons why it is preferable to consecrate unleavened bread. And *De sacramentis ecclesiae (The Sacraments of the Church)* discusses several minor ceremonial issues that regard the Eucharist. Anselm's last treatise, *De concordia (The Harmony of the Foreknowledge, the Predestination, and the Grace of God with Free Choice),* treats the three controversies alluded to in its title.

All things considered, Anselm's treatises—because of their conciseness and directness—provide an excellent introduction to medieval theology in general and to early medieval philosophy in particular.

Anselm's main intellectual source was Augustine; yet, often he simply borrowed a topic or an idea from Augustine and went on to develop it in his own way. He was also influenced by his teacher Lanfranc; by Boethius' translations of, and commentaries on, Aristotle's *De interpretatione* and *Categories;* and by Cicero's *Topics,* though perhaps not by Boethius' commentary thereon. Among his pupils who made some intellectual mark of their own are Gilbert Crispin, Eadmer, Honorius Augustodunensis, and Ralph, abbot of Battle.

BIBLIOGRAPHY

Editions. Franciscus S. Schmitt, ed., *Opera omnia,* 6 vols. (I, 1938, repr. 1946; II–VI, 1940–1961), all vols. reprinted in 1968, with an introduction by Schmitt drawing together his articles on Anselm; Schmitt, "Ein neues unvollendetes Werk des hl. Anselm von Canterbury," in *Beiträge zur Geschichte der Philosophie und Theologie des Mittelalters,* **33** (1936); Richard W. Southern and Franciscus S. Schmitt, eds., *Memorials of St. Anselm* (1969).

Recent English Translations. Joseph M. Colleran, trans., *Why God Became Man and the Virgin Conception and Original Sin* (1969); Maxwell J. Charlesworth, trans., *St. Anselm's Proslogion* (1965), includes *Proslogion, On Behalf of the Fool,* and *Reply to Gaunilo;* Eugene Fairweather, ed. and trans., *A Scholastic Miscellany: Anselm to Ockham* (1956), includes *Proslogion, Reply to Gaunilo* (excerpt), *De incarnatione Verbi* (excerpt), *Cur Deus homo, De conceptu virginali* (selection), and two letters to Pope Paschal II (excerpts); Desmond P. Henry, trans., *The De Grammatico of Saint Anselm: The Theory of Paronymy* (1964), republished in Henry's *Commentary on De Grammatico* (1974); Paschal D. Honner, "Letters of St. Anselm to His Monks at Bec," in *American Benedictine Review,* **14** (March 1963) (letters 98, 116, 118, 147, 148, 151); and "Letters of St. Anselm to the Community of Bec, II," in *American Benedictine Review,* **14** (June 1963) (letters 156, 157, 164, 165, 166, 173, 178, 179, 199, 205, 468); Jasper Hopkins and Herbert Richardson, trans., *Anselm of Canterbury,* 3 vols. (1974–1976) (the complete treatises); Anselm R. Pedrizetti, "Letters of Saint Anselm and Archbishop Lanfranc," in *American Benedictine Review,* **12** (December 1961) (letters 1, 14, 23, 25, 27, 30, 32, 39, 49, 57, 66, 72, 77, 89, 90, 103, 124); Benedicta Ward, trans., *The Prayers and Meditations of Saint Anselm* (1973), includes *Proslogion,* all meditations, all prayers, letters 10, 28, 147. Other English translations are listed in Jasper Hopkins, *A Companion to the Study of St. Anselm* (1972), and in *Anselm of Canterbury,* I and IV.

Studies. Richard J. Campbell, *From Belief to Understanding: A Study of Anselm's Proslogion Argument on the Existence of God* (1976); Norman F. Cantor, *Church, Kingship, and Lay Investiture in England, 1089–1135* (1958); Eadmer, *The Life of St. Anselm, Archbishop of Canterbury,* Richard W. Southern, ed. and trans. (1962); *Eadmer's History of Recent Events in England,* G. Bosanquet, trans. (1964); Charles Hartshorne, *Anselm's Discovery: A Re-Examination of the Ontological Proof for God's Existence* (1965); Desmond P. Henry, *The Logic of St. Anselm* (1967); Jasper Hopkins, *op. cit.,* IV: *Hermeneutical and Textual Problems in the Complete Treatises of St. Anselm* (1976); John McIntyre, *St. Anselm and His Critics: A Reinterpretation of the Cur Deus Homo* (1954); Richard W. Southern, *Saint Anselm and His Biographer* (1963); Jules Vuillemin, *Le dieu d'Anselme et les apparences de la raison* (1971).

JASPER HOPKINS

ANSELM OF LAON (*ca.* 1050–1117), theologian, conducted the cathedral school of Laon with his brother Raoul (Radulphus) and died in that city. In 1113 or 1114, Peter Abelard attended Anselm's lectures; judging Anselm senile and his teaching sterile, Peter began to lecture on theology himself. Anselm's literary legacy has been in process of recovery for nearly a century, and there is now a body of texts in critical editions, not all of which are of unchallenged authenticity. Georges Lefèvre inaugurated modern textual scholarship on Anselm with his edition of the *Liber pancrisis* in 1895. Recent scholarship has established that it is no longer possible to ascribe the interlinear glosses of the *Glossa ordinaria* to Anselm and the marginal glosses to Walafrid Strabo, but Anselm is still credited with the gloss on Paul, on the Psalter, and possibly that on the Fourth Gospel. His brother Radulphus is held to be the author of the gloss on Matthew.

Three stages can be discerned in recent scholarly opinion on Anselm's work and influence. A first enthusiasm assigned to him a long list of "sentences" and of isolated theological discussions from which it was inferred that he stood at the fountainhead of both the summary (*summa*) and of the disputed questions, literary forms conspicuous in later theology. A second stage assigned much of this writing not to him but to the School of Laon, that is, to a group of theologians affected by the work of the two brothers. Finally, Valerie Flint has made the revisionist claim that the term "School of Laon" can be used correctly only of the cathedral school, not of the alleged crowd of geographically far-flung disciples.

The juxtaposition of Anselm with Abelard has been illumined by Ermenegildo Bertola's insight that the former represents the "erudite" theological lecture, whereas the latter represents—or is at the origin of—a more personal and more speculative reading of the "sacred page." It is safe to say that Anselm was an early participant in the theological movement of the twelfth century, seeking to employ in orderly fashion the views (*sententiae*) of Church Fathers in order to read Scripture with greater understanding, above all by reconciling apparent contradictions among authorities through a discreet use of rationality. The claim that theology as a scientific discipline began with Peter Abelard and Hugh of St. Victor is thus yielding to the view that the true pioneers were Anselm at Laon and William of Champeaux at Paris, both in turn indebted to Manegold, "the master of modern masters," who had taught at Paris and died around 1110 at Lauterbach.

BIBLIOGRAPHY

Sources. The *Liber pancrisis* was edited by Georges Lefèvre as *Anselmi Laudunensis et Radulfi fratris eius sententiae excerptae* (1895); Franz P. Bliemetzrieder published *Sententie divine pagine* and *Sententie Anselmi* as "Anselms von Laon systematische Sentenzen," in *Beiträge zur Geschichte der Philosophie des Mittelalters,* **18** (1919); Odon Lottin, "Nouveaux fragments théologiques de l'école d'Anselme de Laon," in *Recherches de théologie ancienne et médiévale,* **11** (1939), **12** (1940), **13** (1946), **14** (1947); Heinrich Weisweiller, "Le recueil des sentences 'Deus de cuius principio et fine tacetur' et son remaniement," in *Recherches de théologie ancienne et médiévale,* 5 (1933).

Studies. Ermenegildo Bertola, "Le critiche di Abelardo ad Anselmo di Laon ed a Guglielmo di Champeaux," in *Rivista di filosofia neo-scolastica,* **52** (1960); and "La 'Glossa ordinaria' biblica ed i suoi problemi," in *Recherches de théologie ancienne et médiévale,* **45** (1978); Valerie I. J. Flint, "The 'School of Laon': A Reconsideration," in *Recherches de théologie ancienne et médiévale,* **43** (1976); Joseph de Ghellinck, *Le mouvement théologique du XIIe siècle* (1948), 113–148; Artur M. Landgraf, *Introduction à l'histoire de la littérature théologique de la scolastique naissante,* Albert M. Landry, ed. (1973).

EDWARD A. SYNAN

ANSELM OF LIÈGE (*d.* 1056), chronicler, was born near Cologne and studied in Liège. His history of the diocese of Liège, the *Gesta episcoporum Tungrensium, Trajectensium et Leodiensium,* was written at the request of his aunt, the Abbess Ida of St. Cecilia in Cologne. Bishop Wazo of Liège held Anselm in high regard and is included in Anselm's history.

BIBLIOGRAPHY

The *Gesta* was edited by Rudolf Koepke in *Monumenta Germaniae historica: Scriptores,* VII (1846), 134–234, and XIV (1883), 107–120; and is also in *Patrologia latina,* CXXXIX (1880), 957–1102. See also Maximilianus Manitius, *Geschichte der lateinischen Literatur des Mittelalters,* II (1923), 372–375; and Franz-Josef Schmale's biography in *Lexikon für Theologie und Kirche,* I (1957), 596–597.

NANCY A. PORTER

ANTAPODOSIS. See **Liutprand of Cremona.**

ANTELAMI, BENEDETTO. See **Benedetto Antelami.**

ANTEPENDIUM, the covering on the front of an altar, often richly decorated. First made of costly fabrics or tapestries, antependia were introduced during the early Christian period to veil altars with open fronts. During the Middle Ages, more elaborate antependia were constructed of painted panels or precious metals, often decorated with repoussé figures (for example, the Basel antependium, now in the Musée de Cluny, Paris).

LESLIE BRUBAKER

ANTHEMIOS OF TRALLES, a Byzantine engineer and mathematician who, with Isidoros of Miletus, designed the domed Justinianic church of Hagia Sophia, Istanbul, built between 532 and 537. Anthemios may have died in 534 before the church was finished.

LESLIE BRUBAKER

ANTHOLOGIA LATINA. In a narrow sense, the term frequently refers to a collection of short poems and excerpts that appears to have been made in North Africa about the time of the Vandal kingdom's collapse in 534. This anthology has come down to us, wanting its first portion, in the so-called *Codex Salmasianus* (Paris, Bibliothèque Nationale, MS lat. 10318) of the late seventh or early eighth century. It contains selections from classical poets, trick forms of poetry (acrostics and the like), the riddles of Symphosius, the poems of Luxorius, the *Pervigilium Veneris,* and much other material. Many of the pieces reappear in other manuscripts.

There is no warrant, however, for speaking more broadly of "the Latin Anthology" as though there were one standard collection, entitled *Anthologia latina* and frequently copied during the Middle Ages. Such a use of the term, though common, is misleading. Various manuscript anthologies of verse, reflecting the tastes and backgrounds of those responsible for them, share some poems with the *Salmasianus;* yet they are not multiple copies of the same collection.

BIBLIOGRAPHY

No treatment of the *Salmasianus* anthology is totally free of the confusion described above. See Morris Rosenblum, *Luxorius: A Latin Poet among the Vandals* (1961), for the most complete discussion in English, along with useful bibliography. The *Salmasianus* is edited in Franciscus Buecheler and Alexander Riese, *Anthologia latina, sive poesis Latinae supplementum,* 2 vols. (1894–1926; repr. 1973). The edition fails to respect the orthography of the manuscript.

DAVID R. TOWNSEND

ANTHOLOGIES. The words "anthology," "florilegium," and "excerpt" are all closely connected and derive from the image of plucking flowers; "florilegium" *(flores + legere)* is simply the Latin equivalent of Greek *anthologia* (ἄνθους + λεγειν), and "excerpt" comes from *ex-carpere,* "to pluck." In modern critical terminology, however, anthology is usually distinguished from florilegium: the former is a collection of complete texts, the latter consists of extracts or excerpts from longer works. One might describe the *Golden Treasury of English Verse* as an anthology but the *Oxford Book of Quotations* as a florilegium.

FLORILEGIA

There are florilegia of both prose and verse. Prose florilegia are usually collections of wise sayings excerpted from philosophers and theologians, and often amount to collections of proverbs: indeed, the Old Testament Book of Proverbs (usually ascribed to Solomon) was a kind of model. In late antiquity the works of Seneca were culled for wise sayings, which were rearranged into collections, such as the *De paupertate honesta* and the *Liber de moribus* (also called the *De institutione morum*); these were popular throughout the Middle Ages. Similar collections were made from the works of the Latin Fathers, Augustine, Gregory, Jerome, and so on.

The great *summae* of the later Middle Ages (such as John of Bromyard's *Summa predicantium,* intended for the use of preachers) were in effect florilegia organized by subject heading. Students of medieval literature must be cautious in interpreting references to, or quotations from, ancient authors as indications of direct knowledge of the whole of that author's works, as the source may well have been a florilegium; literary interpretations that depend on the original context of an allusion are very dangerous.

Not all prose florilegia are moral: in the thirteenth century Laurent, a monk of St. Omer, compiled the popular *Liber floridus* (not a "flowery book" but a book consisting of extracts) of geographical selections, accompanied by maps and diagrams and some verses. The *Florilegium Angelicum* (from San Angelo) was a popular collection of the sayings of classical and patristic authors, and directly influenced writers such as Giraldus Cambrensis.

Florilegia of verse, based on both classical and medieval poets, were used for teaching: they seem to have been planned as much for their meter, grammar, and style as for their content. Extracts varied in length from a single line (often modified grammati-

ANTHOLOGIES

cally so that it would stand alone) to long passages, such as Vergil's description of Fame, or Ovid's House of Rumor (perhaps used to teach the arts of description). Many classical poets, such as Tibullus and Propertius, were known to the Middle Ages mainly through florilegia rather than from complete texts of their works. Verse florilegia could vary in content according to the knowledge and interest of the individual scribe or compiler, but some had a kind of separate existence: the *Florilegium Gallicum* ("French florilegium") exists in many copies that contain essentially the same extracts.

ANTHOLOGIES

Anthologies of prose are, of course, rare; few pieces of prose are short enough to be anthologized. Some collections were made, however, for specific purposes, such as collections of letters for teaching epistolary composition. Collections of medical recipes have an obvious practical application, but many of them are so disorganized that they appear to have been gathered together as anthologies rather than as usable manuals. Short chemical and technical recipes were collected in a fluid composition known as the *Mappae clavicula.* At the end of the Middle Ages Konrad Kyeser composed a lavishly illustrated book of military inventions called *Bellifortis*; many parts are from a much earlier collection of magical and pseudochemical recipes. The *Bellifortis* was thus itself an anthology of sorts, and copies made from it add and subtract both text and illustrations.

Verse anthologies are as old as literature itself. Most short poems, other than a few scribbled on flyleaves or quoted in prose works, have come down to us in collections, often of hundreds of poems. In some respects the history of medieval lyric poetry (or of short poems) is a history of anthologies: books, chapters, and articles are devoted not to authors or genres but to collections, such as the poems of the Exeter Book (Old English), the *Carmina burana* (Latin), and the Harley Lyrics (Middle English). This is due partly to the anonymity of most medieval short verse: in the absence of a known author the literary historian is almost obliged to use the anthology as his own organizing principle.

Perhaps fewer than five percent of medieval short poems even in Latin—and still fewer in vernacular languages—can be assigned to specific authors. The anonymity of the short poems results in part from the nature of the collections themselves: their compilers were not interested, as we are, in individual authors but in making readable collections of poems. Even where names are given, they are often no more than guesses by scribes. With great difficulty and only mixed success modern editors have managed to disentangle the poems of, for example, Walter of Châtillon, Hildebert of Le Mans, Petrus Pictor, Marbod of Rennes, and others from the anthologies; their names are given in very few of the manuscripts. Scarcely any vernacular poems have been successfully attributed to known authors.

The anthologies are much more fluid in content than the florilegia; although we can occasionally group together a set of anthologies because of their shared poems, the texts that they share rarely form more than about a quarter—if that—of the total content of each manuscript. They appear to draw on a common fund of popular poems; some may have been compiled in universities. The methods of compilation can sometimes be inferred from their physical makeup: some collections were written down from end to end, but many were written in booklets (often consisting of only a single quire or gathering of eight or ten leaves). Many anthologies "grew" over a long period, even centuries, by the addition of further quires and the entry of more poems on blank leaves and in blank spaces; some apparently uniform collections were copied from collections that had grown accretively, and the detection of blocks of material sometimes indicates common authorship of a group of poems (this method has helped in the establishment of the canon of Walter of Châtillon's poems).

The oldest medieval anthology is the *Anthologia latina,* the nucleus of which is contained in the so-called Codex Salmasianus; this is probably of North African origin and contains in its various forms both pagan and Christian poems and epigrams. It was copied frequently, and pieces of it turn up in anthologies throughout the Middle Ages. The manuscript is of the seventh or eighth century, and the collection was made earlier, probably sometime around the Vandal kingdom's collapse in 534.

From the eleventh century on we have many important anthologies. In ten leaves at the end of Cambridge University Library, MS Gg. 5. 35, written in Canterbury in the mid eleventh century (itself an important collection of major Christian Latin epic poems), is the collection of over forty poems known as the "Cambridge Songs." These include sacred and profane, comic and erotic, metrical and rhythmical spring celebrations and funeral laments. A chance reference by the satirist Sextus Amarcius to a minstrel whose repertoire included some poems that can be identified with the Cambridge collection makes it probable that it was originally a songbook: some of the items are provided with neumes (an early musical notation); from the contents it is clear that the Canterbury text was copied from an original collection made in the area of the lower Rhine. Also from this period is the Exeter Book, a unique collection of vernacular Old English poems.

In the second half of the twelfth century Petrus Riga, author of the *Aurora,* composed a collection of short poems known as the *Floridus aspectus.* The nucleus of this collection is preserved in Arsenal MS 1136 (Paris), but the collection is more important in that pieces from it are often found in a series of related anthologies of the works of Hildebert of Le Mans and Marbod of Rennes. One of the biggest collections of this group is known as the "Saint-Gatien" anthology (formerly Tours, Bibliothèque Municipale, MS 890, now lost); many manuscripts show affinities to this collection, such as British Library MS Add. 24199 (from Bury St. Edmunds) and Cotton MS Vitellius A. XII. From this period we begin to see the major satirical collections, such as Oxford, Bodley MS 603, containing some of Walter of Châtillon's satires against the papal Curia.

The thirteenth century is undoubtedly the greatest period for the compilation of Latin anthologies. Its most famous product is the Codex Buranus (Munich, Staatsbibliothek, MS clm. 4660), containing the *Carmina burana.* This collection includes satire, an unsurpassed collection of love songs, some drinking and dicing poems, and some religious drama; a few of the poems are in German. Important though the Buranus is, it should not be allowed entirely to eclipse other great anthologies of the period, such as the "Florence Antiphonary" (Florence, MS Laurent. plut. 29. 1), a massive musical collection. Related to these is the small songbook known as the "Later Cambridge Songs" ("Die jüngere Cambridger Liedersammlung," MS Ff. 1. 17 in the Cambridge University Library). Other important anthologies include one from the library of Queen Christina of Sweden, originally probably compiled in France and now in the Vatican (MS Reg. lat. 344), and Paris, Bibliothèque Nationale, MS 11867, perhaps compiled in England.

England certainly produced several important verse collections: the "Bekynton Anthology" (Oxford, Bodleian Library, MS Add. A. 44) is an English rival to the Buranus for its length and catholicity of taste; in the fifteenth century it belonged to Thomas Bekynton, bishop of Bath and Wells and Henry VI's chancellor, who had it indexed and amplified. Among other English satirical anthologies are Cambridge, Trinity College, MS 0. 2. 45 (from Cerne Abbas, Dorset) and British Library, MS Harley 978 from Reading (incidentally famous for its text of the English poem "Sumer Is Icumen In"). In addition to Latin satire (the major contents) these two collections also contain French verse, and from this period onward we begin to see the emergence of collections of vernacular poetry, such as the Codex Regius, which is one of our main sources for the Icelandic Eddic poems.

A well-known anthology from the early fourteenth century is the collection of Harley Lyrics, the English and French poems in British Library, MS Harley 2253, which includes satire, religious verse, and love poems. This manuscript is also notable for having been written in a script previously reserved for legal documents (rather than in a normal book hand), but a collection of Latin satire compiled about 1310 by a Durham lawyer (Cambridge, Corpus Christi College, MS 450) is also in a legal hand. Other parts of Britain produced anthologies, such as Wolfenbüttel, Herzog. August. Bibliothek, MS Helmst. 628 (from St. Andrews in Scotland), and Madrid, Real Biblioteca, MS 2 N 4 (compiled for Margaret of Dumfries). From a Franciscan library in Ireland came the interesting trilingual anthology (now British Library, MS Harley 913) that contains the burlesque "Land of Cockaigne" as well as French and Latin satirical prose and verse. Shorter collections of Latin lyrics continued to appear, such as the Arundel Lyrics (now British Library, MS Arundel 384). Toward the end of the fourteenth century we see the massive Vernon Manuscript (now in the Bodleian Library, Oxford), which contains not only many short religious lyrics but also long texts such as *Piers Plowman;* it is closely related to the Simeon Manuscript, now British Library, MS Add. 22283.

Latin anthologies continued to appear throughout the fifteenth century. Sometime after 1469 John Wilde, precentor of Waltham Abbey and author of a treatise on music, produced a fine collection of prose and poetry, much of it dealing with British history (it begins with Trojan history and ends with poems on the reign of Henry V); it is now in the Bodleian Library, MS Rawlinson B. 214. In Bohemia—which had ties with England through Richard II's wife, Anne of Bohemia, and because of the political links between the English Lollards and the Bohemian Hussites—the English satirical tradition took on a new life, and many Latin anthologies of

Bohemian provenance can be related textually to English ones.

The influence of the professional bookseller was considerable. In the fourteenth century a bookseller probably in Oxford produced a set of small booklets, some scientific, some poetic, each of which sold for two or three shillings; this is now Bodleian Library, MS Digby 166. A London bookseller compiled the Auchinleck (pronounced Afflek) Manuscript, a well-known collection of English verse romances. In the fifteenth century booksellers may have produced anthologies to order (a "bespoke" trade); this seems to have been the case with the "Grete Boke" of Sir John Paston, prepared by the bookseller William Ebsham; it contained works of chivalry and romance. The most famous English "publisher" was John Shirley, who is responsible for many of the "aureate" collections of poetry by Chaucer, Lydgate, and others; of these fine books the most famous is the Fairfax Manuscript, now in the Bodleian Library. Such collections were made into the sixteenth century; here we may note the Scottish anthology known as the Bannatyne Manuscript, which contains both Middle English and Middle Scots poetry.

Most anthologies, even those clearly associated with monastic houses, were probably compiled by individuals purely for their own amusement (though some may have been used for teaching rhetoric and metrical composition, such as the thirteenth-century anthology now in Glasgow, Hunterian Museum, MS V. 8. 14); many probably belonged to students. The nature of the contents probably depended more on editorial inertia than on deliberate planning—that is, compilers probably drew on existing anthologies to make up their own books. Some collections, however, were clearly made by individuals for specific purposes: some have a clear theme (such as mortality lyrics), others may have been designed to provide material for sermons. Sometimes the contents of a manuscript were not planned in advance but were entered into a book of blank pages according to the fancy of the compiler—these are what we call "commonplace books." At the other extreme, we may note the highly organized Bohemian collection known as the *Summa recreatorum,* a fifteenth-century compilation of prose and verse designed specifically for entertainment, which drew on earlier anthologies.

Anthologies, particularly of medieval Latin poems, can be used by modern readers simply as sources for the discovery of previously unknown poems, but they should also be studied as cultural documents in themselves. Frequently they can show the continuing popularity of works long after they were originally written: fifteenth-century collections often contain not only contemporary poems but goliardic satire of the twelfth and thirteenth centuries, and even works from the *Appendix Vergiliana* and the *Anthologia latina.* An anthology can thus serve as a kind of index to the taste of an age, and the selection and organization of its contents can sometimes also give a glimpse into the imagination and literary values of the compiler.

BIBLIOGRAPHY

A. G. Rigg, "Medieval Latin Poetic Anthologies," in *Mediaeval Studies,* **39** (1977), **40** (1978), **41** (1979), **43** (1981). The first article in this series contains a full bibliography of published anthologies.

A. G. Rigg

[See also **Anthologia Latina; Cambridge Songs; Carmina Burana.**]

ANTHONY OF PADUA, ST. (*ca.* 1195–1231), Franciscan preacher and saint, was born in Lisbon and died at Arcella, near Padua. Anthony was an immensely popular figure as a preacher in his own lifetime in northern Italy and southern France, and as a saint after his death, both in his native Portugal and in his adopted city and region of Padua in northeastern Italy.

Born into a family of the lesser military nobility and baptized Ferdinand, he received his first formal education at the Lisbon cathedral school and then at age fifteen he joined the regular canons of São Vicente in Lisbon. He had himself transferred to a study house of his order at Coimbra, where he became proficient in the study of biblical literature and theology.

In 1220 the relics of five Franciscan missionaries killed in Morocco were paraded about the towns of Portugal, including Coimbra. Ferdinand was so impressed that he joined the Franciscan Order, with a resolve to carry on the mission of those martyrs. He took on the Franciscan habit (and probably then changed his name to Anthony) in the friary of San Antonio at Olivares, near Coimbra. He set out on his mission to Morocco, but illness forced him to alter his plans and on the return trip from North Africa his ship was thrown off course and landed in Sicily.

Anthony took part in the Franciscan "Chapter of

Mats" at Assisi in 1221. From there he was sent to a hermitage near Forlì, still unknown and still perhaps a stranger in a foreign culture. But on the occasion of an ordination when he was called upon to speak, he so overwhelmed his auditors with his erudition and rhetorical skill that he was immediately catapulted to an important role in his order and to fame.

Saint Francis of Assisi commissioned Anthony to serve as lector of theology for the order, the first to hold such a post. He taught subsequently at Bologna, Montpellier, and Toulouse. He was called on to preach against the Catharist heretics in several places in northern Italy and southern France, and he briefly held administrative posts in his order at Le Puy and Limoges as well as in the Romagna. From 1227 until his death in 1231 he preached indefatigably; this steady round of preaching included a session at the papal court in March 1228 at the request of Pope Gregory IX.

The same pope canonized Anthony within a year of his death, and from that time on the Franciscans have honored him as a Doctor of the Church. The life *(Legenda prima)* of Saint Anthony was written probably by one of his confreres at Padua, possibly in connection with the canonization, in any case close to the time of the subject's life.

Saint Anthony's preaching focused on the fundamental evangelical virtues; its more contemporary emphases included the humanity of Christ, the Eucharist, the sacrament of penance, exhortations to restore or maintain civic peace, pleas for the extension of political rights to the urban poor, and attacks against usury, theft, simony, and the imprisonment of nonfraudulent debtors. The principal collections of sermons are the *Sermones dominicales per annum, Sermones in solemnitatibus sanctorum,* and *Sermones in laudem et honorem beatae Mariae Virginis.*

BIBLIOGRAPHY

Sophronius Clasen, *St. Anthony, Doctor of the Gospel* (1961); Léon de Kerval, ed., *Sancti Antonii de Padua vitae duae* (1904); Beda Kleinschmidt, *Antonius von Padua in Leben und Kunst* (1931).

LESTER K. LITTLE

[See also **Franciscans; Francis of Assisi (St.).**]

ANTICHRIST. According to medieval tradition, Antichrist was a thoroughly evil human being (not a devil) who was expected to reign in Jerusalem in a hideous parody of Christ's ministry before the Last Judgment. Since ecclesiastical writers assumed that many evil people were already preparing the way for Antichrist's reign, precursors and ministers of Antichrist could also be called antichrists. A third use of the word was more theological: just as Christ was the mystical head of his body, the church, so Antichrist was the mystical head of the human body of evil.

The ultimate source for medieval Antichrist doctrine was the New Testament. The name Antichrist appears only in the first two epistles of John (1 John 2:18, 22; 4:3; 2 John 7), which make a clear distinction between the coming great Antichrist and his precursors—"as ye have heard that Antichrist shall come, even now there are many antichrists." Richer sources for the development of subsequent medieval Antichrist lore were passages in Second Thessalonians and the book of Revelation. In 2 Thess. 2:3–8 St. Paul referred to a "man of sin" or "son of perdition" whom medieval commentators understood to be Antichrist. This evil figure would not come until "a falling away" had taken place. Then he would sit in the temple of God until the Lord would destroy him. Revelation's "beast from the sea" and "beast from the earth" (chapter 13) were also widely understood by medieval exegetes to stand for Antichrist. Accordingly, medieval commentators believed that Antichrist would reign for forty-two months (Rev. 13:5), would deceive men by performing "great wonders" (13:13), but would finally be defeated by the power of the Lord and cast into "a lake of fire burning with brimstone" (19:20).

Patristic and early medieval commentators expatiated on these and a few other biblical texts (sometimes rather arbitrarily) to create a full-scale Antichrist myth. Important contributions to the developing lore and theological interpretation of Antichrist's career were made by Hippolytus of Rome, St. Jerome, Pseudo-Methodius, the Venerable Bede, and Haimo of Auxerre. The first Latin writer to assemble all the major prior elements of the Antichrist story into one treatise—virtually a life of Antichrist—was the tenth-century Burgundian monk, Adso of Montier-en-Der. Adso's tract quickly became extremely popular and influential, but it was by no means the only Antichrist tract to gain wide circulation: among numerous other popular ones written in the High Middle Ages were those of Hugh Ripelin (written around 1265 and originally part of Hugh's *Compendium of Theological Truth*);

the "Passauer Anonymous" (mid thirteenth century); John of Paris (1300); and Hugh of Novocastro (1319). Although writers disagreed about particular points of interpretation, the broadest outlines of Antichrist lore remained more or less constant from the time of Adso until the end of the Middle Ages.

Most medieval commentators believed that St. Paul's "falling away" referred to the end of the Roman Empire and that Antichrist would therefore not come until it was destroyed. But since medieval tradition assumed that the Frankish and German empires of the Middle Ages were direct continuations of the Roman Empire, medieval authorities usually concluded that Antichrist's advent would occur only after the reign of a final medieval Western emperor. Often this emperor was expected to be a marvelous messianic hero, who would unite the world and reign in peace before laying down his crown in Jerusalem in expectation of Antichrist's coming.

Around the time of the Roman Empire's decline or fall, Antichrist would be born in Babylon from the incestuous union of a father and daughter; while still in his mother's womb the devil would take possession of his soul. He would be called Antichrist because he would be contrary to Christ in all things. In his youth he would learn to perform magic, and in his thirtieth year he would appear openly in Jerusalem. Then he would reign triumphantly for three and a half years. He would deceive the Jews by telling them he was the Messiah and would deceive many Christians by saying he was Christ come to judgment. His evil or deluded followers would worship him sacrilegiously, and he would keep them enthralled by performing many bogus miracles.

In order to hearten the faithful and counteract Antichrist's wiles, the Lord would send "two witnesses" clothed in sackcloth (Rev. 11:3–11) to preach against him. Almost all medieval commentators agreed that these witnesses were to be Elijah and Enoch because the Lord had said at the end of the Old Testament, "Behold, I will send you Elijah the prophet before the coming of the great and dreadful day of the Lord" (Mal. 4:5), and because both Elijah and Enoch (Gen. 5:24) did not die in the body but were believed to have been transported to the hidden earthly paradise. The two witnesses would preach steadfastly against Antichrist, but finally, after 1,260 days, he would kill them. Their bodies would then lie for three days in the streets of Jerusalem without burial because all would fear to bury them, but the two would be resurrected on the fourth day (Rev. 11:11).

After three and a half years of triumph, Antichrist himself would be killed on the Mount of Olives either by Christ directly or by Christ's power exercised through the agency of the Archangel Michael. But human history would not end immediately. A span of time, usually expected to be short, would follow for the penitence of those who had wavered in their faith during Antichrist's ascendance. In some accounts this final period would also see the conversion of the Jews and heathens, and the renewal or spiritual improvement of the church. Only thereafter would come a final evil onslaught of Gog and Magog (Rev. 20:8), the Last Judgment, and the end of the world.

BIBLIOGRAPHY

Adso Dervensis, *De ortu et tempore antichristi,* D. Verhelst, ed. (1976); Adso's tract is translated in Bernard McGinn, *Apocalyptic Spirituality* (1979), 89–96; Klaus Aichele, *Das Antichristdrama des Mittelalters, der Reformation und Gegenreformation* (1974); Wilhelm Bousset, *The Antichrist Legend, a Chapter in Christian and Jewish Folklore* (1896); Richard K. Emmerson, *Antichrist in the Middle Ages: A Study of Medieval Apocalypticism, Art, and Literature* (1981); Robert E. Lerner, "Refreshment of the Saints: The Time After Antichrist as a Station for Earthly Progress in Medieval Thought," in *Traditio,* **32** (1976); Alexander Patschovsky, *Der Passauer Anonymus* (1968), 157–168; D. Verhelst, "La préhistoire des conceptions d'Adson concernant l'Antichrist," in *Recherches de théologie ancienne et médiévale,* **40** (1973).

ROBERT E. LERNER

ANTIFEMINISM. In the Prologue to Chaucer's Wife of Bath's Tale, the Wife states:

> For trusteth wel, it is an impossible
> That any clerk [cleric] wol speke good of wyves,
> But if [unless] it be of hooly seintes lyves,
> Ne of noon oother womman never the mo.
> (III, 688–691)

There is a great deal of truth in her accusation. Monasticism provided a congenial atmosphere for misogyny, and works written by clerics were a major source of the antifeminism of the Middle Ages.

Most antifeminist literature was based at least in part on works by the church fathers, who blamed woman for the Fall and considered Eve the prototype for all women. Tertullian's attitude in *De cultu feminarum* (Of the Training of Women), written around 200, is typical.

> You give birth, O woman, in pains and anxieties; and your desire goes to your husband, and he will lord it over you. And do you not know that you are Eve? God's judgment over this sex continues in this eon; its guilt must also continue. You are the gate of the devil, the traitor of the tree, the first deserter of divine law; you are she who enticed the one whom the devil dare not approach; you broke so easily the image of God, man; on account of the death you deserved, even the Son of God had to die.
>
> (1:1)

Like Tertullian, most of the church fathers had a low conception of women's motives and functions. They feared their attractiveness and exhorted them to hide their beauty. Rather than considering men responsible for their own sexual desires, they placed the blame on women. Asceticism and antifeminism were closely connected. The church fathers disparaged motherhood and saw virginity as superior to marriage. They believed that woman could rise above her sinful, earthbound nature only by retaining her virginity. Most of them wrote works in favor of virginity, including Tertullian, Cyprian, Ambrose, Jerome, and Augustine.

Jerome's *Epistle Against Jovinian* (393), a particularly popular authority, was written to refute the contention that a virgin is no better than a wife in the sight of God. Jerome quotes the *Golden Book on Marriage* by Theophrastus, a supposed disciple of Aristotle. This work survives only in Jerome's quotation, but his paraphrase became immensely popular and led an independent existence of its own. Theophrastus states that a wise man will not marry, for philosophy and marriage do not go together. Wives make many material and emotional demands and lecture their husbands all night long. Men learn of their wives' faults only after marriage, since—unlike horses, mules, cattle, slaves, and household objects—wives are not tested until after the bargain is consummated. Theophrastus goes on to show that whether a woman is rich or poor, beautiful or ugly, she will bring misfortune to her husband.

Theophrastus was quoted by many later writers, including Walter Map, John of Salisbury, Abelard, Deschamps, and Chaucer. Much of the literature characterized as antifeminist is in fact antimatrimonial.

Another important source for the low opinion of women inherited by the Middle Ages was the medical and scientific literature of antiquity. Believing that he had scientific evidence, Aristotle held that women were physically, intellectually, and morally inferior to men. He claimed that in nature, the male of the species was always larger, stronger, and more agile; therefore, men were meant to be dominant. Even in reproduction, he claimed, the male played the active, effective role—the female the passive one: contributing soil to nourish the male seed. He went so far as to claim that the female was an incomplete male produced by a defect in the active force of the semen.

Medieval Christian theorists rejected this last point, believing that women could not be misbegotten since they were created by God. Nevertheless, they followed most of Aristotle's points regarding the inferiority of women. Thomas Aquinas passed on much of Aristotle's lore in his *Summa theologica,* where he claimed that women were meant to be subject to men since reason predominates in men. He too saw men as playing the more active, important role in reproduction. Averroës claimed that women were less efficient than men in most activities. Medieval Latin writers agreed with this assessment, seeing women as weaker, less capable, and less reasonable.

Medieval satirists thus had a number of theological and scientific authorities to draw upon to support their antifeminism. They did not initiate antifeminist satire but formalized it and developed it as a separate genre. Independent satires first appeared in Latin in the twelfth century, including Walter Map's popular *Letter from Valerius to Rufinus Against Taking a Wife* (*ca.* 1181). In this work, Walter, under the pseudonym of Valerius, exhorts his friend not to marry, warning him about the evils of women and the inconveniences of marriage. *De coniuge non ducenda* ("Do Not Take a Wife"), written at the beginning of the thirteenth century, remained popular until the sixteenth. In this satire, the author is saved from marrying by a vision of three angels, who warn him about the evils of women. The work was translated by John Lydgate in the fifteenth century as *The Payne and Sorow of Evyll Maryage.* A Continental satire on women and marriage, *The Lamentations of Matheolus,* was occasioned by the Council of Lyons (1274) and written to support the cause of clerical celibacy. The work was used to support more general misogynistic feelings and won a broader audience in the French translation done by Jean Le Fevre in the fourteenth century.

Antifeminist satire in Latin also appears as parts of works written for other purposes. In his *Historia calamitatum* ("The Story of My Misfortunes"), written in 1135, Peter Abelard used his life as an exemplum so that the reader could see how small his problems were in comparison and could thus bear them more easily. Among Abelard's misfortunes was his love affair with Heloise, which resulted in her vengeful uncle having him castrated. In the *Historia,* Heloise argues against getting married, using Jerome and Theophrastus as authorities. In *Policraticus* John of Salisbury provides many examples of women who brought misery to their lovers or husbands and cites Cleopatra and Dido as examples of the disastrous consequences of female rule. John attacks marriage in a section on "The Annoyance and Burdens of Wedlock," quoting Theophrastus. John claims that women are frivolous, unreasonable, cruel, and lecherous. In Richard de Bury's fourteenth-century *Philobiblon,* clerics are advised to flee from a certain "biped beast" named woman and to fear her more than the asp or basilisk, for she reviles books, condemns them as superfluous, and wishes to exchange them for expensive clothes. Richard acknowledges that her antipathy is justified, if one considers the contents of books such as Ecclesiasticus, Theophrastus' *Golden Book on Marriage,* and Walter Map's *Letter to Rufinus.*

Satires were also written in the vernacular by clerics. One of the most influential was Jean de Meung's section of *The Romance of the Rose,* written in the latter part of the thirteenth century. Jean uses the speech of Le Jaloux, the jealous husband, to introduce the commonplaces of antifeminist and antimatrimonial literature into his work. His sources represent the central texts of the tradition: Juvenal, Ovid, Jerome, Theophrastus, Abelard, and Walter Map. The accusations made by these authors are set forth in the dramatic context of a vituperative tirade addressed by Le Jaloux to his wife. The confession of La Vieille (the Old Woman), the duenna of the Rose, regarding her own tricks and those of other women, provides evidence for the truth of Le Jaloux's accusations. Since *The Romance of the Rose* was one of the most popular works of the Middle Ages, Jean's use of antifeminist material was particularly influential. Christine de Pisan, the first woman writer to speak up for the female sex, attacked Jean de Meung as the representative of antifeminist clerics in the *Letter to the God of Love,* written about 1400 and translated by Thomas Hoccleve as the *Letter of Cupid* about 1402.

Antifeminism was not merely a product of the cloister but was also expressed by authors who addressed a courtly audience of men and women. In these works, antifeminism was one side of a rhetorical game of coquetry played out between the sexes. The idealization of courtly love was balanced by the satire of antifeminism, and the same writers often expressed both sentiments. Many authors who wrote idealistic love poems in which they played the role of the servile, courtly lover also wrote poems of rebellion in which they attacked their ladies. Outbursts of antifeminism can be found in the midst of courtly romances such as *Sir Gawain and the Green Knight* (*ca.* 1375–1400), when Gawain, the paragon of chivalry and courtesy, utters a tirade against women after finding out that he has been tricked by the lady of the castle. Eustache Deschamps (1346–1406), the author of many courtly lyrics, also wrote the *Mirror of Marriage* (*ca.* 1381–1389), a satire in the dissuasion-against-marriage tradition.

Antifeminism as a kind of game is apparent in the debates, often between birds, on the value of women. The earliest example in English is *The Owl and the Nightingale* (*ca.* 1200), where women are defended by the courtly nightingale and opposed by the ascetic owl. In *The Thrush and the Nightingale* (*ca.* 1275), the thrush gives examples of evil women, but the nightingale defeats him with an appeal to woman's perfection as shown by the Virgin Mary. A similar argument is conducted by a man and a woman in the fifteenth-century *Debat de l'omme et de la femme* by Guillaume Alexis, translated into English as *Interlocucyon with an Argument betwyxt Man and Woman, Whiche of Them Could Proue to be Most Excellet.* The man cites evil examples such as Delilah, Bathsheba, Solomon's wives, and Helen of Troy; whereas the woman opposes him with Esther, Judith, and the Virgin Mary.

The debate form is also used in the Holly and Ivy carols. The origin of the strife between these two forms of Christmas greenery appears to be connected with the survival of a pagan fertility rite associated with the celebration of Yule. Since Holly is masculine and Ivy feminine, these songs become a contention over what the Wife of Bath called "maistrye." Sometimes Ivy wins, and other times Holly is victorious. In the later Middle Ages, the argument became a game in which one of the features was the exclusion of Ivy from the hall.

Punctuation poems are an obvious literary game. The following example is feminist if read according to line division but antifeminist if read according to punctuation.

> In women is rest peas and pacience
> No season. for-soth outht of charite

Bothe be nyght & day. thei haue confidence
All wey of treasone. Owt of blame thei be
No tyme as men say. Mutabilite
They haue without nay. but stedfastnes
In theym may ye neuer fynde y gesse. Cruelte
Suche condicons they haue more & lesse.
(*Secular Lyrics,* p. 102)

The game aspect of antifeminism also emerges in the coy apologies to ladies set forth by some authors. A master of this kind of rhetorical game, Chaucer plays it in his own voice in the Prologue to *The Legend of Good Women,* where the God of Love accuses him of antifeminism because of his translation of *The Romance of the Rose* and his narration of *Troilus and Criseyde,* a tale of an unfaithful woman. He plays it in the voice of the Nun's Priest in the Nun's Priest's Tale of the Cock and the Hen. The Nun's Priest utters a bit of antifeminism in front of the Prioress, his superior, but then disclaims responsibility: "Thise been the cokkes wordes, and nat myne" (VII, 3265). Chaucer's good-natured portrait of the Wife of Bath turns the entire antifeminist tradition into a game and exposes some of its absurdities. Her husband Jankyn's "book of wikked wyves" is a veritable anthology of antifeminist literature:

He hadde a book that gladly, nyght and day,
For his desport [amusement] he wolde rede
alway;
He cleped [called] it Valerie and Theofraste,
At which book he lough alwey ful faste.
And eek [also] ther was somtyme a clerk at
Rome,
A cardinal, that highte [was named] Seint
Jerome,
That made a book agayn Jovinian;
In which book eek ther was Tertulan,
Crisippus, Trotula, and Helowys,
That was abbesse nat fer fro Parys;
And eek the Parables of Salomon,
Ovides Art, and bookes many on,
And alle thise were bounden in o volume.
(III, 669–681)

The Wife is a clever preacher who refutes these authorities and reveals many of the absurdities of the antifeminist tradition, particularly its one-sided attack on sexuality and marriage. Although she has many of the faults criticized by antifeminists, she is a thoroughly likeable character, modeled on La Vieille in *The Romance of the Rose* but with none of her bitterness or vengefulness. In his complex portrait of her, Chaucer uses the antifeminist tradition and parodies it at the same time.

BIBLIOGRAPHY

Primary Sources. Peter Abelard, *The Story of My Misfortunes,* Henry A. Bellows, trans. (1972); Guillaume Alexis, *Oeuvres poétiques,* Arthur Piaget and Émile Picot, eds., I (1896); John W. H. Atkins, ed., *The Owl and the Nightingale* (1922); Diane Bornstein, ed., *The Feminist Controversy of the Renaissance* (1980); Richard de Bury, *The Love of Books,* E. C. Thomas, trans. (1888; repr. 1966); Geoffrey Chaucer, *The Works of Geoffrey Chaucer,* Fred Norris Robinson, ed. (1957); Richard L. Greene, ed., *The Early English Carols* (1935); Jerome, *The Principal Works of Jerome,* W. H. Fremantle, trans. (1893); *The Stateman's Book of John of Salisbury,* John Dickinson, trans. (1927); Guillaume de Loris and Jean de Meung, *The Romance of the Rose,* Charles Dahlberg, trans. (1971); John Lydgate, *The Minor Poems of John Lydgate,* H. N. Mac Cracken, ed. (1934); Walter Map, *De nugis curialium,* Frederick Tupper and Marbury B. Ogle, eds. (1924); Russell H. Robbins, ed., *Secular Lyrics of the Fourteenth and Fifteenth Centuries* (1952).

Secondary Literature. Vern L. Bullough, "Medieval Medical and Scientific Views of Women," in *Viator,* **4** (1973); and *The Subordinate Sex* (1973); Joan M. Ferrante, *Woman as Image in Medieval Literature* (1975); William Matthews, "The Wife of Bath and All Her Sect," in *Viator,* 5 (1974); Robert P. Miller, "The Wounded Heart: Courtly Love and the Medieval Antifeminist Tradition," in *Women's Studies,* **2** (1974); and "The Antifeminist Tradition," in *Chaucer: Sources and Backgrounds* (1977); Sarah B. Pomeroy, *Goddesses, Whores, Wives and Slaves* (1975); Katharine M. Rogers, *The Troublesome Helpmate: A History of Misogyny in Literature* (1966); George H. Tavard, *Woman in Christian Tradition* (1973); Francis L. Utley, *The Crooked Rib* (1970).

DIANE BORNSTEIN

[See also **Family.**]

ANTIOCH (modern Antakya in southern Turkey), was one of the great centers of classical culture in the eastern Mediterranean. Seat of one of the five patriarchates of the Christian church, it played a major part in the theological and Christological controversies of the fourth and fifth centuries and remained an ecclesiastical center of some importance even after its conquest by the Muslims.

It suffered a series of unparalleled disasters—fire, earthquake, sack by the Persians, and the bubonic plague—in the sixth century. Rebuilt by Justinian on a reduced scale, it never regained its ancient splendor. After a long Persian occupation (611–628), Heraclius recaptured Antioch only to lose it definitively to the Arabs in 638. Under Umayyad, Abbasid, Tulunid (878–898) and Hamdanid (944–969) rule, Antioch declined as trade routes shifted eastward, but remained an intellectual and military center; in the tenth century it was the headquarters of the al-ᶜAwāṣim military organization, a strategic zone of frontier fortresses.

In 969, the Byzantines recaptured and rebuilt the city, introducing a poorly known period of reoccupation terminated in 1084 by the Seljuks, who in turn yielded to the Norman crusaders in 1098 after a long siege. The struggle between the Normans and Byzantines in the late tenth and eleventh centuries was one of the important factors in the growing tension between eastern and western Christendom.

Antioch then became the capital of a feudal principality, with Normans and a Latin patriarch ruling a largely Greek Orthodox and Monophysite population. The city covered a vast area of about two square miles, not densely occupied but including many gardens and pastures, all protected by the walls of Justinian and the Byzantine citadel. Internal dissent weakened the state, which was under constant pressure from Muslims, Armenians, and Byzantines.

Although twice forced to recognize imperial suzerainty and briefly occupied by the Armenians (1216–1219), Antioch maintained its independence and an ever-shrinking territory until its destruction by the Mamluks in 1268. The vast booty then seized reveals the commercial success and prosperity of Antioch at that period, but the city never recovered from the devastation. Under the Mamluks (1268–1517), it became a small and inconsequential town. Constantly rising ground level, warfare, and neglect have covered or destroyed most of the city's monuments; of medieval Antioch only the citadel and some walls remain.

BIBLIOGRAPHY

Claude Cahen, *La syrie du nord à l'époque des croisades et la principauté franque d'Antioche* (1940); Glanville Downey, *A History of Antioch in Syria: From Seleucus to the Arab Conquest* (1961); Maurice Gaudefroy-Demombynes, *La Syrie à l'époque des Mamelouks d'après les auteurs arabes* (1923).

CLIVE FOSS

[See also **Baybars; Bohemond; Crusades and Crusader States to 1199; Nikephoros II Phokas; Saladin.**]

ANTIOCH, SONG OF. See **Cancun D'Antioche.**

ANTIOCHENE RITE, in patristic times the liturgy observed by the Church of Antioch and by those churches that were under its direct liturgical influence. In modern times the term designates the liturgical rites that derive, at least substantially, from the patristic Antiochene rite, that is, the Armenian, Byzantine, Maronite, and Syrian rites. A number of local intermediate rites can be called Antiochene, especially those of Asia, Pontus, Georgia, Cilicia, and Tagrit, but except for meager remnants of the last named, they have not survived into modern times, and the evidence furnished by historical documents does not suffice to give a clear picture of their relationships to the rite of Antioch.

The same is true of the relationship between the rites of Antioch and Jerusalem. Although we have more surviving documents from the ancient rite of Jerusalem (for example, the Armenian and Georgian lectionaries and the accounts of early pilgrims), these tend to point up only the peculiarities of the practices of Jerusalem that were connected with particular holy places. They do not indicate the more general similarities and differences between the usages of the two great ecclesiastical centers regarding the celebration of the Eucharist, the sacraments, and other ceremonies and offices in patristic times. We can say of the modern Antiochene rites that they have been strongly influenced by Jerusalem, yet the extent to which the patristic rite of Jerusalem was similar to or influenced by the rite of Antioch, or vice versa, is uncertain.

Scholars often divide the Antiochene rite into West Antiochene (Armenian, Byzantine, Maronite, and Syrian) and East Antiochene (Chaldean) rites. This is a mistake. The West Antiochene rites all show basic similarities that can best be explained by derivation from a common source, the patristic rite of Antioch. The Chaldean rite is basically different, with only a few secondary similarities due to mutual borrowings. The case of the Maronite rite is singular, however. It has a much greater resemblance to the Chaldean rite than do the other Antiochene rites. Mutual borrowings can explain some of the similarities, but others suggest a derivation from a common source. A probable explanation is that the Maronite rite originally derived from the same source as the Chaldean rite, which was presumably the rite of the Church of Edessa. Subsequently, the Maronite rite borrowed so extensively from the Syrian rite that it became Antiochene.

Little is known about the liturgical usages of Antioch before the fourth century. We do have the Didascalia of the Apostles from Syria of the third century, but it gives disappointingly few details. The fourth century, by contrast, provides three important documentary sources, the Antiochene homilies of John Chrysostom, the catechetical homilies of Theodore of Mopsuestia, and Book VIII of the Apostolic Constitutions. The order of ceremonies for the Eucharist and baptism in the three sources is fundamentally the same, but some secondary differences can be noted, possibly because the homilies of Theodore may reflect the usages of Cilicia, rather than those that he knew in Antioch. Book VIII of the Apostolic Constitutions is thought to have been composed by Apollinarists and may reflect the usages of Laodicea. Still, the discrepancies in both cases are so minor that we are fully justified in speaking of a single liturgical rite with local variations.

This one rite seems to have been observed in the Greek-speaking cities of the patriarchate of Antioch and to have been widely imitated outside, in Asia Minor, Armenia, and especially in Constantinople. John Chrysostom's homilies delivered in the imperial capital bear witness to some differences from the liturgy of his Antiochene homilies, but the similarities are even greater. To what extent Chrysostom himself may have been responsible for the similarities is not known. The Aramaic-speaking portion of the patriarchate of Antioch, on the other hand, seems to have enjoyed greater liturgical autonomy, to judge by the scanty documentary evidence that has survived. These areas adopted Syriac, the Aramaic dialect of Edessa, as their liturgical language. This, the formative influence of the hymns of St. Ephrem, and the Semitic culture tended to produce an independent liturgical rite.

This liturgical situation was profoundly influenced by the great ecclesiastical controversies of the fifth, sixth, and seventh centuries. First, the Nestorian movement led to the establishment of an independent church in the Persian Empire under the highly centralized authority of the katholikos of Seleucia-Ctesiphon. This church, which had numerous adherents in the Roman Empire, seems to have followed the liturgical usages of Edessa, which had crystallized by the middle of the seventh century into the Chaldean rite.

The Monophysite schism next affected large numbers of churches in both the Greek-speaking and Aramaic-speaking portions of the patriarchate of Antioch. When it was possible to organize an independent church in the sixth century, the Greek-speaking cities were under the control of the Orthodox emperors, and the Monophysite patriarchs were often obliged to establish their monasteries in Aramaic-speaking areas. As a result the liturgy was a sort of marriage between the Antiochene usages of the Greek speakers and the Edessene usages of the Aramaic speakers; the former prevailed generally in the liturgy of the Eucharist and the sacraments, whereas the Edessene usages tended to prevail in the divine office, in which Syriac hymns were chanted. From this marriage of usages came the Syrian rite.

The Monophysites also established a separate hierarchy in Persia among the Christians who rejected the theology of the Nestorians. Their chief bishop, called the Maphrian, had his see in the city of Tagrit on the Tigris. At first, their liturgy was presumably the same as that of the Nestorians, but the need to distinguish themselves liturgically from their rivals must have facilitated the early acceptance of Antiochene usages. Already in the ninth century, the commentary on the eucharistic liturgy by Moses bar Kefa presupposes an Antiochene liturgy that differs little from the modern Syrian rite. Today, one can still speak of a rite of Tagrit, but it amounts to no more than a local variation of the Syrian rite.

The Monophysite movement also won over the Church of Armenia, which already had its own autocephalous hierarchy under a katholikos. This church was able to maintain its own liturgy relatively intact for a time. After the Islamic invasions, the Armenians felt the need to ally themselves with their Christian neighbors, first with the Byzantine Empire and later with the Latin Crusader states, and these political ties were reflected in the liturgy. The Mass, in particular, was Byzantinized to the point that some have considered the Armenian rite a purely local variation of the Byzantine. Latin influence was much more superficial and was limited to such externals as episcopal headdress and the position of the Creed.

Within the Roman Empire, many of the Aramaic-speaking churches opposed both the Nestorians and the Monophysites. As a result of the Monothelite schism and the Islamic invasion, their ecclesiastical loyalties were divided: some maintained ties with the Orthodox churches of the Byzantine Empire, while others did not. The first ended by adopting integrally the Byzantine liturgy translated into Syriac or Palestinian Aramaic and later into Arabic. The others organized themselves into an autonomous church called the Maronite church, which has also had difficulties in maintaining its liturgical independence. First, under the crusaders, communion with the

Latin church was reestablished and Latin miters were adopted. After the departure of the crusaders, a reconciliation with the Syrian Monophysites occurred and a Maronite was even elected patriarch of the Monophysites.

The manuscripts of the fifteenth and sixteenth centuries bear witness to a progressive Syrianization of the Maronite Mass that virtually obliterated the earlier similarities to the Chaldean rite. Syrian anaphoras were introduced, some bearing the names of their Monophysite authors. This threat from the Monophysites led to a vigorous reaction from Rome that was exercised especially through Franciscan and Jesuit missionaries. Although this renewed Latin influence tended to concentrate on theology, canon law, and personal piety, the liturgy was also affected with regard to the use of unleavened bread, communion under one species, the multiplication of Masses on holy days, the adoption of a form of low Mass, and so on.

The hallmark of the Antiochene rite is the characteristic form of its eucharistic anaphora. This raises the question: What was the ancient eucharistic prayer of Antioch that would have corresponded to the Anaphora of Mark for Alexandria and the Roman Canon for Rome? It cannot have been the actual principal anaphora of the Syrian rite, the Anaphora of James, which has clearly been borrowed from Jerusalem. The most probable candidate seems to be the Anaphora of John Chrysostom, which formerly did not bear this title and may possibly have acquired it because it was introduced by him into Constantinople. The Syrians have a modified form of it and call it the Anaphora of the Twelve Apostles, but the Byzantine form seems older.

The Antiochene anaphora begins with a dialogue that has the Pauline Blessing (2 Corinthians 13:13) instead of "The Lord be with you," and "Let your minds (instead of "hearts") be on high." The eucharistic part of the anaphora that follows is characteristically divided into two prayers: a theological prayer that praises God and his creation and terminates with the Sanctus, and a Christological prayer that praises the work of redemption by Christ and terminates in a narration of the Last Supper. The narration, as in other, non-Antiochene anaphoras, is followed by an anamnesis and an epiclesis. The intercessions, unlike the non-Antiochene anaphoras, follow the epiclesis and terminate directly in a doxology.

There are few other distinctive characteristics of the Antiochene rite. Since it became the imperial rite, it was widely imitated. One feature, the litany, should be mentioned. The Byzantine rite may have exaggerated its use, but it has also preserved its ancient form and even many of the ancient petitions that are also found in Book VIII of the Apostolic Constitutions and the Antiochene homilies of John Chrysostom.

BIBLIOGRAPHY

Eusèbe Renaudot, *Liturgiarum orientalium collectio*, 2nd ed. II (1847); Heinrich Denzinger, *Ritus orientalium, Coptorum, Syrorum et Armenorum, in administrandis sacramentis*, 2 vols. (1863); F. E. Brightman, *Liturgies Eastern and Western*, I (1896); Alphonse Raes, *Introductio in liturgiam orientalem* (1962); Anton Baumstark, *Comparative Liturgy* (1958); William F. Macomber, "A Theory on the Origins of the Syrian, Maronite and Chaldean Rites," in *Orientalia Christiana periodica*, **39** (1973); Pierre Gemayel, *Avant-messe maronite, histoire et structure* (1965), esp. 43–88; Franz Xaver von Funk, *Didascalia et Constitutiones Apostolorum* (1905, repr. 1959); Franz van de Paverd, *Zur Geschichte der Messliturgie in Antiocheia und Konstantinopel gegen Ende des vierten Jahrhunderts* (1970); Theodorus, *Les homélies catéchétiques*, Raymond Tonneau and Robert Devreesse, eds. (1949); see also the bibliography in J.-M. Sauget, *Bibliographie des liturgies orientales (1900–1960)* (1962).

WILLIAM MACOMBER

[See also **Armenian Rite; Maronite Church; Monophysitism.**]

ANTIPHON, a word that seems to describe the early Christian practice of "sounding" short lyrical texts "against" psalms in a refrainlike manner. The antiphon was originally sung between every verse of a psalm or canticle: in the later Middle Ages normal procedure was to sing the incipit before the psalm and the whole antiphon only at the end. The term can refer to the whole item, psalm and refrain, but more properly signifies only the refrain.

At first, the text was one verse of the psalm, perhaps slightly paraphrased, and the antiphon would probably have usually been sung with that psalm. As the liturgy grew more complex, the connection disappeared and any antiphon could be used with any psalm. Some antiphons were drawn from other parts of the Bible. Gradually, nonscriptural sources such as saints' vitae provided the source for the texts, and poetic forms became more common. Introits, invitatories, communions, and offertories, all of which once had psalm verses, are special kinds of antiphon. Even though communions and offertories lost their psalm verses, these antiphons are not independent but are "psalm antiphons." The "refrains" of responsorial items are not called antiphons.

Other antiphons, composed or adapted later in the Middle Ages, were independent of a psalm and are best qualified by their function, for example, as processional or votive antiphons. Among the latter are the four famous Marian antiphons, *Alma Redemptoris mater, Regina caeli laetare, Salve regina,* and *Ave regina caelorum.* Some psalm antiphons were also used independently.

The first word or two are sung by a soloist, to set the pitch, and the choir then continues to the end. Despite the term "antiphon," the method of performance has nothing to do with antiphonal singing. Musically, the ferial day-to-day antiphons are very simple, restricted in range, and largely syllabic. There are several thousand, using a much smaller number of formulaic melodies; they are found in the choir psalter. Introit, invitatory, communion, and offertory antiphons are a little more elaborate; and the offertories, in particular, exhibit some unique features of melodic repetition. Invitatory antiphons occur in only a few of the melodic modes. Proper antiphons of all kinds are more florid, and the antiphons for the gospel canticles (Magnificat, Benedictus, and Nunc dimittis) are often highly ornamented and melismatic. Independent antiphons, especially processional and Marian ones, often have exuberant melodic characteristics quite unlike those of traditional tunes. Proper antiphons are given in the antiphonal or gradual.

BIBLIOGRAPHY

Willi Apel, *Gregorian Chant* (1958); Andrew Hughes, *Medieval Music: The Sixth Liberal Art,* rev. ed. (1980); and *Medieval Manuscripts for Mass and Office* (1982); Peter Wagner, *Introduction to the Gregorian Melodies,* Agnes Orme and E. G. P. Wyatt, trans., 2nd ed. rev. and enl. (1901, repr. 1962).

ANDREW HUGHES

ANTIPHONAL (ANTIPHONER, ANTIPHONARY), used in its most general sense, refers to a book that contains liturgical texts sung to melodic chants. Thus, prayers, lessons, psalms, and other texts sung to reciting formulas are not included. It is implicit that the chants are present, although this is not always guaranteed, even in modern usage. Prior to the twelfth century, the book giving the musical items of the services was sometimes called a cantatorium, and it is not clear that the *antiphonarium* was really different. The disappearance of the former word perhaps coincides with the reform of liturgical books and their contents in the twelfth century, when the antiphonal and responsorial chants were sometimes in separate books. Although the association of the former chants with the Mass and the latter with the offices is misleading, the books seem from this date to have been distinguished in this more practical way. Antiphonals containing only antiphons have no special name: most medieval books called antiphonals do contain the responsorial items, and the term needs to be used more carefully.

Excluding late additions such as tropes and sequences, the sung texts of the liturgy are in the Mass:

> *Agnus dei,* alleluia, communion,*Credo*
> *Gloria,* gradual, introit, *Ite missa est*
> *Kyrie,* offertory, *Sanctus,* tract

in the offices:

> antiphon, hymn, invitatory, responsory.

Books that contain the items for the Mass are sometimes called *antiphonaria missarum.* When abbreviated to *antiphonarium* or antiphonal, as it frequently is, this term can lead to considerable confusion, since "antiphonal," without qualification, refers to the book that contains the items from the offices. A more accurate title for the Mass book would nowadays be gradual. Whatever the title, Mass books may not include the italicized items; these are the ordinary of the Mass, the texts of which are mostly invariable. They are usually contained in the kyriale, which is a separate book or section of the gradual.

There are eight offices a day but, for most of the year, only one Mass a week. The book giving office items is therefore much larger, even though the hymns are usually written in a separate hymnal. Some books contain only antiphons and invitatories: these were presumably paired with a responsorial, containing the responsories. Such pairs of books seem more common in certain areas, especially Spain. Another slightly different separation is into a book for matins and lauds, the nocturnal, and one for the day offices, the diurnal.

Antiphonals usually contain only the proper items for the liturgical year, the incipits of the associated psalms, and sometimes a separate section, the venitarium, giving the tones for the invitatory psalm. Other ferial items are normally in the choir psalter. Rubrics sometimes appear, especially in English books. Less often there are chapters or prayers. Even when separated into summer and winter books, antiphonals have the Temporale, Proper, and Common of Saints in the usual liturgical order, but not often a Kalendar.

For catalog descriptions, the general definition as "the book containing the sung items of the offices" should be qualified by a more accurate identification of the contents.

BIBLIOGRAPHY

Virgil Fiala and Wolfgang Irtenkauf, "Versuch einer liturgischen Nomenklatur," in Clemens Köttelwesch, ed., *Zur Katalogisierung mittelalterlichen und neueren Handschriften* (1963), 105–137; P.-M. Gy, "Typologie et ecclésiologie des livres liturgiques médiévaux," in *La Maison-Dieu,* **121** (1975); René-Jean Hesbert, ed., *Antiphonale Missarum sextuplex* (1935); and *Corpus antiphonalium officii,* 4 vols. (1963–1970); Andrew Hughes, *Medieval Music: The Sixth Liberal Art,* rev. ed. (1980), nos. 502–525; and *Medieval Manuscripts for Mass and Office* (1982); John Plummer, *Liturgical Manuscripts for the Mass and the Divine Office* (1964).

ANDREW HUGHES

ANTIPOPE, someone said to hold the office of the Roman pontiff on the basis of a false or illegal claim. As many as fifty such individuals have been identified by scholars, although most would argue for a somewhat shorter list.

As good a working list as any was published by the Vatican scholar Angelo Mercati in 1947; it contains thirty-eight names:

Hippolytus, 217–235	Honorius II, 1061–1072
Novatian, 251	Clement III, 1080–1100
Felix II, 355–365	Theodoric, 1100
Ursinus, 366–367	Albert, 1102
Eulalius, 418–419	Sylvester IV, 1105–1111
Lawrence, 498–505	Gregory VIII, 1118–1121
Dioscorus, 530	Celestine II, 1124
Theodore, 687	Anacletus II, 1130–1138
Pascal, 687	Victor IV, 1138
Constantine, 767–769	Victor IV, 1159–1164
Philip, 768	Pascal III, 1164–1168
John, 844	Calistus III, 1168–1178
Anastasius, 855	Innocent III, 1179–1180
Christopher, 903–904	Nicholas V, 1328–1330
Boniface VII, 974	Clement VII, 1378–1394
Boniface VII, 984–985	Benedict XIII, 1394–1423
John XVI, 997–998	Alexander V, 1409–1410
Gregory, 1012	John XXIII, 1410–1415
Benedict X, 1058–1059	Felix V, 1439–1449

The antipopes in Mercati's list may be roughly divided into types by chronological periods: those with doctrinal differences (third to sixth century), those in the age of secular control of the church (ninth to mid eleventh century), those of the papal-imperial struggle (mid eleventh to late twelfth century), and those of the Great Schism (1378–1415).

Like all such lists, this one has problems, and a few examples will demonstrate certain limitations. The first antipope on the list, Hippolytus, so strongly opposed what he perceived as the heretical views of the reigning pontiff, Calistus I, that he set himself up, with the aid of sympathizers, as a rival pontiff. Then, during a wave of persecution, he was deported to Sardinia to work in a mine. At the time of his death, he had been reconciled with the second of his opponent's successors, Pontian, and henceforth the Roman church honored him as a saint and martyr.

There are a few cases where an individual challenged the existing pope by claiming the papacy and then outlived the man he had challenged and received full support for his claim to the papal office. By some counts, such persons were antipopes before acceding to the papacy. Sergius III, officially regarded as the legitimate pope from 904 to 911, perhaps was claiming to be pope beginning as far back as 898, or so some controversial evidence would suggest. If that evidence were proved sound, then Sergius would have been an antipope for six years, unless he was legitimate from that earlier time, but that would turn four intervening claimants to the papal throne into antipopes.

When Nicholas II issued the papal election decree of 1059, the German court and many of its political allies in Italy rejected this innovation and held to the traditional methods of selection. Two years later the cardinals elected Alexander II, and the Roman partisans of the emperor chose Honorius II. Because the revolutionaries of the papal reform party won out, Honorius is considered an antipope.

The disputed election of 1130 produced two claimants to the throne, Innocent II (1130–1143) and Anacletus II (1130–1138). Neither showed any sign of yielding to the other; each regarded the other as illegitimate. When Anacletus died, his supporters elected Victor IV. Only when Victor IV resigned, not long after his election, was the issue settled—retroactively and entirely in favor of Innocent.

With reference to the Great Schism, during which rival claimants excommunicated one another, some scholars think it preferable to speak of popes of the Roman line, popes of the Avignon line, and popes of the Pisan line, rather than to single out some as popes and others as antipopes.

"Antipope," it should by now be clear, is a hostile term used to discredit the legitimacy of someone who claims (or claimed) to exercise the office of pope. It is not a term such a claimant would use or accept in reference to himself. While the precise term, an obvious echo of "Antichrist," appears to date from the late twelfth century, there were earlier equivalents such as *perturbator* (troublemaker) and *pervasor* (usurper).

In simple and straightforward legal definition, an antipope would be one who usurped the papal office or in some way held it by virtue of an illegal or uncanonical claim. Yet such a definition is inadequate because there is no clear legal definition of papal legitimacy that is uniformly valid throughout the centuries of papal history.

Where the charge of illegitimacy is made against a living, contemporary claimant, the definition of legitimacy prevailing at that particular time would presumably apply. But the problem is compounded because the charge is often made retroactively, well after the problematic claimant's lifetime. Whereas the issue of a contemporary charge would probably have immediate political implications, in what we may call a posthumous charge the issue would still be political but in a more complex way. It would arise because of a need to establish a precise, unbroken line of legitimate holders of the papal office from the very beginning to the present. The establishing of an officially recognized legitimate line of succession surely serves not only a political purpose but also the psychological needs of list makers and above all the compelling human, societal need for genealogies.

The *Liber pontificalis* is just such a compilation of names. It appeared in several redactions over the centuries, with its origins dating back surely as far as the seventh century and perhaps, as some would argue, as far as the fifth. In late antiquity and early Germanic Europe (but not only then, of course), a genealogy was a fundamental source of authority. Thus where there had been two popes or two rival claimants to the papacy at one time, it was necessary to declare one legitimate and the other illegitimate.

It would be simpler (and more honest) to call everybody pope who had ever claimed seriously and with a lucid mind to be the pope and whose claim was taken seriously by other people. Then one could mark all those on the list whose legitimacy had ever been seriously challenged. They would then be the antipopes, and the list would include some names not usually found there, such as Boniface I, Innocent II, Alexander III, Eugene IV, Martin V, Urban VI, or Gregory VII.

BIBLIOGRAPHY

Geoffrey Barraclough, *The Medieval Papacy* (1968); G. Jacquemet, ed., *Catholicisme,* I (1947), 653–658; Angelo Mercati, "The New List of the Popes," in *Mediaeval Studies,* 9 (1947).

LESTER K. LITTLE

[See also **Papacy, Origins and Development of; Pope; Schism, Great.**]

ANTIQUARIANISM AND ARCHAEOLOGY. In the modern sense of the word there was no archaeology in the Middle Ages, for there existed neither the inclination nor the methodology to investigate ancient peoples systematically by means of scientific study of their cultural artifacts. Conversely, in the original sense of the word (ἀρχαῖος = ancient, early + λογία = word, writing), archaeology existed in the Middle Ages, albeit with a decidedly Christian bias.

In the early twelfth century Bernard of Chartres paid due respect to the ancient writings on which medieval theology was based when he proclaimed, "We are as dwarfs on the shoulders of giants; we can see farther and farther into the distance than could the ancients, not by virtue of the keenness of our sight or by the size of our bodies, but because we are supported and elevated by them as giants" (John of Salisbury, *Metalogicon,* III, 4). Medieval Europe preserved a considerable amount of pre-Christian and non-Christian literature and scientific writing. Vitruvius' *De architectura* was copied at least half a dozen times in monastic scriptoria, the oldest surviving example being a copy made in Northumbria, possibly at Jarrow, in the eighth century (British Library, MS Harleian 2726). Given the paucity of classical Roman architecture built in Northumbria at that time, copying Vitruvius was not a pragmatic act with practical consequences but an example of respect for ancient authority.

If in the Middle Ages there was no archaeological practice as currently defined, there did exist the five prerequisites to modern archaeology in its most esoteric and scientific sense: interest in ancient writings, travel to distant sites and accounts thereof, collecting of ancient artifacts, epigraphic study, and premeditated excavation to obtain specific artifacts. These activities were frequently carried out in isolation from one another and were subsidiary to other endeavors. Thus, ancient literature generally was studied and of interest to the degree that it could be made to parallel or to support Christian exegesis; travel accounts and diaries were produced as byproducts of travel for commercial, military, or religious purposes; collecting artifacts most often meant use of spolia, looting, or souvenir hunting; epigraphy was indifferently and only occasionally practiced; and the discovery of antiquities was made, as is always the case, more by accident than by design.

This article focuses on those instances within these five categories—however isolated and exceptional these examples are—that prove that there existed in the Middle Ages an incipient antiquarianism that culminated in the eighteenth century with the establishment of learned societies and academies and the creation of the principles of modern archaeological practice.

TRAVELERS AND THEIR ACCOUNTS

Being the "Land of the Bible," the Near East throughout the Middle Ages attracted the attention of Christian, Muslim, and Jew. From the time of the *Peregrinatio ad loca sancta Silviae,* a narrative of her visit to the Hold Land at the end of the fourth century by the abess Aetheria of Gaul (or Spain), or the even earlier account of the so-called Pilgrim of Bordeaux *(Itinerarium Burdigalense,* 333), Christian visitors to the holy sites recorded their experiences.

The Arab geographer al-Mas˒ūdī traveled to Nineveh in 943 and observed that it was to that city that Allah had sent Jonah. He commented on the ruined walls of the city and noted that "one finds [there] stone statues covered with inscriptions." In 1166 the Spanish rabbi Benjamin of Tudela, after visiting Rome and Constantinople, traveled throughout the Near East and ultimately to China. He visited Babylon and Nineveh, describing the remains of both places, as well as those of Birs Nimrud (the Biblical Kallah). Benjamin's account was published in Constantinople in 1453. In the fourteenth century the Berber geographer Ibn Batuta visited Nineveh, identifying it as the city of Jonah and describing its walls. Ibn Batuta also traveled to what is now Russia, India, Ceylon, and China.

In the West the best-known travel account was that of the Venetian Marco Polo, who visited China between 1271 and 1295 on business with his father and uncle. Fascinated with Chinese life and customs, Marco Polo made no mention whatsoever of the Great Wall of China. Between about 1316 and 1330, the Franciscan friar Oderic de Pordenone traveled to China via Persepolis and on his return to Venice in May 1330 dictated a widely circulated account of his adventures. Proof of the fascination with faraway places in the later Middle Ages is typified by the celebrated *Voyage of Trivaile of Sire Jehan de Manderville, Knight,* written between 1357 and 1372. Popular for its detailed descriptions, including "dragonns, grete serpentes, and dyverse venymous bestes" that afflicted Babylon, this account was a fabrication by a Liège physician named Jean à la Barbe who never left Europe but simply embellished the accounts of Oderic and others with examples of his own lively imagination.

Not until the late fifteenth century, when the Venetian ambassador to Persia, Giosophat Barbero, visited and described Persepolis around 1472, was there a change in tone in travelers' accounts. Barbero visited Bīsitūn and was the first European to mention the inscriptions of Darius found engraved on the cliffs there.

There is an occasional example of travel to a distant place not merely on pilgrimage or business but for the specific purpose of studying something. About the year 1000, Bishop Meinwerk of Paderborn sent Abbot Wino of Helmarshausen to the Holy Sepulcher in Jerusalem to obtain measurements that were to serve as the basis of design for a church to be built in Paderborn. The church was built, but the Holy Sepulcher measurements were either inaccurately recorded or not carefully followed.

Inhabited cities as well as those long deserted fascinated medieval travelers. To Westerners no city was more impressive than Constantinople. Fulcher of Chartres, a member of the First Crusade, saw Constantinople in May 1097—and his praise was lavish: "Oh what a noble and beautiful city is Constantinople! How many monasteries and palaces it contains, constructed with wonderful skill! How many remarkable things may be seen in the principal

ANTIQUARIANISM–ARCHAEOLOGY

avenues and even in the lesser streets!" (*Historia Hierosolymitana,* I, 9).

Although no longer a center of art or learning, Athens attracted the attention of the pilgrim Niccolo da Martoni, who visited there in 1395 on his way to the Holy Land. His description of the city still survives.

Rome never lost its attraction to northern Europeans. Bede chronicled the visits to Rome of English churchmen and recounted the purification of the Pantheon as the Church of the Virgin and Holy Martyrs (*Historia ecclesiastica gentis Anglorum,* II, 5). Bede appears to have been the first writer to note the pilgrim's motto that so long as the Colosseum stands Rome shall stand, and so long as Rome stands the world shall stand, an idea known to most people from Byron's *Childe Harold's Pilgrimage.*

Rome as pilgrimage center produced a special genre of medieval literature, the guidebook for travelers. Inspired by comparable productions of classical antiquity, most notably Pausanias' *Periegesis* (second century A.D), medieval guidebooks combined anecdote, folklore, history, itinerary, myth, and topography in equal measure. The best example of the type is the *Mirabilia urbis Romae* compiled in the mid twelfth century, based on firsthand observations and on earlier guides, including the first such guidebook, the early seventh-century *Notitia ecclesiarum urbis Romae* from the time of Honorius I. Although full of inaccuracies—identifying the Pyramid of Gaius Cestius as the tomb of Remus, for example—Gregory the Englishman's *Mirabilia* is notable for decrying the destruction of ancient monuments.

The principal European rival to Rome as an object of pilgrimage, the Tomb of St. James Major at Santiago de Compostella, also generated a guide for pilgrims. The fifth book of the *Liber sancti Jacobi* was composed by Aymery Picaud, a monk from Parthenay, in 1138. Picaud had made the pilgrimage to Compostella around 1120 and observed that "all kinds of iniquity and fraud abound on the road of the saints."

Medieval guidebooks failed consistently to illustrate accurately sites to be visited. Maps with vaguely indifferent drawings of buildings existed throughout the Middle Ages, such as the *Tabula Peutingeriana* in Vienna, copied in 1265 at Colmar from possibly a third-century original; or an itinerary from London to Jerusalem in Matthew of Paris' (d. 1259) *Chronica majora* (Cambridge, Corpus Christi College Library, MS 26, fols. 1–6). But nothing resembling accurate topographical views existed. According to Einhard, Charlemagne possessed two tables, one showing Constantinople and one showing Rome (*Vita Caroli,* V, 33), but both have disappeared. The *Itinerarium einsidelense* of the first half of the eighth century contained a view of Rome, now lost, that possibly was related to Charlemagne's tables.

Until the middle of the thirteenth century miniaturists were incapable of representing actual buildings accurately. The oldest view (early fourteenth century) of Stonehenge shows that complex as square or rectangular (Cambridge, Corpus Christi College Library, MS 194, fol. 57). Two early fourteenth-century views of Rome, the seal of Ludwig IV of Bavaria (1328; Dresden, Staatsarchiv) and Paulinus the Minorite's map, (1320's; Venice, San Marco, MS HS Zan. 399, fol. 98), prove both the late medieval interest in and the shortcomings of topographic views.

COLLECTING ARTIFACTS

The acquisition of artistic artifacts of earlier periods in the Middle Ages falls into three categories: use of spolia, looting, and collecting. There is not always a clear distinction among these, but the first is used here to indicate removal of materials in peacetime for reuse, as distinct from acquisition of booty through military conquest.

The ancient practice of using the monuments of the past as ready-made quarries and supply sources of materials for construction and decoration continued in the Middle Ages. Between 792 and 795 Charlemagne obtained from Pope Adrian I authorization to strip churches and palaces in Rome and in Ravenna of marbles and mosaics for reuse in the emperor's building projects north of the Alps (Einhard, *Vita Caroli,* II, 26; *Codex Carolinus,* no. 67). Adrian pulled down the Temple of Ceres in the Forum Boarium lest it collapse on the Church of St. Maria in Cosmedin and relocated the Church of Sts. Sergius and Bacchus in the Forum Romanum because of the impending collapse of the Temple of Concord.

In 1066 Abbot Desiderius of Monte Cassino "set out for Rome and, appealing to those who were generous, and at the same time opportunely paying out money with a liberal hand, he bought in large quantity columns, bases, and both white and many-colored marble" (Leo of Ostia, *Chronicon monasterii Casinensis,* III, 26). These materials were shipped from Ostia and hauled up the mountain to the re-

ANTIQUARIANISM–ARCHAEOLOGY

construction site of the abbey. For transport of the first column the faithful served as beasts of burden, a significant and influential example of the so-called "cult of carts" phenomenon in the eleventh and twelfth centuries.

When rebuilding the abbey church at St. Denis outside Paris in the 1140's, Abbot Suger considered transporting from Rome columns of the Baths of Diocletian, which he had seen and admired. But he ultimately abandoned this idea as too costly, risky (because of Saracens), and time-consuming (Suger, *Liber alter de consecratione ecclesiae sancti Dionysii,* 2). However, many churches of medieval France contain spolia from nearby Roman sites: the south arm of the transept of Soissons cathedral employs five Roman column shafts.

Roman marbles were hauled as far as England to be reused. The tomb of Abbot Richard of Ware contains the inscription: HIC PORTAT LAPIDES QVOS HVC PORTAVIT AB VRBE (This [tomb] carries stones which he [Richard of Ware] carried here from the city). It was unnecessary to state that the city was Rome.

From time to time there was protest, and even legislation, against collecting spolia and against outright vandalism. For the most part these outcries and laws had little effect. On 11 July 458 the Roman emperor Majorian decreed that anyone caught destroying an ancient building would have both hands amputated. The Ostrogothic emperor Theodoric I issued a similar decree against vandalism, but without the drastic penalty. Theodoric had the astonishingly modern idea that if a locale were used and its buildings restored, vandalism would cease. To this end he undertook repair of buildings in, and appointed a guardian of, the Forum Romanum (Cassiodorus, *Variae* [*Epistolae*], IV, 30).

The popes of medieval Rome by and large were more protective of the classical *fabrica* of the city than were their Renaissance successors. Both Calixtus II, in 1119, and Alexander III, in 1162, issued decrees against vandalism of the triumphal columns of Marcus Aurelius and Trajan; and Calixtus undertook restoration of some classical buildings in the city. The column of Marcus Aurelius was annually rented to the highest-bidding monk of Sts. Dionysius and Silvester in Catapauli, who derived income from charging pilgrims and tourists to climb the stairs to the top.

There is one haunting example from the twelfth century of someone's reusing ancient marbles not merely for their practicality or ready availability but also for their beauty and historical value. The house (actually the base of a tower) of Niccolo Crescentius near the Forum Boarium is studded with ancient fragments and an inscription stating that Niccolo was "induced to build this dwelling . . . by the desire to restore the splendor of ancient Rome." Typically, medieval guidebooks identified it as Pilate's house, possibly because the judgment scene in passion plays was enacted in or in front of it.

Despite these occasional efforts to protect or even to restore ancient monuments, the Middle Ages produced neither an effective nor a universal concept of preserving antiquities, let alone a policy of restoration.

Throughout history one aspect of archaeologically related activity has been the looting of conquered territories. The Romans, beginning with the sack of Syracuse by Marcus Claudius Marcellus in 211 B.C., had perfected looting as state policy by the time Lucius Cornelius Sulla sacked Athens around 86 B.C. Thus, when Constantine I the Great dedicated Nova Roma (Constantinople) on 11 May 330, it was altogether customary for him to have pillaged Greek cities, notably Athens and Delphi, to decorate the new capital. He also transported an immense amount of statuary from Rome to his new foundation.

The above citation of Fulcher of Chartres indicates the attraction that Constantinople held for Westerners. Nonetheless, their admiration did not protect the city during the Fourth Crusade. When the French and Venetians turned their wrath on Constantinople in 1204, their pillage was indiscriminate and pitiless. Both Byzantine and Western writers—for example Robert de Clari and Geoffroi de Villehardouin—documtneted the artistic carnage, termed "a work of darkness" by Pope Innocent III.

The most detailed record of the events of April–May 1204 is found in the account of the Byzantine historian Nicetas Chionates. Nicetas accused the Westerners of barbarism, claiming that they "had no love of what was beautiful, but coined art into money, exchanging what was beautiful for what was vile." His detailed inventory of what was destroyed or removed demonstrates that, despite disasters such as the riots in 532 during the reign of Justinian I, Constantinople had preserved a large amount of the ancient statuary brought there from various places in the Byzantine Empire.

The Crusaders were more interested in relics and in the physical value of looted materials than in art objects as such. But the numerous ivories, manu-

 ANTIQUARIANISM–ARCHAEOLOGY

scripts, manuscript covers, and reliquaries transported back to Europe after 1204 had a classicizing impact on Western art in general, and French art in particular, during the following two decades. There is one well-documented case of art objects being admired and removed with care to the West from Constantinople: the Venetians transported and installed on the facade of the Basilica of San Marco in Venice the four bronze horses still found there. Having no religious significance, this particular statuary must have appealed aesthetically to the Venetians.

While it is self-evident that war is not good for art, invaders are not always the villains in their treatment of monuments and statuary. When the Goths besieged Rome in February 537, the defenders of the city broke up and threw down statues from the Mausoleum of Hadrian onto the invaders (Procopius, *De bello gothico,* V, 22).

MEDIEVAL COLLECTORS AND COLLECTIONS

Antique statuary presented a special problem to the medieval Church because so much of it depicted pagan deities in the nude. Nonetheless there emerge, from an almost complete lack of documentation, occasional indications that ancient statuary was admired and even collected. In the mid twelfth century Henry of Blois, bishop of Winchester, transported statues from Rome for his palace at Farnham. Because these statues do not survive or cannot now be identified as those collected by Henry, one cannot be certain that the worldly bishop actually collected figures of nude pagan deities. Certain proof of fascination during the Gothic period with antique nude statuary is found in drawings made in the second quarter of the thirteenth century by the Picard artist Villard de Honnecourt (Paris, Bibliothèque Nationale, MS fr. 19093, fols. 6, 11v, and 22). Villard's models have been identified as classical bronzes. He could have had no possible practical application for these drawings; one must conclude therefore that his interest was curiosity about something he found unusual.

The ancient artifacts most prized in medieval Europe were gems of various kinds, especially cameos and intaglios. For the most part they were put to practical use or reuse, as for example, in the cameo bust of Augustus set into the Lothar Cross of *ca.* 985–990 (Aachen, Domschatz) or the famous Gemma Tiberiana set into a reliquary of the Ste. Chapelle in Paris in the fourteenth century (Paris, Bibliothèque Nationale, Cabinet des Medailles). The beauty of this precious object attracted the attention of Peter Paul Rubens, who made a drawing of it in 1622 (Antwerp, Stedelijk Prentenkabinet). Matthew of Paris drew the splendid cameo that was presented to Saint Albans by Ethelred the Unready (London, British Library, Cotton MS Nero D.I, fol. 146). According to Matthew, the cameo had been intended for a shrine at the abbey but was not so employed due to its great use to women in childbirth.

Ancient gems, and often coins, were collected simply for their own sake, without any practical application. Suger of St. Denis bragged (*De rebus in administratione sua gestis,* 32) of having paid less than fair value for a collection of gems that had once been owned by Henry I of England, "who had collected them throughout his lifetime in wonderful vessels." Inventories show that Charles V of France owned fifty-two cameos in 1380 and that his son Charles VI had increased this collection to 101 by 1390. Papal inventories record that in 1295 Boniface VIII owned about fifty cameos. Francesco Petrarch gave his collection of Roman coins to the Holy Roman emperor Charles IV at Mantua in 1354.

Another product of antiquity highly valued in the Middle Ages was vases. Greek black- and red-figured vases were little known, if at all; but vases of rich material were prized. The best-documented example concerning such vases is associated with Suger of St. Denis (*De administratione,* 34), who was given an Egyptian crystal vase by Eleanor of Aquitaine. The abbot had it and three other antique vases, one of which "had lain idly in a chest for many years," converted by goldsmiths into various eucharistic vessels. The two most celebrated of these are a porphyry eagle ewer in the Louvre Museum and a fluted sardonyx chalice in the National Gallery of Art in Washington, D.C.

Suger and other medieval patrons understood fully that art could increase the significance as well as the value of mere material, for Suger paraphrased Ovid's expression *opus materiam superabat* ([their] workmanship surpassed [their] material) (*Metamorphoses,* II, 5) in connection with his metalwork products at St. Denis. In May 1244 Pope Innocent IV used the same expression to praise the Ste. Chapelle of Louis IX the Saint, a building that he had never seen.

Finally, the Middle Ages had a passion for collecting and preserving manuscripts. As noted above, Vitruvius' *De architectura* was copied at least half a dozen times during the Middle Ages. Pliny's *Historia naturalis* exists in several medieval copies in which portraits of the author and presentation

ANTIQUARIANISM–ARCHAEOLOGY

scenes reflect antique prototypes in iconography while being altogether contemporary in style (for example, Le Mans, Bibliothèque Municipale, MS 263, fol. 10v). The Utrecht Psalter (Utrecht, Rijksuniversiteit Bibliotheek, MS 32), made at Reims around 820 or in 832 as a copy of an earlier manuscript, was itself copied at least twice in England: at Canterbury, around 1000 (London, British Library, MS Harleian 603) and again around 1150 (Cambridge, Trinity College Library, MS R. 17. 1). The Utrecht Psalter was copied a third time around 1200, either while still at Canterbury or at St. Bertin, after having been returned to the Continent (Paris, Bibliothèque Nationale, MS lat. 8846).

Manuscripts were valued for several reasons. One was the authenticity of their texts, and this would appear to have been the basis of five trips to Rome between 653 and 684 by Benedict Biscop to purchase manuscripts (Bede, *Historia ecclesiastica gentis Anglorum,* IV, 18; V, 19). Another was the significance of previous owners, although this consideration cannot be clearly isolated from artistic merit. Two psalters exist containing notations that they had belonged to Louis IX the Saint (Leiden, Rijksuniversiteit Bibliotheek, MS lat. 76^{A}; Paris, Bibliothèque Nationale, MS lat. 10525). The notation in the Leiden psalter states that it was from this psalter that the young Louis learned to read.

As is the case with coins and gems, there were secular collections of manuscripts. One of the earliest documented cases, apart from Charlemagne's, is that of Oliviero Forza (or Forzetta), a wealthy merchant of Treviso, in the late thirteenth century. Even before his brief reign (1350–1364), Jean le Bon of France assembled a collection of manuscripts. Charles V of France collected manuscripts as well as coins and gems, and in 1379 presented a fine Ottonian evangelistary (Paris, Bibliothèque Nationale, MS lat. 8851) to the Ste. Chapelle. Jean, Duc de Berry owned an extensive collection of manuscripts as well as coins, gems, medallions, and other antiquities.

EPIGRAPHIC STUDIES

A fundamental prerequisite to antiquarianism and archaeological investigation is the ability to interpret accurately the languages of the past. On this count the Middle Ages generally was inadequate. To be sure, ancient texts were preserved to prove ancient claims, but the number of successful forgeries (most notably, perhaps, the *Donatio Constantini*) proves that at any given time even the most learned could be tricked. Gregory of Tours' lament in the sixth century that "the pursuit of letters is truly dead" (*Historia Francorum,* preface) makes the point quite well indeed. The most eloquent, and modern, plea for knowledge of foreign and ancient languages comes from Roger Bacon, who wrote both Greek and Hebrew grammars.

The eighth-century *Itinerarium einsidelense* mentioned above contained copies of ancient inscriptions, but this was not a usual practice. The honor of being the first to attempt to understand the past by means of its inscriptions probably belongs to the Roman tribune Cola di Rienzi, who collected, restored, and studied inscriptions on Roman monuments in the 1340's. Rodolfo Lanciani calls Cola "the real founder of the modern archaeological school." In fairness, Lanciani notes that Cola made mistakes but that, compared to Petrarch's serious errors in copying inscriptions ("from an archaeological point of view, monuments of ignorance"), Cola was most successful.

PLANNED ARCHAEOLOGICAL EXCAVATION

Deliberate archaeological excavation was very rare during the Middle Ages. Then, as in all periods, the majority of archaeological discoveries were made accidentally as the fortuitous by-products of other activities, such as plowing or clearing a site for construction. A good example of the latter type occurred in Paris in 1186. While clearing the foundations of the old cathedral of St. Étienne preparatory to construction of the facade of the present Gothic cathedral of Notre Dame, workmen unearthed a hoard of relics including the hair of the Virgin, the stones employed in the lapidation of St. Stephen, and the cranium of St. Denis. These relics were turned over to Philip II, who subsequently presented them to the bishop of Paris, an event recorded in a dado relief of the west facade of the cathedral.

There were at least three documented instances of sites intentionally excavated with the reasoned expectation of discovering specific artifacts. The best-known and earliest example of such archaeological fieldwork concerns St. Helena (d. *ca.* 327) and the relics of the Passion. According to a number of early western writers (St. Ambrose of Milan, Tyrannius Rufinus of Aquileia, Sulpicius Severus of Tours—though no contemporary Eastern historian gives an account—St. Helena visited Jerusalem shortly before her death. As recounted by Jacobus de Voragine in the thirteenth century Helena tortured a Jew named Judas (later bishop of Jerusalem under the name of Cyriacus) into revealing the location of the burial place of Christ (*Legenda aurea* [*Legendae sanctorum*], 3 May). Helena caused this site to be excavated to a depth of twenty feet, destroying a Hadrianic temple of Venus in the process. In the grotto were found the True Cross and, through subsequent investigation, the nails employed in the Crucifixion.

In the ninth century extensive excavations of the catacombs of Rome were undertaken. Possibly because of the decree of church councils in 801 and again in 813 that any altar lacking a relic be destroyed, the demand in northern Europe for relics of Roman martyrs became insatiable. The greatest prize was the body of St. Sebastian, which Abbot Hilduin secured in 826 for his abbey of St. Médard at Soissons, making that city an important site of pilgrimage. Not to be outdone, Charlemagne's biographer, Einhard, contracted in 827 with the most successful relic-procurer of the century, the Roman deacon Deusdona, to secure for him the bodies of St. Peter and St. Marcellus from the catacomb bearing their names on the Via Labicana. Deusdona transported the relics to Einhard's monastery at Mulinheim (Seligenstadt), as Einhard recounts in his *Translatio et miracula sanctorum Marcelli et Petri.*

From about 826 to 836, Deusdona and his brothers systematically excavated various Roman catacombs to supply northern churches with the coveted relics. The specific details of their archaeological activities are not recorded, but it is documented that they employed church archives to locate specific entombments. They apparently excavated during the winter months, then in spring and summer made the journey north with the newly excavated relics. The Romans took a dim view of this removal of their patrons and protectors, and it is recorded that Deusdona and his brothers changed the site of their activities each year "to avoid the wrath of [Roman] ecclesiastical officials."

The third and most fascinating medieval example of successfully excavating a specific site to a specific end took place at Glastonbury, England. In 1190, according to Giraldus Cambrensis and Adam of Domerham *(Historia de rebus gestis Glastoniensibus),* Abbot Henry of Sully caused the old cemetery of the abbey to be excavated, and the remains of King Arthur and Queen Guinevere were found. Adam of Domerham was a monk at Glastonbury, and while his account was written about a century after the event described, his words have an extraordinary tone of authenticity. He posits that Abbot Henry knew both what he wished to find and where to find it: "He [Henry], frequently urged to dispose more fittingly of the famous King Arthur (for he had lain for 648 years [that is, since 542] near the old church, between two pyramids, once magnificently carved), one day surrounded the place with curtains and ordered that the digging should be carried out. . . ." Giraldus provides additional details: that the bodies were at a depth of sixteen feet, that they were buried in a hollow tree trunk, and that a lead cross was found with the following inscription: HIC IACET SEPVLTVS INCLITVS REX ARTHVRVS IN INSVLA AVALONIA (Here lies buried the famous King Arthur in the Island of Avalon).

It is of course now impossible to verify the details of this archaeological undertaking, let alone that the bodies found were those of Arthur and Guinevere. The bodies were reburied in a new tomb in the new church. This tomb was opened in 1278 in the presence of Edward I, when lavish reburial was made. Subsequently lost, this tomb was rediscovered in 1931. Excavations undertaken in this century confirm that the old cemetery at Glastonbury was excavated around 1200. The inscribed lead cross, long preserved at Glastonbury, is also lost. An engraving of it was published in the 1607 edition of William Camden's *Britannia,* on the basis of which most authorities agree that the inscription is earlier than 1190—that is, that it was not forged at that time and planted in the burial.

There are isolated mentions in medieval documents of excavations not of relics but of ancient marbles, for example, at Modena around 1100, but it is impossible to tell whether their discovery was accidental or planned. When such mentions occur, it is equally difficult to be certain that the event is not simply removal of spolia.

Throughout the Middle Ages there was interest in, and occasionally fascination with, the classical past, especially in ancient literature and sculpture of various types; but investigation of this past and its artifacts was sporadic and unsystematic. Not until the fourteenth century did there begin to appear, especially in Italy, a consistent and sustained effort to study ancient monuments and their inscriptions and to collect and preserve artifacts—in short, to study methodologically the wonders of history. This activity, coupled with increased travel and travel accounts, led to the humanist undertakings of the fifteenth and sixteenth centuries, which in turn developed into the antiquarianism of the seventeenth and eighteenth centuries. This antiquarianism, of which the beginnings are to be found in medieval Europe, produced scientific archaeology as it is practiced today.

BIBLIOGRAPHY

There exists no study of archaeology in the Middle Ages, even in encyclopedias. The data in this article have been taken from a variety of sources; when available to the author, medieval sources for specific quotations have been given in the text.

General Studies. On Rome in the Middle Ages the best sources are Rodolfo A. Lanciani's two basic studies, *Ancient Rome in the Light of Recent Discoveries* (1888, repr. 1967) and *The Ruins and Excarvations of Ancient Rome* (1897, repr. 1967); Margaret R. Scherer, *Marvels of Ancient Rome* (1955) is especially useful for the medieval period; Richard Krautheimer's *Rome: Profile of a City, 312–1308* (1980), a study of Rome from the time of Constantine to the period of the Avignon papacy doubtless will provide much essential information.

Brian Fagan, *Return to Babylon* (1979), surveys briefly the history of early European visitors to the Near East. Useful information is to be found in "Geography," "Itinerary," "Map," and "Pilgrimage" in the *Encyclopaedia Britannica,* 11th ed. (1911).

A convenient summary of medieval interest in ancient literature, containing a chart showing when, where, and by whom ancient scientific writings were translated in the West, is in A. C. Crombie, *Medieval and Early Modern Science,* I, *Science in the Middle Ages, V–XIII Centuries* (1959), 33–64.

Specialized Studies. For an account of the intention to employ measurements of the Holy Sepulcher at Paderborn, see Sergio Luis Sanabria, "Metrics and Geometry of Romanesque and Gothic St. Benigne, Dijon," in *Art Bulletin,* **62** (1980).

The quotation from Aymery Picaud is taken from Kenneth J. Conant, *Carolingian and Romanesque Architecture, 800 to 1200,* 2nd ed. (1966), 92. The basic study of the Santiago de Compostella pilgrim's guide is Jeanne Vieillard, *Le guide de pèlerin de Saint-Jacques de Compostelle* (1938).

The inscription on the tomb of Richard of Ware is taken from Charles H. Haskins, *The Renaissance of the Twelfth Century* (1927), 120.

The quotation of Nicetas Chionates is from Judith Grant, *A Pillage of Art* (1966), 25–29, which contains a good summary of the sack of Constaninople in 1204. On the bronze horses of San Marco, Venice, see the Metropolitan Museum of Art exhibition catalog of that title (1980).

Henry of Blois' collecting of statues in Rome for his episcopal palace at Farnham is reported in a number of writings, none of which cites proof of this claim. On the sources of Villard de Honnecourt's drawings of nudes, see Jean Adhémar, "Villard de Honnecourt," in *Influences antiques dans l'art du moyen âge français* (1939), 278–280.

Discussion of the St. Albans cameo, called the Kaadmau, is in M. R. James, "The Drawings of Matthew Paris," in *The Walpole Society, Oxford, England,* **14** (1925–1926).

On the collections of Jean Duc de Berry, as well as those of Charles V and Charles VI, see Millard Meiss, *French Painting in the Time of Jean de Berry* (1967).

The discovery of the relics of Notre Dame is treated in detail in William M. Hinkle, "The King and the Pope on the Virgin Portal of Notre-Dame [in Paris]," in *Art Bulletin,* **48** (1966); Hinkle suggests that the site was not the old cathedral of St. Étienne but the church of St. Étienne des Grès across the Seine from the cathedral.

The most detailed account of the activities of Deusdona and his brothers is in Patrick J. Geary, *Furta Sacra, Thefts of Relics in the Central Middle Ages* (1978). The significance of the Roman relics to the northern churches is discussed by Richard Krautheimer, "The Carolingian Revival of Early Christian Architecture," in *Art Bulletin,* **24** (1942), reprinted in *Studies in Early Christian, Medieval, and Renaissance Art* (1969), 203–256.

For a summary of the excavations in 1190 at Glastonbury, including the quotations in the text, see Geoffrey Ashe, *The Quest for Arthur's Britain* (1968), 119–127.

CARL F. BARNES, JR.

[See also **Classical Literary Studies in the Middle Ages; Classical Scholarship in the West; Geography and Cartography, Western Europe; Travel and Transport; Travel and Transport, Islamic.**]

ANTI-SEMITISM, a term in many ways inappropriate to the Middle Ages, was coined toward the end of the nineteenth century. It reflects new views of the Jews as a racially defined group that allegedly posed dangerous threats to European society. Nonetheless medievalists have utilized the term extensively. While this usage has been loose and idiosyncratic, it has generally focused on the set of irrational beliefs that portrayed the Jews as a diabolical and powerful force committed to the destruction of the established order. It was particularly in Western Christendom that these convictions emerged most strongly, a result of both a venerable theological tradition and special socioeconomic circumstances.

In antiquity the Jews and Judaism came into conflict with a variety of political groups and religious faiths. Such natural conflict was, in the case of the Jews, intensified by their monotheism, which made them both difficult to understand (because of their

 ANTI-SEMITISM

uniqueness) and objectionable (because of the exclusiveness of their commitment to one deity alone). With the rise of other monotheistic faiths, the situation of the Jews became more, rather than less, complex. While it is true that the Western monotheisms—Judaism, Christianity, and Islam—understood each other better than the pagan faiths understood them, such comprehension did not result in more cordial relations. The general monotheistic intolerance of others was exacerbated by the sense of one authentic religious heritage initiated by the vision of Abraham, a heritage claimed by all three groups.

This special intergroup tension was particularly pronounced in the relationship between Judaism and Christianity. The earliest stages of Christian history took place within the Jewish community of Palestine. During a period of political, social, and religious upheaval the young Christian sect, like other Jewish sects of the period, saw the ruling authorities in Palestinian Jewry as perverters of the true faith, while viewing itself as the upholder of the authentic Israelite religious vision. As this sectarian Jewish group began to attract non-Jewish adherents, first in an informal manner and then in a more formal way (Acts 15:1–35), it increasingly perceived itself and was perceived by others as a separate faith community.

As a distinct religion, however, Christianity was unwilling to abandon the claim to serving as the correct upholders of the earlier Israelite covenant. Thus it continued to see itself as the True Israel, the grafting of a new physical branch onto the old and authentic Israelite stock. This view relegated post-Christian Judaism to a position of nullity—it became the outmoded heritage of a biological group that failed to comprehend properly the covenant to which it had once been heir. The New Testament portrayal of this displacement is intensified by the charge of deicide; the Jews are depicted as responsible for the crucifixion of Jesus, overtly and gloatingly accepting guilt for themselves and their successors. Thus Jews are seen as more than benignly misguided; they are blind to the true faith and malevolent in their treatment of its messiah and deity. These are motifs with a vast potential for inciting violent anti-Jewish feelings, particularly since recollection of the Crucifixion plays such a central role in Christian ritual and liturgy.

With the achievement of political authority in the Roman Empire during the fourth century, Christianity reached a new stage in its relationship to Jews and Judaism. Possessed of power, Christianity now had to adopt a broad theoretical stand toward Jews and Judaism and to adumbrate a practical program as well. On the theoretical plane, Judaism, despite its nullity, was recognized as a legitimate religion, affording its adherents the untrammeled right to practice their faith as they understood it. On the practical level, Jews were to behave in such a way as to pose no threat to the ruling Christian community or to present any challenge to it. In a less specified way Jews were to live in a manner that would make it obvious to all observers that they were the devotees of a superannuated and secondary religious faith.

This set of fundamental Christian views was increasingly well articulated and had enormous impact upon the situation of the Jews in all of Western Christendom. For an understanding of medieval anti-Semitism, the special circumstances of medieval northern European society, the scene of the most radical manifestations of this anti-Semitism, must be borne in mind. This northern area was, first of all, a late addition to the Christian camp. The relatively sudden intensification of Christian identity in heretofore backward northern Europe resulted in, on the one hand, rapid and brilliant cultural and religious creativity and, on the other, significant excesses.

The Jews were to feel the brunt of much of this tendency toward excess. Indeed, it was a special Jewish community that developed in northern Europe. As this area began to develop demographically, economically, and socially, Jews were invited northward, primarily to play the role of innovative urban settlers. From the first, these Jews appeared as a strange, alien, and highly limited group. There was an artificiality in this settlement that distinguished it from the older forms of Jewish life in the Byzantine Empire and in the Mediterranean areas of the Roman Catholic sphere. It is therefore not surprising that this region was the locus of the most rigorous efforts to enforce ecclesiastical limitations upon the Jews, the most damaging outbursts of anti-Jewish violence, and the most significant reflections of medieval anti-Semitism.

The fundamental element in medieval anti-Semitism was the image of the Jew as the implacable foe of Christendom, an enemy that, in the popular mind, would one day pay a heavy price for its unrelenting hostility. It is this view of the Jew as the inveterate adversary of Christendom that inspired unruly bands of Crusaders to attack the major Rhineland centers

ANTI-SEMITISM

of Jewish life in 1096. It is important to note that the organized military forces of the First Crusade remained true to the accepted ecclesiastical policy of preservation of Jewish life and property. The unruly German bands, however, gave vent to more popular feelings. Reported by both Jewish and Christian observers, their battle cry upon assaulting a Jewish neighborhood was: "Behold we embark upon a long journey to seek the sepulcher and to take our vengeance upon the Muslims. But the Jews, whose ancestors killed and crucified Jesus groundlessly, dwell among us. Let us first take vengeance upon them. Let us wipe them out as a people; the Jews' name will be mentioned no more. Or else let them become like us and acknowledge Jesus."

This is a striking example of negative popular motifs breaking through the protective shell of official Church doctrine. There can be little doubt that the view of the Jews as enemy so forcefully expressed in these crusading assaults was central to the anti-Semitism destined to develop. Indeed, in a certain sense, the powerful Jewish rejection of the conversion alternative offered by the rampaging Crusaders seemed to buttress the original perception that the Jews were implacably opposed to Christianity. To the extent that Christian observers were aware of the radical lengths to which the beleaguered Jews and Jewesses went in order to avoid this conversion—culminating in suicide and the slaughter of their own youngsters—these Christian onlookers saw something deeply sinister in such behavior.

The notion of Jewish enmity was embellished during the twelfth century in northern Europe into the ritual-murder allegation. This slander first surfaced in England in 1144. In the town of Norwich the Jews were alleged to have maliciously killed a twelve-year-old tanner's apprentice, a Christian youngster named William. The crime involved more than simply murder; it involved mutilation and torture inflicted upon a young innocent, culminating in his crucifixion. This dastardly behavior was supposedly motivated only by a generalized hatred for Christianity and Christians and a perverse desire to reenact the historic Jewish crime of deicide. Thomas of Monmouth, the chronicler of the life, death, and miracles of the young William, asserts that this act was not simply a vicious act perpetrated by a specific group of Jews; he claims rather an international Jewish conspiracy to wreak vengeance upon the Christian world. While the authorities interceded on behalf of the Jews of Norwich and protected them against the fury of the mob, the story of St. William was carefully written and subsequently elaborated in art.

The notion of Jewish malicious murder as undertaken out of loathing for Christianity and reflecting a criminal compulsion to repeat the classical sin of deicide, spread quickly throughout northern Europe. The elements in it are constant: a pure and virtuous Christian youngster, a nefarious Jewish plot, proximity to the Easter season, a horrible murder, discovery of the crime, and sanctification of the child martyr. In general, the authorities rejected the charge and protected their Jews. Occasionally, as for example in Blois in 1171, complications could lead to governmental support of the allegation and a resultant disaster for the Jews. In this incident, some thirty Jews were burned because Count Theobald of Blois chose to accept a murder charge for which there was not even the evidence of a corpus delicti. Not surprisingly, the Jews of northern France embarked upon a feverish campaign to secure official repudiation of his actions and of the charge in general. Such disavowals were achieved but had little impact on popular thinking.

During the thirteenth century, a series of shifts transformed the ritual-murder allegation into the blood libel. The religious festivity that served as the occasion for it changed from the Christian Easter to the Jewish Passover, generally celebrated at approximately the same time; the core of the accusation shifted from a reenactment of the Crucifixion to ritual utilization of Christian blood. Once again the allegation circulated widely among the lower echelons of society, with both ecclesiastical and secular authorities rejecting the charge and urging protection of the Jews. In the most famous effort to stem the slander and the animosity that it provoked, Emperor Frederick II convoked a panel of experts in Jewish law in 1236. The conclusions of this investigation were couched in unequivocal terms:

> When their findings were published on this matter, then it was clear that it was not indicated in the Old Testament or in the New Testament that Jews lust for the drinking of human blood. Rather, precisely the opposite, they guard against the intake of all blood.... We can surely assume that, for those to whom even the blood of permitted animals is forbidden, the desire for human blood cannot exist, as a result of the horror of the matter, the prohibition of nature, and the common bond of the human species in which they also join Christians. Moreover, they would not expose to danger their substance and persons for that which they might have freely when taken from animals. By this sentence

ANTI-SEMITISM

> of the princes, we pronounce the Jews of the aforesaid place [Fulda] and the rest of the Jews of Germany completely absolved of this imputed crime.
>
> (MGH, Legum Section IV, vol. II, p. 275.)

Such was the power of the increasingly irrational view of the Jews and Judaism that neither this sharp repudiation of the charge nor the equally clear stance of the papacy against it sufficed to lay the slander to rest.

During the thirteenth century the ritual-murder allegation was twisted in yet another direction. In this instance the notion of Jewish hostility toward Christianity and the compulsion to reenact the Crucifixion was transferred to the Eucharist. It was claimed that the Jews furtively gained possession of a Host wafer or wafers and subjected them to abuse and physical torture. As in the case of the ritual-murder charge, these alleged crimes were uncovered, usually in miraculous fashion, with the incident often resulting in the establishment of a local memorial shrine.

In these ritually oriented slanders, Jewish malevolence was supposedly focused upon single adherents of Christianity, who in their purity and innocence were reminiscent of Jesus, or upon the Host wafer, which was seen as the mystical embodiment of Christ. In a broader way, Jewish animosity was alleged to express itself against all of Christian society; imputed to the Jews were acts designed to harm all of Christendom. The most prominent of these slanders was the suggestion that Jewish hostility led to large-scale plots that could endanger an entire Christian population. Already during the First Crusade (1095–1099) one of the major Rhineland assaults was sparked by the charge that Jews had poisoned wells:

> It came to pass on the tenth day of Iyyar, a Sunday, that they [the burghers of Worms] took counsel against them [the Jews]. They took a Christian corpse, which had been buried thirty days earlier, carried it through the town, and said: "Behold what the Jews have done to our companion. They have taken this Christian, boiled his body in water, and then poured the water into our wells in order to kill us." When the crusaders and the burghers heard this, they cried out . . . and said: "Behold the time and season have come for wreaking the vengeance of the Crucified, whom their ancestors slew. Now let not a remnant remain, not even a youngster or a suckling in the crib."
>
> (Neubauer and Stern, *Hebräische Berichte über die Judenverfolgungen während der Kreuzzuge,* p. 49.)

In addition to graphically depicting the first known medieval allegation of well poisoning, this quotation reflects once again the perception of Jewish animosity inextricably linked to the fateful crime of deicide. Well-poisoning accusations surfaced occasionally during the twelfth and thirteenth centuries, but during the bubonic plague of the mid fourteenth century the slander proliferated, with frightful consequences for European Jewry. Faced with an uncontrollable calamity of momentous proportions, European society sought to propitiate the deity through intense religious penitence, while attempting to identify the causes or carriers of the disease. Of all the suspected agents, no group recommended itself more readily than the Jews. The allegation that poisoned wells had triggered the plague spread quickly through most, although not all, affected areas. In some instances, the result was popular assault upon the Jews; in others it was precipitate court proceedings in which confessions were extracted through torture and from which a series of condemnations and executions ensued.

Underlying the allegations, and at the same time nourished by them, was the belief that Jews were in some sense less than human. This perception is widely reflected in the art and folklore of medieval Western Christendom. Jews are depicted in a variety of animallike forms or with a series of bestial features. They were supposed to give off an especially offensive odor. More significant and more damaging than the view of Jews as subhuman was the contention that they were linked in an inhuman alliance with the pervasive forces of evil personified in the devil. Especially telling is the identification of Jews with the devil in the Gospel according to John (8:44–45), where Jesus chides a group of Jews for not comprehending the revelation brought by him from God. The reason for this failure is that these Jews are not in fact God's children: "Your father is the devil and you choose to carry out your father's desires. He was a murderer from the beginning and is not rooted in the truth; there is no truth in him. When he tells a lie, he is speaking his own language, for he is a liar and the father of lies. But I speak the truth and therefore you do not believe me." To most medieval readers, this was a broad assertion about and condemnation of the Jews in general.

During the Middle Ages, as the sense of the incontrovertible truth of Christianity deepened, the almost incomprehensible failure of the Jews to accept this truth was increasingly attributed to their satanic nature. In this view, not only were the Jews outside the normal human pale, they were dangerously powerful as well. The Jews seen as disposed to and capable of evil made conceivable the slander that began to develop in the twelfth century, in which the Jews were identified as Satan's henchmen. Although some of the excesses of this identification were combatted by ecclesiastical spokesmen, clearly these radical allegations drew much of their strength from normative church teachings.

Medieval anti-Semitism developed throughout the Middle Ages, intensifying in periods of general societal unrest and accumulating new motifs and weight. Its impact on modern anti-Semitism is incontrovertible, although there is uncertainty and disagreement as to the precise dimensions and nature of this lamentable influence.

BIBLIOGRAPHY

Shmuel Almog, ed., *Sinat Yisra'el le-doroteha* (1980); Salo W. Baron, *A Social and Religious History of the Jews,* 2nd ed., XI (1967), 122–191; Gavin Langmuir, "Anti-Judaism as the Necessary Preparation for Anti-Semitism," in *Viator,* 2 (1971); and "Prolegomena to Any Present Analysis of Hostility Against Jews," in *Social Science Information,* 15 (1976); Koppel S. Pinson, ed., *Essays on Antisemitism* (1946); Léon Poliakov, *The History of Anti-Semitism,* 3 vols. (1965–1976); Joshua Trachtenberg, *The Devil and the Jews* (1943).

ROBERT CHAZAN

[See also **Jews and the Catholic Church; Jews in Europe (to 900); Jews in Europe (900 to 1500); Jews in Papal States.**]

ANTON PILGRIM. See **Pilgrim, Anton.**

ANTONINUS, ST. (1 March 1389–2 May 1459), archbishop of Florence, theologian, and reformer, was born Antoninus Pierozzi. He made his profession in the Dominican order at the age of sixteen and was ordained eight years later. Toward the close of the Western Schism, the Dominican brothers of Fiesole (of whom Antoninus was a member) lost their convent for not recognizing Alexander V, elected at the pseudo-Council of Pisa (1409). As a result of this disturbance, Antoninus had to fend for himself in obtaining an education, and he received formal training only in logic. In 1431 he was appointed auditor general of the Rota, and between 1432 and 1445 he served as vicar-general for Dominican houses of strict observance in Italy. With Cosimo de' Medici's help Antoninus founded in 1436 or 1437 the convent of San Marco at Florence. He was consecrated archbishop of Florence on 12 March 1446. As archbishop he was concerned with social reform and with prudent observance of canon law within the Church. His writings include theological and pastoral tractates. Antoninus' major work, *Summa moralis* or *Summa theologica,* is a tract in four parts that is concerned largely with ethical, political, and social questions.

BIBLIOGRAPHY

Bede Jarrett, *St. Antonino and Mediaeval Economics* (1914); Raoul Morçay, *Saint Antonin, fondateur du Couvent de Saint-Marc, archevêque de Florence, 1389–1459* (1914).

JOHN C. MAGEE

ANTONIO DA VINCENZO, Bolognese architect, born *ca.* 1350, died 1402. First mentioned as fortifications architect for Bologna, 1382. 1383 paid for fortress in Cento and worked on Porta Saragozza of Bologna. 1384 renewed Bologna's city walls and designed windows for the Palazzo de'Notai, Bologna. 1386 worked with Giovanni da Siena on S. Proculo-Bastion, Faenza. 1388 received commission to redesign church of S. Pretonio, Bologna, begun 1390 and considered his major work. 1390 submitted drawings for Duomo, Milan. 1397 paid for foundation work on S. Francesco, Bologna, and worked on its sacristy.

BIBLIOGRAPHY

Igino Supino, *L'architettura sacra in Bologna nei Secoli XIII e XIV* (1909); Igino Supino, *L'arte nelle chiese di Bologna. Secoli VIII–XIV* (1932); Ulrich Thieme and Felix Becker, eds., *Allgemeines Lexikon der bildenden Künstler* (1908); John White, *Art and Architecture in Italy: 1250–1400* (1966).

ADELHEID M. GEALT

ANTONIO VENEZIANO (*fl.* 1369–1419), cognomen of the Florentine painter Antonio di Francesca da Venezia, whose earliest activities involve decorations, now lost, for the Siena cathedral, documented in 1369. He is most famous for his work on the Pisa Camposanto frescoes. Between 1384 and 1386 he is recorded completing the *Life of St. Ranieri* frescoes for the Camposanto, which were begun by Andrea da Firenze. Damaged in 1944, they survive only in fragments; but they still demonstrate Antonio's great gifts as a draftsman, narrator, and composer. Antonio's only signed panel is the *Flagellation of Christ* (Palermo, Museo Dioce Sano), dated 1388. Only the now-ruined frescoes for the Torre degli Agli depicting the Deposition, Last Judgment, and Death of the Virgin reflect what must have been extensive activity in Florence.

Shaped by the art of Giotto, Nardo di Cione, Taddeo Gaddi, and the Sienese (principally Ambrogio Lorenzetti), Antonio's work ranks him among the most gifted and important painters of the late Trecento. His painting forms a significant link between the art of Giotto and that of Masaccio.

BIBLIOGRAPHY

Eve Borsook, *The Mural Painters of Tuscany,* new ed. (1980); Richard Fremantle, *Florentine Gothic Painters* (1975); Richard Offner, *Studies in Florentine Painting* (1927, repr. 1972).

ADELHEID M. GEALT

ANTRUSTIONES, the elite personal bodyguard of a Merovingian king and the only permanent military force at his command. They were recruited broadly from the Frankish and Gallo-Roman population regardless of class or prior social standing. The oath that an antrustion took to serve the king set him apart from the rest of society. This elevated status is recognized in the *Lex Salica* by the stipulation of a triple *wergild* price paid for the murder of an antrustion. The role of the antrustions was similar to that of the *comitatus* described by Tacitus. Toward the end of the Merovingian period some antrustions served outside the royal household in military colonies. Their decline in importance parallels the decline of Merovingian royal power. In the later eighth century, as vassalage to the Frankish kings became the norm and was highly sought, especially in return for a landed estate, there was no longer the need to maintain antrustions as a separate class.

BIBLIOGRAPHY

Bernard S. Bachrach, *Merovingian Military Organization* (1972); Maximin Deloche, *La trustis et l'antrustion royal sous les deux premières races* (1873); Samuel Dill, *Roman Society in Gaul in the Merovingian Age* (1926); François L. Ganshof, *Feudalism,* Philip Grierson, trans., 3rd ed. (1964); John Michael Wallace-Hadrill, *The Long-Haired Kings and Other Studies in Frankish History* (1962).

THOMAS KEEFE

[See also **Feudalism; Merovingians.**]

APOCALYPSE. See **Millenialism.**

APOCALYPSE, ILLUSTRATION OF. Beginning in the early Christian period, a number of eschatological visions from the Apocalypse were depicted as isolated scenes in monumental art and on sarcophagi. Individual motifs described in Revelation (for example, the Alpha and Omega) were also common. Although the earliest preserved Apocalypse texts with illustrations date from the ninth century, two manuscripts, now in Germany and France (Trier, Stadtbibliothek, codex 31; Cambrai, Bibliothèque Municipale, MS 386), may copy a complete set of il-

The Second Coming of Christ. Detail of a 12th-century illumination of manuscript of Beatus of Liébana. THE PIERPONT MORGAN LIBRARY (MS 429, f.21)

lustrations to the Book of Revelation from the fifth century.

During the Middle Ages, isolated visions from the Apocalypse, especially the *Majestas Domini,* continued to be popular in both monumental art and manuscript illumination. During the Carolingian period, the Apocalyptic *Agnus Dei* was favored in manuscripts, while in Romanesque and Gothic ecclesiastical sculpture the Last Judgment dominated central portals, as at the cathedrals of Autun and Chartres. In addition, many sets of Apocalypse illustrations are preserved from the medieval period. Between the tenth and the twelfth century, artists from Mozarabic Spain and southern France illustrated copies of the late eighth-century commentary on the Book of Revelation by Beatus of Liébana with up to sixty scenes drawn from the Apocalypse.

Various twelfth- and thirteenth-century encyclopedias or compendia, such as the *Liber floridus* and the *Hortus deliciarum,* also included short Apocalypse miniature cycles. The majority of illustrated Apocalypse manuscripts belong to the Gothic period. In the first half of the thirteenth century, influenced by widespread unrest and possibly stimulated by the writings of the Italian monk Joachim de Fiore, English illustrators created a set of approximately ninety miniatures to accompany the Apocalypse (see, for example, the Trinity Apocalypse, Trinity College, Dublin). Over seventy copies of this series, called the Anglo-Norman cycle, are preserved from England and the continent.

Byzantine theologians considered the Apocalypse to be noncanonical; although isolated motifs from the Book of Revelation were depicted, complete cycles of Apocalypse illustrations are, with the exception of one post-Byzantine manuscript (Chicago, University Library, codex 931, of the seventeenth century), unknown in the east. From the eleventh century on, increasingly elaborate representations of the Last Judgment were depicted (for example, the paraklesion of the Kariye Djami, Constantinople), and in the post-Byzantine period copies of western Apocalypse illustrations were made at Mount Athos and various other sites.

BIBLIOGRAPHY

Frederic van der Meer, *Apocalypse: Visions of Revelation in Western Art* (1978).

LESLIE BRUBAKER

[See also **Agnus Dei; Anglo-Norman Literature; Manuscript Illumination.**]

APOCALYPTIC LITERATURE AND MOVEMENT, JEWISH. The development of Jewish apocalyptic and messianic literature in late antiquity and the early Middle Ages is closely linked to the development of Jewish mystical literature of that time. One of the earliest surviving apocalyptic documents is the martyrological and mystical Story of the Ten Martyrs, which forms part of a mystical work of the talmudic period, *Heikhalot rabbati.* According to this document, which probably originated in the third or fourth century A.D., a Roman emperor decided to execute the ten most prominent rabbis of the tannaitic age. When the group heard about this decision they sent one of the rabbis, Ishmael ben Elisha, "the high priest," to the celestial palaces, in order to inquire whether this decision was merely a whim of the emperor or a divine decree. *Heikhalot rabbati* is Ishmael's report of what he saw on this trip; most of it is a mystic's report of a visit to the seven divine palaces *(heikhalot),* the songs of the angels that he heard, the various roles of the different celestial powers, and methods of mystical ascension.

But the answer to Ishmael's question was given by a report of a dialogue between God and Samael, the archangel representing Rome. In this dialogue Samael insisted that the ten martyrs should be tortured and executed as punishment for the sin of Joseph's ten brothers, who sold him into slavery in Egypt. God accepts the argument but insists that Samael must agree, in compensation, to the complete destruction of Rome. Samael accepts, and a detailed, apocalyptic description of the city's fate is given. Clouds of pestilence and a rain of plague will fall upon it, destroying not only all human and animal life but even stones and metals. Corpses will cover the earth, and should Rome and everything in it be offered for sale on that day, no one will pay a penny for it. Thus the work expresses Jewish feelings of hatred toward Rome, describes the forthcoming divine revenge, and raises messianic hopes, although messianic ideas are not discussed in detail.

The most important Hebrew apocalyptic work of this early period is the brief Book of Zerubbabel, probably written in the early seventh century, before the Islamic conquests, though a definite date cannot be ascertained. The work is in the form of a revelation by an angel (called Michael or Metatron in different versions) to Zerubbabel, the last ruler of Judea of the house of David. The language is deeply influenced by the style of the revelations to Ezekiel and Daniel. Zerubbabel is shown a vision of the messianic era, at the beginning of which the Messiah sits among the beggars and the wounded at the gates of Rome, suffering and waiting. A messianic staff handed down from generation to generation reaches Hephzi-bah, the Messiah's mother, who assembles an army to fight for the liberation of Israel, headed by a second messianic figure, the Messiah son of Joseph.

The book contains a detailed description of the rise of an Antichrist, a satanic figure named Armilus (possibly derived from Romulus), whose monstrous appearance is described. Armilus is the son of the devil, Belial, and his mother was a stone statue of a beautiful Roman woman. Armilus became the king of Rome, preached a new religion, and conquered the whole world before beginning to fight the Messiah. In the ensuing battle, which was held at the gates of Jerusalem, the Messiah son of Joseph was killed, and only then did the Messiah son of Judah appear, join his mother, and defeat Armilus. The various stages of these apocalyptic wars, depicting the remnants of Israel against the entire Christian world, are described chronologically in great detail as visions shown to Zerubbabel by the angel. After the victory, the return of the exiles proceeds, followed by the resurrection, the rebuilding of the temple in Jerusalem, and the messianic era.

The Book of Zerubbabel became the prototype of Jewish apocalyptic works in the Middle Ages, especially since it could not be characterized as typifying any specific Jewish ideology. It is a perfect apocalypse in that it describes in a visionary way a future that is independent of any human deeds. The work preaches no specific way of life, faith, or behavior that can enhance or delay the process of redemption. The future depends only on divine decisions, and the actors in the eschatological drama will be messianic and divine figures. Thus, even though in the Middle Ages different ideologies and theological systems were developed within Judaism, all of them could still accept and rely upon the Book of Zerubbabel because it did not contradict any of them. During the great messianic upheaval of the seventeenth century, the work was still quoted, although more than a thousand years had passed since its composition.

Although several sporadic Jewish messianic movements occurred in the Middle East during the early Middle Ages, none of them left any apocalyptic or ideological literature. All that survives are brief descriptions of their founders in the works of Jewish and Arabic historians. At the same time a sizable literature developed following the basic outlines of the Book of Zerubbabel. There are several works describing the signs of the messianic era, listing the main events of the messianic wars, and computing the time of arrival of the Messiah. The Greek literature following the visions of Daniel had some Hebrew counterparts, probably from early tenth-century Byzantium, describing past and present events and dealing with the future in an apocalyptic manner. Still, at this time there is no unity between messianic and apocalyptic literature and a movement: the two seem to be following parallel lines without combining vision and action.

Medieval Jewry developed three major theological systems, which differed significantly in their attitude toward apocalyptic creativity and messianic speculation and activity. The rationalistic philosophers usually did not emphasize the apocalyptic element in their eschatological expositions, though they were not consistent in this respect. The tenth-century scholar and writer Saadiah Gaon in Babylonia included a summary of the Book of Zerubbabel in the eschatological chapter of his major work, The Book of Faiths and Beliefs; while Moses Maimonides insisted on denying any supernatural element in his description of the redemption, maintaining that messianic activity will follow natural, historical lines. But on the whole, rationalistic philosophy, the ideology of the intellectual class of Jews in Spain and Italy until the fifteenth century, deemphasized messianic and apocalyptic elements.

The second major theological movement, which developed in central Europe—mainly in Germany—in the twelfth and thirteenth centuries, was the mystical and pietistic movement of the Ashkenazi pietists *(ḥasidim).* In their speculations there is a steady element of messianic speculation and a belief in imminent divine redemption. But the teachers of this movement did not reveal their complete messianic picture, and most of the extant material is in the form of obscure hints. It is quite clear, however, that their theology did not contribute to the creation of an apocalyptic literature.

From the thirteenth century, the main impetus for the creation of apocalyptic and messianic literature, which gave an ideological basis to such movements, was the cabala, the third major Jewish theology of the Middle Ages. Early cabala, the mysticism that began to develop in southern France and Spain late in the twelfth century, did not contain messianic or apocalyptic elements; the mystics who developed it were interested mainly in the esoteric meaning of the process of the Creation. The change that occurred in the second half of the thirteenth century, however, brought apocalyptic and messianic speculation to hold a central place in cabalistic literature.

The first major work to reflect this change was a treatise by the Spanish cabalist Isaac ben Jacob ha-Kohen written about 1265 in Castile and called "A Treatise on the Emanations on the Left." To the ordinary cabalistic system of ten divine powers *(sephirot)* Isaac added another ten, divine in character but governed by Samael and Lilith, the male and female powers of evil, and parallel to the divine powers of good. Isaac's dualistic system offered the first explanation in Jewish theology of evil as emanating from a satanic divine system. The good "right" divine powers are in constant struggle with the evil "left" ones; and the struggle of the past and present turns, in the concluding chapters of the work, into a description of the future. An apocalyptic war is to be fought between the representative of evil and the messianic "sword," which God will send to vanquish the evil powers. These wars will culminate in a messianic era of revenge followed by a period of peace and bliss.

Most of Isaac's contemporaries and followers did not accept his apocalyptic and dualistic mysticism; but the most important cabalist of the next generation, Moses ben Shem Tov de Leon, author of the Zohar, the major mystical work of the cabala, incorporated his symbols and attitudes in this work. The Zohar thus became an enduring source of apocalyptic and messianic symbolism, which remained a main characteristic of the cabala. Many Jewish mystics of the fourteenth and fifteenth centuries did not emphasize these zoharic elements in their work, but they remained within the pages of the Zohar awaiting the historical circumstances that could reawaken Jewish apocalyptic and messianic thought.

One of the most important components of Jewish apocalyptic literature in the late Middle Ages was the myth of the ten lost tribes. Detailed descriptions of an independent, powerful, and deeply committed kingdom of these tribes circulated throughout the Middle Ages, based on the writings of Eldad ha-Dani. This traveler appeared in Babylonia in the late ninth century and gave descriptions of powerful African and Asian kingdoms, whose hundreds of thousands of soldiers were ready to rescue Judaism when needed. While Eldad's reports are not messianic in character, later Jewish storytellers and messianic activists relied on them when describing the imminent apocalyptic redemption. Stories circulated about the deliverance of a certain community from hardships caused by Christian rulers with the assistance of a powerful magician who was called from beyond the legendary Sambatyon River, where the tribes lived. When messianic expectations became acute in the late Middle Ages, stories reporting a sighting of the armies of the ten lost tribes served as an incentive to messianic beliefs and activity.

During the late fifteenth and sixteenth centuries, especially following the expulsion of the Jews from Spain in 1492, a marked increase in messianic and apocalyptic speculation occurred throughout the Jewish world. An early example is *Nevu'at ha-yeled* ("The Prophecy of the Child"). The short story is set in an early period and tells of a wonderful child, Nahman Ktofa, who composed a series of prophecies in difficult and symbolic language. The prophecies themselves—if not the entire story—were probably written by a late fifteenth-century cabalist, who included veiled references to major contemporary historical events and described a messianic apocalypse. Commentaries on these prophecies added to the general messianic tension of the period and offered a major sacred source to rely upon.

Another important story reflecting this atmosphere is that of the messianic attempt by a cabalist, Joseph della Reina, who reportedly attempted to enchain Samael and Lilith using magical formulas. The attempt failed at the last minute, when Joseph in his mercy offered the bound devil sustenance, a gesture interpreted as an act of idolatry. Joseph was probably a late fifteenth-century cabalist, whose other works reflect messianic endeavor. He was very close to a circle of cabalists who produced several important mystical works that influenced the development of cabalistic messianism after the expulsion from Spain.

BIBLIOGRAPHY

Judah Kaufman, *Midreshey geulah* (1954), in Hebrew; Gershom Scholem, *Major Trends in Jewish Mysticism,* 3rd ed. (1954); and *The Messianic Idea in Judaism* (1971); Isaiah Tishby, *Netive emunah u-minut* (1964), in Hebrew.

JOSEPH DAN

[See also **Cabala; Philosophy-Theology, Jewish.**]

APOCRYPHA, IRISH. Although no comprehensive study of medieval Irish apocrypha has yet been made, the available evidence suggests that Ireland may well possess the richest store of vernacular apocrypha in Western Europe. Irish sources occasionally provide the earliest witness to an apocryphal text and, in a few cases, the only witness in the Western church to a text otherwise found only in Greek or in Near Eastern versions. The survival of such unusual apocrypha in Ireland has been interpreted as evidence of that church's eccentricity and its fascination with bizarre and uncanonical matter. More likely, however, these remains resulted from the historical and geographical isolation of the Irish church from Western Christendom in the early stages of its development. In any case the Irish primarily used apocrypha for the same reasons that obtained elsewhere—to supplement the meager details of canonical Scripture wherever necessary and to embellish interesting characters and events, especially those concerning the life of Christ and the Apostles.

Identified apocrypha occur in Irish works in two forms: directly, in excerpts, quotations, and translations into Irish; and indirectly, through their use as subordinate sources of information in biblical commentaries, saints' lives, devotional poems, canonical texts, and the like. Irish apocrypha fall into three broad categories, each with its own chronology: (1) Hiberno-Latin, 600–850; (2) Middle Irish, 900–1100; (3) Medieval after 1100.

The Hiberno-Latin apocrypha were produced by the monastic schools, which during this period cultivated Latin learning and culture. Among the direct apocryphal witnesses are the earliest known Latin fragment of the Gnostic *Acts of Thomas,* used as a hymn in the Mass for the Feast of the Circumcision, which survives in a Gallican-Irish sacramentary written around 650, and the *Epistle to the Laodiceans,* an apocryphal letter attributed to St. Paul, found in the Book of Armagh (807). But the bulk of the evidence for apocrypha in this period comes indirectly from extracts, stories, and exempla incorporated into nonapocryphal works. For example, a story from the *Acts of Thomas*—the cursing of an insolent steward who subsequently dies—occurs in the Hiberno-Latin *Collectio canonum hibernensis,* as supporting evidence that the infliction of death by malediction is justified in certain circumstances. Likewise, the apocryphal *Gospel According to the Hebrews* is cited by Irish biblical exegetes to provide greater detail about the miracles performed by Christ and to supply the names of the Magi. One exception to the dominance of Latin during this period is an Old Irish verse translation composed about 700 of the apocryphal *Infancy Gospel of Thomas.*

The Middle Irish apocrypha, virtually all composed in Irish, also differ from those of the first period in displaying greater originality and a more skillful handling and elaboration of Latin apocryphal sources. Eschatology ranks as the favorite subject, reflecting Irish interest in the otherworld, already a characteristic feature of certain genres of secular Old Irish literature. The best-known eschatological work, the *Fifteen Signs Before Doomsday,* composed in Ireland probably in the tenth century, enjoyed great popularity in both Latin and vernacular versions in other parts of Western Europe.

Another, related genre, the *fís,* or vision of the otherworld, is attested as early as the seventh century in the Latin account of Fursa's vision given by Bede in his *Historia ecclesiastica.* The best-known example, the *Fís Adamnáin* ("The Vision of Adamnán"), a composition of the tenth or eleventh century, provides graphic descriptions of hell and heaven, partly based on apocrypha such as the *Apocalypse of Thomas,* the *Transitus Mariae,* and the *Visio Pauli.* The other most important Irish eschatological works are the *Scéla Laí Brátha* ("Tidings of Doomsday") and *Scéla na h-Esérgi* ("Tidings of the Resurrection"). *Saltair na Rann* ("The Psalter of Quatrains"), composed in verse around 988, incorporates apocryphal matter on the Creation, the Fall, and Judgment Day from such apocryphal texts as the *Book of Adam and Eve*, the *Apocalypsis Mosis*, the *Apocalypse of Thomas,* and other as yet unidentified sources.

Medieval apocrypha after 1100 are preserved (mostly uninvestigated) in the great Irish codices of the late fourteenth and fifteenth centuries such as the *Leabhar Breac* and the Yellow Book of Lecan. A considerable part of this material represents reworking or transmission of apocrypha composed or elaborated during the second period. The Norman invasion (1169) and the reform of the Irish church in the twelfth century brought Ireland into closer contact with Europe and facilitated the propagation of later medieval apocrypha such as the *Legenda aurea* and the pseudo-Bonaventure's *Meditationes vitae Christi.* Two fundamental intermediaries for the transmission of such European apocrypha into Ireland were the Irish bardic poets and the preaching orders, especially the Franciscans.

BIBLIOGRAPHY

For a catalog of identified Irish apocrypha and an extensive bibliography, see Martin McNamara, *The Apocrypha in the Irish Church* (1975); see also reviews by D. N. Dumville, in *Journal of Theological Studies,* **27** (1976); and Dáibhí I. Ó Cróinín, in *Éigse,* **16** (1976), for additional references.

PÁDRAIG P. Ó NÉILL

[See also **Airdena Brátha: Fifteen Tokens of Doomsday** and **Saltair na Rann: The Psalter of Quatrains.**]

APOLLINARIUS, "the Younger" (*ca.* 310–*ca.* 390), was born at Laodicea (Syria). Educated in both pagan and Christian thought, Apollinarius was an outspoken advocate of Nicene theology. He was excommunicated in 342 by George, the Arian bishop of Laodicea, for his support of Athanasius, but was subsequently elected bishop of Laodicea by its Nicene community in *ca.* 360.

An eloquent speaker and prolific writer, Apollinarius produced biblical commentaries (noted by Jerome, who heard him speak at Antioch), apologetical works against Porphyry and Julian the Apostate, and polemical and dogmatic works. It is in the dogmatic writings, especially the *Proof of the Incarnation of God According to the Image of Man* (*ca.* 376–380), that he presented his Christology.

Apollinarius was concerned with the metaphysical problem of how two beings, God and man, could unite in such a way as to produce a unity, and with the soteriological problem of the necessity of Christ's sinlessness for the efficacy of the Redemption. He solved both problems by maintaining that Christ's humanity was incomplete: Christ had human flesh but his human soul as vivifying principle (*ψυχή*) and as rational principle was replaced by the divine Logos. Thus the unity of both Christ's nature (*φύσις*) and his person (*πρόσωπον*) was maintained. Further, since the Logos and not a human principle of rationality chose between good and evil, Christ was necessarily sinless and the efficacy of the Redemption guaranteed.

This Christology was condemned by Pope Damasus I at a synod in Rome (377), a verdict subsequently affirmed by synods at Alexandria (378), Antioch (379), and finally the First Council of Constantinople (381). Refutations were written by Athanasius, Basil, Gregory of Nazianzus, and Gregory of Nyssa. Apollinarius' writings are extant primarily in fragmentary form, except for a few dogmatic works circulated by his pupils and ascribed by them to Gregory Thaumaturgus, Athanasius, and Pope Julius I.

BIBLIOGRAPHY

R. Hübner, "Gotterserkenntnis durch die Inkarnation Gottes. Zu einer neuen Interpretation der Christologie des Apollinaris von Laodicea," in *Kleronomia,* 4 (1972); Charles Kannengiesser, "Une nouvelle interprétation de la christologie d'Apollinaire," in *Recherches de science religieuse,* 59 (1971); Hans Lietzmann, *Apollinarius von Laodicea und seine Schule* (1904); Ekkehard Mülenberg, *Apollinaris von Laodicea* (1969), with bibliography; Johannes Quasten, *Patrology,* III (1960), 377–383, bibliography.

John F. Boyle

APOLLONIUS OF TYANA, a neo-Pythagorean philosopher and magician, was born at Tyana in Cappadocia and died at Ephesus about A.D. 100. In the third century Philostratus wrote a highly rhetorical biography of the wonder-worker, attempting to portray him as a Christ figure for the pagans. In an anti-Christian work which he wrote during the reign of Diocletian (284–305), Hieracles of Nicomedia used Philostratus' *Life* to make an unfavorable comparison between the miracles of Apollonius and those of Christ. This work was refuted by the Church historian Eusebius of Caesarea in his *Contra Hieraclem.*

BIBLIOGRAPHY

P. de Labridle, *La réaction paiënne: Étude sur la polémique antichrétienne du premier au sixième siècle* (1942); G. R. S. Mead, *Apollonius de Tyane: le philosophe réformateur du premier siècle de notre ère* (1906).

Deirdre Baker

[See also **Eusebius of Caesarea.**]

APOLOGETICS. See **Polemics.**

APOLONII GESTA. See **Gesta Apollonii.**

APOLONIO, LIBRO DE, an anonymous mid-thirteenth-century poem of 656 stanzas composed in the *cuaderna vía* (four-line strophes of monorhymed alexandrines), the prevailing erudite meter of thirteenth-century Castile. The work is preserved in a single manuscript (Escorial MS III-K-4) dating from the late fourteenth century. Aragonese linguistic traits point to a scribe from that region, but there is no doubt that the language of the original text was Castilian.

It has been demonstrated that the source of the *Libro de Apolonio* is a version of the anonymous Latin *Historia Apolonii Regis Tyri.* The *Historia* clearly belongs to the tradition of the Greek romances and, in addition to the conventional motifs of shipwrecks, kidnappings, and separated families, incorporates such folkloric elements as the theme of incest and the trials that the hero must undergo in order to obtain the hand of a princess. The tale's conjugation of stock romance and folkloric motifs must at least partially explain its popularity throughout the Middle Ages.

The Spanish poet is extremely faithful to the plot of the *Historia,* and his mastery of Latin is most evident where he is merely translating his source. More often than not, however, in accordance with his own spiritual and artistic criteria, he paraphrases the *Historia,* transforming the lean prose of the Latin text into a vivid poetic narration. His suppressions and additions tend to give greater coherence to the story, removing inconsistencies and unnecessary repetitions.

Often the amplifications are part of the process of medievalization that the *Historia* undergoes. The source's Greco-Roman gymnasium becomes a medieval ball game (a kind of field hockey) in which Apolonio demonstrates his inherent nobility. The Latin *Historia* mixes pagan and Christian elements; the Spanish *Libro* intensifies that process of Christianization, incorporating a series of pious digressions and underscoring the role of Divine Providence in human affairs. The Spanish poet emphasizes the goodness of Apolonio and the wickedness of Antíoco, and this polarization of values is evident in the portrayal of the secondary characters as morally good or evil, a technique absent in the *Historia.* The Apollonius tale is set in a clearly Christian frame of reference in which Divine Providence causes good to triumph and evil to be punished.

The Apollonius legend stands apart from epic poems and chivalric romances in that it relegates bellicose activity to the antagonist, Antiochus. Apollonius is an intellectual hero who triumphs not through the force of arms, but through the exercise of his intelligence and his trust in Divine Providence. The Spanish poem gives special emphasis to Apolonio's ingenuity in solving Antíoco's riddle, to the intern's skill in reviving Apolonio's wife Luciana after her apparent death while giving birth to their daughter Tarsiana, and to Tarsiana's carefully planned education.

Through his choice of a protagonist and his manner of highlighting the powers of the intellect, the poet reveals his pride in his clerkly craft. In the introduction to his work he announces that he will compose "un romance de nueva maestría," a clear indication of his faith in his own intellectual powers and in his ability to handle the difficult and rigorous *cuaderna vía* meter. At the end of the poem, when Apolonio has been reunited with his family and restored to his kingdom, the poet looks forward to a heavenly reward. Apolonio has in a sense become the poet's literary double, for the author, like his protagonist, may expect a suitable recompense for the virtuous exercise of his intelligence.

BIBLIOGRAPHY

Manuel Alvar, ed., *Libro de Apolonio* I, *Estudios* (1976); Joaquín Artiles, *El "Libro de Apolonio," poema español del siglo XIII* (1976); Wilfredo Casanova, "El *Libro de Apolonio:* Cristianización de un tema clásico" (dissertation, Yale University, 1970); Charles Carroll Marden, ed., *Libro de Apolonio,* I (1917); Ronald E. Surtz, "The Spanish *Libro de Apolonio* and Medieval Hagiography," in *Medioevo romanzo* (in press).

RONALD E. SURTZ

[See also **Spanish Literature; Spanish Romances.**]

APOSTASY, from a Greek noun meaning defection, departure, or revolt. Hence, in general, an apostate is a person who renounces the Christian religion. In the Middle Ages the word was often used of a priest or a monk who renounced his vows. See examples in J. E. Niermeyer, *Mediae Latinitatis Lexicon Minus* (1976), and Charles D. Du Cange, *Glossarium Mediae et Infimae Latinitatis* (many editions), under the headings *apostasia, apostatare.*

JOSEPH R. STRAYER

APOSTOLIC CONSTITUTIONS, probably a fourth-century work, presents itself as the work of the apostles published by Pope Clement I in the first century. The unknown author, most likely an Arian writing in Syria or Constantinople, has been identified with both Pseudo-Ignatius and Pseudo-Clement. The *Apostolic Constitutions* is, in fact, a compilation drawn from earlier pseudo-apostolic writings. The first six of the eight books are based upon the *Didascalia*, but reflect a greater liturgical development. Book I deals with morals and customs; book II with clergy, penitence, and liturgy; book III, widows and deacons; book IV, orphans; book V, martyrs, feasts, and eschatology; and book VI, schism, heresy, Jews, and burial practices.

The first thirty-one chapters of book VII are taken from the *Didache*; the remainder is a collection of Jewish prayers and the Antiochene rites of baptism and confirmation. Chapters 1 to 27 of book VIII deal with charismatic gifts and formulas for conferring orders according to the Antiochene liturgy. Chapters 5 to 15 contain the oldest complete extant Mass. The remainder of book VIII is a collection of eighty-five canons. Known as the "Apostolic Canons," they are presented in the form of conciliar decrees dealing with various aspects of the clergy. In the West, Dionysius Exiguus (late fifth century) translated the first fifty canons into Latin, including them in his *Collectio Dionysiana.* In the East, Johannes Scholasticus (mid sixth century) included all eighty-five in his collection. The *Apostolic Constitutions*, excluding the Apostolic Canons, was condemned by the Quinisext Synod (692) for unorthodox content. As the largest such collection from late antiquity, it is particularly important for the study of developments in church order and liturgy.

BIBLIOGRAPHY

Franz Funk, *Didascalia et Constitutiones Apostolorum* (1905); James Donaldson, *Ante-Nicene Fathers* (1888, American Edition), VII, 391–505, English translation; Johannes Quasten, *Patrology* (1953), II, 183–185.

JOHN F. BOYLE

[See also **Books, Liturgical; Dionysius Exiguus; Liturgy, Treatises on.**]

APOSTOLIC SUCCESSION, a doctrine of the Catholic Church that states that the power to teach, rule, and consecrate, which Christ conferred upon the Apostles, has been transmitted from generation to generation, in accordance with his intentions, through the succession of bishops. The doctrine allows that Christ committed the pastoral mission of the Church to his disciples, understanding that they were mortal and that others in turn would succeed to their responsibilities. Initially perceived in literal terms, by the end of the second century the notion of a historical succession became increasingly subsumed under a sacramental interpretation, that of episcopal consecration.

The New Testament did not specifically provide a practice or mandate concerning the way the apostolic mission was to be continued after the deaths of the Apostles, although the pastoral Epistles to Timothy and Titus, for example, indicate that others chosen by the Apostles were carrying their work forward. This had been the practice from the earliest days of the Church. In order to provide unity, continuity, and authority within the growing Church, this first-century practice needed to be clarified and affirmed.

The first claim for authority based on apostolic succession came from Clement of Rome writing in the last decade of the first century. Forced to deal with the problem of schismatics, Clement wrote that the Apostles, inspired by Jesus, knew that the time would come when the Church would need clearly established figures of authority. Thus they appointed certain men to follow them, who in turn were succeeded by others when necessary. In Clement's understanding, the Church might be presided over by a group of such men, and the succession was joint. He called the persons charged with the direction of the church "bishops" (overseers) and "deacons" (servants or ministers), sometimes, however, referring to the bishops as "presbyters" (elders). These men had apostolic authority. They did not receive any authority from the congregation, so it could not depose them.

By the second century the challenge to the Church was not only one of authority but also of doctrine, and arguments that advanced the notion of apostolic succession came from churchmen who were writing to counteract proliferating heresy, Ignatius of Antioch, Tertullian, and Irenaeus. Such heresy was to be controlled by a single strong authority. The collegial church organization known to Clement was no longer typical in the experience of Ignatius among the churches in Syria and Asia Minor. Here a "monarchical" church was well established and it was the monarchical bishop who became universally acknowledged as successor to the Apostles during the second century. Whereas Clement had found authority in the apostolic succession of the group, Ignatius appealed to the authority of the bishop by virtue of his unique position.

These two notions were joined in the writings of Irenaeus and Tertullian, who were the first to place emphasis on the uninterrupted chain of bishops who unite the present church with apostolic times. Irenaeus and Tertullian developed the concept that the Apostles were the depositaries of the true faith; that they communicated it to their best disciples; and that they made these men their successors in the episcopacy of the churches they founded. These disciples did the same with their own followers, establishing a single unbroken line that still continues. Moreover, not only churches founded by Apostles possess the true faith, but all churches that follow the same practices are apostolic.

BIBLIOGRAPHY

Arnold Ehrhardt, *The Apostolic Succession in the First Two Centuries of the Church* (1953); P. Etienne *et al.*, "Comme le père m'a envoyé, moi aussi je vous envoie," as well as other articles on the apostolic succession, in *Verbum Caro,* **15** (1961); Antonio M. Javierre, *El tema literario de la sucesión* (1963); Kenneth E. Kirk, ed., *The Apostolic Ministry* (1946, repr. 1957); Einar Molland, "Irenaeus of Lugdanum and the Apostolic Succession," in *Journal of Ecclesiastical History,* **1** (1950); H. B. Swete, ed., *Essays on the Early History of the Church and the Ministry* (1918).

ANN K. WARREN

[See also **Clergy, Grades, Ranks, Titles, Privileges of; Pope.**]

APPANAGES. In the strict sense, appanages were grants of land made by the kings of France to their younger sons in order to provide for their maintenance while also compensating them for their inability to inherit the throne. Their stated purpose was to preserve love and peace in the family. More broadly, however, the term is often used to describe similar inheritance practices observed by other royal and noble families all over Europe. In the French case, though not elsewhere, such grants always carried inheritance restrictions limiting enjoyment of an appanage to direct heirs of the original holder; in their default, the land returned to the crown and the royal domain.

Appanages came into being as a solution for the family problems created by the evolving fortunes and changing conceptions of monarchy. Since under Carolingian rule kingdoms had been divisible, younger sons needed no special treatment. In 987 Hugh Capet stopped dividing the kingdom and began what became a system of primogeniture. Given the relative poverty of his early successors, few made provisions for their cadets beyond advantageous marriages, but when Philip Augustus (1180–1223) vastly increased royal holdings—and when his son, Louis VIII (1223–1226), had seven sons of his own—it became clear that a new approach to family property was needed. The solution adopted, borrowed from the practices of the northern French nobility, was to grant the bulk of the new acquisitions in appanage.

The appanage system lasted down to the nineteenth century, finally ending two years after the overthrow of Charles X in 1830. It also underwent remarkably few changes, the principal ones coming early in the fourteenth century as a reflection of changes in the monarchy itself. Thus, for example, as royal blood became ever more sacred, appanaged princes began to be made peers of the realm. Similarly, when women began to be excluded from the throne in 1316, they were simultaneously denied the enjoyment of new appanages as well—though here the granting of Burgundy in 1364 with no such restriction was a late and important exception.

Critics have charged that appanages had pernicious consequences insofar as their creation deprived the monarchy of the benefits flowing from its new acquisitions, but the case can easily be overstated. Under the Capetians, the appanaged princes served the king loyally and well, their close family ties and imitation of royal administrative practices serving to introduce large areas of France to a quasi-monarchical rule that facilitated rapid acceptance of the king himself. If later appanages, notably Burgundy, were to cause the Valois endless grief, the problem appears to have arisen not so much from defects in the system itself as from the consequences of a situation in which princes began to receive delegations of royal sovereignty and were often forced to operate in a power vacuum created by kingly weakness and insanity. Such difficulties apart, appanages proved a useful tool of monarchy and family alike.

BIBLIOGRAPHY

Andrew W. Lewis, "Anticipatory Association of the Heir in Early Capetian France," in *American Historical Review,* **83** (1978); and "The Capetian Apanages and the Nature of the French Kingdom," in *Journal of Medieval History,* **2** (1976); Ferdinand Lot and Robert Fawtier, *Histoire des institutions françaises au moyen âge,* vol. II (1958), 122–139; Charles T. Wood, *The French Apanages and the Capetian Monarchy 1224–1328* (1966).

CHARLES T. WOOD

[See also **Inheritance, Western Europe.**]

APPRENTICE/APPRENTICESHIPS. See **Guilds.**

APSE, an architectural projection, usually semicircular in plan, surmounted by a half dome. Of Roman origin, the apse was adopted along with the basilican plan by the early Christians (Old St. Peter's) to house the altar. Usually located at the east end of the church on axis with the nave, in some Carolingian and Ottonian churches (Fulda) apses appear at both ends. They may also terminate transept arms. Western apses were often raised above a crypt (Hildesheim); in Byzantium (and occasionally in the West) the main apse may be flanked by two smaller ones (prothesis, diaconicon). Romanesque and Gothic apses are often surrounded by an ambulatory from which issue chapels; in the Gothic period the ambulatory, chapels, and apse were united into a single spatial unit (chevet).

LESLIE BRUBAKER

APSE ECHELON, a number of small chapels grouped on either side of an apse; the depth of each chapel is progressively increased so that a steplike arrangement, culminating in the apse, is achieved. An apse echelon, or apse *en échelon,* is usually found at the eastern end of a church.

LESLIE BRUBAKER

APSIDAL CHAPEL. See **Chapel, Types of.**

AQ QOYUNLU (Turkish, "white sheep"), a Turkoman confederation in Eastern Anatolia (1378–1502). Their ruling clan derived from the Bayundur of the Oghuz. In the mid fourteenth century they figured in the affairs of Trebizond through marital ties with the Comneni. Fully emerging under Qara Yülüg Osman (d. 1435), they became allies of Tamerlane and were given Diyarbakir. Uzun Ḥasan (1453–1478) made best use of this legacy, crushing the Qara Qoyunlu (1467), defeating the Timurids (1468), and extending his authority to Iran and Iraq. The Ottoman threat forced him to support the Karamanids and seek alliances with the West. His successors, however, torn by family bickering and dissension created by Shiite propaganda, fell to the Safavids.

BIBLIOGRAPHY

Sources. Jalâl ad-Dîn Davvânî, *'Arẓnâma* in *Millî Tetebbular Mecmuası,* V (1331/1912–1913); Vladimir F. Minorsky, "A Civil and Military Review in Fars in 881/1476," in *Bulletin of the School of Oriental and African Studies,* **10** (1938); Abū Bakr-i Ṭihrānī, *Kitāb-i Diyārbakriyya,* ed. Necati Lugal and Faruk Sümer, 2 vols. (1962–1964); Michael Panaretos, *Peri tôn tês Trapezountos Basileôn:* see Gyula Moravcsik, *Byzantinoturcica,* I (1958), for complete bibliography of this source.

Studies. Walther Hinz, *Irans Aufstieg zum Nationalstaat im fünfzehnten Jahrhundert* (1936); Vladimir F. Minorsky, *La Perse au XVe siècle entre la Turquie et Venise* (1933); I. H. Uzunçarşılı, *Anadolu Beylikleri ve Akkoyunlu Karakoyunlu Devletleri* (1969); John E. Woods, *The Aqquyunlu, Clan, Confederation, Empire: A Study in 15th/9th Century Turko-Iranian Politics* (1976).

PETER B. GOLDEN

[See also **Trebizond.**]

AQUILEIA, RITE OF, the early liturgy used by the patriarchate of Aquileia, which originally included only Venetia and Istria but extended from the Danube to the Po by the fifth century. The oldest liturgical evidence dates from around 400, at which time Rufinus was living in Aquileia. Something of the liturgy is known from the tracts of Bishop Chromatius and from Rufinus' commentary on the Symbol (the phrase "descendit ad inferna" was already recorded for the Church of Aquileia at the time). Chromatius may also have compiled the so-called *series romana* (psalms-collects), which was widely used in the early Middle Ages, as well as a response book that survives, together with parts of a requiem mass and prayers for the morning office, only in a few isolated pages from a fifth- or sixth-century copy. A distinguishing characteristic of the rite is that the Sanctus is still missing from the eucharistic prayers. A lectionary, which in its original form may date from the fourth-century Bishop Fortunatianus, is preserved in an eighth-century copy, with pericopia of the church year.

As in the rest of Upper Italy, the Mass in the Aquileian patriarchate was originally celebrated according to the Gallican rite. Apart from the aforementioned fragment and a qualification test for prelates (now in the Ambrosian Library in Milan), nothing from this early period has survived. Although the synod held around 700 may have brought a gradual turning toward the Roman rite, later liturgy books retain elements of the original rite, such as the interpolation of Patriarch Paulinus in the canon of the Mass, which is preserved in the sacramentary of Brescia.

Surviving fragments of sacramentaries from the period of the Roman-Ravennan rite are characteristic of the entire patriarchate and are of a type otherwise not attested. The most important manuscripts are the sacramentary of Salzburg (shortly after 800) and of Padua (mid ninth century). They belong to the group of mixed Gelasian sacramentaries, which had emerged in Upper Italy, presumably in Ravenna, in the seventh century and represent a link between the Gregorian sacramentary and older Ravennan missals. The Aquileian manuscripts are distinguished from other mixed Gelasian sacramentaries particularly in the preface of the Mass and in the inclusion of orations from the Gregorian missal.

Although parts of the patriarchate had belonged to the Byzantine Empire for centuries, there is virtually no discernible influence of the Eastern liturgy, apart from the Greek akathistos hymn, which was translated and disseminated by Bishop Christophorus of Rivoalto (Venice) around 800. Influences in the artistic sphere are generally known, especially as they are revealed in the cathedral of St. Mark in Venice.

The later patriarchate rite differs from the preceding by the greater emphasis on the plenary missals, which were in general use throughout Italy during the High Middle Ages. It is preserved in printed editions from around 1500, such as the *Missale pro S. Aquileiensis ecclesiae ritu* (1494, 1517, 1519) and the *Sacramentarium patriarchale secundum morem S. Comensis ecclesiae* (1537). Individual differences are insignificant; differences from other rites are more easily recognizable in the rituals, in the *Agenda dioecesis Aquileiensis* (1454), and in books for the chancel office. A thirteenth-century manuscript of a book for the chancel office (Trieste, Biblioteca Civica) bears the title *Ordo breviarii secundum consuetudinem Aquilegensis et Tergestinae ecclesiae per anni circulum.*

The patriarchate rite was abolished in 1594–1595 as a consequence of the Council of Trent and was replaced by the new Roman missal (1570) of Pope Pius V. Liturgical books predating that time were generally destroyed or sold as junk; only a few copies remain intact.

BIBLIOGRAPHY

Fernand Cabrol, ed., *Dictionnaire d'archéologie chrétienne et de liturgie,* I (1907), 2690. Klaus Gamber, *Codices liturgici latini antiquiores,* 2nd ed. (1968), 81–83, 187–189, 287–291, 397–405, with complete bibliography; and "Fragmente eines oberitalienischen Liturgiebuches aus dem 6. Jh. als Palimpsest im Codex Sangallensis 908," in *Florilegium Sangallense* (1980), 165–179; Archdale A. King, *Liturgies of the Past* (1959), 1–51; Joseph Lemarié, ed., *Sermons de Chromace d'Aquilée,* I (1969), 82–108; Bernardo Maria de Rubeis, *Monumenta ecclesiae Aquilejensis* (1740); and *De antiquis Forojuliensium ritibus* (1754).

KLAUS GAMBER

AQUINAS, ST. THOMAS (1224–1274), was born Thomas d'Aquino at Roccasecca Italy, into a family of minor nobility. At the age of five, he was presented as an oblate to the monastery of Monte Cassino, where he remained from 1230 to 1239 and where he began his studies. When the monastery became unsafe because of war, Thomas was sent to Naples, where he continued his studies (1239–1244). During this period he met his first Dominicans and felt drawn to this new order, which, like that founded by St. Francis, embraced poverty and represented reform. Thomas' family, seeing in a vocation to the Order of Preachers the loss of family benefits from his religious profession, was violently opposed to his becoming a Dominican. But Thomas prevailed, and in 1245 he set off for the north in the company of Dominican confreres.

Thomas continued his studies in Paris, then was sent to Cologne (1248), where he studied under Albert the Great, famous for his openness to Aristotle. Doubtless Thomas had already been introduced to the writings of Aristotle at Naples, but Albert's enthusiasm for the new learning was an important influence. Thomas prepared Albert's commentary on the *Nicomachean Ethics* for publication and, perhaps with the exception of some minor logical works written during the year his family detained him in the hope of dampening his desire to become a Dominican, this is the first product of his pen.

After his stay in Cologne, Thomas returned to Paris, where he remained from 1252 to 1259. For four years he lectured on the *Sentences* of Peter Lombard, the twelfth-century bishop of Paris whose collection and arrangement of fundamental theological topics provided the material that, along with

AQUINAS, ST. THOMAS

Holy Scripture, the apprentice theologian had to discuss. In 1256, Thomas became master of theology, and he and St. Bonaventure, his great contemporary, were appointed to chairs reserved for mendicant friars. There was opposition from secular masters, and it was only in 1257 that Thomas became *magister regens.* (By that time Bonaventure had been called to high office in the Franciscan Order.)

It was during this time in Paris that Thomas began his first great summary of theology, the *Summa contra gentiles* (1258–1264). Thomas spent the years 1259–1268 in Italy, where, after being attached to the papal court for several years, he taught in Dominican houses at Rome, Viterbo, and Bologna. He then returned to Paris, where he remained from 1269 to 1272, resuming his chair and continuing work on the *Summa theologiae,* which he had begun to write in Italy. The final period of Thomas' life (1272–1274) was spent in Naples. He was on his way to the Council of Lyons when he fell ill and was taken to the Cistercian monastery at Fossanova, south of Rome, where he died on 7 March 1274.

Thomas was a Christian, a Dominican, and a theologian; this meant, among other things, that he believed God had revealed himself to men in the scriptures and in his son Jesus. Owing to original sin, man's will has been weakened and his mind clouded, but grace and revelation both restore the natural destiny and elevate men to a new and supernatural one. While men can by their natural powers arrive at some knowledge of God, revelation puts them in possession of truths about God that could never be achieved by natural reason. Truths that can be achieved by natural reason are known in the sense that they are derivable from self-evident truths by way of an argument such that if one accepts the premises as true, one must accept the conclusion as true. Believed truths are held to be such on the basis of the authority of God's say-so. The distinction is one between faith and reason, belief and knowledge, and it gives rise to a distinction between philosophy and theology. Thomas Aquinas is of peculiar importance in the Middle Ages for the carefulness, subtlety, and precision with which he handled this question. The following passage provides what may be called the motto of his intellectual effort:

> On this matter I want first to warn you that in arguing with nonbelievers about articles of faith, you should not try to devise necessary arguments on behalf of faith, since this would derogate from the sublimity of faith, whose truth exceeds the capacity not only of human but also of angelic minds. These things are believed by us as revealed by God. However, because what comes from the highest truth cannot be false, nor can what is not false be impugned by necessary arguments, our faith can neither be proved by necessary arguments, because it exceeds the human mind, nor, being true, can it be impugned by necessary argument.
>
> (*De rationibus fidei,* 2)

Thomas' receptivity to pagan thought, his serene confidence that known truth cannot be in conflict with believed truth, his conviction that faith is the culmination and perfection of intellectual inquiry, led to what has fittingly been called the Thomistic synthesis, a breathtaking effort to show the continuity and compatibility of philosophy and theology, and to use what he took to be the achievements of natural reason to cast light on revealed truths.

THEOLOGY AND PHILOSOPHY

In the prologue to his exposition of the *Sentences* of Peter Lombard, Thomas, as had many expositors before him (notably his mentor Albert the Great), discussed the nature of theology. He returned to this subject in his two great theological summaries, the *Summa contra gentiles* and the *Summa theologiae,* as well as in other works. Because of its central importance to his teaching, it is useful to consider closely his abiding thought on this matter. (It is of great historical interest to compare this preliminary discussion with the corresponding expositions of Lombard made by Albert the Great and St. Bonaventure.) Since Thomas' definitive position is to be found in the *Summa theologiae,* we will be guided principally by that work.

The first question that arises is why there should be need for any doctrine beyond that contained in philosophy. This question assumes two things: that philosophy is the name of any and all knowledge acquired by man's natural faculties, and that the classical Greek conception of philosophy as comprising knowledge of God, as well as of man and the world, is the correct one. Thus, Thomas is asking: If philosophy includes all knowledge of anything whatsoever, what need is there for any cognitive discipline or science over and above philosophy? In reply, Thomas says that man requires a special teaching in order to be apprised of the end beyond the reach of reason to which he has been called. Man is called to a supernatural happiness, but this had to be made known to him by divine revelation. Furthermore, Thomas holds that the human mind needs faith and revelation even concerning things we can naturally know, "because only a few men come to rationally

AQUINAS, ST. THOMAS

acquired truth about God, and this after a long time and with the admixture of error" (*ST* 1, q. 1, a. 1).

Theology as a discipline over and above philosophy is necessary because faith and revelation put us in possession of truths that could not be arrived at by natural reason. As a discipline or science, theology, accepting as true whatever God has revealed, uses argumentation to see, for example, what might be implied by the conjunction of belief A and belief B. The characteristic note of Scholastic theology is its employment of philosophical truths and method in reflecting on revelation. Thus, when he speaks about the subject of theology, when he asks if theology is a practical or a speculative science, when he speaks of theology as a subalternate science, Thomas is developing a concept of theology that depends on a whole series of features of Aristotle's thought. Whether this should be done is a question Thomas put to himself. This is his answer:

> Just as sacred doctrine is founded on faith, so philosophy is founded on the natural light of reason; hence it is impossible that those things which are of philosophy should be contrary to the things of faith, but they do fall short of them. Nonetheless, they contain similitudes and preambles, just as nature is the preamble to grace. If something contrary to faith should be found in philosophy, this is not philosophy but an abuse of it due to a defect of reason. Therefore one can, employing the principles of philosophy, refute an error of that sort either by showing it to be in every way impossible or at least not necessary. Just as the things of faith cannot be demonstratively proved, so too some things contrary to them cannot be demonstrated to be false, but they can be shown not to be necessary. Therefore philosophy can be used in three ways in sacred doctrine. First, to demonstrate the preambles of faith, . . . (what things in faith it is necessary to know), those things about God which can be proved by natural argument, such as that God exists, that God is one, and the like (as well as other truths about God and man proved in philosophy which faith presupposes). Second, for making known by way of similitudes those things which are of faith, as Augustine in his work *On the Trinity* uses many similitudes taken from philosophical doctrines to manifest the Trinity. Third, for resisting things said against faith either by showing them to be false or by showing them not to be necessary. (*Exposition of Boethius' "On the Trinity,"* q. 2, a. 3)

FAITH AND REASON

The conception of preambles of faith is of great importance to Thomas' doctrine on the compatibility of faith and reason. If we believe a proposition to be true, we accept its truth on the basis of an authority, someone's say-so. Thus, if we think of a proposition as minimally the ascription of a property to a subject—S is P—the link between predicate and subject, when the proposition is believed, is initially supplied by an authority. For example, I first take someone's word for the fact that the Seine is a more beautiful river than the Tiber. Then I look at the two and assert the truth of this comparison on my own.

Thomas interprets knowing a proposition to be true as either immediately seeing that S is P or deriving this from truths already held, and ultimately from self-evident or immediate truths. To know mediately that S is P is to have a middle term that connects them. In short, Thomas' conception of knowing is connected with syllogism. Propositions immediately known to be true function as principles or starting points. "The whole is greater than its part" and "Equals added to equals give equal results" are examples of immediately known truths. To know what a whole is and what a part is is to know the truth of the first claim, just as knowing what equality and addition are suffices for the second.

Something first taken on authority can subsequently be accepted or rejected on the basis of knowledge, but religious faith is different. If I accept a proposition as true because God reveals it, I am accepting something I cannot know. To hold that Jesus Christ is a single person, human and divine in nature, is not to hold a self-evident truth or one that could be proved by appeal to known things. The believer must always in this life hold such a truth on the basis of revelation. Thus, religious belief is not seen as something replaceable by knowledge in this life.

Although the realms of knowledge and faith thus seem quite distinct, with no overlap possible, the concept of preambles of faith seems to blur the sharp distinction. Preambles of faith are exemplified by "There is a God" and "God is one." These are truths that Thomas believed as a child but that as an adult he felt he could prove to be true. Some of the things God has revealed are knowable. The revealed truths that can be known are not so much matters of faith as preambles of faith. Matters of faith, what is *de fide,* are mysteries. The sharp distinction between religious belief and knowledge applies only to the mysteries.

Thomas finds it significant that God has revealed to us truths we can in principle know. That we need special help even to grasp knowable truths indicates how the human mind has been weakened by sin. But one can also say that if some of the things God has

 AQUINAS, ST. THOMAS

revealed can be known to be true, it is reasonable to accept as true the rest of what he has revealed. This argument on behalf of the reasonableness of religious faith is not, of course, an argument on behalf of a particular datum of revelation, as if one were proving its truth.

In a famous passage Thomas (*Summa theologiae,* 1a, q. 2, a. 3) describes five ways in which the existence of God can be demonstrated: from an analysis of motion, from an analysis of efficient causality, from an analysis of the possible and the necessary, from the grades of nature, and from the governance of things. In some of these arguments it is clear that Thomas is simply taking over an earlier philosophical position. For instance, the proof from motion is taken from Aristotle. For Thomas it was simply a fact that some philosophers had arrived at truths about God of the sort he calls preambles. Once more we are confronted with Thomas' conviction that philosophy and theology are compatible, that the latter depends in various ways on the former.

ARISTOTLE

Faith preceded the study of philosophy for Thomas, but he held that the study of philosophy must precede theology. When Thomas speaks of philosophy, he means the thought of Aristotle. Although, in the early Middle Ages, Aristotle was known only through a few of his logical writings, namely the *Categories,* and *On Interpretation,* toward the end of the twelfth century, a flood of Aristotelian works translated into Latin came onto the scene from centers in Spain, Sicily, and elsewhere. The influx of so impressive an amount of pagan thought, accompanied by Muslim commentaries and interpretations—Avicenna and Averroës playing an important if subsidiary role—presented problems of digestion for the Christian West.

The traditional educational system, grounded on the seven liberal arts—grammar, rhetoric, logic, arithmetic, geometry, astronomy, and music—with the standard *auctores* to be read, could scarcely be unaffected by a system that divided intellectual labor differently and was conveyed in works of overwhelming mastery. The natural works of Aristotle—the *Physics,* the *Parts of Animals, On Heaven and Earth*—when accompanied by Arabic works on medicine and mathematics, represented a veritable earthquake. But such works were only part of the vast Aristotelian system. Knowledge, Aristotle held, is either speculative or practical, and that is the first division of philosophy. Practical philosophy contains three basic divisions: ethics, economics, and politics. Speculative philosophy is first divided into natural science, mathematics, and metaphysics. How does one go about acquiring all this?

> The intention of philosophers was chiefly this: that they might arrive at knowledge of first causes from consideration of all other things. So they put the science of first causes last and devoted the final part of their lives to its consideration. Beginning first with logic, which provides the method of the sciences; moving second to mathematics, of which even children are capable; third to natural philosophy, which requires time and experience; fourth to moral philosophy, of which the young are not appropriate students, they came finally to divine science which considers the first causes of beings.
>
> (St. Thomas, *On the Book of Causes,* proemium)

LATIN AVERROISM

Thomas studied Aristotle at Naples, Paris, and Cologne, but as a master of theology he would not have lectured on the writings of Aristotle as such. It is, therefore, a matter of great significance that he commented on so many Aristotelian works. One reason may well have been the use to which some masters of arts at Paris put Aristotle. Two extremely polemical works by Thomas, *On the Eternity of the World* and *On the Unicity of Intellect Against the Averroists,* were aimed at what he took to be misunderstandings of Aristotle and/or the implications of Aristotelianism.

Aristotle, in proving the existence of the Prime Mover, assumes that the world is eternal. The clear teaching of scripture is that the world had a beginning and is not eternal. Thomas' views, as we have already seen, will not allow that a philosophical truth can be in conflict with a truth of faith. Since he believes the world is not eternal, he knows that "The world is eternal" is false. Can he show it to be false? He doesn't think so. He thinks that, from a purely philosophical standpoint, the matter is undecidable. Furthermore, he argues that Aristotle himself regarded the matter as debatable.

In the work on the unicity of the intellect, Thomas argues that Averroës' interpretation of Aristotle to the effect that there is but a single mind through which all men think, a sort of satellite in the ontological skies that survives the coming and going of individual men, is wrong. Thomas does not simply assert this. The little work is a textual analysis meant to show that Aristotle held that each man has a soul that will continue to exist after his death. The Latin Averroists maintained the following, accord-

AQUINAS, ST. THOMAS

ing to Thomas: "By argument I conclude necessarily that there is numerically one intellect; however, I firmly hold the opposite on faith." What is one to make of such a position?

> He [The Latin Averroist] therefore thinks that faith bears on things whose contrary can be proved with necessity. Since only what is necessarily true can be proved with necessity and its opposite is the false and impossible, it follows from the above remark that faith bears on the impossible, which not even God can make be, nor can the ears of the faithful tolerate it.
>
> (*The Unicity of Intellect,* ch. 5, n. 123)

Clearly, this sort of response to the influx of Greek and Muslim thought had to be countered. Holding that what Aristotle taught is compatible with Christian faith was not simply an abstract policy for Thomas. His commentaries on Aristotle exhibit this in detail. This is not to say that there is any overt reconciling of knowledge and faith in the commentaries; rather, there is the painstaking effort to clarify precisely what Aristotle means.

COMMENTARIES ON ARISTOTLE

Thomas commented on the following works of Aristotle: *On Interpretation* (incomplete), *Posterior Analytics, Physics, On the Soul, On Heavens and Earth, Nicomachean Ethics, Politics* (incomplete), *Metaphysics,* and some minor works. There has been discussion as to the significance of this vast output for the evaluation of Thomas' own teaching. When Albert the Great embarked on the gigantic task of paraphrasing the whole work of Aristotle, he said that that was all he was doing, setting forth Aristotle's views, not his own. Some have felt that the same motto can be put over Thomas' commentaries on Aristotle. Given the two little polemical works—*On the Eternity of the World* and *On the Unicity of Intellect*—this seems unlikely. Indeed, Thomas' statements about philosophy indicate that what he is interested in is the truth of propositions, not just historical accuracy.

Perhaps he finds truths in Aristotle that are not there? Some students of Aristotle contest Thomas' rejection of Averroës' interpretation of Aristotle on the human mind. It is sometimes said that Thomas baptized Aristotle—that is, that he read the great Greek philosopher with Christian eyes and found compatibilities the text will not support. Those who maintain this do not suggest that Thomas deliberately distorted Aristotle. Obviously there is no way in which such claims can be assessed other than by the careful study of the commentaries and the texts of Aristotle. When this is done, it becomes impossible to take Thomas as simply setting forth things he does not himself accept. When he says an argument is sound and cogent, he clearly means that without qualification; he does not mean Aristotle thought it sound and cogent. Nor are there any major instances of misunderstanding and distortion. Thomas called Aristotle *the* philosopher, and it would be impossible to understand his writings without knowing Aristotle. That his interpretations differ from others is true enough, but we have the text of Aristotle as the basis for deciding on their accuracy.

THOMAS AND PLATONISM

If Aristotle was *the* philosopher, he was not the only philosopher. In recent times increasing attention has been paid to the Platonic and Neoplatonic elements in the thought of Thomas Aquinas. Thomas commented on two works of Boethius, *On the Trinity* (incomplete) and the so-called *De hebdomadibus.* He also commented on the *Book of Causes,* proving that it was compiled of selections from Proclus. He also commented on the *On the Divine Names* of Pseudo-Dionysius, whom he took to be Dionysius the Areopagite, converted by St. Paul. It has been held that such concepts as that of participation and such signal teachings as the composition of essence and existence in every being other than God are indications of the Platonism of St. Thomas. Some have gone so far as to say that Thomas is more a Platonist than he is an Aristotelian. Surely that is an exaggeration. No one can read the commentary on the *Book of Causes* and fail to be struck by the way in which Aristotle serves as the measure in assessments of the basic claims of the work. Furthermore, insofar as Platonism and Aristotelianism are distinguished on the basis of differing positions on the problem of universals, there is little doubt where Thomas stands.

The problem of universals, so much discussed in the early Middle Ages, consisted of three questions formulated by Porphyry in his *Introduction (Isagoge)* to the *Categories* of Aristotle. Do common nouns like "man" refer to something real or to a figment of the imagination? Is the real thing they refer to corporeal or incorporeal? Is the real, incorporeal thing they refer to associated with bodies, or separate from them? It can be seen that the sequence of questions incorporates certain answers and suggests a solution to the problem. Plato can be said to have held that "man," while a common noun with respect to Plato and Socrates and Alcibiades, is the proper

AQUINAS, ST. THOMAS

name of an entity distinct from these changing, evanescent individuals. The Ideas or Forms exist apart from particulars, and are their ontological ground as well as the possibility of knowledge.

In *On Being and Essence,* a youthful work, Thomas develops his own position by distinguishing the following propositions: Man is rational; Man is seated; and Man is a species. The first is true essentially; to be human is to be rational; rationality is part of the definition of man, part of his essence. The second is true because it happens that one or more men are seated. To be human and to be seated are only accidentally conjoined. The third is true because the human mind forms a concept of humanity and refers that concept to a variety of individuals. "Species" is one of the five predicables Porphyry discusses in his *Introduction;* the others are "genus," "difference," "property," and "accident." These are five instances of universals. A universal is some one thing that is said of or predicated of many. Species is a universal predicated of many numerically distinct things.

Thomas holds that the unit predicated is a consequence of human understanding. To-be-said-of or to-be-predicated is not part of man's essence. But insofar as we formulate a concept of the nature, there is some one thing that can be predicated of many. If being seated is an accident of the nature or essence thanks to material individuals, then to be a species is an accident of essence thanks to the character of human knowing. There is a real similarity between individual men, and this is the basis in reality for the formation of the concept "man." But it is only as conceived that the nature or essence is something one-over-many. Thomas' position on universals is called moderate realism. He does not think that natures exist apart from individuals (realism) or that there is no basis in individuals for the formation of the concept (nominalism).

On this basic point, then, Thomas opts for Aristotle as against Plato. But in the following passage he states what may be taken to be his basic policy toward Platonism. Having summarized Platonic realism, Thomas remarks:

> This argument of the Platonists agrees with neither truth nor the faith with respect to separated natural species, but, with respect to what it says concerning the First Principle of things, their opinion is most true and is consonant with Christian faith.
>
> (*On the Divine Names,* proemium)

That is, Thomas wishes to distinguish between the view that there is a separate entity Man over and above men, a separate entity Horse over and above horses, and so with all natural species, which he rejects, and the claim that there is a separate Being, Goodness, One on whom all other things depend. Platonism is a bad way to interpret the import of the common nouns with which we speak of creatures, but it a most fitting way to speak about God.

In somewhat the same way, Thomas compares Aristotle and Plato on separated substances or angels. Aristotle's talk about immaterial beings other than God has the great merit to be grounded on sound argument. Plato's argument for immaterial being is deficient. But what is appealing in Plato is the vast number of immaterial beings he speaks of, whereas Aristotle, rightly bound by experience, can formulate arguments for only a small number of separated substances.

HYLOMORPHISM

Since Plato did not regard the things of this world as really real or as adequate objects of knowledge, he did not develop a natural science. The *Timaeus* can hardly be compared with the sequence of natural writings that came from Aristotle. One of the oddities of the transmission of classical texts is that in the twelfth century, Plato was known as the physicist. By the time of Thomas there was no longer any confusion as to which of the great pagan philosophers had devoted himself to natural science. Thomas' understanding of the nature of physical objects is derived from Aristotle.

His treatment of the constitution of physical objects—that is, objects that come to be as the result of a change—can be found in his commentary on the *Physics* and in the opusculum *On the Principles of Nature.* Besides these formal treatments there are many other works in which Thomas recalls the basic doctrine; it is safe to say that the bulk of what he says would be unintelligible without an understanding of this conception of the constitution of physical objects.

One of the consequences of the Aristotelian maxim that art imitates nature is that one can look to art to cast light on nature. So too in analyzing change, Aristotle first refers to changes wrought by the human artisan, as opposed to those brought about by nature, using the former as a way to understand the latter. And he can look at the change involved in a human being's acquiring a skill or art.

 AQUINAS, ST. THOMAS

Thus, he says, consider the following statements: (1) A man becomes skilled; (2) An unskilled man becomes skilled; (3) The unskilled becomes skilled. These are meant to be three different expressions of the same change. The artifact of language too may, when analyzed, cast light on what language is about.

There are two basic ways in which we can express a change: "A becomes B" or "From A, B comes to be." (1), (2), and (3) are all stated in the "A becomes B" form. Could each of them be reexpressed as "From A, B comes to be"? Thomas suggests that we would feel comfortable doing that with (2) and (3), but not with (1). The grammatical subjects of (2) and (3) do not express the subject of the change except accidentally; but the grammatical subject of (1) directly expresses the subject of the change. What is meant by "the subject of the change"? That to which the change is attributed and which survives the change.

This analysis leads to the claim that in any change there must be a subject, and that the subject acquires a characteristic it did not have earlier. It is because of an example Aristotle used that the subject came to be called "matter" and the acquired characteristic "form." If wood is taken and shaped into boards, a material has acquired a new form. The Greek words here are *hylē* and *morphē*. Thus, the theory that whatever has come to be as the result of a change is a complex of matter and form—that is, the subject and its acquired characteristic—is dubbed the hylomorphic theory.

When this analysis is applied to natural changes, it yields the view that things, from not being in such-and-such a place, come to be in such-and-such a place; from not having quality, come to have that quality; from being small, become large; and so on. The analysis, in short, provides a first way of interpreting changes in place, quality, and quantity. The subject to which such changes are attributed seems to be an entity of a more important kind than are the qualities, places, and quantities it loses and acquires. The Greek word for that subject is *ousia,* which becomes the Latin *substantia,* the latter term retaining the context of the analysis of change; the substance "stands under" the forms acquired in change, not unlike the way the subject of a sentence stands under the predicate. Thus, the application of this analysis of change to natural things comes down to saying that it explains the way substances can take on new accidents (things that befall or inhere in substances).

For Aristotle, the great problem confronting natural science in the fourth century B.C. was whether substances themselves come to be as the result of a change. He felt this had been denied because of the influence of Parmenides. Being cannot come to be: what is, is; what is not, is not. This should have stopped all talk of accidental change, but the line was drawn by saying that nothing really real, no substance, comes to be. Talk of change is all right as long as it does not suggest real novelty, that new being comes to be. Aristotle opted for substantial change—that is, for the view that substances, too, come into being as the result of change.

Thomas accepts the view that there are substances and that they come to be as the result of a change. Both these are givens, not a matter of theory. There are basic units in the world, things like Socrates and Plato and an olive tree. Once these things were not, and now they are; and it was by a process of change that they came to be. The problem, therefore, is not to prove that substantial change occurs—only a theory would lead one to deny it—but to ask how the analysis and terminology of accidental change can be adapted to talking about it. If the subject to which a substantial change is attributed (for example, "Xanthippe is born") were itself a substance, it would not be a substantial change, the coming into being of a new substance, but merely the modification of a substance that survives the change. The subject of substantial change cannot be a substance. If we call it the matter of the change, we must set it off from the subject of accidental change. "Prime Matter" is the term devised to name the subject of substantial change. The form it takes on is called a substantial form. Thus, not only is the product of the change whereby the Green Knight becomes tan describable as a complex of matter and form, but substances themselves are compounds of matter and form, of Prime Matter and substantial form.

ANALOGY

Words like "matter" and "form" and "nature" pervade the writings of Thomas Aquinas. The contexts of their use make it difficult to think that they are meant to be understood in the same way all the time. Thus there seems to be a constant threat of equivocation. This is a difficulty we ought to have when reading Thomas, if only because it makes his justification for so limited a vocabulary more interesting.

Already in the discussion of accidental and sub-

AQUINAS, ST. THOMAS

stantial change, words like "matter" and "form" have several meanings. When he wished to speak of the matter of substantial change, Aristotle said we should think of it on an analogy with the subject of accidental change. Thomas is going to put the matter–form dyad to a variety of uses, as in his analysis of knowing, but the retention of these terms is meant to incorporate similarities as well as differences in the things talked about. If there are connections among the things talked about, if our knowledge of one is dependent on our knowledge of another, then the use of the same terminology to speak of these various things can itself reflect these epistemological and ontological connections.

Thomas distinguishes three major ways in which things can share a name. If I say that Socrates is a person and Xanthippe is a person and Cyrus is a person, the recurring predicate here is shared, and presumably we would give the same account of "person" in these three occurrences of the word. Thomas calls such a shared term "univocal." On the other hand, the Latin *volo* means both "I wish" and "I fly" and *liber* means both "book" and "free." Thus, *volo* in "*Volo hodie*" can receive quite different and unrelated accounts. Thomas calls such a shared term "equivocal." Of course there is nothing about "*volo*" and "person" as such that makes them equivocal or univocal; we could easily find uses of "person" in which it would be equivocal and uses of "*volo*" that would be univocal.

There is another way in which a term can be shared, which Thomas says is midway between univocation and equivocation. He calls it "analogy," and he exemplifies it by "healthy" in the following situation. We say that Fido is healthy, that exercise is healthy, and that a sleek coat is healthy. Here we are unlikely to say either that "healthy" has exactly the same account in all these occurrences or that it has entirely different and unrelated accounts.

An analogous term is one that has a variety of accounts or meanings, and these accounts are partly the same and partly different. In what does the sameness and in what does the difference consist? The adjective "healthy" may be defined as "that which has health," and this may be made yet more abstract as "——— health." Then we can say that any account of "healthy" will include the abstract term "health" (that is, the element of sameness), but that the accounts differ because what fills in the blank differs. What can fill in the blank? Subject of; preservative of; sign of. Fido is the subject of the quality "health," exercise is preservative of it, and a sleek coat is a sign of it. In sum, the many meanings of the analogous term are partly the same—all include health—and partly different—each expresses a different mode or way of referring to health.

There is more to Thomas' theory of analogous names. One account takes precedence over the others, is prior to them, is the primary analogate. The primary analogate of "healthy" is "subject of health" because that is understood when we say "preservative of health" (in the subject of health) and "sign of health" (in the subject of health). The analogous name not only has a variety of accounts that are partly the same and partly different; one of those accounts is primary in the way just described.

When he commented on the fifth book of Aristotle's *Metaphysics,* a work often referred to nowadays as a philosophical lexicon, as if it merely set down a technical vocabulary, Thomas Aquinas saw it as a basic manifestation of the way in which words whose natural habitat was the physical world become analogous, as accounts for them are fashioned that enable us to use them to speak of immaterial things. After we have seen how Thomas uses the language of hylomorphism to analyze knowledge, we will return to that metaphysical use of analogy, particularly as it enters into his discussion of how we can speak meaningfully about God.

KNOWLEDGE

In his analysis of what knowing is, Thomas emphasizes such statements as "Socrates came to know such-and-such." To possess knowledge, in short, is to be in a condition that is the result of a change. This is why he can apply the language of change to knowing.

To be a thing is to be a kind of thing, and while there are many things of the same kind, there are also different kinds; thus A, being the kind of thing it is, does not have what B, a different kind of thing, has. If a thing comes to be as the result of a change, it is the completion or perfection of the process of change. Thanks to its kind, a thing has the perfection it does, and of course it does not have the perfections of other kinds of thing. Thus, in a certain way, though a thing is perfect of its kind, it is imperfect, only a part of the total perfection of the universe.

> Hence, in order that there might be a remedy for this imperfection, another mode of perfection is found in created things, thanks to which the perfection proper to one thing is found in another. This is the perfection of the knower as such, for thus it is that something is

AQUINAS, ST. THOMAS

> known by the knower, that what is known is in some way with the knower. That is why Aristotle says in *On the Soul,* book three, that the soul is in a certain way all things, because it is fashioned to know all things.
> (*Disputed Question on Truth,* q. 2, a. 2)

If coming to know is thought of as a kind of change, a way of coming to be, then knowledge will be thought of as taking on the form of another. Now, in natural change, to take on a kind of form is to become a thing of a certain kind. In acquiring the form of redness, a thing becomes a red thing. Furthermore, it ceases to be the kind of thing it was before the change occurred. Thomas wants to speak of knowing as having-the-form-of-another-as-other—that is, having another's form without the knower's ceasing to be himself. Seeing red, as a species of knowing, is to have the form of the red thing; it is not to become another red thing.

The change that knowing is thought to be is an intentional rather than an entitative change. The form acquired by the knower is a means whereby the known thing is present to it. Thus, the form stands for (intends) the thing whose form it is. Furthermore, though knowing is a change, it is not to be thought of as passive, as something that happens to the knower. The knowing powers are faculties of the soul that enable the living thing to initiate activity. There is, however, a passive element in knowledge. For example, when our sensory apparatus comes into contact with things, an entitative change occurs. When I touch something warm, the temperature of my hand alters. That change is not cognition.

"There is nothing in the mind that was not first in sensation." This maxim incorporates the empiricism of Thomas Aquinas. The human soul is man's substantial form; its faculties or powers belong to a form actuating matter. The proper object of the human intellect is the quiddity or essence of the material object. Sensation is the indispensable condition for intellectual knowing. The ideas that the mind forms are ideas of physical objects, of sensible things. Thomas' theory of concept formation is Aristotle's. The agent intellect, a faculty of the soul, abstracts a form from sense data, and it is this form that actuates the passive intellect and permits the activity of knowing to take place. The concept is as form and the passive intellect is as matter.

This analysis of knowing permits Thomas to make use of terminology already fashioned in speaking of natural changes, but of course knowing is a change of a special kind. Thus there is continuity as well as variation in the use to which Thomas puts an amazingly small basic vocabulary, and it is his theory of analogous signification that saves him from the charge of equivocation.

METAPHYSICS

Being is the first thing grasped by the intellect. Being as being is the subject of metaphysics. Understanding the relationship between these two fundamental Thomistic tenets is of the utmost importance. Their conjunction would seem to suggest that a man can become a metaphysician without difficulty. Yet for Thomas, as we have seen, metaphysics is the last of the philosophical sciences to be studied.

Thomas' theory of knowledge, according to which it is the nature or essence of physical objects that is the proper object of the human mind, entails that, until proved otherwise, to be and to be material are identical. If there is immaterial being, we do not have direct access to it, because of the nature of human knowing, and its existence will have to be knowable through what is known of physical objects. The ways of proving God's existence formulated by Thomas all employ as premises truths about material things.

When Thomas speaks of a science, he has in mind an argument or syllogism of a certain kind. The subject of a science will be the subject of the conclusion of such a demonstration; the object of a science is the conclusion. There can be a network of demonstrations making up a single science if their subjects are all defined in the same way. That is, sciences will differ formally insofar as their modes of defining differ.

The notion of demonstrative syllogism that Thomas takes from Aristotle involves two notes: necessity and immateriality. Necessity, because really to know is to know that something is true and that it could not be otherwise. Immateriality, because of the nature of the faculty of knowing. The intentional reception of a form is different from the entitative; it is unlike the reception of a form in matter. If the object of theoretical knowing is necessary and immaterial, there can be different speculative or theoretical sciences insofar as there are formally distinct removals from matter and motion. What has matter can be otherwise, since matter is precisely the potentiality for forms other than the one currently actuating matter.

Some things require matter both in order to be and in order to be defined. Physical objects are by definition composed of matter and form, and their appropriate definition will express this fact. Natural science is concerned with things of this kind. Other

AQUINAS, ST. THOMAS

things require matter in order to exist, but they can be thought of without thinking of matter. For example, line and circle and square can be defined without mentioning sensible matter, but this does not commit us to the claim that lines and circles and squares exist apart from material things. Mathematics is concerned with things of this kind.

Yet other things are such that they require matter neither in order to be nor in order to be defined, either because they never exist in matter (such as God and angels) or because they sometimes exist in matter and sometimes do not (such as being, act, potency, cause, and such). Just as, from a philosophical point of view, that there is a God or that there are angels must be proved, so it must be proved that some beings are immaterial. In order for metaphysics to be a possibility, what Thomas calls a judgment of separation must be made—that is, a judgment that something exists apart from matter and motion—and such a judgment must be the conclusion of an argument. Such arguments are found in natural science. The proof of the Prime Mover and the argument that the human soul does not cease to exist at death, the first found in the *Physics* and the second in *On the Soul,* are, for Thomas, the warrant for commencing a science whose subject is being as being.

THEOLOGY

If there is a philosophical theology, there is also a theology based on Sacred Scripture:

> Theology or divine science is twofold: one in which divine things are considered not as the subject of the science but as principles of the subject, and this is the theology pursued by philosophers, which by another name is known as metaphysics; another, which considers divine things themselves as the subject of the science, is the theology which is treated in Sacred Scripture.
>
> (*Exposition of Boethius' "On the Trinity,"* q. 5, a. 4)

Either sort of theology, and Sacred Scripture itself, will speak of God, and the question arises as to how this is possible. Human language is the expression of human knowledge, and human knowledge bears on physical things as its commensurate object. Our language is fashioned to talk about things so different from God that it seems to be an inadequate, even a misleading, instrument for the task of revelation and theology.

Since God's essence is not the essence of a material thing, he is not an appropriate object of human cognition. Such knowledge of him as we have will be indirect, grounded in our knowledge of other things; and words fashioned to speak of those other things will have to be extended by way of analogy to express, however inadequately, what God is.

> It was shown above that God cannot be known by us in this life in his essence, but He is known by us from creatures, because of the relation of principle and by way of excellence and remotion.
>
> (*ST* 1a, q. 13, a. 1)

God can be known by us through his effects and by the concept of a perfection found in creatures but considered in mode excelling the creaturely by removing from it the limitations that attend it in creatures. At the root of this is a proof of God's existence, and it is in the proof that our language is extended to refer to him. Consider the bare bones of the proof from motion.

> It is certain and evident to the senses that in this world some things are moved. Whatever is moved, however, is moved by another. But nothing is moved if it is not in potency to that to which it is moved: something moves to the degree that it is actual. To move is nothing else than to lead something from potency to act; but something can be reduced from potency to act only by a being already in act, as the actually warm fire makes wood that is potentially warm to be actually warm, and in this way moves and alters it. It is impossible that a thing be simultaneously in act and in potency in the same respect, but only in respect to different things. What is actually warm cannot be at the same time potentially warm, but it can be potentially cold at the same time. Therefore it is impossible for something to be in one and the same respect moving and moved, or that it move itself. Whatever is moved, therefore, must be moved by another. If, then, that by which it is moved should itself be moved, it must be moved by something else, and that something else by something further. But this cannot go back infinitely, for then there would be no first mover, and consequently no other mover, because secondary movers move only insofar as they are moved, as the stick is moved only when it is moved by the hand. Therefore one must come to some first mover, itself unmoved, and this all understand God to be.
>
> (*ST* 1a, q. 2, a. 3)

What justifies the extension of the term "mover" to God is the truths adduced about moved and moving things in the world. That God is not a mover like any other is captured by adding "prime." The whole sense of the term "prime mover" is read off the world, and the proof is what grounds the denotation of the phrase.

Thomas analyzes the meaning of terms applied to

God by taking them to be shared terms, common to God and creature. Furthermore, he assumes that while we can more or less easily explain what a term means as applied to creatures, the difficulty arises in extending it to God. Thus "God is wise" and "Socrates is wise" exhibit the shared term "wise." When we say "Socrates is wise," we mean he has acquired the ability to assess all things with reference to what is first and best. Clearly the term cannot be shared univocally by God and Socrates; nor does it seem to be an equivocal term.

In taking the shared term to be analogous, Thomas finds the primary analogate in creatures. He does not take "God is wise" to mean only that God is the cause of wisdom in creatures, but rather that wisdom, found in creatures in a limited and incomplete way, is found in God fully and excellently. Thomas sees three stages in such talk about God: God is wise, God is not wise, God is wise in a manner that exceeds our ability to understand. The affirmation bears on the quality "wisdom," the negation bears on the created way of being wise, and the final way of putting it admits that we can have no idea of the divine mode of wisdom.

One sign of the inadequacy of our knowledge of God's possession of wisdom is that in him wisdom is identical with Himself and with the other attributes. In God, wisdom and justice and mercy and unity are one simple reality. This does not mean that "wise" and "just" and so forth, when affirmed of God, mean the same thing, as if we would give the same account of each, but they refer to the same entity. For every creature, to be is to be in a limited and restricted way; God is unlimited perfection. Furthermore, there is no necessity that any creature be, whereas God is such that he cannot not be. It is these and other things that Thomas has in mind when he says that the least inadequate way of referring to God is as subsisting existence: *Ipsum esse subsistens.* Any creature has existence; God, so to speak, is existence.

Thomas' remarks on the reach of our knowledge and language in the matter of God make it clear that we are here at the very limit of our capacity. Finally, he wrote, what we know of God is that we do not know what God is. Human knowledge is always imperfect and inadequate in its attempt to think about God. This does not mean either that it is unimportant to seek precisions or that it matters little what we say of God. But, in the phrase of Nicholas of Cusa, man's knowledge of God seems to be a learned ignorance.

THOMAS AND SCRIPTURE

It would be misleading to view Thomas' work as a theologian solely in terms of the *Summa theologiae* and the *Summa contra gentiles.* These justly famous efforts to produce systematic summaries of theology were not products of Thomas' teaching, but were undertaken by him independently of his academic tasks. The three academic tasks of the theologian were *praedicare, legere, disputare:* to preach, to lecture, to dispute. The *Quaestiones Quodlibetales* are records of the free-for-all disputes Thomas conducted at specified times in Advent and in Lent. The *Quaestiones Disputatae* of Thomas contain some of his most important treatments of various subjects. His *Disputed Questions On Evil,* those *On Truth* and *On the Power of God,* are indispensable sources for his thought. The literary form of the recorded disputation clearly provides the model for the *Summa theologiae:* A question, a proposed answer with a number of arguments on behalf of it, followed by the citation of an authority indicating that the opposite of the proposed answer is true. Then a magisterial resolution of the question, after which the arguments offered on behalf of the first solution are dealt with singly. The *Summa theologiae* thus appears a closet drama when compared with the records of university disputations, however edited these may be.

Legere means literally to read. What texts was the theologian held to read and explicate? Chiefly the books of the Bible. The medieval Master of Theology was first of all a *Magister Sacrae Paginae,* one who had mastered Holy Writ. We have seen how Thomas, in his systematic description of theology, states that its starting points are to be found in what God has revealed. Thomas' lectures on Scripture were given throughout his academic career. In the Parisian custom, he probably alternated a work of the Old Testament and a work of the New. These are the biblical works for which we have Thomistic commentaries: Isaiah, Matthew, Canticle of Canticles, Lamentations *(In threnos Jeremiae),* Jeremiah, Paul's Epistles, Job, John, the Psalms. A distinction is made among these between those which are *reportationes* and those which are *ordinationes.* The difference is that the former were taken down by others and not checked by Thomas, whereas the latter were checked by Thomas. Sometimes a *reportatio* is called a *lectura* and an *ordinatio* an *expositio.*

Thomas learned from Augustine the various "senses of Scripture" (Cf. *ST* 1, q. 1, a. 10). A human author can make the word for one thing mean an-

AQUINAS, ST. THOMAS

other thing, but God can make the thing meant by a word another thing. Thus, in reading Scripture, we first attend to the things meant by the words: this is the historical or literal sense. The sense according to which those things refer to other things is the spiritual sense of the text. The spiritual sense is subdivided into the allegorical (the way the Old Testament prefigures the New), the moral (the way Christ's deeds indicate how we should behave) and the anagogical (the way the text signifies what will be in eternal glory).

The preeminent commentary on Job was Gregory the Great's *Moralia*. St. Gregory emphasizes the spiritual and moral senses of the book. Indeed, it came to be thought that it was impossible to find a literal sense for some passages in Job. In any case, the tradition of interpretation was heavily allegorical. Thomas, as the editors of the Leonine edition point out, explicitly breaks with this tradition.

> We intend to give an exposition of that book said to be *Of Blessed Job* as compendious as we can and according to its literal sense, trusting in divine aid; for its mysteries have been laid open for us so subtly and fully by Blessed Pope Gregory that he seems to have left nothing further to say of them. (*In Iob,* prologue)

It should be noted that Thomas will include the figurative or metaphorical sense under the literal. "And although spiritual things are proposed under the figures of corporeal things, what is intended of spiritual things through the corporeal figures should not be assigned to the mystical sense but to the literal, because the literal sense is what is first intended by the words, whether it is expressed properly or figuratively." (*In Iob,* ch. 1, ll. 229–234)

MORALITY

If speculative philosophy is divided into three sciences on the basis of different modes of defining, practical philosophy is divided into three sciences on the basis of the difference between the goods or ends aimed at. Ethics is concerned with the perfection of the individual; economics is concerned with the good shared by the members of a domestic community; politics is concerned with the good shared by the members of a state.

Thomas' views on morality may be described as both eudaemonistic and incorporating the theory of natural law. Man's happiness consists in achieving the end or good that is perfective of his nature. There are some things that are good for men but that are not peculiarly human goods. Thus, simply to be and to survive are good; food and sex are good; but these are goods pursued by beings other than man. The good for man is to be found in the perfection of his distinctive activity, rational activity. Other creatures pursue goals, but man alone consciously directs himself to goals he judges are perfective of him.

But "rational activity" is a phrase that covers a wide variety of types; consequently, doing it well will be various and man's perfection or happiness is made up of a plurality of virtues. Rational activity can mean mental activity as such whose end is truth, and the perfections of it in this sense are called intellectual virtues. Some human acts are rational because desires and activities other than reasoning come under the sway of reason. To feel anger or sexual desire is neither good nor bad as such; it is the way man conducts himself when he feels such passions or emotions that determines the moral good or evil. Acting well in this way is productive of moral virtue. Constituents of the human good are the cardinal virtues—temperance, courage, justice, and prudence—as well as intellectual virtues. Thomas recognizes a vast number of subsidiary moral virtues as well.

Natural law is the peculiarly human participation in God's eternal law, whereby man directs himself to the end perfective of the kind of agent he is. Thomas held that it is comparatively easy for any person to recognize the basic values constitutive of human perfection and to formulate judgments that these are to be pursued and their opposites avoided.

> Because the good has the note of a goal and evil the contrary note, all those things to which man has a natural inclination, reason naturally apprehends as goods, and consequently to be striven for, while their opposites are seen as evils to be avoided. Therefore, according to the order of natural inclinations, there is an order in the precepts of natural law. First, there is an inclination in man toward the good of the nature he shares with all other substances, since any substance seeks to preserve itself in existence as the kind of thing it is. On the basis of this inclination there pertain to natural law all those things through which man's life is preserved and its opposite impeded. Second, there is in man an inclination to more special things because of the nature he shares with other animals. According to this inclination those things "which nature teaches all animals" are of natural law, such as the union of man and woman, the rearing of children, and the like. Third, there is in man an inclination to the good of reason that is peculiar to him; thus men have a natural inclination to know the truth about God and to live in society. Things that look to this inclination pertain to natural law, for example, that

AQUINAS, ST. THOMAS

man avoid ignorance, that he not harm those with whom he must live, and other like things.

(*ST* 1a2ae, q. 94, a. 2)

Natural law precepts are the starting points of moral reasoning; the moral task is to pursue the goods they incorporate in the fluctuating and altering conditions of our lives.

Unlike Abelard, who maintained that any action is morally neutral and becomes good or bad only because of the intention with which we perform it, Thomas held that there are objectively good and bad actions. Indeed, if there were not, he felt it would be difficult to know what a good or bad intention would be. Intention is the soul of morality, but good intentions are those that aim at performing good acts.

CONCLUSION

Thomas Aquinas was principally a theologian, and the vast majority of his writings consists of commentaries on scripture and discussion of the mysteries of the Christian faith, as well as sermons. Many of his writings arose naturally out of his duties as master of theology; besides the kinds just mentioned there are a great number of *Disputed Questions* and a volume of *Quodlibetal Questions.* Among his writings we find a goodly number of responses to requests made to him for the discussion and solution of vexing theological and ecclesiastical questions. His theory about the propaedeutic necessity of philosophy for theology is everywhere evident in his vast literary output. But Thomas was not merely an intellectual; he was also a saint. His biographers tell us of the time he spent in prayer, begging for the light with which to see his way in his studies. In the last year of his life, as the result of a mystical experience, Thomas stopped dictating, telling his intimates that after what he had been shown, his writings seemed as mere straw. And yet, on his deathbed, at the request of the Cistercians at Fossanova, he undertook a commentary on the Canticle of Canticles.

Thomas' thought came under censure after his death. Several teachings associated with him found their way onto lists of condemned propositions. But this was a momentary, and indeed local, setback. Thomas quickly became the preferred author of Dominicans engaged in the study of theology, and over the centuries his teaching has attained an authority among Roman Catholics all but unequaled by any other author. Pope Leo XIII, in 1880, established a commission to edit and publish a definitive edition of Thomas' work. This (Leonine) edition is still incomplete. Whether he is regarded simply historically as one of the most important medieval theologians or is taken as a personal guide, Thomas Aquinas continues to be read and written about. In 1974, the seven-hundredth anniversary of his death, there were meetings, conferences, special editions of journals, and volumes of studies devoted to his thought. If few have read everything Thomas wrote, it is becoming humanly impossible to read everything written about him. The bibliography below thus contains only a sampling of the literature.

BIBLIOGRAPHY

Primary Sources. Good lists of Aquinas' works are provided by I. T. Eschmann, "A Catalogue of St. Thomas' Works: Bibliographical Notes," in Étienne Gilson, *The Christian Philosophy of St. Thomas Aquinas* (1956); and "A Brief Catalogue of Authentic Works," in James Weisheipl, *Friar Thomas D'Aquino* (1974).

Collected editions include *Opera omnia,* the Leonine edition (Rome, 1882–)—vol. XLII of a projected 50 appeared in 1979; and *Opera omnia,* 25 vols. (1852–1873, repr. 1948–1950).

Editions of individual works include *Aquinas on Being and Essence,* Joseph Bobik, trans. (1965), with commentary; *Aristotle on Interpretation: Commentary by St. Thomas and Cajetan,* Jean Oesterle, trans. (1962); *Aristotle's De Anima with the Commentary of St. Thomas Aquinas,* Kenelm Foster and Silvester Humphries, trans. (1951); *Catena aurea,* Mark Pattison et al., trans., 4 vols. (1841–1845), commentary on the Gospels collected from the writings of the Church Fathers by Thomas; *Commentary on Aristotle's Physics,* Richard J. Blackwell et al., trans. (1963); *Commentary on St. Paul's Epistle to the Ephesians,* M. L. Lamb, trans. (1966); *Commentary on St. Paul's Epistle to the Galatians,* Fabian R. Larcher, trans. (1966); *Commentary on the Metaphysics of Aristotle,* John P. Rowan, trans., 2 vols. (1964); *Commentary on the Nicomachean Ethics,* C. I. Litzinger, trans., 2 vols. (1964); *Commentary on the Posterior Analytics,* Fabian R. Larcher, trans. (1970); *Compendium of Theology,* Cyril Vollert, trans. (1947); *The Division and Methods of the Sciences,* Armand Maurer, trans. (1953); *On Charity,* Lottie H. Kendzierski, trans. (1960); *On Spiritual Creatures,* Mary C. Fitzpatrick and John J. Wellmuth, trans. (1951); *On the Eternity of the World by St. Thomas Aquinas, Siger of Brabant, and St. Bonaventure,* Cyril Vollert et al., trans. (1964); *On the Power of God,* Lawrence Shapcote, trans. (1952); *On the Principles of Nature,* Robert J. Henle and Vernon J. Bourke, trans. (1947); *On the Truth of the Catholic Faith (Summa contra gentiles),* Anton C. Pegis, J. F. Anderson, et al., trans., 4 vols. (1955–1957, repr. 1975); *On the Unity of the Intellect Against the Averroists,* Beatrice H. Zedler, trans. (1968); *On the Virtues, in General,*

John Patrick Reid, trans. (1951); *On Truth,* R. Mulligan, B. McGlynn, and R. Schmidt, trans., 3 vols. (1952–1954); *The Soul,* John Patrick Rowan, trans. (1949); *Summa theologiae,* Thomas Gilby, exec. ed., 60 vols. (1964–); *Treatise on Separate Substances,* Francis Lescoe, ed. (1963), a critical edition that includes the Latin text; and *The Trinity and the Unicity of the Intellect,* Rose E. Brennan, trans. (1946).

Secondary Literature. James F. Anderson, *The Bond of Being* (1949); Ross A. Armstrong, *Primary and Secondary Precepts in Thomistic Natural Law Teaching* (1966); Dennis Bonnette, *Aquinas' Proofs for God's Existence* (1972); Vernon J. Bourke, *Aquinas's Search for Wisdom* (1965); David Burrell, *Analogy and Philosophical Language* (1973); and *Aquinas: God and Action* (1979); Steven Cahn, *Fate, Logic and Time* (1967); Gilbert K. Chesterton, *Saint Thomas Aquinas* (1933); Mary T. Clark, *Aquinas Reader* (1974); Frederick C. Copleston, *Aquinas* (1970); Eric D'Arcy, *Conscience and Its Right to Freedom* (1961); James Doig, *Aquinas on Metaphysics* (1972); Cornelio Fabro, *Participation et causalité* (1961); and *Esegesi Tomistica* (1969); Kenelm Foster, *The Life of St. Thomas Aquinas* (1959); Réginald Garrigou-Lagrange, *Reality: A Synthesis of Thomistic Thought* (1960); Peter Geach, *Mental Acts* (1957); and *God and the Soul* (1969); Peter Geach and Elizabeth Anscombe, *Three Philosophers* (1961); Étienne Gilson, *Being and Some Philosophers* (1952); and *The Christian Philosophy of St. Thomas Aquinas* (1956); Desmond P. Henry, *Medieval Logic and Metaphysics* (1972); Harry V. Jaffa, *Thomism and Aristotelianism* (1952); Anthony Kenny, *Aquinas: A Collection of Critical Essays* (1969); and *The Five Ways* (1969); John King-Farlow and William N. Christensen, *Faith and the Life of Reason* (1972); George Klubertanz, *St. Thomas Aquinas on Analogy* (1960); Charles de Koninck, *Ego sapientia: La sagesse qui est Marie* (1943); *De la primauté du bien commun* (1943); *La piété du Fils* (1954); and *The Hollow Universe* (1960); Hampus Lyttkens, *The Analogy Between God and the World* (1952); Jacques Maritain, *Angelic Doctor* (1931); and *The Degrees of Knowledge* (1959); Eric L. Mascall, *Existence and Analogy* (1949); Ralph McInerny, *The Logic of Analogy* (1961); *Thomism in an Age of Renewal* (1966); and *St. Thomas Aquinas* (1978); Battista Mondin, *The Principle of Analogy in Protestant and Catholic Theology* (1963); and *Il problema del linguaggio teologico* (1971); John Naus, *The Nature of the Practical Intellect According to St. Thomas Aquinas* (1959); Thomas O'Brien, *Metaphysics and the Existence of God* (1960); Joseph Owens, *The Doctrine of Being in the Aristotelian Metaphysics* (1951); *St. Thomas and the Future of Metaphysics* (1957); and *St. Thomas Aquinas on the Existence of God* (1980); Anton Pegis, *Introduction to St. Thomas Aquinas* (1948); Josef Pieper, *The Silence of St. Thomas* (1953); *Guide to Thomas Aquinas* (1962); and *Belief and Faith* (1963); Victor Preller, *Divine Science and the Science of God* (1967); Frederick J. Roensch, *Early Thomistic School* (1964); Heinrich Rommen, *The Natural Law* (1947); James F. Ross, ed., *Inquiries into Medieval Philosophy* (1971); Edward Sillem, *Ways of Thinking About God* (1961); Yves Simon, *Introduction à l'ontologie du connaître* (1934); James Weisheipl, *Friar Thomas D'Aquino* (1974).

RALPH MCINERNY

[See also **Abelard, Peter; Albertus Magnus; Aristotle in the Middle Ages; Boethius; Bonaventure, St.; Dionysius the Pseudo-Areopagite; Peter Lombard; Philosophy, Thirteenth-Century Crisis; Philosophy-Theology, West European (Twelfth Century to Aquinas; Late Medieval); Rushd, Ibn (Averroës); Scholasticism, Scholastic Method; Theology, Schools of.**]

AQUITAINE, a pre-Revolutionary province in southwestern France, and a kingdom, duchy, and principality before annexation by the French crown in 1422.

By 482 the Visigoths held the region from the Pyrenees to the Loire River and from the Atlantic to the Rhone River. They were conquered by the Merovingian Franks in 507–508. The Gascons invaded from Spanish Navarre, and by 581 had penetrated the valleys of Gave de Pau and Adour. In 602, Theodibert II and Theoderic II imposed suzerainty over them while recognizing their conquests and leaving them their own duke. Further battles ensued, and in order to contain the Gascon advance, Dagobert I created a state for his brother, Caribert, in 628. This was the genesis of the kingdom of Aquitaine. Its beginnings were short-lived, for the territory reverted to Dagobert upon Caribert's death in 632. During the sixth and seventh centuries Merovingian Aquitaine was a center for the preservation and transmission of late Roman culture.

In 781, following the defeat at Roncesvalles, Charlemagne had his third son, the three-year-old Louis the Pious, consecrated as king of Aquitaine. The kingdom of Aquitaine embraced the four ecclesiastical provinces of Aquitania Prima (metropolitan: Bourges; other major cities: Clermont-Ferrand, Rodez, Albi, Cahors, Limoges, Mende, Le Puy), Aquitania Secunda (metropolitan: Bordeaux; other major cities: Agen, Angoulême, Saintes, Poitiers, Périgueux), Aquitania Tertia (metropolitan: Eauze; other major cities: Dax, Lectoure, St.-Bertrand-de-Comminges, St.-Lizier, Argenteyres, Béarn, Aire, Bazas, Tarbes, Oloron-Ste. Marie, Auch), and Narbonensis (metropolitan: Narbonne; other major cities: Toulouse, Béziers, Nîmes, Lodève, Uzès)—a ter-

AQUITAINE

English Possessions in France 1154–1223

ritory covering approximately twenty-five of the ninety-five departments of modern France.

The kingdom reverted to the status of a duchy when Louis II became king of France in 877. In 889, Ramnoux II, count of Poitiers, laid claim to the title of duke, and the history of the duchy as such began. In the following century the counts of Bordeaux became dukes of Gascony. Gascony is the region bounded on the south by the Pyrenees, on the north and east by the Garonne River, and on the west by Landes. The line of Gascon dukes ended with the death of Sanche Guillaume in 1032, and the title of duke of Gascony became merged with that of duke of Aquitaine.

In 1137, Guillaume X died without a male heir, leaving his vast dominions to his daughter, Eleanor. In the same year Abbot Suger of St.-Denis, the first great French ecclesiastical statesman, who has been called "the architect of the French monarchy," arranged the marriage of Eleanor to Louis VII, thus adding the duchy, her dowry, to the royal domain. The marriage was not a happy one, but so long as Suger lived, it held together. His death in 1151 and Eleanor's scandalous behavior during and after the Second Crusade led to her divorce, on grounds of consanguinity rather than adultery, in 1152. According to feudal law her dowry, undiminished, was restored to her, with the provision that she hold it of her former husband as a fief.

In the same year Eleanor married Henry of Anjou, duke of Normandy and claimant to the throne of England, which he ascended in 1154 as Henry II, thus linking the fortunes of southwestern France to the English crown. But it was not until 5 February 1156 that Louis was constrained to receive Henry's homage for Normandy, Anjou, and Aquitaine. The territory of Eleanor's dowry extended to the Loire River and included, besides Gascony, the counties of Poitiers, Saintonge, Angoulême, Limoges, Périgord, Ventadour, Turenne, Quercy, Rouergue, and Auvergne, in addition to claims of suzerainty over the entire county of Toulouse.

In 1169, Henry gave the duchy to his son Richard, a boy of twelve, who ruled jointly with his mother until her imprisonment in England, at her husband's command, in 1173. From 1174 until his father's death in 1189, Richard was sole ruler, but he acted more as the king's lieutenant than as one exercising final authority. In 1189, Eleanor was restored, and continued to hold the duchy until her death in 1204 except for the years 1196–1198, when it was granted to Richard's nephew, Otto of Brunswick. The feudal link between the dukes of Aquitaine (also in the thirteenth century called Guyenne, a variant of Aquitaine) and the kings of France was severed in 1202 by the condemnation of King John of England by the court of Philip II for a breach of the feudal contract. It was restored by the Treaty of Paris (1259) between Henry III and Louis IX, but at the cost of Henry's abandoning the titles of duke of Normandy and count of Anjou and his claims to Maine, Touraine, and Poitou. It was broken again in 1294, when, as a result of maritime disputes, Edward I renounced the homage he had done to Philip IV; and it was again restored by the Treaty of Paris of 1303. In 1324, because of the War of St.-Sardos, Charles IV confiscated the duchy. It was returned the following year, but by this time English holdings in the duchy had been reduced to little more than part of Gascony itself. Its reconfiscation by Philip VI in 1337 was the immediate cause of the Hundred Years War.

From the reign of Edward I on, the aim of English kings was to achieve unchallenged sovereignty over the duchy of Guyenne. This was done, at least for the space of ten years, by the Treaty of Brétigny (1360). On 19 July 1362, Edward III created the principality of Aquitaine and bestowed it on his eldest son, Edward, the Black Prince, retaining supreme sovereignty and the right of hearing appeals. The prince behaved like a foreign conqueror. His sumptuous court, a reflection of his father's, and his misguided munificence were galling to unruly, independent nobles and costly to towns and peasantry. A disastrous expedition into Castile led to the ruin of the prince's career. With his return a horde of companies of unpaid soldiers, rapacious and violent, was let loose on the land. His demand for a hearth tax in 1368 (the fourth such he levied) was the occasion for general revolt. Charles V, acting quite illegally, heard the resulting appeals and confiscated the territory in 1369, thus abrogating the Treaty of Brétigny. The prince returned to England ill and exhausted, and on 5 October 1372 he surrendered the principality into his father's hands. There followed the victories of Bertrand Du Guesclin, constable of France, in Guyenne, Saintonge, Poitou, and Limousin. When Bordeaux fell in 1453, at the close of the Hundred Years War, all of the English possessions in France except Calais had been surrendered to the French crown.

The acquisition of Gascony (the name is synonymous with Aquitaine during English rule) by the English marks the beginning of the Angevin or Plantagenet empire. Its importance was clearly economic. Some idea of its wealth is furnished by a record of revenues, rents, and dues from the royal demesne in the duchy for the period Michaelmas 1306–Michaelmas 1307, which amounted, in round figures, to 84,000 *livres bordelais*. The bastides of Agenais alone brought a rent of 1,500 *livres tournois* in 1272, and those of Périgord and Quercy, 1,458 *livres tournois* in 1304–1305. Between 1181 and 1350, 124 bastides were founded in Gascony, sixty-three of them during the reign of Edward I; this town plantation is a clear indication of further economic exploitation. The salt mines of Agenais were valuable, but wine, still famous today, constituted the principal article of commerce and the most important source of revenue. The great custom on wines at Bordeaux, for example, yielded roughly 39,355 *livres bordelais* in 1310.

Many experiments were tried in the government of Gascony, including the disastrous one of 1248–1252, when Simon de Montfort served as king's lieutenant and infuriated practically every important vassal in the duchy by his highhanded and dictatorial methods. But except for the abortive essay in dependent government under the Black Prince, the administration of the duchy was firmly fixed by the regulatory ordinances issued by Edward I at Condom in 1289. These established the seneschal of Gascony as the chief administrative officer, with a subseneschal in Saintonge and another in Périgord, Limousin, and Quercy. Agenais was organized separately. The constable of Bordeaux was the chief financial officer and keeper of the archives; after 1293 he rendered his accounts yearly to the exchequer in London, where they were heard by the treasurer and barons, and enrolled on the pipe rolls. The seneschal had his court with its seal, and under him and the subseneschals was an elaborate array of officials such as baillis, prévôts, castellans, military engineers, controllers, receivers, collectors of customs, scribes of bailliages, notaries, proctors, advocates, and clerks.

These people saw to the day-to-day administration, but it is clear from the entries on the Gascon rolls, which begin in the reign of Henry III and continue until 1453, that the king–duke exercised a constant and a very real control over the affairs of the duchy. He insisted on his ultimate right to hear and decide appeals, and his parliaments received and heard Gascon petitions. Important documents originating in the duchy were issued in duplicate, one copy being sent to England and the other kept in the treasury at Bordeaux, which was housed in the castle of L'Ombrière.

The possession of Gascony by the English was incompatible with the policy of every king of medieval France, beginning with Philip Augustus, to achieve absolute sovereignty over their realm. The position of the English king was anomalous; as king of England he was sovereign by right of conquest and heredity; as duke of Aquitaine he was a feudal vassal of the king of France, and as such subject to the decisions of the court of his overlord. Even so, it was not until 30 March 1331, seventy-two years after the treaty that had stipulated it, that an English king agreed to the precise terms of the homage he owed and recognized it as liege. No other vassal of the French king was in exactly the same position as the king of England. By the thirteenth century the situation was exacerbated by a growing tendency to distinguish between the person of the king and the crown as an office of state. Gascony was held to belong to the English crown. Thus in 1258 Henry III revoked the grant of the island of Oléron by the Lord Edward to Gui de Lusignan, on the ground that it represented an alienation of the island from the crown. Three years later he issued letters patent granting that Oléron should never be separated from the crown of England.

The king of France claimed the exercise of *ressortum et superioritas* in the duchy of Aquitaine. This was implemented by reserved cases *(cas royaux)* and appeals. Appeals constituted the most powerful weapon for meddling in the administration of the duchy. French seneschals along the borders of the duchy sought to undermine the authority of the duke by encouraging his vassals to appeal grievances to the parlement de Paris, the French court. During the period 1259–1337 there were 269 such cases, a dozen of them dragging along from the reign of one English king to that of his successor.

Little wonder, then, that Edward I's ordinances of 1289 provided for the appointment of "a discrete clerk, learned in law, as king's proctor in the court of France" at the annual salary of 50 *livres bordelais* "and reasonable expenses going to Paris, remaining there, and returning." Decisions in these cases were almost always inimical to the interests of the king–duke. Herein lies the real cause of the Hundred Years War, the first national conflict in western European history and the first to be fought over the issue of sovereignty.

In 1422, Aquitaine (or Guyenne, as it was known) was definitively reunited to the French crown and became one of its administrative areas. In the seventeenth century it was combined with Gascony to form one province, which it remained until the reorganization of France into departments during the French Revolution.

BIBLIOGRAPHY

Léonce Auzias, *L'Aquitaine carolingienne (778–987)* (1937); Bernard S. Bachrach, "Military Organization in Aquitaine Under the Early Carolingians," in *Speculum,* **49** (1974), 1–33; Richard W. Barber, *Edward, Prince of Wales and Aquitaine: A Biography of the Black Prince* (1978); Paul Courteault, *Histoire de la Gascogne et de Béarn* (1938); George P. Cuttino, *English Diplomatic Administration, 1259–1339,* 2nd ed. (1971); George P. Cuttino, ed., *Gascon Register A (Series of 1318–1319),* 3 vols. (1975–1976); John B. Gillingham, *Richard the Lionheart* (1978); Amy R. Kelly, *Eleanor of Aquitaine and the Four Kings* (1950); Eleanor C. Lodge, *Gascony Under English Rule* (1926); Frank B. Marsh, *English Rule in Gascony, 1199–1259, with Special Reference to the Towns* (1912); Yves Renouard, *Bordeaux sous les rois d'Angleterre* (1965); Jean Paul Trabut-Cussac, *L'administration anglaise en Gascogne sous Henry III et Édouard I de 1254 à 1307* (1972); Malcolm G. A. Vale, *English Gascony, 1399–1453* (1970).

GEORGE G. P. CUTTINO

[See also **Angevins, France, England, Sicily; Edward the Black Prince; Eleanor of Aquitaine; Henry II of England; Philip VI de Valois; Richard the Lionhearted; Simon de Montfort; Suger, Abbot of St. Denis.**]

ARABESQUE, an overall decorative pattern based on stylized leaf- and scrollwork; the stylization of the plant forms often results in geometric patterns. The arabesque was developed under the Umayyad dynasty in the eighth century; by the tenth and eleventh centuries it had spread throughout the medieval world. Arabesques were most frequently used to decorate borders or, especially in architectural sculpture, to cover small flat surfaces.

LESLIE BRUBAKER

ARABIA. The following article is in two parts: I. **Pre-Islamic Arabia**, by A. F. L. Beeston; and II. **Islamic Arabia**, by George Rentz.

I

PRE-ISLAMIC ARABIA. Central and northern Arabia form part of an arid belt stretching from the Sahara into central Asia, albeit with scattered oases of cultivable land. The south of the peninsula belongs to the Indian Ocean monsoonal climatic zone, with rainfall that is abundant though, as in India, subject to occasional failure of the monsoon. Hardly anything is known about the prehistoric inhabitants of the peninsula; sporadic traces of their Stone Age culture (artifacts and rock drawings) are not datable, and we know nothing about their racial affinities. All that we can say is that by the historic period, from the first half of the first millennium B.C., various Semitic languages were spoken throughout the peninsula, but the demographic movements that produced this result are unknown. The south, and the central and northern oases, probably had farming populations from an early date; the deserts became habitable only with the domestication of the camel, usually thought to have been toward the end of the second millennium B.C.

In the southwest (modern Yemen and South Yemen) the farming populations achieved a high level of culture, the written records of which extend from the fifth century B.C. to the sixth century A.D. in a large collection of inscriptions on stone, and the material remains of which are still to be seen in the ruins of impressive buildings and irrigation installations, as well as (from the second half of the total time period) fine sculptures and bas-reliefs. The favorable climatic conditions fostered an advanced agriculture with sophisticated irrigation techniques; the area was also a pivotal point in trade between India and the Mediterranean. Furthermore, southern Arabia is one of the two areas in the world (the other being the Horn of Africa) where frankincense and myrrh are produced. Both these indigenous products and reexported Indian goods reached the north by two great trade routes, one up the west coast from Najrān to Gaza, the other crossing the peninsula diagonally from Najrān to Gerra near the east coast (in the modern province of al-Ḥasā), and thence to Mesopotamia.

From the fourth to the second centuries B.C. these trade routes were in the hands of a south Arabian people, the Minaeans; thereafter Minaeans disappeared from history and the trade routes apparently were taken over by north Arabian peoples. The Minaeans; the people of Saba (biblical Sheba), centered in the northern highlands of present-day Yemen; the people of the kingdom of Hadhramaut; and the people of Qatabān, in the Wadi Bayḥān of modern South Yemen—are the four groups of whom the third-century B.C. Greek geographer Eratosthenes (cited by Strabo) spoke as the principal "folks" *(ethnē)* of south Arabia. All of them were situated on the inland side of the mountain chains that run parallel to the coasts of the Red Sea and the Indian Ocean.

The most florescent period of this highly developed south Arabian civilization was from the first century to the third century A.D. But the same period saw new developments. Independent Qatabān disappeared from history, probably early in the third century; and from the turn of the Christian era we begin to hear of two important new powers in the coastal regions: the Himyarites (Greek, *Homeritai*), in the southwest, and the Ḥabashat, on the west coast of Arabia (the relationship between the latter and the African "Ḥabashat" or Abyssinians is obscure). At times, bitter wars raged between the Sabaeans on one side and the Hadhramites, Himyarites, and Ḥabashat on the other; at other times Sabaeans and Himyarites were in alliance against the others. However, around A.D. 300 a Himyarite dynasty (known to Muslim writers as the Tubba^{c} kings) gained the throne of Saba, conquered Hadhramaut, and fused the whole southwest of the peninsula into one realm.

Trade links with the north kept this civilization in close touch with the Hellenistic-Roman-Byzantine world, and features such as coinage and art forms show an evolution in south Arabia that faithfully follows the trends in the north. In religion also, the crumbling of polytheism characteristic of the fourth century in the Mediterranean lands had its echo in south Arabia, where polytheistic cults were the rule up to the third century. The majority of the fourth- and fifth-century texts display a neutral monotheistic cult (resembling what has been called "philosophical monotheism" in the Mediterranean world), in which the deity is styled Raḥmān "the Merciful One" (later adopted by Islam as an epithet of Allah). Two or three texts prove the presence of a Jewish community, and there is at least one that still invokes a deity of the polytheistic pantheon; but explicitly Christian texts are not found until the sixth century. Byzantine claims of an evangelization of south Arabia in the mid fourth century therefore are, if not altogether unfounded, at least overoptimistic.

The social structure of the south Arabian agricultural-irrigational civilization was based on the village community; a cluster of such communities formed a unit that is commonly referred to by European scholars as a "tribe." It is important to realize that "tribe" here is used in the anthropologists' sense of "any social unit intermediate between the village and the nation," and not in its everyday connotation associating it with nomadism or a low level of cultural achievement.

Compared with our fairly ample records concerning south Arabia, the center and north are sparsely documented. There is a wealth of inscriptions, but the vast majority of them are simply graffiti scratched on the rocks by passing bedouins and contain little more than personal names and a few stereotyped formulas. These attest a surprisingly widespread acquaintance with the arts of reading and writing; and the type of script used, which is similar to that of the south Arabian inscriptions, suggests some degree of cultural affinity with the south. On the other hand, in patterns of social organization and behavior the bedouin nomads were widely different from the south Arabian farmers, especially in that the "tribe" was genealogically and not geographically based.

The oasis populations depended either on date palm cultivation, as in the chain of oases stretching northward from Medina (called by the Greek and Latin authors "the Palmgroves") and the east coastal regions, or on agriculture, as in Taif to the southeast of Mecca, the Hail region in the center of Nejd, and other areas. But the agriculturalists were regarded as socially inferior by the camel-raising nomad tribes (a dictum attributed to Muḥammad is that "A plowshare outside a man's dwelling degrades him"); and to judge by the Muslim writers, even the oases tended to be dominated by the social patterns of prestige groups affiliated to the camel-nomads. On the other hand, trade was a high-prestige occupation, since it was conducted by camel caravaneers.

Apart from a tiny handful of east Arabian texts, which reveal very little, the only indigenous records that we have from an oasis are those of Dedan (modern Al-ᶜUlā in northern Hejaz). Here, during the period of Minaean florescence, there was a Minaean trading post that coexisted with some sort of local polity; after the withdrawal of the Minaeans, there was from approximately the first century B.C. to the second century A.D. a kingdom of Liḥyān (Latin, Lechiani) that left a group of inscriptions in a type of script differing only minimally from that of the bedouin; these texts reveal that the Lihyanites engaged in date palm cultivation and in the caravan trade.

The architectural monuments of the Lihyanites were heavily influenced by those of their immediate neighbors to the north, the Nabataeans, who probably moved in on Dedan after the disappearance of the Lihyanite kingdom, though their main centers were at Petra and at Egra (Arabic, al-Ḥijr; modern Madāᵓin Ṣāliḥ, only a few miles north of Al-ᶜUlā). The Nabataeans had a history as an independent people from the third century B.C. to the second century A.D., and as a people under Roman rule their fame, particularly as skillful agriculturalists, lasted long after that. But they belong only marginally to "Arabian" history, since in their heyday their territory covered all of present-day Jordan, parts of southern Syria and northwest Saudi Arabia, and the Negev Desert. Their inscriptions are Aramaic in language and script.

From about the early third century A.D., south-central Arabia was dominated by the bedouin tribal confederation of Kindah under a "king," a title that in the early Arabian context probably implied little more than a loose hegemony over several tribes. In northern Arabia a certain Umruᵓ al-Qays, who died in 328, called himself "king of all the Arabs" (which in early times signified bedouins) and claimed to have subdued the tribal group Madhḥij, which had close links with Kindah. But his precise relationships with Kindah are obscure; he was able to maintain friendly relationships with both Rome and Persia as a result of the peace treaty of 298 between those two powers. Bedouins from west-central Arabia, including Kindites, furnished mercenaries for the kingdom of Saba, and those from east-central Arabia for Hadhramaut, during the third-century conflicts between those two kingdoms.

Indigenous sources provide little information about central Arabia during the next two centuries, while Byzantium and Sasanian Persia extended their influence over the northern areas adjacent to their realms through the medium of Arab chieftains. This led to the founding of the Ghassanid dynasty in the northwest, allied to Byzantium, and that of the Lakhmids of Hira in the northeast, siding with Persia.

In the south early in the sixth century, a member of the Himyarite dynasty named Yūsuf embraced Judaism, conducted military campaigns deep into central Arabia, and persecuted the Christian population of Najrān. This provoked a retaliatory invasion from the Christian kingdom of Aksum in the Horn of Africa, with encouragement from the Byzantine emperor Justin I, whose motive, according to Procopius, was less religious than that of gaining a hold on a trade route to India that would bypass Sasanian Persia.

Yūsuf was killed and was succeeded on the throne by two Christians. The second of these, Abraha, was of non-Arabian origin but had a long and successful reign; he claimed to have received embassies from Aksum, Byzantium, Persia, Ghassān, and the Lakhmids and (like Yūsuf) campaigned into central Arabia. These campaigns appear to have led to the breakup of the Kindite kingdom. Around 570, after Abraha's death, the Persians conquered Yemen, and although after a time they were expelled by a native rising headed by Sayf ibn Dhī Yazan (of a Hadramite family), there was no attempt to revive the ancient Sabaeo-Himyarite kingdom. Toward the end of the century, moreover, Ghassanids and Lakhmids were beginning to lose their influence; the last Lakhmid king was deposed and imprisoned by the Persians in 602. The collapse of the kingdoms in both north and south left a power vacuum into which there was a central folk ready to step.

Four generations before Muḥammad—that is, around 500—his tribe, Quraysh, under the leadership of a certain Quṣayy, settled in Mecca. Once established, they took control of the west-coast trade routes, sending annual caravans to Syria and Yemen. Besides being in a position to command the trade route, Mecca had the advantage of being the site of two ancient cults, one centered on the Black Stone, later built into one wall of the Kaaba in the town itself, the other on the hill of Arafat just outside the town. According to the Muslim account, the motivation for the Yemenite incursions into central Arabia was an attempt to destroy this shrine and divert the pilgrims to a Yemenite shrine. Although it probably tells only half the story, this account does suggest that the growing significance of Mecca as a cult center under the aegis of Quraysh was a cause of anxiety to the Yemenites.

The Meccan cult was polytheistic, and the deities worshipped were regarded as patrons and guarantors of the caravan trade. It is therefore not surprising that Muḥammad's monotheistic preaching aroused antagonism among the Quraysh, and he moved to

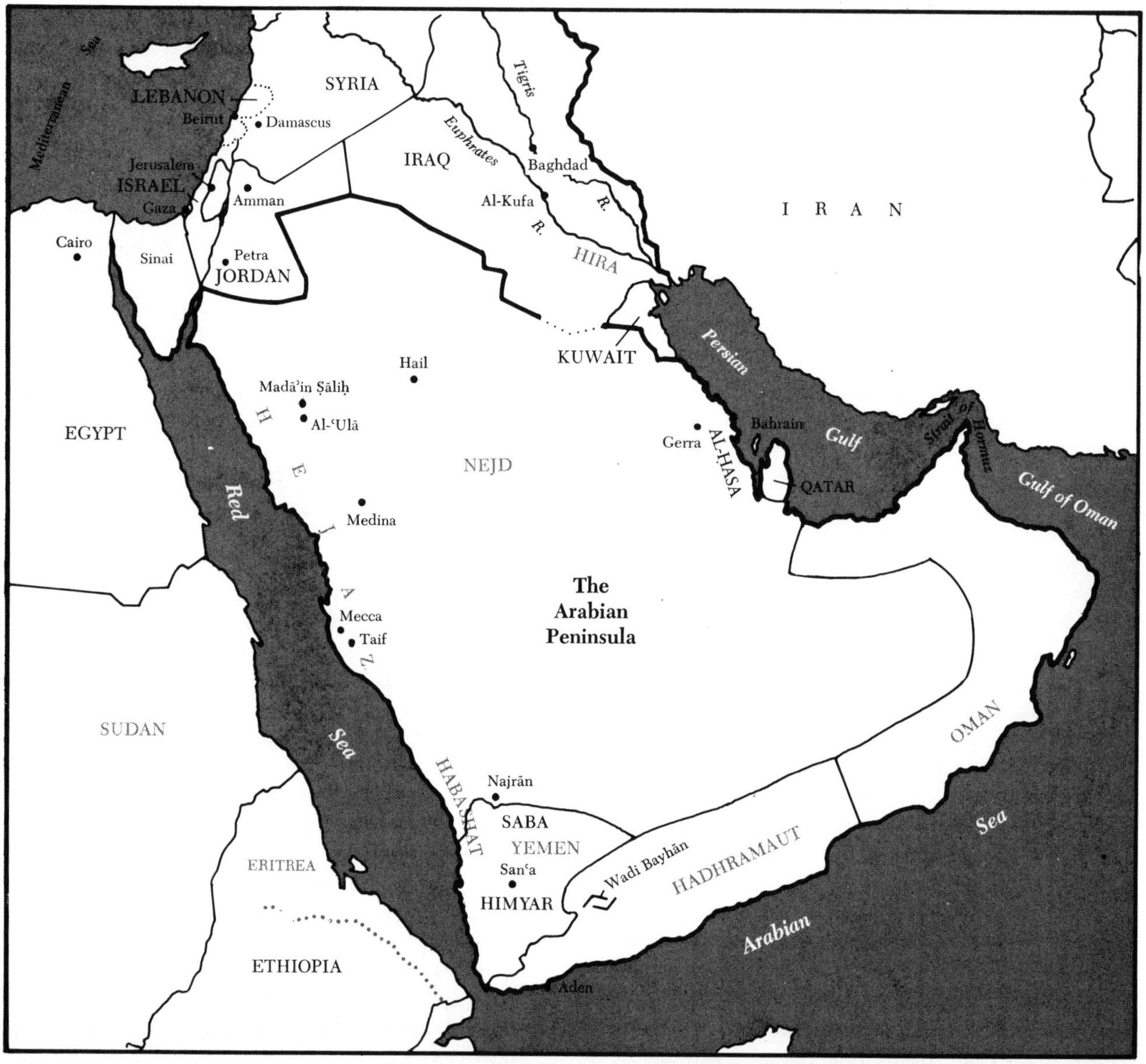

 ARABIA

Yathrib (subsequently renamed Medina). Here, even before he had an opportunity to preach his faith, he was welcomed as an arbiter to put an end to feuding between the two principal tribes of the oasis. Without minimizing the effect of his religious message, it is possible to suggest that the arrival there of "delegations" *(wufūd)* from all over the peninsula to make their submission was, in the first instance, due to weariness with the savage intertribal warfare that ravaged the peninsula and to the lack of such stabilizing influence as the northern and southern kingdoms had been able to provide before their collapse.

In the end the Quraysh submitted; thereafter Arabia, unified for the first time in history, was able to embark on its astonishing career of conquest outside the peninsula. The background presence, within living memory, of the highly developed antique Yemenite civilization is a factor in the formation of the Islamic state to which hardly sufficient attention has been paid.

BIBLIOGRAPHY

It is impossible at the moment to give an adequate bibliography of the subject. The results of the latest research are to be found only in some hundreds of articles, each dealing with some highly specialized topic and aimed only at experts. More general surveys, accessible to nonexperts, are with very few exceptions out-of-date and unreliable.

Bernard Lewis, *The Arabs in History*, 2nd ed. (1954), still has value as a clear and sober account; Irfan Shahid, "Pre-Islamic Arabia," in *Cambridge History of Islam, I* (1970), is good on North Arabia, but the material on the south is based on outdated secondary sources and hence is unreliable. John Spencer Trimingham, *Christianity Among the Arabs in Pre-Islamic Times* (1979), has much of interest but is dominantly concerned with the Arabs outside the boundaries of the Arabian peninsula.

For the south, an important collectaneous work is Joseph Chelhod, ed., *L'Arabie du sud, histoire et civilisation* (1982). Brian Doe, *Southern Arabia* (1971), is a good account of the land and extant physical archaeological remains but must not be relied on for the interpretations proposed, many of which have been negated by later research.

A. F. L. BEESTON

II

ISLAMIC ARABIA. The year of Muḥammad's move (hegira) to Medina, A.D. 622, was later taken as year 1 of the Islamic calendar. With the occupation of Mecca, the Muslims took control of the pilgrimage to the Kaaba. When they prayed, they faced toward Mecca, which in this regard had replaced Jerusalem. Medina, however, remained the capital of the Islamic state.

In Medina the Prophet continued to receive revelations, later written down as the Medinan suras of the Koran. Longer and more prosaic than the Meccan suras, they provided guidance for Muḥammad as head of state. The Koran became the heart of the Sacred Law, or *sharīʿa*, supplemented by records of the sayings and acts of Muḥammad and his pious companions and by devices of the legists. During Muḥammad's lifetime most of western and central Arabia and Oman in the far northeast recognized the authority of Medina. This spread of the new religion was accomplished in good part by missionary endeavors, not by force of arms.

Muḥammad died in 632, two years after the occupation of Mecca, without having designated anyone to take his place as head of state. The influential members of the community ("the people who loose and bind") chose the venerable Abū Bakr as the first caliph, or *khalīfa* ("successor"), in preference to ʿAlī, Muḥammad's cousin and son-in-law, who had considerable support. With Muḥammad gone from the scene, some of the tribes repudiated the allegiance they had sworn to him, but Abū Bakr's captains, chief among whom was Khalīd ibn al-Walid, "the sword of God," brought them to heel. Among the Muslims who fell in the campaigns against the rebels were men who had memorized the revelations received by the Prophet. Their loss pointed up the need to reduce the text of the Koran to writing, which was done at the order of Abū Bakr's successor.

In the time of ʿUmar, the second caliph (also elected instead of ʿAlī), decisive victories by Muslim armies over the Byzantine and Sasanian empires, then the strongest powers in the region, brought extensive lands outside Arabia under Islamic rule, and many Muslim Arabs left to settle in them. During the rule of the third caliph, ʿUthmān (ʿAlī having been passed over once again), the wealth acquired as booty tended to temper, and in some instances to undermine, the austerity of very early Islamic society, Mecca and Medina not excepted.

While Muslim tribesmen from Arabia moved into the newly occupied countries to seek their fortune and to rivet the hold of Islam there, non-Arabs came to Mecca every year in throngs for the pilgrimage. Many went on to visit the Prophet's tomb in Medina, and some stayed on to live and die in the holy land. The conversion of African blacks to Islam and the religion's tolerance of slavery helped to make the population of Arabia more cosmopolitan.

ᶜAlī was finally elected caliph, the fourth of "the Rightly Guided," in 656. When the Muslim governor of Syria rose against him, Iraq became the battleground, and ᶜAlī moved his capital from Medina to Al-Kufa. Condemning the conduct of ᶜAlī in an arbitration with the rebel, extremists among his followers forsook him, whereupon they were called Kharijites ("Outgoers"). One of them assassinated ᶜAlī, whose older son, Hasan, was then recognized as leader of his party *(shīᶜat ᶜAlī)* the Shiites, who preferred the title imam to caliph. Hasan soon renounced the title, which the party then bestowed on his younger brother Husayn. The rebel governor of Syria, by proclaiming himself caliph, became the progenitor of the hereditary Umayyad dynasty of Damascus (the Umayyads were a clan of Ḳuraysh), and troops of his successor slaughtered Husayn and his family at Karbala in Iraq.

Under the Umayyad caliphate the Sunnites ("those who follow the Prophet's example," as if other Muslims did not) commanded a majority in the Islamic realm, probably including Arabia, though Shiites held their ground in some parts of the peninsula, particularly in the east. The Umayyads appointed governors for Mecca and Medina and, with their freer outlook, tolerated or even encouraged formerly forbidden pleasures there. The two sects differed fundamentally on the basic qualification for the head of the community. The Shiites insisted that the imam must be a direct descendant of the Prophet through his daughter Fatima and her husband ᶜAlī, while Sunnite doctrine required simply that the caliph be a member of the Prophet's tribe Ḳuraysh.

The Umayyads virtually completed the expansion of the early Islamic state. From Central Asia and the borders of India in the east it reached across North Africa to the Atlantic in the west. Most of Spain and Portugal were subdued in the eighth century. The main thrust across the Pyrenees was halted by Charles Martel at Poitiers (Tours) in 732.

Near the end of Umayyad rule, dissident Kharijites seized Mecca and Medina, but the Umayyads quickly recovered the cities. Supplanting the Umayyads in 750, the Abbasids, also Sunnites from Ḳuraysh, built a new capital for the caliphate in Baghdad. The first Abbasids enjoyed effective authority in the holy cities, which they adorned with handsome structures, and sometimes in other places in Arabia. Hārūn al-Rashīd's wife Zubayda lavished care on the main pilgrimage route to Mecca from the east, which still bears her name.

In the eighth century Kharijites filtered into Oman and made their version of Kharijism, called Ibadism, the dominant faith there. Unlike the Sunnites and Shiites, the Ibadites held that any Muslim with the necessary qualifications of piety and learning could be elected imam. They also accepted an interregnum if no suitable candidate could be found. For four centuries many Ibadite imams were elected, and few interregnums occurred. The Ibadites of Oman kept in tenuous touch with other Ibadite groups in faraway East Africa and North Africa.

During the Umayyad regime the Alids—both descendants of Hasan and descendants of Husayn—were in the main quiescent in Arabia, but they became active there after the advent of the Abbasids. The Hasanid al-Nafs al-Zakiyya ("the Pure Soul") was hailed as the Mahdi in Medina, only to be killed by Abbasid forces. Following the death of the sixth Shiite imam, a dispute arose over the succession between the supporters of his older son (later called the Twelvers), whose line of imams was to end with the occultation of the twelfth, and the Seveners, or Ismailis, who looked upon his younger son, Ismail, as the seventh imam (the Ismailis subsequently recognized many other imams). As a militant minority the Ismailis appealed strongly to the oppressed and discontented elements in society.

Yemen proved fertile ground for the Alids, who won the favor of al-Shāfiᶜī, the founder of one of the four Sunnite schools for the interpretation of the Sacred Law. A Husaynid made himself master of Mecca, and a Hasanid did the same in Medina. The waxing of Alid influence induced an Abbasid caliph to name the eighth imam of the Twelvers as his heir apparent, but the imam died before he could accede. Abbasid power in Arabia was declining, and the first independent dynasty there arose in Yemen, though not with an Alid as its head. This was followed by other independent dynasties in various regions, including one inaugurated by a Hasanid in Nejd.

The Abbasids were further weakened by a serious uprising of the Zanj, black slaves who toiled in the salt marshes of lower Iraq, the effects of which reached Mecca and Medina. Ismaili missionaries worked hard to spread their doctrines in the Persian Gulf area and in Yemen, where an Ismaili leader held Sanᶜa for a time. The Ismailis, however, encountered a new enemy in the person of the first Zaydite imam. The Zaydites were Hasanids whose beliefs were more moderate than those of the Ismailis.

At the end of the ninth century, Ismailis established a state in eastern Arabia. The term "Qarmatian" was applied to these Ismailis, who soon became the terror of Arabia and Iraq. In 930 they raided Mecca, removed the sacred Black Stone from the Kaaba, and carried it off to their new capital in the east. Sweeping over Nejd and Oman, they brought most of the peninsula under their sway. In this disturbed time a Hasanid moved from Iraq to Hadhramaut, where his descendants were the sayyids, destined to wield great influence in the religious and political life there.

Other Ismailis moved into North Africa and founded the Fatimid dynasty, which took its name from Fatima, the Prophet's daughter and mother of Hasan and Husayn. On good terms with the Qarmatians at first, the Fatimids induced them to return the Black Stone to Mecca twenty years after its removal, but when the Fatimids invaded Egypt, the two factions turned against each other. The Qarmatian chief took Damascus but failed in expeditions against Egypt, where he could not reach the new Fatimid capital of Cairo. The Qarmatian state in eastern Arabia was governed in its later stages by a council of six sayyids, who administered, according to an eyewitness account by a Persian traveler, a sort of communistic society. The heyday of the Qarmatians was past by the late tenth century; they lost Oman, and tribesmen humiliated them in their home territory. By the last quarter of the next century, a local dynasty completed their overthrow. No trace of Qarmatian beliefs can now be detected in their former strongholds; the Shiites there are Twelvers, ancient rivals of the Sevener Qarmatians.

About the middle of the tenth century Hasanids established the sharifate of Mecca, which was to last nearly 1,000 years. Beginning with the Fatimids, the sharifs were usually nominal vassals of more powerful rulers outside Arabia, but the affairs of the city and surrounding areas fell largely within the province of the sharifs. An attempt by one of them to assume the caliphate was foiled by the Fatimids. Husaynids bore the title of emir of Medina until the fifteenth century.

Another Ismaili dynasty, the Sulayhid, fixed its capital at San^{c}a in Yemen, with the Fatimids as nominal overlords. The most noteworthy figure was a woman, as-Sayyida Arwā, who received Aden as her dowry, ruled on behalf of her husband, and was recognized by the Fatimid imam as "suzerain of the kings of Yemen." After her death in 1138 the Sulayhid dynasty faded away, but a minor Ismaili dynasty ruled Aden for some years thereafter.

The growth of the various branches of Shiism stirred up a Sunnite reaction, led initially by the Seljuk Turks. Putting the Abbasid caliphs under their thumb, though they allowed the caliph's name to continue to be mentioned in the Friday prayers in Mecca and Medina, the Turks crossed into Oman. The line of Ibadite imams there was broken in the middle of the eleventh century; for well over 300 years only one imam was elected, but the imamate revived in full force in the early fifteenth century.

In the middle of the twelth century the Zaydite imam in Yemen was supreme in his capital Ṣa^{c}dah, in San^{c}a to the south, and in the valley of Najrān to the north. Numbers of Jews dwelt in Yemen and Najrān, and Christians had once been strong in Najrān, even though the second caliph, ^{c}Umar, reportedly ordained that none of these scriptuaries ("the People of the Book," the Old and New Testaments) should be allowed to live in Arabia, which was Islam's preserve. After the Middle Ages a new branch of Ismailis acquired power in Najrān.

The Fatimids of Egypt gave way in 1171 to the Sunnite Ayyubids. Saladin, the most illustrious representative of the new dynasty, received recognition as sultan in Mecca. Although his main concern was to wage war against the Crusaders in Palestine, he did not neglect his interests in Arabia, sending his brother south to annex Yemen to his domains. Sunnism was now well along the road to gaining the upper hand over Shiism in Arabia, though Ismailis retained a foothold (without real political control) in Yemen until the sixteenth century, after which time many of them migrated to India.

The Crusaders posed the first Christian military threat to Islamic Arabia, but it did not prove very serious. Reginald of Châtillon raided the oasis of Taymâ, north of Medina, and dreamed fruitlessly of attacking Medina itself. He sent war vessels into the Red Sea, where they did some damage to Muslim shipping.

The Sunnite Rasulids, who claimed descent from the old Arab tribe of Ghassān but were actually of Turkoman origin, succeeded the Ayyubids in Yemen in 1229, beginning a rule that was to last more than two centuries, one of the brightest periods in the history of medieval Yemen. They promoted scholarship, erected charming buildings, and received embassies from as far away as China. The writ of an early Rasulid ran from Mecca to Hadhramaut. San^{c}a was taken from the Zaydites and held for a century and a half. One of the Rasulids tried to make himself caliph after the execution of the Abbasid caliph in Baghdad by Hulagu, but the response beyond Yemen was negative.

In Egypt the Sunnite Mamluks overcame the last Ayyubid in 1250 and continued the Egyptian practice of exercising suzerainty over the holy cities in Arabia, with Mecca in particular prospering under their aegis and the administration of the sharifs. In Cairo the Mamluks maintained shadow Abbasid caliphs whose line ended (with that of the Mamluks) when the Ottomans conquered Egypt in 1517.

By 1500, Arabia was more Sunnite than Shiite. The Ismailis were reduced to a minor role, while the Ibadites remained in place in Oman. The second Christian threat came after Vasco da Gama discovered the sea route to India in 1498. In the early sixteenth century the Portuguese took Oman and Bahrain, but in time they lost out in the Persian Gulf to the Ottomans, the Persians, the British, and the Dutch.

BIBLIOGRAPHY

A. J. Arberry, ed., *Religion in the Middle East* (1969); Cornelis van Arendonk, *De Opkomst van het Zaidietische Imamaat in Yemen* (1919); Thomas W. Arnold, *The Caliphate* (1921); C. E. Bosworth, *The Islamic Dynasties* (1967); Rudolf Brünnow, *Die Charidschiten* (1884); Leone Caetani, *Annali dell'Islam*, 10 vols. (1905–1926, covers the period A.H. 1–40/A.D. 622–661), *Chronographia Islamica* (1912, covers the period 622–1517); D. M. Donaldson, *The Shi^{c}ite Religion* (1933); H. A. R. Gibb, *Mohammedanism, a Historical Survey*, 2nd ed. (1953); M. J. de Goeje, *Mémoire sur les Carmathes du Bahraïn*, 2nd ed. (1886); Philip K. Hitti, *History of the Arabs*, 10th ed. (1970); P. M. Holt *et al.*, eds., *The Cambridge History of Islam* (1970); Derek Hopwood, ed., *The Arabian Peninsula* (1972); Christiaan S. Hurgronje, *Mekka*, 2 vols. (1888–1889); Bernard Lewis, *The Origins of Ismā^{c}īlism* (1940); William Muir, *The Caliphate*, 3rd ed. (1898); A. S. Tritton, *The Rise of the Imams of Sanaa* (1925); William Montgomery Watt, *Muhammad at Mecca* (1953); and *Muhammad at Medina* (1956); Julius Wellhausen, *Die religiös-politischen Oppositions-parteien* (1901); Heinrich Ferdinand Wüstenfeld, *Geschichte der Stadt Mekka* (1861); Eduard de Zambaur, *Manuel de généalogie et de chronologie pour l'histoire de l'Islam* (1927).

GEORGE RENTZ

[See also **Abbasids; Agriculture, Islamic; Alids; Ayyubids; Commerce, Islamic; Fatimids; Geography and Cartography, Islamic; Hasan ibn ^{c}Ali; Husayn ibn ^{c}Ali; Ismā^{c}iliya; Kaaba; Ḳuraysh; Mamluks; Mecca; Medina; Muḥammad (Prophet); Nabataeans; Shi^{c}a; Sunni; Umayyads; Yemen.**]

ARABIC LANGUAGE. Arabic belongs to a linguistic family termed Semitic; other Semitic languages are Hebrew, Aramaic, some of the Ethiopian languages, and various others now dead. Until the great conquests of Islam in the seventh and eighth centuries, Arabic was confined to the Arabian Peninsula, and did not even cover the whole of it; for in the south there were, and today still are, Semitic languages not classifiable as Arabic. Moreover, a mass of pre-Islamic graffiti found throughout the peninsula, and ranging probably from the fifth century B.C. to the fifth century of the Christian era, are in dialects that can only dubiously be called Arabic, since their definite article ("the") is *ha-* or *han-*, not the typically Arabic *al-*. This feature has analogies with Hebrew; but at the same time the alphabets in which these graffiti are written are of a south Semitic type markedly different (particularly in possessing a larger range of letters) from the north Semitic scripts exemplified in Hebrew and Aramaic.

From about the third century of the Christian era onward we have a handful of inscriptions that do contain the article *al-* and are unmistakably Arabic. In the south and east of the peninsula, and in the northwest, they are written in scripts of the southern type; but in the extreme north they appear in a script having strong affinities with the Aramaic one, though probably not directly derived from it. It is from this northern alphabet that Arabic script as we know it has evolved.

A considerable obstacle to the linguistic evaluation of a Semitic language (apart from those still spoken today) is that Semitic alphabets normally do not record short vowels, being in principle consonantal, with some limited facilities for recording long vowels. The scripts have, it is true, in the course of time developed ancillary means of full vowel notation, but (except in Ethiopia) these extra aids are never used in normal writing. Hence there is a great deal of ambiguity in the actually recorded forms of words.

For the ordinary European a particular difficulty of the Semitic languages in general is that they pos-

ARABIC LANGUAGE

sess some half-dozen consonants pronounced in a way wholly unfamiliar to European speech habits; this gives rise to a disconcerting variety in the modes of representing Arabic words and names in European script.

In addition to the above-mentioned early inscriptional records, there was in the sixth and seventh centuries a flourishing body of poetry transmitted orally and not written down until the eighth century. In literary prose the earliest record in writing is the Koran, revealed to the Prophet Muḥammad in the early decades of the seventh century. The records of the Prophet's life and sayings, and of the events of the beginning of Islam—the Tradition *(ḥadīth)* literature—were partially written down during the course of that century, but the great bulk was, like the poetry, transmitted orally and is known to us only in compilations of the eighth and ninth centuries. All this material represents the linguistic expression of an essentially bedouin culture, for which the language was fully adequate; but there remained large areas of human experience and thought wholly alien to the bedouin.

The eighth century brought great changes as a result of the widespread conquests of Islam. Arabs were settled in the garrison cities—Basra and Al-Kufa in lower Iraq, Al-Fustāt immediately to the south of modern Cairo, and (later) elsewhere. The conquered populations, who had been speakers of Greek, Aramaic, Coptic, Berber, Iranian, and other languages, tended, at least in the upper social strata, to adopt the language of the conquerors. This necessarily had a considerable impact on Arabic: the language had to be adapted to the needs of an urbanized culture and to the expression of modes of thought long familiar in the Byzantine and Iranian civilizations, but strange to the bedouin.

Adaptation showed itself both lexically and grammatically. The lexical needs were met partly by loanwords from Greek and Iranian (a few loanwords from Aramaic had already appeared in Arabic before Islam), but to a larger extent by developing the resources of Arabic itself. One facility for the creation of neologisms lay in the Arabic verbal system, which permits the formation, from a basic root, of a series of derived stems, each with a special nuance. Another noteworthy example of the process is the evolution of a termination *-iyyah,* serving to generate abstracts such as quantity, quality, humanity, and spirituality (and also, in the modern language, many English *-ism* terms); this ending is simply the feminine of a termination used in the bedouin language for denoting tribal affiliation or geographical association.

In the domain of grammar, a new sophistication was achieved by assigning precise functions to grammatical tools and forms that in the older language had been imprecise and ambivalent.

Thus developed, Arabic became an extremely subtle medium for the expression of sophisticated ideas in philosophy and science. A vigorous translation program through the eighth and ninth centuries, part of it directly from Greek or Iranian into Arabic, part by way of Syriac (a variety of Aramaic), made the Arabic-speaking world familiar with most of the essentials of Hellenistic philosophy and science: Aristotle, Galen, Dioscorides, Euclid, and Ptolemy are particularly well represented, though Platonism was better known in its Neoplatonic than in its original form.

On this foundation the Islamic world went on to make an independent contribution to the development of science and philosophy. In science the camera obscura, the circulation of the blood, and the parasitic origin of scabies, to name only a few phenomena, were familiar in Arabic long before they were "discovered" in Europe. The system of place notation for arithmetical operations, though derived ultimately from India, was mediated through Arabic to Europe, where it did not become current until the end of the Middle Ages. Algebra was entirely an Arabic science, unknown to the Hellenistic world. In philosophy the role played by the Arabic writings of Avicenna (Ibn-Sīnā) and Averroës (Ibn-Rushd) in the history of European philosophy can hardly be overestimated.

Furthermore, Arabic scholars of the eighth and ninth centuries set themselves to describe and analyze their language, achieving a number of highly sophisticated insights into general linguistics that were wholly unknown in Europe until worked out independently by linguisticians in the twentieth century. For example, the principle of what is now called "ultimate constituent analysis" was basic for the Arab grammarians.

Virtually every language has various "levels," ranging from the speech of everyday life to the high-prestige diction of literature and formal speech. At present the cleavage between these two extremes in Arabic is exceptionally wide; what the difference was in earlier times is a debatable problem. The difficulty of arriving at any firm conclusions rests in the nature of our sources. To an overwhelming extent these sources reflect the formal language of poetry, belles-lettres, science, philosophy, and history. Some minimal indications of popular speech can be gained from letters and similar documents on papyrus ranging from the seventh to the ninth century, and in later times from writings by non-Muslims who remained outside the Muslim educational framework based on the Koran. Yet even these sources are contaminated by a certain amount of striving by the writers after a prestigious form of language. It could be thought that the Tradition literature represents the everyday speech of Mecca at the time of the Prophet, but in this case, too, evaluation is hampered by the inadequacies of the Arabic script system.

One point around which scholarly dispute has especially raged is that of the case system of nouns; this manifests itself principally in short vowel terminations, and is thus, to a large extent, not recorded in writing. Although the case system has always been part of the most formal language, it does not exist in the modern vernaculars, and there are indications that it was not present in the everyday language from the end of the seventh century on. Some European scholars have claimed that the system was not in everyday use even in the early seventh century; nevertheless, the current trend seems to hold that the system was in use in all forms of the language until the urbanization following the Islamic conquests and the influx of non-Arabs into the Arabic linguistic community.

The spread of Arabic throughout the Islamic empire was a gradual process. Greek, which had always been mainly a language of the towns in Egypt and the Levant (Asia Minor did not become Muslim until centuries later), disappeared quite rapidly. Outside the towns, although from an early date Arabs settled on the land side by side with the preconquest populations, Coptic remained in use in the Egyptian countryside well into the Middle Ages; Berber is still used in large parts of the North African countryside; and Aramaic long lingered in Syria (there are a few pockets where it is still spoken today.)

In Iran, on the other hand, the situation evolved quite differently. For the first few centuries of Islam, the Persian educated classes enthusiastically adopted the Arabic-language culture, and a great deal of the best writing of that period in Arabic is the work of authors of Persian stock. But from about the tenth century, Persian staged a comeback unparalleled in the rest of the Islamic world. The historian Rashīd al-Dīn (d. 1318) published his works simultaneously in Persian and Arabic, but thereafter Persian became the language of literature as well as of everyday life in Iran, and only religious works continued to be drafted in Arabic; even these were sometimes in Persian. The same is the case in other non-Arabic-speaking parts of the Islamic world, such as Turkey, the Indian subcontinent, and the East Indies: Arabic is cultivated as a learned language for religious purposes only.

Cultural contacts between the Arabic-speaking world and the West certainly existed in the Latin Crusader kingdoms and in Norman Sicily (especially under Roger II), but influences due to these contacts hardly appear in the language and literature—unless one holds the highly dubious thesis that Dante's *Purgatorio* was inspired by an Arabic original. It was primarily in Spain that really fruitful linguistic exchanges took place, with a vigorous outburst of translations of Arabic philosophical and scientific works (themselves either original or ultimately derivative from Greek) into Latin by a number of western scholars such as Adelard of Bath, and in the scientific work of Alfonso X (called el Sabio, "the Wise") in the thirteenth century. Thus a large number of Arabic technical and scientific terms were borrowed into medieval Latin, and thence into modern European languages: such as alcohol, algorism, and many others.

Spain was also the birthplace (about the tenth century) of a tradition of Arabic lyrical poetry that bears strong resemblances to the work of the Provençal and Catalan troubadors; whether direct inspiration of the latter from the Arabic can be admitted is a subject of dispute.

Maltese occupies a unique position. In spite of heavy infiltration of loanwords from Italian, it is fundamentally and without question an Arabic dialect. But the two centuries of Arab occupation did not lead to Islamization of the island, which therefore remained cut off from the Islamic-Arabic mainstream in North Africa. When finally, in the eighteenth century, it became a written and literary language, an orthography in the Latin alphabet was devised for it.

BIBLIOGRAPHY

Mary C. Bateson, *Arabic Language Handbook* (1967); A. F. L. Beeston, *The Arabic Language Today* (1970); Anwar G. Chejne, *The Arabic Language, Its Role in History* (1969); J. Fück, ᶜ*Arabīya* (1950); Charles Pellat, *Langue et littérature arabes* (1952).

A. F. L. BEESTON

ARABIC LITERATURE, PROSE

ARABIC LITERATURE, PROSE

THE FORMATIVE PERIOD: 700–900

The pagan Arabs had developed a rich poetic tradition, but Arabic prose literature is a product of Islamic civilization. In the eighth century, religious and legal needs demanded, and cultural rivalry between Arabs and non-Arabs spurred, great scholarly enterprises in law and hadith (sayings of the Prophet and reports about him by his companions), in philology and history. Literary prose, too, began in response to a need: The "secretaries" who manned the bureaucracy of the Muslim empire, inheritors of Sasanian polish and protocol, composed in Arabic, mostly by loose translation, a variety of didactic and historical works.

Most of this early literature is lost. We have several works by its chief figure, the Persian Ibn al-Muqaffa^c (d. 756[?]) among them an Arabic adaptation from the Middle Persian of the originally Indian fables of Bidpai *(Kalīla wa-Dimna;* French trans. by André Miquel, 1957) and a short book of practical ethics for princes and courtiers *(al-Adab al-kabīr).* This book takes up general counsels of happiness (how to pick one's friends; how to know one's own faults), but it is also a manual for survival at a despotic court (how to avoid the often fatal suspicion of the ruler; how to induce a wicked ruler to correct his faults of his own accord; how to stay unperturbed when a friend keeps company with an enemy). The author was executed in 757.

The ninth century saw the true foundation of Arabic art prose. There was much to draw on. A vast amount of material had been accumulated by scholars of Arabic philology: both texts (chiefly pre-Islamic poems) and the lexical, historical, and ethnographic information needed for understanding them. Materials were abundant on the past of the Arabs and their neighbors. Translations of Greek science and philosophy existed. Jurists and theologians had identified their chief problems and sharpened their distinctions. Wealth and power fostered learning and the arts. The civilization of this time found its prose reflection in the works of two great writers: al-Jāḥiẓ and Ibn Qutayba.

Al-Jāḥiẓ (d. 869) was born and educated in Basra, one of the foremost cultural centers of that time. His intellectual curiosity was limitless, his pen fluent, his life long. Some thirty of his many works survive, among them two large compilations (with a personal touch) of humanistic learning, a book of character sketches, and numerous essays. Well-turned phrases and speeches make up the body of the *Book of Eloquence and Exposition.* The chapter headings show al-Jāḥiẓ's frequently uttered principle of mixing the serious and the entertaining: There is a famous section on the eloquence of ascetics, and another on the memorable repartees of people thought to be demented.

The principle of diversity is also evident in al-Jāḥiẓ's greatest work, the *Bestiary* (*Kitāb al-ḥayawān*; selections trans. in Charles Pellat, *The Life and Works of Jāḥiẓ*, 1969). After a prefatory section in praise of books, the discussion of the nature of various animals begins (by way of zoology, legend, and anecdote), but al-Jāḥiẓ delights in straying from topic to topic, and the adventitious subjects are often the most intriguing. He discusses why man is a microcosm, why babies cry and how they should be soothed gently; he speaks of the virtues of hybridization, the nature of fire, the psychology of eunuchs; he tells us why some professors write obscure books (would anyone come to their lectures if the books explained all?), that there is no evidence for rains of frogs, and so forth. The *Book of Misers*, a late work, is full of anecdotes of contemporary life. The dialogue seems direct; the characters, authentic (French trans. by Charles Pellat, *Le livre des avares,* 1951).

Among the essays of al-Jāḥiẓ some are concerned with gratuitous subjects chosen for argument's sake ("Speaking Is Better Than Silence"), but others mean to engage in serious argument ("Against Christians"). He excelled at the sketching of manners, fashions, and humors. This is done with delicious gusto in "On Singing Girls" (trans. in Pellat, *Life and Works of Jāḥiẓ*) in which he pokes fun at courtesans, lovers, and procurers alike, not without a good-humored affection for them all.

In theology al-Jāḥiẓ was of the rationalist Mu^ctazilite school. An idiosyncratic position is reported of him: that he thought God sent no one to hell, that something in the sinner's constitution would draw him to the nature of fire, and that he would not suffer pain without end (rather, in time sinner and fire would become a single substance). This notion has a blend of rational form, humanity, and perhaps irony that would be characteristic of al-Jāḥiẓ.

Less probing but better organized, al-Jāḥiẓ's younger contemporary Ibn Qutayba (born in Merv; died at Baghdad, 889) created a type of book that had many imitators. His *Choice Stories* (*^cUyūn al-akhbār)* is an encyclopedic source book of *adab:* urbanity and *humanitas* (partial trans. are Josef Horovitz, in *Islamic Culture,* vols. IV and V, 1930–1931;

ARABIC LITERATURE, PROSE

and Lothar Kopf and F. S. Bodenheimer, *The Natural History Section from a 9th Century "Book of Useful Knowledge,"* 1949.) Through exemplary stories and pithy sayings the book teaches manners and describes types of human character. A man's *adab* will show in social intercourse: He will be decorous, temperate, and judicious in his management of affairs and in dealings with others. It will show in his pursuit of happiness, for knowledge of human nature and of the lot of mankind will give him a broad view and freedom from compulsion. Thus the same book will discuss how to pick a good police chief and how to resign oneself to the will of God. *Adab* is a humanistic complement to the religious charting of human conduct (which also, as the hadith collections show, ranges from the believer's heart and mind to his table manners).

The sources are diverse: Sasanid or Indian maxims are side by side with anecdotes about the Prophet and his companions, and are followed by stories about bedouin chiefs, slave girls, or Muslim princes. *Adab* represents the triumph of a catholic Islamic culture over various local cultural patriotisms *(shuᶜūbīya)*. The topics of Ibn Qutayba's *ᶜUyūn* are gathered under ten headings, ranging from government and war to friendship, food, and women. Anecdotes, maxims ("I never use my sword when my whip will do, never my whip when my tongue will do"), catalog-style wisdom ("the ten bad qualities of women"), and observations of social life are used.

The goal of such a work is twofold: The stories and quotations are didactic, but they also have a cultural value in their own right. You do not learn the moral and forget the tale. The *ᶜUyūn* means to be didactic, but also entertaining and a source book for speakers and writers. Therefore it includes some matters that are independent of manners and morals but ought to be known (for example, natural history).

The book is aimed primarily at the bureaucratic class—as is especially evident from the sections on government and style—but it and the *adab* literature it engendered served all educated men and women.

THE TENTH CENTURY AND LATER

The writing of *adab* continued as an important literary activity. As in other areas of medieval literature, the authors relied heavily on each other, relishing the maintenance and elaboration of a shared culture. There were specialized *Etiquettes* such as several *Manners of the Drinking Companion* and encyclopedic *adab* books. These later books tended to be longer than the earlier ones. Especially well-known such works are the *Unique Necklace (ᶜIqd al-farīd)*, by the Spanish Arab writer Ibn ᶜAbd Rabbih (d. 940), and the *New Book of Polite Accomplishments (al-Mustaṭraf fī kull fann mustaẓraf*; French trans. by G. Rat, 2 vols., 1899–1902), by the Egyptian al-Ibshīhī (d. after 1446). In the latter book, chapters of factual information—on divination, on the properties of metals and precious stones, on the marvels of the seas—complement the core about man and manners.

The art of the anecdote was practiced widely and well. The stories are presented as narratives of fact, although wit and dramatic flair must have contributed. Writers of anecdote books often had a didactic aim in view. There are anecdote books organized according to human types (anticipated in al-Jāḥiẓ's *Misers*) or types of event. Of the first group are the "Clever Madmen" of al-Nisābūrī (d. 1015) and the books by Ibn al-Jawzī (d. 1200), *Fools and Gullible People* and *Clever Men and Women* (German trans. by Oskar Rescher, 1925). Tragic lovers people the *Lovers' Disasters* of al-Sarrāj (d. Baghdad, 1106) and several similar books.

Of the second group is the *Deliverance After Distress* of al-Tanūkhī, an excellent storyteller who lived in Iraq, was a judge, and died in 994. Several authors wrote books of pious optimism on this motif. Al-Tanūkhī also wrote—with no guiding principle other than holding the reader's attention—what may be the most enjoyable anecdote book in Arabic: the *Food for Entertainment* (*Nishwār al-muḥāḍara;* partial trans. by D. S. Margoliouth, *The Table-Talk of a Mesopotamian Judge,* 1922). It ranges from stories about princes and viziers to the young girl of Ramleh who digs up fresh graves and collects shrouds for a pastime. Good and evil deeds are repaid in *The Book of Just Rewards* by another tenth-century author, Ibn al-Dāya. Ribald anecdotes and verses fill the erotic anthology *Nuzhat al-albāb,* by the North African al-Tīfāshī (d. 1253). (There is a French trans. by René Khawam, *Les délices des coeurs,* 1971.) Anecdotes for religious edification are collected in the anti-Sufi *The Devil's Deceit,* by Ibn al-Jawzī and the pro-Sufi *Garden of Fragrant Plants (Rawḍ al-rayāḥīn),* by the South Arabian al-Yāfiᶜi (d. Mecca, 1367). There are several "Legends of the Prophets."

Between specialized branches of the humanities (history, biography, philosophy) and belles lettres it

ARABIC LITERATURE, PROSE

is often profitless, in the Middle Ages, to look for a hard and fast line. Sharpness of character and incident, vitality of language, and interest in addressing a public having a general humanistic education give literary worth to many works in these fields. Only a few examples can be given here. The historian al-Masᶜūdī (d. 956), in his *Murūj al-dhahab,* or *Golden Meadows* (a history, beginning with the Creation, of the Muslim world and its neighbors), delights with an eye for the memorable detail. His drawing of the concrete is worthy of the pen of Jean Froissart. (There is a French trans. by Barbier de Meynard and *Pavet de Courteille, Les prairies d'or,* 9 vols., 1861–1877.)

The *Book of Songs,* by Abuᵓl-Faraj al-Isfahānī (*d.* 967), is a vast work devoted to the lives of poets and musicians. It is of great value as a source of literary history, but also offers page after page of vivid narrative. As often happens in medieval books, fact is at times adjusted by a moral perception that heightens its matter to drama. We cannot be sure that the caliph really resolved to test whether a mortal could spend a day of unmarred happiness, and that his favorite, with whom he meant to spend it, choked that night on a pomegranate seed and died, but it makes a powerful story. The tenth-century philosophical encyclopedia of the "Sincere Brethren" contains a long fable on the hierarchy of creatures and man's moral nature (trans. by L. Goodman, *The Case of the Animals Versus Man Before the King of the Jinn,* 1978).

In the *Kitāb al-imtāᶜ waᵓl-muᵓānasa* (the title has been rendered *The Book of Enlivenment and Good Company*), Abū Ḥayyān al-Tawḥīdī (d. 1023) purports to set down the intellectual conversations held at a vizier's salon. Great issues of philosophy and theology (there are chapters on the nature of the soul and on free will and predestination) meet *adab* material (from curiosities about animals to people whom lines of verse threw into unseemly agitation).

Two autobiographies stand out. Al-Ghazālī (the Latin Algazel, d. 1111) gives, in his *Rescuer from Error* (trans. in W. Montgomery Watt, *The Faith and Practice of Al-Ghazālī,* 1953), a glimpse of his intellectual crisis and turn from law and scholastic theology to mysticism. The *The Contemplation of Experience (Kitāb al-iᶜtibār),* by the Syrian notable Usāma ibn Munqidh (d. 1188), is much occupied with memories of hunting, but is especially delightful in its observations of the Crusaders' daily life in peacetime (trans. by Philip K. Hitti, *An Arab-Syrian Gentleman,* 1929). Their odd or boorish customs—their trials by ordeal, their lack of pudicity—supply Usāma with vigorous subjects, and he treats them with gusto, in straightforward Arabic.

There is an extensive literature on the nature of love: its psychological and moral aspects and its forms, from brute lust to the stylized love where life imitates art. In these books, such as the *Ring of the Dove* by Ibn Ḥazm of Córdoba (d. 1064) (trans. by A. J. Arberry, 1953), we get a picture of the elegant sensibility of the age, romantic or earthy vignettes, and serious moral arguments smoothly blended with poetry, *adab,* and gossip.

The learned literature of the Arab Middle Ages admitted few types of outright fiction. Works to point a moral occasionally used fictive characters or fables. The Sicilian exile Ibn Ẓafar (d. 1170) did so in his *Consolation,* a book of pious and philosophical wisdom for princes in distress. So did also Ibn ᶜArabshah (d. 1450), in his *Fākihat al-khulafā,ᵓ* a book that promotes simple virtues in a ponderously ornate style.

An unusual work in which a fictional situation—the author's conversations, in heaven and hell, with various Arab poets—serves as a vehicle for much philological erudition and some humor is the *Epistle of Forgiveness,* by the poet al-Maᶜarrī (*d.* Syria, 1057). A contemporary, the Spanish Arab Ibn Shuhayd, wrote a book of conversations with jinn who had inspired poets (*The Treatise of Familiar Spirits and Demons,* trans. by J. T. Monroe, 1969).

Fictional incidents are treated, finally, by the *maqāma* (lit. "assembly"). This important genre was devised by al-Hamadhānī (d. 1008). He invented a hero, an itinerant confidence man who has a way with words, and put him into a picaresque series of brief episodes. Al-Hamadhānī cast in alternations of verse and rhythmical rhymed prose the speeches of the narrator and his vagabond hero. The great appeal of his *maqāmāt,* and those of his equally famous successor al-Ḥarīrī (of Basra, d. 1122), perhaps came from their using an elaborate style—extravagant in vocabulary, lush in tropes, fluent though artificial—for the description of everyday events, often of humble or ludicrous circumstances. (Trans. are *The Maqāmāt of Badīᶜ al-Zamān al-Hamadhānī,* by William J. Prendergast, 1915; *The Assemblies of al-Hariri,* by Thomas Chenery and Francis Steingass, 2 vols. 1867–1898.)

After the Mongol devastation of the eastern Muslim world in the mid thirteenth century, there was no lack of intellectuals in the Arab lands. There were lucid, systematic compilers, but also original thinkers like Ibn Khaldūn, the great philosopher of history (b. Tunis, 1332; d. Cairo, 1406). There were some vivid books, like the *Travels* of the world traveler Ibn Baṭṭūṭa (b. Tangier, 1304; d. Morocco, bet. 1368 and 1377). (Three volumes have been trans. by H. A. R. Gibb, 1958–1971.) But the vital age of Arabic belles-lettres had passed. Perhaps the ahistorical nature of *adab* and of the anecdote collections, which at first made possible the goal of selecting from history the universally valid exempla, at length sapped the life of such literature. Ibn al-Jawzī's clever people are those of Tanūkhī, two centuries before him, or characters from the dawn of Islam. Al-Qalqashandī (d. 1418) inserted into his monumental manual for secretaries a "contention between pen and sword," a theme that poets of the ninth century had treated.

At any rate, the decline had begun before the Mongols. Once the secretaries had put on their clever style, they wore it as a badge of class. In the eleventh century, Iranians had begun to use Persian rather than Arabic as their literary language, and in the post-Mongol age the cleavage was complete. In many intellectual disciplines success was fatal: inquiry yielded to the careful stating of a school's accepted answers. Schoolmen seemed to be writing for schoolmen. In the ninth and tenth centuries there was an educated public that had striven, perhaps lightheartedly, for elegance of mind. In the later Middle Ages gravity descended.

It was, however, in the post-Mongol age that the chef d'oeuvre of Arabic entertainment literature, the *Thousand and One Nights,* gradually assumed the general form in which we know it. The tales have various origins: Indian, Arab, Persian, Greek. Some of them (including the frame story) are known to have existed as early as the ninth and tenth centuries.

Those with a literary education held these stories in low esteem, scornful of language without artifice and of mere fabulation. Nevertheless, there is no work of classical Arabic literature that approaches the best of the *Thousand and One Nights* in weave of narrative or grasp of moral complexities.

Among cycles of popular narrative that originated in the Middle Ages are the romance of chivalry relating the exploits, from pagan times to the Crusades, of the warrior and poet ᶜAntar (partial trans. in Terrich Hamilton, *Antar, a Bedoueen Romance,* 1819–1820), and the saga of the Banū Hilāl, a nomadic tribe that invaded North Africa in the eleventh century.

BIBLIOGRAPHY

Mia I. Gerhardt, *The Art of Story-Telling* (1963), on the *1001 Nights;* H. A. R. Gibb, *Arabic Literature* (1963), an excellent introductory survey with extensive bibliography of Arabic works translated into European languages; Gustave E. Von Grunebaum, *Medieval Islam, a Study in Cultural Orientation* (1953), highly informative, though colored at times by the author's nostalgia for the culture of antiquity; Zakī Mubarak, *La prose arabe au ivᵉ siècle de l'hégire (xᵉ siècle)* (1931); Udo Steinbach, *Dāt al-himma, kulturgeschichtliche Untersuchungen zu einem arabischen Volksroman* (1972), which contains much information about popular romances of chivalry in general.

Of the English translations of *1001 Nights,* that of Richard Burton is bizarre, and E. W. Lane's is bowdlerized. The uninspiring text by John Payne (13 vols., 1882–1889) is complete. Perhaps the best modern translation is Enno Littmann, *Die Erzählungen aus den tausendundein Nächten,* 6 vols., (1921–8, re-edition 1953). A good selection is N. J. Dawood, ed., *Tales from the 1001 Nights* (1973).

ANDRAS HAMORI

ARABIC NUMERALS. Historically Arabic numerals are more properly referred to as the system of Hindu-Arabic numerals and reckoning. As we know it today and use it in calculating—less and less since the advent of computers—it has been at the center in the advance of mathematics during the last millennium and a half, two-thirds of which belongs to the Middle Ages.

ORIGINS AND EARLY RECEPTION

The ingenious and eminently simple system of representing any quantity by the device of nine figures in decimal place value arose in India during the fifth century of the Christian era, if not earlier. Such an origin was universally recognized by medieval users of the system: Arabs, Latins, and Byzantines. Only a few Western scholars have attempted in recent centuries to deny an Indian origin, either contesting the historical evidence, or crediting the Greeks with the invention, or expressing mere disbelief: none of these rejectionist views have prevailed, and today the Indian origin is universally accepted by serious scholars.

We must distinguish, however, between number representation and methods of calculation. For the latter we have only indirect information, since the

ARABIC NUMERALS

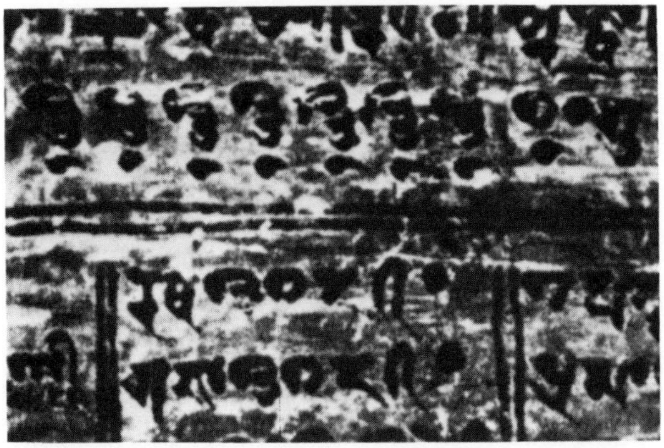

Detail of a Hindu manuscript showing the three and the zero, indicated by heavy dots. COURTESY, NEW YORK PUBLIC LIBRARY

original Indian treatises, and even those of the early Arab imitators, have not survived. Al-Khwārizmī's description of the Indian methods of reckoning, which he introduced about 825, must be reconstructed from their use and imitation by later Arab authors, such as Kūshyār ibn Labbān (*fl. ca.* 1000), Abūᵓl-Wafāᵓ (late tenth century), and al-Uqlīdisī (*fl. ca.* 952), but especially through some twelfth-century Latin translations or adaptations that claim to follow al-Khwārizmī's original work, the exact title of which is not known, but which must have been something like *Calculation with the Hindu Numerals* or *Method of Calculation of the Hindus.* (This aspect of the question, which will not be treated here, belongs to the "science of reckoning" [Arabic, *ᶜilm al-ḥisāb*], and is properly labeled *ḥisāb al-hind,* or "calculation according to the Indians.")

Our subject is the Hindu-Arabic system of number representation, especially its symbols (Arabic, *al-ḥurūf al-hindī*), in its origin and diffusion throughout the Middle Ages. It is legitimately called Hindu-Arabic because the invention has definitely been traced to India, while its main agent of diffusion was the Arabic civilization. Three principal characteristics gave it its originality: decimal notation as the basis; use of only nine symbols (there was no zero at first) to represent any quantity; and place value. Each of these features may have existed separately elsewhere and earlier, but never attained the efficacity and the durability of the Hindu system, which for the first time fused the three factors into one coherent and comprehensive system.

Place value proved to be the key, its particular significance in the Hindu invention coming from its exclusive association with the decimal notation. It thus required only nine symbols or figures for the entire system (no particular symbol for the twenties, thirties, . . . hundreds, thousands, and so on, as in older systems of number notation). No zero was included among the nine symbols at the origin, and neither the Indians nor the Arabs needed one for several centuries afterward. This historical fact reveals a state of mathematical conceptions that included only positive quantities. Zero is not a positive quantity, so it did not belong to the system, or at least could not be conceived in the same way as positive quantities and occur alongside the nine symbols. In the early Hindu system of place value, only the absence of any quantity in a given order had to be indicated, and this could be done by any number of devices, including a blank space, or a dot or other indicator placed above or below a symbol to indicate a certain rank (tens, hundreds, and so on); the dot or indicator was sometimes placed on the line itself, along with the other symbols. But in any case such an indicator did not belong to the nine positive quantities. Provided the absence of a quantity from any given order was sufficiently indicated, the system could and did operate without the need for a special symbol for zero. The blank space (*śunya* in Sanskrit; *ṣifr* in Arabic) was always noted.

The historical record shows that for several centuries after its appearance among the Arabs, the Hindu system of number notation did not gain general acceptance, at least among scientists. The overwhelming evidence in surviving ancient Arabic manuscripts, in astronomy and astrology in particular, is proof of this: authors and scribes express quantities by writing them in words—ten, fourteen, one hundred—or by resorting to the *abjad* (letters of the alphabet given numerical value). Furthermore, the arithmeticians proceeded in largely the same way.

The solution to this apparent enigma must be sought in the fact that in ancient times, and until very late in the Middle Ages, practical arithmetical calculations were performed on dust boards. These boards, which contained a layer of fine-grained sand on which arithmetical calculations were made, allowed for plenty of erasures during the operations. As ordinarily required, only the final result had to be neatly transcribed onto parchment or paper. Final transcriptions were more regularly made in traditional number systems: *abjad, zimām* (administration), full words, or any other system, the operations being performed on erasable tablets or boards in any system at all, including the Hindu system when its

ARABIC NUMERALS

diffusion had spread further. This dichotomy in practice—one notation system for permanent records, the other merely functional and ephemeral—may explain why progress in the diffusion of the Hindu-Arabic system among calculators (*ḥussāb:* in the West, abacists) could, and did, go on for a long time without much notice in the permanent documents, and why the traces of progress are so hard to find.

Astronomers and astrologers, who used numbers extensively in their texts and sets of tables, supply confirming evidence of the slow acceptance of the Hindu numerals among the Arabs. None of the ancient copies of their works contain them; rather, numbers are written in words or in the system of the *abjad.* In my research on Arab astronomy and astrology, I have encountered but one ancient manuscript making partial use of the *zimām* (Coptic numerals, used in early Arab administration records) in numbering the pages. In the text itself the numbers are written in words, and the *abjad* is used in the tables. This manuscript, dated 938, is preserved in the Süleymanie Library at Istanbul (MS Garullah Efendi 1508). Another manuscript (Berlin, Sprenger 1829) follows a similar practice, but is from the thirteenth century at the earliest.

MEDIEVAL ARABIC TRADITION

How scanty and unsustained the interest in the Hindu numerals was among early Arabs may be perceived from their treatment in the *Fihrist* of Ibn al-Nadīm (*ca.* 987), the very well-informed and generally reliable record of all the literature of the Arabs to the end of the tenth century. Although a few works on the *ḥisāb al-hind* are recorded, the fundamental *Calculation with the Hindu Numerals* is not even listed among the works of al-Khwārizmī. Furthermore, in his presentation and explanation of the Hindu symbols, which still lack the zero but have subscript dots to indicate rank orders, Ibn al-Nadīm shows a slight acquaintance with the numerals themselves, describing them as letters *(ḥurūf)* and nearly assimilating them with the *abjad* for their representative function. He gives no hint of the particular methods of reckoning they make possible and shows no awareness of their distinct advantage and simplicity.

This relatively meager record among Arab bibliographers could have resulted from the inferior status at which arithmetical operations were held as belonging to the realm of practical *(ᶜamali),* in contrast with theoretical *(naẓari),* mathematics, which indulged in abstract speculation but also favored numerology and magical practices. We are perhaps confronted here with the same problem that the lack of distinction between mathematics and mathesis represented for the medieval West: the common origin was Hellenistic, probably Hermetic speculation. But the early record of Hindu arithmetic is also lean. Yet the record could have been lost for technical reasons. Dust-board calculations were impermanent by their very nature, cumbersome at any rate, and rendered obsolete as soon as the results were duly registered in more permanent form. In addition, as early as the tenth century, mathematicians such as al-Uqlīdīsī and Abūʾl-Wafāʾ proposed to get rid of the more cumbersome methods of erasures involved in the use of tablets or dust boards, apparently signaling a transition from the dust board to ink and paper for arithmetical operations. M. Levey and M. Petruck observe: "There must have been many texts of Kūshyār ibn Labbān's arithmetic at one time, but with the change from use of the dust board to a more permanent form of writing, the technique for algorisms changed, and the earlier texts probably lost much of their usefulness" (Kūshyār ibn Labbān, *Principles of Hindu Reckoning,* p. 5). One may venture to suggest, though, that the vast number of surviving manuscripts in Oriental libraries, the inventory of which has just begun seriously, may still hold many surprises.

The fact remains, however, that among medieval scientists, both Arabs and Latins (they drew on the same Greek sources), mathematical sciences as we understand them did not receive sufficiently concentrated and sustained attention, and thus were not given room for rapid development. Furthermore, abstract speculation frequently succumbed to the attraction of numerology and "magic" use of numerals. In the present state of our information, the number of Arabic (and other Oriental) manuscripts that use the Hindu numerals for divination and for magic far exceeds those that deal seriously with mathematics proper.

Although he spent the last decades of his life in the East, Ibn Khaldūn acquired most of his culture among Western Arabs. Writing in North Africa toward the end of the fourteenth century, he showed himself in his *Muqaddima* to be well acquainted with the flourishing practices of the astrologers and diviners who used different systems of numerals. Among his prefatory discussions in the first chapter he devotes a long passage to the various processes of divination using numbers, among which he lists geo-

ARABIC NUMERALS

mancy *(khaṭṭ al-raml),* another system called *ḥisāb al-nīm*, and finally the *zāʾiraja,* a magical circle drawn on paper and filled with letters and numbers in many of its subdivisions. Ibn Khaldūn explains that the *zāʾiraja* uses three different types of numerals: the Arabic letters *(abjad),* the *ghubār* "letters," and the *zīmam* "letters." There is no mention of the Indian figures, which are replaced by the *ghubārs.* On Ibn Khaldūn's testimony, therefore, we must conclude that the divinatory practices of his time in the Maghrib used the form of the Indian symbols known as *ghubār.* We shall see later that similar divinatory practices in the East were using the Oriental form of the Hindu figures instead of the *ghubār.* Both practices testify to the actual diffusion of these alternative forms of the Hindu ciphers in the Arab world during the Middle Ages, the *ghubār* form being more prevalent in the Maghrib.

Another divinatory practice described by Ibn Khaldūn is *ḥisab al-nīm,* which was an offshoot of astrology. After adding numerical values of the letters of a given name and dividing the result by nine, the remainder was used by casters of lot in this tradition to determine certain outcomes of human actions. Ibn Khaldūn adds characteristically that these rules of the *ḥisāb al-nīm* were transmitted on the authority of "the leading Maghribi scholar in astrology as well as letter magic Abūʾl ʿAbbās ibn al-Bannāʾ (*ca.* 1256–1321)." Ibn al-Bannāʾ is known to have been an important writer on arithmetic who influenced Arab generations after the fourteenth century.

The connection between genuine mathematics and the pseudosciences in those times, at least for the individuals who practiced both, must not be regarded with a mind steeped exclusively in the twentieth-century mathematical categories. The historian's task is not primarily to vindicate or to apologize, but to report accurately and fully, to describe as best he or she can. Moral and spiritual self-righteousness, as well as feelings of cultural superiority, must be banned from evaluations.

Ibn Khaldūn had no such prejudices respecting the Arab civilization of his times. In book III of his *Muqaddima* he describes the magical *zāʾiraja* in the same tone of serenity as he does all other "sciences concerned with numbers." It is instructive to read his descriptions of the "craft of calculation," algebra, and "business arithmetic." On the craft of calculation, which he defines as "the art of 'combining' and 'separating,' " he makes an interesting remark: "This craft is something newly created. It is needed for business calculations. Scholars have written many works on it. They are used in the cities for the instruction of children. . . ." Further on, when describing "business arithmetic," he mentions textbooks on this subject (presumably taught in the schools) composed by Spanish authors—al-Zahrāwī, Ibn al-Samḥ, and Abū Muslim ibn Khaldūn (surely an ancestor)—all of whom were disciples of Maslama al-Majrīṭī (*ca.* 1000), the author of a much-quoted commentary on the *Astronomical Tables* of al-Khwārizmī.

Ibn Khaldūn's descriptions of the Arab arithmetical sciences of his time and his candor, totally free of the modern distinction between genuine sciences and pseudosciences, constitute an invitation to examine the nature and range of use of numeral figures in medieval Arabic manuscripts.

The Istanbul manuscript Aya Sofya 2672, dated in its various sections between 1287 and 1296, contains several works by Kūshyār ibn Labbān (940–1025), one of them purely astrological: *Majmūʿa rasāʾil fī aḥkām al-nujūm* (fols. 1v–36v) in four *magālāt,* the last one being *ikhtiyārāt* (Elections). Another is his *Kitāb al-asṭurlāb* (fols. 37v–64r). There follow some extracts from Abū Maʿshar and Māshāʾallāh. Throughout the codex the numerals employed are of the *abjad* type. Another Istanbul codex, Aya Sofya 4857, is dated 1283 (fol. 283r); this is the manuscript containing the unique copy of Kūshyār ibn Labbān's *Uṣūl ḥisāb al-hind.* It also contains another astrological work by Kūshyār (fols. 195–266), *Kitāb min Uṣūl ṣanāʿat al-aḥkām,* which is divided into four *maqālāt: Mudkhal* and *Uṣūl* (Introduction and Principles); *Ḥukm ʿalā amwār al-ʿālam* (Judgment about world events); *Ḥukm ʿalāʾl-mawālīd wa taḥwīl sinīhā* (Judgment on nativities and the revolution of their years); *ʿaml al-ikhtiyārāt.* As can be seen, this is a genuinely astrological work; but, surprisingly, while the manuscript section that contains Kūshyār's *Hindu Reckoning* (fols. 266ff.) uses the Hindu numerals, the section that contains the same author's astrological works is entirely free of them, although innumerable occasions for their use occur in the course of the works. In the astrological sections the scribe uses the *abjad* (see fols. 257v–258r in particular). We incline to see in this manuscript a standard example of how the astrological tradition among medieval writers remained staunchly attached to older systems of number representation (here the *abjad*), while genuine mathematical works, at a relatively late date, dabble somewhat with the still strange Hindu system. In sheer quantity though, the astrological works far outnumber the mathematical ones.

Two other Istanbul manuscripts of approximately the same epoch, Fatiḥ 3426 and Fatiḥ 3427 (the latter dated 1309 [fol. 112v]; no date could be found in 3426, although in structure and handwriting it is very similar to 3427), show a sporadic use of Hindu numerals in a context dominated by the *abjad.* Fatiḥ 3426 contains the *Kitāb al-mudkhal* (astrology) of Kūshyār ibn Labbān (fols. 1–90) and a work by Abū Maᶜshar (fols. 90–154) on the influence of "the superior celestial individuals" (heavenly bodies) upon the things created. This is not Abū Maᶜshar's *Book of Great Conjunctions,* despite the opening words, which are nearly identical; many paragraphs begin with "Qāla al-Ḥakīm" ("Said the philosopher"), which clearly refers to Abū Maᶜshar. A Paris manuscript (BN Arabe 2588), dated 1212 by William MacGuckin De Slane, contains *Book of the Revolutions of the Years of Nativities* by Abū Maᶜshar with a prologue of which the first three lines are identical with the opening words of Abū Maᶜshar's text in Fatiḥ 3426, fol. 90v, except that Paris has *al-sufliya* instead of the *al-mahluqa* in Fatiḥ. Because of the presence of Kūshyār's astrological work in the early portion of the Fatiḥ manuscript, the text ascribed to Abū Maᶜshar may be Kūshyār's own summary of some work by Abū Maᶜshar. The numerals used in Fatiḥ 3426 are predominantly of the *abjad* type, save for a few Hindu numerals near the end of Abū Maᶜshar's text (fols. 152r–152v, 154v).

Fatiḥ 3427 offers an astrological hodgepodge by a certain al-Ḥasan ibn ᶜAlī al-Qumȳ (presumably of Qum in Iran) al-Muhannī bi Abī Naṣr al-Munajjim, probably transcribed at Baghdad in 1309 by a Christian physician named Abdallah ibn Mawhub (fol. 112v). A few Hindu numerals in Oriental style appear on folio 69r in the discussion of *numudar* (a Persian technical term relating to nativities) "according to Hermes and Baṭalmiūs" (Ptolemy); all other numbers are given in *abjad* form.

But, more interesting still, in the middle of Kūshyār's work (fol. 40v) comes a series of numerals written in the *abjad,* with a correspondence for each term of the series in Hindu numerals, written underneath, that is totally unarithmetical; rather, it is cabalistic. The correspondence is close, though not exactly similar to the *ḥisāb al-nīm* from Ibn Khaldūn's *Muqaddima;* both, however, are akin in astrological purpose. One thing manuscript Fatiḥ 3427 makes clear: the Hindu numerals in their Oriental form were known to some scribes in the East, but they were used preferably in divination practices, while the system of the *abjad* was followed in mathematical contexts.

The example from manuscript Fatiḥ 3427 reveals that the divination with numerals described by Ibn Khaldūn for the Maghrib in the late fourteenth century was thriving in a closely similar form in the eastern Arab world at the beginning of the same century. The particular form in Fatiḥ 3427 reappears in a series of Arabic manuscripts dating from the sixteenth and seventeenth centuries now preserved at the Bibliothèque Nationale in Paris (BN MS Arabe 2582, 2584, 2587, and 2718). In these manuscripts *abjad,* Hindu, and *zimām* numerals are arranged in parallel series with correspondences between them of a nonmathematical order. The discernible pattern is twofold and is labeled *al-jummal aṣ-ṣaghīr* (the little calculus) and *al-jummal al-kabīr* (the great calculus), expressions that were not used in Ibn Khaldūn's description.

In *al-jummal aṣ-ṣaghīr*, also labeled in one instance (MS Arabe 2587, fol. 1r) *bi-ḥisāb al-ᶜarabī* (according to Arab calculus), a first row contains the entire series of numerals of the *abjad* in the proper order of units from one to nine, then the tens, the hundreds, and 1,000, using all twenty-eight letters of the alphabet. Under the *abjad* numerals, in a parallel line, are the Hindu numerals in their Oriental form. But the progression in the second line is not regular, as in the line of the *abjad.* For after reaching 10 in parallel with the *abjad* line, the values in the second line begin to decline through even numbers back to 2, which thus appears under *nun* (50) of the *abjad;* under *sin* (60) is written the word *sāqiṭ* (drop), marking a first interruption. Then the sequence resumes in the second line with 10 in Hindu form under ᶜ*ain* (70), and proceeds in declining order again through even numbers down to 4 and then back to 8, followed by another *sāqiṭ.* At this point the parallelism with the *abjad* line has extended to *shin* (300). For the rest of the *abjad* sequence from 400 to 1,000, the Hindu 4 and 8 are used, first under 400 and 500, respectively, then under 700 and 800, separated by a *sāqiṭ* under 600; another *sāqiṭ* is under 900, then the line closes with a Hindu 4 under *ghain* (1,000). Two of the Paris manuscripts (BN Arabe 2582 and 2584) add to the two parallel lines of this *jummal aṣ-ṣaghīr* a third one containing the *zimām* numerals in a similar matching scheme that is not clear to me.

The second type of arrangement is called *al-jum-*

mal al-kabīr, further labeled *bi-ḥisāb al-hindī* in BN Arabe 2587 (fol. 1r). This time the progression is normal in each line and the correspondence between the *abjad* and the Hindu numerals is perfect. MSS 2582 and 2584 add a third line for the *zimām* numerals, maintaining the exact correspondence with the numerals of the other two lines.

BN Arabe 2582 (fol. 2r) states that the arrangement is of astrological application: "Description of the science [*ma*ᶜ*rifa*] of the great calculus in order to know the ascendant of a human [being] male or female" *(tal*ᶜ*i al-insān d̲ikrān kāna aw unt̲ā).* The same manuscript contains the above-described schemes of number correspondence in two widely separated portions. First, in folio 2r there are the three sets of numerals, including the *zimām*, followed by a passage on astrological letter magic that distributes the letters of the alphabet among the four natural elements: fire, earth, air, and water.

The second appearance of the scheme of corresponding numerals is at folios 77v–79r. It has both *al-jummal al-kabīr* and *al-jummal aṣ-ṣaghīr*, but no *zimām* numerals, and is entitled "Description of the *jummal al-kabīr* that facilitates the 'abundant flow' of the sciences [ᶜ*alā midrār al-*ᶜ*ulūm*]." The passage concludes: "Tamma al-jummal al-kabīr waᵓl-jummal aṣ-ṣaghīr waᵓl-abwāb ᶜiddati." *Adwāb* ᶜ*iddati* (chapters on quantity) introduces a piece on numbers overpowering others, and concludes (fol. 79r): "Tamma ḥisāb aṭ-Ṭālib waᵓl-Maṭlūb wa yuqālu ḥisāb al-taīm" (Here ends the calculus of the Seeker and the One Sought After, and it is called "calculus of the *taīm*"). *Taīm* means the enslaved one, but it may also stand for "a pair" (from the root *taw*ᵓ*ām;* twins). Either interpretation suits the scheme that considers one pair of numbers representing two opponents and tries to determine, on the basis of the numerical values of their names and other circumstances, which one will overpower the other. This is the system described in Ibn Khaldūn in the *Muqaddima* under the label *ḥisāb al-nīm.* Either Rosenthal's reading of *al-nīm* in the manuscripts of the *Muqaddima* should be corrected to *al-taīm*, or the manuscript BN Arabe 2582 should be emended to read *al-nīm*: the Arabic writing of the consonants *ta* and *nun* are very easily confused.

As Ibn Khaldūn had stated, the ultimate authority behind the *ḥisāb al-nīm* (or *al-taīm*) was the well-known North African mathematician Ibn al-Bannāᵓ (thirteenth–fourteenth centuries). MS BN Arabe 2582, dated in the sixteenth century and containing mostly nativities by Abū Maᶜshar, is shown to be of Oriental origin by the form of the Hindu numerals; this is also the case for the other Paris Arabic manuscripts mentioned here. Astrological numerology constituted a vast field for the use of Hindu numerals (or *ghubār* in western Islam) hitherto little noticed, while the purely arithmetical or mathematical works rarely made use of these numerals until relatively recent times.

In addition, in all the above-cited manuscripts from the Bibliothèque Nationale in Paris, the rendering of the Hindu numerals by the scribes is clumsy and inconsistent, especially the placing of the dots (our zeros) indicating rank among the units, tens, hundreds, and thousands. In BN Arabe 2582 the dots are placed either in a row on the line and to the right of the symbol or slightly above the line; the three dots for 1,000 are placed in a triangle to the right. In BN Arabe 2584 the dots are placed either to the right and in a vertical row when there is more than one (1. = 10; 1: = 100, 1⁝ = 1,000) or within the body of the figure under the superior arm for 2, 3, and 4 (٢. = 20; ٢: = 200; ٣. = 30; ٣: = 300; ٤. = 40; ٤: = 400), on the right at the bottom or top for 5 (٥. = 50; ٥: = 500), distributed on both sides of the figure for 6 (.٦ = 60; ٦. = 600; .٦: = 6,000), above for 7 (٧̇ = 70; ٧̈ = 700), and under the figure for 8 (٨̣ = 80; ٨̤ = 800). It is obvious that the scribes, even at this late date, were not familiar with the Hindu system of number representation and place value, although it was originally conceived as a simplified system to help in arithmetical calculations.

GHUBĀR (TOLEDAN) NUMERALS

Ghubār ("dust" in Arabic) is the historical term under which the nine Hindu figures were most frequently designated among the western Arabs at least from the eleventh century on. Solomon Gandz claims that the oldest such appellation is found in the writings of Judah of Barcelona (*ca.* 1100). But D. E. Smith and L. C. Karpinski (p. 65) cite an anonymous Tunisian author of about 950 who speaks of his "gobar calculations." Similarly, in their translation of *Kūshyār ibn Labbān,* Martin Levey and Marvin Petruck write (p. 6) that the expression *ḥisāb al-ghubār* occurs in the *Sefer Yezirah* of Abū Sahl ibn Tamīm (*d.* 950), but they appear to have culled their information from J. T. Reinaud's *Mémoire sur l'Inde* (1849). At any rate, the advent in Europe of the new

ARABIC NUMERALS

algorisms during the twelfth century caused the term *algorismus* to be substituted. The Hindu figures in the West were called *ghubār* because of their direct link with the dust board (Latin, *abacus*), which was in general use for reckoning.

Much has been written on the *ghubār* figures since their modern rediscovery by Silvestre de Sacy (*Grammaire arabe,* 1810), but with little regard for solid historical evidence. We shall limit ourselves here to the highlights of evidence available thus far, and incidentally to refuting some of the errors that still have currency. We shall do this by offering and demonstrating four main propositions that appear to sum up the principal evidence and to answer most problems.

Proposition 1: The appellation *ghubār* is applicable to the nine Hindu figures only in the form current among western Arabs. The methods of calculation for which they were developed belong to the *ḥisāb al-hind* (Indian reckoning) and are not particular to the *ghubār.*

Proposition 2: Although ultimately of Indian origin, the *ghubār* figures must be historically linked with the spreading of al-Khwārizmī's *Calculation with the Hindu Numerals* (*ca.* 825).

Proposition 3: The *ghubār* figures in their definitive shape could have developed only in Spain.

Proposition 4: The *ghubār* figures cannot be earlier than the ninth century.

PROPOSITION ONE

To demonstrate the first proposition, one must begin by comparing the Oriental and the *ghubār* figures.

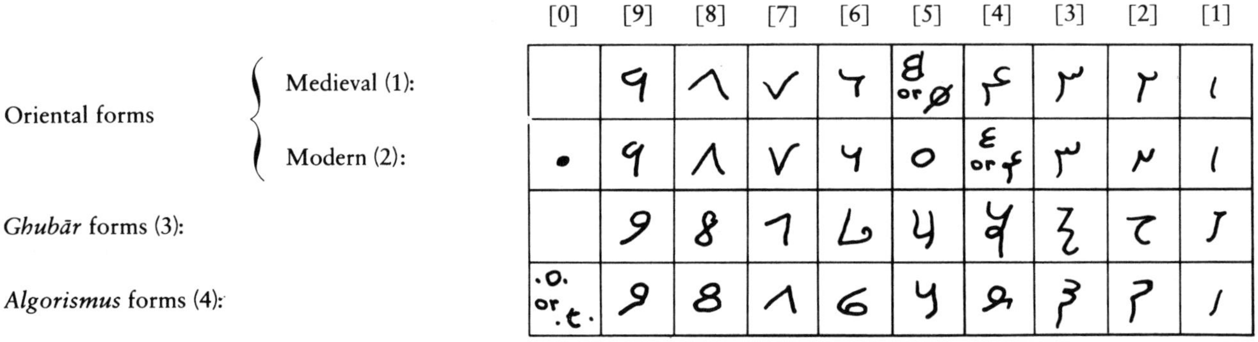

(1) Kūshyār ibn Labbān, *Principles of Hindu Reckoning,* p. 47, facsimile, second line of the text.

(2) From D. E. Smith, *History of Mathematics* II, 70. We have added ۴ for 4 because it is still frequently encountered, although the ٤ form predominates in general use and in printing.

(3) From the manuscript of the monastery of Albelda (976). Compare Zacarias García Villada, *Paleografía española,* 97, n. 23; 186, n. 51. I have drawn my figures from their reproduction in D. E. Smith, *History of Mathematics* II, 75. Smith (II, 74) offers several other examples of alleged *ghubār* forms, but two series in this table (example 3 in the third line and example 4 in the fifth line) are obviously not of the *ghubār,* but of the Oriental type: the revealing test is found in the figures for 5, 7, and 8, which are there Oriental, not *ghubār.* It will be noticed in our table that the *ghubār,* in its earliest form (976 in Spain), had no separate symbol for zero. Silvestre de Sacy's specimens of *ghubār* (*Grammaire arabe,* pl. VIII) have dots above or to the right of the figure to indicate place value.

(4) From John of Seville's *Liber Alghoarismi* (twelfth century), combined with a specimen of *ghubār* in a Munich manuscript (CLM 18927). See Richard Lemay, "The Hispanic Origin of our Present Numeral Forms," figs. la, 5. In presenting the symbols John includes only nine of them, without a zero, although he uses a circle, so named by him, to indicate a vacant place ("preposito circulo in primo loco versus dextram scriptoris ut per hoc prima differentia vacua esse ostendatur"). Other twelfth-century algorisms are more explicit in presenting a double form for zero: "O vel .t. sunt cifre."

It is clear that *ghubār* and *algorismus* are morphologically identical, taking into consideration paleographical evolution, which in some instances was also influenced by "rotation of the apices." Apices were separate and movable counters on which the *ghubār* were inscribed for use in the columns of the the Latin abacus; the effect of rotation is clear in the case of 2, 3, and 4 in Gerbert's apices. Paleographical evolution is sensible in the early forms of the 2 and 3, written 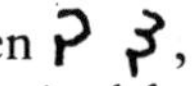, before it was realized that the long tails inherited from the Oriental 2 and 3 (٢ ٣) were no longer essential for identifying the symbols in the context of a Latin script. Also, a symbol for zero was absent in the early *ghubār,* a situation still reflected in John of Seville's presentation of the "nine sym-

ARABIC NUMERALS

bols," although John uses a zero that he calls a circle in the rest of his text. From the widespread use of *ghubārs* in astronomical tables inspired by the Arabic science coming from Spain during the twelfth century, one can easily see how *.o.* and *.t.* came to be presented as alternative symbols for zero, as stated in twelfth-century *algorismus.* This entire and unique tradition can be traced to the diffusion of the *ghubār* from the West.

By comparison, the *ghubār* and algorism of the West show significant differences from the Oriental Arabic forms of the Hindu numerals. This is abundantly clear for the 5 and 6, which in the *ghubār* were mere transfers of the Roman V and VI of the archaic Visigothic script (V [5] written ; VI [6] a ligature 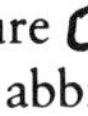 that easily resembled a capital G) or for 8, an abbreviation of Latin *octo,* written with a single *o* and another *o* superscript. These symbols 5, 6, and 8 in the *ghubār* have no morphological relation whatsoever to the Oriental 5, 6, and 8. Only the *ghubār-algorismus* 7 has a direct ancestor in the Oriental Λ [8], which, after the introduction of a Roman *octo* into the *ghubār* symbols, could be shifted to the place of the 7: all early forms of the *ghubār* 7 shows that they are some modification in position of the one symbol, used upright (V) for the 7, or upside down (Λ) for the 8 in the Oriental form of Hindu numerals. The *ghubār* forms, in their *algorismus* evolution and with the zero added, were to become the modern Arabic numerals after further slight variations due to manuscript transmission before the spread of printing in the fifteenth century. After that they became practically fixed in their present form.

Once the *ghubār* forms were absorbed into the twelfth-century Latin algorisms, both their tradition and their appellation in Europe and in the Maghrib began to diverge. The expression *ghubār* remained attached to these figures among the western Arabs, while the designation *algorismus* prevailed among Latin Europeans, obviously because they had been introduced to the Hindu system with the nine symbols through the translations of the work of al-Khwārizmī. They evolved slightly differently during the remainder of the Middle Ages, but not enough to obliterate their single origin in the West. A trace of this relationship between *maghrebī ghubār* and Latin *algorismus* can still be perceived in the title *Introductorius Liber qui et pulveris dicitur in mathematicam disciplinam* given to a fourteenth-century remake of John of Seville's *Liber alghoarismi de pra[c]tica arismet[r]ice* (twelfth century). It was de Sacy's wondering at the resemblance of the *ghubār* figures to modern Arabic numerals, together with their shared striking difference from the Oriental Arabic forms, that led him, without further proof, to the assumption that the Arabic and *ghubār* numerals represented two different systems, both of which were presumed to have originated, independently from one another, in India.

Apparently in the wake of de Sacy's hypothesis, Franz Woepcke made great efforts to establish a separate tradition for the transmission of the *ghubār* from India to Spain independently of, and prior to the arrival of, the Arabs in Spain. Following Woepcke, and later Nicholas Bubnov, Solomon Gandz sought to link the *ghubārs* directly to the tradition of the Roman abacus, of which the Arabs of Spain would be the continuators.

All these efforts would have been unnecessary if sufficient attention had been given to the denominations *ghubār* and "Indian figures" as used by Arab authors, and to the context in which the terms were used. The figures in the *ghubār* were always designated by the expression *ḥurūf al-ghubār* in the Maghrib, where they were principally diffused. The Hindu figures in the rest of the Islamic world were called *al-ḥurūf al-hindī.* In both cases the term *ḥurūf* referred to the symbols exclusively, and not to the methods of calculation associated with them, as the example of Ibn al-Nadīm further confirms. The facts that there were just nine *ḥurūf,* that they indicated quantity by place value, using a dot in several ways to indicate that place when otherwise some places were vacant, and that in every instance—except for numerology and magic (this development came much later)—they appear in the context of the Indian methods of reckoning (the *ḥisāb al-hind*) originally presented by al-Khwārizmī all leave no doubt that the *ghubār,* like the Oriental forms of Hindu numerals, originated in the diffusion of the Hindu system of reckoning to the Arab world, principally through the agency of al-Khwārizmī. Until now no evidence has been found that the evolution to the Arab on the one hand, and to the *ghubār* forms on the other, of the nine symbols is not contemporary with that diffusion. The difference was geographical region, in consequence of which cultural variety produced different experiences within a single broad stream. In point of historical fact, the appellation *ḥurūf al-ghubār* appeared later than the appellation *ḥurūf al-hindī.* The scribe of the oldest dated *ghubārs* (Albeldense codex of 976) expressly notes their Indian source, but does not call them *ghubār.* On the other hand, although there may have

 ARABIC NUMERALS

been a few early treatises on Indian arithmetic (tenth century) that occasionally mentioned the *ḥisāb al-ghubār,* the works on that subject listed in the *Fihrist* of Ibn al-Nadīm all carry the expression *ḥisāb al-hind* in some form in the title (even those employing the *ghubār* numerals). As late as the fourteenth century, when describing the *ghubār* used in numerology, Ibn Khaldūn clearly hints that he means solely their design: "*bi rushūm* (or *bi-rashm*) *al-ghubār al-muta*^{c}*ārafat*" (in the design of the ordinary *ghubār* figures).

But why should the *ghubār* figures be so labeled in Spain and not in the rest of the Arab world, where the dust board was also in general use? Guy Beaujouan explained (1948) how the "rotation of the apices" accounted for the seemingly distorted shape of the Hindu numerals in Gerbert's school and among the abacists of the eleventh century. If one examines the shapes of the *ghubār* numerals in the Albeldense codex, one will notice that some of the figures have suffered deformation by rotation. This is obvious for the 2 and 3, which must be turned counterclockwise ninety degrees to restore the pure Arabic 2 and 3. Similarly, the 4 can be likened to the Arabic 4 (٤) if rotated clockwise ninety degrees. Probably the 7 should also be considered in the same way: it is the Arabic 7 (٧) turned clockwise 180 degrees or so. Four instances out of nine possibilities is a rather high proportion.

Considering the general phenomenon described by Beaujouan, which was historically linked to the use of an abacus with movable counters called apices (in contradistinction to an abacus in the sense of dust board), one is led to conclude that Vigila, the scribe of the Albeldense codex, knew his *ghubār*s through their use on an abacus with movable counters, like those used in Christian Europe at the time of Gerbert. Like their brethren elsewhere in Europe, the Christians in northern Spain used an abacus with movable counters, while the Arabs of medieval Spain remained faithful to the abacus in the sense of dust board, and hence used the term *ghubār* (dust) to designate the Indian numerals that they were using in their perishable arithmetic operations on the dust board. In Andalusia this practice must have involved the work of merchants, but also qadis, secretaries, *muḥtasib,* surveyors, and others.

The Muslim cities of Andalusia, stretching as far as Saragossa and Huesca, were thriving centers of commerce and learning, involving a mixed population of Christians, Jews, Arabs, Berbers, Saqalibi, and Africans. These bustling centers, thriving under the relatively stable protection afforded by the emirs, then caliphs, of Córdoba until the middle of the eleventh century, provided an atmosphere conducive to rapid advance in all fields of endeavor. Since the markets, city administration, and schools in Arab Spain formed a complex eminently favorable for practical arithmetical operations, and since these operations normally were performed on an abacus of the dust-board type, the nine symbols developed at home from the methods of Hindu arithmetic came to be designated by the term *ghubār,* recalling the name of the abacus on which they were performed, and which in medieval Andalusia took an orientation different from that of the rest of the Arab world at that time.

From Andalusia, where they had already undergone the influence of a mixed Romano-Arab tradition, the new *ghubār* symbols made their way to the monasteries of northern Spain, where they were used on the movable counters of an abacus with columns, in the way the monk Vigila preserved them in the Albeldense codex, and where Gerbert discovered them in the late tenth century. Our explanation of the diffusion of the *ghubār*s to northern Spain renders improbable the hypothesis that the monks of Ripoll near Barcelona, or of San Millán de la Cogolla in Castile, where Vigila wrote his manuscript, would have derived their knowledge of the *ghubār* numerals through mercantile sources rather than from the dust-board practice of Andalusia.

PROPOSITION TWO

The *ghubār* figures must be linked historically to the arrival in Spain of al-Khwārizmī's *Calculation with the Hindu Numerals.* Two arguments that supplement each other will be followed here. The first is the historical reality of the enormous popularity of al-Khwārizmī's book in twelfth-century Spain. In the interval of a few decades in the early twelfth century, four or five translations or adaptations were produced in Latin (as were Hebrew adaptations) to satisfy the avid demand in the Latin world, which had recently discovered the wealth of Arabic scientific literature available in Spain. Among the books on Indian arithmetic in Arabic, only al-Khwārizmī's received attention, with the ultimate result that these various Latin adaptations and translations preserved his text, which is not known to have survived in Arabic. Unless contrary evidence is found some day, it must be assumed in the present condition of our knowledge that Leonardo Fibonacci's acquaintance with the *Algebra* of Abū Kāmil (early tenth century)

ARABIC NUMERALS

and its possible use of Hindu methods must have come to him not through a Latin translation of Abū Kāmil's work, of which there is absolutely no trace, but through Leonardo's familiarity and personal contacts with the Arab world.

Furthermore, in light of Ibn Khaldūn's testimony that practical, business arithmetic of the Indian type was taught in the schools of Spain, and that several Spanish authors had composed textbooks for that purpose since the time of al-Majrīṭī (*ca.* 1000)—who also adapted the *Astronomical Tables* of al-Khwārizmī to the meridian of Spain—there would appear to exist compelling motives to credit Andalusian scholars for their admission of al-Khwārizmī's authority in the field of mathematical, astronomical, and geographical sciences; his *Astronomical Tables* apparently were more highly regarded than his arithmetic; some sections of his *Geography* were known to Spanish scholars; his *Algebra* was twice translated into Latin during the twelfth century. This testimony to the wide popularity of al-Khwārizmī's works in Spain, together with the unquestioned presence of the *ghubār* form of numerals in the twelfth-century Latin translation of his work on Indian arithmetic, establishes a strong link between al-Khwārizmī's *Calculation with the Hindu Numerals* and the appearance of the *ghubār* numerals in the West.

Our second argument will be taken from the opposite end of the time scale: al-Khwārizmī's work is dated approximately to 825. Prior to that date there has been discovered absolutely no trace of the *ghubār* numerals in Spain, nor anywhere else in the Arab world. Not a shred of evidence of any kind has yet been found that the *ghubār* existed in Spain before the appearance of al-Khwārizmī's works, let alone before the arrival of the Arabs in Spain, as was sometimes claimed. We shall have the opportunity to explain how this had to be so while demonstrating proposition 4.

PROPOSITION THREE

The *ghubār* figures could have developed only in Spain. Unless proposition 2 is proved false, the conditions leading to the development of the *ghubār* clearly imply a link with al-Khwārizmī's book on Indian arithmetic and its diffusion through the medieval learned communities. Mere opportunity for travel, without actual evidence of its role in diffusion, will not constitute a decisive argument, nor will geographical proximity or even indentity of intellectual interests. An illustration of this more delicate argument may be derived from the embassy to Baghdad conducted for the Byzantine emperor Michael III by Photius in 855 (Photius was made patriarch of Constantinople in 858). Photius was surely one ot the most learned men of his time, as his *Bibliotheca* demonstrates (René Henry, ed. [1959]). His prolonged stay in Baghdad on the occasion of his embassy offered an opportunity to meet the main scientific personalities of that city, or to learn of their reputations and their works, especially since at that time the most famous Arab scientists were assembled in the Bayt al-Ḥikma (House of Wisdom) created by al-Ma$^{\supset}$mūn. Even though under al-Mutawakkil (caliph from 847 to 861) the Bayt al-Ḥikma may have been reduced in its activity, this period in Baghdad witnessed the height of scientific endeavor in Islam. Al-Khwārizmī and Sind ibn $^{\subset}$Alī, the first known commentator on al-Khwārizmī's arithmetic, may have died shortly before the arrival of Photius, but their reputations and accomplishments in science still dominated the intellectual life in Baghdad. Yet the Hindu-Arabic numerals and the methods of Indian reckoning remained unknown in Byzantium until an anonymous work on Indian arithmetic (1252) that influenced Maximus Planudes, who is generally credited with the introduction of Indian reckoning and the use of Indian numerals into Byzantium. This was amply demonstrated by André Allard in his *Le grand calcul selon les Indiens de Maxime Planude* (1972).

The fact that the Byzantine Empire and the Islamic world shared an extended frontier provided numerous opportunities for trade and eventually for cultural exchanges. Travels by learned men from Baghdad to the Byzantine lands and to Constantinople were frequent. Ḥunayn ibn Isḥāq, the famous translator of Greek scientific works into Arabic, was sent to Byzantium to procure Greek scientific codices, as stated by Ibn al-Nadīm in his *Fihrist,* Bayard Dodge, trans., II (1970).

Perhaps the most revealing instance of opportunities missed by Arabs and Byzantines alike is revealed by the story concerning Leo the Mathematician, told by Louis Bréhier in *La civilisation byzantine* ([1950], 465–467). A brilliant philosopher and mathematician versed in all the sciences, Leo became known to the caliph al-Ma$^{\supset}$mūn through one of his former students, who had been captured in a skirmish with the Arabs. Al-Ma$^{\supset}$mūn invited Leo to teach in Baghdad. The caliph's letter was shown to Emperor Theophilos, who thus discovered his brilliant mathematician and offered him a position in

ARABIC NUMERALS

Constantinople. The emperor's answer to the caliph was that "it was not customary among the 'Greeks' to trade in philosophers." After inevitable troubles due to his iconoclastic opinions, Leo was finally appointed director of the "Philosophical School" founded at Constantinople by Caesar Bardas about 855. Chairs in geometry, astronomy, and grammar were subsequently created for Leo's disciples.

The channels of communication, therefore, both material and intellectual, were open between Byzantium and Baghdad in the time of al-Khwārizmī and long after him. During the era of Photius and of Leo the Mathematician, however, Byzantine learned men experienced severe attacks by the monastic establishment upon secular sciences, but the restoration under Bardas and the presence of Leo should have engendered an exceptionally favorable atmosphere for scientific exchanges. Yet the history of the intellectual relations between Byzantium and Islam during the early period of the diffusion of the Hindu arithmetic among the Arabs shows a trend operating in only one direction: from Byzantium to Baghdad. The Arabs were "pillaging" Greek scientific tradition, while the Byzantines remained attached to ancient Greek tradition in learning, and to monastic ideals in social and religious matters.

So the Byzantine culture remained unaffected for more than four centuries by the diffusion of the Indian system of reckoning among their Arab neighbors after its introduction by al-Khwārizmī. This situation provides an irrefutable argument against the hypothesis that the Indian numerals had penetrated the Roman Empire through Alexandria about 450, and from there had spread throughout the Mediterranean basin. If indeed the Hindu numerals had been known that early in Alexandria, it is inconceivable that Constantinople, whose intellectual dependence on Alexandrian learning in the fifth through seventh centuries is a matter of record, would not have become familiar with the Indian numerals before Maximus Planudes in the thirteenth century. Meanwhile, Baghdad, whose dependence on Alexandrian scholarship until the ninth century is also a matter of record, was made acquainted with the Indian numerals and reckoning not through Alexandria, but probably after the arrival of a learned Indian (Kankah?) at the court of Caliph al-Manṣūr (*ca.* 773), and surely through the work of al-Khwārizmī (825).

We must therefore conclude that travel alone, or intellectual exchanges such as there could have been between Byzantium and its Arab neighbors, were not conducive to an early diffusion of the Indian arithmetic in general, nor of al-Khwārizmī's work in particular, to the Byzantine Empire. On the other hand, al-Khwārizmī's work was central in the transmission of Indian arithmetic to the Islamic lands as far as the Maghrib and Spain, whence it was carried by the same vehicle to Latin Europe in the twelfth century, and from Europe to Byzantium in the following century.

The historical outline makes Arab Spain, with its mixed culture, the focal point of the diffusion east and north of a modified form of the Indian numerals, the *ghubār,* and, most important, of the methods of calculation that were associated with them. The *ghubār* forms in which the Indian numerals spread to Europe and Byzantium carry an unmistakable trace of Latin influence, especially in the figures for 5, 6, 8, and 0, which they had already acquired in the mixed culture of Spain. Moreover, some distinctly Visigothic characteristics of a paleographic nature that are traceable in the evolution of the forms of the *ghubār* make the Spanish location of their origin inescapable, and further explain their limited diffusion among the Arabs of the Maghrib nearly exclusively. Neither Egypt and Alexandria, nor the various regions of North African Islam offered such conditions as Spain did for the development of the *ghubār.* Arab Sicily would hardly qualify either: the Arab presence there came late; it was long a shaky one; and the level of cultural exchanges between Aghlabid conquerors and the native Latins or Greeks did not reach the intensity and durability experienced in Spain. As seems to have been the case for the influence of Arab medicine upon neighboring Salerno, the Sicilian cultural mix began to work effectively as a focus of scientific transmission only after the Norman conquest in the late eleventh century.

PROPOSITION FOUR

The traces of the Visigothic script and abbreviation system recognizable in the development of some of the *ghubār* numerals, together with the close association between the developing *ghubār* and the diffusion of al-Khwārizmī's mathematical and astronomical works in medieval Spain, force the conviction that the *ghubār* numerals cannot have appeared before the ninth century.

On the one hand, the *ghubār* figures for 2, 3, 4, and 9, being direct borrowings from the "Arabic" figures of al-Khwārizmī, with but slight paleographical modifications required to suit a Western scribe's hand, are demonstrably the continuation of the

ARABIC NUMERALS

Hindu figures introduced by al-Khwārizmī, and consequently cannot have appeared earlier, even in Spain. Otto Neugebauer's statement in *The Exact Sciences in Antiquity* (2nd ed. [1969], p. 5) that "Our present number symbols for 2 and 3 originated from = and ≡ by connecting lines in cursive writing" has no paleographical support that I know of, but on the contrary stands against all the paleographical evidence that these symbols came from the Arabic 2 and 3.

On the other hand, the *ghubār* symbols for 5, 6, and 8 (, G, and 8, respectively) are shown paleographically to be the survival of the older Visigothic script for V (5), VI in ligature (6), and *octo* abbreviated by the contraction . While Visogothic forms V and VI existed somewhat earlier than the ninth century, their preservation as symbols for the Roman 5 and 6 is of more than antiquarian interest after they were used in place of "Arabic" 5 and 6 in the *ghubār* system. As for the 8 being an abbreviation of the Latin word *octo,* such methods of abbreviation did not occur in European handwritings before the Carolingian renaissance.

Before the advent of the Arabs in Spain, these Visigothic symbols for some simple numbers belonged to the Roman system of numerals, never associated with a series of only nine symbols or with place value. Another number symbol for 40, and its extension to 90, appeared in Visigothic script, possibly before the arrival of al-Khwārizmī's work. The Roman XL (40) was written in ligature thus: 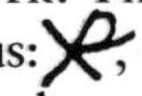, a combination of X and 2 (L). (Numerous examples are in García Villada, *Paleografía espanola;* and in Joaquim M. de Navascuès, *La Era " . . . AS"* [1951], lamina II, 11, "Epitafio de Marcella.") Combined with L (50), the same symbol could be used in the Roman figure for 90 (XC) and written thus: 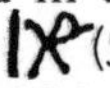(50) + 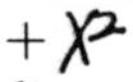(40) = 90. The symbol 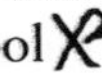(40) thus could help dispose of two cumbersome subtractive numbers of the Roman system. But at no time before the knowledge of al-Khwārizmī's work are these Visigothic symbols used with place value, which is an essential feature of the Indian system. In addition, a special symbol for 40, or 90, is indication enough that the system of nine symbols only, another essential feature of the Indian system, was unknown.

Excellent Roman paleographer though he was, Jean Mallon failed to grasp these indispensable features of the Hindu-Arabic system when he claimed that "our system of numerals, which we find in use in Spain as in the rest of the Latin world in the sixth century, is a survival of a Latin script that had become obsolete for a long time" ("Pour une nouvelle critique . . . ," p. 25). Mallon produced several specimens from this "obsolete" script preserved as number symbols: (VI) for 6, as in 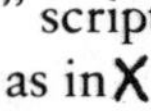(XVII); 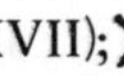(XL) for 40; and so on. But without the essential features of nine symbols and place-value characteristic of the Hindu system, these isolated Visigothic symbols are but a refinement in the Roman system of numerals, and do not imply any knowledge of the Hindu symbols, let alone the Indian method of calculations with the nine symbols.

Latin paleographers have concentrated almost exclusively on literary texts. There is no serious, systematic study available of the scientific manuscripts, particularly those in astronomy and astrology, which are full of examples of the use of numbers in medieval times. Such manuscripts dated prior to the twelfth century are relatively rare in Europe, perhaps a little more abundant in Spain. The early European scientific manuscripts depend exclusively on the Roman system of numerals. But under the kings of Ta⊃ifas in the eleventh century, The Iberian Peninsula rapidly acquired numerous scientific writings, particularly in astronomy and astrology, that were discovered by Latin scholars—various Englishmen and Italians, Hermann of Carinthia and Rudolph of Bruges—who were the vanguard of a movement in Europe that avidly sought the "sciences of the Arabs." In Spain they encountered Arabs, Jews, and Christians who willingly joined in an increasingly large movement of transfer. A host of scientific manuscripts, containing treatises in translations, astronomical and mathematical tables, and original works based on such translations and tables were produced and later diffused in the rest of Europe, which involved a sudden growth in the use of numerals.

In this new crop of manuscripts are found the most telling testimonies of the rapid evolution of numeral symbols. There was an initial period during which the Roman system of numerals was still adhered to. But the avalanche of numbers pouring into these scientific texts, especially the astronomical tables, soon led to the realization that the Roman system was rather cumbersome. We then observe some specific improvements brought into its number symbols: suppression of all subtractive forms, either by use of ancient Visigothic symbols, such as  in the forties and nineties, or of the acrophonic principle with the initial letter standing for the units from three to nine (*t* = 3; *q* = 4; *Q* = 5; *s* = 6; *S* = 7; *o* = 8; *n* or *no* = 9), thus permitting the elimination

ARABIC NUMERALS

of repeated strokes for III, IIII, VII, VIII, VIIII; and finally expression of a void in astronomical number sequences (zodiacal signs, degrees, minutes, seconds, and so on) by a .t., which was occasionally transferred as zero in the *ghubār* (but soon was eliminated in favor of the circle).

The overwhelming impression created by this extensive deployment of numbers in twelfth-century manuscripts is one of determined adherence at first to the old Roman system (after all, the intended Latin audiences had to be able to decipher all these tables of numbers), then a rapid yielding to an inclination to modify it drastically. Based on the handling of a large (but by no means exhaustive) number of such manuscripts, it can be concluded that manuscripts originating directly in Spain—and many copied directly from them in other European regions—indulge less in this modification of the Roman system and often favor the discrete introduction of *ghubār* numerals. For in Spain the *ghubār* were by then relatively well known, less so in Latin Europe; and the scientific manuscripts, even those originating in Spain, being destined for Latin use at large, thus remained faithful to the Roman system of numbers. Conversely, the modifications brought into the Roman system as described above appear mostly in manuscripts produced elsewhere in Europe (France, Italy, England, Germany).

Meanwhile, in Spain scientists of all cultural backgrounds, sharing in the renewed activity of the eleventh and twelfth centuries, when applying themselves to mathematical subjects undoubtedly performed many of their arithmetical operations on the abacus or dust board, independently of the final transcriptions on parchment. It must have been in such a context that several symbols inherited from the old Visigothic script for Roman numerals were substituted for the few potentially confusing Hindu symbols of al-Khwārizmī: ٦ (6), which could easily be taken as the Tironian note for *et;* the ٧ (7), easily confused with the Roman V (5); or even ٨ (8), which if turned slightly clockwise, could look like a capital *A* without a middle stroke. The Arabic script that required joining most letters (as in our cursive hands) was relatively immune from these potential confusions, but in the Latin script the Khwarizmian symbols listed above were definite handicaps.

Thus, when the first Latin versions of al-Khwārizmī's *Calculation with the Hindu Numerals* appeared before the middle of the twelfth century, their lists of nine symbols uniformly contained for 5 and 6 the Roman numerals V and VI stylized from ancient Visigothic script, together with the 8 *(octo)* abbreviated by contraction. These three symbols of Hispanic origin joined the Khwarizmian symbols—9 unaltered; 2, 3, and 4 slightly modified by the ductus of a Latin hand; and the slightly rotated 7—to produce the list of *ghubār* numerals. When the .t., standing for *terminus* (or the equivalent of zero in the cyclical values of the astronomical tables), was added to the series of nine symbols, the *ghubār* system, save for the circle, which soon replaced the .t. for zero, henceforward remained unaltered and spread to Europe and North Africa.

The presence of a zero in the *ghubār* was a clear outcome of the use of the system in astronomical tables: When a circle like the zodiac (twelve signs) was traversed from beginning to end, or the progression of degrees, minutes, seconds, and so on reached the limit of the category (thirty degrees for a sign of the zodiac, a total of sixty minutes in a degree, sixty seconds in a minute, and so on), and before the next series started, the exact value in the tables was null, and so was indicated by .t. In many twelfth-century astronomical tables where this value had to be indicated, the circle was avoided because it often stood already for 8 *(octo)* in the acrophonic system described above. Therefore the presence of a .t. for zero in the *ghubār* reflects the scientific activity of the eleventh and twelfth centuries, and is not likely to have existed earlier. Similarly, the presence in the *ghubār* of the form 8, which is a late abbreviation by contraction, dates the appearance of the *ghubār* not earlier than the ninth century.

Outside Spain, although in close dependence on its production of scientific manuscripts, scribes seem to have advanced much further in their attempts at "salvaging" the Roman system of numerals, the only one with which they were at first familiar. There is, for example, virtually no trace of the diffusion of the apices of Gerbert to astronomical or astrological manuscripts. But the improved Roman system observed in Spain found a larger scope in astronomical manuscripts—as evidenced, for instance, in two particularly important manuscripts, probably of French origin, preserved at the Bibliothèque Nationale in Paris (BN lat. 14704 and BN lat. 16208, both of the twelfth century). The numerous astronomical tables in these manuscripts are replete with Roman numerals of the improved type, while the texts accompanying them use the regular Roman system. Yet BN lat. 16208, being later than the middle of the twelfth century, was written some time after the appearance of the Latin versions of al-Khwārizmī's *Calculation*

ARABIC NUMERALS

with the Hindu Numerals (I do not believe that the *Liber ysagogarum alchorismi ... a magistro A. compositus* is by Adelard of Bath). It appears likely that al-Khwārizmī's work on the arithmetic of the Indians was overshadowed, in Spain and abroad, by his *Astronomical Tables* (drawn from the *Sindhind*), which were adapted in Spain to a Western meridian, commented upon, translated into Hebrew and Latin, and widely diffused in the twelfth century. His *Algebra* also attracted much attention, and Paris MS BN lat. 14704 (containing, among others, the *Tables* of Raymond of Marseille) contains a bit on longitudes and latitudes of many cities that claims to be drawn from al-Khwārizmī's adaptation of Ptolemy's *Geography.*

A fact is clear: despite the knowledge of al-Khwārizmī's *Calculation with the Hindu Numerals* among Latin authors and scribes from shortly before the middle of the twelfth century, scribes of scientific manuscripts in Latin Europe continued depending upon and refining on the Roman system of numerals. Some late-twelfth-century manuscripts show an inclination to transfer to the *ghubār* system, but only hesitatingly and in a manner of suggestion: numerical values included in Roman numerals in the text are sometimes represented in margins with their equivalent in *ghubār* numerals. And throughout the thirteenth century, astronomical texts continue to use the Roman numerals, at least in their text if not always in the tables that accompany them.

There were probably psychological motives for this. The potential for confusion when using the acrophonic principle in the improved Roman numerals was constant: these letters standing for the numbers ($t = 3$; $q = 4$; $o = 8$; n or $no = 9$) in a running text could always be taken in their literal, rather than numerical, meaning. Hence the textual part of astronomical works remained bound to the strictly traditional Roman numerals, while the astronomical tables tended to indulge in a seemingly uncontrollable scramble to simplify the cumbersome Roman numerals. But, significantly, only rare attempts were made during the twelfth century to introduce the full *ghubār* system into scientific manuscripts, except of course when the subject was the *algorismus,* and during the twelfth century such treatises among Latins were few and far between.

MEDIEVAL EUROPE

Once the term *ghubār* and the objects it signifies are placed in their proper historical context, most of the controversies that have plagued the question of its origins disappear. Such controversies arose from insufficient familiarity with scientific currents in the early medieval centuries and from a weak regard, sometimes a total disregard, for paleographic evidence. After eliminating the traces of these controversies, the general historical account offered by D. E. Smith and L. C. Karpinski, *The Hindu-Arabic Numerals* (1911), stands nearly unaltered. In particular, the major stages of the history of the penetration and diffusion of the numerals in Europe have been very adequately outlined in their work. We may be allowed, however, a brief recapitulation with a view to proposing a different emphasis respecting the end of the medieval period.

First, the Hindu-Arabic numerals were developed in their *ghubār* form in Spain during the tenth century, perhaps the ninth century at the earliest. There is absolutely no trace of them as an independent system before that time, except in some instances of Roman numerals that were later absorbed into the *ghubār,* which is itself directly connected with the diffusion of al-Khwārizmī's *Calculation with the Hindu Numerals.*

Second, the nine numerals in their *ghubār* form were communicated to Europe in a first stage (as the apices) by Gerbert about 980, but Gerbert remained totally ignorant of the Hindu methods of reckoning. Used in the Roman abacus by Gerbert and his disciples, the *ghubār* numerals—despite distortion of their shape through exaggeration in their design and through the effect of "rotation"—introduced a semantic shift into the meaning of the abacus tradition. Called apices because they were inscribed on movable counters, the new numerals were at last likened to the abacus itself. Thus Leonardo Fibonacci gave the title *Liber abaci* to his famous book (1202), although in that book he rejected the methods of the abacus in favor of the Indian methods of reckoning.

Third, a number of Latin translations and adaptations of al-Khwārizmī's *Calculation with Hindu Numerals,* done in Spain during the twelfth century and soon diffused throughout Latin Europe, introduced the Hindu methods of reckoning, together with the nine *ghubār* numerals, and added a zero represented by either 0 or .t. The new numerals and the methods of using them in calculation were hence called *algorismus,* from the warped name of al-Khwārizmī in these Latin works. For more than a century a struggle ensued between the abacists and the algorists, the latter making no real headway. The conservatism of the Western schools (and later, universities) long favored the abacists, for the propen-

ARABIC NUMERALS

sity of the Scholastics toward abstractions and speculations found more nourishment in the *Arithmetic* of Boethius, which dominated school curricula. The latter work was totally lacking the Hindu calculations and the nine numerals.

Fourth, in 1202, Leonardo Fibonacci of Pisa brought out his *Liber abaci,* of which he published a second, revised edition dedicated to Michael Scotus in 1228. This was the work that eventually proved to be the most influential in gaining acceptance for the nine-numeral Hindu system of arithmetic among Latin scholars. From a mercantile and culturally varied background (he traveled to North Africa, where his father had commercial interests), Leonardo fully understood the advantages of the Hindu system for mathematical operations, and he brilliantly and convincingly displayed them in his voluminous work. The influence of the *Liber abaci* in spreading the Hindu-Arabic system in the West was strong and durable, although limited at first to circles of "specialists." The popular diffusion was enhanced by two much simpler presentations, certainly influenced by Leonardo's work: *Carmen de algorismo,* a poem in verse by Alexander of Villa Dei (*ca.* 1225), and the *Algorismus vulgaris* by John of Sacrobosco (mid thirteenth century). It was probably through these popular works, soon current in the universities and schools, that Chaucer learned about the *augrym* (medieval French vernacular for *algorismus*).

Fifth, the struggle of the algorists for recognition and acceptance went on throughout the thirteenth and fourteenth centuries. Most manuscripts on mathematics and related subjects continued to use Roman numerals, although an increasing number contained the *ghubār* numerals. Some had a mixture of the two, without much coherence. Place value was frequently misunderstood by scribes, most of whom obviously remained ignorant of the principles of the Hindu-Arabic methods of reckoning. Readers and editors of these texts occasionally would insert *ghubār* numerals in the margins, to express in the new fashion quantities already written in Roman numerals in the text. This conservative resistance, fostered by ignorance of the system, helps to explain the official prohibitions against the use of "ciphers" in Florence and Padua during the thirteenth and fourteenth centuries. In Florence bankers were forbidden to use the new numerals. At the University of Padua in the fourteenth century, booksellers were directed to keep lists of books for sale, with the prices marked "non per cifras sed per literas claras" (G. G. Neill Wright, *The Writing of Arabic Numerals* [1952], 126).

Sixth, in the fourteenth century there occurred a development of a broader nature, but of paramount importance, that signaled the final stage in the general acceptance of the Hindu arithmetic with the nine figures we now call "Arabic numerals." This was the rise of a deep interest in mathematics for the understanding of nature, a movement traditionally associated with Merton College, Oxford (the Merton School). Scholars like Thomas Bradwardine, Richard Swineshead, and the Oxford "Calculators," soon joined by their followers at the University of Paris—Nicole Oresme, Themo the Jew, Albert of Saxony—heralded an entirely new approach to natural science and the role of mathematics in Latin Scholasticism.

Abandoning the worn concept of *doctrina-mathesis* inherited from Greek philosophy and still adhered to by Roger Bacon and Robert Grosseteste, for instance, the fourteenth-century Merton School transformed traditional problems of action, passion, and motion in Aristotle's *Physics* into genuinely mathematical queries such as velocity, intensity, acceleration, time, and space. Its members soon realized that such problems, involving above all mathematical measurements, had to be handled by a sort of arithmetic different from that offered by Boethius. We know, for instance, that Oresme went as far as to use graphs to study motion or intensity; the tendency toward a new mathematics is clearly perceptible. At their disposal and wondrously fitting their needs stood the Indian methods of the algorithm, so convincingly argued and masterfully displayed by Leonardo Fibonacci a full century earlier.

Thus the hitherto slow penetration of Leonardo's concepts made a new start, and within less than a century after the rise of the Merton School, the Indian methods of reckoning and the nine numerals of the algorism had pretty much replaced the antiquated and cumbersome Roman system of the abacus and Roman numerals among scientists.

The tool had been slowly developed in Europe, as well as among the Arabs and Indians, but an intense demand from scientists and mathematicians for such a system to study nature had not previously emerged to any significant degree. In short, the Hindu-Arabic system of number representation and reckoning, once it was applied to the solution of problems in the mathematical study of nature, produced a quantum change in the progress of mathematics, just as the advance of computer technology is doing today to our traditional arithmetic.

BIBLIOGRAPHY

David Eugene Smith and Louis Charles Karpinski, *The Hindu-Arabic Numerals* (1911), gives ample information on the previous literature with a keenly critical approach, and has retained nearly all of its authority. The results of their work were incorporated by Smith into his *History of Mathematics,* 2 vols. (1925). Karpinski has written two articles that bear directly on the present subject: "Hindu Numerals in the Fihrist," in *Bibliotheca mathematica,* 3rd ser., **11** (1911); and "Two Twelfth Century Algorisms," in *Isis,* **3** (1920–1921).

An extremely valuable catalog of Arabian mathematicians, astronomers, and astrologers, together with an extensive list of their works, manuscripts, and editions, and an up-to-date bibliography, is Fuat Sezgin's *Geschichte des arabischen Schrifttums,* 7 vols. to date, esp. V (1974), on mathematics; VI (1978), on astronomy; and VII (1979), on astrology, meteorology, and related subjects. Sezgin treats all this rich material historiographically, but his historical interpretation contains some weaknesses. Two Soviet historians also have shown a specialized interest in Islamic mathematics: A. P. Youschkevitch, *Geschichte der Mathematik im Mittelalter* (1964) originally published in Russian (1961); and "Ueber ein Werk des Abū Abd Allah Muḥammad ibn Mūsā al-Ḥuwārizmī al-Mağūsī zur Arithmetik der Inder," in *Schriftenreihe für Geschichte der Naturwissenschaften, Technik und Medizin: Beiheft zur 60. Geburtstag von Gerhard Harig* (1964); and A. P. Youschkevitch and Boris A. Rosenfeld, "Die Mathematik der Länder des Ostens im Mittelalter," in Gerhard Harig, ed., *Sowjetische Beiträge zur Geschichte der Naturwissenschaften* (1960).

On the history of mathematics in India, see Bibhutibhusan Datta and A. N. Singh, *History of Hindu Mathematics,* 2 vols. (1935; 2nd ed., 1962).

Among the nineteenth-century writers the works of Léon Rodet contain interesting insights: *Sur la véritable signification de la notation numérique inventée par Âryabhata* (1881) and *Sur les notations numériques et algébriques antérieurement au XVIe siécle* (1881).

On the paleographical evolution of the *ghubār* numerals, see Richard Lemay, "The Hispanic Origin of Our Present Numeral Forms," in *Viator,* **8** (1977). A more general work on paleography that deals with Visigothic forms is Zacarías García Villada, *Paleografía española,* 2 vols. (1923; repr. 1974). A paleographer who displays a keen perceptivity that goes beyond mere recording is Bernard Bischoff, "Paläographie, mit besondere Berücksichtigung des deutschen Kulturgebietes," in W. Stammler, ed., *Deutsche Philologie im Aufriss,* I (1957); also see his "Die sogenannten 'griechischen' and chaldäischen Zahlzeichen des abendlandisches Mittelalters," in *Scritti di paleografia e diplomatica in onore Vincenzo Federici* (1945).

The problem of Pseudo-Boethius' *Geometry,* in which Hindu numerals were long thought to have existed in Europe before Gerbert, has been handled critically by Menso Folkerts, *Boethius' Geometrie II* (1970).

On the methods of reckoning associated with Hindu numerals, see Alfred Nagl, "Ueber eine Algorismus-Schrift des XII. Jahrhunderts und über die Verbreitung der indisch-arabischen Rechenkunst und Zahlzeichen im christlichen Abendlande," in *Zeitschrift für Mathematik und Physik,* **39**, no. 4 (1897). Maximilian Curtze, Über eine Algorismus-Schrift des XII Jahrhunderts," in *Abhandlungen zur Geschichte der Mathematik,* **8** (1898). These are partial editions of the text generally known as *Liber ysagogarum alchorizmi,* which, with John of Seville's Latin translation of the original work of al-Khwārizmī, has been edited by André Allard as *Les plus anciennes versions latines du 12e siècle issues de l'Arithmétique d'al-Khwārizmī* (1975). Also on the same theme are Suzan R. Benedict, *Comparative Study of Early Treatises Introducing into Europe the Hindu Art of Reckoning* (1916); and Julius Ruska, *Zur ältesten arabischen Algebra und Rechenkunst* (1917). The early twelfth-century *algorismus* entitled *Liber Algoritmi de numero indorum,* once presumed to be an anonymous Latin translation of the lost Arabic original of al-Khwārizmī, was printed together with John of Seville's nearly contemporary elaboration entitled *Liber algorismi de practica arismetrice* in Baldassare Boncompagni, ed., *Trattati d'aritmetica* (1857). The anonymous *algorismus* was published again, together with a facsimile of the unique manuscript by Kurt Vogel, as *Mohammed ibn Musa Alchwarizmi's Algorismus: Das früheste Lehrbuch zum Rechnen mit indischen Ziffern* (1963).

For the connection between the progress of algorism and the teaching of arithmetic in the universities of the thirteenth and fourteenth centuries, see Guy Beaujouan, "L'enseignement de l'arithmétique élémentaire à l'Université de Paris aux XIIIe et XIVe siècles," in *Homenaje a Millás Vallicrosa* (1954). On the abacists in the schools of the tenth to the twelfth centuries, see Gillian R. Evans, "From Abacus to Algorism: Theory and Practice in Medieval Arithmetic," in *British Journal for the History of Science,* **35** (1977); and "Schools and Scholars: The Study of the Abacus in English Schools c. 980–c. 1150," in *English Historical Review,* **94** (1979); also see her "*Difficillima et ardua:* Theory and Practice in Treatises on the Abacus, 950–1150," in *Journal of Medieval History,* **3** (1977).

On the mathematical sciences in medieval Spain, see José M. Millás y Vallicrosa, *Estudios sobre historia de la ciencia española* (1949) and *Nuevos estudios sobre historia de la ciencia españalo* (1960). Also see George F. Hourani, "The Early Growth of the Secular Sciences in Andalucia," in *Studia islamica,* **32** (1970).

The following are relevant in the illustration of some

of the Arab tradition: *The Fihrist of Ibn al-Nadīm*, Bayard Dodge, ed. and trans., 2 vols. (1970); Kūshyār ibn Labbān, *Principles of Hindu Reckoning*, Martin Levey and Marvin Petruck, trans. (1950).

On the *zimām* figures described by Ibn Khaldūn, which were used in early Arab administration and remained in Fès (Morocco), see Ibn Khaldūn, *Muqaddima*, Franz Rosenthal, trans., I, 238–245; G. S. Colin, "De l'origine grecque des 'chiffres de Fès' et de nos 'chiffres arabes,'" in *Journal asiatique*, **222** (1933); Giorgio Levi della Vida, "Appunti e quesiti di storia letteraria araba," in *Rivista degli studi orientali*, **16** (1933); J. A. Sánchez-Perez, "Sobre las cifras Rūmīes," in *Al-Andalus*, **3** (1935).

On some sensitive issues concerning early *ghubārs* and apices, see Guy Beaujouan, "Étude paléographique sur la rotation des chiffres et l'emploi des apices aux Xe–XIIe siècles," in *Revue d'histoire des sciences*, **1** (1947); Solomon Gandz, "The Origin of the Ghubar Numerals . . . ," in *Isis*, **16** (1931); Jean Mallon, "Pour une nouvelle critique des chiffres dans les inscriptions latines gravées sur pierre," in *Emerita* (Madrid), **16** (1948).

For the introduction of the *ghubārs* in Byzantium, consult André Allard, *Le grand calcul selon les Indiens de Maxime Planude, sa source anonyme de 1252 et les additions du XIVe siècle*, doctoral thesis, Univ. of Louvain (1972).

RICHARD LEMAY

[See also **Bardas, Caesar; Khaldūn, Ibn; Leo the Mathematician; Mathematics, Islamic and Western European; Nadīm, Ibn al-Photius.**]

ARABIC POETRY

FORM

Classical Arabic poetry uses a variety of meters based on the alternation of long and short syllables. Rhyme is obligatory, and in most types of poem a single rhyme must cap each line. Rhyme words must not be repeated, unless they can be used in different senses. The Semitic derivational system, in which root consonants are combined with vowel patterns and affixes, makes it possible to sustain such rhyming over eighty or one hundred lines without artificiality. In the Islamic period, couplets were occasionally used with the easiest iambic meter *(rajaz)*, but in versified histories and textbooks rather than serious poetry. Simple stanzaic forms appeared in the Abbasid age, but did not, in the East, become more than a curiosity. In Spain, however, poets developed strophic poems melodious and intricate in rhythm and rhyme *(muwashshaḥ)*. Another strophic form popular in Spain, the *zajal*, was written in dialect rather than standard literary Arabic.

PRE-ISLAMIC POETRY

In the pre-Islamic age poetry was, as a rule, not written down, but memorized and performed by professional reciters *(rāwīs)*. Muslim scholars, chiefly of the eighth century, fixed the written texts. The poems stem from the century and a half before Islam. No poems survive in which either form or conventions are rudimentary. Some eighth-century collectors of old texts had a fine hand for forgery, but there is no reason to doubt the basic authenticity of the collections that scrupulous medieval scholars regarded as trustworthy.

There were Arab cities and courts, but the poetry belongs to the warrior–nomads of the desert. Some of the poems were written "to build up high the fame" of the poet's tribe for the possession (or to deride a rival tribe for the lack) of noble lineage, hereditary virtues, and bold achievements. Some served the personal fame of the poet–hero. There are panegyrics to protectors or patrons, and poems of mourning for friends or kin. Some of these last were written by women. There was no truly narrative poetry. Some poems were satisfied with conventional topoi and the general ascription of certain qualities; others singled out events in which these qualities were displayed. However, even when an event occasioned the poem, it was not so much narrated as flashed, in vivid sketch, at the audience, as if meant only to refresh its memory.

The medieval Arab philologists divided the surviving poetry of the pagan Arabs, according to manner of composition, into odes *(qaṣīda)* and fragments *(qiṭ^{c}a)*. In fact, many of the "fragments" must have been independent brief poems, and some of the odes may owe their final form to *rāwis* who combined short poems into longer ones. The *qaṣīda* consists of a string of loosely connected scenes. In its full form (from which many *qaṣīdas* deviate) such a poem opens with a recollection of the parting between the poet and a lady whose tribe had lived next to the poet's, but is now far away. Commonly the occasion for this recollection is the deserted campsite where traces of human habitation remain, but which has reverted to wilderness. The lady is often described in detail, according to conventional canons of taste. The next scene shows the poet riding through forbidding deserts. Here his camel may be described at length, its speed and endurance painted in conventional long similes. While the lady is as-

ARABIC POETRY

sociated with a sheltered life, indolence, and pleasure (and possesses the appropriate languor, and luxuriance of figure), the journey scene (with its description of the lean, strong animal) speaks of privation and danger. The length of these tableaux varies greatly.

The second half of the poem is devoted to praise or satire, with illustrative scenes. The hero is proud and generous, a protector of the weak, impetuous in battle and in pleasure. Prudence, perhaps the rule of everyday life, is despised in poetry. The hero spends his blood and wealth carelessly, for "you who reprove me because I fling myself into battle and pleasure alike, can you keep me forever alive?" Except for dim and perhaps short-lived ghosts, no ideas of an afterlife are entertained, no gods are mentioned, no myths are related. As important as courage and generosity is patient fortitude, *ṣabr.* ᶜAmr ibn Maᶜdīkarib (*d.* 641) writes:

Many a good companion have I lowered with my own hands into the grave.
I did not flinch, my spirit did not break. To weep brings not the least thing back.
I clothed him in his shroud—I was made steadfast when I was made.
I stand in the place of those who are gone; the foe accounts me the equal of many.
Gone are those I loved; I am alone as a sword.

As in other heroic traditions, the enemy too, may be a respected warrior.

As though to balance the prospects of poverty and violent death, scenes of pleasure—wine, the hunt, women—are drawn in many *qaṣīdas.* Here is the theme of a risky visit to a woman, in its version by Imruᵓ-al-Qays:

On my way to her I passed the watchmen and then the rest of her tribe, who would have been happy to stab me in the back.
The Pleiades were by now broad in the sky, like a woman's sash set with cowries and precious stones.
When I arrived, even she was ready to go to sleep, and, near the tent-flap [that is, still on the lookout], had stripped down to her shift.
"Good God," she cried, "no trick will get you out of this! I see your foolishness has not let up."
I raised her up and took her outside, and there she followed me, erasing our footprints by trailing her embroidered skirt along the ground.
When we were past the tribe's enclosure and reached a glen hidden among the heaped-up hills
I pulled her side-tresses so that she leaned toward me. . . .

The intensities, not the middle ground of life, form the topics.

The selection of experience painted by the ancient poets—much of it in ritualistically repeated emblematic scenes—gains vigor from extraordinary riches of diction and exactness of detail.

In this passage by Bishr ibn abī Khāzim (translated by Charles Lyall), description supports the first, direct statement:

We occupy at will the highest region of Najd when the rains fail [and famine comes],
With led mares, all pressing on, frisky, prancing out of the road in wantonness, made lean and spare by constant duty in places of danger and distant raids,
Striving against the reins, unquiet as though in each of them there were a locust in a cloud of dust, yellow in color,
Thrusting back with their elbows the girth, with the space between their teats stopped up with dust;
Thou mayst see them gray from the sweat dried upon them—here a plentiful flow, there only a little.
In every place of soft soil, wheresoever they wheeled about, is a well-like footprint of the hoof with the sides crumbling in. . . .

A journey scene from ᶜAbda ibn al-Ṭabīb:

When the company's journey grows arduous along the beaten track that resembles a palm branch stripped of leaves, the kind woven into mats in Yemen;
Along a distinct road on either side of which you can see handfuls of eggs that look like glass phials in the hollows the *qaṭā*-birds have dug for them,
Glass phials filled with oil and without any palm-leaf cover on them;
When, after a long journey of much exertion and no rest, little is left in the big communal water bags and only residual moisture in the men's own water skins,
While the last drop of stored strength is squeezed out of the white camels, some prodded by sticks or by the riders' heels,
Some urged on gently, a little at a time, their saddles loaded on other beasts and the removable parts of equipment carried by the travelers,
Then a she-camel [the poet's] that is accustomed to be first leads the caravan, mindful of the road even as the rugged and rocky ground and the milestones grow burning hot.

The concrete binds its spell on the poetry through metonymies (for weapons, animals, and such) and similes—corpses with skin swollen like tragacanth bark after rain; date palms whose "topmost heads of foliage waving in every wind are like girls that pull at one another's hair" (Lyall's translation). Some

ARABIC POETRY

long similes are conventional; others paint scenes both vivid and fresh. Everywhere are objects that might be barely touched on, being incidental to the main drift of the passage, but that draw to themselves the poet's attention and, as the objects in Homer, astonish, engage, and delight. A poet speaks, at a lean time, to his querulous wife (Lyall's translation): "Then possess thyself in patience—it may be that yet shalt thou be happy, and milk thy herds into a great milk-skin—the skin of a sheep tanned with acacia-bark."

The outlaw Shanfarā's poem of solitude ends:

I squat or stand on a peak, while the dark yellow
mountain goats come and go about me like maidens in
trailing garments,
Until at dusk they stand about me motionless, as if I
were a white-legged, crook-horned one, with a twist
in the legs, a scaler of summits.

THE ISLAMIC MIDDLE AGES

Islam broke the pagan heroic ethos: the gain of empire changed its material underpinnings. Death was no longer the end of experience. The balance of pleasure and want had shifted agreeably. Nevertheless, there was no abrupt break in the poetic tradition. In the first Islamic century, the old conventions of the *qaṣīda* still govered the panegyrics of the Umayyad court poets (Jarīr, al-Farazdaq, al-Akhṭal) and the satires they aimed at one another. A truly heroic strain survived for a while in the poetry of the Kharijites, an implacably puritanical group of sectaries whom outrage at the worldliness of political power pushed into civil war, ferocity, and an ardor for martyrdom.

While retaining many of the old conventions, the poetry of the Umayyad period (650–750) also enlarged the stock of forms. The chief innovation was the independent love lyric. The poems of ᶜUmar ibn abī Rabīᶜa, who lived in Mecca and Medina and died about 720, already show many of the motifs of elegant love used in the golden age of Arabic poetry, but occasionally retain the Bedouin backdrop.

Authentic love songs, romantic forgeries from two centuries later, and perhaps folklore are inextricably mixed in the poetry celebrating "ᶜUdhrī love" (after the tribe of ᶜUdhra, "those who die when they love") —ardent, chaste, hopeless, incapacitating. By convention the ᶜUdhrī lover rejects counsels of moderation, quite as the old heroic persona had, for love is his danger and to suffer it, his point of honor. The motifs of religion may be appropriated: for Jamīl (*d.* 701?) love is the holy war, and the man who dies for love is a martyr.

The classical forms of the Arabic poetry of the Islamic Middle Ages developed in the hundred years or so after 750. With the accession of the Abbasid dynasty, the center of the Muslim empire moved eastward, away from Damascus and the Syrian desert where the Umayyad rulers had felt at home. There arose a cosmopolitan, urban culture, in which the Arab heritage was blended with that of the conquered lands, especially Iran. The riches, elegance, and intellectual vigor of the new Abbasid capital, Baghdad (founded 763), attracted the best writers and assured them of patronage. There was a public that appreciated charm rather than grandeur.

The poets obliged, writing love poems to singing girls, wine songs, witty descriptions. The delicate love poems of Bashshār ibn Burd (*d.* 784); the brilliant lyrics of love, wine, and the hunt by Abū Nuwās (*d.* 813/815); but also the pious exhortatory verse of Abū'l-ᶜAtāhiya (*d.* 826) come from this period. The "new poets" of the early Abbasid period let go of that part of the old poetic vocabulary that was no longer readily understood, and they did not yet embrace rhetoric with an excessive fervor. This is not to say that their poems are devoid of rhetorical figures or conventions of motif and wording. But the conventions of love and pleasure seem fresh and the rhetoric sits lightly.

It was, however, not long before the celebration of rulers and patrons claimed the chief place in the work of the most famous professional poets. The literary marketplace pushed, the lure of a grand style pulled them in this direction. It was not all for the best. Panegyrical poetry chose a stately idiom for its vehicle (which in part meant difficult syntax and obscure vocabulary), and invited exhibitions of rhetorical skill. The critics of the tenth century noted the dangers of artificiality. Medieval comparisons of Abū Tammām (*d.* 845/846) and al-Buḥturī (*d.* 897) illustrate the fluency of the latter and the rhetorical overload in the former.

Throughout the Middle Ages the lyric style and the grand, public style both remained in use. The poetry of the golden age (lasting from the mid-eighth to the mid-eleventh century in the East, starting and ending later in Spain) is conventional enough to be adequately described, without further periodization, according to the types of subject matter treated in the poems.

The conventions of the love poem are not unfamiliar. Conflicting emotions are set down in neatly

 ARABIC POETRY

antithetical phrases. The sentimental lover submits to the whims of the beloved, who is made of much sturdier stuff; discretion fails because watering eyes betray hearts on fire; ill turns are done by people who malign the lovers to one another and gossip about them to others; the faithful lover grows thin, falls ill, and stays trapped between hope and despair; the beloved is fickle and, worse luck, unafraid of the divine wrath that must avenge a lover's death.

Some poets write of chaste longings (such as al-^{c}Abbās ibn al-Aḥnaf [*d. ca.* 807], of the "sinful glance and pure conscience"); some have real tenderness (such as the Cordoban Ibn Zaydūn [*d.* 1070]). There is at times a restrained sensuousness as with this unknown poet:

Three things prevent her visit, would tip off meddlers
gagging on envy:
The dazzling forehead, her whispering jewels, ambergris
drifting through her cloak.
Yes, with a broad sleeve she could dim her face, she
could leave off her pendants.
What could she do about the third, the drops of sweat
on her skin?

Some poets can poke mild fun at the sentimental conventions. Others—such as Abū Nuwās or the brilliantly vigorous Spanish poet Ibn Quzmān (*d.* 1160)—can be sharply ironic or ribald.

The prose literature on love tells us that love conduces to virtue, but the poets do not much bother their heads about such things. They stress not virtues but sensibility. A tenth-century book on *elegantiae* (the *Kitāb al-Muwashshā*) holds that such tremulous sensibility is part of the elegant behavior of people of fashion. The sensibility was also known for a charming pretense. Ibn Ḥazm of Córdoba (*d.* 1064) explains that the lover's speeches of humble submission to the beloved are not unmanly (which they would be in different circumstances), for it is understood that in reality the beloved is the lover's social inferior. This was a love poetry addressed to slave girls, and boys (although not without exception: Ibn Zaydūn's Wallāda was a princess).

Many poems deal with such pleasures as hunting and drinking parties. Among the latter the wine songs of Abū Nuwās stand out, as much for their perfection of language as for their ironic knowledge that to seize on pleasure as a refuge from the warnings of time and changing fortune is both impious and futile.

Wine songs that were explicitly impious (for intoxicants are forbidden in Islam) and love songs that were implicitly so (for sensibility to the detriment of sense, as the Muslim moralists saw, was no religious good), as well as poems recounting pleasant but illicit adventures could be defended by citing the Koran: "The poets say that which they do not do." So censure was turned into shield. "Poetry," it was further said, "and religion are things apart." Such opinions made for much literary saturnalia.

Description occupies a place of the first importance. There are long descriptive passages in poems of all kinds, but poems may also be entirely devoted to description. Many of these are very short, consisting of a few, at times subtly related, similes, as in the verses of Ibn al-Mu^{c}tazz (*d.* 908): "The star in the black night is like an eye stealing a glance when the watchers [set over a girl] have grown lax./ [Then] morning rises from under the dark, as gray hair shows in a black lock." Other descriptive poems—of gardens, of seasons, of objects—are longer. Description is often an excuse for fanciful conceits. It often adorns the natural world with metaphorical jewels and perfumes. At times the older aim of precision is still kept in view. As is generally the tendency of mannerism, there is a kind of disinterest in the moral implications of the topic: A swaying anemone affords as good a subject for the poet's metaphorical alchemy as a dead body raised on a cross.

There are many poems of pious exhortation. They speak of the snares of this desirable world ("the world is an enemy in the guise of a friend"), and of the need to repent. Mortals must be reminded of mortality: "Like coins in its hand, time spends us as it will," writes Abū'l-^{c}Alā al-Ma^{c}arrī (*d.* 1057), the blind Syrian poet famous for the extravagant formal difficulties of his verse, his gloomy compassion for all fellow creatures, and his "fierce hatred of injustice, hypocrisy and superstition" (R. A. Nicholson).

Elegies for public figures provide occasions for stately mediation. Al-Mutanabbī (*d.* 965) mourns his patron's mother:

In spite of us, you have moved to where you are far from
the south wind and the north.
The scent of lavender is hidden from you and the soft
rains are kept away;
In a house whose every tenant is a stranger, in a far
country, his strings of affection snapped;
A house in which is a person pure as rainwater, with
whom secrets are safe and who speaks the truth.

The loss of a child or parent may yield poems in which personal emotion and circumstance blend strikingly, and on the modern reader's first acquaintance oddly, with conventional perceptions and the formulas of gnomic wisdom.

Mystical poetry is not as important in Arabic literature as in the Persian, but it is not lacking. Yearning for, and intoxication with, the divine is the theme of the great allegorical odes of Ibn al-Fāriḍ (*d.* 1235) or the more delicate love songs of al-Shushtarī (*d. ca.* 1212). There are other poems of religious feelings in praise of the Prophet, or, by poets of Shī^{c}a sympathies, in commemoration of those of the Prophet's family who perished in the battle of Karbala at the hands of the Umayyad soldiery.

Satire, aimed at individuals or tribal groups (not at social types or the like), ranged from friendly raillery to scurrilous gibes. It is at times still amusing, as with Ibn al-Rūmī's (*d.* 896) wicked association of an imposing white beard with an ass's feedbag.

Panegyrics were of the first importance in the estimation of the medieval poet and his public, for they could unite solemnity of language to grandeur of subject. For the modern reader they are harder to approach. Bacon's opinion that hyperbole is comely only in love would not have been approved. The patron is a sea of generosity, a lion in battle, and on and on. Medieval critics noted that some early poets had praised people only for the qualities they really had, but as poetry turned into a moneymaking profession, such scruples were abandoned. Certainly there is much luxuriant flattery (though we must take into account the ceremonial conventionality of many tropes). The rhetoric can be obtrusive. Nevertheless, some of these poems have linguistic sparkle, sensory vividness, or real enthusiasm for bold action.

There are of course many poems—humorous, elegiac, or contemplative—that do not fall into these basic categories.

The Arab critics of the later Middle Ages agreed that the line of great professional poets—those one cannot hope to emulate—had run out in the eleventh century. There are exceptions, but it is true that the poetry of later centuries is mostly recombination and a parade ground for rhetorical drills. There are many possible reasons. The Seljuk Turks took Baghdad in 1055; the Mongols sacked it in 1258. The intervening centuries saw much political instability. There were nomadic incursions. There were foreign rulers who cared little for Arabic literature. Yet, this cannot be all. Cairo, prosperous until the Black Death, did not become another literary Baghdad. Simply, and most importantly, there was no change in what poetry was expected to say and do, and short of such change the only drift could be toward further verbal intricacy.

COMPOSITION AND CONVENTION

Three facts made for looseness of composition: apart from brief idylls, there was no strong tradition of narrative in poetry; a poetic subject was associated with a ready store of topoi and conceits that the audience expected to see in new dress; and a good line of verse was (with few exceptions) to be end-stopped and meaningful in itself. A panegyric, in which a catalog of virtues might do the job, could do without cogency of relation among its verses; a love poem, too, might present the traditional topoi in a fairly random order. But there is no lack of poems in which logical or temporal progression is observed, or in which the end-stopped lines enter into large, syntactically complex units. Recurrent motifs, echoes, congruent images, contradictions, and the like often hold poems together, even where an obvious linear progression is absent.

The pre-Islamic poets relied heavily on stock phrases adaptable to the different meters, as well as on predictable syntactic structures. Unavoidably, this caused problems of attribution and produced many equally acceptable variants when the medieval scholars collected the archaic poems. It has been suggested that these scholars imposed their own notions or authorship on the material they had gathered, and that the pre-Islamic poetry was, in fact, largely anonymous and collectively composed. This is not an inevitable conclusion. Quite as likely, even in the pre-Islamic age, poems making conventional statements with conventional tableaux, images, and phrases were attributed to individual authors, and on the whole it was remembered which poets had more vigor of language or more moments of invention.

Conventional situation, imagery, and phrasing persist in the poetry of the Islamic period. The thematic boundaries of poetry were, it was felt, fairly well established. One might, to be sure, find a new object of description for a witty conceit. An unusual event might give a description unusual freshness. Ibn al-Mu^{c}tazz writes of a flood in Baghdad:

The Tigris, when it came, paid me a call. No sea could match it!
My walls tilt, bow in prayer, or touch face to ground.
The ceiling rains, springs burst the flagstones,
And in the hollows that were pleasure gardens, the frogs praise God.

But the themes and attitudes of love, praise, mourning, and the like had, it was felt, all been found. Not excellence of thought, but excellence in expressing it, the judges agreed, marked the good poet.

Plagiarism became a thorny critical problem. There was much debate on what was conventional enough to be in the public domain and, when an image was not obvious common property, what constituted sufficient improvement in it to secure from the charge of plagiarism the poet who reused it. But in its best age Arabic literature was not without poets and poems of marked individuality, even though poets and public candidly recognized, and treasured, the interdependence of all poems; found nothing odd about compiling florilegia of topoi or similes, or discussing who wrote the best lines about fidelity, or roses, or the Pleiades; and assumed that what had often been well expressed could not likely be better thought. A fully conventional lyric might be woven with complex harmonies of sense and sound.

In some cases linguistic brilliance, coupled with strength of personality—as with the defiant libertinism of Abū Nuwās or the pride of al-Mutanabbī—gives poetry an individual stamp. Personal history may shape a poet's work; for example, Abū Firās (*d.* 967) had the literary good luck of being captured by the Byzantines and not being ransomed by his powerful relatives. From captivity he wrote a series of poems, some of them powerful and moving. Panegyrics often treat particular details with vigor. The ceremonial and personal aspects of poetry sometimes blend, as in al-Buḥturī's poem of real grief and outrage over the assassination of the caliph al-Mutawakkil. The knowledgeable medieval audience no doubt derived much pleasure from the rhythm of convention, variant, rhetorical invention, and individual detail.

BIBLIOGRAPHY

Translations. Pre-Islamic poetry—Charles J. Lyall, *The Mufaḍḍalīyāt; an Anthology of Ancient Arabian Odes* (1918) and *Translations of Ancient Arabian Poetry* (1930), with an excellent introduction; and A. J. Arberry, *The Seven Odes* (1957), a translation of the much-admired poems known as *muᶜallaqāt.* Poetry of the Islamic period—René Khawam, *La poésie arabe* (1960); and A. J. Arberry, *Arabic Poetry, A Primer for Students* (1965), bilingual, with a brief preface on rhetorical figures. There are selections from, or complete renderings of, the works of several poets, including Abū Nuwās, in the text of Ewald Wagner's *Abū Nuwās* (1965); al-Mutanabbī, in A. J. Arberry, *The poems of Al-Mutanabbi* (1967); Bashshār ibn Burd, in A. F. L. Beeston, *Selections from the Poetry of Baššar* (1977); and, in French, Andreé Roman, *Baššar et son experience Courtoise* (1972); from Spain, Ibn Zaydūn, in French, by August Cour, *Un poète arabe d'Andalousie, Ibn Zaïdoun* (1920); and Ibn Quzmān, in Spanish, by Emilio García Gómez, *Todo Ben Quzman,* 3 vols. (1972).

Histories. Régis Blachère, *Histoire de la littérature arabe des origines à la fin du xve siècle de J.-C.,* 3 vols. (1952–1966); H. A. R. Gibb, *Arabic Literature* (1963). For Spain, see the introduction to James T. Monroe, *Hispano-Arabic Poetry* (1974).

Studies. Jamel-eddine Bencheikh, *Poétique arabe* (1975); Gustave Edmund von Grunebaum, *Kritik und Dichtkunst, Studien zur arabischen Literaturgeschichte* (1955)—most of these studies were first published in English (dates and places given in the book); Gustav Edmund von Grunebaum, ed., *Arabic Poetry, Theory and Development* (1973); Andras Hamori, *On the Art of Medieval Arabic Literature* (1974); Wolfhart Heinrichs, *Arabische Dichtung und griechische Poetik* (1969); Renate Jacobi, *Studien zur Poetik der altarabischen Qaṣide* (1971); Raymond Scheindlin, *Form and Structure in the Poetry of al-Muᶜtamid Ibn ᶜAbbād* (1974); and Michael Zwettler, *The Oral Tradition of Classical Arabic Poetry* (1978).

ANDRAS HAMORI

[See also **ᶜAbbās, Al-; Abū Nuwās; Akhṭal, Al-; Arabic, Persian, and Hebrew Rhetoric; Farazdaq, Al-; Ḥazm, Ibn; Imruᵓ-al-Qays; Jarīr; Maᶜarrī; Mutanabbī, Al-.**]

ARAGON (800–1137). The kingdom of Aragon arose from the efforts of Hispano-Visigothic chieftains to reorganize an upland population against the Muslims of the Ebro valley. Confined to valleys above the river Aragon (barely 600 square kilometers), the Aragonese were dominated in the early ninth century by Aznar Galindo (*ca.* 809–839), who was recognized by Charlemagne. Culturally as well as politically, the early county was oriented toward Frankland, easy of access through the Hecho and Confranc passes. The Benedictine house of Siresa was nourished by the Frankish monastic reforms.

This orientation proved short-lived, chiefly because the Aragonese ceased to be seriously threatened by the Muslims in the ninth century. Even in the Ebro valley there survived a considerable Mozarab population, whose Arabic-speaking masters had long since quarreled among themselves. The Christians of Saragossa retained their bishop. Although the mountaineers were subject to tribute, the effective Moorish domination reached no further northeast than Huesca, Barbastro, and Monzón. A sister of Galindo Aznar II (893–922) married the *wāli* of Huesca. But the most influential factor was Aragon's dynastic involvement with Navarre. Galindo Aznar I (*ca.* 844–867) could secure his father's claim to Aragon only at the price of dependence on the king of the Pamplonese; his son Aznar II Galindo (867–893) married the daughter of King García Iñiguez. In the tenth century a new line of Navarrese kings threatened to swallow up Aragon entirely. The Navarrese fortified devastated lands south of the Aragon River, thus encroaching severely on Aragon's zone of natural expansion. Aragon was to be virtually incorporated in the kingdom of Pamplona until the death of Sancho the Great of Castile (1004–1035).

Nevertheless, the county of the Aragonese retained its social and administrative identity: the land of the "Aragonese barons" or "lords." In the tenth century San Juan de la Peña, on the rugged frontier south of Jaca, replaced Siresa as the religious center of Aragon. Traditionally associated with the arrival of Christian refugees from Saragossa, the foundation of San Juan encouraged not only a restoration of Visigothic culture but also a patriotic militancy soon to be turned against the Muslims. And in 922 an Aragonese bishop was established. The location of his see in the valley of Borau points to a growth of population in the upper valleys increasingly protected by military resettlement south of the Aragon. Life in the latter zone, Aragon's first frontier, already contrasted starkly with that of farmers and shepherds in the unwalled hamlets of the mountains.

In the eleventh century Aragon became a kingdom. Ramiro I (1035–1063), who had ruled Aragon as his father's deputy "kinglet" since 1015, conceded his brother's supremacy in Navarre. He was in turn permitted to extend Aragonese authority deep into the frontier area formerly fortified by Navarre, a policy that resulted in a permanent enlargement of Aragon. The incipient realm grew, indeed, to more than six times the territorial extent of the original county. Nor was this all, for in 1044, Ramiro annexed Sobrarbe and Ribagorza, remote lands east of Aragon. If Ramiro did not quite claim to be king (using the expression "as if . . . king"), he nonetheless had manifestly assumed leadership in the struggle against the Moors, whose strongholds now faced his own across a long frontier. Ramiro's precedence in the dynastic patrimonies was confirmed when his nephew became king of Pamplona (1054); his son Sancho Ramírez (1063–1094) submitted Aragon to papal protection, a dependence converted into vassalage in 1089; and when Sancho succeeded his cousin in Navarre in 1076, the supremacy of Navarre was ended. Sancho styled himself "king by God's grace of the Pamplonese and Aragonese."

This political success was enhanced by singularly favorable circumstances. The Muslim cities, while continuing to prosper economically and culturally, lost the military initiative to strengthened contingents of mounted knights on the Christian side. With the pressure thus reversed, so was the flow of gold. Sancho Ramírez derived great wealth from the Moorish tribute of Huesca, Tudela, and Saragossa. Meanwhile, Christian Aragon became a crossroads. The Gascon passes carried a swelling throng of merchants and pilgrims; the former traded cloth, weapons, and hardware for Muslim spices, fruits, and manufactures, while the latter found Jaca a convenient stage on the route to Santiago de Compostela. The tolls of Canfranc and Jaca produced spectacular profits for the Aragonese monarchy and church. In a land hitherto lacking cities, Jaca became an "instant city." It attracted settlers not only from its environs but, especially, from Gascony and Toulouse. Sancho Ramírez encouraged this movement, granting Jaca a charter of liberties (1077) and instituting a national coinage.

So transformed, the first city of Christian Aragon naturally became its ecclesiastical capital. Restoration of the Aragonese church was inaugurated in a synod at Jaca (1063) attended by the archbishop of Auch and other prelates from both sides of the Pyrenees. The episcopal see was relocated to Jaca and grandly endowed. Its canons received the Augustinian Rule, which was also instituted in royal chapels at Siresa and elsewhere; the monastic customs at San Juan and San Victorián (Sobrarbe) were reformed; and churches throughout the realm gave up the Visigothic observance for the Roman liturgy.

In 1068 the king restored the old episcopate of Roda (Ribagorza). The religious revival combined with economic prosperity to revolutionize ecclesiastical architecture. The splendid cathedral at Jaca was the first edifice in Spain built in the French Romanesque style. There were similar innovations in the renovated churches at Iguácel (1063–1072), San Juan (1094), and elsewhere; little survived of the traditional, undecorated style save, here and there, the Hispanic arch. Artists from southern France introduced new meaning and elegance to the sculpture of interiors and cloisters.

By the later eleventh century Aragon seemed to

 ARAGON (800–1137)

have come of age. Yet the young kindgdom, so precociously expansive and receptive, was then only on the eve of conquests that would enlarge its territories nearly tenfold during the next two generations. There was nothing fortuitous about this renewed expansion. Jaca's designation as an episcopal see seems to have been provisional, pending the conquest of Huesca. Ramiro I died in conflict with the Muslims near Barbastro in 1063, an event that contributed to a hardened perception of the Moors as enemies of the Christian faith. French and Catalan knights were soon fighting alongside the Aragonese in this zone of the frontier, and such expeditions came to be promoted as pious works and, finally, as crusades. But progress remained slow. The Muslims retained a string of fortified places well upland from the Ebro, extending from lower Ribagorza to Tudela. Moreover, the kings of Pamplona and Castile for a time supported the *taifa* of Saragossa against the Aragonese. In the last quarter of the eleventh century the tide turned. The death of Sancho IV of Pamplona in 1076 ended the debilitating competition of Navarre, while Muslim leadership itself faltered with the death of al-Muqtadir of Saragossa in 1081.

So a new wave of Aragonese conquests began in the later years of Sancho Ramírez. Acting as viceroy in Sobrarbe and Ribagorza, his son Pedro captured Estada in 1087 and Monzón in 1089, opening the way to rapid advances southward in the Cinca valley and as far east as Almenar (taken in 1093). Progress toward Barbastro and Huesca proved more difficult. Although Montearagón, within view of the city, fell in 1088, it was not until November 1096 that Huesca surrendered to Pedro I (1094–1104), now king of Aragon. Barbastro capitulated in 1100, leaving only Lérida unconquered among cities of the eastern

Aragon (800–1137)

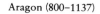

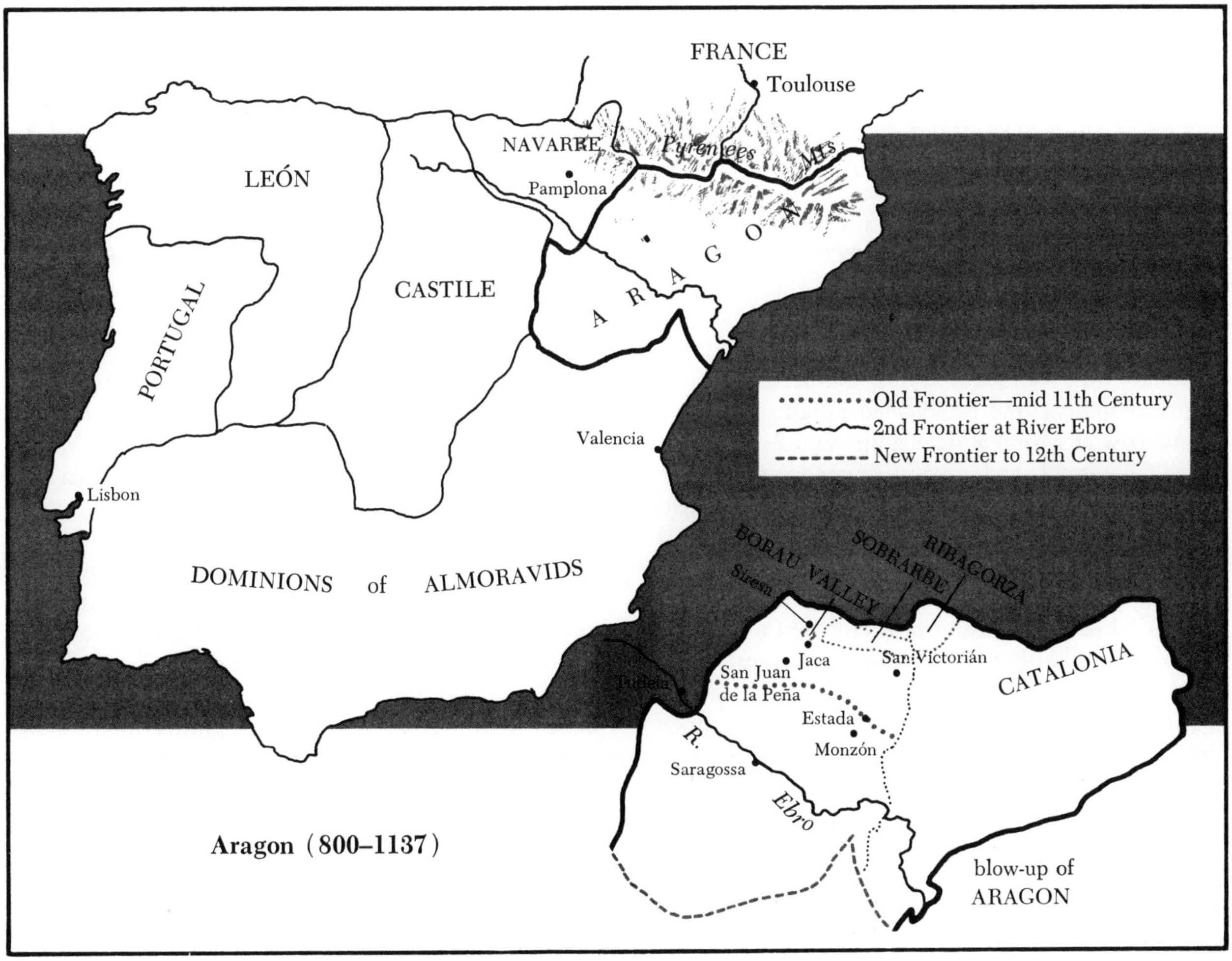

frontier. Meanwhile, progress along the sparsely settled Gallego River had been equally spectacular. By 1101, Pedro's forces were in control of strong points virtually under the walls of Saragossa and Tudela.

At this point the campaign was slowed. Alfonso VI of Castile, who had previously resisted Aragonese expansion as a threat to Castilian destinies, was moved by the conquest of Huesca to renew his aid to the Muslims. The Aragonese, while breaching the enemy frontier, had failed to secure the lands behind their advance positions. Nor could the kings of Aragon yet safely commit all their resources to this enterprise. They had felt obliged to collaborate in Castilian expeditions to the lower Ebro and to Valencia, so as not to jeopardize their own claims to rich coastal domains. Preoccupation with Castile continued during the reign of Pedro I's brother, Alfonso I (1104–1134), whose stormy marriage to Alfonso VI's daughter Urraca ultimately failed to effect a dynastic union. Not until 1117 was Alfonso prepared to renew the campaign against the Muslims.

Inspired by the crusading ideal then in its flower, he welcomed papal support in the form of indulgences and military aid from foreign knights, notably the duke of Aquitaine and the viscount of Béarn. Saragossa fell in 1118 after a long siege, followed in 1119 by Tudela and Tarazona. In 1120, Soria was resettled and Calatayud was besieged. News of a counterattack on Saragossa diverted the king to the Valencian borderland, where in June 1120 his forces routed the Muslims in battle. Soon thereafter Alfonso captured Daroca and Calatayud. The destruction of the Moorish realm of Saragossa was almost complete. Alfonso secured his southern positions against Valencia, and established knights under religious vow at Monreal del Campo and Belchite. To the east he established a new frontier extending virtually from Morella to Mequinenza, seriously threatening the Moors of the Cinca and lower Ebro. For all this success Alfonso was frustrated in his ambition to conquer Lérida and Tortosa, which lay in zones marked out for annexation by the Catalans. In 1134 he lost a battle at Fraga and died several weeks later.

Alfonso I "the Battler" ranks among the great kings of the Spanish Reconquest. His victories substantially defined the medieval realm of Aragon, establishing borders with Catalonia, Valencia, and Castile. Under him Aragon lost the defensiveness of her upland origins and assumed an expanded role as liberator of oppressed Christians. "No king of Aragon was inflamed with a spirit so authentically religious and crusading as the Battler king," according to José María Lacarra. It is in light of these circumstances that most historians have explained the strange will by which Alfonso, childless and probably sterile, bequeathed his kingdom to the military orders of the Holy Land—an exalted but unrealistic act. But it seems possible that this will, which was composed in 1131 and confirmed shortly before the king's death in 1134, was a shrewd contrivance intended to have almost precisely the consequences that ensued.

The defeat at Fraga touched off Muslim uprisings in which the southeastern frontier collapsed. Saragossa was saved from recapture by forces of Alfonso VII of Castile (December 1134), who had a good dynastic claim to Aragon and Navarre. The purpose of the will may have been to neutralize papal influence in support of this claim. The Aragonese magnates set aside the will in favor of the Battler's younger brother, the monk Ramiro, who was married to Agnes of Aquitaine in order to beget the required heir. The Navarrese rejected this arrangement, choosing a king of their own. Ramiro II (1134–1137) retired to the monastic life after fathering a daughter, Petronilla, who was promptly betrothed to Count Ramon Berenguer IV of Barcelona. Aragon had escaped Castilian domination—at what cost, it remained to be seen.

Enormous problems of organization faced Alfonso I and his successors. Their domains, which involved a compounding of frontiers, had multiplied too fast to be assimilated. South of the original nucleus of Aragon lay the "old frontier" *(vieja extremadura),* dating from the tenth century. Next came the "new land" conquered at the end of the eleventh century, the key points of which were Huesca and Barbastro.

Relatively densely inhabited, this frontier was organized in military tenancies awarded to barons who had contributed service and men in the campaigns, while its extension west of the Gállego remained an incompletely subjugated no-man's-land. Imported from the old frontier, the tenancies of the "new land" were devised to support fighting men on the produce of peasants who became progressively less free. That the king was obliged to create baronies in lands over which he claimed sole dominion points to a characteristic weakness in his position. The military obligations of (old) Aragon, having become customary at a level suited for defensive service, were

ARAGON (800–1137)

too light to sustain the prolonged campaigns and sieges of the twelfth century. The king had to persuade and to pay. Less a popular than a royal idea, the expansion of Aragon obliged the king to raise up powerful tenants-in-chief in the "new land."

The Ebro valley, with its cities, gardens, and orchards, posed a different problem. It had to be secured and exploited without destroying its prosperity. The solution was to clear the cities for Christian resettlement while allowing the Muslims to retain their movables and rural property. Every effort was made to preserve the structure of obligations and irrigation in the countryside. The king compensated his knights with properties confiscated in Saragossa and Tudela, and enticed settlers from the old Aragonese lands—Catalonia, Gascony, and Castile, even Christians from Granada—to share in the spoils. Although many Muslims—especially administrative officials and expropriated landlords—abandoned these homelands, the masses of peasants and artisans remained, enough so that the Mudejars long outnumbered the Christians.

Finally, there was the "new *extremadura*" established by Alfonso I on the borders of Castile and Valencia. Arid and rugged, it was organized in military zones projecting from towns such as Soria, Medinaceli, Calatayud, and Daroca. These places, generally commended to the king's barons, were settled on unusually liberal terms, including freedom from prosecution for felonies. Castilians, Navarrese, and Gascons joined the Aragonese and other immigrants to this frontier. These were communities of peasant warriors: foot soldiers and mounted men shared a common status. Governed by customary statutes *(fueros)* and by councils, the early settlers were resistant to seignorial exploitation.

Aragon was, therefore, far from being a homogeneous state at the death of Alfonso the Battler. Although "Aragonese" were fighting and settling on all the frontiers, the term "Aragon" continued to be reserved to the old homeland, and the king's authority remained a cluster of lordships: over Aragon, Sobrarbe, Huesca, Saragossa, and the rest. The process of assimilation was beginning, to be sure. Settlers in Barbastro received the same privileges as the knights of Sobrarbe. Alfonso I encouraged his followers to serve him, regardless of local custom. That is why in 1134 the "knights and barons of Aragon" insisted on having their customs confirmed as they had been in the time of Pedro I. Moreover, the clergy supported the royal view that the war was a reconquest. Bishops' churches were to be restored where they once existed—in Tarazona as well as in Huesca and Saragossa, for example—and they were endowed in similar ways, often by expropriation of mosques. Upland churches became annexes of restored sees: Jaca, of Huesca; Roda, of Lérida.

Yet the monarchy as institution had evolved very little. Alfonso I, like his ancestors, was a warrior-king. He dominated and rewarded followers, who derived status and privilege from association with him; through men of his court, their functions unspecialized, he exploited his estates in the old Aragonese lands, and his rents, justice, and tolls everywhere. While the common military obligation was derived from an ancient conception of public order upheld by the king, the prevailing forms of service, obligation, and right were essentially personal and patrimonial. The king retained the initiative while the expansion continued; few military tenancies were yet hereditary in the early twelfth century. But the stability of this royal-baronial condominium remained to be tested.

BIBLIOGRAPHY

Sources. The sources for the early history of Aragon are chiefly ecclesiastical charters preserved in originals or isolated copies, and principally in cartularies in various repositories, notably in the Archivo Histórico Nacional (Madrid), Sección Clero. Numerous cartularies have been edited, some rather hastily, in *Textos medievales* (1960–1981). A fundamental collection is "Documentos para el estudio de la reconquista y repoblación del valle del Ebro," José María Lacarra, ed., in *Estudios de edad media de la Corona de Aragón,* 2 (1946), 3 (1949), and 5 (1952), indexed.

Secondary. Geronimo Zurita y Castro, *Anales de la Corona de Aragón,* 6 vols. (1562–1580), Bk. I. This is a great work of its kind, citing numerous texts now lost, although less useful for this than for later periods; it is best used in the new edition by Angel Canellas López, 6 vols. (1967–1975), or in the modernized Castilian and annotated version by Antonio Ubieto Arteta and María Desamparados Pérez Soler, 4 vols. (1967–1972). Also see José María Lacarra, *Aragón en el pasado* (1972), 11–73; Elena Lourie, "The Will of Alfonso I, 'El Batallador,' King of Aragon and Navarre: A Reassessment," in *Speculum,* 50 (1975); Lynn H. Nelson, "The Foundation of Jaca (1076): Urban Growth in Early Aragon," in *Speculum,* 53 (1978), with useful maps; José María Ramos y Loscertales, *El reino de Aragón bajo la dinastía pamplonesa* (1961).

THOMAS N. BISSON

[See also **Alfonso I; Spain, Christian-Muslim Relations; Spain, Moorish Kingdoms of.**]

ARAGON, CROWN OF (1137–1479). The marriage of the heiress of Aragon to the count of Barcelona inaugurated a dynastic union that would last for centuries. It is customary to speak of this union as the "Crown of Aragon" (although the term itself dates from later times) and of its rulers, who never ceased to style themselves "count" in Catalonia, as "count-kings."

THE EARLY COUNT-KINGS (1137–1213)

The greatest of the early rulers (although he refused the title "king") was Ramon Berenguer IV (1131–1162). Not the least of his achievements was simply to secure Aragon according to the terms of 1137. The marriage itself could not take place for many years; the dispossessed military orders had to be compensated and the pressures of Castile resisted; the papacy had to be reconciled. Most of these requirements were met by 1143, when a legatine council at Girona [Gerona] ratified the agreement by which the Templars were promised a tithe on all royal revenues and a fifth of lands conquered from the Moors. Ramon married his sister to Alfonso VII of Castile and conceded the latter's lordship over Saragossa.

Ramon Berenguer IV demonstrated his fidelity to his suzerain as well as his capacity to lead and reward by his conquest of Almería in 1147. He had little trouble securing support for campaigns against Tortosa and Lérida. The Genoese were promised a third part of Tortosa, as was Guillem Ramon de Montcada, while other military contingents from Catalonia, Occitania [southern France], and Aragon joined the campaign, which Pope Eugenius III declared a crusade. After a long siege Tortosa fell in December 1148. The Moors were allowed to retain their customs and commercial rights, while Christian settlers were granted personal and civil liberties in charters of 1148 and 1149. The count-prince exploited the momentum of this success to attack Lérida, which he captured on 24 October 1149. The leading coadjutor there was Ermengol VI of Urgell, who became, like Guillem Ramon at Tortosa, colord for one-third of the city. Christian resettlement was patterned (charter of January 1150) on that of Tortosa.

These conquests definitively secured a vast frontier for Catalan expansion. The bishoprics of Tortosa and Lérida were restored; the reorganization of Christian Tarragona was accelerated; and in 1154 the pope prescribed the primacy of Tarragona over all the sees of Catalonia and Aragon. Saracen strongholds at Miravet and Siurana fell in 1152–1153. Rural churches were built; mosques were converted. Cistercian monks from southern France founded the monasteries soon to be known as Poblet and Santes Creus, which were endowed by the count and other magnates. The lords of the frontier—count, archbishop, Templars, and others—encouraged immigration by granting liberal terms of settlement. Settlers came from all parts of Christian Catalonia, from Occitania, even from England. Many Muslim hamlets remained, and new ones arose in the suburbs of Lérida and Tortosa, where the early prosperity owed much to the maintenance of the Moorish economy.

His victories in New Catalonia strengthened the count-prince abroad. Tribute flowed from Valencia once again, and in 1151 Alfonso VII recognized a sphere of prospective Catalan-Aragonese conquest comprising Valencia and Murcia. Béarn became a dependency in 1154. In Occitania, Ramon Berenguer IV exercised lordship over Montpellier and Narbonne, and acquired the fealty of Trencavel of Béziers in 1150. Only in Provence was there trouble. Acting as protector of his nephew Ramon Berenguer I (1144–1166), the count-prince fought repeatedly against the counts of Saint-Gilles and the castellan lineage of Les Baux. In 1162 he secured his nephew's title to Provence by an act of Emperor Frederick Barbarossa.

These successes, coupled with the collapse of Castilian hegemony at the death of Alfonso VII (1157), left Ramon Berenguer IV the most powerful ruler in Spain. In Catalonia, where his policy is most clearly visible, he strove to rebuild the public order weakened in the eleventh century. A high court was reestablished, while legal experts produced the *Usatges of Barcelona,* a code that stressed the regalian authority of the count. Ramon Berenguer IV was the first Catalan ruler to conceive of a uniform fiscal administration for his aggregated counties. A remarkable survey of Old Catalonia, carried out in 1151, was intended not only to improve the accountability of bailiffs but also to evaluate the old domain as potential collateral for credit in the postconquest years when the old counties ceased to be the count's main resource.

Alfonso II (Alfons I in Catalonia, 1162–1196) was a child of five at his father's death. Nominally the protégé of Henry II Plantagenet, he was supervised for many years by advisers both Aragonese (notably the queen mother) and Catalan, whose vigilance in external affairs did much to secure the monarchical union in its early years. By negotiating first with Leon and Navarre, they managed to forestall the Castilian claim to suzerainty over the "kingdom of Saragossa." By 1170, Alfonso II could ally with Alfonso VIII of Castile on favorable terms, reserving a common loyalty to Henry II and securing for the count-king a restoration of Valencian tribute.

Alfonso II exploited this solidarity as he came of age. With the foundation of Teruel (1171) and the death of King Lop (1172), he was prepared to attack Valencia, only to be diverted by the belligerence of Navarre. In 1177, having married Sancha of Castile, he aided Alfonso VIII in the conquest of Cuenca, where a new treaty confirmed the territorial integrity of Aragon. The climax of this alliance came in the treaties of Cazola (1179), in which these militant young kings not only proposed to partition Navarre but also delimited their prospective zones of Moorish conquest. Aragon was to have Valencia, leaving Murcia to Castile.

The Plantagenet alliance nurtured in Castile was deployed chiefly in southern France against the perceived threat of an expansionist Capetian monarchy allied with the count of Toulouse. In this sector Alfonso's policy was related to the progressive consolidation of his counties to form an independent administrative unity: the resumption of Roussillon (1172) and lower Pallars (1192), the promulgation of a territorial peace for Catalonia as such (1173–1198), and the decision in 1180 that scribes should henceforth employ the year of the Incarnation instead of the regnal year of France.

There was nothing imperialistic about Catalan interests across the Pyrenees. Provence might have remained under a cadet branch of the dynasty of Barcelona had not Ramon Berenguer III been killed

Crown of Aragon

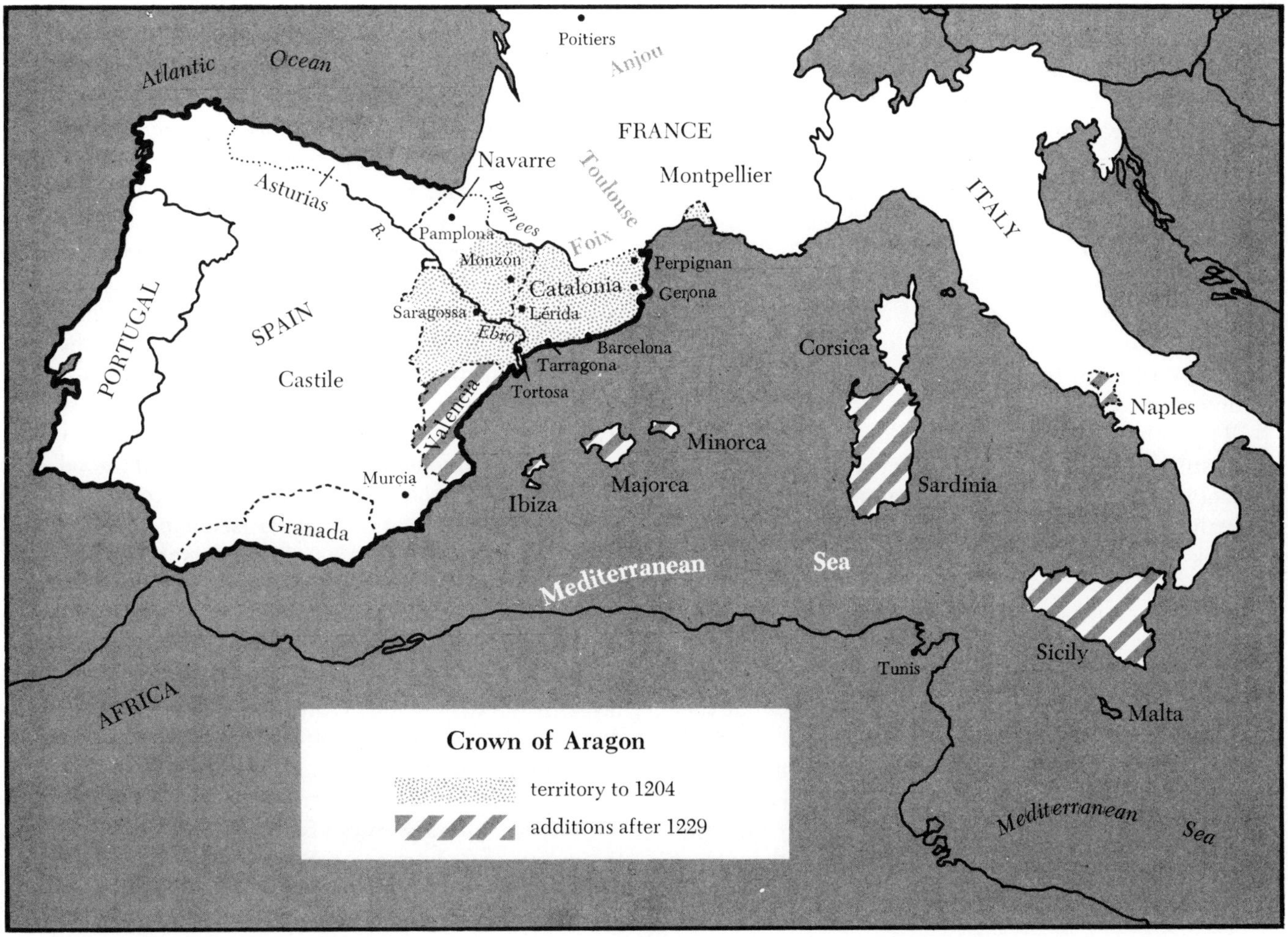

ARAGON, CROWN OF (1137–1479)

(1166) without leaving a male heir. Thereupon Alfonso's advisers, goaded by Guillem VII of Montpellier, seized Provence in defiance of the claims of the late count's daughter, who had been betrothed to the count of Toulouse. So was renewed the old conflict between Toulouse and Barcelona. The count-king secured recognition of his rights by compensating Raimond V of Toulouse (1176), appointed his brothers successively to the countship of Provence, and then (1185) assumed for himself the title "marquis of Provence" and governed the county through a procurator. Alfonso was aided by the rise of legitimist sentiment in Provence founded on the rights of his grandmother Dolça, a development that enabled him likewise to vindicate his dynastic claim to Millau, Gévaudan, and the Carladès adjoining Gévaudan on the west.

But his success in Provence cost the count-king support elsewhere in the Midi. By 1176 most of the magnates of lower Occitania, including the viscount of Béziers, had aligned themselves with Toulouse. To counter these defections, Alfonso secured the vassalage of Béarn (1170) and Bigorre (1175) and the fidelity of Foix. Such was the situation when, in November 1179, having become vulnerable to the Church's decision to combat heresy actively, Roger II of Béziers upset the Toulousan hegemony by commending himself and his lands to Alfonso, thus renewing an old tie and bringing Catalonian influence in Occitania to a new peak.

Strengthened on his Pyrenean frontiers, Alfonso II returned to Hispanic affairs in his later years. He abandoned the alliance with Alfonso VIII, who had continued to be tempted by Aragonese borderlands, and entered into agreements first with Navarre (1190), then with Leon and Portugal (1191), against Castile. But the Almohad victory at Alarcos (1195) lent urgency to a papal effort to unite the peninsular realms against Islam, a project in which Alfonso took the lead, but which was frustrated by his death in 1196.

Pedro II (Pere I in Catalonia, 1196–1213) succeeded his father in Aragon and Catalonia as well as in most of the Occitanian suzerainties; his brother inherited Provence, Millau, and Razès. But while the concept of a solely peninsular union thus survived intact, Pedro was to be at once more ambitious and less successful across the Pyrenees than his father had been. He broke with tradition by allying with Raimond VI of Toulouse. In 1204 he married the heiress Maria of Montpellier, and a few months later had himself crowned at Rome by Pope Innocent III, to whom he agreed to pay an annual tribute. Despite the latter engagement it can be shown that this event was cannily planned by the count-king to enhance his prestige among Christian monarchs. It led logically to Pedro's spectacular role in the united crusading army that crushed the Almohads at Las Navas de Tolosa in 1212.

But the Aragonese-papal entente failed badly in Occitania during the Albigensian Crusade. Pedro tried to mediate; he accepted Simon de Montfort's fealty for Béziers; he gave Simon the custody of his infant son; and his sister married Raimond VII of Toulouse. When he obtained the commendation of the counts of Toulouse, Comminges, and Foix, and the people of Toulouse allied themselves to him in January 1213, Pedro achieved a pinnacle of political success in Occitania. He had challenged Simon de Montfort, leader of the Albigensian Crusade, and a claimant to the county of Toulouse. It was not to last. On 12 September 1213 the victor at Las Navas lay dead on the battlefield of Muret, his lately enlarged designs shattered by his own tactical imprudence and by Montfort's well-drilled knights. The Catalan lordship of Béziers-Carcassonne collapsed.

It is easy to exaggerate the import of this disaster. The Occitanian suzerainties had never been regarded as extensions of Catalonia, and if Pedro II envisaged the dynastic conquest of Occitania, he was the first of his house to do so. But the defeat precipitated internal issues critical to the constitutional formation of the Crown of Aragon. It came at a time when the old aristocracies felt threatened by social and economic trends. In both Catalonia and Aragon the continued growth of population was linked to sustained agrarian expansion and commerical prosperity; Alfonso II promoted resettlement and local order by granting innumerable charters. A class of "good men" rose to predominance in the older towns; in Lérida, Cervera, and Barcelona semiautonomous councils emerged about 1200. The secular clergy became better organized under the archbishops of Tarragona and the Roman See; the older Benedictine houses, while retaining their traditional dynastic affiliations, saw royal and popular preference shift in favor of the Cistercians, Hospitalers, and Templars. An artificial Provençal culture flourished in the count-kings' courts; Alfonso II, himself a poet, patronized many of the ablest troubadours of the age.

Only the military elites of Aragon and Old Catalonia had ceased to prosper as in the past. Their dissatisfaction with the slackened pace of the Reconquest may be discerned in the apparition of a pseudo-

ARAGON, CROWN OF (1137–1479)

Alfonso the Battler about 1174. Barons in both lands led the opposition to King Pedro's extravagance, presuming to represent popular opinion in the enlarged courts now more frequently convoked. To support the rising costs of their expanded retinues, Alfonso II and his son tried to turn compensations for the maintenance of monetary stability and the peace into territorial subsidies, but in the process they abused precedents and violated custom. In 1205 the Catalonian barons tried unsuccessfully to impose a charter on Pedro II, who countered desperately by imposing a money-tax (ostensibly a compensation for maintaining the coinage stable) not only on Catalonia (for the second time in his reign) but also, for the first time ever, on Aragon.

Another cause of aristocratic discontent was the rise of an administrative elite recruited from clergy, knights, and the lower classes. The territorial peace was made the basis for a higher jurisdiction, hostile to baronial courts, entrusted to vicars responsible to the count-king. About 1178, Alfonso II employed Ramon de Caldes, dean of Barcelona cathedral, to reorganize the comital archives for more efficient access in suits against castellans feigning independence; this work led to the compilation of the "Great Book of Fiefs" (1192–4), one of the earliest administrative registers of a medieval monarchy. But the shift from patrimonial exploitation to fiscal administration was slow and erratic. Curial officers, like the *mayordomo* in Aragon or the seneschal in Catalonia, remained primarily domestic servants and their titles tended to become honorific; untitled barons and scribes supervised the farmers and auditors (*merini* in Aragon, bailiffs in Catalonia; they were peasants, merchants, and Jews) who managed the king's estates. In Catalonia this fiscal accounting was tightened under the direction of Ramon de Caldes (1178–1194), a reform that collapsed, however, in the reign of Pedro II.

THE AGE OF JAMES THE CONQUEROR (1213–1276)

The minority of James I (Jaume I in Catalonia) was a time of reconciliation. Pope Innocent III persuaded Simon de Montfort to deliver the child to his legate and Aragonese and Catalan notables, who in 1214 presented him to an assembly of prelates, barons, and representative townsmen at Lérida to receive their professions of fidelity. James was brought up in the custody of the Templars at Monzón while his uncle Sanç supervised the regency. But Sanç was committed to avenging Muret, a cause that collapsed under papal pressure in 1218. Sanç gave way to procurators in Catalonia, Montpellier, and (probably) Aragon, who strove to recover alienated domains. In 1220 the Templars were commissioned to direct the accounting in both realms.

Only the barons remained disaffected. To deal with them, James was obliged to create factions of his own as he came of age. In Catalonia his most notable early success came in 1228, when he defended the heiress of Urgell against Gerald of Cabrera, rendering Urgell an annex of Barcelona. In Aragon troubles escalated after an unsuccessful siege of the Saracen stronghold at Peñíscola in 1225. Nobles banded with the townsmen of Jaca, Huesca, and Saragossa against the king, who prevailed only with difficulty in 1227. This league not only betrayed discontent with policies thought partial to Catalonia, but revealed a new potential for political expression in Aragon.

It was in the general courts (or *cortes*), which met frequently after 1214, that Aragonese barons and towns began to associate actively, and the towns represented in the league had been convoked to these assemblies. In both realms the king's men used such occasions to justify subsidies—the money tax in Aragon, the peace tax in Catalonia—thus encouraging political debate of a kind that might easily be carried on independently of the king. After 1225, Jaime convoked *cortes* less often, and then only to seek support in popular causes: for example, to secure the fidelity of Aragon to his infant heir Alfonso (February 1228), and ten months later to mobilize the Catalans against Majorca.

In his resolve to renew the Hispanic Reconquest, James I satisfied his barons, the Templars, and the pope alike. Catalan merchants, harried by Moorish pirates, influenced the decision to attack Majorca first. The expedition was carefully planned. Catalan prelates and barons agreed to furnish determined numbers of knights and foot soldiers on condition of receiving proportionate shares of conquered properties. A *bovatge* (tax for the maintenance of the peace) was ordained, and the peace and truce were renewed in the great *cort* of December 1228. Contingents from southern France but relatively few Aragonese joined the expedition, which was declared a crusade.

Sailing from Cape Salou and neighboring ports in some 150 ships, an army of 800 knights and 1,000 foot soldiers landed in Majorca on 9 September 1229, besieged the city until it fell on 31 December, and overran the island. Among the Christians' few casualties were Guillem and Ramon de Montcada, their family's emblem becoming symbolic of Catalonian valor. Catalans, notably men from the Empordà (northeastern Catalonia), dominated the resettlement; Marseilles obtained 300 houses; Barcelona, Genoa, and Pisa received privileges in Majorca. The *Usatges of Barcelona* were introduced together with the urban liberties in effect at Tortosa. The isle of Minorca became tributary; that of Ibiza fell in 1235 to the archbishop of Tarragona.

Having had the marriage with Eleanor of Castile annulled in 1229, James waited until 1235 to marry Iolanda (Violant) of Hungary, whose holdings in northern Europe seemed to an approving pope to pose no threat to Capetian interests in the south. Meanwhile, impatient Aragonese barons had forced the king's hand in Valencia. Morella fell to Blasco of Alagón in 1232, followed by the capture of Burriana and Peñíscola in a preliminary royal campaign (1233). A more urgent (and dangerous) motive for the Valencian conquest arose from the king's engagement to cede the Balearic Islands and Valencia to the sons of his second marriage.

The new campaign was projected in the *cortes* of Monzón (1236), which granted a money tax for the purpose. Operations began with the capture of Puig de Cebolla (1237), followed by the surrender of Valencia city (28 September 1238) on terms permitting the Moorish ruler and his followers to leave in peace. James was obliged to guarantee this agreement against his own men bent on pillage; but a more serious difficulty arose when the Aragonese, who had marked out Valencia for their own, found themselves outnumbered by Catalans in the Christian resettlement.

Aragonese custom had prevailed in charters granted during the earlier phases of the conquest (1232–1238), and continued to be prescribed in some borderland settlements thereafter. But about 1239 the king ordered a new territorial custom drawn up for Valencia, which was thus established as a realm in itself. The *Furs* (or customs) of Valencia, eclectic and Romanist in content, were composed in Latin, then (1261) republished in Catalan. Settlers came chiefly from the plains of Lérida and Urgell, in considerable numbers, but remained the minority in a predominantly Mudejar population. Expropriations were exceptional, the king confirming Muslim law and religion in many communities. The conquest was virtually completed with the capture of Játiva (1244) and Biar (1245), although there would be uprisings thereafter.

With the annexations of Majorca and Valencia, James I fulfilled the design of his forefathers. He had dramatically enlarged the Crown of Aragon in God's service, and his conquest of Murcia on behalf of Castile in 1266 proves that political opportunism did not replace the altruism traditional in his lineage. Nor had any public concern for administrative unity overtaken the conception of the royal inheritance as a proprietary condominium. If he reserved the patrimonial kingdoms for his first-born Alfonso in a provision for his second son Pedro (Pere in Catalan) (1241), James seriously proposed, in a second partition occasioned by the birth of a third son (1243 or 1244), to separate Aragon and Catalonia. This scheme reflected the king's increasing estrangement from Alfonso, whose Castilian sympathies grew stronger as his political ambitions were thwarted; moreover, James favored Catalonia (and Pedro) against Aragon by extending its western limits to include Lérida and its environs. Nor was this the end of partitions, since the birth of Ferdinand (1248) and the death of Alfonso (1260) occasioned new arrangements.

The Conqueror's success in Spain was offset by setbacks in southern France. In Béarn the heiress of Gaston VII was married to Alfonso of Aragon, but their brief union was fruitless, and the viscounty later passed to Foix. More ominous was the failure of the counts of Toulouse and Provence to bear male heirs, for the sons of James I were too closely related to the heiresses to compete for their hands with Capetian princes. Despite protracted negotiations to prevent it, James saw Provence pass to Charles of Anjou (1246) and Toulouse to Alphonse of Poitiers (1249). But while some lament was heard for the passing of native dynasties in the Midi, notably from the troubadours, there is no evidence that the Conqueror viewed the king of France as other than a fellow crusader. By the treaty of Corbeil (1258) James renounced all his rights and claims in Occitania, save that over Montpellier, while Louis IX gave up his claim to the counties of the former Spanish March. To complete this diplomatic reversal, which recognized Capetian expansion almost to the Pyrenees, James engaged his daughter Isabel to Philip, the heir to the throne of France.

But it was one thing to treat with Saint Louis, quite another to allow Charles of Anjou a free hand in the Mediterranean. In 1262 the Infante Pedro married Constance of Hohenstaufen (Constance of Sicily), the daughter of Charles's enemy Manfred, an event that stirred a pro-Catalan reaction in Provence.

 ARAGON, CROWN OF (1137–1479)

James assured France and the Holy See that no disloyalty to Charles or the pope was thereby entailed; but Pedro himself, principal heir since his elder brother's death in 1260, made no promise. By a new partition Pedro was designated to inherit Aragon, Catalonia, and Valencia, while his younger brother would succeed to the Balearic Islands, Montpellier, Roussillon, and Cerdanya [Cerdagne] (the aggregate of lands later to be known as the kingdom of Majorca).

James found it harder to govern in peace than in war. His barons were dissatisfied with a military program that reduced them to fighting Castile's Moorish wars for the benefit of Castile; and when he treated their violence leniently, he ran afoul of his more demanding son Pedro, who served as procurator from 1262. Pedro feuded with his half brother Ferdinand Sanchez, who finally betrayed his father by siding with the dissident Aragonese. This event reconciled James with Pedro, who crushed the revolt (1275). In 1269 the king had led an overseas crusade intended to cap his life's work. Its failure—James himself got no farther than southern France—was symptomatic of his loss of confidence. Disorders in Valencia city escalated into a general Saracen rebellion (1275), which the king tried to subdue before falling ill. He died at Valencia on 27 July 1276. The Infante Pedro restored order.

James the Conqueror was an outstanding ruler in an age of famous kings. A great warrior, he knew when (and where) to negotiate. No king in medieval history ever revealed himself better to posterity, and in writing (or inspiring) the *Book of Deeds,* James celebrated his peoples as well as himself in the glow of their most durable triumphs. His crusading piety was matched by his humanity: an impressive integrity in dealing with foes and fellow rulers alike, and a notorious weakness for women. His reign was marked by continued institutional growth. After the conquests the royal court began to keep registers of administrative correspondence. Among new forms of delegation, the procuratorships exercised by the king's sons and others pointed the way to the late medieval vice regencies. The *cortes,* becoming an instrument of political influence in Aragon and Catalonia, was instituted in Valencia.

In local government royal judges supplemented the vicars, who remained officers of justice, police, and muster in Catalonia. James I actively promoted urban life. A series of charters to Barcelona (1249–1274) attributed increasing administrative autonomy to the elected counselors and the assembly; the "Council of One Hundred" dates from 1265. The commercial law of Barcelona was codified in the *Libre del consolat del mar* (Book of the Sea Consulate) one of a remarkable series of legal compilations in the mid thirteenth century that include the customs of Valencia, Aragon, and Lérida, and the *Commemorations* of Pere Albert. The Franciscans and Dominicans spread from Barcelona and Perpignan throughout the Crown of Aragon.

MEDITERRANEAN EXPANSION (1276–1336)

Pedro III (Pere II in Catalonia, 1276–1285) succeeded his father a grown and tried ruler. It took him more than a year to put down the Valencian revolt, during which time he left Valencia only long enough to be crowned at Saragossa (November 1276), taking care not to use the royal title until then. But when he tried to collect a *bovatge* in Catalonia without first promising to uphold Catalan privileges, he met general resistance that, momentarily appeased (1278), was followed by risings of west Catalonian barons. Supported by the counts of Pallars and Foix and the viscount of Cardona, Ermengol X fought for a claim to Urgell so clouded that the king had virtually controlled the county since 1270. Pedro III captured the rebels at Balaguer (1280); won their loyalty in generous negotiations; and soon released all except Roger Bernard of Foix, who had induced the king's brother, James of Majorca, to join the rebels. Of James, Pedro demanded no less than homage and fealty for his inherited lands, relenting only on condition that James's successors render such submission. Pedro clearly intended to restore the unitary administration of his father.

Pedro now took bold initiatives. He tried to neutralize Castile and France at a stroke by seizing the Infantes de la Cerda, the disinherited grandsons of Alfonso X and the sons of Blanche of France. He projected a Portuguese marriage for his daughter and an English marriage for his son. He arranged a truce with Granada and renewed his protectorate over Tunis. And it is clear that he was thinking of Sicily when he prepared fleets for service on the Tunisian coasts in 1281 and 1282; his court had long harbored Hohenstaufen dissidents. When the Sicilians rose against the Angevins on 30 March 1282, Pedro readied himself for their call, and landed at Trapani to an enthusiastic welcome five months later. Having received the Sicilians' fealty and confirmed their customs, he drove the Angevin fleet from Calabrian waters.

Never had a realm been so easily annexed to the

ARAGON, CROWN OF (1137–1479)

Crown of Aragon—or so precariously. Charles of Anjou challenged Pedro to regulated single combat at Bordeaux, an engagement that Pedro prudently evaded (1 June 1283). But the (French) pope Martin IV excommunicated Pedro for attacking Sicily (a papal fief), relieved his subjects of their fealty, and conferred his lands on Charles of Valois. Pedro had now to deal with his own peoples. In a stormy *cortes* at Tarazona (September 1283), the Aragonese protested that they had not been consulted about the Sicilian project and that they were being taxed unlawfully; they also demanded that the *Fueros* of Aragon be made obligatory in Valencia. When the king's reply was found inadequate, the nobles and towns united at Saragossa to demand a general confirmation of their privileges, which the king was obliged to accept (October 1283).

Thus originated the Aragonese "Union," which was to have constitutional influence for decades; from this time, too, dates the power of the *Justicia* to mediate between the king and the Aragonese. The Catalans were no less angry before Pedro finally convoked them in December 1283 at Barcelona. It was there laid down that prelates, barons, knights, and towns should be assembled in Catalonia once a year, and that legislation should have their consent. The Catalans, too, had formed a representative union, but had contrived to render their general *cort* the instrument of its expression.

Not all discontent was allayed. In the spring of 1285 a demagogic uprising of workingmen at Barcelona was cruelly repressed. The count-king was unable to persuade the Aragonese to mobilize in Catalonia against the French. James of Majorca chose to support the French in an expedition labeled a crusade. In the late spring of 1285, Philip III crossed the eastern Pyrenees with some 8,000 men, forcing Pedro into defensive positions in the Empordà. Girona fell to the French after a long siege that gave Pedro time to harass the enemy, and his admiral Roger of Loria time to bring his fleet from Sicily. When Loria destroyed Philip's ships in the Gulf of Roses (3 September), the French position became untenable. Battered by the Catalans, the Capetian forces struggled back to Perpignan, where Philip III died in October. Pedro acted vigorously to deprive his insubordinate brother of Majorca, but, before he could do so, died on 11 November 1285.

"Peter the Great had triumphed over all his enemies," said Ferran Soldevila. He had gained Sicily, and pacified and defended his realms. But he had fundamentally altered the constitution by conceding baronial and municipal autonomy only after such resistance that he was forced to allow the power of the estates to be institutionalized. And it remained to be seen whether the Aragonese could be reconciled to an expansionist regime partial to Catalan interests, and whether Sicily could be defended against Angevins, Capetians, and popes.

These problems clouded the reigns of Alfonso III (Alfons II in Catalonia, 1285–1291) and his brother James II (Jaume II in Catalonia, 1291–1327). Alfonso, having inherited all the realms except Sicily, which passed to his brother, had also to contend with his rebellious uncle James. Negotiations with France were stalled as long as Charles of Salerno (captured in 1284) was imprisoned, and went badly once he was released (1288). In 1291, Alfonso agreed to withdraw support from his brother in Sicily and to offer obedience to the pope, who would lift the longstanding sanctions against Aragon.

This agreement collapsed upon the king's death in June 1291; James of Sicily succeeded, leaving his younger brother Frederick as lieutenant in Sicily. But when James found the Catalans unwilling to insist on sovereignty over Sicily at any cost, he revived his brother's initiative. He agreed (Anagni, June 1295) to convey Sicily to the Holy See in return for the lifting of sanctions, to marry the daughter of Charles II of Naples, and to restore Majorca to his uncle James on condition of his holding it in vassalage. To compensate for Sicily, Boniface VIII invested James II with Sardinia and Corsica in 1297. But the Sicilians refused their fate and elected Frederick king (1296), a fait accompli that neither the pope nor James II could undo. At Caltabellotta (August 1302) it was settled that Frederick should reign in Sicily for life, after which that realm should devolve on Charles of Naples. So Sicily remained effectively Catalan (-Aragonese), attracting numerous settlers from Catalonia and developing commercial ties with the homeland; and in 1322 the Sicilians defied Naples by swearing fealty to Frederick's son Pedro.

James II acted with energy and caution on all his frontiers. When Alfonso de la Cerda was excluded from the Castilian succession in 1295, James sent an Aragonese army against Castile while he himself overran Murcia. He subsequently abandoned the Cerda cause and compromised on Murcia, retaining Alicante and other places north of the Segura (1304). In North Africa, James promoted military and commercial interests, notably in Tunisia, but also, during the Castilian war, in Morocco, and even as far east as Egypt, where a treaty in 1293 virtually rendered

ARAGON, CROWN OF (1137–1479)

the count-king the protector of Christians in the post-Crusade Levant. James's second marriage, to Marie of Lusignan, was designed to enhance this east Mediterranean role, for Marie was a prospective heiress to Cyprus and Jerusalem; but this prospect collapsed when she was disinherited in favor of a nephew.

Catalonian influence reached Greece as the result of a spectacular exploit. In 1302, Catalan mercenaries idled by the end of the Sicilian war agreed to aid the Byzantine emperor against the Turks in return for concessions that soon led to their settlement in Greece. After 1311 the Catalan duchies of Athens and Neopatria became dependent on Sicily, and the custom of Catalonia was introduced; but the colonies descended from Catalan warriors were never more than a precarious outpost of the Crown of Aragon (1311–1388). As for Sardinia, where Genoese and Pisan resistance was inevitable, James II bided his time for a quarter-century before entrusting its conquest to his son Alfonso, who carried it out in 1323–1324. Here the Catalans had to dominate as colonial masters, like the Angevins in Sicily, and their rule was seldom secure.

If his grandfather was the great conqueror of his dynasty, James II was arguably the greatest of its rulers. In his time the Crown of Aragon became the foremost Mediterranean power while prospering economically and culturally. Rejecting the policy of dynastic partition, James prescribed (*corts* of Tarragona, 1319) that his realms be henceforth indivisible. He was attentive to the Aragonese, encouraging them to share in the conquest of Sardinia. He established a university at Lérida (1300), the most central of his peninsular cities. James loved administration. Through tireless diplomacy he recovered the Val d'Aran from France (1295–1312), dissolved the Templars without losing their property, and secured the homage of Sanç of Majorca (1321).

Templar and Hospitaler holdings in Valencia were consolidated in the Order of Montesa (1317). The royal court became more professional, with increasingly specialized delegations for the several lands. The *Mestre Racional,* first appointed after the conquest of Sicily, supervised finance and accounting; the patrimonial administration was strengthened. Perhaps most remarkable, James defused political opposition by working through the *cortes,* which evolved rapidly in his time. In Catalonia the counties of Urgell (1314) and Empúries (1322) were annexed to the comital patrimony.

For all the king's solicitude for the federation, Catalonia dominated the expansion. Western Mediterranean trade—grain from Sicily, salt and silver from Sardinia, cloth from Catalonia—fell increasingly into Catalan hands. Perpignan and Majorca, as well as Barcelona, opened commercial consulates in Mediterranean ports. The wars of Sicily, Greece, and Sardinia were fought chiefly by the dreaded *almogàvers,* mercenaries originally from the old Catalonian frontier. The leading cultural figures were also Catalans: the Franciscan writer and missionary Ramon Lull (*ca.* 1232–1316), the physician Arnald de Vilanova (d. 1311), the chroniclers Desclot (*d.* 1288) and Muntaner (1265–1336). James II, himself a vernacular poet, became deeply interested in medicine, and his court was suffused with Franciscan piety in the time of his wife Blanche of Anjou (*d.* 1311). His marriage to Elicsenda de Montcada in 1322 seems to have been a programmatic expression of Catalan patriotism. The spacious grace of Catalan Gothic architecture spread through the kingdom of Majorca and abroad.

The short reign of Alfonso IV (Alfons III in Catalonia, 1327–1336) was troubled by his marriage (1329) to Leonora of Castile, who wished to endow her own sons at the expense of those from her husband's first marriage, of whom Pedro was designated the heir. To evade the act of union, the king was induced to cede towns, such as Tortosa and Albarracín, an unpopular policy. He allied with Castile against Granada, a campaign from which he was recalled by a revolt in Sardinia.

PEDRO "THE CEREMONIOUS" AND HIS SUCCESSORS (1336–1410)

During the long reign of Pedro IV (Pere III in Catalonia, 1336–1387), the Crown of Aragon attained its apogee as a federative state. Pedro was molded curiously of past and present: assiduous, cultivated, pompous, vindictive, militant without a personal taste for combat, he took pride in his divine and dynastic destiny and his public obligation. He began with lofty intentions. Although only sixteen, he insisted on crowning himself in an otherwise traditional ceremony at Saragossa, thus rejecting papal pretensions founded on the precedent of 1204. He antagonized the Castilians by withholding his half brothers' inheritance and the Catalans by failing to confirm their customs according to precedent; he also tried to replace the Catalonian custom of revocable castellanies with the Castilian custom of heritable ones.

His great early success was the reconquest of Ma-

ARAGON, CROWN OF (1137–1479)

jorca from his brother-in-law, James III. When the latter antagonized France, Pedro contrived to summon him to a *cort* at Barcelona that he could not attend, thus opening the way to charges, and then a suit, against James. There was violence on both sides, and in February 1343, Pedro declared Majorca and James's other fiefs forfeited. In May, Pedro seized Majorca, and in the following year conquered Roussillon and Cerdanya as well. James, having first surrendered into a harsh captivity, later escaped, sold the lordship of Montpellier to France, and was killed in a vain attempt to recover Majorca (1349).

Pedro worked deliberately to reintegrate the kingdom of Majorca into the Crown of Aragon. Nevertheless, the rebellious spirit smoldered, and Pedro's absence from his western realms, together with attempts to exclude his brothers from the succession, resulted in a revival of the Unions in Aragon and Valencia. In the *cortes* of Saragossa (1347) Pedro had to capitulate to the Aragonese; in 1348 he was virtually a captive in Valencia. Meanwhile, Pedro's Catalan adviser Bernart de Cabrera had formed a party of Aragonese royalists that joined with Catalan forces under Lope de Luna to shatter the Unionist cause at Epila (July 1348). In October 1348 the king personally destroyed the privileges of the Union in a new *cortes* at Saragossa, and a similar act of ritual destruction was ordered in Valencia.

It was a troubled victory. Pedro's first wife had died in childbirth in 1347; his second died of plague barely a year later; only in 1350 was the consolidation of the Crown of Aragon completed by the birth of an heir to the king's third wife, Eleanor of Sicily. Economic misfortune had preceded the Black Death: the "first bad year" (1333); then the "year of the great hunger" (1347), which conceivably lessened resistance to the disease, which struck Majorca, Barcelona, and Valencia in May 1348 and swept inland. The plague diminished later that year, but revived each summer until 1351, and hit yet again—especially children—in 1362.

Pedro IV was soon caught up in more costly and less successful wars. In Sardinia the heavy-handed rule of Catalan officials caused an uprising in sympathy with the Genoese, against whom Pedro allied with Venice in 1351. In 1352 a Catalan-Venetian-Byzantine fleet won a costly battle with the Genoese in the Bosporus; in 1355 the king himself campaigned in Sardinia, captured Alghero, and resettled it with Catalans. But the king's forces were weakened by malaria, desertion, and a lack of sustained support from the homelands, where a Castilian war, still more burdensome and dangerous, had broken out.

Relations with Castile had been uneasy since the Aragonese penetration into Murcia (1304). Pedro IV's struggle with his Castilian kin was virtually repeated in reverse when Pedro I ("the Cruel," 1350–1369) succeeded his father in Castile at the expense of *his* own half brothers. When Pedro IV negotiated with the latter, there could be no turning back. Tarazona fell to Pedro the Cruel in 1357, and by 1363 much more of Aragon was lost. Nevertheless, the Aragonese objectives still remained viable, for by agreements with Henry of Trastámara (1363, 1366), Aragon was to acquire numerous cities of eastern Castile in return for supporting Henry's bid to conquer Castile.

But Pedro IV miscalculated when he gave up this alliance in favor of a treaty with Navarre providing for the partition of Castile. By the late 1360's it was becoming clear that Aragon lacked the resources to defeat Castile decisively, and when Henry of Trastámara supplanted his half brother in Castile (1369), he understandably refused to honor the old treaties with Pedro IV. The war continued until 1375, when Pedro secured the territorial integrity of Aragon and an indemnity while giving up Molina and Murcia. In a further agreement of transcendent if unforeseen importance, the Infanta Leonora of Aragon was betrothed to Juan of Trastámara.

Pedro's political hopes were now confined to the Mediterranean, itself an uneasy horizon. Unrest among the knights of Catalonia was exploited by James IV, who made a last attempt to recover his father's title to Majorca (1374). Sardinia remained turbulent; war with Genoa continued. More promising was Sicily, where the death of Frederick III, leaving a daughter as heiress (1377), fairly invited Pedro's intervention. But the Sicilians had come to think of the main Catalan line as foreign, and Pedro had difficulty securing custody of the heiress. Moreover, he failed to persuade his son Juan to marry her, and thus achieve a dynastic reunion of Sicily and Aragon. Ultimately, she married the son of Pedro's second son, Martín, who in 1380 assumed the administration of Sicily in his father's name; and in the same year the Catalan duchies in Greece, which were to be overthrown a decade later, submitted to Pedro IV. So for a few years at the end of his reign Pedro the Ceremonious achieved the administrative integration of a Crown of Aragon dramatically expanded to the east.

ARAGON, CROWN OF (1137–1479)

Yet the king's real power had declined. The customs of the older realms made no provision for extended military service or expansionist wars against Christian realms. Unable to match his rivals' ability to pay professional soldiers, Pedro IV became so reliant on the *cortes* and *corts* during the Castilian war that he lost the initiative in policy and finance. In 1359 he was obliged to cede judicial supremacy to the *corts* of Catalonia in return for a subsidy, and from then on the Deputation of the Generality functioned as an administrative committee of the *corts.* The royal patrimony had been dissipated in sales, pledges, and gifts. Thus the ruler who had begun his reign by attempting to enhance his prerogative with principles of Castilian law ended up bound by balanced constitutions in his peninsular realms.

Pedro was more successful in administration and culture. He justified (and exaggerated) his achievements in a brilliant vernacular *Chronicle.* He organized the royal court, the chancery, and the archives; rebuilt his palaces at Barcelona, Saragossa, and Valencia; and promoted universities at Perpignan and Huesca. He patronized scientific, historical, and poetical writing, translations into Catalan, cartography, and the revision of maritime law.

Pedro's sons succeeded him in turn: Juan I (1387–1395) and Martín I (1395–1410). Juan was a self-indulgent man of courtly tastes who took little interest in government. Influenced by his French wife, he was accused of favoritism and fiscal mismanagement. When the count of Armagnac invaded Old Catalonia, claiming title to Majorca (1389), Juan relied on his brother Martín to drive him out. He also left it to Martín and his son (who had married the heiress) to conquer Sicily, an expedition carried out in 1392, although it took years more to pacify the island. Martín I, while not unlike his brother, worked hard to recover alienated domains, and took serious interest in the economic and cultural needs of his realms. His lone success abroad was the pacification of Sardinia (1409). With the death of his son Martín in 1409, it seemed that Sicily might devolve to the principal royal line, a prospect that was dashed by the death of King Martín himself—without heirs—in 1410.

THE TRASTÁMARAS (1412–1479)

This breach of the direct succession brought on a constitutional crisis. Among numerous contenders for the crown, the favorite in Catalonia was James of Urgell, grandson of James II in the male line. But James antagonized the Aragonese, opening the way for the candidacy of Ferdinand of Antequera, grandson through his mother of Pedro IV, and the uncle of the king of Castile. In the spring of 1412, electors chosen by parliaments in the peninsular realms met at Caspe and decided in favor of Ferdinand I (1412–1416). James rebelled, but was captured in 1413 and died in prison twenty years later.

It was a fateful turning point, the dynastic ratification of Castile's demographic and military superiority. Ferdinand and his sons ruling after him were Castilians who married Castilians and appointed Castilians, and they were in real and constant danger of losing touch with their subjects. Ferdinand found it easier to govern as he had been accustomed to do in Aragon and Valencia than in Catalonia, where the estates exacted a high fee for support against James of Urgell. Meeting at Barcelona in 1413, the *corts* refused to grant the lesser nobility the status of a fourth estate, rejected a measure to alleviate the condition of the *remensa* peasants (serfs subject to onerous obligations) in Old Catalonia, and forced the king to recognize the Deputation as an independent authority for defense of the customs of Catalonia.

Ferdinand was more successful elsewhere. He helped to end the Great Schism by abandoning the obstinate Aragonese pope Benedict XIII (1416); made peace with Genoa (1413); restored order in Sardinia (which had revolted yet again during the interregnum); and placed Sicily, which he declared united to the Crown of Aragon, under the governance of his son Juan. He planned to link Sicily and Naples by marriage.

Alfonso V (Alfons IV in Catalonia, 1416–1458), like his father, met resistance in Catalonia, where the *corts* granted aid only on conditions that nullified royal mediation between oligarchical factions. There was trouble over appointments of Castilians; and the king flouted the *Fueros* of Aragon. His costly efforts to maintain his family's interests in Castile were unpopular in the Crown of Aragon. Only in the Mediterranean could he—sometimes—escape these constraints. From 1420 to 1423 Catalan fleets helped him increase royal power in Sardinia and Sicily; he also made progress in Corsica. In Naples he secured for himself Queen Giovanna's recognition as her heir, then lost that fragile prospect to Louis III of Anjou, whose brother René finally succeeded her in 1435. After a time in Spain (1423–1432) Alfonso returned to Sicily, and through tortuous negotiation and fighting conquered Naples (1436–1443).

He never returned to Spain, despite incessant appeals. He ruled his other realms through lieutenants general—such as his wife in Catalonia—and viceroys, and made some effort to centralize his federative administration, establishing a supreme fiscal jurisdiction and audit in 1455–1456. But Naples was not for him so much a unit of the Crown of Aragon as a preserve for his illegitimate son Ferdinand and a base for dynastic hegemony in Italy. Often tempted by still more distant ventures in the East, in the end Alfonso achieved little more than self-commemoration in his beloved Naples. He made some effort to revive Hohenstaufen administrative efficiency; patronized literature, music, and theology; squandered Catalonian and Sicilian money—and retained his Castilian habits and friends. His death was a signal for revolts in Sicily as well as in Naples.

Things were much worse in his Spanish realms. Aragon bore the financial brunt of Prince Juan's self-serving yet futile conflicts in Castile. Majorca was set back by the renewed war with Genoa, and suffered agrarian disorder. Only Valencia seemed relatively immune from the social unrest and economic dislocation that afflicted the other realms, Catalonia above all. Without firm direction the Catalan *corts* had fallen prey to searing antagonisms: of the lesser knights against the old nobility, of merchants and artisans against the urban patriciate, of greater landlords against the *remensa* peasants or against royal agents striving to recover alienated patrimony. At first Alfonso sided with the old aristocracy, but as their financial support dwindled, he revived—opportunistically—the traditional royal program of agrarian reform.

In the 1440's he negotiated with a syndicate of peasants from the Gironès (northeast Catalonia), offering them freedom for a grant of 100,000 florins, only to suspend the concession when the *corts* voted 400,000. In the towns Alfonso tried to alleviate social conflict by imposing the *insaculació*, or electoral lottery, which was introduced at Játiva in 1427 and spread widely thereafter. The patricians resisted this threat to their control of offices. At Barcelona the problem was compounded by economic troubles, creating a split between the "honored citizens" and landlords (called the *Biga*) and the merchants, artisans, and laborers (the *Busca*). Supported by the governor Galceran de Requesens, the *Busca* organized a "syndicate of the three estates," and in 1454–1455 gained control of the city councils. Once in power, the Busca tried to devalue the coinage and to protect the shipping and textile industries, delicate matters over which their leaders soon split. In the *corts* of 1454–1458 royal support of the *Busca* and the *remensas,* together with an effort to enlarge the representation of the urban estate, galvanized the opposition of nobles, prelates, and patricians. There could be no compromise in the absence of the king, who died in 1458.

The accession of his aging brother Juan II (1458–1479), who had been lieutenant general since 1454, did nothing to improve matters. Juan retained his Castilian ambitions, and he promptly abandoned the (Catalan) blockade of Genoa. Moreover, his refusal to approve his son Carlos of Viana's inheritance of Navarre led to a domestic quarrel that polarized the political cleavage in Catalonia. Carlos received a tumultuous welcome from all except his father when he came to Barcelona in 1460; he negotiated with his father's rival Henry IV in Castile; and he was arrested by Juan at Lérida (December 1460), an event promptly denounced as a violation of Catalonian liberties. The Deputation, the *Biga,* and the *Busca* moderates united in outspoken defiance of the king. Winning support throughout the Crown of Aragon, a council representative of Catalonia not only secured Charles's release, but imposed a "Capitulation" on Juan by which he conceded the Deputation's authority and promised to recognize his son's right of universal succession.

But the accord was too extreme, even perhaps for Carlos, who died in September 1461. The unanimity he had inspired soon collapsed. Queen Juana managed to win support for the king and their son Ferdinand, and when the *remensa* peasants revolted in 1462, a general civil war broke out. The Council of Catalonia raised an army to quell the uprising, while the queen first tried to impose a settlement on the peasants and then allied with their leader, Francesc de Verntallat. Meanwhile, King Juan's pledge of Roussillon and Cerdanya to Louis XI in return for French intervention fired a resurgence of antiroyalist patriotism. But the Catalonian cause (so to call it) failed to elicit much response in the other realms; its forces were inadequate, and its desperate bids to replace Juan with foreign rulers all miscarried.

Juan was not much better off, but he was patient and resourceful. After a reversal of alliances in 1466, the French supported Barcelona no better than they had the royalists. Girona and Barcelona surrendered in 1472, and Juan granted a general pardon conceding all Catalonian privileges except the Capitulation

ARAGON, CROWN OF (1137–1479)

of 1461. Moreover, Juan lost no time moving to regain Roussillon and Cerdanya, a politic but inconclusive effort, for money was still owing to France by the treaty of 1462; and Perpignan was lost again in 1475. The *remensa* conflict continued, as did disorders in Aragon, Valencia, and Sardinia. Juan's son Ferdinand, having married Isabel of Castile in 1469, became king consort in Castile at the death of Henry IV in 1474; and he succeeded his father in the Crown of Aragon in 1479. The old dream of Hispanic hegemony was realized at last—in favor of a Castilian dynasty.

SOCIETY, ECONOMY, AND CULTURE IN THE LATER MIDDLE AGES

The troubles in fifteenth-century Catalonia, while in some respects the result of peculiar circumstances, were symptomatic of structural problems characteristic of the Crown of Aragon. Everywhere society was oligarchic and jealous of the "liberties" by which it defended the incomparable advantages of birth and inheritance. Neither in *cortes* nor in municipalities were merchants, artisans, or peasants adequately represented; in some places even the lesser nobles were politically excluded. Yet the federation as a whole was remarkably urbanized: in Catalonia and Valencia some thirty percent of the population inhabited towns or cities. Only Aragon, where Saragossa, with some 15,000 inhabitants in the fifteenth century, was by far the largest place, formed an exception to this pattern. Thus the townspeople, the most dynamic social class, whose wealth the kings sought most urgently to tap, was also the most restricted and most vulnerable in its power and rights. Everywhere the nobility, including that of the "honored citizens," was thought to possess an innate right to command, a presumption that lent credibility even to political groups, like the *Biga,* without a viable cause.

The population of the peninsular Crown of Aragon is estimated to have totaled somewhat more than one million before the Black Death. This figure alone, when compared with Castile's six million, goes far to explain the rise of Castile to peninsular dominance. Catalonia, with some 500,000 inhabitants, was for long the most populous and prosperous of the realms, having more than twice the population of Aragon (about 250,000) or Valencia (200,000) in the early fourteenth century. As late as the 1450's Alfonso V saw fit to request 400,000 florins from Catalonia, 120,000 from Valencia, and 80,000 from Aragon.

Jews made up six or seven percent of the total population before 1348; Mudejars, mostly in Valencia, perhaps twenty percent; and there were several thousand slaves concentrated chiefly in the seaboard cities. The Black Death struck hard in the Crown of Aragon, notably in Majorca and Catalonia. A mortality of two-thirds has been discovered in the Plain of Vic. The result was to intensify social conflict. In Aragon the *cortes* regulated prices and wages to protect the nobility, clergy, and patriciate; in Catalonia the aristocracy was weakened as peasants fled to the towns. After numerous recurrences of plague, the fifteenth century saw demographic recovery in all the realms except Catalonia, where the population, reduced by war, disease, and emigration, stood at about 300,000 in 1497. During the civil war Valencia outstripped Catalonia, its capital of 75,000 becoming the largest city in the Crown of Aragon.

Nevertheless, mercantile prosperity had persisted strongly. In maritime enterprise Barcelona and Majorca competed effectively with Italian cities into the fifteenth century. Commercial protection and investment were promoted by the institution of funded debts at Barcelona, Perpignan, and Majorca city. Strength in trade was supported by the growth of a textile industry, notably in Catalonia, which drew in part on wool exported from Aragon and Valencia. But the competition of Genoa, together with rural depopulation, left Catalonia increasingly dependent on imported cereals; and imbalances of trade were reflected in overvalued currencies. These demographic and economic difficulties contributed to social unrest.

The Mudejars of Aragon, protected by the king and the lords, maintained themselves as farmers and artisans; those of Valencia, more than half the population and less well assimilated, declined in numbers and were persecuted in the fifteenth century. The Jews, mostly physicians, artisans, and moneylenders, were heavily taxed by the crown while exempt from municipal obligations. They were persecuted after the Black Death, especially in 1391, when massacres occurred at Valencia, Majorca, Barcelona, and elsewhere, inspired by fiscal, social, and religious motives variously compounded. The breakdown of religious *convivencia* (harmony) continued in the fifteenth century, when the fiery sermons of Vincent Ferrer resulted in conversions of Jews and Moors. As for the *Busca,* the setting aside of their program not

ARAGON, CROWN OF (1137–1479)

only invited civil war but accelerated the economic ruin of Catalonia. The *remensa* peasants, having agitated against seigneurial exploitation for a century, won freedom to leave their lands and exemption from the "bad customs" in the Sentence of Guadalupe (1486). Aragonese peasants, less well organized but often no less miserable, obtained no such relief.

Contemporaries lamented the strife that weakened the traditional order. But their very values were in conflict: sumptuousness for the ruling classes, poverty for the rest. As elsewhere, the friars were outspoken about disorder in the Church; the Valencian Dominican Vincent Ferrer (d. 1419) was preeminent among popular preachers. The traditional monastic life weakened, although the Cisterican house of Poblet retained an exceptional vitality. Vernacular literacy spread in the nobility and mercantile society, the tradesmen having a penchant for moral treatises; Francesc Eiximenis wrote much about civic functions as well as about constitutional order. There was a new interest in classical and secular moralities: the royal secretary Bernat Metge (d. 1413), having started out writing in traditional style, produced the first work of humanist prose in Catalan (*The Dream,* 1399).

Italian influences, manifest in Catalan painting from 1330, may be seen in the gracefully arched mercantile exchanges built at Valencia, Barcelona, and Perpignan, and more obviously in the court culture of Naples. France contributed to courtly manners, dress, and literary taste from the late fourteenth century. More distinctively Catalan was the sculpture of Jordi Johan, whose son Pere Johan (1398–after 1458) brought this art to high perfection in the portal of the Generality in Barcelona (1418), and later worked at Tarragona, Saragossa, and Naples. In the same period the Valencians Ausias March (*ca.* 1397–1458) and Joannot Martorell (*ca.* 1413–1468) introduced a new naturalism into Catalan literature. The high culture of the Crown of Aragon remained predominantly Catalan.

BIBLIOGRAPHY

Sources. The archival sources, mostly unprinted, survive in enormous quantity. The most important collections are preserved in the Archivo de la Corona de Aragón, Barcelona, where deposits of the chancery, monasteries, and military orders are very rich; for the thirteeneth and later centuries the outstanding resource is the series of chancery registers beginning about 1250. See generally *Guía del Archivo de la Corona de Aragón* (1958); and, for local resources, Josep Baucells i Reig et al., *Guia dels arxius eclesiàstics de Catalunya-Valencia-Balears* (1978). The main published sources are gathered chiefly in *Cartas de población y de franquicia de Cataluña,* José María Font Rius, ed. (1969); *Colección de documentos inéditos del Archivo General de la Corona de Aragón,* Próspero de Bofarull y Mascaró, ed., 48 vols. to date (1847–1977); *Cortes de los antiguos reinos ed Aragón y de Valencia y principado de Catalunya,* 26 vols. (1896–1922); Ferran Soldevila, *Les quatre gran cròniques* (1971); *Els nostres clàssics* (1925 to date); *Textos medievales* (1960 to date).

Secondary. Among general works dealing with the whole period, see especially Gerónimo Zurita y Castro, *Anales de la Corona de Aragón,* 7 vols. (1967–1979); and José María Lacarra, *Aragón en el pasado* (1972), 73–176, brief but sure. H. J. Chaytor, *A History of Aragon and Catalonia* (1934), is readable but dated. For the later period J. N. Hillgarth, *The Spanish Kingdoms, 1250–1516,* 2 vols. (1976–1978), is well informed with fine bibliographies; Ferran Soldevila, *Història de Catalunya,* 2nd ed. (1963), superbly informed but tendentiously pro-Catalan.

The Early Count-Kings (1137–1213). There is no thorough study of this period. See provisionally Soldevila, *Història;* chs. 7–10; and articles collected in *VII Congrés d'Història de la Corona de Aragó* (1962). On major topics: Ramon d'Abadal, "A propos de la 'domination' de la maison comtale de Barcelona sur le Midi francais," in *Annales du Midi,* **81** (1964); Thomas N. Bisson, "The Problem of Feudal Monarchy: Aragon, Catalonia, and France," in *Speculum,* **53** (1978), and "The Organized Peace in Southern France and Catalonia, *ca.* 1140–*ca.* 1233," in *American Historical Review,* **82** (1977); José María Font Rius, *Orígenes del régimen municipal de Cataluña* (1946); A. J. Forey, *The Templars in the Corona de Aragón* (1973).

The Age of James the Conqueror (1213–1276). There is a mediocre translation of the *Libre dels feyts* (original ed., Soldevila, *Els quatre grans cròniques*) by John Forster, *The Chronicle of James I, King of Aragon,* 2 vols. (1883). See generally Soldevila, *Història,* chs. 11–13; Lacarra, *Aragón,* pp. 84–125; Hillgarth, *Spanish Kingdoms,* I, 233–251; and for the present state of research, *Jaime I y su época,* (X Congrés d'Història de la Corona de Aragó, 1979). On consultation in the early years, see Thomas N. Bisson, "A General Court of Aragon (Daroca, February 1228)," in *English Historical Review,* **92** (1977); and for the annexation of Valencia, Robert I. Burns, S. J., *Islam Under the Crusaders: Colonial Survival in the Thirteenth-Century Kingdom of Valencia* (1973).

Mediterranean Expansion (1276–1336). The great primary narratives are Bernat Desclot and Ramon Muntaner, whose chronicles are both edited by Soldevila, *Els quatre grans cròniques,* and are respectively translated by F. L. Critchlow, *Chronicle of the Reign of King Pedro III of Aragon,* 2 vols. (1928–1934); and Lady Goodenough, *The Chronicle of Muntaner,* 2 vols. (1920–1921). See generally Soldevila, *Història,* chs. 14, 15; Hillgarth, *Spanish Kingdoms,* I, 251–286. Four major studies are Charles Emmanuel Dufourcq, *L'Espagne catalane et le Maghrib au XIII*[e] *et XIV*[e] *siècles* (1966); Luis González Anton, *Las Uniones aragonesas y las cortes del reino (1283–1301),* 2 vols. (1975); Juan Reglá Campistol, *Francia, la Corona de Aragón y la frontera pirenaica,* 2 vols. (1951); Vicente Salavert y Roca, *Cerdeña y la expansión mediterránea de la Corona de Aragón, 1297–1314,* 2 vols. (1956).

Peter the Ceremonious and His Successors (1336–1410). The main narrative sources include *Crónica de Pere el Cerimoniós,* Soldevila, ed., in *Els quatre grans cróniques* (a translation by Mary Hillgarth is announced); *Crònica dels reys d'Aragó e comtes de Barcelona,* A. J. Soberanas Lleó, ed. (1961), of which the Latin version is edited by Antonio Ubieto Arteta (1961). See generally Ferran Soldevila, *Història,* chs. 16–21; and the remarkable essay by Ramon d'Abadal i de Vinyals, "Pedro el Ceremonioso y los comeinzos de la decadencia política de Cataluña," in *Historia de España,* Ramon Menéndez Pidal, ed., XIV (1966). Also Hillgarth, *Spanish Kingdoms,* I, 347–371 (and, for citations of other works, 431–432); and studies in *La Corona de Aragón en el siglo XIV,* 3 vols. (VIII Congrés d' Història de la Corona de Aragó, 1969–1973).

The Trastámaras (1412–1479). For archival material and sources, see Hillgarth, *Spanish Kingdoms,* II (1978), 655–656; and bibliographies in works by Batlle, del Treppo, Vicens Vives, and Vilar cited below. For general secondary discussions, see Angel Canellas López, "El reino de Aragón en el siglo XV," in *Historia de España,* Menéndez Pidal, ed., XV (1964); Hillgarth, *Spanish Kingdoms,* II, 215–299; Lacarra, *Aragón,* chs. 6, 7; Ferran Soldevila, *Història,* chs. 22–26; Jaime Vicens Vives, *Juan II de Aragón* (1953) and *Els Trastàmares (segle XV)* (1956). On government, see José María Font Rius, "The Institutions of the Crown of Aragon in the First Half of the Fifteenth Century," in *Spain in the Fifteenth Century, 1369–1516,* Roger Highfield, ed. (1972); and Alan Ryder, *The Kingdom of Naples Under Alfonso the Magnanimous* (1976). On the *corts,* see Peter Rycroft, "The Role of the Catalan 'Corts' in the Late Middle Ages," in *English Historical Review,* 79 (1974); and Santiago Sobrequés Vidal, "Los orígenes de la revolución catalana del siglo XV: Cortes de Barcelona de 1454–1458," in *Estudios de historia moderna,* 2 (1952); and for the *cortes* of Aragon, Luis González Antón, *Las Cortes de Aragón* (1978).

Society, Economy, and Culture in the Later Middle Ages. Hillgarth, *Spanish Kingdoms,* II, pt. 1 provides a good survey; see bibliography. Among modern works fundamental to the discussion of the nature and chronology of socioeconomic change and of the place of Catalonia in the history of the later Crown of Aragon, see especially Carmen Batlle y Gallart, *La crisis social y económica de Barcelona a mediados del siglo XV,* 2 vols. (1973); Claude Carrère, *Barcelone, centre économique à l'époque des difficultés, 1380–1462,* 2 vols. (1967); Mario del Treppo, *I mercanti catalani e l'espansione della Corona d'Aragona nel secolo XV* (1972); Jaime Vicens Vives, *An Economic History of Spain,* F. M. López-Morillas, trans. (1969); Pierre Vilar, *La Catalogne dans l'Espagne moderne,* 3 vols. (1962), and "Le déclin catalan du Bas Moyen Age: Hypothèses sur sa chronologie," in *Estudios de historia moderna,* 6 (1956–1959).

THOMAS N. BISSON

[See also **Alfonso I; Almogavares; Angevins, France, England, Sicily; Castile to 1474; Languedoc; Montpellier; Pedro El Ceremonioso, Literary Court; Sicilian Vespers; Sicily, Kingdom of.**]

ARAKS RIVER (classical Armenian, *Erašx;* Greek, *Araxes;* Arabic, *al-Rass;* Persian-Turkish *Aras*), the only one of the four main rivers of Armenia that remains on the Armenian Plateau for most of its course. The Araks—as "Mother Arax" an Armenian national symbol—rises in the mountains south of Erzurum in Turkey and, flowing east to the Soviet border, then turns in a large arc to the southeast, forming along the way the Soviet boundary with Turkey and Iran. After joining the Kura, the Araks flows another 60 mi. (100 km.) to enter the Caspian Sea. In antiquity the Araks entered the Caspian as a separate river, and after a flood in 1897, a branch formed a secondary outlet south of the mouth of the main course. Its total length is about 650 mi. (*ca.* 1,080 km.).

BIBLIOGRAPHY

Guy Le Strange, *The Lands of the Eastern Caliphate* (1905; repr. 1966); Henry F. B. Lynch, *Armenia: Travels and Studies,* 2 vols. (1901; repr. 1965).

ROBERT H. HEWSEN

[See also **Armenia (Geography); Kura/Mtkvari.**]

ARARAT, MOUNT (Armenian, *Masis;* Greek, *Baris;* Persian, *Koh-i-nuh* ["Mountain of Noah"]; Arabic, *Aghri* [or *Eghri*] *Dagh;* Turkish, *Ağri Daği* ["Painful Mountain"]), an extinct volcano in Turkish Armenia, at *ca.* 16,900 ft. (5,172 m.) the highest mountain of western Asia. An Armenian national symbol, the mountain rises 14,000 ft. (4,267 m.) above the plains. Due south of Great Ararat lies the smaller, more perfect volcanic cone of Little Ararat (12,877 ft., 3,396 m.). Connected by a saddle (8,800 ft., 2,677 m.), their summits are seven miles apart.

Ararat has been associated with the story of Noah's Ark since at least the first century A.D. although this recently has been claimed to be a misreading of the biblical text, and many other legends concern the mountain. Ararat was first climbed successfully by Friedrich Parrot in 1829 and there have been many ascents since, in search of the Ark.

BIBLIOGRAPHY

James Bryce, *Transcaucasia and Ararat,* 4th rev. ed. (1896), 211–310; Henry F. B. Lynch, *Armenia: Travels and Studies,* I (1901; repr. 1965), 156–199; Friedrich Parrot, *Reise zum Ararat* (1834), trans. by W. D. Cooley as *Journey to Ararat* (1846); Gwyn Williams, *Eastern Turkey; a Guide and History* (1972), 238–240.

ROBERT H. HEWSEN

ARARAT (PROVINCE). See **Ayrarat.**

ARATOR, a Christian poet, was born in Liguria before 500 and died about 550. His father was probably a rhetorician. After being orphaned, he was educated by Bishop Lawrence of Milan. In his youth he knew the poet Ennodius and also studied in the school of Deuterius, an admirer of Ennodius. He became an advocate, and brilliantly pleaded a case before Theodoric the Great in 526. Soon afterward Athalaric became king and Cassiodorus wrote to Arator, asking him to serve in the king's court.

In 533, Justinian I began his campaign to reconquer the Western Roman Empire. The Ostrogoths suffered badly under the repeated assaults, and by 540 their empire was near collapse. Arator was profoundly affected by these events and was ordained as a subdeacon. In his *Epistula ad Vigilium* he says that after he had saved his body, he began to think about saving his soul. Thus inspired, he forswore writing pagan poetry and produced the Christian epic poem *De actibus apostolorum,* in 2,326 hexameters, modeled on the *Carmen paschale* of Sedulius. The poem covers selected acts of the apostles from the ascension of Christ to the visit of Paul to Rome. When it was finished, he wrote three dedicatory letters, to Pope Vigilius, Abbot Florian, and his friend Parthenius.

In the *Epistula ad Vigilium,* Arator justifies Christian poetry by noting that the Psalms, Jeremiah, and Job are in verse. He read the poem aloud to a large crowd of clerics, noblemen, and peasants at the basilica S. Petri ad Vincula (St. Peter's in Chains). The audience received it well, applauding and demanding encores. To a modern reader it seems tedious and poorly constructed, full of frequent rhyme and flawed prosody. Arator combines his knowledge of rhetoric with his new-found interest in Christian allegory and the mystical interpretation of numbers. The work was popular during the Middle Ages. Joannes Fuldensis, a Carolingian writer, placed *De actibus apostolorum* just beneath the *Aeneid.* Arator is listed among famous poets in the *Ars lectoria* of Aimeric of Angoulême (eleventh century).

BIBLIOGRAPHY

Berthold Altaner, *Patrology,* trans. by H. Gaef from the 5th German ed. (1960), 600–601; Maximilianus Manitius, *Geschichte der lateinische Literatur des Mittelalters,* I (1911), 162–167; Artur P. McKinlay, ed., *Corpus scriptorum ecclesiasticorum latinorum,* LXXII (1951); J. P. Migne, ed., *Patrologia Latina,* LXVIII, cols. 45–252; Frederic J. E. Raby, *A History of Christian–Latin Poetry,* 2nd ed. (1953), 117–120.

NANCY A. PORTER

[See also **Ennodius; Sedulius Scotus.**]

ARAXES/ERASX. See **Araks River.**

ARBEO OF FREISING (bishop 764–783) was born into the Bavarian family of the Huosi, raised in the household of Bishop Ermbert of Freising, later educated in Italy, and in 763 made abbot of Scharnitz. His lives of two locally venerated saints, Emmeram of Poitiers, venerated at Regensburg, and Corbinian, the first bishop of Freising, whose remains Arbeo ordered translated to Freising, are the first works known to have been written in Bavaria; the Latin in which they are written is characteristic of the period before the Carolingian reform. Under Arbeo, Freising drew closer to the Frankish political and religious orbit.

BIBLIOGRAPHY

Arbeo of Freising, *Arbeonis episcopi frisingensis vitae sanctorum Haimhrammi et Corbiniani* (1920); Bernhard Bischof, *Leben und Leiden des Hl. Emmeram* (1953); Wilhelm Wattenbach and Wilhelm Levison, *Deutschlands Geschichtsquellen im Mittelalter, Vorzeit und Karolinger,* (1952), 144 ff.; W. Wunder, "Aribo von Freising," in *Die deutsche Literatur des Mittelalters Verfasser Lexikon,* 1, 2nd. rev. ed., K. Ruh et al., eds. (1978), 100–107.

LEAH SHOPKOW

ARCADE, BLIND. See **Arch.**

ARČĒŠ (Urartaean, Argishtiuna; Greek, Arsissa or Arsessa; Latin, Aretissa; Arabic, Arjīsh; Turkish, Erçiş). A town on the northeast shore of Lake Van in eastern Turkey, Arčēš lay in the old Armenian principality of Aḷiovit-Aṛberani, belonging first to the House of Gnuni and then, after 772, to the Kaǰberunids. In the mid ninth century the town passed to the Qaysite emirs of Malazkirt and in the tenth century to the Kurdish Marwānids.

Captured by the Byzantines about 1025, Arčēš fell to the Seljuks in 1055/6, then passed to the shahs of Armenia in the twelfth century and to the Ayyubids in the thirteenth. Destroyed by the Georgians in 1208–1209, Arčēš recovered under the Mongols, who fortified it. As the earlier trade routes across the Armenian Plateau shifted to the south, Arčēš became highly prosperous because it was an important point on the road from Iran to Mesopotamia via Xoy, Van, and Bitlis. In the late thirteenth century Marco Polo counted "Arziz" with Erzurum and Erzincan as one of the three major cities of Armenia. A possession of the Black Sheep Turkomans in the fifteenth century, Arčēš passed to the Ottomans in the sixteenth century, and has been Turkish ever since. In the early nineteenth century the old town was permanently inundated by the rising waters of Lake Van.

BIBLIOGRAPHY

H. F. B. Lynch, *Armenia, Travels and Studies,* 2 vols. (1901), I, 26–27; Hakob A. Manandyan, *Trade and Cities of Armenia in Relation to Ancient World Trade,* Nina G. Garsoïan, trans. (1965); S. T. Eremyan, *Hayastanē ēst "Ašxarhacᶜoycᶜ "-i (Armenia according to the "Geography")* (1963); C. Toumanoff, *Studies in Christian Caucasian History* (1963); T. X. Hakobyan, *Hayastani patmakan ašxarhagrutᶜyun ("Historical Geography of Armenia"),* 2nd ed. (1968); A. Ter-Ḷewondyan, *The Arab Emirates in Bagratid Armenia,* Engl. trans. by Nina G. Garsoïan (1976).

ROBERT H. HEWSEN

[See also **Armenian Muslim Emirates.**]

ARCH, a curved construction that spans an opening, usually composed of wedge-shaped stones called voussoirs that are held together by mutual pressure and are supported only at the sides. The Mycenaeans developed an early form of the arch by corbeling, with each successive rectangular block of stone projecting beyond the one below it and held in position by the weight of the superstructure, but these arches were not load-bearing. The arch proper was devised by the Etruscans or Romans and was used extensively in early Christian and medieval architecture.

Blind arch: A decorative arch set directly against a wall surface with little if any supporting function.

Diaphragm arch: A round or pointed arch that spans the nave of a church from a pier or column on one wall to its counterpart on the opposite wall. The diaphragm, or transverse, arch helps to support the ceiling and was used extensively in Romanesque churches to isolate visually each bay unit. It was also used by Gothic architects, but they no longer distinguished it visually from a rib.

Equilateral arch: A pointed arch in which the radius of the arc is equal to the span of the arch; an equilateral triangle fits exactly within the opening.

Horseshoe arch: A round or pointed arch with an inner surface extending more than 180 degrees, most common in Islamic architecture but also found in some Byzantine and Lombardic buildings.

Lancet arch: A pointed arch in which the radius of the arc is larger than the span of the arch, resulting in a slender opening surmounted by a tall, steeply pointed arch. Also called acute arches, lancet arches were especially popular in thirteenth-century High Gothic churches in northern France.

Lombard arch: A form of surface decoration composed of pilasters that extend up the entire wall surface of a building and are joined at the top by a series of blind arches. Lombard arches decorated brick buildings in Ravenna during the fifth and sixth centuries (the Orthodox Baptistery) but received their characteristic stone form in the early Romanesque buildings of Italy, France, and Yugoslavia.

Ogee arch: An arch with a profile that describes a double curve, the lower portion concave, the upper portion convex. The ogee, or ogival, arch was introduced in the late thirteenth century and was especially popular in England (Ely Cathedral, Lady Chapel).

Pointed Arch: An arch produced by two or more arcs that culminate in an angle at the top. The pointed arch is more stable than a round arch because its halves lean against each other and are mu-

Diaphragm

Lintel

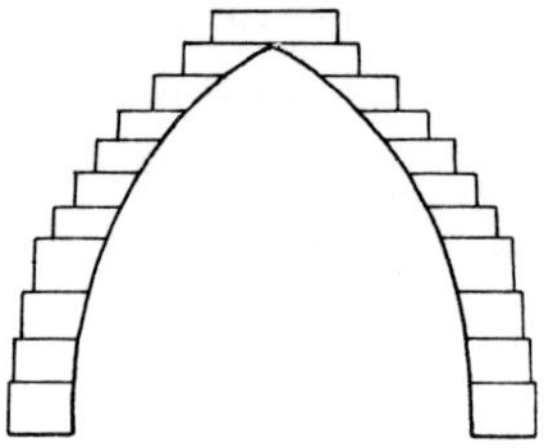

Corbelled

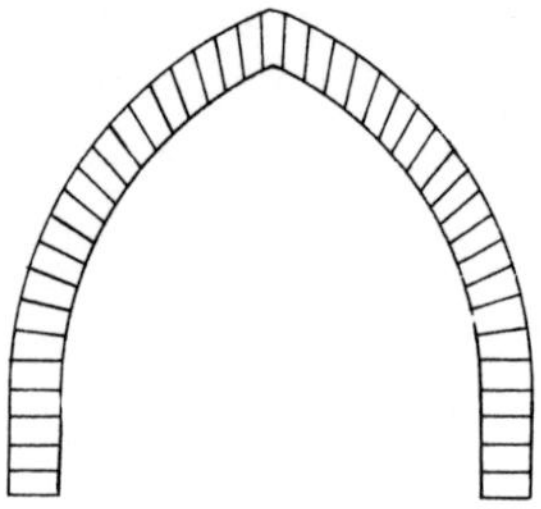

Pointed

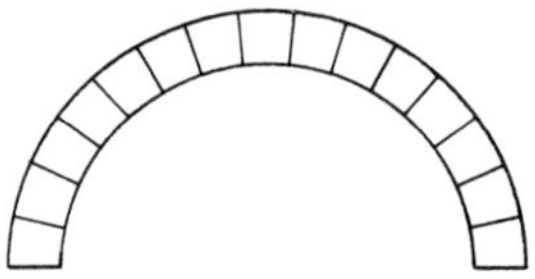

Round

Lancet

Blind or Lombard

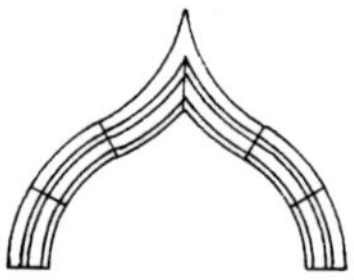

Ogee

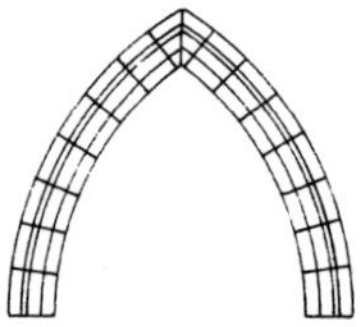

Equilateral

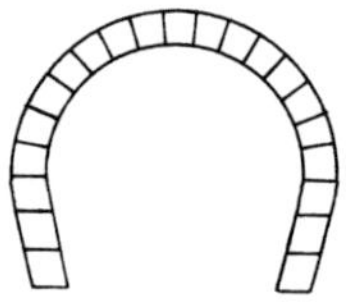

Horseshoe

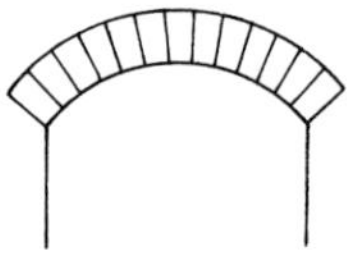

Segmental

Relieving

Flying Buttress
(Quadrant Arch)

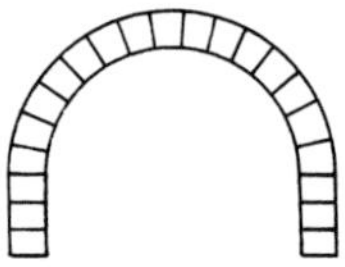

Semi-Circular Stilted

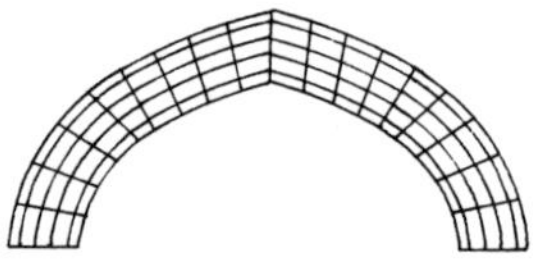

Tudor

TYPES OF ARCHES

tually supporting; much of the lateral thrust on the arch is also channeled down rather than out. First regularly constructed by the Arabs, the pointed arch was disseminated from Islam to Byzantium, where it was rarely used, and to the West, possibly by Crusader architects. Some Romanesque churches contain pointed arches (Autun), but they did not become characteristic features of western architecture until the middle of the twelfth century. The elaboration and refinement of the pointed arch was at least partially responsible for the increased verticality and decreased wall surface of Gothic cathedrals.

Quadrant arch: Half of a round or pointed arch, used as a buttress by Romanesque and Gothic architects.

Relieving arch: An arch, usually of rough construction, built as part of the wall surface above another arch or opening to relieve it of much of the imposed weight of the superstructure. Relieving, or discharging, arches were first used during the Roman period.

Round arch: A semicircular arrangement of voussoirs that converge toward the same point and are held together by mutual pressure. Until the Gothic period, the round arch was the most common form; both the barrel vault and the dome are based on the principles developed in it.

Segmental arch: A single arc that is less than 180 degrees, also called depressed arches.

Stilted arch: An arch in which the curve begins above the impost rather than springing directly from it; the vertical masonry between the impost and the springing line resembles stilts.

Tudor arch: A late medieval, rounded or pointed, elliptically shaped arch in which the curve begins by describing nearly a quarter-circle before continuing to the apex in a straight, or almost straight, line.

BIBLIOGRAPHY

John Fitchen, *The Construction of Gothic Cathedrals* (1961); John Fleming and Nicholas Pevsner, *A Dictionary of Architecture;* Paul Frankl, *Gothic Architecture* (1962).

LESLIE BRUBAKER

ARCHAEOLOGY OF MEDIEVAL MONUMENTS. Examination of the physical structure and decoration of medieval architectural monuments, for the purpose of dating and placing them in the general context of the development of medieval architecture, is a practice developed in the second half of the nineteenth century in Western Europe. This traditional archaeology, which is frequently conducted above ground and involves no actual excavation, is inconsistent and inadequate to its goals. Only during the last quarter of the twentieth century has a truly scientific methodology for the study of medieval monuments begun to be developed and practiced with some consistency.

TRADITIONAL ARCHAEOLOGY AND ITS SHORTCOMINGS

Architectural history is a subspecies of art history and employs the latter's methodology of analysis of style and technique, modified only as required to take into account techniques of masonry and timber construction. The underlying assumption of all stylistic analysis is that different details of design (projects for execution) and forms (executed projects) and different techniques of execution were employed by different individual designers and craftsmen and, like fingerprints, can be used to identify these individuals. A corollary to this assumption is that style and technique evolve in logical, discernible sequence and that plotting these progressions can reveal the order of creations of a given individual or of known or unknown individuals working in a given style or technique.

Neither of these assumptions is false; but neither is as sound—let alone as scientific—as their practitioners believe or would have others believe. At all times in all types of medieval monuments there were too many variables in design and execution to permit accurate plotting of linear development centuries after the fact. Moreover, many other assumptions by historians of medieval architecture have proved to be simplistic and have resulted in untenable conclusions.

The most erroneous simplistic assumption of architectural historians is the "one design = one designer" thesis, which holds that in any medieval building in which a change in design, material, or technique is observed, a change in designers occurred. The most extreme practitioner of this approach is the Australian, John James, who postulates that as many as thirty different designer-masons built Chartres Cathedral over a period of about thirty years (1194/1195–1225) but that no single designer or architect was ever in charge of the project's continuity.

Individual designers of all periods, including the medieval period, altered their designs due to considerations such as personal creative growth, simple changes of mind, changes of patron, fluctuations in funding, and availability of materials. The nave of Troyes Cathedral provides an especially well-documented case of one designer's having more than one design: in the 1450's Antoine Colas employed two rib profiles and two different pier designs.

Another simplistic assumption of architectural historians, that of a linear life cycle of stylistic development, was inherited from the "Father of Art History," Johann Joachim Winckelmann (*Geschichte der Kunst des Altertums,* 1764), and was promoted in the twentieth century by Henri Focillon (*Vie des formes,* 1924). George Kubler (*The Shape of Time,* 1962) has proved that styles are not independent of one another and that in any given style period there exist constant, simultaneous, and contrasting formal or stylistic trends in interaction, the more dominant being modified by the less dominant and, occasionally, replaced by it. In short, Kubler has clearly shown that the notion of a linear development of style is untenable, a finding that must be taken into account if the history of medieval architecture is to reflect historical reality.

Historians of medieval architecture have traditionally relied on medieval documents for textual evidence to correlate stylistic evidence. This practice has serious deficiencies, as the Pantheon in Rome proves. The inscription on that building refers to Marcus Agrippa, who died around 12 B.C., and the Pantheon was dated to his time until archaeologists found that the bricks in the building bore Hadrianic stamps. Only then was it realized that the Pantheon had been rebuilt during the reign of Hadrian (A.D. 117–138) and rededicated to Agrippa.

Few medieval documents of any nature focused either on the history or style of the buildings to which they refer. There are notable exceptions to this generalization—for example, Suger of St. Denis's account of his building activities in the 1140's and Gervase of Canterbury's account of the construction of the Gothic choir of Canterbury after a fire in 1174. However, most references to architecture in medieval annals and chronicles are formulas by writers who may never have seen the buildings in question. Accounts of fires frequently employ a stock formula of exaggeration for effect: for example, "1096. The Church of St. Martin at London with a large part of the city burned." Architectural historians have been far too prone to take such texts as being literally true and as proof that the church in question was totally consumed by fire (a rare occurrence in masonry construction, as the case of Canterbury shows) and that new construction was begun immediately or shortly thereafter.

The single most consistent abuse of medieval documents has been misuse of the expressions *ad opus ecclesiae* and *ad opus fabricae,* meaning "to the work of the church" and "to the fabric of the church." Donations *ad opus ecclesiae* were generally made to support the pious works of the church. Donations *ad opus fabricae* were made to the "fabric agencies" of churches, special accounts set aside for funding ordinary maintenance and repair and, as required, reconstruction of churches. But donations could be made to the fabric agency at any time. Texts recording specific donations to the *fabrica* by no means ensure that construction was either being considered or was underway when the donation was made (which was rarely the same time when it was recorded). Only if a text recording a donation is specific as to its purpose ("for the construction of the tower," "for the new vault," "for the windows in the chapel") is it safe to assume that construction was anticipated to begin shortly or was actually in progress. And it is by no means certain that funds were always disbursed for the purpose specified in the act recording the donor's intention.

Even texts and inscriptions providing exact dates for the laying of cornerstones or the consecration of altars are unreliable for dating construction, as the case of the Pantheon inscription proves. In medieval Europe as now, the laying of a cornerstone was the symbolic act of acknowledging construction, not the commencement of construction itself. The official *fundatio* or "establishment" of Cluny III in 1088 took place three to five years after construction of the great church had been started. Altars could be consecrated when someone of sufficient status happened to be available, and such altars were neither necessarily installed at the time of consecration nor put into service immediately afterward. The choir of Cluny III was neither complete nor in use on 25 October 1095, when Urban II happened to be at Cluny and consecrated the altars destined to be placed in the radiating chapels.

Architectural historians have long relied on another assumed principle now known to be unsound. This is the belief that all major architectural innovations, whether structural or decorative, originate in major centers of creative impulse, usually cities, and diffuse to less sophisticated areas. Two major examples of the reverse process in medieval architecture expose the inaccuracy of this diffusionist principle. The celebrated A-B-A three-story interior of main arcade, band triforium, and tall clerestory, which is characteristic of French High Gothic architecture, originated not in or around Paris but in small churches in the valley of the Aisne (Bony, 1957–1958). Bourges Cathedral, a French High Gothic building with a very different interior elevation, confirms Kubler's thesis that at all times there were alternatives to the norm. In 1980 Walter C. Leedy, Jr. proved decisively in *Fan Vaulting* what others had long suspected: the celebrated fan vault of late English Gothic architecture originated not in or around London and the royal court projects but in the West Country.

Finally, a major failure of medieval architectural historians has been their refusal to consider seriously the question of the simultaneous autonomous invention and development of similar forms of techniques. While anthropologists have rightly questioned the diffusionist theories of Vere Gordon Childe, many architectural historians doggedly maintain that every known motif originated in a specific time and place and spread to or was subsequently adopted elsewhere. This dubious proposition has led to a search for "firsts" as an end in itself; worse, searchers have confused "oldest known" with "first," seriously distorting what is known.

The issue of "firsts" was especially acute in the nineteenth century because many attempts to discover them were motivated more by nationalistic chauvinism than by a search for historical truth. Nationalistic claims of priority set scholar against scholar: the French and the English argued over who had the earliest ribbed vaults and who first employed the ogee arch; the French and the Germans argued over whether the hall churches *(Hallenkirchen)* of Germany were an autonomous development or the importation of an idea from Poitou.

It is clear that traditional stylistic analysis is an imperfect means of precisely dating historic monuments or of accurately plotting their places in the sequential development of style. Medieval documents often are unreliable for the purposes for which archaeologists have attempted to use them. Some of the most basic principles espoused by architectural historians are manifestly suspect. Only gradually have historians of medieval architecture begun to borrow methodologies from more scientific disciplines in an effort to improve the accuracy of their findings and interpretations.

EARLY ARCHAEOLOGY OF MEDIEVAL MONUMENTS

The goal of architectural history is to place monuments accurately in a historical context. For medieval monuments two interrelated contexts are involved, one purely architectural, the other socioreligious.

Until the second half of the nineteenth century the predominant focus of scholars was the socioreligious context. Investigation of medieval history centered on the interpretation of documentary evidence; monuments were of interest only to the extent that they played a role in understanding the setting of the evolution of Christianity in medieval Europe. The study of medieval architecture in 1840 was little advanced beyond the state of study in 1140. When Suger of St. Denis rebuilt the church of the abbey in the 1140's, he had neither the inclination nor the means to verify the tradition that the old church dated from the time of the Merovingian king Dagobert I (629–*ca.* 639)—the church in fact dated from the time of Charlemagne (*d.* 814)—or the belief that Christ himself had consecrated it.

This uncritical approach had not changed in France in the eighteenth century. The scholarly Congregation of St. Maur, established in 1621, set about to investigate systematically the history of French ecclesiastical foundations. In this effort scholars first began to take an interest in medieval buildings. The leader of this study was Dom Jean Mabillon, whose *De re diplomatica* (1681) is still considered the first great work on paleography. Mabillon's follower, Dom Bernard de Montfaucon, combined paleography and diplomatics with the study of medieval monuments and their sculptural programs. His most famous work, *Monuments de la monarchie française* (1729–1733), reveals clearly the shortcoming of studying monuments through documents. Whenever Montfaucon had a Merovingian or Carolingian document relating to an ecclesiastical foundation, he commonly dated any extant building on the site to the Merovingian and Carolingian dynasties, as he did with the twelfth-century portal of St. Germain des Prés. Montfaucon employed a personal and crude iconographic and stylistic analysis to misdate a number of twelfth-century sculptural programs. His conclusions were frequently based on examinations of drawings and engravings of sculpture rather than on examination of the sculpture itself; and in cases where a monument did not fit his theory (for example, the portal at Ivry), he simply ignored it.

By the nineteenth century, when his errors were

ARCHAEOLOGY

exposed, Montfaucon's tragic role had been played out: his misidentification of many portal statues of Old Testament kings and queens as Merovingians and Carolingians had led to their destruction in the antimonarchy rage of the French Revolution.

The first monographic studies devoted to specific French medieval buildings focused more on religious than on architectural history, and their content was based more on interpretation of documents than on firsthand examination of buildings. The first study of this type was Sébastien Roulliard's *Parthénie, ou Histoire de la très-auguste ... église de Chartres* (1609). Roulliard's claim that the "Polyclituses of yore would throw down their chisels" were they to see the sculpture of Chartres reveals his sensitivity to the famous sculpture of that building as well as his classical antiquarianism. Roulliard provided a walk-around tour of Chartres, including measurements taken from the inner faces of walls, a practice still employed by archaeologists.

In 1617 Oseas Schadaeus published a guide to Strasbourg Cathedral that included six engraved views of the building and the claim that it was the eighth wonder of the world. In Italy attention was directed to the study of early Christian monuments, the first great work being Giovanni Ciampini's *De sacris aedificiis a Constantino Magno constructis* (1693). Ciampini concentrated on Roman buildings that he knew firsthand, but he also included Constantinian foundations in the Holy Land, illustrated with thirty-five large folding engravings.

The most important seventeenth-century study of medieval monuments was the three-volume *Monasticon Anglicanum* (1655–1673), a collaborative effort of William Dugdale, who took most of the credit, and the philologist Roger Dodsworth, who did most of the work. The focus of this study was the history of the foundations, but the engravings in volumes 2 and 3 by Wenceslaus Hollar are considered among the finest ever done of medieval buildings. The *Monasticon Anglicanum* has been termed by Paul Frankl *(The Gothic)* "the first illustrated history of a medieval style [of architecture]," and it was the first instance of antiquarians studying medieval architecture as seriously as they had studied classical architecture. In France, Dom Michel Germain had the drawings made for a publication entitled *Monasticon Gallicanum* before his death in 1694, although they were not engraved and published until 1871. The focus of the work was its 169 plates rather than its text; and since many of the abbeys illustrated have since been destroyed or modified, these engravings are very valuable records.

The seventeenth century firmly established the practice of illustrating monuments studied. The eighteenth century continued this practice but made few advances in the scientific approach to monuments. Johann Wolfgang von Goethe's celebrated essay, *Von deutscher Baukunst* (1772), is an unusual early example of praise of the Gothic style but in fact was intended to extol the architect of Strasbourg Cathedral, Master Erwin [von Steinbach?] more than the building itself. The primary eighteenth-century example of a more inclusive study is Browne Willis' two-volume *Survey of the Cathedrals ...* (1727–1742), dealing with ten of the most famous English foundations and describing with some accuracy their principal architectural features. By the end of the century, the study of medieval monuments had become a respected scholarly activity. The format of the illustrated documented study was firmly established. Although the focus remained ecclesiastical history first and architectural history second, the groundwork had been laid for a different approach to medieval monuments.

THE FIRST TRUE ARCHAEOLOGY OF MEDIEVAL MONUMENTS: THE NINETEENTH CENTURY

In the nineteenth century a "new" archaeology of medieval monuments came into being for two reasons: a romantic fascination with the Middle Ages, accompanied by a religious revival; and a widespread effort born of nationalism to restore and even to complete unfinished medieval buildings. The two great accomplishments of the century were the compilation of complete inventories of medieval buildings and the first successful attempts to distinguish among the various styles of medieval architecture.

England led the way with romantic interest in the Middle Ages and in the revival of ecclesiastical or liturgical ritual. A sham Gothic ruin was built at Hagley Park as early as 1747, although London's Houses of Parliament, designed by A. W. N. Pugin and Charles Barry in 1835, represented a serious approach to the Gothic revival style. Pugin's *Contrasts* (1836) and *True Principles* (1841) illustrate clearly the emotionalism of the theory that "the medieval style of architecture is equivalent to true Christian faith."

Germany took the lead in completing unfinished Gothic cathedrals, most notably the nave and upper parts of the west facade and towers of Cologne

(1842–1880, on the basis of plans of *ca.* 1320) and the west spire of Ulm (completed in 1890 to a plan of *ca.* 1474–1492 by Mathäus Böblinger). In Italy the facades of the cathedrals of Florence and Milan were both finished in the nineteenth century.

France led Europe in the restoration of medieval monuments threatening ruin, through the direction of the Commission des Monuments Historiques, founded in 1839. By 1871 the commission had funded the restoration of 379 classified historic medieval monuments. The most famous, energetic, and controversial restorer-architect employed by the commission was Eugène Emmanuel Viollet-le-Duc, whose extensive restoration projects gave him an intimate knowledge of every aspect of all styles of French medieval architecture and permitted publication of his most celebrated work, the ten-volume *Dictionnaire raisonné ...* (1854–1868). Although distorted by his rationalist interpretations of medieval construction and decoration, the *Dictionnaire raisonné* remains an unrivaled study.

Viollet-le-Duc understood the different phases of medieval architectural style, including regional variations. Elsewhere such understanding was lacking. In England in 1817 Thomas Rickman published his *Attempt to Discriminate the Styles of English Architecture ...*, establishing the stylistic phases of English Gothic architecture still accepted with only minor modifications. John Britton's five-volume *Architectural Antiquities of Great Britain* (1807–1826) did for England what Viollet-le-Duc later did for France and, in the words of Kenneth Clark, "killed ruins and Rococco ... with an accuracy and detail [of text and illustration] never before achieved." The English had three other notable achievements in the study of medieval monuments: publication of a series of monographs in which documentation and firsthand investigation were reconciled—the best examples are George Gilbert Scott's *Gleanings from Westminster Abbey* (1861) and Robert Willis' studies of Canterbury (1845), Winchester (1846), and York (1846); study of domestic architecture, most significantly the five-volume *Some Account of Domestic Architecture in England* by Thomas Hudson Turner and John Henry Parker (1851); and investigation of foreign medieval architecture. Willis' study of Italian medieval architecture (1835) and George Edmund Street's study of Spanish Gothic architecture (1865) stand as monuments of a broad interest rarely imitated elsewhere in the nineteenth century.

In France important archaeological data resulting from their restoration activities were published in two forms by architects of the Commission des Monuments Historiques: monographs such as Jean-Baptiste-Antoine Lassus's study of Chartres (1837–1867) or regional studies such as *Architecture normande ...* (1884–1889) by Victor Ruprich-Robert. The Société Française d'Archéologie, founded by Arcisse de Caumont at Caen in 1834, provided an outlet for studies of individual buildings in its *Bulletin monumental* and an annual study of monuments of a specific city or region in its *Congrès archéologique.* As early as the 1840's the Société sent individuals to select sites to use the then new medium of photography to record specific monuments.

In Germany the pattern of investigation was comparable to that in England and France. In 1842 a transplanted Parisian, Sulpize Boisserée, followed up a monograph on Cologne Cathedral (1823) with *Monuments d'architecture ... du Rhin inférieur.* In this pioneering effort to study the architecture of five centuries, Boisserée was surprisingly accurate and unprejudiced, except for the claim that the Gothic style may have originated in Germany. The same allegation had been made in the first history of German architecture, Ludwig Steiglitz's *Von altdeutscher Baukunst* (1820). No one took either claim very seriously, but Boisserée and Steiglitz represent one of the sorriest aspects of nineteenth-century archaeology of medieval monuments, that of chauvinistic claims of national priority. The only interest of such petty arguments today is that they reveal that even before 1850 the pointed arch was taken to be the chief distinguishing feature of the Gothic style. The ribbed vault generated as much petty bickering as did the pointed arch, not merely pitting German claims against French claims, but pitting Frenchman against Frenchman. Anthyme Saint-Paul defended Poissy, and Eugène Lefèvre-Pontalis championed Morienval as having had the earliest known ribbed vaults. This dispute attracted the attention of John Bilson, bringing him into the fray with the claim (1898–1899) that Durham's ribbed vaults were even earlier. Even in the twentieth century the English and the French have argued over who first employed the ogee arch.

Happily, by the end of the nineteenth century most scholars were above such petty parochialism and demonstrated a wider range of interest in medieval architecture, establishing a seminal pattern of investigation. The finest example of late nineteenth-century internationalism is Georg Gottfried Dehio

ARCHAEOLOGY

and Georg von Bezold's two-volume *Die kirchliche Baukunst des Abendlandes* (1887–1901), with 601 engraved plans and elevations of medieval buildings of all periods. Auguste Choisy's *L'art de bâtir chez les Byzantins* (1883) proves that by the end of the century interest in medieval architecture had developed broad perspectives.

THE FIRST TRUE ARCHAEOLOGY OF MEDIEVAL MONUMENTS: THE TWENTIETH CENTURY

Study of medieval monuments in the twentieth century has continued and elaborated on the practices of the previous century with, however, two very significant differences: for the most part, the nationalistic search for "firsts" has been abandoned, and during the second half of the century the first steps toward a truly scientific archaeology have been taken.

Throughout the century monographs have been produced, as well as studies of entire styles or of regional variants. Great catalogs continue to appear, most notably Richard Krautheimer's five-volume *Corpus basilicarum christianarum Romae* (1937–1977) and Hans Kubach and Albert Verbeck's *Romanische Baukunst an Rhein und Mass* (1976), three volumes containing over 3,700 illustrations. These works demonstrate what a true inventory of monuments should be. Both avoid a major fault of earlier catalogs, for example, Robert de Lasteyrie's *Architecture religieuse en France* volumes (Romanesque, 1911; Gothic, 1926–1927), that of making lists and thereby linking in linear series features such as pier or window forms that had no historical connections. More recent archaeologists make every attempt to distinguish between "like" and "related."

An especially laudable aspect of twentieth-century study of medieval monuments is the serious investigation by Western scholars of medieval architecture outside Western Europe, starting with Alexander Van Millingen's *Byzantine Churches in Constantinople* (1912). The studies of Islamic architecture by Giovanni Rivoira (1914) and K. A. C. Creswell (1932–1940) are comparable examples of breadth of interest.

The maturity of the study of medieval monuments in the twentieth century is perhaps best proved by two developments. One is that scholars such as Henri Focillon, Hans Jantzen, and Hans Sedlmayr have written not on the structure of buildings but on their meanings. The other is that a number of scholars have felt sufficiently secure to write surveys of entire styles of medieval architecture, usually as part of a series such as the Pelican History of Art or the History of World Architecture series. These sweeping surveys present grave difficulties on two counts: within a given series the studies themselves, being by different individual authors, are uneven; and at best they represent the state of the art at the time of publication and are very quickly outdated by subsequent detailed investigations and publications.

It is the monographic study that most frequently invalidates or forces revision of status quo knowledge about medieval monuments. From Georges Durand's three-volume monograph on Amiens (1901–1903) through Dethard von Winterfeld's on Bamberg (1979), the "definitive monograph" has been a peculiarity of twentieth-century scholarship. This is explained by several considerations. Many such studies originated as doctoral dissertations; and many scholars have come to realize that the complexities of a single great building require a lifetime of investigation and reflection. Von Winterfeld studied Bamberg for fifteen years before publishing his monograph. Walter Horn and Ernest Born collaborated for more than thirty years prior to publishing *The Plan of Saint-Gall* (1979), a "paper monument" since the famous plan was never executed as drawn. Kenneth J. Conant devoted a full career to excavation and study of Cluny, publishing reports along the way but not summarizing the totality of his conclusions until 1968, after forty years of work.

Monographs are always welcomed, for they invariably make the objects of their attention newly or better understood, and the new data presented and interpretations offered ultimately enter the more general literature. Nonetheless, such studies invariably present two inherent problems. The complexity and sheer bulk of many monographs make them appear to be definitive, leaving others with the feeling that nothing remains to be said on the subject; and a monographic study can be intensely personal, and therefore controversial, in its interpretation. One reviewer said of John James's interpretation of Chartres, "If John James is right, then nearly everyone else is wrong." Another reviewer said of Hans Reinhardt's monograph on Rheims (1963), "Reinhardt's Reims is a building I have never seen."

There are two remedies for the personal-interpretation monograph, other than authors' eschewing writing of them. One is for readers to recognize that interpretation of evidence is inexact and subjective,

ARCHAEOLOGY

and to insist that all interpretation be as objective as possible. The other is for authors to employ new technologies to augment traditional stylistic analysis.

THE NEW TECHNOLOGIES

The extensive damage to many medieval buildings during World War I and II permitted archaeologists to observe structural and design "secrets" for the first time since the buildings themselves were completed; Gilman's memoir on Rheims and Soissons (1920) is only one of many examples. Excavations undertaken preparatory to reconstruction revealed foundations of earlier churches at Rheims after World War I and at Rouen after World War II, to cite only two examples. Since World War II exceptional discoveries have been made either through intentional efforts or as the accidental result of restoration or of urban renewal projects. A prime example of the former is the discovery of the sixth-century (and later) church of Santa Reparata under Santa Maria del Fiore in Florence during the extensive archaeological campaign of 1965–1974. Dramatic examples of the latter were the discovery in April 1977 of 364 fragments of sculpture from the Cathedral of Notre Dame during excavations for the foundations of a new bank in Paris and the discovery in 1974 of the eleventh-century synagogue of Rouen under the courtyard of the Palais de Justice during the course of repair to the pavement.

Beginning in the 1960's and the 1970's, excavators of medieval monuments began to borrow from anthropological archaeologists their techniques and methodologies, including physical and chemical means, of dating finds.

The best known of these is radiocarbon dating, devised in the 1940's by the astrophysicist Willard F. Libby. Reduced to simple terms, the complex principle of radiocarbon (C^{14}) dating is that all living organisms take in radioactive carbon until death, at which time absorption stops and the radiocarbon begins to disintegrate or reduce. Since the rate of disintegration is measurable, the time of death can be determined; thus burials can be plotted chronologically, and the time when a specific piece of timber was cut can be known. The technique has become so sophisticated that even the carbon in soot on an iron cooking pot—not itself datable by this process since the iron pot never absorbed C^{14}—can be dated. It has been determined that the amount of radioactive carbon in the atmosphere has not always been constant, as had originally been assumed, and certain adjustments have had to be made in deriving dates from C^{14} analysis; but the system itself is not suspect. Carolyn Marino Malone is an example of an archaeologist who employed C^{14} analysis of mortar, excavated at St. Bénigne at Dijon, to corroborate dating based on stylistic analysis and other documentation (1978).

A more recent means of physicochemical dating of architecture is thermoluminescence (TL) testing. The theoretical principle, first enunciated by Robert Boyle in 1664, is that when clay is fired the radioactive energy in certain minerals in it is locked into place, "setting the clock to zero at the time of firing." Refiring the clay under carefully controlled laboratory conditions releases this stored energy in the form of heat and light, which can be measured in such a way as to determine the time between firings. TL testing was performed on mortar from sixteenth-century Venetian villas, accurately dated by other means, to verify the accuracy of TL dating. Cross-verification not only confirmed it but also revealed new data about certain of these structures not known from other documentation (Geodicke *et al.*, 1981).

A third means of dating historic monuments is that of dendrochronology, developed by the astronomer Andrew Ellicott Douglass in 1901 and since refined. Dendrochronology is based on the dating of timber growth and harvest by measuring the unique pattern of annual growth rings in trees. Starting with newly cut timber, then matching growth rings backward from timber removed from progressively older buildings in the same geographic area, year-by-year chronologies can be worked backward for centuries and even for millennia in areas of continuous timber growth and use. Oak grown in Britain and in southern Germany has been employed to establish chronologies of approximately 1,000 years.

Dendrochronology's obvious advantage over either C^{14} or TL dating is that it yields absolute chronologies. The others give relative chronologies, there being uncertainty factors in both processes, for example A.D. 1200 $\pm$ 150, or a period between 1050 and 1350. There is an obvious caveat involved with all of these physicochemical means of dating: any one may show when an individual died, a brick was fired, or a beam was cut. But they tell nothing about reburial in a later structure when a cemetery was removed (a common medieval practice) or about the reuse of bricks or timber from an earlier building in the construction of a later building. Scientists and historians agree that all of these scientific methodologies provide cross-checks and can be useful adjuncts to traditional stylistic analysis and textual documentation; but no one of them replaces traditional methodologies. It is clear that scientific methodology has not and cannot replace common sense.

In addition to analysis of remains to determine or verify dates, engineers have become involved in the study of medieval structure. Best known in this effort are Jacques Heyman and Robert Mark. An engineer at Cambridge University, Heyman has done analysis of medieval vaults (1968) and medieval timber roofs (1976). Mark is an engineer from Princeton University who has analyzed medieval structure in a novel way. He has constructed small epoxy models of medieval buildings (Amiens, Bourges, and Chartres cathedrals, among others) and has attempted to replicate various stresses on the actual buildings, for example, vault thrust and wind pressure or loading on roofs. The replicated stress pattern is baked into the model and can be seen in polarized photographs. Mark has received wide attention by publishing in popular magazines as well as scholarly journals. The scholarly community has been slow to accept his conclusions because many doubt that his small epoxy models "work" exactly like masonry structures weighing millions of tons. Mark has also turned to mathematical computer modeling of medieval vaults (1977). It is certain that the methodologies of the engineer, no less than those of the physicist and chemist, have come to stay in the study of medieval monuments.

Finally, a solution has been found to the abiding critical problem of obtaining truly accurate measurements of medieval buildings. This is photogrammetry, first employed at Bamberg in 1903, a system of employing three cameras to record images of the same subject from three different, carefully controlled angles. The results are then simultaneously projected onto a special screen, from which composite a very detailed contour map showing variations of millimeters can be drawn (Crosby, 1980). Photogrammetry is much more accurate than steel tapes or even the use of theodolites but, like the physicochemical dating methodologies, is expensive, requires special equipment operated by trained specialists, and does not give on-the-spot results.

CONCLUSION

From the seventeenth century until the second half of the twentieth century the investigation of medieval architectural monuments demonstrated few methodological advances. Aboveground and underground archaeology, beginning in earnest in the nineteenth century, have added immeasurably to our knowledge. Focus on architectural history as an end in itself rather than as an adjunct to ecclesiastical history was a significant step forward. Yet it has become clear—if only reluctantly acknowledged by architectural historians—that traditional stylistic analysis is merely an imperfect art. Practitioners have finally realized that only through the integrated collaborative efforts of architectural historians, laboratory scientists, paleographers, and other experts can the archaeology of medieval monuments hope to become true science. Only when documentation, connoisseurship, and physicochemical interpretations verify one another can one feel confident in the results of investigation and interpretation.

BIBLIOGRAPHY

No one has yet written the history of the archaeology of medieval monuments, for which reason there is no specific—let alone standard—bibliography. However, several works require special citation. Paul Frankl, *The Gothic; Literary Sources and Interpretations Through Eight Centuries,* Priscilla Silz, trans. (1959), is of much wider scope than its title suggests and is the best summary of the study of medieval architecture from the twelfth through the twentieth centuries. For developments in England, Catalog 14, *The Gothic of Gothick, English Church Building in Nineteenth Century Theory and Practice,* B. Weinreb (n.d. [but after 1960]), is most valuable. For France the key source is the centennial volume (vol. 97) of the *Congrès archéologique de France* (1934), which traces the history of the Société Française d'Archéologie and the Commission des Monuments Historiques.

Much of the information given above under "The New Technologies" is summarized from Rainer Berger, ed., *Scientific Methods in Medieval Archaeology* (1970). Only recently have specialized studies of the new methodologies begun to appear in scholarly journals; likewise, specific "how to" texts, such as Michel de Bouard, *Manuel d'archéologie médiévale* (1975), are a recent phenomenon.

Works cited above include John Bilson, "The Beginnings of Gothic Architecture," in *Journal of the Royal Institute of British Architects,* 3rd ser., 6 (1898–1899); Jean Bony, "The Resistance to Chartres in Early Thirteenth-Century Architecture," in *Journal of the British Archaeological Society,* **20–21** (1957–1958); Kenneth J. Conant, *Cluny: Les églises et la maison du chef d'ordre* (1968); K. A. C. Creswell, *Early Muslim Architecture,* 2 vols. (1932–1940); Sumner McK. Crosby, "Some Uses of Photogrammetry by the Historian of Art," in *Études d'art médiéval offertes à Louis Grodecki* (n.d. [1980]); Georges Durand,

Monographie de l'église Notre-Dame, cathédrale d'Amiens, 3 vols. (1901–1903); Christian Geodicke *et al.,* "Thermoluminescence Dating in Architectural History: Venetian Villas," in *Journal of the Society of Architectural Historians,* **40** (1981); Roger Gilman, "The Theory of Gothic Architecture and the Effect of Shellfire at Rheims and Soissons," in *American Journal of Archaeology,* **24** (1920); Jacques Heyman, "On the Rubber Vaults of the Middle Ages, and Other Matters," in *Gazette des beaux-arts,* **71** (1968); and "An Apsidal Timber Roof at Westminster," in *Gesta,* **15** (1976); Carolyn Marino Malone, "Les fouilles de Saint-Bénigne de Dijon (1976–1978) et le problème de l'église de l'an mil," in *Bulletin monumental,* **138** (1980); Robert Mark *et al.,* "The Structural Behavior of Medieval Ribbed Vaulting," in *Journal of the Society of Architectural Historians,* **36** (1977); Augustus Welby Northmore Pugin, *Contrasts; or, a Parallel Between the Noble Edifices of the Fourteenth and Fifteenth Centuries and Similar Buildings of the Present Day* (1836); and *The True Principles of Pointed or Christian Architecture* (1841); Hans Reinhardt, *La cathédrale de Reims* (1963); Giovanni Rivoira, *Architettura musulmana* (1914); George Edmund Street, *Some Account of Gothic Architecture in Spain* (1865); Eugène Emmanuel Viollet-le-Duc, *Dictionnaire raisonné de l'architecture française du XIe au XVIe siècle,* 10 vols. (1854–1868); Robert Willis, *Remarks on the Architecture of the Middle Ages, Especially of Italy* (1835); Dethard von Winterfeld, *Der Dom in Bamberg* (1979).

CARL F. BARNES, JR.

ARCHANGEL, the second lowest of the nine orders of celestial beings. Gabriel, Michael, and Raphael are the only archangels specifically named in the Bible and Apocrypha, though their order traditionally consists of seven members. Represented in both Christian and Islamic art, archangels are usually nimbed and may hold a staff, labarum, scepter, or globe to symbolize their dominion over the terrestrial world.

LESLIE BRUBAKER

[See also **Angels and Angelology.**]

ARCHBISHOP. See **Clergy.**

ARCHDEACON. See **Clergy.**

ARCHES, COURT OF. Medieval England was divided into two ecclesiastical provinces, Canterbury and York. In the former, central ecclesiastical jurisdiction was exercised in two courts, the Audience Court of the archbishop, a peripatetic court that followed the archbishop (or his household) and heard cases both in first instance and on appeal, and the Court of Canterbury, also known as the Court of Arches because it sat in London at the Church of Saint Mary-le-Bow which had a spire supported by arches or bows. The Court of Arches likewise heard cases in first instance and on appeal. The lines of authority in these courts, and in the courts for the diocese of Canterbury (the consistory court and the Court of the Archdeacon) were established with some clarity only in the late thirteenth century.

BIBLIOGRAPHY

Brian L. Woodcock, *Medieval Ecclesiastical Courts in the Diocese of Canterbury* (1952).

RICHARD KAEUPER

ARCHIEPISCOPAL CROSS. See **Cross, Forms of.**

ARCHIMANDRITE (Greek, ἀρχιμανδρίτης), literally "head of the sheepfold," title given to a monastic abbot in the Eastern Church. Used interchangeably with *hegumenos* ("leader"), it appears frequently in documents of the fifth and the sixth centuries, particularly in the legislation of Justinian. In later centuries the title was reserved for the heads of a few important monasteries. (In the modern period it is used very widely to designate any unmarried priest in the Greek church.)

JOHN MEYENDORFF

[See also **Clergy, Ranks, Titles, Privileges of, Byzantine.**]

ARCHIMEDES IN THE MIDDLE AGES. Medieval geometry rested primarily on the *Elements* of Euclid. Yet there was a modest but persistent knowledge and use of some phases of the more mature geometry of Archimedes (*ca.* 287–211 B.C.) during the high and late Middle Ages. To understand the limits and sources of this knowledge one must first exam-

ARCHIMEDES IN THE MIDDLE AGES

ine the early stages of the transmission of the works of Archimedes.

Our knowledge of Archimedes' works depends primarily on the interest taken in them at Constantinople from the sixth through the tenth centuries. Before that time the individual works were studied at Alexandria and were often cited by Hero, Pappus, and Theon. But it was with the activity of Eutocius of Ascalon, who was born toward the end of the fifth century and studied at Alexandria, that the textual history of a collected edition of Archimedes began. Eutocius composed commentaries on three of Archimedes' works: *On the Sphere and the Cylinder*, *On the Measurement of the Circle*, and *On the Equilibrium of Planes*, presumably Archimedes' most popular works at that time.

The works of Archimedes and the commentaries of Eutocius were studied and taught by Isidorus of Miletus and Anthemius of Tralles, Justinian's architects of Hagia Sophia at Constantinople. Isidorus was probably responsible for the first collected edition of the Archimedean works and Eutocian commentaries then being studied. Later Byzantine authors seem gradually to have added other works until the ninth century, when Leon of Thessalonica prepared the compilation given in Greek manuscript A (adopting the designation used by the modern editor, J. L. Heiberg).

Manuscript A, which appears to have been a codex of the ninth or tenth century, contained all of the Greek works of Archimedes now known except *On Floating Bodies*, *On the Method*, *Stomachion*, and *The Cattle Problem*. It was one of two Greek manuscripts available to William of Moerbeke when he made his Latin translations in 1269. It was the source, directly or indirectly, of all the Renaissance copies of Archimedes before its disappearance sometime after 1564. A second Greek manuscript, which I have called B in place of Heiberg's 𝔅, included only the mechanical works: *On the Equilibrium of Planes*, *On the Quadrature of the Parabola*, and *On Floating Bodies*. It too was available to Moerbeke but has been missing since a reference to it in a catalog of 1311. Finally, there is a third Greek manuscript, C, a Byzantine palimpsest in a hand of the tenth century, that was not available in the West until its identification by Heiberg in 1906 at Constantinople. It contains large parts of *On the Sphere and the Cylinder*, almost all of *On Spirals*, parts of *On the Measurement of the Circle* and *On the Equilibrium of Planes*, almost all of *On Floating Bodies*, a part of *Stomachion*, and, most important of all, *On the Method of Mechanical Theorems*.

At the time that the texts of Archimedes were being collected in Byzantium, the Arabs began to study Archimedes. It seems unlikely that the Arabs possessed any Greek manuscript as complete as manuscript A. Still they often brilliantly exploited the methods of Archimedes and brought to bear their fine command of conic sections on Archimedean problems. Of the genuine works of Archimedes the following seem to have been translated into Arabic: (1) *On the Sphere and the Cylinder* and at least a part of Eutocius' commentary on it. A poor early translation was revised in the ninth century, first by Isḥāq ibn Ḥunayn and then by Thābit ibn Qurra. It was reedited by Nasīr al-Dīn al-Ṭūsī in the thirteenth century and was on occasion paraphrased and commented on by other Arabic authors. (2) *On the Measurement of the Circle*, translated by Thābit ibn Qurra and reedited by al-Ṭūsī. There is some evidence that Eutocius' commentary on it was also available. (3) A fragment of *On Floating Bodies*, consisting of a definition of specific gravity not present in the Greek text, a better version of its basic postulate than exists in the extant Greek text, and the enunciations without proofs of seven of the nine propositions of Book I and the first proposition of Book II. (4) Perhaps *On the Quadrature of the Parabola*—at least this problem received the attention of Thābit ibn Qurra. (5) Some indirect material from *On the Equilibrium of Planes* found in other mechanical works translated into Arabic, such as Hero's *Mechanics*, the so-called *On the Balance* attributed to Euclid, the *Liber karastonis* of Thābit ibn Qurra, and others.

Various other works found in Arabic bear Archimedes' name but have no known source in Greek. Of these works, the *Lemmata (Liber assumptorum)* and *On the Division of the Circle into Seven Equal Parts*, though surely not by Archimedes in their extant forms, betray techniques that seem Archimedean in character.

Knowledge of Archimedes came into the Latin West from both Byzantium and Islam. There is no trace of earlier translations imputed by Cassiodorus to Boethius. The only Archimedean knowledge that circulated in the West before the twelfth century was some hydrostatic information found in a *Carmen de ponderibus* (present in several codices of Priscian's grammatical work) and in a fragment, *De probatione auri et argenti*, that circulated independently

ARCHIMEDES IN THE MIDDLE AGES

and was absorbed in slightly emended form in the well-known medieval collection of recipes *Mappae clavicula*. But this material is in no way directly related to the works of Archimedes. It bears, rather, on the crown problem the solution of which by Archimedes is described by Vitruvius in his *Architecture*.

In the twelfth century the translation of Archimedean works into Latin was first made from Arabic. *On the Measurement of the Circle* was translated twice. The first, a rather defective translation that may have been done by Plato of Tivoli, bears the title *Liber Ersemidis in quadratum circuli*. There are many numerical errors in the extant copies, and the second half of Proposition 3 on the calculation of π is missing.

The second translation, also from the twelfth century, was executed by the celebrated translator Gerard of Cremona. It was complete and indeed included a corollary on the area of a sector of a circle attributed by Hero to Archimedes but missing from our extant Greek text. There were two traditions of this translation, *Liber Arsamithis de mensura circuli* and *De quadratura circuli tractatus*. In at least one manuscript of the second tradition the author's name is given as Archimenides, which became the most popular form of the great geometer's name during the Middle Ages. Not only was Gerard's translation widely quoted by medieval Schoolmen such as Gerard of Brussels, Roger Bacon, and Thomas Bradwardine, but it also served as the point of departure for a whole series of emended versions and paraphrases during the thirteenth and fourteenth centuries.

Among these are the so-called Naples, Cambridge, Florence, and Gordanus versions of the thirteenth century; and the Corpus Christi, Munich, and Albert of Saxony versions of the fourteenth. These versions were expanded by the inclusion of pertinent references to Euclid and by the detailing of geometrical steps that are only implied in Archimedes' text. In addition, we see attempts to specify the postulates that underlie the proof of Proposition 1. For example, in the Cambridge version three postulates (*petitiones*) introduce the text: "[1] There is some curved line equal to any straight line and some straight line to any curved line. [2] Any chord is less than [its] arc. [3] The perimeter of any including figure is greater than the perimeter of the included figure." Furthermore, self-conscious attention was given in some versions to the logical nature of the proof of Proposition 1. Thus, the Naples version immediately announced that the proof was to be *per impossibile*, that is, by reduction to absurdity.

Another trend in the later versions was the introduction of inept physical justifications for postulates. In the Corpus Christi version, the second postulate to the effect that a curved line may be equal to a straight line is supported by the assertion that "if a hair or silk thread is bent around circumferencewise in a plane surface and then afterward is extended in a straight line in the same plane, who will doubt—unless he is harebrained—that the hair or thread is the same whether it is bent circumferencewise or extended in a straight line and is just as long the one time as the other?"

Finally, in regard to the many medieval versions of *On the Measurement of the Circle*, it can be noted that the Florence version of Proposition 3 (*ca.* 1400) contained a detailed elaboration of the calculation of π. One might suppose the influence of Eutocius' commentary, except that the arithmetical procedures in the Florence version differ widely from these of Eutocius. Furthermore, no Latin translation of Eutocius' commentary appears to have been made before 1450, and the Florence version must surely be dated before that time.

In addition to translating *On the Measurement of the Circle*, Gerard of Cremona also translated the Archimedean work entitled *Discourse of the Sons of Moses (Verba filiorum)* composed by the ninth-century Arabic mathematicians, the Banū Mūsā. This translation introduced important Archimedean procedures and conceptions into the Latin West, and particularly those relevant to Archimedes' *On the Sphere and the Cylinder*.

It includes a proof of Proposition 1 of *On the Measurement of the Circle* that differs slightly from that of Archimedes' tract. It has further calculations of π similar to those found in Eutocius' commentary. It includes theorems with demonstrations for the area and volume of a cone as well as theorems with demonstrations of an Archimedean character concerning the area and volume of a sphere. It uses a formula for the area of a circle equivalent to $A = \pi r^2$, in addition to the more common Archimedean form $A = \frac{1}{2} cr$. Instead of the modern symbol π the authors use the expression "the quantity that when multiplied by the diameter produces the circumference." Finally we should note that the *Verba filiorum* introduced into the West two of the classic Greek geometrical problems, the finding of two

ARCHIMEDES IN THE MIDDLE AGES

mean proportionals between two given lines and the trisection of an angle.

The *Verba filiorum* was, then, rich fare for geometers of the twelfth century when compared with the handbook geometry of the Roman *agrimensores* or the geometry of Gerbert at the end of the tenth century. Still the handbook tradition, with its collections of formulas (but without much attention to demonstration), continued vigorously in the Middle Ages and the Renaissance with only occasional influence from the Archimedean works that were circulating.

The *Verba filiorum* was quite widely cited in the thirteenth and fourteenth centuries—indeed, it was known to Regiomontanus in the fifteenth century. It was used by Leonardo Fibonacci in the early thirteenth century and somewhat later by the author of the longer version of the *De triangulis* attributed to Jordanus de Nemore. For example, the author of that tract extracted the solution of the trisection of an angle from the *Verba filiorum* but in addition made the perceptive suggestion that the *neusis* involved in the solution of this problem can be solved by the use of a proposition from Ibn al-Haytham's *Optics* in which a similar *neusis* was solved by conic sections.

Further interest in Archimedean geometry was stimulated by the appearance about 1200 of *Liber de curvis superficiebus Archimenidis*. In one tradition it bears the name of Johannes de Tinemue and was either translated from the Greek or composed on the basis of a Greek tract. A second tradition has the colophon: "Explicit commentum Gervasii de Essexta [*or* Assassia]." The tract contains ten propositions and several corollaries. These are concerned, for the most part, with the surfaces and volumes of cones, cylinders, and spheres; and thus the treatise has the same basic objective as *On the Sphere and the Cylinder* of Archimedes.

The author employs a form of the method of exhaustion that differs from that of Archimedes. It simplifies the proofs of Archimedes' main conclusions by assuming that to any plane surface there exists some equal conical, cylindrical, or spherical surface; and that with two surfaces given there is a surface similar to one of the given surfaces and equal to the other. Furthermore, with two volumes given there exists a solid similar to one of the given solids and equal to the other. These assumptions are coupled with the principle that an "included figure" cannot be greater than an "including figure." The including figure for this author always surrounds the included and in no way touches it (compare Euclid, *Elements*, Proposition XII.16). The method that the author used may have been suggested to him by the proof of Proposition XII.18 of the *Elements*. We should also note that the author of the *Liber de curvis superficiebus* substituted rectangular measures of figures bounded by curved lines or surfaces for the circular measures that appear in *On the Sphere and the Cylinder*.

The *Liber de curvis superficiebus* was a very popular work and was often cited by later authors. In fact, along with the translation of *On the Measurement of the Circle*, it initiated a mild flurry of Archimedean geometry. In one version of *De curvis superficiebus* (represented by manuscript *D*), two original propositions were added; and to another version (in manuscript *M*) three further propositions were added. In the first proposition of this latter set, the Latin author applied the method of exhaustion to a problem involving the surface of a segment of a sphere, revealing that at least this author had made the method his own. The techniques and propositions of this work were taken over and brilliantly extended in the sixteenth century by Francesco Maurolico under the title of *On the Sphere and the Cylinder*.

About the same time as the appearance of the *Liber de curvis superficiebus*, an unknown geometer named Gerard of Brussels composed *Liber de motu*, which extensively employed the conclusions and techniques of *On the Measurement of the Circle* and the *Liber de curvis superficiebus*. From the latter Gerard took its modified form of the method of exhaustion and used it often. Also noteworthy was his skillful technique of comparing geometric magnitudes and their motions by comparing their corresponding line elements, a technique reminiscent of a rather similar method used in Archimedes' *On the Method*. However, it is clear that Gerard could not have seen the Archimedean work, which had long since disappeared. It is probable that Gerard's method of the summation of infinitesimals came from extending Euclid's Proposition V.12 to infinite sets of corresponding line elements. The *Liber de motu* was quite influential on the development of kinematics at Merton College, Oxford, in the first half of the fourteenth century, a development that seems ultimately to have influenced Galileo.

In 1269, some decades after the appearance of the *Liber de motu*, the next important step was taken in the passage of Archimedes to the West: much of the Byzantine corpus of his works was translated from

ARCHIMEDES IN THE MIDDLE AGES

the Greek by the Flemish Dominican, William of Moerbeke. In this translation Moerbeke employed Greek manuscripts A and B, which apparently had passed into the papal library in 1266 from the collection of the Norman kings of Sicily. Charles of Anjou seems to have given this collection to the pope after Manfred's defeat at Benevento.

All the works included in manuscripts A and B except for *The Sandreckoner* and Eutocius' *Commentary on the Measurement of the Circle* were rendered into Latin by William. Needless to say, *On the Method*, *The Cattle-Problem*, and the *Stomachion*, all absent from manuscripts A and B, were not among William's translations, though he included at the beginning of his codex two pseudo-Archimedean works: *Liber de speculis comburentibus* (written by Ibn al-Haytham and translated by Gerard of Cremona) and the *Liber de ponderibus* [*Archimenidis*], a hydrostatic work of mixed Latin and Arabic origin. Although William's translations are not without error, they present the Archimedean works in an understandable if literal way.

We possess the original holograph of Moerbeke's translations in MS Vat. Ottobonianus lat. 1850. This manuscript, being in William's hand and exhibiting many marginal words and notes that reveal his hesitation and puzzlement concerning the Greek text, gives us a unique view of the great translator at work. This codex was not widely copied. The translation of *On Spirals* was copied from it in the fourteenth century (MS Vat. Reg. lat. 1253, 14r–33r); several works were copied from it in the fifteenth century in an Italian manuscript now at Madrid (Bibl. Nac. 9119), and one work *(On Floating Bodies)* was copied from it in the sixteenth century (Vat. Barb. lat. 304, 124r–141v, 160v–161v).

But, in fact, the Archimedean translations of William of Moerbeke were more influential than we would expect from this paucity of manuscripts. They were used by several Schoolmen at the University of Paris toward the middle of the fourteenth century. Most noteworthy was their use by John of Murs, an astronomer and mathematician whose works were quite widely read in the fourteenth and fifteenth centuries. He appears to have been the author of a hybrid tract entitled *Circuli quadratura*, which consisted of fourteen propositions. The first thirteen were drawn from Moerbeke's translation of *On Spirals* and were just those propositions necessary for the proof of Proposition 18 of *On Spirals* (= Proposition 13 of the *Circuli quadratura*), which demonstrates that a tangent to a spiral of first revolution intercepts on a perpendicular drawn from the origin of the spiral a line equal to the circumference of the first circle of the spiral.

The fourteenth proposition of the hybrid tract was Proposition 1 from Moerbeke's translation of *On the Measurement of the Circle*. Thus the author realized that, by the use of Proposition 18 of *On Spirals*, he had achieved the necessary rectification of the circumference of a circle preparatory to the circle's final quadrature accomplished in Proposition 1 of *On the Measurement of the Circle*.

Incidentally, the hybrid tract did not merely use the translations of William of Moerbeke in near-verbatim fashion but also included considerable commentary. In fact, this medieval Latin tract is the first known commentary on Archimedes' *On Spirals*, a commentary that was at times exceedingly perceptive. For example, in one place the commentator suggests that a *neusis* introduced by Archimedes in Proposition 7 of *On Spirals* could be solved by means of an *instrumentum conchoydeale*. The only place in which a medieval Latin commentator could have learned of such an instrument was in that section of Eutocius' *Commentary on the Sphere and the Cylinder*, Book II, Proposition 1, where Eutocius describes the quite different use of this instrument in Nicomedes' solution of the problem of finding two mean proportionals. Hence it was an act of some cleverness for the author to suggest its use in *On Spirals*.

There is further evidence that John of Murs knew Eutocius' *Commentary* in the translation of William of Moerbeke, for the Parisian mathematician used sections from this commentary in his *De arte mensurandi* (Chapter VIII, Proposition 16) in presenting three of the many solutions of the means problem given by Eutocius. John also incorporated the whole of the above-noted *Circuli quadratura* into Chapter VIII of his *De arte mensurandi*. Furthermore he quoted verbatim in Chapter X of that work many propositions from William of Moerbeke's translations of *On the Sphere and the Cylinder* and *On Conoids and Spheroids* (he misapplied the latter work to problems concerning solids generated by the rotation of circular segments). It is worth noting also that the treatment of spiral lines in *Circuli quadratura* seems to have influenced the accounts of spirals found in the *De trigono balistario* composed by the Venetian physician Giovanni Fontana in 1440 and in the *Quadratura circuli* of Nicholas of Cusa, dated December 1450.

Two other Schoolmen at Paris used the Archi-

 ARCHIMEDES IN THE MIDDLE AGES

medean translations of William of Moerbeke; they were Nicole Oresme and Henry of Hesse. The more interesting was Oresme's quite extensive use of Moerbeke's translation of *On Floating Bodies.* In his *Questiones super de caelo* Oresme joined the dynamic definition of specific weight (perhaps derived from the *Liber de ponderoso et levi*, a peripatetic work translated from the Arabic in the late twelfth or early thirteenth century) with the Archimedean considerations of *On Floating Bodies.* It was just such a juxtaposition of ideas that appeared in Niccolò Tartaglia's Italian translation and commentary on Book I of *On Floating Bodies* (included in *La travagliata inventione*, 1551). This confluence of Aristotelian and Archimedean ideas may have led Giovanni Battista Benedetti in 1553 to his modified form of the peripatetic law of motion, namely that bodies fall with a speed proportional to the excess in specific weight of the falling body over the medium. In fact, a century earlier Leone Battista Alberti had made observations much like Oresme's and Tartaglia's, though without citing *On Floating Bodies* directly.

In summary, toward the middle of the fourteenth century the following Archimedean translations of William of Moerbeke were known and used: *On Spirals, On the Measurement of the Circle, On the Sphere and the Cylinder, On Conoids and Spheroids, On Floating Bodies,* and Eutocius' *Commentary on the Sphere and the Cylinder.* Though no direct evidence exists concerning the use of the remaining three translations, an Archimedean-type proof of the law of the lever appeared in a Parisian manuscript of the fourteenth century (Bibl. Nat. lat. 7377B, 93v–94r) that may have been inspired by Archimedes' *On the Equilibrium of Planes.*

Other influence of Archimedes on medieval statics appears to be indirect, through such works as the anonymous *De canonio* (translated from the Greek in the late twelfth or early thirteenth century) and the *Liber karastonis* of Thābit ibn Qurra (translated from the Arabic by Gerard of Cremona). Both tracts reveal an Archimedean type of geometrical demonstrations and the geometrical form implied in weightless beams and weights that were really only geometrical magnitudes. They give specific reference in geometrical language to the law of the lever, and in the *De canonio* the law of the lever is explicitly attributed to Archimedes. They also reflect Archimedes' doctrine of centers of gravity when they follow the practice of substituting for a material beam segment a weight equal in weight to that segment but hung from the middle point of the weightless segment used to replace the material segment. These two tracts were important in stimulating the impressive statics associated with the name of Jordanus de Nemore.

A further question arises concerning the use of Moerbeke's Archimedean translations. Did the rather extensive references to conic sections therein have any significant influence on the development of a geometry of conic sections in the Middle Ages? While the answer to this question seems to be no, investigation of unpublished manuscripts shows that there was a modest development of that subject, largely, but not entirely, in the context of optical studies. This development may be briefly described by singling out the works listed below.

(1) The *De speculis comburentibus* of Ibn al-Haytham mentioned above. Prefaced to this work was a fragment translated by Gerard of Cremona from the Arabic version of Apollonius' *Conics.* In the Latin version of Ibn al-Haytham's work we find the first appearance of the expression *latus rectum* to denominate the parameter of a parabola. Further, it was that work which contained the earliest treatment in Latin of the focus of a parabola.

(2) *De duabus lineis semper approximantibus sibi invicem et nunquam concurrentibus*, translated in the early thirteenth century from the Arabic by John of Palermo, a *notarius* at the court of Frederick II. The objective of this tract was to demonstrate the asymptotic property of a hyperbola. This the author did without naming either the hyperbola or its asymptote.

(3) The *Perspectiva* of Ibn al-Haytham (available in Latin from the hand of an unknown translator in the early thirteenth century).

(4) The *Perspectiva* of Witelo, derived from the work of Ibn al-Haytham. Witelo's work appears to have depended to some extent on the Greek text of Apollonius' *Conics* (and perhaps also on the Greek text of Eutocius' *Commentary on the Conics*). A case can be made that one or both of these works were available to Witelo in translations provided by his friend William of Moerbeke. At any rate, Witelo introduced into Western geometry the terms *parabola, hyperbola,* and *ellipsis*, or at least he took them from William of Moerbeke and introduced them into discussions of conic sections.

(5) An original Latin work entitled *Speculi almukefi compositio* (the original title of which was probably *De speculis comburentibus*), a work attributed (but falsely it seems) to Roger Bacon. The highlight

 ARCHIMEDES IN THE MIDDLE AGES

of this tract was its proof in Conclusion 4 that the *latus rectum* of a parabola generated from a right-angled right cone is double the segment of the axis of the parabola that extends from the vertex of the parabola to the axis of the cone. In this conclusion we also find a proof of Proposition I.11 of the *Conics* of Apollonius, which, however, differs from Appollonius'. It is worth pointing out that the measure of the *latus rectum* here established was the one several times given by Archimedes, though this author makes no mention of Archimedes. This tract was reworked and tightened in the fifteenth century by Regiomontanus, who appended some highly original notes.

(6) The *Libellus de seccione mukefi*, composed by the French instrument maker Jean Fusoris in Paris, in all likelihood prior to 1400. In it he developed a method of describing a parabola as the locus of all points that reflect to a single focus the totality of rays that are parallel to the axis, the focus being located at a given distance from the vertex of the section. This is a method, then, that essentially freed the generation of a parabola from the cone itself in favor of a two-dimensional generation dependent only on the focus and its distance from the vertex of the section.

These six medieval tracts, and some others, influenced a number of authors in the Renaissance, including Johann Werner, Oronce Fine, Francesco Maurolico, and Francesco Barozzi. It was only after the preparation and publication of Latin versions of Apollonius' *Conics* by Giambattista Memmo (1537), Francesco Maurolico (prepared in 1547, published in 1654), and Federigo Commandino (1566) that the medieval traditions of conic sections fell into disuse.

As for medieval influences on the mainstream of Archimedean studies in the Renaissance, it should be realized that knowledge of Archimedes began to expand toward the middle of the fifteenth century. A new source for Archimedes appeared, namely the Latin translation made by Jacobus Cremonensis about 1450 by order of Pope Nicholas V. Since that translation was done exclusively from Greek manuscript A, it failed to include *On Floating Bodies*, but it did include the two treatises in Manuscript A that had been omitted by William of Moerbeke from his translations: *The Sandreckoner* and Eutocius' *Commentary on the Measurement of the Circle.*

It seems almost certain that this new translation was made with an eye on Moerbeke's translation. It achieved some popularity in the second half of the fifteenth and the first half of the sixteenth century. There are at least nine manuscripts of it. One was written by Regiomontanus and brought to Germany about 1468 (the Latin translation published with the *editio princeps* of the Greek text in 1544 was made from this copy). Regiomontanus' copy was particularly interesting because he made a large number of corrections of the translation by referring to the Greek text, and his copy contains numerous marginalia. Unfortunately only the corrections of the texts themselves were reproduced in the *editio princeps*, and hence the rich marginal notes have to be examined directly in Regiomontanus' manuscript.

Despite the new translation of Jacobus Cremonensis, both the translation of William of Moerbeke and the various works done from the Arabic continued to exert some influence in the sixteenth century on such authors as Leonardo da Vinci, Francesco Maurolico, Niccolò Tartaglia, Federigo Commandino, Francisco de Mello, Pierre Forcadel, and others, and these various influences have recently been examined in great detail. Furthermore the medieval versions played some modest role in the publication of Archimedean texts. The earliest printed texts of any of the works of Archimedes were the Moerbeke translations of *On the Measurement of the Circle* and *On the Quadrature of the Parabola* published by L. Gaurico (*Tetragonismus, id est circuli quadratura . . . ,* 1503) from the Madrid manuscript mentioned above.

In 1543 Tartaglia republished directly from Gaurico's work the same two translations and, in addition, from the Madrid manuscript two further translations of Moerbeke: *On the Equilibrium of Planes* and Book I of *On Floating Bodies.* In this publication Tartaglia left the erroneous impression that he himself had made these translations from a Greek manuscript. But this is not so since he merely repeated the texts of the Madrid manuscript with almost all of its errors. Incidentally, Curtius Troianus, in 1565, published from the legacy of Tartaglia both books of Moerbeke's translation of *On Floating Bodies.* Finally we should note that Commandino reworked in an exceedingly skillful way Moerbeke's translation of that work, publishing it that same year. His version quickly displaced Tartaglia's version.

The medieval Archimedes had now run its course. The *editio princeps* of 1544 and other Archimedean translations of Commandino (published in 1565) were now everywhere cited as an increasing number of authors turned to Archimedean problems. A new and splendid edition was published by Joseph Torelli at Oxford in 1792. It served students of Archimedes well until the publication a half-century later of the modern editions of J. L. Heiberg.

BIBLIOGRAPHY

This article is based largely on Marshall Clagett, *Archimedes in the Middle Ages,* 4 vols. (1964–1980); a fifth volume is in preparation. Extensive bibliographies can be found in vols. I, III, and IV; there is also a bibliography in Marshall Clagett, "Archimedes," in *Dictionary of Scientific Biography,* I (1970). Other studies include Marshall Clagett, "The *Liber de motu* of Gerard of Brussels and the Origins of Kinematics in the West," in *Osiris,* **12** (1956); and *The Science of Mechanics in the Middle Ages* (1959, repr. 1979), 85–93; and E. A. Moody and M. Clagett, *The Medieval Science of Weights* (1952, repr. 1960), 55–117.

To the items on the Arabic Archimedes should be added Juan Vernet and M. A. Catalá, "Dos tratados del Arquimedes árabe: *Tratado de los circulos tangentes* y el *Libro de los triángulos,*" in *Publicaciones del seminario de historia de la ciencia de la Real Academia de buenas letras,* no. 2 (1972); Yvonne Dold-Samplonius, "Archimedes: Einander berührende Kreise," in *Sudhoffs Archiv: Zeitschrift für Wissenschaftsgeschichte,* **57,** no. 1 (1973); and Fuat Sezgin, *Geschichte des arabischen Schrifttums,* V (1974), index.

MARSHALL CLAGETT

[See also **Anthemios of Tralles; Gerard of Cremona; Isidorus of Miletus; Mathematics, Islamic and W. European; William of Moerbeke.**]

ARCHITECT, STATUS OF. This brief article will be confined to building from the twelfth through the fifteenth centuries. To get a proper perspective on the Gothic architect, we must dissociate from our notions about architectural design many characteristics of modern professional architects as well as certain features that derive from the artist-architects of the Italian Renaissance. To be sure, we should recognize that, by the end of the Middle Ages, Gothic builders were using many design techniques and practices that are fundamental in modern architectural practice, such as building plans, elevations, shop drawings, presentation drawings, building models, drafting rooms, and contracts with detailed specifications for construction. Given these similarities, it is tempting to equate the nature and status of the Gothic architect with that of his modern counterpart. But to do so is to misunderstand some of the fundamental features of Gothic design and building practice.

The correct perspective can be maintained only if we recognize that virtually all Gothic architects were master craftsmen. This circumstance determined much of their behavior as designers and supervisors of construction, affected their relationships with patrons and other masters and journeymen of the building crafts, and determined their general social and economic status.

Because architects and journeymen builders were all craftsmen, the designers and executors within each building craft not only spoke the same technical languages—verbally, graphically, and in terms of architectural forms—but they also largely depended on and worked closely with each other in both design and construction processes. Within this setting, for many buildings there was no one "architect" in the modern meaning of the word. Certainly for buildings constructed primarily in stone the master mason came closest to serving this function. But on a Gothic cathedral he did not design many important elements. The wooden roofs were designed by the master carpenter, the glazing of the huge windows by the master glazier, and the intricately carved wooden choir stalls by the master carver or joiner. Perhaps even the design of the statues and tympana of the church portals was assigned to the master sculptor. With the design of so much of the building in the hands of various master craftsmen, one must think of the master mason as the architect only in a very special, very medieval way. In effect, he designed the stone structure that provided the physical setting and the spatial limits for the efforts of the other master craftsmen, who worked in wood, glass, iron, and lead.

On such projects the master mason was probably considered the first among equals, the equality being reflected in his salary, which was often the same as that of other master craftsmen. Furthermore, their salaries were derived from the wage scales of journeymen building craftsmen. Hence in terms of this economic indicator, the master craftsmen as architects were only somewhat more valued than the journeymen, since ecclesiastical or royal officials associated with building projects received salaries that were "off the scale" of wages for journeymen builders.

The relationship of Gothic architects to their patrons is difficult to analyze briefly, for in addition to designing buildings they also served as construction supervisors and sometimes as administrative officials or building contractors. In the complexity of these roles they were indispensable, and the rapport between patrons and building masters was often greater and more favorable to the craftsmen than is sometimes the case today. This rapport existed not only in personal terms but also in technical matters of design, where the architects worked closely with the patrons on the building site throughout the design and construction process. Direct and frequent consultations between architects and patrons was the norm in medieval building practices.

On the other hand, the various roles of Gothic architects did not change the basic condition of their relationship to the patrons: the architect was a master craftsman, a building technician (in medieval terms, a practitioner of one of the mechanical arts), hired to perform skills that the patrons did not possess. The architect was neither a professional (like a medieval theologian, lawyer, or physician), nor an artist, humanist, or gentleman architect in the way these terms came to be applied during the Renaissance.

The personal status of Gothic architects varied enormously. Many developed only local careers and were little distinguished from journeymen; others acquired widespread reputations and were much sought after. Regardless of their reputation, their social status remained pegged to that of the building crafts. Sons of successful master builders, for example, might pursue careers affording higher social status, but sons of mercantile or feudal lords seldom entered the building crafts in order to aspire to the rank of master builder. That, at least, is one measure of the social status of the Gothic architect.

BIBLIOGRAPHY

See Martin S. Briggs, *The Architect in History* (1927); now largely outdated by Spiro Kostof, ed., *The Architect* (1977); Paul Booz, *Der Baumeister der Gotik* (1956); John Harvey, *The Mediaeval Architect* (1972); and Pierre Du Colombier, *Les chantiers des cathédrales* (1973). On the economic status of master masons, see Louis F. Salzman, *Building in England down to 1540* (1952); and Douglas Knoop and Gwilym P. Jones, *The Mediaeval Mason,* 3rd ed. (1967).

Specialized studies include Nikolaus Pevsner, "Terms of Architectural Planning in the Middle Ages," in *Journal of the Warburg and Courtauld Institutes,* 5 (1942); and "The Term 'Architect' in the Middle Ages," in *Speculum,* 17 (1942); and Lon R. Shelby, "Monastic Patrons and Their Architects," in *Gesta,* 15 (1976).

LON R. SHELBY

[See also **Artist, Status of.**]

ARCHITECTURE. See individual articles: **Gothic, Romanesque,** etc.

ARCHITECTURE, LITURGICAL ASPECTS. The history of architecture includes not only the evolution of structural forms but also the functional purposes of these forms. In the realm of medieval religious architecture, this amounts to an investigation of how architecture, in its external and physical shape, accommodated the liturgy. This area of study lies between architecture and liturgy, and sheds light on both disciplines. For the liturgy must be understood not simply as a collection of texts, but as a concrete and living action involving movement, color, and dramatic symbol, unfolding in a real physical setting. At the same time, medieval architecture was not intended as abstract sculpture, but as housing for certain very specific activities; understanding these activities takes one a long way toward understanding the architecture.

Research in this interdisciplinary area is still in its infancy, but a methodology for dealing with the subject has begun to develop and the main problem areas of the material have begun to emerge. Methodologically, the first step is to distinguish the buildings by the functions for which they were principally intended—for clearly the rites that explain a baptistry are not going to explain a chapter house, for example. The second step involves classifying buildings by the separate local liturgical observances. This means more than just placing the architecture in the large divisions of rite, such as Roman or Slavonic; for within each rite separate traditions must be distinguished by province or by separate monastic usage (for instance, Cistercian as opposed to Franciscan). The third general rule requires understanding the dynamics of a rite's evolution. Despite the conservative nature of religious practices in general, liturgy is always in a gradual process of change. While the overall lines of the evolution may be clear, it is often very difficult to fix the precise stage of that evolution embodied in a given architectural monument.

This brief review of the liturgical aspects of architecture concerns liturgy in the strictest sense of the term—that is, the liturgy of the Mass or the Eucharist. The celebration of the Eucharist is historically the most important focus of the Christian community's cultic life, to the extent that when one speaks of church architecture without qualification, one is speaking of buildings intended for the Eucha-

 ARCHITECTURE, LITURGICAL ASPECTS

rist. This aspect of liturgy has therefore received more scholarly attention. But research ought to be conducted on the architectural setting of the other aspects of liturgy, from baptism to the coronation of kings.

EARLY PERIOD

The origins of Christian church planning seem to lie not in pre-Christian religions but in the secular realm, for one of the most basic distinctions between early Christian worship and pre-Christian cults lay in the public character of the Christian church. In ancient Greek and Roman cults the temple was regarded as the dwelling of the god, housing his statue; it was therefore treated as a sanctuary to which only the priests of the god had access. Public worship would take place outside at the altar, which was generally erected before the facade of the temple. By contrast, the church was first of all a place for assembly, and the Greek word for assembly, *ekklēsia,* could mean either the church building or the community that gathered in it.

This assembly-hall character of the church is clearly something that the Christian religion inherited from its Jewish background in the synagogue, yet the planning of the church shows little debt to the synagogue. Instead, the church seems to have looked to the secular public hall, particularly the law court, for its model. Here the *praetor* or magistrate sat on a *sella curulis* on an elevated dais in the apse with judges on *subsellia* beside him, while a barrier of *cancelli* separated his place from the public. In similar fashion the bishop took his place on a *cathedra* in the apse of the early Christian basilica with his clergy in the *synthronon* beside him, separated from the congregation in the nave by low chancel barriers. Where the *praetor* would have a desk before him the bishop had before him the *mensa* or *trapeza* (the table or the altar). While in modern times the preacher usually stands while his congregation sits, in early Christian times the bishop sat in his place of authority in the apse while the congregation stood.

Eastern and Western church planning show marked differences from the outset. In the earliest Roman plans a portion of the east end of either aisle, called the *senatorium* and the *matroneum,* was set apart for offertory and communion of men and women, respectively. In the center of the nave a reserved processional way, or *solea,* was provided for the solemn entrance and exit of the bishop and his attendants. In the East, however, the offertory was assigned to deacons from earliest times: hence they were provided with a separate place for preparing the vessels containing the bread and wine; in Constantinople this was in a nearby building, the *skeuophylakion,* while in Syria it was in a sacristy adjoining the sanctuary. The Eastern churches tended also to give greater architectural prominence to the readings of the liturgy. In Constantinople and Greece a two-staired *ambo* (pulpit) accommodated the reader and the candles and incense that accompanied him; in Syria a platform, called a *bema,* was set up in the middle of the nave. However, despite these differences between East and West, there are some striking general parallels in the medieval development of liturgical planning in two important aspects: the gradual withdrawal of the liturgical action from the public, and the eventual multiplication of chapels for semiprivate celebration of the Eucharist.

LATER MEDIEVAL PERIOD

Whereas the early liturgy was shaped around a large measure of public participation in processions of entrance, offertory, communion, and recessional, the medieval liturgy tended to be shaped around a series of appearances of clergy who emerged from their sacred, and eventually secret, functions behind the chancel barrier. In the West the first step toward removing the sanctuary from the public consisted in elevating it to afford room underneath for the veneration of relics. In the late sixth century, at St. Peter's in Rome, a crypt underneath the sanctuary provided for circulation of pilgrims to the saint's tomb under the altar. This separation of crypt functions from the properly liturgical activities of the church is one of the central developments of medieval architecture, and the press of boisterous crowds to visit relics was one of the reasons for removing the sanctuary more completely from lay access.

The Enlightenment was responsible for destroying the furnishings of many of the great churches of Europe, but an old engraving preserves the appearance of the thirteenth-century sanctuary at Chartres, which was more or less typical. From the nave of the church one's view was completely obstructed by an enormous *jubé,* called in English the "rood screen" because of the great cross, or rood, that surmounted it. The Gospel and Epistle readings and the sermon were delivered from the top of the rood screen, and in front of it, at appropriate seasons, the mystery plays were presented. The Mass, however, and the

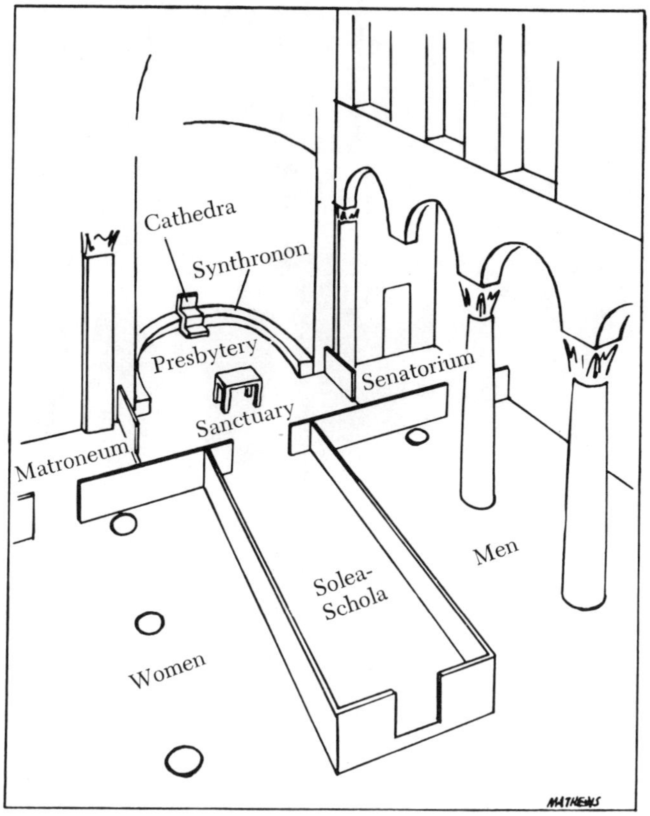

Interior plan of an early Roman church. DRAWING BY THOMAS MATHEWS

The *jubée* of Chartres, 13th-Century engraving. BIBLIOTHÈQUE NATIONALE

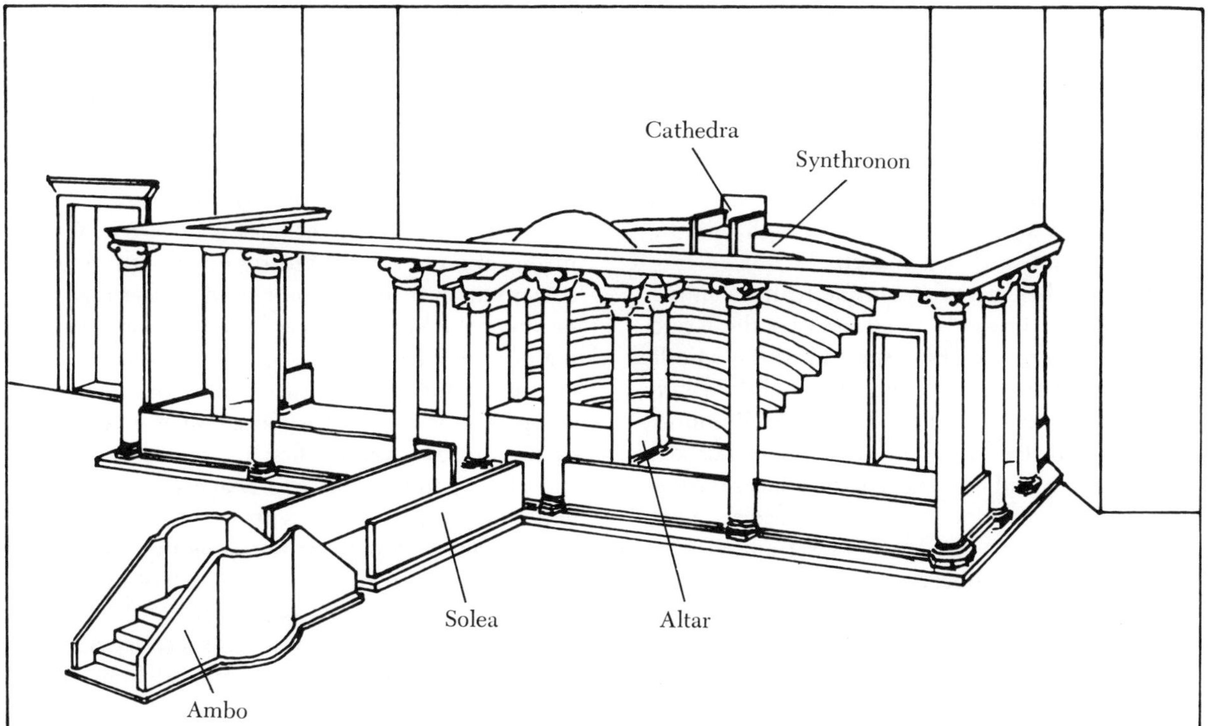

Interior plan of an early Greek church. DRAWING BY R. NAUMANN

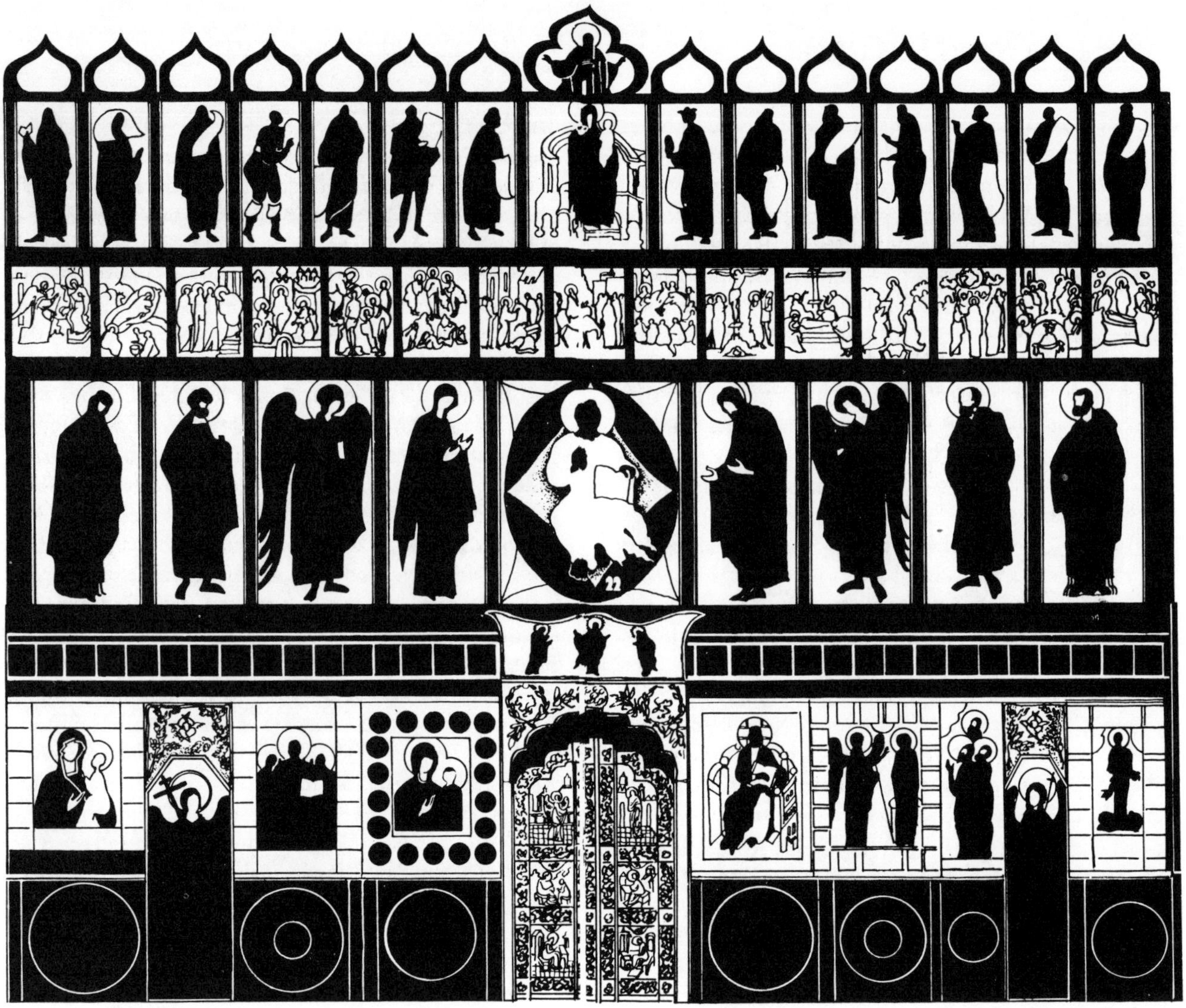

Byzantine iconostasis of the late Middle Ages. Cathedral of the Annunciation, Moscow. FROM Y. KOZLOVA, *CATHEDRAL SQUARE IN THE MOSCOW KREMLIN: A GUIDE*

chanting of the Divine Office went on virtually in secret, for the entire nave east of the crossing was hidden behind a wall some twenty feet high, creating a veritable church within a church.

In the churches of the Byzantine realm a similar screening of the liturgy was effected by the iconostasis (icon screen), which by the end of the Middle Ages closed off the eastern end of the church with tier upon tier of icons. Participation in the Byzantine liturgy was achieved by unceasing public response in song and prayer, and by the dramatic appearances of the clergy from the doors of the iconostasis at set intervals. The processions of the Lesser and Greater Entrance were now abbreviated so that the Gospel and the bread and wine were brought out through the north door and returned to the sanctuary through the holy door in the center. The *ambo* was eliminated and readings were done directly before the holy door; the sermon fell into disuse.

Although both in the East and in the West the medieval architectural setting of the liturgy evolved toward an ever more remote and mysterious presentation of the Mass, another development in liturgical planning tended, on the contrary, to make the rite ever more intimate and accessible: that was the development of chapels for the semiprivate celebration of the liturgy. Popular first in monastic settings in the Holy Land, subsidiary chapels on ground and gallery levels became a regular part of medieval Byzantine church design. At the same time the aisles of the great monasteries and cathedrals of the West accommodated a growing proliferation of altars. This phenomenon must be linked to a variety of factors. While in early Christian times the celebration of the

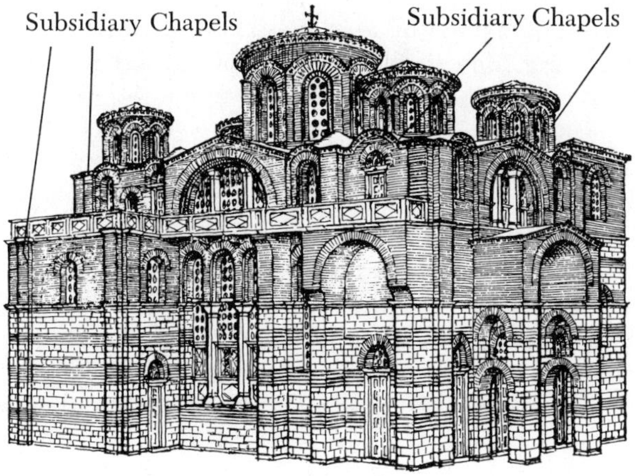

Reconstruction drawing of Theotokos Church of Constantine Lips, Constantinople. A.H.S. MEGAW, DUMBARTON OAKS

Eucharist was restricted to Saturday and Sunday, the veneration of saints gradually began to fill out the calendar with feasts for the whole year. Separate altars and separate chapels for saints and their relics were one aspect of this development. Another factor was certainly the erection and dedication of chapels under private sponsorship, with endowment for set numbers of Masses. A demand for more frequent Masses for the dead also contributes to this trend, as did the tendency of priests to celebrate privately for their own spiritual welfare. The end of the Middle Ages, then, presents one with a wide variety of architectural accommodations to ever more fragmenting liturgical practices.

BIBLIOGRAPHY

Gregory Dix, *The Shape of the Liturgy,* 2nd ed. (1945); Angelus A. Häussling, *Mönchskonvent und Eucharistiefeier: Eine Studie über die Messe in der abendländischen Klosterliturgie des frühen Mittelalters und zur Geschichte der Messhäufigkeit* (1973); Thomas F. Mathews, "An Early Roman Chancel Arrangement and Its Liturgical Functions," in *Rivista di archeologia cristiana,* 38 (1962); and *The Early Churches of Constantinople, Architecture and Liturgy* (1971); Robert F. Taft, *The Great Entrance: A History of the Transfer of Gifts and Other Preanaphoral Rites of the Liturgy of St. John Chrysostom* (1975).

THOMAS F. MATHEWS

[See also **Altar and Altar Apparatus; Basilica; Cathedral; Chapel; Early Christian and Byzantine Architecture; Ecclesia and Synagoga.**]

ARCHIVES are collections of the documents and records generated or received in the course of routine activity by any agency, office, or person, public or private, and retained as legal or historical evidence of that activity. The term is derived through Latin and French from the Greek *archeion* (governmental property), the name applied by the governing councils of Athens to the store of their records, kept in the temple of the Metroön.

Ancient Rome stored its public records in the *aerarium* or treasury in the temple of Saturn; and copies of important testaments, contracts, and similar instruments were preserved in collections called *archia, archiva,* and *tabularia* that served municipal, provincial, and military communities. The city *archiva* also served as libraries of deposit for texts that were regarded as public treasures. The similar Latin word *arca* (a chest or strongbox) encouraged the development of connotations of family or private documents, and also the notion of secrecy that was enshrined in Isidore of Seville's mistaken explanation (*Etymologiae* 20:9): "The *arca* is so called because it shuts out *(arceat)* and forbids vision; hence 'archives' and 'arcane,' that is, secret." Byzantine imperial practice continued the archival tradition of Rome as legislated in the Code of Justinian, but no imperial record collections survive.

The Christian church played several important roles in the history of archives in Europe. Having inherited the sacral functions of the Roman state, the church also retained in some form its administrative practices and the terminology associated with them, for preserving the authentic texts of the Scriptures and for safeguarding the documents that proved ownership of land and buildings, the precious articles and rights that made up its sacred patrimony. Archival collections of various church offices and communities coexisted with their secular counterparts throughout the Middle Ages. Religious establishments, especially monasteries, provided a secure place for royal and territorial authorities to deposit records. Both the ecclesiastical and the secular archives were maintained almost exclusively by clerics, who exercised, in Latin, a nearly total monopoly of literacy and written documentation until the fifteenth century.

In the Middle Ages, three major forms of archival institution emerged, all bearing some mark of their derivation from the ancient world but responsive to changed conditions: archives of state, notarial or communal archives, and private or house archives.

There were secular and ecclesiastical versions of each of these functional types.

Archives of state preserved formal documents and records incidental to the acts of government: laws, decrees, judicial sentences and the records of the processes that created them, treaties and other political correspondence, letters of privilege in the form of preparatory briefs or registers, records of taxation and other incomes, statements of expenses, and lists of government personnel. State archives included those of the Holy Roman Empire, kingdoms and territorial lordships, city councils and communes, and the Church of Rome and other major churches. From the tenth century the typical monarchy, which was feudal and military and bound to a rural economic base, was constantly traveling, carrying some of its most important records along with it. Those departments of government that settled permanently in the capital generated the earliest consecutive archives that survive today; the Pipe Rolls of the English Exchequer, beginning in 1130, are an outstanding example. The major European monarchies began keeping registers of a major portion of their correspondence during the thirteenth century; the papacy had begun this practice during the combative pontificate of Innocent III (1198–1216), whose example was followed by his chief secular adversaries. The Muslim states generated archival materials, chiefly tax and judicial records, in imitation of the Byzantine administration as they supplanted it; but only fragments survive before the sixteenth-century archives of the Ottoman Empire.

The function of Roman municipal archives was continued by notarial or communal archives, which were intended to preserve the documents of private acts that had or might eventually have public or legal consequences—such as contracts of partnership and sale, marriage settlements, testaments, and adoptions. Especially widespread in Italy and Provence, the Mediterranean heart of the old Roman world, this form of archive found new impetus when the Code of Justinian was introduced into European scholarship, courts, and administration in the eleventh century, reviving the profession of notary or *tabellio*. Notarial archives are made up of registers containing full, formal copies of notarial instruments or simply the accumulated *notae* or preparatory briefs. These public records had the power of proof in a court of law without having to be proven themselves by the summoning of their original witnesses; they were a "matter of record." The ecclesiastical equivalent of the notarial archive is the parish register of baptisms and burials. Similar records were maintained by the Jewish communities of Europe, but almost all were destroyed in the violent persecutions of the later Middle Ages.

Private, family, or dynastic archives were devoted to maintaining the documentary evidence of a house's property, rights, rank, and powers. Original charters and grants of privilege, deeds of purchase, testaments, court sentences and similar documents, and their copies in registers (often called cartularies) fill the typical dynastic archive or "muniment room." Under pressure of the canonical presumption that they were mere stewards, not owners, of church property, abbots and monastic communities, bishops and the incorporated clergy of cathedrals and other large, "collegiate" churches also kept cartularies and original documents to defend their ownership—and financial accounts to explain their uses—of property. Commercial families and companies, which greatly increased in number, wealth, and importance from the thirteenth century, also maintained international correspondence and financial records. Usually it was in a company's interest to destroy such records after their immediate usefulness ended; but one fourteenth-century trading magnate, Francesco di Marco Datini, endowed a permanent archive preserved in his house in Prato, near Florence.

These three types of archives are now frequently found together, embraced as historical documents by a national or regional archive regardless of their origins. The Apostolic See was both a governing authority that granted privileges and a vulnerable institution that received them; consequently the Vatican Archives include *munimenta* as well as registers of state papers.

Another inveterate confusion persists between archives and libraries. The two kinds of repositories have frequently been intermixed not only because they both contain handwritten parchment and paper but also because an establishment, abbey, cathedral, or princely house sometimes used the same scribes and clerks to maintain both archives and libraries in the same secure, dry rooms and even on the same shelves. After the middle of the fifteenth century the confusion eased because most library books were then printed. For earlier periods, however, it is necessary to distinguish between archival materials and library books. A formal imperial or papal decree and its registered copy, for example, are archival documents; a code of such laws assembled for school or court use is a library book. A narrative history is a library item, even though it quotes documentary ma-

ARCHIVES

terial that the author may have found in an archival collection.

Archives are of practical importance as the files of working government departments, the daily registers of busy and litigious urban societies, and the record of the acquired wealth of ambitious families. Eventually, they become historical treasures, highly prized for the light they can shed on the past. Most losses occur between these two periods of high attributed value, when archival collections have become obsolete as current files but have not yet acquired the value of unique historical witnesses. They often become waste paper or reused parchment, used for wrapping, packing, or fuel; or they may be broken up or jumbled, losing their original, natural, and meaningful order. Only a few long-enduring and physically stable government offices, which needed to refer to their own records over generations and which carried on their functions through political revolutions, were able to keep their archives nearly intact into the modern age.

The credit for major leadership in the modern development of medieval archives belongs to France. In France, dynastic and ecclesiastical establishments already possessed large archives before the thirteenth century, when the Capetian monarchs began accumulating records of state in Paris, judicial records from the Parlement de Paris, and fiscal records from the Chambre des Comptes. The *trésor des chartes* (documents received), some of its 14,000 items dating from the reign of Philip IV (1285–1314), was listed in an inventory for Charles V, decades before similar inventories in the papal and English royal archives. The crown jurisdictions outside Paris, the *bailliages* and *sénéchaussées,* were assembling parallel records; and other lordships, secular and ecclesiastical, were preserving the documents of their property and of its financial and judicial management.

A scholarly debate developed in the sixteenth century about the authenticity of certain contents of those nonroyal archives, the supposed Merovingian charters belonging to Benedictine monasteries. From that courteous quarrel emerged Jean Mabillon's *De re diplomatica* (1681), the foundation of the scientific study of archival documents. When the French Revolution had destroyed feudal privileges, the family and church archives that recorded them were nationalized, becoming a permanent patriotic historical treasure. The Archives Nationales were established in Paris in 1789 to house the records of the central government past and future; in 1796 the Archives Départementales were given responsibility for the regional records of the *ancien régime.* To exploit the opportunities thus opened and to try to solve some of the problems of organization and historical science raised by this embarrassment of riches, the École Nationale des Chartes was founded in 1821. The French example in each of these developments was widely imitated, even by nations allied against Napoleonic France.

There is a great advantage for the scholar of medieval history in such a national archival system, which has responsibility for the preservation and accessible order of historical records and also of the files created by existing government departments. The old records receive the same appropriate housing and security that any state requires as a matter of course for its own storage facilities; such services as printed inventories and microfilming become readily available; and the researcher, even if a foreigner, can take advantage of the collaboration of a national school of archival administration and research. One of the most valuable contributions of the French enterprise is the principle of *respect des fonds* that governs most current archival practice. Adopted in 1841 in a reform of the operations of the Archives Départementales, the phrase signifies in this context very nearly what it would mean in archaeology—minimal disturbance of the ground. According to this principle, the archivist should not rearrange the material committed to the archive, because no other arrangement promises to be as historically useful as the order imposed by the department or agency that originally generated or received the documents. The order of the records is, in itself, historical information. An inventory of personal property, for example, if found among the documents of a fiscal department, strongly indicates a confiscation; separated and neatly located among other inventories of personal property of similar date, it loses its full potential as a historical source.

Belgium, politically united to France in 1797, had a system of departmental archives imposed on it that began to receive the records of the medieval territorial lordships of modern Belgium and Luxemburg. Today the Belgian system consists of the Archives Générales du Royaume in Brussels and provincial Archives de l 'État, but because the process of central deposit was never completed, there is considerable medieval material still in municipal and church archives. Similarly, the Bundesarchiv of Switzerland in Bern contains only material generated since its own creation in 1798; for historical records the federated cantons have their own Staatsarchive, which operate

ARCHIVES

independently. In the federal Netherlands, alongside the reigning queen's private archive of the house of Orange-Nassau, we find the Orange dynastic archives of the county of Holland as the nucleus of the Algemeen Rijksarchief in The Hague. Ten other rijksarchieven are responsible for the archives of old lordships and some urban records as well; but the municipal archives of such major cities as Amsterdam, The Hague, Utrecht, and Rotterdam contain a wealth of medieval material.

Italy also imitated the French pattern, but also not slavishly. In 1875, shortly after national unification, the Archivio di Stato di Roma was established as receiver of current state files, and the existing archives of the earlier independent cities and states were adopted as Archivi di Stato and national historical deposits without being moved. Medieval materials are therefore normally housed near their place of origin. Church archives persist, and those of the Apostolic See and the preunification Papal States are found in the Archivio Segreto Vaticano.

As the center of the Christian church in Europe, the Church of Rome had by the eleventh century developed many of the characteristics of a monarchy with international scope, legislative and judicial functions, administrative and fiscal offices, and masses of written documents. Pope Innocent III, who greatly advanced the political powers of the Apostolic See, also improved its archival support system with the regular registration of papal letters and the safe deposit of important documents received, such as privileges and deeds of donation. When the Apostolic Camera became a major office of state responsible for finance and household at the beginning of the fourteenth century, it began to accumulate its own records. The Vatican library, built in the fifteenth century, housed some of the archival material, notably chancery registers; the *munimenta* were in safeguard in the Castel Sant'Angelo, and the Camera had its own archives. In 1610, Pope Paul V began the Archivio Segreto Vaticano and ordered the assembly there of archives from the three major deposits and all other holders. When Napoleon occupied Rome in 1798, he ordered large quantities of the papal archives transported to Paris for a central imperial archive; they were returned, minus documents lost, stolen, or destroyed, after the Congress of Vienna. Since 1881 the Vatican archives have been open to historical research; as a state without a nation, the Vatican depends on the work of national schools at Rome, notably the German, French, and British, for the scientific exploitation of its archival wealth.

In England, King John "Lackland" began the registry of royal letters in 1199, in parchment rolls. Those rolls and the administration responsible for their creation and maintenance in the chancery provided the medieval matrix for a sophisticated archival system, recording the activities of the royal courts, chancery, and exchequer. In 1838, the old system was converted into the Public Record Office, charged with the reception of new archives from the central government. This office did not have to learn the principle of *respect des fonds.* County, family, and church archives remain outside the state system. The archives of Eire and Northern Ireland and Scotland follow the same system.

Central state archives were not so neatly applicable in the Iberian Peninsula. The Archivo Histórico Nacional in Madrid contains some records of defunct monasteries and military orders, but the royal archives of Castile are at Simancas near Valladolid, those of Aragon in Barcelona, and those of Navarre in Pamplona. Rich regional archives, of Valencia and Majorca for example, survive, and the church archives remain with the churches. Chancery registers dating back as far as 1248, with other royal documents, formed the nucleus of the Antiga Casa da Corõa, now in the Portuguese Arquivo Nacional in Lisbon; the ancient port towns of Portugal keep valuable municipal archives as well.

The vast territory of the medieval Holy Roman Empire, although conquered by Napoleonic armies and crystallized during the nineteenth century into large national states, never centralized its medieval archival riches into large state deposits. The surviving medieval archives of the empire and its constituent kingdoms and duchies are mostly to be found in the regional German Staatsarchive, usually close to their location at the end of the Napoleonic wars, since the unification of Germany in 1866 did not create a retrospective national archive system. Many municipal archives retain their medieval holdings, and in the Federal Republic of Germany church and family *munimenta* remain private.

The central Haus-, Hof-, und Staatsarchiv in Vienna grew around the dynastic archives of the Hapsburg family (other portions of the family records are in the Landesarchiv of the Tyrol in Innsbruck). The Landesarchiv of Salzburg holds the records of the archbishopric and the monastery of St. Peter. Private archives still exist for the Schwartzenberg family of Vienna and the monastery of Klosterneuburg. The Magyar Országos Levéltar in Budapest, successor to the Hungarian royal archive, holds the bulk of the surviving royal records, some dating from the thirteenth century.

In Scandinavia, the centralization of royal records took place nearly simultaneously with the Reformation, so that the archival systems of both the monarchy and the medieval church are found together.

BIBLIOGRAPHY

The best short survey of the history and current state of European historical archives, with very useful bibliography, is Robert-Henri Bautier, "Les archives," in Charles Samaran, ed., *L'histoire et ses méthodes* (1961). Adolf Brenneke, *Archivistica,* Renato Perrella, trans. (1968), is very thorough for archives of state, especially in German-speaking areas, with fine topical and national bibliographies. Vivian H. Galbraith, *An Introduction to the Use of the Public Records* (1934), shows the organic history of the English records. Leonard E. Boyle, *A Survey of the Vatican Archives and of Its Medieval Holdings* (1972), has historical sketches of each *fondo.* Jean Favier, *Les archives,* 3rd ed. (1975), reviews the whole field, with good detail on the French archives. Up-to-date bibliographies appear in *Archivum: Revue internationale des archives,* published annually under the auspices of UNESCO at Paris; see especially the combined vols. 22–23 (1972–1973), entitled *International Directory of Archives.*

DANIEL WILLIMAN

ARCHIVOLT, the molding that frames an arch, often used loosely as a synonym for the voussoirs. In Romanesque and Gothic architecture, each one of a series of arches, often decorated with relief sculpture, that frames the tympanum is called an archivolt.

LESLIE BRUBAKER

[See also **Arch, types of.**]

ARCHON TON ARCHONTON (prince of princes), called *išxan išxanac*ᶜ in Armenian and *biṭrīq al-baṭā riqa* in Arabic, the title of the senior prince of Armenia in the ninth century. The Arabic is probably the original form, since the Abbasids first conferred it upon Bagarat II Bagratuni, the Armenian prince of Taron (826–851), and then upon his nephew Ašot Bagratuni. The Byzantines recognized Prince (later King) Ašot and his two successors, Kings Smbat I and Ašot II, as *archon ton archonton* of Armenia. In the 920's the title was taken from the Bagratids and given to Gagik Arcruni, the king of Vaspurakan. After his death it was probably restored to the Bagratids, and the Arcruni kings were referred to as *archon ton archonton* of Vaspurakan. The holder of the title was called the *philos hyios* (beloved son) of the emperor and was honored with a chrysobull of three solidi.

BIBLIOGRAPHY

Josef Markwart, *Hay Bagratuneac*ᶜ *Čiwłagrut*ᶜ*iwnə* (1913), 63–64; Cyril Toumanoff, *Studies in Christian Caucasian History* (1963), 107, n. 165; 205, n. 200.

KRIKOR H. MAKSOUDIAN

[See also **Arcrunis; Bagratids/Bagratuni.**]

ARCHPOET, pseudonym of the author of ten secular Latin poems, nine of which are found in the same, unique Göttingen manuscript. We do not know the Archpoet's real name, and his origin and personal data must be inferred from his poems. He was a German or possibly French cleric of knightly origin who wrote between 1159 and 1165 and belonged to the entourage of Rainald of Dassel, archchancellor of Emperor Frederick Barbarossa and archbishop of Cologne. On the basis of his "Confession" the Archpoet was already being called a Goliard in the thirteenth century, but if the term is meant to imply that he was a wandering scholar then it is not apposite. His goliardic image is suggested by his efforts to present himself as a hard-drinking, immoral, and gambling poet who drew inspiration for his poetry from his vices. He also pretends to suffer from poverty and to live on what he can obtain by begging from his patron, Rainald. All of this, however, is most likely traditional poetic fiction ably presented in highly lyric poetry in which even human weakness and vice are made to appear quite attractive.

It is assumed that the ten existing poems represent only a fraction of the Archpoet's total output. Three of them are especially noteworthy: his "Imperial Hymn" to Frederick, his famous "Confession," and his "Minor Confession." Although he does not give the impression of being an ardent political partisan, his "Hymn" is an impressive tribute to Frederick's imperial policy. The images dealing with the emperor and his adversaries are built around two contrasting centers: the emperor represents the idea of the divinely ordained *rex Christianus,* portrayed in expressions drawn from the Bible and Christian tradition. His adversaries are presented as godless titans, in images borrowed from pagan mythology. The emperor is *dominus mundi,* a world leader who is an exponent of Christian universalism rather than of German nationalism. His victories in Italy are stepping stones toward the realization of a *sacrum imperium* in which there is no place for the temporal power of the pope.

In the "Hymn" the Archpoet translates the imperial doctrine of Frederick and Rainald into a poetic language; but elsewhere he refuses, like Horace, to lend himself to writing an imperial epic. Most of his other poems have a more personal character about his real or pretended relationship to Rainald and about his so-called goliardic way of life. He depicts himself as an oversexed, pleasure-seeking, unabashed bon vivant, a twelfth-century exponent of *Diesseitsstimmung,* the orientation toward earthly happiness and enjoyment. The basis of this image is not a poetic application of the idea of the power of nature as understood by the School of Chartres and applied by Scaglione to Boccaccio's outlook but, rather, the idea borrowed from St. Paul about the two laws dominating the human heart.

The "Confession" is a religious parody, an inversion of the sense of the Christian confession. Lighthearted humor and even cynicism are mixed in the eschatological scene of his death in the tavern. He achieves great poetic effect by leaving the reader in doubt about whether he takes his way of life seriously. In a clever turn the Archpoet, begging for Rainald's pardon, relieves the tension by alluding to the lion, the king of beasts, who shows mercy to his subjects. This is, of course, a playful parable for Rainald, but with this device the ethical problem is taken out of the moralistic framework and transposed into the sphere of the contemporary satirical beast epic.

The Archpoet created well-balanced and organized poems, superb in language and style, displaying a wide knowledge of the world of Latin poetry and employing both metrical and rhythmical verse forms with equal skill. He used poetic and rhetorical devices, the *colores rhetorici,* and was a master of adapting Biblical and religious images to his purpose. The term *archipoeta* was applied in the thirteenth century to various poets, such as Henry of Avranches, to indicate their excellence—enduring tribute to that of the Archpoet.

BIBLIOGRAPHY

"Archipoeta," in Karl Langosch, ed.,*Verfasserlexikon des deutschen Mittelalters,* V (1955); Ernst R. Curtius, "Der Archipoeta und der Stil mittellateinischer Dichtung," in *Romanische Forschungen,* 54 (1940); *Die Gedichte des Archipoeta,* edited and revised by Heinrich Watenphul and Heinrich Krefeld (1958); Willibrord Heckenbach, "Zur Parodie beim Archipoeta," in *Mittellateinisches Jahrbuch,* 4 (1967); W. T. H. Jackson, "The Politics of a Poet: The Archipoeta as Revealed by His Imagery," in Edward P. Mahoney, ed., *Philosophy and Humanism* (1976); Karl Langosch, ed., *Politische Dichtung um Kaiser Friedrich Barbarossa* (1943), 97–140; Frederic J. E. Raby, *A History of Secular Latin Poetry in the Middle Ages,* 2nd ed. (1957), II, 180–189; Otto Zwierlein, "Antike Motive beim Archipoeta und im 'Lingurinus,'" in *Mittellateinisches Jahrbuch,* 7 (1972).

J. SZÖVÉRFFY

[See also **Goliards; Latin Literature; Rainald of Dassel.**]

ARCN (or Artzn; Assyrian, Arzanibia[?]; Byzantine, Artzke; Turkish, Arzan) a large mercantile center of northwestern Armenia of the Bagratid period (884/5–1046), located about nine miles from Theodosiopolis on the caravan route from Ani to Trebizond. An entrepôt for the exchange of goods from Syria, Persia, India, and elsewhere in Asia, Arcn was a cosmopolitan city and, with Dwin, Ani, and Kars, was one of the four great commercial centers of Armenia at that time. Arcn owed its rise to the Byzantine campaigns of the tenth century that ruined Theodosiopolis, and it was originally settled by refugees from that city, whose role as a center of economic importance it acquired. In 1049 the city, which was not fortified, was attacked by a marauding razzia of Seljuk Turks and, after a six-day siege, was completely destroyed. The surviving population took refuge in Theodosiopolis, which thereafter came to be known as Arzan ar-Rūm "Land of the Romans" (now Erzurum), to distinguish it from Arzan in southern Armenia.

BIBLIOGRAPHY

Hakob A. Manandyan, *Trade and Cities of Armenia in Relation to Ancient World Trade,* Nina G. Garsoïan, trans. (1965), 139, 141, 144–146, 148–149, 155, 179, 181; Aram Ter-Ghewondyan, *Arabakan amirayut^{c}yunnerě Bagratunyac^{c} Hayastanum* (1965), trans. by Nina G. Garsoïan as *The Arab Emirates in Bagratid Armenia* (1976), 115, 123, 131–132, 139–140.

ROBERT H. HEWSEN

ARCOSOLIUM, an arched tomb niche excavated in the wall of early Christian catacombs to shelter a sarcophagus. The sarcophagus might have been used as an altar if it contained a martyr's body. Arcosolia were often decorated, usually with wall paintings, although stucco decoration was occasionally employed.

LESLIE BRUBAKER

ARCRUNIS, Armenian feudal family whose ancestral homeland was the district of Aɫbak in Vaspurakan, in the region of Bashkale. Movsēs Xorenac^{c}i in his *History of the Armenians* claims that they were descended from Sennacherib, king of Assyria. Modern scholars derive the family name from the Urartian toponym Arṣuniuni. The Arcruni onomasticon, however, and information from the medieval sources indicate an Iranian-Orontid origin.

Nothing is known for certain about the Arcrunis before the fourth century A.D. During the rule of the Armenian Arsacid dynasty, they probably held the position of *bdešx* of Adiabene as their hereditary office. Their relationship with the Arsacids deteriorated during the second half of the fourth century, when they chose to pursue a pro-Persian policy. After the fall of the Arsacids in 428, the Arcruni expanded into the neighboring territory of Mardpetakan, which had formerly belonged to the grand chamberlains. During the eighth and ninth centuries they absorbed most of the minor feudal families in Vaspurakan and annexed their territories.

The Arcrunis survived the Abbasid atrocities of the early 850's and emerged as the archrivals of the Armenian Bagratids. In 908, Xač^{c}ik-Gagik, son of Grigor Derenik, severed Vaspurakan from the Bagratid kingdom of Armenia, and accepted the crown sent to him by Yūsuf, the Sājid emir of Azerbaijan. After Gagik's death in 943, the Arcruni kingdom lost its significance, and his successors became the vassals of the Bagratid kings of Ani. Senek^{c}erim, the last king of Gagik's line, fearing a Seljuk onslaught, turned over his realm to the Byzantines and emigrated to Sebastia in 1021. His descendants ruled there until 1080. Not all of the Arcrunis forsook Armenia; some remained in Vaspurakan, while others settled in Ani. Among their descendants were the Arcrunis of Mahkanaberd, who played an important role in twelfth-century Georgia, and the patriarchal dynasty that occupied the see of Aɫt^{c}amar until the seventeenth century. The main branch of the family probably became extinct by the end of the thirteenth century.

BIBLIOGRAPHY

S. G. Barkhudaryan, "Urartskoe proiskhozhdenie armyanskogo nakhararskogo roda Artsruni," in *Issledovania po istorii kultury narodov Vostoka* (1960); Cyril Toumanoff, *Studies in Christian Caucasian History* (1963), 164–165, 199–200; and *Manuel de généalogie et de chronologie pour l'histoire de la Caucasie chrétienne* (1976), 87–95.

KRIKOR H. MAKSOUDIAN

ARDEŠĪR (ARDASHIR, ARTAXERES) I, son of Pāpak, grandson of Sāsān, and founder of the Sasanian dynasty in Iran, reigned from about 224 to 240 (241?). Under the rule of the Parthian Arsacids, Pārs (Greek, Persis), the home of Ardešīr, had been a semiautonomous vassal province. Pāpak, whose family were hereditary guardians of the temple of the goddess Anāhīd at Istaxr, apparently overthrew the Arsacid governor. Having inherited his father's newly won domains, Ardešīr took advantage of the chaos caused by a war of succession between the two brothers and candidates to the Arsacid throne, Valaxš (Vologases) V and Ardawān (Artabanus) V, to seize power over all the provinces of Iran.

The investiture scene in the bas-reliefs of Naqš-i Rustam at Persepolis shows the supreme god of Zoroastrianism, Ahura Mazda (Ormazd), extending the divine and kingly glory to Ardešīr; the mounts of God and king trample the Evil Spirit (Ahriman) and the defeated Ardawān respectively. The foundation of the Sasanian dynasty was seen as a victory of Zoroastrianism over heterodoxy and as the restoration of the legitimate sovereigns of Iran over usurpers. The Sasanians claimed descent from the Persian Achaemenid dynasty overthrown by Alexander the Great five centuries before. The same foundation myth is repeated in a Pahlavi literary work composed toward the end of the Sasanian period, the *Kārnāmag ī Ardešīr ī Pāpakān* (Chronicle of Arde-

AREITHIAN PROSE: PROSE RHETORICS

šīr the son of Pāpak). Although similar romanticized accounts of other kings existed, this legend of the founder of the dynasty was obviously the most important, for it is the only one preserved and was translated into foreign languages. A Greek version, apparently translated from Armenian, is found at the beginning of the Greek recension of the *History of the Armenians* of Agat^{c}angełos.

Under Ardešīr the Zoroastrian church was centralized in Pārs, the written canon of the Avesta (the Zoroastrian sacred texts) was fixed, and important reforms were instituted in the calendar of religious feasts. Images of the Iranian gods in temples were destroyed and replaced by sacred fires. These changes were supervised by the high priest Tansar, whose works and orthodoxy are praised in the *Dēnkard,* a religious encyclopedia compiled in the ninth century. In his own time, however, Tansar encountered bitter opposition from other Iranian Zoroastrians, as indeed did Ardešīr; and his defense of his reforms, in response to the protests of a local ruler conquered by Ardesīr, are set forth in the *Tansarnāme* (Letter of Tansar), a medieval Persian document that derives from a Sasanian original.

In 240 (241?) Ardešīr abdicated in favor of his son, Šābulhr (Sapor) I, who continued his father's policies of conquest and religious centralization.

BIBLIOGRAPHY

Primary sources include *Kārnāmag ī Ardešīr ī Pāpakān,* Darab P. Sanjana, ed. and trans. (1896)—for other editions, studies, and manuscript sources, see Mary Boyce, "Middle Persian Literature," in *Handbuch der Orientalistik* (1968), 60 and note 2; and *The Letter of Tansar,* Mary Boyce, trans. (1968)—see the introduction for Persian editions and citations from the *Dēnkard.* The secondary literature includes Mary Boyce, *Zoroastrians: Their Religious Beliefs and Practices* (1979), 101–109; Arthur Christensen, *L'Iran sous les Sassanides,* 2nd ed. (1944), p. 91, fig. 2; and S. H. Taqizadeh, "The Early Sasanians, Some Chronological Points Which Possibly Call for Revision," in *Bulletin of the School of Oriental and African Studies* (University of London), **11** (1943–1946).

JAMES R. RUSSELL

[See also **Agat^{c}angełos; Sasanian Dynasty.**]

AREITHIAN PROSE: PROSE RHETORICS. The Welsh term *areithiau* (singular: *araith*) is applied to a type of brief prose piece in which various aspects of verbal dexterity are highlighted. Written primarily in the fifteenth and sixteenth centuries, a period that saw production of a large number of treatises on grammar (Latin and Welsh), metrics, and traditional bardic lore in the medium of Welsh prose, the *areithiau* probably served as model exercises for students of the poetic craft. Many of the handbooks of rhetoric popular throughout the Middle Ages include such models: Geoffrey de Vinsauf's widely circulated *Poetria nova,* for example, contains sample treatments of subjects culled from myth, legend, the Bible, and current events. Similarly, most of the *areithiau* are organized around subjects that would confront a poet working in the Welsh tradition: lists of things hated or loved; accounts of dream visions; and descriptions of a beloved woman, a patron, or desired gifts provide a framework through which the poet could gain facility in *inventio* (finding the appropriate thing to say), *dispositio* (ordering his material), and *elocutio* (finding the right words).

The *areithiau* stress skill in verbalization, particularly in the coining of the strings of compound words that are a hallmark of Welsh poetic diction, and in the handling of alliteration, rhyme, and rhythm. It has been suggested that passages of alliterative rhythmic prose found in the *areithiau* classified as parodies (of earlier romantic tales) reflect the oral technique of the Welsh storyteller, the *cyfarwydd.*

Most *areithiau* are found in several copies, suggesting that they enjoyed fairly wide circulation. They exhibit a pleasure in the manipulation of words that belies their modern editor's opinion that they represent finely adorned "emptiness of spirit." The *areithiau* are jeux d'esprit, the work of poets at play with their medium of expression, the Welsh language.

BIBLIOGRAPHY

Edition. David J. G. Jones, ed., *Yr Areithiau Pros* (1934).

Secondary Works. Harold I. Bell, *The Nature of Poetry as Conceived by the Welsh Bards* (1955); F. Loth, "Une parodie des Mabinogion," in *Revue Celtique,* **19** (1898); Thomas H. Parry-Williams, "Welsh Poetic Diction," in *Proceedings of the British Academy,* **32** (1946); Brynley F. Roberts, "Tales and Romances," in *A Guide to Welsh Literature,* vol. I, Alfred O. H. Jarman and Gwilym R. Hughes, eds. (1976).

HEATHER HENDERSON

[See also **Ars Poetica; Welsh Literature: Poetry.**]

ARENA CHAPEL (Padua), a small building originally attached to a now destroyed family palace, housing Giotto's most renowned fresco cycle illustrating the life of the Virgin and the life of Christ. According to a lost inscription, the cornerstone was laid in 1303, the chapel consecrated in 1305, and Giotto's work done between 1305 and 1312, under the patronage of Enrico Scrovegni, who is shown on the end wall, offering the chapel to the Virgin, as an expiation for the sin of usury.

BIBLIOGRAPHY

Bruce Cole, *Giotto and Florentine Painting* (1976); James Stubblebine, *Giotto: The Arena Chapel Frescoes* (1969).

ADELHEID M. GEALT

[See also **Giotto.**]

AREOPAGITE. See **Pseudo-Dionysius the Areopagite.**

ARGUN. Mongol ruler of Iran (1284–1291). He was the grandson of Hulagu, founder of Mongol power in the Middle East, and the son of Abaqa. He took the throne from his uncle Tegüder (Aḥmad), a convert to Islam who had previously seized the crown from him. He reversed Tegüder's pro-Islamic policies and promoted closer ties with the Christian West. These largely took the form of abortive projects for Mongol–Christian invasions of Mamluk lands. Most notable of these was the mission in 1287 of the Uyghur Nestorian Rabban Sauma to the West, where he met with Popes Honorius IV and Nicholas IV, Philip IV of France, and Edward I of England.

BIBLIOGRAPHY

J. A. Boyle, "Dynastic and Political History of the Īl-Khāns," in J. A. Boyle, ed., *Cambridge History of Iran,* V (1968), 368–372; Igor de Rachewiltz, *Papal Envoys to the Great Khans* (1971).

PETER B. GOLDEN

ARIANISM, the widespread fourth-century Trinitarian heresy that denied the divinity of Christ, took its name from the Alexandrian priest, Arius (*ca.* 250–336). In spite of several disputes with Archbishop Peter over doctrinal matters, Arius was nearly elected archbishop of Alexandria in 312; in 313 he was put in charge of the Baucalis church there. Contemporaries describe him as tall, urbane, and well educated, renowned for asceticism and quick to engage in disputations. About 318, he became embroiled in a dispute with Archbishop Alexander about the relationship of Christ, the Word (Logos), with God the Father. Arius argued that since the Godhead (that is, the Father) was by definition unoriginate, uncreated, and unchangeable, the Word could not share the same divine substance with the Father. The Father in fact created the Word as an instrument for the creation and redemption of the world, the bridge across the gulf that separates God from the world. Christ is at best a kind of demigod, the firstborn of all creatures. When he comes into the world, he inhabits a body that is not completely human because it has no rational soul of its own.

Arius' opponents saw this formulation as a neopagan attack on the very core of Christian doctrine. In 320, Archbishop Alexander called a synod of the Egyptian bishops, which excommunicated Arius in 321. But Arius had some powerful sympathizers among the bishops in the East, especially in Syria and Palestine. He took refuge with Eusebius of Nicomedia and produced a prose poem, *Thaleia* (the Banquet), to disseminate his ideas. The continuing dissension convinced Emperor Constantine to call the first general council of the Church, which assembled at Nicaea in 325. The defense of orthodoxy fell largely to Alexander's assistant, the young archdeacon, Athanasius. The council produced the Nicene Creed, which embodied the central teaching of the council that Jesus Christ was consubstantial *(homoousios)* with the Father. Arius and those of his supporters who refused to subscribe to the creed were banished, the first instance of civil punishment for heresy. Athanasius succeeded Alexander as archbishop in 328.

Although Constantine attempted to reinstate Arius at least twice, in 331 and 336, Athanasius' refusals prevailed. But when the emperor died in 337, a period of instability followed in the East, where Emperor Constantius II supported Arianism. Athanasius went into the first of a series of exiles, and orthodox bishops were replaced by Arians or their sympathizers. Arianism itself was split into factions. The radical faction, called Anomoeans or Heteroousians, held the strict Arian teaching of different substance for Father and Word; the middle ground was held by the Homoeans or Semi-Arians, who taught that the substances were similar. From 330 to 362, at least twelve synods were held in the East and the West in an attempt to settle matters, usually by some sort of Semi-Arian compromise. In 361, Constantius died, and the indifference of Pope Julius I gave the orthodox some respite. Still, by 364, when the Arian Valens became emperor, Arianism had all but prevailed, at least among the upper classes.

The vindication of orthodoxy was begun by the Cappadocian fathers, Basil the Great, Gregory Nazianzus, and Gregory of Nyssa, who kept up the struggle after Athanasius' death in 373 despite harassment from Valens. In 379, the Spaniard Theodosius I, who was raised in the Nicene faith, succeeded Valens. Gregory of Nazianzus came to Constantinople and through his eloquence reconciled the city to Nicene orthodoxy. The Council of Constantinople (381) reaffirmed the Nicene creed and affirmed the divinity of the Holy Spirit. Besides the work of the Cappadocians, the monastic movements in Egypt and Syria, which were increasingly identified with the orthodoxy of Athanasius and Basil, helped to turn the tide against the Arians.

Support from the West came from Rome and from Ambrose of Milan. This time the civil arm was against the Arians, and a decree of Theodosius (July 381) gave over all church property to the orthodox. Disestablished by law, Arianism quickly ceased to be a significant force inside the empire, and the emphasis shifted from Trinitarian questions to the relationship between divinity and humanity in Christ.

Outside the empire, the situation was different. Through the zealous missionary work of Ulfilas (Wulfila), who was born of captive Cappadocian parents among the Goths, the latter were converted to a Homoean form of Arianism. Ulfilas, while in Constantinople, had been consecrated as a missionary bishop about 340 by Eusebius of Nicomedia, who was then archbishop of that city. He was sent out to convert the Goths, for whom he made a translation of the Bible. He also composed an Arian confession, parts of which have survived. As a result of his efforts, Arian Christianity spread among the Germanic tribes, where it became a symbol of their independence of imperial jurisdiction. When these tribes invaded the empire, they brought their Arianism with them. With the notable exception of the Vandals in North Africa, the Germanic kings tended to rule their Arian and orthodox subjects impartially. When persecutions of the orthodox did take place, political intrigue almost always lay at the root of the trouble.

A crisis was precipitated in Italy by the persecution of Eastern Arians by Justin and Justinian in the early sixth century. When diplomacy failed, Theodoric, the Ostrogoth king, jailed Pope John I and killed some Roman senators. Justinian eventually invaded Italy and destroyed the Gothic kingdom. The same move against the West saw the liberation of the Church in North Africa from the Arian Vandals (429). Another blow to Arianism was the conversion to the Nicene faith of the Frankish king Clovis (496). He eventually drove the Visigoths out of France into Spain, and by the end of the sixth century they had abandoned Arianism. Other Germanic tribes (the Suevi in Spain, the Burgundians in France, and the Lombards in northern Italy) were all converted by the mid sixth century. Arianism as a living faith ceased to exist.

BIBLIOGRAPHY

The primary historical sources are the ecclesiastical histories of Socrates, Sozomen, and Theodoret of Cyr; English translations edited by Philip Schoff are in *Nicene and Post-Nicene Fathers,* 2nd ser., II–III (1973–1979). On Arius, see Johannes Quasten, *Patrology,* III (1975), 3–17. For a general overview, see Henry M. Gwatkin, *Studies in Arianism,* 2nd ed. (1900); and Hubert Jedin and John P. Dolan, eds., *History of the Church,* II (1980), 16–77. On the theological aspects, see John H. Newman, *The Arians of the Fourth Century,* 5th ed. (1888); Jaroslav Pelikan, *The Christian Tradition,* I (1971), 172–225, and bibliography, 369–371; and Harry A. Wolfson, "Philosophical Implications of Arianism and Apollinarianism," in *Dumbarton Oaks Papers,* **16** (1958).

D. W. JOHNSON

ARISTAKĒS LASTIVERTC^c I, eleventh-century Armenian cleric and historian. Unlike earlier Armenian historians, Aristakēs had no patron and was not writing a eulogistic account of the role of a particular noble family in Armenia's history. His *History Regarding the Sufferings Occasioned by Foreign Peoples Living Around Us,* written between 1072 and 1079, opens with a poetic summary of some of the disasters befalling the Armenian people in the eleventh century and continues with a prose narration of events from 1000 to 1071. It is a prime source for Byzantine-Armenian relations, the Seljuk invasions, and the T^{c}ondrakrc^{c}i movement in the Armenian Church. Aristakēs' material on Byzantine attempts to subjugate the Armeno-Georgian district of Tayk^{c}/T^{c}ao (1000–1022), on conflicts and cooperation among Armenian and Georgian princes, and on the fall of the Bagratid kingdom of Ani confirms and supplements what is known from Byzantine, Arab, and Iranian sources. He was the first Armenian historian to describe the Seljuk invasions from 1047 to the capture of Ani (1064) and the battle of Manazkert (1071), providing considerable information on the nature of the invasions, the routes, and the participants. The work of a patriotic historian who heaped scorn upon those clerical and lay Armenian lords whose actions the author regarded as detrimental to Armenia's national church and to the preservation of Armenian polities, this *History* displays equal aversion to Armenia's foreign overlords, Byzantine and Seljuk.

BIBLIOGRAPHY

The critical edition of the classical Armenian text was published by K. N. Yuzbashyan, *Patmut^{c}iwn Aristakisi Lastivertc^{c}woy* (1963), to which is appended a full bibliography by H. A. Anasyan. Marius Canard and Haïg Berberian, eds., *Récit des malheurs de la nation arménienne* (1973), is the French translation and contains additional bibliography. See also K. N. Yuzbashyan, "The Daylamites in the *History* of Aristakēs Lastivertc^{c}i," in *Armenian Review,* **31** (1979).

ROBERT BEDROSIAN

ARISTOTELES UND PHYLLIS, a thirteenth-century Middle High German verse tale *(Märe).* In it King Philip of Greece retains Aristotle as tutor to his son Alexander, whose progress is halted when the young man falls in love with Phyllis, one of the queen's ladies. Aristotle reports to the king, who orders the lovers separated. The enraged Phyllis plans her revenge on the old teacher. Making well-calculated use of her womanly charms, she arranges to be seen picking flowers outside his study. The old man is so stirred by love and desire that he first offers her money but then yields to her one condition: Phyllis insists on riding outside on the philosopher's back. Fitted with a saddle and with her silk belt between his teeth, the old man crawls through the park, carrying the singing girl on his back. The scene is witnessed by the queen and her court, and the humiliated philosopher subsequently embarks for the island of Galicia, where he writes a huge tome on the wiles of women.

The dialect of the anonymous poet, a narrator of some talent, especially in his description of the alluring Phyllis, is Alemannic. But the recently discovered Benediktbeuern fragments (*ca.* 1200) show rhymes indicating an earlier Rhenish-Franconian stage according to Hellmut Rosenfeld. It also appears that the previously known Strassburg text (*ca.* 1287) is an adaptation of the Benediktbeuern version expanded by some 200 lines with lengthy reflections on love, borrowed from Gottfried von Strassburg's *Tristan* (*ca.* 1210), as well as with verses from other thirteenth-century authors.

Similarities with French treatments of the same theme (Henri d'Andely's "Lai d'Aristote" and Jacques de Vitry's Latin exemplum in his "Sermones," both *ca.* 1230) suggest a common source. In origin the motif is Oriental; it occurs in the Old Indian *Panchatantra.*

Although the poem is basically a farce *(Schwankmäre),* the introduction of Alexander (genealogy, elaborate praise) shows influence of the chivalric tale, while the attached moral exhibits the misogynic tendency present in some exempla of biblical provenance—for example, Adam and Eve, Samson and Delilah.

The intriguing story of the famous philosopher literally brought to his knees by the wiles of a vindictive woman also enjoyed great popularity in Shrovetide plays (compare Hans Sachs), as well as the visual arts (drawings, paintings, and frescoes in numerous churches).

BIBLIOGRAPHY

See Hanns Fischer, *Schwankerzählungen des deutschen Mittelalters* (1967), 5–15, for modern German translation; and *Studien zur deutschen Märendichtung* (1968), 280–298f., for listing of manuscript transmission, printed editions, and scholarly studies; Hellmut Rosenfeld, "Aristoteles und Phillis: Eine neu aufgefundende Benediktbeurer Fassung um 1200," in *Zeitschrift für deutsche Philologie,* **89** (1970); and Otto Springer, "A Philosopher in Distress: A Propos of a Newly Discovered Medieval German Version of *Aristotle and Phyllis,*" in Frithjof A. Raven, et al., eds., *Germanic Studies in Honor of Edward Henry Sehrt* (1968), which contains extensive bibliographical notes.

KLAUS W. WOLLENWEBER

[See also **Antifeminism; Jacques de Vitry.**]

ARISTOTLE IN THE MIDDLE AGES

ARISTOTLE IN THE MIDDLE AGES. One of the most influential philosophers of all time, Aristotle was born in the Greek colony of Stagira (whence named "the Stagirite") in 384 B.C. and died at Chalcis, Euboea, in 322 B.C. Only portions of his writings were known to the Latin West in the early Middle Ages, but in the twelfth and thirteenth centuries the remainder reached, then inundated, the universities of Europe and profoundly influenced developments in their faculties, especially those of philosophy and theology. Previously Aristotle's teachings had been studied and had elicited commentary from Greek, Arab, and Jewish scholars, undergoing subtle transformations at their hands. The resulting movement of Aristotelian thought as understood, interpreted, and developed across the centuries is known as Aristotelianism. This article traces its history from 500 to 1500, with particular attention to the high point of its influence, 1250–1350.

For twenty years Aristotle studied in the Academy at Athens under another great philosopher, Plato, and then formed a school of his own there, the Lyceum, whose members were known as Peripatetics—presumably from their walking about while engaged in philosophical discussion. Aristotle composed several treatises that are now lost; indeed the only writings of his that have survived are those developed as lecture notes, in Greek, for the Lyceum. These are characterized by their lack of literary style and their cryptic expression—understandable in terms of their origin, but nonetheless inviting liberties on the part of translators wishing to make them intelligible in other vernaculars. Various theories of chronology and development have been proposed for these writings, mainly in terms of their relationship to Platonism, but none has secured universal acceptance.

All of Aristotle's works are philosophical in content, considering that for him philosophy had a much broader significance than it enjoys in the present day. The major treatises cover logic, natural philosophy, metaphysics, and ethics, to which are appended substantial tracts on rhetoric and poetics and on natural and political science. The logical works, known collectively as the *Organon* (meaning instrument), are intended to serve the needs of investigation and reasoning in the remaining subject matters. They include the *Categories, On Interpretation, Prior Analytics, Posterior Analytics, Topics,* and *Sophistical Refutations,* the last four being concerned with the analysis (or unraveling) of complex reasoning processes, and the first two with the modes of being and types of judgment, respectively, that such processes presuppose. Usually assimilated to these works are the *Poetics* and the *Rhetoric,* the former of importance for literary criticism and the latter for persuasive argumentation.

The fundamental text for natural philosophy is the *Physics,* which treats of nature and related topics: matter, form, motion, time, place, infinity, continuity, and the First Mover. Such generalities understood, succeeding works take up topics now treated under the natural sciences. *On the Heavens* offers a primitive astronomy and astrophysics; *On Generation and Corruption* develops a theory of the elements; *Meteorology* studies phenomena in the atmosphere; *On the Soul* establishes principles for dealing with life and knowledge; and various related treatises have applications mainly to the animal kingdom. The *Metaphysics,* by contrast, extends Aristotle's generalized thought into the regions "beyond physics" to develop a first philosophy, or science of being, in complete abstraction from matter. It investigates concepts such as being, substance, causality, potency, actuality, unity, and pure thought, and so lays the groundwork for theological speculation.

Aristotle's practical interests are manifested in his moral philosophy, or ethics, which survives in three versions: the *Nicomachean Ethics,* the *Eudemian Ethics,* and the *Magna Moralia*—all explaining human conduct and its perfection in the good as attained through virtuous activity. The themes of the first work are continued in the *Politics,* which examines the state and various forms of government, and uses the ideal of the common good to adjudicate between them. Apparently Aristotle also studied the constitutions of various cities in some detail, but only his *Constitution of Athens* survives—discovered in the late nineteenth century and therefore unknown in the Middle Ages.

Although all of the resulting teachings provoked thought and discussion, two in particular were to attract special attention in later centuries because of their obvious relation to religious themes. The first was Aristotle's treatment of separated substances or intelligences in his *Metaphysics,* which led him to speculate about the existence of a supreme immaterial being or Intellect, "Thought Thinking Itself," endowed with various attributes usually associated with the God of revelation. Aristotle does not speak of this being as the Creator—indeed, there is no doctrine of creation in his writings—since he thought that the world and motion existed from all eternity. Yet he clearly establishes elements of dependence

ARISTOTLE IN THE MIDDLE AGES

between the Supreme Intellect and other intelligences that he regarded as movers of the celestial spheres, and also between it and the terrestrial world made up of the four elements, for which it serves in somewhat disinterested fashion as First Cause and First Mover. One could therefore say that Aristotle's first philosophy, which he himself termed the "divine science," provided the basis for constructing a natural theology that would have points of contact with revealed religion, though in an indeterminate way that left full room for further development.

The second teaching occurs in the third book of Aristotle's *On the Soul,* wherein he attempts to join his more empirical analysis of human knowing with speculative elements deriving from Plato in order to explain how man can transcend the world of matter and sense to arrive at knowledge of universal and necessary ideas. Here Aristotle discourses about an active or agent intellect and a passive or possible intellect, both of which must function to provide human intellectual knowledge and, in the process, seem to confer on the human soul a special immateriality, or even immortality. Unfortunately, Aristotle's text here is brief and his treatment somewhat ambiguous, with the result that one is left in doubt whether these functioning intellects are really powers of the human soul or separated intelligences after the fashion of the celestial movers. Here too there was considerable room for interpretation and emendation on the part of those interested in developing a theology of man, particularly in relation to the problem of individual immortality, as will be seen.

ARISTOTLE IN THE GREEK AND ARAB WORLDS

Aristotle's immediate Greek disciples continued to elaborate his synthesis of the empirical and the speculative, generally concentrating on detailed scientific studies and adding new treatises on plants, colors, sounds, and mechanics to the body of his writings. In the second century of the Christian era, Ptolemy and Galen extended these researches into astronomy and medicine, respectively, and so may be regarded as Aristotelians in the broad sense. The more speculative elements in Aristotle's thought lay dormant up to this point, though a few developments in logic had resulted from interaction with Stoicism. Alexander of Aphrodisias (*ca.* 160–200) then initiated a systematic revival in psychology and metaphysics, summarizing Aristotle's teachings, focusing on problems inherent in his texts, and reporting fragments of his earlier writings that otherwise have not survived.

Neoplatonic Influences. Paralleling this effort by Alexander were the syntheses of Plotinus and Porphyry, both essentially Platonist in their own commitment and concerned to develop elements in Aristotle's thought that resonated with those of Plato. Plotinus (205–270) is best known for his theory of emanation, wherein Intellect (conceived on Aristotle's model) proceeds from the One and the Good and is itself the repository of the Ideas of Forms (all Platonic conceptions). From Intellect there comes forth Soul, which is related to a World Soul and to individual human souls; the latter become virtuous by turning, through contemplation, from material needs to the sphere of Intellect.

Plotinus rejected Aristotle's ten categories (or modes of being, including substance, quantity, quality, and relation), among other teachings, but Porphyry (*ca.* 234–*ca.* 301), his student at Rome, accepted them and enhanced their value by composing a treatise on the five predicables (or modes of predication: genus, species, difference, property, and accident), entitled the *Isagoge* (meaning introduction), which later came to be regarded as an integral part of the *Organon.* Porphyry also attempted to show that Aristotle's teaching was basically the same as Plato's; in his account, apparent discrepancies arose from Aristotle's starting points in the world of nature, as opposed to Plato's in the world of Ideas. Fourth-century thinkers who furthered these lines of thought were Iamblichus and Themistius, the latter of whom is important for his efforts at Constantinople to present Aristotle's thought in more intelligible dress.

The most proficient of the fifth-century Neoplatonists at Athens was Proclus (410–485), who drew from Aristotle's works to combat Christian beliefs regarding creation and providence, and who in his *Elements of Theology* presented a pagan cosmogony employing doctrines of emanation and participation—the latter explaining temporal diversity (the many) in terms of eternal unity (the One). Other scholars at Alexandria, under the influence of Ammonius, son of Hermias, and less inimical to Christianity, advocated a rationalist theology that interpreted revealed religions as poetic expressions of a transcendent truth at which they had independently arrived. Simplicius, who studied there in the early sixth century, wrote masterful commentaries on the *Physics* and *On the Heavens,* then taught at Athens. And when the Academy there was closed in 529, he brought Alexandrian teachings to Persia. A contemporary Alexandrian, John Philoponus, who was a

ARISTOTLE IN THE MIDDLE AGES

Monophysite Christian, refuted Proclus' arguments for the eternity of the world; he also argued in favor of the creation of matter and the immortality of human souls. In an important commentary on the *Physics,* he emended Aristotle's teaching by proposing a theory of impetus that was to be revived in the fourteenth century, with important consequences for the rise of modern science.

By the mid sixth century such scholars at Athens and Alexandria, notwithstanding their Neoplatonism, had produced an impressive series of Aristotelian commentaries; and, as in the case of Philoponus, these had already begun to influence Christian theology. Earlier, Nemesius of Emesa (*fl.* 400) had used Aristotle's *On the Soul* for his own teachings on that subject, and the Pseudo-Dionysius had employed the logical terminology of the *Organon* to explicate his mystical theology. Treatises on God and the Trinity began to employ more substantive Aristotelian concepts in theological contexts, as in the writings of John of Damascus (*ca.* 675–*ca.* 750). During the ninth-century Byzantine renaissance this trend developed into a Greek Aristotelian scholasticism that was to continue through the eleventh and twelfth centuries, and even into the Renaissance.

Arabic and Islamic Syntheses. The initial development of Aristotelian thought understandably took place in the Greek culture and language, with little impression being made on the Roman world. Simplicius' influence in Persia has already been noted, and this is significant, for the Persians and the Syrians quickly manifested an interest in Greek philosophy. Between the fifth and the eighth centuries a considerable absorption of Aristotelianism, in particular, was triggered by translations and commentaries in Syriac. With the overrunning of these areas by Islam, further translations were made into Arabic, both from Syriac versions and from original Greek texts. The consequent Arab assimilation of Aristotelian learning was probably the most thorough ever effected, rivaling even that of the Latin West, as will be detailed.

The principal Syrian Christian translators were Hunayn ibn Isḥāq al-ᶜIbādī (Johannitius of Bagdad, *ca.* 809–873) and Qusṭa ibn Lūqā (Costa ben Luca, 864–923), the latter of whom composed a work on the difference between spirit and soul that was later translated into Latin as *De differentia animae et spiritus.* These and others made available not only the main writings of Plato and Aristotle, but also two spurious works, the *Theology of Aristotle* and the *Liber de causis,* drawn mainly from Plotinus and Proclus but attributed by later generations to Aristotle himself. Such writings were studied by Muslim theologians, some of whom saw in them ways of explicating the teachings of Muḥammad and others, a threat to religious orthodoxy.

In this setting al-Kindī (*ca.* 805–873), known as "the first Peripatetic in Islam," undertook the exposition of Aristotle's thought to the Arabs, covering the entire corpus in some 260 treatises. In his writings on the intellect, influenced by Alexander of Aphrodisias, he speculated that a first intelligence, always in thought, was situated above human souls and helped explain their intellectual activity. This teaching was taken up by al-Fārābī (*ca.* 870–950), the foremost political philosopher among the Arabs, who continued the harmonization of Plato and Aristotle with his own theory of emanation. Human knowledge, in his account, arose partly by abstraction from sense experience (following Aristotle) and partly from intuited Forms (following Plato): the mediation was effected by an agent intellect, or separated spiritual substance, that acted on human souls and actualized their knowing capabilities.

As a systematizer of Muslim, Aristotelian, and Neoplatonic thought, the Persian Avicenna (Ibn Sīnā, 980–1037) had no equal. He was a physician of note, and his *Canon of Medicine* served as a textbook in medical schools through the Renaissance; in addition, his compendious *Al-Shifāᵓ* (The Cure) organized all of logic, mathematics, physics, psychology, and metaphysics into a whole that had great appeal for later, Christian theologians. There are Stoic elements in Avicenna's logic, which prefers hypothetical reasoning over Aristotle's demonstrative ideal; and his metaphysics ranges far beyond Aristotle's to serve, under Neoplatonic inspiration, beliefs propounded by Muḥammad. One such belief is the unity of God as a being that is necessary and yet stands in some kind of relation to the world; another is the dependence of all creatures on God for their actual existence.

Avicenna met these demands by proposing a real distinction between essence and existence and by developing a comprehensive theory of emanation proceeding from God as the One. From this Necessary Being's reflection on self emanates a Pure Intelligence, and from this come forth other Intelligences, all in a necessitated series that gives rise to the various celestial spheres together with their movers or animating principles. The process terminates with a tenth or last intelligence, the agent intellect, which not only begets human souls and the four elements

ARISTOTLE IN THE MIDDLE AGES

of the sublunary sphere but also plays a role thenceforth in human psychology. Although one for all humans, as in al-Fārābī's account, the agent intellect gives rise to various ideas in the minds or possible intellects of individuals. Each human soul, moreover, has annexed to it a "form of corporeity" and thus inhabits a body, which serves as its instrument; on death the soul returns to the world of intelligences, its natural home.

Avicenna's efforts in service of Islam, though well intentioned, were not appreciated by another Persian theologian, al-Ghazālī (Algazel, 1058–1111), who has been called "the Muslim Saint Augustine." Concerned with orthodoxy and mysticism, he searched through the writings of al-Fārābī and Avicenna, first to summarize their doctrines, then to write a companion treatise, "The Incoherence of the Philosophers," which pointed out their errors and inconsistencies. The two treatises unfortunately became separated, with the result that thirteenth-century Christian thinkers, having access to the first without the second, regarded al-Ghazālī as a follower of Avicenna rather than his adversary, as he truly was.

With the spread of Islam into Spain, the western part of the Arab empire produced a number of philosphers who, while in doctrinal continuity with the East, were soon to exert an unparalleled influence in the Latin West. Among the first of these was Avempace (*d.* 1138), who wrote commentaries on Aristotle and is best known for an interpretation of Aristotelian physics that allowed for the possibility of motion in a void—a possibility not countenanced by Aristotle himself. Another was Ibn Tufail (Abubacer, *ca.* 1105–1185), who wrote discerningly on the problems of faith and reason, a topic that continued to disturb Muslin intellectuals.

The most famous of Spanish Arabs was Averroës (Ibn Rushd, 1126–1198), born at Córdoba and introduced into court circles there by Ibn Tufail. Like Avicenna, Averroës wrote a treatise on medicine (the *Colliget*) that later served as a textbook. He is more respected, however, for his extensive commentaries on most of Aristotle's works, which summarized and critically discussed earlier Greek and Arab expositions, and strove to establish a definitive interpretation of "the Master"; so successful was Averroës in these efforts that later generations referred to him as "the Commentator" par excellence.

Critical of Avicenna's attempts to placate Muslim theologians, Averroës taught that the universe was eternal, despite religious belief that it had a beginning and was created from nothing. He also rejected the Avicennian theory of emanation and the real distinction between essence and existence. Yet he was willing to concede that God is the cause of all being, and thus that the believer has grounds for asserting that the world is dependent on an eternal "Creator." Particularly disturbed with the extreme orthodoxy of al-Ghazālī, Averroës wrote a detailed refutation of the former's second treatise, which he pointedly entitled "The Incoherence of the Incoherence." His own view was that the philosopher alone can discern truths that are hidden from the common man, whereas the believer can be concerned only with symbolic interpretations; the diversity of such interpretations fostered by Islamic theologians, not the true teachings of philosophers, was the real problem.

Another Averroist doctrine that was to stimulate later controversy relates to the unity of the human intellect. Concerned to explain the universality of human knowledge, Averroës went beyond the Avicennian teaching that the agent intellect is one for all persons. Not only this, he maintained, but also the possible intellect that had been attributed to individuals is actually separated from all matter and is likewise one for the human race. The best that individual souls can do, says Averroës, is prepare percepts (called phantasms) on which the separated intellect works to produce its universal ideas. This teaching seemed to deny the human person any truly spiritual capacity, and was rejected by later thinkers as an implicit attack on belief in a personal immortality.

Jewish Philosophy. Largely in association with Islamic thinkers, a number of Jewish philosophers addressed problems of interest from the Hebrew religious perspective and developed views that engaged Christian thinkers as well. The earliest of these from the viewpoint of Aristotelianism was Isaac Israeli (*d. ca.* 932), a native of Egypt, who composed in Arabic a number of medical treatises and short books on definitions and on the elements, all later translated into Hebrew and Latin. Actually a Neoplatonist, Isaac attempted to reconcile the Hebrew creation account with a theory of emanation.

A more developed Neoplatonism was articulated in Spain by Ibn Gabirol (Avicebron, *ca.* 1021–*ca.* 1058), whose major treatise, the *Fons vitae* (Fountain of Life), attracted considerable attention in later centuries. Without concern for biblical exegesis, he presented a doctrine of matter and form in an emanationist setting: proceeding from God as the First Essence, the Divine Will became for him the source

 ARISTOTLE IN THE MIDDLE AGES

from which flow primary matter and first form in a voluntary, as opposed to a necessitated, fashion. All else, including intelligences, therefore have matter and form as constituent principles—thereby implying a doctrine of "spiritual matter" that would have great appeal for Franciscan theologians. Ibn Gabirol's views were so severely criticized by Abraham ben David (Ibn Daoud or Avendouth *ca.* 1110–1180), another Jew who was theologically oriented but more professedly Aristotelian, that they thenceforth passed out of the Hebrew tradition.

The preeminent Jewish Aristotelian of the Middle Ages was Maimonides, or Rabbi Moses ben Maimon (1135–1204), who was born at Córdoba but spent most of his life in North Africa because of persecution of Jews. Well educated in medicine and in rabbinical teaching, Maimonides undertook to dispel the doubts of learned believers in his masterwork, the *Guide of the Perplexed,* which attempted to define biblical terms and to evaluate arguments against the Mosaic law. He was opposed to the use of positive attributes in describing God, but was not averse to negative or action attributes. He thus accepted proofs for God's existence based on Aristotelian metaphysics, seeing God as the Unmoved Mover, the Uncaused Cause, and the Necessary Being behind all the world's contingency. On the question of the world's eternity, Maimonides rejected Aristotle's arguments; he opted for the position that human reason alone cannot decide the question of the world's temporal origins, and so must leave its resolution to biblical authority. Otherwise he endorsed Aristotle's cosmology, seeing the intelligences and heavenly movers as analogues of the angels. He taught also that personal immortality comes about through human union with the agent intellect, which he conceived, in Avicennian fashion, as the tenth or last intelligence that reduces the individual's possible intellect to act.

Following Maimonides the most important Jewish philosopher was Levi ben Gerson (1288–1344), who taught in France and generally tried to improve on Maimonides' teaching. He allowed the use of positive attributes in describing God, and held that God created the world from eternally existing matter, thereby rejecting Neoplatonist emanation theory. Later, in Spain, Hasdai Crescas (1340–1410) reacted to such Aristotelian influences on Jewish theology, retaining only the proof for God's existence based on necessary being, thus effectively bringing the scholastic phase of Jewish philosophy to an end.

ARISTOTLE IN THE LATIN WEST

The early growth of Aristotelianism took place in the Roman Empire—curiously, without any extensive translation into the Latin language. Undoubtedly Cicero (106–43 B.C.), Varro (116–27 B.C.), and Seneca (4 B.C.–A.D. 65) read Aristotle in the Greek, and thus were able to reflect his ideas in their own Latin compositions. Cicero, in particular, shows acquaintance with early writings of the Stagirite that have not survived; he found Latin equivalents for many Greek philosophical terms, and composed a *Topics* related to Aristotle's work of the same title. The pagan rhetorician Apuleius (*ca.* 124–*ca.* 170) translated some Platonic treatises and the pseudo-Aristotelian *De mundo* (On the Universe) into Latin, and imported Peripatetic logical teachings with Stoic overtones in that language into North Africa.

Then, as Greek culture became less influential in the Roman Empire from the fourth to the sixth centuries, Latin translations became more numerous—though still largely confined to Aristotle's logical writings. Gaius Marius Victorinus (*d.* after 363) translated the *Categories* and Porphyry's *Isagoge;* Praetextatus (*ca.* 320–384) adapted parts of Themistius' paraphrase of the two *Analytics;* and Martianus Capella (*fl.* 410–439) summarized the *Categories* and *On Interpretation* in his writings. Finally Boethius, a Roman scholar and statesman (*ca.* 480–*ca.* 524), decided to translate all of the works of Plato and Aristotle to show their basic agreement, but never got beyond Aristotle's *Organon.* His own inclination was toward a Neoplatonic Aristotelianism, and he wrote a number of theological tractates that imported technical Latin terms into discussion, for example, of the Trinity.

Boethius' versions of the *Categories, On Interpretation,* and the *Isagoge* were known in northern Europe from the ninth century on, and became the basis for a dialectical movement in theology that reached its culmination at Paris with Peter Abelard (1079–1142). Aristotelian categories were there applied to the problems of universals, the Eucharist, and the Trinity with results that satisfied some but alarmed others. The full influence of Aristotelian thought was not felt, however, until the remaining works were available in Latin. This eventuated in the mid twelfth century through the efforts of James of Venice (*d.* after 1142), who traveled to Constantinople and translated the *Posterior Analytics, Physics, On the Soul, Metaphysics,* and minor works from the Greek; others contributed versions of the *Ethics* and new readings of the logical works before

1200. A better translation of the *Nicomachean Ethics* was made about 1240 by Robert Grosseteste (*ca.* 1168–1253), along with *On the Heavens.* The entire Latin corpus was completed in the third quarter of the century by William of Moerbeke (*ca.* 1215–1286), who was the first to translate the *Politics* and *Poetics,* together with the treatises on animals, commentaries, and scientific classics of Greek antiquity.

A lesser translating effort from the Arabic took place in the late twelfth and early thirteenth centuries; this was centered in Spain and Sicily, and came about largely through the efforts of Gerard of Cremona (*ca.* 1114–1187) and Michael Scot (*ca.* 1175–*ca.* 1253). Although later than, and not so widely circulated as, the translations from the Greek, these made available alternative readings of Aristotle's text, and thus contributed to its better understanding.

Reception in the Universities. The arrival of Aristotelian learning in the Latin West coincided approximately with another important event there, the rise of the universities. Groups of students and masters emerged as self-governing associations (somewhat similar to guilds) at Bologna, Paris, Oxford, and other universities toward the end of the twelfth century, and by the beginning of the thirteenth had begun to replace monastic and cathedral schools as the principal institutions for the communication of knowledge. The liberal arts, the Bible, law, and medicine were the main subjects of instruction, and as courses developed, the universities formed recognizable faculties. The arts faculties were the first beneficiaries of the new knowledge, for Aristotle's natural science provided an admirable complement to instruction in the liberal arts, which up to that point had been confined to the trivium (grammar, rhetoric, and logic) and the quadrivium (arithmetic, geometry, music, and astronomy). Rather early the ecclesiastical authorities at Paris recognized that elements of the new learning could be inimical to the Christian faith, and in 1210 forbade "any public and private reading at Paris, under penalty of excommunication, of the Books of Aristotle on natural philosophy and their commentaries." Fortunately this prohibition was restricted to the arts faculty and did not prove completely effective, for in April 1231, Pope Gregory IX commanded that the books on nature prohibited in 1210 be purged of their errors so that they could henceforth be studied without detriment to the faith. By 1255 all of Aristotle's treatises then available in Latin translation, plus the *Isagoge,* the *Liber de causis,* the *De differentia animae et spiritus* of Qusṭa ibn Lūqā (translated from the Arabic in the twelfth century), and some works of Boethius were the prescribed texts for the arts curriculum at the University of Paris. Other universities, such as Oxford, unaffected by the action of 1210, were already using the Aristotelian texts in the first decades of the thirteenth century.

One of the earliest forms of university Aristotelianism—known variously as eclectic, Augustinian, or Neoplatonic Aristotelianism—was pioneered at the University of Oxford by the master who is recognized as its first chancellor, Robert Grosseteste. Educated at Oxford and probably at Paris, he composed the first Latin commentary on the *Posterior Analytics* and quickly saw the possibilities of its "new logic" for the systematic treatment of Christian truths. Though not a Franciscan, he taught in the Greyfriars' house of studies at Oxford and greatly influenced the community there, especially Adam de Marisco (*d.* 1258) and Roger Bacon (*ca.* 1214–1294).

Like most theologians of his day, he was well versed in the Bible and in the thought of Augustine, and thus tended to read Aristotle against the background they provided. The themes of light and illumination, so pervasive in Augustinian thought and themselves compatible with Neoplatonic theories of emanation, abound in Grosseteste's writings. They serve to explain the special interest of the English Franciscans in optics and the "metaphysics of light," bearing fruit in the works of Bacon and John Peckham (*d.* 1292).

Grosseteste also commented on the *Physics,* and later, as already noted, translated the *Ethics,* the *On the Heavens* with the commentary of Simplicius, and some shorter works from Greek into Latin. The syncretist theology he elaborated, selectively employing Aristotelian teachings to buttress a basic Augustinianism, characterizes the thought of such Oxford Franciscans as Adam of Buckfield (*d.* before 1294), Thomas of York (*d. ca.* 1260), and Roger Marston (*ca.* 1245–*ca.* 1303), and almost equally that of the English Dominicans Richard de Fishacre (*d.* 1248) and Robert Kilwardby (*d.* 1279).

A similar eclectic Aristotelianism is discernible in the writings of the early Franciscans and Dominicans at the University of Paris, as the masters there, mendicant and secular alike, attempted to go beyond the dialectical applications of the "old logic" to develop theology as a systematic discipline. The first masters among the Franciscans, Alexander of Hales (*d.* 1245) and John of La Rochelle (*d.* 1245), began by using Aristotelian terminology, as did such early Do-

 ARISTOTLE IN THE MIDDLE AGES

minicans as Roland of Cremona (*d.* 1259) and Hugh of St. Cher (*ca.* 1200–1263), while remaining committed to traditional Augustinian views. The same could be said of William of Auvergne (*ca.* 1180–1249), a secular master, and later of St. Bonaventure (1221–1274), who, though paying more lip service to Aristotle, was basically suspicious of attempts to place his thought at the service of the Christian faith.

The attitude of such theologians is easily explained in terms of the suddenness with which the newly translated works impinged upon the university world, offering as they did a self-contained system of thought that stood in complete independence of the Bible and yet provided reasonable answers to some of the very questions that had exercised Christian scholars for centuries. Some of Aristotle's teachings—the eternity of the world, the absence of creation, the substitution of a First Mover for a personal God, the problematical status of the human soul (on knowledge of which Augustine had based so much of his synthesis)—seemed threatening to the faith, to say the least. Others were difficult to understand, and thus invited the use of commentaries; and in the early 1200's those available in Latin translation were Neoplatonic in inspiration, deriving from Plotinus, Proclus, and Avicenna, and actually never far from the themes found in Augustinian theology.

As the century moved on, and particularly after 1230, when the commentaries of Averroës became available in Latin and ecclesiastical censorship was relaxed, a new kind of Aristotelianism began to appear. This saw more promise in the enterprise of reconciling the pagan Greek with the Christian faith, and on this account is usually referred to as orthodox Aristotelianism. Its foremost proponents were Albertus Magnus (*ca.* 1200–1280) and Thomas Aquinas (1225–1274), both Dominicans, the latter the student of the former.

Before becoming a friar, Albert had been an astute observer of nature and had studied liberal arts at Padua. He studied theology in Germany, after which he taught during the 1230's at various priories in northern Europe, traveling and making extensive observations. Around 1241 he was sent to the University of Paris to become a master of theology; here he encountered the vast influx of Aristotelian writing and commentaries, and found in them a systematic framework on which he could organize his vast empirical knowledge. For the next several decades Albert worked on a monumental Latin paraphrase of all human knowledge—including the entire Aristotelian corpus, related works by Greeks and Arabs, and substantial additions of his own—which earned him the title "the Great" even in his own lifetime.

Whereas previous Christian thinkers had sought to reconcile Aristotle with Augustine by stressing Platonic elements common to both, Albert came instead to value Aristotle's distinctive approach to man and the physical universe that allowed for a truly scientific study of nature. Plato and his followers had claimed that science could be found only in mathematics and in the world of pure Forms, dismissing all attempts at constructing a physics as little more than a "likely story." Aided by the newly available commentaries of Averroës, Albert could make a stronger case for the validity and autonomy of the *scientiae naturales* ("sciences of nature"), and so reject "the error of Plato," which he saw as weakening the claims of reason in works of earlier thirteenth-century Aristotelians.

The immediate fruits of Albert's efforts were seen in the magnificent synthesis produced by his disciple Thomas Aquinas. The latter turned out to be an excellent expositor of Aristotle's thought, although, oddly enough, most of his commentaries were written in his last years, when the groundwork was already in place for his theological writings. Thomas' basic conviction, no doubt deriving from Albert, was that reason and faith played complementary roles in making the whole of knowledge, both human and divine, available to mankind. Reason was the prior and necessary requirement, for without it nothing could be understood, not even the teachings of the Bible. But the power of human reason was not unlimited, and in particular areas, such as knowledge of the human soul and of God, it would need to be supplemented by another source. Divine revelation, grasped in the light of faith, could then come to the aid of reason and assist it in penetrating age-old religious mysteries.

For Thomas, therefore, the whole of philosophy could be organized as a unity of human sciences in the Aristotelian sense, and beyond this the whole of theology could be similarly organized as a science by systematically applying Aristotelian concepts and canons (the latter as found in the *Organon,* and particularly the *Posterior Analytics*) to the data of revelation. Thomas' eminence as a theologian derives from this basic inspiration, which led him to "baptize" Aristotle, as it were, and to see the latter's thought as a handmaiden rather than an enemy of Christianity. In carrying out his theological project, especially in his two summaries, the *Summa contra Gentiles* and the *Summa theologiae,* Thomas made

ARISTOTLE IN THE MIDDLE AGES

use of his own distinctive interpretations of Aristotelian texts, aided in some cases by the superior translations of his Dominican confrere William of Moerbeke, but in others reading Aristotle benignly, stretching his thought to the limits of its elasticity to show its basic accord with Christian truths.

The Crisis of Averroism. The resulting Thomistic Aristotelianism had instant appeal to many theologians at the University of Paris, and has continued to attract adherents to the present day. But at the very time that Albert and Thomas were engaged in elaborating their syntheses of faith and reason, another movement was taking place in the arts faculty of the university that was to undo, at least temporarily, the results of their labors. This new movement was likewise associated with the rediscovery of the commentaries of Averroës, which were being studied by masters in the faculty of arts to cast light on Aristotle's text and its rational interpretation, rather than to establish any concord with revealed truth. Because of this orientation some have referred to the movement as radical Aristotelianism; others, stressing its negative relation to religious orthodoxy, know it as heterodox Aristotelianism.

The champion of the new movement, which may also be described as Latin Averroism, was Siger de Brabant (*ca.* 1240–*ca.* 1283). He and others taught the eternity of the world and its necessary existence apart from God's free creative action, and the unity of some separate intellect that, serving as both agent and possible intellect for all people, would not require individual humans to have immortal souls. Coupled with these theses was the allegation that the Latin Averroists were holding a theory of double truth—maintaining that one thing could be true in philosophy and its opposite true in theology—if not the more serious type of rationalism wherein philosophical inquiry would hold primacy over religious belief and theological modes of investigation. Such teachings, of course, elicited speedy reply and refutation from Albert, Thomas, Bonaventure, and others in the faculty of theology, but such efforts apparently were not sufficient to silence their proponents.

In that atmosphere the bishop of Paris, Étienne Tempier (*d.* 1279), motivated by the Franciscans and conservative Augustinian theologians at the university, decided to impose his ecclesiastical authority on the disputants, and on 10 December 1270 he condemned thirteen philosophical errors of the Averroists. Among the errors listed were the oneness of the intellect, the eternity of the world and of the human species, the mortality of individual souls, the denial of Divine Providence, and the necessitating action of the heavens on the sublunary regions. Even this step did not produce the desired results, for on 18 January 1277, Pope John XXI asked Tempier to identify the errors still being circulated at Paris and those responsible for them.

Tempier's reply to the pope is unknown, but on 7 March 1277, three years to the day after Thomas Aquinas' death, he issued his own condemnation of 219 propositions, mainly Averroist and including those just mentioned, but also specifying a few taken from the writings of Thomas. The list apparently was drawn up hastily, without any consultation or serious theological consideration on Tempier's part. It seems indisputable, however, that the questioning of Thomas' teachings did not come from Tempier alone, for on 18 March 1277, Robert Kilwardby, archbishop of Canterbury and himself a Dominican, condemned a similar list of thirty propositions, including several not mentioned by Tempier but known to represent Thomas' stand against positions of the Franciscan school.

With strong support from the Dominicans, reinforced by the canonization of Thomas Aquinas in 1323, the type of Christian Aristotelianism known as Thomism (the basic tenets of which will be sketched later) was able to survive these and other attacks. Yet the condemnations at Paris and Oxford had a significant effect on the direction Aristotelian studies were to take in the later thirteenth and early fourteenth centuries. By then Aristotle's texts were too entrenched in the universities to be abandoned, but they began to be read more critically and skeptically than before.

Henry of Ghent (*ca.* 1217–1293), a secular master, reacted against both Latin Averroism and Thomism to propose a more Avicennian position that effectively rejected Aristotle's main theses; possibly in reaction, Godfrey of Fontaines (*d.* 1306), another secular who was probably Henry's student, returned to a more Averroist reading that, while eclectic, made him basically sympathetic to Thomistic interpretations of the Stagirite. The most influential thinker of the period, however, was an English Franciscan, John Duns Scotus (*ca.* 1266–1308), whose teachings (also to be discussed later) register the full impact of the condemnations. No longer intent on assimilating philosophy into theology, as Albert and Thomas had done, Duns Scotus concentrated instead on freeing theology from any encroachments by naturalist and rationalist thought. Apparently he found in Henry of Ghent both an adversary and an inspi-

ARISTOTLE IN THE MIDDLE AGES

ration, for his own synthesis, while more Aristotelian than, and critical of, Henry's, yet shows the heavy influence of Augustine and Avicenna that characterizes the work of the Flemish master.

Later Developments. Educated in the Franciscan order and critical of the Scotism then being taught there, William of Ockham (*ca.* 1285–1347) reacted even more critically to the doctrines prevalent at Paris before 1277. A logician by inclination, he commented on most of the *Organon* and on the *Physics,* and discovered in these works a new interpretation of Aristotle, the *via moderna* ("modern way"), that drastically changed the course of medieval scholasticism. Whereas followers of the *via antiqua* ("old way"), such as Thomas Aquinas and Duns Scotus, had taken Aristotle's logic to imply some form of realism (in which, for example, all categories and even predicables were taken to have ontological counterparts as modes of being), Ockham argued for a position that has since come to be known as nominalism or terminism. In his view categories are merely names (*nomina,* whence "nominalism") or terms (*termini,* whence "terminism") that indicate our ways of speaking or thinking about things, and not necessarily things themselves.

Consistent questioning of linguistic usage in this manner led Ockham to invoke a principle of economy (later called "Ockham's razor"), according to which entities should not be multiplied without necessity. The real sciences, as he saw it, were not concerned with things, but with terms that stand for things; through careful and critical analysis, therefore, they could be purged of much of the metaphysical content that had proved so troublesome for theology. He thus initiated a program of philosophical study, analogous to that of the analytical and linguistic schools of the present day, that took its basic inspiration from Aristotle, yet permitted a complete rethinking of the entire Aristotelian corpus. Not only would the difficulties of Latin Averroism thenceforth be avoided, thought Ockham, but philosophy itself could be purified of the Platonic and Neoplatonic accretions that had encumbered it through the ages, and henceforth could permit a more empirical and positive investigation of the world of nature.

Ockham's program (the essentials of which are outlined below) had great appeal for philosophers and theologians alike throughout the remainder of the Middle Ages. It was received with enthusiasm in England, particularly at Merton College, Oxford, by a group of thinkers (called Mertonians) who combined logical with mathematical interests to make substantial progress in the study of motion. Under the leadership of Thomas Bradwardine (*ca.* 1290–1349), later archbishop of Canterbury, writers such as William Heytesbury (*ca.* 1313–1372) and Richard Swineshead (*fl.* 1340–1355) proposed various mathematical laws that related the velocities of motions to the times and distances traversed and to the forces and resistances associated with them.

Such studies were based on Aristotle's *Physics* and showed a sophisticated awareness of the contributions of Avempace and Averroës, but went considerably beyond them to develop concepts, such as that of instantaneous velocity, that prepared for the mathematical physics of the seventeenth century. Bradwardine's investigations of the continuum and the problems of infinity were particularly original in this regard. He also showed himself a competent theologian in taking up the cause of God's sovereignty against the Pelagians of his day, addressing problems of grace, free will, and predestination that were later to occupy the attention of the Reformers.

Fourteenth-century Paris likewise benefited from the nominalist influence. Jean Buridan (*ca.* 1295–1358), rector of the university there, commented on the entire *Organon* in order to work out the implications of Ockham's reform in logic. He and his disciples are generally credited with anticipating, as a result, the logic of propositions that is now taught in modern symbolic notation.

Buridan also composed commentaries and questions on most of Aristotle's other works, ameliorating the extreme nominalism of Nicholas of Autrecourt (*ca.* 1300–*ca.* 1350), and occasionally departing from Ockham's views. His most significant departure came in his studies of the causes of local motion, which he, unlike Ockham, regarded as a real entity distinct from the body being moved. To account for the continuation of a projectile's motion after it had left the projector and for the acceleration experienced by falling bodies, Buridan developed a theory of impetus along lines previously suggested by John Philoponus. This concept, a forerunner of that of inertia, played an important role in the genesis of the new mechanics and astronomy that were to emerge in the scientific revolution.

Otherwise, Buridan's nominalist ideas found fertile ground in new universities then springing up in Germany, where his students Albert of Saxony (1316–1390) and Marsilius of Inghen (*ca.* 1330–1396) quickly assumed leadership roles. They and another disciple, Nicole Oresme (*ca.* 1320–1382), combined

ARISTOTLE IN THE MIDDLE AGES

Buridan's dynamical concepts with the mathematical formulations of the Mertonians, and further advanced the progress of late medieval physics.

As the fourteenth century moved on, nominalist Aristotelianism took its place among the various schools claiming allegiance to Aristotle—usually some type of scholasticism being promoted by religious orders, especially the Augustinians, Dominicans, and Franciscans—in the universities then mushrooming all over Europe. Moreover, despite the condemnations at Paris, Averroist thought there had not died, as witnessed by the writings of John of Jandun (*ca.* 1275–1328), who in his commentaries on Aristotle continued to advance all the theses of Latin Averroism, even more strenuously than Siger de Brabant had done. His friend and associate Marsilius of Padua (*ca.* 1278–1342) developed a political philosophy that was Averroist in inspiration, and strongly influenced thought in this period.

Earlier, Thomas Aquinas had distinguished between the Church and the state, regarding each as a type of perfect society; his disciple John of Paris (*d.* 1306) had then championed the integrity and natural character of the state against those arguing for absolute papal authority even in temporal affairs. Marsilius pushed this reaction to papal temporal dominion further still, proposing in his *Defensor pacis* (Defender of the Peace) a radical secularism that denied the pope any jurisdiction whatever, even in ecclesiastical affairs. His political views were much discussed in later centuries, and no doubt contributed to the antipapal polemics of the Reformation.

Others were not so extreme, and found in Averroës' commentaries on Aristotle a continued source of knowledge and inspiration. This was particularly true in the universities of northern Italy, where faculties of medicine (rather than the faculties of theology, as at Paris and Oxford) exercised the dominant influence over the teaching of arts, and a more secular ambience permitted the unfettered development of Aristotelian thought.

Paul of Venice (*ca.* 1369–1428) is representative of this tradition; an Augustinian friar who had studied at Oxford and taught at Paris, he was well acquainted with the "new logic" and recent developments in natural philosophy. He commented on Aristotle's works, favoring Averroist interpretations but situating them in the context of the *via moderna.* One of his students, Cajetan of Thiene (1387–1465), was particularly expert at combining the Averroist with the terminist tradition, and kept the mathematical methods of the Mertonians alive at Padua long after they had ceased to be of interest at Oxford and Paris.

VARIETIES OF ARISTOTELIANISM

There was no single, uniform body of knowledge that can be labeled simply as the Aristotelianism of the Middle Ages. The manner in which Aristotle's texts arrived in the Latin West, as well as the diverse circumstances in which they were studied and elicited interpretation—to say nothing of the institutional settings that encouraged some lines of development and discouraged others—all contributed to the formation and perpetuation of "schools," each with its own way of integrating Aristotle into its distinctive synthesis. It is difficult to characterize the teachings that came to be associated with the resulting varieties of Aristotelianism, for generalization is usually made at the expense of oversimplification and at risk of error in particular cases. This understood, however, the following may furnish some idea of the doctrinal diversity that came to be associated with the name of Aristotle in the high Middle Ages, especially in the century from 1250 to 1350.

Augustinian Aristotelianism. This eclectic and attenuated form of Aristotelianism, as has been seen, was the earliest to arise, and never did achieve systematic status. There are a number of themes, however, that take their origin from Augustine and were developed by later medievals, mainly Franciscans and Augustinians, in conjunction with their study of Aristotle's texts, and serve to identify this school. These center on its approach to knowledge, some special teachings about the physical world, and an extensive development relating to the human soul and spiritual reality.

In the sphere of knowledge the distinctive note is the rejection of rationalism and related attempts to separate reason from faith, with the result that philosophy loses its autonomy and is worked out in an ambience dominated by faith. Knowledge is thought to be acquired primarily through divine illumination, since God is the source of all truth and is man's ultimate good. The light of God's truth, participated in by man's intellect, is the source of human concepts; as a consequence the divine ideas, the exemplars according to which the world was created, serve to guarantee the certitude of man's knowledge of creation. The human soul itself is likened to an incorporeal light that illuminates its own being, and so can provide direct and immediate knowledge of its inner nature.

The physical universe is therefore unintelligible

ARISTOTLE IN THE MIDDLE AGES

without a doctrine of creation. Not only is the fact of creation in time knowable by faith, but it can be demonstrated using Aristotelian canons of proof once these are properly applied. The *Fiat lux* ("Let there be light") of the biblical account of creation further provides a way of understanding Aristotle's doctrine of matter and form: just as there is a first or primary matter, so there is a first form—light itself—that by its autodiffusion can serve to explain the mathematical form (and intelligibility) of the universe. And primary matter need not be regarded as completely passive and inert, as many interpret Aristotle's teaching; it can be seen as endowed with *rationes seminales* ("seminal reasons") through which God guides the creative process and brings the universe to its ultimate perfection, with minimal reliance on creaturely causality.

The perfection of philosophy, however, is found in its knowledge of the spirit world, where its principal objects of study are God and the soul. The human soul is a complete substance in its own right, and therefore it must be composed of matter and form; its matter, however, is of a special kind: pervasive throughout spiritual creation, common to souls and to angels, and able to individuate human souls independently of the bodies they animate. The powers Aristotle attributes to man's soul, such as intellect and will, are really identified with the soul's essence; and, contrary to Aristotle's view, the will and affective powers are superior to the intellect and cognitive powers. The rational soul, moreover, is not the unique substantial form in man; rather, a plurality of forms enter into his essential composition, including the Avicennian "form of corporeity," which can survive in the body even after a person's death.

Thomistic Aristotelianism. In contradistinction to the foregoing Aristotelianism—which effectively rejected Aristotle by "correcting" his main theses but nonetheless remained in dialogue with his thought—that elaborated by Thomas Aquinas and his disciples (mainly Dominicans) professed an essential fidelity to Aristotle's teaching while supplementing it with insights and interpretations consonant with revealed truth. In a number of particulars the resulting Thomism stood in conscious opposition to the Augustinian tenets just enumerated, and on this account was suspect (and at least temporarily condemned) by proponents of the earlier doctrine.

All natural knowledge, for Aquinas, arises from sense experience, and thus nothing exists in the intellect that was not first known in the senses. (To be sure, truths can be known by faith, but these fall outside the ambit of philosophical consideration.) Man comes to know universal ideas not by divine illumination, but by a process of intellectual abstraction wherein the agent intellect illumines sensible particulars and extracts from them their intelligible or universal content. The human soul, on this accounting, does not know itself directly, but only in its knowledge of other things. Yet the soul's cognitive powers are superior to its appetitive powers, for contemplation is man's highest achievement and explains why his soul is referred to as rational.

All physical bodies, following Aristotle, are composed of primary matter and a unique substantial form that actualizes the pure potentiality of the matter and confers existence on the composite. Each physical body, moreover, is rendered numerically one by its determinate or quantified matter, and not by any special intervening form. Such matter is thus the principle of individuation and of corruptibility, and cannot exist in spiritual substances; therefore, there is no such thing as "spiritual matter," nor can there be numerically distinct angels within a given species—rather, each separate substance constitutes its own species. In all created substances, moreover, the powers and activities are really distinct from the natures or essences. In man the rational soul is the single substantial form of the body, its manifold powers replacing the plurality of forms advocated by earlier thinkers. Again, each human soul has its own agent and possible intellects, as well as a will that freely determines its activities. From such activities one can demonstrate, using Aristotle's own canons, the spirituality and immortality of the soul.

Study of the material universe enables the human mind to rise to knowledge of God as the author of nature, first mover and first cause, supreme exemplar, and final cause of all creation. God's nature lacks limitation of any kind and is pure actuality, *ipsum esse subsistens* ("subsistent being itself"). His essence is thus identical with his existence, whereas in every creature there is a real distinction between its essence and the existence it borrows, one might say, from the Creator. As a consequence the term "being" *(ens)* cannot be predicated of God and creatures in precisely the same way, but only analogically. And though man can demonstrate the fact of creation, he cannot know by reason that it took place in time, but accepts this as a datum of revelation.

Scotistic Aristotelianism. Developing after the condemnations of 1277, and within the Franciscan order, Scotism revives the characteristics of an Ar-

ARISTOTLE IN THE MIDDLE AGES

istotelized Augustinianism, though exhibiting its own distinctive form—which can be sketched briefly by setting it against the Thomistic Aristotelianism just described. Rather than make being an analogous concept, as Aquinas had done, Duns Scotus argued for its univocity and maintained that it is the proper object of the human mind. As such, it grounds the science of metaphysics, which becomes the prerequisite study for man and precedes any work in the specialized sciences. In terms of this univocal concept, God and creatures can be known as two modes of being, the first infinite and the second finite. With regard to God, special emphasis is placed on his freedom and love; correspondingly, man's affective powers are given preeminence over his cognitive powers.

Where Thomas Aquinas argued for a real distinction between the soul and its powers, and the earlier Augustinians had held for no distinction at all, Duns Scotus proposed a formal distinction between them—a distinction so fine that it earned for him the title "Subtle Doctor" *(Doctor subtilis).* He denied both the pure potentiality of primary matter and the real distinction between essence and existence in creatures, and held for a plurality of forms (called *formalitates*) in natural substances. To account for individuation he proposed a special formality, *haecceitas* ("thisness"), which in his view combined with a "common nature" to account for the way individuals differ numerically within a given species.

Scotistic Aristotelianism grew out of these and similar teachings, as Duns Scotus' followers (mainly Franciscans) commented on the works of Aristotle and in so doing attempted to develop a consistent synthesis. The movement never exhibited the doctrinal unity of Thomistic Aristotelianism, and served mainly to articulate a theological position intermediate between Augustinianism and Thomism, though closer to the former.

Nominalist Aristotelianism. The essential difference between nominalist, or Ockhamist, Aristotelianism and those already sketched is the theory of knowledge that underlies it. As already explained, nominalism focuses on the terms that enter into any proposition; these are taken to signify concepts, and so can stand indifferently for one thing or for many. What other philosophers call "universals" are for nominalists only terms or concepts that stand for many: their universality is entirely functional, and is not to be found in any "common nature," such as Duns Scotus thought was possessed by many things independently of the mind's consideration. Reality is nothing more than a collection of singulars the basic components of which are substances and qualities; all else is a modification or way of speaking about such components.

Man can have an intuitive grasp of individual things that affect his senses, but apart from this his knowledge must remain abstract and largely conjectural. Furthermore, singulars depend for their being on the will of God, and since God can do anything that does not imply a contradiction (such as producing an effect without its proper cause), there are no necessary connections on which to base abstract knowledge. Arguments for the existence of God or soul, or of the human soul's immortality, can therefore yield little more than probability.

Consistent application of such principles to the Aristotelian corpus, particularly in commentaries and questionaries that were produced in great numbers in the fourteenth and fifteenth centuries, yielded a somewhat eclectic body of knowledge—frequently combined with elements deriving from systems as diverse as Thomism, Scotism, and Averroism—that may be described as nominalist Aristotelianism. Like the Scotistic variety, this served theological purposes as much as it did philosophical inquiry, and seems to have exerted special influence on the *novatores* of the Protestant Reformation.

Averroist Aristotelianism. The distinctive features of Averroism that proved troublesome in thirteenth-century Paris and Oxford and led to its characterization as heterodox Aristotelianism have already been discussed. This movement was also called radical Aristotelianism, a label that perhaps explains why it received increasing attention with the waning of the Middle Ages. An astute student of Aristotle, Averroës had composed three sets of commentaries on the Stagirite's works: an epitome that summarized the essentials, an intermediate exposition with examples, and an exhaustive commentary divided into brief numbered passages that thoroughly elucidated the text.

With the invention of printing these commentaries received wide diffusion, and the third, the "great commentary," quickly became the standard guide to Aristotle's teachings. Generally its interpretations were insightful and accurate, but in a number of instances Averroës removed the obscurities and ambiguities in the original and thereby impeded any further development of Aristotelian thought. This led to a conservatism, reinforced by the humanists' philological interest in the Greek text, that typified many later Aristotelians and served to alienate them from

ARISTOTLE IN THE MIDDLE AGES

the more progressive thinkers of the fifteenth and sixteenth centuries.

In matters relating to natural philosophy, for example, Averroists generally held for a strict geocentric universe surrounded by concentric celestial spheres, refusing to grant any physical reality to Ptolemy's eccentrics and epicycles, and, a fortiori, to the innovations of Copernicus; they regarded the medium as essential for both projectile and natural motions, rejecting theories of impetus and ruling out every possibility of motion in a void; they insisted that mover and moved must always be in contact, and so would not countenance action at a distance; and they were averse to the application of mathematics to nature, thus hindering the development of mathematical physics. Such doctrines partly explain why founders of modern science such as Galileo were so opposed to the Aristotelian professors who held chairs of philosophy at Padua and elsewhere, most of whom drew their inspiration from Averroës. Scholastic Aristotelians, on the other hand, were usually more open to innovation, and so could not only "correct" Aristotle but also be disposed to modify, or reinterpret, his teachings to take account of empirical discoveries and other advances in knowledge.

Aristotle's writings were consistently a factor in molding the intellectual life of the Middle Ages, and even as the medieval period came to an end, Aristotelianism was still a dominant philosophy in western Europe. This dominance continued throughout the sixteenth century, when the Greek commentators on Aristotle were fully translated into Latin and all the riches of the text, together with the emendations of the Greeks, the Arabs, and the Latins, realists and nominalists alike, were placed at the disposal of scholars. At the end of the century, Aristotle, "the master of all who know," was still firmly entrenched in the universities of the West. It would take a tremendous effort to dislodge him from that place of eminence. Even those who eventually were able to do so, the fathers of the "modern philosophy" that would emerge in the seventeenth century, owed a great debt—possibly greater than they realized—to this thinker whose ideas had proved so attractive to medieval minds.

BIBLIOGRAPHY

Apart from standard histories of philosophy, a number of books on medieval philosophy provide useful overviews of Aristotelianism: Frederick C. Copleston, *A History of Philosophy,* II (1950; repr. 1962); and *A History of Medieval Philosophy* (1972), the best one-volume account in English. Briefer treatments are Julius R. Weinberg, *A Short History of Medieval Philosophy* (1964); and Paul Vignaux, *Philosophy in the Middle Ages, an Introduction,* E. C. Hall, trans. (1959). Gordon Leff, *Medieval Thought: St. Augustine to Ockham* (1958); David Knowles, *The Evolution of Medieval Thought* (1962); and C. S. Lewis, *The Discarded Image* (1964) are helpful for situating Aristotelianism within the general context of medieval intellectual history.

More detailed studies of Aristotelianism treat the different periods of its history or its interaction with various cultures and civilizations. The Greek development is well treated in Klaus Oehler, "Aristotle in Byzantium," in *Greek, Roman, and Byzantine Studies,* **5** (1964); and in Paul Moraux, *D'Aristote à Bessarion* (1970). Geoffrey E. R. Lloyd, *Greek Science After Aristotle* (1973), has a compact treatment of scientific achievements under Aristotelian influences. See also Morris R. Cohen and Israel E. Drabkin, eds., *A Source Book in Greek Science* (1958), for representative selections in English translation.

For the reception in Islam, the sources are listed in Francis E. Peters, *Aristoteles Arabus: The Oriental Translations and Commentaries of the Aristotelian Corpus* (1968); general accounts are given in his *Allah's Commonwealth: A History of Islam in the Near East, 600–1100 A.D.* (1973); and Majid Fakhry, *A History of Islamic Philosophy* (1970). Interpretive literature is contained in Richard Walzer, ed., *Greek into Arabic: Essays on Islamic Philosophy* (1962), as well as in Thomas W. Arnold and Alfred Guillaume, eds., *The Legacy of Islam* (1931; 2nd ed., 1974).

Jewish Aristotelianism is amply discussed in Isaac Husik, *A History of Mediaeval Jewish Philosophy,* 2nd ed. (1930; repr. 1969).

For the encounter with, and assimilation within, Christianity, a basic work is Richard P. McKeon, *Aristotelianism in Western Christianity* (1939). Descriptions of manuscripts and printed sources containing Latin commentaries on Aristotle have been compiled by C. H. Lohr, "Medieval Latin Aristotle Commentaries," in *Traditio,* **23** (1967); **24** (1968); **26** (1970); **27** (1971); **28** (1972); **29** (1973); and **30** (1974).

Important studies of Latin Aristotelianism include Étienne Gilson, *Reason and Revelation in the Middle Ages* (1950), which examines Augustine, Anselm, Averroës, and Aquinas in detail; and two works by Marie D. Chenu: *Nature, Man, and Society in the Twelfth Century,* Jerome Taylor and Lester K. Little, trans. (1968); and *La théologie comme science au xiiie siècle,* 3rd ed. (1957), which document the religious and theological ambience. The crisis of Averroism is treated in masterly fashion in two works by Fernand van Steenberghen: *Aristotle in the West: The Origins of Latin Aristotelianism,* Leonard Johnson, trans. (1955); and *Thomas Aquinas and Radical Aristotelianism* (1980). For the later development and decline of scholasticism, see Meyrich H. Carré, *Realists and Nominalists*

(1946; repr. 1950); and *Phases of Thought in England* (1949; repr. 1973), supplemented by Gordon Leff, *The Dissolution of the Medieval Outlook* (1976).

Medieval logic has been the subject of numerous studies, among which Philotheus Böhner, *Medieval Logic: An Outline of Its Development from 1250 to ca. 1400* (1952); and Ernest A. Moody, *Truth and Consequence in Mediaeval Logic* (1953), are most helpful. For speculative grammar and the philosophy of language, see Jan Pinborg, *Die Entwicklung der Sprachtheorie im Mittelalter* (1967).

Science and natural philosophy in the Middle Ages have received much attention in recent years. The best introductory work is *Science in the Middle Ages,* David C. Lindberg, ed. (1978), which includes essays by specialists on all aspects of medieval science; this should be complemented by Edward Grant, ed., *A Source Book in Medieval Science* (1974), with extensive selections in English translation. Natural philosophy is amply treated by James A. Weisheipl, *The Development of Physical Theory in the Middle Ages* (1959); and by Olaf Pedersen, "The Development of Natural Philosophy, 1250–1350," in *Classica et Mediaevalia,* **14** (1953). Volumes that document contributions to the physical sciences are Edward Grant, *Physical Science in the Middle Ages* (1971); and Olaf Pedersen and Mogens Pihl, *Early Physics and Astronomy* (1974).

For detailed discussions of issues pertaining to metaphysics and natural theology, the most comprehensive treatment is that of Étienne Gilson, *History of Christian Philosophy in the Middle Ages* (1955). Psychology and ethics are surveyed in Odon Lottin, *Psychologie et morale aux xiie et xiiie siècles,* 6 vols. (1942–1960). For political thought in the Middle Ages, see George H. Sabine, *A History of Political Theory,* 4th ed. (1973), together with the readings in Ralph Lerner and Muhsin Mahdi, eds., *Mediaeval Political Philosophy: A Sourcebook* (1963).

WILLIAM A. WALLACE

[See also **Albertus Magnus (St. Albert the Great); Aquinas, Thomas (St.); Duns Scotus, John; Maimonides, Moses; Ockham, William of; Philosophy-Theology, Islam; Philosophy-Theology, Jewish/Islamic World; Philosophy-Theology, Western Europe; Rushd, Ibn (Averroës); Sina, Ibn (Avicenna).**]

ARK OF THE COVENANT, the rectangular chest that contained the tablets of the law received by Moses, and possibly other objects (Exodus 25 and 37; I Kings 8:9). From the early Christian period the ark was represented with either a flat or rounded top in a variety of contexts: as part of the Exodus narrative (Santa Maria Maggiore, Rome, nave mosaics); in schematic diagrams of the Temple or tabernacle (Codex Amiatinus, Florence); or, in Byzantium from the thirteenth century, as a symbolic image of the Virgin.

LESLIE BRUBAKER

ARMA CHRISTI, in art, the instruments (the cross, the crown of thorns) or specific manifestations (the wounds) of Christ's Passion, or objects connected with it (Veronica's veil). In early medieval images the *arma Christi* were incorporated into larger compositions, usually apocalyptic, to symbolize Christ's conquest of death and to suggest his powers of salvation. Throughout the Middle Ages, but especially on French portal sculpture of the twelfth and thirteenth centuries, angels are shown carrying the instruments of the Passion as symbols of Christ's authority.

Coinciding with an increased number of relics of the Passion in the West after the Fourth Crusade (1202–1204), and an escalating sense of personal spiritual involvement, the number of instruments included in representations increased markedly, especially in the fourteenth century. They were often depicted independently as an aid to meditation on Christ's suffering or combined with images of Christ as the Man of Sorrows.

BIBLIOGRAPHY

Gertrud Schiller, *Iconography of Christian Art,* J. Seligman, trans., II (1971), 184–197.

LESLIE BRUBAKER

[See also **Iconography.**]

ARMAGH, Irish metropolitan see founded, according to Irish tradition, by St. Patrick in the mid fifth century, toward the end of his career as an evangelist. St. Patrick apparently intended to establish a diocesan administrative structure for the Irish church, with Armagh as the first metropolitan center. After his time, however, the great monastic movement of the sixth century created an abbatical rather than episcopal system of ecclesiastical administration in Ireland.

Armagh also had become a monastic center by the mid sixth century but continued to claim primacy over the other churches of Ireland. The Irish annals record a vigorous campaign, particularly in the eighth century, to extend its area of jurisdiction. There are numerous references to its abbots and other ecclesiastics throughout the early medieval period. Frequent references to its scribes and teachers mark it as an academic as well as religious center of note. Armagh's prominence made it a target for raiding; its churches were periodically plundered and burned.

From the late tenth to the early twelfth centuries (*ca.* 965–1134), the abbacy of Armagh was held by the powerful Airgialla family Clann Sínaigh. In the early twelfth century under Abbot Cellach O'Sínaigh and his successor, St. Malachy, Armagh became a center of the reform movement that brought the Irish church into conformity with the Continent, establishing a diocesan system and introducing the newer monastic orders into Ireland.

At the Synod of Rathbreasail in 1111, Ireland was divided in half with the northern sees under Armagh and the southern ones under Cashel. The Synod of Kells in 1152 modified this arrangement by making it a fourfold plan, adding the centers of Dublin for the east and Tuam for the west. Under both these divisions, Armagh retained primacy.

In the twelfth and early thirteenth centuries the Augustinians, Dominicans, and Franciscans established themselves in Armagh, though the Dominicans did not have a community there. Two communities of nuns, Temple-breed and Temple-na-Ferta, became communities of Augustinian canonesses around 1144; the Abbey of Sts. Peter and Paul had become Augustinian about five years earlier. These communities were finally suppressed in 1562. The Franciscan friary founded by the Dominican Archbishop Patrick O'Scanlain around 1263–1264 lasted until it was raided and destroyed in 1587.

BIBLIOGRAPHY

Aubrey O. Gwynn, *The Medieval Province of Armagh, 1470–1545* (1946); Katherine Hughes, *The Church in Early Irish Society* (1966); R. Buick Knox, *James Ussher, Archbishop of Armagh* (1967); Hugh J. Lawler and Richard I. Best, "The Ancient List of the Coarbs of Patrick," in *Proceedings of the Royal Irish Academy,* **29c** (1911); J. Ryan, ed., *Essays and Studies Presented to Professor Eoin MacNeill* (1940), 319–334, 394–405.

DOROTHY AFRICA

[See also **Irish Church; O'Sínaich, Cellach.**]

ARMAGH, BOOK OF. See **Patrick, St.**

ARMENIA, GEOGRAPHY. The physical outline of the Armenian highlands is clearly identifiable. The region that has been called the "Armenian Fortress" or "Armenian Island" is a high plateau with an area of some 300,000 square kilometers, formed as the east-west Syrian and Pontic chains draw closer together between 37° 30′ and 41° 30′ north latitude. Towering over both the South Caucasian plain in the north and the lowlands of Mesopotamia in the south, it is linked with Asia Minor to the west and Iran to the east, primarily through the valleys of the upper Euphrates and Araks rivers. It is bounded in the north by the Pontic chain and in the south by the Taurus and the mountains of Kurdistan south of Lake Van.

The general altitude of the plateau ranges from 1,000 to 2,000 meters, and its fortresslike character is reinforced by the higher mountains of the periphery, which average 3,000–4,000 meters. Within the plateau the "spine" of Armenia (consisting of a series of west-to-east chains culminating in Mt. Ararat [about 5,205 meters], then turning southward by way of Mt. Tendürük [3,548 meters] and running down between Lakes Van and Urmia to lose itself in the Zagros Mountains) divides the Armenian highlands into northeastern "Araksine" and southwestern "Vannic" Armenia. Within these broad divisions, chaotic mountain formations with numerous volcanos (Sip^{c}an, 4,176 meters; Nemrut, 2,910 meters, near Lake Van; and the fourfold Aragats, 4,180 meters, north of the Araks), higher plateaus, and isolated, restricted plains (of which the largest is formed by the valley of the Araks) create small units for which communication even with close neighbors is extremely difficult.

The rivers, except for the Araks (flowing from west to east to join the Kura before both empty into the Caspian Sea), are normally mountain torrents rushing through all-but-inaccessible canyons. This is true even of the mighty Euphrates and Tigris within Armenia. The approaches to the major Armenian lakes, such as Sevan in the northeast (1,916 meters altitude, 1,416 square kilometers) are equally restricted by formidable mountain formations. Finally, the harshness of the relief is intensified by a severe climate with temperatures oscillating between extremes of +40°C. and −40°C. Winter snows close the mountain passes up to eight months of the year,

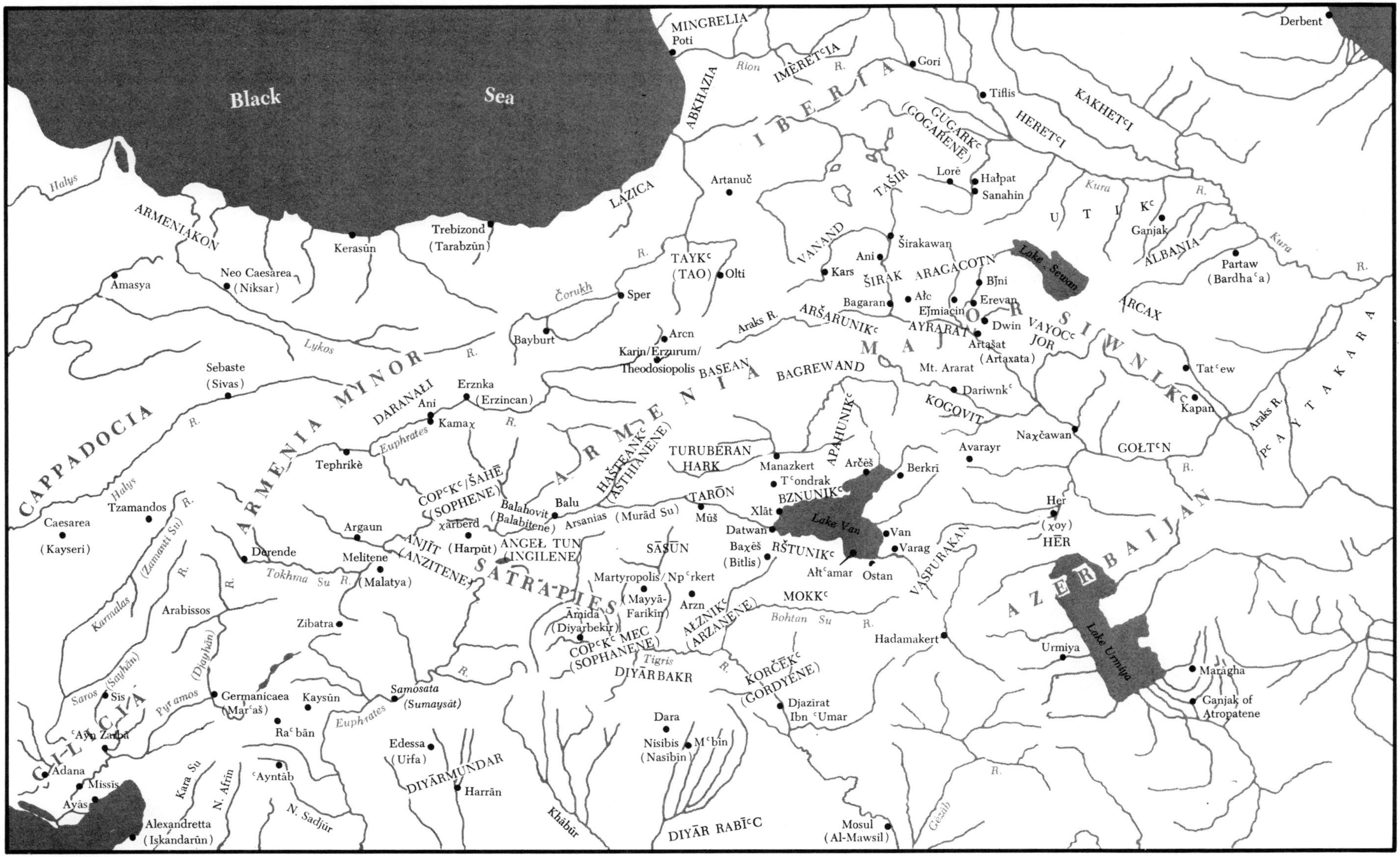
Black Sea
MINGRELIA
Poti
ABKHAZIA
IMERETᶜIA
IBERIA
Gori
Tiflis
KAKHETᶜI
HERETᶜI
GUGARKᶜ (GOGARENE)
Derbent
Loṙē
Hałpat
Sanahin
TAŠIR
Artanuč
LAZICA
Trebizond (Tarabzūn)
Kerasūn
ARMENIAKON
Neo Caesarea (Niksar)
Amasya
Halys
TAYKᶜ (TAO)
Olti
Sper
Čorukh
Bayburt
Arcn
Karin/Erzurum/ Theodosiopolis
VANAND
Kars
Ani
Širakawan
ŠIRAK
ARAGACOTN
Bagaran
Ałc
Ējmiacin
Bjni
Erevan
Dwin
Artašat (Artaxata)
AYRARAT
VAYOCᶜ JOR
SIWNIKᶜ
Lake Sevan
U T I Kᶜ
Ganjak
ALBANIA
Kura
Partaw (Bardhaᶜa)
ARCAX
Tatᶜew
Kapan
Araks R.
PᶜAYTAKARAN
Mt. Ararat
Dariwnkᶜ
KOGOVIT
Naxčawan
GOŁTᶜN
Avarayr
ARŠARUNIKᶜ
BASEAN
BAGREWAND
MAJOR
ARMENIA MAJOR
Sebaste (Sivas)
Lykos
ARMENIA MINOR
CAPPADOCIA
DARANAŁI
Ani
Erznka (Erzincan)
Kamax
Euphrates
Tephrikè
COPᶜKᶜ/ŠAHĒ (SOPHENE)
Balahovit (Balabitene)
Balu
xarberd (Harpūt)
ANGEŁ TUN (INGILENE)
ANJIṬ (ANZITENE)
HAŠTEANKᶜ (ASTHIANENE)
TURUBERAN HARK
Manazkert
APAHUNIKᶜ
Arčēš
Berkrī
Tᶜondrak
BZNUNIKᶜ
Xlāt
Lake Van
Datwan
Van
Varag
Ostan
Ałtᶜamar
RŠTUNIKᶜ
Baγēš (Bitlis)
TARŌN
Mūš
Arsanias (Murād Su)
SASUN
Martyropolis/Npᶜrkert (Mayyā-Farikin)
Arzn
AŁZNIKᶜ (ARZANENE)
MOKKᶜ
Bohtan Su
VASPURAKAN
Her (xoy)
HĒR
AZERBAIJAN
Lake Urmiya
Urmiya
Marāgha
Ganjak of Atropatene
Hadamakert
SATRAPIES
Amida (Diyarbekir)
COPᶜKᶜ MEC (SOPHANENE)
Tigris
DIYĀRBAKR
KORČĒKᶜ (GORDYENE)
Djazirat Ibn ᶜUmar
Dara
Nisibis (Nasibin)
Mᶜbin
DIYĀR RABĪᶜC
Mosul (Al-Mawsil)
Gēzāb
Khābūr
Edessa (Urfa)
DIYĀRMUNDAR
Harrān
Samosata (Sumaysāt)
Euphrates
Kaysūn
Raᶜbān
Germanicaea (Marᶜaš)
Zibatra
Melitene (Malatya)
Argaun
Tokhma Su
Darende
Arabissos
Tzamandos
Caesarea (Kayseri)
Zamanti Su
Karmalas
Sayhān
Saros
Sis
Pyramos
Djayhān
ᶜAyn Zarba
CILICIA
Adana
Missis
Ayās
Alexandretta (Iskandarūn)
Kara Su
N. Afrin
ᶜAyntāb
N. Sadjūr

ARMENIA

ARMENIA, GEOGRAPHY

but the burning summer heat, aided by the fertile volcanic soil, allows the raising of considerable crops where the relief of the land permits and the rainfall (greatly reduced by the Pontic Mountains' halt of rain clouds carried by winds from the Black Sea) is adequate.

The sharply accented and austere character of the highlands has considerably influenced Armenian history. The lofty "Fortress" rising above the Mesopotamian plain has repeatedly provided refuge from attacks, and its strategic position has not escaped the notice of Armenia's powerful neighbors over the centuries. The fragmentation of the country into small, isolated units has continually impeded attempts to create a centralized state. The relative accessibility of the "Armenian Fortress" from the east and the west both increased its vulnerability to invasion and enhanced its cultural variety and its role in international trade. Finally, the close proximity of high mountains and plains within the country fostered the simultaneous development of two nearly irreconcilable socioeconomic systems: sedentary agriculture and nomadic pastoralism.

Whereas the physical elements of Armenian geography are clearly identifiable, its political and administrative aspects still present numerous problems. The sources are often unclear: classical, Armenian, and Muslim authors use different names for the same area, while the same term has often been used, as we shall see, for different areas at different times. Consequently, extreme care must be taken to avoid serious misunderstandings.

From antiquity the term Armenia has included several subdivisions. 1) Greater Armenia/Armenia Magna or Maior, east of the Euphrates River, extended between the latter and the confluence of the Araks and the Kura to the east, and between the middle Tigris in the south and the Čoroχ and the Kura in the north. This portion reached its maximum expansion under the Armenian Arsacids. According to the seventh-century *Armenian Geography/Asχarhac^{c}oyc^{c}*, formerly erroneously attributed to the historian Movsēs Xorenac^{c}i, Greater Armenia (*Mec^{c} Hayk^{c}* in Armenian) consisted of fifteen countries *(asχarhs)* with imprecise boundaries, containing various numbers of districts *(gawaŕs)*. In a generally counterclockwise order, beginning in the northwest, they were Barjr Hayk^{c}/Upper Armenia, on the upper Euphrates (nine districts); Čorrord Hayk^{c}/Armenia IV (borrowing a Byzantine term discussed below), in southwestern Greater Armenia, east of Melitene (eight districts); Ałjnik/Arzanenē (in Greek), north of the upper Tigris (ten districts); Turuberan, east of Armenia IV, extending from the upper Euphrates-Arsanias to the north and west of Lake Van (sixteen districts); Mokk^{c}/Moxenē, south of Lake Van (nine districts); Korčēk^{c}/Gordyenē (in Greek), south of Mokk^{c} (ten or eleven districts); Parskahayk^{c}/Persarmenia (in Greek-Latin), around Lake Urmia (nine districts); Vaspurakan/Basprakania (in Greek)/Busfurradjān (in Arabic), from south of Lake Van, east of the lake and up to the Araks (thirty-five districts); Siwnik^{c} or Sisakan/Sunitai (in Greek), southeast of Lake Sevan and south to the Araks (twelve districts); Arcaχ, northeast of Siwnik^{c} (twelve districts); P^{c}aytakaran/Baylaqān (in Arabic), east of Arcaχ (twelve districts); Utik^{c}/Otenē (in Greek), north of Arcaχ and of Lake Sevan (seven districts); Ayrarat (the central royal domain), in the valley of the Araks (sixteen districts); Gugark^{c}/Gogarenē (in Greek)/Somχet^{c}i (in Georgian), northeast of Ayrarat on the upper Kura (nine districts); Tayk^{c}/Tao (in Georgian), northwest of Ayrarat on the Čoroχ (eight districts). This Greater Armenia formed the kingdom of the Armenian Arsacids until the partition of 387.

2) Lesser Armenia/Armenia Minor, west of the Euphrates (not to be confused with Cilicia, to which this name was also given in the eleventh century). It gradually spread south to Melitene and west to Sebaste/modern Sivas and Caesarea of Cappadocia. Incorporated into the Roman Empire in the first century of the Christian era, it became the separate province of Armenia Minor with Melitene as capital under Diocletian at the end of the third century. A century later Theodosius I divided this province in two: Armenia I, with capitals at Sebaste and, later, Salala, and Armenia II, with its capital at Melitene.

3) The Armenian satrapies/*ethnē* (in Greek)/*gentes* (in Latin)—also called "the Other Armenia"—between the Euphrates-Arsanias and the Tigris in the southwest. Their territory, status, and number varied. Five or six are recorded in the sixth century: Anzitenē/Anjit (in Armenian), Ingilenē or Angelenē/Angeł-tun (in Armenian), Asthianenē/Hašteank^{c} (in Armenian), Sophenē/Cop^{c}k^{c} Šahuni or Šahē (in Armenian), Sophanenē/Mec Cop^{c}k or Sup^{c}an (in Armenian), Balabitenē/Balahovit (in Armenian). These territories, which were autonomous until the end of the fifth century, shifted from the Iranian to the Byzantine sphere of influence, and disappeared as separate units in Justinian's reform of 536.

In 387, Arsacid Greater Armenia was partitioned

ARMENIA, GEOGRAPHY

between Byzantium and Persia along a line stretching from Theodosiopolis/Karin in the north to Dara, west of Nisibis, in the south. To the west the new Roman territories had three subdivisions. In addition to its former territories—the two provinces (Armenia I and II) created from the earlier Armenia Minor, and the satrapies—Byzantium now acquired eleven districts from Arsacid Greater Armenia. These lay just east of the Euphrates and consisted of the entire Upper Armenia/Barjr Hayk^{c} of the *Armenian Geography* plus two districts taken from Armenia IV. This new unit was, confusingly, also called Greater Armenia/Armenia Magna (like the much larger Arsacid unit from which it had been taken), although writers of the period also refer to it as Armenia Interior. On the Persian side, to the east of the border, former Arsacid Greater Armenia, still called Mec Hayk^{c} by the Armenians but now known to Western sources as Persarmenia, lost most of its borderlands to its neighbors. Of its fifteen *ašχarh*s listed above, it retained only the central six: Ayrarat, Turuberan, Mokk^{c}, Vaspurakan, Siwnik^{c}, and Tayk^{c}.

The sixth century brought major changes to the administrative subdivisions of Byzantine, or Western, Armenia.

In 536 a new law of Emperor Justinian (*Novella* XXXI) totally reorganized his Armenian holdings into four provinces: Armenia I was composed of the previous Greater or Interior Armenia plus the northwestern territories of the old Armenia I (in Armenia Minor) and some Pontic lands. It lay between the upper Euphrates and the Black Sea, and included Theodosiopolis/Karin. Its capital was the new city of Justinianopolis, the location of which is still disputed. Armenia II (southwest of Armenia I) was composed of the rest of the old Armenia I and other Pontic districts. The capital was Sebaste/Sivas. Armenia III (south of Armenia II) coincided exactly with old Armenia II. Its capital remained at Melitene. Armenia IV (east of Armenia III) coincided with the former satrapies. The capital was Martyropolis/Np^{c}kert (in Armenian)/Mayyāfāriqīn (in Arabic).

A new partition of Armenia in 591 moved the frontier east to a line running from Gaṙni (southeast of modern Erevan) in the north to Aṙest at the northeast tip of Lake Van in the south. The imperial districts were again reorganized to include the newly acquired Armenian territories in six or seven provinces. The new Armenia I was equivalent to Justinianic Armenia III. Armenia II remained unchanged. Armenia III consisted of Justinianic Armenia I plus new territories including most of Arsacid Ayrarat and Turuberan. The new Armenia IV presents problems. Some scholars equate it to the Justinianic Armenia IV, although it was now occasionally given the name of Upper Mesopotamia. Others, like Nikolai Adonts, postulate a second Armenia IV: Armenia IV altera, also known as Justiniana IV, though this hypothesis has been disputed. Finally, two more provinces were created from the newly acquired territories: Armenia Interior, between Karin and Kars, and Lower Armenia/Armenia Inferior, to the east between Kars and Lake Sevan. These administrative divisions were to last about half a century.

The Arab conquests of the mid seventh century brought other changes to Persarmenia, the western boundary of which moved back toward the Euphrates although its precise position fluctuated. The new Arab administrative term *Armīniya* should not be taken as an equivalent for Armenia, even in its widest extension. *Armīniya* included most of the lands of Caucasia, from the Caucasus chain in the north to the mountains of Kurdistan in the south; from the Euphrates, Čoroχ, and Black Sea in the west to Lake Urmia, the lower Kura, and the Caspian Sea in the east.

Some Arab writers, such as al-Balādhurī and Ibn Khurradādhbih, follow the Byzantine practice of subdividing the region into four parts, but these divisions are composed of totally different territories. For them Armīniya I consisted of Caucasian Albania (that is, Utik^{c} and Siwnik^{c}) and eastern Caucasia; Armīniya II, of Georgia and western Caucasia; Armīniya III, of the Armenian heartland (Širak in the northwest, the Araks valley, and Vaspurakan); and Armīniya IV, of western Armenia from Karin to the north of Lake Van. Other geographers speak of Interior Armīniya (Karin, Dwin, Naχčawan) and Exterior Armīniya (around Lake Van), or of Greater/Armīniya al-Kubrā and Lesser/Armīniya aṣ-Ṣughrā, around Xlat^{c}/Akhlat and Tiflis, respectively.

The autonomous Armenian territories recognized by the caliphate still centered on Ayrarat, but western districts remained Byzantine while southern ones were absorbed into Mesopotamia. With the creation of the Bagratid kingdom at the end of the ninth century, however, a number of lost borderlands in the north were recovered. The new kingdom consequently extended over ten of the original fifteen Arsacid *ašχarh*s—Turuberan, Mokk^{c}, Vaspurakan, Siwnik^{c}, Arcaχ, P^{c}aytakaran, Utik^{c}, Ayrarat, Gugark^{c}, Tayk^{c}—and some territory in Parskahayk^{c}, although its borders were unclear and much territory in the southwest around Lake Van and even the valley of the Araks was controlled by Muslim emirates.

After the fall of the Bagratid kingdom in the mid eleventh century, the name Armenia passed to Cilicia, or Armenia Minor. It was also perpetuated in that of the Byzantine theme of Armeniakon, created in the late seventh century from most of the lands of the original Armenia Minor west of the Euphrates up to the Halys, but subsequently reduced to a central strip running south from the Black Sea around Sinop. Additional, though short-lived, themes came into being on Armenian territory as a result of the Byzantine reconquest: Tarōn, in the southwest, in the late ninth century and, in the eleventh century, Theodosiopolis, around Karin; Mesopotamia, between the main Euphrates and the Arsanias, west of Tarōn; Iberia, from Tayk^{c} to the vicinity of Ani in Širak; and Basprakania, in Vaspurakan.

With the Seljuk invasions of the mid eleventh century, the Armenian highlands could no longer be separated politically or administratively from the adjacent lands of Azerbaijan or Asia Minor. No fixed boundaries could be maintained in the prevailing chaos of the twelfth through fifteenth centuries; and in general only temporary local units, some limited to a single city, can be identified. Exceptions are the administration of the Zak^{c}arids, who held much of north-central Armenia during the early thirteenth century, and the twelfth-century realm of the Shāh, stretching north of Lake Van on either side of the capital of Xlat^{c}. The eastward expansion of the Ottomans in the late fifteenth and early sixteenth centuries once again divided the Armenian highlands, this time between Turks and Persians along a north-south line that moved sharply with the fortunes of war, but often came to rest west of present-day Erevan and east of Lake Van.

BIBLIOGRAPHY

Nikolai Adonts, *Armenia in the Period of Justinian,* N. G. Garsoïan, ed. and trans. (1970), pp. 7–182, 234–251, *103–*246; R. Blanchard, "L'Arménie," in P. Vidal de la Blache and L. Gallois, eds., *Géographie universelle,* VIII (1929), for the best succinct account of the physical geography; Sowren T. Eremyan, *Hayastan ast "Asχarhac^{c} oyc^{c}* (1968), for the fullest discussion of the seventh-century *Armenian Geography* and the best map of seventh-century Armenia; R. Hewsen, "Armenia According to the Ašχarhaçoyç," in *Revue des études arméniennes,* n.s 2 (1965), for a summary of Eremyan's work; and "On the Date and Authorship of the Ašχarhac^{c}oyc^{c}," in *Revue des études arméniennes, n.s.* 4 (1967); Ernst Honigmann, *Die Ostgrenze des byzantinischen Reiches von 363 bis 1071* (1935), with maps; Heinrich Hübschmann, *Die altarmenischen Ortsnamen* (1904; repr. 1969), for place names and a useful map; J. Laurent, *L'Arménie entre Byzance et l'Islam depuis la conquête arabe jusqu'en 886* (1919; new rev. ed. by M. Canard 1980), pp. 39–75, for a useful summary and updating; Hakob Manandyan, *The Trade and Cities of Armenia in Relation to Ancient World Trade,* N. G. Garsoïan, trans. (1965), pp. 23, 47–52, 90–116, 155–172, 187–202, with maps (for the main transit routes); Josef Markwart, *Ērānšahr nach der Geographie des Ps. Moses Xorenac^{c}i* (1901); *Südarmenien und die Tigrisquellen* (1930); and "La province de Parskahayk^{c}," ed. G. V. Abgaryan, in *Revue des études arméniennes,* n.s. 3 (1966); Arsène Soukry, ed. and trans., *Géographie de Moïse de Corène* (1881), for the text and a translation of the seventh-century *Armenian Geography.*

In addition to the maps indicated in the above works, see H. F. B. Lynch, *Armenia: Travel and Studies,* 2 vols. (1901; repr. 1965)—the map in the original edition is far more legible than its reproduction. Also see William M. Calder and George E. Bean, *A Classical Map of Asia Minor* (1957); *Haykakan SSR Atlas* (1961); A. H. M. Jones, *The Cities of the Eastern Roman Provinces* (1971), map of Mesopotamia and Armenia for the satrapies; and Heinrich Kiepert, *Karte von Kleinasien in 24 Blatte* (1902).

NINA G. GARSOÏAN

[See also **Ani (in Širak); Ararat (Mt.); Armenian Muslim Emirates; Ayrarat (Province); Caesarea (Capadocia); Theodosiopolis; Van, Lake.**]

ARMENIA: HISTORY OF. From antiquity, Armenia's geographical position at the meeting point of the Greco-Roman and Iranian worlds created a situation that favored the country's cultural life, enriching it with two major traditions but playing havoc with the continuity of its political history. As a general pattern, therefore, Armenia flourished only when the contending forces on either side were in near equilibrium and neither was in a position to dominate it entirely. This instability, characteristic of the entire medieval period, was compounded by a number of factors and has led to historiographic misconceptions likewise deriving in large measure from the geographical conditions, at least in the earlier period.

The term "Armenia" has been used loosely to indicate any portion of the Armenian plateau and even adjacent areas. In the fourth century this indefinite "Armenia" consisted of three main sub-divisions.

ARMENIA:HISTORY OF

Armenia Minor (Lesser Armenia), was a Roman province west of the Euphrates that remained politically and largely culturally, though not demographically, outside the sphere of Armenian history. Armenia Magna or Maior (Greater Armenia) was the buffer kingdom east of the Euphrates ruled by a junior line of the Irano-Parthian Arsacid royal house but under Roman protectorate since Nero's coronation of the first Armenian Arsacid king, Trdat (Tiridates) I, in A.D. 66. It is this portion that is most commonly equated with the general term "Armenia" by contemporary sources and modern scholarship. The autonomous Satrapies of southwestern Armenia (north of the Arsanias River) consisted of five or six separate units that had in large part entered into the Roman sphere of influence at the end of the third century as autonomous political and fiscal units *(civitates foederatae liberae et immunes)*, which were required only to coordinate their foreign policy with that of the empire. Nevertheless, Armenian sources ignore them and their autonomy, treating most of this region as part of the Arsacid kingdom of Greater Armenia.

This geopolitical fragmentation was greatly intensified by those internal divisions of the Armenian plateau that favored the centrifugal tendencies of the magnates *(naχarar)* who asserted their hereditary prerogatives against any centralizing policy. Thus although Armenia Minor increasingly followed a divergent path from that of the eastern portion, and the Arsacid kingdom disappeared in 428–429 and the Satrapies in 536, Armenia can rarely be treated as a single unit. The internal fragmentation of the plateau, intensified through the mutual antagonism and perpetually centrifugal aims of the *naχarars*, may not be ignored, since the individualism of northern and southern districts continually asserted itself in the particularism of Vaspurakan, Tarōn, Siwnikᶜ, and Taykᶜ. Centrifugality and fragmentation are constants in Armenian medieval history, and they impeded all attempts, internal or external, to achieve a politically centralized state.

Equally serious for Armenian historiography has been the question of sources. Not only are Armenian texts unavailable before the fifth century A.D., insufficient or lacking in a number of cases, and riddled with problems of dating and attribution, they also normally present very definite and limited points of view. Characteristically they manifest an inalterable antagonism to all manifestations of Iranian culture or Byzantine Chalcedonian Orthodoxy; with few exceptions they seek to obliterate the political, religious, and cultural importance of sourthern Armenia; they overstress the importance of the particular noble house—Mamikonean, Bagratuni, Arcruni—that they support, while overlooking or denigrating others; and they disregard the important demographic changes brought about by the Arab, Iranian, and Turkish invasions of the Armenian heartland. Thus, they present a unified but greatly oversimplified view of the complex development of Armenian history.

As a result of these distortions and of the paucity of supporting archaeological evidence, much of the history of early medieval Armenia, especially its chronology, still requires considerable investigation. The overthrow of the Parthian Arsacid dynasty in Iran by the Sasanians (around A.D. 224) made the Arsacid Armenian kings the enemies rather than the kinsmen of the Persian ruling house, at the same time that it rekindled the war between the Roman and Iranian empires. Battered between the two world powers, and probably divided for a time, Greater Armenia did not regain a measure of stability until the enthronement with Roman support of the Arsacid heir Trdat III/IV over the whole of this region and the transfer of the allegiance of the autonomous Satrapies to Rome. These events most likely occurred as a result of the Peace of Nisibis, concluded in 298 between Rome and the Sasanian king of kings, Narseh, whom inscriptions name as the former ruler of a portion of eastern Greater Armenia.

During the reign of Trdat the Great, Christianity became the official religion of the Arsacid kingdom with the conversion of the king and the consecration of the patriarch, St. Gregory the Illuminator, at Caesarea of Cappadocia in 314. This conversion is traditionally presented as the inauguration of Armenian Christianity, although the new faith had undoubtedly penetrated into the southern area of the autonomous Satrapies considerably earlier. This is attested by a passage in the *Ecclesiastical History* of Eusebius of Caesarea, by the persistent memory of the Apostolic or Edessene origin of the Armenian church, and by the assertion that "Armenia" had been the first officially Christian realm. Consequently, no single date seems warranted for the Christianization of all the Armenian lands, but the conversion of the Arsacid kingdom of Greater Armenia unquestionably marked a watershed in its history. It turned the country sharply away from its Iranian past. At the same time, the increasingly powerful national church provided both a durable focus for the cultural

ARMENIA:HISTORY OF

and even political unity of Armenia and, on occasion, a challenge to the authority of its king.

Much of the political history of Armenia remains unclear during the fourth and early fifth centuries. Armenia Minor, divided into two provinces by the emperor Theodosius I, was totally absorbed into the Roman Empire. Almost nothing is known concerning the autonomous Satrapies beyond the fact of their existence. In Greater Armenia the allegiance of the Christian Arsacid rulers (314–428/429) vacillated between Rome and Persia, although the Roman historian Ammianus Marcellinus considered them "faithful friends" of the empire.

Probably the most outstanding among them, Aršak II (350?–367) sought to maintain a precarious balance between the two great powers. His attempts to curb the autonomy of the Armenian magnates by making their hereditary prerogatives subject to royal control and by creating at least one urban center, as well as his support of the Arianizing religious policy of Constantine's successors, earned him the antagonism of the rigidly Nicaean Gregorid patriarchs and of much of the nobility. Abandoned by Rome, as a result of the unfavorable peace concluded by the emperor Jovian in 363 and by the southern satrap Meružan Arcruni, who sided with Persia, Aršak II was defeated by the king of kings Šāhpuhr II, and deported to Iran, where he commited suicide in the "castle of oblivion," while the Persians overran Armenia and destroyed its cities.

With Aršak's disappearance the Arsacid dynasty, dominated by the powerful Mamikonean house, rapidly declined. His son, Pap, was murdered in 374 by the very Romans who had reinstated him on the throne a few years earlier, and with the probable connivance of some of the nobles outraged by the king's assassination of the great Gregorid patriarch, St. Nerses I (353–373). Seemingly by 387, although the date has been disputed, Rome and Iran agreed to a partition of Greater Armenia along a line running east of the Euphrates from the northern city of Karin, soon to be renamed Theodosiopolis, down to Dara in western Mesopotamia.

This division left the western fifth of the kingdom in the hands of a powerless Roman client, Aršak III, while the far greater eastern portion became a Persian protectorate under another Arsacid candidate, Xosrov III/IV, who kept the royal capital of Dwin. Even this compromise solution was not lasting. In the western portion, the Arsacid dynasty ended with the death of Aršak III, whom the Romans eventually replaced by a primarily civilian official known as the *comes Armeniae*. In eastern "Persarmenia," it lingered until 428–429, when the self-serving Armenian magnates themselves urged the Sasanian king of kings to put an end to the autonomous Armenian kingdom.

With the disappearance of the independent Arsacid state, the lands of Armenia entered into an intermediate period of some two centuries, known in Armenian historiography as the *marzpanate*, during which they continued to be divided and disputed between Byzantium and the Sasanians. In the absence of an internal political focus, the increasingly independent church provided the only element of unity and continuity, while the *naχarars* pursued their individual interests, forming continually changing alliances that coalesced periodically around the Mamikonean leaders of the proimperial party or the supporters of Persia, the princes of Siwnik^{c}, and eventually the Bagratunis. The earlier contemporary sources, Ɫazar P^{c}arpec^{c}i and Eɫišē, presented the Armenian opposition to Sasanian Iran in the light of a crusade; but from the sixth century on, the political and religious policy of Byzantium aroused a similar antagonism in the native historians, and recent investigations have tended to show a highly complex situation.

Fundamentally, the Armenian social structure fitted far more satisfactorily into the similarly aristocratic Iranian "feudalism" than into the centralized and bureaucratic Byzantine state; and most of the privileges of the *naχarars* were maintained by the Sasanians, who merely sent a viceroy, or *marzpan*, to Dwin as governor of their Armenian territories. Yet the national historians systematically stress the constant rebellions of Armenia against Iran, branding as archtraitors the leaders of the pro-Persian party, Vasak and Varazvaɫan Siwni.

There is, to be sure, no question that Sasanian policy was oppressive at times and that the ill-advised attempt of Yazdgard II to reimpose Zoroastrianism on Armenia provoked the violent reaction that united the clergy and most of the magnates around the hereditary commander in chief of the Armenian army *(sparapet)*, Vardan Mamikonean, in the great revolt of 450. Not even the decimation of Vardan and his supporters at the memorable battle of Avarayr (2 June 451) and the martyrdom of the religious leaders halted the guerrilla opposition of the country, which exploded again in the successful rebellion of Vardan's nephew, Vahan Mamikonean (481–484), at a time when the Sasanians were distracted by war with the Hephthalite Huns on their eastern border.

ARMENIA:HISTORY OF

In 571 Vardan II Mamikonean rose again against Xusrō I Anōšarwān until the absence of help from the emperor Justin II forced him to take refuge in Byzantine territory. Nevertheless, Persarmenia often flourished under the Sasanian *marzpans*, especially under the native princes Vahan Mamikonean and his successors Vard Patrik and Mžež Gnuni (485–548?), who followed the successful outcome of the rebellion of 484, and a vigorous national culture grew apace.

As the Armenian church increasingly turned against the Chalcedonian Orthodoxy of Constantinople, it became more acceptable to the Sasanians, who no longer viewed it as a fifth column and a focus of hostility to their state. The Armenian patriarchs, or *kat*^{c}*ołikoi*, preferred to reside in the *marzpan*'s capital of Dwin rather than on imperial territory; and the benevolence of later Sasanian rulers toward the Armenian church is reflected in the apocryphal stories of their secret conversions to Christianity found in contemporary Armenian sources. Simultaneously, the numerous favors shown by Xusrō II Aparwēz to Smbat Bagratuni, *marzpan* of Hyrcania, known as *Xusrō šnum* ("the Joy of Xusrō"), and to his son Varaztiroc^{c} won over much of the Armenian military nobility, which had already helped Xusrō II defeat the usurper Vahrām Čobēn in 591. Hence, with the passage of time, the weakening of the Sasanian dynasty in the seventh century and the development of a deep-rooted Christian culture after the creation of the Armenian alphabet early in the fifth century ensured that the *naχarars* would preserve a considerable part of their prerogatives and that Persarmenia would not be absorbed into the Iranian world.

The pressure of Byzantium on the lands it controlled as a result of the partition of 387 rarely led to explosions of violence, but it was perhaps more insidious and ultimately more damaging. Little is known of the precise functions of the *comes Armeniae*, but the constant policy of Byzantium seems to have been the total integration of its Armenian territories into the empire, as had been the case for Armenia Minor. Before the end of the fifth century, the autonomous Satrapies that had backed an unsuccessful candidate for the imperial throne lost their right of hereditary succession, but the major transformations were introduced by Justinian I. The entire eastern border of the empire, from its main anchor point, Karin (Theodosiopolis), in the north to Dara, was heavily fortified, thus reinforcing the division of former Greater Armenia.

More important, in 536 the autonomous Satrapies were abolished altogether; and all of Byzantine Armenia, including Armenia Minor, the Satrapies, and the newer territories east of the Euphrates, was transformed into four imperial provinces, all called Armenia and subject to Roman law and customs. The rights and privileges of the magnates were abolished, and the entire region was set on a rigid path of denationalization.

Critical as was Justinian's legislation for Armenian social and administrative history, the religious policy of the empire was equally damaging. Like most of the East, the Armenian clergy had come to reject the doctrine promulgated by the Council of Chalcedon (451), which it considered "Nestorian," but as head of the church the Byzantine emperor could tolerate no dissent within his realm. As a result, religious pressure to ensure the adhesion of the Armenian church to the faith of Constantinople reinforced Byzantine policy and aroused a growing antagonism in the native clergy and in the population. Some attempts at compromise were made by the Justinianic Council of "The Three Chapters" in 553, but the situation of Armenia took a sharp turn for the worse after 591.

In return for the support received from the emperor Maurice in the recovery of his throne, the Sasanian king of kings Xusrō II ceded to the Byzantine Empire a large portion of Persarmenia. The line of demarcation between the two empires moved markedly eastward—to the Azat River just west of the capital of Dwin in the north, and to the northeastern tip of Lake Van in the south. The new lands were again incorporated into imperial provinces, and the Byzantine policy of de-Armenization applied to them as well. Armenians had long staffed the imperial armies and rebellious magnates had been deported to Cyprus; now, massive transportations of Armenian troops and settlers to the Balkans helped secure the imperial Danube frontier but drained Armenia of both population and leadership. Even more serious, Maurice's attempt to force Chalcedonianism on Armenia split the country and precipitated a twenty-year schism (591–611), during which rival *kat*^{c}*ołikoi* at Dwin and Awan confronted each other over the Azat frontier. Simultaneously the national Armenian church broke with the northern church of Iberia, which returned to communion with Constantinople (607), leaving Armenian and Syriac Christianity isolated in the midst of the imperial ecclesiastical world.

With the beginning of the seventh century, the

ARMENIA:HISTORY OF

situation of Armenia became even more difficult. After the brief Persian reconquest following Maurice's murder in 602, the rapid disintegration of the Sasanian dynasty left the country increasingly in Byzantine hands. The emperor Heraclius used Armenia repeatedly as a base for his retaliatory campaigns against Persia (622–629). Disregarding the traditional Armenian pattern of hereditary offices, he bypassed the Mamikonean commanders in chief to confer imperial titles such as curopalate and patrician and even the supreme internal dignity of prince *(išχan)* on the lesser houses of the Saharuni and the Ṙštuni.

Exploiting the considerable Chalcedonian elements still remaining in Armenia, he continued the oppressive religious policy of Maurice. Hence, as a result of the break in the international balance of power between Byzantium and Persia following Heraclius' victories, Armenia in the early seventh century seemed destined to be absorbed into the political and cultural world of Byzantium. This seemed inevitable even though the antagonism of the clergy and the remaining magnates had been exacerbated by the imperial policies, and even though a national consciousness centered on the church in the absence of internal political leadership, as well as on social and cultural institutions, had come into being within the country.

Before Byzantium had succeeded in its attempted integration of the entire Armenian plateau, the international equilibrium was unexpectedly broken again by the Arab invasions, which apparently reached Armenia by 640. Numerous problems, primarily of chronology, are still connected with the Arab conquest; the contemporary Armenian sources (Sebēos followed by Łewond the Priest) often disagree with the basic Arab historians (al-Balādhurī or al-Ṭabarī), and modern scholarship has been equally divided. The first attacks seem to have been hit-and-run raids from neighboring Mesopotamia and Azerbaijan, although the capture of the capital of Dwin on 6 October 640 was unquestionably a severe blow. The seriousness of the incursions rapidly increased, so that by 652 the *išχan* Theodore Ṙštuni thought it wise to accept the favorable terms, recorded by Sebēos, that had been offered by the future caliph Muᶜāwiya, then governor of Syria.

A brief return of Byzantine domination occurred under Constans II, who again antagonized the Armenian clergy by his forcible imposition of Chalcedonian doctrine during the winter of 652–653, which he spent at Dwin. The Arabs under Habīb ibn Maslama then began the systematic conquest of Transcaucasia. Most cities were captured, including Karin (Theodosiopolis), the capital of Byzantine Armenia; Dwin, with whose population a new treaty (preserved by al-Balādhurī) was concluded; as well as Tiflis in Iberia and Derbent in Azerbaijan, which commanded the northern passes of the Caucasus. In 655 the Arabs named a new *išχan*, Hamazasp Mamikonean, and by 661 the magnates of Armenia, as well as those of Iberia and Caucasian Albania, had recognized the suzerainty of the Umayyad caliph.

Like many of the disaffected Christians of the East embittered by the imperial religious policy, the Armenian *naχarars* do not seem to have offered a prolonged resistance to the Arab conquest. The contemporary historian Sebēos complains that the princes "made an accord with death and an alliance with Hell." The submission of Theodore Ṙštuni seems to have been voluntary, and even the traditional leaders of the pro-Byzantine party, Hamazasp Mamikonean (655–658) and his brother Gregory (662–685), accepted the title of *išχan* from the conquerors. The church in the person of the *katᶜołikos* Nersēs III (641–661) acquiesced.

In fact, the early period of Arab domination seems to have been relatively favorable for Armenia. The conquerors needed Armenian contingents, especially the famous cavalry explicitly noted in the treaties for the continuing war with Byzantium and its threatening Turkic allies, the Khazars, who were raiding southward through the passes of the Caucasus. Southern Armenia was tied into the developing system of fortified border zones *(thughūr)*. Hence, in the second half of the seventh century, Armenia found most of its territories, which had been split asunder since the partition of 387, again reunited, according to the description given by the contemporary *Armenian Geography*.

Religious freedom was conceded to the population upon the payment of the taxes required by Muslim practice (*kharāj* and *jizya*); and the autonomous church, freed from imperial coercion, consolidated its authority and developed its own institutions. Despite the claim of Arab sources that Armenia was under Arab government, native magnates such as the Mamikonean and subsequently the Bagratuni (Ašot, 685–688 and his nephew Smbat, 693) seem to have held internal authority as *išχans* through most of the century, and no foreign troops were quartered in the country.

ARMENIA:HISTORY OF

The well-being of Armenia during this period should not be overestimated, however. The rivalries of the *naχarars* and the Arab-Byzantine war continued to convulse the country—especially the great Khazar raids beginning in 684 or 685 and the reoccupation by Justinian II (685–693), whose troops pillaged as though in enemy territory, according to the native historians. Nevertheless, Armenia seems to have enjoyed relative autonomy during this early period; and the extensive architectural program, especially fostered by the *kat*ᶜ*ołikos* Nersēs III the Builder, attests to the economic prosperity and artistic vitality of the times.

Both Armenian and Muslim sources note a sharp downward turn in Armenia's fortunes toward the end of the seventh century. The precise dates of the changes cannot always be ascertained, but the sources normally place them in the caliphate of ᶜAbd al-Malik (685–705). Beginning in 694 the campaigns of Muḥammad ibn Marwān, intended to bring Armenia back into submission after the temporary Byzantine reconquest, ravaged the country. The creation of the new administrative district of Armīniya, including eastern Iberia and Caspian Albania as well as Greater Armenia, must have followed soon afterward. From an autonomous if tributary state, Armenia became a province of the caliphate, and an Arab governor *(ostikan)* resided first at Dwin and subsequently at Bardhaᶜa (Partaw) in Azerbaijan. Arab garrisons were installed at Dwin and Karin as well as other Armenian cities around Lake Van, and at Tiflis and Derbent, to guard the Caucasian passes.

The resistance of the Armenian *naχarars*, now alarmed by the loss of their prerogatives, was drowned in blood. Summoned to Naχčawan in 705, the magnates were locked into their churches, which were then set on fire. A brief reconciliation in the face of the common Khazar danger was followed by further oppression. A new census taken in 724–725 greatly augmented the Armenian taxes. The Mamikonean attempt to exploit the difficulties of the late Umayyads and raise a new revolt in 743–750 failed in the face of internal disunity and the continuing rivalry between the Mamikonean and the more favored Bagratuni.

The victory of the Abbasid dynasty in 750 increased the gravity of the situation. The pro-Byzantine Mamikonean suffered particularly, but even the Bagratuni paid for their loyalty to the Umayyads. The famous Armenian cavalry was now compelled to serve without pay, and taxation grew steadily heavier. The withdrawal of Byzantine troops from the east left Armenia without hope of support from outside, and the caliphate strengthened its hold by refortifying the western border fortresses of Karin and Melitene/Malatya. The third great Armenian revolt of 774, uniting the traditional rivals Mušeł Mamikonean and the *sparapet* Smbat Bagratuni, again failed to unite the country, and both leaders together with their supporters died a martyr's death on the battlefield of Bagrewand in 775.

The aftermath of the disaster of Bagrewand was particularly damaging. The Bagratid heir, Ašot, found refuge in his distant northwestern domain, but the Mamikonean were decimated and one of their last heiresses was reduced to seeking safety in a marriage with a local Arab chieftain. Numerous *naχarar* families died out or abandoned their land in flight to Byzantium. The more stringent Muslim policies of the Abbasids imposed forced conversions on the defeated princes, leading to martyrdoms such as that of the southern Vaspurakan princes Sahak and Hamazasp Arcruni in 785. The resultant depopulation of Armenian territories, especially in the southwest, was accompanied by the settlement of northern Arab tribes, which gradually carved permanent principalities for themselves around Lake Van, thus aggravating the country's fragmentation and inaugurating its demographic transformation. All internal cultural and artistic life seems to have come to a stop.

The eighth century marked the nadir of Armenian fortunes under Arab domination. At the beginning of the ninth century, distracted by the long revolt of Babak (809–837), the Abbasids began to relax their hold on Armenia, from which the Arab governor had already been removed to Bardhaᶜa in 789. Amid the prevailing rivalries and chaos the major remaining great families—the princes of Siwnikᶜ entrenched in their northeastern mountains and collaborating with Babak, the growing Arcruni of Vaspurakan of which little is known before 850, and especially the Bagratuni heir Ašot Msaker "the Man-Eater"—began to reconstitute their power.

A last attempt to crush the reviving Armenian nobility was made in 852, when the caliph al-Mutawakkil sent his Turkish general Bughā the Elder on a bloody campaign that ended with the deportation in 855 of the surviving magnates to the Abbasid capital of Samarra, where they were offered the choice of death in captivity or conversion to Islam. But the external circumstances had already shifted. The growing threat of the Byzantine armies in eastern Asia Minor in the second half of the century forced al-Mutawakkil to release the captive *naχarars* and in 862 to recognize as *išχanac^c išχan* (prince of princes) the son of the *sparapet* Smbat Bagratuni "the Confessor," who had died at Samarra. The murder of the caliph in 869, followed by the rapid decline of the Abbasids, further improved the situation of Armenia and especially of the Bagratuni house.

The fortune of the Bagratids had been a long time in the making and was based on a number of favorable factors. Their distant domain in Sper and Tayk^c made them inaccessible to Arab retaliations. Their almost invariable policy of supporting the caliphate and its governors usually made them acceptable to the Muslims, who repeatedly named them *išχan*, thus increasing their internal authority. The disappearance of many noble houses in the disasters of the eighth century led to the concentration of power in a few hands. The wealth of the silver mines of Sper allowed the Bagratids to purchase the adjoining districts of Aršarunik^c and Širak from the ruined Kamsarakan early in the ninth century, while the eclipse of the Mamikonean permitted the annexation of Bagrewand in the south.

The martyr's death of Smbat *sparapet* at Bagrewand and his grandson and namesake's confessor's death at Samarra for refusing conversion to Islam erased the memory of former pro-Persian and pro-Arab policies and gave to the ninth-century Bagratids a spiritual prestige that finally matched that which had long been enjoyed by the Mamikonean through their *tanutēr* Vardan, the champion of Avarayr. After a temporary check due to the division in mid-century of their lands and offices between the *išχan* Bagarat of Tarōn in the south and his brother the *sparapet* Smbat the Confessor in northern Tayk^c, the Bagratids finally found the leader who was to carry them to power in the Confessor's son, Ašot I the Great.

Every circumstance seems to have favored Ašot's career. He held a secure territorial base and had inherited his father's spiritual aura. The renewed external balance, between the reappearance of Byzantine armies on the Euphrates and the fragmentation and decline of the caliphate, was propitious to Armenia. There was tension between the increasingly restive local emirs and the attempts at control of the caliph's representatives. And the surviving Armenian *naχarar* houses had disappeared or were rife with internal rivalry, especially the powerful Siwni and Arcruni, which were split between the returning prisoners of Samarra, disgraced by their apostasy, and a younger generation, which had seized power in their absence.

Ašot exploited all of these factors with consummate skill. With the *ostikan* he continued to play the role of the caliph's loyal supporter, thus gaining a free hand in his spoliation of neighboring emirs. Simultaneously his profession of uninterrupted allegiance to the empire earned him the counterbalancing favor of Byzantium. Internally, he backed the powerful church, the only focus of national unity in this critical period, against the pretensions of independence of the northern church of Albania and the renewed pressure from Constantinople, thus earning the church's support, as is evident from the praise of the contemporary historian John the Kat^cołikos. Skillful dynastic marriages transformed Siwni and Arcruni princes into his sons-in-law and made him the arbiter of their quarrels, as well as of those of the junior Bagratid branches of Iberia and Tarōn. The title of prince of princes granted him by the caliph extended his authority over Muslim as well as Christian lords effectively replacing that of the distant *ostikan* residing in Azerbaijan. In 886 (or more likely 884, as has been shown by recent scholarship) Ašot received from the *ostikan* a crown sent by the caliph al-Mu^ctamid, while Emperor Basil I hastened to send similar gifts and regalia.

The solemn coronation of Ašot I in 884 by the *kat^cołikos* George II was assisted by the bishop of Siwnik^c and attended by a multitude of magnates in Bagaran. Its recognition by the two adjacent empires is traditionally greeted as the beginning of a new era and as the restoration of the independent kingship, which had vanished from Greater Armenia more than four centuries earlier with the fall of the Arsacid dynasty. The thesis of the paramount importance of the royal coronation on the history of Armenia has been contested by a number of scholars, however, and an evaluation of the entire Bagratid period still requires considerable research.

But the impressiveness of Ašot I's achievements remains undeniable. As the caliph's representative; as the lord of a considerable domain; as the *tanutēr* or head of the entire Bagratid clan in Iberia and Tarōn, as well as in the lands under his direct control; as the secular arm of the church; and as the senior of the Armenian princes, he had long held de facto a quasi-royal position, as was observed by John the

ARMENIA:HISTORY OF

Kat^{c}ołikos. In that sense, the coronation at Bagaran added little to his power. Internationally his position remained unaltered de jure since the titles conceded to him by the caliphate *(baṭrīḳ al-baṭarīḳa)* and the empire *(archōn tōn archontōn)* were merely precise translations of the title of *išχanac^{c}išχan*, (prince of princes), which had been his for more than twenty years. The sending of crowns was a frequent diplomatic courtesy of the period. Even after his coronation, Ašot continued to pay tribute to Baghdad, and neither he nor his successors presumed to appropriate the sovereign right of issuing his own coinage; the mint at Dwin struck coins in the name of the caliph or of local emirs as before. In Byzantium, official sources stressed that the Bagratid king was the emperor's servant *(doulos)*, and the false pedigree linking Basil I to the early Arsacid kings might well have foreshadowed the claim of the Macedonian dynasty to the Armenian crown.

Internally, a number of serious problems remained unsolved. Neither Ašot I, who preferred to remain at Bagaran, nor his successors at Širakawan, Kars, or Ani ever gained full control of the central Araxes valley with its capital at Dwin; the city had been the residence of the Arsacids, *marzpans*, and *ostikans* and a major commercial center but its overlordship was increasingly preempted by local emirs. Consequently, the domain of the Bagratids always remained tangential, an excellent refuge in critical times but not a central base for the unification of Armenia. The country remained fragmented by the presence of powerful Arab emirates, especially the Qaysites of Manazkert ruling over much of the land west and north of Lake Van, as well as by local emirs at Dwin, Karin, Naχčawan, and Gołt^{c}n in the Araxes valley, Arčēš, Xlat^{c}, and Berkri. These states served as advanced bases for Muslim incursions, especially from Azerbaijan, and hindered internal communications among the Christian principalities.

The centrifugal aspirations of the Armenian magnates, especially of the Siwni and Arcruni, had in no way abated; and they formed constant nuclei of opposition, often in alliance with their Muslim neighbors. To them, the king was at best the first among equals, despite the blessing of the church and the apocryphal descent from the royal house of David now claimed by the Bagratuni. Nothing in ancient Armenian tradition provided for a king who was not an Arsacid; the growing system of appanages for younger sons undercut the solidity of the royal domain, and the absence of a clear hereditary principle from father to son invited recurring crises in the transmission of power. Despite these evident or still latent dangers, however, the brilliance of Ašot the Great's prestige struck all the contemporaries, *naχarars* and emirs, the church, Byzantium, and the caliph, who ceased to appoint *ostikans* for Armenia. His dominant personality clearly emerges from the pages of John the Kat^{c}ołikos.

Unhappily, some of the inherent weaknesses of the Bagratid kingdom manifested themselves as early as the reign of Ašot's son, Smbat I the Martyr (890–912/914). Immediately after his father's death, Smbat's uncle, the *sparapet* Abas, sought to dispute the succession, and two years passed before Smbat's coronation in his city of Širakawan. For twenty years thereafter, he fought energetically to maintain the integrity of the Bagratid kingdom continually threatened by the disruptive activities of Arab emirs or Armenian *naχarars* bent on carving independent principalities for themselves with the support of the Turkish Sājid emirs of Azerbaijan, who continually harried Armenia from Dwin, which they seized after the devastating earthquake of 893/894.

The fragmentation of Smbat I's sphere of authority began with the proclamation of the kingdoms of Caspian Albania to the north in 893 and of Abkhazia on the Black Sea early in the tenth century. As a result, his kinsman and loyal ally, the *curopalates* Adarnarsē II, who had been crowned king of Western Iberia by the Armenian king in 899, now turned against him. Most damaging of all, Gagik Arcruni, prince of Vaspurakan, making the most of Armenia's difficulties with Azerbaijan, sought the support of the Sājid emir Yūsuf, who crowned him king in 908.

Gagik's policy is vehemently defended by his relative Thomas Arcruni, whose *History of the Arcruni House* provides a useful check on the generally pro-Bagratid account of John the Kat^{c}ołikos. Nevertheless, the Armenian realm had been split and the traditional particularism of southern Armenia had been reinforced and institutionalized by the creation of the kingdom of Vaspurakan. By the second decade of the tenth century Smbat could no longer withstand the advance of Yūsuf, who had been ravaging Armenia since 909. Abandoned by most of his supporters, Smbat was compelled to surrender to Yūsuf, who had him executed one year later, following his refusal to convert to Islam, and had his body exposed on a cross in the city of Dwin (914 or more probably 912 according to Adontz).

The martyrdom of Smbat I brutally awakened the Armenian princes. King Gagik Arcruni now assumed the defense of Armenia, diverting Yūsuf against Vaspurakan; while Smbat's son Ašot II Erkatᶜ, "The Iron King" (912/914–928/929), returning to his family's traditional policy, retired to his remote domain of Taykᶜ, from which he conducted a successful guerrilla war. Ašot was supported by the *katᶜołikos* John the Historian, who obtained for him the recognition and military help of Constantinople which the young king visited in 914 (as is clear from the Byzantine sources and not in 921, as has often been assumed), and by Adarnarsē II of Iberia, who had him crowned. Ašot II relentlessly proceeded to reestablish his power despite Yūsuf's attempt to raise a rival in the person of his cousin, the *sparapet* Ašot, at Dwin.

The "war of the two Ašots" lasted two years; but Yūsuf, weakened by his own rebellion against the caliph, was forced to reverse his policy and send the crown to Ašot II. With Yūsuf's imprisonment and exile, the Sājid power began to crumble. The antiking Ašot made his submission, and in 922 the caliph recognized Ašot II as *šahanšah* ("king of kings"), thus raising him once again above all local Armenian rulers. Ašot was somewhat undercut late in his reign by the growing hostility of Byzantium, which twice attacked Dwin and granted the title "prince of princes" to Gagik Arcruni, as well as by the withdrawal of the *katᶜołikos* who also settled in Vaspurakan. Nevertheless, the Bagratid kingdom recovered much of its power and prestige under the "Iron King."

A measure of Ašot II's success can be seen in the relative peace and unquestionable prosperity of the kingdom under his successors Abas (928–952/953); Ašot III Ołormacᶜ, "the Merciful" (952/953–977); Smbat II Tiezerakal, "the Master of the Universe" (977–989/990); and Gagik I (989/990–1017/1020), celebrated by Stephen of Tarōn (usually known as Asołik), who continued the *History* of John the Katᶜołikos. External and internal circumstances were propitious at the time. The caliphate was powerless in the area, and Armenia seems to have stopped paying taxes by the mid tenth century. Byzantium's attention was usually diverted further to the south. The great emirates, the Qaysites of Manazkert and the neighboring Ḥamdānids of Mosul and Aleppo, were beginning to weaken by the end of the century. Despite recurring incursions the Threat of Azerbaijan, which was split by the rivalries of local Iranian (Kurdish or Daylamite) chieftains, was temporarily less critical. Pressed by Byzantium and the Ḥamdānids after Gagik's death in 937, Vaspurakan broke up among the Arcruni heirs of his son Abusahl in 972 and presented less of a threat.

In the new capital of Ani, where he was crowned in 961 by the *katᶜołikos* returned from his wanderings in Vaspurakan, Ašot III and later Gagik I figured again not only as the heads of the Bagratid house but also as the suzerains of all the Armenian principalities. On several occasions Dwin acknowledged the overlordship of the king of Ani, whose domains stretched into the valley of the mid-Araks, the center of Arsacid Armenia, although Iranian dynasties, Salārids or Musāfirids, Rawwādids, and eventually the Kurdish Shaddādids continually reestablished themselves in the old capital.

Convoked by Ašot III to Harkᶜ in 974 in the face of a possible threat posed by the advancing army of the emperor John I Tzimiskes all the normally insubordinate Armenian nobles—even the princes of Siwnikᶜ and Vaspurakan—responded to the royal summons. The greetings sent by Tzimiskes to his "beloved son" Ašot, preserved by the historian Mattᶜeos Uṙhayecᶜi (Matthew of Edessa), reflect the wariness of Byzantium in the face of the strength and unexpected unity of Armenia. Firmly supported by the king against the separatist tendencies of the sees of Albania and Siwnikᶜ, the powerful heretical movement of the Tᶜondrakecᶜi, and the recrudescence of Chalcedonianism condemned once again by the Council of Ani in 969, the Armenian church continued to collaborate with the crown, and the *katᶜołikos* returned to the vicinity of the court, first at Argina, before settling at Ani in 992.

The splendor of the royal capitals—Kars under Abas and above all Ani, "the city of 1,001 churches," surrounded by the formidable fortifications erected by Smbat II, as well as the Arcruni capital on the island of Ałtᶜamar in Lake Van; the proliferation of vast monastic complexes at Sewan, Hoṙomos, Narek, Hałbat, Sanahin, Varag, Makenocᶜ, Ałtᶜamar, Tatᶜew, and elsewhere testify to the royal protection and the wealth of Armenia enriched by the international trade between Byzantium and the East in the tenth and early eleventh centuries.

A parallel cultural explosion surged forth from the contemporary courts and monasteries. The reputation of scholars and miniature painters trained in monastic academies at Sanahin and Tatᶜew among others, and the fame of Armenian architects such as

Trdat of Ani, who was entrusted with the repairs of the dome of Hagia Sophia in Constantinople, bear witness to the international standing of Bagratid Armenia. Archaeological evidence makes it clear that the population of Ani far surpassed that of western capitals.

The only serious shadow cast on this prosperous picture was the result of the Bagratids' own policy. Following contemporary custom, and perhaps seeking to avert all too common family rivalries, Ašot III erected the western district of Kars (also known as Vanand) into a kingdom for his brother Mušeł in 961/962, and that of Loři-Tašir to the north into one for his youngest son Gurgēn (or Kiwrikē) around 972. Following suit, prince Smbat II of Siwnik^{c} proclaimed himself king by 987. Barely a century after the coronation at Bagaran, five kingdoms had replaced the single realm of Ašot the Great.

The powerful personality of Gagik I successfully maintained and even enlarged the Bagratid territories in the early eleventh century, but the tide of external circumstances was once more running against him. The impotence of the distant caliphate at Baghdad and the disappearance of the great emirates, except for the Kurdish Shaddādids established at Ganjak from 970 and at Dwin in 1022, left no counterweight for the steady eastward expansion of Byzantium under the Macedonian dynasty.

The disappearance of the medieval Armenian kingdoms has led to considerable debate among scholars and is obviously far too complex to derive from a single cause. Their decline was unquestionably hastened by the fratricidal struggle between Gagik I's heirs, Yovhannēs-Smbat at Ani and his brother Ašot IV K^{c}aǰ, "the Brave," and by the separatist policies of the Bagratid kings of Kars and Tašir or occasionally Iberia, whose religious union with Byzantium pulled it away from its Armenian kinsmen. Other factors included the parallel morcellation of Vaspurakan after 972 among Abusahl's three sons, aggravated by the subsequent usurpation of the youngest, Senek^{c}erim-Yovhannēs (1003–1021), who deprived his nephews of their patrimony, and endemic rivalry among the magnates. But the most immediate threat to Armenian autonomy in the first half of the eleventh century seems to have come from the West.

The political theory of the Macedonians, spelled out by Constantine VII Porphyrogenitus in his treatise *On the Administration of the Empire* and echoing the earlier formulation of Eusebius of Caesarea, saw in the emperor the icon of Christ on earth. Temporary diplomatic concessions might be made by him for the sake of expediency; but ultimately he could tolerate no autonomous ruler outside his realm, which was to mirror the unity of the Heavenly Kingdom. In the case of the Bagratids, Byzantium's basic opposition was exacerbated by the reaffirmation of Armenia's rejection of imperial Orthodoxy in the tenth century and the intransigent positions of the *kat^{c}ołikoi* Anania Mokk^{c}ac^{c}i (944/945–967/968) and Xač^{c}ik I (973–992), threatened by the renewed strength of Chalcedonianism in Armenia, as well as by the intransigence of the imperial clergy in Cappadocia.

Having consolidated his power, Basil I, followed by his successors, turned to the reconquest of lost imperial territories in the east as well as in the west. As early as 872, the heretical Paulician state on the upper Euphrates had been destroyed. By the 920's Byzantine armies had twice attacked Dwin, and in 949 they retook the strategic northern fortress of Karin (Theodosiopolis) from the local emirs. The pressure increased late in the century. The small southwestern Bagratid principality of Tarōn was annexed by 967/968, and the Marwānid successors of the Qaysites of Manazkert were crippled two years later. Only the united front of the "Assembly of Hark^{c}" in 974 probably kept John Tzimiskes from the main Bagratid lands.

The crucial step was taken by Basil II (976–1025). One of the junior Iberian Bagratid princes, David of Tayk^{c} (or Tao), was rewarded for his support of the imperial side during the great revolt of Bardas Skleros (976–979) with the title of *curopalate* and an enormous domain. The latter stretched across western Armenia from his own domain of Tayk^{c} on the Armeno-Iberian border, by way of Karin, Basean, and Hark^{c}, to include the north shore of Lake Van with Manazkert, which David retook from the Muslims in 990. Unfortunately, David backed the wrong party in the new revolt of Bardas Phokas (987–989) and was compelled by Basil II to will all his lands to the empire. When David died in suspicious circumstances, probably murdered by a proimperial faction among his nobles, Basil immediately attacked. Gagik I was sufficiently powerful to withstand personally the emperor's first campaign in 1001; but by 1021/1022, after the Armenian king's death, Basil II, having refortified the city of Karin, successfully annexed the entire inheritance of David of Tayk^{c} despite the resistance of Iberia supported by the local nobles,

ARMENIA:HISTORY OF

and turned it into a regular imperial province known as the Theme of Iberia.

Equally damaging for the Bagratids was the situation in Vaspurakan. Alarmed by the first raids of the Daylamites accompanied by Turkish contingents from the east, King Senek^{c}erim-Yovhannēs Arcruni surrendered his kingdom to Basil II in 1021 in exchange for the imperial title of *magistros* and extensive domains in Cappadocia around Sebaste/Sivas, while his son David received Caesarea. Vaspurakan, together with the northern Vannic cities of Manazkert, Arčēš, and Berkri, was turned into the imperial Catepanate of Basprakania next to the Theme of Tarōn. Hence, two years after the death of Gagik I and on the eve of the Seljuk invasions, his domains were held in a pincer of increasingly threatening imperial territories. Hindered by the constant opposition of his brother Ašot IV and compromised by his anti-Byzantine stand during Basil II's latest campaign, King Yovhannēs-Smbat Bagratuni in turn willed his kingdom to Byzantium in 1022 in a testament carried to Constantinople by the *kat^{c}ołikos* Peter I Getadarj.

Difficulties at Constantinople following Basil II's death in 1025 momentarily distracted the attention of Byzantium, but on the almost simultaneous deaths of Ašot IV and Yovhannēs-Smbat in 1040/1041, Michael IV claimed the kingdom of Ani. The situation in the Armenian capital was tense, as reported by the contemporary historian Aristakēs Lastivertc^{c}i. The pro-Byzantine faction, led by the *vestes* Sargis, first seized power; but his opponents under prince Vahram Pahlawuni succeeded in driving him out and crowning Gagik II, the son of Ašot IV, in 1042. Imperial armies repeatedly failed to take Ani, even with the help of the Shaddādids of Dwin, whom they had called, or after the departure of the young king, who sought to negotiate personally at Constantinople despite the opposition of Vahram Pahlawuni, and left his capital in the hands of the *kat^{c}ołikos*. Understandably alarmed by the Turkish raids now reaching into central Armenia—or self-serving, according to the accusation of Aristakēs Lastivertc^{c}i—Peter Getadarj surrendered Ani to Byzantium in 1045. Detained in Constantinople and accepting the fait accompli, Gagik II also relinquished his kingdom, in exchange for a Cappadocian domain, as had the Arcruni. Ani with its territories was incorporated into the Theme of Iberia, of which it became the capital.

Byzantine domination of Greater Armenia did not last. The rhythm of the Seljuk invasions accelerated in the mid eleventh century, though their precise chronology remains debatable. The kingdom of Kars was devastated in 1054 and Sebaste in 1059. In 1064 Ani fell to the sultan Alp Arslan. The able king of Kars, Gagik-Abas, briefly saved his capital by submitting to the sultan but in turn took the road to Cappadocia, abandoning the city to the Seljuks in 1064–1065. Even the Muslim Shaddādid emirs were swept from Dwin, though they survived at Ani, which they bought from Alp Arslan in 1072. All Byzantine attempts to defend their Armenian territories ended with their defeat at Manazkert in 1071.

With the murder of Gagik II and the suspicious deaths of the heirs of Kars and Vaspurakan in 1080, almost nothing remained of the Armenian principalities. In the north, Loṙi-Tašir flourished briefly under David Anhołin "the Landless" (989–*ca.* 1048) and his son Kiwrikē I (*ca.* 1048–*ca.* 1089), who saved himself by giving a daughter in marriage to Alp Arslan. But from 1113 his descendants clung only to scattered fortresses in the northern mountains, where they survived until the thirteenth century according to late inscriptions. Similarly, eastern Siwnik^{c}, protected by its inaccessible terrain, lingered into the twelfth century.

The disintegration of the Bagratid kingdoms was accompanied by profound geographical, social, and demographic transformations. The mainstream of Armenian life moved generally southward with the Seljuk conquest. There, occasional and little-known Armenians first held individual cities for a time—like Gabriel at Melitene, T^{c}at^{c}ul at Marash, and T^{c}oros at Edessa—or attempted to create principalities—as T^{c}ornik did in Sasun or Goł Vasil ("Basil the Robber") around Kesun and Raban near the mid-Euphrates. Some of these principalities survived in isolated southern mountain districts, such as Sasun or the Arcruni *kat^{c}ołikosate* of Ałt^{c}amar.

The ablest of these chance leaders, the Armenian Chalcedonian Philaretos Varažnuni, duke of Antioch, united much of Syro-Mesopotamia and Cilicia for some fifteen years after the Byzantine defeat at Manazkert; but in 1086 he too was forced to submit to the Seljuks. Only the Rubenid princes succeeded in creating a more lasting state in Cilicia, to which both the political focus of Armenian life and the residence of the *kat^{c}ołikos* had been transferred by the end of the eleventh century—together with the name of Armenia Minor, which now took on a new meaning.

The resettlement of Senek^{c}erim-Yovhannēs Ar-

ARMENIA:HISTORY OF

cruni in Cappadocia "together with 14,000" followers, who probably included a sizable portion of the nobility of Vaspurakan, as well as the similar migrations of Gagik II of Ani and Gagik-Abas of Kars, produced a major re-Armenization of ancient Armenia Minor west of the Euphrates, but they deprived Greater Armenia of much of its ruling class. Armenians likewise fled from the invasions of Iberia, Mesopotamia, Syria (where they populated the Amanus region), Edessa, and even Antioch. Armenian vizirs served the Fatimid caliphs at Cairo. Earlier Arab and Iranian settlements in Bagratid Armenia had introduced demographic changes; but as late as the tenth century the contemporary Arab geographers al-Muqāddasī and Ibn Ḥawqal wrote that Armenians were still the majority in the Araxes valley and in the cities of Dwin and Naxčawan despite the presence of Muslim local rulers. The massive exodus of the Armenian upper classes in the tenth and eleventh centuries, the devastation of war, and the steady influx of Turkoman nomads following in the wake of the Seljuk raids inaugurated a gradual shift in the balance between Christian Armenians and Muslim (Kurdish or Turkish) elements on the Armenian plateau.

Despite the survival of various minor principalities, the disappearance of the kingdom of Ani marked the end of the last major political unit in Greater Armenia for centuries to come. Nevertheless, some portions of the region recovered following the Seljuk conquest and the final withdrawal of Byzantium. Ani generally prospered under Shaddādid rule (1072–1199) despite repeated Georgian attacks, as did Xlat^{c} under that of the "Philochristian" Armenized Seljuk dynasty of the Šah-i Armen (1100–1207). Armenian historians unanimously praise the beneficent rule of the sultan Malikshāh (1072–1092). But the failure of the Seljuks to maintain a stable state in the area resulted in anarchy that lasted throughout the twelfth century, insofar as can be gathered from the scarce and fragmentary sources of the period. Individual emirs held single cities, such as Kars, Karin/Erzurum, or Erzincan. Artukids ruled Harput and Diyarbakir. Ayyubids replaced the Šah-i Armen at Xlat^{c}. Seljuks of Rum and Danishmendites fought over central Asia Minor.

The Indian summer of Greater Armenia came at the beginning of the thirteenth century as medieval Georgia reached its apogee. Nearly a century earlier, the Georgian Bagratid king David the Builder had succeeded in occupying Ani (1123–1126), and the expanding Georgian state retook the city from the Shaddādids in 1161 and 1174, though it did not succeed in holding it. Finally two viceroys of Queen T^{c}amar (1184–1212), the Christianized Kurds the *amir-spasalar* Zak^{c}arē and his brother the atabeg Iwanē *Mχargrzeli* ("Long Hand"), reconquered Ani in 1199 and Dwin in 1203, together with much of the Bagratid territory to Manazkert and Arčēš north of Lake Van, as well as eastward along the Araxes valley through Naχčawan to Azerbaijan.

For some thirty years, Zak^{c}arē and his son Šahanšah ruled the northwestern portion of the reconquered territories—Loṙi, Širak, Aragaçotn, Bagrewand—with Ani as his capital; while Iwanē further east held Dwin, Bǰni, Siwnik^{c}, and part of Arcaχ. A remarkable renaissance attended the Zak^{c}arid reconquest. New *naχarar* families, such as the Dop^{c}ean, the Xaŕbakean/Pṙošean, the Vač^{c}utean, and the Hasan J̌alalean, joined the ancient houses of the Arcruni, Pahlawuni, and Orbelean to recreate the traditional pattern of Armenian social life. The enormous prosperity that Ani derived from international trade is best seen in the rise of a new nobility of wealth, the *mecatun*; its best-known example, Tigran Honenc^{c}, willed multiple villages and estates to the church that he had built and adorned in the capital. The buildings and dedicatory inscriptions of the Zak^{c}arids covered the countryside.

The degree of Armenian dependence on Georgia during this period is still the subject of considerable controversy. The numerous Zak^{c}arid inscriptions leave no doubt that they considered themselves Armenians, and they often acted independently. Armenian sources attribute mixed Armeno-Georgian titles to the contemporary nobility. The Muslim Abu^{c}l Fida unexpectedly styles Zak^{c}arē "king of Georgia." Yet a considerable portion of Tašir and adjacent territories were incorporated into Georgia, and Queen T^{c}amar used Dwin as a winter residence. The relationship between the queen and her "viceroys" seems to have been ambiguous at times, but their full autonomy seems equally questionable.

Whatever its precise character, the Zak^{c}arid principality, which lasted barely one generation, marked the end of any Armenian political autonomy in the north. It ended with the destructive raids of the Khwarazm-shāh Jalāl al-Dīn (1225–1231) and the appearance of the Mongols. The first Mongol raids in 1220–1221, which preceded the attacks of the Khwarazm-shāh, and the more permanent conquering expeditions of the 1230's led to the incorporation

ARMENIA:HISTORY OF

of most of Greater Armenia into the realm of the Mongol Ilkhans of Iran by 1256. Like the southern Cilician kingdom, the northern Armenian homeland became part of the vast Mongol empire. At first, much of the socioeconomic life lingered on. A number of the *naχarars* submitted to the Mongols and were duly rewarded, according to the historians Kirakos Ganjakec^{c}i and Stephen Orbelean. Iwanē Mχargrzeli's daughter T^{c}amt^{c}a, the widow of one of the Šah-i Armen, continued to rule at Xlat^{c} under Mongol protectorate until 1231. Some Armenian cities still prospered for a time from the great transit trade crossing the Mongol empire to the Far East. But any suggestion of an autonomous Armenian state had come to an end in the area. Armenian contingents were incorporated into the Mongol armies, and the country was subject to Mongol taxes. As the Ilkhans converted to Islam at the beginning of the fourteenth century, the situation was aggravated by religious persecution. Battered by the constant rivalry between the Iranian Ilkhanids and the northern Golden Horde, and burdened by increasingly heavy taxation, the social fabric began to give way altogether. The *naχarar* families were destroyed or fled; the cities, repeatedly sacked, were ruined and depopulated. The fleeing population created new Armenian colonies in the fourteenth century in the Crimea, especially around the Genoese trading center of Caffa/Theodosia, in the Balkans; and eventually in the Ukraine and Poland, where Armenian centers arose and gradually assumed intellectual leadership. But the eclipse of Armenian historiography in the fourteenth century is an index of the cultural collapse of Greater Armenia.

The disintegration of the Ilkhanid realm after 1335 removed the last form of stable government, and the entire region from Tabriz in Azerbaijan to Konya in Asia Minor became a no-man's-land for a long time to come. The rivalry of the Mongol Cubānid and Jalāyirid clans and of the various Turkoman groups intensified the chaos. By the time of the devastating campaigns of Tamerlane (1386/1387, 1394–1396, 1400–1403), the lands of southern and central Armenia were held mostly by the Turkoman confederation of the Qara-Qoyunlu (Black Sheep), from whom they were later wrested by the rival group of the Aq-Qoyunlu, who briefly controlled the entire region as far north as Georgia in the mid fifteenth century. The Ottomans already controlled the western regions of Sivas and Erzincan. "Armenia" had become little more than a geographical term, and only the return of the *kat^{c}ołikosate* to the valley of the Araks in 1441 after the fall of the Cilician kingdom gave a semblance of focus to a population bereft of any political life.

BIBLIOGRAPHY

At present the best introduction in a Western language to Armenian medieval history is the brief summary by Cyril Toumanoff in the *Cambridge Medieval History,* J. M. Hussey ed., IV, pt. 1 (1966), ch. 14, which also contains a useful bibliography. A useful companion is the survey by Sirarpie Der Nersessian, *The Armenians* (1969), which concentrates on cultural aspects. Considerable information can also be obtained from Ernst Honigmann, *Die Ostgrenze des byzantinischen Reiches von 363 bis 1071* (1935). Most other accounts are inadequate and dated, since, aside from other factors, they do not include the archaeological material that is only beginning to become available. Although more up-to-date, the multivolume history of the Armenian people (1971–) published in Armenian by the Academy of Sciences of the Armenian S.S.R. (see below) remains incomplete, lacking the volume on the early medieval period. Consequently, studies on particular periods and subjects must be consulted until a suitable synthesis becomes possible.

Sources. For the relevant Armenian sources see the article on "Armenian Historiography." The main pertinent classical sources are Ammianus Marcellinus, *The Surviving Books of the Histories,* John C. Rolfe, ed. and trans., 3 vols. (1950); Procopius, *Works,* Henry B. Dewing and G. Downey, ed. and trans., 7 vols. (1940); and Constantos VII Porphyrogenitos, *De administrando imperio,* Gyula Moravcsik, ed., Romilly H. Jenkins, trans., 2 vols. (1949–1962; repr. 1967). The other important sources, such as Theophylakt Simokattes, Theophanes Confessor and his continuator, Skylitzes, have not been translated into English. The main surviving Sasanian inscriptions are translated in Ernst Emil Herzfeld, *Paikuli,* 2 vols. (1924); and Martin Sprengling, *Third Century Iran: Sapor and Kartir* (1953).

The most accessible Muslim sources are al-Balādhurī, *The Origins of the Islamic State,* Philip Hitti, trans. (1916, repr. 1968); Ibn Hawqal, *La configuration de la terre,* J. H. Kramers and G. Wiet, trans., 2 vols. (1964); Bagrat Khalateantz, *Textes arabes relatifs à l'Arménie* (1919); Joseph Muyldermans, ed. and trans., *La domination arabe en Arménie* (1927), drawn from the thirteenth-century *History* of Vardan the Great; and al-Ṭabarī, *Geschichte der Perser und Araber zur Zeit der Sasaniden,* Theodor Nöldeke, trans. (1879, repr. 1973). Texts relating to Armenia are translated in some of the secondary sources dealing with the Arab period (see below). Syriac sources, mostly untranslated, are also pertinent.

Secondary Literature. On the Arsacid period and the marzpanate, see Nikolay Adontz, *Armenia in the Period of Justinian,* Nina Garsoïan, ed. and trans. (1970); Pascal Asdourian, *Die politischen Beziehungen swischen Armenien und Rom von 190 v. Chr. Bis 428 n. Chr.* (1911); Gérard Garitte, ed., *La Narratio de rebus armeniae* (1952); Nina Garsoïan, "Politique ou orthodoxie? L'Arménie au quatrième siècle," in *Revue des études arméniennes*, n.s. **4** (1967); "Quidam Narseus—A Note on the Mission of St. Nersēs the Great," in *Armeniaca* (1969); "Armenia in the Fourth Century: An Attempt to Re-define the Concepts 'Armenia' and 'Loyalty,'" in *Revue des études arméniennes*, n.s. **8** (1971); "Le rôle de l'hiérarchie chrétienne dans les rapports diplomatiques entre Byzance et les Sassanides," *ibid.*, **10** (1973–1974); and "Prolegomena to a Study of the Iranian Aspects in Arsacid Armenia," in *Handes amsorya*, **90** (1976); Paul Goubert, *Byzance avant l'Islam*, I (1951); and Cyril Toumanoff, "Christian Caucasia Between Byzantium and Iran," in *Traditio*, **10** (1954); "Introduction to Christian Caucasian History: The Formative Centuries (IV–VIIIth)," *ibid.*, **15** (1959); *Studies in Christian Caucasian History* (1963); "The Third Century Armenian Arsacids," in *Revue des études arméniennes*, n.s. **6** (1969); and *Manuel de généalogie et de chronologie pour l'histoire de la Caucasie chrétienne* (1976).

On the period of the Arab conquest, see Mkrtitsch Ghazarian, "Armenien unter der arabischen Herrschaft bis zur Entstehung des Bagratidenreiches," in *Zeitschrift für armenische Philologie*, **2** (1904); Joseph Laurent, *L'Arménie entre Byzance et l'Islam depuis la conquête arabe jusqu'en 886* (1919), rev. and enl. ed. by Marius Canard (1980); H. Manandyan, "Les invasions arabes en Arménie," H. Berbérian, trans., in *Byzantion*, **18** (1946–1948); and Richard F. Vasmer, *Chronologie der arabischen Statthalter von Armenien unter den Abbasiden von as-Saffach bis zur Krönung Aschots I (750–887)* (1931).

The only recent general work on the Bagratid period is the Armenian history of the Armenian people, *Hay žołovrdi patmut^{c}yun*, III (1976). Much of the work dates from the nineteenth century, for example A. Daghbaschean, *Gründung des Bagratidenreiches durch Aschot Bagratuni* (1893); as well as Hagob Thopdschian, *Die inneren Zustände von Armenien unter Ašot I* (1904); and "Politische und Kirchengeschichte Armeniens unter Ašot I und Smbat I," in *Mitteilungen des Seminars für orientalische Sprachen,* **8**, pt. 2 (1905). See Sirarpie Der Nersessian, *Armenia and the Byzantine Empire* (1945), especially for the cultural life of the period; and Joseph Markwart, *Osteuropäische und ostasiatische Streifzüge* (1903). See also the various studies of Nikolay Adontz collected in his *Études arméno-byzantines* (1965); V. Hakobyan, "La date de l'avènement d'Ašot premier roi bagratide," in *Revue des études arméniennes*, n.s. **2** (1965); Vladimir Minorsky, "The Caucasian Vassals of Marzuban in 344/955," in *Bulletin of the School of Oriental and African Studies*, **15** (1953); and K. N. Yuzbashyan, "K khronolgii pravleniia Gagika I Bagratuni," in *Antichnaya drevnost i srednie veka*, **10** (1973), in Russian. See also the relevant sections of various works on Byzantine-Arab relations. Marius Canard, *Histoire de la dynastie des H'amdanides de Jazîra et de Syrie* (1951); Steven Runciman, *The Emperor Romanus Lecapenus and His Reign* (1929); Gustave Léon Schlumberger, *L'épopée byzantine à la fin du Xe siècle*, 3 vols. (1896–1925); and Alexander A. Vasiliev, *Byzance et les Arabes*, Marius Canard, trans., 3 vols. (1935–1968). The archaeological evidence on the city of Ani is presented in Nikolay Marr, *Ani* (1934), in Russian.

On the period of the Byzantine annexation of the Armenian states and the Seljuk invasions, see V. Arutiunova-Fedanian, *Armiane-Khalkedonity na vostochnykh granitsakh Vizantyskoy imperii (XI v.)* (1980), in Russian; Z. Avalichvili, "La succession du curopalate David d'Ibérie, dynaste de Tao," in *Byzantion*, **8** (1933); R. Bartikyan, "La conquête de l'Arménie par l'empire byzantin," in *Revue des études arméniennes*, n.s. **8** (1971); C. Cahen, "La campagne de Mantzikert d'après les sources musulmanes," in *Byzantion*, **9** (1934); and "La première pénétration turque en Asie Mineure," *ibid.*, **18** (1948); Marius Canard, "La campagne arménienne du sultan salǧuqide Alp Arslan et la prise d'Ani en 1064," in *Revue des études arméniennes*, n.s. **2** (1965); G. Dédéyan, "L'immigration arménienne en Cappadoce," in *Byzantion*, **45** (1975); Joseph Laurent, *L'Arménie entre Byzance et les Turcs seljoucides jusqu'en 1081* (1914); Vladimir Minorsky, *La domination des Dailamites* (1932); J. Shepard, "Skylitzes on Armenia in the 1040's," in *Revue des études arméniennes*, n.s. **11** (1975–1976); and K. N. Yuzbashyan, "Deylemity v 'povestvovanii' Aristakesa Lastivertsi," in *Palestinsky sbornik*, n.s. 7 (1962), in Russian, with French résumé by Marius Canard in *Revue des études arméniennes,* n.s. **3** (1966); "L'administration byzantine en Arménie aux Xe–XIe siècles," *ibid.*, **10** (1973–1974); and "Skilitsa o zakhvate Anyskogo tsarstvo v 1045 g.," in *Vizantysky vremennik*, **40** (1979), in Russian.

On the late medieval successor states in Greater Armenia, see Lewon H. Babayan, *Hayastani soc^{c}ial-tntesakan ew k^{c}ałak^{c}akan patmut^{c}iwne XIII–XIV darerum* (1964), in Armenian, with Russian trans. (1969); Claude Cahen, *Pre-Ottoman Turkey* (1968); Vladimir Minorsky, *Studies in Caucasian History* (1953); and *History of Sharvān and Darband in the 10th–11th Centuries* (1958); Vladimir Minorsky and Claude Cahen, "Le recueil trans-caucasien," in *Journal asiatique,* **237** (1949); Speros Vryonis, *The Decline of Medieval Hellenism in Asia Minor* (1971); and John E. Woods, *The Aqquyunlu: Clan, Confederation, Empire* (1976). Histories of the Mongol and early Ottoman empires should also be consulted, although they contain little on the conquest of Armenia.

NINA G. GARSOÏAN

[See also **Ani; Aq-Qoyunlu/White Sheep; Armenian Alphabet; Armenian Church; Caesarea (Capadocia); Van, Lake**;

Armenian Muslim Emirates; Armenian Social Structure; Arsacids; Aršak; Ašot; Bagratids; Dwin; Gagik; Karin; Marzpan; Naχarar; Ostikan; Sasanians; Smbat; Tanutēr; Trdat; Vardan.]

ARMENIA, SOCIAL STRUCTURE. The social structure of medieval Armenia has been the subject of considerable study and discussion; nevertheless, a number of problems still await clarification. To some degree the difficulties have been compounded by confusion in the Armenian sources, none of which precede the fifth century, when the Armenian alphabet was invented, and thus throw no direct light on the formative period. Moreover, the earlier scholars Nikolai Adonts and Hakob Manandyan were so strongly influenced by patent similarities to Western feudalism that they tended to underestimate the individuality of the Armenian system. The parallel Iranian institutions are still insufficiently studied. The simultaneous presence of two elements, dynasticism and feudalism, identified by Cyril Toumanoff, has required a closer and subtler analysis of the existing pattern.

Nearly all studies up to now have understandably focused almost exclusively on the "classical" period of the fourth through seventh centuries, for which there is considerable evidence, to the detriment of the later medieval period (ninth through thirteenth centuries), of which little is known, so that the evolution of existing institutions still needs considerable research. Finally, as elsewhere, most of the available information bears on the upper strata of society, the landed military nobility; thus, little can be learned of the structure of the lower classes, be they peasants or city dwellers.

The origins of the major social pattern of medieval Armenia, the so-called *Naχarar* system, are still unclear, but scholars trace them to the disintegration of the early clan structure, which they have tended to push increasingly further back, to the Hellenistic period or even considerably earlier. By the fourth century, Armenian society, probably helped by the fragmented character of the physical setting, was clearly aristocratic. That is, it was strongly decentralized into units capable of surviving under either native or foreign rulers, but highly resistant to all forms of unification. The pervasively Iranian origin of its social vocabulary suggests obvious parallels, if not necessarily direct evolution or borrowing of institutions.

As in the Iranian world, Armenian society was basically divided into three classes or estates. 1) The magnates or high nobility, the "mightiest lords" *(mecameck^{c}, gahereck^{c})*, were commonly described by such terms as *išχan, tēr, tanutēr,* and *naχarar.* In practice these could be identified as "senior" *(awag)* or "junior" *(krster),* and although they were ranked according to a rigid order of precedence, all were equal de jure. 2) The *azat*s, or minor nobility, usually were seen as the vassals of the magnates, with whom they were not confused. The composition of this class was at times mixed, but it was unequivocally ranked within the nobility. 3) The *ṙamik,* or "third estate," included all the "nonnoble" *(an-azat)* population: merchants and artisans as well as peasants *(šinakan),* who were the overwhelming majority.

The clergy does not seem to have formed a separate estate. Priests were assimilated to *azat* rank, while the hierarchy, from bishops to the patriarch, was usually drawn from the high nobility. Two groups at the opposite extremes of society lay, in a sense, outside this threefold division. At the top the four great *bdešχs,* or "marcher lords," who do not seem to have survived the fifth century, stood above the magnates. At the bottom the slaves *(struk)* were separate from the *ṙamik,* who were all personally free even where they were bound to the soil like the *šinakan*s. A fourth class, found in contemporary Sasanian Iran, the *dibīr* ("clerks"), does not seem to have existed in Armenia. *Dpir*s are mentioned in Armenian sources, but on an individual rather than a class basis, possibly because their function was taken over by the clergy, or because Arsacid Armenia failed to develop the elaborate Sasanian bureaucracy.

The magnates were unquestionably the dominant class of this society and, interestingly, reflected its double aspect, in that they were simultaneously autonomous sovereign lords or dynasts, and dependent vassals of the king.

The great autonomous "houses" *(tun)* preserved the prerogatives of an earlier age. Their lords (*tanutēr* or simply *tēr*) had sovereign administrative, legislative, and judicial authority within their "lordship" *(terut^{c}iwn);* they commanded the military contingents of the *tun;* and their position was hereditary, passing through agnatic seniority, usually in *primogeniture.* Other members of the *tun* were known as its *sepuh*s (not to be confused with the *azat,* as has sometimes been done). The *tēr* was, however, only the administrator of the unalienable and indivisible lands belonging jointly to all members of the *tun,* whether they were the common patrimony *(hayrenik^c)*, acquired lands *(k^c sakagink^c)*, or granted benefices *(pargewakank^c)*; and he ruled with the help and advice of the *sepuhs*, of whom the "senior" *(awag sepuh)* was normally his heir. Each *tun* seems to have had its *ostan* (court or nucleus) and perhaps a group of *ostanik^c* (retainers), although considerable controversy centers on this term, which some scholars take as referring to tenants of royal lands.

The signatures on conciliar acts show that the great houses also had their own bishops who were their religious representatives and spokesmen as the *tēr* was the political and military one. As in Iran, the great houses held hereditary offices, which were likewise unalienable. These included *sparapet* (commander of the army), held by the Mamikoneans; *t^c agadir* (coronant), by the Bagratuni, and *hazarapet* (seneschal), set over the third estate, by the Gnunis. The religious office of patriarch was likewise hereditary in the Gregorid house of the descendants of St. Gregory the Illuminator until its extinction in 439.

The order of precedence of the houses was strictly set according to a Rank List *(Gahnamak)*, of which no example has survived. However, it is evidenced in contemporary sources and later copies reflect an earlier reality. This precedence probably related to the size of the military contingents of each house as given in later Military Lists *(Zōrnamak)*. Despite its rank, however, every *tun* was sovereign and theoretically equal to every other. In this sense the Armenian king was but the first among his equals. As such, he was the *tēr* of the Arsacid *tun* and of its *sepuhs*, and the administrator of its lands; his hereditary office was the kingship.

At the same time as the *tanutēr* was an autonomous dynast, he was also a *naχarar*. This term is also derived from Iran, and Toumanoff has translated it "duke." The important point is that the *naχarar* was bound to the king by parafeudal ties called "service" *(caṙayut^c iwn)*, and his official position was delegated to him. As royal delegate he was an "official" *(gorcakal)* rather than a "lord" *(tēr)*, though the relation between these terms is still unclear, and there seem to have been more *gorcakals* than *tanutēr-naχarars*. Feudal homage was unknown in Armenia, but the oath of fidelity *(uχt)* is recorded and the *naχarars* received from the king the rank and insignia *(gah* and *patiw)* of their office as well as benefices *(pargewakank^c)* connected with it. In return they owed military service in wartime *(paterazm* and *aspatak,* equivalent to Western *ost*

and *chevauchée),* guardianship of castles, and counsel.

The king had judicial rights over the *naχarars* that theoretically could lead to the forfeiture of their estates and supervision over their succession. Similarly, although some of the *azats* held allods, most were *χostakdars.* That is, they received conditional land tenures *(χostaks)* in return for military service in the *naχarar*'s contingents, and some cases of subinfeudation also occurred. The clergy likewise received the use of *χostaks* whose ultimate ownership remained with the church, in exchange for the performance of religious services.

Little is known of the lower classes of society. The majority was composed of the peasants *(šinakan),* as might be expected in a predominantly agricultural society, but they should not be confused with the *ṙamik,* who included all other nonnoble groups as well. Like all *ṙamiks,* the *šinakan* was personally free, but bound to the land of his lord. He owed various taxes *(hark),* of which *sak* and *baž* (probably poll and land taxes) are best known, as well as work similar to the Western corvée *(bekar)* and some military service. Although heavy, these obligations were not unlimited, but regulated by church canons, and later by laws. The fines applied to *šinakans* were half those levied on *azats* in similar cases. A minimal village organization must have existed, since "heads" *(dasapet, geljawag)* are recorded in the sources. On very rare occasions *ṙamiks* and *šinakans* participated alongside the nobles in the councils of the realm.

We have practically no information on the status or size of the other, urban, *ṙamik* groups, since most of the Armenian cities were destroyed by the Persians in the 360's and much of their population deported. Slaves *(struk)* are mentioned, but were not as common as in the classical world. They were in the main prisoners of war, though some were defaulting debtors. They occasionally worked on the land, but were mostly used as household servants.

The dual dynastic and feudal character of the Armenian social structure has led to many disagreements among scholars, not all of which have been resolved. Nevertheless, it seems possible to say that the dynastic aspect prevailed, at least in the early period. This is best exemplified by the rigorously hereditary character of the *tun* in terms of its office and its lands. The Armenian kings failed in the attempt to impose the centralizing policies of their Sasanian neighbors in Iran. At best the king ratified the succession of a *tanutēr* to the prerogatives of his

ARMENIA, SOCIAL STRUCTURE

predecessors. The sources give instances when this ratification was dispensed with or the king's will was disregarded. Lands personally forfeited by an individual *naχarar* reverted to his *tun,* which continued to hold and administer them as long as a single male member survived. If there was no surviving male member, a female transmitted them to her husband's house. The entrenched arrogance of the magnates, "the lords with contingents and banners," constantly reflected in the contemporary sources, is the best proof of their independence vis-à-vis the crown.

The strength of this dynastic aristocracy is evidenced by its survival long beyond the political structures of either the Arsacids or the Bagratids. Many of its aspects were present in the more feudalized Cilician state, and traces survived as late as the eighteenth century. The persistently centrifugal tendencies of the *naχarar*s asserting their prerogatives against the ruler ultimately defeated all attempts at centralization while preserving the social fabric of the country during periods of foreign overlordship. Nevertheless, the system evidently evolved and partially disintegrated, although, as already noted, we know far less about its subsequent development than about its classical stage.

In Byzantine Armenia the application of Roman law mandated by the Justinianic reform (536) rapidly destroyed the autonomous units by identifying the *tanutēr* rather than the whole *tun* as the possessor of the domain (thus dispossessing the *sepuh*s) and by making the female members of the *tun* coinheritors (thus rapidly fragmenting the territorial units into extinction). Not even the names of the houses based on the imperial side of the border have come down to us. In eastern Persian, then Arab, and ultimately Turkish Greater Armenia, many *tuns* likewise vanished. Of the forty-two families identified by Toumanoff in 400, only twenty can be found by 800. This disappearance was unquestionably due largely to wars and massacres, but some of the attrition probably stemmed from the gradual emancipation of the *sepuh*s. This process cannot be traced, but we know that the *sepuh*s gradually acquired appanages of their own, a system known to tenth-century historians, and even became vassals of lords outside their *tun.*

The pattern of hereditary offices began to break down, with many vanishing altogether. Only the command of the army *(sparapetutᶜiwn),* after passing to several houses following its loss by the Mamikoneans, came to rest by the eighth century in the Bagratid house, where it became the prerogative of the ruler's brother. This institution survived until the twelfth or thirteenth century in Cilicia and Zakᶜarid Armenia under the Georgian form, *amir-spasalar.* Vertical inheritance from father to son increasingly gave way to lateral succession, resulting in the constant opposition of brothers or uncles and nephews that weakened the Bagratid kingdom. Senior princes *(išχans)* now dominated lesser ones, and the emergence in the ninth century of a "prince of princes" *(išχanacᶜ išχan)* created a hierarchical structure in which even the Muslim emirs were de jure vassals of the Armenian ruler. The *azat* cavalry survived as a military unit, but its clear class distinction from the magnates gradually disappeared.

Despite this evolution, much of the traditional *tanutēr-naχarar* structure seems to have survived under the twelfth- and thirteenth-century Zakᶜarid viceroys beneath the overlay of Georgian, Turkish, and subsequently Mongol terms and institutions. The old terminology—*tun, tanutēr, išχan, gorcakal, hayrenik, pargewakan*—is still found, but a detailed analysis of its content and meaning in this period needs to be made. Many of the Zakᶜarid *naχarar*s were new men appointed by the viceroys, and consequently were far more closely tied to their lords, to whom they owed their position and whom they repaid with both military and monetary service. The official aspect of the *gorcakal*s—chamberlains *(hečup*s*),* lieutenants with administrative and judicial powers *(kołmakaḷ*s*),* and such—is much clearer than in the early period, and their offices were no longer hereditary.

The most important transformation of Armenian society derived from the growth of cities, from the Bagratid period to the fourteenth century. By the tenth century there were some forty-five "cities," some of considerable size, in Armenia. At first these were the possessions of feudal, especially Muslim, lords *(išχan*s, emirs), who resided in them with their officials and retainers. Only at Dwin, and perhaps Ani, can one distinguish city "elders" who played a role in moments of crisis. Gradually, however, the cities became emancipated, and artisan and merchant classes emerged under the stimulus of the transit trade.

At their apogee in the twelfth and thirteenth centuries, the cities showed a wide social diversity, ranging from the lowest proletariat (beggars, slaves, temporary bondsmen and bondswomen, hired unskilled laborers [*varjanankᶜ*], and seasonal workers [*mšak*], who might own small plots near the city) through apprentices, journeymen, and premasters to the master craftsmen and merchants with increasingly active and powerful guilds *(ham-k^c arut^c iwn, ełbayrut^c iwn).* A council of leading citizens *(glχawork^c k^c ałak^c in),* headed by a mayor *(amira),* administered city affairs and grew steadily more independent. The growth of the economy altered traditional patterns so that even the *šinakan* paid their dues in money rather than in kind. Most interesting is the rise of a new class, the *mecatun* (big house), which seems to have been drawn from the wealthiest urban group and from city officials appointed by the local lord. Inscriptions show that some of the *mecatun* had enormous wealth, which they invested in land, as well as in buildings, hostelries, mills, barns, and oil presses, thus transforming themselves into a new noble class without links to the past.

The Zak^c arid and early Mongol periods are the last in which the Armenian social structure is still discernible. Political chaos, warfare, heavy taxation, and the overlay of foreign institutions obscure it thereafter. Nevertheless, some dynastic elements survived even beyond the Middle Ages, especially in the church. For example, the patriarchate of Caspian Albania remained a hereditary office of the Hasan-Djalalian house into the nineteenth century.

BIBLIOGRAPHY

The classic studies of the Armenian *naχarar* system are Nikolai Adonts, *Armenia in the Period of Justinian, the Political Conditions Based on the Naχarar System,* N. G. Garsoïan, ed. and trans. (1970), pp. 183–371; R. Kherumian, "Esquisse d'une feodalité oubliée," in *Vostan,* **1** (1948–1949); Hakob Manandyan, *Feodalizm hin Hin Hayastanum* (1934); Aleksei G. Sukiasian, *Obshchestvenno-politichiskiĭ stroĭ i pravo Armenii v epokhu rannego feodalizma* (1963); Cyril Toumanoff, *Studies in Christian Caucasian History* (1963), pp. 33–273.

Also see Nikolai Adonts, "L'aspect iranien du servage," in *Recueils de la Société Jean Bodin,* **2** (1937); B. N. Ařakelyan, *K^c ałak^c ner ew arhestneř Hayastanum IX–XIII dd* ("The Cities and Crafts of Armenia, IX–XIII Centuries"), 2 vols. (1958–1964); Lewon O. Babayan, *Sotsial'no-ekonomicheskaia i politicheskaia istoriia Armenii v XII–XIV vekakh* (1969); Émile Benveniste, *Titres et noms propres en iranien ancien* (1967), and *Le vocabulaire des institutions indo-européennes,* 2 vols. (1969); M.-L. Chaumont, "L'ordre des preséances à la cour des Arsacides d'Arménie," in *Journal asiatique,* **248** (1960); N. G. Garsoïan, "Prolegomena to a Study of the Iranian Aspects in Arsacid Armenia," in *Hantes Amsoria,* **90** (1976); Hakob Manandyan, *The Trade and Cities of Armenia in Relation to Ancient World Trade,* N. G. Garsoïan, trans. (1965), pp. 40–43, 69–72, 136–150, 153–155; Anait G. Perikhanian, "Drevnearmianskie vostaniki," in *Vestnik Drevneĭ istorii* (1956); A. Ter Ghewondyan, *The Arab Emirates in Bagratid Armenia,* N. G. Garsoïan, trans. (1976).

NINA G. GARSOÏAN

[See also **Sparapetut^c iwn.**]

ARMENIAKON, THEME OF, Byzantine army corps that gradually developed into a theme district from the army of the *Magister Militum* (Master of the Soldiers) for Armenia. *Armeniakoi* is the earliest recorded form of reference to the theme of Armeniakon. The name probably referred to the soldiers as well, most of whom were of Armenian origin. Its *strategos* (commander with the rank of *patrikios*) appears to be mentioned in the 640's and eventually acquired responsibility for what remained of Byzantine Armenia and Pontus. From it were later created the themes of Chaldia, Koloneia, and Charsianon. It was the second largest theme, a rival of the Anatolikon, but suffered heavily from Arab raids during its apogee in the seventh and eighth centuries. Its headquarters was probably Amasya or Koloneia.

BIBLIOGRAPHY

Constantine VII Porphyrogenitus, *De Thematibus,* ed. and comment. by A. Pertusi, *Studi e testi,* 160, Biblioteca Apostolica Vaticana (1952), 117–120.

WALTER EMIL KAEGI, JR.

[See also **Themes.**]

ARMENIAN ALPHABET. The testimony of Koriwn, a fifth-century Armenian historian, implies that Armenian was not a literary language until the beginning of the fifth century, when a monk by the name of Mesrop Maštoc^c invented the alphabet still in use today. Maštoc^c's creation had thirty-six symbols, representing all of the phonemes in Classical Armenian. Two additional characters, *ō* (the omega) and *f* (phi), were borrowed from Greek in the twelfth and thirteenth centuries, and placed at the end of the alphabet. Loan words from Western languages made these additions necessary. In time, *ō* replaced the classical diphthong *aw.*

The direction of the Armenian script is from left to right. Documents in the opposite direction are very rare and not old. The alphabetical order of the

ARMENIAN ALPHABET

letters follows that of the Greek, with the fifteen additional phonemes interspersed among the twenty-one that follow the pattern of the Greek alphabet. The method of arrangement is such that letters with similar shapes and designs are grouped together.

Certain scholars have raised questions about the possibility of the existence of an older script and a lost literary tradition. Moreover, they have expressed contradictory views concerning the origins of the present script. In fact, many questions about the Armenian alphabet remain unanswered. For example, we know neither the exact date nor the place of Maštoc^{c}'s invention, since direct evidence is lacking. Problems such as these stem from the many flaws, corruptions, and arguable passages in the text of Koriwn's *Life of Maštoc^{c}*, our only source. Lack of concrete evidence, and the similarity—if not identity—of the early fifth-century literary idiom with the spoken language of the period exclude the possibility of any kind of pre-Christian or early Christian literary tradition in Armenian. From Koriwn we learn that Maštoc^{c}, after failing in his attempt to adapt the presumably Armenian characters that had been acquired from a certain Syriac bishop called Daniel, traveled to the northern Mesopotamian cities that were known as centers of learning. In either Samosata or Edessa he invented the Armenian alphabet. In Samosata he employed the services of a Greek calligrapher by the name of Rufinus who helped him give the final artistic touches to the shapes of the characters. The dates of these events can be conjectured from the chronological epilogue of Koriwn's work as 404–406. However, the discrepancies between the epilogue and the text of Koriwn have made many scholars wary of accepting the veracity of the chronology.

There is still a great deal of controversy about the origin of the artistic design of the characters. The majority of scholars agree upon its derivation from the Greek. The Armenian script has, however, undergone change and development ever since the time of Maštoc^{c}. In the oldest manuscript fragments and inscriptions, dating from the late fifth through eighth centuries, the uncials (called *erkat^{c}agir*) were used universally. In the eighth century a smaller majuscule script made its appearance; it evolved into a third style sometime during the following century. The characters in the last style were not only smaller, but also rectangular at the corners. During the course of the eleventh century, the style changed from uncials to the cursive *(šełagir)*, but this did not last long, because a minuscule script *(bolorgir)* was employed beginning in the tenth century. At a much later date, in the seventeenth century, a smaller cursive style (called *notrgir*) was developed.

In addition to their use as phonetic symbols, the letters of the Armenian alphabet have been employed as numerals. Like the Greek alphabetic system, the Armenian numerals *A* to *T^{c}* represent 1 to 9; *Ž* to *Ł*, 10 to 90; *Č* to *J*, 100 to 900; *Ṙ* to *K^{c}*, 1,000 to 9,000. For numerals 10,000 and over, a special sign placed over any letter multiplies it by 10,000.

The Armenian Alphabet

Ա	A	1	Մ	M	200
Բ	B	2	Յ	Y	300
Գ	G	3	Ն	N	400
Դ	D	4	Շ	Š	500
Ե	E	5	Ո	O	600
Զ	Z	6	Չ	Č^{c}	700
Է	Ē	7	Պ	P	800
Ը	Ě	8	Ջ	J̌	900
Թ	T^{c}	9	Ռ	Ṙ	1,000
Ժ	Ž	10	Ս	S	2,000
Ի	I	20	Վ	V	3,000
Լ	L	30	Տ	T	4,000
Խ	X	40	Ր	R	5,000
Ծ	C	50	Ց	C^{c}	6,000
Կ	K	60	Ւ	W	7,000
Հ	H	70	Փ	P^{c}	8,000
Ձ	J	80	Ք	K^{c}	9,000
Ղ	Ł	90	—		10,000
Ճ	Č	100	Օ	Ō	
			Ֆ	F	

BIBLIOGRAPHY

Hrač^{c}eay Acaṙean, *Hayoc^{c} Grerě* [The Armenian Characters] (1928; repr. 1968); A. Hovhannissian, "L'alphabet arménien et son action historique," in *Revue des études arméniennes,* n.s. 2 (1965); Josef Markwart, *Ueber den Ursprung des armenischen Alphabets* (1917); Paul Peeters, "Pour l'histoire des origines de l'alphabet arménien," in *Revue des études arméniennes,* 9 (1929); Anait G. Perikhanian, "K voprosu o proiskhozhdenii armianskoi pis'mennosti," in *Peredneaziatskii sbornik,* vol. 2, I. M. D'iakonov, ed. (1966).

KRIKOR H. MAKSOUDIAN

ARMENIAN ART essentially began with the establishment of Christianity as the official religion in the early years of the fourth century. Very little has survived from the pre-Christian period because of the ravages of time and the destruction of pagan temples and idols, as described by historians, after the conversion to Christianity. The rare survivals display characteristics of late Greco-Roman art: for example, the temple of Garni (now reconstructed) in its plan and frieze sculpture, the pavement mosaics in the bath of the adjoining palace, coins struck by Tigran II the Great (95–55 B.C.), and a few pieces of sculpture.

The three most creative periods of Armenian art coincide with those of national independence or semiautonomy. The first, or classical, period dates from the fifth to the mid seventh century, the time of the Arab conquest. The second, from the late ninth to the mid eleventh century, began under the Bagratids and ended with the Seljuk conquest. The third, from the late twelfth to the mid fourteenth century, corresponds to the period of semi-independence in the northern provinces, when Armenian princes, the Zakᶜareans, ruled under Georgian or Mongol suzerainty, and to the life-span of the independent kingdom of Cilicia.

ARCHITECTURE

Armenian architecture is noted for its technical mastery of the problems of stone construction and its creativity in developing a rich variety of building types. Structural problems presented by the use of stone vaults and domes in Christian church architecture were solved in Armenia earlier than in the West, and in ways that created a distinctive national style. Unlike the West, which limited itself for the most part to the longitudinal basilican plan for its churches, Armenia soon abandoned that form and experimented with different kinds of centralized longitudinal churches and truly centrally planned buildings. A remarkable number of churches were built throughout the country from the fifth to the fourteenth century, many of them firmly dated through inscriptions or contemporary chronicles.

The churches were constructed of native volcanic stone carefully cut into thin slabs, polished, and used as a facing on the exterior and interior of a core of rubble masonry. The natural coloring of the tuff stone (yellow, rose, gray, and other tints) creates a handsome effect of shading on the facades.

The earliest Christian structure extant in Armenia is the mausoleum at Ałcᶜ, dated at least as early as 346, its crypt composed of a vaulted chamber, horseshoe apse, and two lateral arcosolia. According to archaeological finds, the earliest churches in Armenia were vaulted, longitudinal basilicas with one nave, a semicircular or horseshoe apse, and sometimes one or two lateral rooms. The oldest extant churches, vaulted basilicas with one or three aisles, date from the fifth and sixth centuries Širvanǰuł, Ereroykᶜ). This type, used throughout most of Armenia during this period, soon gave way to a centralized plan with a dome covered on the exterior by a conical roof. This became the predominant form from the sixth century on, possibly even in the fifth, according to evidence of an earlier church revealed by excavations under the cathedral of Ēǰmiacin.

The architects devised imaginative variations of central-plan churches that provided sufficient support for the dome and satisfied liturgical needs at the same time. For the interior the simplest form consisted of a central square covered by a dome set on corner squinches buttressed by four vaulted apsoidal niches, one on each side (Agarak). In one variation the number of niches around the central square increased to eight with the addition of four small cylindrical spaces in the corners under the squinches (Ēǰmiacin, St. Hřipᶜsimē). In other churches the central area was encircled with eight apsoidal niches of approximately the same size (Zoravar). Other plans include a cross inscribed in a rectangle, the central dome supported by four freestanding piers (St. Gayianē, Mren); trefoils (Kamsarakan Church at Tᶜalin); quatrefoils (Zvartnots); octagons (Irind); and other forms.

The complexities of the interior plans usually are not revealed by the exterior forms. For example, the interior space of St. Hřipᶜsimē, which consists of four large apsoidal niches plus four small ones that lead to four corner chambers, is sheathed on the exterior by rectangular walls. The only indication of the interior division of space consists of pairs of triangular recesses carved on each exterior wall to mark the position of the four large niches. The exteriors of other churches take the following forms: rectangle with one, two, or more projecting apses (Bagawan, Tᶜalin Cathedral); freestanding cross with rectangular arms (Lmbatavankᶜ) or polygonal arms (Alaman); circular exterior (Zvartnots); hexagon; octagon; and other polygonal shapes. Armenian architects displayed technical virtuosity of the highest level in their ability to combine the different internal and external geometric forms of a church into an organic whole.

ARMENIAN ART

The Cathedral at Ani (989–1010), interior and exterior views. PHOTOGRAPHS BY THOMAS F. MATHEWS

In the second and third periods, the interest in diversity and experimentation continued. A new form became the most widespread type: the domed-hall church, which elevated the aisle vaults and expanded and unified the interior space by using engaged instead of freestanding pillars to support the dome. Most of the earlier plans were repeated, but with modifications and an accent on verticality. In the now-ruined medieval capital of Ani, there is no duplication of ground plan or exterior design among thirteen of the surviving churches. Different architectural types appeared, such as two-story churches (Eɫvard, Noravank^{c} at Amaɫu), three-story bell towers, and the *gavit*^{c}, a large assembly hall for both religious and secular functions, generally erected adjoining the west facade of a church.

In addition, new modes of construction were invented. The cathedral of Ani, built by the architect Trdat, who was invited in 989 to rebuild the fallen dome of Hagia Sophia in Constantinople, displays at a much earlier date (1010) features associated with Gothic architecture in the West: clustered piers, pointed arches, and slightly pointed, ribbed ceiling vaults. In other churches, innovations included a new framing system of ribs and arches to support the weight of ceiling vaults. The Shepherd's Chapel at Ani (late tenth or early eleventh century), an early example of an ogival structure, uses six arches to support the heavy vault of the first story, each arch springing from wall colonnettes to the hanging keystone at the center of the church. Later stages of development include the construction of pairs of intersecting arches running the length of a *gavit*^{c} to bear the weight of the ceiling. Large monastic complexes, made up of several churches and, in some cases, a library, refectory, and bell tower (Haɫbat, Sanahin), were erected or restored. Many of the surviving examples of secular architecture—palaces, fortifications, caravansaries, bridges—date from the later period and display the technical ingenuity seen in church construction.

Drawing on late-classicial building types or those of Persia and Mesopotamia as sources, as well as on local building traditions, Armenia created an architecture so original in its forms and technically so inventive that it holds a major place in the history of medieval art.

SCULPTURE

Very little survives of Armenian pagan sculpture aside from the coinage of Tigran the Great and the stone heads found at Dwin. With the advent of Christianity and extensive church construction came the beginning of a continuous and innovative tradition of architectural sculpture in stone. The use of both figurative and ornamental relief sculpture on church facades distinguishes Armenian from Byzantine and all other East Christian art except Georgian. Floral, geometric, and figural motifs are carved over the windows, between the arches of blind arcades, and on the tympana and lintels of the doorways. Another characteristic form of Armenian sculpture is the commemorative stele carved in low relief. Examples first appear both as tall, obelisk-shaped pillars and as smaller, cubic slabs with reliefs on several sides. Beginning in the second period, a different type, referred to as a *khatchkᶜar* (cross-stone), takes the form of a rectangular slab with a large, usually ornate cross carved on the face and framed elaborately.

The earliest examples of Christian relief sculpture appear to be in the fourth-century mausoleum at Aŀcᶜ and include the scene of Daniel in the lions' den. During the early period, the religious images found on the churches and stelae include representations of Christ, the Virgin, saints, angels, and ecclesiastics, as well as scenes of the Virgin and Child (Ōjun), Christ with the apostles (Ptŀni), a limited selection of biblical compositions taken almost entirely from the Old Testament (Hařič), and other scenes that are unique in Christian art (Mren, Dwin).

In addition to these saintly figures there are his-

A *khatchkᶜar,* or cross-stone (thirteenth century), Monastery of Gosavankᶜ. PHOTOGRAPH BY LUCY DER MANUELIAN

torical personages such as King Trdat (Ōjun) or more contemporary rulers (Mren), architects and stonemasons (Zvartnots), praying figures (Tᶜalin), and princely founders of churches (Mren, Sisian), some identified by inscriptions. Sometimes the secular rulers are introduced into traditional Christian compositions found in both East and West, and shown in contemporary dress. The interest in secular figures is manifest in the different types of founder portraits, some of which remained in use into the fourteenth century: one or two figures holding the model of the church; a founder-prince shown hunting; founders depicted with Christ or the Virgin and Child; and portrait busts. The figure style is almost geometric, and there is an absence of modeling.

The outstanding example of Armenian architectural sculpture appears in the second period at the Church of the Holy Cross, built by King Gagik I between 915 and 921 on the island of Aŀtᶜamar in Lake Van. It is the first medieval stone monument in the art of both East and West to be entirely covered with sculptured reliefs. On the dome and four walls there are large figures of Christ, the Virgin, saints, prophets, apostles who preached in Armenia, historic Armenian personages, and scenes from the Old Testament. Sculptured friezes depict real and mythical animals amid fruits and vines, and scenes of hunting, harvesting, and feasting—an unusual feature in a Christian sculptural program. King Gagik (989–1020), as the founder, is shown offering a model of the church to Christ. Similar portraits, but with two princes, are found throughout the second and third periods (Sanahin, Hařičavankᶜ).

During these periods single and paired birds and animals are carved in prominent locations on the churches, sometimes beside crosses (St. Gregory, erected by Tigran Honencᶜ, Tᶜanahat). Such churches usually have richer ornamentation, with intricate floral and geometric interlacing on window frames and portals, often with blind arcading or large crosses on the wall surfaces. Some of the carving, particularly on large *khatchkᶜars* beside church portals, is in the lacelike openwork technique.

A group of splendid monastic churches of the early thirteenth century, built by the Zakᶜarean princes and their vassal nobles, display a variety of representational and ornamental motifs amid the blind arcading of the drum (Geŀard, Ganjasar). In the province of Siwnikᶜ, in the late thirteenth and early fourteenth centuries, a series of elaborately carved tympanum compositions appear (Areni, Spitakavor), including the unique and complex depiction of the

Architectural detail, Church of the Holy Cross, Ałt^{c}amar in Lake Van. King Gagik I *(left)* offers a model of the church to Christ. PHOTOGRAPH BY THOMAS F. MATHEWS

Ancient of Days (St. Karapet of Noravank^{c} at Amału). The figures on these tympana are more fully modeled than the earlier examples. In general, however, and even though the chapels at the monastery of Gełard, masterfully carved out of the cliffs, attest the skill of Armenian sculptors, a disinterest in naturalistic representation is more characteristic.

PAINTING

The development of monumental painting in Armenia is difficult to trace, since very few examples of mosaics and mural painting survive. Remnants of frescoes at some churches (T^{c}alin, Mren) indicate that images of Christ, the Virgin, and saints, and scenes from the Gospels were depicted on the interiors of Armenian churches from an early period. During the later periods there are only isolated examples (Hałbat, St. Gregory of Tigran Honenc^{c}), of which the most interesting is the extensive cycle at Ałt^{c}amar. In addition to New Testament scenes, Ałt^{c}amar has the only narrative cycle from the Old Testament to be found on a medieval monument in the Christian East.

It is through the study of illustrated manuscripts that the development of Armenian painting can best be traced. We have an almost continuous series of high-quality illuminated manuscripts stretching from the ninth to the end of the seventeenth century, many of them dated and often signed. The only illuminations extant from the early period are the four sixth-century miniatures included at the end of the ninth-century *Gospel of Ējmiacin* (Erevan, Matenadaran 229). For the Armenians commissioning, copying, or donating a manuscript was considered a pious act, and increased the hope of salvation.

Armenian illuminations are notable for their rich and imaginative ornamentation. Real and imaginary birds and animals, intricate floral and geometric motifs are painted in vivid colors against a gold background on the canon table pages of Gospel manuscripts—on the headpieces, in the margins, and, shaped like letters, in the text as well. There are often full-page illustrations of scenes from the life of Christ, based on compositions developed in early Christian and Byzantine art, grouped at the beginning of these manuscripts. But they are often distinguished from Byzantine and other examples by the addition of new elements that make the Gospel story more real and immediate: more dramatic interpretation of the emotional content; vignettes painted in the margins; the use of familiar details from everyday life, including contemporary costumes; and the introduction of historical Armenian personages.

Two different artistic trends coexist in Armenian miniature painting: the first is an Eastern style with an emphasis on abstract ornamental design and a disinterest in the natural appearance of figures and objects; the second, influenced by Byzantine art, blends naturalism with the native Armenian tendency toward abstract form. The latter, more elegant style is predominant in the sumptuous manuscripts commissioned by the kings and prelates of Armenian Cilicia.

Manuscripts as early as the tenth and eleventh centuries demonstrate movement toward the evolution of a national style. Both trends appear in the famous *Gospel of Queen Mlk^{c}ē* of 862 (Venice, Biblioteca Armena dei PP. Mechitarista, San Lazzaro MS 1144), while the *Gospel of 966* (Baltimore, Walters Art Gallery MS 537) is an example of the more abstract style. In the eleventh-century *Gospel of King Gagik of Kars* (Jerusalem, Armenian Patriarchate MS 2556), the Byzantine influence becomes more apparent in the figural scenes but is accompanied by richly innovative ornamentation. Yet, the figures in the *Gospel of Mołni* (Erevan, Matenadaran MS 7736) are

 ARMENIAN ART

depicted in a markedly linear, abstract style. In most cases luxury manuscripts produced for the court, high church dignitaries, and wealthy patrons reveal Byzantine influence, while those illustrated in outlying or conservative monasteries in Armenia proper preserve the native, popular style.

In the later period the school of painting in Cilician Armenia had its roots in the style of the eleventh-century luxury manuscripts of Armenia proper, and soon developed along original lines. Contacts with the Latin West and the Far East inspired highly imaginative works. Thirteenth-century Cilician manuscripts attained such a high degree of excellence that they rank among the best examples of medieval illumination, East or West.

T^{c}oros Roslin, the head of the patriarchal scriptorium, whose signed works date from 1256 to 1268, was the foremost painter of the period. His innovative and lively interpretations, interest in narrative, and subtle coloring are among the finest achievements of the age. He found new ways to illustrate

Dedication page by T^{c}oros Roslin for Second Constantine Gospel, with King David. HROMKLA, JERUSALEM ARMENIAN PATRIARCHATE MS 251

Gospel passages (*Gospel* [1268], Erevan, Matenadaran MS 10675; *Ritual* [1266], Jerusalem, Armenian Patriarchate MS 2027); he enlivened traditional representations by adding scenes from daily life (*Gospel* [1262], Baltimore, Walters Art Gallery MS 539); he emphasized emotion through subtle and dramatic means (*Gospel* [1265], Jerusalem, Armenian Patriarchate MS 1956); and he invented new types of decorative compositions (*Gospel* [1265], Jerusalem, Armenian Patriarchate MS 1956).

Cilician painters often included portraits of the sovereigns of Cilicia with their children in scenes with Christ and the Virgin Mary (*Gospel of Queen Keran* [1272], Jerusalem, Armenian Patriarchate MS 2563; *Gospel of Prince Vasak* [thirteenth century], Jerusalem, Armenian Patriarchate MS 2568), just as Armenian sculptors sometimes carved founder portraits on their churches. The difference is that Cilician rulers are never shown presenting the manuscripts they commissioned; they gesture toward the holy figures. Like the sculptors, painters varied the iconography of donor scenes, and were interested in creating accurate portraits, particularly in details of dress. As a result these religious compositions take on a feeling of immediacy and the saintly figures are brought closer to the people of the time.

Despite the destruction of the Cilician kingdom in 1375, manuscripts continued to be illustrated in Armenian monasteries as well as in various centers outside the native country. Different schools with a considerably wider range of styles were developed, some of them highly original, as in the provinces of Siwnik^{c} in the fourteenth century and Khizan, near Lake Van, in the fifteenth century. In the eclectic art of the seventeenth century, the forms and style of Cilician painting were revived and entire cycles, such as Genesis and the Book of Revelation, were taken over from Western art.

The art of goldsmiths and silversmiths, and of silk and carpet weavers, was highly developed in medieval Armenia. But very little survives apart from a few silver reliquaries, thirteenth- and fourteenth-century manuscript bindings, and textile fragments.

Throughout the centuries, medieval Armenia created a legacy of architecture, monumental sculpture, and manuscript painting remarkable in originality, diversity, and high quality of execution. Armenia's most outstanding contribution to the history of art is in the field of architecture, but the significance of its artistic creations as a whole for an understanding of Christian art is in the process of becoming recognized.

ARMENIAN CHURCH, DOCTRINES

BIBLIOGRAPHY

Architettura medievale armena, Roma—Palazzo Venezia, 10–30 giugno, 1968 (exhibition catalogue) (1968); Sirarpie Der Nersessian, *The Chester Beatty Library, a Catalogue of the Armenian Manuscripts; with an Introduction on the History of Armenian Art,* 2 vols. (1958); *Aght'mar, Church of the Holy Cross* (1965); *The Armenians* (1969), pp. 97–154; *Armenian Manuscripts in the Walters Art Gallery* (1973); and *Armenian Art* (1977), with useful bibliography; Levon Azargan, *Khatchkars arméniens* (1973); Mesrop Chanashian, *Armenian Miniature Painting of the Monastic Library of San-Lazzaro-Venice* (1966); *Documenti di architettura armena,* 8 vols. (1968–1977), monographs on Armenian churches and monasteries; Lidiia A. Durnovo, *Armenian Miniatures* (1961); Varaztad Harouthiounian, *Monuments of Armenia* (1975); A. Khatchatrian, *L'architecture arménienne du IVe au VIe siècle* (1971); Richard Krautheimer, *Early Christian and Byzantine Architecture* (1975), pp. 338–348; Bezalel Narkiss, *Armenian Art Treasures of Jerusalem* (1979); Nona Stepanian and Arutyun Tchakmaktchian, *Art décoratif de l'Arménie médiévale* (1971); and *Studi di architettura medioevale armena,* 4 vols. (1971–1973), monographs on Armenian churches.

LUCY DER MANUELIAN

ARMENIAN CHURCH, DOCTRINES AND COUNCILS. The Armenian church shares with the other Eastern churches the basic dogmas evolved in the first three ecumenical councils: the Trinity, the Incarnation, and the Redemption. They constitute the foundation of the teachings of the Armenian church and are professed in the final Armenian version of the Nicene Creed (post seventh century), which is recited during the Divine Liturgy.

The Armenian Fathers, who distinguished dogma from doctrine, derived all their teachings from the Holy Scriptures, the first three ecumenical councils, the early local councils, and the pre-Chalcedonian patristic literature (both Greek and Syriac). The doctrines of the Armenian church are very similar to those of the other Monophysite and Eastern Orthodox churches.

The earliest councils of the Armenian church were devoted to disciplinary matters. We learn from the historian P^cawstos Buzand (fifth century) that the bishops of Armenia held synods in the town of Aštišat in Tarawn. The earliest of these, the Council of 365 over which Bishop Nersēs I (353–373) presided, made provisions to establish order and uniformity in the churches. The Council also decided to found hospitals, asylums, and leprosaria. The earliest Armenian canons are those of the Council of Šahapivan (444). Besides the bishops of districts and the clergy, princes and members of the nobility also participated in this council. Such participation became a common pattern in the Armenian tradition. The purpose of Šahapivan was to complement the ecumenical councils and the local councils. The individual canons provide penalties for various offenses and deal with subjects such as immorality, magic, witchcraft, lamentation over the dead, monastic life, acquisition of ecclesiastical offices through bribery, relics of martyrs, excommunication, clerics accused of *mcłnēut^ciwn* (Paulicianism?), and bishops and priests who protect criminals.

Shortly after Šahapivan, another important council met at Artašat in 449. The edict of the Sasanian King of Kings Yazdagird II (439–457) ordering the Armenians to convert to Mazdaism prompted this gathering of seventeen bishops, priors, and priests and eighteen princes, who were accompanied by several cadets. The participants wrote an official letter in which they reaffirmed their political allegiance to the King of Kings, but refused to carry out his order.

The earliest doctrinal questions that attracted the attention of the Armenian fathers concerned the teachings of Theodore of Mopsuestia, the teacher of Nestorius and an author greatly honored by the Nestorians. The Latin sources speak of a council of Armenian bishops about 427–429, where the works of Theodore and the letters of Bishop Rabula of Edessa and Bishop Acacius of Melitene were carefully examined. The Armenians, unable to come to a decision about the orthodoxy of either Theodore or his opponents, sent representatives to Constantinople to ask for the opinion of Proclus, the patriarch. The fifth-century Armenian historian Koriwn states that Bishop Sahak and Vardapet Maštoc^c rejected the teachings of Theodore and banned his books from Armenia.

The Armenian bishops could not attend the Robber Council of 449 and the Council of Chalcedon in 451 because most of the Armenian prelates, the katholikos, and many of the leading presbyters participated in the Persarmenian rebellion against the Persians. Most were taken captive and exiled to remote areas in Iran. Soon thereafter, they were martyred for their faith. (The Armenian participants at Chalcedon came from Byzantine Armenia and Armenia Minor; they could not represent the Armenian church, since they were not subject to the Armenian katholikos.) At a later date the Armenian fathers re-

ARMENIAN CHURCH, DOCTRINES

jected the teachings of Chalcedon and the Tome of Leo. Some scholars regard this act as the cause of the schism between the Armenian church and the see of Constantinople. In fact, the Armenian church had already severed her ties with the see of Caesarea about 373.

At about the end of the fifth century, the Armenians acquired the text of the *Henotikon* of Zeno; they must also have been aware that the Monophysite beliefs of Emperor Anastasius prevailed throughout the Byzantine Empire. In view of these developments, the Armenians, who had earlier rejected the teachings of Theodore of Mopsuestia, resorted to the provisions of the first two ecumenical councils. In 506 the Monophysites of Persia, who had been greatly annoyed by the Nestorians and were asked by the King of Kings to supply a profession of their faith, sent a delegation to Armenia to seek help. There a council of bishops and princes was already in session in Dwin, the capital. The council studied the teachings of the Nestorians (which they associated with those of Chalcedon) and anathematized them. The Armenian katholikos Babgēn and his bishops formally announced their decision and acknowledged the orthodoxy of the *Henotikon* of Zeno in a pair of letters addressed to the Persian Christians. Although they did not directly anathematize the teachings of Chalcedon, they were very sensitive toward its Christology.

The rejection of the "Three Chapters" (the writings of Theodore of Mopsuestia, Ibas, and Theodoret) by the Fifth Ecumenical Council (the second council of Constantinople held in 553) did not satisfy the Armenians, who continued to identify Nestorianism with the teachings of Chalcedon. This is evident in the documents from the Armenian Council of Dwin (554). Despite the testimony of certain sources, the Armenian Fathers did not anathematize the Duophysite doctrine and Chalcedon in this council; the canons of Dwin do not deal with doctrinal issues.

The partition of Armenia under Emperor Maurice in 591 was a very important event in the development of ecclesiastical relations, since for the first time the greater part of Armenia came under direct Byzantine control. In 591 the emperor forced the twenty-one Armenian prelates within the Byzantine borders to hold a council and accept the teachings of Chalcedon. The Armenian katholikos Movsēs, who resided in Persian-occupied Dwin, refused to participate. In retaliation, Maurice appointed an antikatholikos, Yovhannēs of Bagaran. The schism within the Armenian church ended only after the conquest of Armenia by the Sasanian King of Kings Khosru II in 611. Prior to that, however (in 607), the Armenian bishops from both the Byzantine and Persian sections of Armenia gathered in Dwin and set canons that made provisions for all the bishops, priors, and presbyters who had complied with Maurice's orders and accepted the orthodoxy of Chalcedon. The participants in the council were asked to supply written proof of their orthodoxy. Soon thereafter, the bishops presented to Smbat Bagratuni, the viceroy of Vrkan, a document in which they officially anathematized the Council of Chalcedon and the Tome of Leo. A similar document was also presented to Abraham, the recently elected katholikos.

These events probably caused the schism between the Armenian and Georgian churches in 608. The Church of Georgia, originally under the jurisdiction of Antioch, had developed close ties with the Armenian church from the fourth and fifth centuries. According to the Armenian sources, the katholikoi of Georgia and Albania received their episcopal ordination from those of Armenia. Katholikos Kiwrion of Georgia, who was responsible for the schism, was the presbyter of the cathedral of Dwin and was ordained bishop by the Armenian katholikos Movsēs. Despite these credentials, Kiwrion had a non-Armenian background; he was educated in Nikopolis on the Byzantine side of the border, where he learned Greek and probably adhered to the teachings of the Byzantine church. During his pontificate, his friendship toward the Nestorians and Chalcedonians aroused the suspicion of Bishop Movsēs of C^{c}urtaw, the capital of Gogarene, who informed against him to the Armenians. The religious orientation of the Georgian church greatly threatened the authority of the Armenian katholikos. The efforts of the Armenians were of no avail to dissuade Kiwrion from his determination to accept the doctrines of the Byzantine church. When all negotiations failed, Katholikos Abraham excommunicated Kiwrion and the Georgian church. Relations between the two churches, however, were not entirely severed. The Armenian katholikoi continued to exercise some spiritual control over Georgia, especially during the Arab period (seventh to tenth centuries), when the Georgian katholikate had presumably lapsed.

During the third decade of the seventh century, the Monothelite doctrine temporarily resolved the Christological controversies between Byzantium and the Monophysite East. Although the Armenian sources do not specify the official acceptance of this

ARMENIAN CHURCH, DOCTRINES

doctrine by the Armenian church, they are aware of a council that met in 631 or 632 in Karin (Theodosiopolis), where the Armenian katholikos Ezr and the emperor Heraclius established communion between the Imperial and Armenian churches. The acts of this council have been lost; and the Monothelite doctrine, now considered to be an important teaching of the Armenian church, is no longer associated with the name of Heraclius and the Council of Karin. Heraclius' attempt to reconcile the Armenians did not succeed, since communion with the Byzantines aroused much opposition in Armenia.

According to the seventh-century Armenian historian Sebēos, Constans II sent a copy of the *Type of Faith* (he calls it a *hrovartak,* "edict") to Armenia. In 648 or 649, a council of Armenian bishops and princes met at Dwin. In their official letter addressed to the emperor, they tactfully avoided mentioning the Monothelite doctrine, but openly rejected the Council of Chalcedon and the Tome of Leo, arguing that these were not in agreement with the Christology of the first three ecumenical councils. However, they quickly changed their minds when in 652 Emperor Constans, victorious against the Arabs, entered Dwin and forced the Armenians to unite with the Imperial church. This 'watery union' did not last long, since the feudal lords of Armenia accepted the terms of peace offered by the Arabs, and entered the service of the caliph in 653.

In 690 the Byzantines once again tried to force union on the Armenians. During the brief Byzantine occupation of Armenia at the time of Justinian II, the Armenian katholikos Sahak III and some of his bishops went to Constantinople, where they accepted the teachings of the Byzantine church; but soon after their return to Armenia, they changed their minds and returned to Monophysitism. Three decades later, the efforts of the Byzantine patriarch Germanus to approach the Armenians were terminated when he was deposed in 730. The iconoclastic controversy and the Arab domination of Armenia throughout the eighth century and the first half of the ninth put a temporary stop to Armeno-Byzantine church relations.

The theological discussions between Byzantium and Armenia were resumed only after Prince Ašot Bagratuni had ascended to power in Armenia in the 850's. The subsequent exchange of correspondence between the Armenians and Patriarch Photius led to a council that met at Širakawan in 862. The canons of the Council of Širakawan dwell on the doctrines of the Trinity, the Incarnation, the hypostatic union of natures in Christ, the Virgin Birth of Christ, the theopaschite heresy, docetism, and more.

The treatment of Chalcedon is indeed unique: the thirteenth canon pronounces anathema against all those who believe that the teachings of Chalcedon are contrary to those of the first three ecumenical councils, but refuse to reject Chalcedon. The fourteenth canon is the reverse: those who recognize Chalcedon and the fifth, sixth, and seventh ecumenical councils as being in agreement with the teachings of the first three, but dare to reject them, shall be anathematized. These canons, which appear to contradict each other, were intended for the purpose of maintaining the religious status quo in Transcaucasia and for providing a modus vivendi for the Monophysite and the Duophysite parties. Such an agreement was consonant with Ašot Bagratuni's master plan of creating a Bagratid Caucasia, which required as a prerequisite an atmosphere of religious tolerance. It was this atmosphere that made it possible for the Armenian katholikos to play the role of spiritual leader throughout Caucasia. Even the Byzantine church recognized this: Nicholas Mysticus, in his letter of 915 to Katholikos Yovhannēs of Armenia, refers twice to the Armenians, Georgians, and Albanians as part of Yovhannēs' spiritual flock.

The political fragmentation of Caucasia in the tenth century put an end to this kind of mutual tolerance. Relations with Byzantium deteriorated, and in the early 970's, the attempt of Katholikos Vahan of Siwnik to correspond with them and discuss doctrinal questions resulted in his dethronement at the Council of Ani.

The Eastern policy of Emperor Manuel Komnenos and his interest in Cilicia form the background of the eleventh-century Armeno-Byzantine discussions on church unity. The negotiations between the two sides continued for a number of years (1165–1179), and were terminated at Manuel's death. The result of this attempt of union was that the Armenian Fathers at the Council of Hřomklay (1179) expressed willingness to relinquish the formula of "one nature" for the sake of church unity, although they never acknowledged the acceptance of the Chalcedonian formula. The official documents of this council never reached Constantinople. Subsequently, there was correspondence between the Armenian katholikos Grigor Tłay and Emperor Isaac Angelos (*ca.* 1185), but it bore no fruits. The journey of Nersēs Lambronac^{c}i, the bishop of Tarsus, to Con-

ARMENIAN CHURCH, DOCTRINES

stantinople in 1197 and his discussions with the Greek theologians also had no consequences. A final effort on the part of the Armenians to revive relations failed, since the response of the Greek patriarch Isaiah (1321–1332) was not conciliatory.

The Armenian church councils of the Cilician period (1198–1375) usually dealt with various questions arising from liturgical and doctrinal differences between the Armenian and Roman traditions. Since the kingdom of Cilician Armenia was a vassal state of both the Holy Roman Empire and Rome, union with Rome was a prerequisite for such a status. The Council of Tarsus in 1198, shortly before the coronation of Levon I, had formally accepted such a union. The political expectations of Levon I from the West played a major role in the decision of the Armenian fathers. In the earlier stage of her relations with the Armenians, Rome did not show any interest in discussing Christological questions; she only demanded certain minor liturgical changes and adaptations which did not alienate the Armenians. The Roman demands, however, gradually increased. In the second Council of Sis (1243), the Armenians were asked to introduce the sacrament of Extreme Unction, and interpolate the words "Christ Our Lord" into the prayers that precede the chanting of the *Trisagion,* so that the phrase "Who wast crucified for us" would be taken for the Son of God and not the Trinity.

It was not until the third Council of Sis (1251) that the Armenian fathers were compelled to deal with a doctrinal question. Pope Innocent IV had sent a letter requesting that the Armenians define their formula about the procession of the Holy Spirit. The theological treatises that the Armenian doctors produced on this occasion curiously avoided using the *filioque procedit* formula. On several occasions, however, they used the *filioque* with verbs that refer either to the consubstantiality of the Spirit with the Father and the Son or to the temporal mission of the Spirit.

From the point of view of doctrine, much more serious was the Council of 1307, which also met at Sis. Under the pressure of the Armenian court, the participants of the Council decided to profess the doctrine of "two natures," "two wills," and "two energies" in Christ; to interpolate the word "Christ" into the text of the *Trisagion;* to accept the first seven ecumenical councils; to introduce several Western liturgical and calendrical traditions. The canons of the Council met much opposition in both Cilicia and especially Greater Armenia, and an unofficial popular gathering of bishops, clerics, and laymen in 1309 rejected them. As a result, the Cilician court was forced to hold another council in Adana in 1316, which reinforced the rejected canons of the Council of 1307; but it fared no better.

The demands of Rome and the efforts of the Armenian court to draw the Armenian church closer to the Latin rite were very unpopular with the Armenians. The Council of Sis in 1342 rejected as unwarranted a list of 117 errors, which Rome had demanded that the Armenians correct. In 1361 another council at Sis returned to the older Armenian tradition of using unmixed wine with the host; the Council of 1307 had introduced the Latin tradition of mixing water.

Besides the usual Christological issues, the Armenian fathers also discussed other doctrinal questions in their councils. The Council of Manzikert in 726, which was held jointly with the Syriac church, dealt with the question of the corruptibility of the body of Christ. A little earlier, in 719, the Armenian fathers of the Council of Dwin set canons concerning the sacrament of marriage, fasting, worshiping the cross, holy chrism, the text of the liturgy, the holy offices, ordination, baptism, and so on—most of them of a ritual, liturgical, or disciplinary nature. The last canon anathematizes and excommunicates the Paulician heretics. This indicates that the reemergence and spread of the Paulician heresy in the seventh and eighth centuries was the reason why the Armenian bishops, especially Katholikos Yovhannēs of Awjun, strove to give a canonical and doctrinal basis to the liturgical and ritual practices of the church, since the Paulicians adhered to a more primitive form of Christianity.

Unique among the councils of the eleventh and twelfth centuries are those of Sew Leaṙn (1113) and Sis (1204). In the first, a large assemblage of bishops and princes anathematized the see of Aḷtʿamar, the bishop of which had assumed the title of katholikos. This was the first time that a bishop of the Armenian church had dared to attach the honor, authority, and title of katholikos to an episcopal see. Aḷtʿamar remained on and off under anathema until about 1409. Subsequently it continued as a local patriarchate with limited jurisdiction. The Council of 1204 made a number of concessions of liturgical, calendrical, and dietary nature to please the Zakʿarid princes of northeastern Armenia, who were the vassals of the Georgian kings; the Chalcedonian milieu of the Armeno-Georgian armies made certain adaptations (such as portable altars) necessary.

The Council of Vałaršapat in 1441 and the transfer of the patriarchal see from Sis to Ējmiacin were crucial for the future of the Armenian church, since the permanent residence of the katholikoi was now located deep in Armenian territory. It is not clear why the last katholikos who resided in Sis did not go to Vałaršapat. After his death, the successors to his see occasionally contested the supreme ecclesiastical authority of the Katholikoi of All Armenians. However, their jurisdiction was gradually confined within the immediate boundaries of Cilicia and neighboring areas. In the Council of 1651 in Jerusalem, P^cilippos, Katholikos of All Armenians, and Katholikos Nersēs of Cilicia met and set canons defining the limits of the jurisdiction of the two katholikates.

The Armenian church, like the Eastern Orthodox church, never formally defined the number of her sacraments. The general understanding is that there are six of them; unction of the sick has fallen out of use. The Armenian doctrine of the veneration of saints and icons is more archaic than that of the Orthodox church, since the Armenians do not accept the Second Council of Nicaea. We know from the works of Yovhannēs of Awjun (early eighth century) that the Armenians anointed their icons with holy oil and venerated them. We also know from earlier sources that they prayed to the saints asking for their intercession. The Virgin Mary was greatly venerated as *Astuacacin,* a compound word derived from the Greek *Theotokos.* The earliest use of the term in Armenian literature seems to be located in translations of the works of Cyril of Alexandria. The Armenians, like the Greeks, commemorated the conception of the Virgin on 9 December. The feast of her Assumption has eclipsed the commemoration of her Dormition since the Cilician period.

The Armenian doctors of theology always boasted that they were faithful to the words of the Holy Scriptures and the early Fathers of the Church. They were very conservative about doctrinal questions and protective of the traditions of their church. New terminology, formulas, and interpretations did not please them. The ancient traditions and teachings of the Church that the Armenians had acquired during the course of the fourth, fifth, and sixth centuries became part of the national heritage and identity of the Armenian people. Any attempt to introduce changes in their church was regarded as a treacherous act against the nation. This may explain the conservatism of the Armenian church.

BIBLIOGRAPHY

Alexandro Balgy, *Historia doctrinae catholicae inter Armenos unionisque eorum cum ecclesia Romano in Concilio Florentino* (1878); Clemens Galanus, *Conciliatio Ecclesiae Armenae cum Romana* (1690); Gérard Garitte, *La narratio de rebus Armeniae* (1952); Nina Garsoïan, *The Paulician Heresy* (1967); Malachia Ormanian, *The Church of Armenia,* 2nd ed. (1955); *Azgapatum,* vols. I–II (1912–1914); and Pascal Tekeyan, *Controverses christologiques en Arméno-Cilicie dans la seconde moitié du XIIe siècle (1165–1198)* (1939).

KRIKOR H. MAKSOUDIAN

[See also **Councils, Byzantine (787–1453); Councils, Western (869–1274); Henotikon; Koriwn; Monophysitism; Paulicians; P^cawstos Buzand.**]

ARMENIAN CHURCH, STRUCTURE. The structure of the Armenian Church is founded on principles derived from the episcopate of the third and fourth centuries, the early church councils, and the prevailing sociopolitical pattern in Armenia. The episcopate was established in Armenia before the Council of Nicaea (325). During the fourth century it gradually adapted to the social structure of Arsacid Armenia and became completely feudalized. The episcopal hierarchy defined in the Nicaean and post-Nicaean councils remained unknown to the Armenians until the fifth century, when the Armenian Church had already become autocephalous. Nevertheless, the fathers of the Armenian Church accepted the first three ecumenical councils as the supreme authority in matters of dogma, doctrine, and discipline. Decisions concerning doctrinal questions and disciplinary matters were made by the collective body of the ecclesiastical and feudal hierarchy; the first Armenian council of this type met at Šahapivan in 444. The clerics and laymen participating in such councils had the authority to elect (also to try and depose) katholikoi, to excommunicate disobedient bishops, to anathematize heretics, and to draw up new canons.

The hierarchic order before the eighth century comprised the following ranks: katholikos of Greater Armenia, bishops of districts and chorepiskopi, presbyters, deacons, subdeacons, and readers. The katholikos, who presided over the councils, was

ARMENIAN CHURCH, STRUCTURE

the spiritual head of the church. In the fourth century the Arsacid king of Armenia selected him from the members of the house of St. Gregory the Illuminator, and the metropolitan of Caesarea conferred episcopal ordination upon him. His title was "chief bishop" *(glxawor episkopos),* and later "katholikos of Greater Armenia." Even in the fourth century the chief bishop of Armenia had the right to ordain bishops for the districts under his jurisdiction, which originally extended over the Armenia Magna of the period of King Tiridates III (early fourth century).

The relationship between the katholikos and the other bishops was analogous to that between the Arsacid king and the feudal lords. The katholikos was primus inter pares among the bishops and exercised his episcopal authority in Ayrarat, the royal province. After the fall of the Arsacid dynasty in 428, and the expiration of the line of bishops descending from St. Gregory the Illuminator, the office of the chief bishop probably became elective. Its jurisdiction now extended over Persarmenia and certain other districts of the historical Armenia Magna. The katholikoi of fifth-century Armenia also acquired ascendancy over the bishops of Iberia and Albania, and had the right (at least in the sixth century) to apppoint and ordain them bishops over their respective jurisdictions.

From the early sixth century the Armenian katholikoi also championed the cause of the Monophysites in the Sasanian Empire. It was perhaps to sanction their presumed role and extended jurisdiction over territories outside of Persarmenia that the liturgical tradition of ordaining the newly elected katholikoi was introduced into the church ritual; the first evidence for this practice comes from the early seventh century. The practice of anointing the katholikoi probably began in the ninth century. In a document from the same period the katholikos is actually called "the vicar of Christ."

In a geographically, politically, and socially fragmented country such as Armenia, the office of katholikos emerged as the only one vested with universal authority. The presiding princes and royal dynasties of Armenia and Cilicia tried to use the katholikoi to their political advantage, and always sought their presence in or near their capitals. Consequently, the see of St. Gregory, which was located in Vałaršapat until the second half of the fifth century, was transferred from one site to another; it was finally returned to its place of origin in 1441.

Before the eighth century the Armenian church did not recognize any high ecclesiastical ranks other than katholikos and bishop. The reason for this was that the episcopal sees had a feudal, not a territorial, basis. The episcopal jurisdictions were identical with the realms of the major feudal houses, and the bishops were usually members of the feudal families. They were ranked analogously to the feudal hierarchy. Through contacts with the Byzantines, especially in the eighth century, the Armenians acquired the theory that the hierarchy of the church should correspond to that of the nine orders of the celestial hosts. They claimed that the see of St. Gregory was elevated to the patriarchal rank in the fourth century, and that the titles "archbishop" and "metropolitan" given to the katholikoi of Albania and Georgia corresponded to those of the Byzantine hierarchs.

The Abbasid atrocities of the eighth and ninth centuries annihilated most of the Armenian feudal families and their bishops. Despite these adversities the church enjoyed a major revival during the ninth through eleventh centuries. The family bishops were replaced by the priors of important monasteries that were built by the members of the Bagratid royal dynasty, the Siwni, and the Arcruni. Metropolitan bishops began to appear in the new cities of Armenia. The katholikoi exercised greater and more direct control over the new prelates, and even ventured to curb the centrifugal tendencies of the bishops of Siwnikᶜ and Anjewacᶜikᶜ.

Twelfth-century documents indicate that the prelates of the larger cities bore the title "archbishop." Foremost among them was the bishop of the city of Ani, the capital of the Bagratid kingdom. At the end of the thirteenth century, the title "metropolitan" was conferred on the bishops of Siwnikᶜ, who had replaced those of Ani in rank of importance.

The dispersion of the Armenians in the eleventh century, the rise of the Cilician kingdom at the end of the twelfth century, and the existence of numerous communities outside of Armenia were the cause for the emergence of a number of new episcopal jurisdictions that had a territorial basis.

After the fall of the Bagratid kingdom in 1045, bishops who were motivated by personal ambitions and the political ambitions of their patron princes occasionally challenged the authority of the patriarchs and declared themselves katholikoi. Important among the early antikatholikoi were the bishops of Ałtᶜamar, whose patriarchal jurisdiction over the re-

ARMENIAN CHURCH, STRUCTURE

gion of Lake Van was later recognized and sanctioned. After the transfer of the patriarchal see from Cilicia to Vałaršapat in 1441, the Cilicians continued the tradition of electing their own katholikos. The territorial jurisdiction of the katholikoi of Ałtᶜamar and Cilicia was limited, but they both were recognized as katholikoi, and had the right to ordain bishops.

The Armenian bishops of Jerusalem used the title "patriarch" as early as the fourteenth century. In the sixteenth century, the Ottoman Sublime Porte granted the same title to the Armenian bishops of Constantinople, who were also recognized as "ethnarchs" of the Armenian community living under Ottoman rule. Neither of these bishops had the right to ordain bishops or exercise the authority of the katholikoi.

Prior to the ninth century the bishops of the different districts in Armenia had chorepiskopi as their assistants. The function of these clerics was to administer to the spiritual needs of the villages. They may also have served minor feudal families as prelates. The office disappeared in the eighth century.

The higher hierarchic orders in the Armenian church were reserved for the celibate clergy. The priesthood, however, was open to married men. The recommended age for ordination was between thirty and fifty years. The priests belonged to the *azat* class, the lowest-ranking order of noble status. Like the episcopate, the priesthood was hereditary.

In addition to their ecclesiastical duties, the katholikoi, the bishops, and the priests had judicial functions. The katholikos decided major issues concerning kings and the higher nobility, the bishops sat on tribunals within their districts, and the priests tried cases that had to do with the *azat* order and the lower social classes.

The minor ranks of the ecclesiastical hierarchy were originally three: deacon, subdeacon, and reader. The term "psalmist," which is occasionally seen in the sources, was a general designation and not a separate order. Contacts with the Latin West in the twelfth and thirteenth centuries were responsible for the introduction of three additional minor orders: porter, exorcist, and acolyte.

The kings and the nobility participated in the church councils and signed documents along with the bishops. Otherwise, laymen had no legitimate authority in ecclesiastical matters. Christianity in Armenia was in its infancy when the Arsacid kingdom fell and left the church without lay rivals. For that reason caesaropapism was unknown in Armenia. The kings and presiding princes usually tried to impose their will through the legal channel of church councils, which did not always decide in their favor. The Cilician kings occasionally resorted to brute force, but they always tried to conceal their actions under a veil of legitimacy.

Armenian monasticism, which went back to the fourth century, was also part of the church structure. The pre-tenth-century sources speak of different types of institutions: monastery, cloister, hermitage, and so on. Among these the early *vankᶜ* (monasteries), which were usually located within city limits or near places of habitation, appear to have been dominant in church affairs. The celibate priests (*abełay*, a Syriac loanword) living in these institutions rose to the ranks of bishop and katholikos. In the ninth and tenth centuries monasticism underwent important changes. The new monasteries emerged as large, self-contained, feudal complexes that began to play a vital role in the administration of the church, as the centers of episcopal sees. In contrast with the Western tradition, each Armenian monastery was an independent unit under the jurisdiction of a prior, who was either the prelate of the region or subject to the bishop of its diocese. The monasteries were founded on feudal lands; the feudal families financed their construction. The longevity of a monastic institution was dependent on that of its patron family.

In the fourteenth century, with the rise of the monastery of Tatᶜew, an academic hierarchy of fourteen ranks, or degrees, was introduced. The first four ranks conferred on a celibate priest made him a *vardapet* ("teacher" or "doctor"); the remaining ten degrees raised him to the rank of *mec vardapet* (senior *vardapet*). In contrast with the modern practice in the Armenian church, the academic hierarchy remained separate from the ecclesiastical.

The economic structure of the Armenian church was also feudal. The "church lands" were really feudal lands under the control of the family bishops. The lavish donations made by the feudal lords were not really alienated from the family possessions. Like the feudal houses, the episcopal sees, monasteries, and cathedrals all subsisted on an economy dependent on the mandatory labor of serfs who cultivated the "church lands." In addition, the priests collected the tithe (*ptuł* or *ptłi*; literally, "fruit"), which was a head tax paid in kind. The priests were required to make an annual contribution to the bishop of their district and to support the chorepiskopi. Since there

ARMENIAN HELLENIZING SCHOOL

was no separation between church and state, the feudal lords implemented the rules and regulations of the church.

BIBLIOGRAPHY

Koriwn, *VarkᶜMaštocᶜi* (1941); Agatᶜangełos, *History of the Armenians, Robert W. Thomson, trans. (1976); The Teaching of Saint Gregoṙy: An Early Armenian Catechism,* translation and commentary by Robert W. Thomson (1970); Pᶜawstos Buzand, *Patmutᶜiwn Hayocᶜ* (Venice, 1889); *Kanonagirkᶜ Hayocᶜ* vols. I–II (1964–1971); *Girkᶜtᶜłtᶜocᶜ* (1901); Łazar Pᶜarpecᶜi, *Patmutᶜiwn Hayocᶜ* (1904); Yovhannēs Drasxanakertacᶜi, *Šar hayrapetacᶜn hayocᶜ*, in Samuēl Anecᶜi, *Hawakᶜmunkᶜ i grocᶜ patmagracᶜ* (1893); and *Patmutᶜiwn Hayocᶜ* (1912); Movsēs Dasxurancᶜi, *The History of the Caucasian Albanians,* C. J. F. Dowsett, trans. (1961); Maštocᶜ Vardapet, "Tᶜułtᶜ aṙ Gēorg A. Gaṙnecᶜi," in *Ararat* (1902); Maghakᶜia Ōrmanian, *The Church of Armenia* (1955); M. Ormanean, *Atᶜoṙ Hayastaneaycᶜ* [The Armenian See] (1886, repr. 1972); M. Ormanean, *Azgapatum,* vols. I–II (1912–1914); Nikolaĭ Adonts, *Armenia in the Period of Justinian,* trans. with partial revisions, a bibliographical note and appendices by Nina G. Garsoïan (1970); N. Akinean, *Kiwrion Katᶜołikos Vracᶜ* [Kiwrion Katholikos of Georgia] (1910); V. Hacᶜuni, *Katᶜołikosakan ĕntrutᶜiwn ew jeṙnadrutᶜiwn patmutᶜean mēǰ* [The election and ordination of katholikoi in history] (1930); H. Manandyan, *Kᶜnnakan tesutᶜiwn hay žołovrdi patmutᶜyan* [A critical history of the Armenian people], vol. II, part 2 (1960).

KRIKOR H. MAKSOUDIAN

ARMENIAN HELLENIZING SCHOOL (*Yunaban dprocᶜ* in Armenian) is a modern term that scholars use to single out a group of sixth- to eighth-century Armenian translations from Greek and Syriac. Unlike the earlier writings in Armenian, the Hellenizing School comprises works that are technical in nature. The Armenians felt the need for such literature because of the theological, christological, dogmatic, and liturgical issues that arose in their discussions with the Greeks, Georgians, and Syrians. The Hellenizing School was responsible for the creation of a new idiom that served as a vehicle for translating grammatical, rhetorical, theological, philosophical, scientific, and physiological works into Armenian. The distinctive characteristics of the Hellenizing idiom lay in its precision, whereby the translations could remain slavishly faithful to the Greek or Syriac original; its technical vocabulary; its structure, which emulated Greek syntax, and word formation, which was realized by the use of artificial prefixes derived from Armenian prepositions; its introduction of certain morphological changes and innovations.

The Armenian translation of the *Grammar* of Dionysius Thrax is believed to have been the foundation of the new idiom. This work was followed by an adaptation of Aphthonius' and Nicolaus Rhetor's *Progymnasmata,* which bore the title *Girkᶜ Pitoyicᶜ (Peri Chreias).* The studies by Manandean revealed that these works, and the Armenian translations of Philo and Irenaeus, were the earliest texts in the Hellenizing tradition, since their language is less technical and much closer to that of the late fifth- and early sixth-century documents.

Dating the beginning of the Hellenizing School is very difficult, but quite vital for determining the approximate periods of a number of authors and works. Unfortunately, the earlier documents give no hints. The only solution to the problem is Timothius Aelurus' *Against Those Who Say Two Natures.* From the testimony of seventh- and ninth-century sources we know that this work was translated in the 550's. Manandean convincingly demonstrates that the technical idiom used in this treatise employed newly formed prefixes unknown to the translators of the *Grammar* of Dionysius Thrax and the other early translations. From this he correctly concludes that Timothius' book belonged to a group of Hellenizing writings that were later than the *Grammar* of Dionysius, the *Girkᶜ Pitoyicᶜ,* and the translations of the works of Philo and Irenaeus. The other works in the later group were the *Progymnasmata* of Aelius Theon, the *Definitions of Hermes Trismegistos to Asclepius,* the *Isagoge et in Aristotelis Categorias commentarium* of Porphyry, the *Categories* and the *De interpretatione* of Aristotle, a commentary on the *Categories* of Aristotle, and another one on his *De interpretatione,* both of which are attributed to Iamblichus. These translations, according to Manandean, were popular among the Monophysites. A third group—in a style distinct from that of the first two—comprising five dialogues of Plato, four philosophical commentaries attributed to the Neoplatonist David, an anonymous commentary on the *Categories,* the mythological *Scholia* of Pseudo-Nonnus, *De mundo* and *De virtutibus* of Pseudo-Aristotle, Zeno's *De natura,* Eutychius, patriarch of Constantinople's *On the Distinction of Nature and*

Person, and two anonymous commentaries, one on rhetoric and the other on the definitions of philosophy, was apparently the product of an Armenian Chalcedonian milieu.

From the end of the seventh and the first half of the eighth century two names of translators—P^{c}ilon Tirakac^{c}i and Step^{c}anos Siwnec^{c}i (*d.* 735)—are known. Their translations constitute a fourth group in the Hellenizing School: George the Pisidian's *Hexaemeron,* Socrates Scholasticus' *Church History,* Nemesius' *De natura humana,* Cyril of Alexandria's *De incarnatione unigeniti dialogus,* Gregory of Nyssa's *De opificio hominis,* and Dionysius the Areopagite's *De caelesti hierarchia.* The activities of the school probably ceased shortly after the death of Step^{c}anos Siwnec^{c}i.

The Hellenizing School played a major role in the history of Armenian literature by opening the channels of philosophical and theological thought for Armenian intellectuals. Although all the works in the Hellenizing idiom are translations, their terminology was widely used in original writings. The immediate influence of the school was still strong in the twelfth century, and even later.

BIBLIOGRAPHY

Sen Arewšatean, "Płatoni erkeri hayerēn t^{c}argmanut^{c}ean žamanakě," in *Banber matenadarani,* **10** (1971); Yakob Manandean, *Yunaban dproc^{c}ě ew nra zargac^{c}man šrannerě* (1928); and A. N. Muradean, *Yunaban dproc^{c}ě ew nra derě Hayerēni k^{c}erakanakan terminabanut^{c}ean stełcman gorcum* (1971).

KRIKOR H. MAKSOUDIAN

[See also **Dionysius the Pseudo-Areopagite; Philosophy-Theology, Byzantine; Socrates Scholasticus.**]

ARMENIAN LANGUAGE, an independent branch of the Indo-European languages, closely related to the Iranian, Hellenic, and Balto-Slavic languages. Very little is known about its history before the fifth century A.D. Before that time Armenian was influenced by a number of ancient Indo-European, Asianic, and Semitic languages such as Hittite, Old and Middle Persian, Parthian, Greek, Hurrian, Urartian, and Syriac. The influence of the Iranian languages was particularly great, since Armenia had intermittently been both politically and culturally under Persian control from the middle of the fifth century B.C. to the third century A.D.

Armenian was probably introduced into the Armenian highlands as early as the twelfth century B.C., but according to the Greek geographer Strabo, its usage did not become widespread throughout the Armenian plateau until the second century B.C. The language did not possess an alphabet until the fifth century. The court language, which was identical with that of the central provinces, was adopted as the basis of the literary idiom.

The phonetics of Armenian is rich with consonants; Classical Armenian has thirty-six phonemes. It is a highly inflective language with a very complicated system of declensions. The conjugational patterns are comparatively simple; there are only four conjugations (and the vestiges of a fifth), which have a highly defective passive system. One of the characteristics of the earliest literary language is the great abundance of idiomatic expressions that were later replaced by nominal verbs: *patasxani aṙnel* ("to answer"), for example, yielded to *patasxanel.* The grammar of Classical Armenian is very similar to that of Greek and other classical languages, but the rules of syntax are lax and less complicated than those of Greek and Latin.

The works written in the early fifth century are characterized by simplicity, a lack of technical terminology, the complete absence of jargon, and traits of an oral tradition. Yet works written toward the end of that century already betray a greater dependence on the literary tradition. During the sixth and seventh centuries the need to express sophisticated philosophical, theological, and technical concepts forced Armenian intellectuals to seek the necessary linguistic flexibility. Using Greek patterns, the Armenian Hellenophile school created a new idiom that was used not only in translations but also in original works.

While these changes were taking place, the spoken language had gone its separate way, becoming distinct from the literary idiom. By the ninth century there was a marked difference between the vernacular and the written language. A close examination of extant ninth- and tenth-century texts in Classical Armenian reveals that their authors were no longer writing in a living language, but, rather, in a bookish and dead idiom, which remained in use until the nineteenth century. Works in that language, which formed the majority of the corpus of medieval Armenian literature, were accessible only to the learned. Later writers emulated the style of fifth-century writers and translations. Since medieval doctors were required to memorize the entire Bible, they readily drew upon scriptural idioms and expressions. Thus one would find biblical citations and allusions even in nonreligious texts.

The medieval texts are stylistically divided into two categories: those written in a highly rhetorical language and those simple in style. It was fashionable for people of high social and ecclesiastical status and for men of letters to display their erudition and write in flowery language. This style reached its peak in the tenth and eleventh centuries. The simple style was more popular especially among the post-tenth-century historians. Side by side with the classical language, which became identified as *grabar* (literary language), the spoken language was also utilized in writing from the twelfth century. In the course of several centuries the vernacular had changed considerably; the phonetic structure, morphology, and syntax of Armenian had undergone major changes. Agglutinative suffixes had replaced certain case endings, and new words had entered the vocabulary. Some of these were native words that had been hitherto unrecorded in literature, but there were several others that were loan words from Arabic, Turkish, Modern Persian, and French.

A large number of inscriptions, colophons, medical texts, historical works, and poems were written in this idiom, which is now identified as Middle Armenian. Unlike its classical ancestor, this language is based not on one but, rather, on several dialects. Middle Armenian lacks uniformity; dialectial variations are detectable in the texts. The time span of Middle Armenian is also a matter of controversy, since scholars disagree about the date of its termination and the beginning of Modern Armenian. For example, the Middle Armenian texts from the Armenian kingdom of Cilicia are all in the same dialect and date from the twelfth to fourteenth centuries, but elsewhere we find a variety of dialects and a time span extending beyond the fourteenth century.

The fourteenth through seventeenth centuries present a chaotic period in linguistic matters. Adding to the confusion of idioms and dialects, Roman Catholic missionaries and their Armenian followers tried to create a new idiom based on Latin grammar and produced several translations and original works in this style. The Latinophile school, however, made no impact on the Armenian language. Soon after its activities had begun, the Armenians, both in Armenia and abroad, either adopted the modern dialects or returned to the classical language.

The earliest evidence for Modern Armenian dates from the fifteenth century, and its usage was already widespread in the seventeenth century. Like Middle Armenian, early Modern Armenian was not based on a single dialect.

BIBLIOGRAPHY

Hrach^{c}eay Acharhian, *Hayoc^{c} lezui patmut^{c}iwn,* 2 vols. (1940–1951).

KRIKOR H. MAKSOUDIAN

[See also **Armenian Alphabet; Armenian Hellenizing School; Armenian Literature.**]

ARMENIAN LITERATURE.

THE EARLY PERIOD

The origins of the Armenian literary tradition go back to the early fifth century, when the vardapet Maštoc^{c} invented a phonetic alphabet for Armenian. Assisted by his colleague Bishop Sahak of Armenia and his students, Maštoc^{c} translated many of the writings of the Syriac and Greek fathers. The earliest translations (*ca.* 406–440) comprised biblical, hermeneutical, patristic, canonical, martyrological, and liturgical texts that were used for teaching and missionary purposes. The language of these works appears to be very close to the spoken idiom of the fifth century; it is relatively uninfluenced by either Greek or Syriac. These early Armenian translations are of great value since the originals of some have not survived. Several others are based on Greek and Syriac originals that are earlier than the orthodox editions that have reached us.

Besides the Armenian versions of the Septuagint and the New Testament, the list of the earliest, or "Golden Age," translations includes: the Euthaliana, the *Prologus galeatus* of St. Jerome, a spurious work attributed to Epiphanius of Salamis, many of the commentaries and homilies of St. John Chrysostom, nine homilies of Bishop Severian of Gabala, fifteen discourses of Eusebius of Emessa, some of the works of Cyril of Alexandria, Cyril of Jerusalem's *Catechetical Lectures,* Basil of Caesarea's *In Hexaemeron* and his *Divine Liturgy,* several works of Evagrius of Pontus, Eusebius of Caesarea's *Chronicon,* his *Ecclesiastical History,* and so on, the *Chronicon* and another work by Hippolytus of Rome, Gregory Thaumaturgus' (the Wonder Worker's) *Discourse on the Nativity of Christ,* the letter of Patriarch Proclus of Constantinople to the Armenians, the letters of Bishop Acacius of Melitene to the Armenians and to

Bishop Sahak of Armenia, Aristides of Athens' *Apology,* most of the works of Ephraim the Syrian, the homilies of Aphraates, Bishop Zenobius of Amida's four homilies, Bishop Aithallah of Edessa's discourse, five of the Pseudepigrapha, the canons of Nicaea and the local councils, the *Lives of the Egyptian Fathers,* the *Lives of the Persian Martyrs,* and approximately thirty saints' lives.

The numbers of original works from the same period are very limited. The short list includes the canons of the Armenian Council of Šahapivan (444), the letters of Bishop Sahak of Armenia to Patriarch Proclus and Bishop Acacius of Melitene, another letter from Eznik of Kołb to Vardapet Maštoc^c explaining the theology of the Council of Ephesus, and a fragment of a treatise on divination attributed to Vardapet Maštoc^c. Besides these, there are four major works from the mid fifth century that are stylistically related to the earliest translations. The first is the *Life of Maštoc^c* by Koriwn, who was his pupil and close associate. The life has the structure of a work that belongs to the hagiographical genre; it is, nevertheless, an important historical source on the fifth century. Koriwn's work is also useful for the cultural history of Transcaucasia.

The History of the Armenians by Agat^{c}angełos is a composite work comprising hagiographical, homiletic, catechetical, historical, and epic elements, which the otherwise unknown author has pieced together in order to narrate the story of the conversion of the Armenian people to Christianity. Related to this work is the now-lost life of St. Gregory the Illuminator, which has reached us in several non-Armenian versions. Another important historical work is the *Buzandaran Patmut^{c}iwnk^c* (Epic Stories) by P^{c}awstos Buzand, which is a major source on fourth-century Armenia. It is a compilation of historical, epic, hagiographical, and even liturgical elements.

The last work from the mid fifth century is a treatise by Eznik of Kołb. There is much controversy about the nature of this work: scholars have variously suggested that it is a refutation of sects, a treatise on the nature of God, a treatise on the problem of good and evil, and a philosophical treatise on free will. Eznik's work is a mosaic of citations and excerpts from the works of the early Fathers, which the author has integrated into a unified Christian thesis on free will.

Armenian translations and original works from the second half of the fifth and the early decades of the sixth century still reveal an Armenian style that is free of heavy Greek influence. The language of

these works lacks some of the oral qualities that are characteristic of the earlier literature; the new generation of writers was removed from the oral tradition, and learned the literary language in school. Among the important translations of this period are: Pseudo-Callisthenes' *History of Alexander,* the writings of Gregory Nazianzus, Hesychius' *Commentary on the Book of Job,* the Lectionary of Jerusalem, the lives of St. Anthony and St. Macarius, the epistles of St. Ignatius, St. Nilus of Ancyra's *Sententiae,* some of the writings of Athanasius, Zeno's *Henotikon,* the Edict of Anastasius I, and the spurious correspondence between Acacius of Constantinople and Peter Mongus (the Fuller).

The most important writer of this period is the historian Łazar P^{c}arpec^{c}i, whose work covers the period of Armenian history from 387 to about 485. The author was a priest and a pupil of Ałan Arcruni, who in turn was a pupil of Maštoc^c. Łazar was also a schoolmate of Vahan Mamikonean, the marzban (governor) of Armenia (485–505), and so he was very favorably disposed toward the Mamikonean clan. Despite this, his history is a very reliable source on the antecedents and aftereffects of the great anti-Sassanian rebellion of 451. P^{c}arpec^{c}i's work is a straightforward and unpretentious narrative of the contemporary events that the author has either witnessed in person or verified from reliable sources. It is probably the earliest example of classical historiography in Armenian. From the same period we also have three discourses by Katholikos Yovhannēs Mandakuni (478–490). The first of these is on lent, the second on the Trinity, and the third on martyrs.

The sixth century marks the beginning of the theological disputes with the Duophysites. Most of the literature of the period consists of correspondence that has been salvaged in the *Book of Letters (Girk^c T^{c}łt^{c}oc^c).* Among these are the two letters of Katholikos Babgēn (490–516) to the Persian Monophysites, Katholikos Nersēs II of Bagrevand (548–557) to the Syriac Bishop Abdišoy, Katholikos Yovhannēs Gabełean (558–574) to the bishops of Siwnik^c and Albania, Bishop John of Jerusalem to Katholikos Abas of Albania, and Macarius II of Jerusalem to Bishop Vrt^{c}anēs of Siwnik^c. The letter of Bishop Grigor of the Arcruni (*ca.* 564) is about the liturgy; it is addressed to the Armenians and urges them to celebrate the Presentation of the Lord on 14 February.

From the early or middle decades of the same century we have a collection of twenty-three homilies that bear the title Yačaxapatum Čaṙk^c. Tradition at-

ARMENIAN LITERATURE

tributes them to St. Gregory the Illuminator; but the doctrine of the Holy Spirit, the reference to the fall of the Armenian Arsacid dynasty (428), and the citation of a canon of the Council of Chalcedon (451) leave no doubt that the work could not have been written before the first decade of the sixth century, when the Armenians first learned of the Councils of Chalcedon and Constantinople. The first two discourses in the collection deal with the doctrine of the Trinity; the remaining twenty-one are about moral issues such as free will, fasting, and so on.

From the fourth quarter of the sixth century we have a very important historical work, Ełišē's *On Vardan and the Armenian War.* The author, whose identity is not known, based his history on that of Łazar Pᶜarpecᶜi, but his purpose is quite different. Ełišē's work is a discourse of epic proportions, seeking to prove that betraying the covenant is destructive on a personal, national, and universal scale.

The sixth century is also well known for the early effects and development of the Armenian Hellenizing School, which continued its activities throughout the seventh century and into the eighth. The language of the fifth- and sixth-century Armenian writers was not sophisticated enough to express with precision philosophical, scientific, theological, and physiological concepts, since Armenian lacked terminology of such nature. A new idiom and a style based on the Greek grammarians and rhetoricians made it possible for the Armenian intellectuals to translate technical works from Greek and Syriac. An early contemporary of the school and a major theologian of the period was Bishop Petros of Siwnikᶜ, some of whose writings have survived, such as his *Discourse on Faith,* his *Discourse on the Birth of Christ* (in fragments), and his *Eulogy on the Holy Theotokos.*

At the end of the sixth and beginning of the seventh centuries the epistolary genre once again began to thrive as a result of the schism between the Armenian and the Georgian churches. The *Book of Letters* contains the correspondence between Bishop Movsēs of Cᶜurtaw and Vrtᶜanēs Kᶜertᶜoł, the *locum tenens* of the Armenian katholikos, and the letters exchanged between the katholikoi Abraham of Armenia and Kiwrion of Georgia. There are also several other letters by Prince Smbat Bagratuni, the viceroy of Hyrcania, Sormen Stratelates of western or Byzantine Armenia, Grigor Kᶜertᶜoł, and Bishop Matᶜusała of Siwnikᶜ.

In the early decades of the seventh century, Katholikos Komitas (617–622) wrote a hymn dedicated to the virgin Hṙipᵓsimē and her companions, who had been martyred at the end of the third century. The katholikos had commissioned the construction of a church over the original martyrium, and probably wrote the hymn on the occasion of this church's dedication. This is the earliest hymn in Armenian in the tradition of the Byzantine *kontakion.* Dawtᶜak, a contemporary of Komitas, is the author of a dirge on the death of Prince Jewanšēr. This is the first poem in Armenian on a nonreligious topic.

Among the prominent writers of the seventh century were Yovhannēs Mayragomecᶜi, Tᶜēodoros Kᶜrtᶜenawor, and possibly Mambrē Vercanoł, who are authors of homilies and discourses. Vrtᶜanēs Kᶜertᶜoł, who lived at the beginning of the century, was a theologian and the author of the earliest treatise on image worship. The major historian of the period is Sebēos, whose work covers the sixth and seventh centuries, from 500 to 662. Sebēos has continued the historiographical tradition of Łazar Pᶜarpecᶜi; his work is important for the history of seventh-century Iran and Byzantium.

The greatest intellectual figure of the seventh century was the mathematician, scientist, and astronomer Anania Širakacᶜi. According to some scholars, he is also the author of the Armenian *Geography of the World (Ašxarhacᶜoycᶜ),* which is based on the works of late classical geographers. The last important writer of the period was Katholikos Sahak of Jorapᶜor (677–703), who wrote discourses, hymns, canons, and theological works. The seventh century proved to be a very productive period: although Armenia was under the nominal rule of first the Byzantines and then the Arabs, the country was actually ruled by the Armenian presiding princes, who promoted cultural activities. This activity continued until the middle of the following century, even though the semiautonomous political status of Armenia had already changed in the 690's and the prevailing conditions were in no way favorable to the advancement of learning.

The leading intellectual figures of the eighth century were the products of the last two decades of the seventh century. Foremost among them was Katholikos Yovhannēs of Ōjnecᶜi, who is the author of theological and liturgical treatises and the first editor of the Armenian canon book. Among his contemporaries were the following: Vardapet Xosrovik, author of a number of theological discourses that deal with the question of the corruptibility of the body of Christ; Grigoris, the chorepiskopos of Aršarunikᶜ, whose commentary on the Armenian lectionary is

 ARMENIAN LITERATURE

still extant; Bishop Movsēs of Siwnikᶜ, who wrote several hymns and a few discourses; and Bishop Stepᶜanos of Siwnikᶜ, the pupil and successor of the latter, who continued his education in Athens and became the most important literary figure of the eighth century. Stepᶜanos was responsible for introducing the tradition of the Byzantine canon into the Armenian hymnal. Among his literary works are several hymns, translations, correspondence with the Byzantine patriarch Germanus, biblical commentaries, homilies, and so on. Stepᶜanos' productive life was cut short in 735; he was killed by a woman of loose morals whom he had admonished. His sister Sahakduxt is the first known woman writer in Armenian; only one of her hymns has survived.

The eighth century is the *terminus ad quem* of a series of hagiographical works that narrate the early evangelization of Armenia by the Apostles Thaddaeus and Bartholomew and their followers. The end of this century or the beginning of the next is also the *terminus ad quem* of the celebrated *History* of Movsēs Xorenacᶜi, the national historian of Armenia. This work covers the history of the Armenian people from the time of the Creation to the end of the 430's. It is really a pretentious genealogy of feudal Armenia. Armenian tradition has assigned it to the mid fifth century, but modern Western scholarship is not at ease with that date, since there are a number of citations in it from post-fifth-century authors and translations. The anachronisms and especially the social order described in the work suggest the last quarter of the eighth century as the most logical date; but assigning it to the period between 750 and 850 presents a serious problem. This was the most barren period of Armenian cultural history; the Abbasids had annihilated most of the Armenian feudal families, the family bishoprics, and the monastic schools. In this atmosphere it is not conceivable how (and for whom) one could compose a sophisticated work like the *History.* The earliest references to it are found in the late-ninth-century historians, who accept it as an established and authoritative source.

THE BAGRATID PERIOD

The revival of literary activity in Armenia was made possible only after 860, when the power of the caliphate had already started to wane and Prince Ašot Bagratuni had emerged as the master of Armenia and later of the rest of Transcaucasia. The epistolary genre was the first to flourish, as a result of the revival of relations with Constantinople. Some of the correspondence between the Armenians and Patriarch Photius have survived. In his history, Katholikos Yovhannēs Drasxanakertecᶜi preserved some of the letters of his predecessor Katholikos Maštocᶜ (*d.* 898); another letter by Maštocᶜ has been preserved elsewhere. Of major importance is the correspondence between Yovhannēs Drasxanakertecᶜi and the Byzantines; this comprises two letters, one by Yovhannēs and the other by the patriarch Nicholas Mysticus, which were written about 915. There are other letters from the tenth and eleventh centuries, notably those of Katholikos Anania Mokacᶜi (*d.* 965), of Vardapets Anania Narekacᶜi and Grigor Narekacᶜi, and of Samuēl Kamrǰajorecᶜ. This literary genre, however, was greatly developed in the mid eleventh century by Grigor Magistros (*d.* 1059), whose collection of letters includes over eighty documents on religious, theological, literary, scholarly, philosophical, and other learned topics.

The Bagratid period is well known for its fine historians. The first and the most unusual figure among these was Prince Šapuh (ninth century), who wrote about the life and times of King Ašot I (884–889). His work, which was written in the vernacular (the spoken as opposed to the literary language), has unfortunately not survived. The great development in this genre is marked by the growing interest in antiquarianism, universal histories, and family genealogy. The history of Yovhannēs Drasxanakertecᶜi is a unique document, since it is based on the recollections of a man of high position who was responsible for shaping Bagratid policy. Stepᶜanos Tarawnecᶜi Asołik's *Universal History* is our major source on the tenth century. Bishop Uxtanēs wrote a history of the Armeno-Georgian schism, and Presbyter Mesrop compiled a biographical history of St. Nersēs, the fourth-century bishop of Armenia. The pretentious histories in the tradition of Agatᶜangełos' and Movsēs Xorenacᶜi's works are also well represented.

The history of Zenob Glak is about the Christianization of Armenia in the early fourth century, and Yovhannēs Mamikonean's work, which is closely related to it, is a compilation of the legendary tales and epics about the Mamikonean princes of the sixth and seventh centuries. Both works are connected with the monastery of St. John the Precursor in Tarawn (Muş), which became the religious center of western Armenia in the mid tenth century. Another history of the same nature, wrongly attributed to Šapuh Bagratuni, contains legends about the Arcruni princes of Vaspurakan. The Arcrunis, however, also had genuine historians—Tᶜovma (Thomas) Arcruni and Tᶜovma Continuatus—narrate their family history. The history of the Bagratid family was written by Yovhannēs Kozeṙn in the eleventh century; only a few fragments of this work survive. The *Primary History* or *Genealogy* of Armenia, which is now attached to the *History* of Sebēos, was also composed in the eleventh century; it seems to be based on a lost earlier document. Another compilation of the late Bagratid period is a history of the Albanians attributed to Movsēs Dasxuranc^{c}i; it is an uneven and composite work, in which some sections are primary sources and others are historically worthless legends, tales, anachronistic details, and the like. Aristakēs Lastiverc^{c}i is the historian of the decline and fall of the Bagratid kingdom of Ani; his work covers the period from 1001 to 1072.

The major poet of the Bagratid period was Grigor Narekac^{c}i, a monk who lived in the monastery of Narek (*d.* 1003), whose *Book of Lamentations* and hymns are among the great literary accomplishments of Armenian literature. The *Book of Lamentations* contains ninety-five discourses in a continuous dialogue between man and God. The hero of the book is man, faced with the choice of eternal damnation or salvation. The pathos in the work arises from the peculiar situation of man, who is made out of flesh and is therefore too weak to make the right choice.

Other genres of literature also flourished in the Bagratid period: Katholikos Zak^{c}aria of Jag (*d.* 876) wrote several homilies; Prince Hamam Bagratuni was the author of biblical commentaries and a scholium on grammar; Xosrov Anjewac^{c}i (tenth century) was renowned for his commentaries on the Holy Offices and the Divine Liturgy; Anania Narekac^{c}i wrote a number of theological treatises; Samuēl Kamrǰajorec^{c}i edited the Tawnapatčaṙ, a collection of discourses arranged according to the order of the church calendar; Anania Sanahnec^{c}i (eleventh century) produced several discourses and commentaries and an important theological treatise against the Duophysites; Grigor Magistros translated some of the dialogues of Plato; and Yovsēp^{c} of Constantinople finished his translation of the Greek synaxary in the 990's (a similar collection of Armenian saints' lives had already been compiled and arranged at an earlier date by Prior Gagik of the monastery of Atom in Anjewac^{c}ik^{c}).

LATE MEDIEVAL PERIOD

After the Seljuk invasions in the middle of the eleventh century, Armenian literature continued to flourish in northeastern Armenia, where the great monasteries were located, and in Cilicia and its neighboring regions. The establishment of an Armenian kingdom in Cilicia in 1198 and the emergence of the Zak^{c}arids in northeastern Armenia greatly enhanced the spread of learning and cultural activity among the Armenians.

At the end of the eleventh century, the traditional historiography was abandoned, and it was replaced with chronicles, such as the works of Matt^{c}ēos Uṙhayec^{c}i (Matthew of Edessa), Grigor the priest, Samuēl of Ani, and Mxit^{c}ar Goš, all twelfth-century writers. The major representatives of that genre in the thirteenth century were Mxit^{c}ar Ayrivanec^{c}i, Mxit^{c}ar Anec^{c}i, Smbat Sparapet, the unknown author of the *Royal Cilician Chronicle,* and Het^{c}um Koṙikosc^{c}i. Besides these, several minor chroniclers flourished, and the genre remained alive as late as the nineteenth century. There was a revival of historiography in the thirteenth century. The authors whose works have survived are Vardan Arewelc^{c}i, Kirakos Arewelc^{c}i or Ganjakec^{c}i, Grigor Aknerc^{c}i, and Bishop Step^{c}anos Orbelean. After the work of Step^{c}anos, historiography came to an inglorious halt: the attempts of Grigor Xlat^{c}ec^{c}i and T^{c}ovma Mecop^{c}ec^{c}i in the fifteenth century represent a sad commentary on the state of that genre. The learned vardapets wrote short chronicles and colophons instead of histories.

Poetry fared very well after the eleventh century, as it became gradually secularized and the spoken language replaced the classical idiom. The most influential and prolific poet of the twelfth century was Nersēs Šnorhali, who was katholikos from 1166 to 1173. Nersēs is the author of several epics, songs, hymns, and religious poems. The historical epic and the lamentation with political undertones that he developed were quite popular with other poets of the late twelfth and thirteenth centuries, such as Katholikos Grigor Tłay, Step^{c}anos Orbelean, Xač^{c}atur Keč^{c}aṙec^{c}i, and Vahram Rabuni.

Xač^{c}atur Keč^{c}aṙec^{c}i was perhaps the earliest Armenian poet to write verses with moral reflections that are based on episodes from Pseudo-Callisthenes' life of Alexander. This genre of poetry was later developed by Bishop Zak^{c}aria of Gnunik^{c} and Grigoris Ałt^{c}amarc^{c}i, in the sixteenth century. Another thirteenth-century poet, who wrote didactic verse of a philosophical and moralistic nature, is Yovhannēs of Erznka. His contemporary, Constantine of Erznka, was the first Armenian poet to be infatuated by nature and physical beauty. Another contemporary, Yovhannēs T^{c}lkuranc^{c}i, was the first to celebrate physical love. One of the greatest poets of the century was Frik, whose poems are about social inequality, poverty, old age, and suffering due to foreign oppression.

Secular poetry continued in the form of popular poetry. In the fifteenth and sixteenth centuries erotic poems became quite popular; a corpus of these appeared in the sixteenth century under the name of Nahapet K^{c}uč^{c}ak. Structurally related to the erotic poems are the laments of the emigrant workers, which express the emotional, spiritual, and physical torments of homesick migrants. The nonsecular mystical poetry never again reached the level attained by Grigor Narekac^{c}i.

The post-Bagratid period witnessed the floruit of hagiography, scriptural hermeneutics, scholia on philosophical and grammatical works, medicine, science, law, and more. Among the major literary figures were Yovhannēs Sarkawag (twelfth century), who wrote calendrical, mathematical, poetical, and religious works; Mxit^{c}ar Herac^{c}i (twelfth century), the author of a medical treatise; Połos Tarawnec^{c}i, Nersēs Šnorhali, and Nersēs Lambronac^{c}i, who were twelfth-century theologians; Dawit^c Alawkayordi, author of a penitential; Mxit^{c}ar Goš, who codified Armenian law in the twelfth century; Smbat Sparapet (thirteenth century), who also prepared a lawbook; Vardan Aygekc^{c}i (thirteenth century), who compiled fables; Grigor Abasean (thirteenth century), who prepared a bibliography; scholiasts Aristakes Rhetor (thirteenth century), Vardan Arewelc^{c}i, Vahram Rabuni, Esai Nč^{c}ec^{c}i, and Yovhannēs Orotnec^{c}i (thirteenth to fourteenth centuries); and Grigor Tat^{c}ewac^{c}i, who was the last prominent theologian of the fourteenth century.

Armenian cultural life suffered greatly as a result of the waning of the Cilician kingdom and the disintegration of feudal society in greater Armenia in the fourteenth and fifteenth centuries. The harassment of the nomadic Turkoman elements in Armenia forced the sedentary population to migrate. The important monastic schools in the northeast and Cilicia were closed; only a small number of monasteries located in the southern and western parts of greater Armenia could keep their schools open. The centers of cultural life were transferred to western Asia Minor and parts of Europe where there were Armenian communities. The impact of the Western cultures was so great on the Armenians that they started to print books in 1512. Despite this disintegration, the influence of the medieval literary tradition persisted as late as the nineteenth century.

BIBLIOGRAPHY

Hakob Anasyan, *Haykakan Matenagitut^{c}yun* [Armenian Bibliography], 2 vols. (1959–1976). A. Łazikean, *Haykakan Nor Matenagitut^{c}iwn* [New Armenian Bibliography], 2 vols. (1909–1912). Manuk Abełean, *Hayoc^c hin grakanut^{c}ean patmut^{c}iwn* [History of Ancient Armenian Literature], 2 vols. (1944–1946). C. J. F. Dowsett, "Armenian Historiography," in *Historians of the Middle East,* Bernard Lewis and P. M. Holt, eds. (1962); Franz N. Finck, "Geschichte der armenischen Litteratur," in *Geschichte der Christlichen Litteraturen des Orients* (1907); Vahan Inglizian, *Die armenische Literatur* (1963); Josef Karst, *La littérature arménienne* (1937); Joseph Muyldermans, "Historiographie arménienne," in *Le Muséon,* 76 (1963); Karl Friedrich Neumann, *Versuch einer Geschichte der armenischen Literatur, nach den Werken der Mechitaristen* (1836); Félix Nève, *L'Arménie chrétienne et sa littérature* (1886); Karekin Sarkissian, *A Brief Introduction to Armenian Christian Literature* (1960); Placido Sukias Somalian, *Quadro della storia letteraria di Armenia* (1829); Hiranth Thorossian, *Histoire de la littérature arménienne* (1951).

KRIKOR H. MAKSOUDIAN

[See also **Agat^{c}angełos; Anania Širakac^{c}i; Aristakēs Lastivertc^{c}i; Armenian Hellenizing School; Ełišē; Eznik of Kołb; Frik; Grigor Magistros; Henotikon; Koriwn; Lazar P^{c}arpec^{c}i; Mesrop; Nersēs Lambronac^{c}i; Nersēs IV Snorhali; Nersēs II of Bagrevand; P^{c}awstos Buzand; Sebēos; Smbat Sparapet.**]

ARMENIAN MUSLIM EMIRATES. The history of the Muslim principalities established on the territory of historic Armenia and its immediate vicinity should be divided into three major periods: 1) The Arab emirates of the ninth and first half of the tenth centuries; 2) the period named "the Iranian interlude" by Vladimir Minorskii in the tenth and early eleventh centuries; 3) the gradual Turkization of the area beginning in the mid eleventh century, punctuated in the mid thirteenth and late fourteenth centuries by the Mongol invasions, and culminating in the control of most of the area by the Ottomans at the end of the fifteenth.

Although the Arabs first appeared in Armenia in 640 and dominated the country by the end of the century, they either raided or established military garrisons in such key cities as Karin, Manazkert,

ARMENIAN MUSLIM EMIRATES

Xlat^{c}, and Arčēš, which served as fortresses in the wars against Byzantium and the Khazars. Massive Arab migrations and settlements do not seem to antedate the reign of the Abbasid caliph Harun al-Rashid (786–809). The earliest colonists may have been drawn from the southern Yemenite tribes, but the northern tribes from Mesopotamia, particularly the Bakr and Qays ^{c}Aylān subgroups, soon dominated. Among the former were the Shaybānids of Ałjnik^{c}, who supplied several governors (or *ostikans*) in the ninth century, and the Zurārids of Arzn; the latter included the Qaysites of Apahunik^{c}, the ^{c}Uthmānids of Berkri, and perhaps the early Djaḥḥāfids.

Benefiting from the weakening of the great Armenian families in the southwestern provinces and occasionally gaining their lands by intermarriage, the Arab chieftains began to carve principalities for themselves in the area. The Djaḥḥāfids, who seem to have been primarily adventurers with no fixed center in Tarōn and Apahunik^{c}, and the Zurārids of Arzn, who assimilated to the point of becoming crypto-Christians, both vanished before the end of the ninth century.

The great punitive expedition of Bughā, followed by the deportation of the leading Armenian princes to Samarra in 855, laid the base for the consolidation and expansion of the Arab emirates. The Shaybānids of Ałjnik^{c} spread to Datwan, on the west shore of Lake Van, in the 860's and remained there until the first quarter of the tenth century; a secondary branch ruled in Sharvān until the eleventh century. The Qaysites succeeded their Sulaym kinsmen in Apahunik^{c} north of the lake and from their center at Manazkert acquired the coastal cities of Xlat^{c}, Arčēš, and Arckē from local emirs. They threatened the Bagratids of Tarōn (present-day Taraun), and by 902 had absorbed the related emirate of the ^{c}Uthmānids of Berkri, thus forming a solid hereditary principality that maintained itself for a century.

In the northwest, Karin/Erzurum was governed by local emirs until its reconquest by Byzantium in 949. To the south the Hamdanids of Mosul and Aleppo threatened Ałjnik^{c} and the Qaysites in the second half of the tenth century. The Armenian capital of Dwin was disputed by the Bagratid kings with various Muslim rulers. The last Arab emirate was created early in the tenth century at Gołt^{c}n in the mid-Araks valley southeast of Dwin, and spread rapidly to nearby Naχčawan. As a result of these settlements the demographic pattern of the Armenian highlands began to alter, although the Arab writer al-Muqaddasī records that Christians still formed the majority of the population at Dwin in the tenth century.

The emirates soon abandoned their early allegiance to the caliphate, and were technically the vassals of the Armenian king after he received the title "prince of princes" from the caliph; as such they shared the interests of local Armenian princes, with whom they allied themselves on numerous occasions. Nevertheless, their alien presence was highly disruptive to the Bagratid kingdom. In addition to their intensification of the endemic civil war of the period by their attempts to extend their domains, they shared the centrifugal tendencies of their Armenian neighbors and prevented the creation of a unified state. The failure of the Bagratids to hold the central capital of Dwin and the presence of Arab wedges splitting Armenian territories irremediably weakened the realm. The settlement of emirs primarily in commercial centers, relegating the Armenian nobles to the isolated, mountainous countryside, gave a Muslim pattern to the layout of Armenian cities and affected their socioeconomic development.

Beginning in the tenth century, new Iranian elements, primarily from Azerbaijan, began to infiltrate into Armenia as mercenaries. They were mainly Daylamites from south of the Caspian, and Kurds. The two groups fought each other for the control of Azerbaijan, and also for Dwin, which passed back and forth in the tenth century from Daylamite to Kurdish hands under the Sallārid, Shaddādid, and Rawwādid dynasties. From the 970's the great Kurdish dynasties began to settle in. The Marwānids took over the lands of the Qaysites, crushed by Byzantium, and those of Hamdānids in Ałjnik^{c} and also the provinces northwest of Lake Van, with Manazkert and Xlat^{c}, which they held until the end of the eleventh century. The Ayyubid ancestors of the great Saladin settled near Dwin. Finally the Shaddādids seized Ganjak in 970/971, soon reached Bardha^{c}a/Partaw, ruled Dwin from 1022, and bought Ani in 1072.

The middle of the eleventh century marked a watershed in the history of Armenia and most of Asia Minor. The Sājids, a Turkic dynasty, had already ruled Azerbaijan between 889 and 929, seized Dwin, and dealt heavy blows to the Armenian Bagratids; but the Turkization of the entire region began in earnest with the destruction of the Armenian principalities and most of the earlier emirates by the Byzantine reconquest, followed almost immediately by the Seljuk invasions. Of the former Arab and Kurdish dynasties, only the Shaddādids maintained themselves at Ani until the end of the twelfth century, although they were swept from Dwin and their holdings in Azerbaijan. With the collapse of the Great Seljuk state after the death of Malik Shāh in 1092, a chaotic constellation of Turkoman emirs fought each other and tried to cling to Armenian and border territories that often were limited to a single city. Dānishmendids in central Asia Minor; Seljuks at Konya, Melitene, Tokat, Sivas, and other cities; Artuqids in Xarpert and Diyarbakir; Saltuqids in Erzurum; Mangujaqids in Kamaχ and Erzincan; Shāh-Armans in Xlat^{c}; Ildenizids in Azerbaijan—the twelfth century presents a picture of almost hopeless confusion.

Gradually, during the first part of the thirteenth century, the Seljuks of Rum reunified Asia Minor, annexing Artuqid territories as well as Erzincan and Erzurum, though not northwestern Armenia around Ani and Dwin, which was held by the Zak^{c}arids. But at the moment of Seljuk apogee, as they reached from the Mediterranean to the upper Tigris and from western Asia Minor to Mt. Ararat, they were totally routed by the Mongols at Köse Daği in 1243. A Mongol protectorate was established over Armenia and Asia Minor, while the Ilkhanid dynasty ruled Iran from Tabriz on the Armenian border. The Seljuk sultanate split asunder and steadily declined as Turkoman dissidents revived and new emirates appeared. The disastrous raids of Tamerlane at the turn of the fifteenth century and the subsequent wars of the Black (Qara-Qoyunlu) and White Sheep (Aq-Qoyunlu) Turkomans reduced all of eastern Asia Minor, including Armenia, to anarchy until the final Ottoman conquest at the end of the fifteenth century.

Not all the Muslim emirates were hostile to the Christians. As noted, early Arab chieftains married Armenian princesses and often collaborated with their Christian neighbors against other emirs or the representatives of the caliph. Later Armenian sources praise the benevolence of the Seljuk, Malik Shah, and Shāh Armans, whom they call "philo-Christians." Nevertheless, the presence of Arab emirates in Bagratid Armenia destroyed all attempts to create a centralized state, and they served simultaneously as advance bases for Muslim attacks from outside. The subsequent failure of the Seljuks to create a stable state resulted in constant warfare between the Turkoman groups that was aggravated by the Mongol invasions. The long anarchy of the twelfth through fifteenth centuries led to a total economic and demographic transformation: from a Christian, Armenian, settled and partially urban world to one that was Muslim, Turkish, and largely nomadic.

BIBLIOGRAPHY

The main study on the emirates in the Bagratid period is Aram Ter Ghewondyan, *The Arab Emirates in Bagratid Armenia,* Nina G. Garsoïan, trans. (1976), which gives a detailed discussion of the various sources. See also his "Dwin (Dvine) sous les Salarides," in *Revue des études arméniennes,* n.s. **1** (1964); and "Chronologie de la ville de Dvin (Duin) aux 9ᵉ et 11ᵉ siècles," *ibid.,* n.s. **2** (1965); J. Laurent, *L'Arménie entre Byzance et l'Islam depuis la conquête arabe jusqu'en 886,* rev. ed. by Marius Canard (1980).

On the "Iranian interlude" see Vladimir Minorskii, "The Caucasian Vassals of Marzubān in 344/955," in *Bulletin of the School of Oriental and African Studies,* **15,** no. 3 (1953); *Studies in Caucasian History* (1953); and *A History of Sharvān and Darband in the 10th–11th Centuries* (1958).

On the last period see Claude Cahen, *Pre-Ottoman Turkey* (1968); Speros Vryonis, *The Decline of Medieval Hellenism in Asia Minor* (1971); and John E. Woods, *The Aqquyunlu: Clan, Confederation, Empire* (1976).

A number of chronological lists of Muslim dynasties, with Muslim dating, are in Eduard K. M. von Zambaur, *Manuel de généalogie et de chronologie pour l'histoire de l'Islam,* 2 vols. (1927; repr. 1955); and a few in the more accessible Stanley Lane-Poole, *The Mohammadan Dynasties* (1925).

NINA G. GARSOÏAN

[See also **Arčēš; Arcn; Aq-Qoyunlu/White Sheep; Bardha^{c}a/Partaw; Seljuks; Theodosiopolis.**]

ARMENIAN PENTARCHY (Armenian satrapies or *gentes*), a group of ten Armenian districts ruled by five princely houses as *civitates foederatae* within the Roman–Byzantine Empire. The territory of the Pentarchy was originally a part of the Armenian Orontid kingdom of Sophenē absorbed by Greater Armenia about 95 B.C. Under Tigran the Great (95–55 B.C.) the former kingdom, minus the districts of Akilisenē (Ekeleac^{c}) and Odomantis (Oromantis?), was organized as the Syrian March, one of the four military viceroyalties defending Armenia from for-

ARMENIAN PENTARCHY

eign invasion—in the case of Sophenē, from Syria and Osrhoenē.

The chief fortress and center of the march was apparently Angł or Karkathiokerta (Hittite, Ingalawa; Armenian, Karkatʿiakert), which in the Arsacid period was one of the royal castles of the Armenian kings housing both Arsacid royal treasures and the tombs of the Orontid kings of Sophenē. Another stronghold was Benabila (Armenian, Bnabeḷ) in Greater Sophenē south of the Tigris, which was also a royal treasury. The commander or viceroy of the march (Latin, *vitaxa*/Armenian, *bdešx*) was the grand chamberlain of Armenia, a eunuch who held the post ex officio.

As a result of the Romano-Persian Treaty of Nisibis (298), the Syrian March, together with several other Armenian lands, was ceded to the Roman Empire, which held it for more than 300 years. Under the Romans the former march first consisted of four princely states ruled by three Armenian dynasties: Greater Sophenē (Armenian, Mec Copʿkʿ), consisting of about 6,861 square miles; Lesser Sophenē (Armenian, Pʿokʿr Copʿkʿ or Copʿkʿ Šahuneacʿ), which included the district of Digesenē (Armenian, Degik) and consisted of about 1,220 square miles; and Ingilene–Anzitenē (Armenian Angł-tun and Hanjit), about 938 square miles and 1,476 square miles, respectively, the latter including the district of Gaurenē or Garinē (Urartian: Gauraḫi; Armenian, Gawrēk). Of these three houses those of Greater Sophenē and Ingilenē–Anzitenē were almost certainly of royal Orontid origin; that of Lesser Sophenē, controlled by the House of Šahuni, may have been Orontid or perhaps was descended from the princes of Šupa of the Hittite period.

Under the Romans and early Byzantines the *civitates foederatae* had fully sovereign status under imperial suzerainty. The princes were accorded the privileges of minor kings, and their regalia included the purple boots worn only by the Roman emperors and the shahs of Iran.

In the period 377–387 two more princely states were added to the original three: Asthianenē (Armenian, *Hašteankʿ*), with about 1,447 square miles, the princes of which, the House of Kaminakan, were cadets of the Arsacids; and Balabitenē (Armenian, *Balahovit*), with about 675 square miles, the princes of which are not named in Armenian sources. If the latter included the neighboring districts of Palisenē (Armenian, *Pałnatun*) and Khorzanē or Khordzianenē (Armenian, *Xorjean* or *Xorcayn*), as seems probable, then its area would be about 2,679 square miles.

Thus, by the end of the fourth century, southwestern Armenia consisted of six states ruled by a pentarchy of princely houses. Referred to as Other Armenia *(Armenia Altera)* to distinguish their joint territory from Lesser Armenia, which had been Roman since A.D. 72, the states of the Pentarchy were officially styled *satrapiae* (satrapies), *gentes,* or *ethne* (peoples). The relative strength of the five houses can be gathered from the number of cavalry they could place in the field: Ingilenē–Anzitenē, 3,400; Lesser Sophenē, 1,000; Asthianenē, 500; Balabitenē and Greater Sophenē, unknown, but at least 100 for the former and probably about 500 for the latter.

The anomalous status of the Pentarchy within the Roman Empire could not be expected to last, and it is surprising that the five houses retained their extraordinary privileges for as long as they did. In 488, as a result of their complicity in the revolt of Illus, the satrapies, excluding Balabitenē, lost some of their sovereign rights—probably their exemption from Roman taxes—and were thus reduced from the status of *civitates foederatae* to that of *civitates stipendiariae.*

Under Justinian I (527–565) a series of imperial documents spelled out the end of all princely prerogatives other than those accorded to any Roman citizen; the princes became mediatized, losing their political and public power and being reduced to the status of landed nobility. In 528 the satrapies lost the right to maintain their own armed forces and their exemption from being garrisoned by imperial troops. Eight years later the satrapies were consolidated into the new Byzantine province of Fourth Armenia (Armenia Quarta), with an area of some 7,292 square miles, under the administration of a Byzantine *consularis* residing at the new capital of Martyropolis (Tigranakert, Npʿrkert, Miyafarkin, or Farkin; now Silvan, Turkey). This represented the dispossession of the five princes as rulers and the abolition of their sovereign rights.

Sometime between 535 and 543, a single edict spelled out in two of Justinian's new laws (*novellae* 21 and 118) ended the agnatic and preordained succession of the princes and replaced it with cognatic inheritance. By these laws the private estates of the princes—their genearchic holdings—were broken up through subdivision among the male and female heirs at the death of each prince. The actual end of the Pentarchy thus occurred between 528 and 535, but probably in 532.

BIBLIOGRAPHY

Nikolai G. Adonts, *Armenia in the Period of Justinian,* Nina G. Garsoïan, trans. (1970), chs. 2, 5–8; S. T. Eremyan, *Hayastanĕ ēst "Ašxarhac^{c}oyc^{c}"-i* (1963), 57, 116; T. X. Hakobyan, *Hayastani patmakan ašxarhagrut'iwn,* 2nd ed. (1968) 229–335; Heinrich Hübschmann, *Die altarmenischen Ortsnamen* (1904; repr. 1969), 245–248, 294–305.

ROBERT H. HEWSEN

ARMENIAN RITE. The importance of the Armenian liturgy for the study of the origins and early evolution of Christian worship cannot be overestimated. From the beginning the Armenian church had close ties with the Syrian communities around Edessa and the Greek church of Cappadocia, so it is not surprising to find Syriac and Greek influence in the Armenian rite. Because of the struggle for survival of the Armenian church throughout the centuries, it frequently mirrors the earliest Syriac form of the liturgy—as in the rites of initiation—and also reflects the Byzantine liturgy—for example, in the Eucharist.

Yet one should not subordinate the Armenian rite to the Byzantine rite, as has often been done. The Armenian baptismal rite, for example, shows no Byzantine influence. The Armenians (and the Maronites) preserved the original character of baptism, reflecting the earliest Syrian baptismal theology. The Syro-Armenian type of baptism is based on the baptismal theology of John 3, and is predominantly pneumatic in its orientation, whereas the Greco-Latin type is inspired by the christocentric baptismal theology of Paul (Romans 6). Thus Paul's christocentric "death mysticism" gave the Greco-Latin type its final shape, whereas the Syro-Armenian baptismal liturgy is rooted in a "Genesis mysticism."

The present Armenian anaphora betrays heavy borrowings from the Byzantine Eucharist. Yet other Armenian anaphoras seem to reflect the pre-Byzantine form of the Eucharist of Cappadocia. According to Catergian and Dashian the Greek anaphora of Basil was translated into Armenian at the beginning of the fifth century. (Later the anaphora became erroneously attributed to Gregory the Illuminator.) Also, Engberding traced the Armenian redaction of the Basil anaphora to one of the oldest versions of the liturgy of Basil. Catergian compared the Armenian text with the present Byzantine version, including in the apparatus the eighth-century *Codex Barberinus* 336. Engberding demonstrated, however, that the Armenian version shows a greater affinity with the Egyptian version of Basil than with the Byzantine text.

Toward the end of the fifth century other Cappadocian anaphoras seem to have been translated into Armenian—according to the Armenian tradition, by Yovhannēs Mandakuni, 478–490—but later attributed to Sahak, Gregory of Nazianzus, Cyril, and Athanasius. At the end of the tenth century or shortly afterward, the liturgy of Basil, as it was celebrated in Constantinople, was again rendered into Armenian. At various places this second translation differs considerably from the first version. In the tenth and eleventh centuries the anaphora of Chrysostom began to replace the liturgy of Basil in Constantinople. Through Byzantine influence the anaphora of Chrysostom also entered Armenia. Aucher (who rendered the Armenian text into Italian) dated the Armenian version in the ninth or tenth century, as Dashian had already suggested. However, the more likely date for the translation is the thirteenth century, as Jacob has shown in his study on the Greek manuscripts of the Chrysostom liturgy.

Between the eleventh and fourteenth centuries two Syrian Eucharistic prayers were also translated into Armenian. Of far greater importance, however, was the Latin influence in this period. With the establishment of the Armenian kingdom in Cilicia, the Armenian rite became to some extent latinized. Nersēs Lambronac^{c}i (1153/1154–1198), who seems to have favored closer ties with the Latin church, normally is associated with the translation of the Latin Mass into Armenian.

The liturgy of the hours of the Armenian church shows some interesting peculiarities. In the Eastern churches the so-called cathedral office (based on psalms chosen according to the time of day) and the monastic office (based on *psalmodia currens*) had been welded into a harmonious unit. That is, the office begins with the recitation of a group of psalms in numerical order (which is of monastic origin), followed by the cathedral practices. For example, the evening office has the following structure in nearly all Eastern rites: monastic psalmody and vespers of the parishes (ritual of the light, Psalm 140 or several evening psalms, intercessions); likewise the morning office consists of monastic psalmody (originally forming the ancient midnight office) and cathedral matins (Psalms 50, 62, 148–150, Gloria, intercessions). Psalm 62 is not used in the Armenian (and East-Syrian) morning office. This is not the only difference. In contrast with the other churches of the Christian East, it seems that in Armenia the monastic psalmody was restricted to the midnight office. Thus the Armenian evening office consists of two juxtaposed cathedral vespers: the first part very likely reflects the evening office of Constantinople, and the second part seems to mirror the original Armenian cathedral vespers.

A similar development took place with regard to the Sunday morning office. In the Eastern rites the Sunday matins have the following structure: Monastic psalmody (= the old *mesonyktikon*), cathedral vigil (or "resurrection office"), and morning office proper. In Armenia we find no monastic psalmody placed before the cathedral vigil. Armenia's cathedral vigil probably consists of two juxtaposed vigils: traces of the older vigil are preserved in the three canticles (Dan 3: 26–45; Dan 3: 52–86; Lk 1:46–55), whereas the Gospel reading was dropped; the later adopted cathedral vigil consists of three psalms and the Gospel of resurrection. The older vigil mirrors some affinity with East-Syria, the more recent one resembles the cathedral vigil of Constantinople. The origins of the cathedral vigil (be it of Armenia, Syria, or Byzantium) lies in the resurrection office of Jerusalem. This Sunday vigil commemorated the three women who came to Jesus' tomb early in the morning. This "resurrection office" was taken over by all the churches of East and West. Yet only the Armenian and Byzantine churches have preserved the original structure and meaning of this cathedral vigil, thus demonstrating the importance of the Armenian evidence for our understanding of the history of Christian worship.

BIBLIOGRAPHY

Rites of Initiation. S. Čemčemean, "Mkrtowt^cean araroghowt^ciwna maštoc^cnerow mēǰ," in *Bazmavep*, **129** (1971) and **130** (1972); Frederick C. Conybeare, *Rituale Armenorum* (1905); Gabriele Winkler, "Zur frühchristlichen Tauftradition in Syrien und Armenien unter Einbezug der Taufe Jesu," in *Ostkirchliche Studien*, **27** (1978); "The Original Meaning of the Prebaptismal Anointing and Its Implications," in *Worship*, **52** (1978); and *Das armenische Initiationsrituale* (1982).

Eucharist. J. Catergian and H. Dashian, *Die Liturgien bei den Armeniern* (1897), in modern Armenian; Hieronymus Engberding, *Das eucharistische Hochgebet der Basileiosliturgie* (1931); Petrus Ferhat, Anton Baumstark, and Adolf Rücker, "Denkmäler altarmenischer Messliturgie," in *Oriens Christianus*, n.s. **1, 3, 7–8**, and 3rd ser., **1** (1911–1927); Paul Vetter, *Chosroae Magni episcopi monophysitici explicatio precum missae* (1880).

Liturgy of the Hours. V. Hayc^cowni, *Patmowt^ciwn Hayoc^c aghot^camatoyc^cin* (1965); J. Mateos, "La vigile cathédrale chez Egérie," in *Orientalia Christiana periodica*, **27** (1961); Gabriele Winkler, "Über die Kathedralvesper in den verschiedenen Riten des Ostens und Westens," in *Archiv für Liturgiewissenschaft*, **16** (1974).

Varia. Sebastiá Janeras, *Bibliografia sulle liturgie orientali (1961–1967)* (1969); M. F. Lages, "The Most Ancient Penitential Text of the Armenian Liturgy," in *Didascalia*, **1** (1971); Athanase Renoux, "Les lectures du temps pascal dans la tradition arménienne," in *Revue des études arméniennes*, n.s. **4** (1967); "Les lectures quadragésimales du rite arménien," *ibid.*, n.s. **5** (1968); *Le codex arménien Jérusalem 121*, 2 vols. (1969–1971); and "Un rite pénitentiel le jour de la Pentecôte? L'office de la génuflexion dans la tradition arménienne," in *Studien zur armenischen Geschichte*, **12** (1973); Joseph Marie Sauget, *Bibliographie des liturgies orientales (1900–1960)* (1962); Nerses Ter-Mikaëlian, *Das armenische Hymnarium* (1905); Gabriele Winkler, "Zur Geschichte des armenischen Gottesdienstes im Hinblick auf den in mehreren Wellen erfolgten griechischen Einfluss," in *Oriens Christianus*, **58** (1974); "Armenia and the Gradual Decline of Its Traditional Liturgical Practices as a Result of the Expanding Influence of the Holy See from the 11th to the 14th Century," in *Bibliotheca ephemerides liturgicae*, subs. 7 (1976); and "Eine bemerkenswerte Stelle im armenischen Glaubensbekenntnis: *Credimus et in Sanctum Spiritum qui descendit in Jordanem proclamavit missum,*" in *Oriens Christianus*, **63** (1979).

GABRIELE WINKLER

ARMENIAN SAINTS. The conversion of the Armenians to Christianity (*ca.* 314) took place soon after the end of the Roman persecutions, when the memory of the "champions of the faith" was still fresh in the minds of the faithful. According to the testimony of the fifth-century Armenian historians P^cawstos Buzand and Agat^cangełos, the establishment of the new religion in Armenia claimed the lives of thirty-three virgins named after their leader, Gayianē. One of them, Hṙip^csimē, rejected King Tiridates III's proposal of marriage and refused to forsake her faith. The king had all thirty-three women executed for supporting Hṙip^csimē and bearing witness to Christ. The same sources also speak of Gregory the Illuminator, a Christian from Caesarea of Cappadocia, as a great champion of the faith. He miraculously survived the tortures applied to him and

ARMENIAN SAINTS

converted King Tiridates and the Armenian people to Christianity.

These saints were among the earliest venerated by the Armenian church. At the beginning of the fifth century, Patriarch Sahak I of Armenia had martyria built at Vałaršapat over the graves of Gayianē and Hṙip^{c}simē. By the middle of the century, there was more than one martyrium housing the relics of St. Gregory; one of them was at T^{c}ordan and another at Bagawan. Their numbers increased in the sixth and seventh centuries.

Agat^{c}angełos and P^{c}awstos provide evidence for the presence of other relics and martyria in fifth-century Armenia. For example, the relics of St. John the Baptist and Bishop Athenogenes were deposited in their martyrium at Aštišat in southwestern Armenia. P^{c}awstos also knew of other relics of John at Bagawan. The same author mentions in passing the repository of the Holy Apostles in Tarawn and the cemetery of the Gregorids (St. Gregory's descendants) in T^{c}ordan. He also states that St. Grigoris, a grandson of St. Gregory and the Illuminator of the Caucasian Albanians, was buried in a martyrium in Amaras (Arc^{c}ax). The early Armenian sources recognized King Tiridates III as a saint, even though he was not a martyr; the Armenian church honored him as Gregory's associate and patron. No martyrium is mentioned for him, since he was probably buried in the royal cemetery of the Arsacids.

In addition to the veneration of the above saints, sources occasionally mention an All Martyrs' Day. They also tell us about the commemoration of the Virgin Mary, who was honored as *Astuacacin (Theotokos)*, on the fifteenth of Navasard, the first month of the Armenian calendar.

The circulation of new relics of saints in the 440's deeply concerned the fathers of the Armenian church. Canon XVII of the (Armenian) Council of Šahapivan (444) forbade anyone to deposit relics, build martyria, or hold gatherings without the consent of the bishop of the district. It also demanded that documentation be presented to establish authenticity of relics. It set the annual commemoration of saints on the day of the arrival (or perhaps deposition) of their relics, and cautioned the faithful not to carry their veneration to excess.

During the general period of the Council of Šahapivan, the Armenian church began to venerate saints who were not martyrs. The translation of the *Lives of the Egyptian Fathers* would have already acquainted the Armenians with the Christian "athletes," men who had reached perfection in this life. Among the earliest of this type of Armenian saints were the monk Maštoc^{c} (*d.* 439), a Christian missionary who devised the Armenian alphabet, and his patron Sahak (*d.* 438), the bishop of Armenia and a descendant of St. Gregory the Illuminator. Koriwn, the fifth-century biographer and student of Maštoc^{c}, speaks of the annual commemoration on the anniversary of Sahak's death at his tomb in Aštišat, and mentions the construction of a chapel over the grave of Maštoc^{c} at Ošakan.

The number of saints was evidently very modest until the end of the fifth century, when the *Lectionary of the Church of Jerusalem* was translated. (It was later adapted for liturgical use.) The *Lectionary* provided scriptural readings for the commemoration of a number of biblical and Christian saints. Included among the latter were Bishop Peter of Alexandria and Abisolom, Anthony the Hermit, the Emperor Theodosius, the Forty Saints of Sebaste, bishops Cyril and John of Jerusalem, Emperor Constantine, and Theodore the Stratelates. To these the Armenians added the celebration of St. Gregory's ascent from the pit. The names of the remaining Armenian saints were not incorporated into the *Lectionary*, since the annual commemoration of each was made at his martyrium.

The great rebellion of 451 against the Persians, and the intolerant attitude of the Sasanids (and later the Arabs) toward converts and apostates, inflated the list of the Armenian saints. According to the historians Łazar P^{c}arpec^{c}i (late fifth century) and Ełišē (sixth century), during the insurrection of 451, Vardan Mamikonean, the commander in chief of the Armenian army, and a number of other dignitaries fell in battle. Soon after the war the Persians executed a number of Armenian clerics who were led by the presbyter Łewond and Katholikos Yovsēp^{c}. Łazar P^{c}arpec^{c}i described how the relics of the martyred priests were recovered and taken to the Armenian feudal lords. With these saints the church associated Šušanik, the daughter of Vardan, whose *Life* was imported from Georgia, where she was originally commemorated.

The historical sources tell of other martyrs. From a sixth-century document in the *Book of Letters*, we learn about a monastery named after Grigor Manačihr Ṙažik ("native of Ray"), a convert from Zoroastrianism, who was martyred in the mid sixth century. The tenth-century historian Katholikos Yovhannēs of Drasxanakert says that the martyrium of sixth-century Persian convert, Astuacatur-Maxož, stood near the cathedral of Dwin and served as the repository of the relics of another Persian convert, Surhan-David, who in 701 was the first victim of Islam in Armenia.

The Armenian prince Vahan of Gołtᶜn was another victim. He had been taken to Damascus at a very young age and raised as a Muslim. Since conversion to another religion was a capital offense under Islamic law, the Muslim authorities seized and executed Vahan, who had returned to his father's faith. The year of the martyrdom is given as 737. The Syrian Christians buried Vahan's body in Ruṣāfah and built a martyrium over his grave. Soon after the building of the martyrium, Artawazd, the prior of Erašxaworkᶜ, wrote Vahan's *Life* after a pilgrimage to Ruṣāfah.

Łewond, the major historian of the Arab domination over Armenia, speaks of two other martyrs during the later eighth century. These were the Arcruni princes Hamazasp and Sahak, who were executed at Dwin and whose reliefs can still be seen on the walls of the Church of the Holy Cross in Ałtᶜamar (tenth century). Katholikos Yovhannēs of Drasxanakert knew about another early martyrium at Dwin that was dedicated to the great martyr Sergius. The structure was burned by the Persians and rebuilt in the mid seventh century. Although it is not clear which Sergius this is, scholars have identified him as St. Sargis the General (of the Church of Persia), whose *Life* was translated from Syriac in the twelfth century.

The christological controversies of the sixth to eighth centuries, and the Byzantine claim of the supremacy of the see of Constantinople, provoked the Armenians to react and emphasize the apostolicity of the Armenian church, the apostolic origin of which was recognized by some Armenian writers as early as the fifth century. Pᶜawstos Buzand refers to the office of the bishop of Armenia as the see of St. Thaddeus. In the sixth century, Katholikos Yovhannēs Gabełean speaks of St. Gregory the Illuminator as the successor of St. Thaddeus.

During the seventh and eighth centuries a new type of hagiography appeared, the essence of which was stories about very early apostolic proselytization among the Armenians. Good examples of such literature were the *Lives* of the apostle Thaddeus, the apostle Bartholomew, and a number of early Christian converts. The major saints among these were St. Sanduxt, the daughter of King Sanatruk of Armenia (*ca.* 75–110); the Roman envoy Oski and his five companions, who were sent on a mission to the court of Sanatruk in Armenia, where they embraced Christianity; Sukᶜias and the seventeen Alan courtesans, who were related to Satᶜenik, the legendary queen of Armenia, and were proselytized by Oski and his companions.

At a later date the Armenian church also recognized as saints and honored King Abgar of Edessa and Addai, the associate of St. Thaddeus, according to the Armenian translation of the *Doctrine of Addai.* It is impossible to establish the historical identities of these saints. Neither their relics nor martyria have been accounted for by the early sources. The first historian to have made use of their *Lives* in his work is Movsēs Xorenacᶜi, whose dates are controversial.

Another group of early but unauthenticated saints is linked with St. Gregory the Illuminator and the conversion of Armenia. Among these are Ašxēn, the wife of King Tiridates III, the virgins Nunē (St. Nino of the Georgians) and Manē, and the hermits Anthony and Kronidēs; the hermits Yovhannēs, Simēon, and their companions are remembered only in the diptychs of the Divine Liturgy. All of these saints are unknown to Agatᶜangełos, who speaks of Xosroviduxt, Tiridates' sister, but does not recognize her as a saint. At a later time she was canonized because of her role in the conversion of Armenia.

Besides these saints the church calendar contains the names of a few others whose lives cannot be authenticated by means of historical methodology. The first among these are Stephen of Ulnia and his companions, who were martyred at the time of Julian the Apostate. Second in chronological order is the Armenian general Atom and his army, whom the Persians slew shortly before the war of 451. From the same period, the anchorites Tᶜatᶜul, Varos, and Thomas were revered for their sanctity. The synaxaria give information about the martyrdom in 604 of seven anchorites who lived at Muš. The same sources contain the *Life* of two Qaysite brothers from Karin (Erzurum), Yovsēpᶜ and Sahak, whose mother was Armenian; they were beheaded in 808 for forsaking Islam.

The historical sources have preserved the names of some pre-eleventh-century national saints whose commemoration has been deleted from the Armenian church calendar. Two groups of martyrs are important: Atom Anjewacᶜi and his companions, whom the Arabs put to death at Dwin in 853, and King Smbat I Bagratuni (*d.* 913) and his contemporaries, who were martyred at the order of Yūsuf, the Sajid emir of Azerbaijan. Both groups were canonized soon after their execution, the first by Katholi-

ARMENIAN SAINTS

kos Yovhannēs Ovayec^{c}i, and the second by (or during the pontificate of) Yovhannēs of Drasxanakert.

These two examples and Canon XVII of the Council of Šahapivan shed some light on the process of canonization in the Armenian church. Verification of martyrdom or sanctity, presence of authentic relics, miracles associated with these, and consensus seem to have provided justifiable reasons for a katholikos to respond to popular demand and set a day of commemoration. The saints were venerated at their martyria, where the ecclesiastic and feudal hierarchy of the land, accompanied by large crowds, attended the Divine Office.

Prior to the eleventh century the Armenians venerated only a small number of non-Armenian saints. The hymns dedicated to Sts. Sergius, George, and Mennas are from the mid eleventh century, which indicates that these saints were venerated before then. St. James of Nisibis, whose *Life* had been translated by the fifth century, and St. Cyriacus appear among the reliefs carved on the walls of the Church of the Holy Cross at Ałt^{c}amar. The colophon attached to the Armenian translation of the Syriac *Life of St. Abdlmseh*, a young Jewish shepherd who converted to Christianity and was martyred in the sixth century, indicates that his commemoration was instituted by Prince Gurgēn Anjewac^{c}i in 873.

The commemorations of the majority of the non-Armenian saints were introduced into the Armenian calendar and the *Lectionary* in the late eleventh and early twelfth centuries. In their joint colophon the katholikos Gregory the Martyrophil (1066–1105) and his associate Kiwrakos Vardapet state that they supplemented the *Lectionary* with seventy-six new entries. We must note that most of the entries contain the names of several saints. The sources that Gregory and Kiwrakos drew upon were the early Armenian translations and compilations, the *Lives* that they commissioned to be translated from Greek and Syriac, and possibly the Greek synaxarion that was rendered into Armenian by Yovsēp^{c} of Constantinople in 991/992. The selections were carefully made so that only the earliest (pre-Chalcedonian) saints would be included. Romanos the Melode seems to be an exception.

The Armenian church discontinued introducing new entries into the calendar and the *Lectionary* in the thirteenth century. The commemoration of the Holy Translators—Maštoc^{c}, the historian Ełišē (sixth century), Movsēs the Grammarian, the philosopher David the Invincible, the mystic poet Gregory of Narek (tenth century), and the twelfth-century theologian, poet, and katholikos Nersēs IV Šnorhali—was probably initiated in the thirteenth century. This is evident from the following: Maštoc^{c} was actually venerated with Sahak on a different day. Maštoc^{c} is commemorated twice. The first day is the Feast of the Holy Translators and the second is that of Sahak and Maštoc^{c} together. The second is the older; grouping little-known and somewhat legendary figures such as Movsēs the Grammarian, David the Invincible, and Ełišē with historical personalities such as Gregory of Narek and Nersēs Šnorhali points to a date after the time of the latter; the hymn of the Holy Translators was not written before the thirteenth century. The commemoration of the Holy Translators may have been one of the last entries in the calendar. Of the twelfth- and thirteenth-century Pahlawuni katholikoi—Gregory the Martyrophil and his descendants—only Nersēs Šnorhali is commemorated in the calendar; the rest are remembered in the diptychs of the Divine Liturgy. This clearly indicates that the *Lectionary* and the calendar of the Armenian church were closed for additional entries by the thirteenth century.

In the eighteenth century, Katholikos Simēon of Erevan revised the church calendar and introduced the names of the eighth-century katholikos Yovhannēs Awjnec^{c}i, the fourteenth-century theologian Yovhannēs of Orotn, and his disciple Gregory of Tat^{c}ew. He also ordered the addition of the sixteenth-century katholikos Movsēs of Tat^{c}ew to the list of saints remembered in the diptychs of the Divine Liturgy.

None of the saints' days in the Armenian church calendar is fixed; they move backward and forward according to the date of Easter. Since Sundays are dominical festivals and Wednesdays and Fridays are dedicated to penitence, saints are venerated only on Mondays, Tuesdays, Thursdays, and Saturdays. Commemoration of saints is observed during the following periods: after the octave of Theophany, twelve days; after the Fast of the Catechumens, nine days; on the Saturdays of Lent, five days; after Pentecost, twenty days; after the Transfiguration, ten days; after the Assumption, eleven days; after the Exaltation of the Holy Cross, thirty-two days; during the fifty days before Theophany, twenty-five days; during the fast before Theophany, one day. All in all, only 125 days in a year are available for commemoration. This calendrical system is quite old, since it was one of the items of discussion between the

Byzantines and Armenians in 1172. In 1307 the Council of Sis tried unsuccessfully to introduce the Western pattern of set dates.

Unlike the hebdomadal pattern of the church calendar, the Armenian synaxaria present the lives of saints according to set dates. This, however, has no liturgical significance, since the hymns and propers of saints are said on the day of veneration according to the calendar, not the synaxaria.

The earliest synaxaria, compiled by Tēr Israyēl and Kirakos Arewelc^{c}i (Ganja), were not composed until the thirteenth century. Subsequently, Katholikos Gregory of Anawarza (1293–1307) and Gregory of Xlat^{c} supplemented the earlier collections with many new *Lives*. Among these are many names that do not appear in the Armenian church calendar. Some are neomartyrs (post-eleventh-century) who were executed by the Muslim authorities. Of these only Goharinos of Sebastia (twelfth century) and his brothers are commemorated. The status of the saints whose names do not appear in the calendar is not clear. The Armenian church traditionally distinguishes between the "commemorated" *(tōneli)* and "remembered" *(yišatakeli)* saints. The latter are those whose names appear only in the synaxaria.

BIBLIOGRAPHY

Primary Sources. Agathangelos, *History of the Armenians*, Robert W. Thomson, trans. (1976); *Čašoc^{c} girk^{c}*, 2 vols. (1873); Ełišē [St. Eghishe], *Vasn Vardanay ew Hayoc^{c} paterazmin* (1957); Ghazar P^{c}arpec^{c}i, *Patmut^{c}iwn hayoc^{c}* (1904); Ghewond, *Patmut^{c}iwn* (1887); *Girk^{c}t^{c}łt^{c}oc^{c}* (1901); Koriwn, *Vark^{c} Maštoc^{c}i* (1941); P^{c}awstos Buzand [Faustus of Byzantium], *Patmut^{c}iwn Hayoc^{c}* (1889); *Yaysmawurk^{c}* (1706), the *editio princeps* of Gregory of Xlat^{c}'s compilation. The synaxary of Tēr Israyēl has not been published; the compilation of Kirakos Arewelc^{c}i was published by G. Bayan, "Le synaxaire arménien de Ter Israël," in *Patrologia orientalis*, **5–6, 15–16, 18–19,** and **21** (1910–1926). The synaxary of Gregory Anawarzec^{c}i was published with revisions at Constantinople in 1834.

Secondary Literature. N. Adontz, "Note sur les synaxaires arméniens," in *Revue de l'Orient chrétien*, **24** (1924); and "Les fêtes et les saints de l'église arménienne," *ibid.*, **26** (1927–1928); Nerses Akinian, *K^{c}nnut^{c}iwn S. Sahaki veragruac kanonneru ew Hayoc^{c} ekełec^{c}akan tarin Ē. daru skizbě* (1950); and "Kirakos Vardapet Gitnakan," in *Matenagrakan hetazewtut^{c}iwnner*, **V** (1953), 231–338; M. Awdalbegean, "Grigor-Vahram vkayasēri 'Tonamak' žołovacun," in *Patma-banasirakan handēs* (1977), no. 4; Sirarpie Der Nersessian, *Études byzantines et arméniennes* (1973), 417–435; Babgen Kiwleserian, *Hayastaneayc^{c} ekełec^{c}cin hingerord darū meǰ* (1912); Maghak^{c}ia Ormanian, *Azgapatum*, I–II (1912–1914); and *The Church of Armenia*, 2nd rev. ed. (1955), ch. 39 of which is dedicated to "the commemoration of saints" and gives a full list of the commemorated saints of the Armenian church; P. Peeters, "Pour l'histoire du synaxaire arménien," in *Analecta Bollandiana*, **30** (1911).

KRIKOR H. MAKSOUDIAN

[See also **Agat^{c}angełos; David the Invincible; Ełišē; Gregory of Narek (St.); Gregory the Illuminator (St.); Koriwn; Łazar P^{c}arpec^{c}i; Łewond; Nersēs IV Šnorhali; Oski; P^{c}awstos Buzand; Romanos Melodos; Sahak (St.); Smbat I, the Martyr; Vardan Mamikonean.**]

ARMIES. See **Warfare.**

ARMILLARY SPHERE, astronomical instrument with rings of brass or wood (diameter six to fifty centimeters) representing the circles of the heavenly sphere. Perhaps known to Gerbert (*d.* 1003), it was later widely used for teaching spherical astronomy. In the Renaissance it developed into a large instrument like its Ptolemaic prototype (*Almagest* 5.1), and was used for observation by Bernhard Walter (of Nuremberg), Copernicus, and Tycho Brahe. Many specimens are preserved in museums.

BIBLIOGRAPHY

Manuel Rico y Sinobas, ed., *Libros del saber de astronomia,* III (1865), is a Castilian treatise of 1276. Also see Friedrich Nolte, *Die Armillarsphäre* (1922); and D. J. Price, "A Collection of Armillary Spheres," in *Annals of Science,* **10** (1954).

OLAF PEDERSEN

[See also **Astrology/Astronomy.**]

ARMS AND ARMOR comprise all types of weapons for offense and defense; offensive arms may be divided into edged weapons (swords, daggers, and the subgroup of shafted weapons, such as lances, axes, maces), missile weapons (slings, bows and arrows, crossbows, with the subgroup of firearms); and defensive armor can be divided into body armor (helmets, cuirasses, etc.) in the narrower sense, and shields.

ARMS AND ARMOR

HISTORY AND DEVELOPMENT

The arms and armor of the early Middle Ages in particular were derived from those used in late Roman times, although some of the edged weapons—such as the *ango,* sax, spatha, or francisc—were of barbarian origin. Several barbarian tribes were even named after their tribal weapons: the Angles after the *ango*, a barbed harpoonlike spear, the Saxons after the sax *(seax)*, a machetelike longknife, the Langobards after their long-handled *Barten* (axes). By contrast, the throwing ax of the Franks was so prevalent among them that it was called *francisca* (francisc) after them, as was the *hunnica,* the ball-and-chain whip of the Huns. The barbarian tribes that carved their own kingdoms out of late Roman territory were mostly Germanic, with an admixture of nomads from the eastern steppes such as the Alani and Sarmatians. These, of the Iranian branch of the Indo-European language family, were horsemen and herdsmen. They wore heavy scale armor of bronze, iron, or horn, including bardings for their horses. They had been used as auxiliary cavalry in the late Roman armies, and their heavy cavalry equipment was adopted by the Romans and Byzantines for their own armored cavalry, the *cataphractarii* and *clibanarii.* These heavily armored horsemen, both Alanic and Germanic, were the ancestors of the medieval knight.

The barbarian warriors of the early Middle Ages wore armor that reflected the mixture of cultures prevalent in the days following the fall of Rome (476). Their helmets were spangenhelms, constructed of an iron or bronze framework filled with segments of iron or sometimes even of horn. Their construction was based on that of the reinforced feltcap of the steppe nomads. Spangenhelms with six straps radiating from an apical disk seem to be of Hunnish origin, while those with two crossing straps may be Sarmatian. A distinctive group of spangenhelms of the radial type is found all over Western Europe; it is thought that they were made at the court armory of the Ostrogothic kings (perhaps in Ravenna) and sent out as diplomatic presents to other barbarian princes.

Body armor consisted either of a short-sleeved mail shirt *(byrnie)* developed from the Roman *lorica* or of corselets with iron, bronze, or horn scales in the eastern style. The scales could be sewn or riveted to a fabric or leather backing, arranged like shingles on a roof, or they could be set in rows, laced together without a backing. This so-called "lamellar armor" had to overlap upward for mobility and so that it could be telescoped for easy storage. Japanese samurai armor was constructed on the same principle until the nineteenth century.

Shields of the early Middle Ages were circular or oval, made of light but tough wood (preferably linden), covered with leather (which would still hold the shield together even after the wood was split under a heavy blow), and reinforced by bronze or iron mountings. In the center of the slightly convex shield body was a circular cutout, bridged by the handgrip on the inside and covered by the iron shield boss *(umbo)* on the outside. Usually the *umbo* was semiglobular, but often, particularly among Germanic warriors, it was conical with a sharp point that could also be used as an offensive weapon. Additional metal mountings were around the shield's rim; others might radiate from the *umbo* all over the shield's surface. These radiating mounts later became stylized as a heraldic charge, the escarbuncle. There was no clear distinction between horsemen's and footsoldiers' shields. The weapons of the early Middle Ages were the spear, sword, ax, and bow-and-arrow. For hand-to-hand combat the preferred weapon was the sword. In contrast to the short *gladius* (about two feet long) of the Roman legionary, the spatha (Italian *spada,* Spanish *espada,* French *épée*) of the early Middle Ages was about three feet long, with a straight, double-edged blade at least two inches wide.

The equipment of a noble warrior in Carolingian times (early ninth century) was declared in the *Lex ripuaria* to have the following values: helmet = 6 solidi, byrnie = 12 solidi, leg armor = 6 solidi, sword with scabbard = 7 solidi, lance and shield = 2 solidi, warhorse = 12 solidi. The solidus was a gold coin equivalent in material value to a milch cow; a solidus was also a month's wages for a *soldatus* (solider). Less expensive, and therefore more likely to be found in the hands of the common warrior, who fought on foot, was the sax (or scramasax), a single-edged longknife.

The ax, too, was carried by foot soldiers; a long-handled ax, significantly called the "Danish ax" by contemporaries, was very popular with the Scandinavian Vikings.

Viking equipment showed many eastern influences thanks to their contacts with Byzantium, following the river route through Russia. Scandinavian helmets, found in the tombs of Vendel and Valsgärde in Sweden, and Sutton Hoo in England, are of

ARMS AND ARMOR

the spangenhelm type with prototypes in Sassanian Persia. It should be pointed out that no horned or winged Viking helmets have been found so far.

The year 1066 has become universally accepted as the date the mounted knight came to England. The Bayeux Tapestry, commemorating the Battle of Hastings (14 October 1066), gives us a detailed picture of the arms and armor of this crucial period. The body armor represented in the tapestry is a byrnie with elbow-length sleeves and its skirts slit fore and aft for an easier seat in the saddle. The hanging parts of the skirt could be hitched around the thighs (earlier historians misunderstood them to be one-piece jump suits with short culottes). Only a few select warriors are shown with mail armor for their legs. The material of the byrnies is certainly mail, although it is represented in various stylizations in the tapestry, which gave rise to elaborate speculations among scholars about "ringed mail," "banded mail," and other purely hypothetical varieties. Several warriors show a square reinforcement element on the breasts of their byrnies. Most byrnies have a hood of mail (coif) attached.

Helmets were conical with a short nasal in front. These so-called "Norman" helmets (they are shown as headgear of the Saxons as well) were sometimes still constructed in segments, spangenhelm-style; but sometimes they were also fashioned in one piece. They were worn over the coif.

Shields in the tapestry are mostly of an elongated almond shape; in Victorian antiquarians' slang they are often called "kite-shaped." Another term is "Norman" shields, but they were universally used by Normans and Saxons alike, with a few old-fashioned round shields still in use. This "Norman" shield was specially designed for combat on horseback with couched lances. It covers the entire left side of the knight, from eyes to knee (the drawn-out point of this shield was intended to protect the knee, a very vulnerable joint in collisions). These long shields were not held by their handgrips alone, like the older round shields; there were now two shield grips. The actual handgrip was moved off-center to the right, and a second carrying loop was added. An adjustable sling (guige) went from the top of the shield around the neck and shoulders of the knight. This arrangement made it possible to brace the shield against the impact of the lance. For fighting on foot this elongated shield offered better protection for the legs against a debilitating blow to the legs. Norse sagas, for instance, are full of descriptions of fighters being

Byzantine shield, 6th century

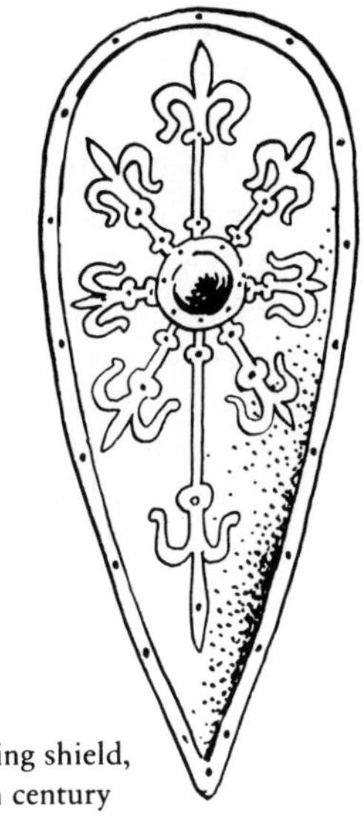

Viking shield, 10th century

Knightly ("Norman") shield, 12th century

Knightly shield, mid 13th century

Late Gothic targe, mid 15th century

"Lithuanian" targe, mid 15th century

ARMS AND ARMOR

cut in the knee or thigh by a sword stroke below the round Viking shield.

Through the shift in position of the handgrip, the shield boss lost its function of protecting the holding hand. Shield bosses and rim mounts, however, were retained for almost another hundred years because of their value as reinforcements against sword cuts, even though the boss interfered with the display of geometrical patterns or animal figures that now became fashionable as shield decorations.

This "Norman" equipment was the armor of the First Crusade (1096–1099). Under the hot sun of the Holy Land mail and helmet might become intolerably hot. For this reason the crusading knights took to wearing a sleeveless surcoat over their mail shirts and put a cloth cover (mantling) on their helmets. These surcoats came to be charged with the crosses that were the distinctive badge of the crusaders and with other cognizances, thus creating the coat of arms. The fashion of the surcoat and mantling was eagerly adopted in Europe because of its decorative value.

Toward the end of the twelfth century a new type of helmet was introduced: it had a flat top and additional side plates that came down to the jawline. In front there were only two small rectangular eye slits and a cluster of breathing holes; otherwise the face was entirely hidden, so that the wearer was unrecognizable. In order to tell friend from foe, it became vital to find an easy means of identification, preferably at a long distance. The largest surface in a knight's equipment, the shield, came to be painted in bright colors with easily recognizable devices, which led to the development of heraldry. Now, despite its usefulness as a reinforcing element, the shield boss was abolished, because it was felt to obstruct the clear view of the vitally important heraldic designs. At the same time, the new flat-topped helmets were equipped with identifying crests.

The added protection for the face afforded by the helmet visor made the highly curved shield top unnecessary; the top was now cut straight and the shield became triangular, the shape we usually associate with a knightly shield. In the spirit of the Crusades and the orders of chivalry this triangular shape was interpreted as a symbol of the Holy Trinity.

During the twelfth century body armor changed too. The mail shirt received long sleeves, even with mittens in one style. The palms of these mail mittens consisted of inset pieces of leather, so that the knight could grip lance shaft and sword hilt firmly. Loops of leather were threaded through the mail fabric around the wrists, where they could be tied for a more secure fit. Often there were slits in the mail sleeves at the wrist, so that the hands could be slipped out for comfort; many representations show knights with their mittens thus dangling from their wrists. Not one mail shirt of this type (now called a hauberk instead of a byrnie) has survived from this period. The only known piece of verifiably Crusader armor is a small lump of rusted-together mail at the Metropolitan Museum of Art, in New York City. It was excavated in 1928 from the ruins of the Crusader castle Montfort in the Holy Land, which was destroyed in 1270 by the Mamluk Sultan Baibars I "the Panther." The earliest datable mail shirt surviving is that of Duke Leopold III of Austria, who was killed in the Battle of Sempach in 1386. This hauberk, of a later type, with long sleeves but without mittens and coif, is preserved in the museum in the City Hall of Lucerne, Switzerland.

Leg armor, too, became more common and complete by 1200. Mail chausses—either long strips of mail to be buckled on the length of the leg, or regular mail stockings—were now worn by most knights. In the middle of the thirteenth century they were augmented by solid kneecops of either hardened boiled leather or steel. This improved protection for the vulnerable knee made the long point of the shield unnecessary, and shields became considerably shorter. There is a direct relationship between the size of the shield and the extent of leg armor worn during the thirteenth and fourteenth centuries. Again, there are no "Norman" shields surviving; the earliest known medieval shields are from about 1200 (shield of Arnold von Brienz, Swiss National Museum, Zurich; shield of a prince of Navarre, Real Armería, Madrid). They are of wood about half an inch thick, covered with thin but tough leather, and painted over a firm foundation of mixed chalk and glue. They are about forty inches long, presumably at least fifteen inches shorter than the "Norman" shields seem to have been.

Mail was a very efficient protection against sword cuts, but because of its flexibility it had no resistance against the crushing force of a blow. In order to absorb the shock of such a blow, which might even break a bone, it was necessary to wear a padded undergarment, the acton (from "cotton"). The drawback of such a garment, which was also necessary to prevent the mail from chafing, was that it was very hot; campaigns had to be planned to avoid the hot-

ARMS AND ARMOR

test seasons. Even so, many chronicles report that knights dropped from heatstroke and heart failure under adverse circumstances.

The main shock-breaker was the shield, but to protect the sensitive shoulder joint ailettes—small squares probably of hard leather or even steel—were attached to the shoulders. These ailettes were usually decorated with the cognizances of the shield. For this reason they are considered by some scholars to be merely decorative appendages; there are no surviving examples to settle the question definitely. But similar squares can be found bound to the knees of mounted knights on effigies, suggesting that they might have been a forerunner of the kneecop.

Horse armor had not been in use in Western Europe since the days of the late Roman *cataphractarii,* but in the early thirteenth century, we find it again. Their armor consists of bardings of mail of the same pattern—hoodlike cover with eyeholes for head, neck, and breast and a separate crupper—as the much more frequent trappings of fabric.

In the first half of the fourteenth century the crossbow had been improved to such a degree that its bolts could pierce the wooden shield and burst through the meshes of a mail shirt. The only possible solution was to design an armor with glancing surfaces to deflect the deadly bolts before they could penetrate. The first attempts used the surcoat as a base and lined it with small rectangular plates about the size of a hand. The rivets fastening these plates show up on the outside as a decorative pattern. The earliest of these coats of plates were in poncho shape, pulled on over the head (and over the hauberk) and buckled at the sides. In eastern and northern Europe there were to be found coats of plates of lamellar type, where the smaller plates (about five inches long and one or two inches wide) were not riveted to fabric or leather backing but were laced together with thongs without any backing or lining. The excavations of the mass graves of the Battle of Visby, in 1361, yielded numerous examples of coats of plates of both types, riveted and lamellar.

Sometimes these early coats of plates have a single larger plate across the chest, where chains could be riveted on. These chains could number up to four and were attached to the hilts of the knight's sword and dagger (to prevent them from being irretrievably lost when the knight was on horseback) and to his helmet and shield. The helmet chain ended in a toggle link that could be inserted into a slot in the lower front plate of the helmet in such a way that the helmet could be worn slung over the shoulder at ease, when not in use. The shield could be similarly secured on the fourth chain.

By the middle of the fourteenth century shields had diminished in size to two feet in length and one and a half feet in width. They were now needed only to protect the vulnerable spot between the chest and the left arm of the knight, where an enemy lance might slip in and break the arm. The shield's reduced size was due to the fact that practically all knights were now wearing extensive leg armor consisting of kneecops, greaves (covers for the shins), cuisses or cuishes (thigh defenses; incidentally, the Spanish term for this thigh armor was *quijote*), and sabatons (shoes of overlapping steel lames).

At this point, a new type of shield, the targe, was introduced. It was roughly square in outline and had a deep cutout, the bouche, in its upper right corner, where the lance could be rested when couched. Another important difference from the older triangular shield, which was convex in its longitudinal axis, was that the targe was concave horizontally. In the fifteenth century targes often had one or several longitudinal ridges; both features were designed to catch an opponent's lance point and prevent it from slipping off. This made the targe an ideal shield for the tournament, where safety was a prime concern. For this reason the targe was also called the "shield for peace," and knights had garnitures of two matching shields of different shapes, triangular and targe, for war and peace, respectively.

After the armoring of the legs with articulated plate armor, the same was done during the second half of the fourteenth century for the arms. They became encased in vambraces (for the forearms), cowters or elbow-cops, rerebraces (for the upper arms), and pauldrons (for the shoulders). The carefully fitted elements were held together by being riveted to inside leather straps. The hands were protected with steel gauntlets with stiff, hourglass-shaped cuffs, and fingers of steel scales mounted on an inner leather glove. The pauldrons and cowters had double eyelets through which were threaded double laces, called "points," sewn to the quilted undergarment, the arming doublet or pourpoint (meaning "for the points"). These points had to be carefully placed and snugly tied, so that the jointed armor elements would stay in place and not hamper the free movement of the arm by shifting position. For this reason, it was most important not to "stretch a point."

The development of full defenses for the arms

ARMS AND ARMOR

made the holding of the shield awkward, and shortly after this full armoring of the limbs was achieved—about 1380—the shield went out of use in the field, although the targe was kept as tournament equipment. One of the best descriptions of the fourteenth-century armor is found in the arming of Sir Gawain in the Middle English poem "Sir Gawain and the Green Knight" (last third of the fourteenth century). English tomb effigies, such as that of Edward the Black Prince (*d.* 1376) in Canterbury Cathedral, are among the best three-dimensional representations. Above this tomb, incidentally, the prince's "shield for war" and "shield for peace" were once hung; today only his triangular "shield for war" is still there—his targe has disappeared.

The helmets worn together with these coats of plates were the bucketlike great heaume, with crest and mantling, the wide-brimmed chapel-de-fer, and the basinet. Of these three types only the basinet was of a radically new design; the other two were older forms. The great heaume was developed from the flat-topped, face-covering helmet of the Crusades. It now consisted of four or five plates riveted together: a slightly domed top plate, a slanting brow plate, a sharply ridged front plate, and one or two rear plates. The junction between brow plate and front plate was partially widened to provide eye slits, with a narrow central bridge to strengthen this potentially weak point. On the right side of the front plate were the breathing perforations, often arranged in a decorative pattern, and a small T- or cross-shaped cutout at the bottom for the carrying chain toggle. One of the finest surviving specimens, the heaume of the Black Prince in Canterbury Cathedral, has the breathing holes arranged in the outline of a crown and also retains its original crest.

The chapel-de-fer, as its name suggests, was an iron hat. It had a high crown, rounded and ridged, and a wide, slightly slanting brim. Sometimes an eye slit was cut into the brim at the base of the crown, so that the chapel-de-fer could be pulled down to cover more of the face. This design was an alternative to the heaume, for claustrophobic knights. In an episode at the Battle of Al-Mansūra (1250), reported in the memoirs of Jean de Joinville, a leader of the sixth Crusade of St. Louis, the king was about to faint under his heavy heaume and Joinville offered him his own chapel-de-fer, which did not obstruct breathing.

The basinet was developed from the coif, the hood worn under the heaume. Since the heaume was carried slung over the shoulder on its chain when not immediately needed, the knights used the coif, reinforced by a steel skullcap, for instant readiness against surprise attacks on the march, ambushes, and so on. This skullcap gradually grew into a close-fitting helmet of pointed ovoid shape; and the mail hood became attached to the helmet's lower edge as the camail, covering chin, neck, and shoulders. Sometimes a triangular nose guard was attached to the camail, which could be hooked upward into a catch in the middle of the helmet's brow. When unhooked the guard hung down from the camail like a small pointed beard. Another variation was the *Klappvisier,* a movable visor attached to a single hinge at the helmet's front. This form was used only from about 1320 to 1340 and almost exclusively in Germany. Later a far more stable attachment was designed, with the visor pivoting on two bolts placed approximately at the temples. The visor had two narrow eye slits and two breathing slits, resembling a smiling mouth. "Breaths," perforations for ventilation, were drilled on the less exposed right side. To facilitate breathing and to streamline the glancing surfaces, the visor was drawn out to a sharp point. The snoutlike appearance of these visors inspired nicknames such as "hounskull" and "pig-faced visor." These visors were detachable from their pivots.

In the knightly tactics of charging with couched lance, it was vital that the enemy's lance did not slip between a knight's body and left arm; this way the arm could easily be wrenched out of its socket or even broken. The safest way to render the enemy lance harmless was to make it snap. This could be achieved if the lance hit a solid surface at a right angle. Once the shield had been given up the knight had to take this impact on his chest; so he needed a solid breastplate. In order to withstand the force of the lance thrust, the knight had to lean forward in his saddle at an angle of about thirty degrees. To create a vertical surface for the enemy's lance to hit and to shatter against, the solid breastplate had to be bulbous, with its upper part slanting at an angle of about thirty degrees (to be vertical, when the knight leaned forward at the optimal angle). At the same time the bulbous breastplate afforded an additional bolster for the vulnerable chest and abdomen.

The first solid breastplates were incorporated into brigandines, short, tight-fitting coats of plates. The breastplates covered the rib cage, with smaller plates riveted to the inside of the fabric coat protecting the abdomen, hips, and back. An excavated and reconstructed specimen (from the Venetian fortress of Ne-

Germanic spangenhelm, *ca.* 500

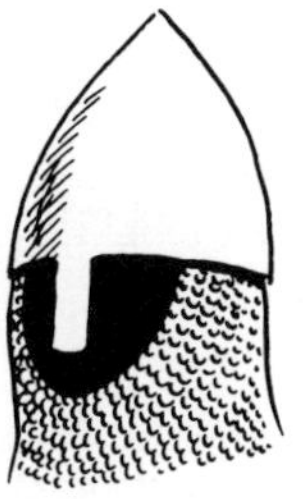

Norman helmet with noseguard, *ca.* 1100

Helmet with noseguard, *ca.* 1150

Kettle-hat or chapel-de-fer, 1300–1450

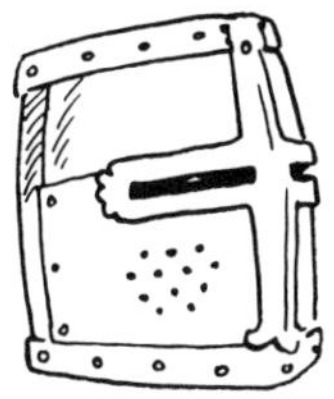

Heaume Topfhelm, *ca.* 1250

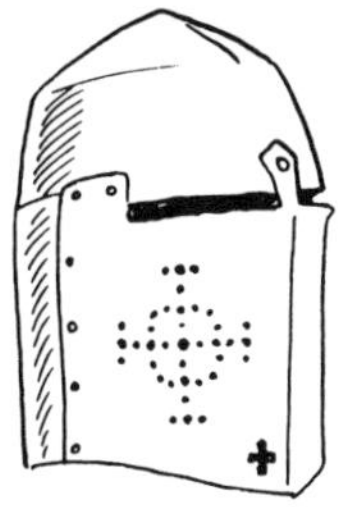

Great heaume, *ca.* 1350

Tilting helmet, *ca.* 1500

Basinet with camail and detachable noseguard, *ca.* 1350

Basinet with camail and Klappvisier, *ca.* 1350

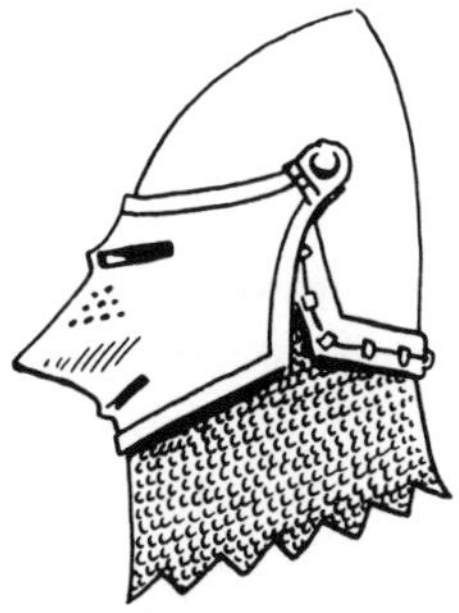

Basinet with camail and pivoted hounskull visor, *ca.* 1400

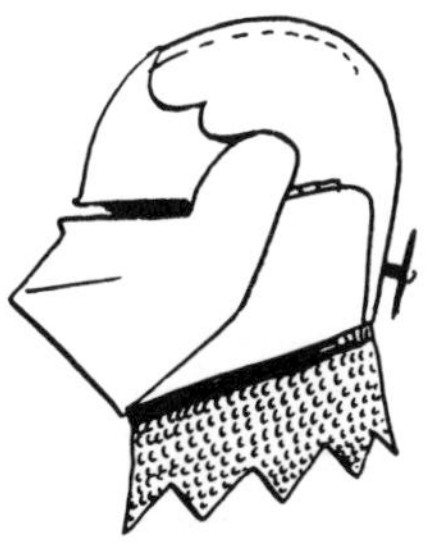

Armet à rondelle, *ca.* 1400–1450

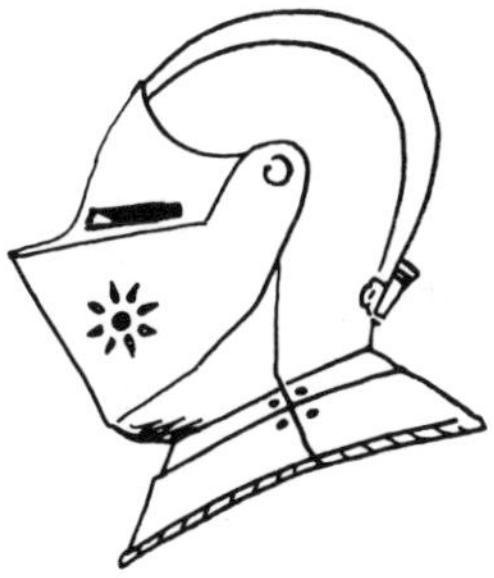

Close helmet, *ca.* 1550

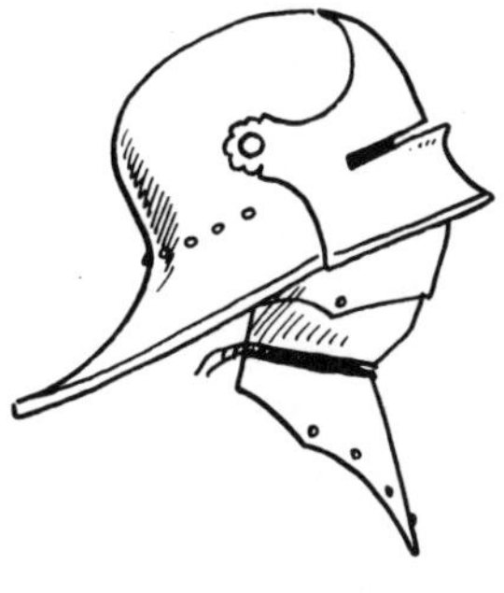

Sallet with bevor, *ca.* 1475

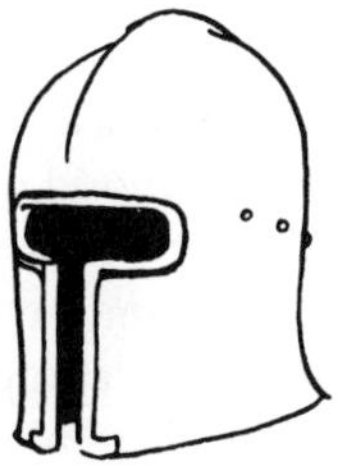

Barbute, *ca.* 1475

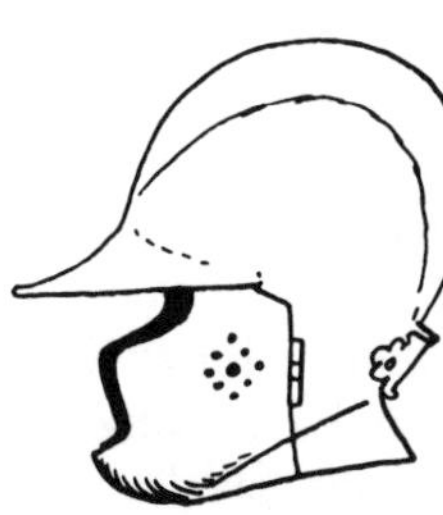

Burgonet, *ca.* 1540

Morion, *ca.* 1560

groponte in Chalcis, *ca.* 1400) at the Metropolitan Museum of Art consists of twenty-seven individual plates, riveted on red velvet. In contrast to the loose-fitting mail shirt, which could be pulled on over the head like a sweater, the plate-lined brigandine had to be tight-fitting, in order to avoid bruising when the plates shifted. For this reason the brigandine was split open in front, with the breastplate divided into two halves, and put on like a modern jacket. In fact, this was the origin of the modern jacket; and the reason that men's jackets are buttoned left over right is that the two halves of the brigandine breastplate had to overlap left side over right, so that a sword blade or lance point would slide off harmlessly, since as a rule all attacks came from the left.

To keep the flat-fitting lower part of the brigandine in its proper position and its hem down, a heavy sword belt *(dupsing),* mounted with studs and rosettes of gilt bronze or silver, was worn very low on the hips. It was also worn as a necessary accessory to the civilian doublet, which was of the same cut as the brigandine. Brigandines were much favored, even after the full plate suit had been perfected, by light cavalrymen, archers, and other troops who depended on mobility. They were equally useful and appreciated in civilian life as a protection against brigands (hence the name)—and possibly also jealous husbands.

After the shield had been given up by the armored mounted knights—everywhere except Spain, where it was still in use at the time of the conquest of Mexico (1519–1521) and Peru (1532)—it was still the main defense for the less well-armored foot soliders. Swordsmen carried bucklers for parrying sword strokes, and crossbowmen had pavises. Bucklers were round, about two feet in diameter, with a central handgrip and shield boss, just like the old round shield of the early Middle Ages. A variant with two shield grips and without boss was the rondache; its wearers were called rondachiers. Pavises were roughly rectangular, with a strong, protruding middle ridge. They were approximately breast high, to be set on the ground as cover for a kneeling crossbowman when he reloaded. In defense, they could be set up as a sort of movable wall around a body of infantry. Small pavises, about two feet long, were used by swordsmen in Bohemia and Germany instead of bucklers, as well as by light cavalrymen. Hungarian hussars had a peculiar shield of basically rectangular shape but with its top cut at a slant; these were eagerly adopted by the Turks. Spaniards, however, took over the *adarga*—a double-oval leather

Pavise,
mid 15th century

shield with four bosses to secure the handgrips—from the Moors. The Mexican *dragons de la cuera* still carried *adargas* against the arrows of Apaches and Comanches in the early nineteenth century.

The introduction of the solid breastplate as an individual element, but an integral part of the plate armoring of limbs and body, marked the beginning of the period of the full suit of armor, the "knight in shining armor" of the popular image. The earliest surviving specimen—and most likely one of the first ever made—is preserved in the ancient armory of Count Trapp in Castle Churburg, in the south Tyrol. It was made around 1380 or 1390 and bears the mark of the armorer Petrajolo dei Negroni da Ello, called Missaglia, in Milan. The solid breastplate made possible another technical improvement, the lance rest, a hook attached to the right side of the breastplate to support the lance in couched position, taking some of the strain off the holding hand. Another new feature was a V-shaped stop-ridge riveted below the neckline to prevent a blade or spear point from slipping upward into the knight's throat.

By the second quarter of the fifteenth century the development of the full suit of plate armor was complete; this important technical step was taken in Milan, the leading industrial center of the period, and probably by the leading Milanese armorer, Tommaso da Missaglia. The earliest surviving homogeneous full suit of plate armor, that of Frederick the Victorious, count palatine of the Rhine, 1451 (now in the Waffensammlung of the Kunsthisto-

ARMS AND ARMOR

risches Museum in Vienna), was ordered from his workshop. From about 1420 on the central element of a suit of armor was the cuirass, consisting of breast- and backplate, and a skirt constructed of horizontal lames, with attached tassets to cover the vulnerable area between skirt and cuisses. The reluctance of knights to be encased in unyielding plate armor (the reason for the long-lasting popularity of the brigandine) showed itself clearly in the construction of fifteenth-century cuirasses: their breastplates, and often their backplates too, were composed of two or more sections flexibly connected by buckled leather straps or sliding rivets. The functional beauty of these early masterpieces of the armorer's craft was such that armor was now worn without even a heraldic surcoat, so as not to spoil the impression of the man in armor as a living metal statue.

At the time that the man's armor was perfected, the same was achieved for his horse. The beginnings had been made in the late fourteenth century, when the existing mail armor for horses was augmented by a chamfrain or chamfron (head armor; the earliest specimen, from around 1370, is in Warwick Castle, England) with attached lames protecting the nape of the neck, and by breast and flank shields of leather. The complete horse armor, developed by about 1450, consisted of steel chamfrain with eye- and earguards, crinet (neck armor of articulated parallel lames), peitrel (breast armor), flancards (side armor), and crupper (rear armor). The armored saddle, with steel plates on saddlebow and cantle, completed the protection of the horse. There exist records, written and pictorial, that especially valuable horses were equipped with cunningly articulated leg armor down to their fetlocks.

Although plate armor was developed in Milan in the first half of the fifteenth century, the northern workshops soon followed in the second half, particularly those of the important German centers Augsburg, Nürnberg, and Landshut in Bavaria; Innsbruck in the Austrian Tyrol; Antwerp and Brussels in Flanders; and Paris and Tours in France. Some of the more important princes set up their own court workshops to produce fine armor for field, tournament, and pageant for themselves and their courts, and in order to secure a supply of prestigious diplomatic presents, because a fine suit of armor soon became the ideal present. The earliest of these court workshops was that of the dukes of Burgundy at Arbois, Bourgogne (*ca.* 1470–1509), staffed with armorers from Milan; later—in the 1490's—the imperial workshop of Emperor Maximilian was set up at Innsbruck. The English royal workshop at Greenwich, established under Henry VIII in 1514, was active until the middle of the seventeenth century; the French royal workshop (so-called "Louvre School") in Paris, under Francis I and Henry II (*ca.* 1540–1559), was particularly renowned for extravagantly lavish parade armor; and the court workshop of the electors of Saxony, at Dresden and Annaberg (after 1545), was active until around 1620.

The armor shops of Milan were organized on a very efficient industrial base and on a vast scale by the standards of the period; the outstanding Missaglia workshop employed up to 500 workmen at times. The German shops, by contrast, were strictly regulated and supervised by their guilds, which permitted only a very limited number of employees—usually not more than five or six—per workshop, in order to spread the work load more evenly among all members. In both systems, however, there was a marked tendency for the shops to be run by the same family for several generations, such as the workshops of the Missaglia, Negroli, and Piccinino in Milan, the Treytz and Seusenhofer in Innsbruck, and the Frawenpreiss and Helmschmied in Augsburg. The industrialized Milanese armor shops employed many specialists, each of whom manufactured only one element of the suit and struck his personal mark on it as a guarantee (and probably also for accounting purposes). Therefore, it is quite normal to have a homogeneous suit of Milanese armor that displays half a dozen different maker's marks in addition to the workshop mark of Missaglia, for instance. On German armor, by contrast, there would be only the mark of the workshop master, together with the mark of the supervising city guild, although there must have been a certain specialization among skilled workers too, as the name of one of the most renowned Augsburg armorer families suggests: Helmschmied = "helmet smith." The first armorer known to have specialized in horse armor was Pier Innocenzo da Faerno of Milan (*ca.* 1450–1460).

Although plate armor was perfected in Milan during the quattrocento, the golden age of the Italian Renaissance, fifteenth-century armor is often called "Gothic armor," because it is styled with an emphasis on the vertical and has—as is especially apparent in the German examples—a certain spiky outline reminiscent of Gothic architecture. The sabatons, for instance, are pointed, with sometimes exaggeratedly long tips; the poleyns (kneecops) have pointedly angled lames overlapping the cuisses and the sharply ridged shinbawdes or greaves; the cow-

ARMS AND ARMOR

ters (elbow-cops) and the knuckle-plate of the gauntlets are spiked; gauntlet cuffs and the lower half of the divided breastplate are cut into sharp points, all adding to the Gothic image.

During the fifteenth century three new types of helmet appeared: the armet, the sallet, and the barbute. The armet encased the entire head closely; it had movable, hinged cheekpieces closed by a lug or hook and eye at the chin. The face opening was covered by a pivoted, detachable visor, similar to that of the now obsolete basinet, though much less pointed. The rounded helmet bowl had a low central ridge, often with a keyhole-shaped cutout at the crown, for the attachment of a crest or plume. The nape of the neck usually was protected by a circular steel disk on a short stem (armet *à rondelle*) against neck-breaking sword strokes.

The sallet was a variant of the chapel-de-fer, with its sides steeply pulled down, an eye slit cut into its front, and its back drawn out into a sharp point. Some sallets had movable (but not detachable) visors. The sallet covered only the upper half of the face. To protect the chin a mail hood had to be worn; or a special chin defense, somewhat in the shape of a ship's prow, called the bevor, had to be strapped on or bolted to the breastplate.

The barbute (sometimes called "Venetian sallet") was a close-fitting helmet shaped in one piece, with a T-shaped cutout as combined eye slit and breathing opening. Its appearance was reminiscent of the Corinthian helmet of classical Greek antiquity. It is most likely that this was a deliberate Renaissance revival. The armet and barbute were created in Italy, the sallet in Germany.

The last technical improvement to effect the full protection of the knight in his armor was the introduction of the colletin, a standing collar of close-fitting lames combined with a shoulder yoke. The colletin closed the gap between breastplate and armet, which had been rather inadequately protected at first by a mail collar, and at the same time the yoke gave a firm foundation to the shoulder straps of the cuirass and made its weight easier to carry. The colletin in its most sophisticated form would have a perfectly circular, lobed rim designed to fit snugly into a matchingly circular, grooved rim of the "close" helmet, thus joining helmet and body armor into one single but flexible unit. The helmet could easily be turned on the colletin but not dislodged. Another useful feature of the colletin was that its yoke made the perfect anchor for the attachment of the pauldrons by means of straps and buckles or bolts and springs. One version even integrated colletin and shoulder guard in one unit, the *spangröls,* where overlapping lames came down from the yoke over the shoulder to join the rerebraces.

The construction of the shoulder guards—pauldrons, *spangröls,* ailettes and so on—was one of the most difficult technical problems that the armorers had to solve. The guards had to be large enough to give full protection, but they should not encumber the free movement of the arm in battle. Italian armorers of the fifteenth century designed huge pauldrons (sometimes large enough to overlap in back) built up of evenly spaced, parallel lames. These pauldrons with evenly spaced lames are later a telltale feature of armor made in the English court workshop at Greenwich, which employed Flemish armorers who learned their craft at the Burgundian workshop, which was in turn established by Milanese experts. In Italy and Germany sixteenth-century pauldrons were of different construction, with one large central lame and several upper and lower side lames. For the fight with couched lance the left pauldron as a rule was far larger than the right one, which also had a cutout to accommodate the shaft of the couched lance. An alternate solution was found by German armorers, who created small, shell-shaped shoulder pieces just large enough to cover the shoulder joint for maximum mobility, particularly for swordplay. The protection of the vulnerable armpit (when the arm was raised for a sword stroke) was left to the mail shirt, which was still worn under the plate armor to cover the chinks in the armor. Small steel roundels, called besagues, were hung in front of the armpits for additional protection. The small shoulder pieces became popular in Italy too, as amor *alla tedesca* (in the German style). The colletin, incidentally, had been invented in Germany too, probably in Augsburg, about 1500. Italian armorers adopted it rather reluctantly during the following two decades.

The technical improvement of the colletin, however, was completely overshadowed by a stylistic change that took place around 1500. In a radical turnabout, all formerly pointed or angular elements became rounded and the emphasis on the vertical, characteristic of "Gothic" armor, was now shifted to the horizontal. The change was most conspicuous in the shape of the sabatons, which abruptly changed from pointed poulaines to blunt and square-cut "oxmouth" shoes, and in the breastplates, which now

ARMS AND ARMOR

became globose with a straight-cut neckline bordered by a thick roped lobe as stop for the protection of the throat.

In German "Gothic" armor flutings had occasionally been embossed into the surfaces of breast- and backplates in imitation of the folds of the tunic of contemporary dress. Similar flutings, but spread over the entire surface of the armor (with the sole exception of the greaves, which always remained smooth), were now used—first in Milan but soon and most enthusiastically in the German shops—as an ingenious way to increase the resilience of the plates (like corrugated iron), and thus to make possible a slight decrease in the thickness of the plates, thereby saving weight. This fluted armor is also called "Maximilian" armor, because it was introduced around 1505 during the reign of Emperor Maximilian (1493–1519), a great fancier of fine armor who was surnamed "the Last of the Knights." The close connection between armor and contemporary costume is apparent in so-called "costume armor," in which the folds, slashings, or fabric patterns of costume are transferred to armor as decorative elements. In extreme cases even the voluminous puffed and slashed sleeves of the German *Landsknecht* (foot soldier) costume were imitated as telescoping sets of steel rings, and the heavily pleated skirts of court costume were converted into steel *tonlets* (Roggendorf and Brandenburg armor in Vienna, Henry VIII's armor in the Tower of London, Radziwill armor in New York). In Italy armor "all'antica" became fashionable; it used elements and motifs of what was considered classical Roman armor, as known from antique statues.

When the fluted Maximilian armor went out of use in the 1530's—probably for reason of its expensiveness due to the additional precision work of fluting—the armor style adapted features of the prevalent Spanish costume, especially a V-shaped waistline with a sharply prominent middle ridge down the breastplate, and a peculiar decoration of three etched ornamental bands that corresponded to the seams of the Spanish doublet. The strange-looking "peascod" shape of the breastplate was again a way of presenting a vertical surface to an oncoming lance point, when the knight leaned forward in the saddle at an angle of thirty degrees.

While the armet helmet became the standard "closed" helmet of the sixteenth century, the sallet went out of fashion by its first quarter. The chapel-de-fer developed into the morion with a high comb and wide brim swept up fore and aft, and the cabasset, with straight and narrow brim and sugarloaf skull. As a new form the burgonet was introduced: this helmet was roughly in the shape of a modern hunter's cap with a peak and movable cheek pieces; its top either came to a point or had high combs (one or three). The face opening could be closed by a special chin defense, the buffe, attached by a hook or strap.

Light cavalrymen (mounted archers), infantry officers, and elite foot soliders (*Doppelsöldner* or double-pay men, who had to stand in the first rank) wore half armor, that is, a cuirass with arm defenses and an open-faced burgonet or a morion. These half armors were distiguishable from the knightly armor because they never had a lance rest and no leg armor.

During the second half of the sixteenth century the changes in armor were only of a stylistic nature. During the 1580's and 1590's the prominent ridge of the "peascod" breastplate was at its highest; the tassets hanging from the cuirass skirt to cover the hips were more and more bulbous in shape to accommodate the fashionable trunk hosen.

During the late sixteenth century an alternate type of cuirass was introduced, the anime, which had the breast- and backplates made from narrow overlapping horizontal lames, for maximum mobility. These animes too never had lance rests and were usually worn with a burgonet. Their tassets often were elongated down to the knees. These long tassets, worn together with a solid cuirass but without greaves, were the characteristic feature of the so-called three-quarter armor, which in the seventeenth century became the standard armor of heavy cavalry, such as the cuirassiers of the Thirty Years' War (1618–1648), who still carried lances. Their headgear was either the "close" helmet or a heavy version of the burgonet, the "death's head" helmet, so named because of its buffe with round eyeholes that resembled a skull.

Seventeenth-century military costume sported enormously bulky trousers, sashes belted high under the armpits and boots with floppy cuffs. The cuirassiers' armor therefore had very short breastplates, bulky tassets down to the knees, and left the protection of the lower legs to the heavy boots. Light cavalry, now equipped with firearms—carbines, harquebuses, or, as in the case of the renowned German *reiters* or *pistoliers,* a pair of long wheel-lock pistols—wore only vestigial armor: a buffcoat of thick buffalo (hence the name) or moose leather, a steel

ARMS AND ARMOR

colletin as protection of the jugulars, and a morion or light burgonet, called *zischägge* (from Turkish *shishak,* helmet) or lobster-tail helmet, because of its long laminated neck guard.

In order to meet the challenge of the firearms, the armorers throughout the sixteenth century had gradually increased the thickness of the plates, particularly of the cuirass. Bullet-proof armor was tested by a pistol shot at twenty paces; the dent of the bullet was left as a mark of proof. By the end of the sixteenth century these bullet-proof armor plates were heavy enough for footsoldiers to refuse to wear them on the march; only in England pikemen's armor, consisting of a short breast- and backplate with huge one-piece tassets and a wide-brimmed pot (chapel-de-fer) was worn until the English Civil War (1642–1648).

It has been repeated over and over again that after the Battle of Crécy (1346), where English longbowmen shot down the flower of French chivalry, the heavily armored knight became obsolete. It was exactly at this time, however—apparently to meet the double challenge of improved crossbows and longbows—that plate armor was introduced. Ninety percent of the surviving armor originates from after 1500, when gunpowder had become an even more serious threat. As mentioned before, by increasing the body area covered by deflecting plate armor the danger from missiles could be counteracted for a while, until the armor plates for the vital areas had to be made so thick that, in order to compensate for the increase in weight, the defenses for legs and arms had to be given up. It should be pointed out here that the total weight of a suit of battle armor should not exceed sixty pounds; this is about the limit of weight that can be tolerated by a man for a long stretch of time—and armor had to be worn for an entire day or longer, if need be. In considering this weight, it had to be kept in mind that full armor was worn only by men on horseback; footsoldiers' armor as a rule was no more than thirty-five pounds. Although after the middle of the seventeenth century only a few elite cavalry regiments still wore cuirasses, they were for protection against sword cuts, not against bullets.

Armor is still worn today, not only for parade, like the helmets and cuirasses of the English Royal Horseguards, or the small shield-shaped gorgets of officers in some armies (the last vestiges of the colletin), but also as steel helmets, flak jackets, and bulletproof vests for combat and police work. For riot control even the long-abandoned shield has made a comeback.

TOURNAMENT ARMOR

A specialized kind of armor was worn for the spectator sport of the Middle Ages, the tournament. Until the thirteenth century there was no differentiation between arms for war and for tournament, with the exception that lances and swords used for this "combat of peace" were blunted. Despite these precautions there were considerable casualties and many fatal accidents. In order to minimize the risks in this very rough sport, additional reinforcement pieces were created: first, a reinforcement plate to the front of the heaume against lance points that slipped over the shield top, and rolls of padding strapped to the saddle in front of the knees as protection against collisions of the horses. A large circular vamplate was attached to the lance as cover for the right holding hand.

The more different from real warfare the tournament became, the more different from field armor the tournament equipment had to be designed. As is often the case with formalizations, the armor for formalized combat in the tournament field preserved archaic types of equipment long after they were abandoned in everyday warfare. The great heaume was transfored into the tilting helm, a ponderous affair bolted to the breast- and backplates, with a wide eye slit over a protruding lip of the ship's-prow-shaped front plate. It was heavily padded to keep the jouster's head stabilized against whiplash. The left arm was reinforced by a special guard on the shoulder, an elbow-cop, and a large, one-piece mitten gauntlet. The most vulnerable spot, the left armpit, where a lance might slip in and break the arm, was covered by an almost square shield of steel or of two-inch-thick hardwood, veneered with polished bone plaques, the tilting targe. The tilting cuirass was asymmetrically built with a boxlike shaping of the right side to accommodate the stout lance rest and its rear extension with a counter-hook, the queue, which held the heavy lance firmly in position without tiring the jouster's arm. Because of the extreme weight of this armor (about 100 lbs.) built strictly for safety, no leg armor was worn with it. The rider's legs were tucked under the huge straw-stuffed cushion bound in front of the blindfolded horse's breast and shoulders as protection against collisions. Another way of protecting the rider's legs was by a high saddle with no cantle but with wooden extensions of

ARMS AND ARMOR

the saddlebow down to the jouster's feet *(Hohenzeuggestech).*

Another very popular form of jousting armor among the approximately twenty-five different versions recorded was reinforced field armor. Here reinforcement pieces were added to the left shoulder and arm, to the breastplate, including a special tasset, and to neck and chin (tilting buffe, often with a little window on the right side for air). In one form, the *Realgestech,* a grand guard flaring out like a little cape covered the left side of the breast and the shoulder down to the elbow and a riveted grid afforded a hold for the lance point to make it easier to snap the shaft.

About 1490 the Augsburg armorer Lorenz Helmschmied designed for Emperor Maximilian what later was called a garniture for field and tournament, a set of armor for man and horse of matching decoration, with exchange pieces for all types of tournament. Grand garnitures of this kind were the most ambitious projects ever undertaken in the field of arms and armor; they could easily comprise several hundred individual elements. In today's values, a fine suit of armor must be compared to a custom-upholstered limousine; such a grand garniture, however, would easily be the equivalent of an executive jet.

For a specific German style of joust, the *Rennen,* the helmet used *(Rennhut)* was derived from the sallet. A large shield, the *Renntartsche,* was molded to the jouster's left front from eye slit to elbow and bolted to the breastplate.

The baston-course was a tournament on horseback without lances, fought with clubs or blunt swords. Here the helmet had a large face opening closed with a grille like a fencing mask's; this was sufficient protection, because the purpose of this course was to knock off the opponent's crest, and to thrust with the sword was against the rules.

For tournaments on foot, special foot-combat armor was designed with wide, flaring skirts of horizontal hoops down to the knees or, as an alternative solution, with cunningly designed, tight-fitting leg armor (hoguine). Foot-combat helmets had sievelike perforated visors for much-appreciated easier breathing. The top of the helmet could be reinforced by a clipped-on pate defense. In the armories of Brunswick and Dresden there were sets of six and more matching foot-combat suits, specially made for "floor shows" in the banquet hall at a princely wedding.

ARMOR MANUFACTURE AND DECORATION

The manufacture of armor was in the hands of highly specialized craftsmen: the mail makers, for instance, were a different group from the makers of plate armor.

Mail was manufactured from drawn iron wire. This wire was wrapped around a dowel in a tight spiral, which then was cut open lengthwise to produce individual rings with slightly offset open ends. By pushing these rings through a funnellike device the ring ends were made to overlap, and then they were pierced and riveted shut by means of an instrument similar to a ticket taker's punch. Within the mail fabric each ring was normally interlinked with four others—two each in the adjacent rows of rings—to create a texture very much like knit fabric. The shaping of a shoulder or elbow rounding was achieved by increasing or decreasing the number of linked rings—linking one ring to five or three others. Mail making was a very time-consuming process; it took a master approximately six months to finish a mail shirt of about 200,000 rings. Mail could not be cleaned ring by ring by hand; its cleaning was done in a tumbler, a rotating barrel (cranked by the knight's squire or page boy), in which the rings would rub each other clean, the rust and dirt to be absorbed by some shovelsful of sawdust in the tumbler.

Plate armor was fashioned from sheet metal hammered from iron ingots under a trip-hammer powered by a waterwheel (rolled sheet metal was not yet available; the hammer marks on the inside of armor plate are one of the criteria for identifying original plates). The shaping of the individual elements (a full suit of armor might consist of up to 200 individual elements) required high technical skill. In order to minimize the weight of the plates, they were worked thickest at their points of stress, such as for instance in the center of a breastplate, and much thinner in places less likely to be seriously hit, such as the sides of the breastplate under the arms. By special heat treatment an almost glass-hard outer "skin" could be created, while the inner portion of the plate remained mild steel and therefore retained its toughness.

The surfaces were either brightly polished (again by specialists), or colored by heat treatment (bluing) or by letting hot oil burn into them (blackening). This blackening was a rust-proofing device; the highly polished "white" armor and the delicate bluing had to be most carefully kept from rusting.

1. Typical 15th-century armor

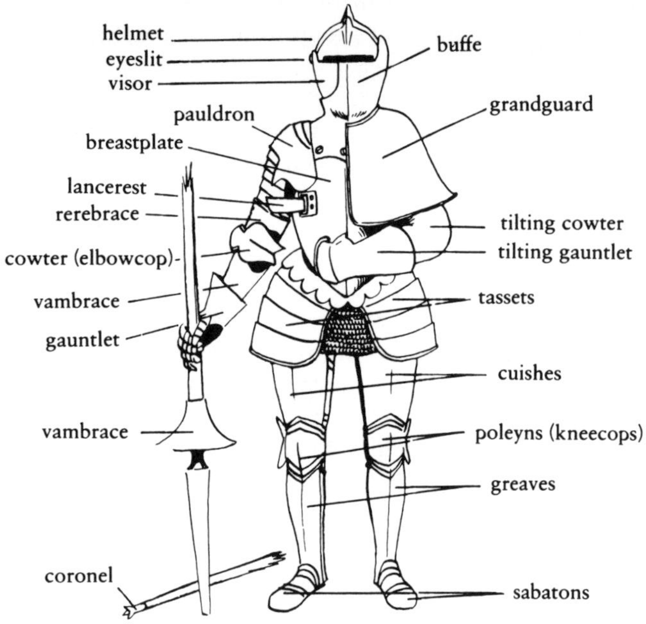

2. *ca.* 500

Alanic or Sarmatian heavy cavalryman scale armor, spangenhelm, leather chamfron

3. *ca.* 1100

Mail, "Norman" helmet and shield

4. *ca.* 1300

Mail, great heaume and kneecops

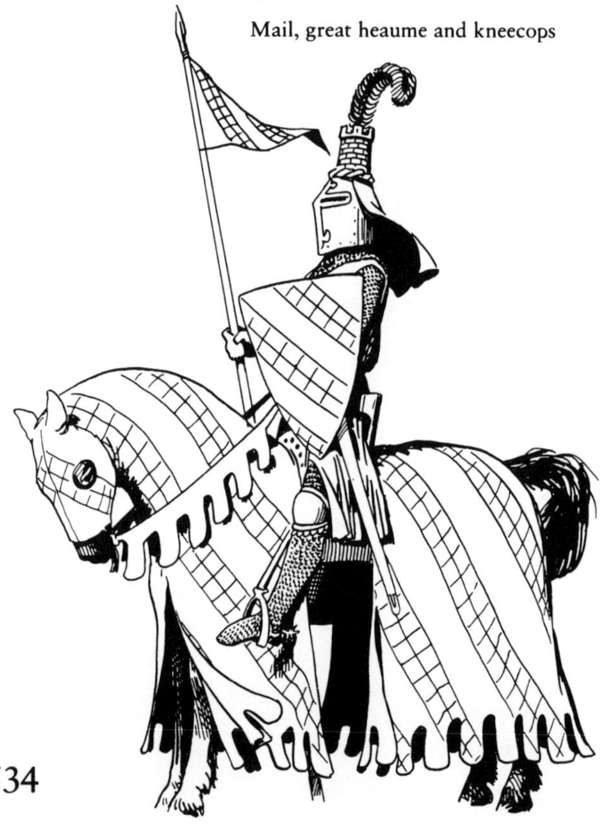

5. *ca.* 1400
Early plate armor with brigandine

6. *ca.* 1450
Complete plate armor

7. *ca.* 1510
Armor *alla tedescha*

8. *ca.* 1540
Armor *all'antica*

All drawings by the author. Figs. 1, 5, 6, 7, 8 from *Gloria Dell Arte: A Renaissance Perspective,* Philbrook Art Center, 1979.

Black armor, therefore, was most appreciated by free lances and other mercenaries (blackguards) who could not afford a squire to polish their armor. Cleaning armor plate was done by wiping it carefully with an oily rag, always in one direction for a fine matte sheen, not in a circular motion, which would result in splotchy reflections.

Decoration of armor could be done by the application of metals of a different color, such as gold or silver. In the early Middle Ages and again in the Renaissance so-called "damascening" was very popular. It was done using two different techniques; in the first, grooves were cut into the surface to be decorated, and gold or silver wires were hammered into these grooves. The second, less durable, method was to roughen the surface by cross-hatching and to hammer the wires of precious metal directly onto the rough surface. The most popular form of decoration of plate armor, however, was etching. There were two different methods employed in this too; they can be used to tell Italian from German workmanship, and to a lesser degree even French technique can be distinguished. The Italian armorers covered the entire surface of the plate to be decorated with an acid-resistant layer such as resin or wax. The design was scratched into this layer down to the metal surface. When acid was poured over this scratched design, it ate into the metal where the wax or resin had been scratched away. After the wax layer had been removed the design showed up etched black into the white surface. For special effect it could be fire (mercury) gilded, which was also an alternative—although very expensive—way of rust-proofing. The German etchers painted the design onto the surfaces with tiny brushes dipped in liquid wax. Their stippled backgrounds, in particular, with every single dot separately applied with painstaking care, are easily distinguishable from the Italians' backgrounds of scratched-in ringlets. French etchers used a combined technique, scratching out blank backgrounds with partially applied patterns. The designs for armor decoration were sometimes made by the greatest artists; neither Leonardo da Vinci, nor Mantegna, nor Albrecht Dürer, nor Holbein felt above doing them.

The most prestigious and lavish kind of decoration was embossing. Here the armor plate was laid upon a wooden block or a bowl of condensed pitch (a steel anvil would be too hard as a base and would crack the finer work), and the design was hammered out in relief from the inside. The delicate details were later worked out from the front. This technique was suited only for parade armor because it defeated the very purpose of plate armor; that is, to present smooth, deflecting surfaces to enemy weapons. The most dazzling examples came from the "Louvre School" in Paris and from an Antwerp master, Elisaeus Libaerts (active around 1563), who apparently once had worked in Paris under the court artist Étienne Delaune.

Of similarly doubtful defensive value was the technique of application of borders of brass, which had been used on early plate armor during the fourteenth and fifteenth centuries. In the sixteenth century, although the Seusenhofer workshop in Innsbruck turned out even armor with silver appliqués, it was used only on parade and pageant armor for colorful effect.

BIBLIOGRAPHY

Howard L. Blackmore, *Arms and Armour* (1965); Claude Blair, *European Armour, Circa 1066 to Circa 1700* (1959); Lionello Boccia and E. T. Coelho, *L'arte dell'armatura in Italia* (1967); Wendelin Boeheim, *Handbuch der Waffenkunde* (1890); Bashford Dean, *Handbook of Arms and Armor* (1930); Ortwin Gamber, *"Die Harnischgarnitur"*, in *Jahrbuch der Kunsthistorischen* (1960); Stephen V. Grancsay, *The Armor of Galiot de Genouilhac* (1937); Guy Francis Laking, *A Record of European Armour and Arms Through Seven Centuries*, 5 vols. (1920–1922); James G. Mann, *An Outline of Arms and Armour in England from the Early Middle Ages to the Civil War* (1960); Paul Martin, *Arms and Armour from the 9th to the 17th Century*, Rene North, trans. (1968); Heinrich Müller and Fritz Kunter, *Europäische Helme aus der Sammlung des Museums für deutsche Geschichte* (1971); Helmut Nickel, *Ullstein-Waffenbuch; eine Kulturhistorie* (1974); A. Vesey B. Norman, *Arms and Armour* (1964); and *Warrior to Soldier, 449–1660* (1966); Harold L. Peterson, *A History of Body Armor* (1968); William Reid, *The Lore of Arms* (1976); Johannes Schöbel, *Fine Arms and Armor—Treasures from the Dresden Collection* (1975); Bruno Thomas, Ortwin Gamber, and Hans Schedelmann, *Arms and Armour; Masterpieces by European Craftsmen from the Thirteenth to the Nineteenth Century*, Ilse Bloom and William Reid, trans. (1964); Bengt Thordeman, *Armour from the Battle of Wisby, 1361*, 2 vols. (1939–1940); Grant Uden, *A Dictionary of Chivalry* (1968).

HELMUT NICKEL

[See also **Bow, Long-bow, Cross-bow, Arbalest; Heraldry; Knights, Knight Service; Lance, Pike, Spear; Swords and Daggers; Warfare, European.**]

ÁRNA SAGA BISKUPS, one of the so-called bishops' sagas, is an Icelandic life of Árni Þorláksson, bishop of Skálholt from 1269 to 1298, written shortly after 1300. Its author was most likely Árni's successor, his nephew Árni Helgason, or someone closely connected with him. The saga, the end of which is missing, is known from two fourteenth-century fragments and a large number of seventeenth-century copies.

Árna saga biskups is considered an important source for the legal and ecclesiastical history of Iceland in the latter half of the thirteenth century, especially after 1264, when the Icelanders had accepted the king of Norway as their ruler. This was a period of legal reform in both church and society, and Bishop Árni spared no effort to instruct secular leaders in the rights of the church. His lessons were little appreciated, and secular leaders found it difficult to abide by the new rules for ownership of church property, which until then had remained largely under lay control. The saga recounts the ensuing legal and political disputes in great—sometimes tedious—detail.

The saga contains a wealth of information believed to have come from archives kept at the see of Skálholt, and it has more references to or quotations from written sources than any of the other bishops' sagas. It also has several passages containing historical information not directly relevant to the main narrative; such information connects the saga with some of the more important annalistic compilations of its day.

Árna saga biskups gives a detailed portrait of a powerful church administrator and accomplished church lawyer, who lived to see the dispute over church property *(staðamál)* resolved in a compromise, ratified in 1297, that was probably not to his complete satisfaction.

BIBLIOGRAPHY

Sources. Biskupa sögur, Jón Sigurðsson and Guðbrandur Vigfússon, eds., I (1858), 677–786; *Byskupa sögur,* Guðni Jónsson, ed., I (1948), 285–457; *Árna saga biskups,* Þorleifur Hauksson, ed. (1972).

Studies. Peter G. Foote, "Bischofssaga," in *Reallexikon der Germanischen Altertumskunde,* 2nd ed., III (1978), 40–43; Jørgen H. Jørgensen, *Bispesagaer—Laurentius saga* (1978), 26–27, 46–47; Magnús M. Lárusson, "Árna saga biskups," in *Kulturhistorisk leksikon for nordisk middelalder,* I (1956), 251; Magnús Stefánsson. "Frá goðakirkju til biskupskirkju," in *Saga Íslands,* III (1978), 109–257.

HANS BEKKER-NIELSEN

ARNALD OF VILLANOVA (*ca.* 1240–1311), Catalan physician, professor of medicine, and religious reformer and spiritual author, perhaps was born at Villanueva de Jiloca, near Daroca, in Aragon; he died at sea off Genoa.

Arnald studied medicine at Montpellier, which was in Catalan territory, about 1260. He married Agnes Blasi of Montpellier, held a prebend in Valencia, and had a daughter, Maria, who became a Dominican nun there. By 1281, Arnald was physician to Pedro III, king of Aragon and count of Barcelona (*d.* 1285), and he later cared for Pedro's sons, Alfonso III and James II of Aragon. In the early 1280's he studied Hebrew and Scripture at the Dominican convent in Barcelona and translated Galen's *De rigore (On stiffness)* from Arabic into Latin.

By 1291, Arnald was established as a master of medicine at the University of Montpellier, where he stayed until 1299 and where he probably knew and was influenced by the Franciscan reformer Peter John Olivi. During the last twenty years of his life, Arnald published extensive and significant medical works, but also became increasingly involved in theological and ecclesiastical controversy. In 1288, while he was still physician to Alfonso III, Arnald composed *De adventu antichristi (On the Coming of Antichrist),* which he kept secret at the time. Once he had moved to Montpellier, Arnald openly published works espousing eschatological prophecies inspired by Joachim di Fiore and the reform of the Church along the lines advocated by the Fraticelli and beghards. He also developed anti-Jewish and anti-pagan (or Moslem) themes, and in 1292 wrote his *Allocutio super Tetragrammaton (Address on the Word of Four Letters),* in which he argued that Hebrew letters YHWH symbolized the Christian Trinity.

Sent to Paris on a diplomatic mission concerning the Val d'Aran by James II in 1299, Arnald defended his work on the coming of the Antichrist—who, he said, would appear in 1378—before the masters of theology of the university. The work was condemned nonetheless, and Arnald was briefly imprisoned. In 1300, Arnald appealed to Pope Boniface VIII, whom he served as a physician; Boniface required Arnald to abjure his heterodox ideas in private but publicly declared the Parisian condemnation excessive. Gratefully, Arnald dedicated to Boniface a magical treatise on astrological images *(De sigillis).*

After submitting to Boniface's successor, Benedict XI, a detailed program for reform, beginning with

ARNALD OF VILLANOVA

the pope, Arnald was imprisoned at Perugia and was only released after Benedict's death. Suspected of having had a hand in poisoning Benedict, who had died of dysentery, Arnald took refuge at the court of Frederick III of Sicily, to whom he dedicated his *Allocutio christiana (Christian Address)* on the reform of the Church. After the accession of Clement V in 1305, Arnald had the support of both the pope and his royal patrons, and served James II as an ambassador to Avignon. Clement followed his advice for the reform of medical education at Montpellier, but in 1309, Arnald created a sensation with a speech at a papal consistory denouncing ecclesiastical errors and calling for reform of the Church, in which he expected James and his brother Frederick to take the lead. Within a year, however, he quarreled with James and again took refuge with the king of Sicily. He died while in the service of Frederick, and was buried at Genoa.

Arnald's knowledge of Arabic and his interest in theory and systems made him the leading figure of his day in the introduction of Greek and Arabic medical theory into the West. He lectured extensively on the Hippocratic and Galenic classics, translated Avicenna (Ibn Sīnā), Albuzale (Abuʾl Salt Umayya), and Avenzoar (Ibn Zuhr Abū Marwān); and in his own writings presented the study of medicine as a systematic science based on Galenic foundations. Although Pope Boniface commanded him, "Immerse yourself in medicine, not in theology," Arnald developed a theological view of natural science. Beginning with the pragmatic sense of a skilled practicing physician, he emphasized the rational nature of medicine, then moved on to develop an abstract, theoretical and quantitative approach. In his treatise *Aphorismi de gradibus (Aphorisms on [Pharmaceutical] Degrees)* Arnald dealt with the mixing of complex drugs as a mathematical science based on a law that the intensity of a compound drug increases arithmetically as the ratio of the opposing forces that produce it (for example, heat:cold) increases geometrically. Although his specific mathematical ideas about compounds were derived from al-Kindi and Averroës (Ibn Rushd), his presentation showed originality and, more important, a determination to base pharmacological analysis on quantitative, and therefore universal, principles rather than on experience or logical, scholastic reasoning. In this respect his medical and religious outlooks were part of the same world view, and his writings may be compared with those of his friend Raymond Lull.

In his own medical practice Arnald appears to have been far more practical, simple, and conservative than his theoretical treatises would suggest. His impact as a teacher and practitioner was great, and a fifteenth-century physician, Anthony Ricart, hailed him as "the pride of the Catalan nation," but his theoretical treatises had little effect on posterity. Instead, his reputation led a number of works, notably such alchemical books as the *Flos florum* and the *Rosarius philosophorum,* to be misattributed to him, and caused a rich variety of legends, such as the idea that he discovered the distillation of alcohol from wine, to grow up about his name.

As one of the earliest authors to write in the Catalan language, Arnald is today honored for his expressive style and rigorous exposition. In his religious writings he reveals a profound mystical inclination. This mysticism coexisted with his medical rationalism and led him to honor intuition and to consider his own finest thoughts to be the result of divine illumination.

BIBLIOGRAPHY

Most of Arnald's medical works in Latin were published in the sixteenth century in various editions of his *Opera;* for a bibliographical guide see Juan Antonio Paniagua Arellano, "La obra médica de Arnau de Vilanova" in *Estudios y notas sobre Arnau de Vilanova* (1962), 1–51. A new edition of the *Opera medica omnia,* eds. L. Garcia-Ballester, J. A. Paniagua, and M. R. McVaugh, is in preparation; vol. II, *Aphorismi de Gradibus,* ed. Michael R. McVaugh (1975), is the only volume to appear so far.

For bibliography up to 1953 see Miguel Battlori, "Orientaciones bibliográficas para el estudio de Arnau de Vilanova," in *Pensamiento,* **10** (1954), 311–323. The best account of Arnald's career available in English is in the introduction to McVaugh's edition of the *Aphorismi de Gradibus,* but McVaugh does not attempt a full biography. John F. Benton, "The Birthplace of Arnau de Vilanova: A Case for Villanueva de Jiloca near Daroca," in *Viator,* **13** (1982) [in press] deals only with Arnau's place of origin. See also J. A. Paniagua Arellano, "Vida de Arnaldo de Vilanova," in *Archivo Iberoamericano de Historia de la Medicina,* **3** (1951), 3–83; Joaquin Carreras y Artau, *Relaciones de Arnau de Vilanova con los reyes de la casa de Aragón* (1955); and Michael McVaugh, "The *Experimenta* of Arnald of Villanova," in *Journal of Medieval and Renaissance Studies,* **1** (1971), 107–118.

JOHN F. BENTON

[See also **Boniface VIII; Clement V; Frederick II of Sicily; Joachim di Fiore; al-Kindi; Lull, Raymond; Medicine; Ibn Rushd; Ibn Sīnā.**]

ARNAUT DANIEL, troubadour celebrated for his virtuosity, about whose life little is known; he claims in one of his poems to have attended the coronation of Philippe Auguste in 1180. Arnaut's songs supposedly date from the late twelfth century, for Peire d'Auvergne made no mention of him in his famous sirventes on the troubadours composed in 1170, whereas the Monk of Montaudon included him among the well-known troubadours in a similar piece produced in 1194. The Old Provençal *vida* for Arnaut describes him as a nobleman from Ribérac, in Périgueux, who was educated to become a priest but chose instead to be a jongleur. His poems, of which eighteen survive (two with music), exemplify the so-called *trobar ric,* for they are studded with rare words, filled with assonance and alliteration, and punctuated with intricate and unusual rhymes. Arnaut is generally credited with the invention of the sestina.

BIBLIOGRAPHY

Ugo A. Canello, *La vita e le opere del trovatore Arnaldo Daniello* (1883); René Lavaud, *Les poésies d'Arnaut Daniel* (1910); Gianluigi Toja, *Canzoni* (1961), a critical edition; and "La lingua di Arnaud Daniel," in *Cultura neolatina,* **29** (1969). For references to studies on specific poems, see Robert Allen Taylor, *La littérature occitane du moyen âge* (1977), 52–54.

ELIZABETH WILSON POE

[See also **Provençal Literature: To 12th Century; Troubadour, Trouvere, Trovadores.**]

ARNOBIUS THE ELDER (*d. ca.* 327), also known as Afer, was born a pagan and taught rhetoric at Sicca Veneria (now Al Kāf, Tunisia) during the reign of Diocletian; his students included Lactantius Firmianus. Around 303, following his conversion to Christianity, he wrote *Adversus nationes* in seven books, an apologetic noted for its invective and satire. Although quoted by Jerome, Arnobius' work had little circulation in the Middle Ages.

BIBLIOGRAPHY

The *Adversus nationes* is in *Patrologia latina,* V (1844), 713–1296; and in *Corpus scriptorum ecclesiasticorum Paravianum,* LXII (1934), with notes by Concetto Marchesi. See also Otto Bardenhewer, *Patrology,* Thomas J. Shahan, trans. (1908), 201–203, for a textural history; and Paul Monceaux, *Histoire littéraire de l'Afrique chrétienne,* III (1905, repr. 1963), 241–286, for further analysis. *The Case Against the Pagans,* George E. McCracken, trans., is a recent translation.

DAMIAN RIEHL LEADER

ARNOBIUS THE YOUNGER (*d.* after 451), a semi-Pelagian African monk who lived in Rome. His *Commentarii in Psalmos,* published by Erasmus in 1522 and wrongly attributed to Arnobius the Elder, contains an attack on St. Augustine's theory of predestination. Arnobius also wrote *Conflictus de Deo trino et uno* (a refutation of Monophysitism), *Expositiunculae in Evangelium,* and possibly several other works.

BIBLIOGRAPHY

The *Conflictus* and *Commentarii in Psalmos* are in *Patrologia latina,* LIII (1865), 239–580. For a critical text of the *Commentarii,* see Germain Morin, in *Anecdota maredsolana,* **3.3** (1903), 129–151. Morin also attributes to Arnobius an anonymous *Liber ad Gregoriam, ibid.,* 2nd ser., **1** (1913), 383–439; and a *Praedestinatus,* in *Patrologia latina,* LIII (1865), 587–672. See also Heinrich Keyser, *Die Schriften des sogenannten Arnobius* (1912).

DAMIAN RIEHL LEADER

ARNOLD OF BRESCIA (*ca.* 1100–1155), radical and dynamic church reformer who insisted on strict clerical poverty and inveighed against the Church's wealth and temporal power. Arnold was born in Brescia, Italy, but little is known of his early life. He was a member of the canons regular of St. Augustine and became abbot of their house at Brescia. Otto of Freising says that he studied with Peter Abelard, but most scholars believe Otto was confused by Arnold's later association with Abelard.

In the early 1130's Arnold incited the populace of Brescia against Bishop Manfred, a new papal appointee; the bishop denounced him as a schismatic at the Second Lateran Council in 1139. Condemned by the council and banished from Italy, Arnold fled to France. There, in vainly defending Abelard's teaching at the Council of Sens in April 1141, he pitted himself against Bernard of Clairvaux. According to John of Salisbury, Arnold accused St. Bernard of vainglory and narrowmindedness. Bernard, who became Arnold's strongest opponent, in turn portrayed

Arnold to Pope Innocent II as Abelard's "shield," joined with him "against the Lord and His Christ." In July, the pope confirmed Abelard's condemnation and condemned Arnold, ordering the two men confined in separate monasteries. When Arnold continued to teach in Paris, Bernard persuaded King Louis VII to expel him from France. Arnold then traveled to Zurich, from which city Bernard's letter to the bishop of Constance prompted his rapid expulsion, and finally to Bohemia. Bernard wrote to Cardinal Guy, the papal legate to Bohemia, describing Arnold's "manner of living as honey and his teaching, poison" and urging Guy to emulate Arnold's previous hosts and expel him. Arnold, however, remained in Bohemia until at least 1145. While there, he was temporarily reconciled with Pope Eugene III, who ordered him to do penance in Rome.

Rome itself was in turmoil. A substantial rebel faction had declared a Roman republic, reestablished the Roman senate, and barred the pope and the cardinals from the city. Finding the rebels' views compatible with his own rejection of the Church's temporal power, Arnold allied himself with them and lent his preaching abilities to their cause. He became a leader of the movement and was excommunicated in July 1148. The revolt continued until the accession in 1154 of Pope Adrian IV. When Adrian placed Rome under an interdict and demanded Arnold's expulsion, the Romans complied. Arnold fled to Tuscany, but the forces of Frederick I Barbarossa, briefly allied with those of the pope, captured him and brought him back to Rome for trial. In 1155, he was condemned and hanged, his body burned, and his ashes spread over the Tiber to prevent their veneration by the populace.

Although Arnold's own teaching was orthodox, if impractical, his followers fell into heresy. The Arnoldists not only preached clerical poverty and unworldliness, but also denied the efficacy of sacraments given by clerics holding worldly possessions. The sect was condemned at the Council of Verona in 1184.

BIBLIOGRAPHY

The main contemporary accounts are the letters of Bernard de Clairvaux, in *Patrologia latina*, CLXXXII (1879); and in *The Letters of St. Bernard of Clairvaux*, Bruno Scott James, trans. (1953), nos. 239, 242, 250, and 251; Otto of Freising, *Gesta Friderici*, George Waitz, ed. (1912); translated by Charles C. Mierow with Richard Emery as *The Deeds of Frederick Barbarossa* (1953); and John of Salisbury, *Historia pontificalis*, Marjorie Chibnall, ed. and trans. (1956).

The most accessible biography is George W. Greenaway, *Arnold of Brescia* (1931). See also Arsenio Frugoni, *Arnaldo da Brescia nelle fonti del secolo XII* (1954); and, for background on the Council of Sens and Arnold's association with Abelard, David E. Luscombe, *The School of Peter Abelard* (1969).

M. S. MILLER

[See also **Adrian IV, Pope; Bernard of Clairvaux (St.); Councils, Western (869–1274); Otto von Freising.**]

ARNOLD OF ST. EMMERAM (*ca.* 1000–before 1050), Benedictine monk and religious writer, made his profession at St. Emmeram in Regensburg. The community's objections to his rewriting of the life of St. Emmeram forced him to leave, but after spending 1030–1033 at Magdeburg, Arnold was allowed to return to St. Emmeram, where he remained until his death. His writings include an office for the feast of St. Emmeram (1030–1031), *De miraculis beati Emmerammi* (1036 or 1037), and *De memoria beati Emmerammi* (1037).

BIBLIOGRAPHY

Patrologia latina, CXLI (1880), *Monumenta Germaniae historica: Scriptores,* IV (1841), 543–574. B. Bischoff, "Literarisches und künstlerisches Leben in St. Emmeram," in *Studien und Mitteilungen zur Geschichte des Benediktiner-Ordens,* 51 (1933).

KRISTINE T. UTTERBACK

ARNOLDI, ALBERTO, sculptor, active Florence 1351–1364. First mentioned in 1351 document concerning windows for the campanile. Member of commission of twelve considering models for modification of the Duomo *ca.* 1350's. 1357–1358 *capomaestro* of Duomo with Francesco Talenti; commissioned to complete tabernacle above central doorway. 1359–1364 sculpted the Virgin and Child with two angels composing the altarpiece for the Bigallo; 1361 (according to documents) executed the relief of the Madonna and Child in the lunette outside the Bigallo; he may well have designed its loggia, built 1352–1358. It is likely that he sculpted the magnificent reliefs of the sacraments of *ca.* 1350 for the campanile, which pushed his talents to their supreme achievement.

BIBLIOGRAPHY

Luisa Becherucci, "I rilievi dei Sacramenti nel Campanile del Duomo di Firenze," in *L'arte,* **30** (1927); Hanna Kiel, *Il Museo del Bigallo a Firenze* (1977); Gert Kreytenberg, "Alberto Arnoldi e i rilievi della Loggia del Bigallo a Firenze," in *Prosepttiva,* **11** (1977); John Pope-Hennessy, *Italian Gothic Sculpture* (1955); Howard Saalman, *The Bigallo: the Oratory and Residence of the Compagnia del Bigallo e della Misericordia in Florence* (1969); Marvin Trachtenberg, *The Campanile of Florence Cathedral* (1971); John White, *Art and Architecture in Italy: 1250–1400* (1966).

ADELHEID M. GEALT

ARNOLFO DI CAMBIO, Italian architect and sculptor, born Colle val d'Elsa *ca.* 1245, died *ca.* 1310. Assistant to Nicola Pisano on Siena pulpit of 1266 and the Arca di S. Domenico, Bologna, 1264. In 1267–1268 he must have become independent. By 1277 he was in Rome, employed by Charles of Anjou, whose seated likeness in stone now in Capitoline Museum probably derives from Arnolfo's shop. The same year Arnolfo produced a small fountain in Perugia near Nicola's Fontana Maggiore. Arnolfo's signature appears on the now reconstructed tomb of Cardinal de Braye (died 1282) in S. Domenico, Orvieto. He also signed two ciboria dated 1285 and 1293 respectively for the churches of S. Paolo fuori le Mura and S. Cecilia, Rome. A now lost inscription assigned the tomb of Boniface VIII in the Vatican to Arnolfo.

In 1296 Arnolfo was in Florence serving as *capomaestro* and designer for the Duomo. Fragments of his facade sculpture *(Seated Virgin, Recumbent Virgin, S. Reparata)* are preserved in the Museo dell'Opera del Duomo. Arnolfo's sure sense of mass and weight, of monumentality and grave simplicity, endowed his sculpture with majesty and his architecture with stately order.

BIBLIOGRAPHY

Luisa Becherucci and Giulia Brunetti, *Il museo dell'opera del Duomo a Firenze* (1969); John Pope-Hennessy, *Italian Gothic Sculpture* (1955 and 1972); Angiola M. Romanini, *Arnolfo di Cambio e lo stil novo del gotico italiano* (1966); John White, *Art and Architecture in Italy: 1250–1400* (1966).

ADELHEID M. GEALT

ARNULF (*ca.* 850–899), emperor of illegitimate though royal lineage, deposed Charles the Fat and succeeded him as king of the East Franks in 887. His reign was marked by an intense struggle with the aristocracy and by the growing influence of several powerful churchmen. His victory over the Vikings at the Dyle River in 891 put a final halt to Scandinavian incursions into eastern France. Generally noninterventionist, Arnulf made Lorraine an independent kingdom and recognized the sovereignty of Odo in France. Having conquered his way to Rome, he was consecrated emperor by Pope Formosus in 896 but suffered a stroke shortly afterward and died three years later.

BIBLIOGRAPHY

Arnulf's official documents were edited by Paul F. Kehr, *Arnolfi diplomata (Die Urkunden Arnolfs)* (1940, repr. 1955); Ernst Dümmler, *Geschichte des ostfränkischen Reiches* (1888), III, 876–918, refers to the narrative sources. See also *Die Entstehung des deutschen Reiches (Deutschland um 900)* (1956), an anthology of articles published between 1928 and 1954; and H. Appelt, "Arnulf von Kärnten und das Karolingerreich," in *Kärnten in europäischen Schau, Hochschulswochen der Universität Graz,* Franz Sauer, ed. (1960).

ALAIN J. STOCLET

[See also **Carolingians and the Carolingian Empire.**]

ARNULF OF MILAN, church historian, whose *Gesta archiepiscoporum Mediolanensium* tells us what little we know of his life; a great-grandson of the brother of Archbishop Arnulf I, he may have been a cleric. His work, which begins in 925 and ends abruptly in 1077, is an important and generally reliable source for local Milanese history and its ramifications in the investiture controversy. Its straightforward account is based on the testimony of credible witnesses, on documents in the ecclesiastical archives of Milan, and, beginning in 1018, on Arnulf's direct participation in the events recorded. In comparison to some parallel sources, it gives an impression of uncontentiousness.

In the latter portion of the *Gesta,* Arnulf moves from pronounced criticism of the ecclesiastical reform movement in Milan to an open endorsement of Roman supremacy in the Church. This shift has engendered a variety of modern descriptions of his stance, marked by differing choices of emphasis, though not by mutual contradiction.

BIBLIOGRAPHY

The *Gesta* was edited by L. C. Bethmann and Wilhelm Wattenbach in *Monumenta Germaniae historica: Scriptores,* VIII (1848), 1–31; and reprinted in *Patrologia latina,* CXLVII (1879), 281–332. C. Violante's notice in *Dizionario biografico degli Italiani,* IV (1962), 281–282, is the most thorough and up-to-date. V. A. Schaefer, *New Catholic Encyclopedia,* I (1967), 848, is less complete but in English.

DAVID R. TOWNSEND

[See also **Milan.**]

ARPENT, the principal medieval measure of land area throughout France; there were three Parisian or state standards. The *arpent de Paris* contained 100 square perches, each perche of 18 pieds in length. It was a square whose four sides were 180 linear pieds each, totaling 32,400 square pieds (34.189 ares or 0.845 English acres). The *arpent des eaux et forêts* (also called the *arpent d'ordonnance,* the *grand arpent,* and the *arpent de roi*) contained 100 square perches, each perche of 22 pieds in length. Also a square, its four sides were 220 linear pieds each, totaling 48,400 square pieds (51.072 ares or 1.262 English acres). The *arpent de commun,* authorized for use in the provinces, was 100 square perches, each perche of 20 pieds. This square had sides of 200 linear pieds each, totaling 40,000 square pieds (42.208 ares or 1.043 English acres). Hundreds of regional variations arose during the Middle Ages, necessitated not only by custom but also by differing soil, topographic, climatic, and crop conditions.

RONALD EDWARD ZUPKO

ARRAN. See **Albania.**

ARRAS, MATHIEU D'. See **Mathieu d'Arras.**

ARRICCIO, the rough plaster layer first applied to building wall, preparing it for the *intonaco,* or smoother plaster, upon which the fresco pigments are applied.

BIBLIOGRAPHY

Cennino Cennini, *Il libro dell'arte, The Craftsman's Handbook,* D. V. Thompson, trans. (1933, repr. 1954).

ADELHEID M. GEALT

ARS ANTIQUA (ancient art), also referred to as *ars veterum, ars vetus,* was used by French musicians in the early fourteenth century to indicate the musical practice of the immediate past in contrast to contemporary practices, which were referred to as *ars nova* (or *ars modernorum*). The word "art" in this context connotes the Greek word *techne*—"technique" or "craft"—excluding modern aesthetic associations of the word.

In its initial usage, for example in Johannes de Muris' *Notitia artis musicae* (1321) and Philippe of Vitry's *Ars nova* (*ca.* 1325), the term was derogatory and referred specifically to a style of composition, rather than to a particular epoch: in the most restricted sense, it referred to the musical notation and style of composition from the last quarter of the thirteenth century.

At the same time, however, the practices of the *ars antiqua* were defended by Johannes of Liège, who in his monumental *Speculum musicae* (*ca.* 1325) upheld the practices of the ancients while criticizing those of his younger contemporaries. *Ars antiqua* theorist-composers mentioned by Johannes are Lambertus, Franco of Cologne, and Petrus de Cruce. Endorsing the authority of these three masters, Johannes leveled specific charges against modern composers: they write only motets and cantilenas, neglecting other important forms such as organum, conductus, and hocket; they emphasize imperfect mensuration (duple rhythm) in their works, whereas the ancients strictly retained the appropriate perfection (triple rhythm); modern composers and theorists divide semibreves into perfect and imperfect groups of minims and semiminims, while for faster notes the ancients divided breves into two unequal or three or more equal semibreves in perfect mensuration, asserting that semibreves themselves were indivisible; and finally, the moderns indulge too much in broken rhythms and capricious melodic movement *(musica lasciva)*, while the ancients retained the constraints of a more refined style *(musica modesta)*. From this, the most authoritative source, we may define the *ars antiqua* as the polyphony of northern France from about 1260 to 1320.

Many present-day writers have extended the use of the term to include the music of the whole Notre Dame period, particularly that of Léonin and Pérotin, thus making the term synonymous with "Gothic" and describing the period from about 1160 to 1320. There is ample justification for this, as the musical forms praised by Johannes, and the development of rhythm and a notation to express them, clearly originated at this earlier time. In fact, the organum and conductus forms had already achieved their fullest development and were already declining by Franco's time, while the motet had reached the midpoint of its early development, characterized by the quickening of the notes with faster textual articulation in the upper parts and a corresponding slowing down of the underlying tempo. It was the later excesses of this trend that Johannes criticized, while praising the restraints of the earlier practice, which dated from well before Franco's time.

The *ars antiqua,* therefore, has two main divisions: French polyphonic music of the Notre Dame school from about 1160 to 1260 and the continuation of this tradition, specifically referred to by Johannes, from about 1260 to 1320. It does not include contemporary practices in liturgical and sacred music, the music of the minstrels and jongleurs, or the vast repertory of vernacular secular music of the troubadours and trouvères, although liturgical music exerted a decisive influence on the initial styles of the new polyphonic music, and the secular repertory greatly influenced the development of the motet, the musical form that dominated the second half of the *ars antiqua* period.

A Scholastic spirit underlay the musical achievements of the *ars antiqua,* which derived considerable impetus from two decisive events: the construction of the new Parisian cathedral of Notre Dame (begun in 1163) and the grant in 1215 of the first statutes to the expanding and influential University of Paris. The Scholastic influences—particularly musical—of these two institutions soon spread to the neighboring abbatial schools at St. Victor, Mont Ste. Geneviève, and St. Germain l'Auxerrois, and by the early thirteenth century they had made their own contributions to the growing school of composers. The university had continued the dialectical instruction established as a tradition in the twelfth-century schools and had also become renowned for its teaching of the seven liberal arts; further, the mendicant orders of Dominicans and Franciscans were granted teaching rights in the 1220's, and from their ranks came some of the most famous university professors: St. Bonaventure, Albertus Magnus, and Thomas Aquinas. Among the university's activities the teaching and practice of music held an honored position, and it is not surprising that the compositions that issued from these institutions were imbued with a Scholastic and mathematical spirit.

In the last third of the twelfth century, there issued from Notre Dame the great cycle of polyphonic compositions for the main feasts of the Parisian calendar set for the responsory propers of the Mass and the office: the *Magnus liber organi de graduali et antiphonario.* In this cathedral chapter, as well as in the university, a rational system of mensural notation was constructed that codified the various rhythmic modes displayed in the vast compositions of this early period: the organa and polyphonic conductus. The development of the motet and the theoretical codification of musical rhythms by John of Garland (*ca.* 1250), Franco of Cologne (*ca.* 1280), and Petrus de Cruce (*ca.* 1290) were very closely connected with the course of study of the University of Paris and the Sorbonne (established 1253).

Ars antiqua composers accepted two basic musical concepts. The first entailed the Scholastic transmission of Pythagorean and Boethian views of the observable world in terms of a harmonious arrangement based on the numerical proportions 2:1, representing the diapason or octave; 3:2, representing the diapente or fifth; and 4:3, representing the diatessaron or fourth. Their second concept, also derived from the Pythagorus and Boethius, entailed the threefold division of music into *musica mundana* (the music of the universe), founded in the harmonious numerical relationships existing between the orbits of the planets and of the stars; *musica humana,* manifest in the harmonious relationships between body and soul; and *musica instrumentalis,* musical sounds produced either by the natural means of the human voice or by artificial means, such as musical instruments.

ARS ANTIQUA

This mathematical and metaphysical approach to music governed the basic structure of the polyphonic compositions that emerged, placing greater emphasis on the techniques employed than on performance (as is evident in contemporary musical treatises) and resulting in the overall structural importance of a vertical harmonic relationship of intervals of the octave, fifth, and fourth.

Yet countering this severe Scholastic understanding of the nature of music were forces that dealt more directly with performance and aesthetic goals. The lyricism of twelfth-century Latin verse influenced not only the texts associated with music but also the style of music itself. The music gradually adopted more songlike qualities, while the rhymed rhythmic inflections of the Latin verse influenced the choice of rhythmic mode used in many works, introducing stronger dance and folk elements. In the texts, too, an interplay between tradition and innovation was evident. On the one hand the patristic symbolic exegesis of Scripture maintained the old tradition; while on the other the practice of adding poetic texts to preexisting music, as in the motet, was of more recent origin. As the century progressed, the growing secularization and loss of political control by the church left an inevitably secular mark on sacred music.

The study of music as a philosophical branch of mathematics, just prior to and during the period of *ars antiqua* composition, is attested by a number of treatises that contain sections on music, written by former students of the university, such as Adelard of Bath (*ca.* 1120), Gossouin (1245), Robert Grosseteste (*fl. ca.* 1250), and Robert Kilwardby; and in his allegorical poem *Anticlaudianus* (*ca.* 1184) Alain de Lille, a teacher at the university, discussed the psychological effects of music as well as of musical intervals. The most important musical treatises to appear during the thirteenth century, however, were those that contain sections describing the new polyphony of the *ars antiqua,* offering discussions of the new mensural notation that was devised to transmit rhythmic values in a clear and precise way.

The first Notre Dame composers and notators took over the ordinary square signs (single notes and ligatures) of plainsong notation and created a rhythmic notation known as "modal notation." By the last quarter of the twelfth century, musicians had at their disposal six rhythmic modes. Groupings of notes, and not their shapes, gave the note values according to one of the rhythmic modes; any attempt to disturb the prevailing rhythmic pattern by lengthening or shortening some of the notes introduced other ambiguous features. Thus the interpretation of the rhythm of texted melodies, which of necessity were notated in undifferentiated single notes, was very ambiguous. Nevertheless, for more than fifty years modal notation served its purpose very well, particularly for notating organa, clausulae, and the melismatic sections of conductus; it was of less value for the texted sections of conductus and the newer motets that proliferated early in the thirteenth century.

An important work that helped to clarify the modal system, the *Tractatus de musica,* was compiled in the late thirteenth century for the use of students by Jerome of Moravia. It includes a chapter on the playing of stringed instruments and four treatises that explain the two main systems ("positions") of mensural notation. One system is outlined in a short treatise on the rhythmic modes, attributed to Robert of Sabilone (*fl.* 1230–1260), and is given extensive treatment in a treatise by John of Garland, which records a very clear and precise approach, now known as "Garlandian notation," to the problems of notating contemporary polyphonic music.

Garland's main contribution was to establish clear and unequivocal note shapes for single notes. He granted them definite values and provided the basis, although not conclusively, for interpreting different ligature shapes; and he also made clearer the total value, although not the exact individual values, of groups of faster notes. He granted long and short notes the "right" *(recta)* values and showed how they could be increased by half their value to become "beyond measure" *(ultra mensuram);* this system laid the foundations of modern rhythmic notation.

The other "position" of notation was that of Franco of Cologne, who in his *Ars cantus mensurabilis* settled the ambiguities in the Garlandian system, so that there could be no doubt about the value of any note: the primary criterion was its shape, and less importance was laid on its context or position. His method was adopted by late *ars antiqua* composers and notators, and it gained the unqualified approval of Johannes of Liège as representing the true *ars antiqua* method. His treatise is briefly excerpted by Petrus of Picardy to provide the fourth mensural treatise for Jerome's compilation.

Other important theorists to use or modify John of Garland's method include the anonymous author of a short treatise (known as Anonymous 7 in Volume 1 of Coussemaker's edition) who, writing about 1270, gives a précis of John's main rules; and a short

ARS ANTIQUA

treatise by Aimerus, *De practica artis musicae* (copied in 1271), which makes some refinements of Garlandian notation in illustrating the best way to notate organa and, in an appendix, clears up further ambiguities in ligature notation. In the decade between the time of Aimerus and of Franco three further treatises appeared, each in its own way attempting to clarify ambiguities in the Garlandian system. The first, dating from about 1270, is a brief treatise by Dietricus; it was followed by a more important work by Lambertus (*ca.* 1275), who by using quicker configurations extends the number of rhythmic modes to nine; and finally in 1279, a somewhat polemical work by the Anonymous of St. Emmeram makes a further attempt to clear up the ambiguities. Only one treatise based on this older system is known to have dated after Franco's work: that of Coussemaker's Anonymous IV (*ca.* 1280), whose conservative approach is valuable in enabling us to determine details of the notation and composition of the early Notre Dame school, even before John of Garland's treatise.

Outside the mainstream of thirteenth-century preoccupation with mensural practices is a very important treatise, *De musica* by Johannes de Grocheo, a teacher closely connected with the Sorbonne. His treatise gives a unique sociological view of *ars antiqua* music at the end of the thirteenth century, discussing its main polyphonic forms and giving us a glimpse of the main secular vocal and instrumental styles of contemporary France, stressing their social functions rather than their musical style. But the apotheosis of all *ars antiqua* theory is the *Speculum musicae* in which Johannes of Liège deals with all aspects of both *musica speculativa* and *musica practica,* and gives us our principal authority for defining the compositions of the *ars antiqua.*

There are three broad groups of musical sources that transmit *ars antiqua* music: central Notre Dame sources using modal notation for melismatic works but unmeasured square notation for texted works; sources using measured notation based on Garlandian principles; and sources using measured notation based on Franconian principles and their later development. Besides a few fragments, there are five main sources from the central Notre Dame area; among them they contain practically all the preserved versions of the great cycle of organa, substitute clausulae, polyphonic and monophonic conductus, and the earliest motets, with both Latin and French texts. Each manuscript in its own way transmits the material in specific groupings, so that it is possible to trace various layers of composition and redaction, and to give some views on the chronology of musical types and styles.

The sources using Garlandian notation contain almost exclusively motets and illustrate the main emphasis of that vigorous period of composition just prior to the influence of the theorists cited by Johannes. These compositions may be designated the "classic" repertory of *ars antiqua* motets. Their tenors are primarily drawn from liturgical chants; they are normally three-part, with two separate texts, Latin or French, or one of each sung simultaneously; the three parts show melodic independence and consistently overlap at their cadence points; their rhythm is temperately constrained within the prevailing system of six rhythmic modes; and their tenors show considerable development in melodic repetitions and variety in their short rhythmic repetitions, thus illustrating the intermediate steps in a development leading to the *ars nova* concept of isorhythm. There are three main sources in this group and one or two fragmentary ones.

Among the manuscripts in Franconian notation are three that contain very interesting transmissions of works from the earlier periods of the Notre Dame repertory. Their clear notation allows us to postulate rhythmic interpretations for these works, which in their earlier transmissions show many ambiguous possibilities. This group of sources also demonstrates quite clearly that even early in the fourteenth century the older forms of organum and conductus were still being performed and understood, although composers were no longer actively cultivating them. The manuscript *Fauvel* is particularly important, for besides works notated in the Franconian system it has other works modified by Petrus de Cruce's innovations and still other works in contemporary (1316) *ars nova* style, notated in the *ars nova* manner of Philippe of Vitry.

In all, these sources transmit an amazing number and variety of musical compositions. Although many manuscripts from this period have been lost, it appears from concordance patterns within the preserved sources that very little of the actual music itself has been lost, and all the musical forms have survived in sufficient numbers to ensure a balanced perspective.

Composition in the *ars antiqua* was stratified. Composers began with a tenor melody, either preexisting or newly composed, and added successive layers of counterpoint above it; as long as each new part was concordant with at least one other part the

ARS ANTIQUA

requirements of discant were satisfied. This method allowed changes and redactions to occur in most styles of composition, and concordances found in several manuscripts often have important differences, either in the form of changed or added upper parts or, particularly in organa, the substitution of one clausula for another.

Ars antiqua composition began with the two-part organa written for the Notre Dame cathedral from about 1180. Many of these were probably written by Léonin. New techniques developed, and the practice was soon extended by Pérotin and Léonin's later contemporaries in the composition of three-part works, culminating in the last few years of the twelfth century in Pérotin's monumental four-part organa set for the masses on Christmas Day and St. Stephen's Day. Chants used for organa were the responsory chants for matins and the gradual and alleluia chants of the Mass for all the main feasts of the Parisian calendar. A complete setting of a chant in organum consists of three separate musical styles, according to the usual liturgical manner of performance. The cantor's opening and closing phrases of the response part of the chant and the psalm verse, all normally sung by the cantor, are replaced by polyphonic settings sung by a soloist for each upper part; the remainder of the chant is sung as usual in unison by the choir.

Two styles of setting are used for the solo sections. In the first, known as "organal style," long-held tenor notes (sung by a few singers or played by the organ, or possibly both) set out the notes of the syllabic phrases of the original chant and support an interweaving and melismatic upper part or parts, organized according to one or more of the rhythmic modes. The second type of setting is known as "discant style"; where the original style of the chant is melismatic, its many notes are organized into short rhythmic units *(ordines),* while the upper part (or parts) continues in much the same manner as in the organal sections. A complete organum setting takes some twenty to thirty minutes to perform; and so these great artistic creations are the first compositions to exhibit balanced structure with extended musical proportions. They represent a high point in musical history.

The short, highly stylized, and self-contained sections of discant became known as "clausulae"; normally they consist of some twenty to sixty measures of music and have a performance time of from one-half to one and a half minutes. Many new clausulae were written to be inserted into the appropriate places in organa, and it seems clear that they were also used as independent instrumental compositions outside the liturgical service. Also, they were treated in a similar manner to tropes of two centuries earlier: the untexted melisma had a sacred Latin text underlaid to it, generally one syllable to a note—only in this case, the Latin text was invariably rhymed and rhythmic. The clausula, thus transformed, was called a "motet," from the French *mot* (word).

Another extended form of early *ars antiqua* composition was the conductus, which was set monophonically, or in two, three, or four parts. In contrast to motets, which are preexisting music to which texts were added, conductus are preexisting Latin poems that were later set to music. At their simplest, the first strophe of the poem is set almost completely in syllabic style, with the added part (or parts) moving in parallel rhythm (a style that has given rise to the term "conductus style") and subsequent strophes sung to the same music.

By far the most common style, however, and the most extended and interesting, are the through-composed conductus *cum caudis*—conductus with long melismatic sections surrounding verse lines of text setting, so that declaimed text alternates with vocalized or instrumental sections. Normally there are three strophes composed in this way, and the average work consists of some 200 measures of music, taking approximately ten or twelve minutes in performance. The longest, of about 400 measures, are great musical structures requiring about twenty minutes.

Around 1230 the motet became the predominant *ars antiqua* musical form. From the earliest simple texted settings, it quickly passed through several stages. A third voice was added in the same style as the *duplum,* taking the same text, to form a conductus-motet. A change to the vernacular then occurred, whereby the original sacred Latin text was simply supplanted by a French secular one in the same rhythmic meter. Next, a separate text was added to the *triplum,* to form the characteristic double motets that make up the greatest proportion of the thirteenth-century repertory: two separate Latin, or two French, or one of each (bilingual) texts were declaimed at the same time. Another type of motet was like an accompanied French song: it was in two parts, with the usual tenor based on a liturgical chant, but with a simple, songlike *duplum* with a French text of the kind typical of the contemporary trouvère repertory.

During the last three decades of the thirteenth

century the main stylistic change came with the introduction of faster notes in the *tripla* of double motets: each note had a separate syllable of text (generally French), so that fast articulation was required, with the result that the lower parts were performed more slowly. It was this later style of motet, under the influence of Petrus de Cruce, both as composer and notator, that led to the innovations of the *ars nova* and consequently into a new period of music history.

The *ars antiqua* also produced some other, minor styles of composition, particularly the later *rondellus*, composed by Adam de la Halle and Jehannot de l'Escurel, the polyphonic examples being based on a free tenor. Another style is that of hocket (truncated voice), whereby the voices stop and start alternately on and off the beat, producing a broken, syncopated effect. These minor styles help to demonstrate the diversity of the musical practice throughout the *ars antiqua* period.

BIBLIOGRAPHY

Edmond de Coussemaker, *Scriptorum de musica medii aevi,* 4 vols. (1864–1876, repr. 1963). Friedrich Ludwig, *Repertorium organorum recentioris et motetorum vetustissimi stili* (1910); 2nd ed., Luther Dittmer, ed. (1964). *Jacobi Leodiensis Speculum musicae,* Roger Bragard, ed., 7 vols. (1955–1973). Heinrich Besseler, *Musik des Mittelalters und der Renaissance* (1931). *Cent motets du XIIIe siècle,* Pierre Aubry, ed., 3 vols. (1908). *El codex musical de Las Huelgas,* Higinio Anglès, ed., 3 vols. (1931). Yvonne Rokseth, *Polyphonies du XIIIe siècle, le manuscrit H 196 de la Faculté de Médecine de Montpellier,* 4 vols. (1935–1948). *The Latin Compositions in Fascicules VII and VIII of the Notre Dame Manuscript Wolfenbüttel Helmstadt 1099 (1206),* Gordon A. Anderson, ed., 2 vols. (1972–1975). William G. Waite, *The Rhythm of Twelfth-Century Polyphony* (1954). Janet Knapp, *Thirty-five Conductus, for Two and Three Voices* (1965). *The Works of Perotin,* Ethel Thurston, ed. (1970). *Motets of the Manuscript La Clayette,* Gordon A. Anderson, ed. (1975). Gordon A. Anderson, *Compositions of the Bamberg Manuscript* (1977); *The Las Huelgas Manuscript,* 2 vols. (1979). *The Montpellier Codex,* Hans Tischler, ed., 3 vols. (1978).

GORDON A. ANDERSON

[See also **Ars Subtilior; Franco of Cologne; John of Garland; Modal Notation; Modes (Melodic); Motet Manuscripts (Thirteenth Century); Musical Notation (West); Musical Treatises (General Overview).**]

ARS DICTAMINIS. See **Dictamen.**

ARS MORIENDI (the art of dying) is the name given to two distinct but related Latin texts that arose in the fifteenth century. Although the need to prepare for one's death was frequently stressed in medieval writings, as in the *Somme le roi* by Frère Lorens d'Orléans, and although medieval literature contains many deathbed scenes, there was no discussion before the fifteenth century of what constituted a good death or how one should prepare for it; and so, to that extent, the *Ars moriendi* represents a new departure. Its only precursor was the section *De arte moriendi* in Gerson's *Opusculum tripartitum* (*ca.* 1400) more concerned with offering help to others who were dying than devoted, as the *Ars moriendi* is, to how an individual should prepare for his own death. Even so, the *Ars moriendi* did make use of Gerson's work as well as of the standard authorities of the church. Its matter is quite traditional, even if the framework is new.

The longer version of the *Ars moriendi,* known as *Tractatus* (or *Speculum*) *artis bene moriendi,* was composed about 1415, probably by a Dominican, on the order of the Council of Constance. It exists in many manuscripts and was translated into most West European languages. An English version, once erroneously attributed to Rolle, was made in the fifteenth century from the Latin. Caxton published two versions at the end of the fifteenth century, one translated from a French version and the other possibly from Latin. The *Ars moriendi* remained a popular text in England, where a literary tradition based on it survived until the seventeenth century.

The longer version consists of six chapters. The first seeks to explain what good dying is, in an effort to console the good man that death need not be terrifying. The second outlines the five major temptations that beset the dying man and their remedies. These are lack of faith, despair, impatience, spiritual pride, and avarice. The third chapter outlines the seven questions to be posed to those on their deathbeds, together with the consolation available to them through contemplation of the redemptive power of Christ's passion. The fourth chapter outlines the need to imitate Christ. The last two chapters are addressed to the bystanders at the deathbed, and promulgate the general rules to be observed by them (chapter 5) and the prayers to be said (chapter 6).

The shorter version, which is linked with the production of block books, made its first appearance about 1450. It is largely adapted from the second chapter of the longer version, and consists of eleven woodcuts with accompanying text. The first ten woodcuts divide into five pairs in which one depicts devils presenting the dying man with one of the five temptations mentioned above and the other shows how the remedy for that temptation is provided by the angels, the Virgin, or even Christ. The final woodcut portrays the man at the point of death when his soul is received by the angels of heaven and the devils rush back to hell in confusion. The woodcuts with their explanatory text are preceded by a brief introduction and followed by a conclusion. The shorter version was as popular as the longer one, though no English version is known. Both versions inspired so many artistic representations that the scene of the dying man is met with as often as the danse macabre.

BIBLIOGRAPHY

Nancy L. Beaty, *The Craft of Dying: A Study of the Literary Tradition of the Ars Moriendi in England* (1970); Frances M. M. Comper, *The Book of the Craft of Dying, and Other Early English Tracts Concerning Death* (1917); Carl Horstmann, *Yorkshire Writers* (1896); Emile Mâle, *L'art religieux de la fin du moyen âge en France* (1922); Edward W. B. Nicholson, *Ars Moriendi* (1891); Sister Mary Catherine O'Connor, *The Art of Dying Well: The Development of the Ars Moriendi* (1942); *A Reprint in Facsimile of a Treatise Spekynge of the Arte & Crafte to Knowe Well to Dye* (1875); and W. Harry Rylands, *Ars Moriendi* (1881).

N. F. BLAKE

ARS NOVA, originally the title of a musical treatise by Philippe de Vitry written about 1320 in Paris. Partly because of the importance of the principles discussed in this document and partly because of the popularity of Philippe's ideas among the next two or three generations of composers, the term "ars nova" has been used to refer to the musical style and repertoire of the entire fourteenth century in Europe. One of his Parisian contemporaries, John of Murs, wrote a similar treatise in 1321 entitled *Notitia artis musicae* (usually called *Ars novae musicae*). The new art was primarily a change in the notation of rhythms, and these principles of measuring note values pervade most of the music of the century. Johannes Wolf, who first used the term in a generic way to describe fourteenth-century music (*Geschichte der Mensural-Notation von 1250–1460* [1904]), did so, therefore, with considerable justification.

The basic principles of the notation of musical rhythm discussed by Philippe were in use a few years before he gave them a thorough description. The earliest musical examples of the notation appear in the extended satirical poem *Roman de Fauvel* (Paris, Bibliothèque Nationale, MS fr. 146). The *Fauvel* romance had musical interpolations added to it in 1316 that include several compositions involving the use of the new, small note value called the minim and examples of a change of meter through coloration (red notes instead of black). Some of the latest compositions in the *Roman de Fauvel* were by Philippe de Vitry, who was in his mid twenties at the time. His treatise describes, therefore, a new musical practice that was already in use by the most advanced composers. It also argued indirectly for a secularization of polyphonic music, which had been the sole domain of church-trained composers who had employed church-related musical forms up to that time. Duple meter, in contrast to triple meter (Trinity-based, according to the medieval mind), was accorded respectability.

The threat to the established style of the previous century, called "ars antiqua," was recognized not only by certain conservative composers and theorists such as Jacques of Liège, but also by Pope John XXII, who issued a papal bull from Avignon in 1324 severely attacking the new practice. Despite this unprecedented intervention by a pope in a debate on musical style, the ars nova movement flourished. The ballade, virelai, and rondeau of the troubadours were given part-settings by the most advanced composers, notably Guillaume de Machaut.

It is for these reasons that the term ars nova is used to refer to the extended period during which part-settings of the popular, secular poetic forms were in vogue. Several modern writers have employed the term very loosely to include the musical repertoire written in both France and Italy during the fourteenth century. The Italian notation and musical forms differ significantly from the French, at least until 1370. Musicologists who insist on preserving this distinction refer to the French practice as ars nova and the Italian style of the fourteenth century as "trecento."

PRINCIPLES OF THE ARS NOVA TREATISE

The rhythmic modes devised by composers in Paris in the twelfth century involved only two values, long *(longa)* and breve *(brevis)*. The long was written as a square note with a stem, the breve as a square note without a stem. This system allowed composers to specify a limited range of rhythms for

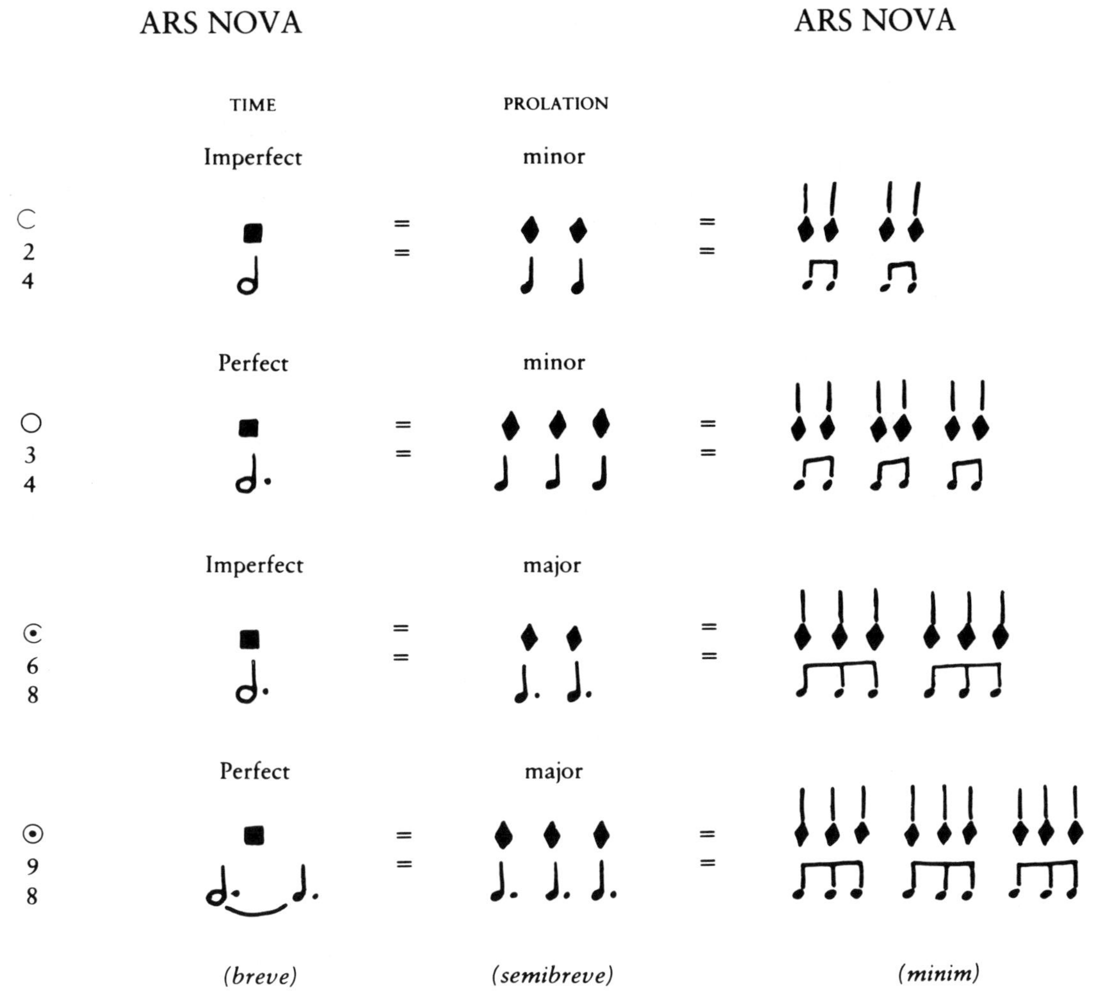

the first time. In the thirteenth century, Franco of Cologne introduced a smaller note value, the diamond-shaped semibreve, which could divide the value of a breve into smaller units from two to nine parts. There was a degree of imprecision in this system because the semibreve did not have a fixed value in relation to the breve. Philippe de Vitry's treatise eliminated this ambiguity by codifying four precise divisions and introducing a smaller value, the minim (diamond-shaped with upper stem). In the thirteenth-century Franconian system the relationship between the long and the breve was called *modus* (mood). The mood was perfect if a long was divided into three breves, imperfect if divided into two.

The *Ars nova* treatise applied this mensural concept to breves and semibreves. *Tempus* (time) refers to the division of the breve into semibreves, with perfection (three) or imperfection (two) being applied as before. The semibreve was also divided into minims. This relationship, called "prolation," was similarly either perfect (major) or imperfect (minor) depending on whether the semibreve was divided into three or two minims. These mensurations function similarly to the time signatures $\frac{2}{4}$, $\frac{3}{4}$, $\frac{6}{8}$, and $\frac{9}{8}$ of our modern musical score. One of the most important factors in this notational system is that duple and triple meter are accorded equal status.

Time signatures to indicate mensuration values were not written at the beginning of a composition, though these values could be determined quite easily by a performer simply through careful observation of the groupings of notes or rests. A change of mensuration was accomplished by writing red instead of black notes—a principle that Philippe de Vitry discussed at some length in his treatise. The usual use of coloration was within the framework of perfect time, in which the black breve is divided into three semibreves; two red semibreves would be equal to three black ones. In modern notation we use three quarter notes for the black semibreves; two dotted quarter notes fill the same time space. Red notes first appear in the *Roman de Fauvel* that appeared about four years before de Vitry's *Ars nova* treatise.

In the last quarter of the fourteenth century, a sys-

ARS NOVA

tem of circles and half-circles, with or without dots in the center to indicate each of the four prolations, gained popularity. The treatise had discussed the use of circles and semicircles for time relationships; it did not mention the use of dots. A circle with three dots in the center signified perfection at the level of time and prolation ($\frac{9}{8}$); with two dots prolation was imperfect ($\frac{3}{4}$). The semicircle with three dots indicated imperfect time and perfect prolation ($\frac{6}{8}$); with two dots both time and prolation were imperfect ($\frac{2}{4}$). This system was usually simplified as seen in the chart above: one dot meant perfection, while no dot in the circle signified imperfection. Obviously, these signs could be—and were—used to accomplish the same effect as coloration.

The rhythm of a composition did not have to remain constant throughout. Composers enjoyed combining various rhythms in different parts that were to be performed simultaneously. As they explored the full range of possibilities inherent in this notational system, more and more complex rhythmic combinations evolved. By the end of the century the mensural signatures and other proportional signs were combined with red notes and even smaller note values than the minim in remarkably complex arrangements, prompting one modern editor, Willi Apel, to refer to the composers involved in that musical practice as a "mannerist school." Ursula Günther used the term "ars subtilior" to refer to the same practice, which flourished primarily in the courts of southern France, Avignon, and Aragon from about 1385 to 1410. Though the notational principles in the *Ars nova* treatise provided the basis for this later development, there were so many new innovations—dots to indicate syncopated position of notes, proportional signs, a variety of new note values acquired from Italian practices—that it is inaccurate to say that consistent notational principles were employed throughout the century. The ideas expounded by Philippe de Vitry did, however, dominate composition to the 1370's, about the time of Machaut's death.

ITALIAN NOTATION

Italian theorists devised a slightly different solution to the imprecise division of the breve, which characterized the late-thirteenth-century notation of Petrus de Cruce. The dots that he placed on either side of a group of semibreves, in order to indicate the number of them that were equivalent to a breve, were preserved in the Italian system. These dots functioned similarly to modern bar lines. They severely limited the possibility of tied notes or syncopation, so by mid century Italian composers turned to French notation for more flexibility.

Marchettus of Padua's treatise, *Pomerium*, written at about the same time as Philippe de Vitry's *Ars nova*, classified a series of three divisions of the breve, which is in some ways like the French practice of mood, time, and prolation. It is actualy quite different in its application, however. The breve was given three divisions on either a binary or ternary basis according to the number of smaller notes within the breve. In the first division, the breve was divided into either two *(binaria)* or three *(ternaria)* semibreves. In the second, the binary semibreves were divided into units of four minims ($\frac{2}{4}$, *quaternaria)* or six minims ($\frac{6}{8}$, *senaria imperfecta*). The ternary semibreves were divided into six minims ($\frac{3}{4}$, *senaria perfecta)* or nine minims ($\frac{9}{8}$, *novenaria)* in this second division. But the Italians devised another dimension, a third division to this pattern, which was not available in Philippe de Vitry's system: a binary semibreve was written as eight minims divided four and four ($\frac{2}{4}$, *octonaria*); the ternary semibreve was similarly divided into twelve minims grouped in three sets of four each ($\frac{3}{4}$, *duodenaria*). A distinctive feature of Italian music of this period when transcribed into modern notation is the recurrence of sixteenth notes grouped in regular patterns of four. The French music appears to have fewer sixteenths but more notes tied over the bar line or in syncopated positions within the bar.

The initial letters of each of the Italian divisions from the second onward (*q*, *i*, *p*, *n*, *o*, *d*) were added to the manuscripts to indicate the mensuration of a composition. An additional innovation involved the creation of a minim with a downward stem (dragma), which had a variable value larger than the minims appearing in the divisions above. This dragma note form, as well as the small note values in the *octonaria* and *duodenaria* patterns, attracted the attention of composers working with the French practice late in the fourteenth century. It was the fusion of these notational schemes that resulted in the extremely complex *ars subtilior* repertoire.

STYLE OF THE FRENCH REPERTOIRE

At the beginning of the fourteenth century the motet was the most popular musical form. By the end of the century composers were providing full polyphonic settings of the musical portions of the Ordinary of the Mass. The motet had evolved during the two previous centuries from the effort of Chris-

ARS NOVA

tian church musicians to elaborate the liturgical service with part music. It remained an important musical form in France throughout the fourteenth century, but the interest of the most able composers shifted rather quickly about 1330 to the secular forms. When we consider Philippe de Vitry's role in the new movement toward secularization, it is strange that there are not extant ballades, virelais, or rondeaux by him, but only motets. That is probably an accident of history, none of his secular compositions having been recorded in the manuscripts that have survived.

The polyphonic repertoire of the ars nova period was usually written in three parts: the cantus, which carried the text to be sung, and two untexted lower parts, the tenor and contratenor. Some four-part writing is represented, Machaut's famous setting of the Mass being a prime example. The fourth voice was identified as a *triplum*—the third part above the tenor. Some compositions, such as the double and triple ballades, have two or even three parts with text. The norm, however, was three parts: cantus, contratenor, and tenor. (The contratenor part received its name because it was usually in the same pitch range as the tenor—therefore, "against the tenor." This part should not be confused with the high male voice called countertenor.)

The two lower, untexted parts appear to have been conceived as instrumental voices. There is controversy over whether they might have been performed by singers, the notes being sung using natural vowel sounds. Some iconographic evidence supports this performance practice; but the extensive collections of instruments known to have been available lends weight, along with other iconographic evidence, to the view that untexted parts were performed on instruments. Extended instrumental (untexted) interludes and postludes are found framing cantus parts, suggesting that a musician may have been expected to both sing and play his part. The difficulties associated with the notation and the problems of combining complex parts argue for a very high level of skill among performers at the time.

The motet and some Mass movements of the ars nova period featured a strong organizing principle: isorhythm. This compositional device, inherited loosely from the groupings of the patterns in twelfth-century rhythmic modes, was essentially an intellectual feature of the music. Because of the considerable length of the repeated rhythmic and melodic patterns, and the relatively slow pace of the tenor where they occur, the ear could not readily perceive isorhythm. Nevertheless, the practice provided a sense of unity, of integration previously unavailable.

Some other stylistic features of the motet repertoire were more obvious to the ear. Hocket involved the fragmentation of a melodic line by interspersing rests with short note values. The melodic line was usually broken up between two voices, one part resting while the other sang a note; the roles were then immediately reversed in the score. This "hiccuping" effect had been a feature of musical practice during the previous century.

Composition according to the rules of successive counterpoint produced unusual simultaneous sonorities in much of the repertoire. The tenor voice had been and still was the primary organizing part against which all other voices were written according to certain rules. The three perfect intervals—octave, fifth, and fourth—were the only harmonic sonorities allowed when part music was first explored, around 900. Thirds, sixths, seconds, and sevenths between melodic lines were tolerated for a time and then were accepted as a means of reaching one of the perfect intervals. Although these principles were not adhered to overtly by ars nova composers, the basic sonority that evolved from the early rules remained unchanged on the Continent throughout the fourteenth century. In England thirds and sixths had more or less equal status with the perfect intervals at this time.

Successive counterpoint, the method of composition apparently employed, involved composing a tenor part first and then the two other parts, not simultaneously but successively, each additional part being justified with the tenor independent of one another. This process often produced strident clashes between the added parts. Occasionally the parts are so diverse in their qualities, so uncomcomplementary, that we must assume that a performance of the work involved one or the other with the tenor, but not both. Although successive counterpoint continued as the fundamental compositional principle of the era, composers increasingly gave consideration to harmonic sonorities as they constructed melodies.

The double leading-tone cadence is a stylistic feature of the ars nova period sufficiently unique to have become an identifying hallmark. A strong sense of repose is achieved musically when the seventh degree (leading tone) of the scale rises a semitone to the eighth degree. In part writing, this melodic gesture was combined with a tenor part that falls from the

ARS NOVA

second to the first degree of the scale. The result is a sixth expanding to an octave. In the fourteenth century, composers compounded this effect by having a third voice rise by a semitone from the fourth to the fifth scale degrees. In the Dorian mode, for example, the tenor would move from E to D, the other two parts from G to A, and C sharp to D, an octave above the tenor. By the rules of *musica ficta* the G and C would be raised to G sharp and C sharp to create leading tones. The G sharp to A is a second leading-tone effect, providing the distinctive ars nova sonority.

PERFORMANCE PRACTICE

The performance practice during the ars nova period placed heavy demands on performers to exercise musical judgment. It is obvious in the manuscript sources that composers did not provide a final and definitive copy of their works. Very often the relationship of word syllables to notes was not clarified with any precision in the copy, because the notes were written very close together to preserve valuable parchment space, the text syllables lying in close proximity below. Singers were required, therefore, to improvise the insertion of the text as they sang. Presumably, certain guidelines for doing this were understood. No one bothered to inform posterity of these principles, if they did exist. Likewise, many melodic and harmonic sonorities were not specified. The flats and sharps provided at the beginnings of lines as key signatures do not carry the consistent force that they have in our modern scores. Different signatures often appear in the parts of one composition, their significance apparently applying as much to the range of the part as to the pitches to be performed. Accidentals, the extra sharps and flats added to a melody, do not always appear immediately before the note to be altered, and we have no way of knowing how long they should remain in force. Modern scholars, intent on discovering decisive rules by which the repertoire was performed, will probably remain frustrated. The bulk of the evidence indicates that performers improvised according to general guidelines that were never consistent enough for us to uncover. The principles of *musica ficta* were discussed by theorists in sufficient detail to allow modern editors to infer that some chromatic alterations were intended, though not specified, at cadences.

The ballades, virelais, and rondeaux are the mainstay of the ars nova repertoire. They are referred to as the *formes fixes* because their poetic and musical structures remained constant. In the majority of poems, the sentiments of courtly love were expressed. Despite close similarities in texts and musical structure, a specific role evolved for each form. Ballades were used to express the sentiments of courtly love, but toward the end of the century their texts became serious, honorific, and laudatory. The grande ballade was employed on occasions of weddings and coronations and to celebrate victory in battle, extolling the virtues and prowess of noble patrons. This role was taken over by the ballade from the motet of a few decades earlier.

The virelai was treated with more freedom both in the extended number of lines used and in the musical style employed. The realistic virelai of northern France often featured imitations of bird calls. The rondeau, on the other hand, remained almost exclusively a love poem. Since the composer usually set his own poems to music, the subtle demands of the repeated-line structure of the rondeau encouraged an equally suave and thoughtful musical treatment.

Though composers were overwhelmingly interested in polyphonic settings, there is an important monophonic repertoire from the fourteenth century. The lais by Machaut provide ample evidence of the beauty of this poetic and musical form. It must be both a feature of personalities and an accident of history that there are lais extant by Machaut, though very few remain by other composers. At the end of his life Machaut had all of his poetic and musical works recorded for posterity in durable manuscripts. Other composers' works were picked up by compilers and copyists for inclusion in collections for wealthy patrons. We assume that, since monophonic works could easily be learned by rote, they were not recorded in these anthology volumes.

STYLE OF THE ITALIAN REPERTOIRE

Secular polyphonic music in Italy in the fourteenth century appeared suddenly and without any apparent antecedents. It is, therefore, not a new art in contrast to an older style as we find in France, but new in being a radical innovation. Italian poets using the Provençal language imitated French troubadour poetic forms in the thirteenth century. Through Dante's influence, the Italian language emerged as a poetic medium at the beginning of the fourteenth century. Italian musicians simultaneously became interested in providing polyphonic settings of the vernacular poetry.

One of the prominent musical forms, the madrigal, apparently derives its name from the fact that the mother tongue, *matricale*, was being given musical setting. The madrigal texts were usually pastoral and rustic, though later in the century amorous and moralizing texts were written. Many madrigals are for two voices. The sixteenth-century madrigal is a very different form and should not be confused with the fourteenth-century madrigal.

The *caccia* was a semiprogrammatic form imitating the hunt; it is closely related to the French *chace*. The text often recounted the events of a hunt and referred by implication to the lover pursuing his lady. Melodic construction in the two upper voices symbolized the chase as well, one part following the other in strict canon at a distance of several bars.

The third prominent form of Italian secular song was the *ballata*, which is akin to the French virelai in structure. Composers such as the blind organist Francesco Landini favored the *ballata* on a ratio of about three to one over all other forms, according to surviving sources.

Keyboard performance emerges as a distinct style of composition during the ars nova period. In the Robertsbridge Codex (London, British Museum, MS add. 28550), keyboard transcriptions of motets from the *Roman de Fauvel* and some dances in Italian notation appear. These pieces date from about 1325, contemporary with the new wave of activity codified in Philippe de Vitry's treatise. Another source, the Faenza Codex (Faenza, Biblioteca Comunale, MS 117) contains keyboard elaborations of French and Italian vocal works. Although this source dates from about 1420, the style and character of the music are closely linked to those of the fourteenth century. Portative organs were considered important artistic instruments at the time in ensemble with other instruments. The new solo repertoire in the Robertsbridge source stands at the beginning of the history of solo keyboard music. Not for another century and a half do we find compositions written specifically for other instruments.

BIBLIOGRAPHY

Willi Apel, *The Notation of Polyphonic Music, 900–1600*, 5th ed. (1961); *Keyboard Music of the Fourteenth and Fifteenth Centuries* (1963); and *French Secular Compositions of the Fourteenth Century* (1970); *L'ars nova, recueil d'études sur la musique du XIV*[e] *siècle* (1959), has several pertinent articles; Peter Dronke, *The Medieval Lyric* (1968); Leonard Webster Ellinwood, ed., *The Works of Francesco Landini* (1939); Gordon K. Greene, ed., *French Secular Music*, vols. XVIII–XXII of *Polyphonic Music of the Fourteenth Century* (1981–); Ursula Günther, "The 14th-Century Motet and Its Development," in *Musica disciplina*, **12** (1958); and "Das Ende der Ars Nova," in *Die Musikforschung*, **16** (1963); Viola L. Hagopian, *Italian Ars Nova Music, a Bibliographic Guide to Modern Editions and Related Literature* (1964); Frank Llewellyn Harrison, *Music in Medieval Britain* (1963); Richard H. Hoppin, *Medieval Music* (1978); W. Thomas Marrocco, ed., *Italian Secular Music*, vols. VI–XI of *Polyphonic Music of the Fourteenth Century* (1967–1978); Leo Plantinga, "Philippe de Vitry's Ars Nova: A Translation," in *Journal of Music Theory*, **5** (1961); Gilbert Reaney, "The *Lais* of Guillaume de Machaut and Their Background," in *Proceedings of the Royal Musical Association*, **82** (1955–1956); "The 'Ars nova' of Philippe de Vitry," in *Musica disciplina*, **10** (1956); "The Development of the Rondeau, Virelai and Ballade Forms from Adam de la Hale to Guillaume de Machaut," in Heinrich Hüschen, ed., *Festschrift Karl Gustav Fellerer zum 60. Geburtstag* (1962); and *Guillaume de Machaut* (1971); Gustave Reese, *Music in the Middle Ages* (1940); *Répertoire international des sources musicales* (1966–1972), vols. B IV, 2, 3, 4, contains an inventory and description of manuscript sources; Ernest H. Sanders, "The Early Motets of Philippe de Vitry," in *Journal of the American Musicological Society*, **28** (1975); Leo Schrade, ed., *Polyphonic Music of the Fourteenth Century*, vols. I–IV (1956–1958), contains the works of Philippe de Vitry and the *Roman de Fauvel* polyphonic repertoire, the works of Machaut, and the works of Landini; Albert Seay, *Music in the Medieval World* (1965); F. Joseph Smith, "Ars Nova—a Re-definition?" in *Musica disciplina*, **18** (1964) and **19** (1965).

GORDON K. GREENE

[See also **Ars antiqua; Ars subtilior; Mensural Notation; Modal Notation; Modes (Melodic).**]

ARS POETICA, the theory of poetic art, in its medieval formulation, draws its basic principles from three popular texts of classical rhetoric: Cicero's early *De inventione,* the pseudo-Ciceronian *Rhetorica ad Herennium,* and Horace's *Ars poetica.* Incomplete versions of Cicero's mature *De oratore* and Quintilian's *Institutio oratoria* were also known to some late twelfth- and early thirteenth-century authors of poetic arts.

In 1924, Edmond Faral published a collection of Latin texts that have become basic to an understanding of medieval poetic theory in western Europe: Matthew of Vendôme's *Ars versificatoria* (*ca.* 1170), Geoffrey of Vinsauf's *Poetria nova* (*ca.* 1210) and *Documentum de modo et arte dictandi et versificandi* (*ca.* 1180; rev. *ca.* 1210), and Everard the German's *Laborintus* (mid thirteenth century). Two other treatises, summarized in Faral's text, have since been published in full: John of Garland's *Parisiana poetria* (between 1220 and 1235), and Gervase of Melkley's *Ars poetica* (between 1220 and 1240). It is of interest to note that the five authors named here had all studied or taught in Paris, and all had connections, directly or through Paris masters, with the schools of Orléans and Chartres, noted centers for the study of classical authors.

Since Geoffrey of Vinsauf's *Poetria nova,* extant in some two hundred manuscripts and the subject of a number of extensive medieval commentaries, was by far the most influential poetic treatise of the period, the following brief summary of medieval *ars poetica* will follow its order of presentation.

Geoffrey opens his treatise with a series of traditional yet striking images that capture fundamental aspects of poetic form: the poem is a "house," an architectural concept, with the poet as designer and builder; the poem is a "journey," a linear concept, with the poet as both traveler and guide; the poem is a "human body" with skeletal structure and adorned outward form, an organic concept, with the poet in the humble role of handmaiden.

The main body of Geoffrey's treatise treats the traditional five parts of rhetoric: invention, arrangement, verbal style, memory, and delivery.

Invention covers the poet's preliminary decision: whether to choose a story already familiar (*materia communis* or *pertractata*) or one not attempted before (*materia nova* or *illibata*). The preferred method is to give fresh and original form to familiar material by adding or omitting episodes, expanding or abbreviating sections, giving a new emphasis or meaning. The poet is advised to keep in mind, as aid to finding fresh material, seven basic questions relevant in any narrative: who, what, where, when, why, and how. Geoffrey's treatise does not discuss invention directly; his contemporary readers, however, would recognize, in the examples he gives throughout his treatise, a source book of invention on subjects ranging through myth, satire, encomium, lament, folktale, comedy, and topical event to an extended passage on paradise lost and regained—a fair if incomplete survey of medieval literary genres.

The second process, organization, directed the poet toward a major decision: did his subject, and his purpose in writing, advise a lengthy treatment, the amplified mode of epic or romance, or the brief treatment usually given to a comic story or illustrative incident? The amplified mode sought richness of texture through clearly defined means: the introduction of lengthy descriptions (of persons, places, times, events), comparisons, apostrophe (stressing the emotional impact of an incident), personification (giving speech to a nation or city or virtue in order to underline the ethical, political, or universal aspects of the story), and digression (for change of narrative pace or tone). Skillfully used, these modes of amplification may give richness and depth, explore motivation, and guide audience response. In Matthew of Vendôme's words, "hearing the story should be equivalent to having the experience" (*Ars versificatoria,* 4:15). Principles of organization also govern the order of events in a narrative. "Natural order" narrates events in their normal chronological sequence; a more effective "artistic order" begins with the middle or end of the action, returning to the beginning through memory and flashback. Well-chosen proverbs or organizing images (exempla) may also provide an artistic beginning if they encapsulate the story's meaning and focus the reader's attention.

The third part of poetic art, verbal expression—the careful refining of word and thought—receives the major attention of the poetic treatises. Invention and arrangement, as Cicero and Quintilian said, are largely matters of intelligence and common sense, but without eloquence in verbal style "all the preliminary accomplishments of oratory are as useless as a sword that is kept permanently concealed within its sheath" (*Institutio oratoria,* 8:15). This most complex area of poetic composition requires the most elaborate formal instruction. Clear, forceful, and elegant use of language requires judgment and skill in adapting style to subject. Aside from the traditional three styles (high, middle, and low), classical and medieval rhetoric recognizes an elaborate system of verbal patterning. The ten tropes (*Poetria nova,* 764–1093) are termed "difficult modes" because they employ words in a nonliteral sense. Of these, metaphor is much the most important; Geoffrey calls it the "star" of discourse, and analyzes its nature and function at great length in his treatises. Aside from tropes, the style manuals recognize some thirty-five figures of diction (modes of auditory, rhythmic, and syntactic patterning), and twenty figures of thought (the conscious patterning of an idea, as through dialogue or rhetorical question). Other suggested modes for developing facility and grace of style, termed "conversions" and "determinations," are the verbal equivalents of finger exercises in music, potentially useful in helping to develop a precise, sensitive, and easy way with words. The goal of this elaborate training is not necessarily an elaborate art—elegant simplicity is a valued norm among the rhetoricians—rather, the goal is to make the craftsman confident, adept, and versatile, ready for any subject (*Poetria nova,* 1707–1708). The last two parts of a rhetorically conceived poetic theory treat techniques of memorizing and reciting the finished poem.

There is another area of medieval *ars poetica,* echoed in the "*status archetypus et sensilis*" ("mode of existence as archetype and as physical entity") of Geoffrey's early lines (*Poetria nova,* 44–49), an area more profound and esoteric than the familiar classical one, developing among scholars at Chartres in the twelfth century. Its techniques of expression are not radically unlike the ones discussed above, but its claims for poetry are more daring. Drawing inspiration from Platonic and Neoplatonic sources, especially from the *Timaeus,* Plato's myth of creation (known in Calcidius' partial translation), the scholars at Chartres saw the poetic possibilities of philosophic myth—the "likely story" of the highly trained mind—as vehicle for the exploration and metaphoric expression of areas where science, philosophy, and theology meet.

BIBLIOGRAPHY

Primary. Edmond Faral, *Les arts poétiques du xiie et du xiiie siècle* (1924; repr. 1962); Ernest Gallo, *The "Poetria nova" and Its Sources in Early Rhetorical Doctrine* (1971) and "Matthew of Vendôme: Introductory Treatise on the Art of Poetry," in *Proceedings of the American Philosophical Society,* **118** (1974); Geoffrey of Vinsauf, *Poetria nova,* Margaret F. Nims, trans. (1967), and *Documentum de modo et arte dictandi et versificandi,* Roger P. Parr, trans. (1968); Gervase of Melkley, *Ars poetica,* Hans-Jürgen Gräbener, ed. (1965); John of Garland, *The Parisiana Poetria,* Traugott Lawler, ed. and trans. (1974).

Secondary. Ernest Gallo, "The Grammarian's Rhetoric: The *Poetria Nova* of Geoffrey of Vinsauf," in James J. Murphy, *Medieval Eloquence* (1978); Douglas Kelly, "The Scope of the Treatment of Composition in the Twelfth- and Thirteenth-century Arts of Poetry," in *Speculum,* **41** (1966); and "The Theory of Composition in Medieval Narrative Poetry and Geoffrey of Vinsauf's *Poetria nova,*" in *Mediaeval Studies,* **31** (1969); James J. Murphy, *Rhetoric in the Middle Ages* (1974); Margaret F. Nims, "*Translatio:* 'Difficult Statement' in Medieval Poetic Theory," in *University of Toronto Quarterly,* **43** (1974); Robert O. Payne, *The Key of Remembrance: A Study of Chaucer's Poetics* (1963); Winthrop Wetherbee, *Platonism and Poetry in the Twelfth Century* (1972).

MARGARET F. NIMS

ARS PRAEDICANDI, or the art of preaching, a term generally applied to manuals of instruction on sermon writing. While the genre's sources reach back to classical and early Christian times, the *ars praedicandi* itself did not appear until the end of the twelfth century.

More than three hundred treatises on preaching have been identified, but fewer than twenty are available in modern editions. Because the popularity of the handbook continued well into the sixteenth century, some medieval treatises are found in early printed books as well as in manuscript. A few first appeared in print. All are in Latin, although in the sixteenth century discussions of vernacular sermon techniques, accompanied by examples, were common.

The textual traditions of *artes praedicandi* are often complex and reflect the different forces that brought the manuals into being. Most of the treatises are anonymous. Some of the better-known ones have spurious medieval ascriptions to such authors as Bonaventure or Aquinas. Questions of authorship may be further complicated because portions of several treatises were gathered under a single title; or, alternatively, fragments of larger works were copied (frequently on blank end leaves) into other homiletic aids such as treatises on virtues and vices, sermon collections, florilegia, theological works, and even assortments of such tracts.

The manuals appear most often in one of two formats: as introductions or epilogues to often elegant, folio-sized collections of sermons or, far more frequently, as sections of quarto-sized or smaller preachers' aids. The latter format could be found in a university library; but it also suggests that such a volume served as a vade mecum for an itinerant preacher or that it rested in the modest library of a parish church or monastery. The longest treatises run to just over 100 quarto leaves; the typical work is less than one fourth of that length. *Artes praedicandi* almost never appear as separately bound pieces.

The *artes* responded to two late medieval needs: they were guidebooks for writing learned, polished sermons as well as basic textbooks for less well-educated clergy. Alan of Lille is often credited with writing the first *ars praedicandi.* His *Summa de arte praedicatoria* (1198) was probably composed and circulated at the University of Paris. Its portrayal of sermon form and content closely parallels the surviving "university" or "thematic" sermons delivered at Paris in the early thirteenth century. The sermons address a cultivated, often clerical audience and reflect the requirement that theology masters regularly demonstrate proficiency in preaching to peers and teachers.

Fourteenth-century handbooks, most notably those of Robert of Basevorn (*Forma praedicandi,* 1322) and Thomas Waleys (*De modo componendi sermones cum documentis,* after 1342), elaborate Alan's prototype to create lengthy guides for writing thematic sermons. These manuals borrow freely from grammatical and, less frequently, poetic treatises for direction on the expansion and illustration of arguments. Although framed as prescriptive guides for sermon writing, the manuals actually describe and codify current preaching practices.

Some earlier treatises, such as those of the English abbot Alexander of Ashby (*De modo praedicandi, ca.* 1200) and canon Richard of Thetford (*Ars dilatandi sermones, ca.* 1260), better reflect the sources of the sermon manual's long popularity. Alexander and Richard probably wrote their manuals for modestly educated priests charged with the care of souls. These treatises were part of a great thirteenth- and fourteenth-century effort, spurred by numerous Vatican decrees and reinforced by such local authorities as Bishop Robert Grosseteste of Lincoln, to improve the quality of pastoral care. Preachers were required to deliver more and better sermons. *Artes praedicandi* and other preaching aids joined a proliferation of catechetical aids to meet the demands of the era's intensified lay spirituality.

The needs of these two classes of preacher did not conflict. A good priest, whether master of theology or parish clerk, was expected to preach frequently and well; and the meaner practitioners surely desired to emulate great preachers like Bonaventure, Aquinas, or St. Francis. The tradition of showcase preaching continued throughout the Middle Ages both in the university and on occasions of high public celebration. But the manuals probably ceased to serve such preaching; they focused on preachers with more elementary needs.

The earlier handbooks were preserved and copied while new shorter, frequently more desultory manuals proliferated well into the sixteenth century. The more complete manuals of the late fourteenth and fifteenth century focus on the problems of preaching to the laity. They continue to advocate thematic sermon structure, but they also consider how audiences steeped in vernacular culture should influence sermon practice. All but the most derivative later manuals take a freer attitude toward appropriate sermon topics—even to the point of encouraging borrowing from popular culture. Some, such as Johann Ulrich Surgant's *Manuale curatorum* (1503), even considered subtle ways to engage audience attention.

The most detailed manuals, written mainly in the thirteenth century, undertook several tasks. They defined preaching and its goals, considered the qualities of a good preacher, reviewed the styles and traditions of preaching, and then outlined the parts of the sermon and discussed methods of proof and embellishment. All but the most fragmentary of the later *artes* preserve these elements in some—often synoptic—form.

This format enabled authors to justify their work. The manual writers frequently quoted St. Augustine—appropriately, because they were extending his reconciliation of classical rhetorical principles and Christian preaching. In the *De doctrina christiana* Augustine adapted the ethical tradition of classical rhetoric, most fully developed in Cicero's *De oratore,* to the priestly vocation. His arguments were repeated frequently throughout the Middle Ages, but the later works that most influenced ethical thought in the *artes praedicandi* were Gregory's *Cura pastoralis* and Rabanus Maurus' *De institutione clericorum.*

Augustine also laid the groundwork for the fundamental distinction between classical and Christian rhetoric: the former relied on a variety of persuasive devices to bring an audience to a particular belief; the latter, possessing the absolute truth of Scripture, laid out and interpreted this authority to move a congregation to greater devotion and better conduct. It remained for the twelfth century to create a type of preaching handbook in which detailed analysis of classical rhetorical devices was coupled with medieval exegetical and etymological analysis. The manuals combined such guidance with reworkings of ancient theories on the proper nature and arrangement of parts in a speech.

There was some sheepishness about the innovation. The *artes* commonly note that the thematic sermon was not used by the Fathers because they did not need it: their superior inspiration enabled them to preach without divisions, subdivisions, and proofs. Less skillful, later medieval preachers and their congregations would profit, they thought, from the more complicated modern sermon style.

The *ars praedicandi* sermon is most fully de-

ARS PRAEDICANDI

scribed in the thirteenth-century manuals attributed to Robert of Basevorn, Thomas Waleys, and "Pseudo-Bonaventure" *(Ars concionandi),* which stress the importance of Scripture. Every sermon must open with a theme, that is, a biblical quotation ordinarily drawn from the day's lection. A protheme follows, combining a salutation with discussion of the importance of the topic broached in the theme. The protheme often includes a scriptural quotation that confirms or elaborates the theme. Then the preacher would pray. Manual writers urge the preacher to establish his audience rapport in these opening sections; and their treatises, drawing on *De oratore,* often devote considerable attention to the proper ethos of a preacher—spiritual intercessor for his congregation, dignified in demeanor, compassionate, and a model of good conduct.

After the prayer, the theme would be repeated and divided. Division fascinated manual writers, and they developed many rules and methods for separating an idea into its component parts. In general, the preacher was to select several—often three—points, based on the theme, to make in the sermon. The writer, for example, might take three phrases in the theme, three key words, three exegetical senses, three "causes," or even three elements representing the contrary of an essential statement in the theme. Each of these divisions in turn received some confirming authority—a quotation from Scripture, the Fathers, the ancients, or even, in the late Middle Ages, from a song or proverb.

After a confirming authority was offered, the preacher was free to expand *(dilatare)* his division. Depending on the audience and the era, the preacher might subdivide his authority—adducing still more confirming authorities. He might demonstrate his point with an exemplum, draw an argument from one of the Fathers, or pursue the Isidorean etymology of a term. One fifteenth-century English writer, Simon Alcock, posed a mnemonic beginning "*ad, quare, propter, hoc . . .*" to help the preacher remember the prepositions and conjunctions that connote each of his suggested modes of amplification *(dilatatio).*

There were also aesthetic considerations in division, confirmation, and amplification. While "external" divisions were proper for laity and less learned audiences, "internal" divisions were regarded as more difficult and more elegant. They required that the words of the theme figure in each partition and that the sermon hew closely to the meaning of the theme. External division could simply use the quotation as a starting point for a lesson. There was also enthusiasm for rhymed, alliterative, or assonantal divisions, grammatically parallel division, and other feats of elocution.

The salient characteristic of the manuals is their conviction that the ends of preaching, "open and public instruction regarding behavior and faith proposed for the formation of man" in Alan of Lille's often quoted phrase, could best be accomplished by dividing a scriptural theme. Toward the end of the Middle Ages doubt appears—some writers suggest that not all lay audiences are best reached through thematic sermons—but for two hundred years, in the handbooks at least, the style prevailed. The *artes* leave the impression that a good sermon is a tightly structured work with three or more internal movements, each offering different arguments but similarly structured. These movements are flanked by an opening that resembles a classical exordium and an ending that, surprisingly, interested sermon theorists hardly at all.

Our understanding of the place of the *artes praedicandi* in preaching and in literary history is hampered by the unrepresentative selection of texts in modern editions. The best-known works, those of Thomas Waleys and Robert of Basevorn, represent the university preaching tradition. Yet evidence in archives suggests that over time the handbooks were most concerned with preaching to the laity.

It is likely that the manuals attempted to codify accepted or effective current sermon practice rather than to promulgate new methods. Medieval preaching was an adaptive art. The sermon manuals, along with the sermons themselves and other preachers' aids, are practically the only sources from which this changing, ephemeral, but essential dimension of medieval spiritual life can be reconstructed. Yet manuals from the most active era of medieval popular preaching, the fourteenth through sixteenth centuries, have been inventoried or studied only in part.

Finally, the medieval manuals must not be read in a vacuum; their development and influence extended well into the Renaissance and they were merely one of several sources of instruction—although the only technical guides to *dispositio*—available to the medieval author. Yet, in part because of the complex textual problems presented by the surviving medieval sermon texts, little recent hard work has been done on the relationship between the theory and practice of medieval preaching or on the relationship

ARS SUBTILIOR

between preaching and other contemporary forms of literary expression. The *artes praedicandi* should be important guides to this study.

BIBLIOGRAPHY

Sources. [See works by Murphy and Caplan below for fuller bibliographies.] Alan of Lille, *Summa de arte praedicatoria,* D. Carolus de Wisch, ed., in *Patrologia latina,* CCX (1855), 111–198; summary translation in Miller *et al.* *(q.v.),* 228–239; Simon Alcock, *De modo dividendi thema pro materia sermonis dilatanda,* Mary F. Boynton, ed., in "Simon Alcok on Expanding the Sermon," in *Harvard Theological Review,* 34 (1941); Pseudo-Aquinas, *A Brief Religious Tract on the Art and True Method of Preaching,* Harry Caplan, trans., in "A Late Medieval Tractate on Preaching," in A. M. Drummond, ed., *Studies in Rhetoric and Public Speaking in Honor of J. A. Winans* (1925), 61–90; reprinted in Anne King and Helen North, eds., *Of Eloquence: Studies in Ancient and Medieval Rhetoric* (1970), 48–76; Pseudo-Bonaventure (in part, Richard of Thetford), *Ars concionandi,* in *S. Bonaventura Opera Omnia,* IX (1901), 8–21; Robert of Basevorn, *Forma praedicandi,* in *Artes praedicandi,* T.-M. Charland, ed. (1936); translated by Leopold Krul in James J. Murphy, ed., *Three Medieval Rhetorical Arts* (1971), 109–217; Thomas Waleys, *De modo componendi sermones,* in T.-M. Charland, ed., *Artes praedicandi* (1936); William of Auvergne (in part, Richard of Thetford), *De faciebus mundi,* A. de Poorter, ed., in *Revue néoscholastique de philosophie,* 25 (1923).

Studies. Harry Caplan, *Mediaeval Artes praedicandi: A Handlist,* 2 vols. (1934–1936); Thomas-Marie Charland, *Artes praedicandi: Contribution à l'histoire de la rhétorique au moyen âge* (1936); Susan Gallick, "*Artes praedicandi:* Early Printed Editions," in *Medieval Studies,* 39 (1977); Joseph M. Miller, Michael H. Prosser, and Thomas W. Benson, eds., *Readings in Medieval Rhetoric* (1973); James J. Murphy, ed., *Medieval Eloquence; Studies in the Theory and Practice of Medieval Rhetoric* (1978), 112–126; James J. Murphy, *Medieval Rhetoric: A Select Bibliography* (1971); Gerald R. Owst, *Literature and Pulpit in Medieval England,* 2nd ed. (1961); and *Preaching in Medieval England: An Introduction to Sermon Manuscripts of the Period* (1926); Woodburn O. Ross, *Middle English Sermons* (1940).

MARIANNE G. BRISCOE

[See also **Preaching, Sermon Literature (Western Europe).**]

ARS SUBTILIOR (a more subtle art), a term first used by Ursula Günther in 1963 to replace the less precise terms "late *ars nova,*" "mannerist school," and "manneristic style" used to describe the music of southern France in the last quarter of the fourteenth century. She chose this term for its positive connotation—"manneristic" has pejorative overtones—and also because *ars nova* music was and is recognized for its subtleties; so the epithet "more subtle" emphasizes a new departure that still retains older forms and some of their features. Willi Apel proposed extreme limits of 1360 to 1420 for the period, but Günther is more cautious, confining the *subtilior* to the time of the Schism, 1378 to 1417. Datable compositions range from 1382 to 1394, while the works of Johannes Ciconia (*ca.* 1335–1411) display many aspects of the style. A more general definition would specify from about the death of Guillaume de Machaut (1377) to the death of Matteo of Perugia (*ca.* 1418).

Ars subtilior style originated at the papal court at Avignon and soon spread to the courts of the French and Spanish nobility. These courts were brilliant exemplars of French social, literary, and musical customs; and although they attracted Italian composers, notably Philipoctus of Caserta, Anthonello of Caserta, and Matteo of Perugia, the language of the texts and musical style of these composers were French. The most notable French composers of these courts include Cuvelier, Galiot, Grimace, Jacob de Senleches, Solage, Suzay, Trebor, and Vaillant. In all, the names of about forty French composers are known.

Only about a dozen sacred pieces (Mass items) and some fourteen motets (mostly with Latin texts) survive in this repertory, but almost 250 French secular compositions are extant, indicating the predominantly secular tastes of contemporary nobles. The French compositions consist primarily of the *formes fixes:* ballades, virelais, and rondeaux, the last group becoming predominant by the end of the fourteenth century. Over twenty manuscript sources preserve this repertory, among which three are outstanding: Chantilly, Musée Condé, MS 564 (formerly 1047); Paris, Bibliothèque Nationale, MS nouv. fr. 6772 (Codex Reina); and Modena, Biblioteca Estense, MS M.5.24 (formerly lat. 568).

Ars subtilior music is characterized by a number of stylistic changes that developed from the compositions of Machaut and his contemporaries. Primarily, one finds greater notational complexities: an increasing use of note values smaller than the minim; caudated notes and *dragmae* that give a variety of special note values; the use of full and hollow red and black notes to produce conflicting rhythms in the several parts; and in all, a profusion of rhythmic complexities and syncopation. It is, in Apel's words, a "style of deliberate diversification, extravagance and utmost complexity . . . with contrasting meters and other types of cross rhythms" (1950, 10–11), often leading to complete rhythmic independence in all three parts. Toward the end of the period a modified "modern style" emerged, which shows triadic melody, a less lively contratenor part, short imitative sections, expressive use of accented discords, and a corresponding lessening of rhythmic complexities and syncopation.

Although it flourished for only four decades, the *ars subtilior* style created and solved the most complex rhythmic problems to emerge in Western musical history until after World War II.

BIBLIOGRAPHY

Willi Apel, *French Secular Music of the Late Fourteenth Century* (1950); *French Secular Compositions of the Fourteenth Century*, 3 vols. (1970–1972); Ursula Günther, *Zehn datierbare Kompositionen der Ars nova* (1959); "Datierbare Balladen des späten 14. Jahrhunderts," in *Musica disciplina*, **15** (1961), and **16** (1962); and "Das Ende der *ars nova*," in *Musikforschung*, **16** (1963).

GORDON A. ANDERSON

[See also **Machaut, Guillaume de; Music in Medieval Society; Music, Liturgical.**]

ARSACIDS/ARŠAKUNI, ARMENIAN. Dynasty descended from a junior branch of the Parthian royal house in Iran. The chronology and history of the entire Arsacid period in Armenia are still confused and open to considerable discussion among scholars. The first Arsacid to rule Armenia may have been the Parthian King Vonones himself in A.D. 12, but the traditional inauguration of the dynasty is usually set at the coronation of Trdat/Tiridates I, a younger son of the Parthian king, by the emperor Nero in A.D. 66, thus initiating a balance between Roman and Persian influence in Armenia. Interruptions in the Arsacid rule of the country continued until the end of the third century, and relations with the Persians were radically altered by the overthrow of the Iranian senior branch by the Sasanians in 224/226, which created a blood feud between the "usurpers" and the Armenian rulers. The Arsacids probably regained power only with the establishment of Trdat III/IV on the Armenian throne by Diocletian about 298.

The conversion of Trdat and his country to Christianity in 314 further alienated the Armenian Arsacids from Iran, while their support of the Arian policy of Constantine's successors antagonized the Armenian church and much of the nobility under Aršak II and his son Pap in the fourth century. Despite constant attempts to preserve a balance between Byzantium and Iran, the Armenian Arsacids could not prevent the abandonment of the country to Persia by the treaty of 364 and its domination by the Sasanians. The partition of Armenia in 387 briefly created two simultaneous Arsacid lines, one in the Byzantine portion and the other in Persarmenia. The Roman branch came to an end in 390 with the death of Aršak III, to whom the emperor allowed no successor. In Persarmenia the dynasty lingered on and a collaboration was reestablished with the Armenian church early in the fifth century, when King Vṙamšapuh encouraged the patriarch Saint Sahak I and Saint Mesrop to create the Armenian alphabet. By 428, however, this branch was likewise abolished and replaced by a Persian governor, or marzpan.

BIBLIOGRAPHY

For the early Arsacid chronology see C. Toumanoff, "The Third-century Armenian Arsacids," in *Revue des études arméniennes*, n.s. **6** (1969). There is no adequate treatment in English of the Christian Arsacids in Armenia. See Pascal Asdourian, *Die politischen Beziehungen zwischen Armenien und Rom* (1911); René Grousset, *Histoire de l'Arménie dès origines à 1071* (1947), 105–162; and Hakob Manandyan, *K^cnnakan testowt^cyown Hay Zoghovrdi Patmowt^cyan*, II, pt. 1 (1957; repr. 1978). A new chronology has been attempted by R. Hewsen, "The Successors of Tiridates the Great," in *Revue des études arméniennes*, n.s. **13** (1978–1979), but it has not yet gained general acceptance.

NINA G. GARSOÏAN

[See also **Arians; Armenian Alphabet; Aršak II; Marzpanate; Sahak, Saint; Sasanians.**]

ARŠAK II, Arsacid king of Armenia (350/351?–367/368) probably son and successor of Tiran. The main sources on his reign are Ammianus Marcellinus (bks. XX, 11; XXI, 6; XXIII, 3; XXIV, 7, 8; XXV, 7; XXVII, 12) on the Roman side, who is favorable to the king, and P^cawstos Buzand (bks. IV, V, 7) and Movsēs Xorenac^ci (bk. III, 18–35) on the Armenian, both of whom reflect the hostile attitude of the contemporary Armenian clergy.

Aršak was considered to be "a constant and faithful" friend by the Byzantine emperor Constantius II, who in 358 granted him immunity from taxation and a bride, Olympias, from the imperial household. Nevertheless, Aršak strove to maintain an equilibrium between his friendship with the empire and his allegiance to Sasanian Iran. The support of Constantius, who leaned toward Arianism, and Aršak's similar religious views antagonized the Armenian clergy, led by the patriarch Nersēs I, and much of the nobility. This antagonism was further increased by the murder of Aršak's nephew Gnel and the king's marriage to the latter's widow, P^c^aṙanjem, who instigated the death of Olympias.

The peace treaty concluded by the emperor Jovian in 364 after the failure of Julian's eastern campaign broke the earlier balance and abandoned Armenia to the Persians. Insufficiently supported by his alienated nobles, Aršak was unable to withstand the onslaught of the Sasanians, who overran Armenia, capturing its cities and deporting the population to Persia. The crown prince, Pap, fled to Byzantium and Queen P^c^aṙanjem continued to resist until her capture and death, but Aršak was finally forced to surrender. He was imprisoned in the "Castle of Oblivion," the names of whose inmates might never be mentioned. According to Armenian tradition he committed suicide there, as did his faithful vassal Drastamat, who had made his way to his lord.

BIBLIOGRAPHY

There is no study in English of Aršak II, and even studies in West European languages are rare and inadequate. See Pascal Asdourian, *Die politischen Beziehungen zwischen Armenien und Rom* (1911); Nina G. Garsoïan, "Politique ou orthodoxie? L'Arménie au quatrième siècle," in *Revue des études arméniennes,* n.s. **4** (1967); René Grousset, *Histoire de l'Arménie dès origines à 1071* (1947), 138–143; Hakob Manandyan, *K^c^nnakan tesowt^c^yown Hay žoghovrdi Patmowt^c^yown,* II, pt. 1 (1957; repr. 1978), 161–193. A new succession and chronology is proposed by Robert Hewsen, "The Successors of Tiridates the Great," in *Revue des études arméniennes,* n.s. **13** (1978–1979), but it has not yet gained general acceptance.

NINA G. GARSOÏAN

[See also **Arsacids/Aršakuni, Armenian; Nerses I the Great, Saint.**]

ARSENIUS AUTORIANUS (b. *ca.* 1200; d. *ca.* 1273) was patriarch of Constantinople in exile in Nicaea (1255–1259), because of the Latin occupation of the Byzantine capital. He resigned his see in a conflict with Michael VIII Palaeologus, who had been made coemperor with the legitimate heir, John IV Lascaris. He recovered his position after the recapture of the capital city by the Greeks (1261). During his second patriarchate (1261–1265) he excommunicated Michael for blinding his ward John IV. But Michael forced Arsenius out of office again in 1265. Arsenius received the support of a numerous party of "Arsenites" who refused to recognize his deposition and the election of subsequent patriarchs until 1310.

BIBLIOGRAPHY

I. E. Troitskij, *Arsenij i Arsenity* (1973).

JOHN MEYENDORFF

[See also **Michael VIII Palaeologus.**]

ART. See individual articles: **Gothic, Romanesque,** etc.

ART, COMMERCIAL TRADE OF. Until the later medieval period virtually all work produced by painters, stonemasons, goldsmiths, and woodworkers was undertaken under contract, in response to the specific demand of a patron. Whether an individual, a cathedral chapter, or a commune, the patron generally stipulated in detail the character of the work required from the artist. Paintings and sculptures were not made by men hoping, at some future time, to find a purchaser for their wares but were created for one particular occasion and place.

In the field of the so-called "minor arts" it is possible that before the twelfth century there was some import into Europe of Moorish lusterwares, Byzantine ivory carvings, and Greek or Islamic silks, but the surviving examples found in the West seem almost always to have been either gifts to or from princes or booty obtained in war. No clear picture of commerce in them can be built up. During the last three centuries of the Middle Ages this situation was to a certain extent modified. The consolidation and expansion of established trade routes within Europe coincided with the emergence of a new class of prosperous townsmen anxious to display their wealth in all aspects of their lives. With these developments, merchants came forward to meet a new demand for

ART, COMMERCIAL TRADE OF

a variety of art wares. However, since merchants themselves very rarely specialized in one commodity—and never in art—and since the trade never assumed such economic importance as that in broadcloths, grain, or salt, information on it is scattered, scanty, and normally to be inferred from casual references in literature of the time and surviving samples rather than from any full documentary record.

For the upper ranks of society, moreover, art was still only rarely an object of trade but remained, as in the earlier Middle Ages, the product of a personal agreement between patron and artist. It follows that besides such high-grade commodities as tooled leather from Spain, glassware (especially mirrors) from Murano, and (from the end of the fourteenth century) Florentine damasks, Venetian velvets, and Valenciennes lace—all of which may be considered crafts rather than art proper—it is likely that any object of quality was made under contract, even when similar goods are known to have been produced for the general market. As a result it is often difficult to decide whether surviving examples of work, found far from their place of origin, are the result of trade or of personal commission.

There are, nonetheless, certain fields in which some element of art dealing can be discerned. The first is that of antique and reproduction cameos, engraved gems, medals, and bronzes. Partly through their classical associations, partly through the belief that Egyptian, Greek, and Roman glyptic art might possess magic qualities in averting evil and preserving health, these articles were valued much more highly than any contemporary painting or sculpture. The Medici's famous collection of these items seems to have been begun with Cosimo the Elder's commissioning of the humanist, Niccolò Niccoli, as his agent to seek them out during his expeditions to Rome. The collections of King Charles V of France, and of his brothers, Louis of Anjou and Jean, duke of Berry, were provided by Italian merchants of deluxe goods who skillfully fostered this Italian upper-class taste in the nobility of northern Europe.

From the beginning of the fourteenth century, too, the unrivaled English embroidery known as *opus anglicanum*, produced by both nuns and professionals, was being exported to richer churches all over the Continent. (The very decline—not in popularity but in quality—of the product in the course of the century may reflect the enlarged market that it was acquiring.)

Tapestries were also by that time being traded. Most of those that have survived were, like the "Apocalypse of Angers" from the firm of Nicolas Bataille, commissioned by specific contracts. Bataille is described as a "dealer" in Saracenic tapestries and, between 1387 and 1400, sold some 250 tapestries and carpets to the royal court of France, as well as other pieces to the dukes of Savoy and Anjou. He must have been an entrepreneur, one who was forcefully promoting the sale of his materials and probably also selling works already made without prior commission.

Tapestry was an art in demand and accessible to those outside the wealthiest nobility and town patriciate. Tin-glazed majolica ware of the fifteenth century falls into the same category. At the end of the fourteenth century all true majolica was imported from Majorca (as its name recalls), probably to meet an exclusively upper-class demand. In the fifteenth century, however, it came to be manufactured in Europe for a wider market, first at Cafaggiolo in the Florentine region and then, from the 1470's, at Faenza (whence the word "faience"). Although Moorish potters were occasionally brought to Europe to teach the techniques and may be supposed to have been influential, the trade in majolica from the Islamic world certainly had equal importance in the European development of pottery. The forms of the drug jars called *albarelli*, for instance, which were made in fifteenth-century Faenza, copy faithfully those that had evolved in the fourteenth century at Sultanabad in Persia (now Arak, Iran). Yet it is doubtful if there was in Italy any large-scale production of ceramics for trade; for as the ability to make true majolica spread, states were frequently found issuing protectionist statutes against imported goods, in the interests of native producers.

Besides such objects of use and display, there was also a large market for domestic painting and statuary. Indeed, they might at that time have been considered things of practical utility, since the Church of the later Middle Ages increasingly recommended the employment of images as aids to religious devotion. Cardinal Giovanni Dominici, for example, in his *Regola del governo di cura famigliare*, written at the beginning of the fifteenth century, urged his bourgeois readers to develop their own and their children's religious sensibilities by placing paintings and statues on sacred themes in shrines in their chambers and gardens.

To meet these needs the wealthier patrons commissioned works from known artists; but most men

ART, COMMERCIAL TRADE OF

had to look to more impersonal means of securing what they sought. As a result more and more minor masters began, often in a mechanical and repetitive fashion, to produce art without previous commission in the speculative hope of future sale.

We meet one of them in a story from the late fourteenth-century *novelle* of Franco Sacchetti about one Mino da Siena, in whose workshop there were always four or five unfinished crucifixes lying around ready for completion. Again entrepreneurs came increasingly to commission work for export. In England a notable example is offered by the production, in the workshops first of Norwich and then of London, of small-scale alabaster figures and reliefs (among which the head of St. John the Baptist was particularly popular). Though often of very high quality they were sold cheaply by itinerant peddlers throughout England and, by the fifteenth century, were extensively marketed in Europe.

England was also remarkable for the monumental brasses from which brass rubbings are now taken. Originating as a large and expensive luxury, monumental brasses were being mass produced by the fifteenth century. No attempt at individual portraiture was made in the representations of the deceased, but the cost was about one tenth of the earlier individualized brasses, and they were produced in enormous numbers (an estimated 100,000 were laid down in all). This phenomenon is the more remarkable in that the latten or alloy from which the effigies were made had to be imported from the Rhineland. At the same time the wealthy merchants of eastern England and Scotland still often thought it worth their while to import brasses from northern Germany that were larger and richer than those of native production.

In the marketing of art, however, it was predictably the Italian merchant houses, whose commercial links were already well established all over Europe, that dominated. In the first quarter of the fourteenth century Italian paintings were on sale in Paris, and Italian stucco figures were being marketed in Amsterdam. The most extensive evidence for commerce in art goods in the medieval period is to be found in the vast surviving archives of the famous firm founded by Francesco di Marco Datini of Prato, which in the second half of the fourteenth century traded with Paris, Avignon, London, Bruges, and Catalonia. Art objects constituted merely a small fraction of the firm's total business, which principally concerned trade in textiles, salt, and arms. Yet in an age of unspecialized commerce nothing that could be thought to yield a profit was neglected. Datini exported to France jewel caskets and painted wedding-chests *(cassoni)* that he had commissioned in Florence (and, on one occasion, in Barcelona). He bought *banquiers* (tapestries to be hung over chairs) in Bruges to be sold in Avignon, and imported a large number of Parisian enamels (in 1371 over 1,300) into Italy. His correspondence shows that pictures on religious themes were also dispatched from Florence to Avignon and bought by all ranks of society from tailors to high curial officials. What Datini sought above all, as a letter of a partner writing from Avignon makes clear, was inexpensive work that would attract customers looking for bargains: "If you don't find good works that are cheap, leave them. They're not much in demand here. You should buy them only when the master's hard up. Do this, for we've no need to take these things on." It is true that painters of some repute in their own day, like Jacopo di Cione and Paolo di Giovanni Fei, were sometimes involved and occasionally even produced large panels for the foreign market. But in general the normal level of demand was for religious objects made by anonymous craftsmen, what later generations came to dismiss as "sacristy" or "St. Sulpice" art.

By contrast one partner in the Datini firm, Domenico di Cambio, while in no way concerning himself exclusively with objets d'art, does stand out for his interest in them and could perhaps be seen as the first documented picture dealer. Between 1390 and 1410 he is found commissioning works for export, with a good knowledge of prices and demand, and acting as agent to visitors to Florence who were seeking paintings. His letters to Datini tell of his negotiations with painters ("They're all liars, and big ones too"). They urge Datini to buy paintings for his own use ("Men who are hard of heart and wrapped up in worldly things need these religious scenes, and you, it seems to me, are just such a man"), and offer him good though neglected advice when Datini found himself in legal difficulties with artists.

No doubt the correspondence of other Italian firms of this period would, had it survived, have revealed much the same minor interest in art as an economic commodity. From the aesthetic point of view trade in art by the end of the fifteenth century probably had some importance in quickening the tempo of stylistic change and in breaking down provincial styles among lesser craftsmen throughout Europe. But it had little effect on "high" art, which then (as perhaps now) could not easily be adapted to the requirements of a mass market.

BIBLIOGRAPHY

There is no general treatment of trade in art in the Middle Ages. The material is normally to be discovered only in the asides of a myriad of works concerned with the aesthetic rather than commercial aspects of the subjects they discuss.

For agreements between artists and patrons, see Michael Baxandall, *Painting and Experience in Fifteenth Century Italy* (1972), 1–27; and John Larner, *Culture and Society in Italy, 1290–1420* (1971), 328–348. For contracts in English translation, see Teresa G. Frisch, *Gothic Art 1140–c. 1450: Sources and Documents* (1971), 82–83, 113–114; Wolfgang Stechow, *Northern Renaissance Art, 1400–1600: Sources and Documents* (1966), 10–11, 77–78, 81–82, 141–145; and David S. Chambers, *Patrons and Artists in the Italian Renaissance* (1970).

For ceramics, see Louis M. E. Solon, *A History and Description of Italian Majolica* (1907), 19–20, 30, 144–145, 195–196.

For English alabaster sculptures, see Lawrence Stone, *Sculpture in Britain: The Middle Ages* (1955), 179–181, 189–192.

For monumental brasses, see Alan C. Bouquet, *Church Brasses, British and Continental* (1956), 18–35.

The large literature on the Datini firm includes Robert Brun, "Notes sur le commerce des objets d'art en France et principalement à Avignon à la fin du XIVe siècle," in *Bibliothèque de l'École des Chartes*, 95 (1934).

JOHN LARNER

ART, THEORY OF. See **Iconoclasm.**

ARTAŠAT (ARTAXATA). Royal residence of the Armenian Arsacid kings located on the north bank of the Araks river some thirty kilometers southeast of present-day Erevan. The site of the city, traditionally set at the confluence of the Araks and the Mecamor rivers by the Armenian historian Movsēs Xorenacʿi and occasionally disputed by scholars in the past, has now been identified through the excavations begun in 1970 by the Institute of Archaeology and Ethnography of the Armenian S.S.R. Academy of Sciences. These have begun to uncover an extensive urban complex of primarily Hellenistic classical type, but containing some artifacts of Iranian inspiration.

The city was founded by Artašes (Artaxias) (223–187 B.C.), a Seleucid ruler now identified through his inscriptions as a native Armenian ruler who proclaimed his independence after the Roman defeat of the Seleucid ruler Antiochus III ("the Great") at Magnesia in 190/189 B.C. According to a tradition known to Strabo and Plutarch but historically unsupported, the plan of the city was designed by Hannibal himself. From its foundation Artašat seems to have been designated as a royal residence and capital, although it was briefly replaced by the new southern capital of Tigranakerta in the first century B.C. and again after the Roman sack of A.D. 163 by Vałarsapat (Kaine-Polis, "New City"). Because of its importance, the city was repeatedly besieged and sacked by the Romans and the Persians, notably in A.D. 58/59, after which it was rebuilt with the help of Roman architects sent by Nero and its name changed to Neroniana for a time; in 163, as noted above; and by King of Kings Šahpur II after the abandonment of Armenia to the Persians in 363/364.

Despite these vicissitudes, Artašat remained the capital of Armenia until it was superseded by the neighboring city of Dwin. The date of this transfer is uncertain, but it probably occurred in the late fourth or early fifth century, after the partition of Armenia between Rome and Persia, although Dwin had been founded earlier. Armenian sources cite the unhealthy location of Artašat in the marshes of the Araks, rather than a political event, as the cause for the shift of the royal residence. As late as 450, Artašat was called a royal city by the church council held there, and the city survived for centuries thereafter.

In addition to its importance as the capital of Arsacid Armenia, Artašat played a key role in the international trade crossing Armenia in the late classical and early medieval periods. It is listed as a major station and junction point in itineraria and maps such as the Peutinger Table of the later fourth century. Its international commercial character may well have been enhanced by the presence of a large Jewish colony that was transferred to Persia after the sack of the city in 364 (according to Armenian sources). Most important of all, Artašat was designated as one of only three authorized transit and customs points on the Byzantine–Persian frontier according to an edict of 408–409 preserved in the Codex Justinianus. This stipulation was repeated in the Justinianic Peace Treaty of 562, thus indicating the continuing international importance of Artašat after the loss of its position as capital of Armenia, despite the growing competition of Dwin. In the period of Arab domination, Artašat was known as the center of the purple dye industry with the local coch-

ARTHURIAN LITERATURE

ineal, and as such was called Kirmiz by Arab historian al-Balādhurī (d. 892), although the center of trade, as of administration, had shifted to Dwin.

BIBLIOGRAPHY

Hakob Manandyan, *The Trade and Cities of Armenia in Relation to Ancient World Trade,* Nina G. Garsoïan, trans. (1965), 44–46, 52, 58, 64–65, 80, 82, 86, 91 ff., 101 ff., 106 ff., 110 ff., 114–115, 153; and Sirarpie Der Nersessian, *The Armenians* (1969), 25, 28–29, 64, 67.

NINA G. GARSOÏAN

[See also **Armenia (Geography); Armenia (History); Dwin.**]

ARTHURIAN LITERATURE. The earliest account of the period of Arthur's supposed flourishing (*ca.* 490–540) is that of Gildas, whose *De excidio et conquestu Britanniae* was composed in the mid sixth century; it does not mention Arthur. Nearly three centuries passed before the personal exploits, the incredible military victories, and the marks of divine favor associated with Arthur and his noble retainers were celebrated in what came to be an outpouring of writings in many tongues and genres. The vogue of Arthur continued throughout the later Middle Ages. The last important medieval contribution to this great corpus of literature is Sir Thomas Malory's *Le Morte Darthur,* completed in 1469/1470 and printed by Caxton in 1485.

THE HISTORICAL ARTHUR

The chronicler Gildas dates his own birth in the year of the battle of Mount Badon, traditionally placed in 516. He credits the victory won by the Britons over the Saxons to the generalship of Ambrosius Aurelianus. Apparently written not more than a generation after the event, Gildas' work possesses special authority, despite the clerical bias evident in his insistence that the immorality and impiety of the British leaders brought woes upon their people, such as the forays of the Picts and Scots, and later the treachery of the pagan Saxons. The same course of events is sketchily rehearsed in Bede's *Historia ecclesiastica gentis Anglorum* (*ca.* 731) and in the *Saxon Chronicle* (*ca.* 800).

The first chroniclers' stark record of these decades came ultimately to be enriched by a far more circumstantial tradition in which the British leader is identified as Arthur and given a more elevated status. No Arthur was known in ancient Celtic lore; but the name was long established in Rome, whence it was transplanted to Britain. For example, Artorius Castor, a distinguished member of the gens Artoria, served as commander of a Roman legion stationed at York in the second century, according to a coffin inscription found in Dalmatia. That the name was adopted by native Britons is readily demonstrated. In particular, Nora Chadwick notes that in Adamnán's life of St. Columba, written before 704, a king of Argyll is reported to have a son named Arthur who met death while fighting the Saxons in southeastern Scotland. But evidence that stories about this dimly historical prince ever drifted south to Wales and Cornwall, along with northern British lore about such figures as Merlin, is lacking.

Nevertheless, that a prototype of some sort once existed is probable. Legendary heroes, of course, are commonly folk creations: some local figure too obscure for historical notice is endowed with a brilliant fictional biography, built up largely of age-old motifs, such as that of the culture hero whose parentage is mysterious and whose career ends not in death but with a journey to the Otherworld, from which he may be expected to return when needed by his people.

It is true that the Old Welsh elegiac poem, the *Gododdin*—the work of Aneirin, who lived in the region of Edinburgh about 600—alludes to an Arthur remarkable for his valor. But the *Gododdin* is preserved only in a thirteenth-century manuscript and includes late interpolations, among which the line concerning Arthur may be included. And the *Annales Cambriae,* compiled in the ninth and tenth centuries, refer twice to Arthur. The entry for 516 informs us that at the battle of Mount Badon, Arthur, bearing the cross of Christ, was victorious after three days of fighting. The second reference, dated 537, records the death of Arthur and Medraut (Mordred) at the battle of Camlann. Leslie Alcock has called the last entry "the irreducible minimum of historical fact" supporting the real existence of Arthur. Yet, Kathleen Hughes raises doubts about the authenticity of the Camlann entry: it, too, could be a later addition.

The first undisputed chronicle reference to Arthur appears in the early ninth-century miscellany conventionally ascribed to Nennius. Besides Nennius' *Historia Brittonum,* in which Arthur steps forward as a valiant *dux bellorum* who fought and won twelve battles, culminating in Mount Badon, the miscellany includes the *Mirabilia,* a catalog of mar-

ARTHURIAN LITERATURE

vels to be found in Britain and Ireland. Among these are the footprint of Cabal, Arthur's dog, and a stream named after Arthur's son Anir. Also appearing in the *Mirabilia* is the forerunner of Merlin, here called Ambrose. Ferdinand Lot believes that the *Historia,* although indebted to the chronicles already mentioned, is to be respected because the author's use of British epithets suggests a firsthand knowledge of the native tradition. As will be shown, later chroniclers testify to the currency of a rich body of Arthurian folklore.

Whether the victor at Mount Badon who so fired the imagination of his countrymen was named Ambrosius, Arthur, or something else would seem to be a matter of slight importance. Yet the name Arthur acquired a nearly irresistible appeal by at least the ninth century, and its luster remains undimmed.

The Arthurian matter in Nennius, if not the somewhat dubious allusions in the *Gododdin* and the *Annales Cambriae,* may well reflect the existence of orally transmitted Welsh, Cornish, and Breton lore. In his *Gesta regum Anglorum* (1125), William of Malmesbury indicates not only an acquaintance with such floating tales but also his mistrust of them when he remarks that the trifling fictions of the Britons rave about Arthur, one who should be celebrated not in lying fables, but in true history.

Such conservatism was lost on Geoffrey of Monmouth, the most influential of all the exploiters of the medieval legend, whose *Historia regum Britanniae* appeared in 1136. His chronicle includes a vastly elaborated account of the Arthurian reign. It is safe to assume that a number of the episodes, such as Arthur's slaying of the giant of Mont-Saint-Michel, and personages, such as Uther, were suggested by Celtic sources, oral or written. Geoffrey himself tells us that he translated his *Prophetiae Merlini* (1135) from the Welsh, just as he claims to have taken his *Historia* from Archdeacon Walter's famous *liber vetustissimus* in the British tongue.

The existence of this "very old book" is doubtful, though Geoffrey had access to native tradition in some form. Certainly chroniclers continued to draw independently on the ravings of the Britons throughout the twelfth century and beyond. Geoffrey Gaimar's *Estorie des Engles* (*ca.* 1150) includes authentic-sounding details of Arthurian episodes not found in Geoffrey of Monmouth. Two other works, Wace's *Roman de Brut* (1155) and Layamon's *Brut* (*ca.* 1200), are essentially renderings of Geoffrey into Old French and Middle English, respectively—though both make significant additions to their original, such as the story of the construction of the Round Table in Wace and the legend of Arthur's fosterage by elves in Layamon.

The popularity of Geoffrey's *Historia* throughout the Middle Ages is proved not only by the two hundred copies extant but also by the numerous translations, adaptations, and summaries that appeared as late as the sixteenth century. Despite occasional adverse criticisms of him as a historian (beginning as early as William of Newburgh's *Historia rerum Anglicarum, ca.* 1198), and especially growing doubts about the old tale of the Trojan ancestry of the British and the Messianic prophecy of Arthur's return, Geoffrey continued to be generally accepted. But at last John Major (or Mair), in his *Historia majoris Britanniae* (1521), declared Arthur, Gawain, and their ilk to be the product of demoniacal art or figments of the imagination. In Book I of his *Anglicae historiae* (1534), Polydore Vergil rejected most of the Arthurian story, and by the time of Holinshed's *Chronicles* (1577), the reign of Arthur had vanished from respectable history.

EVOLUTION OF THE CELTIC TRADITION

A notion of the native tradition of Arthur, drawn on by chroniclers and writers of romance, may be gained from the literary remains in medieval Welsh and Irish. Note has already been taken of Arthurian references in the *Gododdin* and the Latin *Annales Cambriae.* To these must be added the more copious and rewarding Celtic material of later date.

Most of Middle Welsh literature is preserved in *The Black Book of Carmarthen* (*ca.* 1200), *The Red Book of Hergest* (*ca.* 1400), *The Book of Taliesin* (*ca.* 1275), *The Book of Aneirin* (thirteenth century), and a few lesser manuscripts. The fact that we have here copies made as long as three centuries after the presumed dates of composition often renders interpretation difficult and uncertain. That is, genuinely ancient poems and tales are frequently compromised by spurious additions.

A number of short Arthurian allusions occur in pieces considered to antedate Geoffrey's history. The "Verses on the Graves of Heroes" in the *Black Book of Carmarthen* include a comment that Arthur's grave is a wonder forever, which is usually interpreted to mean that the location of his burial place cannot be determined. A poetic dialogue in the same collection speaks of a number of early heroes, among then Llacheu, son of Arthur, noted as a singer of songs. In two of the Welsh collections, we find a poem on Gereint's battle at Llongborth, in which

ARTHURIAN LITERATURE

Arthur's men are said to have participated. The Welsh triads (short stanzas listing three historical or mythical persons or events, or setting forth three aphorisms) evidently represent a conscious effort on the part of poets to preserve, in easily memorized form, the substance of sagas recited by professional bards, as Rachel Bromwich explains. Certain triads concern Arthur, although some of them are not free from suspicion of later interpolations. Other triads have to do with legendary personages who were later drawn into the expanding Arthurian vortex, such as Drystan (Tristan) and Owein (Yvain).

More extended portrayals of Arthur likewise occur in early literature. "The Spoils of Annwfn" in *The Book of Taliesin* describes an expedition of Arthur and his retainers to an Otherworld city in quest of a magic caldron of plenty. In several dialogues Arthur appears as an interlocutor, as in a series of exchanges with his porter, Glewlwyd, taken from the tale *Culhwch and Olwen.* The independent saga of Merlin is represented in some six poems dating, in Jarman's opinion, from the twelfth century. In large part these poems consist of prophecies pertaining to Wales and Welsh struggles against invaders, both Norman and English. The tradition that Merlin lived for a time as a wild man in the Caledonian forest is included here, as it is in Geoffrey's *Vita Merlini* (*ca.* 1151) and in certain romances.

Culhwch and Olwen, written in its present form "not later than 1100," in the view of Ydris Foster, is the most important and widely known early Welsh composition because of its presentation of Arthur. Both *The Red Book of Hergest* and *The White Book of Rhydderch* preserve the tale, although the text is incomplete in the latter manuscript. Lady Charlotte Guest includes the former in her famous edition of the *Mabinogion* (1838–1849). Only one other tale in the *Mabinogion* may be said to represent the early Celtic tradition of Arthur: *The Dream of Rhonabwy.* The three other stories in Guest's collection that concern Arthur are later and are influenced by French romance.

Culhwch and Olwen is the story of Culhwch's long search for his destined bride, Olwen, and his winning of her hand by the performance of nearly forty Herculean tasks prescribed by the chief giant Ysbaddaden, her father. Only with the counsel and active participation of his cousin Arthur and the marvelously gifted members of Arthur's household is Culhwch able to achieve his goal. Several of these retainers come to figure importantly in later romance literature: Cei (Kay), Bedwyr (Bedevere), Hueil (Hoel), and Gware Goldenhair (Gawain). Also, Arthur lists among his treasures his queen Gwenhwyfar (Guinevere) and his sword Caledfwlch (Excalibur).

The key task facing Culhwch is to procure the equipment needed for shaving Ysbaddaden, including the tusk of a great boar. He also must capture a still more formidable boar, Twrch Trwyth, which carries between its ears a magic comb and shears. The second boar is brought to bay only after a strenuous chase by Arthur and his army. Thereafter, Culhwch shaves Ysbaddaden's beard and the flesh on his face. The giant is then put to death, and the couple's wedding can at last be celebrated. The main plot is easily recognizable as a form of the folk type known as the Giant's Daughter.

In the version known to us, *The Dream of Rhonabwy* is considered to date from the early thirteenth century. Rhonabwy, sent out to search for a rebellious prince named Iorwoerth, takes shelter in a filthy shed and sleeps there for three days on a yellow ox hide. The tale consists principally of an account of a dream with which he is visited. Conducted in his vision by Iddawg, who states that he was the instigator of the fateful battle of Camlann, Rhonabwy sees a number of magnificently garbed and accoutered warriors, identified as Cei (Kay), Cadwr (Cador), and the like. He then observes Arthur himself engaged in a chess match with Owein. Bards in attendance chant a song to Arthur, and later tribute is brought to him from Greece. During the chess play, reports are brought of a strange conflict between Arthur's host and Owein's ravens. When informed that his soldiers have been maimed and killed by the birds, Arthur crushes the gold chess pieces to powder in his hands. Owein then lowers his standards and peace ensues. Arthur's royal state and certain details suggest the influence of Geoffrey of Monmouth; nevertheless, *The Dream of Rhonabwy* retains in full measure the Celtic atmosphere of fantasy and unreality.

Two of the three remaining Arthurian tales in the *Mabinogion, Gereint Son of Erbin* and *The Lady of the Fountain,* correspond closely in plot structure to Chrétien de Troyes's *Erec et Enide* and *Yvain,* respectively. Not only in plot but also in settings and narrative tone these late Welsh tales are closer to French romance than to the almost purely Celtic mode of *The Dream of Rhonabwy.* Nevertheless, we may not conclude that Welsh prose writers simply converted these French romances into their own tongue. The fact that on occasion the Welsh version supplies details of, for example, character motivation that are missing in Chrétien strongly indicates that the Welsh redactors and Chrétien drew independently on a common source. One example of a significant narrative element occurring in *Gereint* but not in *Erec* is the revelation that the hero entertains doubts about his wife's fidelity, which provides a clear reason for his otherwise puzzling harshness toward her.

Peredur Son of Efrawg, the third of the later tales in the *Mabinogion,* survives in several rather different texts. It contains features that distinguish it from Chrétien's *Perceval* and the continuations of *Perceval* but that, strangely enough, ally it to later forms of the story in Old French, Middle High German, Middle English, and even Italian. Unique to *Peredur,* however, is the substitution, for Chrétien's bejeweled Grail, of a platter bearing a severed human head, which serves as a feeding vessel in the hall of the mysterious castle of the Rich Fisher. Peredur is told that the head he sees is that of a cousin whose murder he is charged with avenging. An instance of a severed head—and, moreover, one associated with a banquet—occurs in *Branwen Daughter of Llŷr,* another tale in the *Mabinogion.* Toward the end of this tale, Welsh retainers bear the head of their slain king, the Blessed Brân, into a hall, where they hold a joyous feast. That this Welsh episode is an expression of a widespread tradition is shown by a passage in the late thirteenth-century prose *Perlesvaus.* Here, in an experience unconnected with the Grail procession, Perlesvaus is presented with just such a grisly object, also identified as the head of a slain cousin. This and other parallels have been subjected to much study and variously accounted for by James Bruce, Mary Williams, Roger Loomis, Helaine Newstead, and Foster.

The Irish, who possessed the oldest native literature in Europe, were given to recalling traditions concerned with deities and supernaturally endowed persons of their Celtic pagan belief. The Welsh absorbed some of this Irish lore, perhaps from Irish residents in Wales, and occasionally used it to flesh out the legend of Arthur.

An example of such an Irish contribution is furnished by the adventure called *The Phantom's Frenzy,* which may have been written down in the eleventh century. An Irish king, Conn of the Hundred Battles, becomes lost in a dense mist while journeying in Tara. At last he encounters a horseman, who leads him to a hall. There Conn sees a girl, the Sovranty of Ireland, seated on a crystal chair next to the Phantom on a throne. The Phantom, who states that he is the sun god Lug, utters a prophecy, whereupon the girl gives food to Conn and asks the Phantom to whom she should serve the cup of red ale. That these are suggestive parallels to Perceval's experiences in the hall of the Rich Fisher is hard to deny. Perceval, it should be noted, is punished for failing to inquire whom the Grail serves. Moreover, traits of a sun god seem to underlie several motifs carried over into Arthurian romance, such as Gawain's waxing and waning strength.

DISSEMINATION OF THE LEGEND AND THE BRETON LAI

The twelfth-century flowering of Arthurian literature in Old French is proof that Celtic traditions going beyond those found in Geoffrey of Monmouth and Wace had made their way to the Continent by an early date. Roger S. Loomis and Laura H. Loomis have discussed extraliterary evidence of the pervasiveness of the legend, such as the artistic representations of Arthurian characters on an archivolt of Modena Cathedral, executed between 1099 and 1120, and a mosaic pavement in the cathedral at Otranto dating from about 1165. The *Prophetia Anglicana Merlini Ambrosii Britanni,* written in the 1170's and at one time incorrectly ascribed to Alain de Lille, claims that the renown of Arthur has penetrated to the remotest parts of the world. Although so extravagant a statement may be discounted, the fact that Arthur came ultimately to be enshrined as a Christian worthy alongside Charlemagne and Godfrey of Bouillon is a sufficient measure of his international fame.

The migration across the Channel of the oral traditions of Wales and Cornwall could have been effected either by Anglo-Normans maintaining their ties on the Continent or by Bretons at home in French as well as their native Brythonic tongue. Today the Bretons are favored as the intermediaries, in large part as the result of the work of Loomis, who argues that itinerant Breton *conteurs,* plying between their home and Wales and Cornwall, composed songs based on insular traditions, which they performed for their own countrymen. These were soon translated into French for the sake of a wider audience on the Continent, and at the same time were adapted to French literary tastes. A certain Bleheris, mentioned by Giraldus Cambrensis and others, seems to have been such a court performer in France whose repertoire included Arthurian stories. Although a Welshman rather than a Breton, Bleheris could well have found his stock in trade in Brittany, as has been suggested.

The Breton lai is inseparably linked to Marie de France, provisionally considered to have been a natural daughter of Geoffrey IV of Anjou and thus a half sister of Henry II of England. In her later years (1181 to 1216) she was abbess of Shaftesbury. Her lais, composed in standard literary French with some Norman coloration, according to Hoepffner, vary in length from one hundred to one thousand lines in octosyllabic couplets, and contain a number of allusions to Breton originals and to Brittany. In the absence of external evidence, her statements about Breton sources are not verifiable, although she uses Breton words especially in her titles, as in *Laüstic* (The Lai of the Nightingale), and *Bisclavret* (The Lai of the Werewolf). Two of the lais are Arthurian, but only casually or by stipulation. In *Guigemar* the hero, after serving as a page, is knighted by Arthur, and in *Lai de Lanval* the hero dwells in the court of Arthur and Guinevere at Carlyle. A third poem, *Chievrefeuil* (The Lai of the Honeysuckle), briefly relates an episode in the love life of Tristan and Isolt, but the setting is King Mark's court in Cornwall.

The lais of Marie, Arthurian and otherwise, deal with love, its plangent moments, its joys, and sometimes its tragic consequences. Yet, Marie avoids courtly liaisons with their attendant high-flown sentiments and rhetoric. One of her heroines, to be sure, is a married woman (the sad lady in *Laüstic*), but the frustrated love between her and her young bachelor by no means conforms to courtly conventions. Exception must be made for *Chievrefeuil,* but here the love of Tristan and Isolt is very briefly and plainly related.

Several other French lais, all but one of later date, likewise trade on the popularity of the transplanted legend by borrowing Arthurian personal and place names. Their plots differ from Marie's theme of love in that they consist largely of retellings of widely known folk tales. Robert Biket's *Lai du cor,* for example, concerns a chastity-testing drinking horn maliciously presented to Arthur by King Mangons. When Arthur proves unable to drink from the horn without spilling its contents, Guinevere is shamed before the court as an unchaste wife. And Marie's werewolf story, *Bisclavret,* is revived in the anonymous *Melion,* but with the substitution of Arthurian names. Another anonymous lai, *Tyolet,* also garnished with Arthurian characters, exploits several motifs that figure importantly in romance literature, including the unpromising hero reared in a forest and the mysterious quest.

The vogue of these short poems led to translations into several languages. An Old Norse version of most of the lais of Marie de France and of several anonymous lais was composed shortly after 1200. In England, at least by the early fourteenth century, when a ready command of French was becoming less common, English translations and adaptations began to appear. Some nine of these poems, including two of Chaucer's *Canterbury Tales* that claim a Breton background, are known today. No direct French source exists for most of the English lais, but Thomas Chestre's *Sir Launfal* is clearly akin to Marie's *Lanval.*

Chaucer may have drawn mainly on Boccaccio in writing his "Franklin's Tale," but he resorts to the common lai introduction when speaking of "Thise olde gentil Britouns" who accompanied their songs with instrumental music. The story is based on the folk type of the Damsel's Rash Promise, and it also uses with matchless skill such motifs as the trickster who seemingly accomplishes the impossible. Again, Chaucer's "Wife of Bath's Tale" is explicitly associated with the "Britons," although no extant French lai is concerned with its theme of the Loathly Lady, also known as the Transformed Hag. Arthur is the young hero's lord in Chaucer's tale, and Guinevere, who appears in a much better light than in *Sir Launfal,* is shown conducting a kind of court of love.

Several other Middle English poems that are relatively short and claim to be derived from Breton are normally classified as lais. These are *Lai le Freine, Sir Orfeo, Emare, Sir Degare, Sir Gowther,* and *The Earl of Toulous.*

FRENCH ROMANCES

Chrétien de Troyes is the author of the earliest and most prized Arthurian romances; indeed, he was at one time regarded as the inventor of much of the Arthurian story material in his poems. Between 1160 and 1180, Chrétien composed five still-extant Arthurian works—*Erec, Cligès, Launcelot ou le chevalier de la charrette, Yvain ou le chevalier au lion,* and *Perceval ou le conte du Graal.* In addition, as he tells us in the opening lines of *Cligès,* he wrote a now-lost romance "du roi Marc et d'Iseut la blonde": in other words, a *Tristan.*

For the story related in *Cligès,* it must be acknowledged, Chrétien was more indebted to Ovidian and Greco-Oriental themes than to the "Matter of Britain" or corpus of Arthurian tales. Also, the love

ARTHURIAN LITERATURE

of Cligès and Fénice is made into an explicit rebuke of the adultery of Isolt. The romance has been characterized, in fact, as a cerebral, anti-Tristan work that stands apart from most other romances. It owes its Arthurian classification to the facts that the hero is allied by blood to Gawain and that he participates in a tournament with Round Table knights. In contrast, the other four romances are part and parcel of the Arthurian world, and major elements of their plots are traceable to the mother lode of Celtic lore, as shown by Jean Frappier, Loomis, and others. These scholars are in general agreement that Chrétien's principal sources for his romances were tales told by Breton *conteurs,* which may have come to him in the form of French prose narratives.

Certain conventions of twelfth-century courtly love are prominent in Chrétien's narratives, even though *Cligès* reflects a personal distaste for courtly adultery. In representing his heroines as unmarried and the culmination of their love affairs as matrimony (except in *Launcelot* and *Tristan*), Chrétien seems to have established a norm respected in much subsequent literature, Arthurian and otherwise.

Rita Lejeune shows that the troubadours of southern France were more interested in the "Matter of Britain" than is usually recognized. One long poem, *Jaufré,* composed in the *langue d'oc* in the late twelfth or early thirteenth century, reveals a knowledge of Chrétien's works, especially *Yvain,* in Remy's opinion. But apart from another later poem, *Blandin de Cornouailles,* we are made aware of a concern with the legend of Arthur in the South only by passing allusions in lyrics to Guinevere, Gawain, and other "Matter of Britain" personages.

Gaston Paris has observed that not all the provinces of medieval France participated vigorously in the production of literature. During the twelfth century the most sophisticated poetry, especially that concerned with the Round Table, flourished in Champagne and Picardy in the North, in contrast with the relative disregard of such themes elsewhere. Thus we have chiefly in the language of the North, including that of the Champenois, Chrétien, no fewer than thirty-five Arthurian romances in verse and thirty in prose, written by 1300 or only slightly later. The lais are not included in this count. A few of these works are briefly characterized below.

Four French verse romances, if we disregard Marie de France's *Chievrefeuil* and the lost poem by Chrétien, set forth the tale of Tristan and Isolt. A certain Thomas, who may have lived at the English royal court during the third quarter of the twelfth century, wrote the earliest known *Tristan,* of which 3,200 lines survive. Toward the end of the century, Béroul, a Norman, composed another *Tristan,* of which we have nearly 4,500 lines. Two minor poems of later date, both entitled *Folie Tristan,* are concerned with assignations of the lovers. Finally, an extremely lengthy prose *Tristan* of the early thirteenth century has come down to us in two different versions and many manuscripts. Here the adventures of Tristan, enlarged, are interwoven with exploits of Round Table knights. In fact, Tristan is presented as among the most distinguished of Arthur's knights in prowess and in *courtoisie.* The widespread attraction of this story of undying love is well demonstrated by translations into many European languages and also by the Chertsey tiles in England, which illustrate some of the most moving of the lovers' experiences.

The major episodes of the tale are as follows. Young Tristan appears at his uncle's court, where he wins fame as the result of slaying Morholt, the champion of Ireland. Having journeyed to Ireland in quest of a bride for his uncle, King Mark, the hero slays a dragon and also is unmasked as the killer of Morholt. The Irish princess Isolt cures Tristan's wounds, and, since she has accepted Mark's offer of marriage, refrains from exacting vengeance for the hero's dispatch of her kinsman Morholt. The indissoluble love of Tristan and Isolt is sealed by their sharing the fateful potion on the voyage to Cornwall. They carry on their clandestine affair for years after the marriage of Isolt and Mark, but at last discovery leads to Tristan's banishment and then his nominal marriage to Isolt of Brittany. Finally, the hero's serious wounds require summoning the true Isolt to minister to him, and the stage is set for the episode of the white and black sails and the dire conclusion.

Tristan is commonly said to have taken his name from Drust, an eighth-century Pictish prince, references to whom appear in Welsh, as do references to Isolt and Mark. Analogues have been found for Tristan's duel with Morholt and for his love of his uncle's wife in two Irish tales, *The Wooing of Emer* and *The Pursuit After Diarmaid and Grainne.* Such tales apparently migrated to Wales, where they were incorporated into the life of the northern Drust or Drystan, and perhaps given a Cornish setting. On the translation of the expanded legend to Brittany, other motifs were added: the dragon slaying, the lovers' tryst beneath a tree, and the white and black sails. The point at which the well-developed story of Tris-

ARTHURIAN LITERATURE

tan and Isolt was absorbed by the Arthurian epic is uncertain, but the process was probably well under way by the mid twelfth century.

At variance with the widely accepted view, just outlined, of the story's evolution is Eisner's theory, according to which the "Drustansaga" or "Ur-Tristan," associated from its beginning with Arthur, was an eighth-century creation of writers in Dalradian Scotland. Thus, it was a fully developed Arthurian tale that drifted to Wales, where it underwent a few modifications, involving principally the invention of the second Isolt.

A number of writers apart from Thomas and Béroul betray the influence of Chrétien's biographical romances. For example, Raoul de Houdenc's *Meraugis de Portlesguez* and *La vengeance Raguidel,* the latter of which concerns Gawain, date from the early 1200's. Composed at about the same time, *Le chevalier à l'épée* and *La mule sans frein,* though relatively short and lacking Chrétien's sophistication, are reminiscent of his romances. Both of them offer parallels, some of them close, to the Middle English *Sir Gawain and the Green Knight.*

Of more intrinsic worth than the French romances just mentioned is Renaud de Beaujeu's *Guinglain ou le bel inconnu,* of the early thirteenth century. A handsome and strongly built youth without name or known lineage appears before Arthur as a suppliant. In recognition of his nameless state and of his noble appearance, the king bestows on him a sobriquet, "le bel Inconnu" (the Fair Unknown); he also dubs him knight.

In conformity with what may be considered a romance cliché, the untried youth is assigned a dangerous mission, word of which is brought to court by a maiden messenger. The maiden's mistress, the Lady of Sinadon, has been transformed into a serpent by two enchanters, who now hold her castle and realm. Enduring at least initially the contempt of the maiden because of his lack of reputation, the Fair Unknown overcomes preliminary obstacles and then vanquishes the magicians. By planting the Fier Baiser, or Scornful Kiss, on the serpent's mouth, he restores the lady, Blonde Esmerée, to her own beautiful form, and the pair soon become betrothed. The second half of the romance is occupied with a series of delaying actions that mainly revolve around the efforts of the Lady of l'Île d'Or to appropriate the hero for herself. At length he escapes to Esmerée, and the marriage is celebrated. The Fair Unknown is also revealed to be Guinglain, son of Gawain.

Loomis has pointed out analogues to the Transformation by Kiss in Irish tradition and has identified the ruined city of Sinadon with the remains of Roman Segontium, near Carnarvon. The medieval fondness for the Fair Unknown theme is reflected in derivative romances, especially a number written in Middle High German, Italian, and Middle English.

Nearly twenty Old French romances in verse and prose are devoted to the Grail legend. The Arthurian legend as a whole, in fact, may be said to take on a new life—in a sense to become sanctified—upon its assimilation of a profoundly spiritual mission. The quest for the sacred vessel, mysteriously conveyed to Britain by Joseph of Arimathea, there to be secreted for centuries, becomes the predestined objective of the Round Table. That certain pagan Celtic traditions underlie the Grail story is suggested in the earlier remarks about the Welsh *Peredur.*

Even before Chrétien wrote his *Perceval,* the starting point of the Grail romances, tales stemming from a Christianized version of the Celtic legend of Brân could well have been in circulation. These, as Newstead has explained, may have embodied a confusion of the horn *(cors)* of Brân with the blessed body *(cor beneiz)* of Christ. The procession witnessed by Perceval in the castle of the Rich Fisher presents the Grail first as a feeding vessel and later as the container of a consecrated Host: ultimately the hermit advises the hero that the life of his infirm relative was sustained by a Host carried in the Grail. Contemporaries and successors of Chrétien enlarge on this suggestion by presenting the Grail as nothing less than the cup of the Last Supper and the chalice of the first Mass. At last, the history not only of Arthur's reign and the fulfillment of the Grail quest, replete with Eucharistic symbolism, but also of the antecedent period from the time of Joseph of Arimathea, came to be represented in French romance.

Robert de Boron's *Joseph d' Arimathie* and *Merlin,* the latter extant only in a short fragment, were written around the turn of the thirteenth century. Robert may have drawn on a written source, as he claims, but significant features of his poems make his acquaintance with Chrétien's *Perceval* problematical. In particular, the Grail in his work is a chalice filled with Christ's blood, and the Glastonbury or Avalon setting of the Rich Fisher's castle is stressed. Underlying his *Joseph* is the apocryphal Gospel of Nicodemus. We can gain some notion of missing portions of Robert's work from later prose redactions of the *Merlin* and from the so-called *Didot Perceval,* a prose romance.

During the second decade of the thirteenth cen-

ARTHURIAN LITERATURE

tury, various writers produced continuations of Chrétien's unfinished *Perceval.* The earlier of these tend to deal with adventures of heroes other than Perceval, and not until the work of Manessier do we have a conclusion to the main course of action. Including the *Elucidation,* intended as a prologue, *Perceval* with its continuations consists of more than 60,000 lines.

Subsequent Grail romances may be summarily treated. *Perlesvaus,* now thought to have been written about 1212 rather than at a later date, is explicitly linked to Chrétien's *Perceval.* Here it is revealed that Perlesvaus's failure to ask whom the Grail serves is responsible for bringing down evils on the British that only the rediscovery of the sacred vessel by a chaste knight will correct. The quests of several knights are recounted, and in the end the hero joins a community of white monks.

The Vulgate cycle, written before 1250, is a collection of five lengthy romances, the content of which may be briefly indicated. The *Estoire del Saint Graal* relates how Joseph of Arimathea, bearing the cup of the Last Supper, in which he had caught the blood of the crucified Christ, leads his band of evangelists through the Near East and Orient and at last to Britain, where the Grail is installed in Castle Corbenic. *Merlin,* a prose form of Robert's work, develops the theme of the divinely ordained mission of Arthur's reign. *Lancelot* is an extremely long history of Lancelot, baptized as Galaad and a descendant of King David, in which the hero's begetting of Galahad is given special importance. The *Queste del Saint Graal* is the story of the great search for Castle Corbenic and the witnessing therein of the miracles of the Grail that confirm the doctrine of the Eucharist, especially in the form associated with the Cistercians. Only Galahad, Perceval, and Bors prove worthy to serve as guardians of the Grail during the short period before it is taken into Heaven. *Mort Artu* is devoted to the post-Quest history of the Round Table. The revelation of the guilty love of Lancelot and the queen leads to warfare, then to the last battle and the passing of Arthur.

The influence of the Vulgate cycle throughout the later Middle Ages was very great. Not only was it the *locus classicus* of the Grail-oriented Arthurian legend, but it seems to have inspired the writing of sequels of various kinds. The prose *Tristan,* for example, serves the purpose of involving Tristan more deeply with the Arthurian world. The *Suite du Merlin,* purporting to be the work of Robert de Boron, elaborates on the role of Merlin in Arthur's wars against rebel kings, then dwells on a miscellany of Round Table adventures.

ARTHURIANA IN OTHER CONTINENTAL LANGUAGES

Before 1200, a knowledge of and love for the French Arthurian romances had begun to spread into all European countries in which French was understood by at least a few. This phenomenon is best illustrated by the appearance as early as the 1190's of Middle High German adaptations, especially of Chrétien's romances. In countries other than Germany the trend manifested itself somewhat later.

An interesting basis for comparison of the literary cultures of medieval Europe is furnished by romances on widely popular themes. For example, Chrétien's *Yvain,* composed between 1177 and 1181, may be set alongside the *Îwein* of Hartmann von Aue (*ca.* 1202), the Old Norse prose *Ívens saga* (1225), and the Middle English *Ywain and Gawain* (1325–1350). The three derivative works convey Chrétien's story accurately enough, yet each differs from the original, stylistically and otherwise, in its own way. The Yvain story is also represented in the Welsh *Owein* and in a Swedish and a later Danish form as well. The brilliance of Chrétien's writing, particularly his extended similes and metaphors, and his playful banter, internal monologues, and auctorial comments, seem in general to be lost on all these imitators, even though they often display virtues of their own. As would be expected, the foreign redactors aimed at retellings of the story in terms compatible with the expectations of their audiences.

Hartmann von Aue's *Îwein* is the closest of all to the French *Yvain.* Hartmann ignores or considerably modifies Chrétien's figurative language, and he seizes every opportunity to introduce religious sentiments absent from his source. Flights of love rhetoric are prominent in the French poem, and for the most notable of these Hartmann substitutes a rather sober debate between "Vrou Minne" and himself on the exact meaning of the expression "to lose one's heart." In the Old Norse and Middle English versions, French courtly love sentiments are passed over in almost complete silence.

Hartmann's *Erek,* sometimes called the earliest of the German Arthurian poems, is less successful than his *Îwein.* It, too, embodies departures from its source, Chrétien's *Erec et Enide,* occasionally in details that tend to ally it with the Welsh *Owain.* Gottfried von Strassburg's *Tristan und Isolt* of the first

ARTHURIAN LITERATURE

quarter of the thirteenth century claims to be based on the *Tristan* of Thomas, but Gottfried imparts touches of his own, particularly his exalted conception of human love. It has further been pointed out that the drinking of the love potion in his poem portends not only the irrevocable love of Tristan and Isolt but also their death because of love. Such deep significance is lacking in continuations of Gottfried's unfinished work by Ulrich von Türheim and Heinrich von Freiburg. Brother Robert's Old Norse *Tristrams saga ok Ísondar,* also derived from Thomas, is a far less inspired work, but it possesses the virtue of supplying portions of the story missing from the one copy of the Anglo-Norman *Tristan.*

The *Parzival* of Wolfram von Eschenbach is perhaps the best known of the German romances. Completed in the first years of the thirteenth century, it consists of nearly 25,000 lines and brings the story in Chrétien's unfinished *Perceval* full circle. Wolfram alleges that he was primarily following a version by the otherwise unknown Kyot of Provence, yet a number of scholars are content with the theory that the rather numerous innovations in this poem are Wolfram's own. In one famous passage, the hero's hermit uncle states that the object glimpsed by Parzival in the mysterious castle is a miraculous stone, the *lapis exillis,* rather than a precious vessel. It has been conjectured that here Wolfram drew on knowledge of a tale about Alexander the Great involving a wonder-working stone found in the earthly paradise.

In addition to the Old Norse versions of romances about Tristan and Yvain, mentioned above, northern writers produced half a dozen other adaptations of French romances and lais dealing with Perceval, Erec, Lanval, and the chastity-testing mantle. Moreover, Geoffrey of Monmouth's *Historia* was rendered into Icelandic. Most of these saga versions were composed for King Hákon of Norway in the second quarter of the thirteenth century, although the surviving texts are chiefly Icelandic copies dating from at least half a century later.

In yet another Germanic language, Middle Dutch, we have several Arthurian works of consequence. These include the *Historie van den Grale* and *Merlijns Boeck* by Jacob van Maerlant, *Perchevael,* and *De Wrake van Ragisel* (Vengeance of Raguidel), inspired chiefly by the Vulgate cycle. In addition, we have the independent verse romances *Walewein* (Gawain) and *Ferguut,* both apparently adapted from French originals. In general, the Scandinavian and Dutch writers seem to have worked from texts rather than from orally transmitted tradition.

It is perhaps inevitable that in the Middle Ages a literary genre as internationally celebrated as Arthurian romance should come to be represented in Latin. In fact, in addition to a passage derived from an Arthurian lai in Andreas Capellanus' Latin treatise on courtly love, we have three late thirteenth-century romance tales in that language: *Historia Meriadoci, Arthur and Gorlagon,* and *De ortu Walwani.* The first two, considered by Loomis to be the work of the same author, are biographical romances suggestive of Chrétien's poems (although the adventures of their heroes are not matched in known French works). *De ortu Walwani* deals with Gawain's origins and career, preserving some episodes that appear to have originated in Celtic legend. None of the Latin romances found a wide audience, if we may judge from the fact that each is preserved in only a single copy.

The medieval craze for the "Matter of Britain" surmounted both linguistic and religious boundaries, as is illustrated most notably by a Hebrew translation of 1279 called *Melech Artus* (King Arthur), evidently taken from a now-lost Italian prose romance. One of the principal topics in this work is the adultery of Lancelot and Guinevere. Moreover, a Yiddish romance, *Artushof,* based on the thirteenth-century *Wigalois* of Wirnt von Grafenberg, appeared in the late fourteenth or early fifteenth century. According to Robert Warnock, it may have been the work of a professional entertainer who composed it for oral performance at a wedding. Quite naturally, the Jewish author eliminated Wirnt's discussions of courtly love and the Christian religion.

The Modena bas-relief and the Otranto mosaics mentioned earlier are not the only evidence that the "Matter of Britain" was welcomed in Italy at an early date; in addition, we have Godfrey of Viterbo's summary of the pseudo history of Britain, including notice of Vortigern, Merlin, Uther, and Arthur, in a Latin work dated 1186–1191. Moreover, allusions to Arthur and Arthurian characters are common in Italian courtly poetry early in the next century, and before 1300 there appeared the first Italian romance, Rusticiano's *Tristano Riccardiano,* which breaks off incomplete before the tragic death scene. The most important Italian romance, *Tavola ritonda* (1325–1350), was inspired by the French prose *Merlin.* It seeks to encompass the whole legend, but departs from the orthodox story in some respects, as in the events surrounding the last battle. Paolino Piero's

ARTHURIAN LITERATURE

Merlino (*ca.* 1324) is yet another work derived from the prose tradition. Apart from such romances, many trecento and quattrocento works contain allusions to Arthurian figures, including Francesca's famous confession in Dante's *Inferno,* canto V, that a reading of the story of Lancelot led to the love affair, "the book and writer both were love's purveyors."

María Rosa Lida de Malkiel has very lucidly summarized and evaluated the fortunes of the Arthurian legend in the Iberian countries. The earliest evidence of the penetration of the French Arthuriana beyond the Pyrenees is, as in Italy, in the form of chance allusions, such as one by a Catalan troubadour to "mon Tristan" in a poem about 1190. Catalan poets, and perhaps their aristocratic audiences, could be expected to acquire an early acquaintance with literary fashions in France because of the kinship of their language to Provençal. Later translations in the various Iberian dialects had the effect of widening the audience of this literature beyond the upper classes. The first of these translations seems to be the Portuguese *Josep Abaramatia* (1313), which was soon followed by versions of *Merlin* in its expanded form, including the *Estoire del Saint Graal, Mort Artu,* and the *Queste del Saint Graal (Demanda do Santo Grial).* Also preserved are romances based on the French prose *Tristan* and the Vulgate *Lancelot.* The well-known *Amadís de Gaula*, assigned to the late thirteenth century, reveals Arthurian influence chiefly in its citation of proper names and epithets. The large and miscellaneous body of chivalric romances produced in Spain and Portugal from the thirteenth into the sixteenth century appears in general to have been inspired by the French prose cycle.

MIDDLE ENGLISH ARTHURIANA

The first Arthurian work in Middle English, Layamon's *Brut,* is usually dated at the end of the twelfth century, and approximately seventy-five years passed before the appearance of the earliest true romances in English. From the late eleventh century, however, French literature certainly enjoyed an Anglo-Norman audience, and it is possible that stories derived from the French romances circulated in English through the native population long before a demand for committing them to writing was felt. In any case, the survival of some twenty-eight Arthurian verse and prose romances and ballads, not counting variant versions, out of an indefinitely larger number actually written, is sufficient testimony to the success of the genre in English. Included are three of the most distinguished literary works of the Middle Ages and several more of excellent quality.

Many English pieces are obviously adaptations of extant Old French romances and lais, and others are quite likely derivatives of French originals no longer in existence. It must be admitted, in fact, that few are marked by a high degree of originality. Yet, in translating the French sources into their own language, English writers evolved, much as did the German *remanieurs* discussed above, a distinctive type of romance. Perhaps even more than their counterparts elsewhere, they avoided the high style of Chrétien and his imitators, preferring objective detail to figures of speech. The tendency toward greater realism, however, did not extend to the suppression of supernatural and Otherworld phenomena, such as enchantments, fairy mistresses, giants, and the like. The net result is narrative literature characterized by a relatively simple, direct plot line and by characters who reveal their motivation and feelings in action rather than in words.

Rhymed couplets like those in much French romance; various stanzaic patterns, including ballad meter and tail rhyme; alliterative long lines; and prose are all represented in the Middle English Arthuriana. The tail rhyme poems, nearly all of them shorter than works composed in lines of uniform length, are sometimes considered to be minstrel versions, whereas many other works, especially those adhering rather closely to their French originals, could be the products of translator-versifiers in manuscript shops. Even the vernacular works not written by or for minstrels, so far as we can tell, carry over features of oral delivery, such as a constant resort to romance formulas and epithets, the common "Listeneth, lordings!" invocation, and requests to the audience to be quiet. Even so sophisticated a poem as the alliterative *Morte Arthure,* thought by some to be the work of a cleric, contains in the introduction the invocation "You who have a desire to listen or who love to hear about forefathers of days gone by and their remarkable deeds. . . ."

Whether minstrels, clerics, serious poets, or manuscript-shop hacks, the authors of most English romances must have been humble men to whom anonymity seemed natural. If we make exception for Thomas Chestre, the enigmatic Tomas of *Sir Tristrem,* Henry Lovelich, and Malory, they are silent about their identity, thus suggesting that few could boast of their name or social status as could the well-educated Gottfried von Strassburg or the knightly

ARTHURIAN LITERATURE

Wolfram von Eschenbach. Further, the dearth of dedications, such as those occurring in the works of Chrétien, Wace, and Froissart, suggests that not many were so fortunate as to have a patron.

The extant English Arthurian verse and prose works were composed over a period of 250 years beginning about 1250, although those postdating Malory's *Le Morte Darthur* are mostly ballads of negligible value. It is convenient here to classify the romances to be discussed under three headings.

First are several works, the main concern of which is with periods or episodes of King Arthur's reign. The earliest is *Arthour and Merlin* (1250–1275), occurring in the Auchinleck manuscript and also in shorter versions of later date. We find here a reasonably well-ordered story opening with the kingship of Constans and continuing with Arthur's succession to the throne, his betrothal to Guinevere, and his combat with Rion. Apparently the writer worked from a source that patched together the chronicle tradition and a small section of the Vulgate cycle. The alliterative *Morte Arthure,* which concentrates on Arthur's Roman campaign and then the last battle and death of the king, likewise represents the chronicle account; it is one of the most impressive in the entire body of Arthuriana.

The stanzaic *Le Morte Arthur* (*ca.* 1400) should be singled out for notice not only because it served Malory as a source but also because it is a notably well-managed account of the final catastrophe, including the unveiling of the queen's adultery and the last battle. The source would seem to be a special form of the *Mort Artu.* The remaining works in this group are mainly short pieces of little worth, such as the ballad *King Arthur's Death.*

Second are the romances taken ultimately from the French Vulgate *Estoire del Saint Graal* and *Merlin.* The story of Joseph of Arimathea and the early Grail history were warmly received in England, as indicated by the several forms in which they have come down to us. A *Joseph of Arimathie* in alliterative lines (*ca.* 1375) has been preserved in a fragment. Henry Lovelich's incomplete prose translation of the *Estoire* deals mainly with Joseph, and the same writer's lugubrious and inaccurate version of part of the *Merlin* provides a later segment of the story. Shortly after Lovelich's time, an anonymous writer produced a sounder translation of the *Merlin* that takes the account up to the birth of Lancelot. Three later forms of *Joseph of Arimathie* also survive. But only Malory, it is interesting to note, provides a Middle English version of the actual Grail quest.

Finally, about a dozen English works may be considered biographical romances of the type developed by Chrétien de Troyes and emulated by his successors. The seven romances and ballads of this group that are concerned with Gawain are more independent of French Arthuriana than any of the English works just discussed. Conceivably, English partiality for Gawain led naturally to a proliferation of his adventures by English poets, but it is also possible that the prestige of the magnificent *Sir Gawain and the Green Knight* encourages us to misjudge the importance of this hero to fourteenth-century Englishmen. *Sir Gawain and the Green Knight* is known to us in a single manuscript, and our chief evidence that it was appreciated in its own period is a poorly contrived condensation in tail rhyme dating from about 1500 and known as *The Green Knight.* The other Gawain poems, such as *Syre Gawene and the Carle of Carelyle,* are likewise of inferior value.

Several other Round Table knights are celebrated in English biographical romances. The earliest of these is *Sir Tristrem,* written about 1300 by a poet who evidently relied on a faulty memory of the French *Tristan* of Thomas. This work contains some good native touches, however. *Libeaus Desconus,* of the first half of the fourteenth century, is a clearly plotted narrative, the vogue of which is suggested by the fact that six copies survive. The possibility that the author was Thomas Chestre rests on the circumstance that one of these copies occurs in the manuscript containing *Sir Launfal,* which is explicitly claimed by Chestre. The immediate source seems not to be Renaud de Beaujeu's *Guinglain ou le bel inconnu,* mentioned above, but a lost antecedent drawn on by both the French and the English poets.

The excellence of *Ywain and Gawain* (*ca.* 1350), is not to be ascribed simply to its being an adaptation of Chrétien de Troyes's *Yvain,* the work that in Wendelin Foerster's opinion represents the culmination of the French courtly epic. For we must recognize the skill and tact with which the English poet converted his original into a truly English romance. Moreover, the fact that *Ywain and Gawain* includes details foreign both to Chrétien and to Hartmann von Aue, but that appear in the Welsh *Owein,* suggests that a now-vanished romance played a part in the shaping of the English work.

Malory's *Le Morte Darthur,* embracing nearly all the branches of the great legend, is evidence of a lively veneration of the nobility and idealism of a distant age, but it is also a ringing proclamation of the British nationality of Arthur and his Round Table.

BIBLIOGRAPHY

Leslie Alcock, *Arthur's Britain: History and Archaeology, A.D. 367–634* (1971), includes a careful analysis of the chronicles bearing on the Arthurian period and a survey of archaeological studies in Britain; *Annales Cambriae,* John Williams ab Ithel, ed., Rolls Series no. 20 (1860), has two entries of direct relevance to Arthurian backgrounds; *Arthurian Literature in the Middle Ages: A Collaborative History,* Roger Sherman Loomis, ed. (1959), contains forty-one essays by recognized authorities, covering Arthurian backgrounds as well as the medieval literature about Arthur in some twelve languages; *Bibliographical Bulletin of the International Arthurian Society,* **1–31** (1949–1979), an annual publication, lists and annotates scholarly writings in all languages on medieval Arthuriana; James Douglas Bruce, *The Evolution of Arthurian Romance from the Beginnings down to the Year 1300,* 2nd ed., 2 vols. (1958), in many respects outdated, is still useful because of its comprehensive coverage; Nora Chadwick, *Ancient People and Places: Celtic Britain* (n.d.), interprets the scanty evidence bearing on the actual existence of Arthur; R. G. Collingwood and J. N. L. Myres, *Roman Britain and the English Settlements,* 2nd ed. (1937), long a standard history, offers a careful account of fifth- and sixth-century Britain.

Patrick K. Ford, trans., *The Mabinogi and Other Medieval Welsh Tales* (1977), a recent set of translations of value to an appreciation of Celtic backgrounds; Jean Frappier, *Chrétien de Troyes, l'homme et l'oeuvre* (1957), provides an excellent account of the transmutation of Arthurian lore into romance by the leading Chrétien scholar; Kathleen Hughes, "The Welsh Latin Chronicles: *Annales Cambriae* and Related Texts," in *Proceedings of the British Academy,* **59** (1973), includes a skeptical evaluation of entries alluding to Arthur; Kenneth Hurlstone Jackson, *The Gododdin: The Oldest Scottish Poem* (1969), provides a full commentary and a translation; *King Artus: A Hebrew Arthurian Romance,* Curt Leviant, ed. and trans. (1969), a work of 1279 not treated in *Arthurian Literature in the Middle Ages;* Roger Sherman Loomis, *Arthurian Tradition and Chrétien de Troyes* (1949), analyzes the backgrounds, particularly the Celtic, of Chrétien's Arthurian romances, episode by episode; and his *The Grail from Celtic Myth to Christian Symbol* (1963) gives an especially good treatment of the use made by Chrétien and his successors of Irish and Welsh traditions in the development of the Grail story; Roger S. Loomis and Laura H. Loomis, *Arthurian Legends in Medieval Art* (1966), provides a full and interesting discussion of Arthurian sculptures, paintings, drawings, tapestries, and ceramics, with illustrations.

A Manual of the Writings in Middle English, 1050–1500, J. Burke Severs, ed., fasc. I, *Romances* (1967), includes a comprehensive, updated bibliography of the Middle English Arthuriana—see especially Helaine Newstead, "Arthurian Legends," 38–79, 224–256, and Mortimer J. Donovan, "Breton Lais," 133–143, 292–297; Jean Marx, *La légende arthurienne et le Graal* (1952), in the course of a thorough discussion of Grail backgrounds, takes the view that the legend of Joseph of Arimathea in Britain was developed by Glastonbury monks; John Morris, *The Age of Arthur: A History of the British Isles from 350 to 650* (1973), states the belief that Britain retained Roman institutions and civilization into the sixth century, and that Arthur is to be considered an *imperator* of the Roman type; J. N. L. Myres, Review of Morris' *The Age of Arthur,* in *English Historical Review,* **90** (1975), contradicts Morris' theory; *Nennius et l'Historia Brittonum,* Ferdinand Lot, ed. (1934), presents the view that Nennius' work indicates an acquaintance with native Celtic tradition; Helaine Newstead, *Bran the Blessed in Arthurian Romance* (1939), an analysis of Welsh and Irish legend, of particular value in accounting for features of the Grail story; William Albert Nitze, *Arthurian Romance and Modern Poetry and Music* (1940), includes an account of an inscription on a Dalmatian coffin referring to a Roman officer named Artorius; J. S. P. Tatlock, *The Legendary History of Britain: Geoffrey of Monmouth's "Historia Regum Britanniae" and Its Early Vernacular Versions* (1950), provides a useful account of the chronicle tradition of Arthur.

ROBERT W. ACKERMAN

ARTHURIAN LITERATURE, SPANISH AND PORTUGUESE. Although the Matter of Britain had reached the Iberian Peninsula by the late twelfth century, the French prose romances of the thirteenth century—the Vulgate Cycle, the Prose *Tristan,* and the post-Vulgate *Roman du Graal*—became the primary vehicle for the transmission of the Arthurian legend, in both Spain and Portugal. Translations and reworkings of the prose romances, extant in twenty-five manuscript and printed texts, lexically enriched the early Hispanic languages, inspired numerous poets and prose writers, and played a significant role in determining social customs and morals, especially among the aristocracy.

Catalonia, where the earliest Arthurian references are found in troubadour lyrics dating from 1170, was receptive to the greatest variety of Arthurian texts and showed considerable originality in its treatment of the subject. Written in Provençal but of apparent Catalan authorship are *Jaufré,* a verse romance much influenced by Chrétien de Troyes, and *Bladín de Cornualha,* a verse narrative set in Cornwall that emphasizes chivalric adventure over love, like the cyclical romances. *La faula,* by the fourteenth-century Majorcan poet Guillem de Torroella, follows diverse Arthurian sources in recounting the poet's imaginary voyage to a distant island where he meets Morgan la Fée and Arthur. In addition to various extant Vulgate and Prose *Tristan* texts in Catalan, the translation and circulation of the cyclical romances and the importation of other Arthurian texts are attested to in Catalan and Aragonese documents and letters: Arthurian allusions also abound in Catalan and Valencian poetry, historiography, and romance.

In the western part of the Iberian Peninsula, Merlinus was used as a name in Portugal in 1190 (Arthurian names became common in the peninsula in the late Middle Ages). Poets writing in Galician-Portuguese in the thirteenth and fourteenth centuries occasionally treat Arthurian subjects, and allusions are made by later Portuguese poets in Garcia de Resende's *Cancioneiro Geral.* The post-Vulgate *Roman du Graal* was translated into a western Ibero-Romance language around 1313–1314; later versions survive in Galician-Portuguese, Portuguese, and Spanish. The Prose *Tristan* and the Vulgate *Lancelot* were also translated in the West in the early fourteenth century, but only a Galician-Portuguese *Tristan* fragment and a sixteenth-century Spanish copy of the *Lancelot* survive. The *Livro das Linhagens* of Dom Pedro, count of Barcelos, includes Arthurian material from Wace's *Roman de Brut,* based on a lost thirteenth-century Navarrese chronicle and reworked with details from the post-Vulgate texts, like the Spanish *Crónica de 1404* and *Libro de las generaciones.*

The Arthurian legend also took root early in northern and central Spain. Arthur's fatal battle with Modred is recorded in annals attached to a version of the *Fuero general de Navarra* (*ca.* 1196–1212) and the Castilian *Anales toledanos primeros* (1217); references and adaptations of Arthurian material are commonplace in Spanish literary texts from the early fourteenth century. While Spanish versions of the post-Vulgate *Roman du Graal* and the Vulgate *Lancelot* had a western origin, the Prose *Tristan* probably reached Castile via a Catalan or Aragonese intermediary, although the theory of an Italian origin has not been disproved. The Prose *Tristan* inspired a popular medieval Spanish ballad, and two Lancelot ballads seem to derive from a version of the Vulgate text.

The prose romance cycles served as an exemplar for Hispanic society, prompting the mimicry of Arthurian tourneys and jousts and even molding individual behavior. Round Tables (jousting, feasting, and dancing) were held at Valencia, Barcelona, Saragossa, and Calatayud in the thirteenth century. A *Libro de la montería* (*ca.* 1340) chides a Galician noble for hunting a giant called the Black Dragon instead of proper venery. Nuno Alvares Pereira, constable of Portugal, was an avid reader of the Galahad story and emulated his hero's celibacy. In 1434 an extraordinary imitation of chivalric literature took place: with the permission of Juan II of Castile, Suero de Quiñones took control of a bridge over the Órbigo River in León as a tribute to his ladylove. In a series of tourneys, Suero and his companions faced sixty-eight Spanish and foreign knights; one was killed and many wounded.

Some medieval and Renaissance writers condemned the chivalric texts as frivolous, but the Arthurian romances were widely read in the peninsula for more than 300 years. The vogue also gave rise to Spain's most influential romance of chivalry, *Amadís de Gaula,* modeled on the plot and style of the Vulgate *Lancelot* and Prose *Tristan.* The popularity of this and other Hispanic romances, such as *Tirant lo Blanc* and *Palmerín de Inglaterra,* led to a rebirth of the romance of chivalry throughout Europe in the sixteenth century.

BIBLIOGRAPHY

William J. Entwistle, *The Arthurian Legend in the Literatures of the Spanish Peninsula* (1925, repr. 1975); María Rosa Lida de Malkiel, "Arthurian Literature in Spain and Portugal," in Roger S. Loomis, ed., *Arthurian Literature in the Middle Ages* (1959); Harvey L. Sharrer, *A Critical Bibliography of Hispanic Arthurian Material,* I (1977).

HARVEY L. SHARRER

ARTHURIAN LITERATURE, WELSH. Arthurian romance could not have existed without the native British tradition created and developed by Welsh and Breton storytellers. This tradition was the basis of Geoffrey of Monmouth's Arthur in his *Historia Regum Britanniae* written for the Anglo-Norman court about 1136. In turn, his story fueled a great European Arthurian cycle, which, in the Middle Ages, culminated in Sir Thomas Malory's *Le Morte D'Arthur* (completed 1469). Geoffrey's impact was so great that even Welsh *cyfarwyddiaid* (storytellers)

ARTHURIAN LITERATURE, WELSH

incorporated his version of Arthur into the native tradition. Despite all outside influences, however, Welsh Arthurian literature retained a unique flavor—its broadly drawn characters acting and expressing themselves with verve and wit.

The earliest treatment of Arthur in Welsh literature must be pieced together from an array of historical and semihistorical writings, difficult poetry, and the vast repository of Welsh tradition and learning known as the triads. Scholars generally agree that the "historical" Arthur—his existence is still subject to debate—was probably a British war leader who flourished sometime in the fifth or early sixth century. There is no contemporary Latin or vernacular literature about him; indeed, the Welsh language had not yet evolved from its late British antecedent. Thus the first allusions to Arthur in Welsh occur well after his time; how much later is still unresolved. The oldest extant Welsh poetry is the *Gododdin,* preserved in *The Book of Aneirin* (*ca.* 1250). The core of the poem dates from about 600, with many interpolations from as early as the ninth century. One verse praises the fallen warrior Gwarddur with the words, "*ceni bei ef* Arthur" (although he was not Arthur). Interestingly, Gwarddur was not himself the chieftain of the men of Gododdin: this may suggest that Arthur was known and celebrated in northern Britain for military prowess but not necessarily for his rank.

Entries in the *Annales Cambriae* also shed light on stories of Arthur. Gathered from materials from the sixth century onwards, these annals in Latin and Welsh received their earliest written form around the ninth century. Besides crediting Arthur with a victory at a place called Badon, an entry for the year 537 (more probably 539) reads, "The battle of Camlann in which Arthur and Medraut both fell." This is the first historical reference to Arthur's last battle and to Medraut, who in later romance became the villainous Mordred.

Filling in details of Arthur's story is a difficult matter. Very little of the rich oral tradition in Welsh has survived in manuscripts. Nevertheless some stories, poems, and the Welsh triads are preserved in manuscripts such as Peniarth 16 (thirteenth to fifteenth centuries), *The Black Book of Carmarthen* (twelfth to thirteenth centuries), *The Red Book of Hergest* (*ca.* 1375 to 1425), and *The Book of Taliesin* (*ca.* 1275). Although all of these manuscripts date from after the time of Geoffrey of Monmouth, the Arthurian traditions that they preserve revert at least to the ninth to eleventh centuries.

The Welsh triads—short stanzas giving historical or mythical information in sets of three—constitute the largest source of both pre-Geoffrey and post-Geoffrey tradition. The oldest stratum, *Trioedd Ynys Prydein,* reflects a time when the Welsh or Britons inhabited the whole island of Britain. In their terse entries, Arthur emerges as a chief prince of the three tribal thrones of Britain: *Mynyw,* or St. David's; *Celliwig* in Cornwall; and *Penn Rhionydd* in the north. Besides his military prowess he is one of the three *overveird* (a skilled composer of satirical verse) in Britain. He has a son Llacheu, who along with Gwalchmai (Sir Gawain), is one of the "three well-endowed men of the Island of Britain." Among Arthur's companions are Cei (Sir Kay), Bedwyr (Sir Bedivere), and March ap Meirchyawn (King Mark of Cornwall). Arthur's wife is Gwenhwyfar. Medraut is also mentioned as being present at the infamous battle of Camlann, but not until after Geoffrey's writings does he assume an evil role.

The most detailed story of Arthur is found in the triad of the "Three Powerful Swineherds of the Island of Britain." Here, with March's connivance, Arthur, Cei, and Bedwyr try to steal away March's swine while Drystan (Tristan) tends them. What apparently prompts the episode is Drystan's sending March's swineherd off with a message to Essyllt.

Several early poems besides the triads provide hints of Arthurian episodes. Arthur and Gereint (Chrétien de Troyes's Erec and the hero of the corresponding Welsh romance *Gereint Son of Erbin*) are linked to the battle of Llongborth in *englynion* (stanzas of three or four lines in the *englyn* verse form) preserved in *The Black Book of Carmarthen.* This same manuscript contains the first cryptic allusion to the myth of Arthur as the vanished undying hero: "a wonder of the world is Arthur's grave" in the stanzas known as *Englynion y Beddau.*

Arthur is also connected with the legend of another Welsh hero, the poet Taliesin. *The Book of Taliesin* relates a verse adventure in which Taliesin joins Arthur aboard his ship *Prydwen* for a series of raids on fortresses of the Welsh Otherworld.

A few other events are partially preserved in verse dialogues, which unfortunately lack the context for the character's conversation. The earliest, dating from before 1100 and entitled "Conversation between Arthur and Glewlwyd Mighty-grasp," has Arthur regaling the porter Glewlwyd with the feats of his men in order to gain admission to the house that Glewlwyd is guarding.

In *englynion* dated around 1150 Arthur converses

with his nephew Eliwlad, who has assumed the shape of an eagle. This dialogue reveals Uther Pendragon as Arthur's father for the first time in a Welsh story independent of Geoffrey's version.

Another dialogue that survives only in manuscripts from after 1500, but also thought to be from the twelfth century, concerns the abduction of Gwenhwyfar by Melwas (Chrétien's Meleagant). Known as the "Conversation between Arthur and Gwenhwyfar," but more likely to be a dialogue involving Melwas, Gwenhwyfar, and Cei, it seems to be part of an incident found in the Latin life of St. Gildas written by Caradoc of Llancarfan before 1136. According to this story, Gildas helped to mediate the restoration of Gwenhwyfar after Melwas of Glastonbury stole her away.

For the most complete characterization of the native Welsh view of Arthur one must look to the prose narrative of *Culhwch and Olwen,* composed between 1050 and 1120. This lively tale relates the fantastic tasks that Culhwch must perform in order to win the giant Ysbaddaden's lovely daughter Olwen. Culhwch enlists the aid of his cousin Arthur, whose portrayal is the embodiment of the rough-and-ready Welsh chieftain. Generous and warm-hearted to his cousin, exulting in his prowess and abundant wit, this Arthur is a man of action rather than the passive figure of later romances.

Even after Continental and Anglo-Norman influences crept into the native tradition, the Welsh romances of *Gereint Son of Erbin, Owein,* and *Peredur Son of Efrawg* still display the same gusto for adventure, pithy dialogue, and vibrant descriptions that were all so integral to the *cyfarwydd* tradition.

Perhaps the most dazzlingly rhetorical and consciously literary piece is the twelfth-century tale *The Dream of Rhonabwy.* Set in the reign of Madog ap Maredudd (*d.* 1159), Rhonabwy's magical dream of Arthur playing *gwyddbwyll* (chess) at the battle of Badon becomes a brilliant vehicle for political satire.

Much later on, some parts of the Arthurian vulgate cycle were translated almost directly into Welsh: *Y Seint Greal, Perlesvaus, The Birth of Arthur,* and a verse–prose *Ystorya Tristan* all dating from the fourteenth to sixteenth centuries. This last text is an odd mixture of new and old traditions and, unlike the usual Tristan story, has a happy ending.

BIBLIOGRAPHY

A good place to start for further study is with Thomas Jones, "The Early Evolution of the Legend of Arthur," Gerald Morgan, trans., in *Nottingham Medieval Studies,* 8 (1964). Sir John Rhys's introduction to his edition of Thomas Malory's *Le Morte Darthur* (1906) contains translations of early Welsh poetry about Arthur. See also Rachel Bromwich, ed. and trans., *Trioedd Ynys Prydein: The Welsh Triads* (1961, 2nd ed. 1979); Thomas Jones, "*The Black Book of Carmarthen* Stanzas of the Graves," in *Proceedings of the British Academy,* 53 (1967); Mary Williams, "Ymddiddan rhwng Arthur a Gwenhwyfar" ("A Dialogue between Arthur and Guinevere"), An Early Ritual Poem in Welsh," in *Speculum,* 8 (1938); Ifor Williams, "Ymddiddan Arthur a'r Eryr" ("Arthur's Conversation with the Eagle"), in *Bulletin of the Board of Celtic Studies,* 2 (1924–1925); and "Tristan ac Essyllt," *ibid.,* 5 (1930).

For an English translation of the Tristan story see Kenneth Hurlestone Jackson, *A Celtic Miscellany* (1951), where he also translates part of the *Mabinogion* Arthurian texts. For other translations of the texts, see Gwyn Jones and Thomas Jones, *The Mabinogion* (1974), and Jeffrey Gantz, *The Mabinogion* (1977). Kenneth Jackson has an English text and study of the *Gododdin* (1969).

Other studies include Brinley Roberts, "Tales and Romances," in A. O. H. Jarman and Gwilym Rees Hughes, eds., *A Guide to Welsh Literature* I (1976); R. S. Loomis, *Arthurian Literature in the Middle Ages* (1959) and *Wales and the Arthurian Legend* (1956); Glenys W. Goetinck, *Peredur: A Study of Welsh Tradition in the Grail Legends* (1975); Ceridwen Lloyd-Morgan, "The Peniarth MS. Fragment of Y Seint Greal: Arthurian Tradition in the late Fifteenth Century," in *Bulletin of the Board of Celtic Studies,* pt. 1 (Nov., 1978); chapters on *Culhwch and Olwen, The Dream of Rhonabwy* and Romances," in Geraint Bowen, ed., *Y Traddodiad Rhyddiaith yn yr Oesau Canol* (1974); R. M. Jones, "Y Rhamantau Cymraeg," in *Llen Cymru,* 6 (1957); Thomas Jones, "Llenyddiaeth Arthuraidd yn yr Oesoedd Canol," *Llen Cymru,* 8 (1959); and Kenneth H. Jackson, *The International Popular Tale and Early Welsh Tradition* (1961).

Not all Welsh Arthurian texts are available in English, and Brinley Roberts' new editions of "Gereint Fil' Erbin" and "Ymddiddan Arthur a Glewlwyd Gafaelfawr" in his chapter "Rhai Cerddi Ymddiddan" in Rachel Bromwich and R. Brinley Jones, eds., *Astudiaethau ar yr Hengerdd* ("Studies in Old Welsh Poetry") (1978), will undoubtedly change previous translations of these poems.

MARILYN KAY KENNEY

[See also **Welsh Literature.**]

ARTIST, STATUS OF THE. No concept of the artist in the modern sense of the term existed in the medieval period. The Latin *artifex,* the Italian *artista,* were words used to mean artisan and applied

ARTIST, STATUS OF THE

to all manner of craftsmen. (Alternatively *artista* referred to one following the course of the faculty of arts at a university.) The modern idea of creative art and the creative artist, it could be said, was something that came fully to birth only in the eighteenth century. The early medieval world, by contrast, had inherited from Roman civilization a clear distinction between the "liberal arts" (those worthy of a *liber* or freeman), in which no physical labor was involved, and the "mechanical arts" (more suitable for the slave), which required manual activity. Given this antithesis it was inevitable that the painter or sculptor should be seen as Pliny, in the chapters on Greek art in his encyclopedia had seen them and, following him, as the early encyclopedias of the Middle Ages had seen them: men who, while capable of extraordinary achievements, were nonetheless doomed to be considered as much on the level of—it was Seneca who drew the comparison—wrestlers, perfume makers, and cooks.

It was in this spirit that the Fathers of the Second Council of Nicaea of 787 explained that the composition of images did not in any way concern the painter; "to him is entrusted only their execution." The artist was, so to speak, only a hand, subordinate to the directing mind of his priest-patron. Against these formulations the story of the status of the medieval artist is basically one of the attempts made by artists and admirers of art to overturn the crude contrast between the liberal and mechanical arts and to assert that painters and sculptors too could be seen as men of intellectual distinction in their own right. By the eleventh and twelfth centuries this movement can be documented. To cite one of several examples from the period, one Niccolò, who sculpted in the cathedral of Verona in the 1130's, blazoned his claim for esteem in an inscription beneath his work:

> Coming together men will praise for generations
> That Niccolò, the skilled *artifex* who carved these things.

But it was in fourteenth-century Italy, with all its passion for the arts and with its break in some ways from a traditional conservative culture, that such assertions first gained fuller acceptance. Dante, in canto XI of the *Purgatorio,* gave support to the cause by speaking of "the fame" of Cimabue, Giotto, and the manuscript illuminators, Oderigi da Gubbio and Franco Bolognese. Early commentators on the *Divine Comedy* were sometimes shocked by the praise given to these "rude mechanicals," as Benvenuto da Imola calls them, but the celebration of the great painter or sculptor came increasingly to override the categorization of their work as inferior to that of pure thinkers. On the sculpted pulpit that Giovanni Pisano carved in 1311 for the cathedral of Pisa, the artist was permitted to engrave two sets of rhymed Latin verses that exalt the magnificence of his work and at the same time, with their complaints of the "hostile injuries" he has received, offer the first recorded display of artistic temperament: "He who condemns the man worthy of the diadem proves himself unworthy, so he who reproves him shows himself worthy of reproof."

Pisano's impassioned plea for his own work was seconded by the immense fame accorded to Giotto, who, perhaps in large part because he had been praised by Dante, received a public acclaim that no artist had hitherto known. In his lifetime he was hailed as "the distinguished painter," "a skilled and famous man," and "a great master to be held dear in the city [Florence]." It was against this background that the traditional interpretation of the artist's status came to be reformulated. In the series of reliefs portraying "the works of man" executed on the campanile of Florence between 1334 and 1337 the three representations of the fine arts—painting, sculpture, and architecture—were placed in an intermediate position between those of the mechanical and of the liberal arts. From mid century the ever increasing influence of humanism served to raise the artist's status still further. Having read the praise that such writers as Pliny had given to Greek art, Petrarch and Boccaccio and their followers assumed—in fact mistakenly—that the classical world had awarded a high personal esteem to those who had created it. So Filippo Villani, in the chapter on Florentine painters in *Liber de origine civitatis Florentiae et ejusdem famosis civibus (On the Famous Citizens of Florence)* (1381–1382) asserted that "painters are not inferior in mind to those made masters in the liberal arts," that they are indeed in some way superior to them, "since the latter obtain by study and learning in books what is required by their arts, while painters depend only on the high mind [*altum ingenium,* a phrase that comes close to our "genius"] and tenacious memory that is manifest in their art."

Villani's striking defense of the artist bears testimony that, at least in one, most influential part of Europe, the view of the artist as manual worker was giving way to a quasi-modern view of the artist as creative intellectual. This position was forwarded by

Manuel Chrysoloras, who in 1411 wrote of art as "a philosophic activity," and by Leon Battista Alberti, who in his *De pictura* (1435–1436), asserted in forceful terms the artist's nobility and genius. Yet during the fifteenth century more conservative attitudes persisted outside the humanist milieu and were still powerful in the northern world. Even in sixteenth-century Italy, Baldassare Castiglione, in *The Book of the Courtier,* found it necessary to apologize for reference to arts "that today may seem mechanical and inappropriate for a gentleman." For many men the time-hallowed views of the past still held authority.

BIBLIOGRAPHY

The only general work is Andrew Martindale, *The Rise of the Artist in the Middle Ages and Early Renaissance* (1972); on particular aspects, see P. O. Kristeller, "The Modern System of the Arts," in *Journal of the History of Ideas,* **12** (1951), and **13** (1952); and Rudolf Wittkower, *The Artist and the Liberal Arts* (1952). On the influence of humanism, see Michael Baxandall, *Giotto and the Orators* (1971); John Larner, "The Artist and the Intellectuals in Fourteenth-Century Italy," in *History,* **54** (1969); and *Culture and Society in Italy, 1290–1420* (1971), 264–284.

JOHN LARNER

ARTISTS' MANUALS. See **Modelbooks.**

ARTS, SEVEN LIBERAL. A group consisting of the elementary trivium (grammar, rhetoric, and dialectic) and the more advanced quadrivium (music, arithmetic, geometry, and astronomy) that formed the basis of secular education, especially in the early medieval West. The seven liberal arts were established in the early fifth century by Martianus Capella, but were not widely accepted until the time of Alcuin (*ca.* 800). Medieval theologians (for example, Thierry of Chartres in the mid twelfth century) regarded the Virgin Mary as the mistress of the seven liberal arts, which were believed to embody all human wisdom, and thus to be related to divine wisdom. Personifications of the seven liberal arts were often used in a religious context in the medieval West, particularly in the Gothic period, both to show that human knowledge was not possible without the intercession of the Virgin and to indicate the knowledge one must have to approach divine wisdom. Over the right door of the western portal at Chartres cathedral, for example, the Virgin was shown seated in the tympanum with the seven liberal arts surrounding her in the archivolts.

LESLIE BRUBAKER

ARUNDEL PSALTER, an interlinear gloss in Anglo-Norman of the Gallican psalter, dating from the twelfth century, conserved in London, British Library, Arundel MS 230. It begins with Psalm 4:3.

BIBLIOGRAPHY

A. Beyer, "Die Londoner Psalterhandschrift Arundel 230," in *Zeitschrift für romanische Philologie,* **11** (1887) and **12** (1888).

BRIAN MERRILEES

[See also **Anglo-Norman Literature.**]

ASCENSION, the withdrawal of Christ into heaven, witnessed by the apostles, and most fully described in Acts of the Apostles 1:9–11. The Ascension was Christ's last appearance on earth and has been celebrated as a movable feast (on the fortieth day after Easter) since the late fourth century. Representations of the Ascension followed two basic formulas throughout the early Christian and medieval periods. In the first, Christ was shown walking up the Mount of Olives in the presence of at least two apostles (Munich Ascension ivory). The second, and more common, form showed Christ, usually standing within a mandorla and supported by angels, above the apostles and often the Virgin (the Rabula Gospels). In late medieval works, only Christ's feet may be visible, the rest of his body having risen beyond the confines of the composition.

BIBLIOGRAPHY

Ernest T. DeWald, "The Iconography of the Ascension," in *American Journal of Archaeology,* 2nd ser., **19** (1915).

LESLIE BRUBAKER

ASCENSION OF THE PROPHET. The concept of the Ascension of the prophet Muḥammad is traditionally associated with a brief Koranic verse, Sura 17:1, "Praise him who traveled in one night with his servant from the *Masjid al-Ḥarām* to the *Masjid al-Aqṣā* whose surroundings we blessed in order to show him our signs."

Within the Muslim community several different interpretations of this incident have been offered, and the text has been amplified by numerous commentaries and accounts. Some early Muslims felt that this journey was a spiritual one, while others believed that the Prophet was transported physically with miraculous speed. Frequently he was said to have been carried by an equine creature with a human head known as *Burāq*.

There was also a diversity of opinion over the location of the place he visited. Some understood the *Masjid al-Aqṣā* to mean a heavenly sanctuary, while others connected the term with the region of Jerusalem formerly occupied by the Jewish temple. These two opinions were often merged and the Prophet was said to have traveled first to Jerusalem and then to heaven; the first stage is often designated the *isrāʾ* ("night journey"), while the second is called the *miʿrāj* ("Ascension"). Less uncertainty existed about the place from which his journey began, since *Masjid Ḥaram* was customarily used to designate the sanctuary of the Kaaba at Mecca. Since the journey occurred at night, Muḥammad was said to have been awakened from sleep either in the precinct of the Kaaba itself or in a nearby house belonging to his cousin, Umm Hāniʾ, daughter of Abū Ṭālib.

Over the centuries, Koranic commentaries provided many circumstantial details that enriched the brief Koranic text and transformed it into a full-fledged narrative. All versions culminated in the Prophet's communion with, or vision of, the Divine Creator, but the exact stages of his journey were a matter of debate. Frequently the visit to Jerusalem included meetings with earlier prophets such as Abraham, Moses, and Jesus at which Muḥammad led the others in prayer, thus demonstrating his primacy over them. Many accounts also describe the Prophet's meetings with other biblical figures such as Adam, Enoch, Joseph, and Noah. Stress is often laid on his visits to purgatory, where Muslims who fail to observe their religious obligations are tormented, and to hell, where infidels will suffer eternally. He is also given a glimpse of the luxuriant gardens and dwellings reserved for righteous Muslims before coming into the presence of the Divine Creator.

Seven Thrones, mid-16th-century Persian manuscript depicting the journey of the Prophet Muḥammad. COURTESY, FREER GALLERY OF ART

The Prophet's Ascension was given an allegorical interpretation by mystics who saw in it the model of the soul's purification and its ultimate unification with God. In certain periods and regions of the Islamic world, notably fourteenth- and fifteenth-century Iran, the Prophet's Ascension was depicted in manuscripts. Translations and adaptations of traditions concerning it made in Spain during the twelfth and thirteenth centuries are thought to have influenced Dante in his formulation of the *Divine Comedy*.

BIBLIOGRAPHY

Miguel Asín Palacios, *Islam and the Divine Comedy*, Harold Sutherland, trans. (1926, repr. 1968). Ibn Isḥāq, *The Life of Muḥammad*, Alfred Guillaume, trans. (1955).

P. SOUCEK

[See also **Buraq; Mysticism, Islamic.**]

ASCENSION, FEAST OF THE. Since the fourth century the Church has celebrated the fortieth day after Easter or the Thursday after the fifth Sunday after Easter as the feast of the Ascension. Before that time the ascent of Christ to heaven was commemorated either on Easter (following the accounts in Luke 24:50–53 and John 20:21ff.) or in conjunction with Pentecost or the fiftieth day after Easter. But by the fourth century the Church seems to have decided that it should follow in its commemoration the account of Acts 1, in which Christ ascends after having made many appearances for forty days following his resurrection and the disciples' return to Jerusalem from the Mount of Olives.

The narrative of the fourth-century Spanish pilgrim Etheria reports a procession on the fortieth day after Easter to Bethlehem, where a vigil was celebrated; but it is not certain that this is a reference to a celebration of the Ascension. Also, it is reported that St. Helena had constructed a basilica on the Mount of Olives in the fourth century.

By the late fourth and early fifth centuries there are clear witnesses to a celebration of a feast of the Ascension. It is noted in the *Apostolic Constitutions;* John Chrysostom and Gregory of Nyssa preached sermons on Ascension Day; and Augustine of Hippo even reported that it was a festival instituted by the apostles. Moreover, in the earliest liturgical books of all the major rites in the Western church there are formularies and prayers for a celebration entitled either *Ascensa* or *Ascensio.* By the seventh century at least a vigil of the Ascension had been instituted, despite the general rule that there be no fasting during Eastertide; and by the twelfth century there was an octave.

Characteristic of the feast of the Ascension were processions, which probably date from the fourth century. Both Adamnan and Bede report such solemn processions in Jerusalem to the Mount of Olives, and outside Jerusalem it seems to have been the custom to go to a suburb, preferably one with a hill, where a service was held.

Associated with these processions, especially in the high and later Middle Ages, were dramatic interpolations. For example, in the procession before Mass one of the choristers would leave the procession and disappear to sing alone the antiphon "Non vos relinquam"; and priests would raise aloft a cross at the words "Ascendo ad Patrem." Also, in the Mass during the later Middle Ages the paschal candle was dramatically extinguished after the reading of the Gospel.

The most spectacular of these ceremonies were the so-called Ascension plays held in Germany at least from the fourteenth century. In the *Moosburg Ordinarium,* for example, a little drama before vespers is described: a platform was erected with a small replica of Mount Sinai (not the Mount of Olives), in which a wooden image of the risen Christ was kept. After a procession, the image was venerated and censed, and as appropriate music was sung, it was raised by a rope and pulley to awaiting silken "clouds" in the vaulting of the church. Thereafter, those below were showered with eucharistic wafers, drops of water, and rose petals, signifying Christ's continuing presence in the Eucharist and the coming of the Holy Spirit at Pentecost in tongues of fire.

Other customs associated with the feast included the blessing of beans, the eating of birds, and the abusing of specially made images of the devil, which were ceremonially thrown down and beaten with sticks.

BIBLIOGRAPHY

Karl Adam Heinrich Kellner, *Heortology* (1908), 106–109; Alexander Allen McArthur, *The Evolution of the Christian Year* (1953), 141–159; Francis X. Weiser, *Handbook of Christian Feasts and Customs* (1958), 239–246; Karl Young, *The Drama of the Medieval Church* (1933), I, 483–489; II, 532, 537.

ROGER E. REYNOLDS

[See also **Feasts, Festivals, Europe.**]

ASEN, JOHN I; JOHN II. See **John I Asen; John II Asen.**

ASHᶜARĪ, AL-, ABU'L-ḤASAN ᶜALĪ IBN ISMAᶜĪL (*ca.* 873–935), leading conservative theologian in Sunnite Islam, after whom an enduring school of theology is named. Born in Basra, he received the usual Islamic education in the Koran, Traditions, Arabic philology, and *sharīᶜa* law, then studied theology *(kalām)* under the foremost Muᶜtazilite theologian of the Basra school, al-Jubbāʾī. He gained a reputation as an excellent debater on theology in the mosques and wrote works in the rationalist tradition of his master, which have not survived. At the age of forty he changed his doctrinal position to a more traditionalist one and be-

ASHᶜARĪ, AL-

came a strong opponent of the Muᶜtazilites. This event is reported as resulting from two dreams, in the first of which Muḥammad commanded him to defend a more traditional Islam, while in the second he insisted that he should not abandon the dialectical method of *kalām* but should use it to combat Muᶜtazilite rationalism. Then for the rest of his life al-Ashᶜarī championed traditional Islamic theology, moving at some time from Basra to Baghdad, where he died. Among his few surviving works from this later period are two that present in dialectical form his doctrinal positions and arguments, the *Ibāna* and the *Lumaᶜ*, as well as a valuable survey of the sects of Islam, *Maqālāt al-Islāmiyyīn*.

The most distinctive and influential feature of al-Ashᶜarī's new "conservative" theology is its method. This is foreshadowed in the dreams but can be understood better as a synthesis between the positions of two groups prevalent in his time. On one side, the Muᶜtazilites had taken as first principles a few dominant ideas in the Koran, especially the unity and justice of God, and made far-reaching deductions from their principles even at the cost of ignoring or distorting other ideas in the Koran. This had led to serious problems and to growing accusations that Muᶜtazilism was not true Islam but a speculative construction by theologians. In reaction against this system, which he had learned from the inside, al-Ashᶜarī conceived his task as the working out and defense of a theology based more faithfully on the meaning of the Koran and Traditions. "The Koran is to be understood in its apparent meaning. It is not permissible to understand it in any other way, except by proof."

This ruling called for an accurate and wide knowledge of the Arabic language of the Koran; and al-Ashᶜarī was generally able to maintain a high standard of textual interpretation. There were texts for which he sensibly abandoned a literal interpretation, such as anthropomorphic assertions about God. On other points there appeared to be real contradictions in the Koran, on predestination and free will, for example. In such cases he seems to have used another principle of interpretation: to follow the predominant intention of Scripture as a whole. This was in fact the method used by the Muᶜtazilites, but the selection was different, for al-Ashᶜarī emphasized divine omnipotence as the dominant teaching of the Koran. As will be shown, he tried hard to reconcile all the texts, but not without strain.

Much of the theology thus worked out by al-Ashᶜarī was based on doctrines of his traditionalist predecessors. But most of these had taken a different stand against the Muᶜtazilites by refusing to discuss theology at all. Their foremost leader, the great jurist Aḥmad ibn Ḥanbal, had argued that the Koran had not authorized *kalām* and the early Muslims had not practiced it, and that it was therefore a heretical innovation. Good Muslims should settle theoretical problems as far as possible by quotations from the Koran and Traditions, and beyond that maintain silence. Now al-Ashᶜarī, while claiming to be a follower of Aḥmad, broke with the method of his school and used the full technique of argument that he had acquired in his Muᶜtazilite education to do combat with his former associates. Only occasionally did he fall back on the Ḥanbalī answer, "No explaining 'how,'" in face of unfathomable obscurities in the divine message.

The existence of God is briefly affirmed on the basis of statements in the Koran that because man is unable to produce or retard his own growth there must be another maker and governor above him. There is an assumption here that runs throughout Ashᶜarite thought: that physical causes alone are insufficient to produce change; only a living being can be an ultimate cause. The unity of God is similarly supported by a brief Koranic argument: that if there were two (or more) gods, at least one could not be omnipotent. These two principles of theology were accepted by all Muslims.

Concerning the eternal attributes of God, such as knowledge, power, and the many others mentioned in the Koran, al-Ashᶜarī took issue with the Muᶜtazilite position that God is knowing and powerful, but does not have "knowledge" or "power" because these would be eternal beings besides God. He mentions first that these attributes are named in the Koran in their abstract forms and so cannot be denied; he then explains that "having knowledge" means the same as "being knowing," so that the problem is dissolved as one of mere grammar. God has attributes, which belong to him without being himself and without being other individuals.

The Koran is uncreated, contrary to the Muᶜtazilite doctrine. This question is discussed following the attributes, because al-Ashᶜarī understands the Koran as meaning the speech of God *(kalām Allāh)*, primarily in the sense of his power of speaking. This power is eternal and uncreated. The inference from here to the eternity of the product of the power, the spoken or written Koran, is drawn from an unacknowledged ambiguity in the word *kalām*: "speaking" or "that which is spoken." Another argument

ASHᶜARĪ, AL-

is derived from the Koran's assertion that God creates things by his command, "Be!"; since this word is used in all creation, it, at least, must be uncreated.

The problem of human action was formulated in Islamic thought not in terms of free will but of the power to act. On this question the Muᶜtazilites and their opponents agreed on one point: that God creates man and consequently creates in him any power that he has. But beyond that basis they differed.

According to the Muᶜtazilites, two persons cannot have power over the same act. All power is ultimately derived from God, but in creating man he has delegated real power to him to make choices and then to act on them. Further, he gives sufficient grace to everyone, believers and unbelievers, to know what is right and to choose it if they wish. Thus the rewards and punishments of the next life could easily be justified. Support for this straightforward view could be found in many verses of the Koran. But there are many other verses that assert the predestination of all human acts by God, and the Muᶜtazilites had to attempt a reconciliation by interpretations that were sometimes forced.

The earliest opponents of this view, such as Jahm ibn Ṣafwān, had proposed a hard predestination. In this view God is the sole cause of every human act, and any "power" that a man has is to "choose" and do the particular act that God has decided upon for him. But this doctrine was too extreme for most Muslims to accept in face of the Koran as a whole and the problem of divine justice, which it fails to solve.

Another eighth-century theologian had proposed an intermediate view that was to provide the nucleus of al-Ashᶜarī's doctrine: "The ground of the separation of Ḍirār ibn ᶜAmr from the Muᶜtazilites was his view that the acts of the servants [men] are created, and that a single act has two agents: one of whom creates it, namely God, while the other acquires it, namely the servant."

Al-Ashᶜarī took up this view because it suggested the possibility of allowing man's responsibility for his acts and reconciling all the statements of the Koran. His achievement was to formulate an elaborate and subtle exposition that satisfied many Muslims on some crucial and interconnected issues. To begin with, he had to defend the principle that one act can have two agents. Two Bible stories (also narrated in the Koran) were used to illustrate this possibility. In one, Cain was the direct agent of his brother's murder, but Abel was also an agent in a more passive sense, for having allowed Cain to do it rather than retaliate. Similarly, the Egyptian governor imprisoned Joseph, but Joseph had chosen this alternative rather than be seduced by the governor's wife. So God and man can both be agents of the same act (although their relations to it are very different from those in the human examples).

What then are the precise relations of God and man to a human act? Every time a man acts God creates in him the power to choose and the power to carry out his act effectively. Thus man has a "created power," existing only for the moment when he uses it: "No one can do a thing before he does it" ("Two Creeds," arts. 16 and 17; McCarthy, p. 239). Still, with this created power, man carries out the essential act of choosing one act rather than another, and this choice would seem to make him responsible for his acts. Al-Ashᶜarī observes that we know intuitively the difference between God's direct causation of events in nature, including our involuntary transformations such as digestion and sickness, and his "leaving us free" to go and come, to commit sins and all other voluntary acts. Al-Ashᶜarī uses the language of "acquisition" to describe the latter class of acts, defining it thus: "The true meaning of acquisition is that the thing proceeds from its acquirer in virtue of a created power" (*Lumaᶜ*, sec. 92). Thus, because everyone acquires his own voluntary acts, he is sufficiently responsible for them to deserve the rewards and punishments of the next life.

Up to this point, al-Ashᶜarī appears to leave man a free agent by his doctrine of acquisition; "acquiring" the act involves choosing it. But then he takes away the essential feature of choice by denying that we ever have "power" over two alternative and contrary acts, because "it is a condition of created power that its existence include the existence of the object of the power" (*Lumaᶜ*, sec. 126). This conclusion permits a fully predestinarian doctrine of divine grace. God has guided the righteous and made them believers, and he could have done the same for unbelievers. "However, He has willed not to make unbelievers righteous and not to favor them so that they will be believers, and has rather willed [*arāda*, "decided"] that they be unbelievers, as He foreknew, and He abandons them and leads them astray and sets a seal on their hearts" (*Maqālāt* creed, art. 18 in McCarthy). Thus, in spite of his effort to unify everything stated in the Koran into a single doctrine, al-Ashᶜarī seems to end in a real contradiction. But this is not admitted by his followers.

His explicit theory of predestined grace faced the problem of theodicy: how can God be just in punishing for sins that he has predestined? Al-Ash^{c}arī's answer depends on a theory of ethical voluntarism: that the will of God alone *determines* what is good or evil, just or unjust. This theory had already become prevalent in Sunnite jurisprudence, which aimed to base all judgments of law and ethics on revealed sources, that is, on God's approval or disapproval as expressed in the Koran and Traditions, and correspondingly to exclude direct human judgments of right and wrong as authorized sources of Islamic law, except in case of unanimous agreement among jurists. Al-Ash^{c}arī expresses this theory of value clearly in a definition: "A thing is evil on our part only because we transgress the limit and boundary set for us and do what we have no right to do" (*Luma^{c}*, sec. 170). Therefore, when a person commits a sin, he is a sinner only because the act is forbidden by a law *(sharī^{c}a)* of someone in authority over him. But God is not subject to any *sharī^{c}a;* therefore when He wills a man to commit a sin such as unbelief, it does not follow that God is a sinner and is to be accused of injustice, since obedience and disobedience to law are inapplicable to him.

This theory had two advantages for al-Ash^{c}arī as a champion of traditionalist Islam. It does not limit the omnipotence of God by setting up objective standards of value to which he, as God, must conform. (The Mu^{c}tazilites were criticized on this score.) And it provided an answer to the problem of theodicy, because whatever God does to a man, such as withholding grace and then punishing him for his sins, cannot be questioned by any standard. Al-Ash^{c}arī does not shrink from the extreme consequence of such a position, with which his Mu^{c}tazilite opponents challenged him: that lying and other conduct generally considered wicked would have been good acts if God had declared them so and obligatory if he had commanded them (*Luma^{c}*, sec. 171).

Al-Ash^{c}arī was not at first succeeded by well-known disciples. Only in the eleventh century was his doctrine developed by distinguished successors such as al-Bāḳillānī and ^{c}Abd al-Qāhir ibn Ṭāhir al-Baghdādī, both of whom systematized a theory of knowledge and an occasionalist theory of causation supporting God's omnipotence. The school's influence was greatly increased when the Seljuk vizier Niẓām al-Mulk founded colleges of law and theology *(madrasas)* in Neyshābūr and Baghdad and installed two outstanding Ash^{c}arite scholars in their chairs: al-Juwaynī in the former and al-Ghazālī in the latter. Thereafter this theology gradually became predominant in the Mediterranean countries of Islam, but other schools prevailed further east, such as that of al-Ash^{c}arī's contemporary al-Māturīdī in Transoxiana, Ibn Ḥanbal in Arabia, and Shiism in Iran. Asharism is still taught at the Azhar in Cairo and at other colleges of Islamic theology. Al-Ash^{c}arī's thought has had an enduring appeal to Muslims because of its conservative theology based on revelation and its systematization by notable successors.

BIBLIOGRAPHY

Sources. Richard J. McCarthy, ed. and trans., *The Theology of al-Ash^{c}arī* (1953), includes *Kitāb al-Luma^{c}* and other works by or about al-Ash^{c}arī; see also M. M. ^{c}Abd al-Ḥamīd, ed., *Maqālāt al-Islāmiyyīn,* 2 vols. (1950) and Hellmut Ritter, ed., 3 vols. (1929–1933); Walter C. Klein, ed. and trans., *al Aš^{c}arī's al-Ibānah ^{c}an uṣūl ad-diyānah* (1940).

Studies. Richard M. Frank, "The Structure of Created Causality According to al Aš^{c}arî," in *Studia Islamica,* **25** (1966); George Makdisi, "Ash^{c}arī and the Ash^{c}arites in Islamic Religious History," *ibid.,* **17** (1962) and **18** (1963); William Montgomery Watt, *Free Will and Predestination in Early Islam* (1948), ch. 6.

George F. Hourani

[See also **Islam, Religion.**]

ASHKENAZ appears in genealogical lists in the books of Genesis and Chronicles and as a place name in the book of Jeremiah. For reasons that are not at present clear, medieval Jews utilized this term as a designation for Germany, with the related term Ashkenazim referring sometimes in a limited manner to German Jews and at other times to all of northern European Jewry. Ashkenazic Jewry is thus that set of Jewish communities which originated in medieval northern France and Germany, spread westward into England and eastward into Poland, and was destined in modern times to dominate world Jewry demographically.

As a backward area in western Christendom, the northern countries of Europe initially had little attraction for the large Jewish communities that developed all around the Mediterranean basin. Only as northern European civilization began to develop in the eleventh and twelfth centuries were Jews drawn in significant numbers to the nascent urban centers of northern France and Germany. From the outset these Jews occupied a useful but limited niche in the burgeoning economy, encountered substantial popular resentment, and of necessity fell into a protective alliance with the political authorities. In this alliance, the Jews furnished general stimulation to the economy and afforded ready cash directly to their overlords, receiving in exchange guarantees of physical safety and business support. As the experiment with Jewish settlement proved successful, Jews were invited to settle in England and proceeded eastward into Slavic lands as well.

By the thirteenth century, developments in northern Europe conspired to retard the further growth of this vital Ashkenazic Jewry. Political leaders strapped for funds mercilessly exploited their Jews; the Catholic church insisted on an increasingly sharp isolation and limitation of the Jews; the popular sense of national identity enhanced perceptions of Jewish difference; and dangerously irrational anti-Jewish slanders proliferated. Out of these circumstances emerged the expulsion of the Jews from England in 1290 and from France in 1306. Lacking political unity, Germany could hardly follow suit. Indeed, the less mature German economy could and did still benefit from the Jews, despite the serious increase in Jewish insecurity and instability. Ashkenazic Jews tended to move farther eastward, repeating in Poland the pioneering role that they had played in the more westerly countries. By 1500 the major center of Ashkenazic Jewry was to be found in the kingdom of Poland, with enclaves spread throughout the fragmented German empire and Jewish settlement banned in the more advanced areas of France and England.

Ashkenazic Jewry, from the eleventh century on, created its own distinctive set of institutions and mores. Encountering a new and trying environment, the Ashkenazic Jews forged new forms of Jewish self-government, new patterns of religious ritual, and new ideals of intellectual creativity. By 1500 this Ashkenazic tradition had already solidified; it was destined to play a major role in the development of modern and contemporary Jewish life.

BIBLIOGRAPHY

Salo W. Baron, *A Social and Religious History of the Jews,* 2nd ed., IV (1957), 43–88, IX (1965), 135–236, X (1965), 3–117; Robert Chazan, *Medieval Jewry in Northern France* (1973); Bernard D. Weinryb, *The Jews of Poland* (1973), 17–176; Hirsch J. Zimmels, *Ashkenazim and Sephardim* (1958).

ROBERT CHAZAN

[See also **Jews in Europe (900 to 1500).**]

ASMATIKON, liturgical music book probably of Constantinopolitan origin containing a chant repertory performed by the *psaltai,* or select singers, in a choral tradition of the imperial rite at Hagia Sophia. Together with the soloist's *Psaltikon* this collection shows the elaborate chant styles of the urban usage in the eleventh to the thirteenth centuries. A handful of thirteenth-century Greek copies exist, primarily of South Italian provenance. Parts of the *Asmatikon* survive in Slavic *Kontakaria* manuscripts from the eleventh century onward.

BIBLIOGRAPHY

Dimitri Conomos, "Communion Chants in Magna Graecia and Byzantium," in *Journal of the American Musicological Society,* **33** (1980); Simon Harris, "The Communion Chants in Thirteenth-Century Byzantine Musical MSS," in *Studies in Eastern Chant,* II, Egon Wellesz and Miloš Velimirović, eds. (1971); Kenneth Levy, "A Hymn for Thursday in Holy Week," in *Journal of the American Musicological Society,* **16** (1963); and "The Byzantine Communion-Cycle and its Slavic Counterpart," in *XIIe Congrès international des études byzantines, Ochride, 1961,* II (1964); Bartolomeo di Salvo, "Asmaticon," in *Bollettino della Badia greca di Grottaferrata,* **16** (1962).

NICOLAS SCHIDLOVSKY

[See also **Kontakion; Psaltikon.**]

ÁSMUNDAR SAGA KAPPABANA ("the saga of Asmund, the slayer of champions"), a brief Norse legendary saga. Though clearly a product of the late thirteenth or early fourteenth century, the story must have circulated before 1200 in an earlier, oral or written version, since it is also found in Saxo's *Gesta Danorum,* VII, ix, 12–20. The plot combines heroic and supernatural elements. King Buðli of Sweden forces two mysterious smiths visiting his court to forge a pair of extraordinary swords. The smiths curse the swords, one of which is condemned always to yield in battle before the other; they also predict that these weapons will bring about the death of Buðli's grandsons. The king then has the more powerful sword sunk into the sea. His daughter, Hild, bears her first son, Hildibrand, while married to the Viking king Helgi. Later on, when Helgi is away, King Alf of Denmark invades Sweden, kills Buðli, and gives Hild to his champion Aki, with whom she has a second son, Asmund. Hildibrand and Asmund are never told that they are half brothers.

In revenge for the killing of Buðli, his grandfather, Hildibrand kills King Alf. When Asmund later wishes to marry Æsa the Fair, Alf's daughter, she replies that he must first avenge her father, and tells him how to recover the enchanted sword. With this weapon in his power, Asmund travels to Saxland and offers to fight against Hildibrand, who has forcibly wrested much territory and authority from the local dukes. Hildibrand seems to suspect that he may be related to Asmund; to avoid fratricide, he sends his champions, all of whom are described as berserkers, against his challenger. The berserkers confront Asmund in steadily increasing numbers, but he kills them all, so that Hildibrand, who has no more men to send, is finally forced to attack him. The loss of his champions has angered him so much that he kills his own son in a fit of berserk fury.

In the fight between the half brothers, Hildibrand wields the sword that is fated to yield, and it breaks against Asmund's helmet. After killing Hildibrand, Asmund returns to Æsa and finds her listening to another suitor. He kills the suitor and marries her, so the story ends on a happy note.

In Saxo's version, the characters are almost identical in spite of different names: Haldanus (Asmund), Hildigerus (Hildibrand), Guritha (Æsa), Drota (Hild), and Regnaldus (Buðli); the king of Denmark is named Alf in both versions. Saxo has kept the motif of the inherited swords, but without the curse. His account also lacks the sense of an inevitable fate, and brings out the temperamental differences between the half brothers: Haldanus is heroic and conscious of personal honor; Hildigerus has inherited the cruelty of his father, a bloodthirsty pirate. The occasion for the duel between them is also different: Guritha does not demand revenge for her father but wants Haldanus to acquire more fame, for she will not marry an obscure man. It is in the course of a quest for prowess and distinction that Haldanus meets his half brother. Like Hildibrand in *Ásmundar saga,* Hildigerus decides to fight only after all the champions on his side have been killed by Haldanus.

In *Ásmundar saga* the dying Hildibrand recites a death song in six *fornyrðislag* stanzas of four lines, some of which are in a fragmentary condition. Saxo provides a free Latin paraphrase of what is apparently the same song, in thirty-four hexameter lines. Comparison of the Latin death song with the vernacular text in the saga has led Andreas Heusler to the conclusion that the original poem probably had nine stanzas. There are a number of contradictions between the plot of *Ásmundar saga* and the death song, and they seem to indicate that the poem is older than the saga, where the story has been adjusted in some respects to the death song.

The story of the fatal encounter of the half brothers is a late Nordic version of the tragic fight between father and son that constitutes the Hildebrand episode in the Dietrich of Bern cycle. The more famous South Germanic version of the incident is preserved in the Old High German *Hildebrandslied.* There is a verbal echo of the German poem *(suâsat chind)* in Hildibrand's death song: *enn svási sonr* (the dear child/son).

Ásmundar saga contains four other *fornyrðislag* stanzas, recited by Asmund after killing Hildibrand, in which he complains of the unequal battle he has had to fight against his half brother's men. Heusler does not consider these stanzas a unified composition but treats them as *lausavísur* (loose stanzas).

Ásmundar saga is preserved in a vellum manuscript of the early fourteenth century (Royal Library of Stockholm, Holm 7) and partially in a fifteenth-century fragment in the Arnamagnaean collection (AM 586).

BIBLIOGRAPHY

The critical edition is Ferdinand Detter, ed., *Swei Fornaldarsögur* (1891); the standard edition, Guðni Jónsson and Bjarni Vilhjálmsson, eds., *Fornaldarsögur Norðurlanda,* II (1944), 287–308. For Saxo's version, see Carl Knabe and Paul Herrmann, eds., *Saxonis Gesta Danorum,* revised and published by Jørgen Olrik and Hans Ræder, I (1931), 203–206; English translation by Oliver Elton, *The First Nine Books of the Danish History of Saxo Grammaticus* (1894), 291–296. Secondary literature includes Marlene Ciklamini, "The Combat Between Two Half-Brothers," in *Neophilologus,* **50** (1966); and Eyvind F. Halvorsen, "On the Sources of the Ásmundarsaga Kappabana," in *Studia norvegica,* **2** (1951).

JOAQUÍN MARTÍNEZ PIZARRO

[See also **Saxo Grammaticus.**]

ASOLIK. See **Stephen of Taron.**

AŠOT I MEC (THE GREAT) (*ca.* 819–890), founder and first king of the Bagratid kindom of Armenia (884–890), was the second son of prince Smbat the Confessor. Ašot did not play any important role until after his father's exile to Samarra. In 855 he replaced his father as commander in chief *(sparapet)* of the Armenian forces. With the help of his younger brother Abas, Ašot tried to restore the Bagratid family to its former position of power and reestablished the calm that had been disrupted by the Armenian revolts and the punitive expedition of the Abbasid general Bughā in the 850's.

Ašot's careful and circumspect administration earned him in 858 the title and position of prince of princes *(baṭrīḳ al-baṭāriḳa),* which made him, after the Arab governor, the second most powerful man in Transcaucasia. The Bagratid prince gradually reinforced his position at the expense of the Arab emirates and the other Armenian feudal families.

Early in his reign as prince of princes, Ašot defeated Djaḥḥāf ibn Sawāda, thereby preventing the Arab Djaḥḥāfids from becoming established on Armenian soil. The aftereffect of Ašot's action was quite strong on the other Arab emirates in Armenia, all of which accepted his suzerainty. In 879 the failure of the plot of some of these rulers, who were now joined by Muḥammad ibn Khālid, the Arab governor of Armenia, reinforced Ašot's position and made him the sole master of Transcaucasia.

To achieve his long-range goals of establishing a monarchy, Ašot used diplomacy, the traditional resort of the Bagratids. In the 850's he took full advantage of the absence from Armenia of the Armenian feudal lords in exile. After their return, he kept them in line through marriage alliances; he married one of his daughters to the powerful prince of Siwnik^{c} and another to the Arcruni prince of Vaspurakan. He even resolved the internal rivalry between his branch of the family and the southern Bagratids of Tarōn, who were in the service of the Byzantine Empire.

Ašot's foreign policy had always been in line with the pro-Arab orientation of the eighth- and ninth-century Bagratids. In the eyes of the caliphate, he served the court well by keeping peace and order in Transcaucasia. Ašot remained loyal to the caliph at a time when the Byzantines had just begun to restore the eastern territories of the empire on the Euphratene frontier. Realizing the danger that Byzantine expansionism could pose for the outcome of his ambitions, Ašot tried to restrain the Armenian feudal lords from taking sides against the caliphate. He did not refrain from executing a Mamikonean prince who had crossed over to the Byzantine side. Ašot thus pursued an independent policy with the Byzantine Empire. His correspondence with the Byzantine patriarch Photius and the Armenian Church Council of Širakawan in 862 corroborate his far-reaching political aspirations. Recognition from the Byzantine emperor would strengthen Ašot's position in Transcaucasia; the conferral of the title *archōn tōn archontōn* gave him what he sought. In 884 he had himself anointed king of Armenia. The caliph also recognized him as master of Armenia and sent him a crown, although Ašot was still required to pay taxes to the caliphate.

Ašot's kingdom comprised most of the central territory of greater Armenia and southeastern Georgia. As the head of the Bagratid house and the prince of princes of Armenia, he paved the way for Bagratid solidarity in Transcaucasia, enabling the Bagratids to found princedoms and kingdoms throughout the Transcaucasian lands.

BIBLIOGRAPHY

The major source is Yovhannēs Drasxanakertec^{c}i, *Patmut^{c}iwn* [History (of Armenia)] (1867), 166–181. See also Vazgen Hakobian, "La date de l'avènement d'Ašot, premier roi bagradite," in *Revue des études arméniennes,* n.s. 2 (1965); Aram Ter-Ghewondyan, *The Arab Emirates in Bagratid Armenia*, Nina G. Garsoïan, trans. (1976), 51–59; and Hagob Thopdschian, "Die innern Zustände von Armenien unter Ašot I," in *Mitteilungen des Seminars für orientalische Sprachen*, 7, pt. 2 (1904); and "Politische und Kirchengeschichte Armeniens unter Ašot I und Smbat I," *ibid.*, 8, pt. 2 (1905).

KRIKOR H. MAKSOUDIAN

[See also **Armenian Muslim Emirates; Bagratids/Bagratuni (Armenian).**]

AŠOT II ERKAT^{c} (d. *ca.* 929), son of Smbat I the Martyr and king of Bagratid Armenia from 914 to 929. In 896 he was taken hostage and then released by Afshīn, the Sādjid emir of Azerbaijān. Afshīn's successor Yūsuf honored him with the title *išxan išxanac^{c}* (prince of princes) of Armenia. After the martyrdom of Smbat I in 914, Ašot was crowned king of Armenia and succeeded in avenging his father's execution at the hands of Yūsuf. He reinstated the Bagratids in their former position of control over much of Armenia.

In 914–915 Ašot went on a diplomatic mission to Constantinople and asked for Byzantine help and military intervention. On that occasion, the emperor bestowed on him the honorific "son of a martyr" and officially recognized him as his "beloved son"—as *archōn tōn archontōn* of Armenia.

After his return to Armenia, Ašot was confronted

with serious difficulties. Yūsuf set up Ašot's cousin and namesake as king and encouraged him to open hostilities against the legitimate king. Yūsuf's incarceration from 918 to 922 gave Ašot some respite and enabled him to control his rebellious princes. Yūsuf's deputy Subuki conferred on him the title *šahanšah* (king of kings) in recognition of his predominance over all the other kings and princes. Soon thereafter, in 921–922, Ašot's relations with Byzantium were strained, and he probably lost his title of *archōn tōn archontōn.*

After Yūsuf's release from prison, hostilities with the Sādjids were resumed. Ašot was forced to withdraw to the island of Sewan on Lake Sevan, where he organized a strong defense. The ensuing military successes and the gradual decline of the Sādjids helped Ašot to make his kingdom secure from outside intervention.

For his valor and determination, the Armenian historians distinguish Ašot II from his namesakes with the epithet *Erkat*ᶜ ("Iron"). According to the Byzantine sources, his strength was so great that he could bend iron rods with his bare hands.

BIBLIOGRAPHY

Nikolai G. Adontz, "Ašot Erkatᶜ ou de fer, roi d'Arménie de 913 à 929," in *Études arméno-byzantines* (1965), 265–283.

KRIKOR H. MAKSOUDIAN

AŠOT III OŁORMAC (THE MERCIFUL) (*d.* 977), also called Ašot Gagik, the son of King Abas I and grandson of Smbat the Martyr, and fifth king of Bagratid Armenia (953–977). His reign marked the complete exemption of Armenia from paying tribute to the caliphate and the establishment of the Bagratid court in a permanent capital: in 961 he transferred the center of the kingdom from Kars to Ani, a former fortress. Because of the international transit trade, Ani became the largest and the most prosperous city in Armenia. The choice of a new site was perhaps due to Ašot's failure to occupy Dwin, the ancient capital of Armenia, in 953. The move itself was instrumental in centralizing the centrifugal tendencies present in the feudal structure of the Bagratid kingdom.

Ašot's formal coronation immediately following his transfer to his new capital symbolized the establishment of his suzerainty. Shortly thereafter, the patriarchal see of the Armenian Church, which had been transferred to Vaspurakan in 924, was relocated to Argina, a suburb of Ani. With the spiritual head of the Armenian people at his door, Ašot could easily exert pressure on the small kingdoms and princedoms in Armenia to recognize his supremacy and overlordship. His efforts to strengthen the central authority were enhanced by the danger posed by Byzantine expansionism to the continuity of the petty Armenian princedoms. When the Byzantine emperor John I Tzimisces approached the borders of Armenia in 974, all of the kings and princes joined forces with the Bagratid king and confronted the emperor with an army of 80,000 men. Tzimisces had to come to terms with Ašot and, recognizing his predominance, made an alliance with him.

The epithet *Ołormac* ("Merciful") is given to Ašot for his philanthropic deeds. He is said to have shared his meals and living quarters with the poor. Yet despite his piety Ašot was quite active in military matters. He led campaigns against the Caucasian mountaineers and in 959 defeated a certain Hamtun, who was either a Ḥamdānid general, or Sayf al-Dawla in person. These accomplishments gave him the opportunity to secure his territories in the north and west.

Ašot's reign also witnessed the further development of Armenian monasticism and medieval learning. His queen, Xosrovanoyš, founded the monasteries of Sanahin (966) and Hałbat (976), which became important centers of theological learning.

BIBLIOGRAPHY

Vladimir Minorsky, *Studies in Caucasian History* (1953); Aram Ter-Ghewondyan, *The Arab Emirates in Bagratid Armenia*, Nina G. Garsoïan, trans. (1976).

KRIKOR H. MAKSOUDIAN

ASSASSINS, a name given by medieval Europe to a group of Muslim sectaries whom the Crusaders encountered in Syria. The Assassins belonged to a branch of the Ismaili sect, itself a subdivision of the Shīᶜa. They had their main strongholds in the mountains of central Syria, and their leader was known to the Crusaders as the Old Man of the Mountain. The Ismailis separated from the rest of the Shīᶜa in the mid eighth century and took their name from Ismāᶜīl ibn Jaᶜfar, whom they recognized as the seventh imam in the line from the Prophet's son-in-law and kinsman, ᶜAlī. In its heyday, the Ismaili sect achieved very great influence in

Islam. On the one hand it affected many poets, philosophers, theologians, and scholars. On the other, it won a major practical success in the foundation of the Fatimid caliphate, the sovereigns of which based their claim to the headship of Islam on descent from the Prophet through Ismāᶜīl.

A major split in the Ismaili camp occurred toward the end of the eleventh century, when the Fatimid movement had lost its dynamism and the Fatimid state, like others before it, was falling under the control of its own military. In form the split was a dispute over the succession to Caliph al-Mustanṣir, who died in 1094. More than that, it was a conflict between conservatives and radicals. The former supported the new caliph and the old order in Cairo; the latter gave their allegiance to another, ousted son of al-Mustanṣir, Nizār, whom they acclaimed as the sole legitimate heir to the caliphate and imamate. In fact, the Cairo branch abandoned the radical ideas and worldwide ambitions of the earlier Ismailis and became loyal supporters of a local Egyptian dynasty.

The followers of Nizār were mainly to be found among the Ismailis beyond the Fatimid frontier, in the newly created Seljuk Empire in the East. There, under a remarkable leader, Ḥasan-i Ṣabbāḥ, a new phase in Ismaili history began. While the Cairo branch stagnated and eventually disappeared, the Nizārīs entered on a period of intensive development—expressed in doctrine, in a new theology and eschatology, and in action—through a violent challenge to the existing order. Of special significance was their adoption of the tactic that came to be known after them as assassination. Murder as a religious duty was not new to the Middle East. It was practiced in antiquity and was ascribed to the strangler sects of southern Iraq in the eighth century. The Nizārī Ismailis brought the technique of personal terrorism to a degree of perfection without previous parallel.

The open history of the Nizārī Ismailis begins in 1090, when Ḥasan-i Ṣabbāḥ seized the castle of Alamūt south of the Caspian Sea and northwest of Qazvīn. Working from here he was able to acquire other castles in Iran and in Iraq and by the end of the eleventh century commanded a network of strongholds in the east, a corps of fanatical and utterly devoted terrorists known as fidāᵓīs (those who sacrifice), and a fifth column of unknown size in the cities and camps of Islam. By the beginning of the twelfth century, the Ismailis in Persia extended their activities to Syria, where after a few false starts they were able to seize and organize a group of castles and use them, after the Persian model, as a base from which to send their emissaries against the rulers and notables of Islam. Their challenge was to the Sunni state and order, and their main victims were Muslims. Attacks on Christians were comparatively few and were, so to speak, incidental.

At first it was devotion rather than murder that struck the European imagination. As early as the twelfth century, Provençal poets compare themselves to Assassins in their loyalty to their ladies (Chambers, pp. 245–251; Olschki, p. 215; Scheludko, p. 423). But before long it was murder, not devotion, that made the main impact on Western visitors to the Levant and gave the word "assassin" the meaning that it has retained ever since.

Initially, the term was limited to the sectaries in Syria. Most of the Western chroniclers of the Crusades from William of Tyre onward have something to say about the Assassins, and a few striking events spread the fame of the Old Man of the Mountain far and wide. Before long, assassins were alleged to be involved in political murders and attempted murders even far away in western Europe. At some time—it is difficult to say precisely when—the word ceased to have a specifically Syrian and Islamic connotation and was used in the general sense of professional murderer. This would seem to have happened by the thirteenth century. In canto XIX of the *Inferno*, Dante speaks of "the treacherous assassin" *(lo perfido assassin)*; his fourteenth-century commentator, Francesco da Buti, explaining a word that for many readers at that time must still have been obscure, remarks: "An assassin is one who kills others for money." In book IX of the *Chroniche* the Florentine chronicler Giovanni Villani tells how the lord of Lucca sent "his assassins" *(i suoi assassini)* to Pisa to kill a troublesome enemy.

The Assassins appear quite frequently in Western literature. One of the earliest descriptions of them is given in the report of an envoy sent to Egypt and Syria in 1175 by Emperor Frederick Barbarossa. (The report of Gerhard or possibly Burkhard, vice-dominus of Strasbourg, is cited by Arnold of Lübeck in his *Chronica slavorum.*) A few years later William of Tyre included a brief account of them in his history of the crusading states. The murder of Conrad of Montferrat in 1192 made a profound impression, and most of the chronicles of the Third Crusade have something to say about the Assassins, their beliefs, their methods, and their chiefs.

As the stay of the Crusaders in the Levant grew longer, more information about the Assassins became available, and there were some Westerners who met them and talked with them. The Knights Templars and the Hospitalers managed to establish a kind of suzerainty over the Assassin castles and even collected tribute from them. William of Tyre tells of an approach by the Old Man of the Mountain to the king of Jerusalem proposing some form of alliance. William's continuator has a somewhat improbable story about how Count Henry II of Champagne, returning from Armenia in 1198, was entertained in his castle by the Old Man of the Mountain, who ordered a number of his henchmen to leap to their deaths from the ramparts for the edification of his guest and then hospitably offered to place others at his disposal. "And if there was any man who had done him an injury he should let him know and he would have him killed." The polemical purpose of these stories is clear.

Somewhat more plausibly, the English historian Matthew Paris reports the arrival in Europe in 1238 of an emissary from some Muslim rulers including the Assassin chief, seeking help from the Westerners against the new threat of the Mongols from the East. By 1250, when Louis IX led a crusade to the Holy Land, he was able to exchange embassies and gifts with the Assassin chief of that time. Jean Joinville provides an interesting description of these conversations, including a report by an Arabic-speaking friar, Yves the Breton, who accompanied the king's messengers to the Assassins and discussed religion with them. As late as 1332, long after the suppression of the Assassins by the Mongols in the East and the Mamluks in Syria, the writer known as Brocardus, in his advice to Philip VI of France, then contemplating a new crusade to recapture the lost holy places, warned him in particular against the danger of the Assassins, "who are to be cursed and fled." By this time Brocardus sees them simply as hired murderers. "They sell themselves, are thirsty for human blood, kill the innocent for a price and care nothing for either life or salvation."

The Crusaders were aware of the Assassins only as a group of fanatical murderers in Syria. They show little or no knowledge of their place in Islam or of their possible connections with other Islamic groups elsewhere in the Middle East. One of the best informed of medieval Western writers on Islam, Jacques de Vitry, bishop of Acre, noted at the beginning of the thirteenth century that the sect had begun in Persia, but that seems to be the limit of his knowledge. By the second half of the century, new and firsthand information was available concerning the parent branch of the sect in Persia. The informants were European visitors to the Far East taking advantage of the Mongol conquests to establish direct overland contact with the court of the Great Khan.

The first to mention the sect in Persia was William of Rubruquis, a Flemish priest sent by Louis IX of France in 1253–1255. He mistakenly uses the term "assassins," at least as given in the extant text. But this was a local Syrian name, the use of which was confined to the Ismailis of Syria. It was never applied to those of Persia or of any other country. Nor does William connect the Persian sect with their better-known comrades in Syria. This was done by a much more famous traveler, Marco Polo, who passed through Persia in 1273 and described the headquarters of the Persian Ismailis in the mountain fortress and valley of Alamūt. His description includes the celebrated story of the prefabricated gardens of paradise to which the drugged devotees were introduced and given a foretaste of eternal bliss before being dispatched on a mission. He—or his narrator—calls them *ashishim*, refers explicitly to their emissaries in "the territory of Damascus," and even calls their chief the "Old Man."

Marco Polo was right in connecting the Syrian Assassins with the Persian Ismailis, of whom they were an offshoot, but he too was mistaken in calling the Persians "assassins," the name used to describe the sect in Syria. The title "Old Man of the Mountain" that Marco Polo uses of the Ismaili leader in Persia was also purely Syrian and may indeed have been in use only among the crusaders, since it has not yet come to light in any Arabic text of the period. It could be based on a misunderstanding of the Arabic word *shaykh*, which combines the meanings of old man, elder, and chief. Some half a century later a similar account was given by another traveler across Persia, Odoric of Pordenone. From these travel books the stories of the gardens of paradise, the death leap of the devotees, the superlative skill of the Assassins, and the mysterious figure of their chief, the Old Man of the Mountain, became widely known in Europe.

The term "assassin" was for a long time a subject of speculation, and many different interpretations were offered by scholars, some of them fantastic and all of them wrong. The key to the mystery was finally provided by the great French orientalist Antoine-Isaac Silvestre de Sacy, in "Mémoire sur la dynastie des Assassins et sur l'origine de leur nom," presented to the Institute in 1809. Using hitherto unknown Arabic manuscripts, he showed that the word "assassin" was connected with the Arabic *ḥashīsh*. The word *ḥashīsh* in Arabic has the general meaning of grass or herbage and the more specific meaning of Indian hemp. Sacy derived the variant forms in which the word "assassin" was found in the literature of the Crusades from two Arabic forms, *ḥashīshī* (plural, *ḥashīshiyya* or *ḥashīshiyyūn/īn*) and *ḥashshāsh* (plural, *ḥashshāshūn/īn*). In support of this explanation he was able to adduce a number of Arabic texts of the period in which the Ismailis of Syria are called *ḥashīshiyya*, but none in which they are called *ḥashshāsh*. None has since come to light. This is important because *ḥashshāsh* (plural, *ḥashshāshūn/īn*) is the term commonly used in Arabic for a hashish smoker or addict, whereas *ḥashīshī* (plural, *ḥashīshiyya* or *ḥashīshiyyūn/īn*) is a term that does not necessarily indicate actual use of the drug. Moreover, it is a term local to Syria, and even there it was never used by the Ismailis in referring to themselves. It would seem, therefore, that the Western form of the term "assassin" derived from Arabic *ḥashīshī* and not, as Sacy suggested, from *ḥashshāsh*.

There remains the question of why precisely they were called by this name. Sacy explained the use of the term as being due to the secret use of hashish by the sectaries and, in particular, to its use in giving emissaries, about to depart on a mission of murder, a sample of the pleasures that they would enjoy on arriving in paradise as successful martyrs. This explanation seemed to derive support from Marco Polo's story of the gardens of paradise, which also occurs in other sources both Eastern and Western. The earliest version of the story appears to be that of Arnold of Lübeck, dating from the latter part of the twelfth century. According to Arnold, their chief gives them daggers that are consecrated to the mission in hand "and then intoxicates them with such a potion that they are plunged into ecstasy and oblivion, displays to them by his magic certain fantastic dreams, full of pleasures and delights, or rather of trumpery, and promises them eternal possession of these things in reward for such deeds." This story, probably one of the earliest known descriptions of hashish dreams, is repeated with variations by later writers. It is almost certainly no more than a popular tale, and it seems likely that the tale was invented on the basis of a misunderstanding of the term *ḥashīshī* (plural *ḥashīshiyya*). The use and effects of hashish were known at the time and were no secret. Its use by the Ismailis, with or without secret gardens and the rest, is not attested either by Ismaili authors or by serious Muslim authors of other denominations at that time. Arabic writings of the period on hashish make no reference to its use by the Ismailis or to any connection between the drug and the sect. It would seem, therefore, that the name must be otherwise explained. *Ḥashīshiyya* was a term of abuse applied to the Ismailis in Syria by their neighbors. It was probably a comment on their behavior rather than a description of their practices, the implication being that they behaved in a strange and demented way—like hashish addicts.

Scholarly interest in the Assassins seems to have begun in the early seventeenth century with the publication at Lyons of the first monograph on the subject, Denis Lebey de Batilly's *Traité de l'origine des anciens assassins porte-couteaux* . . . (1603). The pagan ethics of the Renaissance had restored murder as an instrument of policy; the wars of religion had elevated it to a pious duty. The emergence of the new monarchies, in which one man could determine the politics and even the religion of the state, made assassination an effective, as well as an acceptable, weapon. Lebey de Batilly's pioneer study attempted no more than to explain the true historic meaning of a word that had recently become current again. It was followed by a number of further monographs, mainly by French scholars.

The beginning of the nineteenth century saw a new rise in interest in the Assassins, no doubt encouraged by the French Revolution and its aftermath and the resulting revival of public interest in conspiracy and murder. Sacy's pioneer study marked a major step forward in the understanding of the subject. It opened the way for further studies, certainly the best-known of which was *Die Geschichte der Assassinen aus morgenländischen Quellen* (1818), written by the Austrian interpreter Joseph von Hammer and published in French (1833) and English translations (1835). Hammer's history, although based on original sources, is very much a tract for the times. Despite its polemical purposes it remained for about a century and a half the main source of information available in the West on the Assassins. Meanwhile, scholarly research had progressed thanks to the discovery, edition, translation, and use of a number of Arabic and Persian texts and, more particularly, through the discovery of the Ismaili communities in Syria, Iran, and, above all, in India and the literature and traditions preserved by them. Archaeological work was also done on the Ismaili castles in Iran and, to a lesser extent, in Syria.

BIBLIOGRAPHY

See "Hashīshiyya" and "Ismā^{c}īliyya," in *Encyclopedia of Islam* (1971, 1978); Marshall G. S. Hodgson, *The Order of Assassins* (1955); Bernard Lewis, "The Sources for the History of the Syrian Assassins," in *Speculum,* **27** (1952); *The Assassins* (1967); and "Assassins of Syria and Ismā^{c}īlīs of Persia," Accademia Nazionale dei Lincei, *La Persia nel Medioevo* (1971); and Charles E. Nowell, "The Old Man of the Mountain," in *Speculum,* **22** (1947). On the place of the Ismailis in Islamic religious development, see Hamilton A. R. Gibb, *Mohammedanism* (1961); Henri Laoust, *Les schismes dans l'Islam* (1965); and William M. Watt, *Islamic Philosophy and Theology* (1962).

On the role of the Assassins in the Crusades, see Kenneth M. Setton, ed., *A History of the Crusades:* I, *The First Hundred Years,* M. W. Baldwin, ed. (1969). On the influence of the Assassins on Provençal poets, see Frank M. Chambers, "The Troubadors and the Assassins," in *Modern Language Notes,* **64** (1949); Leonardo Olschki, *Storia letteraria delle scoperte geografiche* (1937); and Dimitri Scheludko, "Über die arabischen Lehnwörter im Altprovenzalischen," in *Zeitschrift für romanische Philologie,* **47** (1927).

BERNARD LEWIS

[See also **Ismā^{c}iliya; Shi^{c}a.**]

ASSER (d. *ca.* 909), one of the scholars whom Alfred the Great attracted to his court to revive learning in Wessex in the 880's. Originally a monk of St. David's in Wales, he eventually became bishop of Sherborne in Wessex. He aided Alfred in his translation of Gregory's *Cura pastoralis* and possibly also Boethius' *Consolatio philosophiae.* The *Life of Alfred* is generally held to have been written by him in 893, though some have argued that it is a later forgery. The text is poorly organized and may have been only a draft, but it provides information found in no other source.

BIBLIOGRAPHY

Text in *Asser's Life of King Alfred,* ed. William Henry Stevenson, new impression with an article on *Recent Work on Asser's Life of Alfred* by Dorothy Whitelock (1959); Dorothy Whitelock, *English Historical Documents,* **1**, *ca. 500–1042,* 2nd ed. (1979), 289–303 (selections). The authenticity of the text is impugned in Vivian Hunter Galbraith, *An Introduction to the Study of History* (1964), 85–128; and defended by Dorothy Whitelock, *The Genuine Asser* (1968).

DAVID A. E. PELTERET

[See also **Alfred the Great; Alfred the Great and Translations.**]

ASSISI, SAN FRANCESCO, majestic double church erected over tomb of St. Francis (d. 1226, canonized 1228). Commissioned by Pope Gregory IX in 1228, consecrated 1253. Between *ca.* 1240 and *ca.* 1340 scores of artists from Rome and Tuscany transformed the walls of this simple, Latin-cross-planned church into the most sumptuously decorated church in Italy and one of the great puzzles for art historians. Upper church decoration includes stained glass windows in the choir and transepts glazed by Franco-Germans and Italians *ca.* 1240–1295. Illustrating the youth, ministry, and passion of Christ, they form a narrative unit with Cimabue's frescoes of *ca.* 1270–1280 in the choir and transept illustrating the life of the Virgin, and the evangelists, and culminating in two large *Crucifixions* on the transept walls.

The nave, divided into six bays, each pierced by windows glazed *ca.* 1290 by Roman school artists, contains a vast fresco cycle dealing with Old and New Testament scenes and the legend of St. Francis. The upper right walls illustrate sixteen scenes from the Old Testament, the upper left, sixteen from the New Testament. Below to left and right are twenty-eight episodes of the St. Francis legend. Lacking specific documents, dates, and signatures, these frescoes present complex problems of attribution and dating. The first bay nearest the crossing is most often attributed to the S. Cecilia Master; the vault of the second bay to Torriti, the walls to the Master of the St. Francis Legend or Giotto; the vaults and walls of the third and fourth bays to the Isaac Master or Giotto and his shop. Giotto's role is controversial and not easily reconciled with his other accepted fresco cycles in Padua and S. Croce, Florence.

The lower church decoration includes a badly damaged fresco of Madonna and Child and Standing St. Francis on the east wall of the north transept by Cimabue *ca.* 1280. South transept decorations include a Madonna and Child with SS. John and Francis and scenes from the life and passion of Christ by Pietro Lorenzetti. The exact dating and nature of Pietro's involvement in some scenes is open to speculation, but the *Deposition* and *Entombment* of *ca.* 1322–1327 are his greatest surviving works. The Madgalen Chapel and St. Nicholas Chapel preserve frescoes attributed to followers of Giotto, while the St. Martin Chapel, painted sometime between 1320 and 1330 by Simone Martini with scenes from his life, remains one of the most splendid decorative entities to survive from the Trecento. Simone apparently designed the floor, windows, and vaults, as well as painting the marvelously colored, lyrical frescoes. Simone is also credited with frescoes in the transept depicting SS. Francis, Louis of Toulouse, Elizabeth of Hungary, Clare, and Louis of France in bust length, and a half-length fresco of Madonna and Child between two crowned martyrs, all of which are likely the product of his shop or a follower.

S. Francesco is part of a complex including a friary, Sacro Convento with thirteenth-century chapterhouse, an eighteenth-century refectory, a fourteenth-century portico, a fifteenth-century cloister probably designed by Antonio da Como, and a treasury.

BIBLIOGRAPHY

Complete Survey. Beda Kleinschmidt, *Die Basilika San Francesco in Assisi*, 3 vols. (1915–1928).

Architecture. Edgar Hertlein, *Die Basilika San Francesco in Assisi* (1964).

The St. Francis Legend. George Kaftal, *Iconography of the Saints in Tuscan Painting* (1952); Henry Thode, *Franz von Assisi und die Anfänge der Kunst der Renaissance in Italien,* 2nd ed. (1934).

Assisi Problem. Richard Offner, "Giotto, Non-Giotto," in *Burlington Magazine*, **74** (1939); Alastair Smart, *The Assisi Problem and the Art of Giotto* (1971).

General. Bruce Cole, *Giotto and Florentine Painting* (1975); Hayden Maginnis, "Assisi Revisted: Notes on Recent Observations," in *Burlington Magazine,* **117** (1975); and "The Passion Cycle in the Lower Church of San Francesco Assisi: The Technical Evidence," in *Zeitschrift für Kunstgeschichte*, **39** (1976); Carlo Volpe, *Pietro Lorenzetti ad Assisi* (1965); John White, *Art and Architecture in Italy, 1250–1400* (1966).

ADELHEID M. GEALT

ASSIZE. As the English and French monarchies increasingly identified their power and legitimacy with law from the mid twelfth century, "assize" was one of the workhorse terms in their legal vocabulary. Although the original sense of the word is simply a session, in England it came to mean not only a session of the king's court but also an edict made there, the new form of legal action promulgated by the edict, any session of a jury summoned in a case brought by this form of action, and the session of the judges to hear this action. In France the term retained its original sense and its use was thus more restricted, but assize was the name given to sessions of the courts that first brought a significant royal judicial presence into the countryside.

This great use of assize stems initially from the truly remarkable work of Henry II of England. Sometime in the decade before 1166 Henry and his advisers created the assize of novel disseisin, the first and by far most significant of the three assizes (the others were the grand assize and mort d'ancestor) in which jury trial was substituted for trial by battle in settling disputes of land ownership. In contrast to the cumbersome and irrational procedures of old forms of action over land, the new assize was unusually speedy and rational in its mode of proof. Thus it is no surprise that the king's assize became immensely popular and was soon the most frequently used form of action in the king's court. Taking the assizes was one of the most important tasks soon given to justices who went on circuit through the counties on the general eyre. The assize seems amply to have fulfilled what were presumably the king's aims: better protection of freehold property, better keeping of the peace, and increased royal authority.

Certainly the legal advances that Henry accomplished as king in England and duke in Normandy (where novel disseisin was also introduced) appeared an unqualified success to the watchful king of France. Philip II was almost certainly copying his great rival when he established the French royal courts known as assizes sometime before 1190. In that year, as he prepared for the governance of the realm during his absence on the Third Crusade, Philip regulated the work of the baillis, central-court justices who were already going out in groups to hold assizes from place to place. In these assizes the baillis judged not only the freemen of the king's own territories, the royal domain, but also the great laymen and ecclesiastics within a broad radius of the spot where the justices sat. By the mid thirteenth century these itinerant baillis had given way to single baillis or (as in the newly conquered territory in the south) seneschals with a territorial charge. A single judge now presided over the assizes held periodically in the chief towns of his territory. From the beginning the assizes were vastly superior to the older, local courts of the *prévots*, which had lacked competence over the great, or even over rustics, outside the domain. The likelihood of local resistance to the new assizes was lessened by associating leading local men with the king's officers who presided and by paying close attention in the assizes to financial and juridical complaints against the *prévots*. The Capetian kings of France did not have the precocious procedures against disseisin introduced by Henry II, but they had taken a new and important step in establishing the assizes as royal courts with significant local jurisdiction.

The original impulse on either side of the Channel was thus similar, and the initial development of assize in both realms was closely linked. Yet the later histories of assize in France and England diverged sharply, reflecting the basic differences in the law and history of the two countries. By the close of the Middle Ages the assizes were becoming the chief local civil and criminal courts in England, while in France they were withering and would soon die out.

The English eyre had proved so useful for administrative tasks and for civil and criminal justice that the eyre judges were soon heavily burdened and unable to visit the counties regularly. Yet the assizes had to be taken, among much other business. Special, ad hoc panels of local knights or gentlemen to hear individual suits were one solution; panels of professionals specifically charged with the sole task of taking assizes (rather than the full range of eyre business) were another. By the mid thirteenth century the panels of professional assize justices seemed to work best and were preferred, though a professional might take local associates. This system was advanced during the reign of Edward I; assize justices now visited groups of counties in circuits and heard cases by writs of *nisi prius*. But the English government was hard pressed to meet all the demands of litigants and the many requirements of public order, given its reliance on a small body of central justices supervising the work of local men. Thus the crown first experimented with panels of local knights and then began to empower assize justices to deliver the gaols as well, that is to add the important criminal jurisdiction to trying gaoled felons to their already sizable load of civil work in land suits. At first the civil and criminal powers were conveyed by separate commissions, and the gaol delivery circuits did not coincide with the assize circuits. But in 1299 the assize justices were told to remain together after taking the assizes and to deliver the gaols as well. Continued development of the combined civil and criminal competence was delayed, however, by the introduction of trailbaston commissions, which were sent into the countryside from 1305 and absorbed all judicial manpower. Then in the reign of Edward II the link between gaol delivery and assizes was severed. Experiments with various circuits continued for much of the century, and throughout the period the court of King's Bench was on the move, doing work that might have been done by justices of assize.

By the fifteenth century this confused picture had come into sharper focus. Trailbaston commissions were no longer issued, King's Bench settled in Westminster, and the crown no longer put gaol delivery into the hands of local knights (statutes of 1328 and 1330 had linked assize and gaol delivery once again, though practice may have lagged behind crown intent). Newer remedies were replacing novel disseisin in land suits, but the change did not affect the justices who were still said to be holding the assizes. They sat regularly on panels of justices of the peace, thus combining assize, gaol delivery, and peace commissions. By the Elizabethan age these judges monopolized justice in the countryside and stood as chief intermediaries between Westminster and the counties.

The expanding jurisdiction that ensured the triumph of English assize justices ultimately bypassed the assizes of baillis and seneschals in France. Given the press of litigation, the urgent and especially the criminal cases were from an early time more conveniently heard by the baillis outside the ambulatory assizes. These sessions became regular and frequent. But the *bailli* or *seneschal* was too busy an administrator to hold a court all year in a fixed place; he had to appoint special subordinates for justice. Moreover, throughout the thirteenth and fourteenth centuries, especially in the south (with Roman law principles embedded in local tradition and an active Roman law faculty in Montpellier), the idea of a professional judiciary, separate from ordinary administration, gained strength. This professionalism and legal bureaucracy developed much more strongly in France than in England, where the common law was not a university subject and where Roman principles gained little ground. In the south of France the *juge-mage* began taking on the judicial functions of the seneschal from the mid thirteenth century. The process was much slower in the north, but by the late fifteenth century a bailli who was not a law graduate could not preside in court; by that time his judicial functions had been taken over by a special subordinate, the lieutenant general. By the sixteenth century the old French assizes, outmoded courts presided over by nonspecialist officials, were extinct.

BIBLIOGRAPHY

John P. Dawson, *A History of Lay Judges* (1960); Bernard Guenée, *Tribunaux et gens du justice dans le baillage de Senlis à la fin du Moyen Âge* (1963); Alan Harding, *The Law Courts of Medieval England* (1973); Ferdinand Lot and Robert Fawtier, *Histoire des institutions françaises au Moyen Âge*, II (1958); François Olivier-Martin, *Histoire du droit français des origines à la Révolution* (1948); Ralph B. Pugh, *Itinerant Justices in English History* (1967); Eugène de Rozière, "L'assize du baillage de Senlis en 1340 et 1341," in *Nouvelle revue historique de droit*, **15** (1891); Joseph R. Strayer, *The Administration of Normandy Under St. Louis* (1932); Donald W. Sutherland, *The Assize of Novel Disseisin* (1973).

RICHARD W. KAEUPER

[See also: **Law-making, Western European; Law, English Common; Law, French, in North; Law, French, in South.**]

ASSIZE, ENGLISH. The term "assize" comes from the medieval Latin *assisa,* which means in its literal sense a "sitting" or session or assembly. In twelfth-century England it often referred to meetings of the king's council or to the legislation that came out of those meetings. In addition, the word came to refer to specific legal remedies or processes that were contained in such legislation and that first appeared during the reign of Henry II.

Henry II has been called the father of the English common law because he created a large group of remedies for legal complaints that formerly had been treated in various private or feudal courts, and permitted plaintiffs to purchase and to use these remedies in his own royal court. Prominent among the earliest of these remedies was a group of provisions, called assizes, that concerned the nature and possession of property.

In 1164 Henry issued the Constitutions of Clarendon, a large body of legislation in which he sought to regulate matters of possible dispute between the church and the crown. One of these matters concerned land held by the church in free alms, and therefore not subject to secular or feudal service. The king provided that in such a dispute a jury of twelve men of the neighborhood should be instructed to answer under oath before the king's justices whether (Latin, *utrum*) the land was held in free alms or in lay fee. The further disposition of the case would take place in a church court or in a lay court, according to the testimony of the jury. But the determination of the original question took place in the king's court, and by royal writ and process. This was the origin of the assize *utrum,* the first of four petty assizes that originated during Henry's reign.

Whereas the assize *utrum* determined the nature of, or obligations attaching to, a tenement or landholding, the other three petty assizes dealt with possession of land and are called *possessory assizes.* The first of these to appear, and the one destined to become the best known, was given the name *novel disseisin.* Historians are in disagreement about the exact date of its creation: some associate it with the meeting of the king's council at Clarendon in 1166; others believe it may have been slightly earlier.

Henry II came to the throne after a protracted period of civil war in England. He was acutely conscious of restoring stability and order to his newly acquired kingdom, and especially of reestablishing the obligations and ties between lord and tenant in the feudal system. Furthermore, because he had to leave England frequently and for long periods to attend to his lands in France, he wanted to guard against any threat to stability and order during his absences. Disseisin or dispossession or ejectment from land was something that great and powerful men did to lesser men, and often feudal lords did it to feudal tenants for a variety of reasons. The king wanted to create a remedy that would make it impossible, in the later words of Magna Carta, for any freeman to be disseised of his land or free tenement without the lawful judgment of his peers.

Any freeman who claimed to have been unlawfully disseised of his land could come to the royal chancery and purchase a writ that initiated the process known as the assize of novel disseisin. The writ was addressed in the king's name to the sheriff of the county in which the disputed land lay. It informed the sheriff of the complaint and instructed him to take security from the plaintiff for prosecuting the claim. This discouraged persons from making capricious accusations or bringing false suit. The sheriff was to keep the tenement "in peace" until the day set for the assize. But the sheriff's most important duty was to empanel a jury of twelve free and lawful men of the neighborhood and have them view the land in question. He was to have their names written

ASSIZE, ENGLISH

down and to summon them to appear before the king or his justices on the assigned day, prepared to make a statement or recognition concerning the land. The sheriff also demanded pledges from the defendant to assure his presence at the assize.

The outstanding feature and purpose of this assize was the correction and remedy of unlawful disseisin, and it aimed to accomplish this through speed. This characteristic has given this assize in particular, and the other petty assizes in general, the name of summary actions. The delays so common to other lawsuits were not permitted in these actions. In the assize of novel disseisin, the defendant was "attached," not merely summoned, to come on the appointed day. If he could not be found, his bailiff was attached to answer in his place. If neither could be found or, having been attached, refused to come, the assize proceeded without him. It was an action in which the defendant could not act through an attorney, could not essoin himself, and could not vouch anyone to warranty unless he first confessed the disseisin. These tactics, when used in other legal actions, led to delays and adjournments. Nor could the defendant claim that the assize should not be held because he or the plaintiff was a minor; the assize of novel disseisin permitted a minor to sue and to be sued.

This action was not so summary that the defendant was not permitted to be heard or to plead his case. There were many instances in which the jury found that the defendant had not committed an unlawful disseisin. But whatever pleading the defendant did when the suit was brought to trial, the procedure and the judges who managed it sought to prevent him from causing delays and adjournments. Whatever questions he raised about the matter could presumably be answered then and there by the jury of recognition, which was present, which had viewed the land, and which supposedly knew all of the incidental information relating to the case. Ultimately, when the pleading was finished, the judges turned to the jury, which, under oath, said whether there had been unlawful disseisin or not. If there had been, the sheriff saw that the plaintiff was placed in seisin again. If there had not, the defendant was acquitted and the plaintiff was fined for false suit.

Not only did the process aim at speed, but the assize was called "novel" because the disseisin must have been a recent one. The plaintiff could not allege a disseisin that had occurred in the remote past. Time limits were placed on the use of this remedy, although these limits changed from brief periods of less than a year to limits set in the thirteenth century of ten, twenty, or more years, until finally, at the end of the medieval period, the date of the alleged disseisin ceased to be important.

The second possessory assize, the *assize of mort d'ancestor* (death of an ancestor), was created in 1176 in a meeting of the king's council at Northampton. The plaintiff maintained that he should be given possession of his deceased father's land, or of the land of some deceased relative. But his father's lord or some other person had refused to give him possession. When the plaintiff purchased the writ from the royal chancery, the sheriff caused the parties to assemble, and a jury answered the question of whether the "ancestor" of the plaintiff was seised of the disputed land on the day he died. If he had been, the plaintiff was placed in possession of the land.

The date of the third possessory assize, the *assize of darrein presentment* (last presentment), is unknown, but it was probably created sometime after 1179, and concerned the right to appoint a parson or churchman to a church or a church living. The previous incumbent was dead, and two parties contested the right of patronage over the church. Which party should present the next churchman to that church? Henry II wanted to preclude the interference of a bishop in such a matter, and conceived a solution whereby one of the parties could purchase a writ of darrein presentment and have a jury drawn from the neighborhood answer the question of who had presented the last occupant of the church. The party so designated was then given the right to present the new parson.

These three possessory assizes all dealt with the question of possession, or seisin. They did not address the problem of proprietary right, which was related to the concept of ownership rather than of possession. If one person challenged the "right" of another person to land of which the second person was in possession, the challenge customarily had been settled by judicial combat between the two parties or their champions in the feudal court of the lord whose tenants they claimed to be. This was a very doubtful and unsatisfactory way to settle such an important matter; and the king, always desirous of simplifying legal remedy and bringing it under his control, offered a solution about 1179, when he created the process known as the *grand assize.* With this remedy, if a tenant of land had his right to that land challenged, he would not have to offer battle to his adversary; rather, he could purchase the writ that began the process of the grand assize. The writ provided that four knights of his community would elect a jury of twelve knights, who under oath and before the king's justices, would say which of the two parties had the better right to the land. While this was a much slower process than the possessory assizes, it quickly became popular as a means of solving the extremely important question of right in property.

In the late twelfth century these assizes could be heard by itinerant justices on periodic circuit through the counties, or before the king and justices who traveled with him, or even before the sedentary bench at Westminster. Magna Carta at first called for four assize circuits a year to each county, but this was later reduced to one. By the end of the thirteenth century, commissions of assize, composed of judges from the common bench and the king's bench, as well as of lawyers and other legal personnel, heard assizes in the counties two to three times a year.

Of the several assizes, novel disseisin experienced the greatest success and underwent most changes. In the Kent eyre of 1279, when 94 civil cases were pleaded, forty-eight were assizes of mort d'ancestor, forty were novel disseisin, and two each were *utrum* and darrein presentment. In the fourteenth century, mort d'ancestor gradually faded from view, its role being filled by other remedies, and novel disseisin continued strong. Additional actions were covered by novel disseisin even in its early days, and statutory legislation in the thirteenth century further refined its provisions and expanded its scope of action.

In creating these five assizes, Henry II accomplished a conservative revolution. In each case he either invaded the jurisdiction of baronial courts or sharply delineated the jurisdiction of church courts. Thereby he greatly increased the area of action for his own courts and expanded his royal authority. It is correct to say that the assizes played a large, perhaps the largest, role in the appearance and growth of the English royal court system: the justices on eyre, and the courts that later became the king's bench and the common bench. The feudal and freeholder class, including the barons, accepted it because it made justice more certain and objective.

In legal substance, the assizes formed the early foundations of the common law, and especially of land law, which was the most important part of the common law. The name derived from the fact that the assizes made available to the entire population of freemen common legal remedies from a common legal source. The assizes guaranteed the future role of the jury in civil actions, and the general premise that no freeman could be deprived of his land without judgment contributed to the later premise of due process of law.

BIBLIOGRAPHY

Alan Harding, *The Law Courts of Medieval England* (1973); Bryce D. Lyon, *A Constitutional and Legal History of Medieval England,* 2nd ed. (1980), 279–299, and bibliography on 325 f.; Doris M. Stenton, *English Justice between the Norman Conquest and the Great Charter, 1066–1215* (1964), 22–53; and Donald W. Sutherland, *The Assize of Novel Disseisin* (1973).

FRANKLIN J. PEGUES

[See also **Clarendon, Constitutions of; Henry II of England; Land Tenure, Western Europe.**]

ASSIZES OF JERUSALEM is the somewhat misleading title given to the collection of treatises on customary law and court procedure that survive from the Latin Kingdom of Jerusalem and the other states founded in the Near East by the Crusaders. The treatises fall into two groups: those describing the practices employed by the High Court and those describing the practices employed in the burgess courts. The former concern the feudal jurisdiction exercised by the crown and pleas of blood (felonies or criminal acts for which the penalty may be death or mutilation) involving feudatories; the latter deal with the law as it concerned the nonnoble Latin inhabitants of the East and with commercial jurisdiction. All were written in French and were unofficial, private compilations.

Of the works concerned with the operation of the High Court, the earliest is the anonymous *Livre au roi,* which apparently was dedicated to Aimery of Lusignan, king of Jerusalem from 1198 to 1205. The others were composed later in the thirteenth century. The most important are those by Philippe de Novare, who wrote around the middle of the century, and Jean d'Ibelin, count of Jaffa and Ascalon, who was at work in the mid 1260's. Jean d'Ibelin's *Livre des assises et des bons usages dou roiaume de Iherusalem* is by far the longest and most comprehensive and describes the law and procedures of the Kingdom of Jerusalem of his day. One item of par-

ASSIZES OF JERUSALEM

ticular interest that Jean preserved is a detailed list of the military services owed to the king in the period immediately before the destruction of the kingdom by Saladin in 1187.

Philippe de Novare wrote in Cyprus with Cypriot conditions in mind, but since procedures in the High Court of Cyprus were closely modeled on those applied in Jerusalem, it was possible for Jean d'Ibelin to make use of Philippe's work in the final version of his own. Similar treatises are by a knight named Geoffrey Le Tor (fl. 1222–1265) and by Jean d'Ibelin's son, James (d. 1276), but these works are shorter and show less originality. There is also an anonymous work called *La clef des assises de la haute cour du royaume de Jérusalem et de Chypre,* which seems to have been written rather later in the thirteenth century.

Jean d'Ibelin was a prominent nobleman and a member of the most powerful aristocratic family in the East. With Philippe de Navara and Geoffrey Le Tor, he had been a member of the political faction in the East that had opposed the attempts of the emperor, Frederick II, to rule in the Latin Kingdom and exercise suzerainty over Cyprus. Jean, Philippe, Geoffrey, and James would thus all have known one another, and they shared a common outlook on matters of feudal jurisprudence. They agreed in presenting an interpretation of the legal relationship between the king and his vassals that minimizes the capacity of the king to take unilateral executive action against any individual fiefholder. Nowhere is this more apparent than in their treatment of the law of King Amalric (1163–1174), the *Assise sur la ligece.* Originally this enactment had strengthened the crown by decreeing that liege homage was owed to the king by the vassals of tenants-in-chief, but by an elaborate piece of legal sophistry supported by precedents of doubtful validity, these thirteenth-century writers reinterpreted it to provide for legitimate resistance to arbitrary royal actions.

It is clear that the authors of these works were all skilled pleaders in the courts, for whom the subtleties of how to plead were just as important as knowing the substance of the law. Philippe de Novare and Jean d'Ibelin occasionally provide clues as to how customary law had developed, and they have some invaluable reminiscences about the lawyers of a previous generation—notably Jean I d'Ibelin, lord of Beirut, the leader of the anti-Hohenstaufen faction, who died in 1236; Ralph of Tiberias (fl. 1185–1220); and Balian, lord of Sidon (d. 1239)—that reveal how members of the baronage could take a passionate interest in the minutiae of legal procedures and feudal custom.

The *Livre des assises de la cour des bourgeois* is an anonymous compilation of burgess law, its final form apparently dating from the 1260's. It was principally concerned with burgess and commercial law as applied in Acre, and was modeled on a Provençal code grounded in Roman law. One feature of it that has particularly excited the attention of scholars is the lengthy list of commodities bought and sold in Acre and the duties payable on them. A second treatise concerned with burgess courts, the *Abrégé de la cour des bourgeois,* was composed in Cyprus in the fourteenth century.

Some of the manuscripts that contain collections of these treatises also contain the assemblage of genealogical information on the royal and noble families of the kingdoms of Cyprus and Jerusalem known as the *Lignages d'outremer.*

After the fall of the Christian possessions on the Syrian littoral at the end of the thirteenth century, these treatises continued to be read and copied in Cyprus, where in 1369 an augmented version of Jean d'Ibelin's book was accorded official status as a work of reference in the High Court. Various additional materials were incorporated into it at that time, most notably a transcript of the pleading by the two contenders for the regency of Jerusalem in the mid 1260's, a document that affords a rare glimpse of an actual debate in the High Court. In the sixteenth century the Venetian authorities in Cyprus had the treatise by Jean d'Ibelin and the *Livre des assises de la cour des bourgeois* translated into Italian. These two works also survive in a Greek translation.

There is, further, a short treatise from the principality of Antioch that deals briefly with both feudal and burgess law there. It was written during the first half of the thirteenth century, but has survived only in a translation into Armenian.

BIBLIOGRAPHY

For editions of the texts and secondary literature to 1960, consult H. E. Mayer, *Bibliographie zur Geschichte der Kreuzzüge* (1960), nos. 1614–1615. For more recent work see Joshua Prawer, *Crusader Institutions* (1980), and *The Latin Kingdom of Jerusalem: European Colonialism in the Middle Ages* (1972); Jonathan Riley-Smith, *The Feudal Nobility and the Kingdom of Jerusalem, 1174–1277* (1973); Peter W. Edbury, "Feudal Obligations in the Latin East," in *Byzantion,* 47 (1977); and "The Disputed Regency of the Kingdom of Jerusalem, 1264/6 and 1268," in *Camden Miscellany,* 27 (1979).

PETER W. EDBURY

[See also **Commerce, Regulation of; Crusades, Near East; Crusades of the Thirteenth Century; Feudalism; Jean d' Ibelin; Philippe de Novare.**]

ASSIZES OF ROMANIA, the feudal code of the principality of Achaea, or Morea (1205–1430); called in the manuscripts "Book of the Usages and Statutes of the Latin Empire of Romania." It evolved gradually in oral and written assizes that reflected both the "common" feudal law brought from the West and borrowings from the law of Latin Jerusalem. It also included rules of Byzantine law that governed the patrimonial lands of Greek landlords of Achaea and the activities of the Moreote serfs. A private legist, presumably writing in French, codified the law of Achaea between about 1333 and 1346. His redaction survived in a Venetian translation, of which an official version was made at Venice between 1421 and 1453. The Assizes were widely applied in Venetian and other Latin territories in Greece, supplementing Venetian criminal and commercial codes and regulations of Byzantine law.

BIBLIOGRAPHY

David Jacoby, *Le féodalité en Grèce médiévale: Les "Assises de Romanie"* (1971); Georges Recoura, *Les Assises de Romanie* (1930); Peter Topping, *Feudal Institutions as Revealed in the Assizes of Romania* (1949), repr. with corrections in his *Studies on Latin Greece A.D. 1205–1715* (1977).

PETER TOPPING

[See also **Assize; Law, Byzantine.**]

ASSONANCE, in its broadest acceptation, signifies a repetition of vowel sounds in poetry. In medieval prosody, it means more specifically the rhyming of one word with another in which the accented vowels and sometimes the following vowels, but not the following consonants, are identical.

Typical assonances in Old Spanish are: n*o*ch/adurmi*ó*/visi*ó*n/Campead*o*r. Assonant rhyme is thus vocalic rhyme as opposed to full (vocalic and consonantal) rhyme. In Germanic languages assonance did not play any significant role; if it occurred, it did so as impure rhyme. In Celtic languages, however, assonance has always been more important than rhyme.

The medieval Romance area presents a rich and differentiated use of assonance. It is believed that assonance is a more archaic feature of Romance poetry than rhyme, but only in Spanish has assonance maintained itself successfully against rhyme. Assonance has always been used in certain genres of Spanish popular poetry—or rather, poetry in the popular mode—although rhyme triumphed in more learned poetry. Assonance is thus a feature of the twelfth-century *Cantar del mío Cid,* as well as of fifteenth- and sixteenth-century romances (anonymous, narrative, historical, or legendary poems). In Italian, the earliest poetry, such as the *Cantico delle creature* (written by St. Francis of Assisi, *ca.* 1224) was assonanced, but with the exception of some Franco-Italian epics, Italian poetry adopted rhyme. The almost total victory of rhyme over assonance characterizes Old Provençal and Old Portuguese as well. In the former, only epic poetry and ballads in the popular style displayed assonance, or what fourteenth-century Provençal treatises called "bastard rhymes" *(sonansa borda).* In French, the distinction between assonance and rhyme followed not only generic lines (as in Spanish), but also chronological ones. The oldest monuments of French poetry *(Eulalie, Passion de Clermont, St. Legier, St. Alexis)* were assonanced. Early epics were all composed in monoassonanced laisses. But already at the beginning of the thirteenth century, certain epics *(Saisnes, Ami et Amile, Jourdain de Blaye)* present a mixture of assonanced and rhymed laisses. All later epics tend to be rhymed. The French assonanced poetry distinguished more strictly than the Spanish between masculine assonances, where the accented rhyming vowels are final (e.g. am*i*/v*i*s/pr*i*st/hard*i*z), and feminine ones, where the rhyming vowel can be followed by one or even two unaccented *e*'s (e.g. Fr*a*nce/*a*ngele/m*a*rche). The oldest Spanish texts, by contrast, permitted such mixed assonant rhyming as calvag*a*r/v*a*/F*á*ñex/m*a*dre.

BIBLIOGRAPHY

The most general and still most authoritative overview of assonance in the Romance domain is Edmund Stengel, "Romanische Verslehre," in Gustav Gröber, ed., *Grundriss der romanischen Philologie,* II, pt. 1 (1904), 61–64. Georges Lote, *Histoire du vers français,* I (1949, repr. 1970), 96–116, and particularly II (1955), 95–110, offers a detailed history of assonance in French.

On assonance in individual languages, look under "Rhyme" in various histories and manuals of versification such as Rudolf Baehr, *Spanische Verslehre auf historische Grundlage* (1962), trans. and adpt. by K. Wagner and F. Lopez Estrada as *Manual de versificación española* (1970).

PETER F. DEMBOWSKI

ASSUMPTION OF THE VIRGIN, the belief that the Virgin, at her death, was raised into heavenly glory. First expressed in fourth-century apocryphal literature, by the seventh century the Assumption was celebrated as a feast on August 15 in the Greek church and, by the eighth century, in the West as well. In Byzantine art the Assumption of the Virgin's soul, represented as an infant in swaddling clothes, was often depicted as part of her koimesis; in the West the Assumption of her body was represented, often shown orant or within a mandorla, flanked by angels, above the apostles and sometimes above her open sarcophagus. From the twelfth century on, the crowning of the Virgin was frequently combined with her Assumption.

LESLIE BRUBAKER

AŠTARAK (ASHTARAK), Armenian town twenty kilometers northwest of Erevan on the banks of the Kasax River in the province of Aštarak, is noted for its medieval architectural monuments: the half-ruined sixth-century basilica of Ciranawor (S. Astuacacin), the seventh-century Church of S. Karmrawor, the thirteenth-century Church of S. Marinē (S. Mariam Astuacacin), the thirteenth/fourteenth-century Church of Spitakavor, the remains of a twelfth/thirteenth-century bridge beside its seventeenth-century replacement over the Kasax River, and a cemetery with *khatchk*ᶜ*ars* dating from the twelfth to the fourteenth century. (A *khatchk*ᶜ*ar* is a rectangular slab of stone carved for commemorative purposes with a large cross, ornamental motifs, and sometimes figural reliefs on one side.)

Ciranawor, probably erected by the Katholikos Nerses II (548–557) but with traces of an earlier structure, is one of a group of Armenian basilicas with three aisles and four bays (other examples include Kᶜasał and Ereroykᶜ). Only the exterior walls, the apse area, two of the massive T-shaped piers, and the south aisle are preserved. Its horseshoe-shaped

Church of S. Karmrawor, 7th century. PHOTO BY LUCY DER MANUELIAN.

apse and two flanking rectangular chambers are contained within the rectilinear east wall. The north and west walls were doubled in thickness when the church was later transformed into a fortress, and the south facade has been rebuilt.

S. Karmrawor, dated through the donors named on the exterior inscription and preserved intact, is one of a group of small Armenian churches in which the cupola covers the entire central space (other examples include churches at Tᶜalin and Lumbat). Squinches make the transition from the central square below to the base of the drum, which at Karmrawor is octagonal on the exterior. There are wall paintings on the interior.

S. Marinē, dated 1281 by an inscription, is a small, domed church almost square on the exterior, with a tall, polygonal drum carved with a blind arcade. The interior has a two-story chamber in each of the four corners. Spitakavor is a small church with a square plan and a vaulted roof. The bridge is documented by the seventeenth-century Armenian historian Ařakᶜel Dawrižecᶜi, but its design is unknown.

BIBLIOGRAPHY

Architettura medievale armena: Roma, Palazzo Venezia, 10–30 giugno 1968 (1968), 79, 90, 122; Sirarpie Der Nersessian, *The Armenians* (1970), 104; and *Armenian Art*

(1977, 1978), 32, 36; Varaztad Harouthiounian and Morous Hasrathian, *Monuments of Armenia* (1975), 61, 194; Richard Krautheimer, *Early Christian and Byzantine Architecture* (1975), 343–344.

LUCY DER MANUELIAN

[See also **Armenian Art and Architecture.**]

ASTROLABE. The most widely used astronomical instrument of the Middle Ages, the astrolabe is a hand-held device for measuring the height of the sun or a star above the horizon. This is combined with a series of movable plates that can be used for solving graphically otherwise complex geometrical problems of astronomy or astrology. The astrolabe ordinarily consists of a brass body into which are inserted a number of circular brass plates. A decorative extension at the top connects with a suspension for holding the device, and on the back of the instrument a movable sighting bar called an alidade is pivoted on the central axis. The large variety of astrolabes makes generalizations difficult, but the great majority range between 7 and 30 cm. in diameter.

The outermost circular plate, called the *rete* ("net"), serves as a star chart; the metal is cut away to leave an open network with a few dozen stars marked by points in the grillwork pattern. The apparent rotation of the heavens about the earth can be modeled by the rotation of the rete about its center (the north celestial pole). Although the stars remain fixed in their relative positions on the celestial sphere, turning with it once a day, the sun moves eastward through the zodiac along the ecliptic once a year. Hence, instead of a fixed pointer for the sun, the rete contains an eccentric circle that is the projection of the ecliptic, and the user must locate the sun on that circle by means of a calendar relating the day of the year to the sun's longitude along the ecliptic. On some European astrolabes this information is provided by a graph on the back of the instrument.

Held fixed underneath the rete there is generally a horizon tablet, on which is inscribed a series of partial or complete circles, one within the other but not quite concentric, representing the horizon and successive circles of equal angular altitude *(almucantars),* on up to the point directly overhead *(zenith).* By rotating the rete with respect to the horizon plate, it is possible to establish the relation of the stars or the ecliptic to the horizon for any specified moment, or conversely, from the given positions of the sun or stars, to find the time. Since the relation of the stars to the horizon depends on the observer's latitude, an ordinary horizon tablet works for only a single latitude. Generally, however, three, four, or five interchangeable plates provide for a series of different latitudes, thus making the astrolabe much less geographically restricted.

The astrolabe owes its simplicity as a mathematical instrument to the stereographic projection, whose fundamental property causes all circles on the celestial sphere to project as circles on the face of the astrolabe. This allows the instrument to serve as an analog computer for spherical astronomy. A typical astrological problem, simply soluble with an astrolabe, is: given the date, time, and latitude, find the ascendant (that is, the part of the ecliptic just rising).

The circumference of the astrolabe is calibrated in degrees, so that by taking a sight of the sun or other object with the alidade, it is possible to measure its angular height above the horizon (the altitude). A typical astronomical problem would be to find the time of day. The user first lines up the movable alidade with the sun and reads off its altitude from the scale on the rim of the astrolabe. Turning the device over, the user then rotates the rete until the appropriate point on the sun's position on the ecliptic circle lies on the almucantar corresponding to the observed altitude. The line from the center of the astrolabe through the sun's position to the edge of the instrument then gives the time, with noon at the top, midnight at the bottom, 6 P.M. to the right, and 6 A.M. to the left.

The back side of the astrolabe includes a variety of graphical devices for determining trigonometric functions. Islamic astrolabes often display graphs for finding the direction of Mecca. European astrolabes, in contrast, frequently have graphs for finding the position of the sun, or giving the maximum altitude of the sun as a function of season and place. Inside the astrolabe, underneath the horizon tablets, Islamic instruments often have a gazetteer giving latitudes and longitudes of twenty or thirty towns, and, sometimes, azimuthal directions, or *qiblas,* for Mecca.

In addition to the instruments just described, there exist also a few representatives of the universal astrolabe, which is designed to eliminate the use of specific plates for selected latitudes. There is also the spherical astrolabe, represented by a single complete specimen in the Museum of the History of Science at Oxford. A large observing instrument with multiple revolving rings was described by Ptolemy as an

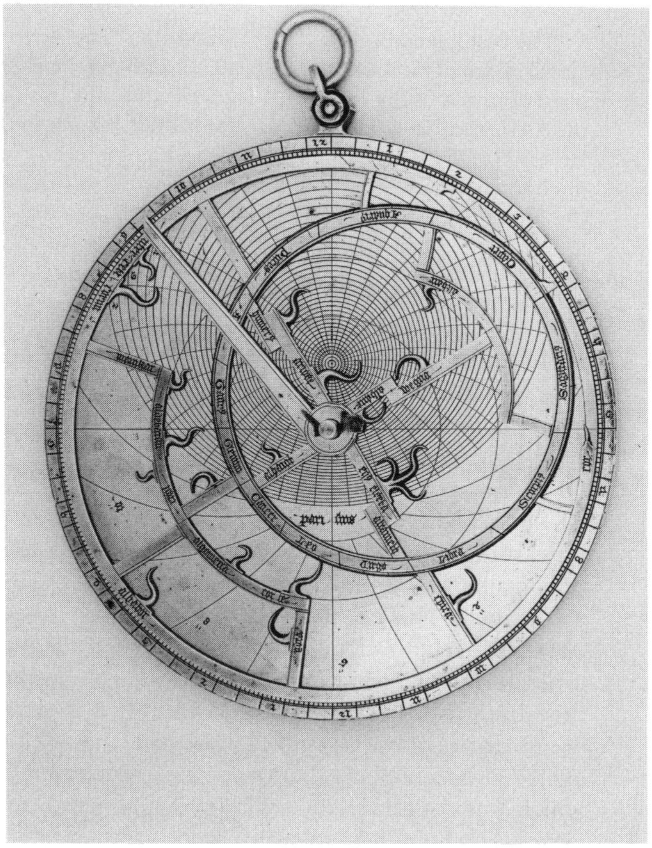

Latin astrolabe, *ca.* 1390, front (left) and back (right). Private collection, ADLER PLANETARIUM, CHICAGO

"astrolabon" but generally today that device is called an armillary sphere.

The largest subclass of astrolabes comprises the mariner's astrolabes, which apparently came into use in the fifteenth century. These consist only of an alidade and graduated scale held to the central pivot with spokes; there are no circular plates because the instrument was designed to be as open as possible and thus less susceptible to ocean breezes. Of the extant mariner's astrolabes, about half were recovered from the sea in a severely weathered state. The most famous is the one lost by Champlain in 1613 in the St. Lawrence River and recovered by chance in 1867.

Although the astrolabe was presumably known in Greek antiquity, the oldest known account of its construction was written in the sixth century by John Philoponos of Alexandria, and the earliest surviving examples are Islamic astrolabes from the tenth century. A computerized checklist made at Yale University lists some 700 Islamic astrolabes, mostly from the seventeenth and early eighteenth centuries, and over 500 Latin astrolabes, primarily from the fifteenth and sixteenth centuries. Only a handful of genuine astrolabes are in Hebrew and a few score in Sanskrit. Because of the Islamic heritage, the basic nomenclature of the astrolabe is directly derived from the Arabic. The outer body is the *mater* (mother), from the Arabic *umm; alidade* and *almucantar* are other words of Arabic origin.

Not only have over a thousand genuine astrolabes survived, but there are also numerous manuscript treatises on the astrolabe. By the fourteenth century, a Latin treatise on the astrolabe (generally but erroneously attributed to Māshā⊃allāh) was considered a regular part of the so-called astronomical corpus, and in making up a standard set of working manuscripts, it was copied together with texts on the sphere, on time reckoning, and on the calendar. Perhaps the most famous astrolabe treatise is the one written in 1392 in Middle English by Geoffrey Chaucer, about two-thirds of which is a translation of the standard Latin text.

BIBLIOGRAPHY

The best general reviews are J. D. North, "The Astrolabe," in *Scientific American,* **230** (1974), with excellent illustration; and Willy Hartner, "The Principle and Use of the Astrolabe," in A. U. Pope ed., *A Survey of Persian Art,* III (1939), 2530–2554. The single most comprehensive modern compendium is R. T. Gunther, *The Astrolabes of the World* (1932, repr. 1976).

OWEN GINGERICH

ASTROLOGY/ASTRONOMY. The following article is in three parts: Astrology (Europe); Astronomy (Europe); Astrology/Astronomy, Islamic.

ASTROLOGY, in general, is the belief that events on earth are caused or influenced in a more or less predictable way by powers emanating from the stars and planets. This belief can be traced to early Mesopotamian civilization, where it flourished among other forms of divination. It was furthered by the prevailing astral religion, which identified the supreme deities of the city-states with the planets. This explains the "public" character of early astrology, which was concerned only with events affecting society as a whole, such as war, famine, pestilence, or even the weather. Reports on celestial omens, interpreted according to codified rules, were regularly addressed to the king by experts in divination who were placed in various cities as salaried officials.

After the middle of the first millennium B.C. the scope of astrology was extended. Public predictions were supplemented by a "personal" or genethliac horoscope that claimed to predict the general circumstances or principal events of an individual's life from the positions of the stars at the moment of his birth or, if possible, conception. Also the history of the world was divided into "great years." These cosmic periods of time were regarded as sharply separated by cataclysmic events caused by spectacular phenomena, such as the "great conjunction" of all the planets in the sign of Aries, wrongly supposed to have occurred in 3102 B.C.

The spread of astrology to the West was furthered by the Persian conquest of Egypt in 525 B.C., the campaigns of Alexander the Great, and the ensuing activity of Berossus and other so-called Chaldean sages in the Mediterranean world, where its way had been prepared by important trends in Greek philosophy. The Pythagoreans had already adopted the idea of a cyclic history of the universe, although the concept of a "great year" was first explicitly mentioned by Plato in the *Timaeus.* Plato also regarded the stars as "visible gods" reigning over individual souls according to an unavoidable necessity already determined before the union of body and soul.

Aristotle also adopted the idea of a necessary connection between the *macrocosmos,* or the world above, and the *microcosmos,* or the world below. Aristotle included the human body in this conception, explaining it in terms of his general theory of material substances as compounds of the four elements. New substances are produced by transmutations, the efficient cause of which is the annual motion of the sun. Consequently such processes are without end, so that the universe "must be cyclical and return upon itself."

In the course of time this theory was applied to alchemy and medicine. Both chemical processes and medicinal cures, as well as surgical procedures such as phlebotomy, had to be performed on specially "elected" days when the configuration of the stars was propitious; this opinion also applied to the conception of a child. But the strongest advocates of astrology among the philosophers were the Stoics, whose conception of the universe as a great organism ruled by an ineluctable fate *(eimarmene)* was easily reconcilable with astrological determinism, as seen in the works of Posidonius.

Thus it was not by accident that the most complete Greek manual of astrology was composed by an eminent astronomer who was also a Stoic philosopher. In his *Almagest,* Claudius Ptolemaeus (*ca.* 142) had developed mathematical theories enabling astronomers to predict celestial phenomena. As a sequel to this work he wrote the *Tetrabiblos,* in order to demonstrate the effect of these phenomena on earthly life. It begins with a rationalistic apology for astrology. Everybody knows that the changing seasons are caused by the sun and that the tides are governed by the moon. Since nature operates in a uniform way it is natural to assume that the other planets also exert specific influences. These effects are described in mathematical terms with few religious overtones.

Thus the *Tetrabiblos* became the basis of a "scientific" astrology cultivated by mathematical astronomers—often simply called mathematicians by ancient writers—in contrast to the vulgar astrological beliefs mixed with magic, demonology, and stellar worship that spread among laymen throughout the Hellenistic world in the wake of Oriental religions. Other important Greek works were the corpus ascribed to Hermes Trismegistus, filled with ideas of Egyptian origin, and the great *Anthology* of horoscopes compiled by Vettius Valens toward the end of the second century A.D.

In Rome astrology became a serious competitor to the established system of divination practiced by the state augurs, and in 139 B.C. as well as on many subsequent occasions the authorities tried to expel the "Chaldeans" from the city. But astrology was favored by many emperors influenced by Stoic ideas, by astral religions from Syria, and in particular by the cult of Mithraism, which was widespread in the army. The planetary names of the days of the week are well attested already in first-century Rome, where much of the astrological literature transmitted to later times was produced. Astrology was expressed in poetic terms in the *Astronomicon* of Marcus Manilius, at the same time that astrological lore was creeping into Seneca's *Questiones naturales* and the second book of Pliny's *Naturalis historia.* A brief summary called *De die natali* was compiled by Censorinus in the third century, whereas the *Matheseos libri VIII* by Firmicus Maternus (*ca.* 336) was a worthy Latin counterpart to the *Tetrabiblos.*

Among the voices raised in protest was that of Cicero—himself an augur and a former disciple of Posidonius. In 45 B.C. there appeared his *De divinatione,* in which natural determinism was carefully distinguished from fatalism, and divination exposed as useless and without scientific foundation. One of his famous arguments is the possibly different fate of twins born under the same stars.

JUDAISM AND EARLY CHRISTIANITY

Despite the fulminations of Old Testament writers against astral religions, astrology also captured the minds of Hellenistic Jews. According to the first-century Jewish historian Flavius Josephus, the destruction of Jerusalem was heralded by a comet. He also credited the Essenes with the belief in a universal fate, a doctrine that he shared and legitimated by his story that astrology was transmitted from Chaldea to Egypt by Abraham himself, whom the Middle Ages accordingly reckoned among the first astronomers.

In the Apostolic church astrology was condemned from the very beginning as a form of astral religion: "Do not be an enchanter nor an astrologer, and do not wish to see [and hear] such things, for they all lead to idolatry," wrote the anonymous second-century author of the *Didache.* At the same time, Ignatius of Antioch explained that the new dispensation had rendered all occult practices obsolete; was not the astronomically inexplicable star of Bethlehem a proof that such arts now had to be abandoned? Around 300, attacks on astral religions were still being voiced by Lactantius and Arnobius the Elder, but the victory of Christianity and the decline of the old beliefs soon compelled the Church Fathers to wage battle on another front. For Basil the Great the vanity of astrology was a moral truth: "If virtuous or vicious acts do not originate from something which is in our own power, but follow by necessity from the circumstances of our birth, to what use are the lawgivers who tell us what we ought to do and what we ought to avoid?"

In patristic times the most violent strictures against astrology came from Augustine, as a consequence of his spiritual experiences on his way to conversion. He first realized that the Manichaean account of the universe was much inferior to the "ratio of the mathematicians," who were able to predict future events without offering sacrifices or prayers to demons. But his personal knowledge of two people born at the same moment and enjoying very different fates convinced him of the futility of nativities (horoscopes of the moment of birth). In a long passage in *De civitate Dei,* Augustine analyzed the argument of twins in more detail, continuing with a historical proof that neither the Roman nor any other empire owed its origin to the stars, and with an argument showing the absurdity of "electing" propitious days.

He ends with four chapters that reveal how deeply intertwined the problem of astrology had become with one of his deepest theological preoccupations—the freedom of man from pagan fatalism versus the universal providence and foreknowledge of God. Supported by a reference to Seneca's remark on those philosophers who rejected stellar fatalism and construed fate as "that connection of causes whereby all things come to pass," Augustine was finally led to confirm that "there is an order of causes wherein the will of God is all in all." This makes possible the scientific study of the world, but "it does not follow that nothing should be left free to our own will because God knows the certain and set order of all events. For our very will is in that order of causes which God knows so surely and has in his prescience."

This theological basis for the traditional Christian hostility toward astrology became normative in the Western church, and it could be left to popes and councils to fight a rearguard action against sects that adopted a more lenient attitude. In 447, Pope Leo I took action against the Priscillians, who subjected both faith and morals to the stars, and previously the first Council of Toledo had condemned believers in "astrology or mathematics." The Council of Braga (*ca.* 561) censured the idea of a certain sympathy between the "twelve signs or stars usually observed by the mathematicians, and the singular organs of the soul and body, designated by the names of the Patriarchs," a phrase that reveals a heretical attempt to lend biblical support to the idea of the microcosmos. In the early seventh century, this attitude was clearly expressed in the *Etymologiae* of Isidore of Seville, who distinguished astronomy from astrology, branding the latter as impious superstition to be avoided by Christians as contrary to the faith.

Nevertheless, at least some astrological beliefs and practices survived ecclesiastical condemnation. The strongest influence seems to have persisted in Byzantium, where the theological schools had absorbed more astrological ideas than had the fathers of the Western church. Moreover, in the fifth century the Platonic Academy of Athens was headed by Proclus, who commented on the *Tetrabiblos* and clearly regarded the stars as the secondary causes of earthly events. These ideas are also found in the anonymous *Theology of Aristotle,* which treats the stars as intermediaries between the soul of the world and the lower regions of the universe.

In 529 Justinian I closed the Academy, and shortly afterward many old and new imperial laws against astrology were incorporated in the new corpus of civil law. The practical effect of these measures was limited, and Byzantine theologians came to terms with a mild form of astrology. Thus John of Damascus in the eighth century explained that although the heavenly bodies do not actually cause events on earth, they nevertheless "induce in us various complexions, and habits, and dispositions" influencing the course of our actions. About the same time a number of astrological, alchemical, and magical works were united into a single corpus. The prolificity of Byzantine astrological literature may be gleaned from perusal of the huge *Catalogus codicum astrologorum graecorum.*

In the West the tradition from Augustine and Isidore kept astrology at bay for several centuries. The best scholar of the eighth century, the Venerable Bede, in *De temporum ratione* briefly mentions the nativities of the "mathematicians" as things to be avoided as completely groundless and contrary to the faith. He also describes the course of the sun through the signs of the zodiac without referring to their astrological significance and mentions the "great year" (after Flavius Josephus) without comment.

The revival of the schools under the Carolingians led to an increased study of the meager inheritance of Latin works on the seven liberal arts, some of which contained a certain amount of astrological lore. This led to crude predictions of a "public" character but, as far as we can see, not to nativities. On the other hand there are frequent references to "Egyptian days" on which certain actions should be avoided. The most comprehensive manual from the schools of this period is *De universo libri XXII* by Hrabanus Maurus of Fulda, written about 844, in which he gives a correct definition of the "great year" but confuses it with the paschal cycle of 532 years. All available evidence suggests that in the eighth century astrology had survived as a disconnected set of vulgar superstitions devoid of scientific trappings and largely ignored by scholars.

THE MUSLIM INFLUENCE

A new epoch was heralded by the first scientific contacts with the Muslim world, which since the foundation of Baghdad in 762 had recovered the principal works of the Greeks and translated them into Arabic with a remarkable scientific renaissance as the result. The Latin world met this movement in Spain, where late tenth-century scholars got the first glimpse of a hitherto unknown world of learning. Soon a faint but ever increasing stream of translations from Arabic found its way to European schools and libraries, resulting in a new interest in natural science.

The wave of translations gained momentum in the early twelfth century, when an important link with the past was established by Plato of Tivoli's translation in 1138 of the *Tetrabiblos* from an Arabic version. It was accompanied by several works originally written in Arabic and often containing doctrines of Persian or Indian origin not found in Ptolemy's work. Among them were al-Manṣur's *Judicia,* Abū Maᶜshar's *Introductorium in astronomiam,* Alī al-Khaiyāṭ's *De judiciis nativitatum,* ᶜUmar al-Ṭabarī's *De nativitatibus et interrogationibus,* the *De significatione planetarum in nativitatibus* of Māshāᵓallāh, and the *Centiloquium,* a collection of 100 astrological aphorisms believed in the Middle Ages to be by Ptolemy himself. The great number of extant manuscript copies of these and similar works shows the fervor with which the schools greeted new astrological texts. That they arrived together with many genuinely astronomical books, often translated by the same persons, increased their status and tended to blur the distinction between astronomy and astrology and to upset the balance established by the Church Fathers.

THE MIDDLE AGES

Thus the question of the relation between astrology and theology was again raised. At first the attitude of the Church was unyielding. Ivo of Chartres included special sections condemning divination in general and astrology in particular in his great collection of canon law, *Panormia,* supported by an array of quotations from Augustine and Isidore and decrees of councils and popes. A similar but more extended section is found in Gratian's more authoritative *Decretum,* written about 1140. But as usual the voice of authority was unable to silence the discussion on a subject that seemed to be part and parcel of scientific progress, and twelfth-century theologians had to work out their own position.

In the eleventh century the idea of man as a microcosm had been presented in at least one manuscript (Paris, BN lat. 7038) but scorned as the "raving of the philosophers." Now Hildegard of Bingen used it as a vehicle for expressing both her physiological ideas and her spiritual visions. It also played a role in *De mundi universitate* by Bernard Silvestre and was taken up by Alexander Neckam in his encyclopedia *De naturis rerum* as a symbolic connection between the seven planets, the seven liberal arts, and the seven gifts of the Holy Spirit. This caused no offense. It seemed more serious when William of Conches in his *Elementorum philosophiae libri IV* adopted the idea of a world soul and described the influences for good or evil of the individual planets; and William of St. Thierry entered a strong protest in a letter to Bernard of Clairvaux.

Other adepts of astrology went even further, while John of Salisbury, in his *Policraticus,* maintained that astrology had outplayed its role when it led the Magi to Christ. Later "astronomers," he held, are dangerous because they seem to rely "upon the firm foundation of nature and sound reason," while their real purpose is to "extend the influence of their own profession," which leads to "error, impiety, and deception."

In the end most theologians adhered to the traditional position, admitting an influence of the stars over the material conditions of man but denying any possibility of predicting *futura contingentia,* events that may or may not happen according to the providence of God. This position was clearly expressed in the *Didascalicon* by Hugh of St. Victor. The most extensive attack on astrology appeared toward the end of the century in a long *Disputatio contra mathematicos* inserted by Hélinand of Froidmont in his huge *Chronica.*

While the discussion in the twelfth century had followed Augustinian lines, the situation changed significantly in the thirteenth century, when the physical and metaphysical works of Aristotle made their way into the university curriculum. Some of these doctrines had become known in the previous century precisely through astrological works. Now the case for astrology was strengthened by the original sources of the theory of elementary transmutations, the heavens as primary causes, and the inherent necessity in the course of nature.

The result of this development can be seen in the attitudes of the great Scholastics. Albertus Magnus admitted that the planets produce general changes among the elements of the lower world, with consequences for conception and birth and for the formation of monsters, and he recommended astrology as general guidance, particularly in medicine. But he clearly exempted the will of man from any stellar influence because the human soul is the image of God, who is free; and he also rejected the "horrible" idea of a cyclical history of the world.

Thomas Aquinas was even more hesitant. He considered the star of Bethlehem as a miracle without astrological significance and gave a long systematic criticism of the doctrine of necessity in his *Summa contra gentiles,* written as a manual for missionaries in Islamic countries imbued with astrology. Horoscopes and elections of propitious days were specially rejected in two brief treatises, *De sortibus* and *De judiciis astrorum.* The outburst of the Italian astrologer Guido Bonatti against "John of Vicenza, that hypocrite among the Preaching Friars, who has dared to say that astrology is neither an art nor a science," shows the open hostility awakened by the cautious attitude of the Dominicans.

A more favorable attitude toward astrology was held by Roger Bacon. A firm believer in both astrological medicine and some forms of "operative astrology" connected with magic, Bacon described the rise of the great religions in terms of planetary conjunctions. The anonymous *Speculum astronomiae* from about 1260 (justly famous for its detailed bibliographical references) went even further. The author seems to accept most astrological practices with a minimum of reserve, regarding astronomy as a prelude to astrology, the latter being a "great science" and a "link between natural philosophy and mathematics."

An attempt to check the rising tide of astrology and other dangerous ideas was made in 1277, when Bishop Étienne Tempier of Paris published a list of 219 propositions that must not be taught at the university. Among them were the statement that "Everything that happens in the sublunary world here below is by necessity governed by the celestial bodies," and the proposition that "Human actions are not guided by the providence of God."

The importance of this censure for medieval science has often been emphasized, but it seems to have had little effect on astrology. In 1305 the cardinals assembled in Perugia greeted Pope Clement V, recently elected in France, saying " . . . you will safely occupy St. Peter's chair and shine with a radiant light . . . for [now] each of the planets has a great force in its own *domus*." Astrology and the fortune of churches were thus connected even by prelates and remained so at least until the Reformation. That it also attained a stronger hold over the fortunes of princes appears from the fact that the official court astrologer, a well-known figure in thirteenth-century Italy, now established himself at one court after another north of the Alps. In 1368 Thomas de Pisan was appointed to the court of Charles V of France, and even ordinary people followed the example of their betters in consulting astrological practitioners on matters of everyday life.

On the other hand, some of the more prominent scholars of the fourteenth century laid the foundations for a remarkable new and scientific attack on astrology. Jean Buridan tried to explain the causes of both terrestrial and celestial motions on the same physical principles, thereby depriving the planets of their "separate intelligences." His successor, Nicole Oresme, made a French translation of the *Tetrabiblos* at the request of Charles V but attacked its doctrines in works of his own written in both French and Latin.

In the treatise *Ad pauca respicientes* he went to the heart of the matter with a new argument based on his insights in the area of natural science. He explained that "A judgment about future events could not be made except by observations of past events" of the same kind. This is why astrologers speak of a "great year," after which the planets return to the same configuration and produce the same effect. The existence of such a period presupposes that the periods of planetary revolution are commensurable; but this hypothesis is not proved in astronomy and is even more improbable because there are so many motions in planetary theory. Therefore, it is "probable that no future configuration is similar to any past configuration, from which it follows that astrology must be regarded as an illusion."

No doubt only a few were able to appreciate a new argument of such mathematical ingenuity, and in their vernacular tracts against astrology lay opponents like Philippe de Mézières found more useful material in Oresme's *Livre de divinacions.* In the university, however, the new critical attitude started an eager discussion between two prominent churchmen and scholars, both of them previously connected with Oresme's Collège de Navarre. Astrology found a strong defender in Pierre d'Ailly, who in *Concordantia astronomiae cum historica veritate* (1410) and *Concordantia astronomicae veritatis cum theologia* relied heavily on Roger Bacon's views. His friend and adversary Joannes Charlier de Gerson was much more skeptical. His *Trilogium astrologiae theologizatae* (419) was written in order to persuade the dauphin (later King Charles VII) not to place his faith in astrologers for several reasons—some of which clearly reveal that Oresme had not worked in vain. One such reason is that, since the earth "according to the faith" is less than 7,000 years old, we have not yet been able to observe a full cycle of the "great year," which is taken to be 36,000 years. Therefore, astrologers have been unable to get "sure and natural experiences" of phenomena, because they have not yet repeated themselves in a sufficient number of times to warrant any conclusions. Furthermore, most of their predictions are patently false, and the few true ones are either due to chance or to the fact that many astrologers are charlatans who secretly obtain information about their clients, pretending to have derived it from the stars.

THE RENAISSANCE AND AFTER

Thus the Middle Ages drew to a close having been unable to solve the problem of whether astrology is true or false. The numerous astrological manuscripts from the fifteenth century seem to indicate that astrology was flourishing more than ever, helped by two new and favorable circumstances. The advent of the printed book afforded printers a profitable market for medieval texts of any kind, including the traditional manuals of astrology, and all of them were in print by 1550. A new genre was the printed almanac or calendar, which usually contained prognostications of various kinds, securing a safe annual income for printers in one town after another. This strengthened popular belief in the more vulgar form of astrology, which went hand in hand with the increasing influence of prophetic movements of various descriptions.

The other stimulus was the humanistic movement, which revived the Greek language among scholars and also heightened their interest in ancient science and pseudoscience. Astrology and magic, as well as Hermetic and cabalistic lore, seemed venerable for their very antiquity itself and gave rise in various combinations to strange, esoteric movements in the sixteenth and seventeenth centuries. It was largely in vain that a humanist scholar like Pico della Mirandola raised his voice in protest in *Disputationes adversus astrologos* (1495), in which he referred to both Oresme and Gerson. Names like Paracelsus, Cardano, Agrippa, John Dee, Kepler, Giambattista della Porta, and Tommaso Campanella testify to the survival of astrology among Renaissance scholars.

It also survived the great religious upheavals of the sixteenth century. In the Protestant camp the humanist, Lutheran scholar Phillip Melanchthon himself produced a new Latin version of the *Tetrabiblos,* printed together with the Greek original (1553). On Catholic soil the Council of Trent condemned occult practices, including judicial astrology, but without any immediate effect, since the decree had to be reaffirmed by papal bulls in 1586 and 1631.

Thus neither scholarly arguments nor authoritative measures were able completely to uproot astrological beliefs. They did finally disappear, not because they were disproved or discredited by unquestionable scientific reasons, but because they gradually became increasingly incredible against the background of the new cosmology. Having removed the earth from the center of the universe, Copernicus placed it among the planets in a position where it was now difficult to regard it as the obvious recipient of influences from other celestial bodies. An attempt by the sixteenth-century Lutheran astronomer Rheticus to create a heliocentric basis of astrology remains an interesting but abortive episode. One century later, when Newton succeeded in giving an account of the mutual interactions of all celestial bodies in terms of light and gravitation, astrology as a serious subject was bound to disappear.

From the historical point of view, astrology was a strange mixture of primitive mythology, Greek physical and cosmological doctrines, and strict, mathematical procedures. Its fall from pseudoscience to pure superstition should not obscure the fact that, in some periods, it was practically the only attempt at giving a mathematical account of natural phenomena. Although this attempt proved to be a failure, it contributed to keeping interest in astronomy alive, furthering the study of both astronomical tables and calculating devices of much more than ephemeral value.

BIBLIOGRAPHY

The literature seems almost inexhaustible, and the following bibliography lists only some important general works and recent studies of particular interest. For editions of astrological texts the reader is referred to the works by Carmody and by Sarton, and to the bibliographies in the books by Neugebauer and Van Hoesen and by Zinner.

Georg-Karl Bauer, *Sternkunde und Sterndeutung der Deutschen im 9.–14. Jahrhundert* (1937); Francis J. Carmody, *Arabic Astronomical and Astrological Sciences in Latin Translation* (1956); George W. Coopland, *Nicole Oresme and the Astrologers* (1952); Frederick H. Cramer, *Astrology in Roman Law and Politics* (1954); Franz Cumont, *Astrology and Religion Among the Greeks and Romans* (1960); Marie-Thérèse d'Alverny, "Astrologues et théologiens au XIIe siècle," in *Mélanges offerts à M.-D. Chenu* (1967); Pierre Duhem, *Le système du monde,* 10 vols. (1913–1959), esp. vol. VIII (1958), chs. 13 and 14; André M. J. Festugière, *La révélation d'Hermès Trismégiste,* I: *L'astrologie et les sciences occultes* (1944); Francis Rarick Johnson, *Astronomical Thought in Renaissance England* (1937); Edward S. Kennedy, "Ramifications of the World-Year Concept in Islamic Astrology," in *Actes du dixième Congrès international d'histoire des sciences* (1964), 23–43; M. L. W. Laistner, "The Western Church and Astrology During the Early Middle Ages," in *Harvard Theological Review,* **34** (1941); Thomas Litt, *Les corps célestes dans l'univers de saint Thomas d'Aquin* (1963); Otto Neugebauer and Henry B. Van Hoesen, *Greek Horoscopes* (1959), with comprehensive bibliography; Martin P. Nilsson, *The Rise of Astrology in the Hellenistic Age* (1943); J. D. North, "Astrology and the Fortunes of Churches," in *Centaurus,* **24** (1980); A. L. Oppenheim, "Divination and Celestial Observation in the Last Assyrian Empire," *ibid.,* **14** (1969); Betsey Parker Price, "The Physical Astronomy and Astrology of Albertus Magnus," in James A. Weisheipl, ed., *Albertus Magnus and the Sciences* (1980); George Sarton, *Introduction to the History of Science,* 3 vols. (1927–1948); Lynn Thorndike, *A History of Magic and Experimental Science,* vols. I–II (1923); and "The True Place of Astrology in the History of Science," in *Isis,* **46** (1955); B. L. van der Waerden, "The Great Year in Greek,

Persian and Hindu Astronomy," in *Archive for History of Exact Sciences,* **18** (1978); and "The Conjunction of 3102 B.C.," in *Centaurus,* **24** (1980); Theodore O. Wedel, *The Mediaeval Attitude Toward Astrology, Particularly in England* (1920); Ernst Zinner, *Sternglaube und Sternforschung* (1953), a popular survey, with bibliography.

OLAF PEDERSEN

[See also **Albertus Magnus; Aquinas, Thomas (St.); Aristotle in the Middle Ages; Augustine of Hippo, Saint; Bacon, Roger; Buridan, Jean; Hrabanus Maurus; Hugh of St. Victor; Ivo of Chartres; John of Salisbury; Manṣur (712–775), al-; Oresme, Nicole; Plato in the Middle Ages; Ptolemaic System, in Astronomy.**]

ASTRONOMY in the Middle Ages was the continuation of a long tradition dating from antiquity. During the last five or six centuries B.C. astronomers in Mesopotamia had developed sophisticated algebraic procedures for predicting certain observable phenomena of the sun, moon, and planets. At the same time the Greeks had taken a different approach, using geometrical models of the solar system to predict the position of all celestial bodies at any given moment.

In Hellenistic times these attempts met with considerable success, and about A.D. 142 their final results were achieved by the Alexandrian astronomer Claudius Ptolemaeus and explained in a great work that became known as the *Almagest.* In it Ptolemy showed how the motion of each planet could be kinematically described as the result of a number of hypothetical circular movements defined by numerical parameters (radii, periods of revolution, etc.), which could be obtained by observations. The behavior of such a model could be presented in a set of tables giving the celestial longitude and latitude of the planet in question as functions of time.

The subsequent history of astronomy is to a great extent the history not only of how the *Almagest* or its theoretical contents were transmitted but also of how astronomers tried to improve upon Ptolemy's methods or results. Because of external, historical circumstances this development took place in different ways in various parts of the world.

Since Greek was the common scientific language throughout the Roman empire, the ancient world produced no Latin versions either of the *Almagest* or of any other work of similar importance. Consequently, when the empire was divided and its western provinces were established as separate kingdoms under "barbarian" rulers, the scientific heritage of the West was reduced to a small number of Latin works of inferior quality compared with the major expositions of the Alexandrians.

One such work was the greater part of a translation made by Calcidius in the fourth century of Plato's *Timaeus,* which became the source of much cosmological speculation and number mysticism in the early Middle Ages. Another was Pliny's comprehensive *Naturalis historia,* book II of which dealt with pre-Ptolemaic astronomy and cosmology. Other sources included the chapters on astronomy in various encyclopedias of the seven liberal arts, such as a commentary on Cicero's *Somnium Scipionis* by Macrobius (*ca.* 400) and *De nuptiis philologiae et Mercurii* by Martianus Capella (*ca.* 470). Some additional information could be gleaned from the writings of Seneca, Varro, and Vitruvius.

Finally, there were a number of astrological manuals with some astronomical contents. These works had one feature in common: they gave a more or less correct exposition of certain results of ancient astronomy without explaining the methods by which they had been achieved. Because they provided no stimulus for further research, astronomy was doomed for several centuries to a rather bleak existence as part of the meager scientific curriculum of the schools of the early Middle Ages and Carolingian period.

The first major scientific work of the Latin West was the encyclopedic *Etymologiae* of Isidore of Seville, who devoted more space to the mythology of the constellations than to the few remarks on the zodiac, the ecliptic, and the motion of the sun and planets that constitute the rest of his astronomy. His much briefer *De natura rerum* is more systematically concerned with bits of astronomical, cosmological, and meteorological lore and was the first of a long succession of similar textbooks. Among them were a tract with the same title by Bede and the very popular *De imagine mundi* by one Honorius Augustodunensis, written around 1100.

Bede's work is better informed than Isidore's and contains the rudiments of a theory according to which the planets move in eccentric circles (without epicycles), as does the sun according to Hipparchus and Ptolemy. But Bede is remembered mainly for his excellent treatise on time reckoning, *De temporum ratione,* which became the basis of the computus as an independent discipline of a high standard and immediate relevance to society.

No Latin work earlier than the twelfth century

ASTRONOMY

reached a similarly high scientific level. Some progress was made in the schools of the Carolingian period, when all the inherited Latin sources were pressed for every possible drop of scientific information. More attention was given to planetary theory, and several manuscripts contain a figure depicting the so-called geoheliocentric system, in which Venus and Mercury orbit the sun, which in turn orbits the earth. Other diagrams give simple, graphic respresentations of the planetary motions in longitude and latitude.

THE ARABIC IMPACT

Because the schools of this period exhausted the available sources, progress depended on an influx of new material. It could be obtained only from the Muslim world, which had experienced a remarkable intellectual and scientific renaissance since the end of the eighth century. Before 1000, Latin scholars had begun to visit monasteries and schools in Spain, returning with books and astronomical instruments of Arabic origin.

One of the first was Gerbert of Aurillac (later Pope Sylvester II), who is said to have introduced the abacus, the armillary sphere, and perhaps the astrolabe as aids for teaching mathematics and astronomy. In the eleventh century the Benedictine monk Hermannus Contractus wrote two treatises, *De mensura astrolabii* and *De utilitatibus astrolabii,* on the construction and use of this instrument, of which a specimen was owned by Radolf of Liège as early as about 1025.

The astrolabe was a small hand-held instrument consisting of a circular brass disk that on the back side carried a circle divided into degrees and an alidade that enabled the observer to take the altitude of a celestial body. On the front side was a fixed *tympanon* or plate, engraved with a stereographic projection of the principal circles of the celestial sphere, and a turnable rete or "spider" in the form of a skeleton map (in the same projection) of some of the brightest stars, and also the ecliptic divided into signs and degrees. This device served as a computer for solving many problems in spherical astronomy and especially for determining the time—by day or by night—from the altitude of the sun or a star as measured by the alidade.

The instrument became extremely popular in the Middle Ages, with Māshāʾallāh's *Tractatus astrolabii,* translated by John of Seville about 1140, as the standard manual. In 1391 Chaucer composed a treatise on the astrolabe for the use of his "little son Lewis." The earliest Latin record of an observation with the astrolabe is from 18 October 1092, when Walcher of Malvern used it in Italy to determine the time of a lunar eclipse.

The introduction of a sophisticated measuring and calculating instrument was a challenge that the schools of the eleventh century had not been intellectually prepared to meet. The scientific prerequisites for understanding it were made available through the increasing stream of translations made in the twelfth century that arrived in Europe in a significant order. Most important for the practical use of such an instrument was a set of tables giving, among other things, the position of the sun for each day of the year.

This demand was first met in 1126, when Adelard of Bath translated a later version of the great *Zīj* (astronomical tables) of al-Khwārīzmī into Latin. It provided scholars with a wealth of new astronomical material but was rather inconvenient in Europe because it was based on the epoch of the hegira and on the meridian of Arim, a mythological mountain in the middle of the world (actually the ancient Indian capital of Ujjain); moreover, it was theoretically based on Hindu *siddhāntas.* As a result Hindu methods sometimes turned up in western astronomy. A *zīj* in the Ptolemaic tradition by al-Battānī was translated before 1145 by Plato of Tivoli under the title *De scientia stellarum.* Tables for various European cities soon began to appear from the hands of Raymond of Marseilles (Marseilles, 1141), Robert of Chester (London, 1149), and Roger of Hereford (Hereford, 1178). Some of them were based on al-Khwārīzmī, others on al-Battānī, while a third group was derived from a now lost *zīj* by the Toledan astronomer al-Zarqālī. These Latin Toledan Tables exist in many variants, usually accompanied by a detailed set of *canones* explaining their use; they still remain unedited.

The astrolabe and astronomical tables enabled astronomers to make observations at precisely determined hours and to compare the results with theoretical values calculated from the tables. But this was insufficient to reveal the theoretical models on which the tables were constructed, just as the geometry of the astrolabe remained unexplained. This latter defect was remedied by a translation made in 1143 by Hermann of Dalmatia of an Arabic version of Ptolemy's *Planisphaerium* (the Greek original is lost), in which the principles of stereographic projection are explained.

Planetary theory was assimilated more gradually.

In 1134–1135 John of Seville produced a Latin version of a brief and rather elementary treatise on the principles of Ptolemaic astronomy by al-Farghānī, *Rudimenta astronomica* or *Liber XXX differentiarum,* which served as an introduction to theoretical astronomy for centuries and was edited as late as 1537 by Melanchthon. Ptolemy's *Almagest* was first translated about 1160 directly from the Greek and then about 1175 from the Arabic by the most industrious of all translators, Gerard of Cremona, whose version became universally used until the Renaissance. In principle this achievement enabled the Latin West to pick up the threads from antiquity and make progress on its own.

The following development reveals the difficulties of introducing the new astronomy into the curriculum of the universities, where astronomy belonged to the basic faculty of arts and had to be taught to young boys with only modest mathematical qualifications. The *Almagest* clearly was much too advanced to be used as a textbook, and a more elementary approach was necessary. Gradually a curriculum was established that led from very primitive questions to rather advanced problems, enabling the student to make use of the classical sources.

It began with three small manuals by the English astronomer John of Sacrobosco, who taught in Paris up to 1250. The first was the *Algorismus vulgaris,* which explained simple arithmetical operations, including root extraction, using the decimal system and Arabic numerals. The *Tractatus de sphaera,* in four brief chapters, gave a nonmathematical exposition of spherical astronomy with a few sections on cosmology and a sketchy final chapter on the motion of the sun and planets. His *Tractatus de computo* was a fairly detailed manual of time reckoning. These three works retained a prominent place in the curriculum for several centuries. They are often found bound together and written in the same hand, forming the kernel of an astronomical corpus to which other treatises were added.

Sacrobosco's works were usually supplemented by an astronomical calendar by Robert Grosseteste or, from about 1300, by Peter Philomena of Dacia and by a treatise on the quadrant. At the next stage the anonymous *Theorica planetarum* was added in order to remedy Sacrobosco's cavalier treatment of planetary theory. The *Theorica* gave a brief survey of the principal features of Ptolemaic astronomy, illustrated by diagrams but without most of the numerical parameters. These could be had, however, from a set of tables also added to the corpus. At first of the Toledan type, from about 1320 they were the so-called Latin Alphonsine Tables with *canones* by John of Saxony. They became the standard astronomical tables of the later Middle Ages and were first printed in 1483.

The corpus was further augmented with four brief treatises by Thābit ibn Qurra. Among them was *De motu octauae sphaerae,* which made the theory of the trepidation of the equinoxes familiar to Latin scholars, introducing the idea that the precession of the fixed stars is not a linear but an oscillating function of time, contrary to the account in the *Almagest.* Final additions included treatises on astronomical instruments and often also on astrology. Much of the astronomical literature of the later Middle Ages consisted of commentaries on Sacrobosco and the *Theorica planetarum,* but also a great deal of original work was done at various centers inside or outside the universities. For about a century after 1220, Paris was the seat of a flourishing school whose members included Campanus of Novara, author of a large *Theorica planetarum.* Of greater value and lesser spread than that of the corpus, it contained a wealth of mathematical parameters, a calculation of the size of the planetary spheres and the universe based on Ptolemy's *Planetary Hypotheses,* and a description of an equatorium for the mechanical calculation of planetary longitudes. He was followed by John of Sicily and then by William of St. Cloud, who in 1290 redetermined the obliquity of the ecliptic and later produced a widely used calendar.

This tradition was continued in the fourteenth century by John of Murs, who in 1318 determined the vernal equinox with a large instrument erected at Évreux; observations elsewhere are also recorded. In 1344 he was called to Avignon with Firmin de Belleval to give Pope Clement VI his opinion on the possibility of reforming the calendar, a question that from then on created a new link between astronomy and the Church. His contemporary, John of Lignères, invented an improved equatorium and, like John of Saxony, worked on the diffusion of the Alphonsine Tables. An interesting figure from the fifteenth century is Jean Fusoris, who had a large workshop in Paris for making astrolabes, sundials, and other instruments.

While these French scholars generally devoted themselves to pure astronomy, their Italian contemporaries were much more interested in astrology, particularly since just before 1300 the University of Bologna had created a special chair for teaching it to medical students. Among its occupants were Thadeus of Parma, who in 1318 produced a huge commentary on the *Theorica planetarum* especially designed for this purpose. One of his successors, the astrologer Cecco d'Ascoli (Francesco Stabili), was burned at the stake in 1327 for heresy. Other notable representatives of the Italian school were Pietro d'Abano, whose *Lucidator astronomiae* from 1310 contains a discussion of alternative planetary theories, and the great Genoese traveler Andalò di Nigro, whose popular *Theorica planetarum* survives in numerous manuscripts.

In Spain, Toledo was the traditional home of the great translators of the twelfth century. During the reign of Alfonso X (1252–1284) it became the center of a team of Jewish, Muslim, and Christian scholars, who under his auspices compiled a monumental collection of treatises on astronomical instruments and tables, known as the *Libros del saber de astronomia.* Written in Castilian, they testify to a growing interest in astronomy outside purely academic circles.

Also in Spain and southern France, a group of Jewish scholars made remarkable contributions to medieval astronomy. Among them were Jacob ben Ma^{c}hir Ibn Tibbon of Marseilles, called Prophatius Judaeus by the Latins, who invented the *quadrans novus,* combining the ordinary quadrant and the astrolabe. In his long treatise *Sefer tekunah* ("Book of Astronomy"), Levi ben Gerson of Bagnols described the cross staff which, through Peter of Alexandria's Latin translation in 1342, rapidly became an important instrument of navigation. He was also the inventor of the transversal division of graduated scales later credited to Tycho Brahe. Around 1365 Immanuel Bonfils of Tarascon compiled a famous set of tables called the "Six Wings." Abraham Zacuto, after the expulsion of the Jews from Spain in 1492, went to Portugal, where his *Almanach perpetuum* became the basis of a set of astronomical tables for the years 1497–1500 used by Vasco da Gama in his circumnavigation of the world.

In England the outstanding name in fourteenth-century astronomy was Richard of Wallingford, abbot of St. Albans. The author of the first original treatise in Latin on plane and spherical trigonometry, he was also deeply interested in astronomical instruments, as seen from his invention of two peculiar devices. The "Albion" was a kind of universal equatorium, while the "rectangulus" was a system of linked rods destined for observation as well as calculation and intended to replace the armillary sphere. An impressive monument to his theoretical and practical ingenuity was the great astronomical clock (now lost) that he built at St. Albans in the last years of his life.

A wealth of unpublished manuscripts of tables, calendars, and commentaries reveals much astronomical activity among the fellows of Merton College, Oxford, such as John Maudith, William Rede, John Killingworth, and Simon Tunsted, the last of whom continued Richard's work on the "Albion."

Around 1400 the teaching of astronomy in universities began to spread to the east. The convinced critic of astrology and of Ptolemaic methods in astronomy, Henry of Hesse, was called from Paris to the newly reorganized University of Vienna. From 1416 to 1425 John of Gmunden lectured exclusively on mathematics and astronomy at Vienna, leaving behind many works, particularly on instruments. His pupil, Georg Peuerbach, wished to reform astronomy after the ways of the humanists by returning to its classical sources. His *Theoricae novae planetarum* (1454) is still in the medieval tradition, but together with his pupil and colleague Johannes Regiomontanus he planned a new Latin translation of the *Almagest.* After leaving the University of Vienna, Regiomontanus set up an astronomical observatory and printing press at Nuremberg. The observations were continued by Bernhard Walther and were published by Johannes Schöner (1544), to be used later by Tycho Brahe and others. The new translation was published as the unfinished *Epitome Almagesti* in Venice in 1496.

The Vienna school was to some extent paralleled at the University of Cracow, which in 1405 created the first regular chair in astronomy outside Italy. It was filled with a succession of professors with astronomical instruments as their principal interest until theoretical astronomy came to the fore in the works of Albert of Brudzewo and John of Glogau at the time when Copernicus began his study at Cracow.

BYZANTINE ASTRONOMY

There is still no comprehensive history of Byzantine science in general or astronomy in particular. Here the initial conditions significantly differed from those of the West. Because the Greek language was used continually, the classical works were both available and studied—as is evident from a long series of commentaries on Ptolemy, Theon of Alexandria, and other astronomers of antiquity. One of the first was due to Stephanus of Alexandria who migrated to Byzantium about 612. Among later commentators were John Tzetzes, Theodore Metochites, Nicholaus Cabasilas, and Issac Argyros.

Another difference was that the contact with Muslim astronomy came much later and by a different route than in the West. It was transmitted in the fourteenth century from Persia via Trebizond by Gregory Chioniades, George Chrysococces, and Theodore Meliteniotes. We get a few glimpses of original work, such as the observation of the solar eclipse of 3 June 1239 by George Ackropolites and of the lunar eclipse of 18 May 1258 by Nicophorus Blemmydes. In 1324 Nicophoras Gregoras proposed a calendar reform that was not carried out.

An interesting episode occurred after 1328, when the Calabrian monk Barlaam of Seminara visited Constantinople and was challenged by Gregoras to calculate solar eclipses in 1333 and 1337. Both astronomers were victorious, proving their competence and familiarity with Ptolemaic procedures. Byzantium was the great repository of Greek literature from whence important manuscripts found their way to the West. In 1158 Emperor Manuel I Komnenos presented William I of Sicily with a tenth-century manuscript of the *Almagest,* and the Vatican *Almagest* once belonged to Emperor Leo the Wise. The increasing traffic in manuscripts in the decades before the fall of Constantinople (1453) had important consequences for Renaissance astronomy, geography, and cartography.

NEW IDEAS

Because medieval astronomy was primarily a subject for teaching, most efforts were doubtless spent on the recovery, assimilation, and exposition of the ancient heritage. But this did not prevent scholars from developing ideas of their own on points where the inherited views seemed insufficient or wrong. Thus planetary theory gave rise to discussions throughout the Middle Ages, beginning with the assumption of simple, circular, and eccentric planetary orbits found in Bede and continuing with the development of the geoheliocentric system of the Carolingians, derived from Macrobius and Martianus Capella. Thus, in a sense, the way had been prepared for the Ptolemaic models even before the *Almagest* or its Arabic recensions became known. From the thirteenth century the overwhelming majority of astronomers adhered to the Ptolemaic models and the corresponding astronomical terminology as defined in the *Theorica planetarum* of the corpus.

Against this consensus only a few choices were heard, mainly from philosophers who took Ptolemy to task for not being sufficiently Aristotelian. This was the case of Ibn Rushd, whose many commentaries on Aristotle were much used in the thirteenth century. His strict Aristotelianism led him to reject the Ptolemaic models because they did not stick to concentric orbits only. His successor al-Biṭrūjī (Alpetragius) tried to develop a concentric theory that became known through Michael Scot's translation, *De motibus celorum* (1217). It led to the same difficulties as Eudoxos' concentric theory of the fourth century B.C. and never did convince astronomers, who were unable to reduce it to tables suitable for predictions. A late echo of this attempt is heard in Henry of Hesse's treatise *De reprobatione eccentricorum et epiciclorum* (1364).

Another objection to Ptolemy was his use of circular motions that were not uniform as seen from the center of the circle itself. For the Aristotelians this was against nature and an aesthetic fault from a mathematical point of view. Albertus of Brudzewo struggled with this problem in his commentary on Peurbach's *Theoricae novae,* and one of Copernicus' reasons for totally abandoning the Ptolemaic system was the wish to avoid such motions.

While most medieval astronomers accepted Ptolemy's planetary kinematics without qualms, they were troubled with his frame of reference for celestial objects. Ptolemy had referred all positions to the ecliptic on which longitudes were reckoned from the vernal equinox, that is, the point where the sun passes from negative to positive declination and day and night are equal. This point moves relative to the fixed stars in such a way that their longitudes increase with time. Ptolemy thought that this "precession of the fixed stars" went on at the constant rate of one degree per century. In the ninth century the astronomers in Bagdhad were unable to verify this by their own observations and concluded not that Ptolemy was wrong but that the rate of precession had changed since his time. Consequently it became imperative to determine this rate as a function of time.

One solution was the theory of trepidation proposed by Thābit ibn Qurra, but several other variants were known. Thus the Alphonsine Tables presupposed that the fixed stars perform an oscillatory motion with a period of 7,000 years added to a linear displacement corresponding to a complete revolu-

ASTRONOMY

tion in 49,000 years. A somewhat similar theory was worked out by Copernicus, who also followed Thābit in replacing the ecliptic by a sidereal frame of reference tied to the fixed stars. Since the sidereal year seemed to be an astronomical constant and thus independent of time, it followed that the length of the tropical year would vary according to the actual amount of precession.

This made the theory of precession of immediate importance to the question of calendar reform and led several astronomers to publish tables of the rate of precession for several years. It was also important to the makers of stellar catalogs, who usually confined themselves to adding the actual value of precession to the longitudes given in the catalog of the *Almagest.*

Strange as they may seem today, such procedures derived from an attitude that marked both Islamic and Latin astronomy throughout the Middle Ages: trust in the reliability and correctness of all observations made by the great astronomers of the past, whose recorded results it seemed dangerous to discard. Consequently the medieval astronomer's task seemed to be to create theories that would account for earlier as well as for more recent observations.

This perhaps explains why the idea of a completely new survey of the heavens as the foundation for a new astronomy did not occur until it was realized by Tycho Brahe. In general, medieval astronomers made occasional observations when they felt the need for redetermining one or more parameters of theoretical astronomy, whereas the idea of compiling long series of systematic records to be stored for later use seems to have been foreign to them. With a few notable exceptions, such as John of Murs, their instruments were small and portable; and the introduction of observatories with large and permanently mounted instruments had to await the sixteenth century.

COSMOLOGICAL DISCUSSIONS

Closely connected with astronomy were the medieval views of the structure of the universe: the inherited belief in the spherical shape of the earth and its immovable position at the center of the universe, surrounded by the elementary spheres of water, air, and fire. In the early Middle Ages the planets were thought to move in a fiery region limited by the firmament containing the fixed stars; above this were the "waters which were above the firmament," mentioned in the Old Testament. This conception was one of the rare examples of the influence of Scripture on medieval cosmology.

In the twelfth and thirteenth centuries this picture was filled out with details from Aristotelian cosmology. The planets and stars were now thought to consist of a fifth element, or "ether," unknown below the inner surface of the moon's sphere. This surface formed a sharp boundary between the two parts of the universe, each of which had its own material constituents and was governed by its own physical laws. In the sublunary world the moving forces were the "natural" tendencies of gravity and levity and the "violent" forces of impact. In the celestial region the planetary spheres were believed to move under the influence of "separate intellects." The outer surface of the outermost sphere was considered the absolute limit of the universe; outside this there was nothing at all—not even empty space. This picture of the universe persisted well into the Renaissance, at least in the popular imagination.

Nevertheless, it was severely questioned on several important points by the critical thinkers of the fourteenth and fifteenth centuries. Dispensing with "separate intellects," Jean Buridan employed the impetus theory to account for planetary motions by the same type of physical forces as those governing the sublunary world. At the same time Thomas Bradwardine conceived the bold idea of an infintite space outside the heavenly spheres.

The physical implications of this conception were examined by Nicole Oresme, who combined thought experiments in physics with mathematical arguments to disprove a number of Aristotelian doctrines, such as the idea of a "natural place" for every body in the universe. Thus gravity became a property inherent in all bodies that could be construed as the *inclinatio ad similes* (inclination toward bodies of the same kind) later adopted by Copernicus as a necessary corollary to the removal of the earth from the center of the universe. In the commentary to his French translation of Aristotle's *De caelo* (1377), Oresme also proved that the hypothesis of the earth's daily rotation would account for all the phenomena usually explained by the diurnal rotation of the heavens and furthermore, that it could not be contradicted either by astronomical or theological arguments. But in the end he himself was unable to believe in it, contrary to Nicholas Cusa, who conceived the earth as a "noble star" among others and visualized an infinite universe everywhere filled with stars of more or less the same physical nature.

But this early statement of the general cosmological principle was premature, and Copernicus still believed in a finite universe centered on the sun—although vastly more extended than had previously been assumed. However, there is no doubt that the cosmological speculations of the later Middle Ages actively prepared the way for the emergence in the sixteenth century of both a new astronomy and a new physics.

BIBLIOGRAPHY

Editions of and literature on astronomers may be found in separate entries on individual scholars and in standard reference works, such as the *Dictionary of Scientific Biography* and George Sarton's *Introduction to the History of Science.* Guides to the MS material include Lynn Thorndike and Pearl Kibre, *A Catalogue of Incipits of Mediaeval Scientific Writings in Latin,* 2nd ed. (1963); and Ernst Zinner, *Verzeichnis der astronomischen Handschriften des deutschen Kulturgebietes* (1925). The following bibliography comprises a brief selection of relevant works on various topics.

Francis J. Carmody, *Arabic Astronomical and Astrological Sciences in Latin Translation* (1956); Pierre Duhem, *Le système du monde,* 10 vols. (1913–1959); B. R. Goldstein, "Levi ben Gerson: On Instrumental Errors and the Transversal Scale," in *Journal of the History of Astronomy,* **8** (1977); Edward Grant, ed., *A Source Book in Medieval Science* (1974); and *Much Ado About Nothing* (1981); Robert W. T. Gunther, *The Astrolabes of the World* (1932, repr. 1976); Willy Hartner, ed., *Oriens-Occidens* (1968), 287–311; and "Trepidation and Planetary Theories," in *Atti dei convegni dell'Accademia nazionale dei Lincei,* **13** (1971); Charles Homer Haskins, *Studies in the History of Mediaeval Science* (1924); Charles W. Jones, "A Note on Concepts of the Inferior Planets in the Early Middle Ages," in *Isis,* **24** (1936); Alexandre Koyré, *From the Closed World to the Infinite Universe* (1957); Claudia Kren, "Homocentric Astronomy in the Latin West," in *Isis,* **59** (1968); David C. Lindberg, ed., *Science in the Middle Ages* (1978), esp. 265–302 and 303–337, with bibliographies; Anneliese Maier, *Zwei Grundprobleme der scholastischen Naturphilosophie* (1951), esp. section 2; and *An der Grenze von Scholastik and Naturwissenschaft,* 2nd ed. (1952), esp. section 2; R. Mercier, "Studies in the Medieval Conception of Precession," in *Archives internationales d'histoire des sciences,* **26** (1976) and **27** (1977); Henri Michel, *Traité de l'astrolabe* (1947); Otto Neugebauer, "The Early History of the Astrolabe," in *Isis,* **40** (1949); and *A History of Ancient Mathematical Astronomy,* 3 vols. (1975); Otto Neugebauer and Olaf H. Schmidt, "Hindu Astronomy at Newminster in 1428," in *Annals of Science,* **8** (1952); John David North, "Medieval Star Catalogues and the Movement of the Eighth Sphere," in *Archives internationales d'histoire des sciences,* **20** (1967); "The Astrolabe," in *Scientific American* (Jan. 1974); *Richard of Wallingford: An Edition of His Writings,* 3 vols. (1976); and "The Alfonsine Tables in England," in M. Schramm, ed., *Prismata* (1977), a *Festschrift;* Olaf Pedersen, *A Survey of the Almagest* (1974); "The Corpus Astronomicum and the Traditions of Medieval Latin Astronomy," in *Colloquia Copernicana,* **3** (1975); and "Some Early European Observatories," in *Vistas in Astronomy,* **20** (1976); Emmanuel Poulle, *Un constructuer d'instruments astronomiques au XVe siècle: Jean Fusoris* (1963); Lynn Thorndike, *A History of Magic and Experimental Science,* I–IV (1923–1934); and *The Sphere of Sacrobosco and Its Commentators* (1949); G. J. Toomer, "A Survey of the Toledan Tables," in *Osiris,* **15** (1968); Ernst Zinner, *Deutsche und niederländische astronomische Instrumente des 11.–18. Jahrhunderts* (1956).

OLAF PEDERSEN

[See also **Adelard of Bath; Alfonsine Tables; Arabic Numerals (Hindu-Arabic); Aristotle in the Middle Ages; Armillary Spheres; Astrolabe; Astrology/Astronomy, Islamic; Calendars and Reckoning of Time; Gerard of Cremona; Silvester II; Grosseteste, Robert; Isidore of Seville; Jean Buridan; Levi ben Gerson; Macrobius; Nicholas of Cusa; Rushd, Ibn.**]

ASTROLOGY/ASTRONOMY, ISLAMIC. The expression *ᶜilm al-nujūm* (science of the stars), as used by most Muslim authors, referred to both astrology and astronomy. More precisely, astrology—defined by the ninth-century astrologer, Abū Maᶜshar, as "the knowledge of the effects of the powers of the stars, at a given time, as well as the future time"—was referred to as *ᶜilmᵓ aḥkām al-nujūm* (science of the decrees of the stars), *ᶜilm alᵓaḥkām,* or simply *ᵓaḥkām* or *tanjīm* (divining by the stars). Astronomy, on the other hand, was commonly referred to as *ᶜilm al-falak* (science of the spheres) or *ᶜilm al-hayᵓah* (science of the [heavenly] configurations).

Early encyclopedists treated both disciplines under the same rubric, with the implication that astrology was the natural sequel to, yet distinguishable from, astronomy, as was expressed by Ptolemy himself. Al-Nadīm around 990 characterized the works of al-Nayrīzī, the commentator on the *Almagest* and the *Elements* of Euclid, as more *hayᵓah* (astronomy) than *nujūm* (astrology).

In the usual classifications of the sciences, the two disciplines were commonly considered as branches of the same science. It is only at a later date, around the thirteenth century, that astronomy was made

ASTROLOGY/ASTRONOMY, ISLAMIC

fully distinct from astrology. Astronomy was thereafter counted as a mathematical science; and astrology was shifted to the applied physical sciences, together with agriculture, medicine, and alchemy.

ASTROLOGY

The early history of astrology in Islam is closely connected with divination. Tradition attests to the presence of astrologers even before the time of Muḥammad. An astrologer named Qays Ibn Nushbah was supposed to have predicted the coming of the Prophet, who later called him *ḥabr qawmih* (chief of his people), a title usually reserved for the learned men of the Jews, the Christians, or the Sabaeans. But the Muslim religious rejection of the ancient Arabian institution of the *kāhin* (diviner priest) had a negative effect on astrology, inasmuch as the latter was identified with that divinatory practice. The Prophet supposedly said that whoever studies anything of the stars *(nujūm)* would have studied some magic, and astrology leads to divination. Other than the divinatory aspect of astrology, the native Arabs probably had a limited knowledge of the lunar mansions and the heliacal rising of certain stars. But by the ninth century several texts had been translated into Arabic from Greek, Pahlavi, Syriac, and Sanskrit. These texts included the masterpieces of Hellenistic astrology, namely the *Tetrabiblos* of Ptolemy and the five books of Dorotheus of Sidon. The latter text had already been translated into Pahlavi sometime during the sixth century, from which source the work became known to the Arabs. The text of Vettius Valens' *Anthologies* seems to have followed the same route but has not survived in Arabic except in scattered fragments quoted by later authors.

Ptolemy's *Tetrabiblos,* on the other hand, was taken much more seriously than any other text and was by far the most influential source of medieval Islamic astrology. It was translated more than once and was paraphrased several times by early writers such as Ibn al-Farrukhān, Ibn al-Ṣalt, al-Nayrīzī, and al-Battānī.

An extensive commentary that became famous during the Middle Ages was made in the eleventh century by Ibn Riḍwān and was later translated into Latin. All of these surviving texts, whether translations, paraphrases, or commentaries, are older than the earliest surviving Greek manuscript (thirteenth century) that was used to prepare the modern Loeb edition of the *Tetrabiblos.* In addition to the Arabic tradition there is also a Syriac fragment (Paris, Bibliothèque Nationale, MS Syriaque 346) containing a paraphrase of book II, 9 to the end. No study has yet been done of these sources and their relationship either to the edited Greek text or to the Greek paraphrases, such as that of Proclus. The negative Muslim attitude toward astrology had taken on a new form by the ninth century, by which time the translations were almost completed. Astrology was now seen as part of a coherent but foreign body of Greek philosophy, primarily that part which dealt with problems such as the eternity of the world and free will.

The religious leaders, feeling that such subjects were within their own domain and already backed by a prophetic tradition against astrology, took a definite position against the new Greek formulation. Their rejection centered on the astrologers' main claim, namely, the ability to foretell the future in a world predetermined by the stars. At times their attacks included the serious charge of atheism. Abū Maᶜshar (Albumasar) was supposed to "have studied astrology until he became an atheist," the implication being that atheism was a natural end of such studies. The suspicion against astrology was not restricted to such passing remarks or the religious men alone. By their association with the "foreign sciences" the astrologers also endangered their colleagues the astronomers, the philosophers, and the physicians. These men in turn had to defend themselves by dissociating themselves from the astrologers.

The earliest known attack on the astrologers came from the famous eighth-century Arabian prosodist al-Khalīl Ibn Aḥmad in a few lines of poetry. A ninth-century poet, Abū Tammām al-Ḥabīb ibn Aws, supposedly celebrated the error of the astrologers, who predicted that al-Muᶜtaṣim would not be able to conquer Amorium in 838, with the famous poem: "The sword is much more telling than the [astrologer's] books. . . ."

Of much greater significance, however, is the attack leveled by the two most prominent men of the tenth century, the famous philosopher al-Fārābī and ᶜAlī ibn ᶜĪsā al-Asṭurlābī the astronomer and astrologist, as his name implies. Al-Fārābī's text comprised a brief introduction and thirty short sections devoted to polemics against astrology.

Al-Asṭurlābī, a convert from astrology to orthodox Islam, is quoted at length, with supplementary remarks, by the Hanbali theologian Ibn Qayyim al-Jawzīyyah. His main argument involves the issue of the eternity of the world, a problem already faced by

ASTROLOGY/ASTRONOMY, ISLAMIC

the ***mutakallimūn*** (speculative theologians?). The astrologers, who are called the atheists (*ᵓahl al-ᵓilḥād* or *zanādiqat*), seem to have held the world to be uncreated, a view diametrically opposed to orthodox Islam.

Abū Ḥayyān al-Tawḥīdī, a tenth-century philosopher and man of letters, devoted two seances of his literary work *al-Muqābasāt* to refuting astrology as a discipline and a profession. In one of the seances an important association was drawn between the astrologer and the physician, a remark already made by Ptolemy in defense of astrology as an "empirical science." The virtue of medicine, al-Tawḥīdī says, is not to be put in any doubt, but it is somehow unfortunate that its method belongs to the same class as that of astrology.

Another philosopher, of comparable stature to al-Fārābī, was Ibn Sīnā (Avicenna), who also devoted a treatise to the refutation of astrology. In his argument against the astrologer's ability to foretell the future, he uses only verses from the Koran and a reported tradition from the Prophet. This may indicate the strength of the religious opposition to astrology: even the philosophers felt they had to dissociate themselves from astrology by appealing to religious dogma.

Al-Bīrūnī, a contemporary of Ibn Sīnā, an astronomer, and a compiler of what remains the best encyclopedic work on medieval Islamic astrology, found himself in a very awkward position. Asked by his patroness to write a text on astrology, but feeling the pressure of religious objections and his own skepticism toward the subject, he could leave only a few remarks throughout the work disavowing astrological doctrines. On another occasion, he even went so far as to attack astrology directly. And in still another work he says that he discussed astrology only to warn the intelligent man away from it. He tolerates it only as a means of livelihood for the astronomer, whose research might otherwise not be supported. From the other end of the Muslim world, medieval Spain, the Zahiri theologian Ibn Ḥazm had a different reason to attack astrology. His chief contention was that any science, especially astrology, that does not serve to understand theology is worthless.

Although Abu Ḥāmid al-Ghazzālī, the most influential theologian and jurist of Islam, devoted a full treatise to attacking the philosophers, in two separate works he seems to accept the validity of astrology inasmuch as he accepts medicine, even though both sciences are conjectural. But in view of the prophetic tradition against astrology, he maintains one can dispense with this conjectural discipline.

Ibn Rushd (Averroës), on the other hand, clearly rejects astrology: it "does not belong to physical science; it is only a prognostication of future events, and is of the same type as augury and vaticination."

Fakhr al-Dīn al-Rāzī was the only philosopher thereafter to have had some sympathy toward astrology. But he could not have any serious impact, for by the early thirteenth century arguments against astrology had become well articulated and formalized, leading in the next two centuries to the most elaborate and comprehensive attack on astrology, by Ibn Qayyim al-Jawzīyyah, and the historian Ibn Khaldūn. It is in these treatises that the "official" orthodox position against astrology is found.

The astrologer's defense was elaborately formulated as early as the ninth century by Abū Maᶜshar. In his main work, *Kitāb al-madkhal ᶜilm ᵓaḥkām al-nujūm* ("Introduction to Astrology"), he fills some twenty folios in defense of astrology against its enemies, whom he classifies into the following types; those who denied the influence of the planets on the sublunar world of generation and corruption; those who believed that the planets influence only general events but not particular ones; traditionalists and speculative philosophers; those who studied the general things (*ᶜilm al-kull*) of the science of the stars (astronomers and philosophers?); those who studied the generals; mathematicians (*ᶜaṣḥāb al-ḥisāb*); those envious of the astrologers; physicians; the general masses (*al-ᶜāmmat*), who do not know the virtue of any science; and the general masses, who are misled by the mistakes of those claiming to be astrologers.

With the exception of the feeble defense of Ibn Ṭāwūs and the sympathies of Fakhr al-Dīn al-Rāzī, there is no other Islamic defense of astrology of the same thoroughness.

Thus astrology seems to have been distinguished from astronomy at an early stage in Islam, although the expression was used to designate both disciplines. The religious reaction to astrology in particular, and to "foreign sciences" in general, forced physicians, philosophers, and mathematicians to dissociate themselves from the astrologers. The religious position most often quoted in the sources is that astronomy is to be considered as permissible and astrology as forbidden. The argument most often presented against astrology is that "God has reserved for himself the knowledge of the future to the exception of his angels and prophets."

ASTROLOGY/ASTRONOMY, ISLAMIC

The attacks on astrology apparently did not stop astrologers from practicing in almost every domain of public life—in the streets, in shops, in the company of armies, on ships, at deathbeds, and in official positions at court. Administrative manuals specify the duties of such astrologers, especially the court astrologers. Sometimes they were carefully tested, and their salaries fixed. The areas of their competence were supposed to include every facet of human existence. The extant sources attest to the following categories of astrological work:

Horoscopic (genethliac) astrology, the most common type, dealt with the problems of the individual, mainly through a reading of the heavenly configurations at his time of birth, starting from the point of the "horoscope," that is, the point of the ecliptic that is ascending at the eastern horizon at that time. In the *Tetrabiblos,* Ptolemy made only an ambiguous reference to that point, as well as to the divisions of the ecliptic known as "houses." With Muslim astronomers, on the other hand, both concepts (as well as others) were all mathematically defined with great precision. In this category one also finds *mawālīd* (nativities). In typical prognostication from one of these texts, if the native is born "with the moon within the limits of Mercury, and Mercury is beholding it from humid places, the native will have the inclination for painting, engraving, embroidering, and the like."

Katarchai, including both the ᵓ*ikhtiyārāt* (elections) and the *interrogationes,* was another common type of prognostication in which the moon plays a very important role. The elections are devoted mainly to determining the opportune time to begin any kind of action: "If you wish to start an alchemical work, or anything requiring fire, or any kind of work you may have to repeat, start that when the moon is in a bicorporeal sign. . . ." A typical example of *interrogationes* is: "If you are asked about an army whether it is small or large, count the signs between the moon and Mercury, and if they come out to be even the army is large, otherwise, it is small. . . ."

World and year's cycles have their origins in the repetitive nature of astronomical phenomena. One such cycle is that of the repeated conjunction of Saturn and Jupiter, which takes place approximately every twenty years on a point on the ecliptic that moves so as to cover the entire ecliptic in 960 years. Political events were assumed to have been determined by such conjunctions. Another cyclical event is that of the return of the sun to the vernal equinox. The planet having the greatest number of "honors" at that moment was called the *aphetis* ("significator") or *hylāj.* The prognostication connected with this phenomenon was called the year's revolution *(taḥwīl al-sanat).* Similarly, the yearly return of the sun to the native's "horoscope" produced prognostications for an astrological birthday. The consideration of such cycles in connection with the native's birth chart, and permutations of these and similar cycles, could increase the astrologer's treasury to meet practically any situation.

Fortune, rays, and lots. The point on the ecliptic that is in the same position to the "horoscope" as the moon is to the sun was called the lot of fortune *(sahm al-sa*ᶜ*ādah).* Once determined, it was used in the same capacity as a planet to foretell a number of events, including the length of one's life. Other lots were similarly defined and allowed to increase beyond reasonable limits. Planets were supposedly able to project rays in order to attack, support, capture, or obstruct another planet. Such concepts apparently stem from the works of Vettius Valens and Ptolemy; Muslim astrologers only gave them a mathematical definition. Other concepts, such as *tasyīr* (astrological computations based on planetary trajectories), "equalization of houses," and transit, were also given similar mathematical formulation.

In all of these problems, and in the type of question the astrologer asked of the astronomer, definite progress was made toward making astrology itself more of an exact science. Al-Bīrūnī's text on astrology, for example, includes a long introduction to mathematics and to mathematical astronomy, a clear indication of the interdependence of these disciplines.

ASTRONOMY

Although a distinction between astrology and astronomy was drawn in early Islamic times, the two disciplines did overlap in more than one area. Astronomers, physicians, philosophers, and mathematicians who were endangered by the religious attacks on astrology were quick to dissociate themselves from the astrologers, thus allowing astronomy to develop as an independent discipline. Its sources are essentially the same as those of astrology and the other "foreign sciences," namely, Indo-Persian and Hellenistic.

Tradition has it that an embassy from the province of Sind visited the caliph al-Manṣūr in Baghdad sometime during the 760's and that this embassy included an Indian astronomer who brought along a

 ASTROLOGY/ASTRONOMY, ISLAMIC

Sanskrit astronomical text known as the *Sindhind (siddhānta).* The caliph supposedly assigned two men to translate an abridged version of this text into Arabic, with the assistance of the Indian astronomer himself. If this tradition is true, it would explain why soon afterward several texts were written in Arabic based on the text of the *Sindhind.* Unfortunately, only one of these texts has survived in extensive form, that of Muḥammad ibn Mūsā al-Khwārizmī, who was also distinguished as the originator of the discipline of algebra. That his text has survived only in a Latin version, and that the others have been all but totally obliterated, clearly indicates the quick neglect of the Indo-Persian tradition.

The Hellenistic tradition, on the other hand, is represented mainly by the transmission of the *Almagest.* Ptolemy's *mathematical collection,* arabized as the *Almagest* through a yet unknown route, was first translated under the patronage of Yaḥya ibn Khālid the Barmacid sometime during the early ninth century. The sources agree as to the unsatisfactory nature of this early translation; and within the next forty-odd years two authoritative translations were made available, by al-Ḥajjāj ibn Maṭar and by Isḥāq ibn Ḥunayn, which was later edited by Thābit Ibn Qurra sometime during the second half of the ninth century.

Once available in Arabic, the *Almagest* generated a tradition of its own, giving rise to epitomes, commentaries, and paraphrases. The relatively new tradition also managed quickly to replace both the Sanskrit tradition of the *Sindhind* and the Pahlavi one represented by the nonextant *Shahrayar zīj.* In the following centuries the astronomical texts that were produced looked at first like mere amalgamations of these traditions, but they very quickly became more and more homogeneously Islamic. Among the most important types are the *anwaᵓ* texts, the *hayᵓah* books, and the *ᵓazyāj,* and works devoted to observational astronomy, instruments, timekeeping for religious purposes, and uranography.

There is no unanimous agreement as to the exact meaning of the word *anwāᵓ* (singular, *nawᵓ*) usually included in the titles of works in this category. But the closest approximation that covers most of the sources is the concept of the setting of one lunar mansion and the rising of another. The material discussed in these texts emphasizes weather prognostications associated with each *nawᵓ*. The pre-Islamic Arab, Indian, Pahlavi, and Greek traditions are also juxtaposed without much coherence or synthesis.

Falak (or *hayᵓah*) books (epitomes of astronomy) constitute a second category of astronomical writings. The text of the *Almagest* was thought of even by Ptolemy himself as comprising three major parts: statements of the general principles and configurations of the heavenly bodies; mathematical proofs (demonstrations) of these principles and configurations; and tables for each planet that allow the prediction of its position. It was Ptolemy who later treated two of these parts in separate books, the *Planetary Hypotheses* and the *Handy Tables.*

In the style of the *Planetary Hypotheses,* several books were written that varied greatly in their contents. A text by Muḥammad ibn Mūsā ibn Shākir (Banū Mūsā), for example, extant in a Damascus manuscript, gives a general description of the major circles on the heavenly sphere and of the star constellations but unfortunately breaks off just before it begins to treat the planets. Muḥammad ibn Kathīr al-Farghānī, on the other hand, wrote a much more extensive text that also dealt with elementary astronomy but included almost all topics treated in the *Almagest.* With time, this genre of literature became more sophisticated and formalistic in structure, and was used as a vehicle to launch criticism of the *Almagest,* as well as to propose new models for planetary theories.

Another type of astronomical writing attempted mainly to summarize the *Almagest* itself and, more often than not, to bring "its terminology more in line with the terminology of the time." Ptolemy's Menelaus theorem, for example, was often replaced by the equivalent sine theorem. That genre too was also formalized with time and reached a standard form with Naṣīr al-Dīn al-Ṭūsī's *Taḥrīr al-Majisṭī,* which was itself the subject of several commentaries.

Those activities that centered on the *Almagest* were also often critical of its contents. Certain phenomena, admittedly of a minor nature, were observed to be at variance with Ptolemy's description. One such phenomenon is the movement of the solar apogee, which according to Ptolemy was fixed at Gemini 5;30°. The reaction of the Muslim astronomers varied from simple corrections of Ptolemy's statement, without further comment, to special attention to the problem and explicit discard of the Ptolemaic value in favor of that found by observation. Bīrūnī went a step further, becoming the first Muslim astronomer to state explicitly that the solar apogee not only partakes of the precession motion, as Ptolemy prescribed for the other planets, but also that it has a motion of its own, totally unknown to Ptolemy. Observations also forced Muslim astrono-

ASTROLOGY/ASTRONOMY, ISLAMIC

mers to correct the precession value adopted in the *Almagest* and to give it a value much closer to the modern one.

More serious criticism of Ptolemy's astronomy was directed at its inherent philosophical contradictions. Ptolemy argued, for example, in the *Planetary Hypotheses* that the planetary spheres were actual physical bodies and not merely a mathematical hypothesis, as he seemed to imply in the *Almagest;* he speaks, for instance, of solid spheres versus empty ones. If the two hypotheses are supposed to be describing the same universe, as they seemed to be doing, then the mathematical hypothesis adopted in the *Almagest* leads to several problems, with the problem of the "equant" being the most outstanding. Put briefly, the planetary models proposed by Ptolemy presuppose the existence of a mathematical point, later called the equant, around which the planetary epicycles were supposed to move at uniform speed. This concept becomes totally absurd when this point is thought of in terms of physical spheres, for then one would have to accept the mechanical impossibility of allowing a physical sphere to move at uniform speed around an axis that does not pass through its center. The realization of this problem in the Ptolemaic theory gave rise not only to several treatises that discussed this point specially but also to books in which this and other problems were treated at great length.

It was Ibn al-Haytham (Alhazen) who devoted a comprehensive treatise to the criticism of Ptolemy, although we are not sure whether he himself produced an alternative system. In a later work he is blamed for "raising doubts; but (failing to) produce anything more than doubts."

In Muslim Spain, the problem of the equant also received some attention, but in the context of several other problems. Jābir Ibn Aflaḥ, for example, criticized Ptolemy for not being rigorous enough and for "taking the center of the deferent [in the model of the upper planets] to be halfway between the 'equant' and the center of the universe without proof." Ibn Rushd, on the other hand, blamed Ptolemy for not being Aristotelian enough, taking him to task mainly in the context of his own commentary on Aristotle's *Metaphysics.* The only Andalusian who attempted to produce an alternative astronomy was al-Biṭrūjī, although it did not meet with much success.

In the eastern part of the Muslim world, sometime during the first half of the thirteenth century, a Damascene named Muʾayyad al-Dīn al-ʿUrḍī wrote a full treatise devoted to a reform of Ptolemy's astronomy. At about the same time, al-Ṭūsī wrote two texts, one in Persian and the other in Arabic, in which he not only argues against Ptolemy's astronomy but also proposes new alternatives to some planetary models that avoid most of its pitfalls. In his discussion of the lunar model, he introduced a new mathematical theorem, now known as the Ṭūsī-couple, which was subsequently incorporated into the works of every original astronomer up to and including Copernicus.

We are not very clear on the works of other astronomers of this period who worked mainly from the Ilkhanid capital city, Maragheh, in northwest Iran. Among them was Quṭb al-Dīn al-Shīrāzī, who proposed one of the most sophisticated models for the motion of Mercury. He also mentions several other texts, which have not yet been studied or even identified, that contain original material.

In the fourteenth century this model-building activity was brought to a very successful conclusion by Ibn al-Shāṭir of Damascus. He not only incorporated al-Ṭūsī's mathematical theorem but also managed to avoid the mistakes of the earlier Ptolemaic reformers. He also drew attention to the need for combining the philosophical treatment, which had characterized most earlier astronomical attempts, with observation and hence produced the first realistic model of the motions of the moon.

These attempts at reforming Ptolemy's astronomy are not totally unrelated to the Copernican revolution. Not only was Copernicus motivated by the same considerations, but recent research has shown that the Copernican model for the upper planets (as discussed in *De revolutionibus*) uses the same techniques proposed three centuries earlier by al-ʿUrḍī, and his model for the moon is identical to that of Ibn al-Shāṭir. Moreover, the similarities between Copernicus and Ibn al-Shāṭir in the Mercury model add one more link in the chain of apparent coincidence to bring the whole issue of independent discovery into question.

The *ʾazyāj* (astronomical handbooks), probably the most extensive genre of Islamic astronomical literature, should be seen as a continuation of the tradition of the *Handy Tables* of Ptolemy. In these works, the authors do not deal with the configuration of the planetary spheres as such but, rather, assume some configuration as given and set out to compute the actual positions of a planet at any given time.

Since all reforms of Ptolemaic astronomy were in

ASTROLOGY/ASTRONOMY, ISLAMIC

essence philosophical reforms, these tables cannot be expected to vary too much from the *Handy Tables,* except for the necessary fixing of calendars, longitudes, latitudes, and so forth. In format, however, these handbooks changed considerably between the ninth century, when they were first computed, and the late seventeenth century, when they started to become scarce. Most of this change was motivated by the concept of "simplicity of use." The ultimate result of simplicity was finally reached sometime in the fifteenth century, when one astronomer managed to change the method of computation and the format of his tables to such an extent that all he required of his reader was the mastery of the operation of addition. One cannot but feel these works were compiled especially for less educated astrologers who were mainly interested in quick determination of planetary positions and not in the kinematics of the celestial spheres as such.

Excluding the treatises on instruments, discussed below, we find a scarcity of texts dealing with observational astronomy. Yet we know that some of the observations produced new parameters, either correcting those of Ptolemy, as in the case of precession and solar apogee, or refining them by applying new methods of observation. An example of these methods is contained, for instance, in the works of Thābit ibn Qurra and al-Bīrūnī, who used the new method of observing the solar declination at midseason instead of at the solstices, as was done by Ptolemy.

Observatories were also established especially for these activities. But although we know some details connected with these observatories as institutions, we do not yet have enough records of the actual observations conducted there or of the methods by which individual parameters were tested and later incorporated into the tables. We are fortunate in this regard to have the text of al-Maghribī, which was wrongly described by Suter as a compendium *(cholasa)* of the *Almagest* with some new observations conducted at Maragheh. The text, which is still extant at Leiden, is not a compendium of the *Almagest* but, rather, a *hay*ᵓ*ah* (astronomy)-type text written in the style of the *Almagest* but based solely on observations conducted in Maragheh between 1263 and 1274. In it we are told in great detail how each parameter, such as eccentricity and epicyclic radius, of each planet was determined. Unfortunately, neither al-Maghribī's text, nor the *Īlkhānī zīj,* nor most of the other texts written in Maragheh during this period has ever been studied in any detail by modern scholars.

Another text that might have been of the same nature, *Ta*ᶜ*līq al-*ᵓ*arṣād* ("Comments on Observations") of Ibn al-Shāṭir, is known only by name. It has not yet been located, nor have we come across anything similar to it from the famous fifteenth-century observatory of Ulugh Beg in Samarkand. All of this evidence—or lack of it—amounts to saying that although observational astronomy managed to attack and solve individual problems, it did not on the whole develop a conceptual framework that analyzed the relationship between theory and observation.

Islamic treatises on instruments were devoted either to large-scale construction of observatories or to individual instruments; of the latter the most popular remains the astrolabe.

Although the theory of stereographic projection was known at least from the time of Hipparchus, and a treatise expounding it was known as early as Ptolemy's time, the theory itself was not put to full use in the construction of the planispheric astrolabe until just before that instrument reached Islam. Once it did, the astrolabe was further perfected and new elements introduced, so that by the early tenth century its capabilities as an observational instrument as well as a slide rule-type computer were fully developed to include some 300 problems in mathematical astronomy, geography, and spherical trigonometry. In the hands of Muslim astronomers the astrolabe became sophisticated enough to be useful for any latitude.

The surviving specimens, dating from the late tenth century to our own, are in most cases superb examples of the blending of precision craftsmanship and fine Muslim metallic artwork. Literary and iconographic evidence scattered over many centuries confirms that the astrolabe became the most popular symbol of the professional astrologer. Quadrants, a further development of the astrolabe and produced by using only one quarter of it, are not known from non-Islamic sources and seem to have been developed by Muslims as a natural consequence of their work on the astrolabe. In this sophisticated form, the quadrant could be used to solve "all standard problems of spherical astronomy."

Spherical astrolabes and celestial globes are much scarcer but, like the planispheric astrolabe, seem to have been of little use in observations and were in all probability intended only to exhibit how the celestial spheres rotated. Connected with this high technology were sundials and equatoria, the former used mainly to determine the time of Muslim prayers,

 ASTROLOGY/ASTRONOMY, ISLAMIC

while the latter exhibited the planetary movements at any given time.

The times for observing the prescribed five daily prayers of Islam were all defined by the daily passage of the sun. Because of this dependence, the time varied from one day and place to another. Muslim astronomers devised several methods that specifically often tabulated their results to simplify the solution of what were essentially problems of spherical trigonometry. Finding the time from the altitude of the sun, for example, was one such problem solved by tables given in the *miqāt* (timekeeping) texts, as this literature was known. Special curves designating the times of prayers were also engraved on astrolabes.

Although there was a religious prohibition on beginning the lunar month of fasting according to the computed time, a *zīj* text often included tables of lunar visibility to answer that problem specifically. Moreover, the beginning of the daily fasting during that month was also astronomically defined by the onset of dawn, a problem that spurred much research of its own.

Following Ptolemy's description of the "fixed stars" in the *Almagest,* Muslim astronomers devoted special texts to describing the constellations. One such work that became very famous in the Islamic world and in Europe, especially because of its artistic value, was *Ṣuwar al-kawākib* of ᶜAbd al-Raḥmān al-Ṣūfī. In these texts old Arabian star names and constellations were matched with those described by Ptolemy, thus allowing pre-Islamic traditions to survive. Through such texts most modern star names still bear the imprint of Arabic.

During the ninth and tenth centuries the religious attacks on astrology began to endanger the astronomers, whose profession had previously been conceived as the same as that of the astrologer. For the sake of survival, the astronomers of the eleventh and twelfth centuries began a process of redefinition of their field that entailed a rejection of the astrologer's craft and a greater emphasis on religious matters.

In this confrontation, the religious authorities seem to have won and hence forced the astronomers to become increasingly dependent on religious patronage. The office of the *muwaqqit* (timekeeper) was introduced into the bureaucracy of the mosque, the main center of the Islamic community, during the thirteenth century.

Most of the astronomical texts thereafter were written by such *muwaqqits*; the net result was less emphasis on astrological subjects and more concern for religious issues. The importance accorded to these issues led to further redefinition of the religious prescriptions, this time in mathematical terms. As a consequence, all problems that had any religious bearing were incorporated into mathematical astronomy and treated in those texts irrespective of the religious injunctions.

Freed from political patronage, the *muwaqqits* could then, in principle, direct their attention to any astronomical problem and no longer had to produce astrological texts. It is still very difficult, however, to assess the significance of this new orientation; for there has never been a full study devoted to the impact of this new patronage on Islamic astronomy.

BIBLIOGRAPHY

An example of the several Arabic texts on the classifications of the sciences is al-Fārābī, *'Iḥṣa' al-ᶜulūm,* Osman Amine, ed. (1968). The English translation of al-Nadīm's *Fihrist* by B. Dodge (1970), should be used with extreme care.

For the sources of Arabic astrology, see Dorotheus Sidonius, *Carmen Astrologicum,* David Pingree, ed. (1976); and Ptolemy, *Tetrabiblos,* F. E. Robbins, ed. and trans. (1971). For overview and manuscript material see M. Ullmann, *Die Natur und Geheimwissenschaften im Islam* (1972); and Fuat Sezgin, *Geschichte des arabischen Schrifttums,* VII (1979).

For a flavor of the texts themselves, see al-Bīrūnī, *Elements of Astrology,* Ramsay Wright, trans. (1934); and the less available work of Abū Maᶜshar, *Kitāb al-madkhal fī ᶜilm 'aḥkām al-nujūm,* Garullah MS 1508.

For a treatment of astrology in Islam, see al-Khaṭīb al-Baghdādī, *Risālat fī ᶜilm al-nujūm,* Asir MS 190. For the social status of the astrologer, see G. Saliba, "The Role of the Astrologer in Medieval Islamic Society," in *Proceedings of the Second International Symposium for the History of Arabic Science* (in press).

Attacks on astrology are numerous, the most extensive being Ibn Qayyim al-Jawzīyyah, *Miftāḥ dār al-saᶜādah, Dar al-Kutub al-ᶜilmiyyah,* II, and Ibn Khaldūn, *The Muqaddimah, F. Rosenthal, trans. (1958). Along different lines, see Ibn Hazm, Marātib al-ᶜulūm,* Ihsan Abbas, ed., (n.d.); and *Kitāb al-faṣl fī al-milal wa-l-'ahwā' wa-l-niḥal,* V (1903). See also M. A. F. Mehren, "Vues d'Avicenne sur l'astrologie et sur le rapport de la responsabilité humaine avec destin," in *Le Museon,* 3 (1884); and Averroës, *Tahāfut al-Tahāfut* ("The Incoherence of the Incoherence"), S. van den Bergh, trans. (1969).

The most extensive defense of astrology is in Abū Maᶜshar's work, *op. cit.,* to which add Ibn Ṭāwūs, Ali ibn Mūsā, *Faraj al-Mahmūm fī ta'rīkh ᶜulamā' al-nujūm* (1949); the former was partially translated in Jean Claude Vadet, "Une defense de l'astrologie dans le Madhal d'Abu Maᶜšar al-Balhi," in *Annales islamologiques,* 5 (1963).

For the "world-year" type of astrology, see E. S. Kennedy, "Ramifications of the World Year Concept on Islamic Astrology," in *Proceedings of the 10th International Congress of the History of Science* (1964), 23–45.

On the mathematization of astrology in Islam, see E. S. Kennedy and H. Krikorian-Preisler, "The Astrological Doctrine of Projecting the Rays," in *Al-Abhath,* **25** (1972); and O. Schimmer, *"Al-Tasyīr,"* in *Encyclopedia of Islam,* 1st ed., IV.

Among the general references for Islamic astronomy are F. Sezgin, *Geschichte des arabischen Schrifttums,* VI (1978), and H. Suter, *Die Mathematiker und Astronomen der Araber und Ihre Werke* (1900).

On the transmission of ancient science to Islam, consult C. A. Nallino, *ᶜIlm al-falak* (1911), translated into Italian in *Raccolta di scriti editi et inediti* (1944), V; and D. Pingree, "The Greek Influence on Early Islamic Mathematical Astronomy," in *Journal of the American Oriental Society,* **93** (1973).

For the important transmission of the *Almagest* and its influence, consult Sezgin, *op. cit.* VI, 88–94; and O. Pedersen, *A Survey of the Almagest* (1974).

For books written in the tradition of the *Planetary Hypothesis* and the *Almagest,* see Muhammad ibn Musa ibn Shaker, *Kitāb ḥarakat al-falak,* Falak 4489; Muḥammad ibn Kathir al-Farghani, *Elementa astronomica* (1969); Baron Carra de Vaux, "L'Almagest d'Abu-lwefa albuzdjani," in *Journal asiatique,* 8th ser. **19** (1892); and for a discussion of the later genre of this literature, J. Livingston, "Naṣīr al-Dīn al-Ṭūsī's al-Ṭadhkirah: A Category of Islamic Astronomical Literature," in *Centaurus,* **17** (1972–1973).

For the term *anwāᵓ*, see C. Pellat, *Encyclopedia of Islam* new ed. I; and for the most comprehensive survey of the *ᵓazyāj* works, see E. S. Kennedy, "A Survey of Islamic Astronomical Tables," in *Transactions of the American Philosophical Society,* **46** (1956); and, for later developments in these texts, G. Saliba, "The Planetary Tables of Cyriacus," in *Journal for the History of Arabic Science,* **2** (1978), which contains a bibliography of the most recent literature on the modifications of the *zīj*.

There are several studies dealing with the Islamic reaction to Ptolemaic astronomy mainly gathered in E. S. Kennedy and I. Ghanem, eds., *The Life and Work of Ibn al-Shatir* (1976); to which should be added O. Neugebauer, "Thabet ben Qurra 'On the Solar Year' and 'On the Motion of the Eighth Sphere,'" in *Proceedings of the American Philosophical Society,* **106** (1962); W. Hartner and M. Schramm, "Al-Bīrūnī and the Theory of the Solar Apogee: An Example of Originality in Arabic Science," in A. C. Crombie ed., *Scientific Change* (1963); G. Saliba, "Ibn Sīnā and Abū ᶜUbayd al-Jūzjānī: The Problem of the Ptolemaic Equant," in *Journal for the History of Arabic Science,* **4** (1980); "The First Non-Ptolemaic Astronomy at the Maraghah School," in *Isis,* **70** (1979); and "The Original Source of Quṭb al-Dīn al-Shīrāzī's Planetary Model," in *Journal for the History of Arabic Science,* **3** (1979); B. Goldstein, *Al-Biṭrūjī on the Principles of Astronomy* (1971); L. Gauthier, "Une réforme du système astronomique de Ptolémée tentée par les philosophes arabes du XIIᵉ siècle," in *Journal Asiatique,* 10th ser., **14** (1909); and for the relationship of these modifications of the Ptolemaic system to the works of Copernicus, see N. Swerdlow, "The Derivation and First Draft of Copernicus' Planetary Theory: A Translation of the Commentariolus with Commentary," in *Proceedings of the American Philosophical Society,* **117** (1973).

For observatories and instruments, consult A. Sayili, *The Observatory in Islam* (1960); W. Hartner, *"Asṭurlāb,"* in *Encyclopedia of Islam,* new ed., I; D. King, "An Analog Computer for Solving Problems of Spherical Astronomy," in *Archives internationales d'histoire des sciences* **24** (1974); K. Schoy, *Gnomonik der Araber in die Geschichte der Zeitmessung und der Uhren* (1923); E. S. Kennedy, *The Planetary Equatorium of Jamshīd ibn Ghiyāth al-Dīn al-Kāshī* (1960).

For astronomical responses to religious questions, see E. S. Kennedy, "The Lunar Visibility Theory of Yaᶜqūb ibn Ṭāriq," in *Journal of Near Eastern Studies,* **27** (1968); and "Al-Biruni on the Muslim Times of Prayers," in Peter Chelkowski, ed., *The Scholar and the Saint* (1975); and with M. L. Davidian, "Al-Qayini on the Duration of Dawn and Twilight," in *Journal of Near Eastern Studies,* **22** (1961).

For Arabic star names and their transmission to Europe, see P. Kunitzch, *Untersuchungen zur Sternnomenklatur der Araber* (1961); and *Arabische Sternnamen in Europa* (1959).

GEORGE SALIBA

[See also **Arabic Numerals (Hindu-Arabic); Astrolabe; Bīrūnī, al-; Fārābī, al-; Ghazzālī, al-; Ḥazm, Ibn; Nadim, Ibn al-; Rāzī, al-; Sīnā, Ibn.**]

ASTURIAN ART reached a high point of sophistication and originality in the ninth century. The monuments of Asturias draw aesthetically and iconographically not only from Visigothic predecessors but also from Spain's Roman past and from the examples of its Carolingian allies. Significant in this period is San Julián de los Prados in Oviedo and the hauntingly beautiful hall of uncertain function at Santa Maria de Naranco. Besides architecture, painting, and stone relief, the Asturians were responsible for fine and delicate metalwork, of which the Victory Cross of Oviedo is one striking example.

BIBLIOGRAPHY

Antonio Bonet Correa, *Arte pre-románico asturiano* (1967), contains excellent photographs, but the text must be taken with some reservations; Jacques Fontaine, "L'art

ASTURIAS-LEÓN (718–1037)

Victory Cross, Oviedo Cathedral. Ninth century. PHOTOGRAPH COURTESY OF FOTO MAS

asturian," in *L'art préroman hispanique* (1973); Helmut Schlunk, "Arte Bisigodo" and "Arte Asturiano," in *Ars Hispaniae*, VII (1947), has solid information, though it is limited in interpretation.

JERRILYN DODDS

ASTURIAS-LEÓN (718–1037). At its inception in the early eighth century, the kingdom of Asturias extended over a few valleys at the western end of the Picos de Europa (a mountain range in the northern part of the present Spanish provinces of Santander and Asturias). In the kingdom's heyday, early in the tenth century and before the rise of the Córdoba caliphate, the Asturian-Leonese kings ruled over an area roughly bounded by the Bay of Biscay in the north, the area of Coimbra and the Tagus River basin in the south, the Atlantic in the west, and the present borders of Old Castile in the east. The beginnings of Asturias as an independent political entity lie partly hidden behind a veil of myths and nationalistic history, the source to this day of unending historiographical controversy.

In 711 the armies of Islam crossed the Strait of Gibraltar and in a series of swift campaigns destroyed the Visigothic empire. In a few years the Muslims imposed their hegemony throughout most of the Iberian Peninsula, establishing without great difficulty a working relationship with the conquered Christian population. Only in the far north, in the mountains of Asturias and Cantabria (northern part of the province of Santander), did a small group of natives and fleeing Visigoths retain their independence. The region had always resisted assimilation and conquest by previous invaders of the peninsula. Its inaccessibility and economic and cultural backwardness made expeditions against these isolated, half-Christianized, primitive outposts as impractical and unappealing for the Muslims as they had been for Phoenicians, Romans, and Visigoths.

This point, made recently by Spanish historians, contradicts the romantic view of the early beginnings of the Reconquest and the heroic colors with which early Asturian history has been painted. Rather than from a desire to reconquer, the expansion of the mountain people into the Leonese and Castilian plain resulted from Muslim indifference to this remote region. The early success of the Asturian realm was not based on religion, or on a desire to revive the Visigothic kingdom. As late as the early eleventh century, Asturias expanded and contracted less by its own efforts than as a result of the frequent political convulsions of al-Andalus (the area of southern Spain, later Andalusia, controlled by Islam). Times of crisis in Córdoba were reflected in Christian gains, but whenever a strong man guided Muslim Spain, its armies usually had the upper hand. As late as 997, al-Mansur, ruler of Córdoba, could strike deep into Galicia and force the Christians he captured to carry to Córdoba the bells and doors of the cathedral of Santiago de Compostela. Nevertheless, in spite of this almost symbiotic link between the two adversaries, the early rulers of Asturias succeeded in surviving, and later in expanding to the point where the Muslims could send punitive expeditions against them but could no longer conquer.

The history of eighth-century Asturias is obscure. Contemporary sources are practically nonexistent, and the chroniclers writing two hundred years later had a vested interest in glorifying the ancestors of their now powerful patrons. The traditional accounts, written late in the ninth century and early in the tenth, relate the story of Pelayo (ruled *ca.*

ASTURIAS-LEÓN (718–1037)

718–737), a member of the Visigothic nobility, or even perhaps of the royal family, who led the Asturians in several losing skirmishes against Muslim troops. His victory at Covadonga on Mount Asueva, however unimportant for his contemporaries, became two hundred years afterward the rallying cry for the Christian kingdoms; and for almost as long Asturian and Leonese rulers traced their ancestry to Pelayo's line.

Unstable conditions in al-Andalus, above all the Berber rebellion and civil war of 741, led the Muslims to withdraw from most parts of Galicia. This region in the northwestern corner of Spain was during some brief periods in the ninth, tenth, and eleventh centuries an independent kingdom, and remained in theory one of the several royal titles claimed by Asturian, and later Castilian, kings. Green and fertile, open to the sea, and with its own rich Celtic tradition and folklore, Galicia, although backward and often ignored, was an important resource for the Asturian rulers. Its perennial surplus population was channeled to the Douro basin in the ninth century, as it is being exported to the factories of northern Europe in the late twentieth.

When the Muslims abandoned Galicia, Alfonso I (739–757), Pelayo's son-in-law, duke of Cantabria and, after the death of his brother-in-law Fáfila (*ca.* 732–739), ruler of Asturias, used the opportunity to take the cities of Lugo and Astorga and to raid the lands of the Tierra de Campos, Álava, the Bureba, and southward to the region of Ávila and Segovia. His armies destroyed Muslim fortifications in the area, carrying the Christian population, Mozarabs (Christians who had accepted Muslim customs and dress but not the religion), back to their mountain strongholds. The Douro River basin became a half-deserted and unproductive land. This buffer zone between Asturias and al-Andalus served as an effective barrier to Muslim attacks. Although the flanks, Galicia and Álava, remained exposed, Asturias was for all practical purposes beyond the reach of invaders. Raids into Muslim territory, stripping the land of its population and wealth, followed by eventual repopulation and creation of a new buffer zone, made up a pattern repeated with some success by many Asturian and Leonese rulers.

Between the death of Alfonso I in 757 and the reign of his grandson Alfonso II (791–842), the kingdom of Asturias enjoyed a period of external peace and probably a moderate growth in population. An expansion of the arable in Galicia and the Asturian valleys was largely due to the more advanced agricultural techniques of the Mozarabs, some of whom had been brought back to Asturias by Alfonso I and others who had migrated to the area during the eighth century. Internally, Asturias suffered continuous political struggles, usurpations of the crown, and a widespread peasant revolt in 774. Although we know next to nothing about the latter, the uprising was perhaps caused by the triumph of a Visigothic elite and their administrative and land tenure patterns over the indigenous pastoral-oriented population, and may have been part of the larger struggle within Spanish history between the mountain and plains people.

The reign of Alfonso II was marked by many important developments. Around 794 he established his court at Oviedo, and although the city was sacked by the Muslims, Alfonso's army inflicted heavy casualties on the invaders as they withdrew from the area. Alfonso's building, or in most cases rebuilding, programs in Oviedo and elsewhere attest to his newfound strength. New monastic foundations; his association with and support of the cult of Saint James at Compostela, perhaps a way of securing Galicia; the claims of the Asturian church to ecclesiastical independence from the adoptionist-tainted see of Toledo; and, above all, the formal reestablishment of Visigothic administrative organization and royal ceremonies gave the king a secure position in the Asturian realm.

Alfonso II's innovations served as the foundations for the so-called neo-Gothic—or, to be more precise, neo-Visigothic—revival of the late ninth and early tenth centuries. The king also sought the cooperation and support of Charlemagne. Spanish historians have argued over the nature and impact that these relations had upon Asturian political developments without fully explaining them. Nevertheless, the establishment of Asturian-Frankish ties influenced, to some extent, the economic, social, institutional, and, above all, ecclesiastical life of the kingdom.

After the usual dynastic struggle that followed Alfonso II's death, the reign of Ramiro I (842–850) witnessed little change in the defensive stance of the kingdom. Under Ramiro's son, Ordoño I (850–866), however, the Christian forces took advantage of the political divisions in al-Andalus and ventured into the Douro basin. The cities of Túy and Astorga were repopulated, and the city of León was resettled in 856 and protected behind its newly rebuilt Roman walls. Further east, Ordoño I encouraged the building of a line of castles protecting the first settlement in the region known as Bardulia, south of the moun-

ASTURIAS-LEÓN (718–1037)

tain areas of Santander and Biscay, which because of its frontier fortifications was soon known as Castile.

Ordoño I's expansionist efforts were aided by the breakdown of Umayyad rule in Muslim Spain. His son, Alfonso III, known to later chroniclers as the Great, fully exploited the political paralysis of al-Andalus, extending his kingdom as far south as Zamora and Oporto. Under his rule, royal and private occupation and resettlement of the entire Douro River basin made Asturias no longer a kingdom perched high in the mountains: it now had access to, and to a certain extent control of, the plains. His convincing victories over Muslim armies at Polvoraria (878) and Valdemora marked a temporary shift in the relations between Asturias and al-Andalus, with Asturias on the offensive. Alfonso III's conscious revival of Visigothic tradition, his territorial claims to the entire peninsula, and his rebuilding program and patronage of culture marked the maturity of the Asturian monarchy after almost two centuries of formation.

At his death (*ca.* 910), Alfonso the Great's lands were partitioned among his three sons. To García (910–914) went the Douro territories with León as administrative center. Spanish historians have seen this year as the point of transition from the kingdom of Asturias to the kingdom of León. Ordoño II (914–924) took Galicia, and Fruela (910–925) kept Asturias, with Oviedo as his capital. Alfonso III's efforts to unite and strengthen the realm were erased by his will.

The infighting among Alfonso's heirs coincided with the revival of al-Andalus. Islamic civilization in Spain reached its high mark in the tenth century, and a great deal of this rebirth of Muslim power was due to ᶜAbd al-Raḥmān III. In 929 he took the title of caliph and brought factional and tribal disputes to an end. While the Umayyad caliphs restored peace and prosperity to al-Andalus, Asturias-León suffered through yet another succession crisis. Regardless of the political problems, and whether as a response to ᶜAbd al-Raḥmān's claims to the caliphate or influenced by the Carolingian example, the Asturian-Leonese kings assumed the title of emperor.

Although the use of this title has generated considerable debate among historians of medieval Spain, the origins or intentions of the imperial title are not clear. From a historical perspective, however, these claims to the imperial dignity were an important addition to the Asturian kings' association with the cult of Saint James and their rejection of Toledo's ecclesiastical primacy. Nevertheless, their mighty titles and political pretensions seldom matched reality. After Ordoño II was able to reunite the realm and even make modest inroads in the area of the Rioja (*ca.* 918), he suffered a severe defeat two years later at Valdejunquera. After 920, al-Andalus launched numerous punitive expeditions that disrupted life in the Christian kingdom. Ordoño II's son Alfonso IV (925–931), unable to stop the Muslim raids, abdicated in favor of his brother Ramiro II (931–950/951).

In Ramiro the kingdom had a ruthless and capable ruler. He secured his grip on the throne by blinding his brother Alfonso and his nephew. In 939, Ramiro II led a coalition of Asturian, Navarrese, and Muslim (provided by his ally, Abu Yahya, the ruler of Saragossa) troops to an important victory against ᶜAbd al-Raḥmān at Simancas. Asturias-León extended its frontier southward, then repopulated the captured area and established a line of fortified places at Salamanca, Ledesma, Los Baños, and other strategic locations along the new border. His successes on the battlefield were somewhat negated by the rise of the Christian kingdom of Navarre and the independent policies of Fernán González (932–970), the count of Castile. One cannot speak of the Reconquest as a concerted union of Christians against Islam, an idealized crusade for their faith. The Christian and Muslim rulers often followed their own particular political interests, and these did not always agree with their religious preferences. Enmity among Christians prevailed more often than cooperation, and alliances between Christians and Muslims against other Muslims or Christians were certainly not uncommon.

After Ramiro's death Asturias-León was beset by civil wars, interrupted by a moment of victory, the sack of Lisbon (955) by Ordoño III (950–955). Fernán González of Castile intervened frequently in the affairs of the kingdom. He was able to influence and sometimes control the succession to the Asturian-Leonese throne. The names of these rulers, kept purposely weak by the Castilian count and other magnates (Sancho I the Fat [956–958, 960–966], Ordoño IV the Bad [958–960]), recall those ninth- and tenth-century Carolingian kings who earned their sobriquets by sheer incompetence. For almost half a century the realm became in fact a client state of the Córdoba caliphs, the kings of León, as was the case with Sancho I, taking the humiliating road to the Umayyad capital to pledge their loyalty to the Muslim rulers in return for their support. Meanwhile, under its able counts Castile had gained a de facto

ASTURIAS-LEÓN (718–1037)

independence from Asturias by maintaining friendly relations with Córdoba.

At the death of al-Ḥakam in 976, control of the Umayyad caliphate passed into the hands of al-Mansur, a brilliant military dictator. He exercised his power from behind the puppet rule of the true caliph, Hisham II. Al-Mansur led more than fifty campaigns against the northern Christian kingdoms. He sacked Zamora, Coimbra, and León, taking and wasting the lands in between. Cordovan troops intervened in Asturian-Leonese affairs, while Castile survived only by accepting al-Mansur's protectorate. The clearest indication of Christian weakness took place on 10 August 997, when the Muslim ruler attacked Compostela, deep in the northwestern region of Galicia, and had the bells and doors of Saint James's shrine carried back to Córdoba by Christian slaves.

Al-Mansur's death in 1002, and that of his capable son ᶜAbd al-Malik in 1008, signaled a return to civil wars and political fragmentation in al-Andalus. The general confusion and decline that followed led in 1031 to the collapse of the caliphate and the emergence of as many as twenty-six *taifas* (small kingdoms). Each of these new political units was too weak to oppose the Christian advance southward alone. Eventually many of these *taifas* were cut up piecemeal or became vassal states to more powerful political units. In the troubled period that followed the death of ᶜAbd al-Malik and the collapse of the caliphate, Castile and not León reaped the benefits. By supporting one faction against the other in al-Andalus, the Castilian counts regained the territories and strong places in Clunia, Gormaz, Osma, Atienza, and Sepúlveda that had been lost to al-Mansur.

Meanwhile, the kingdom of Asturias-León was weakened by the minority of Alfonso V (999–1028). He was two or three years old at the death of his father, Bermudo II (982–999); therefore, during half of his reign he was a minor. Those were years often plagued by unrest among the nobility and Castilian interference. When his time to rule came, Alfonso V's first priority was to check the inroads made by Northmen on the Asturian and Galician shores. He drove them out of his realm and turned to the more pressing needs of the kingdom. In 1017, after his victory over the Vikings, Alfonso V called the magnates of the realm to a meeting at León. This *curia regis* (royal council) enacted the legislation necessary for the reorganization of the kingdom. The *Decretum generale* of 1017 also encouraged the repopulation of León and was accompanied by an active building program. Whether in 1017 or later, as claimed by recent Spanish scholars, the *Fuero* (charter, privilege) of León marks, according to García de Valdeavellano, the first appearance in Spanish legal history of the local community enjoying the privilege of a collective personality.

Alfonso V died before he could set his kingdom on the right path. It is doubtful, in any case, that he would have been successful in balancing the rising power of Navarre and Castile or in restoring the primacy of Asturias-León. The minority of his son, Bermudo III (1027–1037), under the regency of his stepmother Urraca, the sister of Sancho III of Navarre, allowed the Navarrese ruler to extend his influence over León as he had already done to Castile.

Sancho III, a clever and energetic king, had given a warm welcome to the Cluniac order. He had, therefore, opened the peninsula to the new intellectual and religious trends of northern Europe. Institutionally the French feudal model of kingship served as an example for the development of Navarre. After the assassination in 1029 of García, the last count of Castile and last male in the line of Fernán González, Sancho, who was married to García's sister, became the count of Castile. In order to placate Castilian sensibilities, he relinquished the throne of Castile, now raised from county to kingdom, to his secondborn, Fernando. Sancho also seized Leonese territories, incited rebellions by the nobility against Bermudo III, and even assumed the title of king of León on several occasions. In early 1034, Sancho conquered the city of León and claimed the imperial title—and with it primacy over all the Christian kingdoms of Spain. Bermudo fled to Galicia and remained there until after Sancho's death in 1035, when he reclaimed his capital.

Bermudo III lost no time in organizing a military campaign aimed at recovering the lands lost to Navarre. These territories had been appropriated by his brother-in-law Fernando, already discussed as king of Castile. In the valley of Tamarón, near the Pisuerga River, the armies of Asturias-León were defeated by an alliance of Navarrese and Castilian troops. Bermudo died on the battlefield, and Fernando I claimed as his own the rich Visigothic tradition of the Asturian-Leonese realm.

Asturias and León had kings of their own in 1065–1072 and 1157–1230. To the city of León went Alfonso VII (1126–1157) to be crowned emperor of "all the Spains," but the kingdom was caught between Castile and Portugal. Even the wise policies of Fernando II of León (1157–1188) and the energy that

ASTURIAS-LEÓN (718–1037)

his son Alfonso IX (1188–1230) showed in the Leonese repopulation efforts in Extremadura could not prevent the final union with Castile in 1230. After 1037, Asturian-Leonese history became for all practical purposes an appendix to Castilian developments. Castile and not León was the arbiter of northwestern Spain.

ECONOMY AND SOCIETY

Not unlike the rest of Western Europe, Asturias-León was sparsely populated, and remained a predominantly rural society long after 1037. We know little about the Asturian region before 711. Isolated from the centers of civilization in the plain, unconquered by the successive waves of invaders that passed through Iberia, its economy consisted to a large extent of pastoral activities in the mountain grazing lands and cultivation of the soil by free and independent peasants. This pattern of agricultural labor was somewhat changed by the influx of Visigothic magnates fleeing from the Muslims into northern Asturias. These Visigoths became the political and economic elite that ruled the kingdom for centuries to come. They also brought to Asturias their own pattern of agricultural exploitation, cultivation of the land by servile labor. This economic system was not original with the Visigoths, but had been borrowed from the economic models prevalent in southern Spain during the late Roman Empire. In any case, with the Visigoths new economic and social structures came to Asturias.

A word of caution is necessary here. In medieval Asturias-León, as in Castile, the seignorial system was not always accompanied by fully developed feudal ties. The battle over the existence or nonexistence of "feudalism" in Spain has been the subject of endless and unnecessary debates. The opinion of recent historians has been that fragmentation of political authority, with the subsequent exercise of rights of government by local lords, never occurred in Asturias-León. The crown did not lose its regal rights, nor, as Sánchez Albornoz, García de Valdeavellano, and others have shown, did it allow public functions to become hereditary.

In addition to the weakness of feudal ties in the Asturian-Leonese kingdom, the repopulation of the Douro valley by free peasants was an obstacle to the formation of large domains or an extension of the manorial system to the plain. Although this settlement was sometimes carried out under royal auspices or, in the case of Castile, by the initiative of its counts, more important still was the claiming of this open frontier by free peasants. This is the system known to Castilian historians as *pressura (presura).* The Douro region was cultivated mostly by free peasants and not by servile labor, as was the case in other parts of western Europe. Small properties were the norm rather than the exception in the area during the tenth and early eleventh centuries. The importance of this specific type of settlement became evident in the subsequent development of Castilian society.

As elsewhere in western Europe, cereals, wine, and livestock were the basis of Asturian agriculture. However, the kingdom of Asturias missed a great many of the technological innovations that transformed northern rural society in the ninth and tenth centuries. There is little or no indication of the use of the three-field system. Instead, a biannual system of crop rotation was used, and has been used in most parts of Spain until recent times. Similarly, the heavy plow or the widespread use of horses for plowing did not find a willing reception south of the Pyrenees.

The existence of a large number of small properties not always capable of being self-sufficient and the expansion of the arable in the ninth and tenth centuries led to the emergence of local and regional markets, with a subsequent increase in commercial exchange. We cannot assume, however, that the increase in trade led to the emergence of towns in Asturias and León. With the exception of León, the administrative center of the kingdom, where Sánchez Albornoz found evidence of mercantile and artisan activity in the tenth century, and a few episcopal or fortified places, such as Compostela, Asturias-León did not enjoy an active urban development until the twelfth century, when the pilgrimage to Compostela, with thousands of Frenchmen traveling to the tomb of Saint James, served as the catalyst for the formation of the Castilian and Leonese bourgeoisie.

SOCIAL STRUCTURE

The social structure of the Asturian-Leonese kingdom was, in many respects, similar to that of northern feudal Europe. Magnates *(potentates)* and the great barons (counts) owned large expanses of land and held important administrative positions and political influence within the realm. Underneath them were the *infanzones* (knights of good birth), *milites* (knights), and, as a unique development of some Iberian kingdoms, the *caballeros villanos* (nonnoble knights), freemen who fought on horseback and had received special privileges as early as 916 (through the *Fuero de Castrogeriz*). Within

ASTURIAS-LEÓN (718–1037)

these broad categories there were further divisions depending on the nature of vassal ties to the king or on administrative duties. As was the case elsewhere, this dominant group enjoyed the economic, judicial, and social exemptions associated with its status and military obligations.

Below them was a complex structure that included free, semifree, and servile individuals. Among the free, one should count the clergy, a small urban population, and the considerable number of freeholders who owned their lands almost free of seignorial obligations. Other peasants entered into permanent or semipermanent agreements with their lords *(commendatio),* which Spanish institutional historians call *encomendación, comendación, encomienda,* or *patrocinio.* A free peasant would give his land (which he might then continue to hold in exchange for payment of a rent) or a fixed fee to a lord in exchange for protection. One interesting variation of this semiservile tie was the *benefactoría* (later known in Castile as *behetría*), a form of dependence in which the peasants freely selected their lords.

Asturias-León also had a system of hereditary servile labor, serfdom *(colonos, iuniores, collazos).* Slavery, especially in a kingdom perennially at war, also was not uncommon. This short summary only glosses the complex social and economic arrangements present in Asturian society. There were numerous subdivisions in the wide range of the peasants' relations with their lords and the land.

INSTITUTIONS, CHURCH, AND CULTURE

Whether because of Carolingian influence, or because of the pervading Visigothic tradition, as most Spanish historians believe, the Asturian-Leonese kings claimed to be the rightful heirs of the Visigothic empire. As early as the reign of Alfonso II, the kings of Asturias adopted the regal symbols and ceremonies, as well as the administrative organization and offices, once used by the Toledan rulers. The adoption of Visigothic legal *(Liber iudiciorum)* and institutional forms led to a long conflict between the elective (within Pelayo's line) and hereditary principles as to which was the proper form of royal succession. By the tenth century the hereditary principle was reluctantly accepted by the magnates of the realm, but not without lingering doubts and resistance. The survival of such ritual forms and symbols as the acclamation and raising upon the shield of the new king by the great men of the realm is a reminder of the lasting influence of the Germanic elective principle. The failure to set a clear line of succession plagued Asturias, and later Castile, with civil wars in the following centuries. In addition, the organization of the *curia regis* and the revival of the Visigothic court offices *(major domus, spatarius, comes)* were important aspects of the Visigothic renovation under Alfonso II and Alfonso III.

In its institutional formulation the Asturian-Leonese monarchy followed the example of the Visigothic past, and the church of the early Christian kingdoms did not differ much from this pattern. The most important aspect of ecclesiastical organization was that new monastic foundations followed, and often preceded, the repopulation efforts of the ninth and tenth centuries. In one of these new monasteries, the Beatus of Liébana (*ca.* 770) wrote his *Tractatus de apocalypsis,* a theological treatise against the adoptionist heresy of Félix of Urgel and Elipando, archbishop of Toledo.

More important for the development of Asturian society and culture was the rise of the cult of Saint James (Santiago) at Compostela. A long-held belief attributed the conversion of Spain to Saint James the Greater, who after his mission to the West returned to a martyr's death in Jerusalem. As the legend goes, his body was transported by divine intervention back to Spain. Early in the ninth century the body was discovered at Padrón, a small village in remote Galicia. The translation of Saint James's body to Compostela (a few kilometers from Padrón), a site associated with Celtic and Roman religious worship, the expected miracles, and above all the early support of the cult of Saint James by the Asturian kings made Compostela the religious focus of Christian Spain.

After the mid ninth century, peninsular and trans-Pyrenees pilgrimages to the apostle's tomb grew by leaps and bounds until its high point in the twelfth and thirteenth centuries. Toledo's ancient claims to ecclesiastical primacy, already weakened by Muslim domination and Elipando's heretical views, were now seriously challenged by the seat of Saint James. Asturias-León also developed its own liturgy and church organization, the Mozarabic rite, which remained in use until Cluny's expansion into the Iberian Peninsula in the eleventh century.

In art Asturias-León, like the rest of Europe in the ninth and tenth centuries, showed meager accomplishments. Architecturally the Visigothic and Mozarabic influences combined to produce an original Asturian style, of which the churches of San Miguel de Lillo, Santa Cristina de Lena, and Santa María de Naranco are the best examples. Cluny's architectural

ASYLUM, RIGHT OF

style, the Romanesque, falls beyond the chronological boundaries of this essay, and so do the great sculptural works of Romanesque artisans. In the eleventh and twelfth centuries Romanesque found a warm welcome in northwestern Spain.

The Visigothic tradition in goldsmith and enamel work is also evident in the Cross of Angels (808), granted as a gift to the cathedral of Oviedo by Alfonso II, and other crosses and reliquaries of the ninth and tenth centuries. As elsewhere, book illuminations, such as the impressive illustrations of the Beatus' *Commentaries on the Apocalypse,* complete a rather limited list of artistic works.

BIBLIOGRAPHY

Bibliography. Benito Sánchez Alonso, *Fuentes de la historia española e hispano-americana,* 3rd ed., 3 vols. (1952).

General Works. Antonio Ballesteros y Beretta, *Historia de España y su influencia en la historia universal,* 9 vols. (1918–1941); Luis García de Valdeavellano, *Historia de España,* I (1952), 353–1071; Ramón Menéndez Pidal, ed., *Historia de España,* VI (1956); Joseph O'Callaghan, *A History of Medieval Spain* (1975); Ferrán Soldevila, *Historia de España,* I (1952), 110–168; Luis Suárez Fernández, *Historia de España: Edad media* (1970).

Secondary Literature. Louis Barrau-Dihigo, "Étude sur les actes des rois asturiens, 718–910," in *Revue hispanique,* **46** (1919); "Recherches sur l'histoire politique du royaume asturien, 718–910," *ibid.,* **52** (1921); and Armando Cotarelo y Valledor, *Alfonso III, el Magno* (1933); *Estudios sobre la monarquía asturiana* (1971); Antonio Floriano, *Estudios de historia de Asturias* (1962); Justo Pérez de Urbel, *Sampiro: Su crónica y la monarquía leonesa en el siglo X* (1952); and *El condado de Castilla,* 3 vols. (1969); Julio Puyol y Alonso, *Orígenes del reino de León y de sus instituciones políticas* (1926); Justiniano Rodríguez, *Ramiro II, rey de León* (1972); Emilio Sáez Sánchez, "Los ascendientes de San Rosendo (notas para el estudio de la monarquía astur-leonesa durante los siglos IX y X)," in *Hispania,* **8** (1948); Claudio Sánchez Albornoz, *En torno a los orígenes del feudalismo,* 3 vols. (1942); *Estudios sobre las instituciones medievales españolas* (1965); *Una ciudad de la España cristiana hace mil años,* 5th ed. (1966); and *Despoblación y repoblación del valle del Duero* (1966).

TEOFILO F. RUIZ

[See also **Castile to 1474; Cluny, Order of; Fuero; Mozarabic Rite; Navarre, Kingdom; Santiago de Compostela; Visigoths.**]

ASYLUM, RIGHT OF. Although the right of asylum may strike modern sensibilities as wonderfully picturesque, to medieval law officers hot on the trail of an escaping felon, sanctuary must have seemed an omnipresent obstacle. Every consecrated church or chapel, with its churchyard, could give asylum to the fugitive. A number of great abbeys and minsters provided an even more extensive haven, often extending a league beyond the church, with the limits of legitimate pursuit clearly marked by stone crosses. Within certain liberties held in secular hands those fleeing the law could live indefinitely.

But the more common ecclesiastical sanctuary was strictly regulated and limited by provisions of the common law. The fugitive was to confess his wrong, surrender any weapons, and place himself under the supervision of the head of the religious institution to which he had fled. More important, he had forty days in which to make a choice between the two courses of action open to him: he could surrender and stand trial for the crime charged against him, or he could confess his guilt publicly and go into exile. Either choice necessitated the appearance of the coroner as representative of royal justice.

If the fugitive chose to abjure, he confessed his guilt to the coroner in a public act often held at the church gate. His chattels were forfeit to the crown and his land to his immediate lord. He then chose a port (or by the late Middle Ages the coroner chose one for him) and set out for it bareheaded and barefooted, carrying a wooden cross as a sign of the protection of the Church. In theory he kept to the highway, reached his port, and sought passage, even wading into the seas up to his knees daily (in symbolic sign of intent to depart) until he found a ship. In practice we can imagine that most abjurers went a safe distance away, tossed their crosses in a ditch, and tried to make a new life; we can suspect that friends or relatives of the victim saw to it that some of them never had the opportunity. Since a felon who left the highway or who returned from exile without the king's permission could be decapitated, it is likely that communities often exercised their own form of rough justice and later fitted their actions into the requirements of law.

Some fugitives in asylum thus rejected both formal choices and tried to escape before the forty days had passed. They had to contend with a guard of local men selected according to varying local practice. This local guard had to weigh the tedium and even the danger of a strict watch against the fine imposed on those who allowed an escape from sanctuary. A small number of fugitives rejected all choices and were starved out of asylum; after the forty days no one could legally provide the fugitive with food or drink. Breaking into sanctuary, however, was sacrilege, punishable by excommunication.

Henry VIII took several steps to change this system: he introduced branding the abjurer's thumb with the letter *A,* ordered abjurers on pain of death to reside in one of several defined sanctuaries, and radically reduced the list of crimes for which privilege of sanctuary could be claimed. His system was first modified by his son, Edward VI, and then abolished in 1603. A statute of James I in 1623 completely abolished medieval asylum.

BIBLIOGRAPHY

John G. Bellamy, *Crime and Public Order in England in the Later Middle Ages* (1973); J. Charles Cox, *The Sanctuaries and Sanctuary Seekers of Mediaeval England* (1911); Roy F. Hunnisett, *The Medieval Coroner* (1961), esp. ch. 3; Isobel D. Thornley, "The Destruction of Sanctuary," in Robert W. Seton-Watson, ed., *Tudor Studies Presented . . . to Albert Frederick Pollard* (1924).

RICHARD KAEUPER

ATABEG, a Seljuk term (*ata,* father; *beg,* prince) denoting a tutor-guardian for princes during their minority. This position appeared sporadically until the generation after Malikshāh (1072–1092), when it became a frequent feature of administration. As the Seljuk dynasty declined, the atabegs usurped its power and carved out their own domains. They succeeded in making the office and various governorships hereditary. By the mid twelfth century there were atabeg states such as that of the Ildeñizids of Azerbaijan. In the Mongol and post-Mongol periods, the post of atabeg underwent a steady devaluation. From the Seljuk world it spread to Khwarizm, the Ayyubids, and their successors, the Mamluks. It was also adopted by the Georgian monarchy under Queen Tamara (1184–1212). In Georgia an atabeg was a *vazir* (one of five) who was a close adviser to the throne and tutor of the crown prince.

BIBLIOGRAPHY

Ibn al-Athīr, ᶜIzz al-Dīn, "Histoire des Atabecs de Mosul," in *Recueil des historiens des croisades. Historiens orientaux,* **2,** pt. 2 (1876), in Arabic and French; and *al-Tarikh al-bahir fi al-Dawia al-Atabekiya,* A. A. Talaymat, ed. (1963); and Mehmed Altay Köymen, *Büyük Selçuklu İmparatorluğu tarihi,* II (1954).

PETER B. GOLDEN

[See also **Seljuks.**]

ATELIER, French for "workshop." Medieval artists often worked in teams, frequently composed of one master and several apprentices or aides. A single work of art may therefore combine the efforts of numerous craftsmen, usually anonymous, and is thus referred to as the product of a particular atelier. When the identity of the master artist is known, as is increasingly the case from the twelfth century onward, the atelier bears his name; otherwise it is normally identified by the name of its best-known piece (the Ada group, for example, was named after the Ada Gospels). Distribution of labor varied; in some workshops each craftsman was responsible for an autonomous section of the work (such as a single panel from a polyptych), while in others each artist specialized in a particular detail throughout (such as backgrounds or faces).

LESLIE BRUBAKER

ATENIS SIONI. The Church of Zion at Ateni, in the Georgian province of Kartli, is a faithful copy of the Djvari Church. Built by an Armenian mason, Thodosak, it is rich in architectural sculpture executed in various styles of the seventh century as well as of the eleventh, when the church was restored. Among the subjects of the numerous reliefs are the donors and real and fantastic animals such as the senmurv, a composite of bird, dog and peacock. Covering the interior of the church are wall paintings of the later eleventh century that have recently revealed inscriptions of historical significance.

BIBLIOGRAPHY

Giorgi Tshoubinashvili, *Pamiatniki tipa Djvari,* (1948), 44–49, 156–176; Guram Abramishvili, *Stephane mamphalis phreskuli tsartsera atenis sionshi* (1977); and "Dva stroitelnykh periodea atenskogo siona," in *Macne,* **1** (1972).

WACHTANG DJOBADZE

[See also **Georgian Art and Architecture.**]

ATHANASIANS, the supporters of orthodoxy in the controversies between Arians and their opponents. Athanasius (*ca.* 295–373), bishop of Alexandria, was a strong supporter of the Nicene Creed and a vigorous opponent of the Arians. He was exiled several times, but was recognized as the leader of the orthodox doctrine.

BIBLIOGRAPHY

Williston Walker, *History of Christian Thought* (1926), 117–125.

JOSEPH R. STRAYER

[See also **Athanasius of Alexandria, St.**]

ATHANASIUS OF ALEXANDRIA, ST., one of the most prominent fathers of the Church and an active opponent of Arianism. Born around 295 in Alexandria, where he received his education, he was ordained a deacon by bishop Alexander of Alexandria, and served as the latter's secretary. In this capacity he attended the Council of Nicaea (325), where he actively opposed Arius. In 328 he succeeded Alexander as bishop.

As the emperor Constantine turned his support to the Arians, in spite of their condemnation at Nicaea, Athanasius was deprived of his see (335) and sent into exile at Treves, in northern Gaul. Returning to Alexandria after Constantine's death (337), he engaged in a lifelong struggle in defense of the Nicene definition of Christ as the Word (or *Logos*), "consubstantial" (ὁμοούσιος) with the Father. Having been forced into exile five times, he received support in the West, particularly in Rome. However, during the reign of Constantius as sole emperor (350–361), he was practically alone in defending Nicene orthodoxy in the Roman world. Under Emperor Julian, however, he succeeded in convening an orthodox council at Alexandria (362). Exiled again by Julian, then by Valens, he was each time restored to office and died on 2 May 373.

The doctrinal position of Athanasius is summed up by a sentence of the famous tract *On the Incarnation of the Word*, written around 318, before the beginning of the Arian dispute: "[The Word] was made man that we might be made God" (*De incarn.*, chapter 54). Salvation from death and sin is expressed by Athanasius in terms of deification (θέωσις), which implies the participation of man in God's life. Since "God alone has immortality" (1 Tim. 6:16), he is also the only Savior. Consequently, the Arian position, denying the true divinity of Christ, was for Athanasius the denial of salvation itself, as expressed in the Nicene Creed.

During his long episcopate, Athanasius defended his position in the three long *Discourses Against the Arians* and in a number of occasional polemical writings and letters addressed to contemporaries. Some of these writings are of great historical interest and present a living picture of the stormy events in which Athanasius was involved. He also wrote commentaries on Old Testament books, particularly the Psalms. In 357, he composed the *Life of St. Anthony*, the great hermit, who is considered the father of Egyptian monasticism. Following the prevailing custom, Athanasius, as the bishop of Alexandria, made a yearly announcement of the date of Easter to the Christian world. The encyclicals that he published on these occasions contain not only presentations of his theological views but also information about the life and practices of the Church in the fourth century.

BIBLIOGRAPHY

Editions: *Patrologia Graeca*, XXV–XXVIII; H. G. Opitz, et al., eds., *Athanasius Werke* (1935).

Secondary. Johannes Quasten, *Patrology*, III (1960), 20–79.

JOHN MEYENDORFF

[See also **Arians; Councils, Ecumenical; Nicene Creed.**]

ATHANASIUS I, PATRIARCH OF CONSTANTINOPLE (1289–1293; 1303–1309). After a long monastic career renowned for its asceticism, Athanasius was chosen patriarch of Constantinople in 1289 by Emperor Andronicus II. Because of his uncompromising insistence on monastic discipline and episcopal residence, and his intransigent opposition to the schismatic Arsenites, Athanasius was a controversial figure in the Church and was twice deposed from the patriarchal throne. He was, however, a champion of the poor and oppressed, and initiated numerous social welfare projects in the Byzantine capital. After his death, about 1315, his relics became the object of popular veneration, and he was canonized. His memory is celebrated by the Orthodox church on October 28.

BIBLIOGRAPHY

Alice-Mary Maffry Talbot, *The Correspondence of Athanasius I, Patriarch of Constantinople: Letters to the Emperor Andronicus II, Members of the Imperial Family and Officials* (1975).

ALICE-MARY M. TALBOT

ATHENS-THEBES. See **Latin Principalities.**

ATHĪR, IBN AL-. Three brothers constitute the "Ibn al-Athīr family." They lived in the second half of the twelfth century and the first few decades of the thirteenth, associated with the Fertile Crescent and, above all, Mosul. They made their mark to varying degrees in the fields of historiography, literary and religious studies, and political life. Al-Subkī, the fourteenth-century biographer, characterized them as follows: ᶜIzz al-Dīn, "the Koranic scholar and historian"; Majd al-Dīn, "the scholar of Prophetic Tradition *(ḥadīth)* and philologist"; and Ḍiyāᵓ al-Dīn, "the first minister [*wazīr*] and litterateur."

All three were born at Jazīrat ibn ᶜUmar (modern Cizre), on the Tigris north of Mosul. Their father, Muḥammad ibn ᶜAbd al-Karīm, was the chief local administrator of the Zangid regime. The family, of some standing, invested in distant trading ventures and owned land in a village across the Tigris, as well as at Qasr Ḥarb, below Mosul, the latter made the endowment of a Sufi convent founded by the family.

ᶜIZZ AL-DĪN ABU 'L-ḤASAN

ᶜIzz al-Dīn, the middle brother in terms of age (13 May 1160–June 1233), is now the most celebrated. Little is known of his life beyond brief indications in his own works and what is given by Ibn Khallikān in his *Biographical Dictionary.* In his youth he moved between Jazīrat ibn ᶜUmar and Mosul, presumably with his father but possibly also to join his older brother, Majd al-Dīn, once the latter was employed as an official in Mosul. ᶜIzz al-Dīn studied under various teachers in both towns, and after he had performed a pilgrimage to Mecca in 1181, he returned via Baghdad, where he seized an opportunity for further study. An early patron in Mosul was the vizier Jalāl al-Dīn.

In 1188, ᶜIzz al-Dīn spent some time in Syria with Saladin, although it is not known in what capacity. There is no clear evidence that he was ever in government service. The years 1228 to 1231, apart from a visit to Damascus, were spent at Aleppo as an honored guest of the atabeg, Shihāb al-Dīn Toghril. It was there that ᶜIzz al-Dīn met Ibn Khallikān, who found him "perfect in accomplishments, of generous character and of great humility." His other patron in later life was the atabeg of Mosul, Badr al-Dīn Luᵓluᵓ. He died at Mosul.

However useful certain of his works may be, ᶜIzz al-Dīn's fame rests on his historical productions. The *Kāmil fī al-Taᵓrīkh* is a major chronicle that covers the period from Adam to 1231. There is an unusually extended introduction in which the author discusses his aims and methods, and gives some information about the progress of the work's composition. After existing for quite a long time in draft only, the work was prepared for publication at the instigation of Badr al-Dīn Luᵓluᵓ. The writing and study of history are justified, in normal medieval fashion, as a source of vicarious experience and knowledge, an encouragement of public moral accountability, and an inspiration for private piety.

The material for the early centuries of Islamic history is largely derived from the great chronicle of al-Tabarī. The identification of ᶜIzz al-Dīn's sources in general is complicated by the fact that he names them only rarely. A close reading, however, suggests that he selected his sources very judiciously, and one of his great values is that he preserves material from important historians whose works are otherwise lost.

ᶜIzz al-Dīn's explicit purpose is to provide within the scope of one work a comprehensive coverage of both the East and the West of the Islamic world. The breadth of his history is indeed remarkable, although information on the West dwindles progressively throughout the period of the author's lifetime. The last two volumes are notable for the much-used accounts of the long struggle with the Crusader states and of the impact of the first Mongol incursions.

The monograph on the Zangid dynasty, entitled *Taᵓrīkh al-Bāhir,* which was written for the edification of al-Qāhir Masᶜūd between 1211 and 1219, portrays the Zangids as exemplary Muslim rulers. The tone of panegyric is partly explained by the author's acknowledgment of his family's debt of gratitude to the dynasty. Much of the material overlaps with that of the *Kāmil,* but the relationship between the two works has not been fully investigated.

ḌIYĀᵓ AL-DĪN ABU 'L-FATḤ NAṢR ALLĀH

The youngest of the brothers, Ḍiyāᵓ al-Dīn (25 July 1163–28 November 1239), moved to Mosul with his father at the age of twenty. There, in 1189, his son Sharaf al-Dīn was born; he became an author and died in June 1225. In 1191, Ḍiyāᵓ al-Dīn sought service with Saladin, thus beginning a checkered political career. He was soon transferred to serve Saladin's son, al-Afḍal ᶜAlī. After al-Afḍal's succession, Ḍiyāᵓ al-Dīn was his chief minister, and his policies helped arouse opposition to al-Afḍal, who was expelled from Damascus in 1196. Ḍiyaᵓ al-Dīn was smuggled out of Damascus in a chest because of the personal hostility toward him. He continued to serve al-Afḍal at Sarkhad, Egypt, and later at Samosata. He broke with al-Afḍal in 1211 and then served a series of masters at Aleppo, Erbil (in 1214), Sinjār, and then Mosul, where in 1221 he became head of the chancery bureau for the atabeg Badr al-Dīn and the nominal Zangid, Nāṣir al-Dīn Maḥmūd ibn al-Qāhir. He died while on an embassy in Baghdad.

All the known works of Ḍiyāᵓ al-Dīn belong to the category of *adab,* polite literature, and have for later generations eclipsed his political importance. His main writings are treatises on rhetoric and poetics, though they have the practical end of informing the prose productions of the chancery secretaries. A collection of his official and private correspondence is extant.

MAJD AL-DĪN ABU 'L-SAᶜĀDĀT MUBĀRAK

The least celebrated brother is the oldest, Majd al-Dīn (1149–June 1210). He moved to Mosul about 1170 and began his career as an official in the employ of the Mosul vizier, Jalāl al-Dīn ᶜAlī. Later he held the top post in the chancery under the Zangid ᶜIzz al-Dīn Maᶜsūd and his son, Nūr al-Dīn Arslān Shāh, with whom Majd al-Dīn was especially close. A paralyzing illness ended his active career, which had been centered in Mosul. His brother Diyāᵓ al-Dīn collected his *tarassul,* official and private correspondence, and he himself produced a selection of the letters of his former superior, Jalāl al-Dīn.

According to Ibn Khallikān, it was only after his retirement that Majd al-Dīn, with a band of assistants, began to write. Most of his works are in the field of religious studies. His main writings are compilations, justified by the claim that they improve the organization of, and supplement, the material presented.

BIBLIOGRAPHY

On the family in general, see Mehmed Sherefeddin, *Ibn Ethirler* (1904), in Turkish.

ᶜIzz al-Dīn. See Carl Brockelmann, *Geschichte der arabischen Litteratur,* I (1943), 402, 422, supp. I, 565, 587. His works include *al-Kāmil fī al-taᵓrīkh,* C. J. Tornberg, ed., 15 vols. (1851–1876); *al-Lubāb fī tahdhīb al-ansāb* (1937–1940); *al-Taᵓrīkh al-bahīr fī al-dawla al-atābakiyya,* A. A. Tolaymat, ed. (1963); and *Usd al-ghāba fi maᶜrifat al-ṣaḥāba* (1868–1870). On his life and work, see H. A. R. Gibb, "The Arabic Sources for the Life of Saladin," in *Speculum,* **25** (1950); Ibn Khallikān, *Wafāyāt al-aᶜyān,* Iḥsān ᶜAbbās, ed., III (1977), 348–350; D. S. Richards, "Ibn al-Athīr and the Later Parts of the *Kamil,*" in D. O. Morgan, ed., *Medieval Historical Writing in the Christian and Islamic World* (in press); and Franz Rosenthal, *A History of Muslim Historiography* (1952), 332, 413.

Majd al-Dīn. See Brockelmann, *op. cit.,* I, 438; supp. I, 305, 607–609. His works include *Jāmiᶜ al-uṣūl,* Muḥammad al-Faqī, ed. (1949); *Kitāb al-Muraṣṣaᶜ,* C. F. Seybold, ed. (1896); and Ibrāhīm al-Sāmarrā' ī, ed. (1972); and *al-Nihāya fī gharīb al-ḥadīth wa'l-āthār* (1893). On his life and work, see Ibn Khallikān, *op. cit.,* IV, 141–143.

Diyāᵓ al-Dīn. See Brockelmann, *op. cit.,* I, 357, supp. I, 521. His works include *al-Jāmiᶜ al-kabīr fī sināᶜat al-manẓūm min al-kalām wa'l-manthūr,* M. Jawād and J. Saᶜīd, eds. (1956); *al-Mathal al-sā'ir fī adab al-kātib wa'l-shāᶜir,* Aḥmad al-Ḥūfī and Badawī Ṭabbāna, eds., 4 vols. (1959–1965); and *Raṣā'il Ibn al-Athīr,* Anīs al-Maqdisī, ed. (1959). On his life and work, see S. A. Bonebakker, "Notes on Some Old Manuscripts . . . ," in *Oriens,* **13–14** (1961), esp. 186–194; C. Cahen, "La correspondance de Ḍiyā ad-Din ibn al-Athir," in *Bulletin of the School of Oriental and African Studies,* **14** (1952); and Ibn Khallikān, *op. cit.,* V, 389–397.

D. S. RICHARDS

[See also **Arabic Literature; Ibn Khallikān; Mosul; Saladin; al-Ṭabarī.**]

ATHIS UND PROPHILIAS, a Middle High German verse narrative, approximately 1,550 lines of which survive in a series of fragments from three manuscripts. Vocabulary and rhymes indicate a West Middle German, probably Hessian, provenance. This romance of classical antiquity is usually dated around 1210 on the basis of linguistic and stylistic similarities to Otte's *Eraclius* and Herbort von Fritzlar's *Liet von Troya.* The anonymous poet appears to have been very well educated, judging from his use of Latin inflections and unusual participial constructions and from his detailed knowledge of Roman customs, law, and military tactics. His source was the Old French *Li Romanz d'Athis et Prophilias,* composed sometime in the last quarter of the twelfth century by an otherwise unidentified Alixandre. The German version appears to have been much shorter, and was perhaps based on a different redaction of the *Romanz.* The poet adapted freely, adding significant details of what he believed to be ancient life and customs, presumably to lend his story historic "realism." He shows considerable literary artistry and ability, and combines clear syntax, careful meter, and pure rhymes with an admirable rhetorical flair.

Athis und Prophilias recounts the story of the friendship between the Greek Athis and the Roman Prophilias. Both the beginning and the end are missing from the fragments, which relate a complicated series of events in three main sections of the narrative. 1. (A, A^{b-e}): Athis, hiding in a cave outside Rome, witnesses the murder of a young man and laments his death. In despair over his own misfortunes, which have culminated in the failure of Prophilias to recognize him, Athis decides to confess the crime and thus end his life. In accordance with Roman law, he is convicted and put in the pillory for three days. Prophilias eventually recognizes Athis, and claims to have committed the murder himself in an effort to save his friend. The real perpetrators are discovered, and Prophilias explains his act of loyalty: at some (unspecified) time Athis gave his bride Cardiones to Prophilias to save him from dying of love. Athis thanks the gods for his deliverance.

2. (A*–D): Prophilias' sister Gayte laments her imminent marriage to King Bilas, for she has now fallen in love with Athis, but her father refuses to break the engagement. Prophilias swears he will rescue her, and he and Athis muster troops and ambush the king. Athis, strengthened by his love, overcomes Bilas. Athis and Gayte are married in the temple of Venus and then consummate their marriage amid much coy but charming commentary by the narrator.

3. (E, F): When Piritheus is mortally wounded during a fierce battle outside Athens, his father Theseus laments bitterly that his death will mean the city's doom. Piritheus requests that his sister be given to Prophilias, whose wife Cardiones has just died, thinking Prophilias has fallen in battle.

Although it is less well known than other romances of classical antiquity, *Athis und Prophilias* appears to have enjoyed a modest success, as the survival of manuscript fragments from both the thirteenth and fourteenth centuries attests. The heroes are also mentioned in Heinrich von Freiberg's *Ritterfahrt des Johann von Michelsberg* (vv. 26–29).

BIBLIOGRAPHY

Athis und Prophilias, in Carl von Kraus, ed., *Mittelhochdeutsches Übungsbuch,* 2nd ed. (1926); Peter F. Ganz, "Athis und Prophilias," in Kurt Ruh, ed., *Die deutsche Literatur des Mittelalters: Verfasserlexikon,* I (1978).

BONNIE BUETTNER

[See also **German Romance; Middle High German Literature.**]

ATHOS, MOUNT, commonly called the Holy Mountain *(hagion oron)* in Greek, is situated on the southeastern tip of the triple Chalcidice peninsula in northern Greece and served as one of the most influential centers of Byzantine monasticism. Attracted by its natural beauty and relative inaccessibility, monastic anchorites populated the peninsula from the eighth century. In 958 St. Athanasius the Athonite, the spiritual director of the Byzantine general Nikephoros Phokas, retired to Mount Athos to practice asceticism. Once he had assumed the Byzantine imperial throne, which he held from 963 to 969, Nikephoros issued the foundation charter of a new *lavra* (large monastery), of which Athanasius became the first abbot. The foundation and endowment were confirmed by Nikephoros' successor, John I Tzimisces, in 970.

The establishment of this large cenobitic monastery led to conflict with the anchorites ("hesychasts") who had been living on the peninsula in small hermitages *(kellia* or *sketai)* under the leadership of a *protos* ("first" hesychast). A decree of John Tzimisces in 972 defined the respective property rights and other privileges of both the *lavra* of St. Athanasius and the hesychasts. The two types of monasticism—cenobitic and eremitic—coexisted on Mount Athos throughout the subsequent centuries.

In the last decades of the tenth century, six other cenobitic monasteries were founded on the peninsula, following the pattern set by St. Athanasius, under the auspices of high officials who provided endowments. These were the monasteries of Vatopedi, Zographou, Philotheou, Docheiariou (founded by St. Euthymius, a disciple of Athanasius), Xenophontos, and Iviron. The last, founded between 972 and 978, was established by three Georgian (or "Iberian," Greek *Iviroi*) nobles—Ivane, Euthymius, and Tornikios—and became a center of Georgian monasticism.

The eleventh century saw a further multiplication of monastic communities on Mount Athos. Russian ascetics—including St. Theodosios, who later cofounded the monastery "of the caves" (Pechersky) in Kiev—settled in the neighborhood of the newly established cenobium of Esphigmenou (*ca.* 1030). Italian monks from Amalfi created the Latin monastery "of the Amalfitans" that persisted until the thirteenth century, when the sack of Constantinople during the Fourth Crusade (1204) and subsequent rift between the Eastern and Western Churches precluded the coexistence of Latin and Greek monasticism on Mount Athos.

In the twelfth century, a Seljuk prince, belonging to the Kutlumus family and converted to Christianity, established the monastery named after him (Kutlumus). The establishment of another Russian monastic settlement in Xylourgou (1142) led to the founding of a permanent Russian monastery dedicated to St. Panteleimon, known as the Rossikon (1169). Rastko, the son of the Serbian prince Stefan Nemanja, became a monk there in 1186 under the name of Sava (Sabbas) and was followed by his father, who received the monastic name of Symeon. United in their vocation, father and son obtained from the Byzantine emperor Alexis III the right to establish a Serbian community in the abandoned monastery of Khilendar in 1198. In 1219, St. Sava was consecrated as the first archbishop of Serbia.

In the fourteenth century, following a difficult period of Frankish domination, Mount Athos flourished again. Byzantine and Bulgarian emperors, but particularly Serbian *krals,* restored old monasteries and built new edifices. Among the new foundations were the monasteries of St. Paul, Petra ("the Rock"), the Pantokrator, and Dionysiou (the last founded by the emperor of Trebizond, Alexis III). Also during that period, Valachian (Rumanian) princes rebuilt Kutlumus and secured the acceptance of Valachian monks among its brotherhood.

As officially confirmed by a *typikon* (or set of monastic rules) of Emperor Constantine IX Monomachos in 1052, the monasteries of Mount Athos were grouped into a federation with an assembly of representatives from all the foundations gathering regularly in the central village of Karyes. This assembly was presided over by a *protos,* who acted as a supreme abbot for the entire federation. Each monastery also preserved a separate relationship to its imperial or princely founder, or to his successors. In 1312, a more unified canonical structure was established with the formal submission of Mount Athos to the personal jurisdiction of the patriarch of Constantinople. The new, tighter relationship between the holy mountain of Athos and the patriarchate is symbolized by the fact that numerous patriarchs were chosen from among its monks, such as Isaiah (1323–1334), Kallistos (1350–1354, 1355–1363), and Philotheos Kokkinos (1354–1355, 1364–1376).

The various *typika* (or rules) accepted in the monasteries of Mount Athos were generally characterized by ascetic severity. A monk normally practiced perpetual fasting and spent at least a third of his time in the choir, and his daily work schedule was tight. A freer and more contemplative regime was followed in the *kellia,* where the hesychast tradition of constant silent prayer persisted. In the late thirteenth century, it was revived by Nikephoros the Hesychast, who promoted a psychosomatic discipline, a method of constant prayer which connected the invocation of the name of Jesus with breathing, and also by St. Gregory of Sinai, who brought to Athos a similar tradition that had been maintained for centuries in the communities of the Middle East. The method was attacked by Barlaam the Calabrian; but the assembly of abbots, gathered in Karyes in 1341, published the *Tomos hagioreitikos* (Tome of the Holy Mountain), endorsing the theology of Gregory Palamas, who had defended the method's legitimacy. In the following years Gregory Palamas, a monk of the lavra of St. Athanasius, became the major participant in a theological controversy that involved the vision of divine light (the "light of Mount Tabor") and the distinction between the transcendent essence and the "energies" in God. Palamas' theology was approved by several ecclesiastical councils held in Constantinople.

The monasteries of Mount Athos survived the Turkish occupation in 1453 of Constantinople and the Balkan peninsula. They are largely intact today and contain rich depositories of medieval manuscripts and art. No female creature, human or animal, is permitted to enter within the boundaries of the "Holy Mountain."

BIBLIOGRAPHY

The monastic archives of Mount Athos first appeared in print as supplements to the Russian periodical *Vizantysky vremennik,* vols. 10–20 (1903–1913). After World War II, more documents were published by Franz Dölger, Germaine Rouillard, Paul Collomp, Paul E. Lemerle, and others. For a general survey of its history, see Philip Sherrard, *Athos, the Mountain of Silence* (1960); and particularly *Le millénaire du Mont Athos, 963–1963: études et mélanges,* 2 vols. (1963–1964).

J. MEYENDORFF

[See also **Anchorite; Monastery; Monasticism, Byzantine; Mysticism, Byzantine; Sava (St.).**]

ATHOS, MOUNT, MONUMENTS OF. Mount Athos is the site, on a peninsula that projects from Macedonia (Greece) into the Aegean Sea, of a group of Byzantine Orthodox monasteries dating to at least the foundation of the Great Lavra Monastery by St. Athanasius the Athonite in 963. Today the twenty monasteries house a major collection of Byzantine manuscripts and icons; they permit no women or female animals on the peninsula. Other than the Great Lavra, some of the major monasteries at Mount Athos are those of Dionysiou (founded in the fourteenth century), Koutloumousiou (twelfth century), Xeropotamou (late tenth century), Gregoriou (fourteenth century), Iviron (late tenth century), St. Panteleimon (eleventh century), Esphigmenou (late tenth century), and Chilandari (twelfth century).

BIBLIOGRAPHY

Stylianos M. Pelekanides, et al., *The Treasures of Mount Athos. Illuminated Manuscripts,* 2 vols., P. Sherrard, trans. (1974–1975).

LESLIE BRUBAKER

[See also **Monasticism, Byzantine.**]

ATLAKVIÐA is generally considered to be the oldest of the heroic lays in the *Poetic Edda.* It is a stark tale of murder and revenge in 43 laconic stanzas. The Hunnish king Atli, motivated by a desire for gold, issues a deceitful invitation to his Burgundian brothers-in-law Gunnarr and Hǫgni. Despite their sister Guðrún's warning token, and with feigned indifference to the consequences, they undertake the journey. On their arrival, Atli subdues them and demands the location of the Burgundian treasure, but Gunnarr agrees to reveal it only if he is given Hǫgni's heart. Hǫgni laughs under the knife and after his death Gunnarr exults in the assurance that the secret of the treasure is now known only to him and that his lips are sealed. He is cast into a snake pit and dies plucking his harp. Atli returns from the execution to a false welcome from Guðrún, who proffers a festive cup, but serves her unsuspecting husband the flesh of their sons. That night as he lies in bed overcome by drink, she plunges a sword into him, then sets the hall afire, and, as we gather from the elliptical last stanza, perishes in the flames with all the retainers.

Similarities in name (Gunnarr = Gundaharius, *d.* 437; Atli = Attila, d. 454) and circumstance (the Burgundians were decimated by the Huns in 437) suggest that this story derives from Migration Age history. Jordanes in his *Getica* (551) quotes the fifth-century writer Priscus to the effect that Attila died from a hemorrhage as he lay overcome by wine next to a new wife. Later writers (Marcellinus Comes, Agnellus, Poeta Saxo) elaborate the story and report that he died by the hand of a woman. *Atlakviða* appears to be a vernacular offshoot of this legendary development. The Hunnish extermination of the Burgundians has been converted into a story of personal betrayal, and Attila's death is explained as an act of vengeance.

Atlakviða is characterized by a particularly vivid focusing of the scenic and emotional highlights in the narrative—the chill atmosphere at the Burgundian court while the invitation is debated, the mournful farewells, the reckless gallop of Gunnarr and Hǫgni to their destiny, Gunnarr's remorseless sacrifice of his brother to unconditional resistance, Hǫgni's stoic hilarity, Guðrún's grisly revenge and final extinction in the blazing hall. No other heroic poem suppresses human sympathies with quite the same ferocity.

Atlakviða is presented only in the chief Eddic manuscript Codex Regius 2365, 4to (in the Arnamagnaean Manuscript Institute, Reykjavik) from around 1270. The language is poetic and highly colored. There are an unusual number of rare words and collocations, obscure passages, and metrical irregularities. A study by Felix Genzmer, supplemented by Konstantin Reichardt, connected the style of *Atlakviða* with Þórbjǫrn hornklofi's *Haraldskvæði* from the end of the ninth century.

BIBLIOGRAPHY

Text, translation, introduction, commentary, and references to earlier scholarship are provided by Ursula Dronke, *The Poetic Edda,* I: *Heroic Poems* (1969). More recent commentaries are: Carola L. Gottzmann, *Das alte Atlilied: Untersuchung der Gestaltungsprinzipien seiner Handlungsstruktur* (1973); and Piergiuseppe Scardigli, *Un carme dell'Edda: L'Atlakviða* (1974).

THEODORE M. ANDERSSON

[See also **Atlamál; Eddic Poetry; Sagas, Legendary.**]

ATLAMÁL is an Eddic poem of 105 stanzas, which tells a more elaborate version of the same story set down in the older *Atlakviða.* The principal differences are the following: Guðrún's warning token to her brothers becomes a runic message. Hǫgni's and Gunnarr's wives take a considerable part in the discussion of Atli's invitation. The invitation is addressed in the first instance to Hǫgni, not Gunnarr, and it is Hǫgni who rejects all warnings. The journey to Hunland is accomplished at least in part by boat. The arrival at Atli's court is followed by a full-scale battle between Burgundians and Huns. Atli cuts out Hǫgni's heart without Gunnarr's prompting and the point of this motif (Gunnarr's wish to eliminate the only other witness to the location of his treasure) is thus lost. As a result Gunnarr no longer exults over the success of his stratagem. The details of Gunnarr's execution are reduced, but the subsequent acrimony between Atli and Guðrún is much expanded. Hǫgni's son Hniflungr assists Guðrún in her slaying of Atli.

Despite these substantial deviations, it seems probable that *Atlamál* was based on *Atlakviða,* which it occasionally echoes. The order of events is identical, and the expansion from 43 to 105 stanzas is achieved rather mechanically through the insertion of new dialogue, dreams, premonitions, and retrospection. Some of the changes can be accounted for by assuming that the poet knew German versions and attempted to harmonize them with *Atlakviða.* Thus the crossing of a body of water (the Lim Fjord in northern Jutland) on the way to Hunland, the new prominence assigned to Hǫgni, and the regular battle between Huns and Burgundians may be explained from the German tradition that underlies the *Nibelungenlied* and *Þiðreks saga.*

Like *Atlakviða, Atlamál* is preserved only in Codex Regius 2365, 4to (in the Arnamagnaean Manuscript Institute in Reykjavik) from around 1270. Like *Atlakviða*, it is also titled *in grœnlenzko* ("the Greenlandic") in the manuscript, but whereas a Greenlandic origin for *Atlakviða* has never been taken seriously, it has been argued for *Atlamál* on the basis of this poem's parochial and narrowly domestic outlook. Whatever the place of composition, *Atlamál* is generally considered to be a late Eddic poem from the twelfth century, more likely from the end of that century if allowance is made for the infiltration of German variants.

The language of *Atlamál* differs sharply from the poetic style of *Atlakviða.* It is marked by prosaic phrasing, colloquialisms, and down-to-earth references to such matters as the chores assigned to Atli's scullion. The international scope and royal cast of Migration Age heroic poetry have shrunk to the dimensions of everyday life in the North. *Atlamál* seems in fact to share certain features (fuller dialogue, anticipatory devices, emphasis on conjugal relations) with the nascent Icelandic sagas.

BIBLIOGRAPHY

Text, translation, introduction, commentary, and references to earlier scholarship are provided by Ursula Dronke, *The Poetic Edda,* I: *Heroic Poems* (1969). There are two detailed monographs on *Atlamál:* Heinrich Hempel, *Atlamál und germanischer Stil,* in *Germanistische Abhandlungen,* **64** (1931); and D. O. Zetterholm, *Atlamál: Studier i en eddadikts stil och meter* (1934). See also Wolfgang Mohr, "Entstehungsgeschichte und Heimat der jüngeren Eddalieder südgermanischen Stoffes," in *Zeitschrift für deutsches Altertum und deutsche Literatur,* 75 (1938). Two more recent studies are: Theodore M. Andersson, "*Niflunga saga* in the Light of German and Danish Materials," in *Mediaeval Scandinavia,* 7 (1974); R. G. Finch, "*Atlakviða, Atlamál,* and *Vǫlsunga saga:* A Study in Combination and Integration," in Ursula Dronke et al., eds., *Specvlvm Norrœnvm: Norse Studies in Memory of Gabriel Turville-Petre* (1981).

THEODORE M. ANDERSSON

[See also **Atlakviða; Eddic Poetry; Nibelungenlied; Þiðreks saga; Sagas, Legendary.**]

ATLAS MOUNTAINS, the name, of uncertain origin, given to the related mountain ranges of North Africa (see map). The classical Greeks knew the name, but seem to have had only vague ideas about the mountains thus identified. The medieval Arab authors who discuss them also are vague and confused about the extent and placement of the different ranges. With the Sahara Desert to the south and the Mediterranean Sea to the north, these mountains have shaped North Africa's natural and human history.

From Ceuta in the northwest, the Rif Chain runs nearly 300 kilometers to the southeast, melding with the northeast–southwest Middle Atlas range of about 350 kilometers in extent. Roughly parallel to the latter, the High Atlas range stretches from near Morocco's Atlantic coast approximately 750 kilometers to the east northeast. The Anti-Atlas chain to the south runs about 550 kilometers inland from the coast. The Saharan Atlas range extends the High Atlas a further 1,110 kilometers, and its eastern remnants form the majority of Tunisia's mountains. Eastward from Melilla, where the Rif Chain ends, the several chains of the Tell Atlas spread more or less near the Mediterranean coast, while the Hodna and Titeri chains stretch roughly east–west and link the Aurès with the Tell Atlas.

The ranges are much folded; the contrast between the high elevations of many of the chains and the lower plateaus with which they are interspersed is characteristic. This contrast persists throughout

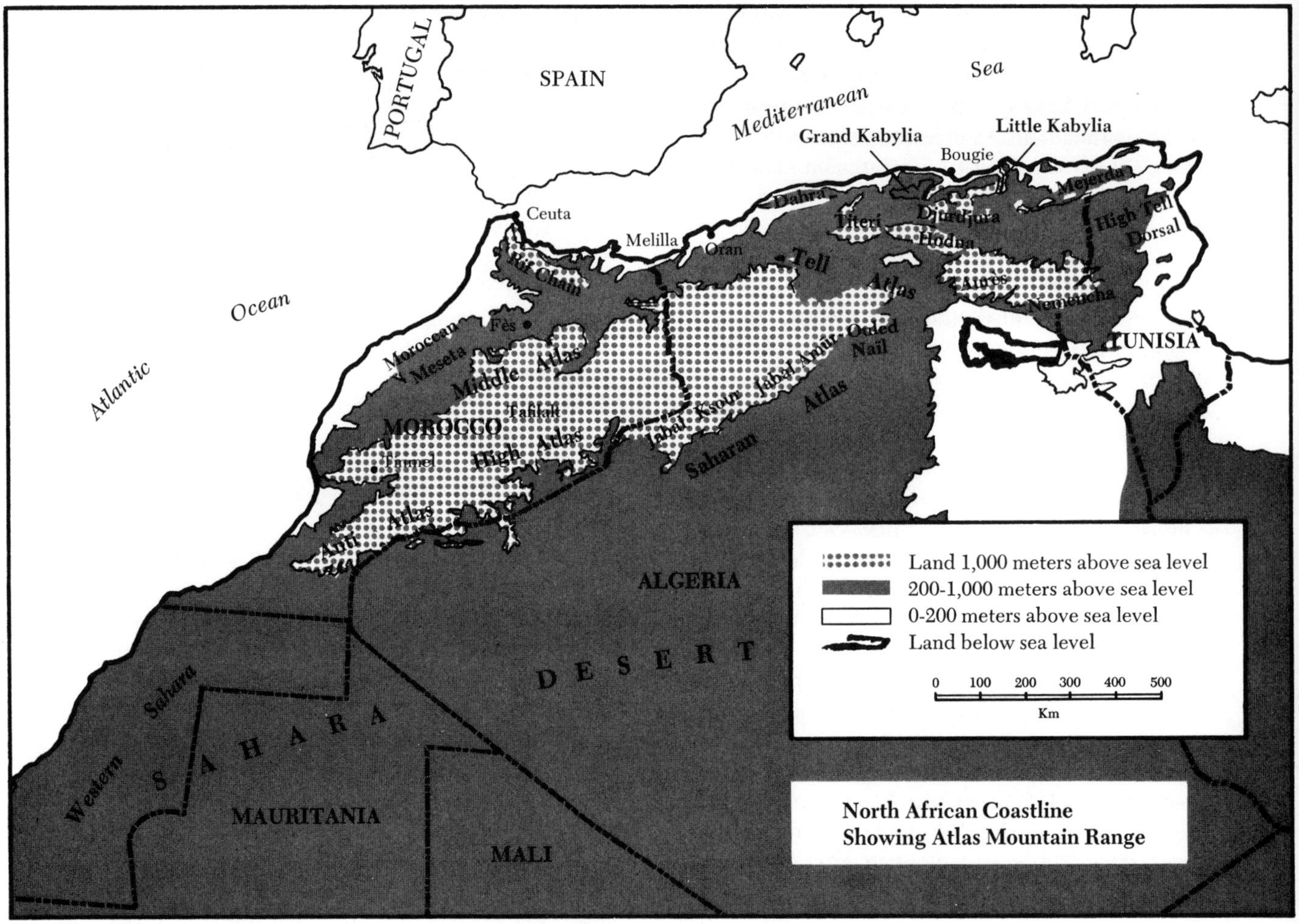

North African Coastline Showing Atlas Mountain Range

North Africa, but the mean elevations generally decrease from west to east. Many of the ranges are of height and length sufficient to cut much of North Africa effectively into compartments, hindering communications between them.

These mountains have had several effects on the North African environment. The presence of the several ranges along or near the northern coast confines the Mediterranean climate largely to the coastal areas, producing an arid, semidesertic climate inland. These coastal mountains, as well as those that limit access to Morocco's Atlantic Meseta (or coastal plateau) from the east and north, also tend to drain much of the moisture from rain clouds originating in the Atlantic. Thus only a few areas of coastal plain and mountain receive sufficient precipitation for unirrigated agriculture.

The Atlas ranges historically have channeled and attenuated lines of communication and diffused coastal regimes' political control over the hinterlands, making North Africa the scene of waves and eddies of tribal coalescence and fission. Justinian's reconquest of Vandal-held North Africa (534) displaced those interlopers, but was unable, because of the necessary expense, to reestablish the extensive border security system *(limes)* with which the earlier Roman rulers protected their upland agricultural plantations beyond the first ranges.

The difficulty of access to the sea enabled the early Muslim regimes (which finally conquered North Africa in 698–711) to establish land-based economies and trade routes, initially without much dependence on shipping. Mountain isolation allowed Muslim religious dissidents to establish long-lived principalities in the early Middle Ages (e.g. the Rustumids at Taher, 776–911, and the Khārijites at Sijilmassa (Tafilalt), 757–909). The Little Kabylia formed the base from which the Shiite Fatimids launched first their proselytizing campaign (893) and then their military conquest of North Africa (902–909). The Almohad movement spread from Tinmel in the High Atlas, whence the mountaineers warred for nearly twenty years (1128/1129–1148) with the Almoravids on the Meseta before finally overcoming them. The mountains also served to weaken the Almohads' hold over their North African empire after their rout at Las Navas de Tolosa in Spain (1212), and made it possible for secessionist dynasties to break away and survive past 1500.

BIBLIOGRAPHY

The *Index Islamicus,* ed. J. D. Pearson (1958, 1962, 1967, 1972, 1977, quarterly since 1976), lists books and articles dealing with both geographical and historical aspects of the Atlas Mountains. See also Jean Despois, *L'Afrique du Nord,* 3rd ed. (1964), 31–72; *Géographie de l'Afrique du Nord-Ouest* (1967), 9–41; and "Géographie et histoire en Afrique du Nord: Rétouches à une thèse," in *Éventail de l'histoire vivante: Hommage à Lucien Febvre,* I (1953); Charles-André Julien, *Histoire de l'Afrique du Nord . . . dès origines à la conquête arabe,* 2nd ed., Christian Courtois, ed. (1951), 256–322, and *History of North Africa . . . from the Arab Conquest to 1830,* 2nd ed., R. Le Tourneau, ed., John Petrie, trans., C. C. Stewart, ed. (1970), 1–219, 351–421.

JAMES L. YARRISON

[See also **Almohads; Almoravids; Fatimids.**]

ATRIUM, an enclosed courtyard, the main court of a Roman house, and, by extension, the forecourt attached to Christian churches. Usually rectangular and on axis with the church, atria were most common in the early Christian period, when they frequently contained fountains. Until the eighth century they enclosed areas in which the congregation gathered to await the bishop or other dignitary. In certain early Christian churches, the unbaptized were restricted to the atrium. Some Carolingian and Romanesque churches, such as the Palace Chapel at Aachen and the Abbey Church at Montecassino, had atria in emulation of early Christian buildings and to provide shelter.

LESLIE BRUBAKER

ATTAINDER. See **Impeachment.**

ATTALEIATES, MICHAEL, eleventh-century Byzantine jurist and historian, left his birthplace of Attaleia (Antalya) and went to Constantinople, where he studied law and held a number of judicial posts. His *Historia,* covering the period from 1034 to 1079/1080, draws on observations made during his judicial career and, with its greater emphasis on military campaigns, complements the *Chronographia* of his contemporary Michael Psellus. The owner of substantial property in Constantinople, Rhaedestus, and Selymbria, he gave much of his fortune to charity and in 1077 founded a monastery and poorhouse.

BIBLIOGRAPHY

Sources. The text of the *Historia* was edited by Wladimir Brunet de Presle and Immanuel Bekker, in *Corpus scriptorum historiae Byzantinae,* L (1853); there is a partial French translation by Henri Grégoire, "Michel Attaliatès Histoire," in *Byzantion,* 28 (1958). The text of the *typikon* (in Greek) was published by Konstantinos Sathas, in *Mesaionike bibliotheke,* I (1872); by Franz Miklosich and Joseph Müller, in *Acta et diplomata Graeca medii aevi sacra et profana,* V (1887); and by Nikolaos Tomadakes, in *Syllabos Byzantinon meleton kai keimenon* (1961).

Secondary Literature. See Herbert Hunger, *Die hochsprachliche profane Literatur der Byzantiner,* I (1978), with good bibliography; and Paul Lemerle, *Cinq études sur le XIe siècle byzantin* (1977), 65–112.

ALICE-MARY M. TALBOT

[See also **Psellus, Michael.**]

ATTO OF VERCELLI (d. 961), bishop of Vercelli from 924. Although he fought clerical concubinage and simoniac bishops, his effectiveness was diminished by a backward-looking caesaropapism. His works include capitularies; *De pressuris ecclesiasticis,* a treatise on church difficulties; *Polypticum,* a treatise on morality; letters; sermons; an exposition on Paul, and his own testament.

BIBLIOGRAPHY

Atto's works are in *Patrologia latina,* CXXXIV (1853), 27–900. See also Augustin Fliche, *La reforme Grégorienne,* I (1924), 61–74; and Suzanne F. Wemple, *Atto of Vercelli* (1979).

EDWARD A. SYNAN

AUBADE (AUBE), an Old French lyrical genre that flourished in the twelfth and thirteenth centuries. Aubade in the narrow sense designates the song sung by watchmen in order to awaken sleepers *(reveillé, mattinata).* As a genre it is a short poem dealing with the separation of lovers at dawn (compare the Provençal *alba* and the Middle High German *Tagelied*). The dawn song was well established in world literature before its treatment in Provençal and Old French. The context of these songs was not necessarily amorous (as in the Provençal and Old French examples) but could be military or Christian.

In Old French, four (or five, depending on the definition) aubades are known. Most likely they were performed musically, their dialogue form lending them a dramatic framework. The poems were often accompanied by musical notation in the manuscripts.

Several characters (the woman, her lover, her husband, the watchman or watchmen, and the jealous onlookers) are involved in the action in different configurations. The woman may be the only one speaking (as in "Entre moi et mon ami" and "Quant voi l'aube dou jor venir"); the lover may engage in an exchange with two watchmen ("Gaite de la tor"); or he may deplore the coming of dawn in a soliloquy ("Est il jors?" and "L'abe c'apeirt au jor").

The lovers' warning also takes different forms in each poem. The warning sign may be birdsong ("Entre moi et mon ami") or the song of the watchmen ("Gaite de la tor"). The impending forced separation gives rise to the lovers' promises and regrets, which form the substance of most aubades.

The designation of these poems as aubes or aubades derives from the presence of the word *alba* ("dawn") in the refrain of most Provençal dawn songs. For Old French, "aube" is used as a critical term in modern scholarship but cannot be traced in this form to any medieval poetic treatises.

BIBLIOGRAPHY

Frederick Brittain, *The Medieval Latin and Romance Lyric to A.D. 1300* (1951, repr. 1969), 29–33; Peter Dronke, *The Medieval Lyric,* 2nd ed. (1977), 167–185; Arthur T. Hatto, ed., *Eos: An Enquiry into the Theme of Lovers' Meetings and Partings at Dawn* (1965), 344–389; Alfred Jeanroy, *Les origines de la poésie lyrique en France au moyen âge* (1889), 61–83.

RENATE BLUMENFELD-KOSINSKI

[See also **Alba; Courtly Love; French Literature.**]

AUBERT, DAVID (*fl.* 1453–1479), calligrapher and translator, was probably from Lille, not Hesdin, as usually asserted. By 1463 he had become clerk to Philip the Good, and in 1469 he helped copy the inventory of his library. He compiled a *Chroniques et conquêtes de Charlemagne,* a *Perceforest,* and a *Chronique des empereurs.* Some twenty signed manuscripts display his large, square cursive script.

BIBLIOGRAPHY

Brussels, Palais des Beaux-Arts (1959), *La miniature flamande,* edited by L. M. J. Delaissé; *Biographie nationale de Belgique,* supp. IX (1971–1972), with full bibliography; Pierre Cockshaw, "La famille du copiste David Aubert," in *Scriptorium,* **22** (1968).

ANNE HAGOPIAN VAN BUREN

AUCASSIN ET NICOLETTE, anonymous work of the late twelfth or early thirteenth century; around 1210–1220 seems most plausible. It has survived in only one manuscript (Paris, Bibliothèque Nationale, Fonds Français 2168), rediscovered in 1752 by the eminent medievalist La Curne de Sainte-Pelaye. Composed in a heavily Picardized Old French, the work is the only known specimen of the genre known as *cantefable* (or *chantefable*). It comprises some forty-one sections of alternating sung (verse) and spoken (prose) passages, which are clearly delineated in the manuscript by such titles as *or se cante* ("now it is sung") and *or dient et content et fabloient* ("now they speak, and tell the story and dialogue"). The *cantefable* resembles the *prosimetrum* (prose verse) genre utilized by Martianus Capella, whose *De nuptiis Mercurii et philologiae* was widely read in schools as far back as Carolingian times and was frequently imitated by such Latin and vernacular poets as Alan of Lille and Chrétien de Troyes. The verse passages, averaging about twenty lines each, are made up of assonanced *laisses,* or stanzas; they recall the *chanson de geste* but in truncated form, since each line contains only seven syllables. With few exceptions the prose passages seldom take up more than a page and a half in modern editions.

The highly contrived simplicity, or naive conventionality, of the plot serves to underscore the text's remarkable poetic sophistication. Aucassin, the son of Garin, lord of Beaucaire, is in love with Nicolette, a captive Saracen maid. His father forbids their mar-

AUCASSIN ET NICOLETTE

riage and has Nicolette imprisoned. Aucassin refuses to help defend his father's castle until promised that he may see Nicolette and obtain a kiss. The father goes back on his word, and Aucassin is also imprisoned. Nicolette escapes and by night sings outside Aucassin's dungeon of her love before fleeing into the forest. Released from prison and disconsolate, Aucassin repairs to the forest, where after several mishaps he finds his beloved.

Together the lovers travel to the castle of Torelore, a "world upside down" sort of place whose king gives birth—or claims to—and whose queen leads an army in defense of the kingdom, with eggs, vegetables, and cottage cheese for ammunition. Aucassin starts to slay his host's adversaries but is halted by the king, who declares that "we are not in the habit of killing each other off here."

The lovers spend three blissful years at Torelore before they are taken prisoner by Saracens. Aucassin is shipwrecked off the coast of Beaucaire and, Garin having died, is made lord by a joyful populace. Meanwhile, Nicolette has been taken to Cartage (perhaps Carthage or Cartagena), where she is recognized as the king's long-lost daughter amid great rejoicing. Not wishing to marry a powerful pagan king, she disguises herself as a wandering minstrel and escapes, at last reaching Beaucaire. Still disguised, she finds Aucassin, who at first fails to recognize her. Eventually the lovers are married.

The Torelore episode furnishes the key to this charming and immensely humorous work: it is built on a systematic reversal of literary conventions, and the literature of the previous half-century is deliberately stood on its head. Even the protagonists' names suggest this reversal: "Aucassin" (al-Kassim?) sounds far more Saracen than the very Christian "Nicolette."

Few Old French genres escape parody in this concise literary encyclopedia. The *chanson de geste* is very much present in the battle scenes at Torelore, the truncated seven- (not ten-) syllable lines, and even in the author's manner of describing himself and his work, as the "amusement" narrated by a *viel antif* (oldster); Veillantif, it should be noted, was the name of Roland's horse in the *Song of Roland.* Garin is the name of an ancestor of Count William in the William of Orange, or Garin de Monglane, cycle, the subject of which was the carving out of fiefs in Saracen-held territory in Provence and Spain. Various lyric genres appear too, and they are similarly if less aggressively turned topsy-turvy. Nicolette's serenade outside Aucassin's window is a kind of pseudo *alba,* or dawn song; her meeting in the forest with the shepherd boys subverts the *pastourelle;* and the theme of distant love *(amor de lonh),* characteristic of much Provençal lyric poetry, is here reversed: the lady is dressed up as a troubadour in search of her beloved.

But the most thoroughly exploited genre is the romance. In order to construct his poetic commentary, the author utilizes the motif of young lovers whose union is frustrated by uncomprehending and prejudiced parents—a theme popularized, for example, by *Floire et Blancheflor* and associated with romances of courtly entertainment. Two bodies of romance text are most consistently undermined here. The first is the mythopoetic narrative epitomized by the *Érec et Énide* of Chrétien de Troyes. Aucassin's encounter with the cowherd during his search for Nicolette in the forest recalls Yvain's—and Calogrenant's—experience in Chrétien's *Le Chevalier au Lion.* Equally important are the many allusions to, and reversals of, episodes pertaining to the *Tristan* legend: the forest exile, the constant travel by sea, the scene during which the disguised and unrecognized Nicolette tells her lover about herself, the last a throwback to the *Folies Tristan.*

These and other references are couched in an apparently naive, popular-styled diction that has deceived many scholars into characterizing the work as a simple, straightforward, and idyllic love story. Rather, this entertainment is to be understood as utterly dependent upon its audience's high degree of literary sophistication. It poeticizes, or thematizes, the extraordinary revitalization of literary practices and generic experimentation that took place in early thirteenth-century France. Furthermore, it is at least possible that by alternating verse and prose passages the poet is poking gentle fun at the ponderous debates of the time concerning the relative merits of these two types of diction.

BIBLIOGRAPHY

Jean Dufournet, *Aucassin et Nicolette, édition critique* (1973), includes the text, a modern French translation, detailed notes, and bibliography. Of the several English translations, the most easily available is Eugene Mason, *Aucassin and Nicolette, and Other Mediaeval Romances and Legends* (1910), frequently reprinted in the Everyman's Library collection. Others include those of August Rodney MacDonough (1880), Francis W. Bourdillon (1887), Andrew Lang (1887), and Laurence Housman (1925).

Of interest to students are Tony Hunt, "Precursors and Progenitors of *Aucassin et Nicolette*," in *Studies in Philology*, **74** (1977); and Joan B. Williamson, "Naming as a Source of Irony in *Aucassin et Nicolette*," in *Studi francesi*, **51** (1973).

KARL D. UITTI

[See also **Alba; Chansons de Geste; Chrétien de Troyes; French Literature; Martianus Capella; Pastourelle.**]

AUDRADUS MODICUS (*fl.* 847–853), priest of St. Martin of Tours, was elevated in 847 or 848 to the rank of suffragan bishop of Sens. He was also the author of a compilation of Latin religious verse interspersed with prose visions about the fate of mankind, the reform of the Church, and the civil strife that followed the death of Louis the Pious in 840. Before he was deposed as bishop by the Synod of Paris in 849, Audradus visited Rome and presented Pope Leo IV with an early version of this work. His later continuations of the visions cover events to 853. These visions were an important source for the years 840 to 853 in the early thirteenth-century world chronicle of Alberich of Trois Fontaines.

BIBLIOGRAPHY

Audradus' works are in *Monumenta Germaniae historica: Poetae latini*, III (1892, repr. 1978), 67–121, 740–745; and A. Gaudenzi, "Un ignoto poema di Audrado di Sens," in *Bulletino dell'istituto storico italiano*, 7 (1889). See also Maximilianus Manitius, *Geschichte der lateinischen Literatur des Mittelalters*, I (1911), 601–603, for background, summaries, and bibliography; Walter Mohr, "Audradus von Sens, Prophet und Kirchenpolitiker (um 850)," in *Bulletin du Cange*, **29** (1959), for a study of the prose visions; and Ludwig Traube, "Audradus Modicus," in *Abhandlungen der philosophisch-philologischen Classe der Königlich Bayerischen Akademie der Wissenschaften*, **19** (1892), for a text and study of the prose visions.

WILLIAM CRAWFORD

AUGUSTA, official title of the crowned Byzantine empress, attested continuously until the fifteenth century, together with that of *despoina.* The augusta could exert considerable political influence and, when a widow, could even assume the supreme powers; she was then also called *basilis* or *basilissa* (ninth and eleventh centuries).

BIBLIOGRAPHY

Elisabeth Bensammar, "La titulature de l'impératrice et sa signification," in *Byzantion*, **46** (1976); Ioli Kalavrezou-Maxeiner, "Eudokia Makrembolitissa and the Romanos Ivory," in *Dumbarton Oaks Papers*, **31** (1977); S. Maslev, "Die staatsrechtliche Stellung der byzantinischen Kaiserinnen," in *Byzantinoslavica*, **27** (1966).

NICHOLAS OIKONOMIDES

[See also **Byzantine Empire.**]

AUGUSTINE OF CANTERBURY (*d.* 604 or 605), saint and missionary to the English, first appears in history in 595 as prior, under Abbot Candidus, of the Monastery of St. Andrew on the Clivus Scauri, Coelian Hill, Rome. He was well known to Pope Gregory I, who had founded this monastery in his family house and had himself been an ordinary monk there. In 595 Augustine was entrusted by Gregory to evangelize the English, who had, Gregory said, been neglected by neighboring clergy, by whom he meant primarily the Gaulish church but possibly also the British (Welsh) church. Legend, as reported by Bede, says that Gregory's idea of an English mission went back to the days when he had watched the sale of English boys in the slave market. The legend is given substance by Gregory's later assigning some of the revenue from the papal patrimony in Gaul to purchasing the freedom of young English slaves. Gregory also records that the English themselves had requested the mission. Legend and documents are not incompatible.

Led by Augustine and consisting of some forty monks, the English mission left Rome in 595 or early 596, taking ship for southern Gaul, where it paused at Lérins, Arles, and Aix. Dissension arose between Augustine and his companions over his leadership and the nature of the hazards of the long journey. He returned alone to Rome for stronger authorization, which Gregory supplied by constituting him abbot over his companions, by sending them a letter of encouragement, and by providing commendatory letters to bishops and others in a position to protect them along their route. These letters, all entered into the Pontifical Register in July 596, indicate a route up the Rhône and down the Loire to Tours, but also passing farther north through one or more of the royal seats: Châlons-sur-Saône, Orléans, Reims, or Paris, so that they could call on Queen Brunhild and her Merovingian grandsons.

The exact places touched by the mission are un-

AUGUSTINE OF CANTERBURY

known, as is the port from which they crossed the English Channel, and the port of landing (traditionally said to be Richborough). Surprisingly even the year of the crossing, which must have taken place in 597, is not mentioned. The oblique evidence for accepting 597 is found in the important letter of Gregory to his friend Patriarch Eulogius of Alexandria written on 29 July 598. It indicates that Augustine had been consecrated bishop of the English while still in Gaul and that the mission was now in England. The same letter also tells how Augustine had on Christmas day 597 baptized "more than 10,000 Englishmen."

The mission's success owed much to King Ethelbert of Kent. When he had heard that Augustine had reached Thanet he asked him to wait there until he came to receive him. Ethelbert was cautious about this meeting at first, interviewing Augustine and his monks in an open field, lest they try magic on him. Having heard their story, he received them warmly and generously, authorizing them to baptize the people of his kingdom, which at that time extended to the Humber. He also allowed them to establish a monastery in his royal city of Canterbury and to build or rebuild churches. Though a pagan, Ethelbert knew something of Christianity from his neighbors, the Gauls and Britons, and also from his Christian wife Bertha and her personal chaplain Bishop Liuthard, who had accompanied her from Gaul at the time of her marriage.

The historian of the actual evangelization is Bede, writing 130 years later in the early books of his *Historia ecclesiastica gentis Anglorum.* Knowing little about the events himself, Bede relied on the materials available to him: eight out of thirty pertinent extant letters of Pope Gregory as recorded in the papal registers; the *Libellus responsionum* (booklet of replies), a long unrecorded letter to Augustine answering his missionary queries; the local traditions of Canterbury and London as relayed by Abbot Albinus of Canterbury and the priest Nothelm of London; and the vita of St. Gregory from the *Liber pontificalis.* (He probably did not use a second available life of St. Gregory by an unknown monk of Whitby.)

Bede's account is not free from errors of fact. He was probably wrong in saying that Augustine returned to Arles for his episcopal ordination; he probably misinterpreted the letter of Gregory to King Ethelbert (601) in which the pope elegantly scolded the king for "postponing" something that Augustine had asked him to do. Bede thought that Ethelbert had not pushed the evangelization hard enough and that there should have been more converts. Modern critics of Bede tend to think that Gregory was complaining about Ethelbert's failure to receive baptism, which Bede said he had received early, possibly in 597. More likely Gregory was scolding Ethelbert for not yet providing for the episcopal see in London, where it was always his intention that it should be.

In 598 (or 600) Augustine sent two of his missionaries, Laurence and Peter, to Rome for reinforcements and to present his now famous questions. They returned to England in 601 with additional missionaries, including Mellitus and Justus, who with Laurence were later ordained bishops and succeeded Augustine at London, Rochester, and Canterbury respectively. They also brought back the *Libellus responsionum* with its nine answers dealing with the disposal of church property, liturgical and customary variations in the churches, marriage legislation, and sexual purity. The authenticity of this document is a matter of controversy among scholars.

Augustine also twice held conferences at Augustine's Oak near the border of Wales, attempting unsuccessfully to achieve uniformity of liturgical, customary, and other practices in the English and British churches. He died in 604 or 605 and was buried near the Church of St. Peter and Paul in Canterbury; when the church was completed his remains were moved into the north chapel. The monument erected gives what is probably an erroneous date of his death as 27 May 605.

BIBLIOGRAPHY

Peter Hunter Blair, *The World of Bede* (1970); Margaret Deanesly and Paul Grosjean, "The Canterbury Edition of the Answers of Pope Gregory to St. Augustine," in *Journal of English History,* **10** (1959); John Godfrey, *The Church in Anglo-Saxon England* (1962); John W. Lamb, *The Archbishopric of Canterbury from Its Foundation to the Norman Conquest* (1971); R. A. Markus, "The Chronology of the Gregorian Mission to England: Bede's Narrative and Gregory's Correspondence," in *Journal of Ecclesiastical History,* **14** (1963); Henry Mayr-Harting, *The Coming of Christianity to Anglo-Saxon England* (1972); Paul Meyvaert, "Bede's Text of the *Libellus Responsionum* of Gregory the Great to Augustine of Canterbury," in Peter Clemoes and Kathleen Hughes, eds., *England Before the Conquest: Studies in Primary Sources Presented to Dorothy Whitelock* (1971).

L. K. SHOOK

[See also **Bede (St.); Canterbury; England, Anglo-Saxon; Gregory I, the Great (Pope); Missions and Missionaries, Christian.**]

AUGUSTINE OF HIPPO, ST. Aurelius Augustinus, with Ambrose, Jerome, and Gregory the Great one of the four major Latin "Fathers of the Church," was born on 13 November 354 at Tagaste, a small Roman municipality in the North African province of Numidia Cirtensis that is the site of the modern Souk-Ahras, Algeria. Augustine died on 28 August 430 as bishop of Hippo Regius in the same province, a city that after Carthage was the most important city in Roman Africa. His father, Patricius, was a landowner and a decurion of limited means who remained a catechumen until a deathbed baptism in 371. Augustine's mother, venerated as Saint Monica, was a simple and extremely devout woman of the same class as her husband. There was a brother, Navigius, and certainly one and probably two sisters.

LIFE

Augustine's best-known work, the *Confessions,* although primarily a prayer of repentance and of praise for God, contains invaluable autobiographical data in the first ten of its thirteen books. On this source is based our knowledge of numerous details that illumine his life and thought: his father's ambitions for Augustine, that Patricius was choleric, unfaithful, and restrained only by Monica's tact from beating her as husbands in their circle were accustomed to beat their wives (*Confessions* 9.9.19). Augustine remarked with disarming simplicity that he had no memory of his own prenatal life and infancy, but that he could infer his beginnings from observation of other infants (1.6.9). Long before Freud, Augustine was struck by evidence of infantile vice: greediness, anger, and jealousy (1.7.11). His adolescent unrest was lucidly remembered and judged severely from the perspective of the bishop he had become at the time the *Confessions* was written; the episode of pears stolen without the excuse of hunger is a classic instance of his psychological insight (2.4.9).

In his own estimate, a year of idleness when his parents could not pay his school fees (2.3.6) and his mother's decision to delay his baptism (1.11.18) accounted for Augustine's youthful moral disorders. The most conspicuous of these was his having taken at age seventeen a mistress whom he never names (4.2.2); by her he had a son, Adeodatus, "Gift from God" (9.6.14; for this name see 2 Samuel [2 Kings] 21:19, which in the Vulgate is Adeodatus, and in Hebrew, Elḥanan). Despite deep affection for his mother, Augustine saw with pitiless clarity that Monica shared his father's excessive ambition for their son's future; this led her to temper concern for his chastity with the notion that a wife might prove a hindrance to his success (2.3.8).

After primary studies in Tagaste, Augustine entered secondary school in nearby Madauros, made famous by the Latin author Apuleius (*b. ca.* A.D. 124). Penury forced the idle year at home, but help from a rich family friend, Romanianus, made it possible for Augustine to resume his schooling, which he completed at Carthage. Augustine's education was a formation in the liberal arts as these were cultivated in late antiquity; it was conducted in Latin, the daily language of Augustine's region, and did not include a full mastery of Greek. He had been taught only enough Greek to make him hate it, by masters who did not love him (1.14.23). Hence, although he was probably of Berber stock and felt that Africans ought not to be ashamed of their Punic tongue (*Letters* 17.2), Augustine was thoroughly Roman by birth, by culture, and in aspiration.

CONVERSION TO "PHILOSOPHY"

Since Augustine's formal education did not go beyond that provided in the school of the rhetorician, he received no training in technical philosophy such as was available at Alexandria or at Athens. Still, at the age of eighteen, and "in the usual course of learning," Augustine came upon a dialogue by Cicero entitled *Hortensius* (now lost), exhorting readers to the philosophic life. Most readers, Augustine thought, were captivated by Cicero's language rather than by his intent, but for him "what was said, not the turn of speech, was persuasive"; his former desires and ambitions suddenly seemed empty in comparison with "the immortality of wisdom" (3.4.7). This replacement of human goals by a love of "wisdom" was the first of Augustine's three great and lasting conversions.

His first impulse was to seek that "wisdom" in Christianity and in the Scripture, both Hebrew and Christian, proffered by his mother's church. If the style of Cicero had taken second place to Cicero's thought, the style of the Bible seemed impossibly crude to the student of rhetoric (3.5.9), and for nine years Augustine searched, with diminishing confidence, among the Manichaeans for wisdom. Meanwhile he began to teach, first at Tagaste and then at Carthage, where he had lately been a student. During his African teaching, perhaps in 380, Augustine produced his first book, *The Beautiful and the Suitable,* already lost when he mentioned it in the *Confessions* (4.13.20). Unruly students and ambitions not wholly eradicated by his devotion to philosophy drove him in 383 from Carthage to Rome (5.8.14). Roman students, however, were careless about paying their fees (5.12.22); the following year Augustine received an appointment as professor of rhetoric on the public payroll in the imperial city of Milan through the influence of Symmachus, prefect of Rome (5.13.23). In addition to teaching, Augustine's duties included delivering panegyrics on the emperor and on the consuls of the year at civic ceremonies (6.6.9).

The aristocratic Ambrose, a celebrated orator, was bishop of Milan. Augustine began to frequent the basilica of Ambrose, reversing the motivation with which he had read the *Hortensius:* Not what Ambrose said, but a professional interest in how he spoke, drew the increasingly skeptical professor of rhetoric (5.14.24). For, having been disappointed by the explanations of the most eminent Manichaean spokesman, Faustus, Augustine had turned once more to Cicero, but this time as transmitter of the skepticism of the New Academy (5.6.10; 5.14.25; 6.11.18): "For the thought even rose under the surface in me that those philosophers whom they call 'Academics' were more prudent than the rest because they held humans ought to doubt everything" (5.10.19).

Meanwhile, the widowed Monica had joined her son at Milan in 385. She did all she could to reinforce his attraction to Ambrose (6.1.1–6.2.2), and arranged for the return of his mistress to Africa (Adeodatus was left with Augustine) and his engagement to marry a girl who was still two years below the legal age (6.13.23). Augustine, in great distress at the departure of his mistress, promptly took another (6.15.25).

Under the influence of dignitaries from the circle of Ambrose, Augustine began to read "Platonic books" in Latin translation (8.2.3; 7.9.13), and it has been argued by Prosper Alfaric that the conversion sealed by Augustine's baptism was in fact a conversion to Neoplatonism rather than to Christianity. Modern scholarship does not favor this interpretation; research has uncovered long paraphrases of Plotinus in sermons delivered by Ambrose, most likely during the very months of 386 when Augustine was listening to his preaching, according to Pierre Courcelle. Augustine seems, thus, to have imbibed an urbane Neoplatonism in the service of Christian faith along with instruction in that faith itself.

In the technically "philosophical" realm the impact of Ambrose and of his associates on Augustine was, first, to free him from any lingering attachment to the doctrinaire materialism of the Manichaeans. The latter held that all reality is material (7.1.2) and that there are two primeval substances (7.14.20), of which one is a god of light and the other a principle of darkness and of evil. Augustine now adopted the view that evil is no more than a privation of good (7.12.18; 7.16.22) and that God is incorporeal Truth (7.20.26). Second, Ambrose and his associates provided Augustine with a Platonic-Plotinian interiorism as the sovereign philosophical method (7.10.16; 7.17.23). In the specifically religious realm the preaching of Ambrose brought Augustine to perceive the "spirit" beneath the "letter" of Scripture (6.4.6), as well as the superiority of the Apostle Paul to Platonist sages (7.20.26–7.21.27). All these positions became fundamentals of Augustine's future thought; and thus two "conversions," intellectual and religious, gave a precise focus to the indeterminate "love of wisdom" that had gripped him thirteen years earlier (6.11.18).

THE GARDEN, CASSICIACUM, BAPTISM

At the end of August 386, Augustine underwent a dramatic and emotional experience in the garden of his lodgings at Milan. The chanting of a child from a nearby house, "Take up and read, take up and read"; his lighting upon the words of Paul in Romans 13:13,14: "Not in revelings and drinking bouts, not in debauchery and vices . . ."; personified vices plucking at his sleeve; and floods of tears (8.8.19–8.12.30) have all suggested literary redaction and exaggeration. Still, the substantial accuracy of Augustine's account can hardly be doubted. Chest pains and labored breathing, coupled with his religious and moral turmoil, prompted him to resign his professorship of rhetoric at the time of the "vintage vacation" (9.2.2; 9.5.13). Augustine retired with his mother, his son, his cousins Rusticus and Lastidianus, his students Trigetus and Licentius, and his friend Alypius to Cassiciacum, the villa of one Verecundus, the non-Christian husband of a Christian woman (9.3.5). There the group spent the fall and winter of 386–387 in reflection, light work, and conversation.

Ambrose had advised Augustine to read the prophet Isaiah, an assignment Augustine found beyond him at that moment (9.5.13). Once more the shadow of Cicero fell across Augustine, for the philosophical dialogues of Cicero are matched by the "Cassiciacum dialogues": *Against the Skeptics,*

AUGUSTINE OF HIPPO, SAINT

The Life of Happiness, Order, and the *Soliloquies.* At Cassiciacum, Augustine set out his plan:

> Let me tell you my whole program briefly. . . . I have turned away from all the things that mortal men consider to be good, and I have set myself the goal of serving the pursuit of this wisdom. . . . We are impelled to learning by a double urge, that of authority and that of reason. . . . My resolve is never to depart from the authority of Christ, for I find none that is stronger. However, I must follow after this with the greatest subtlety of reason. . . . I have an unbounded desire to apprehend truth, not only by believing it, but also by understanding it. In the meantime, I am confident that among the Platonists I shall find what is not opposed to the teachings of our religion. (*Against the Skeptics* 3.20.43; trans. Pegis, slightly modified)

On their return to Milan, Augustine, Adeodatus, and Alypius were baptized by Ambrose at the Easter Vigil of 387, 24–25 April (9.6.14). Having formulated a coherent program at Cassiciacum, Augustine produced the treatise *Immortality of the Soul* and planned a series of works on the liberal arts as preparation for "philosophy," of which the single volume completed is that on music. The choice of music as first of the arts to be discussed may well reflect the aesthetic delight Augustine took in the chanted liturgy established by Ambrose in the church of Milan (9.6.14–9.7.15). Shortly after baptism Augustine went with Monica, Navigius, Adeodatus, and their friend Evodius to the seaport town of Ostia in order to return to Africa. The port was blockaded owing to the revolt by Maximus, and before the blockade was raised, Monica died there in her fifty-sixth year.

At Ostia, Monica and Augustine seem to have undergone a mystical experience that Augustine recorded in heavily Neoplatonic language combined with biblical echoes (9.10.23–9.11.28). His account of Monica's last days, his review of her character and personality, his commendation of her to his readers' prayers (9.12.29–9.13.37) constitute one of the most moving passages in Western literature. Patricius appears there only fleetingly, and it is noteworthy that in the last lines of the account Augustine mentions the "eternal Jerusalem" that in the future would form one pole of his *City of God.*

With the death of Monica the autobiographical portion of the *Confessions* ends. A tenth book devoted to a prayerful essay on memory follows; the eleventh book offers a matchless discussion of time, and inaugurates an exegetical study beginning with Genesis 1:1 and extending to Genesis 2:2 that concludes book 13. For the rest of Augustine's long career a precious source is the *Life of Augustine* by Possidius, bishop of Calama, whose see city was overrun by Vandal invaders late in Augustine's life; Possidius took refuge with Augustine at Hippo in 429 and, while there, was deeply affected by his table talk and especially by Augustine's immense literary production. The biography by Possidius can be supplemented by Augustine's letters and sermons; the study by Frederik van der Meer, *Augustine the Bishop,* demonstrates how much those documents can reveal to a patient and percipient historian.

From Ostia, Augustine and his party returned to Rome in 388. Before that year was out, he had written an essay, *The Quantity of the Soul;* the first book of a three-book treatise, *Free Choice;* and the contrasting *Morals of the Catholic Church* and *Morals of the Manichees.* Late in the same year the party reached Africa. At Tagaste, Augustine established, on land inherited from his father, a community of devout laymen who counted themselves not quite monks, but "slaves of God," *servi dei.* The beloved and promising Adeodatus died around 390.

Conscious as he always would be of his own talents, Augustine was careful to avoid towns in need of a bishop. In 391 he visited Hippo, where there was an elderly bishop of Greek origin named Valerius; standing at the back of the church, Augustine heard Valerius expound on the needs of the local community and, in his own words, "I was seized, made a priest, and through this grade I passed to the bishopric" (*Sermons* 355.1.2). The shouting crowd that pushed him forward misinterpreted his tears as evidence of disappointment that he was to be a mere priest, not a bishop (Possidius, *Life* 4.2), whereas, for Augustine, almost the only consolation was that Valerius allowed him to establish a monastery in the enclosed garden beside the church building (*Sermons* 355.1.2). By 395, Augustine was consecrated a cobishop, and in 396, on the death of Valerius, he succeeded as sole bishop of Hippo; he died in that post during the Vandal siege of 430.

Important works mark Augustine's first years back in Africa: *The Teacher; True Religion; The Usefulness of Believing; "Two Souls:" Against the Manichees;* the two remaining books of *Free Choice;* the text of a public debate, *Acts: Against Fortunatus the Manichee;* and the beginnings of his diverse writings on the Psalms that were later collected and named (by Erasmus) *Accounts of the Psalms, Enarrationes in psalmos.* To the assembled bishops at the Council of Hippo in 393, the newly ordained priest, not without resentment on the part of some of his auditors,

AUGUSTINE OF HIPPO, SAINT

preached the sermon *On the Faith and the Creed.* To the same year belong his *Uncompleted Book on the Text of Genesis* and, a major concession to popular taste, an alphabetical *Psalm Against the Party of Donatus,* as well as *Explanation of 84 Propositions on the Epistle to the Romans, Beginnings of an Explanation of the Epistle to the Romans,* and *Explanation of the Epistle to the Galatians.* This scriptural outpouring was varied with the moral essay *On Lying;* all these works appeared before he succeeded Valerius in the bishopric of Hippo.

BISHOP OF HIPPO

The new bishop took up a range of duties that he would often liken to the heavy knapsack, the *sarcina,* of a Roman legionary (for instance, *Letters* 85.1, 85.2; 86; *Sermons* 340.1). Preaching, debating publicly with opponents of Christianity, adjudicating legal disputes, participating in African church councils, conducting a very extensive correspondence, and writing an unending flow of books made his load crushing—to say nothing of personal involvement with individual believers for whom he felt responsible. Because African churches regularly employed public notaries to take down sermons and debates in shorthand (often with asides on the reactions of the crowd: "'Long live Augustine!' ten times," for instance), we have documents of unparalleled immediacy on Augustine's day-by-day ministry. A few guidelines will serve to order this extensive legacy.

First, from beginning to end he took the word "philosophy" in its etymological sense of "love of wisdom," and applied it to any and all instances of "wisdom"; after his conversion and baptism this was preeminently the wisdom of faith, Church, and Bible. For him the term "theology" could hardly be used to designate reflection on his faith. The term was freighted with unfortunate connotations (*City of God* 8.1) because it had been preempted by unbelievers, Varro at their head, to denote an unpalatable complex (6.5; 8.5): myths concerning "gods" whom the pagans themselves judged to be scandalous in their behavior, a divinized cosmology, and political structures that were both totally sacral, in that they institutionalized pagan cults, and totally vitiated by human pride. Hence he could write "the true philosopher is the one who loves God" (*City of God* 8.1) and "philosophy is not one thing and religion another" (*True Religion* 5.8.25).

On one occasion he used the formula, much debated in modern times among philosophizing Christians, "our Christian" philosophy over against that of pagans as "the only genuine philosophy" (*Against Julian the Pelagian* 5.14.72). Augustine's broad meaning of "philosophy" was to hold the field in Latin Christendom until Abelard in the twelfth century and, against bitter opposition, successfully introduced the term "theology" to name systematic thought on the Christian faith. "Philosophy" thus understood is ultimately concerned with only two themes, in the view of Augustine: God and the human soul (*Order* 2.18.47; *Soliloquies* 1.2.7; 2.1.1). These ultimate concerns left room, however, for speculation on the angels of Scripture, both blessed and damned; on the cosmos as created and developing from "seed-natures," *rationes seminales,* implanted by the Creator; and on material things, seen to be good in themselves, as beautiful, and as intelligible, for they are "full of numbers."

A second guideline is the mistaken translation of Isaiah 7:9 by the Septuagint Greek version and by Latin versions derived from it: "Unless you believe, you will not understand." Augustine knew another Latin version that is faithful to the Hebrew: "Unless you believe, you will not hold out"—that is, without faith in the Lord of history, a Hebrew king could not hope to resist besieging armies. For Augustine this line of Isaiah, taken as the Septuagint invited him to interpret it, grounded a methodology. Beginning in the obscurity of faith, he aspired to anticipate, through some degree of rational understanding, the clear vision of the world to come. Like his understanding of the term "philosophy," his position on this line from Isaiah would have consequences far in the future; we have only to think of Saint Anselm and his *Proslogion* argument, explicitly proffered as an instance of "faith seeking understanding," *fides quaerens intellectum.*

Third, the arrangement of Augustine's numerous writings by Possidius in nine groups to match the opponents against whom they were composed suggests a convenient division of Augustine's career insofar as different opponents—notably pagans, Arians, Donatists, Manichaeans, and Pelagians—tended successively to dominate his thought and work. Possidius included a tenth category that was much larger than his first nine: "works useful for all." Donatists and Manichaeans were strongly organized in what may be understood as counterchurches when Augustine returned to Africa. In 411 a report of Pelagian positions disturbed him, and at his death he left unfinished a treatise directed against the greatest apologist of the movement, Julian, bishop of Eclanum.

As for the Arians, although their claims had been rejected at the Council of Nicaea in 325, a generation before his birth, these paradoxically demanded progressively more of Augustine's attention as he grew older. Goths, Vandals, and Alans were Arian Christians, equipped with the New Testament, if not the whole Bible, in a Gothic translation by the Arian bishop Ufilias (Wulfila, *ca.* 311–382/383). Pagans were always with him and often in high places, notwithstanding the "conversion" of the Roman Empire to Christianity and much repressive legislation. Creative pressure from pagan spokesmen resulted first in long, essay-like letters from Augustine to perplexed Christians that were meant to refute the claim that the sack of Rome in 410 was due to the effects of Christian faith; because he was Augustine, the bishop of Hippo finally answered in the grand manner, twenty-two books called the *City of God.*

PAGANS

Augustine is one of our best witnesses on how and to what degree the old cults of pagan Rome increasingly provoked, yet managed to survive, laws directed against them by the Christian emperors. By the time he had been consecrated bishop, paganism was visibly doomed, and pagans themselves read the signs of the times: "temples abandoned, the shades of ancestors neglected" are phrases from a letter to Augustine, addressed to him before he was a bishop by the pagan grammarian Maximus of Madauros (*Letters* 16.2).

Symmachus, prefect of Rome and leader of the pagan party in the Senate, who had obtained for Augustine his appointment to teach rhetoric in Milan, had suffered defeat at the hands of Ambrose in 385 over an attempt by pagan senators to restore the altar of Victory before the Senate House in Rome, as well as the immunities and revenues of pagan priests and vestals, all of which had been abolished by imperial decrees (*Code of Theodosius* 16.10). Roman conservatism with respect to public games, even those connected with the proscribed pagan rites (*Code* 16.10.17); appreciation of the artistic value of temples and their furnishings, a value recognized by the antipagan decrees (*Code* 16.10.15, 16.10.18); and reduction to the plane of popular symbolism of the grosser elements in cult and myth all conspired to strengthen the case Symmachus made. Last, Symmachus claimed that the safety of Rome, long defended by her gods, was in jeopardy under a Christian regime that suppressed their cult. This claim would be thrown up to Augustine when Rome was sacked by Goths in 410. Like the pagans, Augustine knew that paganism had no future; rearguard actions could only delay its disappearance, even when fought under leadership as formidable as that of Symmachus. As a bishop, however, Augustine could not rest in the long view; pastoral zeal moved him to hasten the inevitable.

Often enough this zeal was exercised on a personal and even friendly plane, as is witnessed by his letters to the pagans of Madauros (*Letters* 232), to Maximus (*Letters* 17), and to Longinianus (*Letters* 233, 234, 235). When the pagans of Calama rioted against the Catholics of their city, in collusion with Donatist heretics, the pagan Nectarius invited the bishop of Hippo to intervene, in the hope that his influence might mitigate the penal measures to be expected (*Letters* 90, 91). Augustine was sensitive to the danger that human punishments could be too severe; questioning under torture, he wrote, ought to be excluded. Still, he thought that the future security of innocent victims demanded present punishment of the guilty (see also *Letters* 95, 133). On another plane, Augustine faced a survival of paganism in popular religious practices. Ambrose had discouraged Monica from one such ambiguous practice, that of ceremonial eating and drinking at the tombs of the dead, which she had brought from Africa with a good conscience (*Confessions* 6.2.2), and Augustine as bishop opposed the same custom in his own jurisdiction (*Sermons* 64.4, 326.1; *Letters* 22.3–6, 29), as did the civil law (*Code of Theodosius* 16.10.19).

MANICHAEANS

Augustine's early involvement with the Manichaeans inspired in him a unique concern for his former coreligionists. "As far as possible," he wrote, "I want them to be healed rather than to be assailed" (*Morals of the Church* 1.2; compare *Against the Letter Called "The Foundation"* 1). For them he was willing to make an exception to his rule that faith and then understanding is the order of speculation. He had experienced the Manichaean thirst for reasoned explanation; in their case he would begin on the plane of reason in the hope of ending on the plane of faith (*Morals of the Church* 1.2.3). The same flexibility can be seen, it ought to be remarked, in a letter he directed to a somewhat "fideist" correspondent (*Letters* 120.1.2–3). Despite Pelagian railing against his austerity (*Incomplete Work Against Julian* 3.170) Augustine never relapsed into a Manichaean contempt for the corporeal. His undeniable moral rigor is free from all ontological implications.

Augustine's basic tenet on the enigma of evil is that God, at once Being and The Good, is the sole author of all "natures" (*Against the Letter Called "The Foundation"* 33, 35); evil is a consequence of sin, not of nature. Whatever, therefore, exists to any degree is good to that degree (*Free Choice* 3.7.21). Despite his often respectful allusions to Plotinus, Augustine could not accept Plotinian matter, conceived as "ugliness, utter baseness, evil without mitigation" (*Enneads* 2.4.16), or the Manichaeans' "god of shadows"; only a perverse created will can be the source of evil.

Even in the area of human sexuality, where Manichaean theory and his personal history combined to make Augustine particularly sensitive, he maintained his balance: "We [Christians] do not term marriage 'good' in the sense that it is good when compared to fornication—else there would be two evils, one of which would be worse than the other. . . . Rather marriage and continence are two goods of which the second is better" (*The Good of Marriage* 8.8). He defended Genesis 1:27 against the alternative proffered by the Manichaeans: "They are of the opinion, and so they preach, that the devil made and joined male and female" (*Against Faustus the Manichee* 19.29).

Augustine's antidualism is transmitted mainly through treatises written against Manichaean doctrine or personalities, as well as through the recorded debates with champions of the religion he had abandoned. Among them was Bishop Faustus, who had failed to convince him that Manichaean faith and Hellenistic science were compatible; their debate, as taken down in 398, is the work *Against Faustus the Manichee.*

There was fearful evil in Augustine's world; whether moral or ontological, his basic tenet remained that evil is a privation of good, and in no sense a reality in its own right. Evil is a gap in being; far from being the result of "confecting," it is a "defect": "From this does the evil of fickle spirits take its origin, the evil by which the good of nature is diminished and depraved. Nothing but a 'defection' results in such a will, a defection by which God is abandoned" (*City of God* 12.9). Thus physical evils result from the original rebellion of Adam against divine command.

Although there is no evil "god" on Augustine's horizon, there is the biblical demon and his legions. As a Christian he retained a lively, not to say credulous, conviction with respect to demonic influence, even though he could not be sure, for instance, about the alleged wonderworking capacities of his fellow African of an earlier generation, Apuleius of Madauros, author of the *Metamorphoses,* or *The Golden Ass.* Augustine was unwilling to dismiss out of hand the tradition that made Apuleius a practicing magician; his best effort was to note that Apuleius had not achieved high office through his putative magical arts, whereas David had risen from shepherd to king without them (*Letters* 138.4.18–19).

DONATISTS

The least comprehensible heresy faced by Augustine was that of the Donatists. It had begun in zealot rigor against the rehabilitation extended by the Church to Christians who, in periods of persecution, had handed over the Scriptures to pagan officials in order to escape martyrdom. This led the founders to reject Bishop Caecilian of Carthage on the ground that he had been consecrated invalidly by one Felix of Apthungi, who was accused of betraying the Christian community during the last of the great persecutions under Diocletian, 303–305. Donatus was the first successor of a schismatic bishop who had been put in place by the assembled bishops of Numidia in 311. His name was given to the movement, and when Augustine became bishop of Hippo, he was faced by yet another rival church, that of the Donatists.

With a dynamism often found in heterodox religious movements, the Donatists proceeded to deny in principle the validity of sacraments, above all that of baptism, at the hands of reinstated "betrayers," the traditors who had "handed over" the Scriptures and those whose orders derived from them. Hence, the Donatists insisted upon the rebaptism of their converts and made the debating point that whereas they rebaptized converts from the Catholic Church, Catholics did not rebaptize converts from the Donatist church—evidence, in their view, of the superiority of Donatist sacraments. Augustine controverted this Donatist practice on the ground that the human minister of a sacrament is but an instrument of Jesus Christ (*Against the Letter of Petilianus* 2.24.57, 2.108.247). Furthermore, the descendants of the original rigorists, the Donatists whom Augustine encountered almost a century after the disputed succession at Carthage, were well-organized vagrants called "cottage-rounders," *circumcelliones,* given to invading the homes of humble Catholics (*Accounts of the Psalms,* Psalm 132.3; *Against Gaudentius* 1.28), beating or killing clergy and laity

AUGUSTINE OF HIPPO, SAINT

alike, then taking their own lives, for they thought suicide guaranteed entrance into paradise.

Social unrest seems to have been an element in this disconcerting religious movement, and imperial decrees against it were extremely severe but not always enforced, perhaps not always enforceable. On the fall of the statesman and general Stilicho in 408, the Donatists proclaimed that his decrees against them had lost all validity and that their sect was no longer bound by law to keep the peace. In response to representations by Catholic bishops, a law was promulgated in 409 that renewed with all possible severity an earlier decree against Donatists, heretics in general, Jews, and pagans (*Code of Theodosius* 16.5.46; compare 16.5.44).

Augustine had been absent from the bishops' council, but he dispatched a letter in favor of their recommendation (*Letters* 95). Henri Marrou has juxtaposed this letter with another, addressed to the proconsul of Africa (named, as it happened, Donatus), requesting that the laws not be administered with unrestrained severity (*Letters* 100), an important exhibition of the distance Augustine was ready to allow between theory and practice in such appeals to the "secular arm." The Donatists were under no illusions as to Augustine's opposition. Their bishop of Cartennae seems to have complained that he had known Augustine as a peaceable student at Carthage, whereas conversion to Catholic Christianity had transformed him into a dedicated controversialist (*Letter* 93).

Augustine would not have been Augustine had he not written extensively against Donatists and their theories, above all the debate conducted in the presence of the emperor's commissioner at Carthage and recorded by notaries under the title *Abridged Report of the Conference with the Donatists.* In 411, having in principle defeated the Donatists and with renewed legislation in place, Augustine was compelled to meet the most difficult of all his opponents: Caelestius, Pelagius, and Julian of Eclanum.

PELAGIANS

In 411, Marcellinus, as imperial commissioner, brought to Augustine's attention the advances at Carthage of the doctrines of an urbane "servant of God" named Pelagius who, like Augustine before him, had come to Africa—in fact, to Hippo—when Augustine was absent and could acknowledge his presence only by a letter (*Letters* 146). He was a vigorously speculating layman, intent upon cultivating an ascetic life, who had long been under the influence of Eastern monks. From then until his death Augustine directed his principal effort against heresy against Pelagius and his defenders; after his death disciples continued the controversy, especially against "the men of Marseilles" whom later theologians called "Semi-Pelagians."

The violence of the controversy has obscured the intent of the participants; Pelagian theory was a "consistent body of ideas . . . in the mind of Augustine, not of Pelagius" is the verdict of Peter Brown, a very erudite modern authority. Although a number of works by Pelagius himself are extant (four, and possibly five, under the name of Augustine, for editors could be confused by collections of letters or essays exchanged between antagonists), they contain views diametrically opposed to those of Augustine, who held that our race is a "condemned mass," *massa damnata* (see, for example, *Enchiridion* 25–27), owing to the sin of Adam.

For Pelagius the glory of our race is our freedom to choose life or death (Deuteronomy 30:19; Pelagius, *Letter to Demetrias* 2). God has given our whole race the power *(posse)* to fulfill his law; to will to do so *(velle);* and to effect what has thus been willed *(esse).* For Pelagius all this remains within the range of human capacities. Grace, he taught, is constituted of a will that is free, of our natural knowledge of divine law and its sanctions, and of revelation, whether on Sinai or in Jesus. Adults, but not infants, may have sins to be remitted. Our destiny is to approach and to attain Christian perfection in freedom through our own unrelenting effort: "Because perfection is possible for man it is obligatory" (*Letter to Demetrias,* cited by Brown, p. 342).

His associate Caelestius drew conclusions more unpalatable to Augustine than were the premises of Pelagius: Infants can be saved without baptism (a point on which Caelestius became more circumspect later), and freedom is incompatible with grace understood as an internal, divine impulse *(On the Doings of Pelagius).* Julian of Eclanum was not only the most capable of the "Pelagians," he was also the most irritating. Julian did not hesitate to write that, thanks to his freedom, "a human being is emancipated from God" (*Uncompleted Work Against Julian* 1.78). He touched a nerve, already touched by Caelestius (*On the Perfection of Human Justice* 6.14), by likening Augustine to a Manichaean because he held that human nature had been wounded by sin and that this is visible in sexual disorders (*Uncompleted Work Against Julian* 1.71, 3.6, 3.14, 5.5).

The controversy is an intricate web of misunder-

AUGUSTINE OF HIPPO, SAINT

standings, or alleged misunderstandings, on all sides. At the end of his career, Augustine held in his *Retractions* that when the "new heretics," the Pelagians, read his *Free Choice,* they thought him an ally of theirs, but in this they blundered (*Retractions* 1.9.4, 1.9.5); indeed, he felt that even though there were "no Pelagians then," he had undercut the position they would adopt in the future (1.9.6). In 412 he began to compose treatises against their excessive optimism on the human condition and their corresponding tendency to minimize divine grace. To his shelf of antiheretical works Augustine added anti-Pelagian essays, the first two of which were *The Deserts of Sins and Their Remission* and *On the Spirit and the Letter.* Both were addressed to Marcellinus, for both had been occasioned by his warnings to Augustine.

Augustine supplemented these first efforts in his anti-Pelagian campaign with a move on the plane of diplomacy. In 414 he sent his Spanish disciple, the priest Paul Orosius, to the Holy Land with the mission of informing the corps of bishops there—and, even more important, Jerome—of the heterodox character of what Pelagius and his associates were teaching, by that date, in the Holy Land itself. This mission was indifferently accomplished, as was a second mission entrusted to Orosius: the collection of factual data on past calamities that had befallen the Roman Empire, perhaps to serve as a source book for Augustine's refutation of the claim that the sacking of Rome in 410 by the forces of Alaric was unprecedented. This Orosius did in his *Seven Books of History Against the Pagans,* making generous use of earlier chronicles and completing his work so rapidly that he was able to consult book 9 of Augustine's *City of God,* available by 417. Augustine eventually finished all twenty-two books without a single reference, implicit or explicit, to the work of Orosius; only *Orosi cuiusdam,* "of some Orosius" (*Retractions* 2.44), is Augustine's chilling turn of phrase.

The anti-Pelagian mission did little but enlist Jerome on the side of orthodoxy; a council of fourteen bishops at Diospolis (Lydda) cleared Pelagius, who defended his views before them. The African councils of Milevis and of Carthage in 416 condemned those views and invoked the judgment of Rome. Innocent I did intervene against Pelagius, but Augustine saw that while Roman rescripts might close the affair as a doctrinal dispute, only a fatuous hope could take that official quietus as the end of the damage that Pelagian teaching was doing. In a passage of which the first sentence is often quoted alone, he wrote: "From there [Rome] too have the rescripts come; the case is at an end. Would that the error might one day end!" (*Sermon* 131.10.10).

The controversy was far from ended. Zosimus, the successor of Innocent, first favored, but then condemned, both Pelagius and Caelestius. Emperor Honorius expelled them from Rome, and in 418 a council at Carthage condemned nine Pelagian propositions. Zosimus ratified the acts of that provincial council, thereby giving them authority throughout the church. The pope renewed the excommunication of the two leaders and demanded the signatures of all bishops on his own *Epistola tractatoria* in 418.

Pelagius disappeared from history, but his quarrel with Augustine continued; Julian of Eclanum pressed him into ever more extreme positions, especially on the issue of predestination—positions more extreme than the Catholic Church has been willing to adopt. Still, the quarrel had its positive side. Augustine has ever since been esteemed as "the Doctor of Grace"—that is, of the freely bestowed gift of divine favor, preceding and rendering possible all human merit in the order of salvation. Both Julian and Augustine were consummate rhetoricians, and modern readers must approach their texts with the knowledge that the "diatribe," the "thorough grinding" to dust of an opponent, was a respectable genre for the rhetoricians of antiquity. Augustine's extreme positions on predestination recommended him to future critics of Rome's refusal to adopt them. Calvinist Protestants and Catholic Jansenists alike considered him their ally, indeed the latter stemmed from the posthumous volume *Augustinus* (1640) by Cornelius Jansen (1585–1638), Catholic bishop of Ypres. Not only Julian, but also the monks of southern Gaul, where John Cassian (*ca.* 360–432/435) had come from John Chrysostom at Constantinople with the traditions of Eastern Christianity, had reservations. As often happens, Augustine's disciples outdid their master in rigor. Prosper of Aquitaine (*ca.* 390–*ca.* 463) in Provence, and then in Rome, saw in Cassian's thirteenth *Conference* a retort to Augustine's *Corruption and Grace.* He applied the punning term *ingrates,* "the ungrateful" or "the graceless ones," to those who, like Cassian, refused to follow Augustine in all respects; Augustine had already applied it to Pelagius (*On the Doings of Pelagius* 25.50). Closer to home Evodius, Augustine's partner in the dialogue *Free Choice* and now bishop of Uzalis, was notably obscurantist when consulted by Abbot Valentinus of Hadrumentum concerning his monks' distress with Augustine's views. Conced-

AUGUSTINE OF HIPPO, SAINT

ing the difficulty (*Letters* 215), Augustine would say: "What we cannot express we are not permitted to pass over in silence; making sounds, we preach what we hardly understand when we think about it" (*Sermons* 215.3).

ARIANS

Mention has been made of the resurgence of Arianism toward the end of Augustine's life, a resurgence due not only to the Vandal invaders but also to the mercenary troops who defended the Roman towns against them; all were Arian Christians. Only after his death did Arianism seriously threaten the Catholic church in Africa, but Arianism enjoyed a vitality that was enough to provoke him to public debates, duly recorded by stenographic notaries. To one such debate we owe the *Conference with Maximus the Arian Bishop* and the treatise *Against Maximus the Arian,* both from the year 428. After a debate that seems to have come to very little, Augustine engaged in correspondence with the Arian Count Pascentius, which is preserved in *Letters* 238–241.

THE CITY OF GOD

The most dramatic challenge posed to Augustine's ontic and moral optimism was the fall and three-day sack of Rome by the Gothic armies of Alaric in 410. From many points of view his great response to that challenge, the *City of God,* is the most influential of his books. In his own words:

> When Rome was devastated as a result of the invasion by the Goths under their "king" Alaric, the worshipers of the many false gods (whom we by custom call "pagans") began to blaspheme the true God with more bitterness and acerbity than usual in their attempt to blame this devastation on the Christian religion. Fired with a zeal for the house of God, I determined to write my work, the *City of God,* against their blasphemies and errors. (*Retractions* 2.43.1)

For not every Christian had felt at ease when pagans ascribed public disasters to outraged civic deities. Augustine undertook first to answer questions posed to his "fellow presbyter, Deogratias" by the pagan Volusianus. Then the Christian count of Africa, Marcellinus, forwarded more questions to Augustine, this time on the delicate subject of alleged incompatibility between Christian ideals and the civic duties of a Roman (*Letters* 135, 136).

The letter Marcellinus received in reply was an essay that might have made the reputation of a lesser man than Augustine (*Letters* 138). His definitive answer, written between 413 and 425, was the monumental reply to those who "prefer their own 'gods' to the Creator" (*City of God* 1, preface). Augustine's *City of God* became the charter for all future Christian speculation on the correlation of politics with faith. Once more an Augustinian theme clearly exhibits his conviction that Greek philosophical wisdom and Hebrew biblical wisdom coincide. Both Plato and the Psalmist have employed the image of "two cities," one heavenly and one earthly; one a pattern to be followed, the other a human construction to be worked out in time and place; one immutable, the other mutable and corruptible.

Plato had suggested the image by speaking in his *Theaetetus* (176E) of "two patterns eternally set before them; the one blessed and divine, the other godless and wretched"; in his *Republic* (9, 592A, B) the image is more explicit: "There is the city of which we are the founders and which exists in idea only. . . . In heaven there is laid up a pattern of it which he who desires may behold, and beholding, may set his own house in order." Augustine found in the Psalter repeated uses of the image "city of God"—for example, Psalm 86(87):3, "Glorious things are said of you, O city of God!"; Psalm 45(46):5, "The flowing of a river makes the city of God rejoice."

Quite apart from his *City of God,* Augustine often used the figure of two cities in his *Accounts of the Psalms;* on Psalm 64(65):1, 2, for instance, he opposed Babylon to Jerusalem:

> . . . two cities indeed, according to the text, two cities truly. . . . Hence that particular earthly city bore the shadow of a certain eternal city in the heavens. . . . And note the names of these two cities: "Babylon" and "Jerusalem." "Babylon" is interpreted to be "confusion," "Jerusalem," "vision of peace." . . . Can we now separate them from each other? They are thoroughly mixed together and from the very beginning of the human race they flow along, thoroughly mixed, even to the end of time. . . . Two loves make these two cities: The love of God makes Jerusalem; love of the world makes Babylon.

It is all there: Love of a common goal by a people constitutes their "city"; to evaluate a city entails the evaluation of the common goal that brought it into being. The "thorough mixture" is a transitory state of affairs and pertains to the body; in the heart the two cities are already two, for their goals are diverse. Eternal peace engenders Jerusalem; temporal peace engenders Babylon (*Accounts,* on Psalm 136[137]).

AUGUSTINE OF HIPPO, SAINT

In the *Instruction of the Uneducated* (400) Augustine had spoken of "two cities," one of the iniquitous and the other of the saintly, now mixed and in the body. At Judgment Day these are to be separated in the body even as now they are separated in the "wills" of their citizens (*Instruction* 19.31). In *True Religion* (391) Augustine wove the imagery of Paul with that of Plato:

> Here one is termed "the old man" and "exterior" and "earthy" even though that one achieve what the mob calls "happiness" in a well-constituted earthly city, whether under kings, or princes, or laws, or under them all. Else a people cannot be well constituted, not even the one that pursues earthly goals, for that sort too possesses a certain measure of beauty that is proper to it. (26.48)

MORAL TEACHING

Augustine drew a comparison between the inner dynamism of the human will and the "weight" that classical physics ascribed to the "four elements." As the "weight" of fire makes it tend toward its own "place," and therefore to rise in the sublunar world, so the "weight" of earth drives it downward. The "weight" of the Augustinian soul is its love: "My weight is my love; by it am I borne wherever I am borne.... By your gift we are set afire and are borne on high" (*Confessions* 13.9.10).

Augustine had experienced the pull of a counterlove: "I did not stand firm to enjoy my God; no, I was drawn to you by your beauty, but immediately dragged down from you by my weight.... This 'weight' was carnality grown customary" (*Confessions* 7.17.23). It was this duality of will on the communal plane that accounted for the two cities, made them into a "people" through the "grouping of a multitude of rational beings, associated by the structure of their concordant love" (*City of God* 19.24). As love of God is love of Being in its highest instantiation, so sin is the love of nothing at all: " ... an ebbing away, not toward evils, but in an evil way, not toward evil natures, but evilly, because it is against the order of natures, away from Him Who supremely is toward what is less" (*City of God* 12.8).

This perception of an "order of natures" led Augustine to a distinction that has been held to contain "all the moral teaching of Augustine ... the fundamental distinction between 'enjoying' and 'using,' *frui* and *uti*" (Marrou, p. 79). By "enjoy" Augustine meant our clinging, out of love, to something for its own sake (*Christian Teaching* 1.4.4), and this can only be God. Lesser goods can be loved, but ought not to be "enjoyed"; their subordination to God demands that they be "used" as means to the possession of God in whom there is a peace "than which a better and a greater cannot be" (*City of God* 19.10). This goal of all morality—the possession of God—is the quietude, the rest, the peace of the human soul. A long passage in the *City of God* (19.13) lists all the instances of "peace" as rest after turmoil that can be verified in the created world; every case is a "tranquillity of order," and for humans, virtue is "an ordering of love" (*City of God* 15.22).

THINGS

Given Augustine's conviction that "philosophy" has but two ultimate themes, the soul and God, appeal must be made to his "interiorism" to see how he could fit a consideration of material things into his perspective:

> Do not desire to go outside, but return within yourself. Truth dwells within and, should you find your nature changing, transcend even yourself. While you thus transcend yourself, be mindful that you transcend a reasoning soul. Strive toward that place where the light of reason is kindled! For where does one who reasons validly journey if not to Truth? Surely Truth does not arrive at Itself by reasoning, rather It is That which those who reason are seeking. (*True Religion* 39.72)

An Augustinian mind thus judges things outside itself and below itself; those things are to be "used" and even loved in an ordered way. One instance of "judging" things is counting them; Augustine was fascinated by the human capacity to manipulate numbers, to find in them universally applicable and unchanging laws. Both things counted and the counting mind are changing and contingent, yet the art of arithmetic discovers the unchanging—indeed, the immutable—and the necessary.

Our knowledge of things starts in sensation: "The human mind first through corporeal senses experiences 'those things which have been made'" (*Genesis According to the Text* 4.32.49). Those things, made by God, are both beautiful and good, but less beautiful and less good than the mind that judges them and still less so than the Creator of them all. Sensations, by which they are known, are instances of vital attention by a human soul to changes in its own bodily organs as material things impinge upon them. In harmony with a human body, things cause pleasurable sensations; out of harmony with a human sense organ, pain is caused by the experience (*Music* 6.5.9).

AUGUSTINE OF HIPPO, SAINT

The whole soul is aware of what goes on in one part of the body, yet a soul does not perceive that episode as occurring in the whole body (*Immortality of Soul* 16.25). Although bodily beauty can move the lustful as well as the wise, that beauty reveals the "numerical structure" *(ratio numerorum)* that grounds both beauty and intelligibility, the work of him who has made us (*Sermon* 243.8.7). All bodies, in the end, shouted to Augustine: "We are not God" and "He made us" (*Confessions* 10.6.9). Basing himself on a Latin version derived from the Septuagint, Augustine read Ecclesiasticus (a book counted apocryphal outside the Catholic church) 18:1 as a revelation that all things had been created "at once," *simul* (*Genesis According to the Text* 4.33.52). The world of things at that moment of creation did not have the shape of our world; a theory of "seed-natures" *(rationes seminales)* accounts for development from a primitive state in which the future was present "invisibly, potentially, causally" (*Genesis ... Text* 6.6.10). "Just as mothers are heavy with their young, so is the cosmos itself heavy with the causes of things coming to birth" (*Trinity* 3.9.16).

SOUL

Augustine was faithful to the tradition that makes the life of beatitude the goal of wisdom. The Epicurean, the Stoic, and the Christian may give diverse answers, but all three respond to the same question: "What makes one happy?" (*Sermons* 150.4.5). He was also faithful to the tradition that urges those who love wisdom to "know themselves" (*Trinity* 10.9.12–10.10.15). Varro provided him with three possible answers to the question: Is a human being a "soul alone" or a "body alone" or a "body and soul"? In Varro's opinion the third option is correct (*City of God* 19.3).

Conceding a certain value to Varro's view, Augustine favored the first answer: a human being is "a rational soul using a mortal and earthy body" (*Morals of the Church* 1.27.52)—or, put another way, "a mind, a certain substance participating in reason, adapted to ruling a body" (*Quantity of Soul* 13.22). "Mind," it should be noted, is used by Augustine interchangeably with "soul," for soul is better than body and mind is what is best in soul; near by nature to immutable Truth, our highest power is rightly called "mind" (*Immortality of Soul* 15.24). Hence the celebrated exhortation "Love intellect very much," for by intellect alone what we hold on faith becomes "useful" to us (*Letters* 120.3.13). "The body is not the good of the mind, but mind is the good of the body . . ." (*Letters* 118.3.14).

The first fruit of self-knowledge defeats skepticism: In doubt, in error, a mind is certain of being, of living, of understanding; "If I err, I am" (*City of God* 11.26; compare *Soliloquies* 2.1; *Trinity* 10.10.13). This "Platonic" human who is a soul-mind did not preexist in a world of forms it now "remembers":

> No, that is not the explanation. . . . The intellectual mind was so made that, being naturally subject to intelligible realities, . . . it sees these truths in a certain incorporeal light of a unique kind. (*Trinity* 12.13.24)

Memory, for Augustine, can bear upon the present as well as upon the past; his disconcerting explanation of this is an exegesis of a line from Vergil: " . . . nor when Ulysses suffered such things / did the Ithacan in peril so great forget himself" (*Aeneid* 3.628–629). On this Augustine commented: "What else did Vergil want understood except that he remembered himself? . . . He was present to himself . . . memory pertains to things present!" (*Trinity* 14.11.14). Those intelligible realities, eternal intelligibilities, *rationes aeternae,* are more than surrogates for Platonic ideas. In "seeing" them we experience the presence of a Light, a "sun of minds" parallel to the earthly sun (*Free Choice* 2.13.36). A human teacher—Moses, for instance—can do no more than direct the attention of his student to truths in the light of that Truth: "To apprehend that what words signify is true demands more than the external teacher can do" (*Confessions* 11.3.5). This is the "illumination theory" according to which Christ, eternal Word of the Father, is the "interior Teacher":

> For knowledge about all things we understand we do not apply to someone speaking audible words outside us, but to the Truth that governs the mind itself within us. . . . It is to our Teacher that we apply for instruction, namely, Christ . . . the unshakable Power of God, the everlasting Wisdom of God. (*The Teacher* 11.38)

Illumination theory, adduced to account for the universality and necessity of humanly perceived truths, leads to God as the "common and public" yet "secret" Light of minds (*Free Choice* 2.12.33).

GOD

Thus things and his own soul drew Augustine ineluctably to God. For him, "God" is the God of the Bible as revealed in Jesus Christ and proclaimed by

AUGUSTINE OF HIPPO, SAINT

the Catholic church. Platonists may have seen the goal from afar but, ignorant of Jesus, they did not know the way (*Confessions* 7.21.27). Augustine had no illusions on the capacity of wayfaring humans to know God: "We say more easily what He is not than what He is" (*Accounts of the Psalms,* Psalm 85(86):12).

"What do I love when I love You?" Augustine asked (*Confessions* 10.6.8), and his paradoxical answer was that God is "One Whom no one is permitted to know as He is, nor yet is anyone permitted to be ignorant of Him" (*Accounts of the Psalms,* Psalm 74(75):9). One thing we know concerning God is that his name belongs only to "that than which it is evident that nothing is superior" (*Free Choice* 2.6.14), a formula used also in *Confessions* 7.4.6, *Letters* 155.4.13, *Christian Teaching* 1.7.7, and *Accounts of the Psalms,* Psalm 32(33):2:15. On this ground God is seen to be the only authentic Being—indeed, "Being Itself" (*Trinity* 5.2.3; *City of God* 12.2). The God of Exodus 3:14 is "substance" or "essence," what "Greeks call *ousia,*" and the ground of this assertion is the perception that God "is immutably." Whatever changes, Augustine saw, ceases to be what it was and begins to be what it was not:

> Whatever can be changed, does not truly exist; true being is not present where nonbeing is. . . . In change, a kind of death has been wrought; destroyed is something which was there and now is not. In the whitening head of an old man blackness has died. (*On the Gospel of John* 38.8.10)

Augustine knew and transmitted the considerations later generations would call "proofs" of the "existence of God." General consent by humankind (*On the Gospel of John* 106.4); the cosmological approach of *Confessions* 11.4.6, in which material things shouted to him that they had not made themselves; the eudaemonic considerations of *The Life of Happiness* 1.11 and the noetic of *Free Choice* 2.2.5–2.16.41 present his reflections on the mystery of divine Being. Finally, in *Sermons* 141.2.2, Augustine formulated what is termed a "teleological" perspective on God. As always, his effort was to attain some understanding of what he believed; he accepted on faith the theophany of Exodus 3:14, and his "proofs" are as many dialectical meditations on the ultimately unknowable Being who alone is truly Being. The God of Exodus is also the triune God of the Gospels, of Paul, and of the great councils of the Church.

Augustine's fifteen-book *Trinity* set out in careful terms his trinitarian teaching, marked by a wealth of analogies with the powers of the human soul, conceived of as traces (in their unity and distinction) of the Creator, Intellect, Memory, and Will. He knew, and was not impressed by, expressions in Plotinian philosophy that others had welcomed as intimations of the Christian doctrine of a triune God: "three principal substances," "paternal intellect," and "soul." "Philosophers," he wrote, "speak using terms with freedom; they do not fear to offend religious ears! For us, however, the right thing is to speak according to an established rule lest freedom in terms beget impious views, even concerning the realities they do signify" (*City of God* 10.23).

The *Confessions, Accounts of the Psalms, City of God,* and the *Trinity* enjoyed wider manuscript diffusion than any other works except the Bible and Gregory's *Books of Morals on Job.* No other author exerted so all-pervasive an influence on the Latin Middle Ages as did Augustine through these widely disseminated works. Augustine saw all his exploitation of Greek philosophical materials (the only work of Aristotle he read seems to have been the *Categories* [*Confessions* 4.16.28]) as a legitimate "despoiling of the Egyptians" (*Confessions* 7.9.15; *Christian Teaching* 2.40.60).

THE RULE OF SAINT AUGUSTINE

A rounded picture of Augustine's impact must advert to his concern with establishing around himself a series of what can only be described as monastic foundations. From the informal grouping at Cassiciacum, that on property inherited from his father at Tagaste, and the monastery in a garden beside the church building at Hippo to that in his bishop's residence, he formed friends and associates into communities designed to evoke the Church of the Acts of the Apostles (*Sermons* 355.1.2). This concern has left written traces, a collection of documents that has circulated from his time to our own under the title "Rule of Saint Augustine." Religious women and men still follow this rule but, as often happens with documents having a long history, its authenticity has been both impugned and defended. Which document, or documents, from among this dossier of directives for the religious life, transmitted in 317 manuscripts, can merit the title "Rule of Saint Augustine"? Luc Verheijen, O.S.A., has subjected the total manuscript tradition to a meticulous examination and has reached scientifically acceptable conclusions, which may be summarized as follows.

The tradition provides a documentation consist-

AUGUSTINE OF HIPPO, SAINT

ing of nine items, each of which has some claim to be, directly or indirectly, a component of St. Augustine's Rule because it can be established as a composition of his, or as a revision of text he had composed, or as a composite of two or more authentic texts and thus, through the mediation of an editor, "indirectly" the work of Augustine.

Three of the nine are brief texts addressed to men. Verheijen has suggested neutral titles to designate them. "The Command" *(Praeceptum)* is the "primitive" text and, with all masculine inflections adjusted, founds the feminine tradition as well. "The Order of a Monastery" *(Ordo monasterii),* with its Oriental flavor and wealth of liturgical directions, is the work of Alypius and is one fruit of his journey from Tagaste to Bethlehem, a journey undertaken to consult Jerome. On his return to Tagaste, Alypius presumably showed his notes to Augustine; the bishop of Hippo added an introduction and an ending. Hence, although not strictly a rule composed by Augustine, "The Order of a Monastery" is a rule in the composition of which Augustine took a significant role. "The Command" seems to have been written later than "The Order of a Monastery," and the two texts were, in any case, combined in the probable order of their composition to form what Verheijen names "The Longer Command" *(Praeceptum longius);* this seems, further, to be the state in which Alypius himself may have made current in Italy Augustine's views on the religious life during the repeated voyages that Alypius made to that country. "The Received Rule" *(Regula recepta)* is simply the text of "The Command," introduced by the first line of "The Order of a Monastery."

To these four documents addressed to men must be added five addressed to religious women. (Here it ought to be noted that Augustine's sister headed a convent of religious women.) "The Rebuke" *(Obiurgatio)* is a letter reprimanding a convent of nuns who had become embroiled with their Superior over their "supervisor" *(praepositus).* "The Training in Lawfulness" *(Regularis informatio)* is nothing but "The Command" with all masculine inflections changed to the feminine. "The Longer Letter" *(Epistula longior)* is a composite of "The Rebuke" and "The Training in Lawfulness." A feminine form of "The Order of a Monastery" is termed "The Order of a Monastery Given to Women" *(Ordo monasterii feminis data).* "The Longest Letter" *(Epistula longissima)* combines a passage from "The Rebuke," the whole of "The Order of a Monastery Given to Women," and a series of passages from "The Training in Lawfulness." Thus the whole collection can be reduced to three basic texts, the oldest from the pen of Alypius and the other two, "The Command" and "The Rebuke," directly from the pen of Augustine.

BIBLIOGRAPHY

Almost every item in the following select bibliography will provide some guidance in the immense sea of Augustinian writing. T. van Bavel continues the bibliographical notices of the work under his name in association with P. Huisman in *Augustiniana;* for readers of English, L. E. M. Lynch, translator of Gilson's work (below), has provided an extensive English bibliographical addition to that work.

Latin Text. In the seventeenth century the Benedictines of the Congregation of Saint Maur produced an edition of all the then-known works of Augustine that is available in J. P. Migne, ed., *Patrologia latina,* XXXII–XLVI (1841–1842); because several inauthentic works are included, the Migne edition ought to be used in conjunction with Palémon Glorieux, *Pour revaloriser Migne, XXXII–XLIV* (1952). Highly scientific texts are provided for many of Augustine's works by the *Corpus scriptorum ecclesiasticorum latinorum,* edited by the National (formerly Imperial) Academy of Vienna; the Corpus Christianorum series, published at Turnhout, has produced a number of important titles; and some works have appeared in excellent editions under other auspices; for example, the Pium Knoell and Martinus Skutella edition of the *Confessionum libri tredecim* (1934) is widely considered the best available text of that work.

English Translations. Many of Augustine's works are in the Library of the Fathers of the Holy Catholic Church Anterior to the Division of the East and West, Translated by Members of the English Church (1838–); these translations are also available in A Select Library of the Nicene and Post-Nicene Fathers of the Christian Church (1886; repr. 1956). More modern translations of certain works are in the series Catholic University of America Patristic Studies (1922 sq.); Ancient Christian Writers: The Works of the Fathers in Translation (1946 sq.), The Fathers of the Church (1947 sq.), and The Library of Christian Classics (1953 sq.). The *Confessions* and *Select Letters* also have appeared in Latin text with facing English translation in the Loeb Classical Library, and a useful collection of Augustinian material has been made by Whitney J. Oates, *Basic Writings of Saint Augustine* (1948). Many works have been translated separately; it should be noted that the works by Bourke and Marrou cited below include tables of all works of Augustine with their dates, the volume of the *Patrologia latina/Corpus scriptorum ecclesiasticorum latinorum* in which they appear, and, in the Marrou volume, an indication of series of English translations, provided by J. J. O'Meara.

Periodicals. Apart from general theological and philosophical journals, a number of periodicals are devoted explicitly to Augustine: *Analecta Augustiniana* (1905–); *Augustiniana* (1951–); *Augustinian Studies* (1970–); *Augustinianum* (1961–); *Avgvstinvs* (1956–); *Revue des études augustiniennes* (1955–).

Studies. Prosper Alfaric, *L'évolution intellectuelle de s. Augustin* (1918); Henri-Xavier Arquillière, *L'augustinisme politique* (1934); Tarsicius J. van Bavel, *Répertoire bibliographique de saint Augustin 1950–1960* (1963); Gerald Bonner, *St. Augustine of Hippo: Life and Controversies* (1963); Vernon J. Bourke, *Augustine's Quest of Wisdom* (1945); Peter Brown, *Augustine of Hippo: A Biography* (1967); Pierre Courcelle, *Recherches sur les Confessions de saint Augustin* (1950); Étienne H. Gilson, *The Christian Philosophy of St. Augustine,* L. E. M. Lynch, trans. (1960); Robert A. Markus, *Saeculum: History and Society in the Theology of St. Augustine* (1970); Henri-Irénée Marrou, *Saint Augustine and His Influence Throughout the Ages,* Patrick Hepburne-Scott and Edward Hill, trans. (1954); Frederik van der Meer, *Augustine the Bishop,* Brian Battershaw and G. R. Lamb, trans. (1961); *Miscellanea Agostiniana: Testi e studi,* 2 vols. (1930); *A Monument to Saint Augustine* (1930); A. C. Pegis, "The Mind of St. Augustine," in *Mediaeval Studies,* **6** (1944); Possidius, *Sancti Augustini vita scripta a Possidio episcopo,* H. Weiskotten, ed. and trans. (1919); and *Vita di S. Agostino,* M. Pellegrino, ed. and trans. (1955); Henri Rondet et al., *Études augustiniennes* (1953); Luc Verheijen, *La règle de saint Augustin,* 2 vols. (1967).

EDWARD A. SYNAN

[See also **Ambrose, Saint; Arians, Arianism, Arius; Cassian, John; Church, Early; Church Fathers; Codex Theodosianus; Donatism; Jerome, Saint; Julian of Eclanum; Manichaeanism/Manichaeans; Orosius; Pelagius.**]

AUGUSTINIAN CANONS, an order of men vowed to the common life under the Rule of St. Augustine. Early in church history, attempts were made to have canons live in common. In the fourth century Eusebius of Vercelli and Martin of Tours founded such communities, but the one founded by Augustine in Hippo became a model and inspiration during the Middle Ages. Augustine's Rule, modeled after the primitive Christian community in Jerusalem, with its general principles of religious life and its insistence on common life and personal poverty, was considered ideal for the canons' active-contemplative life.

The Augustinian canons came into existence in the eleventh century under the influence of the Gregorian Reform. The Rule of St. Augustine was generally adopted in the following century, but only with the adoption of constitutions in the fourteenth century can one properly speak of a religious order. This long period of formation was also the time of the order's most intensive and extensive growth. By the end of the Middle Ages there were more than 4,500 foundations, and in England the Augustinian canons were the largest single religious order of men.

The traditional ministries of the canons were divine worship in their cathedral and collegiate churches, education, hospices, and hospitals. Founded around 1050, the Great St. Bernard hospice in the Pennine Alps, with its ministry of rescue and hospitality, is the best known of the canons' houses.

Two important schools of spirituality arose from among the canons. The earlier, under Hugh of St. Victor, was speculative. Union with God was to be achieved through meditation; contemplation or wisdom, weakened through original sin, could thus be restored. The later movement, Devotio Moderna, founded in the late fourteenth century by Gerhard Groote, was more subjective and moralistic. Thomas à Kempis' classic *Imitation of Christ* has kept alive this antihumanistic and antirationalistic spirituality.

BIBLIOGRAPHY

John Compton Dickinson, *The Origin of the Austin Canons and Their Introduction into England* (1950); Pius Frank, *Canonicorum regularium sodalitates et canonia* (1954), in English, French, German, and Italian.

CYRIL SMETANA

[See also **Augustine of Hippo, St.; Devotio Moderna.**]

AUGUSTINIAN FRIARS, one of the four mendicant orders, trace their spiritual lineage to St. Augustine of Hippo. Although a direct line from Augustine cannot be proved, we know from his first biographer, Possidius, that Augustine's disciples founded monasteries. We know too that persecution by the Vandals forced them from Northern Africa to Sardinia, Spain, and Italy.

The order as such was formed in the twelfth century when several groups of Tuscan hermits banded together with papal approval. Under Richard Annibaldi, their cardinal protector, they held their first chapter in 1244. The Grand Union of 1256 under Pope Alexander IV called on other hermit communities to join this body in their new apostolates of preaching and teaching.

AUGUSTINISM

The first constitutions of the order, ratified in 1290, reflect the pope's directives in their stress on formation and education of candidates. Houses of study were soon founded in the main university centers: Paris, Bologna, Padua, Florence, Oxford, and Cambridge. The constitutions envisage an evangelical and ecclesiastical spirituality, and novices are urged "to read avidly, to listen devoutly, and to study ardently Sacred Scripture."

This scholarly climate produced such reputable theologians as Giles of Rome, James of Viterbo, and Gregory of Rimini. Although influenced by early Scholasticism, they are Augustinian in their themes: Christ, grace, and love. Like Augustine's, their theology dealt with burning issues of the late thirteenth and early fourteenth centuries, church-state relationships and the position of the papacy. A number of Augustinians, friends and mentors of Petrarch and Boccaccio, were recognized humanists in the fourteenth-century Italian Renaissance.

The order early established monasteries throughout the Continent, England, and Ireland. A sixteenth-century source numbers them as 2,000 with about 30,000 friars. This is doubtless an exaggeration, but a report dated 1481 claims that 5,084 friars died in the Black Death. The Augustinian friars weathered the Reformation initiated by one of their members, Martin Luther, and today are found throughout the world.

BIBLIOGRAPHY

Rudolph Arbesmann, "Andrea Biglia, Augustinian Friar and Humanist," in *Analecta Augustiniana,* **28** (1965); and "Some Notes on the Fourteenth-Century History of the Augustinian Order," *ibid.,* **40** (1977); Balbino Rano, *The Order of St. Augustine* (1975); Francis Roth, "Cardinal Richard Annibaldi," in *Augustiniana,* **2** (1952), and **3** (1953); D. A. Trapp, "Augustinian Theology of the 14th Century," *ibid.,* **6** (1956).

CYRIL SMETANA

[See also **Augustine of Hippo, St.; Friars; Mendicant Orders.**]

AUGUSTINISM (AUGUSTINIANISM), a cluster of ideas derived from the work of Augustine, bishop of Hippo, that affected medieval philosophy, theology, and religious communities. Augustine had offered an escape from skepticism, an optimistic ontology, an "illuminationist" noetic according to which truths known by a creature are seen in the light of immutable divine truth, and the conviction that the God of the Bible is the one essence that, because immutable, is truly Being. He had proffered a cosmic theory of seed natures to account for the development of all corporeal things from an undifferentiated primitive state to maturity and an ethico-political concern with the life of beatitude as the ultimate goal of human life.

Philosophical Augustinism was challenged in the thirteenth century by the recovered Aristotelian physics, noetics, and metaphysics, as promoted by Albertus Magnus, Thomas Aquinas, and others against the scholasticized Augustinism of Alexander of Hales, Bonaventure, Kilwardby, Peckham, and Vital du Four. At issue were illuminationism, the plurality of forms, and universal hylomorphism. Of these, the plurality of forms alone survived the thirteenth century—and then only as transmuted by John Duns Scotus, who assigned "formally, but not really, distinct" constituents to all creatures.

Throughout the Middle Ages, Augustine was the preeminent authority on biblical exegesis, thanks especially to his work on the Psalms (the only treatment by a Latin author of the entire psalter) and on speculation, above all on the Trinity, on grace, and on predestination. The rigidity of his views on the last, developed against the Pelagians, was mitigated by successors who emphasized, as he had not, the universally salvific will of God. One who seems to have gone beyond Augustine is the ninth-century theologian Gottschalk of Orbais, who proposed a "double predestination," either to glory or to damnation. Augustine's arguments for the validity of a sacrament apart from the moral status of its human minister, developed against the Donatist practice of rebaptism, had useful application in twelfth-century theological controversy occasioned by reform movements to raise clerical moral standards.

Augustine's clerical household at Hippo, living an austere common life in imitation of the communal living of the Jerusalem Church as described in the Acts of the Apostles, exerted a continuing influence on collegial and cathedral churches throughout the Middle Ages. Until relatively recent times, there was little hesitation in naming a dossier of Augustinian texts on religious communities of both men and women "The Rule of St. Augustine." Those documents set out procedures that had resulted in the devout, self-sacrificing common life recounted by the refugee bishop of Calama, Possidius, in his eye-witness *Life of Augustine.* The prestige of Augustine suggested that his Rule would revive the heroic age

AUGUSTINISM

of the Jerusalem church wherever that Rule might be adopted or adapted. Hence a whole series of religious communities, in some instances for both sexes, were founded to live the provisions of the Hippo community: Canons of St. Victor, Canons of Premontre, the Servites, the Augustinian Friars or Hermits, and even the Order of Preachers ("Dominicans").

BIBLIOGRAPHY

Henry-Xavier Arquillière, *L'Augustinisme politique* (1934); Fulbert Cayré and Fernand van Steenberghen, *Les directions doctrinales de saint Augustin,* rev. ed. (1948); Étienne Gilson, *History of Christian Philosophy in the Middle Ages* (1955); Henri I. Marrou, *Saint Augustine and His Influence Throughout the Ages,* P. Hepburne-Scott and E. Hill, trans. (1957); Fernand van Steenberghen, *The Philosophical Movement in the Thirteenth Century* (1955).

EDWARD A. SYNAN

[See also **Monastery.**]